THE CREATION OF A
NATIONAL AIR FORCE

THE OFFICIAL HISTORY OF
THE ROYAL CANADIAN AIR FORCE
VOLUME II

W.A.B. DOUGLAS

The Creation of
a National Air Force

The Official History of
the Royal Canadian Air Force
Volume II

Editor-in-Chief
Norman Hillmer

Published by University of Toronto Press
in co-operation with the Department of National Defence
and the Canadian Government Publishing Centre,
Supply and Services Canada

© Minister of Supply and Services Canada 1986
Printed in Canada
ISBN 0-8020-2584-6
Government catalogue number D2-63/2-1985E

Printed on acid-free paper

Canadian Cataloguing in Publication Data

Main entry under title:

The official history of the Royal Canadian Air
Force

Includes bibliographical references and indexes.
Partial contents: v. 1. Canadian airmen and the
First World War / S.F. Wise – v. 2. The creation
of a national air force / W.A.B. Douglas.
ISBN 0-8020-2379-7 (v. 1). – ISBN 0-8020-2584-6 (v. 2).

1. Canada. Royal Canadian Air Force – History.
I. Wise, S.F. (Sydney Francis), 1924–   . Canadian
airmen and the First World War. II. Douglas, W.A.B.
(William Alexander Binney), 1929–   . The creation
of a national air force. III. Canada. Dept. of
National Defence. III. Title.

UG635.C2036 1980   358.4′00971   c80-094480-1

Illustrations in this book come from the Public Archives of Canada and the Department
of National Defence; acknowledgment is hereby given for permission to reproduce
them.
Codes appearing at the end of captions represent negative numbers at the PAC (PL, PA, RE)
and DND (RE, PMR, AH, REA, WRF). This volume will also be published in French
translation.

Note: In the writing of this volume the author has been given full access to relevant
official documents in possession of the Department of National Defence. The inferences
drawn and the opinions expressed are those of the author himself, and the department is in no way responsible for his reading or presentation of the facts as stated.

Contents

Appendices

Maps and Illustrations

illustrations

Black and white photographs are placed on pages 2–34, 154–90, 296–340,
430–64, 612–20.

Preface

This book, the second of four projected volumes in the official history of the Royal Canadian Air Force, is about the origins and development of the RCAF as a national institution. The first volume, *Canadian Airmen and the First World War*, recorded a notably generous Canadian contribution to the war in the air from 1914 to 1918.

Several failed attempts to create a national air force out of that contribution formed curious, but important, elements in the early history of Canadian military aviation. Two short-lived organizations, the Royal Canadian Naval Air Service and the Canadian Air Force overseas, both established in 1918, had no institutional links with the Canadian Air Force that came into being two years later. However, the CAF and later the RCAF had unmistakeable connections with the past; thousands of men, from Air Vice-Marshal Sir Willoughby Gwatkin to the youngest airmen qualified during the First World War, created a pool of knowledge, experience, and commitment from which to draw. Aircraft, facilities, and equipment left over from the war provided the initial resources for postwar aviation. Above all, 'air mindedness,' resulting from wartime experience, was a vital prerequisite to winning Cabinet approval for government aviation services of any kind.

Military necessity brought Canada into the air age. In the peaceful 1920s, civil more than military concerns governed the shape, size, and functions of the RCAF; in the following decade the rise of international tensions forced the service to concentrate on its military role. During the Second World War the RCAF grew from a few hundred airmen to a force of some eighty squadrons and nearly a quarter of a million people. RCAF squadrons, wings, and groups took their place beside other Allied air forces in many theatres of the Second World War, and in the process acquired capabilities in virtually every phase of air warfare.

But the roots of the RCAF's growing reputation in overseas theatres – especially in the Northwest Europe campaign – were to be found at home. Responsible for the British Commonwealth Air Training Plan in Canada, the RCAF trained large numbers of other Commonwealth and Allied airmen as well as Canadians. Charged with the air defence of Canada, it built up a big Home War Establishment which played a significant part in the defeat of enemy attempts to destroy Allied shipping, particularly in the Battle of the Atlantic.

A number of RCAF maritime squadrons served on the other side of the ocean in the Royal Air Force's Coastal Command. Their anti-submarine operations have been included in this volume not only for their own intrinsic importance but also to provide a coherent and balanced account of the air war over the 'Atlantic bridge,' which was fought from the United Kingdom and Iceland as well as from Canada and Newfoundland. Most of these overseas squadrons also participated in anti-shipping strikes over the English Channel and North Sea in 1942 and 1943, and in operations directly related to the invasion of northwest Europe in 1944 and 1945. However, those parts of their story have been left for Volume III of this history, which will deal with operations overseas.

It must be remembered that half of the Canadian airmen who served in Coastal Command were not even in Canadian squadrons. They flew with other Commonwealth and Allied units. Their duties were as onerous, the risks they took were as great, and their sacrifices comparable, but to recount the story of their war would involve a comprehensive history of every facet of martime air operations, an approach which constraints of space make impracticable in a volume devoted to the evolution of the RCAF as an institution. Regrettably, a number of other groups – for example, groundcrew, weather and radio technicians, and the Marine and Women's divisions – also deserve more attention than the few references it has been possible to make. They also served and played significant parts in the development of the air force, but economy dictates that their stories, too, give way to those operational functions of organization, strategy, tactics, and procurement that are most central to the thrust of this series.

This book has been written from a wide variety of primary sources. RCAF historians during and just after the Second World War prepared a number of undocumented and somewhat narrowly conceived narratives which nonetheless provided a basis for further research into operations record books and daily diaries, as well as both RCAF and Royal Canadian Navy files held in the Directorate of History and the Public Archives of Canada. British Cabinet, Dominions Office, Air Ministry, Admiralty, and Intelligence records, as well as archival records in the United States, have also been indispensable sources. Some of these documents, particularly British Intelligence files, only began to be available in the later stages of research, and we realize that our use of such sources is far from complete. There must be a limit to all things, and future scholars will have the opportunity of following up leads which may have been revealed by our efforts.

As author of record, I take full responsibility for the accuracy and interpretation of the facts in this book. Like all previous Canadian official histories, however, this has been the work of a closely knit team. I am particularly grateful to Norman Hillmer, senior historian at the Directorate of History and chairman of this volume's editorial committee. Dr Hillmer co-ordinated the entire research, writing, and editorial effort, as well as carrying a good deal of that load personally.

W.J. McAndrew, who has become the authority on the origins of the RCAF and its early growth, wrote the successive drafts of the chapters in Part I, and offered valuable advice during the rewriting process. M.V. Bezeau and Brereton Greenhous carried out the preliminary research and wrote drafts for the section on training in Canada. Captain Bezeau also prepared preliminary chapters concerning the air defence of the east and west coasts, and is responsible for many of the detailed charts and graphs in the volume. Ben Greenhous, whose critical eye has sharpened the perceptions and clarified the prose of so many historians, not just those writing Canadian official history, was an indispensable part of the editorial committee.

Stephen J. Harris wrote the first draft of Chapters 7 and 9, and of Appendix C; his energy and enthusiasm was a great asset as the book was brought to publication. F.J. Hatch, whose *Aerodrome of Democracy: Canada and the British Commonwealth Air Training Plan*, has paved the way for all future studies of this endeavour, carried out his research over many years at the Directorate of History before his retirement. J.D.F. Kealy prepared the first adequately documented studies of Eastern and Western Air Commands, and of RCAF anti-submarine operations. Robert Baglow's statistical analysis of Eastern Air Command submarine sightings in 1942, prepared in co-operation with Mr Kealy, filled a large gap in our knowledge.

Carl Christie, the secretary of the editorial committee, wrote an early draft on 1943 EAC operations, and shares responsibility with Dr Hatch for Appendix D. Roger Sarty, with unmatched persistence, unearthed new material on intelligence and anti-submarine operations for the final part of the book, and prepared the drafts from which much of this section has been written. Marc Milner's contribution to the Battle of the Atlantic section was also a vital one; in addition, he made the preliminary selection of photographs. William Johnston proofread the entire manuscript, verified references, prepared the index, and made astute observations on the use of evidence which has led to important revisions in the text. Major John Armstrong arrived at the directorate in time to assist greatly with the page proofs.

The work of the Directorate of History's cartographer, William Constable, deserves special mention. He has devoted long hours to the preparation of each map, table, and graph in the book. Colonel R.A. Grainger, director of cartography at National Defence Headquarters, and the Canadian Forces Mapping and Charting Establishment, under Lieutenant-Colonel D.T. Carney, provided essential support in the production of maps. Dr M.A. Weinberger and his staff at the Directorate of Mathematics and Statistics were our computer experts, solving our many problems as we developed a statistical data bank on Second World War members of the RCAF. Equally important has been the Directorate of History's senior archival officer, Owen Cooke, as well as David Fransen, Paul Marshall, and others who dug up, accessioned, and catalogued documents. Lieutenant-Colonel David Wiens gave consulting and translation services of signal importance, adding to German language sources so carefully built up by the late Fred Steiger. J.J.B. Pariseau offered useful suggestions in helping to prepare maps for the forthcoming French translation of the book. The complex typing and word-processing requirements for this volume have been handled with their usual efficiency by the directorate secretaries, Gloria

McKeigan, Elsie Roberts, and Loretta Wickens, and by a much put upon word-processing unit at National Defence Headquarters under the supervision of Yvette Landry and Annie Rainville. Over the years, furthermore, students employed for the summer period have made many contributions to the preparation of the volume.

Acknowledgment must also be made to the generous help given by a number of serving and retired officers who have offered constant encouragement and much useful information. General G.C.E. Thériault, recently retired as chief of the defence staff, together with his predecessors, General Ramsey Withers and Admiral R.H. Falls, gave their full backing at every stage of the project. Air Marshal Larry Dunlap and Air Vice-Marshal Clare Annis, as chairmen of the RCAF Memorial, have enthusiastically supported our research. The efficiency and goodwill of Brigadier-General C.J. Gauthier, director-general of the Department of National Defence's Executive Secretariat, has contributed substantially to the preparation of this book. Colonel C.P. Stacey, whose many publications have created a framework for the writing of Canadian military history, was kind enough to comment on portions of the manuscript. The late Air Vice-Marshal G.O. Johnson granted a helpful interview in 1981; so at various times did Air Vice-Marshals Kenneth Nairn, F.V. Heakes, T.A. Lawrence, George Howsam, and Kenneth Guthrie, as well as Colonel R.A. Logan, and many others. Lieutenant-General R.J. Lane read certain chapters in draft and offered valuable comments.

This is a fitting time to pay tribute to Dr W.I. Smith, who recently retired as dominion archivist. Dr Smith and his staff at the Public Archives of Canada, particularly Bernard Weilbrenner, the assistant dominion archivist, and Jerry O'Brien, Barbara Wilson and Glenn Wright of the federal archives division, have performed outstanding service in organizing and making readily available the enormous volume of Department of National Defence records. Air Commodore Henry Probert, head of the RAF's Air Historical Board and his predecessor Group Captain Freddie Haslam, opened the way to Air Ministry documents essential to our research. J.D. Brown, head of the Royal Navy's Naval Historical Branch, generously provided copies of the *BdU* War Diary in translation, and Bob Coppock of his staff answered difficult questions about U-boat operations. R.D. Suddaby, keeper of documents at the Imperial War Museum, London, provided further research assistance. We are also indebted to the Public Record Office, and its keeper, Dr G. Martin. Nor can we forget Major-General J. Huston, the former chief of the US Office of Air Force History and his successor, Dr Richard Kohn. Admiral J.D.H. Kane of the US Navy's Naval Historical Division and Dr Dean Allard, head of the Operational Archives Division, responded promptly and helpfully to various requests, as did Professor Dr Jürgen Rohwer, head of the Library of Contemporary History at Stüttgart, and the members of the *Militärgeschichtliches Forschungsamt* in Freiburg. The staff of the Canadian War Museum was always attentive, Hugh Halliday and Fred Azar in particular, as was Carl Vincent, whose *Canada's Wings* has brought out many titles in Canadian aviation and military history. Professor David Syrett, of the City University of New York, stimulated me to think again about air operations in the Battle of the Atlantic. J. Tuzo Wilson provided us early access to his father's papers. Professor Claude T. Bissell and Dr Hector M. Mackenzie provided us with research materials on the 1939 BCATP negotiations. Our University of Toronto Press editor, Rosemary Shipton, cast her expert eye over the entire manuscript.

As air historians, we owe a great deal to our predecessors, particularly that devoted scholar, Wing Commander Fred Hitchins, the official air force historian from 1946 to 1958, who could not in his lifetime realize his dream of an official history of the RCAF. A special word in this regard must also be reserved for Dean S.F. Wise of Carleton University, Ottawa. All air historians in Canada are in his debt. He provided the inspiration and knowledge for the first volume of this history, introduced the subject to those who would write subsequent volumes, and helped develop the methodology by which they would proceed.

In the final analysis, it is the members of the RCAF themselves who must receive credit for this book. They were worthy successors to that great generation of pioneers who found their way into the field of aviation before a Canadian air force was formed. This volume is therefore dedicated to Canadian airmen in the RCAF from its earliest days, and those who served the organizations which will be described in the pages to follow.

Abbreviations

A/AMAS	assistant air member for air staff
ABC-I	Anglo-us Defence Plan, 1941
ABC-22	Joint Canadian-United States Defence Plan No 2, 1941
AC	army co-operation squadron
ACHQ	Area Combined Headquarters
ACI	Atlantic Convoy Instructions
ACNS	assistant chief of the naval staff (RCN)
ACT	army co-operation training squadron
ADC	Aircraft Detection Corps
Adm	Admiralty records at the Public Record Office, England
AFCS	Air Force, Combined Staff (Washington)
AFGO	Air Force General Order
AFHQ	Air Force Headquarters
AFRO	Air Force Routine Order
AFU	Advanced Flying Unit
Air	Air Ministry records at the Public Record Office, England
AMAS	air member for air staff
AMO	air member for organization
AMP	air member for personnel
AMS	air member for supply
AMSO	air member for supply and organization
AMT	air member for training
ANS	Air Navigation School
AOC	air officer commanding
AOCinC	air officer commanding-in-chief
AOS	Air Observer School
App.	appendix
A/S	anti-submarine
ASB	50 centimetre air-to-surface vessel radar
ASD	3 centimetre air-to-surface vessel radar
ASG	10 centimetre air-to-surface vessel radar
ASV	air-to-surface vessel radar
ASW	anti-submarine warfare

ASWORG	Anti-Submarine Warfare Operational Research Group (US)
ATFERO	Atlantic Ferry Organization
B	bomber squadron
BCATP	British Commonwealth Air Training Plan
B-Dienst	German naval radio intelligence service
BdU	*Befehlshaber der Unterseeboote* (German submarine headquarters)
B&GS	Bombing and Gunnery School
BR	bomber reconnaissance squadron
BS	Cornerbrook-Sydney convoy
BW	Bluie West, Greenland
BX	Boston-Halifax convoy
CAAATC	Coast and Anti-Aircraft Artillery Training Centre
Cab	Cabinet documents at the Public Record Office, England
CAC	coast artillery co-operation squadron
CAF	Canadian Air Force
CAFA	Canadian Air Force Association
CAM	catapult aircraft merchantman
CAS	chief of the air staff
CAHS	Canadian Aviation Historical Society
CCNF	commodore commanding Newfoundland Force (RCN)
CFS	Central Flying School
CGS	chief of the general staff
CHL	chain home low – early warning low flying radar
CinC	commander/commanding-in-chief
CMAB	Combined Munitions Assignment Board
CNA	Canadian Northwest Atlantic
CNS	chief of the naval staff
CO	commanding officer
COAC	commanding officer, Atlantic Coast (RCN)
COMINCH	commander-in-chief, US Fleet
Comm	communications squadron
CTF	commander Task Force (US Navy)
D/AMAS	deputy air member for air staff
DAE	director of aeronautical engineering
DAP	director of air personnel
DCER	Documents on Canadian External Relations
DCNS	deputy chief of the naval staff (RCN)
Defe	class of intercepted German radio messages at the Public Record Office, England
Det	detachment
D/F	direction finding
DHist	Directorate of History, National Defence Headquarters
DND	Department of National Defence
DNI	director of naval intelligence (RCN or RN)
DO	Dominions Office records at the Public Record Office, England
DOC	district officer commanding

DOD	director of operations division (RCN)
DOR	director of operational research (RCN)
DOT	director of operational training
DPO	director of plans and operations
DWT	director of warfare and training (RCN)
EAC	Eastern Air Command
EATS	Empire Air Training Scheme
ECFS	Empire Central Flying School
EFTS	Elementary Flying Training School
F	fighter squadron
FB	flying boat squadron
FIS	Flying Instructors School
FONF	flag officer Newfoundland (RCN)
FTS	Flying Training School
FY	ferry squadron
GMT	Greenwich Mean Time
GP	general purpose squadron
GR	general reconnaissance squadron
GRS	General Reconnaissance School
GS	Greenland-Sydney convoy
HF	high frequency
HF/DF	high frequency direction finding
HMCS	His Majesty's Canadian Ship
HMS	His Majesty's Ship
HNMS	His Norwegian Majesty's Ship
HOMP	Halifax Ocean Meeting Point
HQ	headquarters
HT	heavy transport squadron
HWE	Home War Establishment
HX	fast eastbound transatlantic convoy
IFF	identification friend or foe
IG	inspector general
ITS	Initial Training School
JAG	judge advocate general
JCS	Joint Chiefs of Staff (US)
K	composite squadron
LN	Quebec-Labrador convoy
LORAN	long-range aid to navigation
LR	long-range (aircraft)
MAC	merchant aircraft carrier
MAP	Ministry of Aircraft Production (UK)
MD	Military District
MEW	microwave early warning
MWT	Ministry of War Transport (UK)
NCO	non-commissioned officer
NCSO	naval control service officer

NDHQ	National Defence Headquarters
NHS	naval historian's files
NID	Naval Intelligence Division (RCN or RN)
NL	Labrador-Quebec convoy
NOIC	naval officer in charge
NRO	naval routing officer
NSHQ	Naval Service Headquarters
NWAC	North West Air Command
OC	officer commanding
OIC	Operational Intelligence Centre (RCN or RN)
ON	fast westbound transatlantic convoy
ONM	medium speed ON convoy
ONS	slow speed ON convoy
OR	operational research
ORB	operations record book
OT	operational training squadron
OTU	Operational Training Unit
PAC	Public Archives Canada
PARC	Public Archives Record Centre
PC	order-in-council
PJBD	Canada-US Permanent Joint Board on Defence
Prem	Prime Minister's office files at the Public Record Office, England
PRO	Public Record Office, England
QS	Quebec-Sydney convoy
RAAF	Royal Australian Air Force
RAF	Royal Air Force
RAFDEL	RAF delegation, Washington
RCAF	Royal Canadian Air Force
RCMP	Royal Canadian Mounted Police
RCN	Royal Canadian Navy
RCNAS	Royal Canadian Naval Air Service
RFC	Royal Flying Corps
RN	Royal Navy
RNAS	Royal Naval Air Service
RNZAF	Royal New Zealand Air Force
ROYCANAIRF	cable address for RCAF Overseas Headquarters, London
SAO	senior air officer
SASO	senior air staff officer
B	Sydney-Cornerbrook convoy
SC	slow eastbound transatlantic convoy
SFTS	Service Flying Training School
SG	Sydney-Greenland convoy
SH	Sydney-Halifax convoy
SO	senior officer (of a convoy escort group) or staff officer
SONAR	sound navigation and ranging
SPAB	Sydney-Port aux Basques convoy

SQ	Sydney-Quebec convoy
Sqn	squadron
T	transport squadron or Treasury records at the Public Record Office, England
TB	torpedo-bomber squadron
TCA	Trans Canada Airlines
UK	United Kingdom
UKALM	United Kingdom air liaison mission
US	United States
USAAC	United States Army Air Corps
USAAF	United States Army Air Forces
USN	United States Navy
USNA	National Archives of the United States
USS	United States Ship
VLR	very long-range (aircraft)
WAC	Western Air Command
WEF	Western Escort Force
WESTOMP	western ocean meeting point
WHO	Western Hemisphere Operations
WLEF	Western Local Escort Force
WOAG	wireless operator (air gunner)
WPL 51/52	US Navy hemisphere defence plans
WS	Wireless School
WT	wireless telegraphy/radio
XB	Halifax-Boston convoy
Y	radio wireless service/intelligence (British and Canadian)
Z	naval designator for GMT
ZTPG	series of German naval messages

PART ONE

Between the Wars

Air Commodore A.K. Tylee and C.W. Cudemore, left, arriving in Calgary during the trans-Canada flight, 1920. (RE 20776-19)

Air Vice-Marshal Sir Willoughby
Gwatkin, inspector-general of the
Canadian Air Force, 1920–2.
(PL 117508)

Air Commodore A.K. Tylee, first air
officer commanding the non-permanent
Canadian Air Force, 1920–1.
(PMR 82-189)

A crated Felixstowe F3 arrives at Vancouver, one of the gift aircraft acquired from Britain in 1919–20. (PA 114756)

Curtiss HS2L flying boats at Dartmouth Air Station, 1920–1. The United States Navy turned over a dozen of the versatile aircraft to Canada at the end of the First World War. (RE 17725)

'Eye-e-e-e-e-s Left!' A column of airmen salute the RAF ensign, raised at Camp Borden, 30 November 1921. (RE 13081)

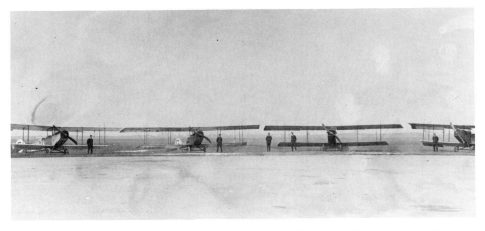

In 1921–2 the CAF's Ground Instructional School at Camp Borden constructed four Curtiss Jennies from spares left at the camp after the war. (RE 12816)

Felixstowe F3s on the slipway at Winnipeg, 1921. These large flying boats, obtained from the United Kingdom at the end of the war, were uneconomical for bush flying. (RE 13548)

Officers of the Canadian Air Force: left to right, Flight Lieutenant A.T.N. Cowley,
Squadron Leader A.E. Godfrey, and Pilot Officer E.L. MacLeod at Jericho Beach,
Vancouver, 1921. (PMR 79-288)

Clair MacLaurin and his Air Board crew in Felixstowe F3 G-CYDI at Jericho Beach,
Vancouver, 1921. (PA 28591)

Jericho Beach, Vancouver, was the principal west-coast air station in the 1920s. (PMR 84-976)

Victoria Beach Air Station, Man., in its early days, with two Felixstowe F3s in the foreground. (PMR 84-975)

Civilian Air Board mechanics change an engine in a Felixstowe F3 flying boat at Victoria Beach in 1922. (PA 053249)

Vickers Vikings being readied for a summer season's civil operations in the Manitoba bush. The RCAF aimed to start flying as soon as the inland waters were free of ice. (PA 53340)

RCAF sub-base, Cormorant Lake, Sask. Through the 1920s forest and photo patrols were extended across the Prairies. (PMR 82-160)

Operating a camera from an open cockpit. This demanding, tedious, and often cold work was the RCAF's contribution to mapping Canada's hinterland. (PA 062960)

The Curtiss HS2L was a workhorse of the air force's civil operations in the 1920s. (PA 140637)

Squadron Leader Robert Logan displays an RAF ensign at Craig Harbour, Ellesmere Island, during his 1922 Arctic expedition. (RE 13080)

Squadron Leader Basil Hobbs and his crew prepare for their extensive 1924 reconnaissance of the water routes in northern Manitoba and Saskatchewan. Their gear overloaded the Vickers Viking, forcing them to remove its wheels and tail skid. (PA 140640)

Avro 504KS on the flight line at Camp Borden. Inspections of the trainees and their aircraft were a familiar occurrence. (PA 140639)

Norway House, the principal base for civil government air operations in northern Manitoba and Saskatchewan. (PMR 82-155)

On 1 February 1927 the RCAF began pilot training courses at Camp Borden for NCO pilots. The first three, A. Anderson, R. Marshall, and A.J. Horner, received their wings on 30 April. (RE 16603)

Three Fokker Universals on the Hudson Strait Expedition, 1927–8, where the open-cockpit, enclosed-cabin monoplanes proved their worth. (RE 13778)

A Fokker Universal readied for an ice patrol at Base 'B' in the Hudson Strait. Engines and oil had to be pre-heated for starting in Arctic temperatures. (RE 13826)

Fordson tractors were used to move aircraft and heavy equipment during the Hudson Strait Expedition. (RE 13772)

Fairchilds on the spring ice at Lac du Bonnet, Man., 1929. (PMR 82-154)

Group Captain J.L. Gordon, director of the RCAF, 1922–4, and senior air officer, 1932–3. (PMR 85-90)

Under the careful eyes of sun-helmeted judges, airmen struggle over – and under – an obstacle course during a sports day at Camp Borden in 1929. (PMR 82-167)

Flying Officer E.A. McNab at left, Flying Officer F.V. Beamish, RAF, centre, and
Pilot Officer E.A. McGowan, members of the RCAF's first aerobatic team, the
Siskin Flight, Rockcliffe, 1929. On 15 August 1940 McNab was the first member of
the RCAF to shoot down an enemy aircraft. (PA 62612)

The graceful Vickers Vedette was the RCAF's main aircraft for mapping and bush flying
by the early 1930s. (PMR 82-162)

A Vickers Vancouver, straining its engines in a futile attempt to pull itself free from an early freeze-up. It later had to be dismantled on the spot. The twin-engined Vancouver was usually used to support operations by the smaller Vedettes. (RE 64-2668)

Airmen's canteen, 119 (Auxiliary) Squadron, Hamilton, Ont. (PMR 77-258)

'Mr Vice – The King.' Observing the military niceties of a mess dinner at Camp Borden. (RE 12821)

J.A. Wilson, secretary, Canadian Air Board, 1920–2, controller of civil aviation, 1922–41, and director of air services, Department of Transport, 1941–5. (PL 117438)

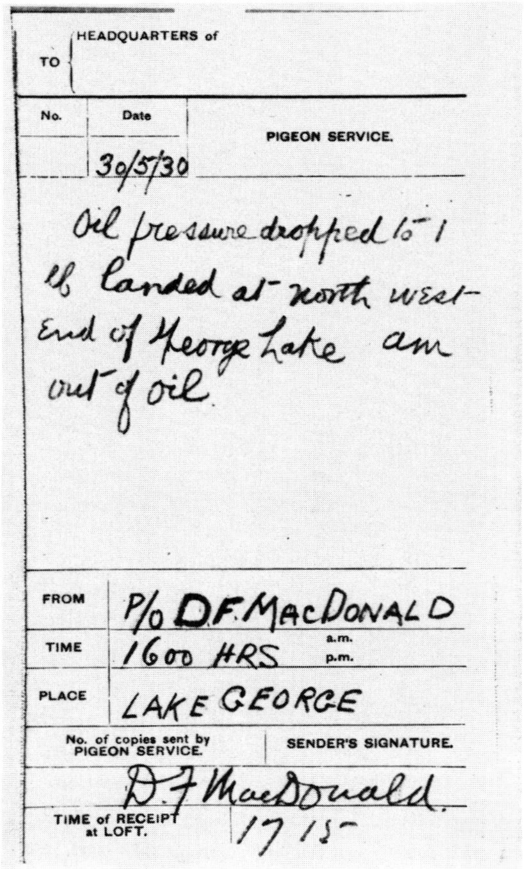

HEADQUARTERS of
TO

No.	Date	PIGEON SERVICE.
	30/5/30	

Oil pressure dropped to 1
lb landed at north west
End of George Lake am
out of oil.

FROM	P/o D.F. MacDonald
TIME	1600 HRS a.m. p.m.
PLACE	LAKE GEORGE

No. of copies sent by PIGEON SERVICE.	SENDER'S SIGNATURE.
	D.F MacDonald

| TIME of RECEIPT at LOFT. | 17 15 |

In an era before the widespread introduction of reliable radio equipment for aircraft, homing pigeons provided an essential means of communication. (PL 9336)

RCAF Station Trenton in the 1930s. (PMR 82-157)

The British airship R-100 at St Hubert, Que., 1930. The runways and other facilities, built to support airship operations, proved more lasting than the dirigible experiment. (PMR 73-562)

Squadron Leader A.E. Godfrey, MC, AFC, in the RCAF's curious interwar full-dress uniform, which included a fur-trimmed leather cap complete with plume. (PL 117416)

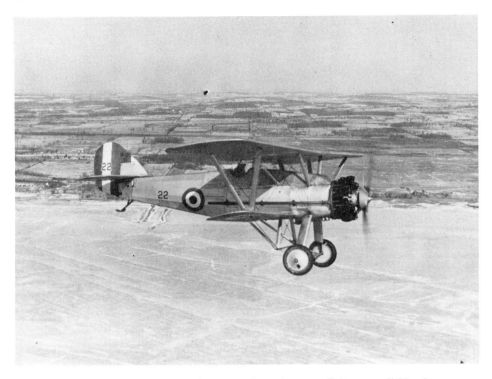

A few Armstrong Whitworth Siskins were the only RCAF fighters until Hawker Hurricanes were purchased in 1939. (RE 64-2646)

The RCAF acquired several Westland Wapitis, the force's only bombers in the 1930s, at bargain-sale prices. 'From the pilot's point of view the aircraft was a beast ... it glided like a brick.' (PA 063307)

Until the Second World War the RCAF used the Armstrong Whitworth Atlas for its army co-operation role, particularly on militia summer manœuvres. The bar and hook arrangement under the fuselage was used for snatching messages from the ground. (PA 063304)

An Armstrong Whitworth Atlas on a message pick-up at Camp Borden. Note the two rifles used to suspend the line. Army co-operation procedures did not advance beyond First World War practice. (PMR 82-183)

Prewar gunnery training, 112 (Auxiliary) Squadron, Trenton, 1936. Pilot Officer A.H. Olloway takes aim at a target simulated range of 200 yards, while Corporal S.C. Martin, the instructor, looks on. (PMR 85-71)

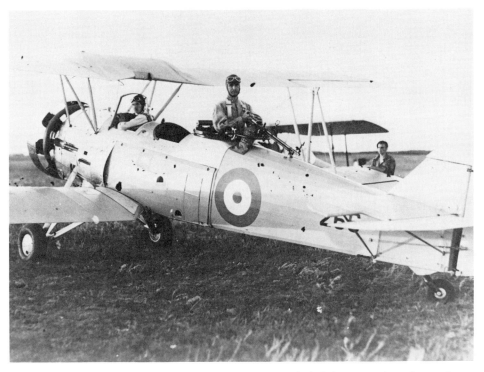

Preparing for war at Camp Shilo, Man., in an Avro 626, July 1939. (RE 18552-1)

Packing parachutes at Trenton, 1939. (PMR 74-275)

A Blackburn Shark drops its torpedo during a training exercise off Vancouver Island in the summer of 1939. (PA 141381)

A Hawker Hurricane of 1 (F) Squadron over Vancouver in the spring of 1939 – one of the first monoplane fighters to fly over Canadian territory. (PA 501526)

Introduction

In the immediate aftermath of the First World War, Canada's need for an air force was not readily identifiable. The country faced no discernible external threat. Canadians had little appreciation of the potential of airpower and little enthusiasm for expenditures on such esoteric military commitments. A minuscule active militia and an even smaller navy had served the national interest in prewar years and would continue to do so, but there was no institutional tradition for an air force to build upon. Thousands of young men had served in the British flying services during the war, but they had served as individuals and they returned home as individuals. A few had briefly become national heroes through their exploits, but memories of their achievements were bound to fade. The short-lived Canadian Air Force, formed in England during the last months of the war, had been left in limbo by the Armistice, without links to the Canadian Corps abroad or the Department of Militia and Defence at home.

The initiative for responding to the challenge of the air age was left to a small group of middle-ranking civil servants in Ottawa. The initial interest of men like J.A. Wilson and C.C. MacLaurin lay in converting the expansive potential of aviation, so clearly demonstrated in war, to constructive peacetime uses, a focus of commitment which coincided nicely with the prejudices of an unmilitary people tired of war and a government bent on economy. The real foundations of a nation's airpower, it was reasoned, lay in the widespread development of civil aviation, including extensive commercial operations and a healthy aircraft manufacturing industry. This in turn would provide the foundation on which a military air force might later be built.

Largely at Wilson's and MacLaurin's urging, the government delegated responsibility for aviation to an autonomous Air Board in the summer of 1919. The board based its approach on a broad, generalized conception of airpower, concentrating particularly on the promotion of civil flying in the more remote and sparsely populated regions of the country. The board's first tentative step towards creating a military air force was to establish a small non-permanent Canadian Air Force along 'militia' lines, firmly tied to the civil sector and intended to be used in close conjunction with it. After the formation of a unified Department of National Defence in 1922–3, the Royal Canadian Air Force emerged as a permanent force, although a directorate of the army. The RCAF did not achieve full independence until 1938, but from the beginning the force granted its own commissions, wore its own light blue uniforms, and used rank titles paralleling those of the fully independent Royal Air Force.

The RCAF's ties with the past remained intact through the officers and men, the originals, who had served with its predecessors during the First World War. Nevertheless, its duties were more closely related to civil than military operations. In its early years, the RCAF found its *raison d'être* in pioneering the application of aviation technology to an array of challenging tasks – forest patrolling and firefighting, aerial surveying and photography, exploratory flights, medical rescue, aerial policing, crop and forest dusting – in hitherto inaccessible areas of Canada. The force had responsibility not only for its own narrow service concerns but also for overseeing the development of the entire field of Canadian aviation. RCAF officers and airmen found themselves with tasks ranging from registering civil aircraft and controlling Canadian air space to supervising the design and construction of machines and attempting to stimulate an indigenous aircraft industry. The RCAF was also significantly involved in, and affected by, the transformation of Canadian aviation in the late 1920s, when in only a few years waterborne aircraft were replaced by wheeled machines using a national airway of interconnected airfields in the populated southern portion of the country.

The RCAF's civil functions were focused inwards, towards the economic development of Canada's hinterland, while the force's service traditions were directed outward to Britain and the Empire-Commonwealth. Even while its primary concern was civil flying operations, the RCAF preserved a measure of military identity by participating in exchanges with the Royal Air Force and by sending officers and airmen to training courses overseas, especially to the RAF Staff College and the Imperial Defence College. Then, when the somnolent 1920s gave way to the international anarchy of the 1930s, the RCAF was converted into an almost exclusively military force. Since it alone had the potential to defend the Atlantic and Pacific coasts from air and sea attack, it became the favoured of the three services, charged with the responsibility for providing Canada's first line of direct defence.

1
The Birth of the RCAF

When the Canadian government decided at the end of the First World War to disband both the Royal Canadian Naval Air Service and the two-squadron Canadian Air Force in Britain, the future of aviation in Canada was left in considerable doubt.[1] Four years of bloody fighting had ushered in the military air age, but few Canadians were aware of the extent or implications of the change. The war had been fought a long way away. The well-publicized exploits of Canadian airmen had generated excitement and pride, but not much understanding of flight or support for the development of a national air policy. A knowledgeable government official lamented that '90 per cent of the people in Canada have never seen an aeroplane and consequently are not alive to the possibilities.'[2]

The government's piecemeal wartime approach to aviation, moreover, had left a badly fragmented inheritance. No single minister, department, or agency had been made specifically responsible for aviation. The scattered aeronautical resources accumulated over the previous four years were disposed of as casually as they had been acquired, except for the air stations at Dartmouth and Sydney. These, together with twelve Curtiss HS2L flying boats, remained the only tangible legacy of the short-lived RCNAS and the 1918 anti-submarine patrols along Canada's east coast. The Royal Air Force soon abandoned all but one of its training bases in Ontario, leaving only Camp Borden to be turned over to the Department of Militia and Defence. The thousands of airmen overseas were demobilized as quickly as they gained release from their British squadrons. The result was that 'every month sees the dissolving and diffusion of this valuable manpower, which has cost millions to consolidate, and will cost millions to re-create at a later date.'[3]

The first object of any postwar aviation policy would be to arrest the drift. In the process the place of military aviation in the country's defence structure would have to be considered, and a suitable relationship between aviation's civil and military sectors sought. There were few guiding precedents. The state of the art had advanced remarkably in the decade since J.A.D. McCurdy took the *Silver Dart* precariously into the air. Bombers – their designs easily modified to civilian purposes – now had a range of 1300 miles with a payload of 7500 lbs, flying at nearly 100 mph at heights of 10,000 feet. Smaller machines could fly higher and faster. War needs, quite naturally, had channelled the course of technological development. The processes of civil design, invention, and production could now be expected to assert themselves.

The immediate post-Armistice months, however, were not a promising time for innovation in Ottawa. Formed in 1917 to implement conscription and fight the war to its conclusion, Sir Robert Borden's Union administration lost much of its credibility, if not legitimacy, with the Armistice. The prime minister himself was preoccupied with international and imperial affairs, spending much of his time abroad, and his Cabinet lacked sustained direction. There was, moreover, little apparent support in Parliament or the government for aviation; certainly the young air veterans were not well placed to have much impact on the people who mattered. One close observer, after discussing aviation with a number of parliamentarians, found that 'with one or two exceptions they know nothing at all … they say "Yes, I have read the stories about our aviators and they are brave men, but about the possibilities of aviation in Canada we know nothing."'[4] Another suggested that the Borden government was 'somewhat skeptical' about aviation.[5]

The prime minister, it is true, had included aviation in the mandate he set for the Reconstruction and Development Committee created in 1917. Among other things the committee was to 'consider the future possibilities of air service for certain national purposes,' under the general rubric of transportation.[6] That same year Borden asserted that the 'formation of the Canadian Air Force would doubtless tend toward giving a greater impetus to the interest which will be taken here in aviation after the war.'[7] Little happened, however. Although he was chairman of the Reconstruction Committee, Borden did not involve himself in its deliberations on policy, leaving the details to his vice-chairman, A.K. Maclean. He received the reports of the British Civil Aerial Transportation Committee in May 1918, but held them for five months before finally passing them along to Maclean without much comment. At the end of the war Borden wrote from London that there should be 'one service for both military and naval purposes';[8] from Paris a few months later he added that 'in any permanent military organization Air Service must have an effective part.'[9] That was the extent of his contribution; a peacetime aviation policy would have to be generated elsewhere.

Participation in the aviation discussions at the Paris Peace Conference in 1919 demonstrated, to begin with, the need for domestic legislation to guide national aeronautical development. In Europe the control of international aerial traffic was already an issue that could not be avoided. Aircraft could take to the air, but there was no mechanism for regulating cross-border flights, monitoring their progress, or setting common safety standards for aircraft and crews. Consequently, the International Commission on Aerial Navigation convened in Paris in 1919 to arrange an international regulatory system. Borden delegated Colonel O.M. Biggar, the judge advocate general, and Arthur Sifton, the minister of customs and inland revenue and a former premier and chief justice of Alberta, to represent Canada in its deliberations.

As in many other areas, Canada's aviation interests diverged from those being pressed by the British government, which incorrectly assumed ready colonial acceptance of strong imperial leadership. Sifton reacted scathingly to British attempts to impose a European-based, centralized system to control international air space, pointing out to the prime minister its irrelevance to North America. 'An International Air Convention,' Sifton wrote in his unruly prose,

is the latest and probably the worst case in which an effort is being made to take advantage of the presence of representatives of different countries here to foist on them an absurd, poorly drawn document, evidently prepared by people without the slightest knowledge of the subject of which they are dealing, aside from the actual flying and that under war conditions when the rights of non-flyers and even states remained in abeyance. The whole subject of air traffic from a commercial standpoint is so utterly unknown, that for anyone to sit down and attempt to draw a treaty for the civilized world is a manifest absurdity, and to attempt without consultation to include a country like Canada where if commercial air traffic is a success it will be of vastly more importance than it is likely to be in any of the countries who are assuming to settle the matter, is a blunder that would generally be called a crime. The only excuse that I have yet heard for the haste is that a factory in Great Britain is very anxious to start work making airships.[10]

Sifton's perspective was that of a jurist and not an airman, but his sense of differing British and Canadian aviation needs was accurate. The British were primarily interested in establishing aerial transportation between European population centres, flying over relatively short distances with ready access to ample ground facilities. Canada's problems were quite different: vast distances, an almost complete absence of ground facilities, and a strong international connection only with the United States. As a result, Sifton concluded, 'I could hardly credit the fact that a country like Canada for instance with a boundary line of four thousand miles over a large portion of which aircraft could start or land without any assistance from an aerodrome and which would be largely interested in air traffic, could ever agree to be governed even in regard to technical matters by a commission meeting in Paris ... and having one representative out of probably fifty.'[11] Yet the international convention finally accepted in Paris provided a convenient framework for Canadian flying regulations adopted in 1920.[12]

Regulations were needed. Before 1914, flying had been informally supervised, where it had been supervised at all, by Canadian affiliates of the *Féderation aéronautique internationale*. During the war, civil flying was restricted under the War Measures Act. When the war ended the Aero Club of Canada had been prepared to assume a supervisory role. In February 1919 it grandly informed the government that its parent, the Royal Aero Club, had delegated it 'entire control for the Dominion of Canada, and [the Canadian branch] is now engaged in issuing aviator's certificates to officers of the Royal Air Force and others who can pass the required flying tests.' In the same letter it also urged the Cabinet 'to enact legislation at an early date, governing flying throughout this country, as in a large measure the future of aeronautics depends on the attitude and policy of the Canadian Government.'[13]

Safety alone demanded more formal control. Early in 1919 the Canadian head of the Imperial Munitions Board, Sir Joseph Flavelle, began to dispose of hundreds of now surplus Curtiss Jennies which Canadian Aeroplanes Ltd had assembled in Toronto. Flavelle, however, 'hesitated to make sales in Canada to sundry persons desiring to buy, until regulations are established in which flying shall be authorized and the necessary repair shops available.'[14] Overcoming his reservations, Flavelle found an American purchaser for most of the obsolete machines who, in turn, sold some of them to sundry Canadians for barnstorming and joyriding across the country.[15] Some aircraft, apparently, ended up in less than responsible hands. A former RAF officer living in Toronto complained a few months later that there was '"stunting" over the center of the city at extremely low altitudes. In fact, yesterday, there was a plane "spinning" not more than a couple of hundred feet above my house. Some day we will have a "proper" crash here and then the "fat will be in the fire."'[16] Not long afterwards an aircraft crashed in Winnipeg killing two passengers and seriously injuring the pilot.[17]

These concerns were readily shared by a small group of officials in Ottawa, and it was they who were the real authors of Canada's postwar aviation policy. The Department of Militia and Defence was the department most directly involved but, as Sir Willoughby Gwatkin, the chief of the general staff, said in 1919, 'Everybody's business is nobody's business. Nearly every Department of State is concerned but no one Department is charged with aviation.'[18] The most immediate difficulty therefore lay in clarifying jurisdictional responsibility. To fill the vacuum Gwatkin drafted an order-in-council for his minister in February 1919 extending the militia department's wartime control and permitting the appointment of an air board to supervise all aspects of aviation development.[19] The Cabinet, however, declined Gwatkin's submission. It seems likely that it was unwilling to confide aviation to military direction while its future was so uncertain.

Gwatkin's interests, in truth, ranged far beyond military aviation. In 1917 he had been opposed to a separate Canadian air force, considering it unnecessary and militarily inefficient, but he thought then that one 'should undoubtedly be formed' after the war. Furthermore, he had pointed out, 'if the C.F.C. [Canadian Flying Corps] is to be a success, it must be something more than a unit of the Canadian Militia. To some extent it should be commercialized, working in conjunction, for example, with the Topographical Surveys, Geographers' and Forestry Branches of the Department of the Interior, perhaps with the Post Office Department, certainly with the Department of the Naval Service.'[20] By early 1919 he foresaw an air board with the widest mandate:

multifarious are the questions with which it would have to deal. Here are some of them: The acquisition of aerodromes, aeroplanes and aeronautical equipment, by purchase or otherwise, from the Imperial Munitions Board; the use to be made of pilots and mechanics trained during the progress of the war; international conventions and domestic legislation; aerial transport in its civil and commercial aspects; the transport of mail, express freight and passengers; the control of private enterprise; industrial development; the standardization and inspection of machines; licenses and certificates; meteorological observations and technical research; air routes, air charts, landing grounds and wireless stations; the establishment of bases, depots and parks; forestry protection and the protection of fisheries; the execution of surveys; excise and police; defence and prohibited areas; co-operation with the Royal Navy; the organization of a Canadian Air Force; the formation of an Imperial Air Staff; the assistance to be rendered towards the establishment and maintenance of an Imperial Air Service.[21]

Ways of adapting aviation to productive peacetime use also interested a few well-placed federal public servants. As early as 1915 Charles Camsell, deputy minister of mines and resources, had proposed using flying boats for transporting geologists to isolated locations. Foresters wished to experiment with aerial patrols to control fires which annually burned uncounted acres of woodland, and both the Ontario and British Columbia governments wrote to Ottawa about airborne fire patrols in 1919-20.[22] Aerial survey intrigued others. Neil Ogilvie of the Geodetic Survey thought that aerial photos could be used in topographical surveys to aid mapping. The surveyor general, Edouard Deville, noted that aerial photo survey was 'more a problem of aviation than a problem of surveying; if the photographs can be obtained economically there is no difficulty in making good use of them for mapping. They would be particularly useful for the exploration of unsurveyed country if the lack of landing places can be overcome.'[23] J.J. McArthur of the International Boundary Survey, whose surveyors were practised in photographing regions from mountain tops, suggested the use of airships, which had the great advantages of range and endurance.[24] Parliamentary support came from Alfred Thompson, the member for the Yukon, who spoke glowingly of the possibilities of the 'largest undeveloped oil field in the world' in the Mackenzie River valley. Mineral deposits in the region promised to be more extensive than those of the Cobalt, Porcupine, and Klondike fields. 'The scientists could by airplanes be taken from almost any part of the northland into the very heart of this country in a few hours, and they could stay there through the summer and come out in the fall. There need be no fear of a lack of landing places. The country abounds in lakes and rivers and an airplane could land on a river or lake almost anywhere.'[25]

These ideas were imaginative but largely unfocused. Nor were they attuned to aviation's technical dimensions until two officials of the Department of the Naval Service gave them a hard, practical edge. J.A. Wilson and Major C.C. MacLaurin had become interested in the peacetime uses of aviation while working together during the war. Wilson had joined the Department of the Naval Service in 1910 and was its director of stores and subsequently assistant deputy minister. MacLaurin was among the first Canadian pilots trained at the Curtiss Flying School and enlisted in the RNAS. He flew coastal patrols off Britain before going on staff in Washington and then Ottawa. He and Wilson worked on the departmental committee which organized the Canadian Naval Air Service. Their experience persuaded them of the almost unlimited potential for using aircraft, especially flying boats and seaplanes, in the Canadian environment. In November 1918 Wilson wrote the first of his many papers on aerial development – 'Notes on the Future Development of the Air Services Along Lines Other Than Those of Defence' – and early in 1919 MacLaurin circulated his 'Memorandum

Regarding the Formation of a National Canadian Air Service.'[26] The papers
shared a number of common themes; both authors freely borrowed ideas from
within the international aviation community and undoubtedly discussed them
with the Ottawa bureaucrats who were thinking along similar lines. Perhaps their
most valuable contribution was to cast theoretical possibilities in a pragmatic
and politically acceptable institutional framework.

Wilson and MacLaurin argued that aviation must be developed at the national
level, and that the federal government should create the necessary regulatory
mechanism. Only Ottawa had the resources to promote development on the
broadest scale. While they took due note of the military factor, both emphasized
the primacy of civil aviation in the postwar years. There were almost limitless
possibilities for employing aircraft – in forestry patrols, surveying, policing,
transportation. These, Wilson pointed out, were 'largely Government operations, and a national air service would very largely pay for its own maintenance
and cost, and the existence of such an organization would obviate the necessity
for subsidizing companies to undertake the work.' Several government
departments, he noted, were already considering how they might utilize aircraft
in their work, but each was faced with large start-up costs in forming its own
aerial organization. A centralized air service made available to interested
departments would be more economical and efficient. Large savings would also
be realized, both Wilson and MacLaurin stressed, if flying boats and seaplanes
were employed, thus avoiding the immense capital costs of constructing
aerodromes for landplanes. 'The whole subject is fraught with so many
possibilities, promises such great developments and the time is so opportune,'
Wilson concluded, 'that it would appear only reasonable that the Government
should take some steps so that the whole problem should be carefully examined
and that some action should be taken without further delay to consider seriously
the whole subject of Aerial Transport, not only within Canadian territory, but
also how it will effect [sic] Canada in her external relations.'

Of the many common features of their proposals – a centralized, federally
controlled air service with multi-purpose civil functions – Wilson's and
MacLaurin's commitment to hydroplanes was perhaps the most significant and
appealing. While climatic extremes and inhospitable terrain naturally restricted
flying in Canada, the biggest topographical asset was provided by an abundance
of lakes and rivers. Both seacoasts, the great lakes system, the major river
networks, and uncounted minor lakes and rivers provided the basis of a national
aerial communication system. There were, of course, plenty of fields and open
spaces where landplanes could take off and land, but building equipped airports
would be prohibitively expensive. Canada already had in place a costly,
overdeveloped rail network, and the possibility of generating the capital
investment which an airway would need was remote. Early action was vital,
MacLaurin concluded; 'The United States is preparing a gigantic Aircraft
policy. Practically every other country in the universe is awake to the
possibilities and is preparing a progressive programme. Should Canada not have
a National Service, a service embodying all the principal branches, a public
utility in connection with aeronautics and an industry that will, within a

few years, compare with motor-car building, shop building, or even rail-roading?'

Both Wilson and MacLaurin were convinced that once civil aviation was developed comprehensively the military sector would follow in good time. A nation's airpower, they reasoned, could not adequately be defined in narrow, purely military terms. Rather, it comprised the sum of aviation's many parts: a viable commercial sector, a healthy aircraft manufacturing industry, widespread training and instructional facilities, technological research, and an active programme of experimental flying operations. Wilson, in particular, had been profoundly influenced by his experience with the Royal Canadian Navy in its formative years. He often cited as appropriate to aviation an analogy with the growth of sea power, emphasizing the close association of the Royal Navy with the Merchant Navy. In Wilson's view, the failure to foster a like relationship had been a fatal flaw in the prewar RCN. 'I spent the best ten years of my life in that endeavour,' he wrote to Charles Grey, editor of *The Aeroplane*, 'and know how true it is that the house was built on sand and had no permanence.'[27] Without a solid civil foundation, Wilson concluded, the navy was never able to muster the material, technological, and moral support it needed to prosper; consequently, it remained an artificial construct imposed on a disinterested public, fighting a continual rearguard action for survival.

Wilson was convinced that a similar fate awaited any attempt to develop Canadian aviation on a narrow military base. As he later explained in the *Canadian Defence Quarterly*, he believed that the First World War had distorted the development of aviation, and that 'there should be an interim period, during which civil aviation might have time to build up [its] organization.' 'Had there been no war, it is probable that the development of the civil uses of aircraft would have preceded the military uses. The natural growth of civil aviation from small beginnings would have resulted in a healthy, sound and useful development as time went on, confidence was gained and new outlets for aviation were discovered. The immense military development has retarded civil aviation not only by stopping it entirely during the war, but also by giving the study of aeronautics an unnatural bent and false direction.' Military aircraft were 'far too costly to operate successfully under peace conditions,' and designers had to turn their attention 'to producing economical, low-powered aircraft, which, by their efficiency, make up for their lack of power.'[28] Concentration on civil aviation would redress the imbalance between civil and military development. Strong public involvement would be required, both to regulate the air space and fly experimental operations until they could be assumed by private companies. The military organization that followed would be able to take advantage of the sound material and technological structure that had been established. Such a structure would, Wilson argued, 'automatically create a self-supporting aircraft industry and a reserve of trained pilots and mechanics for the air defence of the country.' If the government were to adopt Wilson's views as policy, 'there would be little necessity for the maintenance of any permanently embodied Air Force units, other than those existing for staff and training purposes. The permanent Air Force would be almost wholly an organization of that kind, containing the

picked men of all classes engaged in aviation as instructors and staff officers.'[29]
The full development of aviation was a precondition of true airpower, on which
effective military aviation ultimately depended.

These ideas had the force of logic, economy, and consistency. Not content to
leave the future to chance, Wilson and MacLaurin circulated their proposals to
influential individuals and groups. Publicity could also help, and it is likely that
they had a hand in an editorial which appeared in the spring 1919 issue of the
Canadian Forestry Journal. The forestry industry was becoming impatient with
government inaction, and the *Journal* had received 'communications from many
senior aviators who looked upon an aerial forest patrol as a simple, effective and
inexpensive proceeding.' Moreover, the editors 'understood that topographical
survey, the geodetic survey, the Royal Northwest Mounted Police, and the Post
Office Department are thoroughly convinced of the advantage of airplane
service in increasing their efficiency and in certain instances reducing their cost
of operations.' While the bureaucracy was persuaded, however, government
ministers appeared uninterested, and 'a refusal on the part of a Cabinet Minister
to take action gives an instant quietus to the departmental agitation.' The forest
industry could not be similarly ignored: 'Those bodies ... which have taken an
interest in Canadian forest policy are not as sensitive to this official denial and
may be depended upon to intensify their requests until proper consideration is
given.'[30]

Perhaps as a result of such lobbying, perhaps because some action was
necessary, Wilson was asked to prepare legislation for Cabinet consideration in
March 1919. He had a draft ready within two days, arguing for the creation of an
air board to set and implement general aviation policy. Cabinet sent the
document for review by the service chiefs, sitting as the Naval and Military
Committee. Wilson suggested that the board should provide advice to the
government on air defence, but this was unacceptable to the service chiefs. Since
it was still unclear whether any future Canadian air force would be completely
independent or incorporated into the older services, neither the militia nor the
navy wanted to surrender any freedom of action or authority, real or potential.
They therefore advised that the board's mandate be restricted, so that it would do
no more than 'co-operate' with the armed forces until peacetime defence policy
and organization had been settled.[31]

Thus modified, Wilson's paper formed the basis of the government's first
postwar aviation bill, presented to Parliament on 29 April 1919. It stipulated a
five-to-seven member air board with a minister of the crown as chairman, and
representatives of the Departments of Militia and Defence and the Naval
Service.[32] Speaking on behalf of Cabinet, A.K. Maclean admitted that the board
was only a temporary expedient: 'the Government has no settled policy in
respect to aeronautics.'[33] Like the government, opposition members were
content with a flexible enabling authority to experiment and set policy in a field
about which they knew little. They called for only a few additional details and
some assurance that wartime flyers would receive due recognition. The bill
passed after perfunctory debate.

Although Wilson had recommended that board members have technical knowledge and expertise, the better to comprehend, evaluate, and guide programmes and activities, the Cabinet assembled a panel more attuned to the realities of politics.[34] Two Cabinet colleagues joined Arthur Sifton, the chairman, on the board – S.C. Mewburn, minister of militia and defence, and C.C. Ballantyne from the Naval Service – along with R.M. Coulter, deputy postmaster general, and E.S. Busby, a customs officer. O.M. Biggar, as vice-chairman, was chief executive officer and, after a few months, Wilson was appointed secretary. Biggar and Wilson were good choices. Biggar's experience at the peace conference had introduced him to some of the complexities and technicalities of aviation; both men were superb organizers with extensive and influential contacts in Ottawa's political and bureaucractic world.

The Air Board met for the first time on 25 June 1919. A letter from the minister of finance, Sir Thomas White, was immediately put on the record: 'from a financial point of view alone, it was out of the question that aerial services should be generally established by the Government.'[35] Board members, even so, agreed that about $500,000 would have to be spent over the next year. Aircraft would have to be maintained, meteorological and wireless services established, air regulations prepared, and a permanent staff recruited.

The government halved the Air Board's estimate, and in the end the board spent only $100,000 in the first year. This was enough to make a solid beginning. Within a month of the Air Board's first meeting it had settled its internal organization, establishing a certificates branch to license pilots and aircraft and perform other regulatory functions, an operations branch to conduct government flying, and a secretariat. Not long after a technical branch was formed. The board's organization roughly paralleled, and was probably modelled on, the British Air Ministry.

Recruiting for the new organization posed certain problems. Most wartime flyers were still in their early twenties; few had any experience of civilian employment, and the characteristics of an effective combat pilot were not necessarily those of a civilian flyer. The Air Board wanted men with 'good records,' not only as fighting pilots but also as administrators, a requirement that effectively disqualified most wartime flyers who had served as relatively junior officers on squadron service.[36] Furthermore, as a civil agency the Air Board was obliged to hire its staff through the Civil Service Commission, conforming to the normal government career pattern leading to a pension after half a lifetime of service. The board, however, wished to avoid long-term commitments to men who would be too old for operational flying long before they qualified for a pension. It took some time and discussion before the commission could be persuaded that this was a special case, and accepted the principle of making three-year appointments.[37]

Recruiting began in July 1919. Wilson and Lieutenant-Colonel A.K. Tylee, whose wartime experience had included command and staff experience with the RAF's Canadian training organization, formed the selection board, and vacancies were widely advertised. Though the board wished to give preference to wartime CAF members,[38] few applied. Some, like Raymond Collishaw, accepted RAF commissions; others, like W.A. Bishop, W.G. Barker, and R.H. Mulock, had taken up civilian careers. Among those who did join the Air Board was Robert Leckie, whose wartime career included command in 1918 of the short-lived CAF in Britain. He joined the RAF in 1919 and was seconded to the Air Board as director of flying operations. Lieutenant-Colonel J.S. Scott, another of the few air veterans with administrative experience, became superintendent of the Certificates Branch. The salaries of Leckie and Scott were less than those for comparable service rank and responsibility. Scott, for example, received $4500; as a militia lieutenant-colonel he would have earned $4970.[39]

The first Air Board was the object of some criticism because it included neither a military officer nor a representative of the Department of the Interior, the civil department most concerned.[40] In the spring of 1920, as the board began its first season of field operations, its membership was altered. By an order-in-council of 19 April the more 'professional' body recommended by Wilson the previous year received official sanction. The chairman was now Hugh Guthrie, minister of militia and defence, although the board did not function in any sense under that department.[41] Organizational continuity was ensured through the reappointment of Biggar and Wilson. Leckie and Scott represented the board's operational and regulatory functions, Captain Walter Hose the navy's interests, and Edouard Deville those of the Department of the Interior. Finally, there was Sir Willoughby Gwatkin, recently retired as chief of the general staff and now air vice-marshal and inspector general of the new Canadian Air Force.

Despite the inclusion of the quiet, intellectual, witty Gwatkin on the new board, military aviation was to play a subordinate role in the scheme of things, at least in the early stages. In the confused aftermath of war Canada's future defence needs were as vague as the country's external obligations with which, presumably, they had to be co-ordinated. Moreover, defining an appropriate role for military aviation within the shrunken peacetime defence structure was bound to be difficult. Canada's armed forces were still patterned on the British model and, in Britain, wartime arguments supporting the principle of unity of the air, which had led to the creation of the RAF in 1918, were being challenged by both the army and navy.[42] Until that question was resolved and Canada's postwar defence posture determined, the board's military aviation policy remained of necessity partial and temporary.

There was, however, an issue outstanding from the war which forced the board to early action in mid-1919. When the British government formally offered Canada and the other dominions a gift of surplus aircraft in June 1919, a caveat was attached, the 'object of His Majesty's Government being to assist Dominions wishing to establish air forces and thereby develop defence of the Empire by air.'[43] This was sufficiently vague to invite contrary interpretations, and it promptly did. The possibility of obtaining aircraft had first been raised with the RAF in March by the Canadian Overseas Ministry[44] (at the same time that, independently, Wilson was drafting the Air Board Act). Soon afterwards the ministry staff began selecting surplus machines from a variety of combat and training types. They were interested in aircraft suitable for the military air force they had been pressing on Borden since the Armistice. The Cabinet decision not to repatriate the overseas squadrons as a military unit disrupted these plans, leaving the status of the British offer in doubt.

Lieutenant-General R.E.W. Turner, Canada's senior military officer overseas, thought the 'offer may be withdrawn should the Canadian Air Force not be proceeded with.'[45] Consequently, the Overseas Ministry chose to apply the narrowest interpretation to the British condition; that is, that Canada would have to maintain a military air force if it were to be given the airplanes. The ministry informed the Air Board that it had stopped selecting aircraft until 'a definite statement that machines would be accepted in terms of the offer' had been received.[46]

The Overseas Ministry perhaps viewed the aircraft as a convenient lever to pressure the Cabinet into accepting a military air force. Fortunately, the British were flexible. Their chief of the air staff, Sir Hugh Trenchard, told the Canadian liaison officer in London, Major D.R. MacLaren, that 'it is the policy of the Air Council and the Air Ministry to further in every way possible the efforts of Dominions to establish Air Services either for Military or Civil service purposes.'[47] MacLaren, in turn, informed the Overseas Ministry soon after that 'No stipulation has ever been put forward by the Air Ministry that these machines must be used for military purposes only.'[48] When Wilson visited London in October 1919, he found Trenchard was 'rather disappointed with the Canadian Government not seeing their way to maintain a Fighting Force,' but he agreed that 'it was far better to start on a small scale and work up than have a large programme have to be cut down and perhaps disrupted altogether.'[49] Wisely, the British government chose not to involve themselves further in what was clearly a Canadian decision.

The Air Board – barely functioning at this time – wanted the aircraft. While its projected operations were not absolutely dependent upon them, the surplus machines would expand the board's capabilities at little additional cost, and Colonel Biggar became alarmed at the prospect of losing them. He immediately told the Overseas Ministry that 'Terms of Imperial offer thoroughly understood and purpose outlined by Air Ministry is what Air Board has in view,' adding it was 'Most important that machines should be secured.'[50] The types of aircraft initially selected were all landplanes – DH9s, DH9As, Bristol Fighters, SE5s, Dolphins, and Avro trainers – whose utility would be severely limited in Canada by the almost complete absence of adequate ground facilities. The board's primary need was for flying boats and seaplanes, which could be quickly deployed on civil duties. Biggar requested that the discussions with the Air Ministry be reopened with a view to obtaining more flying boats. He also wanted to ensure that sufficient ancillary equipment was included with the aircraft to make them readily operational: 'it is the opinion of the Air Board that they would rather have a small number of machines, and such additional Technical Equipment as to ensure their operations being successful, than to have a large number of machines without such equipment.'[51]

The negotiations with the Air Ministry continued but were only partially successful. Despite Trenchard's apparent support, the equipment staff in the Air Ministry found it did not have enough surplus flying boats to meet all the

Canadian requests.[52] They found eleven Felixstowe F3s, two Curtiss H16 boats, as well as one Fairey IIIC seaplane. Besides these, the final list included sixty-two Avro 504 trainers, twelve each of DH9As, DH4s, and SE5As, along with one Bristol Fighter and one Sopwith Snipe. There were also twelve airships, six kite balloons, and a generous amount of spares and technical equipment. The lot, conservatively valued at more than $5 million, was collected by the wartime CAF's rear party, packed, and shipped to Canada, the first crates reaching Camp Borden early in 1920.[53] As a separate item, the Air Ministry also turned over to Canada a number of captured enemy aircraft. These war trophies, however, were not intended to be used other than for exhibition purpose, as 'what it is desired to avoid is the pushing into prominence of enemy-built aeroplanes ...' Consequently, the Air Board did not take them on its charge and some were given to interested museums.[54]

While the surplus aircraft obtained from Britain did not dictate the form of Canadian aviation policy – it was already being shaped before the British offer became an issue – they did provide the Air Board with the means of equipping a military training organization which would complement and expand the board's overall programme. When Biggar was negotiating the acquisition of aircraft, he had hinted at the type of training organization the board was considering. 'Although the Government has not approved of the establishment of a Canadian Air Force as a permanent force,' he told the Overseas Ministry, 'it ought to be possible to organize some sort of militia force, if the machines are available, without too heavy an investment, and the question of organizing such a force will be one of the first subjects for the decision of the Air Board.'[55]

The idea of forming a non-permanent militia air force was a natural extension of the views of those who were mainly responsible for shaping postwar aviation policy – Biggar, Gwatkin, Wilson, and MacLaurin. It was also an ingenious and pragmatic solution to a perplexing dilemma. Any Canadian air force at this time had to be many things to many people: economical yet efficient, unobtrusive yet effective, unmilitarist yet military. A case for maintaining a new fighting service which promised only to be very expensive was not easily made. As the recently elected leader of the opposition, William Lyon Mackenzie King, asked in the House, 'Where does the Minister expect invasion from? ... defence against whom?'[56] Merely to raise the questions illustrates their complexities. What sort of air force would best suit Canada's defence needs? For what contingencies should it prepare? Against what threats might it concentrate its efforts? How many squadrons and of what types – bomber, fighter, reconnaissance – would it require? A non-permanent militia organization, solidly in the Canadian tradition, would enable the government to skirt the tough political, strategic, and technological obstacles that inhibited the immediate development of military airpower. Moreover, it could be organized quickly by making use of the many wartime flyers who wished to maintain their connection with aviation without taking up flying as a career.

Colonel Biggar sought the Air Board's concurrence to form the Canadian Air Force as a non-permanent service at its sixth meeting, on 28 November 1919. Specifically, he suggested three initial steps: that an invitation be issued to former officers and airmen to enlist on the understanding they would be called for active duty no more than five weeks in any two years; that authority be obtained to form provincial Canadian air force associations to administer the service; and that the British Air Ministry be asked to release RAF reserve officers from their obligations once they joined the CAF. The board members agreed, and asked Biggar to prepare a formal recommendation for submission to the Cabinet.[57]

Biggar's proposal was a significant statement of aviation policy. It began by embracing unreservedly the principle that air forces would play a significant role in any future war, their relative importance increasing progressively 'the longer the period intervening before the commencement of such a war.' Having accepted the need for an air force, the problem lay in determining its most effective form. In Canada's case, the probability of severe financial limitations meant that 'a professional military air force must, by reason of its cost, be so small as to be almost negligible in war, since war strength in the air will, as in other branches, depend primarily upon numbers.' There was also the need continually to turn over flying staffs. Consequently, there would be no place for those 'who are beyond the average efficient flying age for war flying,' making 'the profession of a military air force officer ... a "blind alley" profession from which he must be compelled to retire at a comparatively early age.' In combination, 'these difficulties and objections weigh so strongly against a purely military air force as to practically exclude resort to it.'[58]

Biggar emphasized, however, that aviation employed skills and equipment which, even more than the other services, were 'capable in a large measure of useful exercise in peace.' Relatively few air force officers might perform 'useful civil duties, such as mail carrying and surveying'; most civil flying would be done by commercial companies, whose pilots would constitute an air force reserve. 'It follows, therefore, that war strength in the air must ultimately depend upon civil or commercial air strength; that most of the members of a war air force must normally pursue peaceful occupations (preferably, but not necessarily, in connection with air navigation), that war formations should exist only upon paper and not in the form of embodied units, and that war training should be periodic, intensive and widespread.' Even training and administrative cadres should be made up of 'civilians temporarily assuming military duty.' Biggar acknowledged this would be less efficient than having regular staffs, but 'peace efficiency is not the primary consideration.' In fact, '[a] war organization so constituted as to be comparatively inefficient in peace but reasonably efficient in war is very greatly to be preferred to a war organization which shows a high degree of efficiency in peace but breaks down when it is called upon for war service.'[59]

The government accepted Biggar's reasoning and approved the CAF's formation in February 1920. Rather than framing specific legislation, the Cabinet acted by order-in-council,[60] relying on the permissive authority given in section 5 of the Air Board Act 'to employ such officers and men' as it might require. Their decision was unfortunate. It was a tenuous foundation on which to organize a national air force.[61]

Sir Willoughby Gwatkin became inspector general of the CAF in April 1920. The Air Board wished to offer the position of air officer commanding to Colonel R.H. Mulock, who had commanded the RAF's No 27 Group – the special long-range bombing force formed in England near the end of the First World War, too late to be used.[62] When he declined because of business commitments, the board approached Lieutenant-Colonel A.K. Tylee, who accepted an initial nine-month appointment in the acting rank of air commodore and opened his headquarters in the Air Board offices at 529 Sussex Street in Ottawa on 17 May.[63] He was later joined by Wing Commander R.F. Redpath, Flight Lieutenant G.J. Blackmore, Warrant Officer H.H. Atkinson, Flight Sergeant F. Aldridge, and Sergeant A.H. McKay.[64] All of these, it must be emphasized, were untenured appointments in the non-permanent militia, terminable at will by either party, and conferring no pension rights.

The CAF regulations compiled by this headquarters staff over the summer of 1920 were adapted from those of the RAF.[65] Approved at the end of August, they made the air officer commanding 'responsible to the Air Board through the Inspector General.' The latter's task was to ascertain 'the state of discipline and efficiency in the air force from time to time and report to the Air Board all such matters as in his opinion require to be brought to notice.'[66] Broad policy and day-to-day administration were the work of the Canadian Air Force Association, which was formed in June 1920 by incorporating six members of the Air Board under the Dominion Companies Act.[67] Provincial branches (the Maritime provinces comprised a single branch) of the CAFA were manned by volunteer executive committees, each with a full-time secretary.[68] The central CAFA body in Ottawa set policy, while branches were made responsible for recruiting, maintaining rosters and records, selecting officers and airmen for regular training or for courts martial and other duties, and advancing generally 'the interests of the Canadian Air Force.'[69] This still left a wide array of responsibilities to individual commanding officers, charged (among other things) with promoting 'a good understanding,' preventing disputes, discouraging 'any disposition ... to gamble or to extravagance,' and checking 'any tendency ... to practical jokes ...' among the militiamen who made up their commands.[70]

Unlike their non-permanent army counterparts, all CAF officers and airmen were considered in continuous service but on inactive, unpaid leave except when on refresher training. Provisional commissions granted to suitable applicants in their highest previous RAF rank were confirmed on completion of the first training period. Officers invalided out of the RAF might be enlisted if judged capable of further productive service, and the usual RAF flying age limitations (for example, thirty-two years of age for flight lieutenants) were relaxed to avoid losing the experience of older pilots. When reporting for his first tour of training, each officer selected a specialty, such as administration, photography, or equipment, in which he could be employed when beyond flying age. All officers were eligible for CAF staff and training appointments, which were continuously rotated among those qualified every three to six months.[71] Royal Air Force ranks and traditional army ranks were both acceptable,[72] and apparently used interchangeably at the whim of the holder. Daily pay rates ranged from an air commodore's $9.50 to a pilot officer's $3.00; from a warrant officer's $2.05 to $1.00 for an air mechanic second class. Men on active duty longer than the training period received double rates for up to one year, and after that one and one-half times the norm.[73]

The uniform was distinctive. Styled after army dress, it featured a dark blue serge tunic and slacks, blue or white shirts and black ties, with white wing collars and bow ties for the mess. Army-style rank badges (crowns, stars, and stripes), and all insignia, including pilot and observer wings, were silver. A new CAF crest with the motto *Sic Itur ad Astra* ('This is the way to the stars') adorned cap, collar, and lapels. All ranks could wear either a field service or a forage cap, on the peak of which squadron leaders and above sported a row of silver leaves. Duty officers carried canes.[74] Air Commodore Tylee told the first convention of the Canadian Air Force Association that the uniform was 'democratic and economical'[75] and would enhance the identity of the service, but many incoming officers preferred their wartime ranks and outfits, particularly breeches. No one seemed to mind. As one recalled, 'for the first two years, at least, we were allowed to wear any combination of uniforms while on duty at the aerodrome. This was to permit us to wear out our old R.F.C., R.N.A.S. or R.A.F. clothing. At the Officers Mess we could wear anything (or next to nothing, in the hot weather) at breakfast or luncheon but we were always supposed to be dressed in C.A.F. blue at dinner.'[76]

CAF training was concentrated at Camp Borden, the wartime home of the RAF Canada flying training scheme.[77] It included machine-shops, schools, garages, offices, quarters and messes, a central heating plant, paved roads, a swimming pool, golf course, and tennis courts. Most important, there were eighteen hangars each able to house ten aircraft.[78] But when the newly appointed station superintendent, Captain G.O. Johnson, arrived on a snowy 8 January 1920, he found the buildings deserted, except for a caretaker and his assistant. Johnson and the nine men who reported for duty four days later had to find rooms in the nearby village of Angus, and travel the five miles back and forth to camp in sleighs while they reopened the buildings.

Their task was to prepare the base to receive the gift aircraft then en route by sea from Britain. The first arrived by rail in mid-January, packed in cases weighing two to four tons. These were, Johnson reported, 'lifted from the cars by means of a differential chain tackle, lowered onto a sleigh and drawn into a hangar by horses. It was a very slow and tedious process involving a lot of heavy work but gradually better equipment was acquired. Drifting snow was a great handicap, for every morning it was necessary to cut a roadway through the drifts by hand so that the sleigh could get into a hangar. During the month of February the drifts were from eight to ten feet deep.'[79] The spring thaw slowed unpacking until the men, who had to open up quarters and kitchens between shipments, rigged a wheeled, team-drawn trailer to replace the sleighs.

Hiring casual labour allowed the skilled mechanics to concentrate on assembling aircraft. All had been damaged in transit and needed careful attention before they could be flown, but Johnson had the first, an Avro, fitted with

Curtiss snow skids and test-flew it himself early in March. Johnson tested each of the other machines as it was assembled, including four DH9AS which were then shipped west for the first trans-Canada flight later that year.[80]

An advance party reinforced Johnson's crew for the training season. Sixteen officers and thirty-five airmen joined Squadron Leader F.G. Pinder, who arrived at the camp on 7 June. Of the first instructors, two, Flight Lieutenants A.A.L. Cuffe and N.R. Anderson, later attained air rank in the RCAF, as did two of their earliest students (at the camp for a refresher course), Flight Lieutenants W.A. Curtis and Harold Edwards. The medical officer, Flight Lieutenant H. Norman Bethune, was later a surgeon with the Communist forces in China. The first CAF reservist to complete a refresher course was Wing Commander J.S. Scott, who arrived on 16 August and completed his tour in eleven days before returning to his civil duties with the Air Board. Scott and most Air Board employees, as F.H. Hitchins has pointed out, were 'filling the dual role of civil servants under the Air Board and officers or men in the CAF, [and] represented the only permanent thread through the period of late 1919, when the Air Board began to develop, until April 1924, when the permanent RCAF came into being.'[81] Far outnumbering them, however, were those CAF trainees who were in occupations other than aviation, arranging through their provincial associations to report to Camp Borden when their circumstances allowed.

Subsequently, training was carried out by No 1 Wing, CAF. Formed at Camp Borden on 7 September 1920, it comprised a School of Special Flying equipped with Avro 504K trainers; 1 Squadron with two flights, one of SE5A single-seater fighters and another of DH9A bombers; and a ground instructional section to handle engine and aircraft repairs, wireless telegraphy, photography, gunnery, and navigation.[82] So far as possible both flying and ground training followed the RAF model. The instructors had all passed through the original School of Special Flying in England, which is described in the first volume of this history.[83] Regular refresher training began on 1 October, and by the end of the year 86 officers and 111 airmen had completed courses, and an additional 50 officers and 209 airmen were undergoing some form of training all year round. The camp's total for 1920 was 733 flying hours; for 1921 refresher training totalled 2620 hours.[84]

Camp Borden's informality encouraged initiative. R.A. Logan, who had spent the last years of the war in a German prison camp, was posted to No 1 Wing on 8 September 1920, where he organized the Ground Instructional School. 'When I took over the school,' he recalled, 'I had a big empty building, one or two corporal instructors and no typewriter. On my first trip to Ottawa I asked for a clerk and for a typewriter. I was told that there was not enough work for a clerk and less need for a typewriter. As I left Air Force headquarters that night I picked up a typewriter from one of the desks, carried it back to Camp Borden and kept writing letters to the C.O. to be provided with a clerk so that I would not have to devote so much of my valuable time to typing when I should be lecturing. I got my clerk and it must have been three or four months before the Ottawa office discovered that they had a typewriter missing and that it was at Camp Borden.'[85] Logan and his instructors salvaged useful instructional aids from Borden's considerable stock of wartime aircraft parts. They accumulated enough components to convince two NCO mechanics, Romeo Vachon and C.S. Caldwell, that they could assemble two complete machines. Logan agreed to teach both of them to fly if they were able to make the aircraft airworthy, and 'we eventually had not one but *four* Jennys in good flying condition.'[86]

Unfortunately, there were too few like Vachon and Caldwell. Although the provincial branches had little difficulty filling their officer quotas (1281 of 1340), the recruiting of airmen, especially qualified mechanics, lagged badly. Only 1350 had applied by the end of 1921 for 3905 vacancies,[87] and, at Camp Borden, the problem was aggravated by a lack of continuity and infrequent training periods. The small groundcrew pool, continually rotating through the Training Wing for a month at a time, provided all maintenance and repair, although most of its members had no previous training on aircraft. Only about 12 per cent of the airmen then enlisting in the CAF had air force experience. The small number of mechanics with wartime RAF service had gravitated towards more attractive employment, some with the Directorate of Flying Operations [DFO]. It took an estimated three to six months to train an automobile mechanic to a suitable standard of proficiency on aircraft engines or to convert a carpenter into an efficient rigger. Safety standards were bound to deteriorate unless enough qualified groundcrew were found, but the poor pay and lack of career development opportunities made it difficult to attract them. Meanwhile, aircraft had to be serviced. As Logan, who doubled as a representative of the Maritimes branch of the CAFA, pointed out:

The main trouble in getting the right kind of man here is that there is nothing to attract them ... A man may be here for a year and know as much as a man here for twenty-eight days. Very often a man leaves his own job to come here, and somebody else gets it. Until we can offer him something better, he is going to think twice before coming. We are getting two classes of men. The class out of a job will take anything. All he wants is to hang on until he learns just sufficient to keep him on. There is another class. The one who is coming to learn, who is not worried about the pay. He is considering training, and comes up for all the instruction he expects to get. As soon as he considers himself good enough, he will take up a civil position, because there is nothing to attract him to the CAF at present. As soon as we get a good man, and he gets the offer of a good job, he is gone ... So long as we are trying to run things as we are at the present time, I do not see how we are going to better it. In flying we must depend on mechanics, and nobody wants to fly in a machine that is liable to go to pieces. Good mechanics will not come at the present rate of pay. Most of the men are not here out of patriotism. It is for what they can learn. In the meantime we have got to entrust our lives to these men.[88]

Growing discontent about these unsatisfactory conditions came to the government's notice early in 1921. Two members of the Ontario CAFA, Lloyd Harris and R.W. Leonard, reported complaints made to them by CAF officers at Camp Borden. The problem, they thought, was the Air Board's policy of operating parallel organizations, one for civil and the other for military aviation. Both the DFO and the CAF employed staffs at Borden for equipment and stores, repair shops, and administration and recruiting, but the DFO civilians were much better off. Civil mechanics, for example, received permanent appointments, and their minimum rate of pay was $5.00 per day compared to $2.05 for the same class in the CAF. The immediate need, Harris and Leonard thought, was 'to bring the two branches together with one central authority and direction.'[89] Subsequently, efforts could be made to bring status and salaries into line.

The Air Board was aware of dissatisfaction,[90] but Wilson thought a strong military presence would be detrimental to the development of Canadian civil aviation. Any difficulties which had arisen, he claimed, were not from organizational faults but from the failure of officers employed in the military branches 'to carry out loyally the intention of the Air Board.'[91] He provided no specific examples.

Wilson's arguments notwithstanding, complaints were brought to the Air Board's attention when the CAFA branches convened at Camp Borden in June 1921. The civilian DFO and the CAF, it was argued, needed a professional permanent officer who could command and give direction to the whole of the operational flying system, both civil and military. Moreover, the air force needed a permanent staff. Stability and continuity could not be secured when command and staff appointments were rotated through officers who happened to be available for three- to six-month duty tours. As one of the Manitoba delegates complained:

We have yet to have defined to us the true significance of the Air Force Associations, whether our recommendations or otherwise receive the consideration they are entitled to … Unless we get better co-operation, with a permanent head, and at the same time, with a nucleus of a permanent staff, you cannot expect any one to come down and assume command here for one year and then get their walking ticket. Unless this breach is filled in some way, you are going to have a lot of resignations, the resignation of all the secretaries of the C.A.F.A. This will be done as a protest against the lack of co-operation … It is in the mind of everyone here that there is absolutely no co-operation between the two branches, and we firmly believe it would be in the best interest of flying to have a permanent head to look after the C.A.F. and civil flying.'[92]

Other criticisms were voiced. The DFO had been given a monopoly on civil flying, it was alleged, which eliminated competition and hampered the growth and development of civilian commercial firms. Delegates argued that some operations, for example those being conducted at cost for provincial governments, should be put out to tender with competing civilian aviation firms given preference over the DFO. There were also complaints concerning the board's centralizing training at Camp Borden and the testing of pilots seeking commercial licences by Ottawa-based Air Board officials when qualified CAF pilots in the regions were readily available as examiners.

It was ironic that the strongest arguments for a permanent cadre came from non-permanent CAFA members, while the CAF's only regular officer offered a restraining caution. Air Vice-Marshal Gwatkin warned the delegates that if the association pressed too strenuously, 'people who are jealous of military establishments' would set back whatever progress had been achieved.[93] He had already acknowledged many of the difficulties and was moving to correct them. At an Air Board meeting in March 1921 he had suggested, in the interests of economy, combining the two aircraft repair shops at Camp Borden under the CAF. He had also pointed out that it was not possible to perform repair and maintenance work effectively with a temporary staff employed for short periods of duty, and proposed to employ a regular nucleus of trained mechanics under a permanent superintendent 'who would be responsible not only for the execution of repairs, but also for the technical instruction of air mechanics under training at Camp Borden.'[94] The board had agreed, and Gwatkin now promised the CAFA that he would 'tell the Minister ... that the time has come when the Directorate of Flying Operations and the C.A.F. should be merged in one show, one department, under one head, and that head to be the C.A.F.'[95]

In July 1921 the board enhanced the degree of co-ordination between its civil and military components by making two important joint appointments. Wing Commander J.S. Scott, the controller of civil aviation, became the CAF's third commanding officer as well. At the same time Squadron Leader J.L. Gordon, an assistant director with the DFO, became the fourth commander of No 1 Wing at Borden. This represented only a partial solution. When it had formulated its military aviation policy in the fall of 1920, the Air Board had stressed that 'uncertainty on the point of the primary or ultimate purpose of an organization always results in confusion and inefficiency.'[96] The Camp Borden discussions revealed that many CAFA members were unclear about their role and that the part-time CAF pilots were not getting enough flying time. If the latter could not fly with the small DFO, they could look only to their one month's refresher training periods or to employment with commercial flying companies. The essence of the Air Board's developmental strategy had depended on a strong private sector which would absorb trained flyers looking for an outlet for their flying skills. Commercial aviation, the board expected, would not only make productive use of available pilots, but also create a demand for aircraft which would stimulate a domestic aircraft manufacturing industry. When, in the postwar depression, private aviation failed to prosper, the Air Board's strategy, and the hopes for a vital civil-military relationship which underlay it, were placed seriously into question.

The election in December 1921 of the Liberal government of Mackenzie King brought further problems for the board. The election had inconclusive results, continuing the disruption of the traditional Canadian two-party system which the formation of the Union Government had begun four years before. The new prime minister's chief political concern lay in managing a fragile, minority administration, while his policy preoccupation was to reduce government expenditures. His views on aviation were yet to be formed. Later King gave considerable support to civil flying in the 1920s and then to air defence in the 1930s. To this point, though, he had revealed little of his attitude, if indeed he thought about aviation at all. In opposition King had criticized the Conservatives' aviation estimates, particularly those on 'an air service for military purposes [which] is the height of absurdity.'[97] But it was an isolated reference. His party's emphasis on budget cuts, however, made Gwatkin wary. 'They are pledged to rigid economy; and what their attitude towards the C.A.F. will be, I do not know,' he wrote Trenchard, adding that 'I am a little afraid of an attempt being made to bring it under the Militia Council.'[98]

Gwatkin's antennae were well tuned. Since the war, proposals to integrate military forces had become fashionable. Both the British and American services debated the question, with Canadians as interested onlookers. Sir Arthur Currie, late commander of the Canadian Corps and inspector general of the militia, recommended integration to the government in 1920, but his suggestion was premature in the midst of rapid demobilization. Major-General James H. MacBrien, the chief of the general staff, had also become an ardent advocate of integration while serving on a number of British postwar reorganization committees. Within days of King's election, MacBrien sent him a proposal for consolidating the three military services in a single ministry of defence.[99] MacBrien's submission was strengthened by another from Currie, and a third from Eugene Fiset, the deputy minister of the Department of Militia and Defence. Currie suggested that service integration could 'effect a very large saving.'[100] Fiset was more specific, arguing that 'By such amalgamation a strong and experienced man could save between three and four million dollars a year ... by reducing (by amalgamation and absorption) the four different staffs now administering these different services – in reducing the Permanent Force and Permanent Staff of the Militia Department – the staff and rank and file of the Air Force – and the staff and ratings of the Naval Department.'[101]

King thought Fiset's 'a good suggestion.'[102] He found his 'strong and experienced man' in his one-time leadership rival, George P. Graham, a man with no military background but a reputation as a sound administrator. King issued firm marching orders: 'I want defence consolidated ... a "cleaning up" of the dept. and a "showing up" of expenditures and waste ...' He was, at first, doubtful 'as to Graham being firm enough for that,' but he need not have worried.[103] By mid-February King was able to note that 'a good deal straightened out on consolidation of defence forces.' He seemed unconcerned that one result of the reductions was that 'air force civil end abolished.'[104]

Graham introduced legislation creating a unified defence department in March 1922. Debate was insubstantial; Graham simply informed the House that he wanted 'to have a well organized, snappy defence force that will be a credit to Canada without being too expensive.'[105] The National Defence Act received royal assent on 28 June. It was short and general in nature, setting up the Department of National Defence under a minister of the crown 'charged with all matters relating to defence, including the Militia, the Military, Naval, and Air Services of Canada.'[106] The act was to come into force on 1 January 1923.

While the government's administrative intentions were plain enough, its underlying purpose was anything but straightforward. Military aviation would now come under the Department of National Defence, but the civil sector was set adrift, at least temporarily. Beyond his desire to cut costs, the minister displayed little apparent interest in the subject, and nowhere did he articulate a practicable alternative to the Air Board's approach. There was no attempt by Graham or any other political leader to define the first principles either of air defence or civil aviation. Rumours which had circulated that responsibility for civil aviation would be turned over to a civil department of government proved unfounded.[107] The government simply introduced additional legislation, the Aeronautics Act, which gave to the minister of national defence all the functions previously exercised by the Air Board.[108] Now he and his departmental officials had full responsibility for both military and civil aviation. It remained to be determined what they would do with it.

For the air force, military integration meant less the opportunity for a larger role than a threat of losing the status it had already gained. By this time the Canadian Air Force had achieved a real if ill-defined independent standing as a non-permanent service. Unlike the militia and navy it lacked the institutional advantage of its own separate government ministry, but the air force granted its own commissions, controlled much of its internal administration, wore a distinctive uniform, and, in practice, its headquarters and training staffs served as a regular cadre. Gwatkin had also opened a correspondence with the British chief of the air staff, Sir Hugh Trenchard, from whom he received considerable moral support. Their exchanges had resulted in an agreement for the CAF to adopt the RAF's ensign as its own; at Camp Borden, on 30 November 1921, it was hoisted officially for the first time, an important symbol of the air force's identity and its close relationship with its British counterpart.[109]

Moreover, CAF independence was tacitly acknowledged by the militia and navy, an achievement largely attributable to Gwatkin's enormous personal stature. In January 1920, while he was still representing the militia on the Naval and Military Committee, a joint services body, Gwatkin had suggested broadening its membership to include the Air Board. Colonel Biggar declined at the time, but suggested that the air force be invited once it had been formed. Gwatkin agreed. He also liked Biggar's suggestion that the committee be redesignated as the 'Defence Committee,' 'an embryo, which, after a period of gestation, might develop into an organization second only to the Cabinet in power and importance.' Eight months later, Gwatkin, now inspector general of the CAF, formally requested air force representation. This, and the change in title, was speedily approved.[110]

Gwatkin firmly supported the principle of consolidating Canada's defence forces, judging that it 'would make both for efficiency and for economy.'[111] But the principle of integration was one thing, its implementation quite another. While common administrative requirements might well be rationalized, Gwatkin wrote Trenchard, the CAF should be 'organized and administered as a third service.'[112] In the same vein he told MacBrien that he was 'opposed to the C.A.F. being brought under the Militia Council.' Rather, he wanted 'a Defence Council on which each of the three services would be represented.'[113]

By the end of 1921, then, Gwatkin had become anxious about the CAF's future, and with good reason. MacBrien, who had gained the minister's ear, believed (like most of his British Army peers) that the air force was a subordinate, supporting arm, not an independent military service. He had not participated in the discussions which had led to the creation of the Air Board; his perspective on aviation had been formed within the restricted confines of brigade operations on the Western Front. Especially in Canada, MacBrien wrote, the defence establishment 'will not be large enough to warrant a separate Branch of the Service such as the Royal Air Force, and our Flying Corps should be part of the Army with attachments to the Navy as required.'[114]

MacBrien's concern with the military aspects of aviation was probably confirmed from what he was able to observe of the Air Board's programmes. He had been an attentive listener at the CAFA convention at Camp Borden, observing not long after that 'the present organization of the Canadian Air Force is unsound and extravagant in the extreme. Its unsoundness lies in the association of civil servants and non-permanent airmen in the same Force. A friction of the most acute type is certain ever to be present in such an organization.'[115] Now he gave Gwatkin cold comfort regarding the future status of the CAF. 'If it be the policy of the Government to expand the present C.A.F. and increase the annual expenditure on it,' MacBrien told his old mentor, 'then, in my opinion, separate representation for C.A.F. on the Defence Council might possibly be justified but not otherwise.'[116]

A fundamental factor influencing MacBrien was the organizational imperative of ensuring that Canada's military structure conformed to the greater imperial pattern.[117] The relationship of the CAF to the militia, therefore, was largely dependent upon the fate of the RAF in Britain; if it managed to retain its independence there would be obvious pressures to keep the CAF much as it was. MacBrien was convinced, however, that the RAF's days were numbered. As his deputy, Brigadier-General A.G.L. McNaughton, advised: 'The best opinion inclines to the view that the Air Force is still in the stage of an auxiliary arm; it adds an increment to the power of the Army or Navy, but of itself it can do little. The value of the work performed in the air is in direct proportion to its sub-ordination [sic] to the wishes of the naval or military Commander concerned, and, while it is conceded that the progress of science and invention may ultimately make the Air Force capable of undertaking independent operations, it is recognized that that time is not yet.'[118]

It was MacBrien's intention to establish himself in the Department of National Defence as the senior military adviser to the government, through whom the navy, air force, and others would channel their own views on defence policy to the minister. He proposed making the CAF 'a purely military organization and a Corps of the Active Militia,' with permanent and non-permanent sections, headed by a director responsible to him as chief of staff. DND's new air directorate, replacing the Air Board, Directorate of Flying Operations, CAF Headquarters, and the controller of civil aviation and technical branches, would need a headquarters of only five officers and ten clerks because the air force could call on the more senior and experienced militia staff.[119] Officers would receive common militia commissions (temporarily employing air ranks and nomenclature when seconded for air duties), thus extending their military careers beyond operational flying age.[120] The result would give the CAF a relationship with the army much like that of the Royal Flying Corps to the British Army during the greater part of the war.

The minister, Graham, was content to let MacBrien lead, and in the weeks before Parliament approved the reorganization scheme, the Air Board and CAF, along with the navy, could only fight a delaying action to preserve what they could. The Air Board reiterated that it 'was willing that all services not distinctly aeronautical in their nature should be pooled,' but emphasized that 'any effort made to divide its aeronautical functions among other organizations should be opposed.'[121] This advice was ignored. Biggar and Gwatkin submitted memoranda stressing the need for autonomy and unified direction if aviation was to be effectively developed. Reluctantly, Graham heard them out in a meeting of senior officials, but he was unmoved; 'nothing that can be said will alter the intention of the Government to carry out the proposed consolidation.'[122] With his 'only object ... economy and efficiency,'[123] the aviation budget was slashed 60 per cent to $1 million and, while Graham acknowledged that the navy's objections were making the reorganization 'a much more difficult and irritating task than anticipated,' he remained convinced that 'The co-ordination of the Air Force ought not to be difficult in working out. My colleagues and myself believe the best results can be obtained, and the least friction caused by, as far as possible, utilizing the services of the present Officers, having consideration of their rank, seniority, etc.'[124]

MacBrien's militia staff implemented the reorganization. They ordered the CAF Directorate to move to a location near the new departmental offices. The interim establishment of the force was sixty-nine officers and 238 airmen, recruited from those in the CAF and the DFO who wished to have a permanent military career. The National Defence staff began amalgamating supply, ordnance and equipment, pay, intelligence, medical, engineer, central registry, and library services, leaving the CAF without any direct responsibility but flying and aeronautical technical stores. The air stations operated by the DFO were to be closed following the 1922 summer flying season, replaced by air force training centres at Vancouver, Winnipeg, Camp Borden, and Halifax. CAF flying training at Borden came to an end, and all efforts were directed to the military training of those converting from civilian to service duties.[125]

Consolidation proceeded apace over the summer of 1922. However, even before its statutory authority was formally in place, the plan to incorporate the air force as a militia directorate – such as signals, engineers, and artillery – encountered unexpected difficulties. However much they may have wished to do so, Graham and MacBrien found they were unable to ignore the comprehensive legislative responsibility for all phases of aviation which the department had inherited from the Air Board. The department was the government's sole aviation agency, responsible for both military *and* civil flying. The manner in which it exercised its responsibilities to civil aviation are considered elsewhere; suffice it to say, MacBrien's ideas about the role of the air force as a civil force underwent rapid change.

MacBrien's views on the air force's status as a separate military service also changed. The lead came from London. In March 1922 the British government concluded that 'it would be a retrograde step at this time to abolish the Air Ministry and to reabsorb the air service into the Admiralty and the War

Office.'[126] The decision fundamentally altered the terms of the Canadian debate. MacBrien found himself trapped in his own logic. He and his staff had based their case against a separate air force on what they assumed would be a clear British precedent. The RAF's separate identity was now assured, and it followed that any Canadian air force had to be similarly organized.

On behalf of the CAF, Gwatkin immediately took note of the changed circumstances. He sent MacBrien an extract from the parliamentary debate in which the British government announced its decision, telling him that, in order to ensure imperial standardization, Britain 'has best right to specify the form, the common form, which organization should take,' and 'therefore, that – within limits imposed by local conditions – the Canadian Air Force should be organized on a system uniform with that of the R.A.F.'[127]

MacBrien moved slowly, but eventually asked his judge advocate general to review the legal implications of full or partial air force independence. The JAG reported in October 1922 that the CAF was currently operating under a mix of provisions derived from both the Air Force Act (Imperial) and King's Regulations and Orders (KR and O) for the Canadian militia. Once integration was completed, he pointed out, problems would inevitably arise when members of the militia and air force served together unless they were governed by common regulations. In addition, the jurisdiction over air force personnel by officers commanding military districts would have to be clarified, as would the scope of the Militia Pension Act, if the air force were to be brought under the army. 'The joint administration of both Forces,' he noted, 'might prove difficult and complicated, if it was carried out under an entirely distinct set of legislation, etc, for each Force so administered.'[128]

Whatever regulations were adopted, he went on, depended on the type of air force wanted. There was the British model, based on the premise that 'the functions of an Air Force are so entirely dissimilar to those of a land force that special and distinct legislation is desirable for the government of such force. If such a force was administered under an organization separate and distinct from that administering a land force nothing would be gained by having both forces administered under the one set of legislation.'[129]

If Canada accepted this model of an independent service, it was advisable to have specific legislation for it. The alternative was simply to make the CAF a corps of the militia (under Section 22 of the Militia Act which authorized the Governor-in-Council to create corps as it wished), a course the JAG preferred because both the militia and air force were located in the same government department. He reasoned: 'In Canada ... in view of the creation of the Department of National Defence, the situation is different [from Great Britain], and if, as a result of the amalgamation of the various Departments, the Canadian Air Force will become to all intents and purposes a Force corresponding to what was the Royal Flying Corps, Military Wing, then the administration of both the Air Force and the Militia under one set of regulations appears to be desirable.'[130]

On weighing the two options, MacBrien was apparently more impressed with the need to follow the RAF model. He appointed a staff committee to produce regulations for the air force which would combine the essential provisions of KR and o with those governing the RAF, informing committee members that 'It is considered wisest for the status of the Canadian Air Force to be kept as close as possible to the Royal Air Force.'[131] When the committee reported back early in January 1923 with an acceptable regulatory compromise,[132] MacBrien made his final decision. 'It is intended,' he informed the adjutant general, 'that the Air Force will be a separate Service from the Navy and Militia and that it will be divided into permanent and non-permanent sections.'[133]

MacBrien's departmental fiat was significant in permitting the air force to retain the autonomy it seemed to be losing. However, it by no means finally settled the question of service independence. Until just before the Second World War the air force remained subject to the direction of successive chiefs of the general staff. 'Service as a whole is, at present, administered as a Directorate of the General Staff,' MacBrien wrote in 1923. At the same time, he added, 'It is a separate service, and when its expansion so warrants, its administration will conform to the other services of the Department.'[134] Meanwhile, he wrote:

The objective aimed at in making an Air Force Directorate was to give the newly created Force the benefit of the experience of the senior Officers of the Militia stationed at Headquarters. At the same time it has been the endeavour to organize the Royal Canadian Air Force as a separate branch of the Service, so that it can without hindrance fulfil its full functions in case of war. One of the many reasons for the adoption of a purely military organization was that the Defence Forces of any country cannot be considered complete or effective if they lack a well trained military Air Force. This is generally accepted by all countries in the World in which Air Forces are maintained. Organization is based upon that of the Royal Air Force, so that should war again come to the Empire any unit that might be sent by Canada would be similarly organized and trained to those in other parts of the Empire.[135]

A mark of the air force's renewed status was a change in its title. At the 1921 Camp Borden CAFA conference one of the participants had suggested 'that His Majesty be approached and requested to use the name Royal Canadian Air Force.'[136] The notion gained unanimous support and the Air Board duly submitted such a request. It appears that nothing was done at that time, but in the spring of 1922 the idea was revived by Lieutenant-Colonel E.W. Stedman. He pointed out that the Australian Air Force had been made 'Royal' in the previous year. As he was leaving his post as inspector general of the CAF in April 1922, Gwatkin asked the chief of the general staff to seek permission for the CAF to do likewise, 'as soon as things have settled down ...'[137] Accordingly, on 5 January 1923, an application was sent to the governor general through the Department of External Affairs: 'Such a distinction would be most highly prized by all ranks and would add greatly to the prevailing esprit-de-corps.' Attention was drawn to the thousands of Canadians who had flown with the British flying services during the war, and 'by their efficiency, gallantry and devotion to duty added lustre to the name of Canada.' The survivors of this group had organized the new CAF.[138] After the Department of National Defence received notification of the King's approval, a Weekly Order, No 21/23 of 12 March 1923, placed it formally on record. It was subsequently announced that the Royal Canadian Air Force would adopt the light blue uniform of the RAF and use its motto *Per Ardua ad Astra* ('Through adversity to the stars'). The promulgation of air force regulations, on 1 April 1924, marks the official birthdate of the RCAF.[139]

Not all the pioneers made the transition from Air Board to RCAF. Colonel Biggar remained in government service as chief electoral officer and came back to civil aviation work in the mid-1920s. Robert Leckie resumed his interrupted RAF career, although he returned to Canada after the outbreak of the Second World War, eventually becoming chief of the air staff. Assured that his adopted service would be preserved, Sir Willoughby Gwatkin retired; the death in Britain of this remarkable officer in 1925 went almost unnoticed in Canada.[140] A much younger Clair MacLaurin died tragically in 1922. While station superintendent at Vancouver he took an HS2L into the air on a routine flight. Seven minutes later his machine dived into the sea off Point Grey and he drowned before he could be freed from the wreckage.[141]

Those who did join the RCAF formed a closely knit group whose influence on Canadian aviation flowed far beyond their limited numbers and slender resources. There were just sixty-eight officers and 307 airmen scattered from Dartmouth to Vancouver. All the young officers of the new air force, the most senior of whom were barely thirty, had some First World War experience as well as a postwar association with the Air Board. Over the next two decades they exchanged postings, appointments, and commands in the minuscule service. Thirty-three of the originals rose eventually to air rank, but at the beginning, with their director a mere group captain, they were clearly outranked by their more senior militia colleagues in the defence department. It was perhaps this factor which helped produce an internal cohesion able to surmount the inevitable personal and professional differences in a small, peacetime military force – between those with considerable combat flying and those with more staff and training experience, and between those with quite different backgrounds in naval and military aviation.[142]

Group Captain J.S. Scott, who succeeded Wing Commander W.G. Barker as acting director in May 1924, became the force's first full-time director on 1 April 1925.[143] A veteran of the British air services, Scott had earned a Military Cross on the Western Front before injuries sustained in a crash caused him to be invalided home. After commanding units in both Ontario and Texas as a member of the RAF's North American training organization, Scott left the RAF in 1919 and was soon appointed to the newly formed Air Board as controller of civil aviation. As a former commander of the Canadian Air Force and the first Canadian officer to attend the RAF Staff College, Scott was a logical choice as director. A no-nonsense commander – tough, forceful, and direct – his somewhat arbitrary manner was more apt to generate respect than affection during his four years as the RCAF's senior officer. Retiring in 1928, Scott returned to the RCAF in 1939 as a training officer with the British Commonwealth Air Training Plan.

The RCAF's three assistant directors were Squadron Leader G.O. Johnson (air staff and personnel), Wing Commander E.W. Stedman (supply and research), and J.A. Wilson (secretary). Johnson, the former commander of No 1 Squadron

CAF in England, had originally been appointed an assistant director when the Department of National Defence was formed in 1923. Posted to command RCAF Station Winnipeg in May 1925, Johnson held various commands and appointments including that of acting senior air officer from June to December 1933. As secretary, Wilson retained his responsibilities for civil aviation, and continued to exercise his considerable influence on organizational and operational policy. The RCAF's chief technical officer, Stedman, was a British-born and educated aeronautical engineer who joined the Royal Naval Air Service and ended the war as an RAF wing commander. Afterwards he became chief engineer with the Handley Page firm of aircraft manufacturers before being recruited by the Air Board to organize and head its technical staff. Stedman was intimately involved with all aspects of the RCAF's aircraft selection, testing, and procurement throughout the interwar and war years before retiring as an air vice-marshal in 1946.

Many other senior and middle ranking officers helped shape the air force in the early years of its development. Wing Commander J.L. Gordon, who had previously commanded the CAF as acting director from July 1922 until succeeded by Barker on 1 April 1924, also served as senior air officer of the RCAF from November 1932 until May 1933. A bilingual Montrealer who had attended McGill University, Gordon had joined the Royal Naval Air Service in 1916 and was awarded the Distinguished Flying Cross for his coastal patrols off Britain. He gained valuable experience while employed by the Air Board as superintendent in the Directorate of Flying Operations and commanding officer at Camp Borden. Less abrasive than Scott, Gordon was especially effective in working with the many civil government departments which had an interest in aerial operations. He also graduated from the RAF Staff College and became, in 1931, the first RCAF officer to attend the Imperial Defence College.

George M. Croil flew on operations in Salonika and the Middle East through much of the war, spending part of his time as T.E. Lawrence's pilot on missions into the desert. Released by the RAF in 1919, Croil joined the Air Board the following year and helped to establish the air stations at Morley and High River, Alta. He was sent overseas in March 1925 to serve as RCAF liaison officer at the Air Ministry prior to attending the RAF Staff College. After five years as commanding officer at Camp Borden, he returned to England in 1932 and completed the Imperial Defence College course. Croil succeeded G.O. Johnson as senior air officer in 1934 and became the first chief of the air staff as an air vice-marshal in 1938. Reserved and retiring, Croil's demeanour was in sharp contrast with that of Lloyd Breadner, acting director from 1928 to 1932, and Croil's successor as chief of the air staff in May 1940. Breadner was another former RNAS pilot, a bluff, hearty, and ebullient commander who later directed, in the Second World War, the RCAF's expansion into one of the world's largest air forces. Hired by the Air Board in 1920 as a certificate examiner, Breadner was commander of the RCAF's training centre at Camp Borden when the RCAF observed its official birthday on 1 April 1924.

The matter of the RCAF's status was finally settled, but its future role remained to be identified. The Air Board had found it both prudent and productive to consider airpower in its broadest sense, concentrating its efforts on building a firm civil base while allotting military flying a secondary priority. Now reorganization had eliminated the previously favoured Directorate of Civil Operations, leaving only a skeleton military air force whose actual functions were anything but clearly defined. A directive written at the time of its official inception in 1924 gave the RCAF three tasks: to carry on air force training, to maintain a nucleus around which a military air force could grow if required, and to conduct flying operations for other government departments.[144] The mandate was broad enough to ensure that events, not tidy preconceived doctrine, would determine the service's future.

2

The RCAF and Civil Aviation

It took until 1924 to complete the transition of the air force from a diffuse national movement to a small permanent military service. Although it emerged from the reorganization as the federal government's sole aviation agency, its role was anything but evident. As a military air force it fell heir to the legacy of Canada's fighting airmen of the First World War. It also inherited the Air Board's responsibility to oversee and control the entire spectrum of Canadian civil aviation. Relatively simple in the early years, that task became increasingly unmanageable as the civil sector grew and bush flying was complemented by the construction of an airway connecting Canadian population centres. During its first decade the RCAF attempted with only indifferent success to locate an appropriate balance between the sometimes compatible but often conflicting demands of military and civil aviation. It was an elusive goal, and the relationship between the two sectors was not always an easy one.

By the time the RCAF assumed responsibility for aviation, the Air Board had taken a number of key decisions concerning its development. Initially, there had been some disagreement within the board over the direction Canadian civil aviation might take. Robert Leckie and Colonel O.M. Biggar were attracted for a time by the possibility of using landplanes to carry mail between larger population centres. Biggar was certain that airmail carriage would come eventually and that it was the Air Board's duty 'to investigate, examine, and report on proposals,' but the idea was premature. The Post Office decided not to provide a service which promised only marginal improvement to its existing rail service. J.A. Wilson argued the brief for bush flying, and from the board's first meeting in June 1919 pressed for a forthright commitment that attention should be directed 'for the immediate future, to the question of air services along the natural waterways of Canada by means of flying boats.'[1]

Earlier that year Major C.C. MacLaurin had already proposed a forest survey experiment to the Saint Maurice Protective Association, which controlled the largest timber limits in the province of Quebec. Wilson arranged the loan of two of the Curtiss HS2L flying boats which the Department of the Naval Service had at Dartmouth, and the association hired a former RNAS pilot, Stuart Graham. Graham tested the first boat on 2 June, and three days later, with neither his tachometer nor his air speed indicator working, lifted off from Halifax harbour against a light wind. With him were his wife as navigator and a mechanic, Bill Kahre. Dressed in a pair of drill knickerbockers with puttees and an overcoat, Mrs Graham passed map information to her husband at the controls by a cord and pulley. Their route took them to Saint John, Lake Temiscouta, Three Rivers, and up the Saint Maurice River valley to Lac-à-la-Tortue. Doing their own maintenance, flying on low-grade motor gasoline, and fighting bad weather all the way, their memorable flight covered 645 miles in almost ten flying hours over three days.

Although Graham arrived after the spring fire season, he had a productive summer spotting fires, surveying forests, taking aerial photographs, and transporting company and government officials over vast remote regions. The forest association's manager was highly impressed, finding he was able to sketch timber stands rapidly and accurately from the air. Ellwood Wilson judged that a forester could get a clearer impression of a fifty-square-mile tract in a two-hour flight than in a two-week ground trek. He found that aerial photos could map 200 square miles a day, while a party of two men using a plane table could cover only a quarter of that area in a month. Wilson became an enthusiastic supporter of aircraft operations, and his report of the experiment, published in the British periodical, *The Aeroplane*, undoubtedly influenced others.[2]

The success of the forest survey provided a tangible demonstration of the worth of employing aircraft in remote regions and of the potential utility of similar civil operations. In the fall of 1919 the Air Board commissioned MacLaurin and three other officers, Major A.G. Lincoln and Captains J.W. Hobbs and G.O. Johnson, to conduct a national survey to determine 'what public services could more efficiently, and in the broadest sense more economically, be performed by air than by existing methods.' Each took a separate geographical region, and early in the new year they assembled in Ottawa to report to the board. Unsurprisingly, they recommended 'that the most favourable fields for commencement of operations were the less thickly settled and less thoroughly explored portions of Canada.'[3] The next week the board convened a meeting of departmental officials concerned with resource development to consider how to employ aircraft in their work. At the same time the newly organized Directorate of Flying Operations [DFO] located suitable base sites at Dartmouth, Roberval on Lac St Jean, Ottawa, Morley in the Alberta foothills, and Vancouver. Sub-bases were later added at Haileybury and Sioux Lookout, both communities in Ontario's rugged and sparsely settled Canadian shield. From these bare beginnings, made over the winter of 1919–20, evolved an ever expanding programme of government civil flying operations in the Canadian bush – a programme which was to preoccupy the Air Board, and then the RCAF, for the next decade.

Despite delays in getting aircraft from Camp Borden to their field sites, the DFO made almost 400 flights over more than 33,000 miles in a variety of tasks during the 1920 season. Dartmouth was used primarily to erect and repair seaplanes. From there, two HS2L flying boats were flown to Roberval, where they were employed in forestry patrols, reconnaissances, photographic surveys, and other tasks. Ottawa-based aircraft were flown to Haileybury transporting officers of the entomological branch of the Department of Agriculture on a survey of a large forest tract infested with spruce budworm. From a rudimentary landing strip at Morley, patrols of DH4 and Avro aircraft were conducted over the Rocky Mountain Forest Reserve. The patrols convinced the dominion forestry branch to dispense with the construction of a ground lookout system and to rely on air patrols instead. After securing facilities at Jericho Beach, Vancouver, the Air Board operated an HS2L throughout the fall months on forestry, survey, fishery, and transportation flights for the federal and provincial governments.

A trans-Canada flight, in which the Canadian Air Force would play a prominent part, was to provide a climax to the season's activities. There were, it is true, risks of failure, but it seemed to airmen of the day worth trying to prove the feasibility of transcontinental air transport. Besides, it offered an opportunity to demonstrate the capabilities of aircraft and crews, especially to commercial interests; and there was reason to hope that success would stimulate public support for the fledgling air force.

The Air Board was to complete the Halifax-Winnipeg leg by seaplane or flying boat, the Canadian Air Force taking over the Winnipeg-Vancouver portion of the flight with DH9A landplanes. Wing Commander Robert Leckie, accompanied by another RNAS veteran, Squadron Leader B.D. Hobbs, lifted off from Halifax harbour on 7 October 1920, but high winds buffeted their Fairey Seaplane so severely that its engine cowling came apart near St John, NB. In the HS2L flying boat ferried over to Leckie from Halifax, as a replacement for the seaplane, he had to struggle through driving rain storms all the way to Ottawa. The leg to Winnipeg was less eventful, although fog and radiator trouble caused problems at Kenora, and Leckie finally arrived at Selkirk, Man., a few miles short of his destination, on the morning of the 11th.

Two CAF officers, Flight Lieutenant J.B. Home-Hay and Air Commodore A.K. Tylee, began the second portion of the flight a few hours before Leckie arrived. Forced down by engine failure in Regina, Tylee had to use a replacement aircraft flown in from Moose Jaw by Flight Lieutenant C.W. Cudemore to continue on to Calgary. There they were met by Flight Lieutenant G.A. Thompson in another DH9A, and both aeroplanes set off over the Rockies on the 13th, again after a period of bad weather. Storms caused them to land in Revelstoke, BC, and it was not until 15 October that they were able to leave. A further two-day delay because of weather kept them in Merritt, BC, and it was not until the 17th that they finally arrived in Vancouver, 247 hours after Leckie had departed Halifax. This was by no means the success hoped for, and it taught the lesson that for the foreseeable future weather would determine when flying took place. Even on good days transcontinental operations would not be feasible without an effective ground organization and widespread maintenance and repair facilities.[4]

The 1920 season was a pioneering one, designed above all to demonstrate the potential of aircraft in a huge, diverse, and undeveloped land. The Air Board's major task in its early years was marketing and public relations: persuading potential users of the variety of ways in which aircraft could be put to practical use. Since this could only be done by actual operations, the board accepted almost any task which might produce tangible results. In late November 1920 the board convened a second interdepartmental conference to evaluate the season's results and lay plans for the following year. The attendance clearly indicated widening interest. The Department of the Interior was represented by the surveyor general, the commissioner of dominion parks, and the superintendents of the Natural Resources Branch, Geodetic Survey, and Forestry and Topographical Survey. The Commission of Conservation sent its assistant chairman and chief forester; the Department of Agriculture, the dominion entomologist; Marine and Fisheries, the superintendent of fisheries; and Indian Affairs, the inspector of Indian agencies. The commissioner of the RCMP and the deputy minister of mines also attended. A wide-ranging discussion took place, as a result of which the Air Board prepared a varied and ambitious programme of flying operations for the 1921 season.[5]

Operations in 1921 and 1922 built on those which had been started during the first summer. From Ottawa, photo flights were made over London, Ont., the Welland Canal, and the St Lawrence River system. Little flying was done at Dartmouth, but the Roberval forestry patrols were continued. A new base for forestry patrols was opened at Victoria Beach on Lake Winnipeg during 1921. The following year temporary sub-bases were established further north at The Pas and Norway House. In Alberta, the original base was shifted to High River because of the treacherous and turbulent flying conditions at Morley. Vancouver-based operations included mosquito eradication experiments for the Department of Agriculture and anti-smuggling patrols for the Department of Customs and Excise.[6]

By the end of the 1922 season the operations of the Air Board had developed considerably, and a firm beginning had been made to promote aviation more generally. The Ontario government had organized its own air service and civilian firms had taken root, such as the Laurentide Air Service and the Dominion Aerial Explorations Company which took over contract work for the Quebec government. More requests for aerial services were being received through the annual interdepartmental conference than could be accepted. Standing commitments for forestry patrols and aerial photography forged strong links between the Air Board and its principal user, the Department of the Interior.

The Air Board's burgeoning programme of civil flying operations was placed in some doubt when the Department of National Defence took control of government aviation. As we have seen in Chapter 1, Major-General J.H. MacBrien's initial impulse had been to reverse the civil-military relationship created by the Air Board and form a strictly military air force. The complaints he had heard voiced by non-permanent CAF officers during the 1921 Camp Borden conference had undoubtedly reinforced his own view that the air force should be staffed by regular officers. He therefore ordered the closing of Air Board stations at the end of the 1922 season and their replacement by four air force training bases at Vancouver, Winnipeg, Camp Borden, and Dartmouth.

Although MacBrien and his militia staff may have preferred to place military ahead of civilian development, they could not avoid an active role in the civil sector. The Department of National Defence had assumed the statutory authority originally assigned to the Air Board to regulate and control all aspects of Canadian aviation, and the department had an obligation to provide the necessary means to administer it. Air Vice-Marshal Willoughby Gwatkin, the retiring inspector general of the CAF, had attempted to retain something of the old relationship by suggesting that a civil branch be made directly responsible to either the deputy minister or MacBrien rather than the air force director, in order to maintain a clear separation between the civil and military sectors.[7] MacBrien declined, preferring to make the senior civilian official, J.A. Wilson, one of three assistant air force directors. This solution pleased Wilson least of all. He was so discouraged at first that he sought other employment, but within a few months, he thought that he had detected a change in attitude. 'General MacBrien and his staff are keenly interested in the Air Service and I am sure that things will work out very well in the long run. I do hope, however, that they will not insist on too much Air Force routine and discipline on the stations in the field as an excessive rule for this will certainly spoil the practical usefulness.'[8]

Since the government was determined to create a regular military air force, Gwatkin and Wilson pressed MacBrien to preserve the Air Board's civil flying programme. They were encouraged by his response. However military minded, MacBrien was not averse to civil flying operations which, he readily conceded, constitute 'excellent training for Military Operations.'[9] In April 1922 he asked Wing Commander J.L. Gordon, who was acting as director of flying operations, to draft an outline of the measures which would be necessary to enable the department to continue civil operations from the proposed CAF training bases. MacBrien and his deputy, Brigadier-General A.G.L. McNaughton, were becoming more aware of the potential advantages of an active civil role. McNaughton, in particular, was an ardent advocate of employing military specialists on productive civilian tasks. He seconded engineers to civil work, for example, and sent signallers to operate remote radio links throughout the north. Airmen could perform even more varied tasks, in the process enhancing the visibility and public presence of a barely tolerated military establishment at little additional cost.[10]

MacBrien and McNaughton must also have listened attentively to the parliamentary debate on the CAF's future roles when the minister, George Graham, introduced his aviation estimates in May. Although the government had no definite views on aerial development, the debate made plain that members were more interested in the civil rather than military aspects of aviation. 'What,' opposition members wanted to know, 'does the Civil Aviation consist of?'[11] And how, they asked, was it going to be affected by the reorganization then in progress? The minister's response was unenlightening. His governing principle, he stressed, was to reduce expenditure. Graham attempted to persuade the House of Commons that the budget ceiling of $1 million, which represented a 60 per cent cut-back from the previous year, would allow the CAF to continue the Air Board's civil operations on the same scale. This would be accomplished by charging users the full costs of their flying operations.

The opposition sympathized with Graham's intention of reducing expenditures, but they doubted that his method amounted to anything more than an obfuscating shell game. While the defence budget might be slimmed down, overall aviation costs would remain the same, their details simply buried in other departmental accounts if the level of operations remained as it then was. The government merely wanted 'a way of camouflaging it, of disguising it.'[12]

The parliamentary debate revealed more than Graham's bookkeeping idiosyncracies. It established the primacy of civil over military operations, even if the former were now to be flown by uniformed aviators. Only one opposition member queried the apparent neglect of the military sector. 'Why should men who are acting as fire rangers throughout the country be listed as part of the defence forces of the country?' Donald Sutherland, a future defence minister, asked if 'The air force was going to be a much more prominent feature of warfare in the future than it has ever been in the past.' Graham thanked Sutherland for his intervention, 'because my great trouble during the past two weeks was in the opposite direction. The majority of people complained that I was making this all military and not leaving any civil force.' He denied, however, that concentrating on civil operations would inhibit the development of a military capability. Echoing MacBrien, he pointed to the benefits of a close, continuing civil-military relationship: 'This work which they do in doing civil aviation is for civil purposes, but it gives them possibly the best training they can get. They are really training for defence purposes in the work they are carrying on. For instance, flying over the forests, photographing the ground beneath, is just the work they would be doing on the battlefield. While civil aviation is to be carried on, the bulk of it will be carried on by members of the Civil Aviation Force who will get the best training in air work in that way.'[13]

The path of least political resistance appeared to be in keeping the same pilots in the same aircraft on the same civil tasks as before, even if now the airmen would be in uniform. Pilots had previously been employed by the Air Board in a civilian capacity even though they held commissions in the CAF. The new arrangement meant that airmen would now be full-time air force officers who would spend their summer months flying civil operations. Ends and means were juxtaposed. Instead of having the military air force train pilots for civil operations, civil operations would now be used to train pilots for their ultimate military role. This approach also received the blessing of the British government at the 1923 Imperial Conference. The Air Ministry made it clear to the Canadian prime minister that 'it was preferable to have a military aviation to do the civil flying for the Government than to expect any civil development to serve a military end in time of need.'[14]

Despite their altered status, the fortunes of the military and civil spheres continued to be closely linked. The air force was left not only with the Air Board's programme of civil operations but also with its problems. Many soon surfaced. The board's efforts to persuade government officials of aviation's potential benefits had been all too successful. Requests for a variety of operations proliferated and the air staff found that, rather than having to cajole bureaucrats to use aircraft, it had to arbitrate between competing and equally justifiable demands for more and improved service.

In demonstrating the varied utility of aerial services the Air Board had deliberately chosen to put the overwhelming bulk of its resources directly into operations. By 1923 it had spent all but $160,000 for this purpose, or about 3 per cent of the $5 million appropriated for aviation since the war.[15] The board's reliance on First World War vintage gift aircraft, which allowed it to delay capital expenditures, meant that the air force took over a fleet of rapidly deteriorating aircraft which could no longer be depended upon to provide reliable service when needed. The problem was aggravated by the fact that the board's mechanics had been employed in a civilian capacity, at civilian rates of pay, and were 'not prepared to enlist as privates with small pay in military service.'[16] As a result, most of the board's mechanical staff quit when its civil establishment was abolished and the air force was left with too few groundcrew to service its remaining aircraft properly. Combined with 'financial limitations, adverse weather and the unsettled conditions due to reorganization of the service,'[17] these difficulties badly disrupted the 1923 flying season, leaving a number of dissatisfied civil officials. Government departments which had planned their field programmes on the assumption that aircraft would be available had quickly to improvise alternate plans. It was not a good beginning for the air force in its first operational season.

In November 1923 Wing Commander Gordon, now acting director, met with the interdepartmental committee to review the season's performance. His purpose was to impress upon the members the need for a systematic capital procurement policy. By this time the government had dropped its original intention of splitting aviation estimates among user departments, deciding instead to consolidate them as an air force appropriation. The actual costs of civil flying operations thus remained buried in a politically unpopular military budget. Each civil department simply informed the CAF of its requirements for the following year and the air force prepared estimates and attempted to deploy its dwindling resources to meet them. Gordon pointed out that the service badly needed a storage and distribution depot, a new training base, improved housing and maintenance facilities in the field, and, most important of all, new aircraft. These long-term needs had to be acquired over several years. Gordon asked the departmental representatives to predict the flying hours they might require. The CAF would determine which operations could be conducted with the equipment at hand, and calculate the additional resources needed for the balance. 'A complete record with cost will then be placed before higher authority, and it will then be for the decision of the Governor in Council as to what flying is to be carried out, and what is not to be performed.' It was unlikely, he said, that the Department of National Defence would be able to muster sufficient financing on its own: 'we cannot on our own initiative, get the necessary appropriations for the operations ... the bulk of our flying is for other Government departments, consequently we ask your assistance in obtaining the necessary appropriation.'[18]

Specifically, Gordon suggested that it would be in their own interests if ministers supported aviation estimates when they were considered in Cabinet. As he pointed out, 'When the Minister in Council says, "We will cut off $100,000 from the Air Service," the Minister of the Interior for example is perhaps not aware that that is cutting it out of his own pocket.'[19] Gordon's request seems unexceptionable, but several committee members, perhaps still displeased with the experience of the previous summer, objected. They saw no point in estimating their flying requirements on the assumption that the necessary aircraft would be available. They were concerned with next year, not the long term. The officials wanted Gordon first to guarantee them a specified number of flying hours; otherwise they would make alternative arrangements for their surveys, fire patrols, and scientific experiments. As one representative noted, 'We have to organize our work on the basis of some other [forestry] protection, and we cannot wait until next spring to do that. The time for us to know what to do either way is now.'[20] This uncertainty created an awkward impasse, one that was never fully resolved. The air force could not improve its imperfect service without the funds for an aircraft acquisition programme, and it could not obtain sufficient funding without materially improving its service.

Complaints of interrupted and inconsistent service continued over the next few years while the RCAF tried to obtain the aircraft it needed. In 1926 Parliament was disrupted when the minority Liberal government was temporarily replaced during the summer by a short-lived Conservative administration. New elections then returned the Liberals to power in September. In the political confusion, delay in approving estimates threatened to cut off funds for civil operations. The RCAF was resigned to the situation, making little effort to protect its budget. However, the civil departments whose work depended on aircraft successfully fought to have funds restored. Having taken the initiative to ensure the financing of their civil operations, they then moved to gain more control over the flying programme.

The Committee on Civil Air Operations, formed in May 1926 to rationalize the planning and conduct of the flying operations, was the result. Chaired by Colonel O.M. Biggar, former vice-chairman of the Air Board, its members included the director and secretary of the RCAF, three representatives from the Department of the Interior, the director of forestry, the chief aerial surveys engineer, and the assistant director of topographical surveys. The committee provided the Department of the Interior with a measure of control over RCAF expenditure on civil operations. Its mandate was to 'recommend methods and organization for carrying out all civil air operations; to submit a program for civil operations on a three year basis, including the necessary details as to allocation of bases, aircraft, etc; to analyze the expenditures and progress made in carrying out such program from time to time; when necessary to visit the various stations to study requirements for improving air operations and meeting unforeseen circumstances; and to submit a report each year on the progress made.'[21] The Biggar Committee met frequently over its first year, but its tenure was abbreviated. It was overtaken by events which raised broader questions about the RCAF's relationship with the private sector of aviation.

Until the mid-1920s there had been too little civilian flying to cause concern, although there was a brief flurry of activity just after the war when stocks of wartime Curtiss Jennies were released on the market. A number of adventurous souls took their decrepit machines barnstorming around the country until they crashed or wore out completely, but such enterprises had no commercial future.

Canada's two most famous Victoria Cross flyers, W.A. Bishop and W.G. Barker, persuaded some Toronto and Montreal businessmen to finance a venture aimed at flying passengers between Toronto and the Muskoka Lakes district. 'The Bishop-Barker Company was best remembered for two things; it was a commercial failure and it was a great deal of fun.'[22] The few successful private firms were those which took over the bush-flying experiments in forest survey and aerial photography pioneered by the Air Board.

The board had formulated a policy towards the private sector early in 1921. It cancelled ambitious plans for a regular aerial service in the Mackenzie River valley when it received – and approved – privately sponsored proposals for an air link in the region. Its approach to commercial flying was cautious but not restrictive. 'Wild enterprise' had to be checked to protect the public interest, regulations enforced to limit accidents, and the board's technical expertise made freely available to legitimate interests. The board also decided not to offer public subsidies, a practice many other countries had adopted. Nor would it construct 'terminal air harbours' as 'this would have the effect of stultifying local effort and thus hinder rather than advance general development.'[23] The board, in sum, determined to limit its direct involvement in the aviation market-place, leaving its growth to private initiative. The RCAF inherited this laissez-faire outlook.

For the scale of private investment aviation required, the Air Board had looked to 'the existing railway and steamboat companies,' but they had displayed little 'desire to establish their own services.'[24] The Canadian Pacific Railway Company obtained an amendment to its charter permitting it to operate domestic and international air services but declined to exercise its option for many years.[25] In the mid-1920s there were only fourteen aircraft firms in Canada, with just forty-four registered machines. For most Canadians the world of flight remained romantically unfamiliar; Canadian aircraft were as rare as prairie buffalo.

Within a decade, however, the face of Canadian aviation was transformed beyond recognition. A series of spectacular flights – Charles Lindbergh's 1927 Atlantic crossing was only the most dramatic – stirred the public imagination. In Canada, appropriately, bush flying led the way to growth. In order to exploit promising mineral discoveries at Red Lake, Ont., mining companies hired aircraft to ferry men and equipment to the remote site before freeze-up in the fall of 1925. This tentative beginning sparked the boom in Canadian bush flying which has since become legendary. All phases of aviation prospered. Statistics highlight only part of the story. Between 1926 and 1930 the number of firms operating aircraft in Canada increased to one hundred, while the number of registered civil aircraft rose to 527. Mileage flown and the number of passengers carried multiplied almost twenty times. Significantly, much of the expansion was in land aircraft rather than water-borne planes. In 1926 only fifteen of the forty-four registered machines were landplanes; four years later the number had risen to 318 out of 527. Ground facilities were expanded to keep pace, the number of licensed airports rising from four to thirty-one. Along with another thirty-eight lighted intermediate aerodromes they provided a substantial beginning for the development of a national aerial transportation network, with important military as well as civil implications and benefits.[26]

It was natural that the pace of expansion would raise some very fundamental questions about the civil-military relationship. New companies, most with only one or two machines, began actively to seek contracts for transportation and other work. Bush flying was precarious at best, with high initial capital costs, unpredictable flying conditions, and a short operating season. Small-scale operations needed regular contract work, particularly from government departments, simply to survive. It is understandable that small commercial firms came to view the RCAF as an unfair competitor holding a monopoly on bush flying for civil government departments. The question began to be asked: Did a military service have any role at all in civil aviation?

D.R. MacLaren, a much-decorated First World War flying ace and founder of the one-aircraft Pacific Airways, raised a strong protest about the situation in the spring of 1926. He sent his memorandum, 'Development and Control of Civil Aviation in Canada,' first to the minister of public works, who referred it to his colleague, the minister of national defence. MacLaren complained that the RCAF was 'strangling' the natural evolution of private aviation in Canada, and questioned the legitimacy of the RCAF's conduct of civil government operations beyond the experimental stage. Once the worth of particular operations had been demonstrated, he argued, the RCAF should step aside. Without the RCAF's further involvement, federal government departments would have to contract out their requirements to private firms. This would provide the stable financial commitments they needed to survive. As well as experimenting, the RCAF could assist the private sector by training civilians during the winter months, upgrading flying standards generally, and providing paid employment for pilots while their companies were unable to operate. In turn, the pilots could be enrolled as air force reservists, the foundation on which an effective military air arm could be built.[27]

MacLaren's memorandum percolated through the national defence chain of command until it reached a sympathetic J.A. Wilson. MacLaren's views echoed, in almost identical language, those which Wilson had been promoting since 1919. Wilson referred the director of the RCAF, Group Captain J.S. Scott, to a similar paper on the subject which he had prepared two months earlier, in which he recommended the splitting of the annual aviation appropriation into civil and military segments. A common budget, Wilson argued, was restricting the full development of both sectors. The demand for flying services had outpaced the RCAF's capabilities, and there was no longer any need for a strong central aviation agency. The time had arrived when government departments could either establish their own aviation branches or, as MacLaren argued, contract out their requirements to commercial flyers in order to provide the indirect subsidies they needed to grow. Sceptical about military control of civil aviation, Wilson doubtless welcomed MacLaren's intervention. For some time he had thought the RCAF was allowing itself to be seduced by the obvious attractions of civil operations; in the process it was losing sight of is own long-term interests.[28]

Wilson also agreed that the RCAF should provide winter facilities for civilian pilots as part of a wider training programme. At this time there were no flying schools for civilians, and commercial firms were still relying on pilots trained during the war. The RCAF ran the only primary flying training course in the country at Camp Borden and, while some civilian pilots were given refresher training there, it was not as part of any systematic programme. The lack of facilities to produce the crews needed by an expanding civil sector clearly limited its potential for growth.

Wilson expanded on MacLaren's suggestion that the RCAF train civilian pilots. He proposed that the RCAF give financial support to organize civilian flying clubs across the country which would train a new generation of pilots. With only modest backing, clubs could be formed through which interested individuals would be able to gain easy access to training facilities, and successful graduates would be available to meet the rising demand for pilots. This would be in the public interest because, as MacLaren had remarked, the new pilots would constitute a ready reserve for the RCAF. In addition, by tying the RCAF's financial support to a commitment by the clubs to provide their own ground facilities in conjunction with local municipalities, it would be possible to develop a system of urban aerodromes. The federal government could then link the major airports with intermediate airfields equipped with the necessary ground organization, navigation aids, lighting, and radio services. [29]

Group Captain Scott readily endorsed the flying club scheme. He pointed out to the chief of staff, General MacBrien, that similar projects, made technologically possible by the rapid commercial development of light aircraft, were becoming successful in Great Britain and Australia. When introduced in 1925, the de Havilland Moth, costing only $5000 and economical to operate, had brought flying within reach of the general public. Scott pointed out that as the generation of wartime flyers matured to inactivity, the RCAF would be dependent on civil aviation for reserve pilots. But there were no organized schools of instruction in the country to train them. If primary flying training were delegated to civilian clubs, which could advance trainees to wings standard less expensively than the RCAF, service instructors could concentrate on advanced training. With only a modest expenditure and active supervision to ensure the maintenance of 'adequate standards of instruction and equipment,' the RCAF would be able materially to expand its shrinking base of trained manpower. [30]

To anticipate slightly, the argument proved persuasive. The 1927 estimates provided for two training aircraft for each of sixteen approved clubs in the first year, and one more machine in each subsequent year matched by a similar purchase by the club. A grant of $100 would be given for each private pilot's certificate earned by a club member; in return, clubs had to agree to make available a qualified instructor and air engineer, and to enrol thirty members for flying instruction. Twenty-four communities applied for the first sixteen grants, and by the summer of 1928 fifteen clubs were operating in Halifax, NS; Montreal and Granby, Que.; Toronto, Hamilton, Ottawa, London, and Border Cities (Windsor), Ont.; Winnipeg, Man.; Regina, Saskatoon, and Moose Jaw, Sask.;

Edmonton and Calgary, Alta; and Victoria, BC. Vancouver joined in the following year, along with six other new clubs.[31]

The establishment of flying clubs, however, was only a partial solution. By the fall of 1926, senior RCAF officers agreed with Wilson and MacLaren that there was need for more fundamental change. In September Scott wrote MacBrien, strongly recommending that a clear distinction be drawn between military and civil aviation. He suggested that the common financial appropriation

is at the present time checking the development of aviation in Canada because in peace time it is not to be expected that any large increase of appropriations will be voted to the Department of National Defence for no matter what purpose, with the result that the development of aviation for Civil Government purposes is checked by the fact that the appropriations must be voted for the Department of National Defence.

Our experience has shown that the work required by other Government Departments is increasing so rapidly that at the present time it is impossible to carry out anything like the full program required on the appropriations that are voted for this purpose.

In addition to this, the program of work for other Government Departments requires the purchase of a great deal of equipment, for which funds must be provided, and unless some way can be found for obtaining very much larger appropriations for the Royal Canadian Air Force for Civil Government purposes the natural development of aviation is going to be held up more seriously from year to year.[32]

The first need, Scott claimed, was to amend the Aeronautics Act to relieve the RCAF of its responsibility for general supervision over all phases of Canadian aviation. This would permit other departments either to form their own air branches, or contract out their requirements directly with commercial firms. Not only would this encourage the natural evolution of the civil sector, but the RCAF could concentrate on its military responsibilities. This would be possible 'because while it is very doubtful whether increased appropriations can be expected for National Defence, under the present circumstances, there is on the other hand very little to suppose that with a stable Government the present appropriations would be reduced even if the other Departments had their Air Services. With the present appropriation a very efficient Air Force of small size doing real Air Force training and possessing modern equipment could be operated.'[33]

MacBrien disagreed, but he referred Scott's proposal to the judge advocate general for a legal opinion on the scope of the department's jurisdiction over aviation. His response was that current legislation prevented other departments from forming their own air arms, because the act 'vests in the Air Board [sic] the control and management of all state owned aircraft.' However, the act was 'not so restrictive as to prevent any Government Department making a contract with a civil aviation company for the carrying out of any aerial services which such department might require.' MacBrien sent the opinion to Scott, minuting simply that 'This clears the situation and so there shouldn't be any further misunderstanding on the point.'[34]

Scott, however, was not content to leave things as they were. In January 1927 a canvass of his senior staff confirmed that they shared his misgivings about the existing relationship. Although they approached the problem from different perspectives, each believed that the RCAF had become too involved in civil operations, to the detriment of both sectors. Wing Commander E.W. Stedman's prime concern was with military flying. The RCAF 'as it stands at present is not equipped or manned for its real functions in case of national emergency. It is merely a training organization for the civil operations, whereas the civil operations should be a training organization for the Air Force.' Stedman thought the civil branch would be better placed in a civil department. Wing Commander J.L. Gordon was concerned that the private sector should be given more encouragement. He advised 'that the interest now being evinced in civil aviation throughout Canada foreshadows a rapid development which cannot be taken care of with the present organization. The greater this growth, the greater will be the ultimate strength of the RCAF to this country. The Government should therefore do its utmost to encourage civil development and the fewer restrictions imposed, the more natural and rapid will be the progress.'[35]

If for different reasons, the senior RCAF officers were all equally troubled that the air force had become too preoccupied with civil flying. Scott now approached MacBrien again. The RCAF should discontinue its civil operations, its director recommended, 'as soon as this can be done without disorganizing the present services,' so that the RCAF could 'assume its proper service function of preparing in peacetime for war.' Scott pointed out that twice as many RCAF officers and airmen were being employed on civil as on military duties. This was inefficient, and caused instability in the permanent force as 'Special regulations must of necessity be made applicable to the permanent air force to meet the peculiar responsibilities incurred, many of which do not arise in a civil organization.' Reminiscent of MacBrien's own remarks at the 1921 CAFA conference, Scott felt it 'impossible' to maintain a high standard of discipline or military training in an organization doing civil work which, if it were to be successful, required intimate and continuing contact between officers, airmen, and civil employees of the federal government. Most importantly, he considered that the RCAF had lost sight of its primary responsibility – to prepare for war. In consequence, the permanent force had neither the equipment nor the men to develop essential military skills.[36] 'The first stage' after reorganization, Scott wrote later in the same year, 'should be the building up of a small permanent force, efficient in personnel and equipment. This permanent force will principally exist for the organization and training of a large Auxiliary and Reserve Air Force based on and administered through Military Districts.'[37]

Scott's proposal was still premature. MacBrien remained adamant, replying tersely 'that in spite of disadvantages the present policy is the best.' Parts of the air force's civil activities might be discontinued, he conceded. For instance, forestry patrols could be turned over to the provinces, but aerial survey was valuable training for war when the RCAF could be expected to work closely with survey sections of the Royal Canadian Engineers. MacBrien agreed that the RCAF needed an establishment sufficiently large to allow it to form units able to

conduct proper military training. But, alluding to his recent participation in the
1926 Imperial Conference, he recalled that 'the opinion was expressed ... that it
was a wise policy to use a military air force for work for other Government
Departments, as has been the policy in Canada. It was also stated that it would be
wise to have civil aviation controlled in the same Department as military
aviation, as the two matters were so closely related.'[38]

There the matter seemed to rest. However, at the same time that MacBrien and
Scott were differing over the RCAF's proper role, the civil-military relationship
was raised in Parliament, not of course for the first time. Based on past
experience, the Liberal government knew only too well the potential for political
controversy inherent in the mere discussion of defence issues. The government,
invariably attacked for doing either too much or too little, found the benefits of
civil aviation much easier to justify than the training of young boys for military
service. As Prime Minister King told the British during the 1923 Imperial
Conference, aircraft 'could be used for civilian purposes – surveying, anti-
smuggling, etc. – and the matter could be therefore to some extent disguised.'[39]
Even the most ardent anti-militarist found it difficult to argue with attempts to
eradicate the spruce budworm, stamp out wheat rust, deliver mail to remote
communities, fight forest fires, or map the country.

When he returned to London in October 1926 for his second Imperial
Conference, King once more pledged his support for aviation. Before the
discussions began, he made it clear to his closest advisers that 'at this Conference
emphasis should be laid upon air development and defence.'[40] Later, after
proudly describing the RCAF's civil operations to the delegates, he acknowledged
the close ties between the civil and military branches: 'As civil aviation has a
direct relation to the creation of a Military Air Force and serves to create a
reserve thereto, in this field Canada may be in a position to lend very great
assistance in Imperial Defence. By the Air Force Regulations an individual who
obtains a pilot's certificate automatically becomes a Reservist.'[41]

King's enthusiasm did not lag when the estimates came up for parliamentary
debate in the spring of 1927. On the few occasions when members discussed
aviation in the House their concerns usually centred on the nature of the
civil-military relationship. Was the civil sector being stifled by military control
and a common financial appropriation? Were the RCAF's civil operations merely
a disguise for the build-up of a military air force? Opposition members were
generally in favour of the separation of civil and military aviation. E.J. Garland
admitted that 'the civil air force in this country has been doing a remarkable
work,' but questioned the wisdom of continuing 'the evolution of our civil air
force within a military department.' His recommendation was to remove civil
aviation from the military's control and place it under a newly created
department of transportation. Other members agreed.[42]

In planning the 1927-8 aviation estimates, the Cabinet decided to separate
civil funding from that of the military. The Cabinet discussion on the subject was
one of the few occasions in which the government gave the civil-military
relationship consideration at this level; the prime minister's views on aviation
were normally confined to contemplating the obvious political advantages of

having the RCAF engage in civil flying. King, however, on this occasion demonstrated his commitment to the Wilson view of airpower. The prime minister wanted it 'understood that the Civil work should form the basis of the whole, the military to be an outgrowth rather than vice versa.'[43]

When the estimates were presented to Parliament – $2,222,539 for civil and $1,669,694 for military aviation – it was unclear whether separate funding meant that the government also intended to split the air force into separate civil and military components as well. Members of Parliament were understandably confused. When asked whether he had given serious thought to the issue, J.L. Ralston, the defence minister, replied that the government had the 'general idea' under consideration. King intervened soon after to say that the Cabinet was 'entirely of one mind that the two should be separated, but as to whether they should be under a different minister than the one who now has charge of the Department of National Defence is a matter which we will have to consider further. As to keeping the two services distinct there is but one view in the cabinet.' Later he explained that the government had not had time to complete its plan for reorganizing the aerial services.[44]

MacBrien, who had submitted his resignation as chief of staff after a long battle over his salary and status in the department,[45] was clearly surprised by the prime minister's statement that consideration was being given to separating civil and military aviation. Perhaps worn down by his dispute with the government, perhaps still hoping to win the politicians' favour, MacBrien now reversed his position and immediately submitted a memorandum to Ralston advocating the removal of civil aviation from military control. The memorandum reflected the views of the RCAF's senior officers. It stated that it had been foreseen 'some years ago' that civil aviation would 'possibly' pass through at least two or three stages in its development:

First Stage: In its very early days of development owing to its small size, administration and control to be kept along with that of the Royal Canadian Air Force.

Second Stage: To be controlled under the Minister by a specially elected official with a practicable knowledge of aviation, in the same department of the government, so as to have the assistance of technical officers and experts of the military air service available to assist in the examination of aircraft, inspection and testing of pilots etc., and so save duplication of these important technical advisors.

Third Stage: When commercial aviation had assumed large proportions, then consideration would be given to having it under another ministry such as Railways, Communications, or Transportation.[46]

The time for the second stage had arrived, and a major reorganization of the RCAF took place along these lines. By the spring of 1927, Wilson told his friend Charles Grey, it had become clear that reorganization was badly needed because the government's civil operations were too dominant. While the military was in control, 'there was a disinclination to do anything for the commercial end outside the Government operations. The minute Colonel Ralston took hold, we had a chance to work towards a saner and more practical policy and when

MacBrien resigned the whole structure he had created on a purely military basis collapsed.' Although there is no other evidence of Ralston's role in the reorganization, the change was the kind of reform Wilson had been promoting. 'I am glad to say,' he wrote, 'that everything I fought for in the past five years has been granted and that we get back practically to our old Air Board organization.'[47]

On 1 July 1927, when the new organization came into effect, the RCAF was relieved of the direct responsibility for the control of civil aviation. As Wilson pointed out, the new scheme, in many respects, resembled the old Air Board. Four separate branches were formed. The Directorate of Civil Government Air Operations [CGAO], headed by Wing Commander Gordon, took over all civil operations. The controller of civil aviation [CCA], J.A. Wilson, continued to supervise the administration of air regulations, the inspection and licensing of air harbours, aircraft, and air crews. The Aeronautical Engineering Division [AED], run by Wing Commander Stedman, exercised a general supervisory function over all technical matters. The RCAF, under its director, Group Captain Scott, was left to concentrate on military aviation, especially training. All branches remained in the Department of National Defence; all except the RCAF were placed under the direct control of the deputy minister. The air force remained responsible to the army chief of staff. Units, facilities, aircraft, and equipment were divided. Winnipeg, High River, Dartmouth, and Ottawa (including No 1 Depot and the Photographic Section) became air stations of the CGAO. Camp Borden (three squadrons, the Ground Instruction School, and the RCAF Repair Depot) and Vancouver (two squadrons), along with the Communications Flight were kept as RCAF units. The Committee on Civil Air Operations was reorganized. O.M. Biggar resigned as chairman, and the committee was reconstituted under the direction of the deputy minister.[48]

The 1927 reorganization to some extent met parliamentary criticism by placing 'all government flying operations and the control and supervision of civil aviation under civil control and administration.'[49] But Wilson's initial impression of a fundamental shift proved false. Consideration was given to converting all branches except the RCAF to civilian status, but only the CCA was actually affected. The others remained staffed by the RCAF; the 174 officers and airmen with the CGAO and the seventeen with the AED represented more than half the RCAF's uniformed strength. Although the branches had well-defined duties, the closest co-operation was essential for the wellbeing of each. Frequent cross-postings between them ensured this, but also blurred their separate identities. It mattered little whether a sergeant or flying officer was training others at Camp Borden or flying in the bush, his life went on much as it had before the reorganization. Consequently, while the change produced considerable shuffling of offices and appointments, its effect on flying operations was more apparent than real. Parliamentary critics could still direct their displeasure at having civil aviation located in the Department of National Defence. Commercial operators still objected to the RCAF's monopoly of government flying. RCAF officers who wished to concentrate all their efforts on building a military air force found themselves so restricted by the need to staff the CGAO that their military air force remained a distant dream.[50] Bureaucratic inertia and political indirection combined to limit change. As the annual *Report on Civil Aviation* for 1927 explained: 'The reorganization of the other branches (Civil Government Air Operations and Aeronautical Engineering) is not an easy matter and requires time and the utmost care during the transition period to ensure that their important functions are not interrupted by any sudden change.' There were also 'questions of length of service, pension rights, etc. ... [and] permanent Air Force officers with many years service are entitled to every protection in regard to such matters. The success of the Civil Government operations programme is largely due to them and its continuance on a sound basis is dependent on their experience and knowledge of the work.'[51]

Firm direction from the top could, undoubtedly, have cleared obstacles, but the initial impetus for a clear delineation of the respective spheres of civil and military aviation was not sustained. Major-General A.G.L. McNaughton, chief of the general staff from 1929 to 1935, was a strong believer in the RCAF's participation in civil operations. Group Captain Scott, perhaps disappointed at the lack of substantive change, retired in 1928. The RCAF's senior appointment went to Wing Commander Gordon, who was made head of the CGAO and represented the RCAF on the Defence Council. In a clearly subordinate position was Wing Commander L.S. Breadner, who served only as acting director of the RCAF until 1932.

The government's decision to make Gordon the *de facto* senior RCAF officer reflected its disinclination to make a clean break between military and civil aviation. When estimates were considered in 1929, opposition members returned to their familiar theme of questioning the involvement of the defence department in civil flying. The minister, Ralston, went to great lengths to deny any military intent. The civil flying programme was controlled by the RCAF only because it was more economical to have a centralized aerial agency. It was 'a matter of opinion,' he said, whether the RCAF's service was satisfactory. But, he continued, 'if we placed civil aviation under another department we would be doubling our overhead. Then the Department of the Interior would want an air force, as would also the Post Office Department and the Department of Railways, each with its own organization, and we would be trebling or quadrupling the overhead in that connection, and would not have uniformity of training.' Ralston saw 'another drawback' which he could not 'stress too strongly.' This was that flying required discipline such as could only properly be enforced in a military service:

There is no other activity in which you need more, not the sort of discipline known as parade discipline, saluting and things of that sort, but the sort of discipline which will make men follow a certain line of routing day after day and month after month in order that they may recognize, for instance, the necessity of inspecting a certain part of the machine every morning, whether they think it necessary or not. That condition is more easily attained when you have the men doing those things because they are so ordered rather than leaving it to them to decide whether they will do it or not. For instance they might get the view that 'We do not have to inspect the machine this morning, we inspected it yesterday.' ... it seems to be necessary for the sound foundation of civil aviation in this country to develop that care and caution and ceaseless attention to these matters of detail, which, if not necessary, it is at least desirable that they should be taught by the influence of discipline and routine ... there is no activity where the simple failure to carry out a particular order will lead to such disastrous results as the activity of aviation.[52]

For four more years, until events combined to force yet another reorganization, the RCAF's primary function continued to be the training of pilots and crews for civil flying operations. The pace of training picked up, and the CGAO's activity grew apace under the new arrangement – from 3777 flying hours in 1927-8 to 9372 the next year, and then to a peak of 13,640 in 1930-1. The increase matched the remarkable growth of commercial flying in the period.

The late 1920s also saw the beginning of a fundamental structural transformation in Canadian aviation. In a few years float- and seaplanes were gradually replaced by landplanes, which could make use of an interconnected transcontinental airway system. Although the RCAF was only peripherally involved in bringing about the changes – they were primarily in the domain of the controller of civil aviation – the service was fundamentally affected by them. When the RCAF was eventually freed from its responsibilities to conduct civil operations, it was able to take full advantage of a developed system of aerodromes and ground facilities. It is necessary, therefore, to digress slightly in order to sketch the background of the transformation from a water-borne to a land-based aerial system.

Much of the push for change apparently came from the United States. American federal legislation in the mid-1920s served as 'cornerstones for the development of commercial aviation in America' by permitting the Post Office to let airmail contracts. These provided the indirect subsidies which produced an extremely rapid development of the major US trunk airlines. At the same time, 'a rather liberal policy of placing experimental orders for prototype aircraft' promoted the commercial development and production of aircraft.[53] J.A. Wilson was a close observer of these events. As he noted, the purpose of the US government 'has been threefold, first, to secure better development of this new form of transportation for commercial purposes; second, to create private commercial services which can relieve the post office of its direct expenditure upon air mail, and third, by the creation of a large commercial air fleet with its accompanying personnel and its background of the manufacturing industry to give a fundamental military reserve to the country.'[54] These were uncannily similar to the objectives Wilson wanted to achieve in Canada.

Fast growth in the United States had major implications for Canadian aviation. 'The Americans were expanding aviation at an enormous rate due to very remunerative airmail contracts and also to the enormous expenditure being made by the Department of Commerce in building and organizing airway routes,' Colonel R.H. Mulock, the outstanding First World War airman who was closely involved in commercial aviation, recalled. 'It was the boom period ... It was at this time that we saw the whole of Canadian aviation floating into the hands of the Americans.'[55] In just a few years the major US trunk lines – United Air Lines, American Airways, Transcontinental and Western Air Express, Pan American – had spanned the continent and were establishing international connections in the Carribean, South America, Newfoundland, and Canada. A mail and passenger air service between New York and Montreal was established in 1928, and another connecting Toronto and Buffalo followed soon after. Others were planned.[56]

Like Mulock, Wilson became alarmed at the prospect of Canadian aviation passing by default to American companies. While there was as yet no public demand for airmail and passenger transportation in Canada, he had written prophetically in 1922, it would 'follow inevitably when they succeed in the United States.'[57] Five years later that time had arrived, as Canadian aviation 'may be said to have passed beyond the pioneer stage' and must be prepared for the next, which 'will undoubtedly be the operation of air routes.'[58] This would bring aviation within reach of the bulk of the Canadian population and forestall American expansion, but it required a major policy shift and mobilization of resources. Flying operations in the remote regions, where flying boats and seaplanes had been able to use the almost limitless Canadian inland waterways, had paid large dividends on a very small investment. But the very nature of the water-borne system imposed clear limitations on its development. Such aircraft were unable to function effectively during fall freeze-up or spring break-up; intercity transportation of mail, passengers, and freight had to be regularly scheduled on a year-round basis if it were to gain acceptance over other forms of transport. This meant landplanes, which needed landing fields, ground maintenance facilities, ground control systems, and navigation, meterological, and radio aids. It was predictable that as the scope of operations grew, only ever larger firms would be able to offer the efficiency and economy which characterized successful modern business enterprise. Consequently, the companies operating the aircraft had to be closely linked to the existing transportation network, with access to capital and management skills not needed for bush flying.[59]

Wilson had in mind a three-part approach to promote this new phase of aviation. The first part required flying clubs to train the new generation of pilots needed by a growing commercial sector. The second was related to the section in the clubs' charter that they must provide themselves with a licensed aerodrome and adequate ground facilities. Most clubs were able to construct fields in conjunction with their local municipalities, and by 1929 the combined ground facilities of the twenty-two functioning clubs provided the foundation for a national airway. The government's role was to link the local airports with a network of intermediate airfields equipped with the necessary ground organizations, navigation aids, lighting, and radio services. The third part of Wilson's strategy called for an integrated air mail system. He stressed that an aerial transportation system must be developed in conjunction with existing forms of transport, not competitively as highway transport had challenged railways. Despite the fact that Canada already had a more than adequate rail system, there was a place for a compatible air service for that part of the public which would benefit from an estimated cross-country time-saving of three or four days. Wilson also pointed out to critics of government expenditures that 'Every form of transportation has had state aid ... fast trains are largely paid for by mail contracts.'[60]

Until the late 1920s only unscheduled mail had been carried, as an ancillary service to isolated northern and eastern communities. In 1926, however, the Post Office signalled a change in its attitude and the RCAF was alerted to provide ground support and meteorological facilities. The next year the Post Office appropriated $75,000 for air mail carriage, a new departure and a small but important support for Canadian aviation. The RCAF's function was to prepare the way. Initially two geographical regions seemed most promising. The first was to hasten the delivery of transatlantic mail, the other to serve the Prairies.

Interest in Atlantic mail was part of the more general process of expanding imperial air communications which the 1926 Imperial Conference, an enthusiastic Mackenzie King included, had attempted to promote.[61] Charles Lindbergh's 1927 transatlantic flight had been widely acclaimed as the forerunner of oceanic commercial air transportation. Canada was strategically located astride the great circle route to Europe. Atlantic Canada jutted into the ocean and, west, along the St Lawrence, Canadian territory provided the most direct route between the major population centres of Europe and the American midwest.[62] Airships were one exciting possibility, but proved unworkable. Technological limitations ruled out the early use of long-range aircraft, but even then it was possible to foresee the development of commercially feasible ocean-spanning airliners. In the meantime, a combined ship-aircraft system might fill the gap. Aircraft could meet regularly scheduled ships in the Gulf of St Lawrence, pick up their mail, and quickly deliver it to Montreal. From there it could easily be trans-shipped to its ultimate destination. Hours and perhaps days could thus be saved in delivery time. Commercial companies were to operate the system, but before contracts were let the RCAF flew a series of trials in the fall of 1927 between Rimouski and Montreal. The Post Office was pleased with the results and the following spring awarded a contract to Canadian Transcontinental Airways to continue and extend the connections to Ottawa and Toronto.[63]

The St Lawrence mail flights were able to make good use of a major airport constructed at St Hubert near Montreal. Its origins lay in the commitment made by Mackenzie King at the 1926 Imperial Conference to support the proposed British airship service (a scheme which the RCAF staff considered premature and technologically unsound). At the St Hubert site, selected in 1927, a mooring mast with elaborate docking aids was erected; more important, as things turned out, two hard-surfaced runways and a taxiway for aircraft were added, along with hangars, radios, field lighting, meteorological equipment, and a control tower. In July 1930 the British R-100 arrived at St Hubert on a trial flight, after which it toured parts of Quebec and Ontario to considerable fanfare and public enthusiasm. There were no other flights. That October another British airship, the R-101, crashed and burned in France while on passage from Britain to India. The airship scheme was dead. The sole Canadian legacy of the ill-fated project, and it was a significant one, was a fully equipped airport within easy reach of Montreal and capable of handling all-weather aircraft traffic.[64]

The process of linking St Hubert and the scattered municipal airports with intermediate landing fields and other equipment went on in stages over many years. The CCA divided the country into four geographical regions – the Prairies, the West, the Maritimes, and northern Ontario – and each was intensively surveyed for suitable landing-field sites. The prairie section was easiest to develop. The early objective was to inaugurate a regular service connecting Winnipeg and Calgary. Main and intermediate sites were selected, electric beacons installed, and acetylene lanterns fixed at ten-mile intervals along the route to light the flight path. This section was ready by the end of 1929. The following year the Post Office let contracts with western operators for regularly scheduled deliveries which were maintained on a nightly basis for two years until the Depression forced the Post Office to suspend the service because of lack of funds. Meanwhile, other intercity connections were established by making use of municipal airports, the construction of which the flying clubs had done so much to encourage. In Atlantic Canada, Halifax, Moncton, and Saint John were connected with Montreal and then to Toronto and Windsor. Before the Laurentian Shield was tamed, mail could also be sent by air via the United States to Manitoba to connect with the prairie section. Within a relatively short time the route across the Rocky Mountains was functioning and Vancouver and Victoria were included in the system.[65] By the end of 1929 there were one thousand miles of surveyed air routes for night flying, although the airway was far from being free of difficulties. In 1930 one complaint noted that 'the beacons between Moose Jaw and Swift Current are a disgrace as only an occasional one can be picked up, and then only if the pilot knew exactly where to locate it ... there are only two fields on which it is safe to land between Winnipeg and Regina.'[66]

The transformation of Canada's aviation resources in only a few years was remarkable. The water-borne system of bush flying, which was still opening up the northwest, had been supplemented by a land-based aerial network almost spanning the country. It had not been until 1926, when the possibilities of a new phase of development were first being discussed, that the first cross-country flight by a single aircraft – a seaplane – had taken place. Four years later, on the Prairies alone, fully equipped lighted municipal airports in Winnipeg, Regina, Moose Jaw, Saskatoon, Medicine Hat, Lethbridge, Calgary, and Edmonton joined more than 1300 miles of lighted air routes.[67] The Canadian system also merged with others. 'The magnitude of the air mail services on this continent is seldom realized,' Wilson enthused. 'A correspondent at Aklavik, on the Arctic coast of Canada, can post a letter there and it will be conveyed by air, without a break, to Pembina, thence by American air mail routes to Mexico City, Central America, the islands in the Caribbean Sea, and to any country in South America, as far as Buenos Aires or Valparaiso. The gain in time and convenience is immense and the constant exchange of traffic by air means much to the commerce of the countries on the western hemisphere.'[68]

Although the bulk of the developmental work in the new phase of Canadian aviation was under the direction of Wilson as controller of civil aviation, the

RCAF was involved in all phases of the expansion. It had much to gain from the enlargement of the country's aerial capabilities. The construction throughout the country of facilities able to maintain and service landplanes had military and strategic importance, the full significance of which became clear within a few years.

While this new era of aviation was taking shape, the majority of the RCAF's resources, men, and equipment remained preoccupied with civil operational flying – either flying themselves or training others to do so. There seemed little prospect of drastic change as the interdepartmental committee which oversaw the civil air operations of the RCAF met in mid-January 1932 to allocate the CGAO's aerial resources for the coming season.[69] Those attending – the deputy ministers of the Departments of National Defence and Mines, as well as several branch heads from other user departments and senior RCAF officers – were well aware that worsening economic conditions would probably reduce their estimates further. The committee noted that in the previous year savings of more than $1 million had been realized when the control of their natural resources had been handed over to the Prairie provinces, thus eliminating the RCAF's western fire patrols. It recommended that a further reduction of $301,500 could be achieved by eliminating two photo and one general-purpose detachments, reducing transportation flying by 600 hours, and postponing the purchase of a new, twin-engine aircraft. Although this would mean that fourteen officers and twenty-seven other ranks would have to be let go, the reduction would not affect essential tasks.

The mood of the meeting was cautiously optimistic, noting in particular the growing use and popularity of aerial photography. User departments were satisfied with the work of the RCAF. Except for the Post Office, which contracted out its requirements, departments simply continued to request flying services which the civil government air operations directorate then co-ordinated, approved, and implemented from funds appropriated in the aviation estimates of the Department of National Defence. The director of the Geological Survey, Dr W.H. Collins, commented that 'so long as the RCAF was in a position to undertake operations ... little work would be passed out to commercial companies, as the coordination of civil government air programmes permitted a definite economy which would probably not be realized if departments were to budget their own requirements.' The committee concluded:

The Civil Government Branch of the Royal Canadian Air Force is the central flying organization for the Dominion Service and all operations undertaken by it are for Government Departments. In serving the Departments, a portion of the Air Force obtains practical and valuable training. The Committee commends this policy of combining training and productive work connected with investigation and development of the natural resources of the country particularly in the remote areas which are more or less inaccessible. This policy has already produced an Air Force that compares favourably with those of other countries in general efficiency, that leads in the operation of seaplanes and ski-planes and leads in application of the aeroplane and air photography to exploration and development of natural resources.[70]

Commercial operators outside the meeting, and Wilson in it, objected to the apparent complacency. In the five years since the 1927 reorganization, the civil-military relationship had reverted to its earlier status. The RCAF-CGAO still dominated civil-government flying. The process had been more acceptable during the years when there was enough aviation business to go around, but now, as the economy contracted, the civil sector was being squeezed. On 15 February, exactly one month after the interdepartmental committee's meeting, the government sent word of the cancellation of air mail contracts to private firms, in a stroke undercutting one of the main props of commercial aviation's financial stability. R.B. Bennett, the prime minister, preoccupied with reducing expenditures to meet the increasing charges on the national debt, thought the RCAF could carry the mail at less cost 'due to the fact that they can operate for out-of-pocket expenses,' while the commercial companies had to maintain their profit margins.[71]

Wilson completed yet another of his critical reports, repeating many of his now familiar arguments. The RCAF had strayed from its mandate to experiment only, withdrawing from civil operations once they became commercially viable.[72] The original intention to form reserves from the pool of available commercial pilots had never been fulfilled. Consequently, the RCAF lacked the backing of a significant outside constituency, potentially its strongest support, when it most needed it. Instead, commercial pilots were bound to resent the RCAF's dominance of civil activities. The unfortunate result was to divide the small aviation community, leaving the RCAF isolated from its fellow flyers, who otherwise might have been inclined to support its claims. Nevertheless, the RCAF had no choice but to fly air mails if ordered. For example, in the summer of 1932 it temporarily took over the sea-to-shore route on the Atlantic coast which earlier had been flown by Canadian Airways. During the Imperial Economic Conference of 1932, two RCAF detachments of ten pilots flying seaplanes and flying boats ferried official mail in stages from Red Bay on the Labrador side of the Strait of Belle Isle to Ottawa.[73]

When the prime minister had presented his budget in June 1931, he announced that the aviation appropriation for the fiscal year would be reduced by $2 million as part of the government's commitment to financial retrenchment.[74] This had resulted in some contraction of services, but it was followed the next year by far more drastic economies. For 1932, the combined vote for the RCAF and CGAO was slashed by almost 70 per cent. All phases of training and operations were affected, with a mere $1,750,000 allotted for the service's diverse activities. The Department of National Defence's annual report for 1933 summarized the effects of the 'big cut':

the release of 78 officers, 100 airmen and 110 civilians; vacancies occurring during the year not being filled; curtailment of training in Canada and abroad; normal flying training of provisional pilot officers discontinued; discontinuance of flying for other government departments, except where funds were provided by those departments; no new aircraft or engines purchased; bare maintenance charges only expended; reduction of Ladder Lake and Buffalo Park sub-stations to care and maintenance basis; suspension

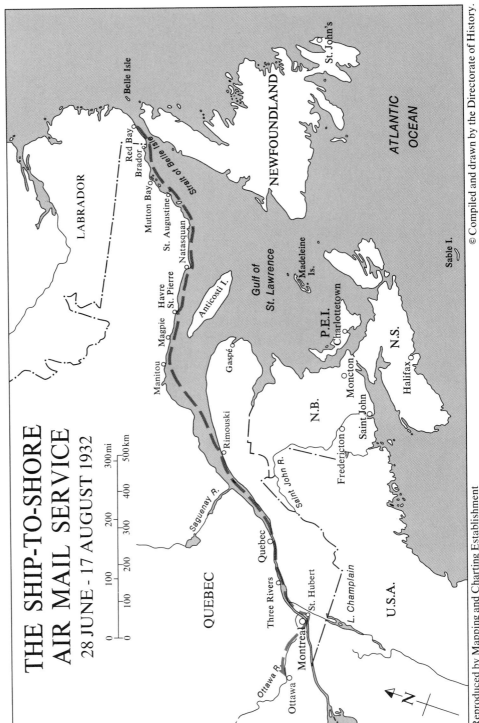

THE SHIP-TO-SHORE AIR MAIL SERVICE
28 JUNE - 17 AUGUST 1932

of construction at Trenton, etc; etc; intermediate aerodromes used for night flying in connection with air mail routes placed on care and maintenance basis; construction and improvement in civil airports suspended; cancellation of air mail contracts; reconditioned or used aircraft issued to flying clubs instead of new ones, etc; etc.'[75]

This severe curtailment of funds and flying services produced yet another reorganization of the air services. When Group Captain Gordon returned to Ottawa from the Imperial Defence College, he was told to organize a new structure to manage aviation. The new scheme, which took effect on 1 November 1932, consolidated the operations of the RCAF, CGAO, and AED. Gordon was given a new title – senior air officer – while remaining responsible to the chief of the general staff. CGAO stations returned to RCAF control, but High River, Dartmouth, and several sub-bases were placed on a 'care and maintenance' basis. Development of the new Trenton base was stopped. Camp Borden remained the main training centre and Station Ottawa controlled a reduced number of mobile detachments. The CCA branch, and Wilson's civilian staff, continued to answer to the deputy minister.[76]

The next few years were lean ones for Canadian aviation. Commercial companies folded as contracts disappeared, again raising fears of American competition. The deputy postmaster general, for example, feared that if air mail were discontinued, all Canadian air mail traffic would become 'subsidiary' to the American system.[77] Aircraft companies which had expanded in the promising climate of earlier days now had to close, and the RCAF found itself presiding over a fleet of obsolescent aircraft which it was unable to replace. But not all was lost. The trans-Canada airway was an early casualty of retrenchment and many municipalities which had committed funds to the construction and operation of their airports were let down. The airway programme, however, was revived when the Department of National Defence was placed in charge of the government's principal unemployment relief scheme. One of the major projects was to clear land and prepare intermediate landing fields across the country, as well as construct a number of terminal airports. By the time the programme was ended in 1936, the unemployment relief scheme had at least partially completed forty-eight fields and built numerous hangars and other buildings at RCAF stations and municipal and provincial airports.[78]

The airway, then, benefited from the Depression. As General McNaughton told a British visitor:

while the route had been settled entirely on economic, geographic and meteorological considerations with a view to serving in the best possible way the civil interests of Canada, particularly as regards the handling of mails between centres of population from the Atlantic sea-board to the Pacific but that as a bye [sic] product the Airway would give us a great military advantage which we did not now possess, namely, the ability to rapidly reinforce by air, our Pacific coast if that were required either on account of our being engaged in war with a trans-Pacific power or by the reason of the maintenance of neutrality in a war between the United States and a trans-Pacific power.

I pointed out that at present if we wished to move the fighting aircraft located at Trenton to Vancouver we would have to dismantle the machines and ship them out by rail or alternately we would have to obtain permission to fly over American routes between Detroit and Winnipeg and again from Lethbridge to Seattle. I said that I anticipated that in a state of tension this permission would be very difficult to obtain. On the other hand when the Trans-Canada Airway was completed and in operation and equipped for night flying and with radio beacons as it would be, we would be able to move our fighting aircraft from Central Canada to the West in the space of 24 hours. I told him that our Post Office schedules contemplate approximately 23 hours from Halifax to Vancouver, and that while fighting aircraft would not be able to make such good time nevertheless with the organization of supply available at intermediate refuelling points they would be able to move very rapidly indeed.[79]

Before then, however, the RCAF's civil flying operations were drastically affected. Some of the more important tasks were continued, albeit on a much reduced level, through strenuous efforts to combine flights and cut down on flying time in order to economize on men and equipment. This was a stop-gap measure, with user departments paying only operating costs and incidental expenses while the RCAF supplied the aircraft and crews. No charge was made for depreciation of aircraft, and the RCAF had to function with existing equipment and no provision for replacement. The situation clearly could not go on indefinitely, but it was better than letting men and equipment stand idle. Although the RCAF continued to perform some civil tasks, especially aerial photography, right up to the outbreak of the war, the government came to the view that the civil sector was too large and complex to keep within a Department of National Defence with growing military responsibilities. In 1936 the new Department of Transport assumed control of civil aviation, and the following year the creation of Trans-Canada Airlines as a national carrier opened a new era of intercity aerial transportation.

Until the mid-1930s, the RCAF had found its affairs touching those of the civil sector at almost all points. On four occasions – in 1918-19 when the the Air Board was formed, in 1922-3 at the creation of the Department of National Defence, and in 1927 and 1932 when events forced major organizational change – the civil-military relationship could have been more clearly defined with benefit to both sectors. It was not. The result, by default rather than design, was that the air force found itself performing civil functions not usually the responsibility of a military service. The impact on the RCAF as a military institution is difficult to gauge. Airmen had little opportunity to prepare for aerial warfare, but this mattered little in the 1920s and early 1930s. It is exceedingly unlikely that the RCAF would have been able to acquire the fighting aircraft and other resources to make it a credible military force. At the least, civil operations gave the RCAF a valid, useful, and politically acceptable role to perform in an unmilitary era.

3

Bush Pilots in Uniform

RCAF pilots wore air force blue, saluted, drilled, and otherwise observed the eternal military verities, even though their day-to-day working lives for most of the interwar years were spent on civil flying operations. The future air marshal and chief of the air staff, C.R. Slemon, recalled that 'I never thought of a weapon; I never saw a weapon or fired a machine gun or whatever. We were just as busy as we could be doing purely civil government flying. We began to get some military training – all along there were military elements, but they were tiny in comparison to the civil government air operations.'[1] 'We were,' another officer recalled, 'bush pilots in uniform.'[2]

Training these 'bush pilots' to fly was the RCAF's primary military function in the 1920s and early 1930s. Air force training remained concentrated at Camp Borden until Trenton was opened in 1931. As far as practicable, training methods were modelled on those used by the RAF for individual flying and ground instruction, and, later, for service or unit training. British course syllabi and training manuals were employed, and officers and airmen sent to RAF courses for advanced and specialist training – flying instruction, army co-operation, photography, armament, air navigation, wireless, explosives, and aeronautical engineering. In time these specialists formed a nucleus of instructors with which the RCAF staffed its own schools.

Recruiting and training airmen, mechanics, and tradesmen had initially proved difficult. When the RCAF became part of the permanent force many skilled men employed as civilians by the Air Board declined to join up, and others were overage or medically unfit. They were not easily replaced. Little in the way of formal instruction for airmen existed in the early years, and the RCAF depended on enlisting men who already possessed related trades qualifications. The recruit then entered into an apprenticeship to learn fitting, rigging, and other skills on the job. He gradually acquired more specific aviation experience and through specialist courses was able to improve his technical grade. Military subjects were injected along the way. In 1927 the RCAF completed arrangements with selected technical training schools to recruit students. Those successful in a trial summer course at Camp Borden were enlisted in the rank of 'boy' for further service until they reached eighteen years of age.[3] As they gained experience, however, many were actively sought by civilian firms with offers of higher pay.

When Wing Commander G.M. Croil commanded Camp Borden in 1928-9, he complained that 'If they do not actually approach them whilst here they do so by letter after their departure from this station and go so far as to pay the sum necessary for the airman to purchase his discharge.'[4]

There was less difficulty attracting officers for the air force. CAF regulations had stipulated that pilot and flying officers would be required to retire at age thirty, flight lieutenants continuing for an additional two years. Officers in these ranks comprised the bulk of the early force's commissioned officers, most of them veterans in their mid-twenties, so there was little problem at first. When new pilots were needed, a training scheme aimed at university students (which had to be deferred for a year during the reorganization) went into effect in 1923. Candidates were required to be members of the Canadian Officers' Training Corps [COTC], enrolled as degree students in applied science or engineering, under twenty-one, and unmarried. The course of instruction consisted of three terms in consecutive years during the university summer break from May until August. While at Camp Borden the pilot trainees were granted temporary commissions as provisional pilot officers in the non-permanent force and received $3.00 a day during the first term, $3.50 the second, and $4.00 the final term. Quarters, rations, uniforms, travelling allowances, and medical and dental treatment were provided. All those successfully completing the course were to be appointed RCAF pilot officers, but with no guarantee of a permanent commission. The terms of the training plan, indeed, emphasized that there would be only a limited number of such appointments. Those not wishing, or not offered, permanent commissions were eligible for appointments to the non-permanent force. Alternatively, they might be transferred to the reserve of officers, which meant that they would have no further direct contact with the RCAF unless called up in time of emergency.

The pilot training programme was scheduled to start with thirty cadets but, because of a late start, undergraduates across the country were not informed of the scheme until too late in the 1922-3 academic year. As a result only nine trainees reported to Camp Borden for the first course on 15 May 1923. One was forced to drop out a month later for medical reasons. The others completed the first term of training at the end of August. Six returned for the second term; four qualified for their wings in December of that year and were awarded commissions in the permanent force. Two of the graduates were subsequently killed in aircraft accidents and one resigned his commission. The fourth was Pilot Officer C.R. Slemon.[5]

The initial flying training scheme produced the first new air force pilots trained in Canada since 1918. Later, to meet shortages, a number of trained flyers were granted short-service commissions, and some university graduates in engineering and applied science courses were enlisted directly. Serving non-commissioned officers [NCOs] provided another source. The first NCO pilot course began in February 1927, and over the next five years thirty of forty-five students attained wings standard.[6] When this scheme had been proposed, Group Captain J.S. Scott enquired about the RAF's experience with NCO pilots. His liaison officer in London reported that 'The scheme is working most satisfactorily. The standard of Airmen Pilots is just about the same in the Royal Air Force as that of the Short Service Commissioned Officer Pilot, but Airmen Pilots in relation to those officers appear to take things rather more conscientiously.'[7] Canadian experience was equally favourable.

In the early phases of pilot training, a great deal of time was spent on ground subjects: the theory of flight, basic areonautical engineering, air pilotage and map reading, aerial photography, meteorology, as well as military organization, administration, drill and physical training, and signalling. Flying began with the student seated in the back of an Avro 504K. The instructor, calling instructions through a speaking tube from the front seat, guided his pupil through a controlled programme over several days, introducing him to the aircraft's flying controls, the basics of level flight, stalling, diving, gliding, take-offs and landings, turning in the air, standard procedures for engine failure and forced landings. Finally the student flew alone. Instructions in side-slips, cross-wind landings, aerobatics, and low flying followed, all leading to wings standard. Once qualified, the new pilot went to Vancouver for a seaplane conversion course. There he mastered the different controls on flying boats and floatplanes, practised landings on heavy seas and glassy calm surfaces, and was introduced to marine navigation, wireless, engine, float and hull maintenance, and the use of carrier pigeons. He was about to become, after all, a bush pilot; a difficult and lonely job where he was dependent upon only his training and self-reliance.

From Camp Borden and Vancouver most new pilots went directly to one of the air force's sub-bases scattered throughout the northwest where they began forest patrolling, the staple of the RCAF's civil flying operations during the 1920s. As we have seen, the Air Board had been highly successful in demonstrating the productive contribution that aircraft could make to the forest industry. Conserving woodland resources with fire patrols was potentially of enormous economic importance. Forest production in 1920 totalled more than $300 million; forests covered almost one million square miles, about half in timber, the rest in pulpwood. Fires regularly destroyed huge sections of forest cover, the equivalent of one-third the annual consumption of standing timber and an additional 1.3 million acres of young growth. Traditional means of forest protection had proved marginally effective at best. In some regions ground systems included lookout towers, telephone networks, fire lanes, guards, and prepositioned equipment and pumps. To an ever greater extent, however, the foresters of the early 1920s still relied on foot, horse, or canoe patrols. Some ranged two to three hundred miles, but unless fires were visible from the waterways or routes used, they were almost impossible to detect. The provincial forester of Manitoba estimated that up to 75 per cent of the forest fires in his area of responsibility remained unobserved or unreported.[8] By contrast, regular air patrols could easily cover vast expanses. 'Even the Ottawa Valley lumberman, than whom no more conservative animal exists, is convinced of the soundness of our ideas,' J.A. Wilson wrote early in 1923. 'Two years ago he did not admit that there was such a thing as an aircraft; one year ago he treated them as a joke; six months ago he was inclined to violently oppose the idea that they were any use and now he admits their presence in the scheme of things but, of course, still objects to their cost even though he sees every year millions of dollars of timber burned, a large proportion of which could be saved by adequate protection.'9

Costs varied from region to region. The Ontario Fire Service concluded that the $125 per flying hour it subsequently paid for detection, suppression, sketching, and survey was amply justified. The federal Department of Forestry projected the cost of protecting its 120 million acres of woodland in the northwest by aircraft at one cent per acre. It judged this reasonable. Foresters reluctantly accepted higher initial expenses because 'an era of high costs is a necessary preliminary to organization on a permanent basis.' The cost effectiveness of aircraft patrols had to be reckoned in the same light as ordinary fire insurance, the premium being measured against the potential economic return.[10]

The aircrews' work included detection, reconnaissance to assist ground firefighters, and the movement of ground parties and equipment. The emphasis given to each task varied by region. In British Columbia an extensive rural telephone network provided the basis for a ground detection system so that in normal circumstances aircraft only supplemented ground crews during peak fire seasons. Their greatest contribution was in transporting fire crews and equipment to remote locations. In Alberta, where few landing sites were available on the forested east slopes of the Rockies, air patrols concentrated on detection. Their introduction in 1920 had been well timed. The dominion forestry service had been about to make a major capital investment to construct an extensive network of ground lookout towers. The foresters were very quickly convinced that aerial surveillance would be more cost effective. Over the foothills, wireless-equipped landplanes were able to communicate with their High River base, which in turn had a telephone link with the forest service. Once the location of a fire was plotted, the district forester could move his ground crews to the scene. Initially, patrols covered only the Waterton Lakes and Rocky Mountain Park areas, but they were gradually expanded to include the Bow River, Crow's Nest, and Clearwater reserves. By the mid-1920s, there was also a sub-base at Grand Prairie in the Peace River district.[11]

The British Columbia and Alberta patrols were important, but they were soon dwarfed in scope by those in the vast forests of the northern Canadian Shield. The Department of the Interior, the responsible department, concluded in 1923 that this area provided the best conditions for the use of aircraft, and 'it is in these regions that their greatest value in fire protection can be secured.'[12] In April 1924 the Departments of National Defence and the Interior formed a joint committee to prepare a detailed plan for extending aerial fire protection to the 120 million acres of forests between the Ontario border and the valley of the Athabaska River in Alberta. They proposed a five-year expansion programme, adding sub-bases annually at locations ever further west. The project began in the 1924 flying season. Once the aircraft were in place each spring, the district forest rangers, after considering weather conditions and the fire hazard, would recommend patrols in specified areas. When a pilot spotted a fire he contacted local rangers, either by wireless or message drop. Supression aircraft might also be sent with crews and equipment. If the fire were spotted before it had time to get out of control, chances were that it would be contained.[13]

A typical operation occurred in June 1924 near Rice River. A flying-boat patrol, carrying the assistant district inspector of forest reserves, spotted a fire late one evening while returning from Norway House to Victoria Beach. The inspector called for a suppression aircraft and fire crew. A Curtiss HS2L dispatched the following morning was able to taxi within 100 yards of the fire. Ten minutes later a pump and 600 feet of hose had been unloaded and the crew was playing a stream of water from the downwind side of the blaze. Later in the day another pilot took photos of the area, confirming that the pump and fire crew were in action at the most effective location. Work continued until late afternoon, when heavy rain clouds to the southeast convinced the fire crew that they could return to base. Two days of rain virtually extinguished the fire. A single fire-ranger was then able to finish the job of extinguishing the large stumps and roots that were still showing flame.[14]

Endless summer patrolling took its toll on the aircraft, and the RCAF was faced with a need to replace them. The Air Board's reliance on the postwar gift aircraft from Great Britain allowed it to delay any capital expenditures for replacements. The Avros were adequate for Camp Borden training. The DH4s employed on Alberta fire patrols, however, were decrepit. An alarming report told how one had failed in the air from 'general deteriorioration.'[15] Wood shrinkage in the laminated main spar had opened up dangerous structural cracks, an especially serious fault in the turbulent flying conditions encountered in the foothills of the Rocky Mountains.[16] Moreover, as one pilot drily commented, the aircraft had its fuel tank between the pilot and observer, making himself 'simply the meat in the sandwich' in the event of a crash.[17] Of the flying boats, the heavy twin-engined Felixstowe F3s and Curtiss H16s were seldom flown because they were too difficult to maintain.[18] The Curtiss HS2Ls were the workhorses, versatile and reliable for bush flying. Yet one station superintendent complained in 1921 that 'unless a new and more suitable type of machine can be produced, there can be little progress made.'[19] RAF practice at this time was to rebuild a wartime vintage aircraft after five years, renewing all its wooden parts, after which it was flown for no more than two additional years. By 1922 the Canadian machines were all more than five years old, and none had been rebuilt.[20]

The Air Board wanted replacements designed and built specially for Canadian conditions. Robert Leckie, the director of flying operations, had noted the environmental and functional factors which were bound to influence the type of machines needed. 'Aircraft in Canada will be used very extensively in the opening up and development of comparatively unexplored land,' he wrote, and both forest protection and photographic exploration demanded long patrolling over rough terrain with few maintenance facilities. Aircraft, therefore, had to be reliable and possess ample range. They needed good short take-off and landing capability in order to operate effectively from small lakes surrounded by trees. They had to be adaptable to wheels, floats, and skis for all-season use. In response to a request from E.W. Stedman, the head of the technical branch, Leckie drew up requirements for three machines: a small and a larger landplane, and a single-engine flying boat.[21]

Designing an aircraft to certain specifications was easier than procuring it. Sources of supply presented a major problem. Once the wartime facilities of

Canadian Aeroplanes Ltd were liquidated, there was no manufacturing or even assembly capability left in Canada, and foreign companies were just beginning to convert to peacetime production. Canadian Vickers Ltd, interested in broadening its Montreal facilities to include aircraft, offered to open up a Canadian branch plant with access to its British parent's technical capacity; it demanded, in return, an exclusive contract to supply the board's aircraft.[22] Stedman was unimpressed. 'This is pure bluff,' he minuted to Wilson. 'If we tied ourselves up to Vickers we should effectually strangle any industry that would otherwise grow up and we should be at their mercy as to price. They should compete with other contractors for our contracts.' Leckie was even more succinct: 'The attached proposal I consider absurd and quite out of the question.'[23] Wilson replied more diplomatically, thanking the company for its interest, but pointing out that the board did not wish to restrict itself to an exclusive contract. He acknowledged that buying from Vickers 'might result in quicker action and faster progress,' but the drawbacks of limiting competition outweighed potential benefits.[24] Moreover, he emphasized, any capable Canadian manufacturer would be given preference. The principle of promoting domestic manufacturing was one to which both the Board and later the RCAF gave continuing priority.

Wilson did not want Vickers to lose interest, however, and tried to impress upon them that aviation in Canada had an unlimited future from which manufacturers might reap substantial rewards. The company, in turn, kept the board aware of its new products. Two in particular were of interest: a flying boat named the Viking, which was just coming into service, and an Avro (Vickers was acting as the Canadian agent of the A.V. Roe Co) modified to take a more powerful Wolseley Viper engine.[25] Stedman kept a close watch on these and other developments in both Britain and the United States, but none of the newer machines seemed entirely suitable without structural alterations. As Stedman recalled, 'we were interested in producing aircraft that, from the start, had been designed to do the work for which they were required and under the climatic conditions that were likely to be experienced.'[26] In the meantime, the only aircraft the Air Board acquired were several more HS2L hulls purchased from surplus American stocks.[27] These were the circumstances which lay behind the aircraft procurement problem, growing to crisis proportions, that faced the RCAF when it displaced the Air Board.

In October 1922 Wing Commander J.L. Gordon, the acting CAF director, informed his superior, Major-General J.H. MacBrien, of the situation. Like Stedman, Gordon stressed that new aircraft should be built in Canada, noting that the wood used by British manufacturers 'undergoes considerable shrinkage due to seasoning when used or stored in this country.'[28] The urgency of the situation was soon made abundantly clear when Gordon called his commanding officers to Ottawa to consider their requirements for the next year. Their reports were gloomy. All of the air force's thirty flying boats were obsolescent; only half would be serviceable for operations. Even if ordered immediately, replacements were unlikely to be found in time for the 1923 spring fire patrols. Gordon needed no persuasion. The next day he suggested to MacBrien that $500,000 be requested in supplementary CAF estimates for an immediate order of twelve flying boats and eight single-seat landplanes. For the former, Gordon recommended the Supermarine Amphibian, which could use Rolls Royce Eagle engines the RCAF had in stock; for the latter he preferred the Avro Viper. MacBrien added an additional $40,000 for radio equipment and sent the proposal to the minister.[29]

The Cabinet authorized half the requested amount in November 1922. Tenders for eight flying boats and six landplanes were immediately called from several British, American, and Canadian firms. Delivery of the first aircraft was to be made by the end of March 1923 and the remainder within two months. Bids were accepted until 2 January and later extended for a month, after protests from some of the companies. Even so, lack of time, both to prepare proposals and deliver aircraft, discouraged a number of prospective bidders. Ericson Aircraft Ltd of Toronto declined, as did the Hall Engineering Co in Montreal. The Ottawa Car Manufacturing Co Ltd tried to locate either a British or American aircraft manufacturer interested in establishing a Canadian branch, but without success. Laurentide Air Service Ltd was more successful and submitted a joint bid with the British Supermarine Co. Nineteen British firms were notified of the competition, and eleven submitted bids. Two American firms, Glen L. Martin and Dayton-Wright, also competed.[30]

The pressure of time eliminated the possibility of waiting for new designs. The Amphibian and Viking were the only two aircraft considered beyond the experimental stage. Stedman confessed a 'slight preference' for the Amphibian, but British Supermarine planned to construct their machines in Britain. Vickers promised more. It would erect the first two Vikings in its British factory, in order to meet the March deadline, and complete the order in a plant to be built in Montreal. Despite an added cost of $6450 to build the boats in Canada rather than at the parent factory, Vickers still offered a significant price advantage – $150,650 compared with Supermarine's $177,400 for eight flying boats. The Vickers bid was accepted, while the order for land patrol aircraft was held over.[31]

Wing Commander Scott, the liaison officer in London, was the target of considerable criticism from unsuccessful British firms when rumours circulated 'that it was a foregone conclusion that Messrs. Vickers Company would be awarded the contract.'[32] But allegations of favouritism were unfounded. The Vickers proposal best fit the tender, even though Scott had his own doubts about the Viking. Reports of its flight trials were mixed. One test pilot cautioned: 'the machine would probably sink as a result of the hull being swamped if it was necessary to taxi at sea with a beam wind for any length of time.'[33] Moreover, its favourable flying characteristics had been achieved with a powerful 450-hp Napier Lion engine. The RCAF planned to install smaller 360-hp Rolls Royce Eagles left over from the British Air Ministry's postwar gift. Scott recommended thorough testing because there were 'great doubts' that such a configuration would meet RCAF specifications.[34]

The order was confirmed, nonetheless, and the first operational machine, Viking ED, was delivered in July 1923, three months late. Scott's reservations were sound. One RCAF mechanic who had already served in three other air forces – the RFC, RAF, and CAF – remembered how 'the *Vikings* were the last thing in flying boats, constructed of beautiful mahogany planking with millions of rivets. Those aircraft had to be beached after every flight and polished every day with cedar oil. The engines were First World War vintage and valve springs were always breaking, mags [magnetos] burning out condensers and points, and they were a mechanic's headache.'[35] They were, as well, underpowered. The Eagle engine was an unimpressive performer. 'On take-off,' wrote one airman, 'I would climb out from the back over the windshield and stand with the photographer up front to change the centre of gravity enough, moving it forward, to get the aircraft up on the step. When she was up and running, we could clamber back to our positions for take-off. It used to take us an hour, on a good day, to get to 5,000 feet with a load of stuff in the aircraft.'[36]

The Viking purchase was an interim response to a long-term problem. The air force wanted domestically designed and built machines because others were technically inadequate for Canadian operating conditions. Stedman reckoned it would take from eighteen months to two years to produce new types. This, however, required long-term planning and funding, luxuries the RCAF did not have. In Britain, the RAF first issued specifications to a number of competitors before narrowing their list to three companies, which would be asked to produce prototypes. Rigorous testing eliminated two, and the survivor then constructed six to twelve machines for service trials, after which suitably modified production models were ordered.[37] By contrast, the air force had no competitive domestic aircraft industry on which to draw, government funding was woefully inadequate, and estimates were restricted to a single fiscal year. In addition, a two-year lead time was out of the question because of accelerating operational demands for the immediate replacement of aircraft in the field.

More Vikings were needed for the 1924 season, as well as an improved, Canadian-designed flying boat, replacements for the DH4s in Alberta, and either new or reconditioned training machines for Camp Borden. Stedman catalogued the requirements and set his technicians to work preparing specifications for them. He described to MacBrien, perhaps wistfully, the ten-year development programme being considered in the United States, which had allocated $15 million annually for aircraft. The Canadian equivalent, he calculated, would be about $1 million a year. Such sums remained elusive. Perhaps, however, because of demonstrated need, perhaps through continued parliamentary and prime ministerial support for civil operations, the air force was able to take its first real steps towards acquiring some of the aircraft it needed in the spring of 1924.[38]

The precise origins of the Vickers Vedette are obscure. Others besides the air force were interested in a Canadian flying boat at this time. In 1923 the Laurentide Air Service flew its own Viking and talked with Vickers about an improved boat. Vickers complied with some preliminary designs. Early the following year the Canadian Society of Forest Engineers formed a committee to draft specifications for the aircraft types it considered necessary for effective patrol work. It recommended two models: a single floatplane, adaptable for skis, for survey and fire detection, and a larger single-engine flying boat for firefighting and other patrols.[39] Stedman's technical branch then redrew the foresters' specifications and sent them along to Canadian Vickers. In April 1924 Stedman asked the firm for an estimate of costs for a prototype of the flying boat; Vickers quoted $15,000, including the installation of the RCAF's own engine. The company added that, if assured of an order, it would bring a designer from England and construct the boat in Montreal towards an October delivery date.[40]

Wing Commander W.G. Barker, who succeeded Gordon as acting director for a few weeks in 1924, continued negotiations with Vickers. Barker disliked floatplanes, considering them unseaworthy, and before leaving to become the RCAF liaison officer in London he reached a verbal agreement with Canadian Vickers to proceed with the construction of two flying boats. The smaller single-engine boat, the Vedette, would carry three and be employed on fire-detection and photo patrols. The larger boat, the Varuna, would carry seven and be used for firefighting and general transportation. A contract was duly let in August, by which time Vickers' designer, W.T. Reid, was already in Montreal and working with considerable dispatch to construct the Vedette by the promised October deadline. He succeeded. The Vedette was taken into the air for its first flight early in November, and further testing and modification continued until the end of the year. Most of the Vedettes later supplied to commercial operators used the American-built, air-cooled Wright Whirlwind J4 radial engine, while the RCAF adopted the Lynx for its production models in the interests of standardizing on British types.[41]

The Vedette was not exactly the flying boat the air force had in mind when it drew up its original specifications. It did not have the high-lift, thick wing construction Stedman preferred, nor was it ideal for aerial photography because of its relatively low load capacity.[42] But it gave good all-round service for several years. Squadron Leader B.D. Hobbs, commanding officer in Winnipeg, reported the next spring that the Vedette was 'exceptionally suitable for Patrol or Transportation service,' and could be used for limited-range photography flights.[43] RCAF pilots flew more than a hundred operational trial hours on the first machine during 1925, and found they could get it off the water in a flat calm in under ten seconds, then climb to 10,000 feet in about thirty minutes. It was reliable, economical, and manoeuvrable in all weather.[44]

The larger boat, the Varuna, which was introduced in the fall of 1925, was less successful. The Varuna was powered by two Lynx engines and carried a photographer in the nose, the pilot and mechanic in a forward cockpit, and four passengers in a rear compartment. Designed primarily for forest-fire suppression, the Varuna was also used for general transportation work, but its need for a lengthy take-off run and a poor rate of climb restricted it to larger lakes. The RCAF bought thirty Vedettes but only seven Varunas.

The Vedettes were not fully operational until the 1926 season. In the meantime Barker's successor as acting director, Wing Commander Scott, found he could not wait for the Vedette's eventual delivery. He had undertaken a cross-country inspection of RCAF bases soon after assuming command in May 1924, in the course of which he was struck by the urgency of the need for new aircraft. He became sufficiently alarmed after talking to RCAF officers in the field to decide that an interim machine was needed until the Vedette was ready, and immediately began drafting plans to supplement the long-range flying-boat development project with other types which were readily available. Scott's three frequently conflicting concerns were quick delivery, economy, and standardization. He concluded that the quickest, least expensive alternative was to fit Avro Vipers with floats. By making them fully convertible to wheels and skis as well, the Vipers could be adopted as a standard patrol type, while the Vedettes were used for aerial photography and the Varunas for fire suppression and transportation. Consequently, the RCAF placed an order for ten float-equipped Avros in December 1924. They were ready for the 1925 season.[45]

The Vipers were themselves far from ideal. They 'were known to throw connecting rods occasionally with disastrous results,' one fitter remembered.

Once when Flying Officer Bill Weaver, flying one of these contraptions, was forced down on tiny Stormy Lake in central Manitoba I was taken in to investigate the damage and found that the engine was a total wreck as two con rods had smashed through the crankcase.

It was a problem to land another aircraft as the lake was only a mile long and a little over 100 yards wide, surrounded by high trees. Flying Officer Frank Wait came in to find out what was required and stalled on take-off; that meant that we had two aircraft in this pothole and something had to be done about it. Joe Maskell was then flown in to Beresford Lake and hiked through the bush to give us a hand. The crashed aircraft was towed to shore by making a winch between two trees. The engine was removed and the mud and slime taken out, the serviceable mags and carburetor were removed from the wrecked engine. One engine was made out of two, installed in Flying Officer Weaver's aircraft, tested and flown out by Flying Officer Roy Slemon.

To fly the aircraft out the fuel was reduced to a minimum, the tail of the aircraft was tied to a tree and when the engine was at full throttle I cut the rope with a sharp axe and the aircraft just made it over the trees.[46]

The new aircraft which the RCAF gradually acquired were put to a remarkable variety of uses. Requests came in constantly: to spray forests for spruce budworm and wheat acreage for blister rust; to take census of reindeer and buffalo herds; to transport geological surveyors, mining engineers, Indian agents, RCMP officers, and medical rescue missions in remote regions; to locate, classify, and sketch or photograph stands of timber; to conduct route surveys for railway construction. Each task was worth doing, but threatened to detract from the primary responsibility of forest patrolling. Since forest fires occurred randomly, forest service officers insisted that the aircraft must be continually on call and not diverted elsewhere. For the forestry branch, 'The essential justification of the use of aircraft in forestry work lies not in any possible economy which may be effected, but in securing a greater degree of efficiency than can be obtained in any other manner. In fire protection nothing short of an organization adequate for all emergencies is worth while for a permanent proposition. The reason for this is that inefficient fire protection is *no* fire protection at all when it is most needed. A properly functioning organization is therefore not an ideal but a necessity.'[47]

Aerial photography, however, was one task that could be carried out without removing patrol aircraft entirely from their primary mission. Air photos were in great demand, and they had potential as an effective means of offsetting the high fixed costs of forest patrol bases by employing their resources more efficiently. Beginning as an off-shoot of forest protection, aerial photography became the RCAF's major civil operational function by the end of the decade.[48]

Aerial photographs, providing basic topographical data, had innumerable uses. Planning of water power developments, irrigation schemes, railway routes, and other engineering projects was simplified. More accurate and rapid surveys of forest and mineral regions were possible, and aerial photography had its widest application as an aid to mapping. The potential wealth of timber and minerals created a demand for accurate maps which could be paid for in part by flying aerial surveys from established RCAF bases. By 1924 the precision and thoroughness of new aerial photo techniques had all but revolutionized map-making in Canada. For the first time it was feasible to map systematically the whole of the Canadian land mass.

The joint DND-Department of the Interior committee, which had earlier prepared a five-year scheme to expand into the west, accepted the principle of using the fire patrol camps as bases from which photo missions could be flown. During the 1924 season, when the lengthy programme to map Canada systematically from the air began, machines based in Manitoba flew more than 160 hours on surveys, covering some 27,000 square miles. The highlight of the season was a major exploratory flight by Squadron Leader Hobbs in the Reindeer Lake-Churchill River district. With Flying Officer D.J.R. Cairns operating the camera, R.D. Davidson (a civilian) acting as navigator, and Corporal J.A. Milne as mechanic, Hobbs flew a pioneer survey of a vast unmapped expanse of forest and lakes, using fuel caches which had been placed the previous winter. He initially planned to run his photo flights at a 5000-foot altitude, taking three pictures every three miles at a ground speed of 60 mph. In the event, he was forced to operate 1000 feet lower because his heavily laden Viking could fly no higher, although Hobbs had removed the wheels and tail skid to lighten the load. Despite bad weather and almost continuous mechanical difficulties with the camera, Hobbs and his crew managed to take about 1700 photographs during their four-week trip.[49]

At first photo missions were conducted when aircraft could be spared from fire patrols, but as more equipment became available, independent photographic detachments, controlled directly by the Ottawa air station, were formed. When topographical surveys and RCAF Headquarters jointly selected a region to be photographed, the flight unit would be briefed so it could position fuel caches. The surveys branch provided a map of the region, if available, and deployed ground parties to locate control points. When lakes and rivers were free of ice in the spring, the photo aircraft would move to their assigned locations and begin flying, following a series of parallel lines related to the control points. On non-operating days the crews maintained their machines, moved supplies, and

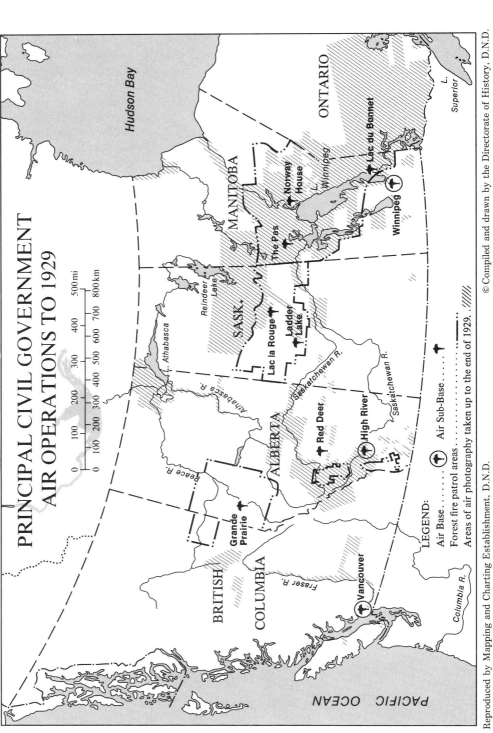

PRINCIPAL CIVIL GOVERNMENT
AIR OPERATIONS TO 1929

LEGEND:
Air Base........✈
Air Sub-Base.....✈
Forest fire patrol areas...........
Areas of air photography taken up to the end of 1929. /////

© Compiled and drawn by the Directorate of History, D.N.D.

Reproduced by Mapping and Charting Establishment, D.N.D.

coped with a variety of unexpected problems requiring a high degree of initiative, patience, and practical intelligence.[50]

Centralizing control of the mobile detachments in Ottawa, where the topographical survey branch had its central photo library, made for easy co-ordination. An effective operating technique gradually developed to meet the increasing demand for photos and maps. Topographical survey formed the central aerial surveying unit, a central clearing house and depository for photographs, which co-ordinated all survey requests from other organizations. By 1927 it had indexed 163,000 photographs covering almost 200,000 square miles.[51]

Photographic patrols over the vast expanses of the Canadian northwest were not without hazard, particularly when air-to-ground radio was inadequate or non-existent. Pilots often relied on pigeons for reporting accidents and forced landings in remote areas, and a number of stations had qualified pigeoniers 'to maintain, breed and train the birds.'[52] During the 1930 season pigeons were dispatched after eight forced landings, and on fourteen other occasions by crews needing assistance or reporting fires.[53] Natural flying hazards were often exacerbated by smoke from forest fires which obscured visibility and could cause pilots to lose their bearings. On a morning patrol in late August 1929, Sergeant J.M. Ready could not find Gordon Lake in the smoky haze of a nearby fire and lost his bearings as he attempted to turn back to Lac du Bonnet. Descending through heavy smoke, he became disoriented and, lacking instrumentation for 'blind flying,' was forced to bail out 500 feet above the water with the machine doing 125 mph. He plunged into Lac du Bonnet, but managed to swim to shore despite the fact that his life preserver failed to inflate. After a five-mile hike to Davis Lodge, he was able to obtain a boat to return to base. This was apparently the first emergency use of the parachute in RCAF history.[54]

Most bush flying was less dramatic. Sub-bases established in the northwest began their operations as temporary, tented camps which were gradually improved each year. They remained small, accessible only by aircraft or boat, and detachment personnel were on their own through the May-to-October flying season. The hours were long, the work hard and usually boring, and the need for ingenuity and improvisation ever present. For the 1926 flying season, the two officers, ten airmen, and three army signallers who comprised the Norway House, Man., detachment operated a Viking flying boat and an Avro 552 floatplane. During the summer the flight crews spotted and took suppressive action against thirty-three forest fires in the district. In addition, they made experimental flights for the Department of Agriculture, transported Indian agents to pay treaty money, flew several emergency medical flights, and conducted survey missions. Although the abnormally wet season reduced flying time, pilots logged more than 271 flying hours before closing up in the autumn.[55]

Keeping the machines in the air was no easy task. When the fire hazard was at its worst, in July and August, the planes were continually on patrol, away from base up to seven hours each day, refuelling from predistributed caches. Maintenance was carried on out of doors with little support equipment. The Viking IV provided few problems, requiring only one engine change during the season, but the Avro 552 detection aircraft was less reliable. Immediately on arrival at Norway House, its engine had to be replaced and the aircraft completely rerigged. The engine problem eventually proved to be the main bearing, which had been improperly assembled when the engine was overhauled during the winter. The engine and spares then had to be stripped down and reassembled in the field.

The Norway House detachment also had to maintain itself, and amenities and support services were anything but lavish. The base had been considered a temporary one when first established, but in the late fall of 1924 a civilian contractor had erected the shells of a cook house, mess, quarters, workshops, and offices. In their spare time over the following season the men of the detachment completed the interior finishings, installing and painting window casings, frames, floors, panelling, and ceilings. They also dug a large cesspool and erected two closed latrines.

But this was only the beginning of their construction tasks. Some years before, the forestry department had installed a sixty-foot dock on the opposite side of the island which the detachment used to unload its summer stores. This meant that every year some 200 tons of freight had to be transported across the island, until the detachment decided to construct a freight and passenger dock closer to the workshop and storage area where it was needed. A seafront built up to dock level and extending back thirty feet provided useful space for unloading heavy supplies and equipment. Next came a new 30 by 100 foot slipway, with a top platform large enough to accommodate four Vikings, so that aircraft could be brought out of the water for maintenance. But first the shoreline had to be cleared by hand of about 150 tons of rock. The men cleared rock from a further fifty feet of beach next to the slipway so that aircraft could be brought to shore for refuelling without interfering with the mechanics working on the maintenance platform. Then came a fifty-foot mooring dock as well as repair and winter storage facilities for the base motor boat. In their spare moments the detachment also cleared, graded, and sanded permanent paths and walks to connect their shore facilities with the base buildings.

All this was done by a very few men. The Norway House commander's 1925 annual report had recommended that the unit's establishment be increased because there were so many non-flying tasks on the remote base. Instead of gaining the four additional men he requested, the detachment was reduced by three. Undaunted, the commander removed the airman cook's helper from the kitchen and put him in charge of the unit's ground equipment. He then hired a civilian for kitchen duties, paying him out of unit funds. The next annual report dryly commented: 'In no other way could the heavy Station construction work of building the slipway and aircraft platform have been carried out by so small a sum of money other than this private employment of civilian labour, as no Government funds were available.'[56] When the unit was unable to obtain more reliable water transport, the detachment made do by hiring a heavy freight canoe (again with unit funds) while the engine of the motor boat was completely overhauled. When yet another engine job on the tired craft proved insufficient, the detachment collected enough mess funds to buy a new boat. Thus RCAF officers and airmen became skilled at improvising and making do with very little.

Such experience stood them in good stead when the RCAF participated in a sustained and difficult operation in the eastern Arctic in 1927-8. The purpose of the Hudson Strait expedition was to determine the nature of ice conditions in the strait in order to assist navigation in Hudson Bay. An aerial reconnaissance of Hudson Strait had first been suggested by C.C. MacLaurin in 1919. The following year, the Department of Railways and Canals requested an ice survey. The Air Board expressed interest in the project but quietly dropped it when the department pursued it no further. During the next seven years little interest was shown in the eastern Arctic – with one exception. In 1922 the air force sent an observer when the Canadian government dispatched an exploratory expedition to the Arctic archipelago to establish a number of police posts. At the urging of the Department of the Interior, the Air Board detailed Squadron Leader R.A. Logan to report on flying conditions in the region. Logan, who had been a dominion land surveyor before the First World War, was an expert in meteorology, navigation, and wireless.[57]

The expedition sailed from Quebec on 18 July 1922 and returned on 2 October, having visited the north end of Baffin Island as well as Bylot, Ellesmere, and North Devon islands. Because of the short season, and because its primary task was to place police posts, Logan was unable to undertake any research or exploration in depth, but his report was full of acute observations. Aircraft, he thought, could play a large part in the orderly development of the region by mapping the inaccessible interior, assisting the RCMP, transporting surveyors and geologists, developing a caribou and reindeer industry, and conducting ice patrols to assist navigation. Logan concluded that coal and probably oil-shale were located in the area, possibly in sufficient quantities to supply any air bases established there, and he judged that ski-equipped aircraft could be used for more than half the year. He recommended that all air patrols be conducted in pairs, each carrying adequate ground survival gear, and that an Inuit always accompany a patrol because 'an Eskimo can find food and direction where a white man would be lost, starved or frozen to death.' Before beginning any major flying operations, adequate preparation was essential. Logan suggested that personnel should travel north to familiarize themselves with climatic conditions, take meteorological observations and tide soundings, and observe surface and air conditions. While on the ground they could also conduct experiments in heating aircraft instruments, starting air and water-cooled engines, and using skis under different conditions.[58]

Logan's recommendations went no further in 1922. The federal government, however, did not completely abandon the possibility of using the Hudson water route as a way of gaining access to the interior of the continent. The idea of an ice reconnaissance in the strait was revived late in 1926, when planning was in progress to complete the Hudson Bay Railway to Churchill. The value of Churchill as a port for shipping western wheat to Europe depended upon the length of the shipping season. Estimates varied all the way from six weeks to six months, and an extended monitoring of ice conditions was crucial. In December

1926 the Cabinet created an advisory board to lay plans for an expedition, headed by N.B. McLean of the Department of Marine and Fisheries, and including Group Captain J.S. Scott, the RCAF director.[59]

The air force had experience in winter flying, but not in severe Arctic conditions. Pilots would need a machine which was versatile, extremely rugged, fitted with a spacious cabin, and equipped with an absolutely reliable engine. The chief engineer, Wing Commander Stedman, and Flight Lieutenant T.A. Lawrence, a staff officer at Headquarters who was promoted to squadron leader and given command of the expedition's flying operations, evaluated several British and American types. None of the British aircraft companies was interested in filling a small order of six specially designed machines within a deadline of three months. The Dutch designer, Anthony Fokker, who had set up shop in New Jersey, agreed to the difficult terms. Fokker and R.B.C. Noorduyn, later the designer of the Norseman, quickly produced and delivered six Fokker 'Universals.' These five-place, high-wing monoplanes had steel-tube fuselages covered with fabric, with wood covering on the wing, an open cockpit and enclosed cabin, and were powered by a Wright Whirlwind engine, capable of a cruising speed of 98 mph with an endurance of four hours. The usual operational load, with crew, fuel, emergency supplies, and cameras, was about 1700 pounds. Purchased by the Department of Marine and Fisheries at about $16,000 each, the aircraft had civil registrations, although the RCAF provided the crews.

Lawrence has recalled that the selection of aircraft divided senior officers. Originally the plan called for modified Avros. When Lawrence strongly objected, Scott sent him to New York to test fly a Fokker. Lawrence liked it, and in the event these seaplanes gave exceptional service. Two problems did surface, however: the floats and fittings proved structurally weak; and all photography had to be carried out through a window in the side door. In addition, the RCAF acquired a float-equipped de Havilland 60 Moth for preliminary reconnaissance flights of possible base sites.[60]

Six pilots and twelve mechanics went on the expedition, as well as a number of civilian specialists: four wireless operator-engineers, three doctors, three storekeepers, and three cooks. They assembled at Camp Borden for instruction in winter flying, meteorology, navigation, engines, first aid, seamanship, snow shoeing, skiing, shooting, dog handling, welding, carpentry, rigging, photography, and instrument servicing. Pilots underwent refresher training intended to 'raise the standard of their ability' and 'to correct any bad habits they may have acquired.' Attention was given to emergency supplies and to the recreational and reading needs of the men, who would be isolated for at least six months.[61]

The expedition set off from Halifax, NS, in the middle of July 1927 aboard two old vessels, the CGS *Stanley* and the ss *Larch*. Jammed in with the aircraft, prefabricated buildings, and a construction crew, expedition members sailed in leisurely fashion up the coast of Labrador, arriving at Port Burwell ten days later. In their reconnaisssance seaplane Lawrence and Flight Lieutenant A.A. Leitch reconnoitered base sites. After thoroughly examining both sides of the strait, they decided to erect camps at Port Burwell (Base 'A') at the eastern end, Nottingham Island (Base 'B') at the western end, and Wakeham Bay (Base 'C') mid-way

THE HUDSON STRAIT EXPEDITION
29 SEPTEMBER 1927 - 3 AUGUST 1928

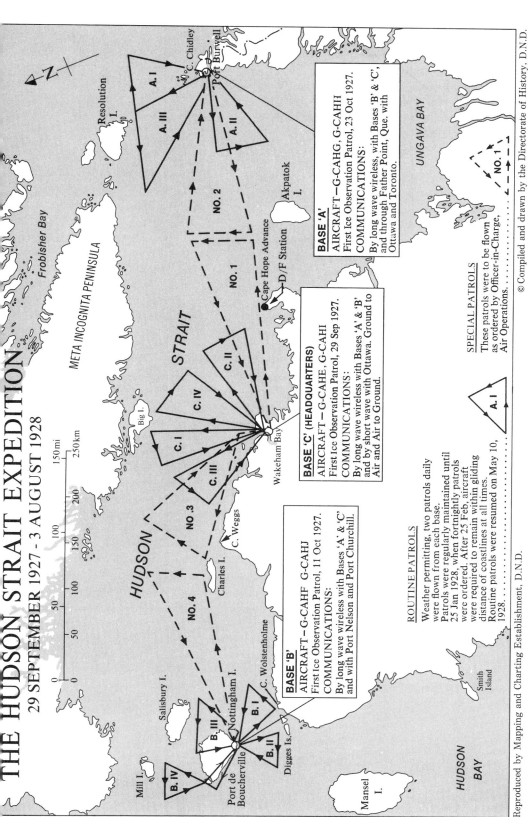

Frobisher Bay

META INCOGNITA PENINSULA

Resolution I.

C. Chidley

Port Burwell

A. I

A. III

A. II

NO. 2

Akpatok I.

Cape Hope Advance

D/F Station

UNGAVA BAY

NO. 1

STRAIT

Big I.

C. II

C. IV

C. I

C. III

Wakeham Bay

NO. 3

C. Weggs

Charles I.

HUDSON

NO. 4

Salisbury I.

Mill I.

B. III

Nottingham I.

B. I

Digges Is.

Port de Boucherville

B. II

B. IV

C. Wolstenholme

Smith Island

Mansel I.

HUDSON BAY

NO. 1

A. I

BASE 'A'
AIRCRAFT – G-CAHG, G-CAHI
First Ice Observation Patrol, 23 Oct 1927.
COMMUNICATIONS:
By long wave wireless, with Bases 'B' & 'C', and through Father Point, Que. with Ottawa and Toronto.

BASE 'C' (HEADQUARTERS)
AIRCRAFT – G-CAHE, G-CAHI
First Ice Observation Patrol, 29 Sep 1927.
COMMUNICATIONS:
By long wave wireless with Bases 'A' & 'B' and by short wave with Ottawa. Ground to Air and Air to Ground.

BASE 'B'
AIRCRAFT – G-CAHF, G-CAHJ
First Ice Observation Patrol, 11 Oct 1927.
COMMUNICATIONS:
By long wave wireless with Bases 'A' & 'C' and with Port Nelson and Port Churchill.

ROUTINE PATROLS
Weather permitting, two patrols daily were flown from each base.
Patrols were regularly maintained until 25 Jan 1928, when fortnightly patrols were ordered. After 25 Feb, aircraft were required to remain within gliding distance of coastlines at all times.
Routine patrols were resumed on May 10, 1928. ....

SPECIAL PATROLS
These patrols were to be flown as ordered by Officer-in-Charge, Air Operations. ....

© Compiled and drawn by the Directorate of History. D.N.D.

Reproduced by Mapping and Charting Establishment, D.N.D.

between. All hands immediately set to work preparing the sites for winter; by the time the ships departed with the construction crews in November the buildings were habitable if unfinished. McLean, a leading figure in the expedition's formative stages, remained on board ship throughout, and did not disembark. Lawrence, who never received written instruction, was left in charge. He concocted his own operation order on the way north.[62]

Lawrence organized a system of routine and special patrols for all three bases, to provide regular and systematic coverage of the strait as well as to ensure the safety of the flight crews. Weather permitting, daily patrols were carried out from all three bases, and aircraft from different bases sometimes arranged to rendezvous, ensuring a continuous monitoring of ice movements. Pilots filed detailed flight reports after each patrol and air photographs provided a permanent visual record. Crews maintained wireless communication with the ground by means of transmitters using trailing antennae. Both voice and key methods were used and a remote control device enabled the pilots to use the radios. While on patrol the crews communicated with their bases regularly at five-minute intervals.

Routine patrols began on 29 September from Wakeham Bay, and continued for almost two months before freeze-up forced a halt. Even so, flights were intermittent: fog, wind, snow, and dangerous shore ice prevented flying on all but ten days in that period. During the three-week freeze-up period, conditions were unsuitable for either floats or skis. Squadron Leader Lawrence reported: 'Some idea of the conditions to be contended with in eventually getting a runway over the rough shore ice to the bay ice can be visualized ... Tons of ice and snow were chopped down, filled in, levelled off and packed into a runway, using the tractor as a roller. At each change of tide, this runway, which extended across a beach about 200 yards long, would heave up and crack until eventually after much labour it became a solid bridge of ice, rising and falling with the tide, but immune to serious damage.'[63] On 12 December more routine patrols became possible with the Fokkers on skis, and these continued until 18 June 1928. A short period again followed when ice conditions prevented the use of either floats or skis. On 29 June 1928 the expedition was able to resume the Wakeham Bay flights with aircraft on floats, and these continued until the expedition completed its work.

Regular patrols from Nottingham Island began on 11 October 1927 and went on until 16 November, when freeze-up set in. Colder temperatures on the island shortened the interval between float and ski operations, and regular flying on skis could be undertaken on 23 November. Floats were refitted at the end of May 1928. At Port Burwell the regular float patrols began on 23 October and continued for thirty-one days. Ski patrols began on 13 December, and these aircraft also reverted to floats in May.

The expedition established three communications systems. Radio technicians from the Department of Marine and Fisheries operated a short-wave link from Wakeham Bay to Ottawa, as well as long-wave links between the three bases. The Royal Canadian Corps of Signals maintained an air-to-ground system. This provided one-way communication only, the aircraft having no receivers, but it enabled pilots to signal ground bases by both voice and key. Messages were always duplicated, transmissions being sent first by key, then voice. Navigation equipment was primitive. Because the aircraft had to remain below cloud cover to carry out their visual reconnaissance, most navigation was simple map reading, using Admiralty charts from the 1830s, on which land contours proved surprisingly accurate. There was, therefore, no need to rely on the two magnetic compasses, the earth inductor compass (similar to the one used by Charles Lindbergh on his transatlantic flight), or the Bumstead sun compass with which each of the Fokkers was fitted.[64]

Pilots and crews soon perfected a procedure for starting the Fokkers in the severe Arctic weather. After each flight the engines were completely drained of oil, which was then stored in a warm place until needed again. To start up, the groundcrew towed the machine to its take-off position, faced it into the wind, and covered the engine with a fitted asbestos cover. They then directed the heat from two or three blow torches through a length of stove pipe into the air space around the engine. After 30-45 minutes heating, during which the mechanic regularly turned over the propeller, the torches were removed and engine oil, having been heated on a stove, was poured into the lines. Finally, and very quickly before the engine cooled, the engine was started. The system worked well, even when aircraft were forced down away from base.[65]

There were three occasions during the winter when aircraft became lost. On 15 December 1927 Flight Lieutenant Leitch and his crew were returning from Erik Cove at Cape Wolstenholme to Nottingham Island. Half way back to base they flew into a snowstorm and lost their bearings. Not sighting land, Leitch landed on a six-inch thick ice-floe and waited out the storm. The crew drained the engine of oil and made themselves as comfortable as possible. That night the temperature dropped to minus 16 degrees Fahrenheit and the men suffered minor frostbite. The following day Leitch calculated his navigational error. Then, using emergency equipment carried in the plane, the flyers warmed the oil, poured it back into the engine, and started up. They arrived back at base with only a quart of fuel remaining.[66]

A second incident occurred on 8 January 1928 when Squadron Leader Lawrence set out from Wakeham Bay en route to Nottingham Island. When he encountered a heavy snowstorm about twenty miles east of Cape Digges, he turned back and landed at Suglet Inlet. The next day he attempted to reach Nottingham but again snow forced him down, this time at Deception Bay. For the next nine days storms battered the area while Lawrence and his crew camped near the Fokker and lived off their survival rations. The weather eased on 16 January. Flying Officer B.G. Carr-Harris from Wakeham Bay located the missing aircraft. By the time Lawrence's crew was able to dig their Fokker out of the snow and make it airworthy, the short Arctic day was almost over. It was therefore necessary to spend another night at Deception Bay. Both aircraft returned to base the following day.[67]

The third occasion on which an airplane became lost was the most serious. It began on 17 February 1928, when Flying Officer A.A. Lewis took off from Base 'A' accompanied by Flight Sergeant N.C. Terry and the usual Inuit guide. Their route for the day was across Hudson Strait to Resolution Island, half-way to Frobisher Bay, and by return course across Grinnel Glacier and the strait to base. The outward passage was routine. When he headed across the strait for home, however, Lewis ran into a blizzard driven by hurricane-strength winds. The snow forced him 'to let down to within a few feet of the ice-pack where accurate navigation became well nigh impossible, what with the local magnetic disturbances, the oscillations of the compass needle, the extreme turbulence of the air and almost zero visibility.'[68] With darkness approaching, and the aircraft rapidly running out of fuel, Lewis began to look for a clear patch of ice, all the while tapping out a message on his radio key to inform base that he was lost and trying to land on the ice pack. Heading the machine into the wind, he could see nothing except rough ice formations on which to land. 'Suddenly I saw immediately below what appeared to be a stretch of clear, greenish ice and fervently praying that it extended ahead at least a short distance I cut the engine whereupon the aircraft dropped like a stone almost vertically and then using the engine for a short burst I set it down on the ice and immediately cut the switches. When we hit the ice, so strong was the wind, that the aircraft stopped almost immediately but the pinnacles were so numerous that we could not avoid hitting one head-on and the aircraft finished up with the tail up in the air and the nose and skis buried in a deep snowdrift against an ice-pinnacle.'[69]

Lewis, Terry, and Bobby Anakatok, the Inuit guide, immediately set to work constructing an igloo, which proved reasonably snug. Their survival kit, fortunately, was not damaged. They had a .303 rifle with fifty rounds of ammunition, rubber raft with pump and two paddles, hard-tack biscuits, six slabs of high-concentrate chocolate, several bottles of Horlicks malted milk tablets, a tin of butter, a can of matches with sealed lid, tea, a snow knife, three jack-knives, fishing line with hooks, a primus stove with a gallon can of kerosene, three sleeping bags, and a bottle of brandy. It was sufficient to keep them alive for a time, even if they were unable to shoot a seal, walrus, or polar bear.

Were they in Ungava Bay or the Atlantic Ocean? Flying into the northwest wind, Lewis had allowed a twenty-degree margin for drift: 'I couldn't reconcile in my mind the fact that any gale would require a greater correction than that.' He concluded they must be on an ice-pack in Ungava Bay, and that by walking east they would reach the shoreline. After a few hours rest the three set out eastwards into continuing strong winds and a temperature of about minus 40 degrees Fahrenheit. Lewis reckoned that the ice conditions would improve as they approached shore, but after two hours he realized that they were in fact getting worse. He called a halt, and they built another igloo. Lewis now believed that they must be in the Atlantic, not Ungava Bay. They would have to retrace their steps. The next day was clear, and Lewis hoped they might be able to sight the range of Labrador mountains which follow the eastern coast:

We were completely surrounded by tightly packed ice-pinnacles and could not immediately sight anything on the horizon, so climbing to the top of one of the pinnacles I was almost afraid to look towards the west for if I saw nothing it would without doubt dash all our hopes for our survival, however when I at last glanced to the west, there clearly etched in the sky, were, what appeared to me to be mountain peaks white with snow, I could scarcely contain my joy at this definite confirmation of my theory. A rough calculation convinced me that we must be about 50 miles out in the Atlantic, for taking into consideration the height of the mountains roughly three thousand feet on a clear day one has a range of vision of approximately 50 miles.[70]

For the next seven days the small party walked westward. Luckily they were able to shoot a walrus to replenish their diminishing food supply. Three times they had to cross open water, the last on an ice-pan after Bobby had quietly abandoned their rubber boat so that he could carry an extra quantity of walrus meat. Finally reaching the coast, the three turned north hoping to find the native village at Eclipse Harbour. After another four days, by now suffering badly from hunger and exposure, they met an Inuit family who helped them to the village. After a short rest and some food, the three set out again with another native escort for Port Burwell, which they reached in the middle of the night of 1 March. Other than frostbite, Lewis and Terry suffered no lasting injury.

The expedition continued patrolling until ice observations ceased on 3 August 1928, when all hands began packing up for the return trip. The plan was to fly the Fokkers back to Ottawa. During the summer a series of fuel caches had been established along the eastern shore of Hudson Bay. The five surviving aircraft assembled at Erik Cove on 24 August. The next morning the Fokkers prepared for take-off despite heavy seas running into the cove from the northeast. Only three got airborne. One failed to take off because of engine trouble, and another crashed with a damaged float. A machine immediately landed to rescue the crews, and Lawrence radioed the ss *Larch* and cgs *Montcalm* for assistance. The remaining aircraft were now examined closely, and it was found that salt water corrosion had weakened both the undercarriage mounts and float fittings on two of them. Consequently, Lawrence decided to evacuate the expedition by sea. The aircraft were dismantled and placed aboard ship for the return journey.[71]

The expedition's long season concluded at the end of November, when the ships reached Quebec. In eleven months of flying the crews had flown 227 reconnaissance patrols over difficult terrain and through weather ranging from bad to impossible. They brought back with them a valuable film record of over 2000 air photographs, a great deal of practical knowledge about working and flying in northern weather, and much information on ice conditions in the strait. In his report, Lawrence noted that ice had first appeared on 16 November at the western end of the strait near Nottingham Island, and did not entirely clear until 3 August the following summer. The weather had been continuously bad, with fog, cloud, and vapour diminishing visibility, and ground conditions were especially difficult during the in-between seasons of freeze-up in the fall and break-up in the spring.

Lawrence's primary recommendation was that an effort be made to prepare accurate maps and charts because the existing ones were 'so inaccurate ... as to present a large and dangerous factor in the development of the strait as a commercial water route.'[72] A hydrographic survey was also needed, but only after a prior detailed aerial survey with vertical photographs. Lawrence thought that a small crew operating from temporary bases at Lake Harbour and Wakeham Bay could photograph both sides of the strait in a summer season. He also noted that at least one aircraft located in the region at all times would be able to give invaluable assistance to ships, informing them of ice conditions by radio, and thus enabling them to navigate through ice-free channels. The ideal machine for Arctic flying, Lawrence thought, would be a twin-engined amphibious flying boat, with air-cooled engines and ski attachments, having an endurance of seven-to-nine hours at about 100 mph, capable of carrying radio equipment and a crew of three or four with full emergency kit and rations for sixteen days.

Lawrence's report was recognized as an important contribution to the development of the Hudson Bay transportation route. Radio stations were established as aids to navigation and in 1930 a government icebreaker, *N.B. McLean*, began regular patrols. Nevertheless, the route's potential remained unrealized and it was not until after the Second World War that interest in the region was revived, and then for strategic rather than economic reasons. Nor did Lawrence and his men gain public acknowledgment until the 1970s, when the National Film Board production, *The Aviators of Hudson Strait*, featured an interview with Lawrence and made extensive use of original film footage taken by the expedition's cameramen. In 1980, belatedly, Lawrence was made a member of the Aviation Hall of Fame.

The purchase of the Fokker Universals for the Hudson Strait expedition had been a significant departure from past procurement practice. Precedent and convenience had previously led the RCAF to rely on Canadian Vickers for its aircraft, but the irregular nature of its procurement policy caused difficulties for both. Lacking other orders which would justify continuous assembly-line production, Vickers had to hire extra tradesmen each winter to meet the air force's latest crisis, and then let them go for the summer. No one knew whether there would be money for more machines next winter or whether the RCAF would have to make do with what it had. It was not a process suited to the retention of skilled workers or the maintenance of good quality control. The result was that Vickers was usually behind with its production, commitments were broken, and the RCAF was left shorthanded. The possible advantages of having one principal supplier were thus largely negated by an unhealthy dependence on one unable to deliver.[73]

The problems came to a head when the RCAF tried to standardize its aircraft fleet around a family of Vickers machines. As the Vedettes and Varunas came into service the force ordered experimental models of the Velos for vertical photography, the Vanessa for general transportation, and the Vigil and Vista as patrol aircraft. The force planned to test the machines early in 1927, and then specify modifications before ordering production models of each for use in the 1928 season. Unfortunately, Vickers was unable to deliver the aircraft in time for proper testing and the procurement timetable was badly disrupted. The Velos prototype, particularly, was an abject failure; it was so overweight that when snow accumulated on its wings, as it lay overnight at its moorings, it sank tail first. Neither it nor the others were taken to the full production stage.[74]

Finding insuperable difficulties in depending on one supplier, the RCAF modified its attempt to standardize and began to look to several manufacturers to fill its needs. It proved impossible to maintain its policy of giving preference to Canadian and British firms. Canadian industry was slow to develop and British companies seemed unable or uninterested in producing aircraft for Canadian conditions, particularly those suitable for civil operations. In the summer of 1929, Group Captain J.L. Gordon asked the liaison officer in London to attend the forthcoming International Aeronautical Exhibition to find prototypes on display which would be useful in Canada. His report was not promising; the only possible patrol type was the Saunders Cutty Sark, which had not as yet been tested. There were no suitable photo machines at all. Ironically, within a few months the British trade commissioner in Canada wrote to the Department of National Defence stressing the desirability of buying British to meet RCAF needs for aircraft equipment. The deputy minister pointed out that the department had already purchased a large amount of equipment in Britain, 'though I am unable to say that this has been quite successful. Questions of prompt delivery and of service within Canada have necessarily influenced the choice of aircraft and firms in the United States have certainly shown greater readiness to meet the needs of the Department than has been shown by British firms.'[75]

One of the American firms well able to meet Canadian needs in the mid-1920s was the Fairchild Co. S.M. Fairchild had begun by building aerial cameras and moved on to designing aircraft to accommodate them. His FC-2 was a high-wing monoplane with heated cabin and large windows for oblique photography as well as a glass panel in the floor, so that a vertical camera could be used.[76] The air force was much taken with the FC-2 and by the end of the 1928 flying season it operated seventeen, including the larger more powerful version, the FC-2W. Further developments of this aircraft specifically for RCAF requirements resulted in the new design, the 71B. Fairchild machines of various types and modifications were used throughout the 1930s for aerial photography and reconnaissance flights. Fitted later with light bomb racks under the fuselage, some of them were even used for practice bombing and army co-operation exercises at Camp Borden in 1937 and 1938.[78]

A Fairchild was the first RCAF aircraft to reach the Beaufort Sea. On 2 July 1930 two planes, under the command of Flying Officer J.C. Uhlman from Station Winnipeg, left McMurray, Alta, to carry Lieutenant-Colonel E. Forde of the Signals Corps and two officials from the Departments of Indian Affairs and Agriculture on an inspection tour of posts along the Mackenzie River valley. The flight stopped at Fitzgerald, Hay River, Fort Simpson, Fort Wrigley, Fort Norman, Arctic Red River, and Aklavik in the Northwest Territories. They also flew to Herschel Island in the Beaufort Sea. By the time they had completed the round trip at McMurray the two Fairchilds had accumulated 140 hours in the air and had flown over 11,000 miles, for the most part over unfamiliar territory.[79]

Even this marathon tour was surpassed by a party leaving Ottawa as Uhlman was flying down the Mackenzie River. On 6 July 1930 Flight Lieutenant F.J. Mawdesley in a brand-new Fairchild 71B, and Flight Sergeant H.J. Winney at the controls of a Vickers Vedette, left Ottawa to explore the main water routes in the Northwest Territories and to inspect the RCAF's gasoline and oil caches along the way. Flying via Lac du Bonnet, Man., Ladder Lake, Sask., and Fitzgerald,

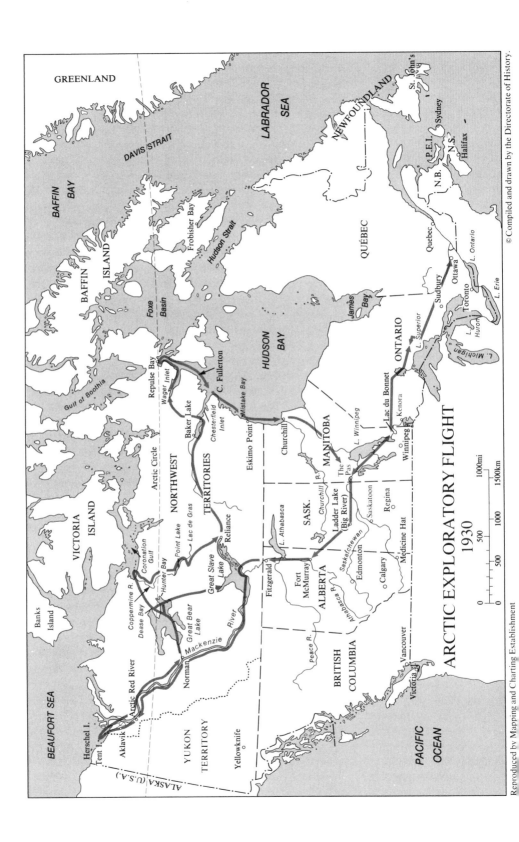

ARCTIC EXPLORATORY FLIGHT
1930

Alta, the two headed north along the Mackenzie to Aklavik, where they landed on 19 July. After fog prevented a flight to Herschel Island, Mawdesley and Winney continued on to Great Bear Lake, Coronation Gulf on the Arctic Coast, and Reliance on Great Slave Lake. After photographing the water routes between Great Slave Lake and Coronation Gulf, they flew east to Chesterfield Inlet and then north as far as Repulse Bay on Melville Island. Having completed the inspection tour, the flight returned to Ottawa through Churchill, Man., along the western shore of Hudson and James bays. When the Fairchild and Vedette touched down on the Ottawa River on 1 October, Mawdesley and Winney's party had flown almost 15,000 miles and taken more than 3000 photographs, the longest exploratory flight undertaken in Canada to that time.[80]

The Fairchild was not the only new workhorse. Another was the Bellanca CM-300 Pacemaker, also a high-wing cabin monoplane, well suited to aerial photography and similar in construction to the Fairchild but faster and with greater load-carrying capacity and/or endurance. Of the thirteen Pacemakers purchased by the RCAF, one remained in service until 1940. In 1931 there were eleven photo detachments in the field flying a mix of aircraft types. Three of the detachments flew Vedettes, seven were equipped with Fairchilds, and one with Bellancas.[81]

All the aircraft were heavily used for a variety of purposes and airmen frequently showed considerable initiative and ingenuity. On 29 March 1931 Flying Officer A.L. Morfee's detachment at Cormorant Lake, Man., received a wireless message to pick up a sick woman at Mile 214 on the Hudson Bay Railway. The railway was not operating, and no knowledge of the woman's condition was available. The nearest hospital was at The Pas. Morfee's Fairchild was lashed to screw pickets driven into the lake ice. He and a crewman poured in hot oil, started the engine, got airborne, and found their rendezvous where they put down safely on a nearby creek. Morfee's starter had been damaged, and so he kept his engine turning over while the patient was carried on a cabin door to the aircraft. A strong crosswind and rough snow hummocks made take-off difficult – almost a series of take-offs, Morfee recalled – and this affected the patient directly. Her baby was born before he could reach the hospital and a very surprised receptionist. The boy, probably the first Canadian aerial baby, was christened Lindbergh Wright Cook.[82]

A much rarer aircraft was the Keystone Puffer, which was used on RCAF crop-dusting operations in the late 1920s. In 1926 the Department of Agriculture had requested that two aerial spraying experiments be conducted, one in Manitoba against wheat rust, the other in Cape Breton against the spruce budworm. In memoranda submitted to the air force, the department reviewed experiments in spraying cotton in the United States, concluding that a special low-speed, low-flying aircraft would be required for both tasks and that the importance of the experiments could hardly be overstated. It was estimated that over 200 million cords of pulpwood in eastern Canada had been destroyed over the previous twenty years by the spruce budworm and that 'no satisfactory methods for immediate direct control of active outbreaks have yet been devised. Airplane dusting with arsenicals offers the only definite hope for a successful direct control of large areas.'[83]

The department initially recommended that the experiment be contracted out to a commercial company in the United States. A debate promptly ensued on the relative merits of conducting the experiment on a contract basis or purchasing the necessary equipment for the RCAF to do it. The director, Group Captain Scott, recommended that a contract would be much more economical than purchasing a special spray aircraft which could not be used for other military or civil tasks. If no suitable Canadian bids were submitted, the contract should be given to an American company, many of which had developed considerable expertise in the field. The chief of staff, Major-General MacBrien, disagreed. The principle that 'generally speaking, all experimental work should be carried out by the R.C.A.F.' should be maintained. Moreover, he was not in favour of a contract being let out to an American firm.[84]

MacBrien's inhibitions about contracting with a US commercial firm apparently did not extend to purchasing aircraft manufactured in that country. Negotiations were opened with the Keystone Co of Bristol, Pennsylvania, for the purchase of two aircraft specially designed for aerial spraying. The Keystone Puffer was a shapely single-seater biplane, powered by the ubiquitous Whirlwind engine, again easily convertible from wheels to floats or skis and fitted with a 600-lb dust-storage tank and a spreading mechanism along the lower wing. In April 1927 Flying Officers J.M. Shields and C.L. Bath were sent to the US Department of Agriculture's cotton dusting laboratory at Talullah, Louisana, for a short training course in aerial spraying. There Shields and Bath were taught the theory of dusting, methods of controlling the rate of spray, and low flying in the aircraft.[85]

The Cape Breton experiment, conducted with a float-equipped Puffer, had limited objectives. As an initial experiment it was primarily designed to overcome the technical difficulties involved in placing arsenic dust accurately in a given area in different degrees of concentration, and in establishing cost data for dusting operations generally. Although hampered by wet and windy weather, the experiment was relatively successful, enabling the dominion botanist, Dr J.M. Swaine, to conclude tentatively that an application of between twenty and thirty pounds of dust would be sufficient to control an infestation of the spruce budworm effectively.[86]

The experiment also exposed some difficulties involved in flying a single-engine aircraft low over treed areas. Unless there were lakes in the immediate area, any engine failure meant that the pilot would have little chance of survival. When the experiment concluded, Flying Officer Bath reported that even an old HS2L would be better for the job because with its much greater wing surface it could be pancaked onto the trees at a much slower speed. Bath also pointed out that the low capacity of the Puffer made it uneconomical; the machine got rid of its dust in about one and one-half minutes but it took half an hour to an hour to reload the aircraft with dust before starting another run.[87] The spruce budworm experiment was continued in June 1929 in the Welcome Lake district of northern Ontario, west of Sudbury. The dangers of low flying prompted the RCAF to obtain a Ford tri-motor for the job. This aircraft had a hopper capacity of 2000 pounds and its three motors made it a much safer aircraft for flying over forests.

On completion of the Welcome Lake experiment the aircraft and crew moved to the province of Quebec where another very successful experiment in spraying to control Hemlock Looper disease was completed near English Bay.

The other major experimental dusting programme was conducted on the prairies to combat wheat rust, which was common throughout Manitoba and Saskatchewan and caused an estimated average annual loss to Western farmers of around $25 million a year. Pending the development of a rust-resistant high-quality wheat, it was thought that aerial dusting with sulphur would be the best, quickest, and most economical way of combating the disease. In 1927 the second Keystone Puffer, this one on wheels, was sent to Winnipeg to conduct the initial experiments. Despite difficulties of weather, problems in locating effective test fields, and the low capacity of the aircraft, the results were moderately successful. Compared with the average yield in the region, all the dusted fields showed considerable improvement both in yield and grade. The experiments were continued over the following years and delivery techniques refined.[88] The results of this research were widely disseminated through scientific journals to a wider community. The collaboration in agriculture research between the scientists and the flying personnel demonstrated another valid use for aircraft within the RCAF's overall aim of promoting aviation.

Another task, anti-smuggling patrols for the Royal Canadian Mounted Police, occupied more than half the air force's civil flying time during the depression years – an incongruous precedent for the anti-submarine patrols which the service would fly in the Second World War. Liquor smugglers had developed a sophisticated system for avoiding RCMP coastal patrols. Schooners and motor vessels plying the West Indies-St Pierre/Miquelon-Maritimes circuit could easily evade authorities until making contact with their associates on shore, who would then dispatch small boats to pick up cargoes. The police lacked the resources to cover the extensive coastline adequately, and early in 1932 Major-General J.H. MacBrien, now the air-minded RCMP commissioner, asked that RCAF patrols be arranged off both coasts to supplement ground and sea policing efforts to reduce smuggling. The air force soon established four preventive detachments, one at Vancouver and the others on the Atlantic coast, where the major problem was located.[89]

On the east coast the RCAF established a joint headquarters with the RCMP in Moncton and deployed detachments at Gaspé, Shediac, and Dartmouth. Using a small number of Vancouver flying boats and Fairchilds to cover the Gulf of St Lawrence as well as the coasts of New Brunswick and Nova Scotia, the RCAF commander in Moncton co-ordinated the patrols, acting on requests from his RCMP counterpart. The pilot determined his own routes and timings according to weather conditions and the capabilities of his aircraft. When they spotted a suspected vessel, the crew, which usually included a local RCMP constable, would plot its location and course and drop a message to the nearest patrol boat or to police headquarters. The air force was prohibited from boarding and searching their targets, although in 1933 three landings were made to allow police constables to do so.[90]

In 1934 the preventive detachments on the east coast were organized as 5

(Flying-Boat) Squadron, and at Vancouver as 4 (FB) Squadron. Although wireless transmitters improved response time, smugglers adapted quickly and began using larger, faster, better-equipped motor vessels. They were able to lurk well offshore for several days, coming in quickly under darkness to unload cargoes onto smaller boats. Flight safety restrictions kept RCAF aircraft within twenty-five miles of shore in daylight, and they could not fly at night or in bad weather. At Dartmouth in 1935, for example, fog and weather grounded patrols for half the summer; moreover, flying had to be discontinued in October. The RCMP found better methods, notably a system of detection which employed radio direction-finding to locate vessels when they communicated with their shore contacts, and the air force withdrew from preventive patrols after the 1936 flying season.[91]

Such civil operations, while a long way from military flying, had their compensations. Two years after returning to the Royal Air Force, Leckie reflected on his time in Canada. His role in the peacetime RAF was 'interesting,' Leckie wrote J.A. Wilson, 'just as interesting, I think as military work can ever be, but frankly the Civil operations interest me very much more. It is distressing to spend one's life and energy assisting in the building up of a machine destined only for destruction, and destruction of a particularly disagreeable nature. I envy you in your simple, honest straightforward problem in Canada, and while I have no doubt you are not entirely free from political and other intrigue, the fascination of the work goes a long way as a recompense for the difficulties of the situation. Canada is too fine a country to stay away from indefinitely, and sooner or later I must return there.'[92] As Leckie said and appreciated, civil operations were visible, productive, and personally satisfying. Beyond this, they were the means by which a generation of officers and airmen learned their craft as commanders, staff officers, pilots, mechanics, storemen, and photographers. Advancing technology rapidly made their aircraft and equipment obsolete, but their experience taught them to handle adversity and improvise in unfamiliar circumstances which could not be foreseen in any training manual. The indispensable military virtues – endurance, flexibility, determination, self-discipline, technical proficiency, professionalism – were nurtured in Canada's remote regions.

4

Towards a Military Air Force

In the postwar years the military potential of airpower seemed almost limitless to many airmen, and there was a surprising unanimity among them about how that potential might best be applied. The two leading theorists were Sir Frederick Sykes in England and Brigader-General Giulio Douhet in Italy. Sykes, who had been the British chief of the air staff at the end of the war, preached a doctrine in which the enemy would be defeated by the strategic action of airpower. He contemplated (in the Lees-Knowles lectures of 1921) that: 'air war ... will be carried into the enemy's country, his industries will be destroyed, his nerve centres shattered, his food supply disorganized, and the will power of the nation as a whole shaken. Formidable as is the prospect of this type of air warfare, it will become still more terrible with the advent of new scientific methods of life-destruction, such as chemical and bacterial attacks on great industries and political centres.' However, to achieve that end it was important that the Royal Air Force retain its hard-won status as an independent service since 'essential independent strategic action would be irretrievably impaired by the reabsorption of the Air into the Army and the Navy ...'[1]

Almost exactly the same views were being expressed at the same time by Douhet, a former chief of the Italian air service, in his seminal work, *Il Domino dell'Aria* (*The Command of the Air*). Douhet proclaimed that the air would be 'the decisive field of action' in any conflict.

In general, aerial offensive will be directed against such targets as peacetime industrial and commercial establishments; important buildings, private and public; transportation arteries and centres; and certain designated areas of civilian population as well. To destroy these targets three kinds of bombs are needed – explosive, incendiary and poison gas – apportioned as the situation may require ...

To have command of the air means to be in a position to wield offensive power so great it defies human imagination ...[2]

Douhet, too, called for independent air forces, 'accorded equal importance with the army and navy ...' In fact, by 1929 he had gone much further; the air force should be the pre-eminent arm, and wise nations would 'concentrate the bulk of all national resources in the decisive field, the air.'[3]

Sir Hugh Trenchard, who succeeded Sykes as RAF chief of the air staff in January 1919 – Sykes sought an air force unacceptably large to his political masters – was a pragmatist, not a theoretician, a man whose success had always been more attributable to character than intellect, though he was well blessed with common sense. As commander of Britain's so-called 'Independent Force' of strategic bombers in 1918, he had become thoroughly disillusioned with the actual strategic capability of airpower at that time, but there was a visionary element in his character which enabled him to see that its prospects might be better in the indefinite future. He adopted a modified version of Sykes' theories while emphasizing the powerful economic argument that airpower was cheaper than either land or seapower; indeed, he was able to demonstrate this in the policing of imperial deserts during the early 1920s. Airpower could make a wilderness and call it peace, either in the natural wildernesses of the Middle East or (he implied) in the urban cornucopias of western Europe.

First World War technology, tactics, and training – which were all still the rule in the RAF throughout the 1920s – were, in fact, quite inadequate for the more complex environments of European war, at least on the strategic level. However, Trenchard made little attempt to develop any of these during his ten years in office. He placed his emphasis on organization and morale and Trenchardian doctrine was never subjected to any kind of rigorous operational analysis. Not until long after his retirement in 1929 was anything practical done in the RAF to implement his explicit final claim that 'It is not ... necessary for an air force, in order to defeat the enemy nation, to defeat its armed forces first.'[4]

Douhet had been just as categorical a year earlier in proclaiming that 'there is no longer any need to break through the enemy's lines to reach an objective ... Armies and navies have lost the ability they once had to protect the nation behind them.'[5] The Second World War would show that both had carried their ideas too far, but their expositions created an intellectual ferment at the highest levels of service thought, some of which doubtless filtered down to ordinary airmen. Some of it even reached the dominions.

Not unexpectedly, perhaps, the RCAF produced no airpower theorists. During the war no Canadian had held an appointment even remotely comparable with those held by Sykes, Trenchard, and Douhet. Very few had ever worked on air staffs at all. They had been combat flyers and now they were 'bush pilots in uniform,' their minds focused on the practical, technical, and administrative problems which beset them on every side. There was no RCAF Staff College to stimulate their thinking on strategy and doctrine, and when merit and good fortune took one or two a year to the RAF college in England, it must have been an exhilarating experience. Those that went absorbed the prevailing Trenchardian strategic doctrine. A 1924 graduate, Wing Commander J.L. Gordon, wrote on his return:

It would appear ... that in stressing the necessity for establishing Air Superiority prior to carrying out aerial operations which may be of vital importance to both an Army and a Navy, the work of these two services must suffer considerably in the opening phases of any campaign. There would appear to be only one practicable means of establishing this very much desired condition, and that is offensive operations against the enemy's means of production ... It should be realized ... that offensive operations in the air, as distinct from purely cooperative measures, should concentrate on what must eventually be their main object. This, it seems, is the principal centres of the enemy, and from the foregoing it will be seen that it is practically impossible, and perhaps inadvisable, to delay the carrying out of these operations until definite Air Superiority has been established.[6]

'The moment war is declared,' Squadron Leader G.E. Wait said in 1931, 'Air Power must be ready to exert direct pressure upon the enemy's internal organization.' Centres vital to the enemy's war-making capacity would be the prime bombing targets, but 'to safeguard her home interests,' the possibility could not be ruled out that Britain might 'be forced into direct air attack on enemy populations.' 'Civilian casualties [would] be unavoidable.' It would never be possible to destroy the enemy's air forces completely, but bombers provided the necessary element of flexibility to take the initiative and force the enemy to respond:

We strike first, then, at another and equally vital point, within range of both our bombers and fighters. Well directed bombing will cause a clamour for protection. The tendency will be for the enemy to divert some, maybe all, of his fighters to defend the threatened point.

But the result will not be a proportional increase in resistance to our attacks. We have the advantage of initiative, choice of objectives, approaches, methods, and times of attack. Also, being forced on to the defensive will react adversely on the morale of defenders ...

Having attained air superiority to-day, does not mean we shall have it to-morrow. Such superiority is never permanent. It must constantly be fought for, and can only be maintained by resolute bombing, *co-ordinated* with equally resolute air fighting. We shall always be operating in the face of hostile air power.[7]

In the same vein, Flight Lieutenant G.R. Howsam attempted to bring bombing theories home to Canadian realities. 'Bombers, supported by fighters,' he wrote, 'are the embodiment of air power which is applied by air bombardment.' While fighters provided the means for defence, which could only be partial at best, bombers were the prime weapons: 'In the last resort air power is one of the instruments whereby a nation is guarded, but without air bombardment an air force becomes an ancillary to the other services. Abolish air bombardment and there is no air power, no air striking force, no air defence and no *Air Menace*.' Canada was not vulnerable to attack, Howsam continued, but technological advance would make coastal raids from carrier aircraft feasible within ten years. Fighters could offer some protection against attacking bombers, but the principal defensive weapons were bombers. They would attack the carriers without which enemy aircraft were useless. Heavy bombers with a 900-mile range could attack up to half that distance. Allowing for ships' night movement during which they would be undetected, 'no carrier or other surface craft can approach unmolested within 150 miles of our shores if protection aircraft (bombers) are employed.' Canada's Pacific coast, he thought, was the more vulnerable. To defend it 'our requirements in military aircraft are bombers, fighters and flying boats for the Air Force proper. These are subject to air strategy and would be employed chiefly in Coast Defence.' Howsam proposed to circumvent the high costs of permanent units by forming auxiliary squadrons with permanent cadres initially on the scale of one flying boat and one bomber squadron for each coast. 'In the 20th Century there may be a Seven Days War – an air war,' Howsam concluded. [8]

It would be misleading to place too much emphasis on these expressions of personal opinion. Junior officers regularly publish their thoughts in military journals, particularly after the intellectual stimulation of a staff course. There RCAF officers could reflect on their military role and exchange viewpoints with their peers free from day-to-day distractions. Years later Howsam recalled: 'We had no Staff College in Canada at all. That level of thinking, that level of doing, was completely unknown. It was a godsend. Without it, we'd have been absolute neophytes.' [9]

The reorganization of 1927 had, in part, been designed to allow the RCAF to become 'purely air force in character and functions' with aircraft that would be 'strictly Air Force or Service types.' [10] As a result, the RCAF purchased nine Armstrong Whitworth Siskins, first-line British fighters, and six Armstrong Whitworth Atlases, the latest RAF army co-operation machines, during 1928-9. They were the first Canadian military aircraft obtained since the British gift aircraft of 1919. Since the reorganized RCAF did not abandon its civil role after 1927, they remained the only military aircraft in the RCAF until ten more Atlases were purchased from the Air Ministry in 1934.

Although they were never used in anger, the Siskins made a big impression. For several months after they were assembled at Camp Borden the Siskins were very carefully tended, rolled out from hangars to tarmac before the envious eyes of trainees. Pilots selected to man the Siskin Flight were a fortunate few; 'It was the realization of every pilot's dream.' [11] In 1929 the flight flew in a number of public air shows, including the Canadian National Exhibition. One pilot recalled:

Two days before the C.N.E. Dave [Harding, a RAF exchange officer and Flight Commander] decided that as the U.S. Air Corps was bringing up a full squadron of Curtiss Hawks we had to do something spectacular so he added to our few manoeuvres, *spinning in formation*. We had one practice at Camp Borden consisting of No. 1 and 2 wing men moving out two spans from the leader, the three aircraft then picked a point on the horizon, put the aircraft in a right hand spin coming out on the picked point on the third turn. It worked! During the years I spent on *flight formation flying* I never heard of any unit in the U.S. or U.K. even contemplating incorporating this manoeuvre in their program, but they didn't have a Dave Harding and two dumb wing men. [12]

The Siskin Flight was organized into a regular aerobatic team and performed until the early 1930s, including displays from Charlottetown to Vancouver with the 1931 Trans-Canada Air Pageant, which the Canadian Flying Clubs Association arranged to stimulate interest in aviation.

Performing aerobatics on Siskin fighters was the closest the air force got to simulated aerial combat. The RCAF was in fact a military air force in name only until the early 1930s, when two unrelated circumstances combined to jolt it out of its largely civil role and begin its tranformation to a military air force. The first event has been described. The 'big cut' of 1931 set in motion a chain of events which led to a structural separation of civil from military aviation. The second was the Geneva Disarmament Conference.

In January 1931 the Council of the League of Nations had announced plans to open its much delayed disarmament conference early in the following year, and it was ironically appropriate that disarmament talks about the efficacy and ethics of aerial warfare got underway as Japanese bombs were falling on China. The interminable posturing and wrangling in Geneva need not concern us here, except to say that the conference ultimately foundered on the fundamental incompatibility of France's demand for security and Germany's for equal status. Germany's withdrawal from the conference in October 1933 set the world on a downward slope to war.

On any international scale Canada's participation at Geneva was insignificant. The process of preparing for the disarmament discussions, however, was important for Canadian defence planning. The government formed an interdepartmental committee to report on the country's defence requirements, whose recommendations in January 1932 framed Canada's negotiating position at Geneva. More important, the re-evaluation of the country's military requirements led to a reordering of its strategic priorities and a fundamental readjustment of the defence structure.

For the chief of the general staff, Major-General A.G.L. McNaughton, the timing of the defence review was fortuitous. After assuming the top militia appointment in 1928, McNaughton had become convinced of the need for fundamental change. By the time the interdepartmental committee met to prepare Canada's position for Geneva, McNaughton's staff had completed an appreciation which concluded that a full-scale reorganization was needed. His principal aim was to reduce the unwieldy fifteen-division militia, which would be next to impossible to recruit or equip, to a more manageable size. The premise on which the outsize establishment had been based – the notion of a North American war and the consequent need for a large Canadian army to fight it – was untenable. As McNaughton noted: 'Provided Canada acts ethically and on the defensive, the United States must spurn the treaty of 1909 (which created the International Joint Commission), defy the League of Nations and forget the Peace of Paris (Kellog-Briand) in resorting to invasion – each and all impossible to conceive under existing world conditions.'

The militia staff foresaw two plausible contingencies: the protection of Canadian neutrality and the need to dispatch an expeditionary force. They were quite distinct, but had a common feature: 'The requirements of either situation call for the rapid mobilization and concentration of a force, not large, perhaps in comparison to the maximum possiblities of Canadian manpower, but equipped and organized on thoroughly modern lines.' McNaughton recommended, therefore, that the top-heavy militia establishment be slimmed down to a level of six infantry divisions with one of cavalry, a force which could be put in the field relatively easily.[13] As Sir Maurice Hankey, the British Cabinet secretary, later observed, 'By this step the Government could take the credit for a large reduction in establishments, and the army would be the more efficient for the reduction.'[14]

McNaughton was also concerned that the air force not be weakened. In the preliminary discussions at Geneva, a proposal was made to freeze existing establishments or budgets as a basis for setting maximum force limits. This, of course, would have left the RCAF with no military capability at all. Another proposal would have restricted the practice of seconding military aviators to civil operations. While aimed at Germany's practice of masking its military aerial development with civilian flying, the effect on the RCAF would have been equally crippling. In the event, neither scheme won general acceptance.[15]

Concerned with preventing unreasonable limitations to its growth, the RCAF for the first time considered seriously the military organization it would need for national air defence. By December 1931 Air Force Headquarters had completed a preliminary review of its requirements,[16] and when Group Captain Gordon returned from his Imperial Defence College course in the spring of 1932 (he was the first Canadian airman to attend),[17] he was relieved of his operational duties to plan in more detail. By mid-July Squadron Leader G.V. Walsh, a member of Gordon's staff, had completed his initial appreciation of the 'Peace Organization and Establishment of the RCAF Considered Necessary to Meet Minimum Requirements for National Defence.'[18]

Walsh considered three contingencies for which the RCAF must plan: direct or home (coastal) defence, the maintenance of neutrality, and, as a lower priority, the provision of squadrons for any expeditionary force which might be raised. The air force's primary responsibility was to defend the integrity of Canada's coasts. This role required forces with both a patrolling and an offensive capability sufficient to detect and attack enemy coastal raiders and monitor ship traffic in Canadian territorial waters. The nature of the threat, which could be mounted with little or no warning, required forces in being; that is, permanent force squadrons in home bases on both the Atlantic and Pacific coasts.[19] As General McNaughton observed: 'The outbreak of hostilities, under present conditions, would today, possibly, and tomorrow probably, be signalised by an immediate attack by air. Indeed, such an attack might be made before a formal declaration of war had been made. It is conceivable that attempted air attack from an aircraft carrier might not be kept secret, but direct attack (by trans-oceanic flight) could easily be kept secret, as the destination of aircraft cannot be gauged as can that of a Naval or Military Force. Therefore, there would not be time for any Canadian Air Force to expand in sufficient time to meet an attack.'[20] The secondary requirements of an expeditionary force, which would have to be mobilized, could be met from non-permanent squadrons.

The specific tasks for coastal squadrons, Walsh noted, included protecting important localities and ports from air raids, intensive reconnaissance and anti-submarine patrols, co-operating with coastal defence artillery, and defending imperial air routes and convoys. Seven permanent squadrons would provide the minimum force level. Two group headquarters, at Halifax and Vancouver, would each control a bomber and a flying-boat squadron. In addition, one army co-operation squadron operating from Ottawa would maintain contact with the latest RAF doctrine and equipment and provide a training cadre for non-permanent units in the event of mobilization. One fighter squadron, with a secondary bombing capability, stationed at Montreal, would be able quickly to reinforce Atlantic defences. A general purpose unit, convertible to either bombers or fighters, would be well placed at Winnipeg to assist on the west coast if needed. Two other group headquarters, at Montreal and Winnipeg, would complete the command structure, and a number of supply and equipment depots would cater to administrative needs.[21]

Walsh's numbers were repeatedly revised over the following years in response to changing events. But the revisions were not fundamental nor were Walsh's basic premises challenged. The primary role of the RCAF remained defined by its mission of home defence, dictated by rapid technological change which was producing ever faster aircraft able to fly further with increased payloads. As airpower developed, North America could no longer assume immunity from attack. Naval patrols could not ensure protection because of the speed and surprise with which air raids could be mounted; and, as McNaughton wrote, 'The Canadian navy as presently constituted is not an answer to any problem of Canadian defence.'[22]

General McNaughton's earlier views on the place of the RCAF in Canada's military establishment had undergone considerable change. Initially regarding the air force as simply an adjunct to the militia, McNaughton became its most influential promoter, believing that technologically advanced airpower ought to have a major impact on Canadian defence planning. His ideal permanent force was a small, well-trained, technically adept cadre capable of providing direction and leadership to reserves of manpower which could be mobilized when needed.[23] The RCAF matched that model.

McNaughton was in Geneva as a member of the Canadian delegation to the Disarmament Conference when he first received word of the 'big cut.' 'The Air Force, of course, is entirely shot to pieces ...' he was informed,[24] and it was no exaggeration. Not only would civil flying operations be virtually eliminated, there would be no possibility of achieving even the modest military aerial capability suggested by the air force staff. McNaughton hurried home from Europe and until the end of his tenure as chief of the general staff in 1935 maintained a continuous, if frustrating, effort to preserve as much as possible of his decimated defence structure. McNaughton had some considerable success in pressing forward with the airway system in conjunction with Ottawa's unemployment relief scheme. He also waged a continuing battle of memoranda as the militia and air force skirmished with the navy for funds sufficient to survive. Here he made fewer gains. Paradoxically, however, as funds declined, defence analyses became sharper, distilled to their bare essentials. And the RCAF found itself taking on the central responsibility for Canada's home defence.

It is difficult to assess in what proportion doctrine and economy were mixed in McNaughton's advocacy of the air force brief. He was more a pragmatist than theoretician, and there is little indication that he thought of airpower in the abstract. The air force could, however, perform an invaluable and practical defence role when inadequate funding forced some extremely hard decisions. He made this clear to Prime Minister R.B. Bennett in June 1933 when he pointed out that further reductions would disband the navy, cripple the air force, and allow the militia only a meagre existence. Because 'the substantial reduction in funds called for could not be whitewashed across the whole three Services,' he stressed, 'having regard to efficiency it would be necessary to concentrate on the absolute essentials, i.e., the Militia Forces and the Air Force.' It would be prohibitively expensive to provide the ships required for an adequate fleet. Moreover, it was 'of the nature of naval forces that they cannot be rapidly expanded to meet emergencies and, in consequence, it seems to me that little purpose is served in maintaining a small nucleus.'[25] He went on:

On the other hand Air Forces even in small numbers are a definite deterrent in narrow waters and on the high seas in the vicinity of the shore; they can be developed with considerable rapidity provided a nucleus of skilled personnel in a suitable training organization is in existence; pilots engaged in civil aviation can be quickly adapted to defence purposes; civil aircraft are not without value in defence, and any aircraft manufacturing facilities are equally available to meet military as well as civil requirements. That is, from a comparatively small current expenditure a considerable deterrent can be created in a relatively short time, and this is particularly the case in Canada where aviation plays a large part in the economic life of the country, a part which is increasing naturally at a rapid rate.[26]

'This being so,' McNaughton concluded, 'it appears to me that the most important element in defence which should be retained is the nucleus Air Force.'[27] It was a significant endorsement of the RCAF from the man who, by force of intellect and personality, dominated Ottawa's defence establishment.

If Bennett accepted McNaughton's logic, it was not made immediately apparent. The RCAF continued to refine its military functions and establishments on paper, but through 1935 expenditure remained at a level lower than that of 1931. The RCAF could neither reach the manpower limits established in the disarmament proposals nor obtain suitable military aircraft. The only service aircraft available in 1930 had been the Siskins and a few Atlas army co-operation machines. Between 1930 and 1935, 143 aircraft were written off because of age, crashes, or general debilitation. Eighty-two replacements were made, leaving a total of 174 in October 1935. Service aircraft comprised eight Siskins, fifteen Atlases, five converted Vancouver flying boats, and four Blackburn Shark torpedo bombers; there were also forty training and forty-five civil types. It was not much from which to fashion a fighting machine capable of carrying out its function as the first line of the country's defence.[28]

On his retirement in 1935, McNaughton wrote an indictment of Canada's defence position, cataloguing its realities and shortcomings, and returning to the theme of the need for a properly manned and equipped air force. In 'The Defence of Canada'[29] he reviewed the accelerating breakdown of international order during the previous years: continuing Japanese aggression and withdrawal of that nation, a First World War ally, from the League of Nations; the rise of Hitler and Germany's pullout from the League; increasing arms expenditures; and the division of Europe into rival systems of armed alliances reminiscent of 1914. Yet 'the Defence estimates provided by parliament have been barely sufficient to keep the mechanism of defence in being.' McNaughton pointed out that the government's failure to maintain the establishment levels it had agreed upon for the Geneva discussions could cause political difficulty. 'Having accepted certain figures for limitation purposes, these figures at once became an "objective" which, at the first breath of danger, the public will recognize as a minimum standard for defence.'[30] However, not even the minimum permanent training cadres were in place. For the air force, personnel strength and expenditures between 1932 and 1935 had remained well below 30 per cent of the ceilings agreed to, despite the most urgent need for an improved system of air defence – urgent enough for action to be taken, if necessary, at the expense of the militia.

I fully appreciate [McNaughton continued] the responsibility I have assumed in not requesting greater provision for the Land Forces at this time, and I do so primarily because I believe that the most urgent requirement is to lay the basis of the Air Force organization which is essential to our defence of the Pacific Coast in the particular contingency which I regard as the most probable, namely the defence of our neutrality in a war in which the USA might be engaged with a Trans-Pacific Power. It seems that in this event we would be friendly with the USA and that our liabilities might be restricted to the enforcement, against the Japanese, of the Rules of Neutrality prescribed by the Treaty of 1872 and also by the Hague. Failure to do so will result in the occupation, by the United States, of the coast of British Columbia and of our islands in the Pacific, following the precedent established during the Great War when the Allied Powers took possession of parts of Greece, and also in consequence of the fact that it will be vital to the safety of the great cities on the Pacific Coast of the United States that no enemy submarine and aircraft bases be established within effective radius of action.

The requirements for Forces sufficient to discharge our obligations for the maintenance of our neutrality in the West are neither extensive nor very costly, and it seems to me that by their absence we are taking a risk to our future wholly disproportionate to the interests we have at stake.[31]

Among its other trenchant arguments, McNaughton's paper made clear that he had clarified his original conception of Canada's role in protecting its neutrality. Rather than attempting to hold the Pacific coast against both belligerents, Canadian efforts would be directed towards Japanese incursions only. It was becoming increasingly clear that Canada could do little to counter an aroused United States. He and the militia staff were probably influenced in this regard by the debate on the future of airpower which was taking place at the time in Washington, more particularly in the House of Representatives Committee on Military Affairs.[32]

Early in the 1920s, Brigadier General William Mitchell of the United States Army Air Corps had noted after a visit to Canada that 'The Canadian frontier from Quebec to Camp Borden dominates our whole area contained in the North East States, Pennsylvania, West Virginia, Ohio, Indiana, and part of Illinois. Hostile aircraft, operating from this line, can render any cities or localities within the above area incapable of use.'[33] In 1935, in Congressional committee hearings regarding proposed legislation to extend the existing system of military airfields in the United States, several Air Corps officers again raised the issue of an attack from Canadian territory. They claimed that the United States could conceivably be subjected to air attack at any time. Even if Canada itself was not actively hostile, one officer emphasized, its neutrality would cause problems. 'Neutrality involves responsibilities as well as rights,' he told the committee, '... flying across Canadian territory would be a violation of Canadian neutrality, and if they did not take steps to carry out the laws of neutrality we would have to do so, I imagine.'[34]

Another officer pointed out that the Douglas Company was building a bomber able to carry a 2500-pound bomb load for 3000 miles at a speed of 225 mph. A hostile coalition of powers, he thought, would be able to establish temporary seaborne logistical bases on the North American continent to supply a fleet of long-range bombers in an attack on the continental United States. 'Fortunately or unfortunately,' he informed perhaps startled or bemused listeners, 'the Creator has given countless operating bases within a radius of action of this country in the vast number of sheltered water areas that are available deep in Canada and far removed from any sphere of action of ground forces.' From James Bay, Labrador, and Newfoundland, down to Bermuda and the Caribbean, small vessels carrying 2000 tons of supplies could establish 'floating railheads' which 'can furnish all the gasoline, all the bombs, oil, and ammunition, spare parts, all the food that is essential to take care of the operating personnel of 15 bombers, as well as the ground personnel for 30 missions, each one of which goes in 1,500 miles and comes back 1,500 miles.' The bombers 'could move from points in James Bay and along the Labrador coast simultaneously and concentrate over any place on the frontiers of this vital area and deliver attack in mass against whatever targets you want.'[35]

The only way to counter such a potential threat, the American officers concluded, was by using bombers against the enemy bases. In order to create this defensive capability, it was necessary to locate and construct more airfields in each of the threatened regions of the country, with sufficient intermediate stations to connect them. Brigadier General Charles Kilbourne, assistant chief of staff in the War Plans Division, was conscious of the sensitivity of the proposal. He wanted to locate one of the airfields in the Great Lakes area but, in order to avoid 'passing away from the century-old principle that our Canadian border needs no defence,' he thought that civilian fields could be constructed. 'I would have been very glad to put in the bill the Great Lakes area because of the Canadian situation,' Kilbourne added, 'but I could not put it in the bill. You will notice No. 7 in my bill is camouflaged. It is called "intermediate" stations for transcontinental flights, but it means the same thing.'[36]

Official reaction in Washington to the leaked testimony was swift and vehement. President Roosevelt, his secretary of state for war, and the State

Department immediately repudiated the suggestion that the United States viewed Canada in any way other than the best of 'good neighbors' or that any resort to force of arms was conceivable. The officers who testified, they made clear, did not set United States' policy, and in no way represented it. The committee had been irresponsible in making private views public. Apologies abounded, but the legislation itself passed the House in June and the Senate a month later, both unopposed, and received presidential approval in August.[37]

Canadian reaction was considerably more restrained. The Department of External Affairs obtained a copy of the hearings and asked the militia staff for comments. The reply was sympathetic to the American military viewpoint, accepting the need for staffs to plan for all contingencies, however unpalatable, and concluding that 'The United States is, in consequence, obliged to contemplate measures to protect itself from attack not by Canada but via Canada.' The staff reiterated that the combination of advancing technology and Canada's large and uninhabited coastline posed potential difficulties for American planners. Moreover, 'there is no record of their having uttered one syllable of hostility towards Canada.' 'No umbrage can properly be taken by Canada at these disclosures. Publicity has simply been given to the fact that is known to the world of Canada's impotence with regard to anti-air defence. Not only are our gates wide open but we have not even the semblance of a fence and our neighbour is, in consequence, obliged to provide against our lack of provision.'[38] The *Ottawa Evening Citizen* agreed, editorializing that the United States had to look to its own interests. If Canada was not doing its share it was because the government had 'virtually disbanded the Royal Canadian Air Force.' Canada could afford to ignore its responsibilities no longer 'unless the pretense of nationhood is to be completely abandoned.'[39]

The inescapable fact was that by the mid-1930s American aviation technology was rapidly closing the historic gap between military intentions and capabilities. By 1933 the B-9 and B-10 bombers, whose radically improved performance was derived through design improvements rather than simply increased power, were in operational service. The following year Colonel H.H. Arnold had led a squadron of B-10s on a flight from Washington to Alaska, stopping at Regina, Edmonton, Prince George, and Whitehorse en route. At the same time the United States Army circulated specifications for an even better aircraft. In 1935 Boeing had its experimental bomber ready. The four-engine XB-17, which the Air Corps tested in August in a spectacular flight from Seattle to Dayton, Ohio, flew 2100 miles at a record-breaking 232 mph. For the first time, it seemed to many aviation theorists, aircraft were coming into service which would be able to match strategic dreams with the means of carrying them out.[40]

Precisely how American airpower would affect Canada remained unclear, except that it would be impossible to mount a military defence against the United States. As the staff noted, the US Army was 'certain at first to be relatively inactive' in a war with Japan and therefore 'if any authentic cases of Japanese infringements, however minor, do occur it is quite probable that United States army authorities, chafing at their inactivity, will bring great pressure to bear on the government at Washington to permit them to take action themselves to supplement alleged Canadian inadequacies ... As Canada is, for practical purposes, incapable of resisting such a United States invasion there would be no course open except the humiliating one of accepting the violation of its sovereign rights.' For this reason it was 'of paramount importance to ensure that the United States Administration is given no basis in fact which would allow it to cite Canadian laxity in enforcing neutrality as an excuse to invade Canada.'[41] When the chief of the general staff, Major-General E.C. Ashton, visited Washington in January 1938 for 'most secret' talks with his counterpart, Major General Malin Craig offered to extend the United States Army's responsibility to include Canada's coastline to Alaska. The United States could supply mobile artillery and aircraft provided there were suitable landing fields. Ashton declined Craig's offer and the compromise of sovereignty it entailed. He pointed out that neutrality remained a distinct option for Canada, not only in her own interests but 'in order to avoid any overt act which might affect Canadian neutrality and thereby react on the other portions of the British Empire.'[42]

Ashton's disclaimer notwithstanding, the notion of holding the ring against all comers to protect neutrality and sovereignty became increasingly untenable in the few years remaining before war. Lieutenant-Colonel M.A. Pope, then the secretary of the Joint Staff Committee, later recalled that there had been considerable doubt among members of the militia staff that Canada would be able to remain aloof from a United States–Japanese war. The United States would simply 'ride roughshod' over Canada 'and make use of our territories and facilities as it pleased them.' Moreover, he thought, 'they would be entirely justified in doing so.' McNaughton thought Canada would inevitably be involved on the American side within thirty days; Pope thought thirty hours was more accurate.[43]

Adjusting defence policy to conform to new continental airpower realities was only one part of the challenge facing Canadian planners. Equally important, as the staff pointed out, 'the Eastern and Western portions of Canada lie on the Great Circle routes from Europe and Eastern Asia to the United States' and 'the continued supposition that Canada is and will remain free from attack by a trans-oceanic power is becoming open to criticism.'[44] The senior air officer was more explicit:

Air action against air-borne attack is a problem that is becoming more complex every day. We have been more fortunate that until the last few years the defence of our sea-borne trade, ports, industries and cities has been a comparatively simple problem compared with that facing us today. The advent and rapid development in the performance of aircraft has immeasurably added to and will continue to add to the complexities of the problem. We are by no means immune to air attack today. Very definitely, at the moment, attack by airships from an overseas base, or by aeroplanes launched from ships, is a probability. Direct attack by aeroplanes from an overseas base is also possible, and it will only be a short time before such will become probable ... if we recollect, the last war proved that aircraft development is considerably more rapid under war conditions, and we have every reason to consider that the same will hold good in any future war. Even if peace continues, records of today will be normal performance five or six years hence.[45]

An active air defence was no longer something for the future. Just as important, it provided a realistic, politically defensible rationale for the country's defence policy. The defence establishment had always been suspect on the grounds that it could be employed overseas in a war in which Canadian interests were touched only indirectly, if at all. But few could fault concern with protecting Canada's coasts, either against hostile assault or in defence of international obligations. Unlike the militia and RCN with their overseas links, the RCAF found itself with a direct defence role which was unassailable, strategically and politically.

This soon became apparent when Mackenzie King's Liberals returned to power in the fall of 1935. The new defence minister, Ian Mackenzie, was sympathetic to the militia staff's arguments about the deficiencies in Canada's defences, but he was unable at first to persuade his economy-minded colleagues.[46] Not until the following summer did the government create the Canadian Defence Committee, a Cabinet-level body to set and co-ordinate policy. The committee – the prime minister as chairman, and the ministers of finance, justice, and defence as members – first met on 26 August to hear detailed presentations from the three service chiefs. The evening before the meeting King briefed himself by reading McNaughton's farewell appreciation of Canada's defences, written over a year before. It disclosed, the prime minister confided to his diary, 'a complete lack of any real defence. I feel we must get aircraft equipment & look after our coasts – defend our neutrality, & be prepared to mobilize industry, and arrange for effective co-operation of Govt. departments.'[47]

The prime minister, however, had to perform an intricate juggling act in fashioning foreign and defence policies amid the many formidable restrictions imposed by political realities. Complicating customary difficulties, latent European antagonisms were smouldering dangerously. In October 1935 Italy invaded Ethiopia while the world stood by; next March Hitler occupied the Rhineland; in July 1936 civil war broke out in Spain. Direct Canadian involvement in overseas conflicts, which would inevitably provoke internal dissension, was most likely to come about through the country's historic ties with Great Britain. King had to tread warily, avoiding specific commitments to Britain which might require Canadian participation in a war not of its own choosing, while taking care not to antagonize those segments of public opinion which thought that the nation could not honourably avoid being actively involved in the world at the side of the mother country.[48] King's task was to locate the elusive point of balance between doing too little and too much. It was not easy. As his biographer has written: 'If Canada did become a belligerent it would need forces that were equipped and trained; the government would be held responsible if the country was unprepared ... Increased defence expenditures, however, might provoke a domestic crisis which would be as dangerous to the government as being unprepared if war came.'[49]

The Cabinet Defence Committee's first meeting confirmed King's worst fears. 'The impression left on my mind,' he wrote, 'was one of the complete inadequacy of everything in the way of defence.' He saw the need for 'changed methods of warfare, of having some coastal armament against raiders, chance attacks by sea and air,' but it was 'going to be extremely difficult to do anything effective without a cost which this country cannot bear. We have been wise in placing our reliance mainly on policies which make for peace. The Military authorities rule out altogether, as useless, any attempt to protect ourselves against the US and were wise in confining their statements to the need of the security of Canada within itself, and defence of our own neutrality.' The prime minister took the question to the full Cabinet that same afternoon: 'Council generally accepted the view we must take action at once, & next step to get a practical scheme for consideration,' despite the minister of finance's 'protest against expense, as something Canada could not face.'[50]

King's views on defence, and more particularly on the air force, were no doubt reinforced by a talk he had with the British prime minister, Stanley Baldwin, during a London visit in October 1936. Baldwin 'thought that we should give attention mostly to air force; while Canada might be the last country to be attacked, the air force would be the most helpful of any in case of attack, and training of men for the air and plenty of air equipment was the essential of modern warfare. He did not seem to think the navy was the thing to be concerned about, nor did he speak at all of the army.'[51] King himself took the same tack when he spoke the next month with the popular Irish Quebecker, C.G. Power, minister of pensions and national health, who had an abiding suspicion that the Canadian military establishment would use any expansion to involve the country in messy European affairs.[52] King spoke again to his cautious and divided Cabinet colleagues at the end of November: 'Excepting Mackenzie, I myself presented, I think, the strongest case for immediate coast defence, taking the ground that as a Canadian citizen, I thought we owed it to our country to protect it in a mad world, at least to the extent of police service, both on sea and in the air, alike on the Atlantic and Pacific coasts. I stated it was humiliating to accept protection from Britain without sharing on the costs, or to rely on the United States without being willing to at least protect our neutrality. That we had no enemies, but owed it to ourselves and subsequent generations to lay foundations on which they would have to build.' King wrote afterwards that he 'got agreement on having Departmental Committee gather information re war supply materials, food transportation facilities, munitions, and facilities for producing such. I drafted this order pretty much in my own way this morning. I spoke very earnestly of the unsettled conditions of the world, and the danger of class struggle extending to Canada ...'[53]

While King was mobilizing his political troops, Colonel H.D.G. Crerar, Commander H.A.C. Lane, and Group Captain L.S. Breadner had been delegated to prepare 'an appreciation of Canada's future military liabilities, outlining the means and arrangements necessary to meet these contingencies, and suggesting the successive steps on the part of each service, which would meet the requirements of a balanced and co-ordinated programme of development.'[54] Their paper, which James Eayrs has termed 'among the key documents of Canadian history,'[55] was ready for submission to the government in early September 1936. The appreciation set out three possible areas in which Canada might find itself obliged to rely on its armed forces: direct defence, preservation of neutrality, and indirect defence through participation in a war abroad. Top priority was given to home defence, and secondary responsibility assigned to an overseas commitment. The main concern was to devise a balanced force of all three services equipped with modern weapons and equipment, capable of being mobilized quickly and deployed to meet any contingency.

The tri-service Joint Staff Committee estimated the cost of rearmament at almost $200 million over a five-year period, with $65 million for the first year in addition to the usual militia vote of around $12 million. King and Mackenzie presented the case for dramatically increased expenditure to the Cabinet, the former arguing 'that we needed at least something that appeared like a protection of the gateway of Canada at the mouth of the St. Lawrence and something which might serve emergency purposes at harbours on the Pacific ... putting most of our expenditure into aircraft which could be available to move from one part of Canada to another, and some anti-aircraft guns at the coast.' Mackenzie recommended a sum of almost $57 million, but the minister of finance's preoccupation with reducing his deficit forced a compromise.[56] In the end, just over $34 million – the RCAF receiving one-third – was allotted in the main estimates. This was about triple the funds directed towards military aviation the year before.[57]

King and Mackenzie next faced the Liberal caucus and subsequently the House of Commons. In the House in mid-February 1937, Mackenzie attempted, with only indifferent success, to dispel any smug assumptions of comfortable isolation:

One of the hon. gentlemen spoke of the impossibility of attack by air. I wonder whether he recalls the great flight of General Balbo's squadron from Italy, over Montreal and on to Chicago, a few years ago. I wonder whether he saw in the press about ten days ago a description of the flight of a squadron of United States battle planes to Honolulu. I wonder whether he read a description which appeared in the press the other day of the manoeuvres at Singapore, with combined operations of the British fleet, the British air force and some other forces. I wonder whether my hon. friend has studied the bill passed by the United States in 1935, which bill particularly provided for the defence of that great republic against air attacks by nations three thousand miles and more distant ...

The hon. member for Vancouver North spoke of vessels making sporadic raids on our Canadian shores, and asked: Does that require any additional defence? Well, Mr. Speaker, the whole theory of National Defence today, with reference to coastal defence, deals with that specific problem, and it is for meeting these sporadic raiders or aircraft carriers that these estimates are compiled. If my hon. friend has read, as he probably has, the most recent pronouncement of those who are competent to make proper observations upon the subject, he would find that the entire conception of Canadian naval, military and aerial defence is based upon the action of sporadic raiders, or upon aircraft carriers. I want to tell my hon. friends this: We are prepared to build a hundred aeroplanes in the country. These, sir, are not necessarily finally localized in any portion of this dominion. They would be machines of high velocity, capable of being moved within a few hours for the defence of any portion of Canada – available for the protection of the great St. Lawrence river, available for the protection of Montreal, available for the protection of Quebec, available for the protection against any raid that might be made on the grain elevators of this country. In this day of aircraft carriers it is quite conceivable that enemy nations might raid this nation, supplying food as a neutral amongst belligerents. Our elevators and our food supplies might be raided, and apart from our essential coast defence our food supplies might be protected in the case of any hostilities.[58]

When the prime minister concluded the discussion on 19 February, he referred to the growing influence of airpower and to his previous and longstanding support of aviation, but kept the threat to Canada well in perspective – 'Relatively our danger is small.'[59] The government could not, however, ignore its responsibilities. These demanded a policy which would appeal to moderate opinion, convince outsiders of seriousness of purpose, and prepare for some future, and largely undefined, participation in collective action to secure peace. The prime minister's words gave hope to all shades of opinion. Isolationists could take heart from his apparent rejection of an expeditionary force,[60] while those who considered an overseas commitment to be inevitable could point to the address as a mandate for action and preparation. 'This speech I read and re-read,' one defence planner recalled; 'it seemed to me the first positive statement on defence policy made by a leader of a government since Confederation. As such I enthusiastically commended it to my friends.'[61] It was hesitant, it was partial, it was a mere beginning, but the rearmament programme sanctioned at the close of the parliamentary debate was probably the most which could be expected in the circumstances. The RCAF, in the process, had been given primary responsibility for Canada's direct defence.

As its responsibilities for the country's defence increased, it was natural that the RCAF began to question its status as a subordinate of the militia. It will be recalled that, whether by oversight or design, the air force's status was imprecisely defined at the time it was absorbed by the Department of National Defence in 1922. The RCAF did, however, exercise a certain autonomy in conducting its affairs, and it seemed to be generally assumed that the air force would become a separate military service 'when its expansion so warrants ...'[62]

In the meantime, a ramshackle administrative system had evolved to accommodate the RCAF. Except for special aeronautical stores supplied by its own technical, research, and supply branch, the RCAF obtained its services – pay, transport, medical, rations, and so on – through regular militia staff channels. Units were under the jurisdiction of regionally based militia districts. In 1932 the RCAF began appointing air staff officers to districts to advise the officer commanding on air matters, especially those pertaining to non-permanent units. On some topics the air staff officer dealt directly with district staffs; others he referred to AFHQ, which would take the question to the adjutant-general or quartermaster-general. Still other issues, such as discipline, lay in administrative limbo. Under the provisions of King's Regulations and Orders, district officers commanding had jurisdiction over RCAF officers and airmen in their districts, but RCAF crews based in one district might well operate in several others while on summer civil operations. It was cumbersome at best to determine where final responsibility lay. In 1935 a new quartermaster-general, Brigadier T.V. Anderson, was astonished to find that he was 'unable to find laid down anywhere what duties the Q.M.G. should carry out in connection with the RCAF.'[63] When the chief of the general staff looked more closely he found that his own authority and that of the adjutant-general was equally cloudy, as 'the situation has never been defined ...'[64]

It became evident, moreover, that the RCAF's military operational requirements differed functionally from the militia's. As the RCAF member on the interservice Mobilization Committee pointed out, the RCAF's responsibilities to defend the coasts against surprise attack meant that, unlike the army, it must have fighting units in place well before any formal declaration of war.[65] In addition, the operational command of air force squadrons could hardly be left to militia districts organized solely for the peacetime administration of static units. On the east coast, for example, seaward air patrols overflew several militia jurisdictions. Clearly an operational headquarters would be needed which took account of the long-proclaimed air force premise that the air was indivisible. Noting the accumulation of differing army and air force needs, the senior air officer, Air Commodore G.M. Croil, proposed in 1935 a full-scale reordering of the existing command and administrative structure.[66]

After reviewing the inadequacies of the current organization, Croil could see two alternatives. The first was to build up all 'the branches of the Air Force Staff, i.e., the Air Staff, Personnel Staff, and Equipment Staff, with armament, photography and signal advisers and the requisite clerical staff in 10 Military Districts.' This, he thought, would be an inefficient use of scarce resources. Instead, he recommended the formation of four air defence areas, each with its own RCAF Headquarters. Decentralization, Croil concluded, would simplify the command and control of air force operations, facilitate local recruiting and mobilization, and take full account of the flexibility of air units. The militia would retain control over common services – medical, pay, engineering, and rations – and provide them on demand to RCAF units from the nearest district.[67] The result would be to give the RCAF co-equal service status with the militia and navy.

For his own unrecorded reasons, the chief of the general staff ignored Croil's recommendation, deciding instead to increase the air staffs of some military districts.[68] When Croil met Ian Mackenzie in 1935, however, the new defence minister told him that he intended 'to make all three services of equal status.'[69] The deputy minister, L.R. LaFlèche, was also sympathetic to the air force's claims, counselling Croil to bide his time and 'continue until change occurred progressively.'[70]

Croil's next opportunity came over the issue of RCAF representation on the Defence Council, which had been formed in 1922 to offer military advice to the government. The chief of the general staff and chief of the naval staff were members, and together with the adjutant-general and quartermaster-general, the director of the RCAF (from 1932 the senior air officer) was an associate member. In 1936 the militia staff proposed that the master-general of the ordnance also be made an associate member.[71] LaFlèche, however, returned the proposal with the suggestion that the senior air officer be elevated to the status of member. When the chief of the general staff demurred, the deputy minister sought the opinions of the navy and air force. The chief of the naval staff was unequivocal: 'as a member of the Defence Council I am of the opinion that the SAO should be the member of that Council.'[72] Croil agreed. Because national defence was the direct concern of all three services, he replied, all must be equally represented in its planning, and 'This co-operation can only be achieved if the requirements and views of the three services receive just consideration. It is felt that each service should be free to express its views and none should be dominated by another. It is clear that unless the Air Force is given a seat on Defence Council, its requirements and views are not brought to the attention of the Minister, and therefore the Government, as clearly and convincingly as those of the other services. As a consequence, the possiblity of a true appreciation of defence requirements is jeopardized.'[73]

The Defence Council considered the matter at one of its rare meetings on 8 July 1936. The RCAF's claim touched a raw militia nerve. Major-General Ashton believed that the air force had no reason 'to develop an inferiority complex' and warned that separating the services would be expensive because 'The tendency of officers of the Air Service, as far as I am aware, is to give little consideration to the question of expenditures ...' He also objected that the change would disturb the seniority list, leaving 'the Adjutant General, Quartermaster General and Master General of the Ordnance, who are his seniors, in the junior position of Associate Members.' Ashton was overruled. The minister elevated the senior air officer from associate member to member within a week.[74] The change was an important symbolic step towards full service independence.

Croil was not content to leave the matter there. He continued to point out to the chief of the general staff that the RCAF needed to control more of its own internal affairs in order to implement its increasing responsibilities. 'The original intention,' he pointed out in 1937, 'in bringing the three Services together into one Department was to effect an economy in the provision of the common requirements. The authority ordering this concentration did not include or suggest any merging of the three Services into one homogeneous whole. That it was intended that each of the three services should retain its individuality and control its policy and administration is apparent. It is presumed that the intention was also that, inasfar as the common provision of the common requirements is concerned, these should when practicable be handled by the Service best equipped to handle the particular work for the other services. This procedure,' the senior air officer cautioned, 'was not intended to embrace all aspects of the "common requirements." For instance, there is no argument in favour of concentrating in the hands of one Service, matters which can be equally well carried out by the existing personnel of the other services. Only where a saving in staff is concerned should concentration be carried out.' Each service had its own concerns. 'Recommendations by the RCAF are purely Air Force in nature until they conflict with another Service,' Croil concluded, and care had to be taken to avoid treading on the prerogatives of others. The danger in limiting one service's growth and autonomy was that it would be unable to attain the 'adequate organization in peace' that would be required in war.[75]

Ashton was too busy to respond.[76] He was preparing to leave for London, in the company of Croil and the chief of the naval staff, as part of the government's delegation to the forthcoming Imperial Conference. Fortuitously, Croil found further leverage in the latest of the general staff's many appreciations of defence needs. Seeing the need for an interdepartmental system for co-ordinating defence planning, Colonel H.D.G. Crerar, the director of military operations and planning, asked for Croil's support.[77] Responding favourably, Croil noted one reservation, a fundamental one. 'The memorandum cannot be supported by me unless it includes a recommendation for the establishment of the RCAF as a separate service along the lines previously discussed. My reason for this stand is that unless the matter is fully dealt with in conjunction with your proposals for re-organization of the Department, it may be difficult to introduce this important point at a later date.'[78] The time for full service independence had come. 'The present organization of the Department of National Defence was ordered by the Minister of the Department at the time of the inclusion of the RCAF when that force was considered to be lacking in the necessary experience to enable it to direct its policies efficiently. Some twelve years have passed since that time and the RCAF now possesses an adequate staff of fully trained officers, well qualified to administer and direct its policy. It is considered desirable therefore that the organization of the Department be now amended so that the fighting services will be on an equal footing; the respective head of each service to be directly responsible to the Minister for the efficiency, administration and control of his service.'[79] Whether persuaded or worn down by attrition, Ashton now agreed. In London the three service chiefs recommended to the minister that 'the respective heads of each Service should each be directly responsible to the minister for the efficiency, administration and control of his particular Service.'[80]

The wheels of change turned slowly, and there was no immediate response to the recommendation. In the fall of 1937 Croil revived his campaign to decentralize control through regional air commands. Reconnaissance of the west coast to fix new base sites had been underway for the past year and the RCAF (unlike the army and navy) lacked any local co-ordinating authority to provide direction. Nor was there an air force headquarters to command permanent and non-permanent units in British Columbia. The non-permanent 111 (Coast Artillery Co-operation) Squadron was under the jurisdiction of the militia district officer commanding for all matters; the permanent No 4 (General Reconnaissance) was responsible to AFHQ for its own training, employment, and technical maintenance, while coming under the district officer commanding only for administration. 'There exists, therefore,' Croil concluded ruefully, 'the unique situation of two units of the same service, intended for the defence of the coast and located in the same place, administered and controlled under two entirely different systems, which is clearly illogical and not conducive to efficiency or economy.'[81]

The deputy minister agreed, as did the minister. They approved a new air force headquarters for the Pacific coast in principle. The deputy minister then presided over several discussions 'in order to find a solution to the points of difference in the proposal to establish an RCAF Western Air Command.'[82] Differences centred on how best to split administrative and command jurisdictions, and whether the officers commanding the military districts and air force commands should be of equal rank. A measure of agreement was finally reached on 15 March 1938, and Western Air Command was formally authorized. Group Captain G.O. Johnson, the commanding officer of RCAF Station Vancouver, assumed command of Western Air Command Headquarters as of 15 April, and took full charge of all air force units on the Pacific coast on 1 August.[83]

The formation of Western Air Command was a major step towards rationalizing the RCAF's command system. The next occurred in September 1938, when the Defence Council again discussed problems of interservice co-operation. The chief of the general staff told the meeting 'that he considered that an immediate decision should be reached defining his responsibilities' for the RCAF. The deputy minister then reminded the meeting, chaired by the minister, of the Joint Staff Committee's recommendation of the year before, and that 'He considered the time had come when the Air Service should be placed in a similar position to the Naval Service.' The minister provided no clear direction, simply informing the service chiefs 'he was prepared to see [them] at any time.' The minutes of the meeting, however, recorded that 'It was presumed that the steps recommended ... will be carried out immediately.'[84]

Within weeks, the minister authorized two additional air commands, Eastern Air Command at Halifax and Air Training Command at Toronto. The former, whose formation was accelerated by the Munich crisis, was to prepare detailed plans for the defence of the Atlantic coast.[85] The latter was 'to permit decentralization from National Defence Headquarters of the multiplicity of detail pertaining to all phases of training at Air Force Training Centres,' because 'the staff at National Defence Headquarters are called upon to deal not only with the major issues of training but to supervise and record so much detail that many important matters cannot be given the attention warranted.'[86] In November the process was completed by Air Force General Order No 2, which provided that 'The control and administration of the Royal Canadian Air Force will be exercised and carried out by the Senior Air Officer who will, in this respect, be directly responsible to the Minister of National Defence.'[87] A third Air Force General Order authorized the Air Council, composed of the senior air officer as president, the air staff officer, the air personnel staff officer, and the chief aeronautical engineer as members. The purpose of the council, a variation on the RAF model, was to afford each of the heads of divisions the opportunity of advising on air force policy, and provide a forum for the exchange of views between the staff branches.[88]

As he considered on the air force's newly expanded responsibilities and unaccustomed affluence, the chief of the air staff, his new title reflecting the RCAF's elevated status, must have had mixed reactions.[89] No doubt Croil was pleased with the public acknowledgment of the RCAF's growing importance in Canada's defence establishment, but the task facing his small command was staggering. Only recently had the RCAF been required to think seriously and specifically about its military task; now it had to move quickly beyond theory to implement plans for the air defence of the country. Resources were few. The 150 officers and fewer than 1000 airmen (with half those numbers again in the non-permanent air force) were spread woefully thin. The RCAF's thirty-one obsolete military aircraft hardly presented a credible deterrent, even to the most faint-hearted enemy.

The 1937-8 estimates had enabled the air force to plan for only six permanent squadrons, each with two flights of military aircraft, and one more with civil machines. Funding levels permitted manning to just 70 per cent of peacetime establishments. Squadrons would require an estimated two years' training before they could be considered operationally effective. Even this assessment was predicated on the availability of aircraft and equipment, and not 'a single item of Air Force equipment required for defence purposes is manufactured in Canada from materials available in the country.'[90] A reliable logistics system remained a distant, elusive goal and, Croil pointed out, aircraft were not sustained in flight by thin air alone: 'There is a large and varied list of equipment which represents a considerable capital investment required before the aircraft can be maintained and operated efficiently. These include, aircraft spares; rations; clothing and necessities; motor transport; motor transport gasoline and oil; marine craft; miscellaneous stores including hand tools; machine tools; work shop equipment; electrical equipment; parachutes; armament stores; bombs and ammunition; barrack stores; wireless telegraphy equipment; photographic equipment; aerial gasoline and oil; overhaul equipment (engines and aeroplanes); printing and stationery, etc.'[91] Once the foundation had been laid, the task of putting operational squadrons in the field was immense:

Briefly, [Croil wrote] this is the situation at present. Although every endeavour is being made to build up the Air Force as quickly as possible, funds are insufficient to bring even this small force up to full peacetime establishment. In actual fact, if annual estimates for the Permanent Force remain on the same basis for succeeding years as for this year, by the end of 1941 it will be possible to completely equip and man to full peace strength only five Permanent Force Squadrons ... In addition five squadrons will be partially equipped. During this period it will be possible to complete the organization of 12 Non-Permanent Squadrons, to equip them with a nucleus of training aircraft, and to partially train their personnel. The Joint Staff Committee, in their memorandum of Sept 5th, 1936, consider that a total of 23 Service Squadrons (11 Permanent and 12 Non-Permanent) represent the minimum number required for the Defence of Canada. The task of organizing and training this force will take considerable time and effort. Unless future estimates are materially increased, and immediate steps taken for the manufacture of Air Force equipment, the possibility of completing the manning and equipment of a force of this size cannot be accomplished.[92]

Money was not the only or even the most vital part of the problem. The RCAF, in its decrepit state, could only absorb so much without clogging the system. A cautious man, Croil chose to be deliberate rather than embark on a crash acquisition programme with a high probability of waste. In fact, Croil pointed out in 1938, 'it is not possible to take full advantage of a sudden and relatively large increase in appropriations. This was demonstrated in 1937–38, when the appropriation was doubled. The Headquarters staff was inadequate to meet the additional strain, with the result that orders for much of the equipment which might have been delivered within that year, could not be placed in time to permit of this ... For this reason it is desirable that where time permits, increases should not be too sudden nor, in comparison to the previous year, too large. It is, of course, realized that in an emergency the disadvantages of rapid expansion must be accepted.' There was little point, therefore, in recruiting large numbers before instructors were available to train them. Nor was the air staff eager to take risks in ordering experimental aircraft whose potential was unclear. Rather, Croil wrote, 'I have consistently resisted anything in the nature of experimental types. We cannot afford to embark upon the manufacture of an aircraft which, when completed, will turn out a failure, therefore we must wait until the Air Ministry have tested the first of the type we desire, in order to be sure that type when completed will be satisfactory.'[93]

The immediate priority was to equip nine permanent squadrons assigned to coast defence with 'modern first-line aircraft immediately available and ready for service.' For a time two other permanent units would have to make do with older types or advanced trainers, as would the non-permanent squadrons. Up to that time fighting units had been formed piecemeal as aircraft and men became available after civil operations were dropped. In 1933 No 4 (Flying Boat) Squadron had been activated from several west coast detachments, and the following year 5 (FB) Squadron was organized in Halifax from crews who had been flying RCMP preventive patrols. In 1935 the Test and General Purpose Flights at Ottawa provided the nucleus for 7 (General Purpose) Squadron, while at Winnipeg 8 (GP) Squadron absorbed detachments located in the Prairie region. That same year the Atlas and Siskin flights became Nos 2 (Army Co-operation) and 1 (Fighter) squadrons, respectively, at Trenton, and authorization was given to form Nos 3 (Bomber) and 6 (Torpedo-Bomber) squadrons. The organization of the first three non-permanent units – No 10 in Toronto, No 11 in Vancouver, and No 12 in Winnipeg – had been begun in 1933. Two years later, Nos 15 and 18 in Montreal, were approved. By 1939 all twelve had been authorized along with three wing headquarters.

Obtaining aircraft for the operational squadrons made the RCAF's earlier procurement difficulties seem simple by comparison. Familiar problems – insufficent funding and the lengthy lead time between ordering and delivery – were more pronounced, and rapid technological change complicated selection. Proven types were already obsolescent by the time they were generally available and choosing experimental machines was risky. Establishing secure sources of supply was another major difficulty. Canada would probably be able to acquire American aircraft in wartime if the United States was an ally, but if not, neutrality legislation would prohibit their export. Moreover, information about American designs was kept classified until the aircraft went into production, and this limited the RCAF 'to aircraft which are already at least a year old, and further, are possibly not the most desirable from military point of view.'[94] Britain was the other potential source, but in wartime the RAF would be a competitor for limited resources. 'There is only one solution to this problem and that is the manufacture of Air Force Equipment in Canada,' Croil concluded.[95]

Unfortunately, the Depression had ruined the promising beginnings of an indigenous aircraft industry. Little choice remained other than to buy British designed and tested aircraft while trying to arrange their construction in Canada under contract. The established policy of standardization wherever possible to British types also pushed the RCAF strongly in this direction. Croil informed the minister:

The Royal Canadian Air Force is organized on Royal Air Force practice, and therefore Royal Air Force equipment fits into the Canadian scheme better then American equipment, e.g., the establishment of a squadron of the Royal Air Force is designed to meet the requirements of the type of equipment used. We use the same establishment, and to get the best results, should use the same equipment. If we change the equipment we must change the establishment, which will result in a certain amount of experimentation until satisfaction is achieved. Similarly, if we change the type of aircraft and go in for the American product, it means that we must also change our supply of bombs, guns, and instruments of all kinds, for the American aircraft are designed to take American accessories of this kind. This is not an insuperable job and could be incorporated in the manufacture if we are building this type of aircraft in Canada. I feel that it is necessary for us to continue to use British accessories, for we have no other supply and these can be purchased through the Royal Air Force from markets which would otherwise be closed to us, and at the same time, we use the Royal Air Force as a proving ground.[96]

In 1935 the RCAF had ordered six Westland Wapiti bombers and four Blackburn Sharks from Great Britain. Neither was impressive. The Wapiti was a modified First World War DH9A with open cockpits for the pilot and an air gunner/bomb aimer. 'From the pilot's point of view,' C.R. Dunlap recalled, 'the aircraft was a beast. It lumbered off the ground and struggled along with very unimpressive performance ... it glided like a brick.' Little wonder, then, that when Wing Commander Breadner asked Dunlap, then on exchange duty with the RAF, his opinion of the machine, he received a blunt reply: 'The Wapiti is without doubt the worst apology for an aircraft that it has ever been my misfortune to fly.' Having recently obtained more Wapitis, Breadner was understandably miffed. 'Dunlap,' he said, 'I am sorry to hear you talking like that about an aircraft ... currently in use in the RAF. You are enjoying the privilege of being here in England, benefitting from everything the RAF has to offer. Therefore, I do not think you have any right to be so critical of the aircraft you are privileged to fly.' It was only after he realized Breadner had purchased the Wapitis at a bargain price because Canada was not prepared 'to spend any money for anything better' that Dunlap understood why his superior had been so defensive.[97] In the event, Canadian Wapitis were used as bomber trainers, and 3 (B) Squadron completed its initial air firing and bombing practice with them in the summer of 1937.

The Sharks destined to equip 6 (TB) Squadron for a strike role were little better. An open cockpit, two- or three-seater, the Shark could operate as a landplane or seaplane on reconnaissance, bomb, or torpedo tasks. Powered with one 770-hp Armstrong-Siddeley Tiger or an 840-hp Bristol Pegasus IX engine, the Shark had a maximum speed of about 150 mph and a cruising range of 500 miles. It could carry 1500 pounds of either bombs or torpedos as well as a fixed forward-firing machine-gun and another movable one in the rear. A contract for additional Sharks was subsequently arranged with Boeing Aircraft of Canada at Vancouver. Enough were eventually ordered for two squadrons.[98]

In 1936 the first five Supermarine Stranraers had been ordered from Canadian Vickers Ltd. The Stranraer, a new flying boat, was meant to fill the need for long-range coastal reconnaissance. Twin-engined, it carried a crew of six or seven with a cruising range of about 1000 miles, which gave it an effective operating radius of about 300 miles. The Stranraer had gun positions amidship and at the rear, as well as room for sleeping quarters. It could also be adapted to carry a torpedo, and was powered by two 875/1000-hp Bristol Pegasus engines. Its endurance was almost ten hours, with cruising speed of 105 mph. The first went into service with 5 (BR) Squadron in late 1938.[99]

When the major increase in the 1937-8 estimates permitted more lavish expenditure on new aircraft, seven more Stranraers were ordered (forty were eventually produced) along with an additional eighteen Wapitis, thirteen Sharks, and two new types, the Bristol Bolingbroke and the Westland Lysander. The Bolingbroke, a Canadian version of the Blenheim IV light bomber, went to 7 and 8 (GP) Squadrons for general reconnaissance tasks. Powered by two Bristol Mercury engines, the Bolingbroke had a cruising speed of 225 mph, a range of 1900 miles, and carried a three- or four-man crew. When fully loaded with its complement of weapons, it had an effective operating radius of about 350 miles. It was constructed in Canada by Fairchild Aircraft of Canada Ltd. The Lysander was a two-seater monoplane, purchased to replace the Atlas on army co-operation duties, especially coast artillery spotting. It was built under contract by the National Steel Car Company in Malton, Ont. It had a single Bristol Mercury XII engine, two fixed forward-firing guns in the wheel fairings, a movable gun in the rear cockpit, and a speed of just over 200 mph.[100]

Fighters had a lower priority than patrol, bombing, or army co-operation aircraft. As Croil pointed out to the minister, the RCAF's need for fighters differed from that of the RAF. Geography left Britain vulnerable to sustained air attack; the RAF needed fighters with rapid climb, fast speed, and high-ceiling capabilities. Canadian conditions, by contrast, required a twin-engined, two-seater with sufficient range and endurance to enable it to overfly vast undeveloped territory with some degree of safety. Such aircraft, however, were not readily available, and in 1938 a few Hawker Hurricanes were ordered instead, the first of which went into service in the spring of 1939.[101]

The RCAF's rearmament programme was not expected to be fully effective – that is, sufficient to implement the Joint Staff Committee's 'Plan for the Defence of Canada' – until the end of 1941. Even then, of the 325 first-line and 202 modern training aircraft considered the 'barest minimum,' only 99 and 127, respectively, would be operational if the current procurement schedule was followed. Moreover, as Croil informed the minister in mid-1938, 'the provision of Service Aircraft is progressing so slowly that some of the types selected will be obsolescent or obsolete before deliveries are made in sufficient numbers to complete the arming of all units.'[102]

During the Munich crisis of September 1938 the inadequacy of Canada's air defences was made all too apparent. Preparations for defending the Atlantic coast in the German war which seemed imminent were as yet incomplete. The RCAF and RCN had quickly to co-ordinate an *ad hoc* emergency plan. It was just as well that it was not tested. The coast artillery co-operation squadron on the east coast had not yet been formed and 2 (AC) Squadron had to shepherd its decrepit Atlases to Halifax to fill the gap.[103] With them went all the other aircraft the RCAF was able to muster: a total of thirty-nine, among them six Sharks, the only remotely modern military types. Thirteen others were obsolete service machines, the rest were civil aeroplanes. Only twelve of the thirty-nine could carry effective bomb loads.[104] These numbers included all available aircraft other than primary trainers and five obsolete machines left on the Pacific coast.

The crisis was almost enough, however, to provide the RCAF with new procurement channels. In mid-September enquiries were made through the Canadian minister in Washington about the availability of American aircraft for quick purchase. On 28 September, as the British prime minister, Neville Chamberlain, met Hitler, Croil obtained authority to create a board of officers to buy as many aircraft from the United States as $5 million would purchase. Air Commodore E.W. Stedman led the group to Washington, where meetings took place with War Department officials and industry representatives over several days. Because of the need for rapid delivery – specified as three months – only aircraft already on contract to the United States Army Air Corps would meet the RCAF's needs. Except for those still classified types not yet released for export sales, the Americans gave the RCAF free access to their own orders. The greatest need was for fifteen reconnaissance aircraft and eighteen bombers with ranges of 1000 miles. The secondary requirement was for fifteen fighters.[105] The most suitable available aircraft were the Douglas 18A bomber, the North American 25 observation machine, and the Seversky P35 fighter.[106]

In the event, the entire exercise went for naught. Stedman's blanket authority was removed when he was told he must first refer his recommendations to Ottawa except if 'it is vitally important to complete the purchase immediately, and no other course seems open to you.'[107] Then, as relief at peaceful settlement of the Munich affair replaced the urgency and panic of late September, the government reverted to its more cautious spending ways. Parliament would now have to be asked to approve any extraordinary expenditures. The Governor General's Warrant, by which the Cabinet originally had granted spending authority to the purchasing mission, was cancelled. Apologies and thanks were extended to the Americans, who had co-operated beyond the bounds of any necessity, and Stedman and his assistants returned home with neither aircraft nor contracts.

Three months later, at the beginning of 1939, the minister asked for a briefing on the RCAF's aircraft. He could hardly have been encouraged by the air staff's response. There were two Stranraers and two Fairchilds in the Maritime provinces; five Sharks and eight other aircraft defended the west coast.

Reinforcement prospects were no more promising. Within one week six Atlases might be found, in two weeks seven Wapitis and three Fairchilds, and in eight weeks two additional Stranraers. In his report to the minister Breadner noted pointedly that fifteen observation and eighteen bomber aircraft could be obtained by July if an order were placed immediately in the United States.[108]

While the attempts to obtain fighting aircraft continued, the British Air Ministry was an interested onlooker. Its concern with the potential productive capacity of the as yet small Canadian aircraft industry developed into a major acquisition scheme which provided a healthy stimulus to the industry. Following discussions at the 1937 Imperial Conference, the Air Ministry had dispatched a delegation to Ottawa in May 1938 for talks on both the training of aircrew and the production in Canada of aircraft for the RAF. The British objectives, in the words of the air minister, were both practical and political: 'The scheme contemplated was one for the creation of a potential capable of providing aircraft in war rather than for the early production of aircraft in peace. Such a scheme, it was felt, would give us a valuable resource in war beyond the range of enemy aircraft, would operate in peace to diminish the tendency in Canada to detachment from concern with imperial defence; and would immediately impress opinion on the continent.'[109] The British opened negotiations with representatives of ten industrial firms, reaching an agreement for the companies to form a central contracting company which would assemble British-designed aircraft for the Air Ministry. In the event, six firms combined to form the Canadian Associated Aircraft Ltd, which assembled airframes from parts and components supplied by the six. In November, immediately after the RCAF's abortive Washington purchasing mission, the Air Ministry let a contract for the assembly of eighty Hampden bombers with an indication of a further order for one hundred more. Coincidentally, the Air Ministry ordered forty Hurricanes from the Canadian Car and Foundry Company of Fort William, Ont.[110] None of the aircraft was ready before war broke out, but these initial orders led to much larger ones later.

The RCAF's deliberate acquisition policy was not without its critics. Non-permanent squadrons were unhappy with their lack of useful equipment, and some of their supporters were influential in business and politics. In the fall of 1938 the minister appointed several of them – W.A. Bishop, R.H. Mulock, A.D. Bell-Irving, H.J. Burden, F.S. McGill – as an Honorary Air Advisory Committee. Its ostensible purpose was to provide the government with an independent source of advice on air force matters. Bell-Irving worried that they were 'expected to be agreeable to the Government rather than helpfully constructive,' and he was unable to 'get away from the thought that the Air Committee are (or is) in danger of being an insignificant preparation of optical hygiene.'[111] Nevertheless, they found much about the RCAF to criticize – questionable policy decisions, inadequate training standards, deplorable staff work, wrong-headed promotions, weak leadership, and endless delays in obtaining new aircraft.[112]

It is impossible to be categorical about the validity of their charges. Non-permanent units have often felt resentful of their second-class status in comparison with regulars. It is true that many prewar policies were quickly outdated, as were most of the RCAF's aircraft. The procurement programme may well have been overly cautious. The decision not to leap a design generation, by consciously avoiding experimental aircraft in a period of technological innovation, condemned the air force to a succession of obsolescent, if not obsolete, types before they were flown operationally. Given the imperfect information available to the RCAF staff at the time, however, as well as the many restrictions imposed on them by circumstances, their policies had an internal logic. The acquisition programme was unimaginative and the product of many compromises, with which few could be entirely content, but it was based on reasonable and defensible premises.

While aircraft were gradually acquired by the RCAF, the cycle of individual and unit training picked up, but with difficulty. Establishments remained emaciated and equipment non-existent or obsolete. One way partially to overcome the problem was to send individuals to the RAF for specialist courses and attachments, a practice which was expanded in the immediate years before the war. It was a valuable exercise, as Air Marshal C.R. Slemon has commented: 'I would say that by 1936 we still had a very low order of military cabability. But from then on we sent more people to the United Kingdom who came back and were instructors and so on, so that by the time the war broke we had a fairly good idea of what was required, even if we didn't have the equipment to carry it out.'[113]

The RCAF had begun sending selected officers to the United Kingdom for specialist training in the early 1920s. Usually, eight to ten were sent annually to the RAF Staff College and schools specializing in aeronautical engineering, air pilotage and navigation, army co-operation, flying instruction, armament, photography, wireless, and explosives. From 1935 each RCAF general list officer, after four years' flying training, chose to specialize in engineering, armament, photography, signals, or navigation. A specialties register was prepared and subsequent course selection and postings were adjusted accordingly.[114] Successful graduates supplied an ever larger cadre of staff-trained officers and specialist instructors for similar RCAF courses.[115] By 1937 the following numbers had been trained (the figures in brackets indicate those trained in Canada): flying instructors – 66 (57); armament – 34 (31); army co-operation – 84 (77); instrument flying – 81 (79); explosives – 14 (13); signals – 10 (8); navigation – 29 (23); seaplane – 74 (73); photography – 36 (36); engineering – 11 (10). In addition, two senior officers had completed, and one more was attending, the course at the Imperial Defence College, and twenty-two others the RAF Staff College. RCAF airmen were attending courses in Britain on automatic controls, armament, instrument repair, and other technical subjects.[116]

As well as specialty training, the RAF and RCAF exchange officer postings afforded Canadian officers an opportunity to gain valuable experience in semi-operational conditions with relatively modern equipment. Squadron Leader F.A. Sampson, for example, was sent on exchange in 1937 to 209 (GR) Squadron based at Felixstowe. After a number of coastal defence exercises, his unit was sent to the Mediterranean, first to Malta, and then to Arzew in Algeria. From Arzew, Sampson's squadron flew anti-submarine patrols to protect shipping in the Mediterranean during the Spanish Civil War. The Short Singapore flying boats of Sampson's squadron were armed with three Lewis machine-guns, two 112-pound bombs, and two 250 pounders. The unit flew three daily patrols, each of eight hours, to locate submarines in the area. The crews could attack if requested by ships under fire, or if submarines were clearly ignoring conventions requiring them to look after the safety of crews and passengers of sunk vessels.[117] When it returned to Coastal Command, Sampson's squadron was re-equipped with Short Sunderland flying boats before taking part in two major air-defence schemes with the Home Fleet. Sampson was able to use this considerable patrolling experience on returning to the RCAF when he was given command of 5 (Bomber-Reconnaissance) Squadron in Dartmouth. Later he was on staff at Eastern Air Command before being posted to command a flying training school and then, during the war, a station of No 6 (RCAF) Group, Bomber Command, in the United Kingdom.[118]

Flight Lieutenant A.A. Lewis, who will be recalled as a participant in the Hudson Strait expedition of 1927–8, went to Britain in 1935 for two years, the first with 13 (AC) Squadron, the second with 7 (B) Squadron. Although he liked 13 Squadron's Hawker Audax aircraft, Lewis was unimpressed with the 'very elementary' training in army co-operation techniques which had not progressed much beyond First World War practice. It was also his 'impression gained during army manoeuvres ... that the higher commanders either did not know how to use the air force or were jealous of its capabilities and would not use it to its best advantages.' Lewis concluded that the average young officer posted to an operational squadron from the RAF School was not as well trained as his counterpart passing out from the RCAF's Army Co-operation School at Trenton.[119]

Lewis's second year was more productive. His bomber squadron was first equipped with Handley Page Heyfords, and then obtained the latest Armstrong Whitworth Whitleys which could carry two tons of bombs. Lewis was able to log considerable day and night cross-country flying as well as bombing practice using both manual and automatic-pilot procedures, all of which helped greatly on his return when he was given command of the RCAF's 3 (B) Squadron. From his exchange experience Lewis had become convinced that 'the supreme test of a bombing squadron is its ability to reach an objective in any kind of weather.' Thus, with No 3, he gave highest training priority to long-range navigation and night flying.[120]

Not all exchanges were fruitful. Air Commodore Croil complained in late 1937 that Flight Lieutenant R.C. Gordon was being misused in flying transportation flights for RAF officers attending air navigation courses. Croil asked his liaison officer in London to have the Air Ministry send Gordon to a squadron 'actively engaged on service training,' so that he would be better qualified to train RCAF officers on his return.[121]

More serious was the problem of training with obsolete equipment and techniques. With few exceptions, until 1939 the RAF trained on a generation of fighting aircraft whose origins lay in the First World War. The technological revolution brought about by mass-produced Hurricanes, Spitfires, Typhoons,

Mosquitoes, Lancasters, and the other powerful, fast, and manoeuvrable machines, as well as the tactics to deploy them effectively, awaited rapid wartime evolution. Consequently, much of the training which RCAF officers received in Britain was soon outdated. One example concerns army co-operation machines. The operational model of army co-operation squadrons, derived from 1914–18, was refined over the interwar years, and aircraft were made ever more sophisticated for the multi-purpose role they were expected to perform. The ultimate machine for the task, the Westland Lysander, was 'built, unfortunately, for the wrong sort of battle.'[122] As it became more powerful and complex it was less immediately useful for its primary role of artillery observation. The Lysander needed relatively large landing fields, which kept it back from the front lines, and while it had a slow enough stalling speed for observation flying, this was achieved by adding external encumbrances which restricted its manoeuvrability. It was also vulnerable, neither slow and light enough to avoid enemy fighters nor sufficiently fast to outrun them. 'Like the White Knight in Alice in Wonderland, it carried around the wherewithal to attempt practically any of the innumerable tasks which an army might at short notice require of it,' but it was less useful for artillery spotting.[123] In the Second World War the army co-operation role was split; close ground support was provided by fast, high-performance aircraft, while artillery observation was taken over by gunners flying slow, simple, Austers. Much of the immediate utility of interwar training in army co-operation was lost.[124]

Flight Lieutenant E.A. McNab had a frustrating experience in learning tactics almost immediately made redundant by technological advance. When McNab was posted in 1937 to 46 (F) Squadron in Great Britain he began flying a new (to the RCAF) machine, the Gloster Gauntlet II. He learned about section and flight tactical-fighter interception with radio ground control, and was pleased when the unit went to armament camp because he 'had never fired a gun in the air before.' Then in the summer of 1938 McNab's squadron was told it would soon be receiving new Hurricanes. The unit continued training with its Gauntlets, but there was no point in his reporting further on this training because the Hurricane's speed, armament, and different maintenance schedules so radically changed procedures that 'anything one might have written would have been obsolete by two or three years.'[125] In August 1940 McNab became the first RCAF pilot credited with downing an enemy aircraft in the Second World War.

When they returned from their overseas courses and exchanges the officers and airmen were slotted into appointments in an expanding staff and training structure. The RCAF was plagued, however, with severe aircraft and equipment shortages which seriously limited all phases of training except for the most basic flying. The number of flying training hours increased dramatically in these years – more than four-fold between 1931 and 1938 – but most flying was pure routine. In 1938, for instance, only 1700 hours were spent on combined operations training, compared to 22,500 hours on such activities as test, transportation, liaison, unit training, and all other types of routine flying. By then almost all individual training was carried out at Trenton where there were also schools for flying instruction, wireless and other technical trades, army co-operation, air navigation, seaplane conversion, and air armament. Courses were run concurrently throughout the year. The flying training school was capable of handling from eighty to one hundred pupils per course, the technical training school about 120 airmen, the wireless school about seventy. The RCAF's only other training establishment was the old station located at Camp Borden. Here, at No 2 Technical Training School, airmen and officers were instructed in a variety of technical trades.[126]

Camp Borden became much more active in 1939 when the system of flying training was completely reorganized to conform to RAF practice. Pilot training was divided into three sixteen-week stages for elementary, intermediate, and advanced training. At the end of the year the graduate would have had flight as well as individual training. The elementary stage was given over to eight civilian flying schools at Halifax, Montreal, Toronto, Hamilton, Winnipeg, Regina, Calgary, and Vancouver. Each was to conduct three courses a year for thirty-two students. From there pupils went on to Borden, and then to Trenton for the final phase. The objective of the revamped programme was to produce 125 trained pilots each year. As part of the programme, a refresher flying instructors' course for club teachers was held at Borden in April. The first elementary school trainees began their course in June 1939; with the threat of war they were moved prematurely to Borden in August. In conjunction with the new scheme, the RCAF began granting most of their commissions on a short service rather than permanent basis.[127]

Service training, such as it was, was carried out by individual squadrons in their bases across the country. The lack of modern aircraft and a limited personnel establishment meant that very little realistic operational training was possible. Service, or unit, training was conducted on the RAF model, and RCAF Headquarters prepared a training syllabus for each unit for the training year. The year was broken into several periods, incorporating phases for individual, flight, and unit training, and exercises with militia or naval units. The training cycle was flexible enough to allow for individual squadron needs. There were common subjects which all squadrons had to master; for example, day and night flying, air pilotage, bombing, reconnaissance and report writing, photo operations, air fighting tactics, ground and air gunnery procedures, and signals. Theory was covered during individual training periods, as well as by specialist courses, and practical training was done in unit training. In addition, squadrons had their own specific subjects. Army co-operation squadrons emphasized ground tactics, liaison with ground units, and other combined procedures.[128] Flying-boat squadrons practised patrolling and prolonged reconnaissance, convoy protection, communications with ships, and recognition of service vessels. Torpedo squadrons had to be proficient in ship recognition and the mechanics of torpedoing as well as the usual subjects.[129]

It is impossible to relate syllabi to the actual quality of training. Units inevitably differed from one another in the type and intensity of their instruction. Moreover, the process of forming squadrons was slow. In 1937 No 1 (F) Squadron had three or four Siskins and could undertake only limited exercises. In that same year 3 (B) Squadron received its first Wapiti aircraft and was just able to begin its service training. It completed its initial air firing and bombing practices that summer. No 4 (FB) Squadron in Vancouver conducted some coastal reconnaissance and anti-aircraft flying. In Halifax 5 (FB) Squadron began its service training early in 1937, having been relieved of its RCMP preventive patrols. No 6 (TB) Squadron obtained its Shark aircraft in 1937, but too late to begin service training. The most active unit was 2 (AC) Squadron. It continued its usual practice of sending detachments to militia training camps for co-operative exercises, and also completed gunnery and bombing practice. Nos 7 and 8 (GP) Squadrons were unable to begin service training operations because they were kept on aerial photo and transportation operations.[130]

In 1938, the final full year before war, the pattern remained much as it had been. Nos 7 and 8 (GP) Squadrons were kept on civil operations, the former on test and transportation flights in Ottawa, the latter with five photographic detachments in the field from Halifax to Vancouver. No 7 Squadron had only three of its eleven officers and had thirteen airman vacancies. The squadron's commander suggested in his annual report that the unit's lack of a clearly defined role on mobilization was causing confusion and affecting morale. The squadron had not yet been given an armament establishment, nor had it been told whether it would operate on land, water, or both.[131] No 8 was still equipped with Bellanca Pacemaker, Northrop Delta, and Noorduyn Norseman aircraft and was employed exclusively on non-military duties.[132] No 3 (B) Squadron moved from Ottawa to Calgary in October and was able to begin training, initially with four Wapiti aircraft and then with four more. The slow, obsolescent biplanes were armed, but only four had wireless. In the training season the machines logged more than 1000 hours and Squadron Leader Lewis was pleased with the standard of formation and night flying. Before flying out to its new Calgary base the squadron participated in army exercises at Camp Borden, flying simulated low-bombing and gas attacks as part of the designated enemy force. It was also able to practise bombing with the camera obscura.[133]

No 2 (AC) Squadron was again the busiest unit, forming detachments to exercise with militia units throughout the country.[134] Its training cycle provided for service training through the fall-winter-spring months and then the squadron participated in various summer camps. Like other units, it was beset with problems of old aircraft and unfilled establishments. It had seven Atlas aircraft serviceable throughout most of 1938, and during the summer sent detachments to Shilo, Petawawa, and St Catharines. In August the squadron joined 3 (B) Squadron at Camp Borden to provide air support for the militia concentration. Two Atlas aircraft crashed during the summer, one a complete write-off. In October No 2 flew to Halifax where it practised coast artillery observation with militia units in the region. On its return, the squadron began individual ground and air training, concentrating on forced landings, message pickups, camera gunnery, night flying (especially for the three new pilots in the squadron), signals, photography, and air-frame and engine mechanics. Detachments also flew tactical demonstration flights for the Army Co-operation School at Trenton. In January and February 1939 the squadron concentrated on two- and three-aircraft formation and night flying. In the spring the commander complained that his schedule was being hampered by the lack of key officers and airmen, as well as by the daily drill parades which were being conducted to prepare for the 1939 visit of King George VI. Nevertheless, service training continued: air firing, bombing, navigation training, air drills, formation flying, and camera gun practice (including practice with towed targets). The squadron also assisted non-permanent squadrons during their summer camps. In July a detachment moved to Petawawa where it conducted eleven artillery observation shoots with sixty-pounder and 4.5-inch howitzers, and flew tactical and photo missions for army units.[135]

No 1 (F) Squadron had other problems. At the end of August 1938 the squadron, under command of Squadron Leader E.G. Fullerton, moved by rail from Trenton to Calgary, taking with it three of the six Siskins remaining in service. The squadron trained ineffectually with the worn-out machines until June 1939, when they were finally sent into storage. Meanwhile, Fullerton proceeded to Vancouver to accept the first of the Hawker Hurricanes delivered there for the RCAF from the United Kingdom. Check-outs on the Hurricanes were interrupted when the first was written-off after colliding with another aircraft on the ground.[136] Not until June 1939 was the first flight of Hurricanes delivered to its home base at Calgary. En route the squadron lost another machine when its pilot, Flying Officer T.G. Fraser, crashed near Mission, BC, and was killed.[137]

Nos 4 and 5 (GR) Squadrons carried out what service training they could in conjunction with surveys on both coasts. In British Columbia 4 (GR) Squadron flew its Vancouver flying boats on numerous reconnaissance flights to locate air-base sites and collect topographical and meteorological information. No 5, equipped with Fairchild seaplanes, flew similar missions from its Halifax base. Both units carried out exercises with the navy and militia and they began to receive new equipment when the Supermarine Stranraer flying boats were delivered in late 1938, first to 5 Squadron, then to No 4.[138]

None of the permanent squadrons, let alone the skeleton non-permanent (renamed 'auxiliary' in December 1938) squadrons, was sufficiently manned, equipped, or free from other tasks to be able to concentrate fully on a balanced and progressive training programme for its war tasks. Those had been detailed in the 1938 Joint Staff Committee Plan for the Defence of Canada which, for the first time, gave direction on service roles for home defence. Drawing on the previous 1936 plan for twenty-three RCAF squadrons, not all of which had been formed when war broke out, it allocated seventeen – including 2 (AC) Squadron, which was to revert to army co-operation duties once selected auxiliary squadrons were adequately manned and equipped – to immediate home defence tasks on the two coasts: reconnaissance, strike, air defence, and coast artillery co-operation. Two other squadrons (three, once No 2 reverted) were to work with an army mobile force. Four more (two bomber and two fighter) were to remain initially in central Canada for general reserve and air defence purposes.[139]

In the late summer of 1939, the RCAF began to mobilize for war. On 24 August Air Commodore Stedman was dispatched once more to Washington to purchase aircraft,[140] and an agreement was quickly reached to manufacture North American Harvards in Canada by Noorduyn Aircraft Ltd of Montreal. On 31

August the three wings and eleven squadrons of the Auxiliary Air Force were called out on a voluntary basis, and instructions were given to bring it and the permanent force to full authorized peace establishment. Two days later all the regular and seven of the auxiliary squadrons were formally placed on active service, and were joined on 5 September by the remaining four organized auxiliary squadrons. At 1430 hours on 10 September the war telegrams were dispatched.[141]

PART TWO

The British Commonwealth Air Training Plan

Negotiators of the BCATP Agreement, Ottawa, December 1939. Front row, left to right: Air Chief Marshal Sir R. Brooke-Popham, RAF; Colonel J.L. Ralston, minister of finance, Canada; Group Captain H.W.L. Saunders, chief of the air staff, New Zealand; Senator R. Dandurand, Canada; Lord Riverdale, United Kingdom; Prime Minister W.L.M. King, Canada; J.V. Fairbairn, minister of air, Australia; E. Lapointe, minister of justice, Canada; Captain H.H. Balfour, undersecretary for air, United Kingdom; N.McL. Rogers, minister of national defence, Canada; Air Marshal Sir C. Courtney, RAF. (RE 12378-7)

BCATP schools being planned in the drafting room of Air Force Headquarters, 28 June 1940. (PL 522)

Clearing the site for B&GS, Mossbank, Sask., October 1940. (PL 1669)

Volunteers learned that line-ups were an inevitable part of wartime service. Winnipeg, October 1940. (PL 1732)

Recruiting poster. (PL 3028)

Security of personal belongings seems to have supplanted sabotage as the concern of the commander of 5 Manning Depot, Lachine, Que., April 1943. (PL 16191)

Polishing buttons at 1 ITS, Toronto, May 1940. (PA 141353)

Air Commodore A.T.N. Cowley, air officer commanding, No 4 Training Command, leads the training flights at the opening of 18 EFTS, Caron, Sask., 2 July 1941. Taking the salute are Prime Minister King and L.J. Martin, the civilian manager of the school. (PMR 84-979)

The ability to withstand drops in air pressure was an essential attribute for aircrew, such as these RCAF recruits undergoing testing in the decompression chamber at the RCAF Medical Investigation Centre, Toronto, in June 1942. (PA 140655)

Instructor and pupil with a Tiger Moth, the BCATP's basic trainer, I EFTS, Malton, Ont., 5 June 1941. (PL 3580)

The Link trainer was a crucial test of a recruit's suitability for pilot training. (PA 140658)

A Stearman, 300 of which were obtained in 1940, at 31 EFTS, De Winton, Alta. The lack of an enclosed cockpit made the Stearman all but useless for winter training. (PMR 77-148)

Oxen towing a Fleet Finch at 17 EFTS, Stanley, NS, in 1940. (PMR 84-977)

A North American Yale, a cousin of the ubiquitous Harvard, sets off from 1 SFTS Camp Borden. (PL 2222)

Groundcrew prepare to start a North American Harvard, while the pilot checks his parachute. (PA 140661)

Canadian-built Harvard trainers over farmland near 2 SFTS, Uplands, Ottawa. (PA 140659)

Cessna Cranes, in their characteristic yellow paint scheme, fly past in formation at 12 SFTS, Brandon, Man., July 1941. (PL 5747)

Defence Minister 'Chubby' Power getting instruction from a pupil at 1 Wireless
School, Montreal, 1940. (PL 1854)

Radio instruction at 19 EFTS, Virden, Man. (PA 140653)

The interior of an Anson, with the two wireless stations at left occupied by air cadets on a familiarization flight, June 1944. (PL 25113)

Fleet Forts of 2 Wireless School, Calgary, Alta. Originally designed for pilot training, the Canadian-built Forts were modified into wireless trainers. (PMR 78-317)

The Fairey Battle, unsuitable for operations, was the mainstay of BCATP bombing and gunnery schools. This aircraft is from 31 B&GS, Picton, Ont., December 1940. (PL 2449)

Trainee navigators take sun-shots at Rivers, Man. (PL 3722)

Sergeants E.M. Romilly, RCAF, W.H. Betts, RAAF, and J.A. Mahoud, RAF, under observer training in an Avro Anson of 1 ANS, Rivers, Man., 4 June 1941. Romilly was later killed on operations. (PL 3740)

Airmen's recreation room at 19 EFTS, in October 1944. Those with white tabs tucked into the front portion of their wedge caps are undergoing aircrew training. (PA 140652)

Leading aircraftman K.G. Spooner, one of two BCATP trainees to win the George Cross: while a navigator trainee at 4 AOS, London, Ont., he took charge after his pilot fainted and ordered the rest of the crew to bale out. Two students did so, but Spooner, the wireless operator, and the unconscious pilot were killed when the Anson plunged into Lake Erie. (PL 112740)

A full complement of de Havilland Tiger Moths at 9 EFTS, St Catharines, Ont., December 1943. (PMR 75-355)

A typical layout for BCATP Service Flying Training Schools: 6 SFTS, Dunnville, Ont.
(PMR 77-610)

Salute for a fallen comrade, 19 EFTS, Virden, Man. (PA 140660)

Pilot error, 19 SFTS, Vulcan, Alta, 23 February 1944. (RE 23061-11)

Wings Parade at 15 SFTS, Claresholm, Alta, 16 August 1941. (PMR 74-280)

176

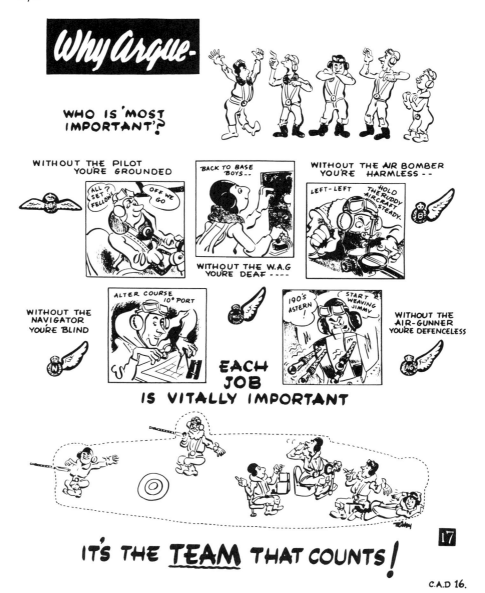

A poster emphasizing the importance of all aircrew – an important morale booster since many volunteers, having failed pilot training, had to swallow their pride and serve as navigators, air observers, gunners, or air bombers. (PMR 85-024)

Flying Officer S.F. Wise, at Summerside, PEI, 1944. (PMR 84-1029)

RCAF Station Trenton, the largest unit in the BCATP, housing the Central Flying School, 1 Instructors School, 1 Composite Training School, and a Reselection Centre for washed-out aircrew. (PMR 79-279)

Prime Minister W.S. Churchill, who took a great interest in the BCATP, during a visit to 2 SFTS, Uplands, in December 1941. (PL 6510)

Fairchild trainers of 'Little Norway,' the Norwegian flying training establishment, over Lake Ontario. (PA 115422)

Not all BCATP students came from the Empire and Commonwealth. Some, such as these Free French Navy air gunners who earned their wings at 9 B&GS, Mont Joli, Que., in September 1944, came from occupied Europe. (PL 25624)

181

Leading Aircraftman J.F. Lazaro, from
Madras, investigating a bombsight,
41 SFTS, Weyburn, Sask., December 1943.
(PL 23215)

Aero-engine mechanics at the Technical Training School, St Thomas, Ont. (PL 1041)

Packing parachutes. Civilian employees at 19 EFTS, Virden, Man., October 1944. (PA 140654)

Polishing the perspex of an Anson at 16 SFTS, Hagersville, Ont., August 1942. (PL 9838)

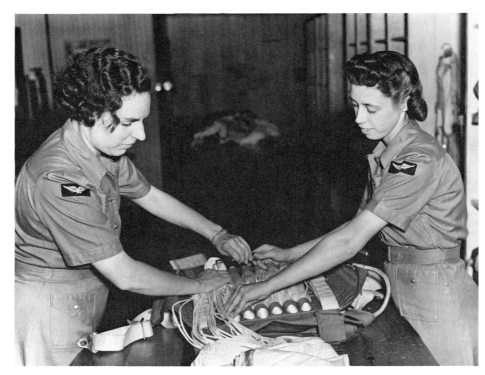

Two members of the Women's Division packing parachutes for the BCATP at Camp Borden, August 1942. (PL 9858)

Air Marshal W.A. Bishop, VC, CB, DSO, MC, DFC, ED, talks to Hollywood star James Cagney during the filming of *Captains of the Clouds,* at 2 SFTS, Uplands, July 1941. (PL 5065)

Rae Stuart working on a Tiger Moth at 9 EFTS, St Catharines, Ont. (PMR 75-363)

F. Patterson, manager of 9 EFTS,
St Catharines, Ont., and A. Parsons, the
secretary treasurer, in their civilian
BCATP uniforms. (PMR 75-368)

Compacting snow at 36 SFTS, Penhold, Alta, often the best solution to the problem of
runway maintenance in the winter. (PMR 84-978)

The long and the short of it: an Avro Lancaster, the RCAF's largest operational aircraft, and a Fairchild Cornell trainer at the RCAF Test and Development Establishment, Rockcliffe, October 1943. (PL 21542)

The sleek de Havilland Mosquitoes of 36 OTU, Greenwood, NS. (PL 24151)

Hurricanes of 1 OTU, Bagotville, Que. (PA 140644)

Liberator crews of 5 OTU, Boundary Bay, BC, practising high-level formation flying.
(PA 132050)

Introduction

The British Commonwealth Air Training Plan had its origins in the prewar strategic requirements of the Royal Air Force, and in the close and longstanding military, political, and emotional ties between Canada and Great Britain. Canada had been the home of an RFC/RAF training establishment in the First World War (when there was no RCAF), and the RAF was inclined to assume that it could still act on the old colonial basis when its prewar expansion plans indicated that overseas recruitment and training would be advisable. It was soon disillusioned. Ottawa firmly opposed anything that might compromise Canada's freedom of action in the event of war. The Mackenzie King government did allow Canadians to be trained or selected at home for service in the RAF and eventually agreed to the training of a few British pilots in Canada. The government refused outright, however, to permit any of the training conducted in the dominion to come under British control. That, to King and his colleagues, would be an infringement of Canadian sovereignty.

The outbreak of war diminished, although it did not remove, King's inhibitions about close Anglo-Canadian co-operation. Canada's prominent – and eventually pre-eminent – role in the British Commonwealth Air Training Plan was dictated by geography and economics on the one hand, demography and politics on the other. The plan's large-scale training commitments required a great many airfields, and clear skies, free from the threat of enemy air activity. Training had to take place within reasonable distance of the likeliest operational theatre, Western Europe, and in close proximity to an industrial base with significant potential for expansion in terms of airframes and engines for training aircraft. Canadian factories were already tooling up in 1939 to produce airframes, and both frames and engines could be obtained from the neighbouring United States. In addition, Canada had a greater population than any of the dominions or 'white' colonies from which to recruit aircrew and provide the human infrastructure for a training system.

A big training plan had clear political advantages. Conscription, brought about by the heavy casualties suffered on the Western Front by the Canadian Corps during the First World War, had come close to splitting the country in 1917. For that reason, if for no other, King was reluctant to see Canada committed to a major contribution of soldiers; he feared that casualties might be as great or greater in a second European war; he sought to avoid another manpower crisis at all costs. Canada's war should be confined as much as possible to the home front, and the overseas effort left to volunteers – as it happened, aircrew were, by definition, all volunteers. Ironically, the course of events in Europe led to substantial air casualties, which was not at all what the government had hoped when it embraced the plan in 1939. Nonetheless, the RCAF never ran short of volunteers.

Article 15 of the BCATP Agreement provided for the possible formation of RCAF squadrons overseas, manned by Canadian graduates of the plan. Putting that article into effect posed all sorts of difficulties, both for British and Canadians, and although a conscious effort was made to form such squadrons, the RCAF never succeeded in creating the separate and distinct identity achieved from the very first by the Canadian Army. The story, however, is essentially one of the RCAF overseas, and will be dealt with in the next volume of this series.

The British Commonwealth Air Training Plan was part of a wider Empire Air Training Scheme [EATS] designed to produce large numbers of trained aircrew. Canada, initially the largest contributor outside of Great Britain, adopted the BCATP designation while the original arrangements were being completed in the fall of 1939. The British and other partners in the plan usually employed the imperial terminology, at least until the BCATP was renegotiated in the summer of 1942, when Canada accepted a still greater part. From that time until the plan was closed out, on 31 March 1945, the Canadian identification was more commonly – but not universally – used.

Any organization's success must be measured by how well it achieves its assigned objectives. No organization which expands to such a size as the BCATP, and as quickly, can be without faults, but in the simplest and most important sense the BCATP met and even exceeded its goals, providing the Allied air forces with more than 131,000 trained aircrew. Of all the Commonwealth aircrew trained during the Second World War, 45 per cent received some or all of their training in Canada. The BCATP was a major contributor to the air supremacy the Allies had achieved in every theatre of war by 1944.

5
Origins

The First World War set a clear precedent for the British Commonwealth Air Training Plan in Canada. Fully two thirds of the 21,000 Canadians who served in Britain's air forces in the First World War entered through RFC/RAF Canada, a recruiting and training organization established in Canada but controlled from London and commanded by a British officer. Over 3000 Canadians completed pilot training by this means; more than 2500 went overseas.[1] The British naturally hoped to receive a similar major contribution in any future European conflict, when both sides could expect very large numbers of aircrew casualties. Success or failure would depend, it was repeatedly emphasized in the interwar years, 'on how rapidly others could be drafted to take their places.'[2] 'Others' inevitably included dominion airmen, who 'would come in a most invaluable form and at the most critical time.'[3] As the deputy chief of the British air staff told Squadron Leader Vernon Heakes, RCAF liaison officer at the Air Ministry, in early 1939: 'All we want of Canada in a war is pilots and aircraft.'[4] Air Vice-Marshal Charles Portal put it even more bluntly: the 'requirement' was for 'bodies.'[5]

Such imperial assumptions had little immediate impact on peacetime recruiting policy. For Canada, the initial flow of pilots was almost exclusively the other way. Partly because of the dearth of flying training facilities, between 1925 and 1928 the RCAF recruited pilots with RAF short-service or reserve commissions.[6] This need for trained pilots was one of the main reasons behind government support of the flying-club movement, and by the end of the decade conditions had changed. As the chief of the general staff observed at the Imperial Conference of 1930, it seemed 'extremely improbable that further enlistments from the Royal Air Force would be required ...'[7]

For its part, the RAF had little need for dominion recruits. It allowed, but did not encourage, outside enlistments, opening only a handful of vacancies to dominion applicants.[8] In 1931 the Air Ministry said that it was willing to extend an Anglo-New Zealand arrangement to grant the director of the RCAF the right to recommend a limited number of fit, educated young men with civil pilot's licences. These candidates had to travel to England at their own expense with no assurance that they would be enrolled. Those without official blessing could apply directly to the Air Ministry, but, the RCAF liaison officer in London warned, it was 'extremely inadvisable for them to proceed to England without first obtaining our opinion as to the likelihood of their acceptance.' Competition was keen; 'only a few vacancies may be expected.'[9]

An understanding on permanent commissions in the RAF was reached in 1932, but the British remained hard to please. Canada could only expect one 'assured vacancy' for all Royal Military College and university graduates, although an effort would be made to find other spots 'if more than one eminently suitable candidate were available.'[10] In the year 1932-3, four Canadian candidates were nominated and accepted for permanent commissions, another was appointed to RAF College, Cranwell, and one was granted a short-service commission. In 1933-4, two Canadians were given permanent commissions.[11]

Then circumstances abruptly changed. After Hitler came to power in Germany and attempts at disarmament collapsed, the British moved to correct the worst deficiencies of their armed services. This resulted, in the words of Sir Maurice Hankey, secretary to both the British Cabinet and the Committee of Imperial Defence, in 'something of a concentration on the Air Force.'[12] The RAF looked to its imperial partners for manpower and the training space needed to support an enlarged force in war.

As one early step, the Air Ministry had suggested a cost-sharing agreement under which Canadian, South African, and New Zealand air force cadets could be granted short-service RAF commissions for a period of five years and then might be returned home for reserve service. Australia already had such an agreement for fifteen officers a year. In November 1934 the British formally placed this proposal before the Canadian government. It was accepted in principle in June of the next year.[13]

The new scheme was to come into effect on 1 January 1937. Dominion authorities were to select Canadians between eighteen and twenty-one years of age, give them appointments in the RCAF, and, after twelve months' training and a medical examination, send them to the RAF where they would be granted short-service commissions. Requests for extensions of service in the RAF reserve or conversions to permanent commissions would be subject to Canadian consent. Without such consent, each officer was to be repatriated after his service and commissioned in the RCAF, where he would be liable for four years' service under Canadian regulations.[14]

Even before the new plan could be launched, the British proposed a wider air training agreement. Many Canadian applicants for the RAF had no air force training. To tap this source, the Air Ministry outlined a scheme 'which would obviate the risk of a candidate being put to unnecessary expense through rejection in this country.' The United Kingdom was prepared 'to accept for appointment to short service commissions a maximum of twenty-five candidates a year who would be finally selected in Canada.' The RCAF was to examine applicants' suitability and medical fitness, and short-service commissions would be granted on Canadian authority without further examination overseas.[15] The Department of National Defence approved this scheme on 27 April 1936, but acceptance at the political level was another matter.[16]

Yet another British proposal had been placed before the Canadian government by the British air minister, Lord Swinton, in March 1936. 'It has occurred to Lord Swinton,' wrote Vincent Massey, the Canadian high commissioner in London, 'that in addition to the Canadian Officers who are being admitted to the R.A.F. under the arrangements which call for their training in England, an additional number might be provided with their preliminary training in Canada and taken on the strength of the R.A.F. after having obtained there certain flying qualifications. The idea was that the course they would receive in Canada would be of a civilian nature in which existing instructional equipment in Canada would be used. The United Kingdom Government would presumably pay the cost of such training just as they do in the case of pilots trained in civilian schools here in Great Britain.'[17]

There were three British air training proposals on the table. One had been accepted by Canada in principle.[18] The Air Ministry hoped for an immediate and favourable response to the other two, but in vain. One reason for the dominion's inaction can doubtless be traced to opposition in the Department of External Affairs, where such schemes were apt to be viewed not as mere Anglo-Canadian military co-operation, but rather as a broad strategic commitment. A senior External Affairs' official, Loring Christie, wrote: 'It seems to me all these schemes are unsound, unless it is to be assumed or decided now that Canada will join Great Britain in any war that may involve the latter.'[19]

While these modest training proposals were circulating within the bureaucracies of London and Ottawa, the Royal Air Force staff was examining other possibilities. Considering potential training sites outside Great Britain, the director of RAF training, Air Commodore A.W. Tedder, wrote in May 1936 that 'Canada has advantages in weather, terrain, accessibility to U.K. etc, over any other overseas location.' He buttressed his argument with a memorandum by Group Captain Robert Leckie, then superintendent of the RAF Reserve. Leckie pointed out the practicability of year-round flying training in Canada, while noting that the country was virtually immune to enemy action and close to both American industrial resources and Great Britain.[20]

That summer Tedder proposed to the visiting minister of national defence, Ian Mackenzie, that the RAF establish a British flying training school [FTS] in Canada. When asked what form it would take, Tedder 'explained that its provision and organization could be adapted to meet the Canadian political considerations. If it were considered desirable to avoid any definite linking of the Canadian Defence organization with the operations of the FTS, the FTS could be supplied and manned entirely from British sources, Canada merely supplying the site. On the other hand, if political considerations permitted, we could employ a percentage of Canadian personnel, material, etc.; or the FTS could even be run on joint lines.' Mackenzie said that he was anxious to co-operate in all such matters and 'personally only too glad to accede' to Tedder's proposal.[21]

Mackenzie did not betray his bias when he took the matter to the prime minister in early September.[22] The Cabinet made its decision a week later. It would be 'inadvisable,' the brief record of the discussion read, 'to have Canadian territory used by the British Government for training school purposes for airmen. It is the intention of the Canadian Government to establish training schools of its own. The situation might give rise to competition between governments in the matter of fields, pilots, equipment and the like.'[23] There the matter temporarily rested for many months, despite an unsuccessful attempt by the Canadian Joint Staff Committee to resuscitate the idea at the time of the Imperial Conference of 1937.[24]

The greatest British concern still continued to be the expansion of existing programmes for the enrolment of Canadians in the Royal Air Force. Sir Francis Floud, the British high commissioner in Ottawa, argued that 'it was going to be extraordinarily difficult to persuade Canada to do anything' for the defence of the empire. The 'best hope of getting any assistance from them lay in such directions as the supply of pilots in time of war.'[25] While in London, Mackenzie had pointed out that there were many more applications for the RCAF than could be accepted, that more publicity would be useful in attracting Canadians to seek British short-service commissions, and that it would be possible to suggest to candidates who were not successful in getting into the RCAF that they should go to England to join the RAF.[26] On 25 March 1937 the Canadian government finally announced complete approval of the November 1935 British 'trained-in-Canada' proposal for the granting of RAF short-service commissions to fifteen Canadian candidates a year. Agreement in principle was also given to the British suggestion for a maximum of twenty-five candidates a year to be fully selected for the RAF in Canada: the 'direct entry scheme.'[27]

Within a month the British returned with far greater direct entry numbers in mind: 'groups of 12 to 20 candidates arriving at regular intervals throughout the year and commencing as soon as practicable.'[28] Political caution, however, prevailed,[29] and British inquiries remained unanswered. In November the British expressed the fear 'that if present quota is not raised, Canadian candidates, finding the quota full, will come independently to England in the hope of being enlisted ... rejected candidates will inevitably feel a sense of severe disappointment at not having been included in scheme of local selection ...'[30] The Canadians responded in late December, saying that they preferred not to increase the numbers beyond twenty-five 'so as not to prejudice the position in Canada should it be necessary at a later date to secure this type of candidate for service in the Royal Canadian Air Force.'[31] In March 1938, in a memorandum directed to the prime minister, O.D. Skelton, the undersecretary of state for external affairs, re-examined the issue after further representations from the British. The views of the Department of National Defence – 'that half the number previously proposed might well be spared, ie, up to 10 per month or 120 per year' – had not changed, and Skelton did not raise any objections.[32] The Cabinet acquiesced, and the good news was conveyed to Whitehall, Mackenzie King adding characteristically that 'it will be understood that this cannot be regarded as a commitment.'[33]

This decision had an immediate impact. Within a year 118 Canadian candidates had been selected and sent to England for RAF short-service commissions under the direct entry scheme. In addition, fifteen men were selected under the trained-in-Canada plan; of this number, nine proceeded to England.[34] In all there appear to have been between four and five hundred

Canadian permanent and short-service appointments by the end of the decade, and a similar number of Canadians who had enlisted as other ranks.[35]

The RAF, however, required trained pilots, not pilot trainees. As the British official history points out, RAF recruiting schemes in Britain were 'successful in attracting a large number of enthusiastic recruits,' but 'there were never enough aircraft and instructors' to train them.[36] If Canada trained the 120 candidates selected under the direct entry scheme before sending them to England, it would relieve the overburdened RAF training organization. In addition, excess training capacity in Canada could be used to train recruits sent out from Britain. Conducting RAF training in Canada held other attractions as well. The British had always viewed an FTS in Canada as a method of attracting more Canadians to the RAF. 'There is in Canada an excellent source of supply for short service officers for the R.A.F. of a type better, in my considered opinion, than we are recruiting today,' wrote Leckie in 1936, 'and the presence of an F.T.S. in their midst would crystallise interest in the R.A.F. and certainly produce excellent applicants if these are required.'[37]

An FTS might also help to break down Canadian reluctance to become involved in imperial defence. Overcoming such Canadian resistance was an important consideration behind the British government's decision to send an air mission to North America in May 1938. The mission, headed by a well-known industrialist, J.G. Weir, was to explore the possibilities of purchasing aircraft from American sources. Although the 'Air Ministry could not hope to make any useful purchases in Canada,'[38] the senior dominion was included on the air mission's itinerary for reasons that were later explained to his Cabinet by the British prime minister. 'If the only object were to get aircraft quicker, the money could be spent more effectively' at home; however, 'if Canada could become interested in the provision of aircraft to this country aloofness of that Dominion from Imperial defence and its dissociation from the problems of the United Kingdom might be reduced. It was not inconceivable that the whole attitude of Canada towards the defence of the Empire might be changed.'[39]

On 13 May 1938 the British government instructed the air mission, then in Canada, to discuss in addition the possibility of establishing one or more schools to train pilots for the RAF. Done at Air Ministry expense, training would 'conform with that now in force' in Great Britain, but it would be left completely in RCAF hands. Canadian pilots were at the heart of the proposal; if the scheme were accepted, it would replace both the direct entry and trained-in-Canada plans, the candidates from these programmes receiving their training at the proposed flying schools. If vacancies existed, British pilots would be trained as well.[40]

The matter was raised by the British high commissioner in two meetings with Mackenzie King on 16 May. Floud stated that the 'problem was really one of air congestion. England was a small country, thickly populated; the spaces available for training pilots comparatively few.'[41] Floud's (and the Air Ministry's) focus was on Canadian candidates, trained by the RCAF for overseas service with the RAF. The possibility of sending British recruits to train in Canadian schools was also raised, but not emphasized.[42] King's concern was that the scheme would 'arouse criticism on the score that an effort was being made to create Imperial forces, and to bring about a condition whereby Canada would be committed to participation in a European conflict.'[43]

King refused to go along with the British training proposal in his first meeting with Floud. The second, with Weir present, simply aggravated him. Although King's own record of the talks contains two references to the British desire to have Canadian pilots trained in the proposed schools, he ignored this aspect when he presented the scheme to Cabinet later that afternoon, talking instead about the training of British pilots in Canada. More importantly, he misinterpreted the approach as a proposal for the establishment of a British-owned and British-controlled military installation in Canada. When Floud said that the British government was prepared to spend large sums of money and thus help Canada's industries and unemployed, King's impression seemed confirmed.

Politics – broad national concerns but also narrow partisanship – were uppermost in the prime minister's mind. In his conversations with Floud and Weir, King expressed his worry that the air training scheme 'would certainly force an issue in Canada at once which would disclose a wide division of opinion … by, first of all, creating disunion in Canada, and secondly, prejudicing in advance the position that might be taken at a later time.'[44] His fears that the training scheme was an attempt to lure Canada into an imperial commitment were not eased by Weir's emphasis on the urgent need for additional training facilities, and the importance of preparing for a 'possible emergency … some time ahead.' The 'value of any co-operation which Canada might be prepared to render when emergency arose would be seriously impaired by a refusal to co-operate now. It would, therefore, in effect be a commitment in a negative sense.'[45]

King's 'very unfavourable'[46] reaction to the air training proposal increased the importance that London placed on the purchase of aircraft in Canada. The dominions secretary informed the Cabinet that he 'laid stress on the real political value of the proposals … He urged that the Mission must be purely technical in character and must avoid touching in any way on politics: otherwise the Prime Minister of Canada, who had already adopted an attitude of antagonism towards proposals for a Training Establishment in Canada, might easily turn against the proposal.'[47] The Air Ministry was particularly 'anxious lest political considerations … may militate against formulation of satisfactory scheme for aircraft production in Canada.'[48] London was doubtless greatly relieved, therefore, to receive word from Floud that 'Political objection to flying school proposals have not prejudiced success of main object of Mission's visit.'[49] Writing to Floud on 20 May, H.F. Batterbee, the assistant undersecretary, explained the attitude of the Dominions Office. 'We could not help being afraid that the political reactions aroused by the flying school proposal might have the result of prejudicing to some extent the consideration of the aircraft proposal. I hope that the form of our telegrams made it clear that we only put up the former proposal because the Air Ministry wanted us to. We were quite clear from the start that the proposal was hopeless, but the Air Ministry were not to be prevented from putting it forward.'[50] As a result of King's attitude, the British government 'hastily dropped all idea of training pilots for the RAF in Canada'[51] and concentrated its efforts on interesting Canada in imperial defence through British purchases from Canadian aircraft manufacturers.

In June 1938, former Conservative national leader Arthur Meighen began making embarrassing enquiries in the Senate. He repeatedly asked if the British had requested permission to set up, at their expense, a flying training school. King was clear in his own mind that no formal approach had been made – he had deliberately sought to keep the discussions tentative[52] – but when Raoul Dandurand, the Liberal leader in the Senate, said that no request had been made 'in any shape or form,' an admission had to be made that 'some informal discussions' had taken place.[53] Floud privately denounced King's 'dishonest wriggling,'[54] but the prime minister boasted to the Cabinet that he 'would ask for no better issue in a general election than one which would seek to have any branch of the British War Ministry undertake establishments in Canada which would be primarily for the purpose of including Canadians to take part in Imperial Wars.'[55]

Floud again spoke to King on 27 June. The British high commissioner attempted, for the second time in two months, to convey to him the essentials of the training proposal; namely, that Canadian and British flyers would be trained in Canadian estabishments. Once again, King misinterpreted the suggestion as entailing the training of British pilots only, but he now understood that the training would take place in Canadian schools.[56] King took this to be a shift in the British position, one that would allow him to steal a march on his critics. 'We will be able to work out,' he wrote in his diary, 'an establishment in connection with flying which will be all to the good so far as Canada's defence is concerned, and will help British defence, but will effectively safeguard against the Tory aim of an Empire control[led] from Britain.'[57] Cabinet had not yet been consulted, but King was prepared for Conservative leader R.B. Bennett when he rose in the House on 1 July to question again the Liberal stand on air training.[58] The prime minister began his remarks by emphasizing 'that in Canadian territory there could be no military establishments unless they were owned, maintained and controlled by the Canadian government responsible to the Canadian parliament and people.' King set out his government's willingness to co-operate in an Anglo-Canadian programme 'to give in our own estabishments the opportunity to British pilots to come over here and train ... controlled by our own Minister of National Defence who is responsible to this parliament.'[59]

King's offer, including the suggestion that a British officer be sent to Canada to discuss the question, was duly conveyed to London on 5 July 1938. The prime minister's words in the House of Commons were quoted: 'We are quite prepared in connection with our own establishments, to help in affording facilities to British pilots if that will be of service to them.'[60]

But immediately – and again – the issue became confused. On 7 July, in a letter to King, Floud referred vaguely to 'the possibility of working out a scheme for the provision of facilities in Canada for training candidates for the Air Force.' In the British House of Commons, on the same day, similar language was used by the secretary of state for air, and again when Floud announced that Group Captain J.M. Robb, commandant of the RAF's Central Flying School, would be sent to Canada to discuss air training.[61]

The British had shifted their ground. The Treasury had raised a number of objections to the possibility of sending British pilots to train in Canada, not the least of which was 'the waste of time and money involved in sending pupils to Canada and bringing them back again.'[62] Robb's mandate was to ascertain if Ottawa were willing to give flying training to at least 135 Canadians (the total of the direct entry and trained-in-Canada schemes) and to enquire about 'additional capacity' up to four hundred. Britain was no longer interested in the possibility of using training facilities in Canada to train British recruits. King's offer of 1 July, however, was strictly 'for British flyers to come to Canada for training in Canadian schools.'[63]

When Skelton again made the terms of the offer clear to Floud in mid-August, the high commissioner argued that it was 'absurd for some hundreds of Canadians to go over to England to train and some hundreds of Englishmen [to] come over to Canada to train.' Although Floud's logic was undeniable, the Canadian government felt it essential to draw a distinction between sending untrained Canadians to the RAF while training Englishmen in Canada, as they proposed, and sending trained Canadians to the RAF, as the British preferred. It was important to the Canadian government that any agreement reached not be viewed as an imperial commitment. Skelton informed Floud that the British plans carried 'the implications of a continuous use of Canada in peace and in war as a basis of training for United Kingdom military forces.' The distinction was exceedingly fine, and Skelton's uncomfortable negotiating position was perhaps reflected in his discussion with the high commissioner when he stated categorically, and in disregard of the facts, that 'there never was the remotest suggestion in any of these conversations of anything other than British flyers being involved.'[64] According to the Canadian definition of their proposal, Canada would be providing limited selection and training assistance, but would not become an imperial training centre.[65]

This subtlety was lost on the Department of National Defence. On 19 July the senior air officer had proposed recruiting and training sufficient Canadians for an output of 300 graduates per year. During a six-month course, the recruits would be given elementary and intermediate flying training before proceeding to the RAF for advanced training. The British were to carry the major financial burden, such as operating Camp Borden.[66] Croil's plan dovetailed nicely with the thinking of Group Captain Robb and L.R. LaFlèche, deputy minister of national defence. The three men met in early August and submitted a revised programme covering three years, and now including all forms of training.[67] The minister of national defence approved the proposal but asked LaFlèche to show it to the prime minister. This LaFlèche did on 8 August.

King's hostility was clearly evident in Cabinet the following afternoon. 'All were impressed,' he told his diary, 'at change of nature of program as set forth by LaFlèche. – I had him come to Council with Skelton. It was clear as he talked that the plan was a *war plan* – to make sure of *a base for training in Canada*, when war comes, – with certainty on part of Defence Department Canada wd. be in it – co-operating in defence of Empire. – I can agree to that – reserving to prlt. decision as to action to be taken, viz., to be in shape to co-operate, if we so decide – but quite different is the proposal to recruit Canadians meanwhile for service in the Br. Air Force in grounds, schools, etc., which will *duplicate* rather than expand our own. I gave LaFlèche as decision of Council to tell Captain Robb who has come from England that our proposal was to afford facilities for training *British* pilots – not recruiting Canadians for Br. service, and to outline what was desired within that compass.' King was outraged later that evening when he read in the *Ottawa Journal* a detailed account of Robb's mission 'as if the matter had been finally settled.' After a fitful night he decided 'that it was the Canadian Defence Dept. – not the Br. Air Ministry that was responsible for advocacy of recruiting Canadians here etc. ... I intend to go to the bottom of this. It is a very dangerous issue ...'

The prime minister now summoned the six members of his Cabinet who were in Ottawa to a meeting in his office, and there they met Croil, LaFlèche, and Robb. The meeting further convinced King that the Department of National Defence – now joined by the Air Ministry, the press, manufacturers, and others interested in contracts and 'imperialistic' programmes – was trying to exert undue pressure on the Cabinet. He claimed in his diary that there was general agreement on this point, and on the importance of following the 'Laurier naval policy in relation to air, of having an efficient service in Canada which, if Parliament so decided, could be made a part of one great service in time of war.'[68]

Robb redrafted and resubmitted the plan, which was also signed by Croil, in September. The new version differed in two major essentials from the original proposal.[69] Nothing was said this time about finances. Robb had been instructed to seek an equal division of costs, but he found that National Defence was making its preparations on the assumption that virtually the whole cost would be borne by the British. Nothing, furthermore, was specifically said about the source of the candidates beyond the 135 Canadians previously agreed to. When King asked how the British expected to make up the balance between the existing schemes and the 300 trainees contemplated in the new one, Floud noted 'his own impression' that all 300 ought, if possible, to come from Canada. The high commissioner's thinking clearly reflected the Treasury view which had taken firm hold of British policy. London was not interested in training British pilots in Canada. What was wanted was 'ready-trained Canadian pilots' for the RAF.[70] 'It was plain,' wrote Skelton, 'that a scheme such as was suggested was purely and simply a recruiting scheme ...'[71] Loring Christie worried that the number of pilots to be trained was so much greater than the normal annual Canadian training programme (of fifty to seventy) that national priorities would be overshadowed. Canadian training might be seen as incidental or supplementary to, or simply the result of, the British scheme.[72]

The Canadian air staff, too, noted that the Robb plan would imply the immediate loss of specially qualified individuals to the training programme, putting back RCAF development for about a year. The advantages, however, outweighed the disadvantages. The British plan would bring into existence, in advance of Canadian requirements, training facilities ready to meet war needs in the event of emergency. There would be a more rapid development of RCAF stations. The plan would ultimately provide a reserve of trained pilots and of instructional and maintenance staff. The aircraft requirements would result in increased Canadian manufacturing capacity, and advanced training aircraft would have military value in an emergency. For greatest efficiency, the air staff proposed to combine RAF and RCAF training. About half the trainees would be RCAF, illustrating that the Canadian service was 'an equal partner in the training scheme, and in no way impelled by the Royal Air Force.'[73]

The air staff's memorandum provided the underlying thrust of a proposal put forward by the Department of National Defence on 5 November 1938. In this plan, Canada would provide the aerodromes and buildings, Britain the initial supply of aircraft, engines, and spares. Remaining costs would be divided in proportion to the number of candidates trained for each service.[74] The British fretted over the costs, but thought that they were not well placed to object: 'We want the ready-trained Canadian pilots; Canada can sit back and demand her price.' The British took some heart that Mackenzie King 'made no suggestion that the training of the existing 135 pupils in Canada would be finally objected to,' and felt that Ottawa could not reject a scheme that was in both Britain's and Canada's interest. They had had sufficient experience in dealing with the Canadian prime minister, however, to realize that 'he would much prefer to adopt no scheme at all.'[75]

The British were themselves unwilling to compromise by agreeing to a scheme that would send British pilots to train in Canada. Their attitude in the negotiations proved disconcerting even to some of their own officials. 'I confess,' wrote a member of the Dominions Office, 'to being perplexed at the way in which ... the whole scheme for establishing flying training schools in Canada has been radically altered backwards and forwards from time to time. I think it would be a fair general criticism to make at the outset if I said that these radical alterations appear to have proceeded from reasons of internal United Kingdom policy, rather than from any developments (important though the latter have been from time to time) which have occurred in Canada.'[76] From this perspective, the assertion of the British official history that the delay in reaching an agreement 'was in no way the fault of the Air Ministry or, indeed, of anyone else in Britain' but 'arose from the political situation in Canada'[77] seems unfair and incorrect. The combination of British intransigence over the source of pilots and King's political concerns cost the two countries any chance they may have had to implement a peacetime agreement that would have allowed both British and Canadian flyers to train in Canada for the RAF.

The November proposal, and a British version submitted on 9 December,[78] were still unacceptable to Mackenzie King. In the Cabinet discussion of the British offer on 15 December his opposition was clear: 'Discussed most of the time new proposal from the Air Ministry in England ... It was not for a British school in Canada, nor was it for training of British pilots in Canada, but it was for recruiting and training of Canadians for 5 years in the Imperial service. This would be certain to provoke a discussion on Canada contributing to forces overseas for war purposes, as contrary to basic principle of Canada's autonomy and the right to reach her own decision on peace and war.' As an alternative, the prime minister advocated an enlargement of the RCAF, 'reserving, of course, the right to Englishmen to come and be trained here, but making the point that it was a supply of trained men that was essential and that we would be co-operating with both Britain and the U.S. in helping to show the strength of the nations that would be against aggressors.'[79]

King's diary entry for that evening reflected his disillusionment with the whole project. 'I must confess,' he wrote, 'I had been deeply disappointed in the manner in which the British Government has shifted its ground, from time to time, with evident design throughout. First a few men have been allowed to go to England seemingly to help co-ordinating services. This has been made a basis for extension of numbers for purposes of enlistment and arrangement to examine men in advance of leaving has been construed as recruiting already commenced ...' The next day, the prime minister recorded in his diary: 'All were agreed we could not possibly undertake to recruit air pilots for Great Britain, but would afford facilities for air pilots to be trained in Canada, meeting all expenses ourselves.'[80]

King formally rejected the British proposal on the last day of 1938. In doing so, he repeated his offer to train pilots from the United Kingdom in Canadian establishments. On 10 January 1939 the new high commissioner, Sir Gerald Campbell, wrote to King to express his government's 'regret that the proposals ... are unacceptable to the Canadian Government.' He also acknowledged the renewed offer with the assurance that the United Kingdom authorities would 'be happy to avail themselves of it.'[81]

Within the Air Ministry the idea of sending Canadian pilots to Britain for training and British pilots to Canada was now thought ridiculous. The seriousness of the international situation, however, precluded further argument. Although unhappy with the 'excessively high' cost of Canadian training, substantially more per pupil than training in Britain, the Air Ministry bowed to Dominions Office pressure and concluded an agreement. By late April the minister of national defence was able to announce that a number of British pilots, not to exceed fifty in any year, would be given intermediate and advanced stages of training under the auspices of the Department of National Defence. The existing Anglo-Canadian air training agreements remained in effect. The Canadian government would purchase the initial aircraft for the training scheme; replacement aircraft would be charged for in an amount paid by the British per pupil. The RCAF would use British aircraft types wherever possible, though no specific commitments were given.[82]

The first batch of pilots was scheduled to arrive in Canada by mid-September 1939. They never arrived. The first days of the month brought the European war that Mackenzie King had been dreading.

In the last few days before the outbreak of war, the British contacted RCAF Group Captain A.E. Godfrey in London (in the absence of Heakes), raising the issue of increased training capacity in Canada. Noting the First World War experience, the Air Ministry suggested that Canada could begin with four training schools, each of which would gradually grow until it produced 468 pupils a year. Godfrey, speaking confidentially, felt that Canada would be 'quite willing to concentrate on training rather than forming additional operational units.'[83]

The British made a formal approach along these lines on 6 September 1939, midway through the week which separated the British and Canadian declarations of war on Germany. Prime Minister Neville Chamberlain telegraphed his appreciation for Mackenzie King's offer of 'action in the Western Atlantic region, particularly in Newfoundland and the West Indies,' but suggested other 'immediate steps': 'provision of naval vessels and facilities and of air force personnel would be of most assistance, and in particular at present time supply of any pilots and aircraft crews available is a capital requirement.' Because of the expected high level of casualties in intensive air operations, Canada could best assist by concentrating on the individual training and dispatching of pilots, observers, and especially air gunners and radio operators, rather than by placing an emphasis on the formation and training of complete air units for sending to Europe with a ground-based expeditionary force. Only when 'sufficient officers and personnel were available in England and France' should the aim become the formation of an RCAF 'contingent.' If such reasoning was accepted, steps should immediately be taken to increase the yearly output of pilots to 2000, to enlist skilled mechanics both for Canadian and RAF purposes, to train as many observers and air gunners as possible, and, perhaps, at a later stage and 'if possible,' to transfer at least four RAF flying schools to Canada.[84]

King's response was an assurance of the immediate, rapid expansion of training, and an offer to dispatch a number of partially trained individuals to the RAF. Coupled to this reply on 12 September was the stated desire that 'Canadian Air Force units' be formed overseas when sufficient trained Canadians were available, and the warning that personnel must be available for transfer back to the RCAF 'if the Canadian Government should later decide upon the organization of distinctive Canadian air units for service overseas.'[85]

By then, Godfrey and Heakes had met with Portal, the British air member for personnel, and other officials, and had been told that the RAF actually foresaw a requirement for three or four times the number of trained aircrew then being produced. A training organization of this size could not be accommodated in the United Kingdom, and the dominions would be asked for major assistance. Portal emphasized the importance of concentrating resources on training, though there was 'no reason at all' why Canadian units should not eventually be sent to England. The Air Ministry conceded that the RCAF would control the organization of the proposed schools. Aircraft would mainly come from Canada and the United States, although the RAF would be prepared to provide some of the equipment. The desirability was underlined of sending a strong mission 'to convince the Canadians of the necessity of an organization on the scale proposed.'[86]

This information led Croil to reconsider his earlier recommendations. Warned that British pilot requests would soon rise to 8000 annually, and armed with

British advice that Canada could best help by the provision of trained aircrew, he reasoned that the RCAF could only meet these objectives if all available personnel were absorbed into the training structure rather than going overseas. Accordingly, in the middle of the month he recommended that training goals be initially set at 1000 graduates per month, with consideration given to future expansion.[87]

In London, meanwhile, a plan of 'impressive magnitude' was being formulated which would dwarf Croil's numbers. On 13 September Vincent Massey, the Canadian high commissioner, Stanley Bruce, his Australian counterpart, Godfrey, and two Australian officers discussed 'the disparity in force & other gloomy features' of Britain's predicament. The group's disquiet was conveyed, later that same day, to the dominions secretary, Anthony Eden, and other British Cabinet members and officials. Massey claims in his memoirs to have decided after the meeting 'that Canada might be able to make a decisive contribution to the common war effort by training Commonwealth airmen,' and to have consulted Bruce, 'who enthusiastically agreed.' Bruce remembered it quite differently, claiming that the idea was wholly his. The contemporary Dominions Office record is probably closest to the truth. It shows that Massey and Bruce jointly put the proposal to a high commissioners' meeting on 16 September, suggesting that 'consideration should be given 'to a scheme whereby Canadian, Australian, and New Zealand air forces should be trained in Canada on 'planes to be specifically built in Canada or the U.S.'[88] An apparently new ingredient had been added to existing Air Ministry training proposals: the creation of a large-scale Commonwealth organization in Canada through which trainees from the several dominions would be channelled for overseas service.

Massey was continually consulted as the plan took shape. He helped to sponsor the plan in Whitehall and to sell it to a notoriously circumspect Ottawa. The high commissioners were shown the telegram which would put the plan to the dominions. Massey edited it and added a personal passage (ostensibly from Chamberlain) designed to attract his prime minister.[89] Legitimate questions might be raised about the propriety of Massey's role in underwriting 'a plan which was likely to have a major effect upon the structure and balance of the Canadian war effort without telling his government what he was doing.'[90] Massey, however, pointed proudly in his diary to the 'important job' he and Bruce had done. What would King say, the Canadian high commissioner wrote, 'if he knew I helped to write what he receives!'[91]

Mackenzie King, as he quickly saw, had been handed a great political prize: 'a form of military effort that likely would not lead to enormous casualties, a positive inducement for French Canada to admire the government's wise management of affairs.'[92] King privately complained that the proposal showed 'how quite unprepared the British ... were in their plans that until now they have not been able to tell us definitely what really is the best of all plans, and which would have saved us having anything to do with an expeditionary force at the start.'[93] To the British he gave immediate approval in principle, adding that his government 'fully' agreed 'that Canadian co-operation in this field would be particularly appropriate and probably the most effective in the military sphere which Canada could furnish.' The prime minister added, however, that Canada

lacked sufficient aircraft and instructors for an expanded air training programme, and also noted that the matter of dividing the costs remained to be
negotiated. King assured the British that Canada would be pleased to play host to
a conference to complete arrangements.[94]

Within the previous two weeks the government had already offered to provide
economic assistance to Britain as well as recruit the 1st Canadian Division; the
Cabinet was unsure whether an air training programme was meant to replace or
supplement these earlier commitments. As the minister of finance, Colonel J.L.
Ralston, remarked, 'the greatly increased emphasis upon the air arm, evident
from Mr. Chamberlain's cable, and the part Canada might be called upon to play
in that sphere, might result in considerable modifications of the Canadian war
programme in other respects.'[95] O.D. Skelton warned the prime minister of the
'*Money factor*. What would be the total training cost? Cost of providing
aerodromes and ground equipment? Cost of training planes? Cost of maintenance and instruction? etc. ... if Britain needs Canadian credits for buying
wheat, she will ask for credits for her air expenditures here ...' Beyond that, the
scheme's long-term implications were worrying: 'it is not merely an air training
scheme. It is an expeditionary air force scheme on a colossal scale. It would be
difficult to train tens of thousands of Canadians as pilots and gunners, etc, and
then restrict ourselves to sending over a dozen squadrons. Australia is sending 6
squadrons in three months. We would be faced with trying to maintain in France
a tremendous Canadian Air Force. What would be the cost of this?'[96]

When the British asked the Canadian government to approve a draft public
statement on the air training plan, there were clear signs that the two countries
might approach the forthcoming planning conference from quite different
perspectives. King cabled Chamberlain that the Emergency Council had three
reservations.[97] First of all, the British note implied that Canada and the other
dominions had originated the air training idea. King insisted that the announcement make plain that the scheme was a British not a Canadian initiative. Second,
the statement 'should also emphasize the fact that this activity constitutes ... the
most essential and effective form of military co-operation open to Canada.'
Third, the draft left an impression that the plan was all but complete. The
Canadian government wanted it made known that no details had been settled;
everything, especially the plan's scale and financing, was open for discussion.[98]
For their part, the British were wary of King's motives and suspected that he was
attempting to manoeuvre them into accepting the air training scheme as
Canada's major contribution to the war, even though 'there was in Canada a
considerable feeling in favour of an Expeditionary Force.' Winston Churchill,
the First Lord of the Admiralty, told the Cabinet that he 'strongly deprecated that
we should lend ourselves to a statement which might encourage the Canadians to
believe that we should be content with little more than a contribution of Air
forces [sic].'[99] The proposed British statement that Canada's involvement in the
air training scheme would be 'a contribution of a high order in line with that
which she is making in all phases of war effort' was unacceptable to the
Canadian government. Ottawa's wording that the scheme would 'constitute the
most essential and decisive effort that Canada could put forward in the field of

military co-operation' was equally unacceptable to London.[100] Although willing to meet Canada's other concerns, the British Cabinet was prepared to omit 'the whole of the relevant section' from the statement rather than concede the second point to King.[101] After some hurried negotiation, the final wording, that 'this co-operative effort may ... prove to be of the most essential and decisive character,' was sufficiently vague to avoid compromising either government's position.[102]

While there was an obvious political dimension to the priorities question, it was inseparable from finances. The Canadian government had little idea of the costs of mobilizing for war. There were strict limits to what was thought feasible or possible; the era of deficit financing still lay ahead. The week before Chamberlain's cable arrived, the governor of the Bank of Canada, Graham Towers, had advised the Cabinet that there were finite limits to Canada's financial capabilities, and only $500 million could be allocated for war expenditures. Any more would risk failure and the breakdown of the war effort.[103]

In many key areas, moreover, the national interests of Great Britain and Canada diverged. For instance, while the British began restricting Canadian imports and bargaining hard for cheaper wheat, thus limiting Canada's ability to pay for its own war effort, they were also asking for financial credits to conserve dollar reserves so they might purchase military equipment in the United States. This made British sense, but it took little account of Canada's needs. As Anthony Eden told his Cabinet colleagues: 'The Canadians will obviously feel that it is wrong that we should be pressing them to supply and even finance purchases in Canada essential to *our* interests while we are taking unilateral action which might damage *their* essential interests.'[104]

The outstanding economic problems were discussed on a number of fronts. The British sent a mission to Canada and the United States to purchase war supplies, and Canada dispatched a senior Cabinet representative, T.A. Crerar, who would be joined by Graham Towers, to London. But the separate talks were bound to be protracted, and it was to prove difficult to weave their common financial threads into mutually acceptable general policies, or to co-ordinate them with the air training talks about to get under way.

The British government appointed Lord Riverdale, a prominent industrialist 'of great experience in business negotiations in Canada,'[105] to head the United Kingdom Air Training Mission which sailed from Liverpool on 7 October. Accompanying Riverdale were Air Vice-Marshal Sir Christopher Courtney and F.T. Hearle, the managing director of the de Havilland Aircraft Company, along with a number of other officials and advisers. Captain Harold Balfour, the parliamentary undersecretary for air, joined the mission later, as did Air Chief Marshal Sir Robert Brooke-Popham. Sir Gerald Campbell at the British High Commission lent his assistance throughout the negotiations.

While en route from Britain, Riverdale's team refined the details of their proposal. The scope was immense – 20,000 pilots and 30,000 other aircrew annually. Since Britain could train less than half, the rest would have to come from the dominions. Canada would provide 48 per cent of these trainees,

Australia 40 per cent, and New Zealand 12 per cent. Each dominion would furnish its own elementary flying training facilities from which the graduates would move on to Canadian-based schools for advanced and specialist instruction. On this projection Canada would have to form seventy-two aircrew schools of all types, as well as a variety of support and maintenance units: repair and recruit depots; aircraft storage facilities; and schools of technical training, aeronautical engineering, equipment, accountancy, and administration.[106]

The scope of the British proposal was, recalled Air Commodore Stedman, the key RCAF figure in the negotiations, 'so far ahead of anything that we had thought of that everyone who had not heard details before was quite taken aback at its magnitude.'[107] The RCAF staff, advised by Riverdale's technical advisers, had 'a very hectic time'[108] putting together specific estimates on the physical plant, equipment, and instructional resources that the plan required; $900 million over a three-year period, they reckoned. Riverdale then took this figure as the basis on which to determine the sharing of costs. Earlier, the Air Ministry had informed him that it would be spending $140 million in Britain on aircraft and equipment for the programme's immediate needs and an additional $81 million for three years' spares and replacements. Riverdale simply assumed the $221 million to be Britain's contribution, allotted Canada half the balance (about $340 million), leaving Australia and New Zealand to share the rest.[109]

In the days before formal negotiations began, Riverdale's mission was restricted to exploring ways of implementing the plan with lower-level officials and the RCAF staff. The prime minister insisted that his ministers not meet with the mission until its formal presentation to the Cabinet, thus emphasizing that initiative was being taken by the British.[110] Unfortunately, this prevented Riverdale from taking 'preliminary soundings' by which he might judge whether his plan was 'likely to be acceptable' to the Canadians.[111] He did speak to Sir Gerald Campbell, who immediately became alarmed at the demands about to be made of Canada. The astonishing costs of the proposal, the high commissioner informed the Dominions Office, 'will amount to about twice the amount provided to be raised by taxation in Canada's war budget for the first year of the war.'[112] Equally disquieting, Campbell warned, the Canadian government was becoming increasingly agitated by London's failure to settle the accumulating financial and economic irritants which were threatening to damage Anglo-Canadian relations.

Canada's most serious complaint concerned wheat. The British understandably wished to keep the price down, while the Canadians wanted much higher rates per bushel in order to finance war expenditures, including those which would be incurred by air training. In the Canadian view, Campbell reported, air training and wheat were inseparable, 'intimately related in their mutual bearing on the question of what economic and financial effort Canada can actually make.'[113] Significantly, when Campbell had first broached the subject of air training with Mackenzie King, 'it was the first thing the Prime Minister brought up in connection with the financial side of the training of pilots scheme.' Wheat was 'acting as a poisonous irritant,' and hard bargaining gave the Canadians the impression that 'we on our side are "chiselling."'[114] This was aggravated by the condescending attitude of some British officials who 'believe that Canada will submit to any demands made of her and to any treatment accorded to her in return without any risk of her good will being forfeited.'[115] The British War Cabinet and Treasury officials acknowledged this problem, but faced financial difficulties of their own.[116] Any expenditures in Canada had to be extracted from Britain's limited treasury, much of which was committed to buying war material in the United States. Therefore, it was in the British Cabinet's interest to persuade Canada to pick up the bulk of the air training bill. 'Lord Riverdale, who knew Canada and the Canadians well could be relied upon to present the matter in the most satisfactory way.' He was told to go ahead.[117]

Riverdale therefore had no specific instructions about how best to proceed. He was given 'only an indication of principles,' and apparently even these were not set out explicitly.[118] The British seem to have assumed an ideal scheme as one which trained Canadian, Australian, and New Zealand students in an organization directed by the RAF and primarily paid for by the dominions. Graduates would then serve in RAF squadrons, perhaps with national identity patches on their shoulders. Riverdale quickly concluded on arriving in Ottawa that 'the Royal Canadian Air Force cannot really organise and control a training scheme of this magnitude.'[119] Consequently, while it would be necessary 'to maintain the Canadian façade ... the scheme would probably have to be run largely by Royal Air Force personnel sent out from the United Kingdom.'[120] This was not a good beginning.

Although much depended on Riverdale's success at reconciling contradictory interests, he lacked a shrewd appreciation of Canadian attitudes. To begin with, he gave the impression that all but minor details had already been settled. He compounded his error by talking about the scheme with the press when he arrived in Canada, an action the Canadian government viewed as 'indiscreet.'[121] Then, when he first met Mackenzie King, Riverdale referred to the proposal as 'your scheme.' Outwardly King was diplomatic, simply pointing out that the scheme was Britain's, not his. Privately he was scathing, objecting to the 'sort of railroading taking for granted style which Riverdale adopted ... It is amazing how these people have come out from the Old Country and seem to think that all they have to do is to tell us what is to be done. No wonder they get the backs of people up on this side.'[122]

When Riverdale and Balfour met with the Canadian Cabinet just before noon on 31 October to present the British air training proposal, it was immediately evident that the two sides had such different views of the scheme that there was bound to be misunderstanding. Emphasizing the huge rearmament burden that Britain had already undertaken, the two British negotiators proposed that Canada finance about 40 per cent of the plan as well as find the majority of trainees. For their part the United Kingdom would be pleased to supply 'without charge ... a contribution in kind towards the cost,' aircraft, engines, and spares – valued at $140 million. The Canadian record of the meeting indicates that Riverdale referred to this equipment as Britain's 'free contribution.'[123]

King was as much irritated by Riverdale's 'airy' manner as he and his colleagues were startled by the size and suggested distribution of the costs. King expected to negotiate as an equal; instead, the British mission seemed to want 'only to tell us what we would be expected to do.' It was, 'in reality, a recruiting scheme for the British Air Force rather than any genuine attempt for any co-operation.'[124] Ralston told the British bluntly that Canada could not come within 'shooting distance' of the 40 per cent – $374 million – and reminded the mission that the programme had to be considered in the context of Canada's other financial commitments. Canada would – had to – look to its own interests.[125]

The discussions, which continued at the working level, were broadened with the arrival of the Australian and New Zealand delegations early in November. Riverdale soon found that they too found his initial proposal wanting. Both judged that it would be more efficient and economical for them to conduct more of their own training at home, and they objected to the numbers of recruits they were expected to raise. While the Australians referred the question to their government, the New Zealanders told Riverdale they could raise no more than 3350 for all categories of air crews annually, just over half the numbers envisaged by the British.[126] The New Zealanders and Australians had been upset by what they regarded as their relegation to second-class status: waiting in ante-rooms until the British and Canadians had finished talking. Facing their own dollar crisis, they also objected to the cost-sharing formula proposed by Canada on the grounds that it was receiving unfair economic advantages from having the bulk of the training plan located there. They therefore proposed that the dominions find suitable recruits on a scale proportional to their populations, a ratio they reckoned at 57 per cent (Canada), 35 per cent (Australia), 8 per cent (New Zealand). For Australia this meant 26,000 pilots and aircrew members over three years, seven-ninths of which they would train at home. The Australians were not prepared to bargain; if their figures were found unacceptable they would then carry out all their air training at home.[127]

The RCAF staff reworked its sums for a third time. Taking into account the shortfall of Australian trainees and cash, Canada would have to provide fewer training facilities but more trainees. The revised total figure was $607 million. Of this total, $68 million was for initial and elementary flying training in Canada to which Australia and New Zealand did not contribute. The United Kingdom's donation of aircraft and equipment amounted to $185 million (a proportion of its original contribution now being directed to Australia), of which $1.9 million was for Canadian elementary training. The remainder, $356 million, was to be divided between Canada, Australia, and New Zealand on the basis of the number of pupils each was expected to contribute: 80.64, 11.28, and 8.08 per cent, respectively.[128]

The negotiations made progress during the last two weeks of November. King's minister of national defence, Norman Rogers, and Balfour reached agreement on the structure and administration of the air training organization, and Ralston informed the Emergency Council on 27 November that he was prepared to accept the financial terms of the scheme. Canada's share was more than originally proposed, but the Cabinet did not complain. By this time they had decided to place an upper limit of $237 million for all Canadian military financial, and other assistance to Britain in the first year of the war, and intended to deduct the first year's air training expenditure from it. The latter was estimated at $46 million but the amount mattered little; it was up to the British to decide how they wanted the money spent.[129]

The scheduled departure of the Australians and New Zealanders at the end of November introduced an element of urgency into the bargaining, all parties thinking it desirable to issue a joint public statement while all the negotiators were still in Ottawa. The British suggested initialling a draft agreement, while they and the Canadians exchanged letters reserving any disputed points for further discussion. Mackenzie King was unimpressed when Sir Gerald Campbell brought him this message on a Saturday morning at his Kingsmere summer home. The prime minister pointed out that there never had been any question about Canada's agreeing to the air training programme: his government 'had accepted the principle of a training agreement before the Missions had left for Canada; that the whole purpose of their being here was the working out of the terms.' Essential to the terms were a comprehensive settlement on all the outstanding economic issues, and a frank statement that the British government gave air training the highest priority among Canada's contributions to the war effort.[130]

The Cabinet's reasons were sound enough. It was necessary to know Britain's priorities in order to allocate Canada's limited resources rationally. There was also a political dimension which the Cabinet wished to contain by carefully avoiding 'any suggestion that [the agreement] had been extracted from the United Kingdom by the Canadian government ...'[131] Otherwise, presumably, those who attacked the government's war policies as unenthusiastic and hesitant would be able to charge that the Liberals were merely trying to substitute the air training programme for other forms of assistance, notably an expeditionary force.

The British chancellor of the exchequer continued to grumble over the problem of British financial credits, and especially at 'King's attempt to tie up the whole question of Canada's contribution with that of a satisfactory price for Canadian wheat,' which 'would mean a steep rise in the cost of living in this country.'[132] The British War Cabinet was wary of the political implications of King's 'troublesome' insistence that the matter of priorities be clarified, and the air minister, Kingsley Wood, suggested that Britain should accede to Canadian wishes because the Cabinet had already agreed that air training must be granted a high priority. Anthony Eden, the dominions secretary, thought it necessary to make a clear distinction between two aspects of the Canadian demands: that of Canada setting its own war priorities, which was entirely its own concern, and King's attempt 'to induce us to give countenance' to whatever priority his government decided. Eden advised that 'we should probably have to take a firm line. The matter was purely a domestic one, which Mr. Mackenzie King must settle on his own responsibility without involving the United Kingdom Government.'[133] After talking with O.D. Skelton a few days later, Campbell reported he had gained the 'clear impression that the Canadian Government intend to avail themselves of the admission that the United Kingdom

Government agree that the Empire training scheme is Canada's main war effort as an excuse for refraining, at any rate in the near future, from despatching [a] second division overseas.'[134] The British ruled in favour of caution: 'The general view of the War Cabinet was that the right way of dealing with this point was to refer to Mr. Mackenzie King's request for an assurance that the Canadian Government's views as to preference of effort was primarily for themselves to decide, and that we would accept their decision in that spirit; to say that we were prepared to give this assurance, as it was for Canada to decide on the priority of her effort, and we should not think of interfering with Canada's opinion.'[135]

Chamberlain's cable to King embodying these sentiments was suitably vague. He suggested that wheat prices and other broad economic issues should be put to one side. 'These we hope to bring to a mutually satisfactory conclusion as soon as possible after Mr. Graham Towers has joined Mr. Crerar here.' As to the priority to be accorded to the air training scheme, the British prime minister assured King that Canadian participation on the full scale proposed was of the first importance, but he declined to say so publicly. Britain, he emphasized, was reluctant to involve itself in the dominion's domestic affairs. Such a declaration, moreover, would cause difficulty with the French, who were pressing for an expansion of the British and Commonwealth land forces to support France's position in northwest Europe.[136]

King evidently accepted Chamberlain's assurance on the wider economic issues. The Canadian prime minister did not raise the matter during a meeting on 27 November of the Emergency Council, which had been called to consider the British request that a draft agreement be initialled before the imminent departure of the Australians and New Zealanders. King, however, refused to do so until the priority question had been settled. As he explained the following day in a cable to Chamberlain, there appeared to be 'some misunderstanding' of the Canadian position. Canada had responded hastily to British requests for assistance, the prime minister noted, and while these initial programmes were just beginning to be implemented the air training proposal had arrived. The plan appealed to the Canadian government but it had to be placed in the broader context of the country's entire war effort. Although Canada would unhesitatingly determine its own policies, 'We also believe, however, that it is essential to consult with our associates in the conflict, and it was for this purpose that from the outset we requested the opinion of the United Kingdom as to what would be the most effective form our effort could take, and as far as conditions permitted, we have adopted the measures proposed.' This was why, King continued, his govern-ment deemed it necessary for the British 'to have it made known that considering present and future requirements they felt that participation in the Air Training Scheme would provide more effective assistance than any other form of co-operation which Canada could give.'[137]

Whether persuaded by the logic of King's case or worn down by diplomatic attrition, the British finally gave way. On 1 December Chamberlain informed King that he could, when announcing the agreement, state:

The United Kingdom Government have informed us that, considering present and future requirements, they feel that participation in the Air Training Scheme would provide for more effective assistance towards our ultimate victory than any other form of cooperation which Canada can give. At the same time they would wish it to be clearly understood that they would welcome no less heartily the presence of Canadian land forces in the theatre of war.

Chamberlain accepted the Canadian prime minister's addition to the last sentence of the words 'at the earliest possible moment' to emphasize timeliness rather than large numbers of troops. Thus amended, King later used the British draft in a broadcast proclaiming the conclusion of the air training agreement.[138]

The essential features of the scheme had in fact been incorporated in the draft agreement that Australia and New Zealand – but not Canada – had initialled on 28 November. This called for the monthly production in Canada (when the programme was in full operation) of 1464 trained aircrew. Canada, Australia, and New Zealand would share common expenses in the ratio 80.64: 11.28: 8.08. Separate clauses arranged for aircraft, instructors, pay and allowances, and sundry administrative details. The RCAF would command and control the programme, with assistance from the RAF. The RCAF was also entitled to fill vacancies in its home defence squadrons with programme graduates up to agreed limits. Other graduates, 'for service with or in conjunction with the Royal Air Force,' would be paid and maintained by Britain, but the dominions were left free to supplement their pay at their own expense.[139]

The protracted negotiations thus far had, understandably, been principally concerned with the air training structure to be built in Canada. Less attention was given to the disposition of the programme's graduates once they were trained; here, as elsewhere, contradictory British and Canadian assumptions led to misunderstanding. Here, also, an incomplete documentary record permits only cautious interpretation, particularly because neither the British nor Canadian principals were entirely consistent in defining their objectives. It is possible, nevertheless, to sketch an outline of the discussions which attempted to determine how air training plan graduates would be committed to operational squadrons when they were judged ready.

It seems likely that the First World War RFC/RAF Canada training precedent was never far from the minds of Air Ministry officials in 1939. Centralizing command and control of all Commonwealth aerial resources in the RAF, by incorporating air training plan graduates as individuals into RAF squadrons, was in purely military terms probably the most convenient, efficient, and economical way to build a large air force. Riverdale thought so; he understood his 'instructions were to endeavour to arrange that they [graduates] should be enlisted in the Royal Air Force.'[140] His mandate was sufficiently broad to permit such an interpretation, but he was perhaps unaware that Air Ministry officials earlier had acknowledged that the dominions would form their own air units in the United Kingdom. Moreover, in his cable of 26 September, Chamberlain had assured King that the scheme 'of course contemplated that the first call on Dominion personnel who had received their training in schools under scheme would be for such air force units of Dominions as their participating Dominion Governments might be prepared to provide and maintain.'[141] The British view suggested that dominion graduates would be posted first to such operational units as their countries were willing to pay for, while the rest went to the RAF. But nothing was settled. As one Air Ministry official remarked, 'the number of operational units to be provided and maintained in the theatre of war by each Dominion out of the pooled training resources would be a matter for discussion.'[142]

It seems doubtful that British officials fully appreciated the desire of Canada to identify its overseas air forces as a national service. Even one so close to the scene as the British high commissioner had difficulty acknowledging national sensitivities. 'All other things being equal, no doubt he [the Canadian] would prefer to be brigaded with his fellow Canadians,' Campbell reported, but it was not vital. 'The average Canadian well remembers the exploits of Canadian airmen in the last war. He knows that they did not suffer from serving in the Royal Air Force. He would undoubtedly say get me to the Front, put me in a machine, and send me up against the enemy: that is all I need to show the world of my Canadian identity.'[143]

Many young Canadians might have agreed with him, but there was little likelihood in 1939 of following the First World War precedent. The chief of the air staff reminded the members of the Emergency Council early in November that 'the end of the last war had seen the beginning of a distinctively Canadian Air Force, in answer to public demand,' and advised that RCAF units should be placed in the field.[144] He pressed this point in a memorandum to the minister two weeks later:

It is considered essential that the R.C.A.F. should participate in overseas war activities and not be restricted entirely to Home Defence and training activities for the following reasons:

(a) It would be detrimental to Canadian prestige as a nation to restrict its official air effort to Home Defence and Training.
(b) The Training Scheme will prepare Canadians for combatant duties in the air but if Canada has no squadrons overseas, the work of the individuals will be merged in the R.A.F. We have every reason to expect that Canadians will do well in the air. If they can serve in Canadian squadrons they will bring credit to Canada as a nation, and build up tradition for the R.C.A.F. and their squadrons.
(c) The Training Scheme involves the employment of 26,000 Canadians, on training work in Canada. This is not in keeping with the temperament of Canadians who prefer to be at the front and they would be dissatisfied unless some provision is made for them to have a chance of getting overseas.[145]

The prime minister had earlier expressed similar views,[146] but the magnitude of the air training scheme overtook events. Once it was functioning there would be no shortage of Canadian aircrew, but maintaining an overseas air force sufficiently large to absorb them all clearly would be prohibitively expensive. Moreover, aircrews accounted for only a small percentage of a unit's establishment, and RCAF groundcrew would be fully committed to air training in Canada. Croil suggested two alternatives:

(a) R.C.A.F. squadrons overseas in which the flying personnel would be Canadian but the ground personnel R.A.F.

(b) R.C.A.F. formations and units overseas in which all personnel would be R.C.A.F., the administrative and ground personnel being released from Training Scheme duties in Canada by the exchange of R.A.F. personnel who have already had overseas service.[147]

But could mixed squadrons of RCAF air and RAF ground crews properly be called Canadian, or would Canada, in Chamberlain's words, 'provide and maintain' them? The demands of finances and national identification pulled in opposite directions, Skelton pointed out. There would be, he noted, 'real difficulty in insisting on the one hand on our right to organize trainees in Royal Canadian Air Force units and on the other on the United Kingdom meeting the costs of the maintenance.' Further, the ambiguity of Canada's interests posed 'some danger of sliding into a position where we would have no answer either to the British Government or to some vociferous elements in the Canadian public if it were suggested that if we call the tune we should pay the Piper.' The piper's fee would be monumental. A projected imperial air force of 196 squadrons would cost some £600 million annually, with Canada's share amounting to about £170 million or $750 million.[148]

Having agreed to provide the major share of air training costs, the possibility now loomed that Canada would have to finance a continually expanding overseas air force in order to absorb its aircrew graduates. The dilemma thus posed, as will be seen, bedevilled attempts throughout the war to formulate a comprehensive Canadian air policy. For the present, Riverdale and his mission embarked on another round of negotiations with the Cabinet. Their starting-point was article 15 of the draft agreement, which was concerned with the identification and national affiliation of pilots and air crews proceeding overseas. 'The United Kingdom Government undertakes that pupils of Canada, Australia and New Zealand shall, after training is completed, be identified with their respective Dominions, either by the method of organizing Dominion Units and formations or in some other way, such methods to be agreed upon with the respective Dominion Governments concerned. The United Kingdom Government will initiate inter-governmental discussions to this end.'

This left open a free range of possibilities – from allowing individual Canadians in RAF units to wear 'Canada' shoulder patches to having Canada form its own squadrons, wings, groups, or even its own autonomous air force. More specific language was needed. In drafting article 15 the parties had considered adding the qualifying phrase 'within the limits of efficient military organization,' but rejected that course, apparently because it did not accurately represent the views of Australia and New Zealand. Before Balfour left for London at the end of November he and Rogers had reached a vague understanding, subject to the British government's concurrence. Rogers, belatedly foreseeing potential trouble ahead, discussed the matter with Riverdale on 8 December, inferring from their conversation 'that you accept as the proper interpretation of this paragraph that Canadian personnel from the training plan will, on request from the Canadian Government, be organized in

Royal Canadian Air Force units and formations in the field.' He asked for written confirmation of this impression, but Riverdale was more cautious on paper than he may have been in conversation. Article 15, Riverdale thought, 'implies' that Canadian requests to incorporate graduates in RCAF units 'will, in all circumstances in which it is feasible, be readily accepted by the Government of the United Kingdom.'[149] The gap between these two positions, of course, was as wide as either party might wish to make it.

Rogers, confined at the time to a hospital bed, rejected Riverdale's interpretation outright, as did the prime minister. Despite having just satisfactorily concluded the much disputed priorities problem, King was determined that there would be no agreement unless the British gave a 'clear and unequivocal statement' that Canadian graduates of the plan would be organized into RCAF squadrons 'at the request of the Canadian Government.' It was a principle, he stressed, that the Cabinet considered 'essential to Canadian participation in the Scheme.'[150] Throughout the weekend, Ralston, Skelton, and Canadian officials conferred continuously with Riverdale, Campbell, and the British mission to find a compromise. The British government, Campbell informed the Canadians, was concerned with the open-ended commitment implied by their interpretation. Would there be no limit on the number of Canadian squadrons? He asked that the Canadians accept British good faith and 'have confidence in the U.K. government that [later] discussions would lead to the "hammering out" of a satisfactory solution of the problem.'[151] Ralston suggested it would be sufficient if the British made clear that they accepted the principle involved, but King was adamant. There would be no compromise. While operational necessity and military efficiency were important, they were not the crux of the problem. The importance of assigning Canadian aircrew to RCAF squadrons was, King said, 'in the broad sense, political, not merely technical.'[152]

Canadian and British delegates were working on another formula. The RCAF was concerned that keeping most of its groundcrew in Canada to maintain air training aircraft would cause morale and recruiting problems. Many would want to get overseas, and in any case the RCAF preferred having its own crews. They suggested posting some of them to the United Kingdom and replacing them in the training scheme with RAF personnel. Then, as complete Canadian air and ground establishments were concentrated in Britain, they would be organized into RCAF squadrons. It seemed a reasonable compromise, so Croil and Brooke-Popham 'proposed the organization of R.C.A.F. squadrons as and when sufficient Canadian air *and ground* personnel should be available.'[153] The Canadians presented their alternative to King and the Cabinet War Committee on 14 December, after which Brooke-Popham, Riverdale, and Campbell were shown into the prime minister's office.

Unfortunately, the RCAF staff had gone beyond the government on the issue and the British delegation was informed that the alternative was 'quite unsatisfactory.' The proposal, King said, 'would result in public criticism that Canadians were being substituted for U.K. personnel in zones of danger.' Moreover, he continued, 'the Canadian government had always assumed that the United Kingdom would provide the ground personnel for Canadian air crews,' and 'that this would not prevent the identification as Canadian ...'[154] Canada was assuming a great financial burden through air training; in return it expected Britain to maintain the air force overseas, including RCAF squadrons with RAF groundcrews.

Not without reason, the British were confused. Despite sound arguments against exchanging groundcrews on the basis of cost and efficiency, they had agreed because they thought it was what the Canadians wanted.[155] How else to define units as Canadian unless most of their personnel were in the RCAF? 'Brooke-Popham pointed out, not without some justice,' C.G. Power recalled, 'that to call a squadron a Canadian squadron, when the personnel attached to it were British in the ratio of about ten to one, would be somewhat of an anomaly.'[156] The bewildered air chief marshal 'expressed the view [to the Cabinet War Committee] that it was surely not suggested that a "unit" was not "one." It must be homogeneous. He had never had the idea that R.C.A.F. squadrons would be otherwise than predominantly Canadian, both as to air and ground personnel.' Riverdale added that if the Canadian proposal were accepted, 'appropriations for ground personnel from the United Kingdom for R.C.A.F. squadrons would have to be provided by the U.K. Parliament.' Extraordinarily, it seems that, during the six weeks of strenuous discussion, each side had been assuming the other would pay for the RCAF's overseas groundcrews. Riverdale was 'dumbfounded' at the Canadian attitude. 'We thought that this was exactly what you wanted,' he told Arnold Heeney, King's principal secretary.[157]

Now the situation was back where it had been. Riverdale was being asked to replace his earlier letter to Rogers with one interpreting article 15 to the Canadian government's satisfaction. The agreement hinged on identifying mutually acceptable words. Riverdale was co-operative, and King also had reason to want to complete the negotiations quickly. The 1st Canadian Division was due to land in Britain in a few days and King wanted to announce the air training scheme publicly before the arrival of the expeditionary force upstaged it. The prime minister of Australia had also informed him that he intended to release a statement on Australia's participation. King responded immediately, urging the Australians to hold back until the agreement was finalized, but his message arrived in Canberra too late. King's government was thereby open to criticism that it was delaying a settlement, and King was all the more outraged when the Australian prime minister informed him that the statement had been prepared in consultation with the Air Ministry. It does not strain credulity to imagine that the British may have been trying to hurry things along. King cabled a vehement protest to Chamberlain. 'I cannot begin to express my amazement that without consultation with the Government of Canada, the United Kingdom Air Ministry should have concurred in the issue of the statement by Australia before agreement had been reached between all parties. I need hardly add that the publication has caused great embarrassment to our Government in relation to other Commonwealth Governments as well as the press and people of our own country.' Chamberlain lamely explained that the mixup was due to a 'regrettable misunderstanding.'[158]

King was also anxious to settle because a propitious occasion was at hand. The prime minister wished to deliver a radio address to the nation on Sunday, the 17th, which happened to be his 65th birthday.[159] He had already calculated, correctly, that his quickest route to an agreement was through Riverdale directly. He had to be separated from 'Brooke-Popham and the technical men,'[160] who were raising the objections, and from the British War Cabinet, which seemed intent on 'objection and delay.'[161] Accordingly, on 15 December, King dispatched Heeney to see Riverdale 'on his behalf as Prime Minister of Canada, [to] urge him, as head of the United Kingdom Mission to do everything in his power to see that the Agreement was signed forthwith.' The Australian announcement, along with the inconclusive meeting the previous day, had 'threatened the entire Scheme. The matter had become even more serious – it threatened good relations within the Commonwealth.'[162]

Riverdale was gloomy when Heeney arrived, feeling that 'we were farther than ever from an agreement.'[163] Nevertheless, Riverdale met at noon with King, Ralston, and Rogers and they jointly produced a letter of understanding on the issue. On the point of signing, Riverdale decided he must first consult his colleagues, and after talking with Campbell concluded he had better await further cabled instructions, expected momentarily, before commiting his government. At King's urging, Riverdale then telephoned London requesting authority to agree in principle with Canada's right to incorporate their graduates into Canadian squadrons.[164] The Air Ministry baulked. Rather, 'the Secretary of State for Air had instructed Lord Riverdale that he must stand fast.'[165] His instructions stipulated that:

> The United Kingdom Government on the request of the Canadian Government would agree to the incorporation of Canadian pupils when passing out from the training scheme into units of the Royal Canadian Air Force in the field ...
>
> It would be a condition that the factor governing the numbers of such pupils to be so incorporated at any one time should be the financial contribution which the Canadian Government have already declared themselves ready to make towards the cost of the training scheme.[166]

The Air Ministry added the condition in order to limit the number of RCAF squadrons it would have to keep in the field. They calculated that, by providing the equivalent of Canada's air training expenditure of $350 million, they could maintain fifteen RCAF squadrons. 'The other Canadian air crews should join the RAF,' L.B. Pearson (indirectly involved in the discussions in London) noted sarcastically in his memoirs, 'and, as a concession to our national feeling, they should be allowed to wear a maple leaf on their caps, or "Canada" on their shoulders, or some such ennobling national device.'[167] King was indignant when he saw the British response. He thought the British were stalling by shifting their ground from the command question to money, which meant that 'the organization of R.C.A.F. units is to be measured by the cold consideration of financial contribution, disregarding entirely Canada's heavy contribution of fighting men in the way of pilots, observers and gunners.'[168]

King summoned Riverdale and Brooke-Popham to his office where, with Ralston and C.D. Howe, they conferred until past midnight, but made little progress. Next morning, 16 December, Riverdale discreetly enquired if the Air Ministry's letter would be acceptable without the last, objectionable paragraph concerning finances. That would help, he was told, but Ralston, in particular, wanted other revisions as well.[169] Ralston and Riverdale conferred, and King increased the pressure by having his minister inform Riverdale that, in view of the need for a public announcement, the matter of timing 'had ceased to be a technical question, and it was one now in which both Governments were deeply concerned; that he, as head of the Mission, should exercise his own authority.'[170] Ralston reported some movement, telling King 'that Lord Riverdale was all right. That he thought he was anxious to have this matter concluded for my birthday [but] ... he was having a very difficult time with Sir Brooke-Popham [sic]. That he wanted further time to think the matter over quietly.'[171]

He then sought out Riverdale, and told him they 'must settle this matter at once ourselves.'[172] The basis of their settlement was the latest draft which Ralston and Riverdale had prepared that day: 'On the understanding that the numbers to be incorporated or organized at any time will be the subject of discussion between the two Governments, the United Kingdom Government accepts in principle as being consonant with the intention of Paragraph 15 of the Memorandum of Agreement, that the United Kingdom Government, on the request of the Canadian Government, would arrange that the Canadian pupils, when passing out from the Training Scheme, would be incorporated in or organized as units and formations of the Royal Canadian Air Force in the field. The detailed methods by which this can be done would be arranged by an Inter-Governmental Committee for this purpose under Paragraph 15.'[173] The offending paragraph relating the number of RCAF squadrons to a financial formula was dropped. Riverdale agreed to substitute the phrasing 'subject of discussion' for the Air Ministry's original 'subject of agreement.' In return he asked that the potentially important 'the' before 'Canadian pupils' be deleted in order to make the term less comprehensive. Finally, a few minutes after midnight, following six weeks of hard bargaining, King and Riverdale signed the agreement.[174]

6
Building the Plan

The primary task of the RCAF in the early years of the war was to meet the challenge of the British Commonwealth Air Training Plan. Only 4000 strong by the end of 1939, the force had to create and administer not only its own Home War Establishment, and an ever-increasing number of overseas squadrons as well, but also a vastly dispersed training organization orginally expected to comprise 33,000 servicemen and 6000 civilians.[1]

At the outbreak of war, the RCAF had only five aerodromes of its own, with six more under construction.[2] Extending the crucial interwar partnership between the RCAF and the Department of Transport [DOT], the chief of the air staff, Air Vice-Marshal G.M. Croil, and J.A. Wilson, controller of civil aviation, agreed on 3 October 1939 to co-operate in the rapid expansion of facilities. DOT would select airfield sites and, after RCAF approval, develop the landing fields. The air force would design and erect the buildings.[3] Site selection and survey work started immediately, before the BCATP Agreement was signed, in order to get as much work done as possible before the onset of winter.[4] The realization of a concrete air training scheme enlarged and accelerated the demand.

The air force had already reached an agreement with the Department of Labour in early 1939 to provide pre-entry trades training under the Dominion-Provincial Youth Training Programme established in 1937 to assist the unemployed. In September 1939 a thousand men were under instruction and another thousand were expected. The two existing technical training schools (No 1 at Trenton and No 2 at Camp Borden) were centralized into a single establishment, located at the Ontario [Mental] Hospital, St Thomas. Youth Training Programme graduates – after May 1940 only aero-engine and airframe mechanics continued in the plan – joined other recruits 'going to the mental hospital for training,' and thus provided enough essential support staff to meet immediate requirements.[5] Groundcrew recruiting never proved a real problem for the RCAF during the war, particularly after women were enrolled in the Canadian Women's Auxiliary Air Force – later called the RCAF (Women's Division) – starting in 1941.[6]

The aircraft requirement had to be met largely from British industry. Britain would supply most of the advanced trainers; the balance, 187 Harvards, was to be provided by Canada, Australia, and New Zealand. Canada was responsible for the cost of elementary trainers, Great Britain for many of the engines. The plan, when fully developed, was designed to turn out 1464 trained aircrew every four weeks. The majority of these graduates would be Canadian, and the RCAF would need to produce 1536 aircrew recruits for each training cycle (allowing for projected failures), or 19,968 per year. From its own graduates Canada could retain a small number each year to fill vacancies in Home War Establishment squadrons. All others were to be made available immediately to the United Kingdom for service overseas.[7]

Conditions of service, other than those of pay and discipline, were those of the RAF. The RCAF had traditionally enrolled pilot recruits as provisional pilot officers, but now all trainees were enlisted as aircraftman 2nd class, the lowest rank in the service. While under specialist training, all pupils were to be leading aircraftmen, and on graduation they would become sergeants. Some pilots and observers were to be selected for commissioning after completing training, and in July 1940, several months before the first pupils graduated, the proportion was set at 33 per cent. A further 17 per cent, chosen from among those who 'rendered distinguished service, devotion to duty and display of ability in the field of operations,' were to be commissioned later.[8] Though RAF regulations provided for air gunner officers, no routine provision was made for wireless operator (air gunner) commissioning until February 1941. Then 2 per cent were commissioned on graduation, and 5 per cent in the field. These rates were both increased retroactively to 10 per cent in August, when rates for aircrew trained purely as air gunners – not included in the original agreement – were established at 5 and 15 per cent. In all cases those commissioned were not given any different or additional training in Canada to prepare them for their officer status. Typically, they were merely informed of their promotion by telegram a few days after graduation. As one pilot and his friend expressed it early in the plan: 'and so, without any instructions as to how to comport ourselves, we became officers.'[9]

The direction and control of the BCATP was vested initially in the Canadian minister of national defence, with the chief of the air staff in executive command. However, it soon became apparent that the operation of the plan – and the administration of a burgeoning RCAF – was a task of such immense proportions that it called for separate administrative arrangements: K.S. Maclachan had held the post of acting associate deputy minister (naval and air) since 8 September 1939, but on 11 April 1940 James S. Duncan, a senior executive of Massey Harris Company Ltd, was appointed associate acting deputy minister for air. German military successes in Denmark and Norway that month served to emphasize still further the importance of air power, and the Cabinet moved quickly to create a separate air minister. C.G. Power, known as 'Chubby,' formerly postmaster general, assumed the portfolio of minister of national defence for air on 23 May 1940. In July another piece of legislation created a similar appointment for the navy.[10]

Despite its high and growing profile in Ottawa, the RCAF remained committed to goals established elsewhere, turning out aircrew to meet the needs of the Royal Air Force. A standing committee of the British Air Council, the Empire

SUMMARY OF 1939 BCATP AGREEMENT

AIRCRAFT REQUIREMENTS: 3540 total
702 Tiger Moths and Fleet Finches (elementary trainers)
  50 per cent with Moth engines at British expense
720 North American Harvards (single-engine trainers)
533 (plus extra engines) at British expense
1368 Avro Ansons (twin-engine and navigation trainers), UK supplied (less wings)
750 Fairey Battles (air gunnery trainers), UK supplied

TRAINING: to follow RAF syllabus

TRAINEE POPULATION
Canada   80.64 per cent of commitment
Australia   11.28 per cent of commitment
New Zealand   8.08 per cent of commitment
United Kingdom
− right to contribute up to 10 per cent of elementary
  flying and air observer trainees
− commitment to make up shortfalls
− Newfoundland trainees to be part of RAF contribution

PRODUCTION TARGETS FOR FULLY DEVELOPED PLAN (every four weeks)
544 service-trained pilots
340 air observers
580 wireless operators (air gunner)
Note: Canadian recruiting requirements to meet these commitments: 1536
      recruits each cycle (allowing for failures), or 19,968 recruits per year

GRADUATES: RCAF graduates to home defence squadrons (maximum per year)
136 pilots
  34 air observers
  58 wireless operators (air gunners)
and to be identified with their dominion by some method to be agreed upon.

ESTIMATED COST TO 31 MARCH 1943: $607,271,210

CONTRIBUTIONS
United Kingdom $185,000,000 in kind
Canada $ 66,146,048 for initial and elementary training in Canada
Remainder $356,125,162 to be divided (based on trainee population):
  Canada   80.64 per cent $287,179,331
  Australia   11.28 per cent $ 40,170,918
  New Zealand   8.08 per cent $ 28,774,913

Air Training Scheme Committee, normally met every two weeks in London, England, to monitor performance and look after the wider interests of the Commonwealth-wide organization as a whole.[11] A Supervisory Board was created in Ottawa, with representation from each of the four countries participating in the BCATP, to oversee the plan's progress in Canada. This board met monthly, at first under the chairmanship of the minister of national defence, but subsequently under the minister of national defence for air. Other Canadian members included the ministers of finance and transport, and the chief of the air staff. A financial adviser was appointed to administer the large number of accounts involved. Each of the three overseas partners established Air Liaison missions in Canada to further safeguard their interests, the United Kingdom Air Liaison Mission being the main channel through which the BCATP was kept informed of operational requirements and changes in plans.[12] Mission members were free to visit any BCATP unit or establishment and to give any observations or recommendations directly to the chief of the air staff or the Supervisory Board.

As in the RAF, elementary flying training schools [EFTSs] were to be organized and run on a civilian-managed, commercial basis. On the outbreak of war, fourteen more flying clubs had been awarded contracts to train pilots, in addition to the eight which had been doing so since June 1939. The clubs' place in the BCATP was soon firmly established. To arrange the details, a committee was formed, chaired by K.S. Maclachlan, and including the chief of the air staff and the president of the Canadian Flying Clubs Association, Major Murton Adams Seymour, who was the driving force on the committee. Seymour had founded the first flying club in Canada (the Aero Club of Vancouver) in 1915, flown in the Royal Flying Corps overseas in 1916 and 1917, and returned to Canada to assist in setting up the RFC Canada training scheme. He remained on the staff of RAF Canada until the end of the First World War. A prominent lawyer in the interwar years, he received the McKee Trophy and an OBE for his work in integrating the flying clubs' training expertise into the BCATP. It was largely Seymour's idea to form twenty-six small elementary flying schools, each operated by one or two flying clubs, in order to distribute the work-load and benefits more evenly across the country than would be possible with the thirteen larger schools originally approved.[13]

With only two exceptions, one at Cap-de-la-Madeleine, Que., run by Quebec Airways, and one at Davidson, Sask., run directly by the RCAF, the participating clubs were reorganized as limited liability companies under the Dominion Companies Act. Each had to raise $35,000 working capital locally as a demonstration of financial stability, community support, and good faith, and satisfy the RCAF that it could provide an adequate instructional, administrative, and technical staff. The entities thus formed were known as flying training companies. Each received a monthly managerial fee, allowances for operation and maintenance, a set payment per flying hour, and a ration allowance, all subject to periodic revision. These payments allowed an efficiently operated company a small profit; a dividend of 5 per cent could be declared, any balance being placed in a government-controlled fund. Aircraft and other major equipment were provided by the government, while the companies were responsible for daily care and maintenance.[14]

The Toronto Flying Club obtained the first contract. Reorganized as Malton Flying Training School Ltd, it operated No 1 Elementary Flying Training School at Malton (Toronto) airport. The training plan was still in some disarray when the school opened in June 1940 under difficult circumstances – for example, all spare parts and tools were for Tiger Moth aircraft; all the twenty-one aircraft supplied were Fleet Finches. In spite of such problems, elementary training in EFTs run by these civilian companies expanded steadily in the ensuing months.[15]

Commercial aviation companies also provided training in aerial navigation. Canadian Pacific Airlines, some of its recently acquired affiliates, and a few independent firms agreed to manage the ten air observer schools [AOSS]. The contracts negotiated were similar to those made with the flying clubs, but with no allowance for profit, payments being adjusted to meet actual expenses. All instruction was done by air force personnel, but the companies provided civilian pilots to fly students and instructors on navigational exercises. Sometimes slightingly called 'taxi drivers' or 'air chauffeurs,' these staff pilots were 'a great source of comfort' to student observers who sometimes 'navigated' their aircraft many miles from their intended path and depended on their pilots to bring them home again.[16]

Finding instructors was difficult. Pilot training schools had to draw on the air force's own small resources to qualify those needed. Only a handful of service and commercial pilots was available, and adequate numbers could only come from new graduates of RCAF training establishments already in existence. Time was short. Course length for each of the current three pilot phases was soon reduced to correspond to the RAF's wartime standard of eight weeks.[17] On the outbreak of war, pupils undergoing advanced training at Trenton were deemed to have graduated and were posted, while those in intermediate pilot training were sent on to the advanced school. This abridgement temporarily freed the intermediate facilities at Camp Borden for more refresher and instructor courses for civilian pilots. In January 1940 the advanced school moved to Camp Borden and joined the intermediate one to form the nucleus of the first BCATP service flying training school [SFTS]; together, the combined school continued both service and instructional training on an interim basis until the plan started. That same month the Flying Instructors School at Camp Borden, which had grown from an instructional flight created in July 1939, moved to Trenton. It was subsequently redesignated the Central Flying School.[18] The few recruits accepted for pilot training under the immediate prewar training scheme worked their way through this system. To their great disappointment, many of the early graduates found themselves posted to the Flying Instructors School, where they were trained for instructional posts in the BCATP instead of going overseas to join operational squadrons.[19]

Air observer and bombing and gunnery school instructors posed a different problem. Fewer were needed, since each could handle fairly large numbers of pupils at a time, but the aircrew categories of air observer and wireless operator (air gunner) were unknown in the prewar RCAF: even in the RAF the employment of specialist observers and air gunners had only been decided on in the last two years of peace, and that policy had not yet percolated through to Canada which had no specialist navigators, bomb aimers, air gunners, or aircrew wireless operators. There were navigation, wireless (radio), and air armament schools before the war, but they taught part of the pilot training course with instructors who were themselves primarily either pilots or ground personnel. These men now provided a small initial staff for the armament and wireless schools, and sixteen university graduates with adequate backgrounds in mathematics were recruited to become navigation instructors for the first air observer schools. In the long run, however, instructors for these specialist branches, as for pilot training, had to come from the plan itself.[20]

Meanwhile, the airfield construction agreement with the Department of Transport was bearing fruit. When the war began Canada had 153 recorded airport sites, over half of which were developed. Many were unsuitable for flying training, being in operational, mountainous, or isolated areas; too close to the international border; or with unfavourable climates. Of the remainder, some could house more than one school. Twenty-four developed sites needed only additional buildings to fit them for immediate use, and eighteen of these sites provided the plan's initial base. Others required extensive work. Each main airfield usually had two subsidiary airstrips, or relief fields, associated with it. These strips lacked the facilities of the main base, but could be used for practicing 'circuits and bumps' and for alternative landings if the main field had to close down. In all, counting both main aerodromes and relief fields, seventy-five separate sites were needed, and DOT field parties, accompanied by RCAF officers, criss-crossed the country to find them. Airfields needed safe approaches; adequate size; level, well-drained, and firm ground; and available public utilities. An adequate supply of potable water, underrated at first but later highly influential in site selection, was essential but sometimes hard to ensure, especially on the prairies, where other conditions were often easily met. Bombing and gunnery schools needed a large training area. Service flying training schools had to have access to smaller practice bombing ranges.[21]

Political pressure, always present, had surprisingly little effect. Decision-making guidelines minimized its impact, and even the prime minister's wishes could be, and were, overruled. Mackenzie King represented Prince Albert, Sask., in the House of Commons. Local and federal representation from that community played a part in the awarding of contracts for EFTS aircraft repair and the operation of 6 AOS, but King's influence did not succeed in reversing a decision to close the school in 1942.[22]

To ensure effective supervision of BCATP construction, the Air Council decided to place it under R.R. Collard, vice-president and general manager of Carter-Halls-Aldinger Construction Company of Winnipeg, who was brought into the air force as deputy director of works and buildings with the rank of wing commander and later rose to air vice-marshal. As the construction programme got under way, engineering sections were established in the field to supervise the work. During the first four-and-a-half years of war, more than one and three-quarter million blueprints were issued, about 33,000 final drawings were

BRITISH COMMONWEALTH AIR

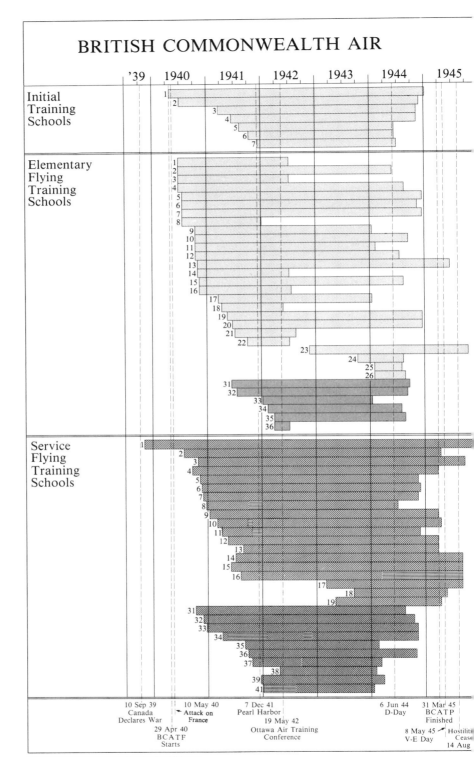

TRAINING PLAN - AIRCREW SCHOOLS

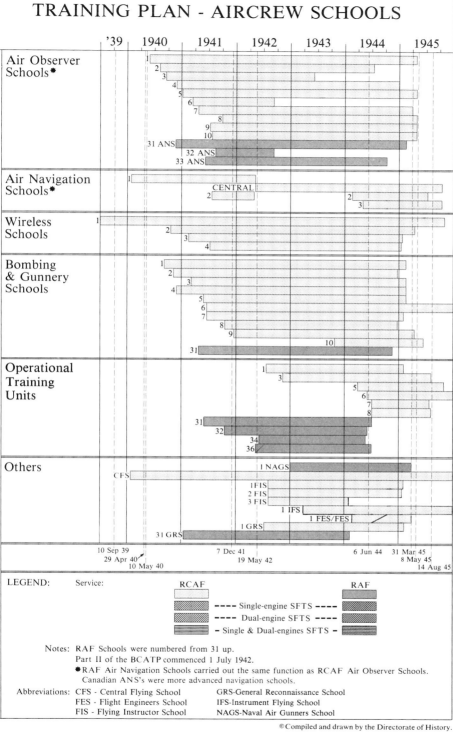

'39 | 1940 | 1941 | 1942 | 1943 | 1944 | 1945

Air Observer Schools*

1, 2, 3, 4, 5, 6, 7, 8, 9, 10, 31 ANS, 32 ANS, 33 ANS

Air Navigation Schools*

1, CENTRAL, 2, 2, 3

Wireless Schools

1, 2, 3, 4

Bombing & Gunnery Schools

1, 2, 3, 4, 5, 6, 7, 8, 9, 10, 31

Operational Training Units

1, 3, 5, 6, 7, 8, 31, 32, 34, 36

Others

CFS, 1 NAGS, 1 FIS, 2 FIS, 3 FIS, 1 IFS, 1 FES/FES, 1 GRS, 31 GRS

10 Sep 39
29 Apr 40
10 May 40
7 Dec 41
19 May 42
6 Jun 44
31 Mar 45
8 May 45
14 Aug 45

LEGEND: Service:

RCAF   RAF

---- Single-engine SFTS ----

---- Dual-engine SFTS ----

- Single & Dual-engines SFTS -

Notes: RAF Schools were numbered from 31 up.
Part II of the BCATP commenced 1 July 1942.
*RAF Air Navigation Schools carried out the same function as RCAF Air Observer Schools.
Canadian ANS's were more advanced navigation schools.

Abbreviations: CFS - Central Flying School   GRS-General Reconnaissance School
FES - Flight Engineers School   IFS-Instrument Flying School
FIS - Flying Instructor School   NAGS-Naval Air Gunners School

© Compiled and drawn by the Directorate of History.

made, and 8300 buildings constructed by the Directorate of Works and Buildings. Although the Directorate served the Home War Establishment as well, most of this work was undertaken on behalf of the BCATP.[23]

Airfields had to be stocked with the myriad items of equipment required by a modern air force. Most RCAF supply had previously been the responsibility of the Royal Canadian Ordnance Corps, itself now strained by the army's expansion, but in late 1939 a new RCAF Equipment (or Supply) Branch took over the procurement and distribution of clothing and non-technical stores. Starting early in 1940, a specially formed Air Force Headquarters section drew up schedules of equipment needed by each type of school to ensure efficient provisioning. Contracts were then let through the Department of Munitions and Supply. In February, Croil was able to tell the Supervisory Board that this work was well advanced and firm orders were in hand for small tools, workshop equipment, barrack furniture, clothing, and miscellaneous items.[24]

These orders did not include the specialist technical equipment, aircraft, and engines which could only come from the United Kingdom. Shipments of these items were irregular, but after discussions with the Air Ministry through the United Kingdom Air Liaison Mission, Croil advised the minister of national defence in April 1940 that no serious delay in the arrival of equipment from overseas was expected.[25] It proved too sanguine a judgment. The disasters of May and June 1940, and subsequent crises in the U-boat war, meant that equipment problems continued to plague the BCATP.

Adequate financial controls were essential, and the RCAF's Pay and Accounts Branch expanded accordingly. The branch's responsibilities were especially complicated since the RCAF had two distinct roles in Canada: air training and home defence. Separate accounts were needed for each since the expenses of the BCATP were shared between the Commonwealth partners and Canada alone was responsible for the Home War Establishment. Those units which served both the domestic squadrons and the training plan had a cost-sharing formula worked out according to the amount of time and effort devoted to each. For example, as of 1 January 1940, it was estimated that RCAF Headquarters devoted about 70 per cent of its effort to the BCATP and 30 per cent to domestic problems.[26]

The prewar Air Training Command, formed in 1938 as an expansion of the Training Group created just three years previously, was manifestly too small to supervise this growing organization. It was redesignated No 1 Training Command in January 1940, and three other geographically based commands were started in March and April, each reporting directly to Air Force Headquarters in Ottawa. Each command was to be as self-sufficient as possible, with its own recruiting and manning organization, supply and repair depots, and air training schools, and sites were chosen accordingly.[27] Because the RCAF could not hope to meet all the manning requirements of these commands, the three overseas partners agreed to provide some of their own staff and instructors.[28] In practice, this meant Royal Air Force support. The first of eighty-five British officers and 182 other ranks, requested in December 1939, landed in January 1940. Eventually, about 300 loaned personnel, including a proportion of Australians and New Zealanders, served in Canada.[29]

In answer to a request for a director of training at RCAF Headquarters, the Air Ministry nominated Air Commodore Robert Leckie. Leckie had commanded the ill-fated, two-squadron CAF in 1919 and, while seconded from the RAF in 1920 and 1921, had been director of flying operations for the Canadian Air Board. Subsequently, his career had taken him to many parts of the globe and had given him experience in all types of air operations; he was air officer commanding, RAF Mediterranean, in Malta when informed of his impending transfer. He was ready and willing to leave with the main party of loaned personnel, but the RCAF was not quite so ready to welcome him back to Canada.[30]

Except for the chief of the air staff, Leckie had seniority over every other officer in the RCAF, including Air Commodore G.O. Johnson, the head of the Organization and Training Division at RCAF Headquarters and Leckie's designated superior. Johnson might have been promoted, or Leckie granted a temporary RCAF commission with a later appointment date, but two other air commodores, E.W. Stedman and L.S. Breadner, were both senior to Johnson, and the RCAF was unwilling to upset their positions and its own promotion procedures. Leckie's seniority, meanwhile, was protected by the Commonwealth Visiting Forces Act. So impossible did the situation seem to the RCAF that Croil cabled the Air Ministry that 'it is apparent another selection should be made in place Air Commodore Leckie to avoid complications.' In reply, he was told that the Air Ministry felt that it 'must insist on ... Leckie's posting remaining unchanged ... [and was] taking the matter up ... through the Dominions Office with the High Commissioner for the U.K. in Canada.' Soon after, Leckie sailed. While he was en route, Croil made another attempt to avoid the problem. He asked that Leckie's appointment be transferred outside of the RCAF's chain of command to the British Air Liaison Mission. This suggestion, too, was rejected.[31]

Leckie arrived in Canada at the beginning of February 1940. He was soon busily at work under Johnson, his junior in rank, years of service, and age. In the event, no problems occurred and in November, largely because of the expanded activities of the Air Training Plan, the Directorate of Training was raised to the status of a headquarters division with three subordinate directorates: Air Training, Technical Maintenance, and Training Plans and Requirements.[32] As air member for training, Leckie, like other division heads, had a seat on the Air Council and was directly responsible to the chief of the air staff.

This headquarters reorganization was only one of several. From the immediate prewar period, Air Force Headquarters had expanded by giving division status (its major organizational element) to those directorates or branches with the greatest new responsibilities, rather than simply enlarging and adding subordinate sections to existing staff branches. In this way it grew to have eight divisions by 1942: Air Staff, Organization, Personnel, Supply, Aeronautical Engineering, Training, Accounts and Finance, and Chief of the Air Staff. This unwieldy organization continued until the last year of the war, when it was consolidated into five: Air Staff, Personnel, Supply and Organization, Research and Development, and Training. This last function was deleted from the organization in August 1945. Leckie had long since left, having been transferred to the RCAF in 1942 and appointed chief of the air staff in January 1944.[33]

Meanwhile, recruiting for the RCAF progressed slowly, surprising those who tried to enlist but not at all surprising in retrospect. In October 1939 the war establishment of the RCAF was set at 1500 officers and 15,000 airmen, and quotas were issued accordingly. During the next few months enrolment was slow, the main concern being to ensure enough skilled tradesmen and professional help for the air force's ground organization. While establishment figures were being decided, recruiting officers confined most of their activities to preliminary interviews, trade testing, and medical examinations. In February 1940 the war establishment was raised to 3500 officers and 41,000 airmen, an elevenfold increase over peacetime strength. It was not possible to recruit and train all these people at once, however, and a limited establishment of 2400 officers and 28,000 airmen was put into effect within this authorized strength. These numbers included personnel for the Home War Establishment (8500 all ranks) and the limited overseas commitments then foreseen (an additional 1000 personnel); the remainder, 20,900, were needed primarily for the Air Training Plan.[34]

Between September 1939, when recruiting centres opened, and 31 March 1940, about 3000 young men applied for aircrew training. Only 229 of these, enough to fill the immediate vacancies at the flying clubs, could be accepted. In addition, a few fully qualified civilian pilots joined as direct entries.[35] These men were not part of the Canadian quota of aircrew recruits for the BCATP; the latter were not accepted until April. In the interim, eager applicants continued to arrive at recruiting centres only to be told that there was 'a waiting list ten miles long.'[36] Recruiters spent hours explaining that a lot of preparatory work was needed before large-scale air training could start. Prospective aircrew trainees were sent home with instructions to hold themselves in readiness for a future call.

There was no waiting list for staff pilots and flying instructors. The Supervisory Board allowed the flying club companies to nominate as instructors, in addition to well-qualified and experienced civilians, promising candidates who were promptly enrolled in the RCAF. Some of these nominees received additional flying experience (to bring them up to a minimum of 150 hours) and a preliminary flying instructor's course at a selected civil school or flying club. They then trained at the Central Flying School for four weeks, were promoted to sergeant, and finally were posted to an EFTS on unpaid leave of absence: enlistment protected the RCAF's investment by discouraging these newly qualified instructors from leaving for more lucrative employment elsewhere. Pre-training of potential elementary instructors at civil schools and flying clubs continued until mid-1941, when a small surplus had been accumulated. The scheme was then terminated and replacement instructors drawn as necessary from regular graduates of the BCATP.[37]

As had happened twenty-five years before, many Americans volunteered for service. The RCAF handled such applications somewhat more delicately than had the British government in the First World War. Those living in Canada or claiming a Canadian address were treated as Canadians. Others were given detailed information only if they visited a Canadian recruiting unit. Initially, Air Force Headquarters examined the files of all volunteers residing in the United

States and tactfully told the best of them that their application would be given 'consideration' if they chose to come north to renew it. Then regulations were changed to allow the enlistment of foreign nationals in the Canadian forces without swearing allegiance to His Majesty the King, and to allow their commissioning in the wartime RCAF.[38]

Simultaneously, Canada quietly consulted American authorities, who secretly confirmed that they did not object to enrolment if it was discreetly handled so as not to antagonize the large isolationist element in the United States.[39] Recruiting was therefore entrusted to a semi-secret organization, the Clayton Knight Committee, which was established for this purpose in the spring of 1940. The committee's principals were three First World War flyers: Clayton L. Knight, C.R. Fowler, and H.F. Smith. The last, commissioned as a wing commander in the RCAF, functioned as the committee's director. By September he had established an extensive organization with headquarters at the Waldorf-Astoria Hotel in New York. Contacts were offered positions in the RCAF or RAF, or civilian jobs as elementary training instructors, staff pilots, or RAF ferry pilots. After warnings from a friendly but correct State Department about overt violations of American neutrality laws, the Canadian government created the Dominion Aeronautical Association Ltd in January 1941 to keep the committee's activities within acceptable limits. Theoretically, the Clayton Knight Committee procured recruits for the association rather than the RCAF, though the former actually functioned as an integral part of the air force's Directorate of Manning.[40] (See Appendix C.)

In April 1940 the air force recalled 166 aircrew applicants to the recruiting centres and sent them to 1 Manning Depot, Toronto. On 'Zero Day,' 29 April 1940, 164 of these men gathered at 1 Initial Training School in Toronto to receive instruction as the first BCATP course.[41] Almost simultaneously, the BCATP faced the only crisis which ever seriously threatened its existence as the Germans followed their attack on Denmark and Norway with an offensive against the Belgians, Dutch, and French that ended with the fall of France in June. In the face of those disasters, there was some discussion of curtailing or abandoning the Air Training Plan in order to provide maximum immediate reinforcements to the United Kingdom. The British position looked desperate, and the new minister of national defence for air, C.G. Power, sided with those who proposed sending as many Canadian pilots as possible to the United Kingdom. The British themselves, however, remained calm. On 20 May they wrote that the 'efficient prosecution of the war can best be achieved by adhering to the plans laid down for the Air Training Scheme and by accelerating them to the utmost.'[42]

This direction, given as German divisions split the Allied forces west of Abbeville in France, driving the British Expeditionary Force back on Dunkirk, was clear enough. Whether it was practicable was another question. On 23 May the United Kingdom advised the Canadian government that 'In view of increased probability that in the next phase of enemy bombing objectives will be air and aero-engine factories in this country, we have regretfully come to the conclusion that export of Battle and Anson aircraft (airframes and engines) should be suspended for 2 months subject to review in the light of war situation.'[43]

There was no shortage of elementary and single-engine advanced trainers. The elementary ones were produced in Canada and their supply was already running ahead of the original requirements. American production of Harvards for the BCATP was also well in hand. Moreover, the stock of single-engine trainers was increased after the French *débacle*, when the United Kingdom took over French contracts in the United States. As far as these aircraft were concerned, the Canadian government could, as requested by Britain, 'continue to exert every effort to make it [training] productive to the fullest practicable extent in the shortest possible time.'[44] Twin-engine trainers, however, were a different matter. The Anson, used in the training of all aircrew categories, was vital, and trained pilot production would be particularly affected by any shortfall. Up to the beginning of June, only fifty-nine Ansons had been received. The shortage of twin-engine trainers meant that some readjustment of training plans was inevitable, and several SFTSs opened as single-engine schools on a temporary basis.[45]

The British implied that the halt in delivery was only temporary, but they were already – and would remain – much behind schedule.[46] It was evident that the long-term solution lay in the construction of twin-engine trainers in Canada. Airframes posed no particular problem – some Canadian firms were already assembling Anson parts and manufacturing wings – but engines were another matter, since Canada produced none herself. Within a few days C.D. Howe, the minister of munitions and supply, had identified a source of suitable engines at the Jacobs Aircraft Company of Pottstown, Pennsylvania. His department immediately began to negotiate an order for 2300 Jacobs engines costing about $10 million. Simultaneously, it arranged to have several Canadian manufacturers share in the construction and assembling of Anson airframes modified to take the new engine and American instruments. The subcontracting of components and the production of finished aircraft became the responsibility of a new crown corporation, Federal Aircraft Ltd, with headquarters in Montreal. Formed in June and given an initial contract for one thousand aeroplanes, the company was expected to deliver its first aircraft in February 1941.[47]

Aircraft were only part of the solution to the war's new demands. Still more aircrew (none of which had yet been produced) would be needed. Taking advantage of its existing surplus of elementary training aircraft, the RCAF boldly decided on 28 May 1940 to open eight EFTSs by 22 July instead of the scheduled two. This was a gamble; there were then only enough advanced trainers and instructors for two SFTSs instead of the five needed to absorb the output of eight elementary schools. By July the RCAF was planning to open eight SFTSs before the end of the year, three more than provided for in the original agreement, despite the delays and shortages of twin-engine trainers. School openings were rapidly accelerated, by averages of just under six weeks for those SFTSs opened in 1940, and almost nineteen weeks for the EFTSs. Aircraft supply did prove inadequate, however. No 7 SFTS, MacLeod, Alta, opened with only three of its allotted thirty-six aircraft, and 8 SFTS, Moncton, NB, which was sixteen weeks ahead of schedule, with only four.[48]

Pilot training was abbreviated, though in measured steps corresponding to training changes in the United Kingdom. There, the SFTS course was revised progressively from sixteen to ten weeks, primarily by transferring such subjects as gunnery and formation flying to RAF group pools – now named operational training units [OTUs] – under the control of Bomber, Fighter, and Coastal Commands. This action was not favoured by the commands, for the OTUs, especially heavy bomber units, were already congested and overworked; they saw a higher standard of basic training as the solution to their problems. The OTUs were equipped with the same front-line aircraft as their parent commands, however. These aircraft, which could not be shipped out of Great Britain, were easier to provide at the time than advanced trainers. Further, there was a shortage of instructors, wireless equipment, and operators at flying training schools, and too few relief fields to allow fully efficient training. Air gunnery facilities were also extremely limited in the United Kingdom, and air firing practice by pilot-trainees had to take second place to that of air observers and air gunners. Hence the OTUs had no choice but to absorb more of the training burden. The syllabi of schools producing RAF pilots were amended accordingly.[49]

Training elsewhere had to be adjusted as well if all SFTSs were to produce a common product. BCATP pilot courses were initially reduced from eight weeks to seven in EFTSs and from sixteen weeks to fourteen in SFTSs in line with British developments. In October the SFTS courses were further reduced to ten weeks. Trainees would no longer spend two weeks of their service flying course at bombing and gunnery schools for live air firing and bombing exercises. Instead, this training was deferred until they reached overseas OTUs. The deletion of this 'applied armament' section from the syllabus removed the major distinction between the intermediate and advanced phases of the service flying course. These phases were therefore amalgamated, and the SFTSs replaced their existing separate intermediate and advanced training squadrons by two identical ones, each covering the same course. After further refinement, these changes boosted each SFTS pilot intake from forty pupils every four weeks to fifty-six every twenty-four days. To keep pace, the number of trainees at elementary flying schools was greatly enlarged. Together with accelerated school openings, these changes meant that BCATP pilot production more than doubled from a 1940-1 forecast of 3196 to an actual 7756.[50] However, the quality of training inevitably suffered at the expense of quantity, and this was especially true of overseas graduates, who necessarily were faced with a much longer period of inactivity between SFTS and OTU in which their newly and hastily acquired skills were likely to deteriorate considerably.

Other aircrew trades did not match the rapid expansion in pilot training. Only slight changes were made in the courses for air observers and wireless operators (air gunner). On 27 May 1940 No 1 Air Observer School at Malton, Ont., and No 1 Wireless School, Montreal, received their first classes. A total of 115 observers and 149 wireless operators (air gunner) graduated in 1940. No provision had been made in the 1939 agreement for training specialist air gunners, but as 1940 wore on the RCAF thought it advisable to train a limited number of such specialists (without giving them wireless training) in order to speed up the production of aircrew.[51] In November the first fifty-four graduated,

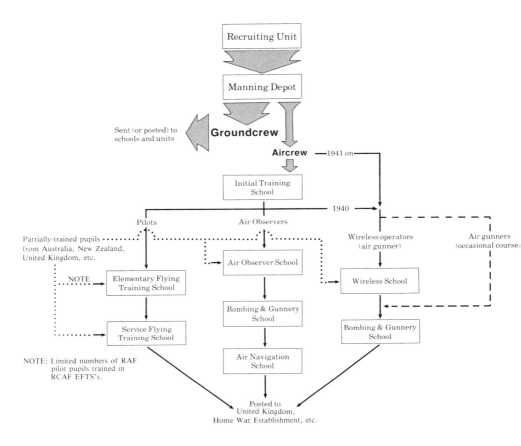

AIRCREW TRAINING FLOW
TO 1942

and all were posted to Home War Establishment positions. Specialist air gunner training was intermittent thereafter until a regular syllabus was established in 1942.[52]

After the fall of France, the British government sought permission to transfer four existing SFTSs en bloc to Canada in order to remove them from what had now become an active war front. Power had assured Sir Gerald Campbell, the British high commissioner, that accommodation for the four schools, and any others the Air Ministry might wish to transfer, could be provided without interfering with BCATP production. The United Kingdom, he stipulated, should bear all operating costs and some of the capital expenditure on aerodrome development, the exact proportion to be agreed later. The British accepted this offer and its conditions, revising the original request to include eight service flying training schools, two air observer schools, one bombing and gunnery school, one general reconnaissance school, one air navigation school, and one torpedo training school. The Canadian government was prepared to receive these units by the end of the year, but the Air Ministry decided to delay the transfer until certain of the outcome of the Battle of Britain.[53] Site preparation was now pushed even faster. Contractors were sometimes asked to begin work without waiting for the required order-in-council. Construction originally planned to take two-and-a-half years was 90 per cent complete by November 1940.[54]

The first British school to move was 7 SFTS for pilots of the Royal Navy's Fleet Air Arm. A site at Kingston, Ont., originally scheduled to be ready in June 1941, was rushed to completion to accommodate the British school. To avoid confusion with BCATP schools, it was renumbered as No 31, thus establishing a sequence of numbering for RAF schools in Canada. Staff began arriving at Kingston on 9 September while painters and carpenters were still putting the finishing touches to the camp. By the end of the month the SFTS was ready, but since the first group of British naval ratings was not due to arrive until January, the school started to train regular BCATP entrants. Two such courses graduated before the instructors turned to training naval pilots. Four more schools moved to Canada in the final months of 1940: 32 SFTS to Moose Jaw, Sask., 33 SFTS to Carberry, Man., 31 Air Navigation School to Port Albert, Ont., and 31 General Reconnaissance School (where aircrew learned maritime patrolling tactics) to Charlottetown, PEI.[55]

The British schools constituted a separate but parallel organization to the BCATP. Governed by the Visiting Forces Acts, they kept their national identity and, to a limited degree, their autonomy. The schools were said to be acting 'in combination' with the RCAF, and the Canadian force possessed extensive powers over them. A Canadian commanding a BCATP training command could, for example, order a British school in his area to alter its training programme or carry out special manoeuvres, or could post RAF personnel to any other unit in the command if necessary. Both RCAF and RAF administrative and disciplinary rules and regulations applied. After a year, in August 1941, the RAF schools were reorganized to make them, so far as practicable, identical in personnel and equipment to BCATP schools.[56]

As more and more RAF schools moved to Canada, Air Vice-Marshal L.D.D.

McKean, who had succeeded Brooke-Popham as head of the UK Air Liaison Mission, grew increasingly apprehensive that the training organization was getting too large for the Canadians. In February 1941 he pointed out to Air Marshal A.G.R. Garrod, the RAF's air member for training, that RCAF air vice-marshals and air commodores actually had less experience than the average RAF group captain. As the training plan expanded, the RCAF would need even more senior officers, and, he feared, '... it rather seems as though they can only produce them by adding stripes to the sleeves of officers already probably "over-ranked." It has been noticeable to me that from the C.A.S. downwards they are now passing through a period of, perhaps, over-confidence in their own powers.'[57] As a hedge, McKean suggested that the RAF should press for as full a measure of control as possible over their own schools. A few weeks later it was too late: the RCAF was already tightening its control over the transferred schools. By the beginning of April, McKean noted 'a clear indication that a strong effort may be made from this side [Canada] in the near future to secure virtually complete control' of the training, even to the point of hearing rumours that 'the Government are seriously considering proposing' that all RAF schools be absorbed into the BCATP. Such a move might cost the RAF schools their identity.[58] He was premature. The real attempt by Canadians to gain complete control over the training organization in their own country did not come for another year.

RAF schools were not the only ones established in Canada after the German successes in Western Europe. The Norwegian government-in-exile, based in London, which had modern aircraft on order in the United States, requested permission to create its own training base. Norway obtained the Toronto Island airport and adjacent property as the site for the Royal Norwegian Air Force Training Centre, colloquially called 'Little Norway.' Later moved to the Muskoka airport, near Gravenhurst, Ont., the centre carried out flying training from September 1940 until early 1945. Though independent of the plan and paying its own way, the Norwegians enjoyed a good deal of support for their flying training from the BCATP.[59]

General Charles de Gaulle also proposed Free French training in Canada, preferably in a self-contained organization similar to that of Norway. In 1941, however, Canada had no facilities for instructing pilots in French – a source of some embarrassment – and discouraged the proposal. Free French airmen were finally sent to Canada, along with other Allied nationals, in early 1942 with the gradual transfer of more RAF schools. All were accepted as part of the RAF quota.[60] The majority were trained at 32 SFTS, Moose Jaw, Sask., and No 34, Medicine Hat, Alta, which soon became quite cosmopolitan. Course No 53, for example, which began training at Moose Jaw on 12 April 1942, included eighteen Norwegians, fourteen Canadians, eight Britons, four Americans, three Czechoslovakians, three Free French, one Pole, and one Belgian.[61]

Meanwhile, in the fall of 1940 students had arrived from the other dominions to make the plan truly a Commonwealth one. The first were Australians. An official welcoming party greeted them when they disembarked from the liner *Awatea* on 27 September 1940. They entrained for 2 SFTS, Ottawa, where, distinctive in their dark-blue uniforms, they were cheered on arrival by Canadian airmen determined 'to show our Australian cousins how welcome they are in our midst.'[62] Graduating on 22 November, they left for Great Britain on 14 December 1940.

While the initial Australian pilot graduates went overseas, the Canadians stayed home. On 30 September 1940, after the first BCATP-trained pilots received their wings at 1 SFTS, Camp Borden, the majority received postings as SFTS instructors. Subsequent classes were similarly employed. Of the 203 Canadian pilots who graduated in 1940, only twenty were posted to Great Britain. A few went to home defence squadrons, but 165 found themselves back in the BCATP which needed more and more flying instructors and staff pilots.[63]

Other aircrew felt themselves more fortunate – or so it seemed at the time. The first air observers, whose training took them from 1 Air Observer School at Malton to 1 Bombing and Gunnery School [B&GS], Jarvis, Ont., and then to 1 Air Navigation School [ANS] at Trenton, completed their training on 25 October. Thirty-seven graduates were immediately sent to Great Britain and arrived on 25 November. One year later, half of them had been killed and several of the survivors were prisoners of war. In December, two other air observer courses, comprising seventy-seven pupils, embarked for the United Kingdom. During November and December, 149 wireless operators (air gunner) and nineteen air gunners graduated from 1 B&GS, No 2 at Mossbank, Sask., and No 4 at Fingal, Ont.[64] All were posted overseas; many were destined to become casualties of the early years of the bomber offensive.

During that first year some important changes occurred in the Air Training Plan's hierarchy. An early bureaucratic casualty was the removal of Air Vice-Marshal G.M. Croil from the key appointment of chief of the air staff. As we have seen, the enormous expansion of the RCAF, much of it directly connected to the creation of the BCATP, had led to the appointment of C.G. Power as associate minister of national defence for air in May 1940. Power, a jovial, chain-smoking, hard-drinking Quebecker and a consummate politician, found it difficult to work with the humourless, 'regimental,' and somewhat puritanical Croil. Power did not dispute Croil's competence, considering him 'an excellent, conscientious, hard-working officer,' but he 'got the impression, rightly or wrongly, that friendly, sympathetic co-operation with him would, owing to our fundamental differences of temperament, be difficult if not impossible. I wanted friendship and co-operation; he, I imagine expected me to give little more than routine supervision, leaving to him the unquestioned authority over the members of the service, and possibly over the purely civilian functions of the department. There was already ... a degree of antipathy between the uniformed members of the forces and the numerous civilian staff. I felt that Croil's influence would lean altogether too heavily on the side of the uniform and so upset the balance that should exist in a department of this kind.' At Power's request, Croil resigned his appointment as chief of the air staff at the end of the month and was shunted off to the specially created post of inspector general of the RCAF. His place was taken by L.S. Breadner – 'an altogether different type ... big, bluff, hearty and congenial, almost at once he became a close friend as well as a valued associate,' wrote Power.[65] Less than two weeks later, on 10 June 1940, the minister of national defence, Norman Rogers, was killed in an air accident while en route from Ottawa to Toronto. He was succeeded by J.L. Ralston, a dour, straight-dealing Nova Scotian with a distinguished record in the First World War, who had held the defence portfolio from 1926 to 1930 and was serving as minister of finance when Rogers died.

These changes at the top made little difference in the daily operation of the Air Training Plan, but the new men had to deal with a number of policy issues looming in the background, some of them long-standing and some the result of uncertainties brought about by the fall of France. The greatest of these concerned British views on the future of the BCATP now that the enemy dominated the whole of continental Western Europe. Had this radically revised alignment, for instance, significantly altered their perceptions about the future of wartime air training? To discuss these and other issues with the British, Ralston flew to the United Kingdom in mid-November. Travelling in an unheated bomber, he caught a severe chill which brought on a bout of sciatica, so that he had to conduct much of his business from a wheelchair.[66] C.D. Howe, the minister of munitions and supply, who sailed to join him in early December, had the misfortune to have his ship, the *Western Prince*, sunk under him somewhere south of Iceland. He spent several hours in a lifeboat, which is no place to be on the North Atlantic in winter, but survived unscathed.[67] In London the two politicians were joined by Breadner, the new chief of the air staff, who attended the discussions leading up to the Ralston-Sinclair Agreement that provided for the formation of twenty-five RCAF squadrons overseas by April 1942, a topic which will be considered at length in the forthcoming third volume of this history. At the same time the Canadian delegation convinced the British government to assume financial responsibility for equipment expenditures made in Canada on behalf of the United Kingdom; the British asked only that such expenditures be approved by the UK Air Liaison Mission before being charged to their account.[68]

However, the Canadians were unable to get any definite assessment of how strategic air requirements were likely to affect the air training organization. Sir Archibald Sinclair, the British secretary of state for air, pointed out that the Air Ministry was too absorbed with combatting the German night-bomber offensive against Britain and preparing for their own spring operations to make any definite decisions about the BCATP. He did give an assurance that all the Canadian air training schools would be fully utilized and explained that Britain was contemplating transferring more schools to Canada. Sinclair felt that it was most important for Canada to concentrate on the production of Anson aircraft, a limiting factor in the expansion of the air training programme.[69]

Unfortunately, Canadian Anson production was in difficulty. There were few engineers in Canada with experience in aeroplane design and manufacture, and the Anson II, the Canadian version, was more than just a copy of the British model. In addition to an American engine and instruments, it had a Canadian propeller, a roomier cockpit, hydraulic air brakes, and a retractable undercarriage. The directors of the new crown corporation, Federal Aircraft, though experienced in general manufacturing, had little knowledge of aircraft design and were, as Howe admitted, 'a bit at sea.' They had lost the confidence of the subcontractors, who confronted Howe on his return from England in January 1941 and asked that Federal Aircraft be dissolved and its functions taken over by de Havilland Aircraft of Canada. Howe stated that he had no intention of disbanding the company, arguing that doing so would only lead to further delays and expense.[70] In the event, he was probably right, and slow progress was made. The first Canadian-built Anson was successfully flown in August 1941. Only one plane was delivered that month, six in September, thirteen in October, sixteen in November, and thirty-four in December, when it was accurately forecast that production would mount rapidly to one hundred per month. Nevertheless, the BCATP was hampered throughout 1941 by a severe shortage of twin-engine aircraft.[71]

Equally important was the lack of spare parts for British-made aircraft. During 1941 many of these planes were due for major overhauls, and a large percentage were grounded because essential items were unavailable.[72] In the United Kingdom, the Ministry of Aircraft Production concentrated on operational aircraft, and less obvious essentials such as trainers and spare parts tended to be neglected. This policy played havoc with the training programme but the problem was deeply rooted in the pattern of British production and could not be easily overcome.[73] As a concession, the British gave the RCAF a freer hand to determine what items could be manufactured in Canada. Lists of the most needed parts were prepared and submitted to the Department of Munitions and Supply, although it took many months to accumulate reasonable stocks. In the meantime, only the initiative and resourcefulness of air force engineers and tradesmen kept the aircraft flying.

Worries over aircraft production were soon compounded by worries over manpower. In March 1941 Power told the House of Commons that although there was no current shortage of aircrew applicants, he was not certain that Canada would be able to meet its future commitments. Aircrew were drawn primarily from the national pool of men in the eighteen to twenty-eight age bracket, fit for high-altitude flying, with good eyesight and two or more years of high school education. There were about 105,000 of these potential candidates, with 15,000 to 20,000 more entering this category every year.[74] Only volunteers could be taken, and not all were available to the air force, because the navy, army, and industry also recruited from this select group. With RCAF requirements in 1941 – some 25,000 recruits – exceeding the number of new entries, there was cause for concern.

Enrolment standards could be, and were, eased. When training began in April 1940, pupils were to be at least 18 and not yet 28 years old for potential pilots, and 18 and 32 for other aircrew categories. In September, as the plan was being accelerated, the upper limit was raised to 31 for pilots. The following January the limit for all except pilots was raised to 33. In October 1942, the age limits were extended again, being reduced to 17½ for all categories, and raised the next month to 33 for pilots (to 35 for other aircrew categories, with special permission from Air Force Headquarters). At the same time, the upper limit for those specifically enrolled as air gunners was raised to 39. Initially, prewar medical standards were applied, but these were ultimately lowered for blood pressure, vision, and heart action, thus allowing increased aircrew enrolment.[75]

Until September 1941 the recruiting process was based exclusively on actual rather than potential academic performance. At first all applicants had to have junior matriculation standing. Too many potential aircrew were being lost because of this academic requirement, however, so in October 1941 special provision was made for suitable applicants who lacked the necessary education. Candidates signed an agreement to enlist for aircrew duties and received a small weekly living allowance while taking pre-aircrew academic training under the aegis of the Dominion Provincial Youth Training Programme to bring them up to the desired academic standard. Starting in 1942, candidates were actually enrolled in the RCAF, and in August they were given air force pay and allowances while undergoing academic training.[76] Then Air Force Headquarters ruled that all aircrew applicants had to take newly developed ability-to-learn and aptitude tests. Based on the work of a joint RCAF-University of Toronto Subcommittee on Personnel Selection, these tests were administered by specially trained manning personnel officers who joined recruiting and medical officers as members of the aircrew selection boards at recruiting centres. In early 1942 an improved version of the ability-to-learn test, the classification test, was adopted for use by all recruits, with a minimum score for each branch and trade. Shortly after, and in conjunction with an educational-achievement test, it replaced the formal education requirements for aircrew selection, and opened a large new source of candidates for the plan.[77]

In other areas, too, recruiting became easier. With the enactment of lend-lease legislation in March 1941, the American government treated the enlistment of its citizens in British and Canadian forces as part of its aid policy and exempted such recruits from its own draft. As of 8 December 1941 (the day after the Japanese attack on Pearl Harbor) 6129 Americans were serving in the RCAF – over 6 per cent of strength. Half of them were aircrew trainees, making up about 10 per cent of regular BCATP intake; almost 900 Americans had already graduated from the plan's schools. Another 650 were employed as staff pilots and EFTS instructors, while 668 had enlisted as ground personnel. Once the United States entered the war approximately one quarter of the Americans in the RCAF chose to transfer to the US Army Air Forces.[78]

The nature of the air war exerted another influence on the BCATP. Winston Churchill was determined to carry the war to the enemy after the fall of France. The only practicable method that seemed available to him, apart from attacking Italian forces in North Africa and the Mediterranean, was to bomb enemy targets in Europe. Daylight raids had proven unacceptably hazardous; night bombing turned out to be deplorably inaccurate. To improve the standard of bombing the British Air Ministry devised a new air observer syllabus in May 1941. The BCATP implemented the new scheme over the following few months. Bombing theory and initial bombing exercises were included in the courses at air observer schools, and these were extended from twelve to fourteen weeks to accommodate the additions. Thereafter, pupils carried out bomb-dropping exercises on the completion of each navigation practice. At the follow-on course at bombing and gunnery school, pupils now trained in night bombing, and practised this skill during navigation training at the air navigation schools they subsequently attended.[79] Together, these changes broadened the knowledge of the air observers in this secondary duty, and increased their proficiency on graduation. Quantity as well as quality was adjusted. In October air observer school enrolments were raised 25 per cent above established levels. Even this number fell short of requirements, so plans were made to double nine of the ten AOSS, increasing the trainee population 90 per cent by March 1942.[80]

Meanwhile, an analysis undertaken by the RAF in 1941 concluded that the emergency reduction in pilot course length implemented in 1940 had seriously impaired training standards and operational efficiency. There had been an alarming increase in the number of air accidents in the training system in the United Kingdom and a monthly toll in operational squadrons equal to 20 per cent of establishment during the winter months of 1940-1. The basic cause appeared to be that training skills had not kept pace with individual advancement to more complicated types of aircraft. Further, pilots from Canada were now arriving in Great Britain faster than they could be taken into the OTUS. During the waiting interval, up to a month or more, they became impatient and unruly, and inevitably forgot some of their previous training. In response, the RAF proposed to increase flying training in Canada and to use the fields in Britain vacated by transferred RAF schools as advanced flying units where newly arrived pilots could be acclimatized to flying conditions in the United Kingdom and continue training without any undue break.[81] Accordingly, in October 1941, the whole pilot training stream was extended: initial training schools and elementary schools from seven weeks to eight, and service schools from ten weeks to twelve. In November, authority was granted to double five elementary schools in size. In December, following another request from the United Kingdom, service flying courses were extended once again to sixteen weeks.[82]

In spite of all the problems, delays, and difficulties encountered in 1941, the air training programme continued to surge ahead. The last of the sixteen initially planned Canadian SFTSS opened on 1 September, placing the pilot training organization seven months ahead of the original schedule. In all, thirty-four BCATP schools came into operation in 1941. By the end of December the programme of school construction provided for in the agreement was complete, less one bombing and gunnery school not yet required, for a total programme gain of four months. Aircrew production, of course, was even more advanced. Trainee intake since April 1940 totalled 39,609, compared to the originally planned 25,120. Canada's share was 83.2 per cent, compared to 80.6 per cent forecast in the 1939 agreement.[83]

At the same time, the RCAF was overcoming major problems of training aircraft supply. April 1942 brought the last Anson Is that the United Kingdom had agreed to provide, but 625 Canadian-built Anson IIs were on hand and there were good prospects of completing the 1000-plane order by the end of October. The last Harvards on Canadian order, also delivered that month, completed requirements until April 1943.[84] Thus, by the spring of 1942, the vast BCATP organization was functioning satisfactorily, churning out the required kinds and numbers of aircrew.

Quality was harder to measure. Perhaps a useful approach is to consider how personnel responded to the training. Candidates were at first enlisted simply as 'aircrew' and were sorted into the various categories at initial training school [ITS]. There they received elementary pre-flight instruction and were separated on graduation into their particular aircrew categories. Four-week ITS courses were gradually extended to ten weeks between January 1941 and October 1942.[85] From the beginning, the ITS's primary function was as a pilot/observer selector. The principal tool used was the Link trainer. This device could simulate an aircraft's motions and was used both to teach the theory of flight and to measure a candidate's pilot potential. In this latter role it was very unpopular. Pupils objected to being eliminated from pilot training by low marks in a machine which never left the ground, pilots on the school staffs were frustrated with the task of administering and marking the tests, and EFTS instructors complained that pupils picked up bad habits which had to be corrected later. In spite of persistent attempts to standardize testing, results were very uneven. In one school, 7 ITS, Saskatoon, Sask., it was even found that 'the percentage of failure [during pilot training] of those obtaining high Link marks is greater than those obtaining low marks.' Essentially, the machines were too temperamental for a closely controlled assessment programme, and the correlation with actual elementary flying was not close enough. The Link was to prove more valuable in teaching the techniques of instrument flying to men who had already learned to fly. Western schools stopped visual Link training in late 1942, and in April 1943 the Link testing programme was moved from the ITSs and placed under the jurisdiction of the aircrew selection boards from manning depots.[86]

With the emphasis placed on selection, the authorities at first paid little attention to the quality of instruction at ITSs. They only issued an outline syllabus before the first course began. Each school determined its own subject content, mimeographed its own precis (lecture notes to be used by the instructor), and set its own examinations. New subjects, such as navigation were added to the course in 1941, but qualified instructors were not brought in at the same time, and the competence of the staff became increasingly suspect Gradually, the training commands identified and corrected these deficiencies but not until the original BCATP agreement had run its course. The RCAF finally issued a standard precis in 1942, but it was not until 1943 that the instructor problem was solved by turning the schools over to specially trained and experienced teachers of the RCAF's Education Branch.[87]

After ITS, pilot candidates advanced to EFTS and their first real contact with an aeroplane. Initially, school capacity was set at forty-eight pupils, but as training was accelerated the schools gradually grew until they were classed as single or double, with a capacity in the former of ninety students and in the latter of 180 By the end of 1941 the number of schools had been stabilized at twenty-two (twenty-six were originally planned). Four were double schools, and approval had been given to increase five more to this size. There were two classes under instruction at all times, and each school graduated one class and took in another every four weeks. The original eight-week syllabus called for about 180 hours of ground instruction and fifty hours of air training, half dual, in which an instructor

ccompanied the student, and half solo. Instruction in the air was by means of a
peaking tube from the instructor to the student, 'a source of irritation to both.'
Pilots who experienced this system both as student and instructor considered that
t 'was very poor ... very difficult to hear – and to give instruction.' Nevertheless,
pupil was expected to be ready for his first solo flight shortly after eight hours
f dual instruction.[88]

The allotted fifty-hours flying time could be expanded if time allowed, and the
minimum by 1942 was sixty hours. The extra time was not to coach slow learners
- 'wastage,' stated the EFTS syllabus, 'should occur in the Elementary stage of
raining rather than at some future date'[89] – because merely learning to fly was
not the goal. Air Vice-Marshal Leckie warned against the lengthy coaching of a
pupil simply 'because he is such a nice fellow.'[90] There had to be stiff standards
o produce potentially efficient service pilots. Although the time to solo was set
as a minimum, 'My instructor mentioned that I would be given, like everybody
else, eight – and only eight – hours of instruction, by which time I would be
expected to go solo,' reported Richard Gentil, who trained at 10 EFTS, Hamilton,
Ont., in 1941. He passed, but others did not. 'One or two needed that extra hour –
that extra hour denied by service regulations so strictly observed by the
authorities – and this I thought was a great pity, for who knows what talent was
likely to be relegated to lesser services by this very stringent rule.'[91] Many got
he extra time, but such strict attitudes throughout the programme allowed
instructors 'to wash out the weaker pupils,' remembered J.M. Godfrey, who
instructed at an SFTS. Otherwise, they 'were the first to become casualties'
overseas.[92]

Ground instruction included engines, airframes, theory of flight, airmanship,
navigation, signals, and armament; all pupils wrote examinations in each of
hese subjects. The June 1940 course reduction from eight to seven weeks was
not accompanied by a reduction in content; the instructors and students simply
had to work harder, a situation not eased until the course was returned to eight
weeks in October 1941. The scope of the syllabus remained generally the same
hroughout the war, though the RAF's increasing emphasis on long-range night
bombing and the growing variety of operational aircraft led to more time being
spent on navigation, armament training, aircraft recognition, and instrument
flying. 'My world shrank to the black-topped stick, the throttle, the rudder
pedals, and the instrument panel in front of me,' Murray Peden later wrote. Such
flying was 'arduous work indeed.' In the spring of that year 'we started night
flying students dual and later on in the year we had to send them solo,' reported
R.E. Baker, who instructed at 13 EFTS, St Eugene, Ont. 'That was tough.'[93]

In spite of the special training programme instituted in 1940, instructor
shortage plagued the elementary schools for the first three years. It was
aggravated by the increased pace of school openings, the move of RAF schools to
Canada, the enlargement of existing schools, and the institution in 1942 of an
average instructional tour length of twelve months. To fill the gaps, opportunity
was given for fully qualified RCAF instructors to take these positions on leave
without pay. In spite of the higher civilian salaries, there were too few volunteers
for what many regarded as dead-end employment. Pilots were therefore posted

as serving members, on air force pay, and under air force discipline. Temporary shortages were made up by loaning instructors from other schools. The long-term solution, however, lay in the creation of additional flying instructors schools to ensure a continued flow of purpose-trained pilots from the BCATP Two new schools were opened in 1942, one of which, No 3 at Arnprior, Ont. was expressly for elementary instructors.[94]

In spite of the shortage, it was still found possible gradually to upgrade the skills of the many elementary instructors trained under the special abbreviated programme started in 1940. They were qualified for elementary training only and were unable to fly any of the more advanced aircraft soon to be encountered by their pupils, who quickly sensed this limitation. To solve this problem, the RCAF proposed to recall them, a few at a time, to air force duty, complete their training, and give them the choice of returning to instruction or serving elsewhere.[95] The schools objected strongly to this policy. 'This school,' angrily wrote the manager of 7 EFTS, Windsor, Ont., 'has a contract with His Majesty' government to train pilots ... and we should not be called upon to procure and train our own instructors and then have them raided by the R.C.A.F. If such a system is to be inaugurated I can foresee nothing but disaster ...'[96] The instructors, however, generally looked forward to the scheme and were impatient with the slowness with which it was implemented. Conversion training started in late 1941 and trickled on over the next two years without apparent disaster. About half of the graduates volunteered to return to their parent elementary school once requalified.[97]

During the winter of 1941-2, the conditions of service of RCAF instructors on leave without pay were made more desirable. They were given permission, for example, to wear their RCAF uniform during off-duty hours. At work, they were essentially civilians, and wore 'the Prairie Admiral's uniform' of their firm. At the request of the British Air Ministry, all instructors at RAF elementary flying training schools in Canada were service instructors, and by July 1941 there were fewer than thirty civilian instructors left at EFTSs, most of whom were overage for the RCAF.[98]

Elementary flying graduates went on to service flying training. Each SFTS was organized into three wings: headquarters, maintenance, and training. In the course reductions and refinements of 1940, the training wing, originally composed of one intermediate and one advanced squadron, became a two squadron/six-flight organization. Every twenty-four days a new intake arrived to be divided between two flights, one in each squadron.[99] At first each SFTS was to give instruction in both single- and twin-engine aircraft, but early in 1940 reflecting supply difficulties and a similar change in the United Kingdom, it was decided to open them either as single- or twin-engine schools.[100] The majority of the former were concentrated in the east, and of the latter in the west.[101] Most students hoped to be sent for single-engine training to become 'a fighter pilot nothing else, a fighter pilot.' After all, the powerful Harvard was a fully aerobatic 'fun airplane,' and one not designed to 'put you in the mood for 30 degree turns or let-downs with the vertical speed nailed on 500 feet a minute. All that rot ... [was] for the Anson crowd' at twin-engine schools.[102]

Although initial plans called for training single- and multi-engine students in the proportions of 1:2, and later of 1:6.5, the early shortages of twin-engine machines made it inevitable that some future bomber pilots had to receive service training on Harvards and Yales. The courses at both types of school were similar, although the time allocated to navigation and armament was less at single-engine schools. Ground school included airmanship, armament, navigation, airframes, engines, photography and reconnaissance, signals, meteorology, and Link trainer practice. A minimum of 75 hours flying time, 40 of which was to be solo, was established, and expanded to 100 hours, half solo, when the course was lengthened to twelve weeks in late 1941.[103] Before receiving his 'wings,' each student had to demonstrate to the chief flying instructor his ability 'to take off and land without damaging His Majesty's property ... to navigate by day or night, to fly on instruments and handle our ships in any average situation.'[104]

Air observer training emphasized navigation, and selection for this vital aircrew category was carried out at ITS. Since mathematics was fundamental to their work, candidates were usually chosen from those recruits with high academic ability. Some recruits requested this category, but most wanted to be pilots. 'We knew, deep inside,' acknowledged J.R. Wood, an air observer trained in 1940, 'that ... the smart boys in maths were tagged to be observers. But secretly we prayed and prayed that we would be chosen to go on for the [pilot's] double wing.'[105]

Specialty training started at an AOS. Here the course, initially twelve weeks long, was increased to fourteen weeks in September 1941 and eighteen weeks in June 1942. It was mainly intensive training in navigation, but also included meteorology, morse code, and, eventually, over a week of instruction in bombing technique, along with the inevitable periods on hygiene, drill, and physical training. There were no rigid passing standards; it was difficult to determine whether an error in a practical exercise was the fault of the observer or of his pilot, who may not have steered according to instructions. Instead, trainees were rated on their general performance. Newly trained instructors, lacking operational experience themselves, were often unsure of the standard they should demand. However, up to the end of July 1942, about 16½ per cent of the pupils had been taken off course, almost precisely the wastage rate allowed for in the BCATP Agreement.[106]

Navigation was the air observer's primary duty, but bomb aiming came next. Air gunnery training was also included so that the observer could share effectively in the defence of his aircraft. After graduating from the AOS, pupils went for six weeks to a bombing and gunnery school to gain these skills. The gunnery portion of their course was similar to that given to air gunners and discussed below. Bombing instruction, however, was central to their operational tasks. At first it was elementary, but soon made rapid strides with the expansion of facilities and improvements in techniques. In the first class of air observers, each pupil flew an average of thirteen hours on bombing practice and dropped thirty-six bombs with an average error of 274 yards. By the summer of 1942, observers were flying an average of twenty-three hours and dropping eighty bombs with an average error of 120 yards. On completing the bombing and gunnery course, graduates were promoted to the rank of sergeant and formally presented with the air observer's badge.[107]

Air observers completed their training with four intensive weeks at 1 ANS Rivers, Man. (moved from Trenton, Ont., in November 1940), or 2 ANS, which opened at Pennfield Ridge, NB, in 1941. (The two schools were amalgamated in May 1942 at Rivers to form No 1 Central Navigation School.) Here observers were brought abreast of recent developments and techniques, and given an astronomical navigation course. On graduation, one-third were commissioned. Selected graduates were retained for qualification as AOS instructors. These candidates were given a four-week navigation instructors course in methods of instruction and classroom control before being posted to the training staff. Starting in June 1940, a few key men were given an even more detailed specialist navigator course to qualify them for chief instructor and flight and section commander positions in the BCATP.[108]

Wireless operators (air gunner) were the third principal aircrew category trained under the 1939 agreement. Except for the initial groups, recruits were enrolled directly into this category. At first they went to ITSs with other potential aircrew, and then to wireless schools for an intensive course which stressed radio theory. Everybody was unhappy with this training sequence, however, and in November 1940 the syllabus was drastically changed. At wireless school much of the theoretical information was dropped, and students were given the essential items of the ITS course and two weeks of bombing and gunnery instruction. This allowed the elimination of ITS from their programme and increased the armament instruction without extending the subsequent training period at bombing and gunnery school. These and other changes affected course length. After cutting back from a proposed twenty-four-week course in the early planning stages, a sixteen-week wireless course proved quite inadequate and was extended while the first group was still under training, settling at eighteen and later twenty weeks in 1940, twenty-four in 1941, and finally twenty-eight weeks in 1942.[109]

Most of the emphasis was on technical classroom work, and trainees spent all too few hours flying. Air time was full. Pupils had to 'handle the trailing aerial, keep busy on the key, keep the log up to date, keep the pilot informed, etc.' 'We used trailing aerials for better reception ... It was a "No! No!" to not reel in the aerial before landing. We heard stories of a few dead cows near the airport and of course, we were green enough to believe it.' Students passed most of these hurdles with the rank of leading aircraftman, having been promoted after ITS or, once direct entry to wireless school commenced, after one month of specialty training.[110]

From wireless school the pupils advanced to B&GS and air-firing exercises. This course, too, was lengthened by 1942 to six weeks from its original four. The first pupils flew about seven hours on gunnery exercises, during which they tried 'to keep from shooting off the tail or wing tips' while firing between 1000 and 1500 rounds from an obsolete Lewis or Vickers gun on a free mount in the open rear cockpit of a Fairey Battle in much the same manner as in the First World

War. In 1941 gunnery training facilities were improved by the introduction of the more up-to-date Browning guns and the arrival of a number of hydraulically operated turret gun mounts from Britain, but these remained in short supply. As late as the spring of 1942, John K. Smith, training at 6 B&GS, Mountain View, Ont., saw only one Browning machine-gun at his unit, 'on display in a cabinet – stripped down.'[111]

Bombing and gunnery school interrupted the wireless practice of the new wireless operators (air gunner), and travel time and lengthy waits before they arrived at their new units overseas led to further deterioration of skill. The British took steps to provide equipment on ocean transports, and suggested that training be undertaken at the embarkation depot and during the voyage. As a result, a policy was adopted in April 1941 of giving graduates further training while awaiting embarkation in order to maintain proficiency. Periodic efficiency checks were also instituted at B&GSs and arrangements made for tests and training during the voyage overseas.[112]

Meanwhile, operations overseas were being developed on a scale, and at a tempo, unforeseen in even the RAF's long-range estimates, while aircraft, equipment, and air tactics were all increasing in complexity. Moreover, it had been obvious for many months that the war would extend beyond 1943;[113] accordingly, an Air Training Conference (to be discussed in chapter 7) was held in Ottawa in May and June 1942, and a new agreement forged to supersede the plan as it then existed. On 30 June 1942 the original BCATP came to an end.

Its results were easy to see. In 1942 air training for the RAF was being carried on in many other countries besides Canada. Australia, New Zealand, and South Africa had schools, as did India and Southern Rhodesia. There were still flying training schools in the United Kingdom, and a number of American schools were training pilots and wireless operators (air gunner) for the RAF. However, the air training organization in Canada was the largest and was paying the greatest dividends. A total of 23,802 aircrew, excluding those trained in transferred RAF schools, had graduated by 30 June 1942. Of this number, 80 per cent or 17,464 were Canadians: 8868 pilots, 2991 air observers, 4183 wireless operators (air gunner), and 1422 air gunners. Most (well over 13,000) had been posted directly overseas to RCAF or RAF squadrons. About 3200 others had gone back into the BCATP or to the staff of RAF schools in Canada, and fewer than 900 to the Home War Establishment. Besides the Canadians, 2934 Australians, 2252 New Zealanders, and 1152 British had graduated from BCATP schools. Many more were still under training.[114]

7

Mid-War Modifications

In 1939 the government had chosen large-scale air training over the dispatch of formed RCAF units overseas, accepting the fact that most Canadian BCATP graduates would be dispersed throughout the RAF. Success in building the British Commonwealth Air Training Plan in Canada, however, did not preclude the need for adjustments to meet the war's changing demands, or eliminate problems relating to broad-based political objectives and the plan's goals. The most compelling consideration – and the one of greatest potential impact – was the issue of the employment of Canadian airmen abroad. At Ottawa's insistence the original BCATP Agreement had included a clause acknowledging that a substantial number of RCAF squadrons (and perhaps even larger formations) might be formed at a later date. This was a vague statement, not a definite promise, but it gave concrete expression to what otherwise might have remained a faint hope that the RCAF would have a significant operational commitment of its own. This issue of 'Canadianization' dominated all Anglo-Canadian discussions about the air war.

It is not easy to determine exactly when the question of RCAF organization overseas became a serious problem. The formation of Canadian squadrons abroad did not play an important part in Ottawa's air policy immediately after the fall of France, and while the Cabinet War Committee discussed the matter in the autumn of 1940, no firm decisions were taken. Perhaps the most sensible advice at that time came from the chief of the air staff, Air Vice-Marshal L.S. Breadner who suggested a gradual evolution to wholly Canadian units abroad. Carried away by a vision of Canadian airpower, however, he optimistically suggested it might be possible to form as many as seventy-seven RCAF squadrons overseas by the end of 1942.[1]

So many squadrons would certainly have strained Canada's resources in aircrew and groundcrew past the breaking point, to say nothing of the burden that would have been placed on the aircraft industries at home and in the United States and Great Britain. Yet Breadner's memorandum illustrated just how unsatisfactory the situation was from the Canadian point of view. This issue was raised during the visit of the minister of national defence, Colonel J.L. Ralston to the United Kingdom in the winter of 1940-1. Having reassessed Canadian manpower potential and estimated the cost of providing completely Canadian squadrons, Ralston suggested that it was realistic to form twenty-five RCAF squadrons overseas to join the three already in England. His proposal was accepted almost immediately by the secretary of state for air, Sir Archibald Sinclair, and an agreement was signed by the two on 7 January 1941. Twenty-five RCAF squadrons would join the British order of battle by April or May 1942 if all went according to plan, and Canadian officers would be posted to them as soon as they were qualified. No special consideration was given to the many Canadians who would still remain in RAF squadrons after these units were formed. Any difficulties encountered in implementing this programme were to be discussed the following September.[2]

The question of Canadianization was again raised during the June 1941 visit to the United Kingdom of C.G. Power, the minister of national defence for air. Unsatisfied with the progress made by then, the minister pressed for the creation of Canadian fighter and bomber groups. He also endeavoured to increase the number of Canadian overseas squadrons, arguing that this would better reflect the dominion's potential. The British replied that a bomber group might well be formed in 1942, though a fighter group was doubtful, and they agreed that making room for more than twenty-five RCAF squadrons posed no problems in principle. However, they also emphasized that it was impossible to make immediate, firm commitments because the ultimate size of the air force depended on the availability of aircraft as well as strategic and tactical factors.[3]

There matters rested until September 1941, when the Air Ministry informed the Canadian government that there was in fact no hope for more than twenty-five RCAF squadrons overseas. The combination of lend-lease commitments to the USSR and the recent decision to increase the aircraft establishment of bomber squadrons meant that no aeroplanes were available for new units. Power promised the Cabinet War Committee on 9 October that he would make every effort to reverse this decision.[4] Otherwise the role of the RCAF in European operations would be severely restricted. Capable of raising the manpower for thirty or forty squadrons for overseas service, Canada had no prospect whatsoever of forming them. Quite apart from considerations of national prestige, the long-term implications were clear. As Breadner noted in October 1941:

Canada, with her present aircraft production (and lack of engine production) and her magnificent air training scheme, cannot be considered in any sense of the term as an Air Power, particularly as most of her training effort is in the elementary or intermediate field, and not operational in the full sense of the word. Abroad her personnel are gradually being organized into Canadian squadrons, some of which are actively functioning in operations, although not through any independent action on Canada's part but entirely, or almost so, through Royal Air Force effort.

The world situation is such that the further continuance of this policy, without the development of air power in Canada, may imperil her position in the future and limit her contribution to the general cause.[5]

Another irritant affecting Canadian perceptions of the BCATP Agreement, one no less important in terms of Canadian self-esteem and identity, was commissioning policy. In December 1939 the question of how many aircrew should be commissioned had been left vague, the provision being simply that 'a number of pilots and observers' would be selected as officers from among BCATP graduates. More definite guidelines were established in July 1940, and Home War Establishment promotions were pegged to lag slightly behind those overseas, as Air Force Headquarters did not want personnel serving in Canada to have any advantages over their comrades in more active theatres.[6] However, the RAF quickly fell behind the commissioning schedule established for Canadians serving in British squadrons. Power was soon aware of this, and of the reasons why. Some squadron commanders were apparently unaware or unsure of the procedures involved in promoting Canadian non-commissioned officers [NCOs], while many more proved simply lethargic. These faults could be corrected in time, and with the proper distribution of regulations, but there was another explanation which was difficult to excuse (at least so far as Canadians were concerned) and for which no ready remedy existed. The RAF, it seemed, was loath to commission Canadian airmen who did not meet the standards set for British officers and gentlemen.[7]

Upset by the RAF's failure to keep its word, by the British attitude to Canadian NCOs, and by his own government's impotence to rectify the situation, Power had sought to amend the commissioning formula when he met Air Ministry officials in June 1941. He failed. Commissioning half of the pilot graduates was 'proceeding too far at present,' the British said; the policy should remain as it was, although its implementation could be improved.[8] Meanwhile, Power continued to receive a flood of complaints from airmen at home and abroad. Of the former, the most deserving were the better graduates of the early BCATP courses who, posted to flying training schools as NCO instructors, were now seeing former students returning to Canada as officers.[9] Like the question of the size of the RCAF overseas, this was not an issue to be brushed aside easily. Nor did the government care to.

The need for a major review of air training policy some time in 1942 or early 1943 was built into the original BCATP Agreement, which was due to lapse automatically on 31 March 1943. The first formal recommendation for negotiations to prolong the training plan seems to have been made by Air Vice-Marshal E.W. Stedman, the RCAF's air member for aeronautical engineering, as early as 7 April 1941. At that time the outlook for the British and their Commonwealth Allies was bleak. France, the Netherlands, and Scandinavia (except for neutral Sweden) had all fallen to the German juggernaut in 1940. Romania and Hungary had been enlisted in the enemy cause and – only the day before Stedman put pen to paper – the Germans had launched attacks against both Yugoslavia and Greece. The United States was still neutral and apparently likely to remain so; Hitler had not yet made the fatal mistake of attacking the Soviet Union; and he was master of Europe. His Italian allies were threatening Malta and his Spanish friends debating whether to attack Gibraltar, the two keys to the Mediterranean. The Atlantic lifelines holding the British alliance together looked particularly insecure in the face of growing U-boat attacks.

Stedman's concern, however, was not with the number or disposition of students who would have to pass through the training pipeline, but with the future availability of aeroplanes in which to train. Manufacturers, he pointed out, had to be informed of future requirements well in advance in order to adjust or retool production lines to provide the appropriate aircraft when needed. Having heard that American factories were fully committed to June 1943, he feared that if orders for more aircraft were not placed in good time the BCATP would find itself without sufficient training machines.[10] Canada could not place orders without consultation with her partners.

'Chubby' Power acted on Stedman's report in June, when he visited the United Kingdom. Although the future status of the RCAF overseas was the major reason for his journey, he told Prime Minister Mackenzie King that he would also pay close attention to the supply of aircraft to the BCATP.[11] His trip was a great success in the latter respect; the Air Ministry was easily persuaded of the urgent need to work out procedures for procuring new aircraft. The British volunteered to contact the other participants in the BCATP and ascertain their views on holding talks to consider the extension of the plan.[12] On 23 October 1941 Malcolm MacDonald, British high commissioner in Ottawa, reported that New Zealand and Australia would also be invited to attend a conference in London.[13]

The Commonwealth's response was a source of great relief to J.L. Ilsley, Canada's minister of finance. All decisions relating to the purchase of new training aircraft could now be safely postponed until after a new cost-sharing formula had been agreed to, he told the Cabinet War Committee. The suggestion that the discussions be held in London was, however, a different matter, and at its meeting of 29 October the committee decided to make representations to the Air Ministry to hold the proposed conference in Ottawa.[14] The government's strong stand on this question reflected the importance of the BCATP as a symbol of Canada's wartime achievement. 'As you know,' Power later wrote to MacDonald, 'the Commonwealth Air Training Plan ... had to be sold to the Canadian people.' 'It was not generally understood,' he continued, 'and until such time as it was in actual operation, it was looked upon with more or less skeptical derision.'[15] The Cabinet doubtless saw the publicity that would result from a major conference on air training in Canada as a useful corrective to such attitudes. Once national objectives of this kind were involved, however, it was unlikely that any meetings on the BCATP's future could be limited to a simple rebalancing of accounts or the supply of aircraft.

On 3 November 1941 the Canadian government suggested to the United Kingdom that Ottawa would be a more appropriate conference site for extending the agreement since so much air training was concentrated in Canada. When no reply was received, the suggestion was repeated on 20 December. Again there was silence until 20 January 1942, when MacDonald reported that his government now believed that the conference should be postponed until the effect on Allied air training requirements of Japanese and American entry into the war could be assessed. There was logic in the British view. It was entirely possible that Australia and New Zealand would have to withdraw temporarily from the BCATP in order to strengthen their own defences against Japan. Moreover, soon after the Americans joined the fight it had been agreed that policy relating to the allocation of aircraft would be a matter for the combined Anglo-American Munitions Assignment Board. Thus a purely Commonwealth conference, even at government level, might be powerless to implement any aircraft supply decisions. This was, after all, the reason why Canada had first proposed talks. However, a limited service-to-service conference might prove useful without interfering with higher Anglo-American planning or offending dominion sensibilities. MacDonald suggested talks on this basis.[16] Its conclusions could be put before the Combined Chiefs of Staff for approval, as with any other staff study. In the meantime, the Air Ministry went ahead with its own Empire Training Conference in London at the end of January, with American observers present.[17]

The Canadians were not dissuaded. The very events predisposing the RAF to put off a substantive review of the agreement had in fact hardened Canadian opinion that the future of the BCATP must be examined forthwith. Possible Australian and New Zealand reassessments of their commitments threatened the plan's continued operation at existing manning levels, as did the probable ending of American recruiting for the RCAF. There was also a good chance that some BCATP airfields would have to be turned over to the RCAF for operational use, which meant that there might have to be an entirely new construction programme. More importantly, the Americans had imposed a ban on the release of aircraft, engines, and spare parts to her allies as a result of Pearl Harbor. If this were not rescinded, any discussion on the supply of training aircraft would be entirely academic. If the ban on shipments continued, Power told his War Cabinet colleagues, it was doubtful whether the BCATP could be expanded, or training maintained, for 1943 and 1944. Finally, he had heard reports that shortages of operational aircraft in the United Kingdom were creating a surplus of pilots there and that the Air Ministry would soon be asking for a decrease in the rate of BCATP output.[18] It was thus in Canada's best interests to go ahead with a conference so that authorities would have a clearer idea of the BCATP's future he told the British on 7 February.[19]

A competing proposal had already surfaced. On 20 December 1941 the American representatives to the Permanent Joint Board on Defence had startled their Canadian colleagues with a recommendation 'that the Canadian and United States Governments should consider the advisability of arranging for a meeting of appropriate representatives of Great Britain, Canada and the United States to make appropriate recommendations for co-ordination of the entire aviation training programs to be conducted in Canada and the United States.'[20] The Americans had been vague, giving neither the reason why nor the extent to which co-operation was desirable. When questioned they said only that there was a need to explore whether North American facilities were being put to the best possible use. In the rarefied atmosphere of the PJBD it was perhaps not good manners to press too hard, and the Canadians had accepted the recommendation on that basis. However, here was an apparent call for action that might interfere with Canada's desire to hold a Commonwealth air training conference.

Things seemed a little clearer in January after the chief of the air staff had had an opportunity to talk with the deputy chiefs of the American naval and air staffs. Asked to explain what 'was behind' the board's 23rd Recommendation, these officers replied that there was nothing 'other than possibly the thought that the R.C.A.F. might like to avail themselves of the mild weather in the Eastern States and establish training stations there for use during the winter months.' Since he saw no reason for this, Breadner suggested that Canada 'should not initiate discussion on this subject.'[21] Power had already come to the same conclusion, and the matter was easily passed over at the Cabinet War Committee meeting of 23 January.[22] In fact, as the Canadian air attaché reported on 10 March, the reasons for American interest were much different. According to Major General Stanley Embick, senior US service member of the PJBD, the Americans feared that there were too few facilities in the United States to support the expansion of its air forces. Later, on 25 March, he reported that while the Americans had room for their own training, they wanted to transfer all British training to Canada.[23]

Meanwhile, Canadian concern grew considerably in February 1942 when it was learned that the American and British navies had been talking about training Fleet Air Arm pilots in the United States without informing Ottawa. Further, the War Department had issued General H.H. Arnold, chief of the US Army Air Forces, with a directive that, to Canadian eyes, looked very much as if the United States wished to assert a measure of control over all air training. Arnold proposed to arrange his own meeting of American and British 'aviation training people' to review all facilities in North America.[24]

Power was extremely unhappy with these American initiatives because they would inevitably 'complicate' things.[25] Canadian leadership in air training would be undermined if a separate Anglo-American agreement were reached, or if the Americans took the lead in a co-ordinated programme of North American training. The obvious solution was to ask the Americans to the proposed conference in Ottawa. This would not only satisfy the spirit of the PJBD's 23rd Recommendation, but also increase the Americans' awareness of the scope and importance of the BCATP to the point where, it was hoped, they could be easily convinced of its need for US training machines.

Unfortunately, the British disagreed. The Air Ministry felt that the development of a comprehensive plan for air training in North America would be sound, but only if it was 'confined to co-ordination with a view to avoiding overlapping and duplication of training effort' and did not involve the Americans in any decisions relating to the BCATP.[26] Unable to reconcile the conflicting approaches, still unsure of American objectives, and unwilling to sacrifice a Canadian-sponsored conference in favour of meetings in Washington, Power decided to caution his staff to 'on no account ... do more than listen to suggestions.'[27] The RCAF was not to propose anything, nor respond to any suggestions Arnold might make.

Arnold's purpose seemed somewhat clearer on 10 March 1942, when the air attaché in Washington reported that the Americans were probably looking for extra training facilities in Canada.[28] However, it was not certain that the Dominion could accommodate them, as Canadians were already hard pressed trying to find space for additional RAF schools which the British wanted to transfer to Canada. With space and new training aircraft likely to be at a premium, there was an even greater need for a conference to set priorities.[29]

The British now took the initiative. While still maintaining that conditions were not ripe for a full air training conference, on 10 March they offered to sort out the aircraft procurement question at an informal gathering in Ottawa later that month. Although Treasury officials would be part of the UK delegation, the talks would be on an almost exclusively service-to-service basis and limited to the supply of training machines to the BCATP. Aware that the Canadian government was likely to view this meeting as an unsatisfactory half-measure the British took care to reaffirm their commitment to a major policy conference when conditions permitted. They also promised that any decisions on procurement taken at the proposed mini-conference would not prejudice subsequent amendments to the plan's cost-sharing formula. Thus insulated against full financial responsibility for new training aircraft, Canada accepted the British proposition.[30]

Power nevertheless had only a slight interest in the upcoming talks. As he told the Cabinet War Committee on 18 March, too many matters of high policy were still outstanding that could only be resolved at a government-level policy conference. The minister therefore proposed to cable the Air Ministry asking it to reconsider its stand.[31] As it happened, a message was received from London the next day which indicated that the British were at last prepared to accommodate the Canadian government. Noting politely that the dominion had been raising the point since the fall of 1941, the deputy prime minister and dominions secretary, Clement Attlee, informed Mackenzie King that it was now time to discuss the extension of the BCATP beyond March 1943 and to work out the best way to complete the transfer of RAF schools to Canada. Opinion in London regarding transferred schools was, he added, beginning to shift to the view that they could be placed under the plan's umbrella.[32]

Attlee's tact was welcome but could not by itself overcome long-standing Canadian objections to the manner in which the British had so far approached the need to amend the air training plan. Anxious to clarify these matters before reply was made, as well as to vent his own frustration at the lack of progress Power sought an interview with Malcolm MacDonald. The Canadian began with a strong statement that he and his colleagues were 'not at all satisfied' with the purely service talks on aircraft supply then underway in Ottawa. As he had predicted, discussion had inevitably involved issues of high policy beyond the competence of the RCAF's representatives and so was of little value. Power then turned to the fact that the British had been talking to the Americans without informing Canada, indirectly challenging the logic of Britain's apparent eagerness to embrace the United States in this instance when, at the same time the Air Ministry objected to including the Americans in the air training conference.[33] MacDonald admitted that Canadian dissatisfaction was justified in many respects. Several issues had to be clarified, among them the status of the RCAF overseas. To this end, he told Power, the Canadian draft reply to Attlee which made all the points that Power was making now, but rather less bluntly hit the mark nicely.[34]

Power then told the high commissioner that Canada was not eager to have more RAF schools because of the administrative burden these would entail. It would be far better to absorb them into the BCATP if and when they were transferred. Finally, the minister turned to the question of commissions and the unsatisfactory pace of promotions for Canadians overseas.[35] MacDonald made no comment on this complaint, but he faithfully reported the Canadian point of view to his government, highlighting two issues: Canada wanted the RAF schools incorporated into the BCATP, and she was determined to have the United States represented at any air training conference.[36]

It was now the turn of the Air Ministry to be upset. H.H. Balfour, undersecretary of state for air, thought (in an internal Air Ministry memorandum) it was unfortunate that Canada was taking such a strong stand on American participation as most of what had to be discussed about the BCATP was of a 'domestic' nature, of interest to the plan's Commonwealth members alone. He warned of morale problems if the RAF schools were brought under the BCATP framework; so far as he could tell the staff and students at these units strongly favoured retaining their RAF identity. Absorption of the RAF schools into the BCATP would increase personnel costs and lead to pay and allowance headaches for the Air Ministry. He went on to assess the Canadian mood fairly accurately; judging from recent correspondence and MacDonald's meeting with Power it was evident that the latter was annoyed and standing firm on what he regarded as first principles. Worse still, Balfour discerned that there was even an element of distrust in the dominion's attitude to the Mother Country.[37]

On 4 April the British informed Norman Robertson, the undersecretary of state for external affairs, that they had at last accepted Canada's request to have the United States represented at the forthcoming conference. MacDonald had to point out, however, that his superiors still insisted that there was no compelling reason for the Americans to be party to negotiations over the transfer of RAF schools, the refinancing of the BCATP, or any other such domestic issue. Accordingly, London was recommending that the conference be organized in two parts, the first to deal with the BCATP, and the second to investigate larger issues such as the co-ordination of North American training. The United Kingdom would nonetheless leave it to Canada to decide whether this was the best course to follow.[38]

Canadian officials were unhappy with the British desire for a split conference. With the United States continuing to press for co-ordination of North American training, and with Canada increasingly dependent on the US for aircraft, engines, and spares, it seemed distinctly unwise to give any impression that there was a Commonwealth 'caucus' whose object was to present the Americans with a 'united front' of carefully worked out positions. Arguing that this was one area where Canada could 'properly take the initiative,' Robertson advised King to reject the British alternative and to insist that the Americans be included from the outset. The British were right in contending that the United States had no business with the internal workings of the BCATP, but there was a simple solution to that problem. Rather than have everything discussed at plenary sessions, it might be better to create a number of subcommittees to handle specific items on the agenda and have these groups report to the full conference. The Americans could be excluded from the pith and substance of purely BCATP discussions without being left out entirely. This seemed reasonable to MacDonald.[39] Less justifiable, in the British high commissioner's view, was Canadian persistence in seeking a more generous commissioning policy. Thus, even though Power (whom MacDonald described as being 'very touchy' on the issue) now offered a small compromise, stating that he would be satisfied if 50 per cent of aircrew received a commission upon graduation from the BCATP, London was advised to pre-empt the Canadian recommendation by instituting strict time-in-rank provisions.[40]

A message from the United Kingdom crossed the one containing this last advice, and so made no reference to Power's latest remarks regarding commissioning policy. However, it indicated that the United Kingdom had at last relented on the question of American participation at Ottawa. The British also accepted the subcommittee formula, although in practice a two-part conference still resulted in May. This removed a major stumbling block.[41] Yet as things turned out, perhaps the most important fact about this message was its time of arrival. Received on 11 April, the British response unknowingly helped Canada to 'ride ... off,' as MacDonald put it, a formal invitation from the United States to attend a multilateral air training conference in Washington on the 15th.[42]

This invitation, sent on 2 April from General Arnold to Air Vice-Marshal Breadner, was the last in a series of somewhat mysterious and even bizarre events reflecting an on-again-off-again American interest in co-ordinating North American air training.[43] With the pressure from Washington having abated Canadian officials appear to have decided that it was best not to mention anything to the Americans about the forthcoming Ottawa conference before the British had approved their participation. Arnold was therefore ignorant of Canadian plans. His sudden invitation to Breadner to take action on the PJBD's 23rd Recommendation in two weeks' time came as a shock to the air staff, not least because the RAF was also invited. It was also unwelcome on this account Although a conference in Washington in April would not prevent Canada from holding one in May, it would nevertheless have to cover much of the same ground and so weaken the impact of the Ottawa gathering. Canada's symbolic position as the leader in Allied air training might also be threatened, particularly if the venue facilitated Anglo-American accords affecting the BCATP.

Whether Ottawa believed that the best response to this unwelcome invitation was to ignore it, or whether it simply took time to compose an appropriate reply is not clear. In the event, nothing was done before the PJBD meeting on 8 April, at which time the Americans took an uncomfortably and disturbingly hard line announcing that Washington had 'serious concern over the non implementation of the [PJBD] recommendation.' The Canadians at once responded that the issue could be settled at Ottawa in May, but this did not satisfy General Embick or his staff. In fact, the US Navy's representative warned, the ban on shipments of aircraft and engines would continue until action had been taken.[44] Breadner was mystified by Arnold's invitation and by the toughness of the American position. Why, he asked, were the US services so adamant about holding a conference in

Washington in April? It took four days to find the answer; apparently the entire American training programme was being held up pending the outcome of the proposed conference. By that time Canada had rejected the American invitation and the United States had decided to proceed on its own with or without an Allied conference.[45]

Malcolm MacDonald was probably right when he reported that the Canadians were buoyed by the British agreement to a May conference in Ottawa, and that this influenced their decision not to go to Washington. Whether this in turn influenced the American decision to go ahead independently with their own training is more difficult to determine. One thing is certain. In his response to Arnold, Breadner had emphasized that Canada was not closing the door on multilateral discussions of air training; it was just that the Canadian government was insisting that they take place at the political level rather than between representatives of the armed forces. All this would be made much clearer when Mackenzie King visited President Roosevelt in one week's time. Meanwhile, Breadner suggested, Arnold and his staff should visit BCATP facilities in Canada as preparation for the Ottawa conference in May.[46] Arnold, who was holding discussions with British officials about aircraft allocations, rejected the invitation. However, Major-General Barton K. Yount, the chief of the USAAF's Flying Training Command, and a small party arrived in Ottawa on 22 April for a quick three-day tour of nearby training facilities.

The prime minister's visit to Washington was crucial in defining the character of the forthcoming air training conference. Invited to attend the first meeting of the Pacific War Council – a purely political forum created to enable representatives of the lesser Allied powers to receive confidential briefings on the course of the war from time to time – King was also asked to come to the White House on the night of 15 April so that he and President Roosevelt could have 'a quiet evening together.'[47] Roosevelt turned out to be in an 'expansive mood,' proclaiming that Canada should have a seat on the Munitions Assignment Board, an offer that was never repeated. King took full advantage of the occasion to describe the BCATP and the benefits of having American participation at the May conference.[48] Roosevelt later told Churchill that he had agreed to the Canadian proposal because 'no harm, and a good deal of probable good' was likely to result, and because King was so 'very anxious to have something to show for his Washington visit.'[49]

King proposed that the meetings take place in Ottawa, not Washington, and that they be attended by both ministers and service representatives. Roosevelt was willing to accommodate King on both scores. However, the president was also determined that the meetings be as broadly based as possible, so that when the prime minister asserted that South Africa, Australia, and New Zealand would have to attend, the president replied that 'other countries of the United Nations ... training pilots on this continent' should also be invited. Norway, China, and the Netherlands were singled out that night, but by the next morning the list of participants had grown considerably. The press release issued by the two leaders explained that 'The Prime Minister of Canada and the President announced today that, at the invitation of the Prime Minister, a conference in which all of the United Nations with Air Training Programmes would be invited to participate would be held in Ottawa early in May ... the Conference developed out of the recognition of the desirability of more closely co-ordinating the British Commonwealth ... Air Training Plan with the greatly extended Air Training Programmes undertaken by the United States and the other ... United Nations ... these will include China, Norway, The Netherlands and several others ... already at war with the Axis.'[50] With both leaders emphasizing the need to co-ordinate air training in North America, Roosevelt had the means to implement the 23rd Recommendation of the PJBD. King, of course, had his conference.

Canadian officials were genuinely surprised by the unforeseen expansion of the conference to include a host of minor powers. The Canadian representative in Washington questioned the wisdom of the last sentence of the release, but feared that it was 'too late to secure its change.' Invitations would therefore have to go to Poland, Czechoslovakia, South Africa, Yugoslavia, India, and the USSR, as well as to those nations mentioned in the communiqué. In addition, Washington was to be asked to recommend which of the Latin American countries would attend, while London would provide information on 'which of the other United Nations have embarked on air training programs.'[51] Eventually the Free French and Belgians were added to the list because they were represented in the RAF schools.[52] The extreme case came when the conference planners had to hold up their invitation to the Greek government-in-exile because they suddenly realized that they did not know if Greece had an air force.

The problem was what to do with all these delegations, most of whom did not conduct their own air training, simply supplying aircrew candidates for others to train. Canada hoped that the majority of countries would be satisfied with having only observers present. As might be expected, however, a number objected to such second-class status. As the Norwegians pointed out, the occupied countries faced one unique problem that would have to be solved some time. Cut off from a guaranteed flow of recruits, they would find it impossible to keep existing squadrons up to strength unless permitted to tap new sources of manpower – nationals now resident in the United States, Canada, and the other Allied powers. Since all these countries would be meeting in Ottawa, the May conference seemed a perfect opportunity to speak to this point. Unwilling to offer equal status to all, but mindful of the Norwegian complaint, planning officials in Ottawa chose to set up a special subcommittee to discuss the situation confronting all the smaller powers. The other subcommittees, agreed to by Canada and Great Britain some time earlier, would deal with major topics including aircraft production, methods of instruction, and co-ordination of training. Care was taken, nevertheless, to ensure that control of the conference remained in the hands of the 'major' powers. A 'conference committee' of Canada, Great Britain, the United States, Australia, and New Zealand, and one European country, would manage affairs and act as intermediary between these subcommittees and the plenary meetings.[53]

As host nation Canada was to prepare the agenda, a fact which gave her the advantage of ensuring that those issues of paramount importance to her would be discussed. So far as the BCATP itself was concerned three specific problems stood out, the most important being the supply of aircraft after March 1943. A cost-sharing formula would have to be arrived at with the British, while the United States had to be fully informed of (and preferably impressed with) the scale of Canadian air training so that there could be no mistaking the requirement for aircraft. The Canadian government also had some qualms about reports that courses would be lengthened in order to reduce the surplus of aircrew overseas, fearing the possibility of severe morale problems when trainees were forced to put in yet more time before their graduation. Canada would have to deal with the consequences, and the Cabinet secretary, Arnold Heeney, asked Mackenzie King to insist upon a full explanation before acceding to any changes proposed in the training schedule.[54] Finally, there was the question of whether and how training capacity in Canada could be increased to accommodate the additional British needs and the possible relocation of some American schools to Canada. Should the RAF schools be absorbed in the British Commonwealth Air Training Plan? And, if the United States wished to conduct training in the dominion, did that mean that the British, American, and Canadian programmes should be fully co-ordinated, permitting free interchange of personnel? Although this prospect seemed increasingly unlikely, there had been no authoritative statement from the Americans that they did not want to train in Canada, and rumours to that effect persisted.

These questions could not be discussed in a vacuum. The flow of students through the BCATP would depend ultimately on the availability of operational aircraft and the need for aircrew overseas, as well as the supply of training machines. Following from this dependency, it seemed essential that the Americans and British disclose their strategic plans, future aircraft allocations, manpower resources, and casualty estimates in order to provide sound statistical underpinning for the conference deliberations. This created problems for both the British and Americans, both of whom were understandably reluctant to broadcast their intentions to such a miscellaneous audience, particularly when they themselves were not in full agreement. In the end each asked Canada not to press for such details, and the information that was made available to Canada was very limited. It did not, for example, deal with expected aircraft production and allocation.[55]

Canadian interest went further than these training matters. It was also important to secure American and British support for the recently approved expansion of the Home War Establishment as they would have to supply most of the aircraft required. Finally, there was the question of the RCAF overseas. The issues of commissioning policy and the formation of Canadian squadrons abroad continued to plague the government and air staff, and since both resulted from the BCATP Agreement the dominion felt that both should be open for discussion and renegotiation at the conference. As Sydney de Carteret, deputy minister of national defence for air, told Norman Robertson, the British must be made aware of Canada's wish to exercise maximum control of the RCAF overseas 'consistent with the maximum efficiency of our united efforts,' and with the principle that 'Canada's quota of squadrons should be increased in keeping with the increased effort and finance that Canada is putting into training.'[56]

That the Canadian delegation would indeed take a strong stand at the conference was practically guaranteed when Air Vice-Marshal Harold 'Gus' Edwards was granted permission to take part. Commanding the RCAF overseas since November 1941, Edwards was a firm and sometimes intemperate proponent of Canadianization, and he announced that his main objective was to elaborate on the 'many difficulties' he had encountered as he endeavoured to carry out the policies of the Canadian government.[57] Although these 'overseas' issues were to play an important part in the Ottawa talks, they did not bear directly on the role and administration of the BCATP and are left for detailed consideration in the third volume of this history.

The British, naturally enough, had their own expectations of the conference. Like Canada, they placed a premium on the co-ordination of air training in North America, although for very different reasons. For where the RCAF hoped to achieve a common standard, whatever it might be, to accommodate American training in the dominion, the Air Ministry and the Admiralty aspired to convince the Americans to adopt British practices so that the RAF and Royal Navy trainees on course in the United States would be ready for operational postings soon after they graduated. Far more serious was Canada's insistence on bringing up the matter of commissions. If, as expected, the dominion demanded commissions for all aircrew, the Air Ministry's position would be all the more uncomfortable, but there was nothing anyone in London could do.[58]

The Ottawa Air Training Conference opened on the morning of 19 May. After reviewing an RCAF Guard of Honour, Mackenzie King welcomed the delegates in the Senate chamber. Noting that 'it would be an advantage to the common cause to have the widest possible use made of the experience gained in Canada, in co-operative air training,' he reminded delegates of the importance of North America to the war. It was, he stated, a centre of gravity on account of its interior lines of communication. The other heads of delegation echoed these remarks. Balfour, representing Great Britain, spoke of Canada as 'the hub of air training around which revolves the ever-widening circle of world battle,' while Robert A. Lovett of the United States passed on President Roosevelt's description of Canada as 'the Aerodrome of Democracy.' Congratulatory remarks followed too from the rest of the countries attending and then, as prearranged, Power was elected as conference chairman and Arnold Heeney as secretary.[59]

The first order of business was to establish the several committees previously agreed to by Canada, the United States, and Great Britain. Power headed the all-important Conference Committee, which would co-ordinate the work of the whole conference; Baron Silvercruys of Belgium led the General Training Committee, the body formed to allow the occupied nations to discuss their problems; the Committee on Standardization of Training was chaired by Air Marshal A.G.R. Garrod, air member for training in the Air Ministry; and his Canadian counterpart, Air Vice-Marshal Robert Leckie, had the Committee on Composition of Aircrew. The other two special committees, Co-ordination of Training Capacity and Manpower Resources, both went to Americans, respectively to Captain A.W. Radford, director of training in the US Navy's Bureau of Aeronautics, and Colonel R.E. Nugent, of the War Department General Staff.[60]

Reversing the suggestion made by the United Kingdom when it had accepted American participation, items of interest to all participants were discussed first, with purely BCATP matters left until later. These initial meetings revealed that there were many similarities in the training carried out in Canada, the United States, and Great Britain, and that the differences found to exist did not call into question the basic approach taken by any one training programme. There were few attempts to standardize or work towards co-ordination of the various training programmes. The British placed the blame for this failure squarely on the United States and its determination to build up a wholly independent air force. American representatives, it seemed, had been given instructions so 'rigid' as to preclude an honest attempt at co-ordination. However, the RAF was just as convinced of the effectiveness of its air training program, no more open to advice, and equally unwilling to make changes.[61] The one bright note came when the special Committee on Co-ordination and Training recommended the creation of a standing committee to work towards increased standardization of air training among the Allied powers.[62] The resolution received unanimous support in plenary session: there was to be an advisory committee in Washington, chaired by a senior American officer, to ensure that North American training capacity was used efficiently and that there was as much co-ordination of effort as possible. Canada, the United States, and Great Britain would be the only permanent members, but other countries could appear before the committee to make requests or to seek solutions to their problems.[63]

The press release issued at the end of the conference stated that 'The Conference has given most careful thought to the means by which the training capacity of the United Nations can be co-ordinated. Alterations in requirements ... may alter the position at any time, thus involving training adjustments of considerable magnitude. With this probability in view, and with the further object of ensuring a rapid and effective interchange of information regarding training generally, the Conference has approved the formation of a Combined Committee on Air Training.'[64] As things turned out, the exchange of information was scarcely 'rapid.' The Canadians were eager enough, choosing their representative, Air Vice-Marshal Leckie, in July, but they ran into a wall of disinterest in Washington.[65] At first the Americans explained that the government had not yet approved the conference report; then the question was apparently 'complicated' by Mexico's entry into the war.[66] Finally, on 23 September 1942, the American ambassador in Ottawa reported that the committee had been approved, that Major-General Yount would chair it, and that Captain Radford would represent the US Navy.[67] This did not mean that an actual meeting was any closer. The British would not call one on the grounds that the initiative should come from the United States since the committee had been established 'mainly to meet announcement by President Roosevelt that Ottawa Conference would promote co-ordination of air training.'[68] Nor were the Americans any readier. When General Yount disclosed in January 1943 that only the director of individual training had authority to convene a meeting, that officer responded that the Combined Chiefs of Staff must make the request.[69] They did not do so, and thus nothing happened until 26-27 April 1943, when the committee finally assembled in Washington. Thereafter it met at least seven times before the end of the war, alternating between Canada and the United States.

The effectiveness of the committee is open to question. C.P. Stacey argues that its work was useful but very limited, as 'North American training facilities were never pooled and ... no US air training was carried on in Canada.'[70] The United Kingdom Air Liaison Mission concluded, however, that the Combined Committee 'provided a link of the greatest value ... and, unquestionably, was a great stimulus to the development of air training on the soundest lines and on approximately a common basis.'[71] 'Approximately' is clearly the important word here. Just as North American training facilities were not pooled, neither were training programmes closely co-ordinated. Simple exchange of information seems, then, to have been the only achievement of the Combined Committee. So far as Canada was concerned, the committee failed in one other area – there is no evidence suggesting that it made the United States any more sympathetic to the dominion's requests for training aircraft.

When the BCATP segment of the Ottawa Air Training Conference got under way, on 22 May, there was unanimous agreement that the plan should be extended beyond March 1943. It was thought that there might have to be some curtailment of training because of shortages of operational aircraft overseas and reduced pilot requirements owing to changed bomber crew composition.[72] Should such curtailment occur, Canada's role as the 'aerodrome of democracy' would be protected by the conversion of some flying schools to operational training units. In the immediate future the need for better trained bomber pilots would add a few more flying training schools to the plan. These and other new and transferred units would expand the British Commonwealth Air Training Plan to seventy-three training schools (of which twenty-one would have double capacity) and four RAF operational training units.[73] As a result, it was estimated that 3000 aircrew could be trained to 'wings' standard each month.

Moreover, all this activity would come under Canadian control. Although the British considered 'that the RCAF lacked the administrative resources to undertake this additional burden,' and had hoped to keep the RAF schools separate from the BCATP, in the end they bowed to Canadian wishes for the incorporation of these units. They were to be brought under the BCATP umbrella and the EFTSs 'civilianized,' although their national character would be protected by the continued employment of uniformed RAF instructors.[74] Canada thus had the total responsibility for air training she had always wanted, while the RAF retained at least some of its separate identity.

The projected costs were staggering (an estimated $1,446,318,000 to carry on training until 31 March 1945), yet the sharing formula was easily devised. The formidable book-keeping involved convinced Canadian officials to accept a more straightforward arrangement. Power may have been leaning in this direction already. He told the House of Commons on 13 May that the simplest course was to consider existing accounts 'all square' and to start again on an uncomplicated per capita or block-sharing arrangement.[75] In the end Great Britain agreed to pay half of the total cost (mostly in kind) less the per capita shares of Australia and New Zealand, which between them amounted to 5 per cent. Canada would look after the rest. Unlike the terms of the initial agreement, the dominion now had the authority to purchase whatever equipment and supplies might be required without consulting her partners. Any expenditures beyond the accepted estimates would be settled after the war.[76]

Most conferences involve conflict and compromise. The Ottawa Air Training Conference was no exception. But before it ended – at 0115 hours on 3 June 1942 – Canada had secured greater control over the BCATP, including the integration of British schools into the plan, and this second Commonwealth air training conference had moved the RCAF some way down the road to maturity and independence. Moreover, it had done so in a spirit of friendly co-operation despite the distrust and ill-feeling that had marked some of the preliminary negotiations. Having expected the worst, Malcolm MacDonald was surprised and delighted by Power's 'constructive' attitude throughout the proceedings; in fact, he reported to Clement Attlee, it seemed that the Canadian minister's 'Irish-French' antipathy to the Air Ministry had been attenuated, and that the United Kingdom had won a new friend.[77] Power came away from the talks in equally good humour, and his concluding remarks about the conference's 'good-will,' 'toleration,' and 'spirit of friendliness and comradeship' had the ring of sincerity.[78] Vital commodities in any coalition war, these qualities were no less important for the harmonious operation of an Anglo-Canadian relationship that could too easily be taken for granted.

The new BCATP Agreement was signed in Ottawa on 5 June 1942 and became effective 1 July. It extended the plan until 31 March 1945. Australia and New Zealand agreed to maintain annual student quotas of 2912 and 1841, respectively. The United Kingdom undertook to provide 40 per cent of the combined establishment's capacity; the British quota was to include pupils from other parts of the Commonwealth and Allied countries, some of whom had already started to arrive with the transferred RAF schools.[79]

The revised agreement also solved the commissioning policy to Canadian satisfaction. Percentage limits were retroactively removed for RCAF pilots, observers, navigators, and air bombers. All Canadian graduates in these trades who were considered suitable could be commissioned, though under rules designed to minimize overseas disruption in the RAF. The commissioning percentages for RCAF wireless operators (air gunner) and air gunners remained unchanged except for some additional flexibility in regulations. These last limitations were removed two years later, in June 1944, but since standards were raised considerably in the interval, the percentage commissioned in these two aircrew trades remained relatively unchanged. When the first course of RCAF flight engineers graduated that year, a percentage received commissions in accordance with existing standards. In late 1944 the standards were raised a final time in order to reduce further the percentage of commissions granted to graduating RCAF personnel. All these changes applied only to Canadians; RAF,

RAAF, and RNZAF members continued to be governed by the pre-June 1942 percentage limitations, though subsequent agreements confirmed the right of Australia and New Zealand to determine their own commissioning standards as well.[80]

Meanwhile, aircrew trades were adjusted to reflect changes in bomber crew composition in the RAF's operational force. Bomber Command was still expanding and experiencing difficulty in obtaining sufficient pilots from its operational training units. Suggestions to solve this problem by using only one pilot in medium and heavy bombers emerged as early as April 1941, and were finally adopted as policy in March 1942 after interim solutions proved wasteful and ineffective. After some discussion, flight engineers, then crew members on many types of large aircraft, were chosen to act as pilot's assistants in emergencies. The work of other bomber crew members was also re-examined. The RAF decided to use only one fully qualified wireless operator in medium and heavy bombers instead of two,[81] and, in a more radical move, split the air observer's trade into its two principal functions: navigating and bomb aiming. Future training was to produce specialists for each task. This last change, designed for the medium and heavy bomber force, was unsatisfactory elsewhere, and some training had to continue for the equivalent of air observers, navigators 'B,' who could carry out both functions, as well as for a new trade combining navigation with wireless operating, the navigator 'w.'[82]

These operational changes were soon reflected in the BCATP. The training of navigators began in March 1942 with the phasing out of the air observer trade. After initial training school, navigators spent eighteen (later twenty) weeks at air observer school in a course which incorporated the astronomical navigation extension formerly taught at the Central Navigation School. The training of navigators 'B' started about the same time. After ITS, these latter attended bombing and gunnery school for six (later eight) weeks (the gunnery portion of the course was dropped in February 1944). After B&GS they took the navigator's course at AOS. Navigators 'B' were intended essentially for coastal operations, and most took a six-week general reconnaissance course before being posted to operational training units.[83]

The adoption of a single pilot in many bomber aircraft, and concurrent OTU course changes, momentarily increased the surplus of newly qualified pilots in the United Kingdom and necessitated slowing the flow from service flying training schools.[84] SFTS courses were lengthened in May. For the first time since the abandonment of the intermediate/advanced squadron system early in the plan, single-engine schools now gave pupils bombing and gunnery training. Subsequently, more emphasis was placed on this subject at all SFTSs. Other course modifications were made as the war progressed, including the addition of training in beam approach – radio landing assistance for lining up with runways in poor visibility – in March 1944.[85]

The first air bombers commenced training in August 1942. After ITS, they took an eight-week (later twelve) course at B&GS for both bombing and gunnery training. As in the case of navigators 'B,' after February 1944 the gunnery portion of the course was dropped. Air bombers completed their training with a

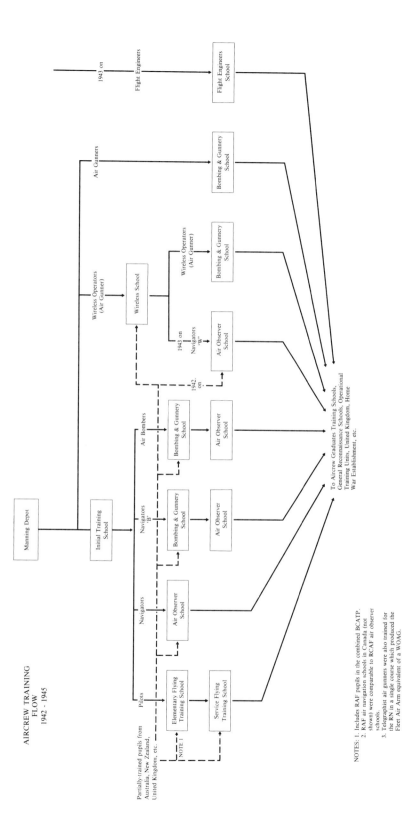

AIRCREW TRAINING
FLOW
1942 - 1945

Partially-trained pupils from
Australia, New Zealand,
United Kingdom, etc.

Manning Depot

Initial Training School

Pilots

NOTE 1

Elementary Flying Training School

Service Flying Training School

Navigators

Air Observer School

Navigators 'B'

Bombing & Gunnery School

Air Observer School

Air Bombers

Bombing & Gunnery School

Air Observer School

1942 on

1943 on Navigators 'W'

Air Observer School

Wireless Operators (Air Gunner)

Wireless School

Wireless Operators (Air Gunner)

Bombing & Gunnery School

Air Gunners

Bombing & Gunnery School

1943 on Flight Engineers

Flight Engineers School

To Aircrew Graduates Training Schools,
General Reconnaissance Schools, Operational
Training Units, United Kingdom, Home
War Establishment, etc.

NOTES: 1. Includes RAF pupils in the combined BCATP.
2. RAF air navigation schools in Canada (not
   shown) were comparable to RCAF air observer
   schools.
3. Telegraphist air gunners were also trained for
   the RN in a single course which produced the
   Fleet Air Arm equivalent of a WOAG.

six-week (later ten) course at AOS. These airmen also acted as assistant pilots on aircraft without flight engineers and were trained to fly straight and level on a given course in an emergency.[86]

Training started for navigators 'w' in the fall of 1942 to produce a combination navigator, wireless operator, and emergency air gunner for night-fighter intruders. At first the courses were composed entirely of RAF personnel, who received an eighteen-week wireless course in the United Kingdom before coming to Canada for twenty-two weeks of navigation training. RCAF navigators 'w' were introduced in December 1943, selected from the top wireless operator (air gunner) pupils graduating from wireless school.[87]

At about the same time, Canadian training began for flight engineers in response to an Air Ministry request for this aircrew category for RCAF heavy bomber crews. The course was twenty-three weeks long, followed by a seven-week 'type' training course on specific aircraft in Great Britain. 'Type' training was conducted in Canada from July 1944 with multi-engine aircraft provided by the Air Ministry. Flight engineers destined for coastal commands received an extra six-week air firing course.[88]

These trade and course changes caused no significant difficulties. The hectic early years were over. By the end of 1942 the largest construction, supply, and instructional problems had all been solved, and aircrew graduates were being produced in satisfactory numbers in every trade. The training war in Canada had been won.

8

The Plan in Maturity

Training an airman, especially in the key role of pilot, was more complex than that for any other category of fighting man, involving a vast infrastructure that demanded great expenditures of time and money. Yet the growth of the air arm was such that thousands more aircrew were needed each year. Sheer output – 'gearing up' the system to produce the numbers of personnel required – had inevitably been the chief occupation of the builders of the British Commonwealth Air Training Plan.

Quantity, however, was only one half of the training equation. Any assessment of the BCATP must also include an examination of the quality of training received by its graduates. The plan was expected to produce a basic kind of airman; in the case of pilots, one capable of flying advanced training aircraft both visually and on instruments. Operational training and conversion to high-performance service aircraft were the responsibilities of operational training units. These were principally in Great Britain, where the RAF brought graduates from the various training theatres to a common standard and prepared them for combat. A certain degree of variance in training was inevitable in an organization as large and diverse as the Empire Air Training Scheme. Training syllabi, produced in the United Kingdom, were common to all the Commonwealth components of the plan, but how closely they were followed and how accurately applied was a matter of national responsibility.

Within Canada, flying standards were set and supervised by the Central Flying School at Trenton. In August 1940 the CFS instituted a programme to report on the quality of instruction in the BCATP's training establishments.[1] Visiting flights of CFS instructors made regular tours of inspection, testing both staff and students of every flying school to determine their shortcomings and suggest remedies. As a result, by early 1942 the officer commanding CFS was able to report that 'the standard expected [for a Class I instructor] is greatly rising and consequently a greater degree of skill is required than possible two years ago.'[2]

Most of those selected for Flying Instructor School [FIS] went there immediately after completing their service training. Although they were the best of the SFTS graduates, they could be posted as qualified instructors with fewer than 300 hours of flying time, most of which had been spent flying training sequences and drills. They lacked the degree of flying experience that would have impressed upon them the importance of each sequence. As No 1 Visiting Flight pointed out in April 1943, a 'large percentage of Instructors have had experience on training aircraft only, and thus fail to appreciate both the necessity and value of some parts of flying training. They also become somewhat disappointed, confused and bewildered when some pupils of theirs write from overseas, saying they are flying this or that Service type of aircraft and telling them of flying characteristics of which they as Instructors have no knowledge.' As a result, instruction was often 'wooden.' It was noted at both EFTSs and SFTSs 'that there is a great tendency on the part of instructors to teach sequences rather than to use sequences and their demonstrations to teach pupils how to fly ...' The instructor became 'artificial and unconvincing, dull and stereotyped because he fails to link up his demonstration with what actually happens while flying. Many Instructors fail to give their pupils the training they should have because they have little or no knowledge of how to teach, but merely present to the pupil a series of sequences taught to them at F.I.S..'[3]

Unfortunately, the most obvious solution to the problem, posting tour-expired pilots from operational commands to SFTSs in Canada, was not feasible. Those fortunate pilots who survived an operational tour and appeared to have instructional qualities were normally sent to OTUs or advanced flying units [AFUS] overseas where their operational experience was more urgently required.[4] The only solution the CFS could offer, the establishment of a visiting flight of service aircraft to give familiarization flights to instructors, was inadequate and could hardly solve the basic problem of having talented but inexperienced pilots teaching trainees flying drills which they themselves had learned but had never had to apply.[5]

These problems could not be overcome by strict adherence to RAF training manuals, even though it was stressed that these books should be regarded as 'the pilot's bible.' For example, in 1941 the visiting flight reported that 'Spinning was causing considerable concern among instructors in several S.F.T.S.s as indicated by their being definitely uneasy about recovering from spins of more than two turns.'[6] Three years later, the problem remained the same, and staff pilots were found to lack 'confidence during the spin and the recovery ... In many case[s] the Examining Officer had to take over to complete the recovery.'[7] Timidity aside, instructors failed to understand fully the purpose of the exercise. 'Instructors invariably leave the impression they are teaching how to spin an aircraft, rather than how to recognize conditions that might cause a spin, and how to recover as quickly as possible. Demonstrations are frequently harsh and quite unlike anything which might happen in actual flight.' Similarly, pupils were 'being taught to stall an aircraft, rather than to recognize conditions inducing stall and to recover before loss of control.'[8] Low flying and single-engine demonstrations suffered as well. 'At all Schools the bad weather low flying sequence is the only one demonstrated and practised. Many Instructors babble on about apparent skid, slip, increased and decreased speeds etc., in no wind conditions. These should only be pointed out when clearly visible to the student ... Instructor's demonstrations and pupils' S.E. flying [single-engine procedure in twin-engine aircraft] shows that much is to be desired in the understanding of s.e. practice. ... The main points noted were that the pupils made a wild scramble in the cockpit on one engine failing, going through a form of cockpit check which obviously meant little or nothing to them.' Inexperience and low morale led to a certain lack of dedication among some instructors as well: 'In spite of the emphasis placed upon the importance of Instrument Flying many Instructors are not keeping up their own Instrument practice and in teaching they are prone to stuff a pupil under the hood long enough to put in the time without teaching him how to fly by instruments.'[9]

These conditions were far from ideal, but the BCATP had no choice other than to use the inexperienced, often frustrated products of its own training system. However, such institutional shortcomings were partially overcome by the pupils themselves who spent much of their training flying solo, practising the sequences demonstrated by their instructors. As the RAF discovered in 1940-1 when they cut the SFTS course to a mere ten weeks, the greatest single factor affecting the quality of graduates was simply the amount of flying time they had been allowed. Course length, though, was beyond the RCAF's control; the training period was set in the United Kingdom according to the RAF's manpower needs.[10] At the end of 1941, the British air member for training, Air Marshal A.G.R. Garrod, took several steps to increase the quality of training, including lengthening courses, though still acknowledging the need for more aircrew. He had recently visited Canada, where he noted that the standard of training 'was good and the instructors generally ... of high quality ... school personnel had shown great enthusiasm and drive in their training duties.' He had toured both transferred RAF schools and Canadian ones, he told the Empire Air Training Scheme Committee in London, and found that 'On the whole there was nothing to choose between the two types of schools from the point of view of efficiency of training.'[11] So long as the BCATP produced the necessary quantity of pilots of sufficient quality to satisfy the RAF, there would be few complaints from overseas.

Initially, comments from the RAF on Canadian-trained pilots were very favourable. They had a 'standard [of] discipline and keenness well above average and refreshing influence on unit personnel.'[12] Air Vice-Marshal Robert Leckie, the air member for training, was not satisfied, however, and requested that the OTUs be canvassed for 'frank criticism.' 'There must be faults in the product,' he noted, 'and I would like to get on top of them as soon as possible.'[13] At the end of April 1941, the chief of the air staff, Air Vice-Marshal L.S. Breadner, received an RAF signal stating that the pilots were 'making favourable impression, only shortcomings [were] basic knowledge navigation below UK standard and signalling knowledge and ability poor.'[14] Two months later, the RAF informed the RCAF that further OTU reports stated that the general standard of flying 'has remained good.' However, 'it has been stressed that pupils cannot have too much instrument flying training in view of difficulty which they experience in accustoming themselves to black-out conditions.' (In wartime Britain street lights were never lit. Vehicles travelling after dark could only do so in the faint glow supplied by heavily-screened headlights, and it was a serious offence for a householder or businessman to allow the slightest glimmer of light to escape through doorways or windows. The intention was to make navigation more difficult for enemy bomber crews, but allied crews flying at night also suffered.) The OTUs also reported the general standard of pilot navigation as 'satisfactory and deficiencies appear in the main to be due to lack of knowledge of modern equipment. Main difficulty continues to be experience in map reading.'[15] A year later, the chief instructor of an RAF air flying unit told Group Captain R.A. Cameron, the RCAF liaison officer, that 'pilots arriving from Canada required only one or two landings by night before being sent solo, notwithstanding the blackout conditions which exist. I was naturally very interested in this comment after all the hull-a-baloo which has been raised about night flying training conditions in Canada.'[16]

In the spring of 1943 the British increased their efforts to gather information on the quality of aircrew being produced by the Empire Air Training Scheme. In May the Air Ministry asked the RAF's Flying Training Command, responsible for all pre-OTU aircrew training in the United Kingdom, to comment upon the skills of pilots trained to service standards overseas and now undergoing more advanced work in Britain. By that time, of course, the BCATP was churning out vast quantities of graduates every month, and eventual Allied victory seemed assured; the Air Ministry could afford to be more choosy about quality. A quarterly return was to be rendered, in order that the ministry might be able 'to give constructive criticism to the overseas training centres.'[17]

The initial Air Ministry return – the bulk of it from 21 Group, whose nine advanced flying units prepared pilots for bomber OTUs, with 23 Group's four AFUS completing the picture – generally found the Canadian-trained pilots' flying ability 'to be low in relation to the flying hours completed.' In addition, navigation was 'found to be of a low standard,' aerobatics were 'generally not well performed,' instrument flying was 'generally below standard,' and the proficiency exhibited during night flying was 'not compatible with the hours of night flying recorded in log books.' By contrast, the Australian-trained pilots were viewed as being 'of a high standard' while pilots from New Zealand and South Africa were of 'nearly as high' a standard as the Australians. The commander of 21 Group, Air Vice-Marshal R.P. Willock, believed that the reports 'help to confirm my contention that the quality of training both in the U.S.A. and CANADA still leaves much to be desired; and I submit that we should neither allow ourselves to be deceived by quantative [sic] production methods nor humbugged by diplomatic or political considerations.'[18]

Subsequent returns continued to assess the Canadian-trained pilots as being of inferior quality to their Commonwealth colleagues. Of particular concern to the British was the reported lack of discipline among Canadians. The director of flying training in the United Kingdom, Air Commodore D.V. Carnegie, wrote to the UK Air Liaison Mission in Ottawa that the 'remarks that worry me most are those under "General Remarks" appertaining both to flying and to ground school, and these refer to the poor standard of discipline.' In fact, discipline standards had previously been noted to be 'very high' in Canada, only suffering 'deterioration' overseas.[19]

Nonetheless, this perception of RCAF pilots clearly influenced the RAF's confidence in the Canadians' ability to be effective aircraft captains. In his first quarterly report, Willock had stated that Australian 'Officers have been selected with a greater regard for the qualities required.'[20] This attitude reflected the Air Ministry's conviction 'that gentlemen made the best aircrew.'[21] They had earlier expressed concern about the decreasing numbers of British aircrew who were 'of the middle and upper classes, [young men] who are the backbone of this country, when they leave the public schools.'[22] As the British historian Max Hastings has pointed out, the RAF attitude to aircrew discipline differed somewhat from that of their Commonwealth colleagues, who 'believed that it was their very intimacy with their crews, their indifference to rank, that often made them such strong teams in the air.'[23] The point to be made is that the British did not consider discipline as a matter that only concerned deportment on the ground; rather, it directly affected their assessment of an airman as an operational pilot.

Different standards of discipline did not, in themselves, mean inferior flying skills. Soon after receiving the first set of quarterly returns from Nos 21 and 23 Groups, the Air Ministry enquired of Coastal Command (whose crews usually went straight from SFTS to OTUS) if it had noticed 'any marked variance ... between those pilots trained in the U.K., Canada, Southern Rhodesia, Australia, etc. If so, your brief comments covering the situation would be appreciated.' The response was very brief indeed. 'The C[oastal] C[ommand] Training Group have found no marked variance between these pilots.'[24]

Coastal Command's conclusion doubtless had something to do with the fact that none of the SFTS graduates had previous experience with the operational aircraft flown at the command's OTUS. This was not the case at twin-engine AFUS which flew Airspeed Oxfords, the same aircraft used in New Zealand, South African, Rhodesian, and many Australian service schools; Canadian pilots trained on Avro Ansons or Cessna Cranes and were therefore initially at a disadvantage.[25] Another explanation for Coastal Command's judgment may be that the pick of the EFTS graduates were selected for single-engine (ie, fighter) SFTSs and the best of the twin-engine SFTS graduates were assigned to flying-instructor training or sent on general-reconnaissance courses which automatically oriented them towards maritime patrol duties. 'The fact that the lower half of each course go to the U.K. immediately after passing out at S.F.T.S.,' read a Bomber Command memorandum of December 1943, 'is evident by the comparatively small proportion of officer pilots undergoing instruction at [Bomber] O.T.U. This is so in spite of the free and easy award of Commissions at S.F.T.S. ... the overwhelming tendency is to post the best pilots to F.I.S.s [flying instructor schools] and the brainiest and more capable pilots to G.R. courses.'[26]

Responding to this complaint, Air Marshal Sir Peter Drummond, the British Air Council's air member for personnel, admitted to Sir Arthur Harris, the air officer commanding-in-chief Bomber Command, that 'When I took over ... I was horrified to find that the practice of creaming off pupils for training as instructors, which no doubt started as an emergency measure, has come to be accepted as a regular procedure. I have been doing my best to put a stop to it as far as possible, but, of course, the difficulty is that there is such a small return of pilots from operational Commands to the training Commands.' He went on to report that the number of general reconnaissance courses being given in Canada had been 'considerably reduced' and were now taking only a small proportion of the SFTS graduates. Moreover, one of Drummond's staff officers had recently visited Canada, arranging with Leckie 'that the major proportion of the best pilots ex-E.F.T.S. were to be fed into twin-engine S.F.T.S's.'[27] He did not add, because doubtless Harris already knew, that these changes would take at least nine months, perhaps a year, to make themselves felt at the 'sharp end.'

As the British were well aware, quarterly reports were impressionistic[28] and based on instructors' assessments of random numbers of students at several different training units. One staff officer had minuted on the original quarterly return that 'These are the first quarterly reports for which we asked. We cannot take action yet, as we must see first if subsequent reports bear out the general assumptions of both 21 & 23 groups.'[29] The reports also lacked consistency. The training in Australia was found to be 'of a high standard'[30] in the first report and 'still weak' or 'rather below average' in the next.[31] What was needed, decided the ministry, was an objective test.

Such a test was instituted in the autumn of 1943 by the Research Flight of the Empire Central Flying School and subsequently given to 764 pilots drawn from the overseas training schemes who had all completed SFTS in the spring and summer of 1943 and were about to commence advanced flying training. The numbers from each training scheme were roughly proportional to the size of the scheme – 153 of them had graduated from both elementary and service RCAF schools, 152 from RAF schools in Canada, 105 from Southern Rhodesian schools, 56 from South African schools, 111 from RAAF schools, 53 from RNZAF schools, 49 from British flying training schools in the United States, and 85 had been trained through various interdominion combinations, such as the Australian pilots who had completed EFTS at home and SFTS in Canada. For various technical reasons, 132 of the total were eventually dropped from the comparisons.

The pilots were tested in groups of twelve, each being tested twice on the same day by a total of fourteen instructors. 'Great care was taken that the officers should achieve a common standard of assessment. The test was thoroughly discussed with them; they flew with each other and in pairs with pilots drawn from a (P[ilot]) A.F.U., and cross checks and comparisons were made until it was found that a satisfactory standard of assessment was being obtained by all.'[32] The candidates trained on single-engine aircraft were tested on Miles Master IIs, machines which none of them had previously flown, while the twin-engine pilots were tested on Airspeed Oxfords. These were the same aircraft flown at the AFUS. All of the New Zealand, South African, and Rhodesian pilots had already trained on these aircraft, while the overwhelming majority of Canadian-trained pilots had flown only Avro Ansons or Cessna Cranes. Consequently, pilots were separated into those who had had experience on Oxfords and those who had trained on Ansons. Fortunately for the purposes of comparison between Canada and the rest of the Commonwealth, the Australian pilots were almost equally divided between the two groups. Scoring was numerical, numbers were tabulated, and a statistical analysis compiled.

Overall, the 'general impression left in the minds of the testing officers was that the ... standard of performance was good, and that the morale of the pilots was high.' The testing officers found that the most noticeable weaknesses, and the ones which required the greatest attention, were common to all of the pilots, regardless of where they were trained. 'The standard was highest on Taxying and Take-off and climb, and lowest on General Engine handling and Aerobatics. Instrument Flying and Airmanship were also below the general level. The weakest points on the whole test were use of throttle, warm air, mixture etc., use of engine in aerobatics, and overshoot procedure on instruments. Control of rate of descent on instruments was also poor, as was the handling of the ancillary controls after landing.'[33] Among wholly RCAF-trained pilots, the one area which was consistently below the standard of other trainees 'was the checking of vital actions before and after take off. They also showed signs of falling short of the standard expected in England in other drills and procedures, and it seems that the training authorities might usefully give special consideration to these points. With this exception there is nothing calling for particular comment.'[34]

Unlike the quarterly reports that Nos 21 and 23 Groups had been submitting at the same time, the ECFS report found that RCAF-trained Anson pilots were as good as RAAF Anson pilots and slightly better than the pilots trained in RAF Anson schools. The marks achieved by RCAF Harvard pilots were somewhat below those of the Rhodesian pilots, who were themselves below the standard of RAF Harvard pilots. These differences are of interest when the make-up of RAF and RCAF schools is considered. Although the RAF schools in Canada had been placed under RCAF administrative control at the Ottawa Air Training Conference, they retained their British character throughout the war, and continued to be staffed almost exclusively by RAF officers and NCOs. RCAF schools, however, were staffed almost entirely by RCAF officers.[35] The fact that the RAF Harvard schools were able to produce the highest quality single-engine pilots may be a reflection of the Royal Air Force's greater familiarity with high-performance single-engine fighters during the interwar years.

When the testers compared RAAF pilots trained on Ansons in Australia with those trained in Canada, specific differences in abilities were apparent.

The Australian trained pilots were inferior in Cockpit check; they tended to be rather less good at Taxying, significantly so at lookout. Their lookout on Steep Turns and their turns in Single Engine flying [flying a twin-engine aircraft on one engine] were below those of the Canadian trained. Their check of the signal area before joining the circuit was very inferior and the quality of their landings was also not up to the Canadian standard.

On the other hand, the Australian trained were much superior on vital actions after take off and their procedure for Single Engine flying was also better. They showed an advantage in their vital actions for landing and in their overshoot procedure, on the instrument circuit. Their handling of the ancillary controls after landing was decidedly better, as was their General Engine handling throughout the test.[36]

Obviously, the ideal was to do well in all skill areas. A pilot whose 'vital actions' on take-off were below average, or whose 'lookout' or check of the signal area was poor, could all too easily kill both himself and his crew either in the course of a routine training flight or on an operational mission. But when coned by searchlights over Essen, or with a night fighter on his tail over Dortmund, monitoring his instruments correctly would momentarily be less important than the ability to corkscrew out of danger; and with one (or even two) engines knocked out by flak, applying the correct procedures for flying on the remaining engine or engines would matter a good deal less than the actual ability to keep the crippled aircraft in the air.

The RAF appears to have been reasonably satisfied with the 'basic training'[37] received by the plan's graduates, despite what the ECFS had earlier termed 'the usual minor faults and omissions' found in student pilots.[38] British concerns with the standard of discipline exhibited by Canadians once they left North America was a separate matter. The director of flying training felt that part of the problem lay with the AFUs and suggested that the Canadians required 'firmer handling' since they tended to relax 'after the strict discipline to which they have been accustomed' in Canadian schools. 'It seems to be the Canadians who throw their notebooks overboard under the impression that they will not be needed again. When they are in this frame of mind, ie, "let's get on with the war," they probably find it all the more difficult to accustom themselves to the long periods of training that still lie ahead.'[39] Discipline aside, by October 1944 the RAF had informed Canada that the 'main deficiencies in overseas training have been eliminated, and it is becoming increasingly difficult to discriminate between the standard of training in one country as compared with another.'[40]

Although it is by no means clear how much of the RAF's other assessments of Canadian standards ever found their way back to BCATP authorities,[41] the ECFS Research Flight report was sent to Ottawa in mid-September 1944. However, by that time the BCATP was rapidly winding down, and there was an enormous surplus of pilots in the pipeline. All but near-perfect pilot candidates were being 'washed out' in order to reduce the flow of graduates.[42] The report seems to have disappeared into some bureaucratic limbo, since there are no indications of action being taken to correct the specific weaknesses outlined in it. Only the report's covering letter now lies in the Public Archives of Canada.[43]

The RAF may have preferred to transmit criticism informally and verbally. However, forty years later Air Vice-Marshal T.A. Lawrence, who held a series of important field appointments in the BCATP between 1940 and 1944 (culminating in eighteen months as air officer commanding of No 2 Training Command), could not remember any 'feedback' at all from RAF operational commands: 'There may have been some comments and criticisms passed to the RAF Liaison Officer in Ottawa, who may have passed them to RCAF Headquarters, but none were passed down to the Command level. At No 2 Training Command they were "pretty much" left on their own, and even RCAF Headquarters did not bother them as long as the training quota was met.' Only once was Lawrence in direct contact with the Royal Air Force's liaison officer in Ottawa, when he requested the dismissal of two RAF school commanders because they were getting behind in their quotas. 'The officers were removed,' he recalled, 'with little fuss.'[44]

As might be expected, the BCATP experienced training problems with other members of the aircrew team as well. At times the pressure to produce the necessary quantity of aircrew meant that some graduates were pushed through simply to meet quotas. In August 1943, for example, the air officer commanding No 12 Operational Training Group, RCAF, complained to the commanding officers of his two general reconnaissance schools that 'It has been noted from recent course reports that some navigators are being allowed to pass out from their G.[eneral] R.[econnaissance] S.[chool] when they have apparently failed the G.R.S. examinations in navigation ... In future all units are to ensure that observers are proficient in navigation before they are passed out as fit to an O.T.U. for operational training.'[45]

Perhaps part of the problem in that case lay with the service bureaucracy and the emphasis on a 'pilot's air force' so often bemoaned by other Second World War aircrew. In October the RCAF's director of operational training noted that restricted establishments for navigation instructors, particularly for those of flight lieutenant or squadron leader rank, meant that many qualified men could not be employed.[46] That was an issue that continued to bedevil navigation training throughout the war – a kind of Canadian 'Catch 22' which seemed to decree that, if a man was ideally qualified to do the job, he was by definition over-ranked for it and consequently could not be used.

With other aircrew trades a lack of operationally experienced instructors was a factor, but problems resulted in the main from the obsolete equipment foisted off on the schools. It was not until the latter part of 1942, for example, that turretted aircraft began to become available to bombing and gunnery schools.[47] When they did, one B&GS promptly reported that 'in general scores are 25% lower from turretted aircraft.' The Air Armament School at Mountain View, Ont. (which stood in a similar relationship to B&GSs as the Central Flying School did to EFTSs and SFTSs) found that 'the difficulties experienced with the turrets have been due to a variety of reasons, ranging from faulty turret design to inexperience on the part of the Instructors themselves regarding the stoppages and difficulties likely to be encountered in a turret exercise.'[48] In May 1943 the chief of the air staff still had to tell his air officers commanding training commands that the RAF had remarked upon the 'insufficient knowledge' of harmonization of turret guns (ie, the setting of the guns to give a certain spread and pattern of bullets at a standard range) and of the Browning machine-gun, which, with its faster rate of fire, was now universally fitted to the turrets of operational aircraft. BCATP graduates were still being trained on the old Vickers GO (gas operated) gun.[49]

Gunnery difficulties were compounded by a blunder in assigning men for training as gunners, as Air Vice-Marshal Leckie was the first to admit. 'When recruiting for the class started, I am well aware that I suggested that educational standards were not necessary and that the local farmer's boy who could use a gun and had the necessary guts, would and should, make a useful air gunner. It now appears as a result of experience, that in this contention I was wholly wrong ... On planning air gunners' courses, a figure of wastage of 10% wa estimated ... Accumulative wastage up to October 9, 1942, was 6.5%. Sinc then the wastage has steadily increased from 6.5% up to 11.1%, the last figure t hand, and it is still rising. I am therefore compelled to recast courses at the B.&G Schools and base them on an anticipated wastage of 20%.'[50]

The BCATP also suffered initial difficulties with its wireless operators (ai gunner). The first 600 to arrive in the United Kingdom were 'definitely belov standard' and had to be given special refresher training before continuing on t OTUS.[51] The low standard was attributed by the RAF to faulty instruction, ol equipment, and a lack of keenness on the part of the trainees, all aggravated b built-in training delays.[52] Bombing and gunnery school interrupted the wireles practice of the new wireless operators, and travel time and lengthy waits befor they arrived at their new units overseas led to further loss of skill. The Britis took steps to provide equipment on ocean transports, and suggested that trainin, be undertaken at the embarkation depot and during the voyage.[53] As a result, policy was adopted of giving graduates further training while awaitin embarkation in order to maintain their proficiency. Periodic efficiency check were also instituted at bombing and gunnery schools, and arrangements made fo tests and training during the voyage overseas.

Air bombing was a new trade, introduced only when the observer functio was split between navigators and air bombers in early 1942. The division o responsibilities had an immediate effect on the standard of air bombing: an average error of 168 yards for high-level (10,000 ft) day bombing and 176. yards for night bombing quickly became 127 yards for day exercises and 15 yards at night. For the new trade of specialist air bomber the increase in accurac was soon even greater – the average error was reduced to 113 yards by day an 136 yards by night.[54] The Air Ministry, however, was dissatisfied with th accuracy of bombing operations, and notified the RCAF in December 1942 tha 'the standard of air bomber training has ... been found to be inadequate an compares unfavourably with that of American bombardiers.'[55]

The RCAF itself was dissatisfied with the method of air bomber training use by the RAF and felt that certain aspects of American training could be adopted i Canada with beneficial effects. Of particular concern to the Canadians was th quality of analysis of air bombing exercises. In September 1942 the RCAF liaiso officer in London reported his findings after examining an RAF school i operation:

I have reserved my comment until such time as I was able to see what was being done i the U.K. for I was always faced with the argument that, 'it was working all right in th U.K. so it was probably just lack of experience.' Well now I have seen, and I am satisfie that the U.K. Schools aren't getting one whit more out of their analysis sections than w are *but* everyone thinks that they are operating smoothly, and producing results. I hav taken the trouble to sit and watch what goes on and it isn't at all impressive – despi what people say ... I recommend that we try the American situation ... they take the re sults of the air exercises to the classroom with the class instructor and do the analys there instead of at the plotting office ... I have mentioned this scheme to experience people in the U.K. and their unanimous comment is that 'analysis must be done immediately after landing to be any use at all.' When I counter this remark by the statement that after 15 years' effort in one direction without spectacular success it's almost worth trying something else which just *might* produce results, the only answer is: 'Well maybe it will' ... I therefore say, new or not, American or not, let's get on and give it a try.[56]

Some of the training difficulties were undoubtedly caused by the fact that when the air observer trade was split into navigation and air bombing, the best mathematicians among the recruits were selected for navigator training while the balance was left to become air bombers. To help overcome these problems, the length of the air bombing course at bombing and gunnery school was extended from eight to twelve weeks in 1942.[57] More time was spent in practice and more bombs were dropped, while training emphasis was changed from 'application bombing exercises,' which judged the proximity of individual bombs to a specified target, to 'grouping exercises,' in which the measure of success was the radius of an imaginary circle encompassing six bombs. Tight groupings measured consistency rather than accuracy and reflected more closely the essentials of the technique of 'area bombing' that obsessed Bomber Command in the strategic air offensive against Germany. To pass their course, air bombers had to register at least two 'close' groups of eighty-yards radius or less (converted to an altitude of 10,000 feet) in six exercises.[58]

The Air Ministry did not request quarterly reports from its observer AFUs on the standard of navigation and air bomber training until May 1944. The first of these was received in September. The AFUs did not find any great variance among training theatres in either navigators or air bombers. Navigators were generally found to be slow in practical work but reasonably sound in the theory of navigation. The greatest problem arose from their unfamiliarity with European conditions in regard to map reading, meteorology, and the navigational aids available in the United Kingdom. It was also found that with 'few exceptions pupils do not at first appreciate the necessity of the AFU course & look upon it as merely another "waiting pool."'[59] The air bombers' scores on bombing exercises were found to be satisfactory 'but on average the standard pupil is only considered as a fair A[ir] B[omber]. Lapse of time between training periods may account for this to a certain degree.' Map reading was 'poor to start with' and the RAF instructors could find little evidence that the air bombers had previously received training in navigation. As with other aircrew, air bombers trained in the dominions experienced difficulty adjusting to European conditions.[60]

Those seeking further statistics and facts concerning the BCATP in all its vast and complex detail can find many of them in another publication of the Department of National Defence, F.J. Hatch's *The Aerodrome of Democracy*.[61] However, a general feeling for the plan in operation can perhaps best be acquired by recounting the experiences and impressions of two students, the first from 1940-1 when the BCATP was in its infancy, the second from 1943-4 when it had just passed its peak. Pilots have been chosen because they constituted the largest single graduating trade, because their training was more complicated, expensive, and prolonged than that of any other aircrew member, and because the pilot was the key member of every crew. In the end, the success of the plan stood or fell on the calibre of pilot training.

Recruiting for the BCATP began in the early spring of 1940. Andrew Robert MacKenzie was one of the first to apply, attracted, like most of his contemporaries, by the 'glamour of the air force.'[62] Aircrew candidates had to be fit males between eighteen and twenty-eight years of age, with at least junior matriculation standing. 'Andy' MacKenzie was nineteen with junior matriculation from Quebec, and most of his fellow pupils were eighteen and nineteen-year-olds – a few were in their early twenties – and high-school graduates. In those early weeks of the plan there was much confusion and uncertainty in enrolment and training patterns. Aircrew trade quotas were known to exist and MacKenzie delayed his enlistment for a week in order to avoid an air gunner quota which he believed was being made up at that time, a delay he later found to be 'a lot of nonsense because we were all recruited as aircrew. The selection was made in ITS ... later on.'

On 7 June 1940 he was taken on strength at 1 Manning Depot, a 'lonely although exciting' experience for a young man who had never been away from home before – 'twelve hundred men all in the same room' in the horse palace on the Toronto exhibition grounds. He received an ill-fitting new uniform and, with others who could afford it, immediately had it 'tailored to look a little nicer,' a vanity that cost each of them about fifty dollars. Just two weeks later, on 24 June 1940, he was posted directly to a four-week course at 1 ITS, located at the Toronto Hunt Club. The school's main function was aircrew trade selection, and the principal tool used to select pilot trainees was the Link trainer, a crude electro-mechanical classroom simulator that tested hand and eye co-ordination. Most volunteers wanted to be pilots, so they concentrated on doing well on the Link. A few preferred to be observers, encouraged by the 'rumours ... that the prestige job was the navigator.' In the end, about half of MacKenzie's course were selected as air gunners. They were the most disappointed. 'Some were heart-broken. Tears.' 'They did a parade down Eglinton Avenue ... saying .. "We've been screwed; we are air gunners."' The problem was, recalled MacKenzie, 'we all wanted to be pilots, and navigators rationalized that they were the smarter ones and they would tell the pilots where to fly. The air gunner had no excuse. They were just going to be sitting in the tail ... it was just not the job they wanted.' None of the pupils felt that they could complain, however, for 'none of us really knew what the criteria were' for aircrew trade selection.

MacKenzie was chosen for pilot training and was posted to 4 EFTS, Windsor Mills, Que., on 21 July 1940. Like other EFTSs, it was civilian-run with civilian instructors and 'the food was nice. They had civilian caterers.' Ground school continued, including more Link training. 'It was certainly valuable ... a little more on the instrument bit ... A little more advanced. I think we expected that and we rather enjoyed it, although Link trainer could never replace the aeroplane.'

MacKenzie 'had never been in an airplane in my life.' The school was equipped with Fleet Finches, one of two elementary trainers initially used by the

RCAF. A fabric-covered biplane, with two open cockpits in tandem, it was powered by a radial air-cooled engine and had a maximum speed of 113 mph. He found it 'a nice, kind, little aeroplane,' though the primitive Gosport equipment used to give dual instruction in the air was 'an absolutely terrible system. It was practically a tube, a flexible tube' through which the instructor talked 'into your ears ... like listening at the end of a hose.' MacKenzie went solo after ten hours. His first solo landing was complicated. As he approached, other aircraft were taking off in front of him, forcing him to go around three times. 'I'll never get this thing on the ground,' he thought. His feelings changed once he was down. 'It was fantastic. Full of elation.'

Although they were given specific manoeuvres to fly while in the air, '99% of us went up and did aerobatics ... instead of practising the set sequences.' Low flying was especially exciting, 'down, kicking the tree tops, flying around just like a high speed car.' The only disconcerting part of the course was watching a fellow pupil 'wash out.' 'You would come back in the barracks and see some kid packing his bags,' he remembered. 'There were no farewell parties. You packed your bags and ... snuck off ... It was a slight and very sad affair.'

Elementary training was followed by service instruction as either a single- or dual-engine pilot. There was no 'special fighter pilot clique' among the pupils, but MacKenzie had always wanted to fly fighters and asked for single-engine training. There was no problem about that in September 1940, with the Battle of Britain at its climax. Although the pilot production ratio was supposed to be one single-engine pilot to two dual-engine ones (already scheduled to change towards a ratio of 1:6.5), twin-engine trainers were in extremely short supply, and the first SFTSs opened as single-engine schools. He was posted to the first transferred RAF SFTS, No 31, just then being established in Kingston, Ont., and intended to train Royal Navy Fleet Air Arm pilots. The first British pupils were not due to arrive until the end of 1940, and, in the interim, two regular BCATP classes were trained at No 31. MacKenzie was on the first of these courses, arriving there on 6 October 1940 and starting work two days later.

He found the school efficient, the discipline 'quite noticeable,' and the instructors stiff. The biggest shock was the 'really strange' British food. 'For instance, one of their favourite breakfasts is semi-cooked bacon, tomatoes, and toast. So, if you go up ... and do air battles ... after you have greasy bacon and stewed tomatoes, oh boy, is it ever tough to keep it down.' Such culture shock worked both ways. The British war diarist at 31 SFTS noted the problem differently.

Our messing in the Airmen's Mess is not satisfactory, due to poor cooking but mainly the difference in the ration issued compared with the U.K. There is no cash element and the rations do not include either Liver, Kidney, Tinned Fruit or Mustard, so these popular dishes are never seen on the menu. They do include, however, Rice, Macaroni and Prunes – all highly unpopular dishes with British Troops.

This is the only country I have served in where both the rates of pay and the standard messing has been different to normal service practice. Undoubtedly the men do not appreciate the changes.

... These pin pricks, are in sum, a serious proposition.[63]

MacKenzie flew Harvards at Kingston. The Harvard was a metal-skinned monoplane boasting enclosed cockpits, a controllable pitch propeller, retractable undercarriage and flaps, with a maximum speed of 180 mph. Moving up to this larger aircraft 'was a tremendous step ... It just scared the daylights out of you.' This feeling did not last long, for the second Canadian course trained on Battles. 'The Fairey Battle was twice as big as a Harvard. Once we got used to flying a Harvard and got over the shock of going from a Fleet Finch to a Harvard, then the Fairey Battle was so much bigger that we were a little bit jealous of the junior course ... [Their aircraft had] been in the Battle of Britain and the Fall of France and ... were real war planes.' Slow and underarmed, the Fairey Battle had proven an operational disaster, however, and was being relegated to training status as fast as the RAF could find better machines.

Link training continued, mostly concentrated on instrument flying 'underhood.' For the first time, MacKenzie flew at night and loved it. 'The whole thing was exciting ... It was much better than going to a party.' They now had more freedom while flying. Officially, they were given the impression that stunting would be punished, but as future fighter pilots they were also 'almost encouraged' to experiment with the aircraft. Inevitably they took chances MacKenzie and two others looped the Thousand Island Bridge over the St Lawrence River in formation one day, a stunt that, years later, 'scares me to look back upon.' During 1941 there were 170 fatal training accidents, forty of them being attributed to unauthorized low flying and aerobatics by pilots whose skills did not match their daring.[64] For MacKenzie and his companions in single-engine schools the hallmark of good flying was 'freedom and bravado.' They got white scarves and flying goggles and taxied and flew their aircraft 'like the Canadian Red Baron.' There was still something of the First World War's adventurism and romanticism in flying, an air of exciting improvisation about the whole experience.

Although steps were already underway to reduce SFTS training to a homogeneous ten-week course, MacKenzie's school had not yet implemented these changes. No 31 SFTS ran a thirteen-week, two-phased course at intermediate and advanced levels, the latter concentrating mostly on formation flying and aerobatics in a separate section under different instructors. In accordance with prewar and initial wartime practice, wings were awarded after the intermediate course. MacKenzie received his without ceremony several days later. 'We got our wings in navigation class. You see our training didn't stop .. Group Captain [A.] Shekleton [RAF, commander of 31 SFTS] came in and said, in his British accent: "Well, chaps, you've made the grade and passed your wing check." He had ... a cardboard box of RAF wings, and he ... said: "Come up here, and if you've got 22 cents in your pocket, that's what they want from stores; 22 cents to pay for the wings. Each of you can take a set, and my congratulations chaps. You've all done well." That was our wings parade.'

All pupils graduated as sergeant pilots and one-third of them were commissioned immediately after graduation. MacKenzie remained a sergeant. The BCATP was still expanding at an accelerating rate and, like the great majority o

Canadian graduates at that time, the whole class was posted to be trained as instructors. 'It was a big surprise ... we were told rather nicely that this was a necessary thing, [that] we needed instructors in the Joint Air Training Plan ... It was one of the most disappointing days of my life ... However, once we got to [CFS] Trenton and started on the instructing course, you just had to make up your mind that you were going to do a good job of that too.'

MacKenzie spent two years as an instructor at SFTSs at Yorkton, Sask., and Hagersville, Ont., and at the Central Flying School at Trenton, winning his commission in March 1942. In that time he trained many pilots who were posted to operational theatres. In February 1943 he finally went overseas, to an operational training unit in the United Kingdom, where he flew Spitfires. He went on to complete an operational tour, being credited with 8¼ victories and winning a Distinguished Flying Cross. MacKenzie remained in the postwar RCAF, served in Korea as an exchange pilot with the US Fifth Air Force, was shot down while patrolling south of the Yalu River, and was held prisoner by the Chinese for two years. He eventually retired from the RCAF in 1966, with the rank of squadron leader.

In the fall of 1942, while MacKenzie was a senior instructor at 16 SFTS, at Hagersville, Ont., a seventeen-year-old high-school student, Sydney Francis Wise, together with fourteen other members of Toronto's Riverdale Collegiate football team, went down to volunteer as aircrew, *en masse*. At the time the only Canadian service carrying the war to the enemy and actually attacking Germany was the RCAF; accounts of fighter sweeps and bombing missions filled the airwaves and the columns of newspapers, painting the air war in tones of excitement and glamour. There was a delay of several months, however, before any of the students were enrolled. They were not surprised; they had been warned that there was a waiting list for aircrew and knew of the RCAF's popularity. A medical examination which revealed spots on Wise's lungs delayed his enlistment further, and he did not join with the rest of the team. He was finally enrolled 12 May 1943, aged eighteen-and-a-half.

Wise was posted to 5 Manning Depot, Lachine, Que. He had been, like all his male high-school contemporaries, a member of a cadet corps, so the military organization and discipline at the depot did not surprise him. He was startled, however, to find out 'how totally your life was controlled by the junior NCOs. That was a shock, because we had been given the impression ... that we were the cream of the crop.' His new masters seemed to look on him as skim milk.

It might be thought that, by this stage of the war, nearly all aircrew would have been teenagers. Not so. 'The exceptions stood out. These were people we thought were vastly older than ourselves. For the most part they would represent about 30% of the intake. They would be people who were either university graduates or had had some university or had in fact been in business for some years. They were clearly, now I think back, in their mid-twenties, but they seemed very old to we 18- and 19-year-olds, which is all we were. Naturally they assumed ... higher status positions than we kids. They were the father confessors and they were the people who set the norms for the group and so on. Not the

NCO's.'[65] When they received the white cap flashes which marked aircrew trainees after basic training, 'we were very proud of them ... we felt it set us apart ... one little distinctive symbol can make you feel first part of a group and then something special.' It was just as well they felt this way, since their post-depot employment was decidedly ordinary. In 1941 and 1942 all recruits waiting to enter aircrew training had been employed on 'tarmac duties' – a synonym for fatigue and internal guard duties that might or might not have anything to do with flying. By 1943 educational standards had been lowered in order to keep up the enlistment rates, and a good proportion of new recruits were academically underqualified for aircrew training. Their time in the buffering pool was now likely to be spent in a classroom, upgrading their academic skills in mathematics and physics, but those like Wise who did not need such tuition still went to tarmac duties.

Wise's course was kept at the manning depot for about two weeks: 'odd jobs shovelling coal and painting barrack blocks and things of this kind.' Although a syllabus had been prepared in December 1941 to give training to pupils during this waiting period, Wise's group received only a little parade-square drill. Attempts to avoid the worst of the make-work projects could easily backfire 'One day our flight sergeant, a French-Canadian, came before our flight and said, "I want two painter." We had been shovelling coal and it was a bloody dirty job. Two fellows ... both of whom were sort of "angles" men and were looking to get out of a tough job, volunteered. That was the last we saw of them, because the flight was posted out, went to ITS, went through EFTS, and then went through SFTS. On the day I got my wings at Centralia, and was going out the gate, [they] ... were coming in the gate ... They had been "painter" ever since ... Quite literally they had fallen six months behind us, because SFTS by that time was running 20 to 24 weeks.'

A few at a time, the recruits left for initial training school. Wise went to 3 ITS Victoriaville, Que., in June 1943. The course had lengthened to ten weeks from the four experienced by MacKenzie in 1940, and the content had been improved A standard précis was now issued, and properly trained instructors provided. There was a good deal of math, and Wise found it 'the toughest intellectual challenge I had faced up to that point.' Throughout the course 'You knew you had to deliver ... Suddenly you were right up against it because you realized the relationship of the performance there to how you were going to be selected at the end of the ITS period. You knew that academic performance was going to have a bearing on this. You also knew that officer-like qualities were being examined and so on. So you were on trial, and I think that there was a common consciousness of this right through the group.'

The final stage of their ITS course was an appearance before an aircrew selection board. 'We all regarded it as *the* key, decisive, fifteen minutes. You were brought before a board which consisted of officers who themselves had had [operational] tours. It was really the first time we had ever been up against what would refer to as the "real" air force, the real fighting air force, instead of training ... They may not have been that old but, my god, they had old faces. It was an extremely serious business ... I can remember that I sweated ... Most people they asked whether or not they would consent to be air gunners, because there was a real demand for that. The correct answer was yes, and then you stood a chance of being selected for something else.' Wise's feeling was that they no longer were really interested in selecting for pilot and were more interested in the other aircrew trades. Whatever the choice, however, pupils accepted it. 'We felt sorry, as a group, for the people who'd been selected air gunner ... first, because we thought the really challenging jobs were elsewhere in aircrew and secondly we knew then what the casualty rates were. We knew very well!' In fact, pilot casualty rates in Bomber Command were the highest of all aircrew categories, perhaps because, in training or operational emergencies, the pilot usually had to 'stick with the plane' until everyone else had baled out. In general at this stage of the war, wireless operators and air gunners were sent straight to specialist training after manning depot, so those selected from his ITS course were probably individuals judged unsuitable for further pilot, navigator, or bomb-aimer training. There was constant reallocation of such pupils throughout the system, but 'it was handled very humanely.' The impression given was that these men had been selected, not rejected.

From Victoriaville, Wise was sent to 11 EFTS at Cap-de-la-Madeleine, Que., on 19 September 1943. Both were francophone communities, but while Victoriaville was hostile – there had been a number of clashes between the townsfolk and service personnel – Cap-de-la-Madeleine was open and friendly. RCAF members had replaced civilian instructors in the elementary flying training system by now, but many aspects of the original civilian EFTS operation remained. The food was excellent, and there were individual tables with chequered cloths and attractive civilian waitresses. Link training continued, but with a difference from Wise's initial contact with that machine when he had found it 'a very specialized form of torture' which 'didn't seem to have much relationship to what we were doing in the air.' The machine was more sophisticated than in MacKenzie's day, and now there was more emphasis on navigational training, working 'blind' under a hood in preparation for the use of such aids as the radio range. The Link was now 'a very considerable test of concentration and capacity to react to new information,' and was 'more benefit ... than I think we quite realized at the time.'

His was the first course to fly the Fairchild Cornell, the elementary trainer scheduled to replace the Finch and DH Moth. Wise had yet to fly. Now 'we were thrilled and filled with anticipation ... the little Cornell ... looked enormous to me.' After the first few hours he thought 'how sweet it was, what a beautiful little aircraft.' Experienced pilots considered it underpowered, but he and his fellow neophytes flew well within its limits, never unduly stressing it, and found it very stable and easy to fly. Perhaps it was just as well that they did not overstress their Cornells, since 'in the last half of 1943 a series of wing structural failures occurred, at least six in the RCAF ... A reinforcement of the centre section main spar corrected the trouble.'[66]

After Wise's first instructor became ill he had a series of substitutes and fell behind his course. In order to keep up, he was sent off solo before he was really ready, but succeeded. As with previous courses, he was then often sent off to practise set sequences on his own. He also received a few hours of dual night flying. The RAF's Bomber Command was very much a night-flying force, and more such training had been placed in the syllabus, even carrying it down to elementary level. In spite of Wise's awareness of flight before he enrolled, this was a new and surprising experience. 'Quite frankly, I didn't think it could be done. It hadn't dawned on me. The first time I was taken up with my instructor and I saw the red and blue lights, I found it very beautiful ... But also I thought that this was pretty ridiculous. The discovery that you could land at night, that was a remarkable discovery. It never ceased to be a somewhat shaky experience until I was well past the wings stage.'

Wise asked for and got twin-engine training – he would probably have been assigned to it anyway – and was posted next to 9 SFTS, Centralia, Ont., in November 1943. There he trained on Anson IIs. It took some time to adjust to handling two engines, and he caught the flu, 'missed some vital hours of instruction ... and came out of the hospital with a temperature to take what was in fact a washout check' to provide formal justification for removing him from pilot training. After a quick flight, to Wise's surprise the instructor sent him off solo 'To have this verdict from the Chief Flying Instructor, who I guess couldn't have given a damn that I'd had a temperature of 102 or something, was enormously heartening. I went off and did my solo right then, ill. When I came back ... I was thrilled and so was the flight. They were all out in front of the flight shack with a cake for me. I leaped out of the aircraft and caught the D-ring of my parachute on the door as I came out and it opened ... There's a lovely picture of the flight rolling about and laughing like hell, and me with this parachute trailing behind It was a wonderful day in my life you know. Then I went back to hospital.'

Wise's service flying course was twenty-one weeks long, compared with MacKenzie's twelve. Included in that lengthened span were more night exercises and long navigational flights. Link training continued as well. It was increasingly complex, but 'most of us regarded the Link training as a diversion from what we were really about, which was accumulating lots of hours in the air.'

These hours were not spent dashing around the skies. While MacKenzie was plotting bridge-loops in 1940, one of his contemporaries, Arthur Wahlroth, was learning that 'the aerobatics I had been painstakingly perfecting [at EFTS] came to nothing, for the next phase of training was on the gentlemanly Avro Anson.'[6] Three years later, Wise also found that 'with your ordinary run-of-the-mill Anson II there isn't a hell of a lot of playing to do.' He did have some freedom to experiment in the air. 'We were permitted to do everything to that aircraft that it was stressed to take and to fly it right to the extent of its capabilities and not one inch beyond. That's what we did. Remember, we were dual pilots and we were trained to fly accurately, straight and level, and to fly precisely. We knew we would be flying bombers, we'd be running a crew with navigators, wireless operators, so precision was our emphasis.' In contrast to MacKenzie's hallmark of 'freedom and bravado' in the early single-engine schools, Wise and his peers were conditioned to fly with precision and 'a sense of professionalism. No military professionalism, really professionalism as a pilot. The sense that you were training for a highly skilled kind of occupation. That's not a proper thing for a service person to feel, and yet it's true. I think one of the effects of the BCATP was to create that sort of sense of professionalism; pride in being a pilot. Their indoctrination reinforced that. The indoctrination had less to do with the RCAF as a fighting unit than it had to do with the creation of an aircrew spirit in which there was a high level of professionalism.'

Wise had close to 250 hours logged on graduation. He found his wings parade both an exhilarating and unusually sobering experience, for the ever-present reality of training casualties intervened (though the BCATP fatal accident rate had declined from 1 in 11,156 hours of flying in 1940-1, to 1 in 20,580 hours in 1943-4).[68] About two hours before the parade he took a last flight with his instructor.

We were approaching the circuit and we could see an Anson taking off. We heard the controller say something, some word of warning, and there was a collision between the aircraft taking off and an aircraft going around again ... I said to my instructor, 'look at the pieces of paper.' He said, 'that's aircraft.' Those two aircraft with four people aboard, two instructors and two students, went down ...

They were all killed ... Whenever there's a fatality on a flying station, there is a certain atmosphere, and so it was within that context that the wings parade took place. So part of my memory of getting my wings is of those four fellows. On the other hand, when we left the station I was wearing sergeant's hooks and my wings, and I felt that everybody in the world was looking at me.

Every new pilot graduated as a sergeant, and those who were selected for commissioning – most of them were as a result of the 1942 Ottawa Conference – were informed a few days later. Wise was commissioned, receiving no preparation or instruction for this new status. He merely put on the uniform. When he received his commissioning scroll he 'read it very carefully,' for he was unsure of what it entailed. Fortunately, he was next sent for commando and local defence training on a course run by army NCOs at 1 Aircrew Graduates Training School, Maitland, NS. By now, in mid-1944, excess aircrew were clogging the system and courses such as this took up some of the slack. Here he got his first ideas of officer responsibilities. The station had a small officer complement, and from them the students received instruction in what it was like to be an air force officer and to be an aircraft captain in an operational situation.

All aircrew trades were at the school, not just pilots, and they were already aware that even if they got overseas or to an OTU in Canada or Great Britain their chances of reaching an operational squadron were 'very small.' In the event, most of Wise's fellow students did go overseas after leaving the school. Few, if any, got on operations. The rest languished in advanced flying units and other training establishments further down the aircrew pipeline. Wise himself was posted to 2 Air Navigation School, at Charlottetown, PEI, where he served for the rest of the war as a staff pilot, flying aircraft in which trainee navigators practised their art. Released from the RCAF in October 1945, Wise went to university, followed an academic path, and held the post of Director of History,

Department of National Defence, from 1966 to 1973. He is the author of the first volume of this history, *Canadian Airmen and the First World War* (Toronto 1980).

In a very real sense, flying is always an 'operational' situation, pitting the airman against an alien element in a battle which may easily be as fatal as one against his fellow man. But service terminology uses the word 'operation' to mean combat against a human enemy. In that sense, Wise never became an operational flyer and thus never experienced the final stage of combat flying training in an operational training unit. MacKenzie, when he eventually went overseas in 1943, did. By that time he could have attended a fighter OTU in Canada, something not possible when he graduated from SFTS in April 1941. OTUs were the last and, for reasons to be explained, least effective part of the aircrew training system to be put into place.

During the First World War and throughout much of the interwar era there had been only moderate differences between the handling and performance of training aircraft on the one hand and operational machines on the other. The improvements that characterized the latter could be mastered at a single step without undue difficulty. Aircrew could, and did, move directly from a service flying training school or its equivalent to an operational squadron. Pilots and observers were expected to complete their training by learning on the job under the supervision of experienced flight commanders and the more senior aircrew.

However, the great advances in aeronautical design that marked the mid-1930s meant that the technological gap between training and operational flying increased substantially and that much greater mental stresses were imposed in successfully piloting and navigating the newest machines. For example, a man who had learned to fly an Avro Tutor, the RAF's standard trainer of the early and mid-1930s, could easily bridge the gap between it and the Gloster Gauntlet, still the commonest fighter in 1937. Both were open-cockpit biplanes, fabric-covered, with the wing loading of the latter being only half as much again as that of the former. Even the heavy night bombers of the time, such as the Vickers Virginia and the Handley Page Heyford, had open cockpits. Indeed, the Virginia's wing loading and performance were almost identical to those of the Tutor; it was much bigger, of course, and boasted two engines. The Heyford, which remained in first-line service until 1939, had a performance very similar to that of the Gauntlet. But the Hawker Hurricane – the first of the monoplane, eight-gun fighters – which entered service in 1937 had a wing loading, speed, and rate of climb very nearly triple that of the Tutor. The Vickers Wellington, which began to replace the Heyford as the RAF's heavy bomber in 1938, had a wing loading four times that of the Tutor when it was fully 'bombed-up' and, although its rate of climb was no greater, it could double the Tutor's maximum speed.[69]

The flying problems posed by these dramatic advances applied most obviously to pilots, especially bomber pilots, and by May 1938 the RAF had come to recognize that 'Training has not kept pace with the increased demands made on the fully trained pilot, due to increase in complexity of modern bomber aircraft. There is an "accident prone zone" following immediately on the arrival

f a pilot at his squadron after leaving F[lying] T[raining] S[chool]. There should
e an interim stage of training between the two.'[70] This stage was provided in
939 by the creation of fighter, bomber, and maritime operational holding units,
iitially called 'group pools,' to provide immediate reserves for the front-line
quadrons while carrying out the needed advanced training. The nomenclature
vas changed to 'operational training units' in the spring of 1940.[71]

The problem of reconciling old and new technologies and training and
perational flying standards scarcely existed for the RCAF. Except for the
lurricanes allocated to 1 Squadron in February 1939, the Canadians had none of
1e new machines and – far removed from the theatre of war – no requirement for
perational training in the tactical sense. However, the climatic and topographi-
al exigencies of Pacific coast flying, which was technically operational, posed
nough of a concern that the air force found it advisable to form a seaplane and
omber reconnaisance school (equipped with Fairchild 71s, Noorduyn Norse-
nen, and Vickers Vancouvers and Vedettes) on the west coast. When it was
lecided to include landplanes as well, the school was redesignated 13
)perational Training Squadron in July 1940.[72] The squadron only trained pilots,
iot complete aircrews, and both machines and equipment were very different
rom those in use in fully operational theatres. None of the instructors had
ombat experience and pupils got no meaningful tactical training.

As early as December 1940, however, Air Vice-Marshal Breadner told the
3ritish air staff that the RCAF was anxious to develop a genuine operational
raining capability, and enquired if OTUs might be included among the RAF
chools about to be transferred to Canada. Air Marshal Garrod had replied that it
vas current policy to retain OTUs in the United Kingdom because the RAF felt that
he further operational training was removed from the operational theatre, the
ess effective it was. That was certainly true, and the principle therefore a sound
ne. As Garrod noted at the time, however, the pressure of operations on air
pace over such a geographically restricted base as Britain might eventually
nake it necessary to shift some OTUs out of the theatre.[73]

In the event, non-operational circumstances were about to force the air staff's
land. Only ten days after Breadner's meeting with Garrod, the Air Ministry's
pecial representative in the United States, Air Commodore J.C. Slessor,
ignalled the chief of his air staff about the problems of ferrying 'large numbers'
)f American-built operational aircraft across the Atlantic. He felt it would be
iecessary to find the crews for these machines from UK Home Commands
'Royal Canadian Air Force may be able to help out with some administrative
personnel but instruct[ors] staff pilots and bulk of ground personnel must be
found by R.A.F.') who would need additional training on American types before
they could attempt the North Atlantic crossing. That, in turn, would require 'an
organisation capable of 2000 hours training a month with say 40 aircraft of types
proportionate to U.S. deliveries.'[74]

Someone in the air staff found a more economical answer. An unsigned
minute of 7 January 1941, attached to Slessor's signal, noted that 'the best way
of meeting it [the need for such an organization] will be to form one or two
O.T.U.'s in Canada.' Selected graduates of the BCATP 'would go through these

O.T.U.'s and do the full course. On completion each individual would be available for one ferrying flight ... We suggest that both the interim training organisation and the O.T.U.'s should be run by the R.C.A.F. We understand that Air Vice Marshal Breadner is in favour of establishing O.T.U.'s in Canada quite apart from this ferrying aspect.'[75]

This advice was taken and, since the ferry route was a maritime one, it made sense that the first RAF OTU to be transferred specialize in maritime reconnaissance. No 31 OTU crossed the Atlantic to Debert, NS, in May 1941 and was able to start training, using Lockheed Hudsons, in August. Because RAF Ferry Command, as the Atlantic Ferry Organization became in July (see Appendix D), was so hard pressed for crews and the airfield at Debert was still unfinished, the full operational training course was held in abeyance until the end of the year. The unit concentrated on preparing pilots, observers, and wireless operators (air gunner) for their transatlantic flights with the emphasis on the instrument flying, navigation, and communications skills necessary for this trip.[76]

Operational training proper commenced in December, with a syllabus which provided for a twelve weeks' course for pilots and wireless operators (air gunner) and eight weeks for observers as the training was broadened to include cross-country flying and navigation, bombing techniques, photography, and 'fighter affiliation' duties – defence against enemy fighter attacks and co-operation with fighter escorts. As each course finished, those crews considered competent to fly the route overseas were posted to Ferry Command at Dorval and subsequently were assigned to fly themselves overseas; the others, with the exception of those posted to Home War Establishment squadrons and those who simply failed the course, were sent to the United Kingdom by sea.[77]

The desire of the British air staff that OTUs should be sited in physical proximity to operational areas was more than realized in No 31's case on 20 April 1942, as 'the Station first became operational.' Upon 'notification of a submarine in the Bay of Fundy, bombs were obtained from 16x [Explosive Depot] and two aircraft were sent in search of it.' The sorties may have been fruitless, but the operational environment they created was invaluable and the Canadian-based trainees were getting experience probably every bit as realistic as that offered by UK-based OTUs.

On the 20th and following days at least three aircraft were sent daily to Dartmouth where they were bombed up and carried out exercises as ordered. Sixteen aircraft [out of 74 on strength] were fully operational for these purposes.

This enabled actual operational patrol practice to be given to the pupils, but some difficulty was found in finding staff pilots to accompany them in view of the shortage of staff for the intensive training already in progress on the Station.[78]

A precedent had been all that was needed to establish the propriety of locating OTUs far from an operational arena. The next OTU to move across the ocean began to arrive at Patricia Bay, BC, early in August 1941, but apparently the idea of using OTUs just to train ferry crews on American aircraft had already been abandoned. No 32 was designated a torpedo-bomber OTU and equipped with

British-designed (and built) Bristol Beauforts. That meant all sorts of delays in providing aircraft and spares and the unit was unable to commence any training at all until 5 December. Even then, it was only pilot conversion training. It was hoped to start operational training with full crews by 1 January 1942,[79] but when the Japanese attacked Pearl Harbor all training activities stopped while the unit stood by for operational duties. By 29 December, when the panic had subsided and training could be resumed, the instructional staff had flown thirty-six operational sorties. As will be seen in chapter 11, they made no contact with the enemy.[80]

Nervousness over Japanese intentions and capabilities kept a striking force of Beauforts on standby at Patricia Bay for the next twelve months while Handley Page Hampdens – another British design, although some were Canadian-built – took up the slack in the training programme. A limited amount of operational training began on schedule, in January 1942, but because of slow delivery and the inevitable shortage of spares the Hampdens did not play a significant role until June. When they did come into service, accident rates were unduly high and the quality of instruction something less than it might have been. Designed as a high-altitude, medium bomber, the Hampden was faster and more manoeuvrable than most machines of the type, but it lacked dual controls, a grave disadvantage when men were being taught to dive almost to wave-top height and then launch a 1600-lb torpedo. Moreover, 'not one of the officers on the staff of this OTU has dropped a torpedo on operations from a Hampden aircraft,' reported the commanding officer at the end of 1942.[81] Nevertheless, 32 OTU became and remained the main source of crew replacement for Coastal Command's three torpedo-bombing squadrons based in the United Kingdom, 144 Squadron, RAF, 404 Squadron, RCAF, and 455 Squadron, RAAF.

No 34 OTU, formed as a light bomber unit to be equipped with Lockheed Venturas, began flying from Pennfield Ridge, NB, in June 1942. Pennfield Ridge had been vacated by 2 Air Navigation School because of the persistent rain and fog which enveloped the station, a quirk of nature which, within reason, made it a peculiarly suitable environment for crews training for operations out of the United Kingdom. But the poor weather, combined with a shortage of instructors and dual-control Venturas, and an excess of serviceability problems, led to the first course of pilots completing only 25 per cent of their scheduled flying hours during the first month of operation. When the first full crews 'graduated,' they had made no cross-country night flights 'owing to lack of dual aircraft in the conversion flight,' and had done no air-to-air firing exercises because of a 'lack of towing apparatus and also because the towing aircraft available – Lysanders – are too slow for the work.'[82] It mattered little. The Venturas were not liked by the RAF and only three operational squadrons were ever equipped with them. For the most part, those graduates of 34 OTU who were posted to the United Kingdom were processed through Boston or Wellington OTUs after their arrival there and subsequently sent to squadrons flying those types of aircraft.

The fourth and final RAF OTU to be transferred to Canada was No 36, which opened at Greenwood, NS, in May 1942 and graduated its first crews on 1

August. Like No 31, it was a coastal reconnaissance unit, equipped with Hudsons, but it seems to have had far fewer problems, a reflection of the Allies' growing strength in men and matériel. Spares for the Hudson, a well-established type in mid-1942, were readily available, and aircraft serviceability was higher from the beginning and rose steadily. Most of the instructors assigned to the unit had completed an operational tour with Coastal Command and had experience on Hudsons. Reporting on the quality of training in November 1942, the director of training at the Air Ministry concluded that 'the crews [coming from 36 OTU] are up to a very satisfactory standard in flying the Hudson, and in Navigation and General Reconnaissance work.'[83]

After the revised BCATP Agreement came into effect in the summer of 1942, all the RAF schools and OTUs already in Canada were promptly incorporated into the plan, retaining their RAF identities and designations but coming under the RCAF for administration and accounting purposes as well as flying training. Meanwhile, the arrival of the first American squadrons in the United Kingdom in May 1942, and the prospect of many more to follow, ensured that air space and ground facilities there were going to become very congested. Whatever the theoretical merits of siting OTUs in proximity to the operational theatre in which their graduates were likely to be employed, there would soon be no room to do so. A total of 127 airfields, some of them currently in use by the RAF and others still to be constructed, would be needed to accommodate the US Eighth Air Force.[84] When additional OTUs were required by the Commonwealth air forces, they had to be established outside the United Kingdom; those created in Canada would be RCAF OTUs and numbered accordingly.[85]

Paradoxically, perhaps, the first such unit established under the revised agreement was one not really needed. When 1 (Fighter) OTU, RCAF, was formed on 14 July 1942, the output of single-seater fighter pilots from OTUs in the United Kingdom was already exceeding the demand.[86] Presumably (there seems to be no direct documentary evidence) the RCAF wanted a fighter OTU to round out its own status as a complete and balanced air force,[87] and used the ready excuse that it could train pilots for the twelve additional Home War Establishment fighter squadrons approved by Cabinet in March 1942, as well as any required replacements. However, even the further squadrons in existing expansion plans could scarcely absorb more than eighteen or twenty pilots a month. The planned output of 1 OTU was forty-five pilots a month and, although that figure was never reached, during 1943 the unit turned out an average of forty a month, all trained on Canadian-built Hawker Hurricanes.[88] Its graduates were mostly shipped overseas, to languish for months in the fighter pilot pipeline or to be cross-trained as multi-engine pilots. It is easy to see now that a complete fighter OTU in the Canadian context was not justified. It used up men and matériel better employed elsewhere. The best that can be said in its favour is that it occupied a considerable number of SFTS graduates who otherwise would have been kept waiting in Canada with nothing to do. However, the decision to create an elaborate organization rather than something less ambitious – one flight in a bomber OTU, for example – was characteristic of RCAF policy in 1942. The Home War Establishment held exaggerated importance in the eyes of the air staff, for reasons discussed in the next chapter.

At the end of 1943 a new demand for pilots of single-engined, high-performance aircraft began to provide an outlet for part of the embarrassingly large surplus of such pilots building up in the United Kingdom. The RAF, faced with irrefutable evidence of the value and importance of close air support for ground forces by experience in the Mediterranean theatre, had finally, if reluctantly, come to terms with the need for a substantial fighter-bomber and rocket projectile (RP) fighter component in its tactical air forces. That would require specialized training quite different from that traditionally given to fighter pilots, although the ground-support experts would still need a competence in air-to-air combat techniques. In June someone suggested that 1 OTU should concentrate on turning out pilots for 'Army support,' but the British authorities foresaw problems with that. Such specialization would be 'undesirable ... at present, [because] it would result in having the whole Army Support Canadianised.'[89] Instead, 'the Army Support fighter role should be known to all Day Fighter Squadrons' and Fighter Command preferred to 'include a little Army Support in all the Spitfire O.T.U.'s and considerably more in the Hurricane O.T.U.'s' As for the graduates of 1 OTU, those 'who have not already served in a Canadian Squadron in Canada, should be split among the [UK] O.T.U.'s and be given one month's acclimatisation course of 25 hours flying. This would have the advantage of giving the Canadian O.T.U. pilots the latest O.T.U. instruction and would also ease the maintenance troubles of each O.T.U. by diluting the intake.'[90]

The RCAF translated these suggestions into another sixteen weeks of OTU training as the syllabus was extended to encompass the mastery of air-to-ground rocketry and dive bombing. 'As a temporary measure ... "the course is to be extended to 12 weeks with the addition of training in the use of Rocket Projectiles as soon as equipment is available" ... In addition a course of 4 weeks duration which will include advanced tactics ... is to be added.'[91] Two weeks of this advanced course were to be spent at Camp Borden, discovering on the ground how armoured formations were equipped, organized, and operated and getting a worm's eye view of the possibilities for close air support, and two more weeks at Greenwood, NS, on air-to-ground firing, low-level, cross-country formation flying, and – ominously – escape and evasion exercises.[92]

The reprieve was brief. Although casualties on fighter-bomber and RP fighter squadrons were to prove heavy during the first few months of the northwest Europe campaign, such was the surplus of trained fighter pilots in the system that by August 1944 the Air Ministry would accept no more from Canada. The Home War Establishment could absorb only six replacements a month. Air Marshal Robert Leckie (who succeeded Lloyd Breadner as Canadian chief of the air staff on New Year's Day, 1944) searched desperately for a way to keep the fighter OTU open, but eventually had to admit that 'replacements for our W[estern] H[emisphere] O[perations] Squadrons do not justify retention of the school even on the smallest possible basis.'[93] No 1 OTU was closed on 28 October 1944.

By that time much of the training organization had closed down. In October 1943, when the Supervisory Board of the BCATP at its regular monthly meeting had considered an Air Ministry request for a further expansion of the plan to train an additional 70 pilots and 136 navigators every two weeks and another 117 air bombers every six weeks, Sir Patrick Duff, the British deputy high commissioner, had astounded everyone by indicating that the British now wanted 'a temporary standstill in the arrangements' while they 'recalculated' their needs.[94] Then, in December, came news that 'the United Kingdom Air Ministry has now advised that the output of Pilots from the [existing] combined training can be reduced.'[95]

Pilots were the very core of the plan, and it was becoming clear that the British had only the vaguest idea how many aircrew they actually had on hand, how many were in the training stream, or how many were now needed. They had, up to that point, been working on the reasonable principle that the more the plan could produce, the better it would be, and that they could not have too many. However, a quick review now revealed that not only could they have too many, but they actually did so. The nearly complete air superiority that had been established meant that casualties were now running at much lower rates than had been forecast, and the *Luftwaffe* was getting progressively weaker. 'Overlord' – the invasion of northwest Europe – was still to come, but there seemed little likelihood that casualty rates would rise again.

In February 1944 Harold Balfour, the British undersecretary of state for air, and Sir Peter Drummond, the RAF's air member for personnel, were dispatched to Ottawa to negotiate major reductions in output. It was a ticklish business, involving assessments of the impact on the Canadian economy, on public enthusiasm for prosecuting the war – still far from won on the ground – and on the morale of men in, or about to enter, the aircrew training flow. However, after much thrusting and parrying with the Canadian government, an agreement was reached to cut back the plan by some 40 per cent over the next year.[96] Probably the only event which could have brought about an upward revision would have been the appearance of a new and exceptionately devastating air weapon on the German side. Even the new rocket and turbojet aircraft that the Germans began to use failed to inflict the damage they might have done because of the success of the Allied combined bomber offensive.[97] Hence the demand for new aircrew continued to decrease. On 27 June 1944 Drummond wrote to Air Marshal Leckie admitting 'that we have gone as far as possible in extending courses and arranging special courses and that if further surpluses occur ... then we can no longer afford to hold the surplus but must transfer it to those categories where it can be readily used, or even to ground duties in or outside the air forces ...'[98]

Power and Balfour had made their 40 per cent cut on the basis of an RCAF component of forty-seven squadrons for the war against Japan, which would still have to be won after the victory in Europe had been achieved. However, the government was quietly cutting back on the proposed contribution to the Pacific war, and it was clear that there was already enough RCAF aircrew for that, too. There were still some commitments to be met in training RAF men, but the other dominions no longer needed Canadian facilities for their own reduced production. On 19 October 1944 the government decided that the plan would be wound up at the end of the current agreement, which extended to 31 March 1945. All RCAF intakes for courses which would not be completed by that date were forthwith cancelled. Those students already in the training stream and past the

ITS stage were to complete their courses, but the ITS men and 4200 seventeen-year-old pre-entry aircrew candidates in the buffering pool were promptly discharged for subsequent enlistment (either voluntarily or compulsorily) in the army, which still had a desperate need for the kind of physically A-1 and relatively well-educated men the air force had been so carefully hoarding.[99] Australia and New Zealand stopped sending pupils to Canada in October 1944 and concentrated instead on supplying their own forces in the Pacific; their graduates returned home except for the few still needed to replace wastage in Article 15 squadrons in Europe.[100]

The British Commonwealth Air Training Plan in Canada was brought to an end in March 1945 having graduated 131,553 of the 159,340 pupils who had begun training. The total included 42,110 RAF (including Allied nationals), 9606 Australian, and 7002 New Zealand aircrew; RCAF graduates numbered 72,835 out of 91,166 entrants, 25,747 of them pilots, 12,855 navigators of one kind or another, 6659 air bombers, 12,744 wireless operators (air gunner), 12,917 air gunners, and 1913 flight engineers.[101]

We will never know how many casualties in the air war might have been avoided if training standards had been higher. But one might equally well ask how many more might have been incurred, both in the air and on the ground, if insistence on higher standards had led to reduced output. And what would have been the effect on the progress of the war as a whole if limitations in the supply of aircrew had restricted the strategic bomber offensive, handicapped anti-submarine operations in the North Atlantic, or limited air support to ground forces in the Italian and northwest European campaigns? These questions cannot be answered. It is clear, however, that despite the imperfections of early BCATP training, the sheer quantity of graduates played a significant part in establishing Allied air superiority at a time when *Festung Europa* seemed impregnable to ground attack. The quality of German aircrew declined during the war (especially during the last two years) while the standard of BCATP graduates rose steadily without a corresponding loss of numbers.

PART THREE

The Air Defence of Canada, 1939–45

Ian Mackenzie, former minister of national defence, about to board a Grumman Goose, 1939. (PA 63538)

Groundcrew of 8 (BR) Squadron servicing one of their Northrop Deltas at Sydney, NS, during the winter of 1940–1. The Deltas were replaced by Bristol Bolingbrokes, one of which can be seen to the left. (RE 20608-1)

The departure of 110 (AC) Squadron for overseas, RCAF Station Rockcliffe, Ont., in the spring of 1940; left to right, K.S. Maclachlan, deputy minister of national defence (air); Air Vice-Marshal G.M. Croil, chief of the air staff; Prime Minister W.L.M. King; Squadron Leader W.D. Van Vliet, officer commanding the squadron; N. McL. Rogers, minister of national defence; and Wing Commander A.J. Ashton. (PA 63634)

To all intents and purposes a First World War aeroplane, this Westland Wapiti was still being used operationally with 10 (BR) Squadron at Halifax, NS, March 1940. It is protected by a nose hangar, which kept the engine dry and warm in winter. (PA 141379)

A Supermarine Stranraer of 5 (BR) Squadron, over an east-coast sailing vessel, 3 April 1941. (PL 2729)

A group of senior RCAF, RAF, and Ferry Command officials in Ottawa in the fall of 1941. At far left, Air Marshal L.S. Breadner; second from left, Air Marshal W.A. Bishop; at the extreme right, Air Vice-Marshal G.M. Croil; and, second from right, Air Vice-Marshal E.W. Stedman. (PMR 85-54)

Canadian-built Grumman Goblins – 'Pregnant Frogs' – of 118 (F) Squadron, seen here on 18 September 1941, were for a time the only fighter aircraft in Eastern Air Command. (PL 5955)

Air Commodore G.O. Johnson,
deputy chief of the air staff, 1941
(PA 141377)

A Lockheed Hudson Mk I, the first contemporary bomber reconnaissance aircraft to be acquired by Eastern Air Command, over a minesweeper, 1940. (PL 1183)

The Air Staff and other senior air officers, probably taken in the fall of 1941. Seated, left to right, Air Commodore A.E. Godfrey, deputy inspector general; Air Commodore A.T.N. Cowley, commander, No 4 Training Command; Air Vice-Marshal E.W. Stedman, air member for aeronautical engineering; Air Vice-Marshal G.M. Croil, inspector-general; S.L. de Carteret, deputy minister of national defence (air); C.G. Power, minister of national defence for air; Air Vice-Marshal L.S. Breadner, chief of the air staff; Air Commodore W.R. Kenny, air member, Canadian liaison staff, Washington; standing, left to right, Air Commodore A.A.L. Cuffe, air member for air staff; Air Commodore A.B. Shearer, commander, No 2 Training Command; Air Commodore G.V. Walsh, commander, No 3 Training Command; Air Commodore N.R. Anderson, air officer commanding, Eastern Air Command; Air Commodore G.E. Brookes, commander, No 1 Training Command; Air Commodore C.M. McEwen, air officer commanding, No 1 Group, Newfoundland; Air Commodore S.G. Tackaberry, air member for supply; Air Commodore G.O. Johnson, deputy chief of the air staff; Air Vice-Marshal H. Edwards, air member for personnel; and Air Commodore R. Leckie, air member for training. (PMR 82-152)

Air Chief Marshal Sir Charles Portal, chief of the air staff, RAF, at right, during a visit to 2 SFTS, Uplands, listens to Squadron Leader S.A. Green, left, while the Canadian CAS, Air Marshal L.S. Breadner, looks on. (PL 6497)

Three senior RCAF officers during a visit to RCAF Trenton, Ont., in 1941: Group Captains F.S. McGill, W.A. Curtis, and J.L.E.A. de Niverville. (PL 5754)

Pilots of 118 (F) Squadron 'scramble' to their Kittyhawks at Dartmouth, 4 April 1942.
(PL 8353)

A Harvard brings Santa Claus to 1 (CAC) Flight, Saint John, NB, Christmas 1942. A
Westland Lysander, which was the mainstay of all coast artillery co-operation flights,
stands at the top of the photo. (AH 67-5)

304

Flight Sergeant Kay Russell of Vancouver at RCAF Station Rockcliffe. (PL 8963)

Air defence for Newfoundland: Hawker Hurricanes of 127 (F) Squadron, Gander, December 1942. Canadian-built Hurricanes were distinguished by large American propellers, which could not be capped by the spinners characteristic of British Hurricanes. (PL 14155)

Group Captain F.V. Heakes, assistant
air member for air staff, 19 January 1942.
(PL6636)

Air Commodore C.A. Ferrier,
air member for aeronautical engineering,
March 1942. (PL 8176)

Dispatch rider cycles past mechanics working on a Canadian-built Hurricane at
133 (F) Squadron, Lethbridge, Alta, September 1942. (PL 12324)

Goose Bay, Labrador, in June 1943: a key link in the transatlantic air route and an alternate field for Newfoundland-based aircraft. The RCAF establishment is at the top of the photo, that of the USAAF to the right. (RE 64-1720)

'Main street,' RCAF Station Goose Bay, Labrador, in May 1943. (PA 141356)

Children making model planes in the 'shop' class of a Montreal area school, June 1942. (PL 9479)

Signallers at 2 SFTS, Uplands, October 1943. (PL 21486)

Women's Division 'Fabric Workers' stitching up a seam at 6 B&GS, Mountain View, Ont., August 1942. (PL 9847)

RCAF Station Yarmouth, the principal airfield for operations south of Nova Scotia, and the home of the Royal Navy's 1 Naval Air Gunner's School, seen here at the top of the photo. (PMR 77-208)

A Liberator transport of 168 (HT) Squadron, laden with mail for soldiers overseas, prepares to take off from Rockcliffe. (PL 37627)

Gander airfield, Newfoundland. The aircraft massed on the American side of the field are on their way to Europe as part of RAF Ferry Command operations. (RE 64-1578)

Whenever possible salvage crews recovered the wreckage of downed aircraft, such as this Ventura being dragged from the woods in September 1943. (PL 20868)

RCAF Marine Service ice boat and crew in the cargo bay of an aircraft, 1945. (PL 28529)

Air Vice-Marshal R. Leckie, on the eve of his promotion to chief of the air staff, January 1944. (PL 23609)

Air Marshal L.S. Breadner, as air officer commanding-in-chief, RCAF Overseas, March 1945. (PL 35325)

A homing pigeon about to be 'launched' from a Canso in January 1944. The use of pigeons proved a remarkably durable emergency communications system. (PL 23625)

Wartime aircraft awaiting disposal at Scoudouc, NB, June 1945. (PA 103048)

RCAF Station Alliford Bay, BC, tucked away in Skidegate Inlet, was the most westerly station in the Pacific coast air defence system. (PA 141383)

The minister of national defence for air, G.C. Power, second from left, and the chief of the air staff, Air Vice-Marshal L.S. Breadner, centre, during a visit to the West Coast in July 1941. Also present are Group Captain F.V. Heakes, assistant air member for air staff, at left, and Air Vice-Marshal L.F. Stevenson, air officer commanding, Western Air Command, second from right. (RE 13833)

Bolingbrokes of 115 (F) Squadron at Patricia Bay, BC, 28 January 1942. The gun-pack which distinguished the fighter version of the Bolingbroke is visible directly under the fuselage. (PA 140638)

A Western Air Command Supermarine Stranraer of 9 (BR) Squadron, July 1942. All three of the aircraft's gun positions are manned, and there are depth charges under the wing. (PL 9601)

An 8 (BR) Squadron Bolingbroke, at Seward, Alaska, during the squadron's move to Anchorage, draws an interested crowd of American servicemen. (PMR 77-98)

Soviet pilots engaged in ferrying aircraft to the USSR pose with allied airmen at Nome, Alaska, in 1942. (PMR 79-617)

This wartime public relations shot taken at Annette Island illustrates an aircrew's 'ready room.' Note the aeroplane on the tarmac outside. (PA 140656)

The maintenance area for fighters at Annette Island, Alaska, in September 1942. The charred skeleton of one of the tents is evidence of a recent fire. (PA 140643)

Flight Lieutenant A. Grimmons, who had flown with pursuit squadrons of the USAAF briefing his fellow pilots of 14 (F) Squadron prior to an Alaskan sortie, 26 October 1942, with one of the squadron's shark-mouthed Kittyhawks as a backdrop. (PL 13098)

A coast watch detachment from RCAF Station Alliford Bay, BC, in the early stages of construction, September 1942. (PA 141360)

Air Vice-Marshal L.F. Stevenson, seen here as an air commodore while commanding the RCAF overseas, was recalled from Britain in January 1942 to take charge of Western Air Command, a post he held until June 1944. (PL 4311)

Squadron Leader K.A. Boomer, of III (F) Squadron, the pilot who shot down a Japanese Zero floatplane over Kiska on 24 September 1942, the only aerial victory by the Home War Establishment and the only victory by an RCAF squadron against the Japanese. Boomer was subsequently killed in action over Northwest Europe, 22 October 1944. (PMR 76-596)

An 8 (BR) Squadron Bolingbroke and work tent at Nome, Alaska, in 1942, the northern-most station used by an operational RCAF squadron during the war. (PMR 79-465)

Kittyhawks of 111 (F) Squadron at Kodiak, Alaska, ca 1942–3. (PMR 80-197)

Wing Commander E.M. Reyno, officer commanding 115 Squadron, and Flight Lieutenant R.A. Ashman, strolling along one of Annette Island's notorious duck-boards. (PMR 79-568)

An RCAF Bolingbroke on Annette Island during the winter of 1942–3. (PMR 79-778)

This smiling member of the Aircraft Detection Corps is busy – for the moment at least – with more down-to-earth matters, June 1943. (PL 17189)

A Canso 'A' and Kittyhawks of 14 (F) Squadron waiting out the fog at Yakutat, March 1943. (PMR 76-382)

Armourers of 111 (F) Squadron servicing the .5-inch guns of a P-40 at Kodiak, Alaska, June 1943. (PL 13129)

A Marine Service rescue launch, picking up the crew of a downed Anson off the West Coast in August 1943. (PL 23075)

Kittyhawks of the short-lived 132 (F) Squadron at Boundary Bay, BC, 1943, along with Bolingbrokes, a Harvard, and a Beechcraft. (PMR 76-123)

Groundcrew in Alaska, September 1943, probably from 111 (F) Squadron, painting Canadian identification serials on a recently acquired USAAF P-40. (PL 13146)

Sergeant Jim Chapman provided baths for his colleagues, in this instance Sergeant
D.D. Harris, during the Aleutian campaign in 1943. (PL 13082)

Annette Island airfield was noted for its swampy terrain, gravel dispersals spread along the runways, and dearth of amenities – characteristics which show clearly in this October 1943 view. (PA 140636)

American P-40s which were flown by pilots of 14 (F) and 111 (F) Squadrons, RCAF, during the Aleutian campaign, waiting in a dispersal on Amchitka Island. (PMR 76-386)

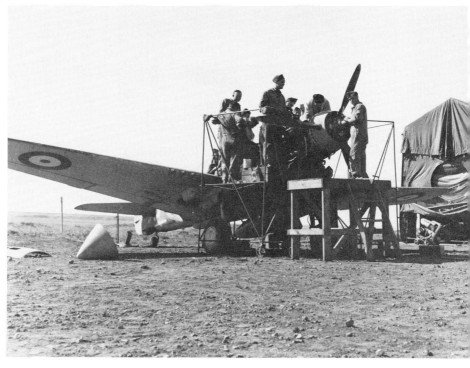

Servicing a Kittyhawk in the field, Alaska, 29 October 1943. (PL 13206)

RCAF accommodation tents in the late summer of 1943, Fort Glenn, Alaska. The arctic landscape offered little cover from the elements or the enemy. (PMR 80-248)

An airmen's hut on Umnak Island, Alaska, 1943, displaying more concern for convenience than military decorum. (PMR 79-538)

A Canso 'A' of 4 (BR) Squadron, Western Air Command, British Columbia coast, November 1943. (PL 21933)

A Canso flying over the west-coast mountains. (PMR 77-14)

RCAF Station Tofino, BC, one of the most important wartime west-coast airfields. By early 1945 it supported fighter and bomber reconnaissance aircraft, including those maintained to guard against Japanese fire-balloons. (PA 140651)

Western Air Command Cansos. (PL 36716)

Venturas of 149 (BR) Squadron neatly arranged on the tarmac at Terrace, BC, in 1944 (PA 139554)

This idle assemblage of Canso 'A's at an unknown Western Air Command base in February 1945 graphically illustrates the winding-down of operations and the surplus of equipment in the last months of the war. (PA 136642)

Introduction

Home defence was the principal justification for the RCAF after 1935. Overseas commitments were not in favour, and only a few squadrons to support an army expeditionary force figured in RCAF plans. The British Commonwealth Air Training Plan, however, became the largest task immediately after the outbreak of the Second World War, and German victories in Europe during 1940 brought a further emphasis on air power – the only significant way in which the Allies could attack the Axis heartlands until mid-1943 – with its consequent demands for more and more aircrew. Home defence now came last; last in men, aircraft, and other operational equipment. The Home War Establishment [HWE] did become a substantial force, but only at a time when the danger of attack on North America was rapidly receding. Paradox, indeed, proved to be the salient characteristic of the RCAF's home defence problem from 1939 to 1945.

The air defence of Canada should have been a simple task. The threat from enemy air forces was remote; calm military assessments consistently foresaw only a danger of naval attacks on maritime trade and isolated coastal raids. The real problem was defence against enemy surface ships and submarines, and the RCAF pressed patrols far out over the Atlantic to defend ocean shipping against a German U-boat campaign that nearly broke the lifeline to Great Britain.

The fall of France in June 1940 created the possibility of a more serious threat to Canadian soil. It appeared that Britain might be defeated as well, removing the shield that the Royal Navy and Royal Air Force provided for North America. That danger brought substantial military collaboration between Canada and the United States (still a neutral power), including the preparation of joint defence plans. Canada, in the meantime, sent assistance to Great Britain at the expense of her own home defences. It was the right decision. In the fall of 1940 the RAF decisively defeated the Luftwaffe's daylight offensive against England, while North America remained an inactive theatre of war. Until December 1941 the danger was concentrated in the North Atlantic, where Canada had assumed responsibility for the defence of Newfoundland.

Improvements in equipment and strength of the HWE occurred at a leisurely pace until the Japanese attack on Pearl Harbor. Unlike the events of 1940, this disaster brought an extraordinary expansion of the HWE that owed as much to an atmosphere of near panic in British Columbia as the actual military threat. Now at war, the United States faced formidable global responsibilities and, without abdicating some of them, could not defend the entire west coast of North America. The RCAF dispatched squadrons to assist in countering a Japanese thrust along the remote Aleutian Island chain just at the time that German U-boat attacks close in to Newfoundland and Nova Scotia, and deep within the Gulf of St Lawrence, placed enormous burdens on the Home War Establishment on the east coast.

The air staff aimed at creating a home air force sufficiently powerful both to defend the coasts against enemy attack and conduct anti-submarine operations in the North Atlantic. Air Defence of Canada plans were devised that called for many more squadrons than were really needed, and senior air officers persisted in their demands even after the United States Navy's victory at the Battle of Midway in June 1942 effectively eliminated any threat to British Columbia.

The RCAF viewed the direct defence of Canada as a purely Canadian concern, but found itself continually bound by the constraints imposed by coalition warfare. With the Americans and British differing over the allocation of scarce resources between the European and Pacific theatres, and competing among themselves for what was available, claims for more squadrons and more aircraft often appeared whimsical. Because of the failure of Canada to develop its own aero-engine manufacturing capacity, the RCAF was in a dependent position, unable to demand, only to plead for, the aircraft needed to equip its squadrons. The HWE, even so, grew too large during the Second World War, particularly in fighter aircraft. Thus arose the paradox of a force too heavily armed with fighter squadrons for which there was no reasonable employment, suffering from a shortage of men and matériel in its vital anti-submarine role as the U-boat war on the Atlantic reached its crisis in 1942–3.

9

Policy and Procurement

As the world learned of the German-Soviet non-aggression pact on 24 August 1939, Mackenzie King's Cabinet met to discuss the deteriorating international situation. 'Canada would participate' in a general conflict involving Great Britain, it was decided, although 'Parliament would decide' the precise nature of its commitment.[1] Within a few days the three armed services had deployed units on both coasts, and the chiefs of staff had submitted to the minister of national defence their recommendations for military operations. The militia and the Royal Canadian Navy strongly advocated direct support to Britain. The chief of the general staff, Major-General T.V. Anderson, proposed at least a one-division expeditionary force, and Rear-Admiral Percy Nelles urged that the navy be placed at the disposal of the Royal Navy. Air Vice-Marshal G.M. Croil, the chief of the air staff, was concerned less with an overseas commitment than the responsibilities the RCAF had assumed for the direct defence of Canada. Of the twenty-three squadrons to be mobilized, seventeen would remain in the country, situated for the most part on the Atlantic and Pacific coasts. The other six squadrons – three bomber and three army co-operation – could be made available to support an expeditionary force.[2]

The eight existing permanent squadrons were already taking up their war stations, and by 5 September eleven auxiliary squadrons had been placed on active service. None of the units was fully manned or equipped. As of 5 September, the air force had only 4153 officers and airmen, far fewer than its authorized establishment of 7259.[3] Of the fifty-three aircraft 'able to take their place on active service,' including eight on the west coast and thirty-six in the east, many were civil types converted with floats for patrol work and most of the others were obsolescent.[4] The outbreak of war, moreover, threatened to curtail the RCAF's supply of aircraft. American neutrality laws might entirely prohibit the export of war matériel from the United States, and with the possibility of RAF requirements outstripping British manufacturing capacity, Canadian orders could not be guaranteed. Even if the domestic aircraft industry could be quickly expanded, as the chief of aeronautical engineering, Air Commodore E.W. Stedman, suggested, no aero-engines were produced in Canada and British supplies were short.[5]

Financial limitations were a further complication. The government enjoined all three services to keep their estimates to a 'very moderate level,' then reduced them considerably. The air force's initial wartime request for $136 million for the period ending 30 August 1940 was pared to $77 million, an amount which, under the best of circumstances, allowed for only 167 aircraft, less than a third of the 574 called for in prewar planning and barely enough to provide the initial equipment for sixteen squadrons, with no provision for reserves, wastage, or training machines.[6]

In light of the dismal prospects for implementing the full twenty-three squadron programme, Air Force Headquarters allocated its limited equipment and manpower to fifteen squadrons and, by early November, had disbanded the rest.[7] Among the units that remained on the order of battle were several originally earmarked to support an expeditionary force. Since prewar plans had concluded that at least seventeen squadrons were required for home defence, a decision had to be made whether any could be spared to accompany the army to Europe.

As Croil grappled with this problem during the first three months of the war, the British proposal for a huge training programme in Canada fundamentally reshaped RCAF planning. When he met with the Cabinet emergency council on 5 September, the chief of the air staff declared that, although there was no firm commitment to dispatch Canadian squadrons overseas, there was also no reason for all RCAF units to remain at home. The 'odd bomb' might fall 'here and there,' but the threat to the dominion was not serious enough to warrant the air force's total concentration in North America. Ten days later, after hearing the British say that training was the best contribution Canada could make, he informed the Defence Council (the minister of national defence's advisory body) that all the RCAF's trained men should remain in Canada as instructors even at the expense of weakening home defence squadrons. On 25 September in another appreciation Croil announced that three squadrons could proceed overseas despite the RCAF's training commitments at home.[8] When Norman Rogers (who succeeded Ian Mackenzie as defence minister) complained on 3 October that sending only three units abroad would not 'satisfy public sentiment,' Croil countered that the Home War Establishment (as the home-based units were now called) could not be weakened further.[9] In the following weeks, however, Croil was apparently persuaded by his minister's views. '[It is] detrimental to Canada's prestige as a nation,' Croil wrote to Rogers on 23 November 1939, 'to restrict its official air effort' to training or to allow its overseas contribution to be swallowed up in the RAF. Canadians by temperament would 'prefer to be at the front' in Canadian units. No fewer than twelve squadrons should go.[10]

By then the larger context within which the RCAF would develop was changing fundamentally. Discussions between the Canadian and British governments over article 14 of the British Commonwealth Air Training Plan Agreement finally guaranteed a limited supply of aircrew to the Home War Establishment, thereby ensuring that the squadrons in Canada could be maintained. More significantly, negotiations on article 15 suggested that a number of Canadian squadrons would be formed overseas from BCATP graduates. It seems likely that Croil was laying a foundation for creating RCAF squadrons overseas, and not

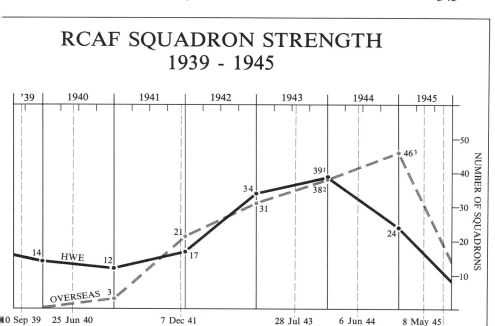

RCAF SQUADRON STRENGTH
1939 - 1945

NOTES: 1. Includes 3 HWE squadrons scheduled to move overseas.
2. Includes 3 HWE squadrons recently moved overseas.
3. Includes 162 Squadron in Iceland.

uced by Mapping and Charting Establishment.   ©Compiled and drawn by the Directorate of History.

ıerely RAF squadrons with Canadian aircrew. Certainly this was the course of
ction favoured by many members of the air staff, who regretted that there had
een no distinctly Canadian squadrons overseas until the very end of the First
World War. If Croil had been converted to the idea of creating a national air force
broad, however, the government was not convinced. Although it agreed to send
10 (Army Co-operation) Squadron to support the 1st Canadian Division, no
ther RCAF units were to go overseas.[11]

By the end of 1939 fourteen squadrons were on active service in Canada, one
ıf which, No 110, was preparing to move to England, taking on additional
ıersonnel from the recently disbanded 2 (AC) Squadron. Only No 1 (Fighter)
vith seven Hawker Hurricanes and 11 (Bomber-Reconnaissance) with ten
Lockheed Hudsons were adequately equipped. Croil therefore submitted
ıstimates for the creation of an operational force of 252 combat aircraft,
ncluding twenty-four Hurricanes, eighteen Bristol Blenheims, thirty-four
Bristol Bolingbrokes, twenty Douglas Digbys, thirty Supermarine Stranraers,
wenty-four Hudsons, sixty-six Westland Lysanders, and thirty-six modern
lying boats and amphibians (flying boats fitted with landing gear to permit

operations from aerodromes as well as from water). For the last requirement the air staff selected the United States Navy's Consolidated PBY, known as the Catalina in the RAF, and, in the variant later built to RCAF specifications, the Canso or Canso A, the amphibious version. To cover wastage on operations, a total of 315 combat aircraft would have to be acquired; Croil hoped the programme could be completed during 1942. Compared to the more than 4000 aircraft needed for the BCATP this was a modest enough request, but one which proved difficult to satisfy.[12]

Despite neutrality laws, some American aircraft found their way to Canada. Since direct delivery by air was specifically prohibited, in December American pilots flew the first two machines to a field in Sweet Grass, Montana, and left them to be towed across the border. A Canadian present at the scene recalls what happened: 'They landed over the brow of a hill where we were waiting and then taxied up to a barbed wire fence separating a Canadian field at Coutts, Alberta, from the adjacent American field. The Americans got out and shook hands with [Squadron Leader R.C.] Gordon; everyone was in civilian clothes. The wire was then cut, a rope thrown across the border to be tied on the aircraft, as a team of horses dragged them over the line. The ground sloped towards our side and the first Digby began to roll quite rapidly causing considerable tension among the bystanders. Fortunately someone managed to get onto the step of the aircraft and after quite a struggle succeeded in putting on the brake.'[13] Eighteen other Digby crossed at Emerson, Man., and No 10 (BR) became the first operational Digby squadron in June 1940.[14]

The international border was the least of the air force's problems. Canada's wartime procurement machinery was a major obstacle, particularly in the period before the Department of Munitions and Supply was formed under C.D. Howe in April 1940. Before that date neither the Defence Purchasing Board nor its successor, the War Supply Board, had placed large enough orders, even though funds were available, and as a result some Canadian factories were forced to lay off men. In part this was because of the unwieldy Defence Purchasing, Profit Control and Financial Act of June 1939, which made it difficult to establish the costs of contracts.[15] At the same time, officials bound by the government's policy of limiting expenditures to avoid massive deficits found that the cost of manufacturing airframes for Canadian needs alone was often prohibitive. The Department of Munitions and Supply was intended to rationalize all production and procurement – a great improvement – but Howe's emphasis on production in quantity did not always work in the RCAF's best interests. The Home War Establishment needed limited numbers of several types of aircraft rather than large deliveries of only a few.

More disturbing, perhaps, though not surprising, was the fact that the Air Ministry in London favoured RAF requirements at the expense of the RCAF. There were few delays in the supply of training aircraft, Air Vice-Marshal Croil noted in April 1940, because the RAF had a vested interest in the success of the BCATP.[16] Canada and Great Britain, however, were competing for the limited supply of fighters, bombers, and maritime patrol aircraft available in the United States and the United Kingdom. The British inevitably and rightly judged their military situation to be more precarious than that of an overseas dominion far removed from the *Luftwaffe*, and after the fall of France in June it was obvious that the coming air battle over Britain was likely to be crucial. No one could deny the RAF's need for replacements, and yet the RCAF too had to expand, and (as it turned out) on a much larger scale than anyone had anticipated.

With expansion came the appointment, on 23 May 1940, of Major C.G. Power as minister of national defence for air. In law there was still a single Department of National Defence whose minister, Colonel J.L. Ralston, had overriding authority, but he confined himself to army concerns. Power, it will be recalled, found that he could not work with Croil and moved the chief of the air staff to the post of inspector general on 28 May, choosing Air Vice-Marshal Lloyd S. Breadner as the new professional head of the RCAF. Early in June the air members for personnel, organization and training, air staff, and aeronautical engineering (Group Captain Harold Edwards, and Air Commodores G.O. Johnson, A.A.L. Cuffe, and E.W. Stedman, respectively) joined Power and Breadner as members of an Air Council to co-ordinate policy, operations, administration, management, and training. This replaced an earlier council, which had not included the minister. Although fundamental policy decisions still appear to have been left in the hands of the chief of the air staff and his minister, the new Air Council nevertheless offered Power easy access to all his senior officers in a collegial atmosphere which he seemed to appreciate.[17]

As the new administration took shape, Britain's increasingly perilous situation overcame the government's reluctance to send additional squadrons overseas. Nos 1 (F) and 112 (AC) Squadrons were dispatched to England on 9 June, and all Canadian Hurricane production was diverted to the RAF. Despite Air Ministry appeals for trained crews from the Home War Establishment to make up for recent British losses, however, neither Power nor the prime minister would go any farther. Concerned about the impact on public opinion, they would not accept a British proposal to divert squadrons from the west coast or relegate those in the east to the status of operational training units.[18]

The air staff shared at least some of the government's concern about the state of Canada's defences. The BCATP and overseas demands had so restricted the growth of the Home War Establishment that only six squadrons were really effective, and that was not enough. On 21 May Breadner gave Air Commodore Cuffe the task of finding American replacements for the Hurricanes that had been offered to Britain, and henceforth the air member for air staff or the deputy chief of the air staff took over responsibility for the Home War Establishment. Within the month Breadner also recommended an increase in Eastern Air Command by five squadrons – two fighter and three flying-boat – to eleven, and of Western Air Command to eight, for a total of nineteen. This was essentially a continuation of the uncompleted prewar plan, with the addition of a fighter and maritime-patrol squadron on the east coast, a reflection of the RCAF's new responsibility for the defence of Newfoundland.[19]

Breadner's appreciation reflected the views of the chiefs of the naval and general staffs. Canada would 'sooner or later ... have to meet the maximum scale of attack' laid down in prewar assessments – bombardment by two eight-inch cruisers or one battleship and landings by small raiding parties – and the three services agreed that the RCAF was 'inadequate' to meet the threat. The Home War Establishment must be expanded, the chiefs of staff concluded, but not at the expense of the BCATP or the air force's existing overseas commitments. The new squadrons advocated by Breadner would therefore not be formed unti September at the earliest, and sometime later than that if aircraft and aircrew were required elsewhere.[20]

The gloom of May and June had brightened somewhat by August. The meeting between Mackenzie King and President Roosevelt at Ogdensburg no only opened the door to military co-operation with the United States, but also confirmed that Canada would not have to stand alone against Germany should Britain fall. The promise of American help meant that the air staff could continue to argue the case for further reinforcements to Britain. Spirits lifted again in September following the defeat of the *Luftwaffe*'s day offensive against the United Kingdom. Still, the need to assist the British remained, and the RCAF held to the view that any increase in the number of squadrons in Canada would interfere unnecessarily with the movement of aircrew overseas. Air Force Headquarters found support for their position from the Canada-United States Permanent Joint Board on Defence [PJBD], formed as a result of the Ogdensburg meeting. The American government, in its pessimism about the prospects for Britain's survival, believed that a major Axis attack on the Western Hemisphere was imminent. After listening to Canadian statements minimizing the threat to North America, however, US members of the PJBD agreed that sizeable forces need not be stationed on the continent. Provided facilities were made ready for American air forces in Newfoundland and Canada's Maritime provinces, the RCAF could establish its own priorities and make its own plans.[21]

These developments were reviewed on 1 October 1940, when Air Vice-Marshal Breadner submitted his outline for the RCAF's 1941 programme Although he stipulated that air training, overseas commitments, and the construction of airfields called for by the PJBD must have priority, he also noted that the time had come to begin completing the nineteen-squadron plan put forward in June. In particular he asked for 200 Martin B-26 Marauders to replace the less capable Bolingbrokes in 8 and 119 Squadrons as well as for new units Replacements for the Hurricanes sent to Britain and for the ancient Blackburn Shark torpedo-bombers and Vickers Vancouver flying boats in the west however, could wait.[22] Unfortunately, Breadner's request failed to take full account of the extent to which Canada depended on Great Britain and the United States for its aircraft and for all of its aero-engines. Air planning could not be done in isolation.

Referring to an earlier RCAF appreciation, the Air Ministry in London had drawn up a 'Target Program for the Dominions' shortly after Breadner submitted his proposals on 1 October. On the basis of British strategic assessments, the Air Ministry concluded that the Canadian Home War Establishment could be limited to no more than nine, and perhaps as few as seven, squadrons, with an initial establishment of seventy-six aircraft.[23] What could have been seen as a British attempt to dictate Canadian home defence policy prompted a mild but firm reply

The RCAF would make no further demands on the British for aircraft, Breadner wrote, but would seek instead to meet requirements from Canadian and American production (except for engines, which were still needed from Britain). At the same time, however, he informed the Air Ministry that the Home War Establishment would grow to nineteen fully equipped squadrons as conditions permitted. This was necessary because a successful enemy raid on Canada made possible by the RCAF's inadequate resources could 'disrupt Canada's war effort' and so play on the public's exaggerated fears that it would 'interfere with the flow of personnel and material to Great Britain.' At the same time, intensified German attacks on shipping had increased the need for air protection in the western Atlantic.[24]

Breadner's contention that a few German aircraft could attack vital points in the Maritimes and that enemy air bases might be constructed at isolated points on the east coast was unlikely to receive a sympathetic hearing from those accustomed to the German bombing of London. At the Washington ABC talks of January-March 1941, the 'Riviera' conference at Argentia, Nfld, in August, and the 'Arcadia' conference in December – at all of which Canadians were conspicuously absent – both British and American staffs agreed that North America was an inactive theatre of war. Little weight was given to matters of purely Canadian concern; the dominion could be supplied on a reduced scale.[25]

Breadner's judgment was also being questioned in Canada. Defence ministers Ralston and Power were stupefied when, in January 1941, the chief of the air staff rejected an offer by the British to give Canada sixty Hurricanes. The minister of aircraft production in England, the expatriate Canadian, Lord Beaverbrook, had earlier declared that allocating such modern fighters to North America would be a 'crime against the Empire,' but Ralston had somehow convinced him to change his mind. Breadner may well have been right to think that the Bell P-39 Airacobra or the Curtiss P-40 Kittyhawk, two American fighters soon to be available, were superior to the Hurricane I and therefore worth waiting for. With their limited range, the Hurricanes were perhaps more useful in Britain, but no matter what their limitations, they were superior to the few Grumman FF-I Goblin biplanes training for service at Halifax, and there were no other fighters in the country. Power overruled Breadner and asked Ralston to obtain the Hurricanes.[26]

Breadner's apparent lack of concern about the speedy expansion of the Home War Establishment – despite his commitment to the idea of nineteen squadrons – continued through February. At the end of the month, two days after a Chiefs of Staff Committee appreciation reasserted the need to strengthen the country's air defences, Breadner reiterated the RCAF's commitment to assist the RAF overseas. It was true, he admitted, that Canadian-based squadrons were understrength and inexperienced because of limits set on the number of BCATP graduates posted to the Home War Establishment, but he expected to make good all manpower shortages by May. Rather more curiously (given what he knew about the Hurricane offer in January), the chief of the air staff also noted that nothing would be gained by rushing the organization of these squadrons since so few aeroplanes were available.[27]

Breadner was caught by conflicting pressures. Determined to maintain the flow of aircrew to Britain, he had to minimize the threat to Canada in dealing with his political masters. Yet to persuade the British and Americans to supply Canada with airframes and engines it was necessary to emphasize the danger that the country faced. Such conflicting signals encouraged Canadian politicians to choose their own course, and since by and large they agreed that Canada's air defences were too weak, they were bound to put the emphasis on defending the homeland. On 2 March 1941 the prime minister intervened directly in deliberations aimed at securing British approval for the nineteen-squadron Home War Establishment programme. Citing the recent Chiefs of Staff Committee appreciation, Mackenzie King told Churchill that he anticipated early delivery of the aeroplanes required to bring all nineteen units up to strength.[28] The British were unresponsive. Great Britain had to be 'fully prepared to meet a large scale attempt at invasion,' replied the British prime minister, while Canada faced only 'tip and run' raids.[29]

King's view eventually prevailed. During a trip to England in April, Air Commodore Cuffe used a PJBD recommendation that fighter cover be provided for the aluminum industry at Arvida, Que., to persuade Air Vice-Marshal Sir John Slessor of the RAF that there was an immediate requirement for Hurricanes to form a new squadron specifically for this purpose. 'It is obviously a very important matter,' Slessor conceded, 'and we should not be lulled into a false sense of security by its distance.'[30] In May, as will be explained in Chapter 12, U-boat operations south of Greenland gave Canada important responsibilities in the northwest Atlantic, and after strong representations from Eastern Air Command the British loaned nine Catalinas to the RCAF. Then, in June 1941 the defence committee of the British Cabinet finally accepted in principle the Home War Establishment expansion plan and agreed to post a large number of BCAT graduates there.[31]

RCAF requirements at this time seemed reasonable enough. If Canadian factories could, as planned, turn out 151 Bolingbrokes, some Stranraers, fifty PBYS, 144 P-39 Airacobras, and 200 Martin B-26 Marauders, and if engines could be secured, the air force would be able to maintain nineteen squadrons at home. But the British, whatever they might have said in June, had their own needs. In September the Air Ministry asked for the return of nine Catalinas loaned in May and, as explained in chapter 10, for an additional fifty ordered by the RCAF. Canada agreed to surrender thirty-six. The next month the British took an even harder line, asking Canada not to undertake licensed production of the Airacobras and Marauders, but to build Avro Lancaster heavy bombers for the RAF instead. At the same time the British refused any early releases to Canada of P-39s on order for the RAF in the United States.[32]

Eagerness to support Britain had placed the RCAF in an awkward position. By agreement in 1939, Canadian factories had concentrated on producing training machines and only a few combat types for the RAF and RCAF, while the Air Ministry undertook to provide aircraft required by the RCAF that Canada had agreed not to assemble. This arrangement had never been wholly satisfactory because, understandably, the RAF became increasingly reluctant to release combat aircraft, especially after the fall of France and the opening of the war in North Africa. Canada had no choice but to look once again to the United States, either by placing orders directly with American firms or by seeking licensing agreements, as Breadner had done with the P-39s and B-26s. The latter alternative also appealed to C.D. Howe, who was anxious to engage Canadian factories in war production. The decision to switch to Lancasters did not upset Howe's plans – Canadian plants would still be busy – but it played havoc with Breadner's. With no domestic supplier for the types it required, and with the British blocking access to the American market without offering anything in return, the RCAF found itself increasingly isolated by Anglo-American co-operation in the allocation of war supplies.[33]

Co-ordinating the allocation of Allied aircraft was the task of the Anglo-American Joint Aircraft Committee [JAC]. Formed on 22 April 1941, and including among its members General H.H. Arnold of the US Army Air Corps, Rear Admiral J.H. Towers, US Navy, and Sir Henry Self and C.R. Fairly of the British Supply Council, the JAC had authority 'to schedule all deliveries ... the production of component parts as well as end products, and ... to make decisions prescribing standardization to be binding on all the parties concerned.'[34] Canada, clearly a concerned party, was not represented on the committee. The RCAF could hope only to influence British and American opinion through the Air Ministry, the PJBD, or other direct military contacts.

This was not easy. At the 'Argentia' conference in August, Admiral of the Fleet Sir Dudley Pound, first lord of the Admiralty, noted with surprise the number of amphibians and flying boats allocated to the RCAF. It may have been his intervention that led the Air Ministry to ask for the fifty Catalinas in September. Later that fall it seemed that the Americans were becoming more sympathetic, the RCAF encountering no difficulty in making arrangements to procure Curtiss P-40 Kittyhawks when P-39 supplies dried up. In November, however, the US chiefs of staff concluded that Canada needed only eight home defence squadrons (four fighter, four bomber), eleven fewer than the RCAF was contemplating.[35]

With the Americans and British together controlling the allocation of engines and airframes to Canada, the future organization of the RCAF's Home War Establishment was in considerable doubt when the Japanese attack on Pearl Harbor brought war in the Pacific on 7 December 1941. The recent acquisition of thirty Kittyhawks had improved the country's fighter defences, but the HWE still numbered only twelve combat squadrons, and of its 160 or so aircraft twenty-eight were obsolete and seventy-three were less than adequate for shipping protection and anti-submarine operations. Moreover, there was little reason to expect new aircraft to replace the Sharks, Vancouvers, Digbys, Bolingbrokes, and Hudsons or to complete the other seven squadrons that remained on the HWE's prospective order of battle.

The broadening of the war dramatically changed Canada's strategic position. Although the United States was now an ally, Canada faced enemies on both coasts, and to many observers seemed open to direct attack as never before. Japan's success at Pearl Harbor shocked Air Force Headquarters, not because

HOME WAR ESTABLISHMENT
OPERATIONAL AIRCRAFT
EASTERN AND WESTERN AIR COMMAND

Very long range patrol A/C (Liberators) ·

Long range patrol A/C (Canso/Catalina) ·

Medium range modern patrol A/C (Ventura, Hudson, Digby, Bolingbroke) ·

Medium range obsolete patrol A/C (Stranraer, Shark, Delta, Anson, Wapiti) ·

Modern fighters (Hurricane, Kittyhawk, Mosquito) ·

Obsolete fighters, etc. (Bolingbroke, Goblin) ·

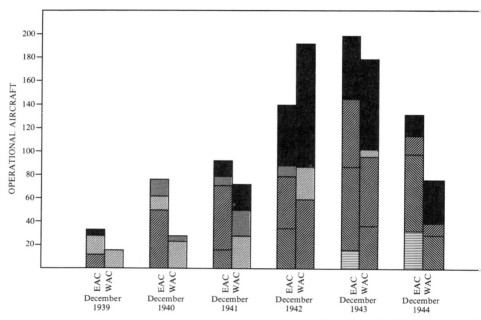

Source: Operational Record Books, DHis

war with Japan was unexpected, but because of the extent of the losses. Senio
officers from all three services had been worried about the state of Canada'
Pacific coast defences, but they had always insisted that the American fleet was
crucial guarantor of the region's security. 'Unless the United States Navy i
seriously defeated or loses its northern bases,' Air Vice-Marshal Croil ha
declared in October 1941, Canada's defence problem in the west could be
limited to 'watchful readiness.' There being little danger of direct attack, the
RCAF could safely limit its role to offshore reconnaissance to detect surfac

raiders.[36] Breadner agreed with Croil. So long as the Americans were in a position to offer effective assistance, the chief of the air staff wrote, it did not matter that the RCAF could not operate against 'larger naval attack, including carrier borne aircraft.'[37]

Not so confident, Power wanted an assurance that the west coast was secure. Breadner told the minister in late November that one fighter and five bomber-reconnaissance squadrons could be made available from Eastern Air Command in an emergency, but at the same time he directed his staff to conduct a more thorough strategic assessment.[38] Carried out between 30 November and 7 December, it too counted on a strong American fleet and discounted any notion of an American defeat. By 10 December, however, the Chiefs of Staff Committee was reporting something quite different: although it had been taken for granted that 'if Japan entered the war … the almost inevitable entry of the United States would more than balance the added threat to this continent – the unforeseen reverses in the Pacific … tended to modify this assumption.'[39] American ships no longer stood guard as anticipated, and to many in Ottawa, especially the political leaders, it now appeared that the Japanese had won a free hand to move about the Pacific at will, even east of Hawaii.

The chiefs of staff did not, even so, want to be 'stampeded' by alarmists, fearing the diversion of attention away from the war against Germany. Furthermore, they believed that Japan's main thrust would be into the south Pacific, not against the western coast of North America. Japan, however, would still be able to mount an occasional air raid, to bombard the shore, or stage small unit raids on shore. Breadner felt compelled to transfer one fighter and one bomber-reconnaissance squadron to the west coast, to complete the personnel and aircraft establishments of Western Air Command units 'as far as possible,' and to prepare Prince Rupert, Bella Bella, and Coal Harbour (on the northwest coast of Vancouver Island) as operational bases. In addition, the RAF's operational training unit at Patricia Bay was put on stand-by.[40]

These measures represented Canada's unilateral and improvised response to an unexpected emergency. The final shape of North American air defence depended ultimately on Canadian-US co-operation through their joint defence plan, ABC-22, which came into force on 7 December.[41] Early Canadian arguments that the Japanese were 'by far too good tacticians' to 'jeopardise their naval superiority' by attacking the west coast did not win American approval.[42] Over the next few months US representatives on the PJBD, 'very frightened' by the prospect of invasion, insisted on providing for the worst possible case, and pushed for American strategic and tactical command of all forces on the coast, a proposition wholly unacceptable to Canada. The Americans also worried about the increased likelihood of German incursions against the eastern part of the continent, urging the necessity of fighter defences at Sault Ste Marie to protect the ship canal there, the busiest in the world, and perhaps even continuous standing air patrols over Great Lakes iron ore traffic to protect it from attacks out of Hudson Bay.[43] On the Atlantic coast the US Army's commanding general in Newfoundland, Major General G.C. Brant, anticipated the fall of Great Britain, German victory in Africa, and 'devastating air raids' against all his installations as a prelude to a 'probable attempt in later stages to capture and hold Newfoundland.'[44]

Pessimism was not an American monopoly. Subordinate commanders on both Canadian coasts did not share the more detached view of the chiefs of staff in Ottawa. Very shortly after the Chiefs of Staff Committee reaffirmed that Canadian objectives were 'unlikely to be included in the probable main strategic aims of the enemy,'[45] Air Commodore L.F. Stevenson, air officer commanding Western Air Command, asked for sixteen squadrons to deal with the maximum scale of enemy attack by battleships, cruisers, and carrier-borne aircraft. Similarly, the Joint Services Committee (Pacific) cautioned that forward airfields planned for the Queen Charlotte Islands should not be built because they could be overrun easily and used by the Japanese to attack Victoria and Vancouver.[46] The air staff treated all such submissions sceptically. The director of plans and acting air member for air staff, Group Captain F.V. Heakes, noted that Western Air Command was failing to show 'any determination to improve any situation that exists or any impression of willingness ... to accept and make the best use of forces and facilities which exist.' Eastern Air Command's need for men and equipment was equally urgent; Stevenson could not expect immediate reinforcement.[47]

Improvements within the scope of available resources were another matter. On 12 February, two weeks before Stevenson asked for sixteen squadrons, the air staff met to consider whether the RCAF required any of the 400 Hurricanes to be built at Fort William. Without committing itself, but 'in the light of the changed war development,' the staff 'was unanimously of the opinion that the air defence requirements of Canada now called for a minimum of not less than 12 fighter squadrons' with 432 aircraft, thus trebling the previous bid for 144 P-39s or P-40s.[48] Subsequently, on 2 March, the Air Council informed Power that the two coastal commands would require a total of ten Canso squadrons with 360 aircraft, which included ample numbers for reserves and wastage, as compared to the forty-five aircraft in the six existing flying-boat/amphibian squadrons. With the additional fighter squadrons proposed in February, this meant that the air staff was seeking to expand the Home War Establishment from nineteen squadrons to thirty to meet the enlarged threat. On 10 March the air member for accounts and finance, Air Commodore K.G. Nairn, informed the deputy minister that the home war personnel establishment as a whole would grow from 1613 officers and 14,300 airmen to 2313 officers and 21,006 airmen.[49]

These were substantial increases, but to the government they no longer seemed enough. Although the chiefs of staff concluded in mid-February that an invasion of either coast was not 'a practicable operation of war,'[50] a rising tide of public anxiety in British Columbia was difficult to resist. Ian Mackenzie, minister of health and welfare but more importantly the minister with political responsibility for British Columbia, complained bitterly to the prime minister about the sorry state of the air force in his home province.[51] In the Cabinet War Committee on 20 February Power 'questioned the soundness of a policy which would provide for the defence of Canada only in order that Canada should assist in the defeat of the major enemy. The defence of Canada,' he argued, 'should surely be a primary objective in itself.'[52] Home defence was also the central issue discussed in a secret session of Parliament held on 24 February. The debate, Prime Minister King recorded in his diary that night, had 'served a useful purpose of giving something in addition in the way of information to members, and I think was helpful in bringing home to Ralston and the Defence Department the necessity of giving more attention to home defence, particularly on the Pacific Coast.'[53] A week later Norman Robertson and Hugh Keenleyside, officials of the Department of External Affairs, exchanged memoranda in which they contended that Japan could strike at British Columbia with relative ease. Canada, they agreed, should therefore look to its own security before sending any more men overseas. On 5 March, a Liberal Party caucus attended by the prime minister echoed these sentiments.[54] Misinformation, prejudice against the Japanese, and the string of disasters at Pearl Harbor, Hong Kong, Singapore, and the Philippines had undermined the politicians' confidence in military advice.

That same day the Cabinet War Committee decided to reinforce home defence rather than supplement its overseas forces. It reversed a decision made the month before to give the British half of the Canadian-built Consolidated Cansos then in production, and directed that initial aircraft go to six west-coast and four east-coast squadrons. Bolstered by General A.G.L. McNaughton's advice that public opinion should be considered in military decisions, the committee told the chiefs of staff to reconsider home defence requirements. On 9 March the RCAF began drafting a new air defence plan, and on 16 March the chief of the air staff submitted a proposal to increase the Home War Establishment to forty-nine combat squadrons. It was approved by the Cabinet War Committee after a perfunctory discussion two days later, along with a programme for a big expansion in the army at home which the chief of the general staff had prepared against his better judgment. The swift formulation of the forty-nine squadron plan represented a dramatic change in policy by the air staff and the Cabinet; as recently as January senior officials from the Department of Finance had strongly advised against a much more modest expansion.[55] Unfortunately, the main planning files kept by the air staff in Ottawa have disappeared, and it is difficult to understand whether the decision represents an independent RCAF reassessment of the threat, a fundamental judgment on the need to reorder and reorganize the air effort, or the product of political direction.

The weight of the available evidence suggests that the forty-nine squadron plan was a response to the perceived threat in the aftermath of Pearl Harbor. One other possible explanation, however, is that the air force intended that the additional squadrons should eventually go overseas. Power and Breadner (among others) had become annoyed at the Air Ministry's reluctance to have large numbers of Canadian squadrons established in the United Kingdom.[56] Forming these units in Canada, ostensibly for home defence, and then offering them for service abroad when conditions permitted was one way around the problem, and it may explain Power's careful words to the Cabinet War Committee on 18 March. Breadner's plan was 'elastic' enough, the minister remarked, to allow the squadrons to be 'used where they were needed.'[57] Air

Commodore A.T.N. Cowley, air member for organization, certainly had this in mind a little over a month later. 'The greatest contribution Canada can make towards ultimate victory', he asserted, 'is to develop overwhelming air strength. But the role of schoolmaster and supplier of fighting men is not enough. Canada should fight – not as a part (however vital that may be) of the great RAF, but as a self-trained, self-equipped, self-controlled RCAF. To do this we must not only continue to train vast numbers of air crews but we must also complete their training through the operational training stage ... We must produce aircraft and engines in Canada. We must complete, equip, and train fighter, bomber, reconnaissance and army-co-operation squadrons, wings, groups, and commands so that as soon as is humanly possible Canada will have a powerful striking force which may be used either for the defence of Canada at home, or in any theatre of war.'[58]

Cowley's views were shared by Air Vice-Marshal Harold Edwards, air officer commanding the RCAF in Great Britain, a passionate nationalist who had told Breadner in February 1942 'that he was prepared to recommend that the RCAF withdraw from Air Ministry Control and that we organize our own air force the Joint Air Training Plan notwithstanding.' Edwards and others in the RCAF wanted a balanced Canadian air force overseas – undoubtedly subject to Allied command and control, but nonetheless recognizable as a national formation;[59] utilizing the Home War Establishment as the foundation for this national air force, if that was the air staff's motive, was not an unreasonable way to achieve it.

Breadner, however, argued his case on the basis of home defence. Canada was now exposed to threats more serious than the 'tip and run' raids that had previously governed the strength of the home forces:

The changing war situation makes it expedient that Canada increase Air Defences to deal more effectively with the following dangers to the Supply Life Line to the United Kingdom and our own existence as a nation:
a. greatly increased enemy U-boat sinkings of our merchant shipping in the Western Atlantic;
b. possible enemy aircraft attacks on vital targets in East and West Coast regions;
c. possible bombardment of East and West Coast ports by enemy naval ships; and
d. possible invasion of Canadian Pacific Coast by enemy seaborne and air-borne forces.[60]

Believing the available forces to be entirely inadequate, Breadner proposed the formation of twelve new fighter and bomber-reconnaissance squadrons in the Atlantic region and eleven in the Pacific. In addition, he asked for fourteen night-fighter flights (one for each fighter squadron), an army co-operation squadron for Western Air Command, and two glider squadrons for each coast, one troop-carrying, the other for light tanks and Universal (Bren) carriers – these latter to permit the army to attack enemy lodgments on Canadian territory. Transport and utility/communications squadrons would bring the total to forty-nine, but that number could be increased to sixty-five by the addition of

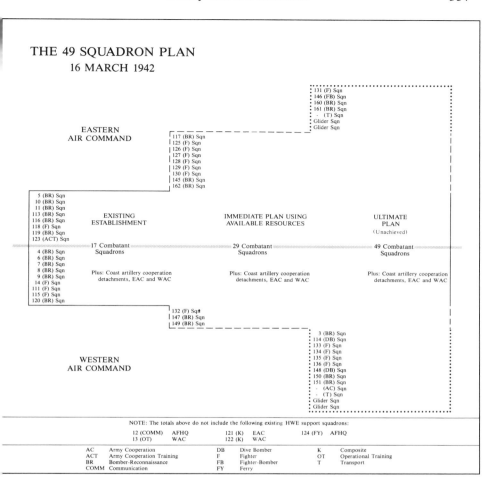

THE 49 SQUADRON PLAN
16 MARCH 1942

EASTERN
AIR COMMAND

131 (F) Sqn
146 (FB) Sqn
160 (BR) Sqn
161 (BR) Sqn
-   (T) Sqn
Glider Sqn
Glider Sqn

117 (BR) Sqn
125 (F) Sqn
126 (F) Sqn
127 (F) Sqn
128 (F) Sqn
129 (F) Sqn
130 (F) Sqn
145 (BR) Sqn
162 (BR) Sqn

5 (BR) Sqn
10 (BR) Sqn
11 (BR) Sqn
113 (BR) Sqn
116 (BR) Sqn
118 (F) Sqn
119 (BR) Sqn
123 (ACT) Sqn

EXISTING
ESTABLISHMENT

IMMEDIATE PLAN USING
AVAILABLE RESOURCES

ULTIMATE
PLAN
(Unachieved)

4 (BR) Sqn
6 (BR) Sqn
7 (BR) Sqn
8 (BR) Sqn
9 (BR) Sqn
14 (F) Sqn
111 (F) Sqn
115 (F) Sqn
120 (BR) Sqn

17 Combatant
Squadrons

29 Combatant
Squadrons

49 Combatant
Squadrons

Plus: Coast artillery cooperation
detachments, EAC and WAC

Plus: Coast artillery cooperation
detachments, EAC and WAC

Plus: Coast artillery cooperation
detachments, EAC and WAC

132 (F) Sqn
147 (BR) Sqn
149 (BR) Sqn

WESTERN
AIR COMMAND

3 (BR) Sqn
114 (DB) Sqn
133 (F) Sqn
134 (F) Sqn
135 (F) Sqn
136 (F) Sqn
148 (DB) Sqn
150 (BR) Sqn
151 (BR) Sqn
-   (AC) Sqn
-   (T) Sqn
Glider Sqn
Glider Sqn

NOTE: The totals above do not include the following existing HWE support squadrons:

| 12 (COMM) | AFHQ | 121 (K) | EAC | 124 (FY) | AFHQ |
| 13 (OT) | WAC | 122 (K) | WAC | | |

AC	Army Cooperation	DB	Dive Bomber	K	Composite
ACT	Army Cooperation Training	F	Fighter	OT	Operational Training
BR	Bomber-Reconnaissance	FB	Fighter-Bomber	T	Transport
COMM	Communication	FY	Ferry		

four fighter and four bomber squadrons to each of the coastal commands if assistance from the United States could not be guaranteed in the event of an invasion.

This plan entailed the purchase of 380 Hurricanes (now apparently acceptable), 244 de Havilland Mosquito night fighters and bombers, twenty-four P-40 Kittyhawks, 144 Canso amphibians, forty Vultee Vengeance light bombers, two hundred gliders, and forty transports, at an estimated cost of $151 million. These were in addition to the aircraft that would be required to complete the current nineteen-squadron establishment. The plan also required the establishment or expansion of airfields and base facilities at Gander and Goose Bay in Newfoundland and Labrador; at Sydney and Stanley, NS; at Pennfield Ridge, Moncton, and Chatham, NB; at Saguenay, Que.; and at Prince Rupert and Vancouver, BC. The additional 989 officers and 11,347 airmen that would be required brought the total cost to about $216 million.[61] The government's quick agreement allowed Breadner to direct his staff to implement the progamme forthwith. At the same time, as a measure of the graveness with which the air staff viewed the Axis threat, work proceeded on Plan 'Vanquo,' for the employment of BCATP schools, operational training units, and civil aviation in the last-ditch defence of the country.[62]

Within three months of the birth of the forty-nine squadron plan, the strategic situation on the Pacific changed dramatically. On 3–4 June 1942 the Japanese bombed Dutch Harbor on Unalaska Island in the Aleutian chain, and then occupied the even more remote and desolate islands of Kiska and Attu. Although the enemy's landings on United States territory caused great public alarm, his presence in limited strength 900 miles west of the Alaskan mainland was not a threat to continental North America. Most significantly, the Aleutian attacks were part of a larger operation that culminated in a decisive victory for the United States Navy over the main Japanese fleet in the Battle of Midway on 4 June.[63] The Japanese advance had been stopped and the Allies began to go on the strategic offensive; an invasion of the Canadian and American Pacific coast was now beyond the enemy's capacity. Although additional anti-submarine aircraft were urgently needed to meet the German U-boat offensive against shipping on the Atlantic coast, the procurement of very large numbers of other types of aircraft projected in the forty-nine squadron plan provided far more than 'a reasonable assurance' against any other form of attack 'likely to be made.'[64] Nevertheless, Air Force Headquarters was reluctant to reduce its expansion plan.

Implementing the plan was difficult, to say the least. Chronic shortages of aircraft, aero-engines, and spare parts continued, while, in the spring of 1942, there were still too few trained aircrew in the dominion to maintain the existing squadrons at full strength. The manpower problem was the easiest obstacle to overcome because it depended entirely on the quota of Canadian BCATP graduates allotted to home squadrons. The Air Ministry could hardly refuse Canada's request to revise article 14 of the BCATP Agreement when there was an acknowledged surplus of aircrew in England. Accordingly, when the question was raised at the Ottawa Air Training Conference in May, the British readily agreed that current regulations were 'not flexible enough' and raised the proportion of pilots posted to the Home War Establishment from 5.6 to 9 per cent of total BCATP output. The allocations of most other aircrew categories to Canada rose as well.[65]

The key provision in the revised BCATP Agreement was the linking of the total Home War Establishment allotment of aircrew to the number of aircraft that could be made available to the RCAF from all sources. Indeed, when Canadians first raised the question of amending article 14, the RAF air member for supply and organization, Air Vice-Marshal W.F. Dixon, asked for more details in order to 'assist the work of the Munitions Assignment Board.'[66] Here lay the RCAF's fundamental problem in carrying through expansion of the home air force. For although the RCAF was guaranteed more aircrew after May 1942, there could be no assurance that it would receive sufficient aircraft for forty-nine operational squadrons whether they were to serve at home or abroad.

The Munitions Assignment Board had been established shortly after the

United States' entry into the war as part of the formal Anglo-American machinery to co-ordinate the Allied war effort. Two Combined Munitions Assignment boards were created as a result of the 'Arcadia' conference, one in London, the other in Washington, and both were charged with the allocation of all the war matériel placed in common Allied pools according to strategic directives produced by the Anglo-American Combined Chiefs of Staff. Discussions on sharing aircraft from these pools took place in January 1942, and the resulting Arnold-Portal agreement – named for Lieutenant General H.H. Arnold, chief of the US Army Air Forces, and Air Chief Marshal Sir Charles Portal, the British chief of the air staff – set basic policy for dividing production between the United States and Great Britain. At that time the British also announced their intention to speak for all the dominions and to count allocations to them as part of the United Kingdom's share.[67]

From the British point of view the RCAF could have chosen no worse moment to ask for aircraft. The RAF was actively engaged all over the world and was already competing with the US army and naval air forces for American-made aircraft. Canada, by comparison, remained an inactive theatre whose large requirements seemed dubious. The British attitude is best illustrated by the Air Ministry's reaction to the forty-nine squadron 'Air Defence of Canada' plan forwarded from Ottawa in April 1942. 'In fact, Vancouver is fighting with its back to the wall,' one official observed drily; another made light of Breadner's assessment that Canada was vulnerable to attack. Of the four threats outlined in the plan only the first – 'greatly increased enemy U-boat sinkings of our merchant shipping' – was considered to be wholly justified. Inevitably, most Canadian bids for aircraft brought before the London assignment board from January to June 1942 were either ignored or rejected out of hand.[68]

All three Canadian services expected to suffer if the Americans and British controlled the distribution of Allied war matériel. As early as 29 January 1942, therefore, the Chiefs of Staff Committee urged the government to secure Canadian service representation on every assignment board. The Cabinet War Committee discussed the matter on 4 February but reached no decision, no doubt because Howe was unhappy with the idea. In his view Canadian participation on these boards would force the country to pool all domestic production, robbing the government of its right to determine the final destination of Canadian-made equipment. This would affect the army, which was to be supplied with Ram tanks manufactured in Canada, in particular. The RCAF's interests differed because the Home War Establishment relied almost exclusively on British and American aircraft. A formal request from the British and Americans for Canada to submit its total war production for allocation by the assignment board in either London or Washington arrived later in February. Howe objected once again, hoping that Canada could retain control over those items destined for the Canadian armed forces while pooling the rest. The British and Americans together opposed any such division of Canadian production, and when the differences could not be reconciled Ottawa did not insist.[69]

The government tried to protect the RCAF's interests. In mid-March the Cabinet decided to place Canadian bids for aircraft in Washington rather than

London, beginning that May. Past experience had convinced Power that the Americans were more likely to give sympathetic consideration 'to the needs of North American defence' than the British. At the same time the Cabinet wished to gain Canadian representation on the Washington assignment board and all its subcommittees; in the interim, the British would continue to speak for Canada in the American capital and allocate aircraft to the RCAF from their share.[70]

The Combined Chiefs of Staff wasted no time in clarifying their views. On 23 March their Directive 50/2 governing the allocation of war matériel rated the defence of North America among the lowest priorities. This meant that the European theatre, Hawaii, Australia, India, and Burma were all favoured over the RCAF Home War Establishment in competition for aircraft from the Allied pool. Prospects for completing the air defence of Canada plan grew still bleaker. Having discovered that their production would not meet the needs of the rapidly expanding US Army Air Forces or the naval air arm, let alone those of their Allies, the Americans imposed a virtual freeze on all aircraft shipments to Canada. The Air Council in Ottawa concluded forlornly that Canada 'would probably be required to accept what is available' rather than the desired numbers and types.[71]

Events in Washington bore out this gloomy prognosis. Taking into account the shortfall in US output, the Arnold-Portal-Towers agreement of 21 June (Rear Admiral John H. Towers, US Navy, represented the interests of American naval aviation) revised existing production-sharing formulae, making drastic cuts in the supply of American aeroplanes to the British Commonwealth.[72] A week later the American Joint Chiefs of Staff proposed an allocation that was eighty-five aircraft short of the RCAF's pre-March establishment, and over 500 below the figure set for forty-nine squadrons. This was significant, the Canadian air attaché in Washington discovered, because Arnold-Portal-Towers had also agreed that Canada came under American strategic control, which meant that the US Joint Chiefs' interpretation of Canadian requirements would carry great weight.[73] Finally, on 4 July, the Anglo-American Combined Planning Staff in Washington found that the US Army Air Forces would not meet their own goals with existing rates of production and decided that, apart from flying boats and maritime patrol aircraft like the Hudson, no American aircraft could be made available to British dominions within American spheres of responsibility.[74] That left out the RCAF, as well as the Australian and New Zealand air forces, despite the fact that under ABC-22 the United States had no right to assert its jurisdiction over Canada.[75]

So far as the Anglo-American Combined Chiefs were concerned, Canada could draw on its own production for the expansion of the RCAF. The Americans seem not to have realized, however, that Canadian industry was not producing aircraft of the types required for home defence because of previous agreements with the United Kingdom. Indeed, the Combined Chiefs' policy would have limited the RCAF's immediate expansion to nine squadrons – two Bolingbroke, four Hurricane, two Mosquito, and one Canso.[76]

The RCAF enlisted the support of the PJBD to challenge the Combined Chiefs' decision placing Canada under US strategic control. But although the senior

American army representative, Lieutenant General Stanley D. Embick, agreed with the Canadian interpretation of ABC-22, the PJBD was an advisory body only, and its recommendations could safely be ignored. They were. Breadner instructed Air Commodore G.V. Walsh, the RCAF attaché in Washington, to point out to the US joint staff that there was a direct threat to North America. Besides, when the Americans had asked for help in strengthening their Alaskan garrison the RCAF had responded willingly and quickly despite its paucity of resources. It was time, Breadner hinted, for the United States to return the favour. In his meeting with the American staff, Walsh also took a firm stand on the question of the strategic direction of Canadian forces, making clear that the Canadian government had never surrendered its sovereign right to exercise such control. The American officers, however, reaffirmed the US Joint Chiefs' intention to assess the merits of all Canadian defence plans through the Combined Munitions Assignment Board. Breadner asked Power to revive the question of securing Canadian representation on the board, but Howe remained adamantly opposed, arguing that any change in the status quo might jeopardize the placing of Allied orders with Canadian firms in the future.[77]

Breadner had little choice but to accept the US Joint Chiefs' evaluation of Canadian aircraft bids before they were passed to the Combined Chiefs and thence to the combined board.[78] With the US freeze on deliveries still in effect, and since the British would do nothing to strengthen the RCAF at the RAF's expense, the only way to ensure the supply of aeroplanes to Canada was to comply with Anglo-American assessments of Canadian requirements.

If ever there was a time for the air staff and the government to reassess the forty-nine squadron plan it was the period after July 1942. In view of the changed strategic situation and Anglo-American reluctance to fill large orders for the Canadian home air force, it would have been both politic and strategically sound for the RCAF to have restricted its demands to anti-submarine types for the Atlantic coast. Instead, the air staff clung firmly to its March 1942 appreciation.

The Canadian attitude contributed even further to Anglo-American scepticism about the RCAF's home war plan. In a study of the dominion air forces, JPS 37/1, that went to the Combined Chiefs of Staff on 3 August 1942, the American War Department joint staff planners readily admitted that the RCAF Home War Establishment would be an 'unbalanced force unsuitable for Canadian requirements' if forced to rely solely on domestic production. However, the planners thought this unimportant, concluding that the Canadians should be limited to twenty-eight home squadrons equipped with obsolescent aircraft unsuitable for other employment. The American commitment to the RCAF stood at sixty-one Hudsons and fifteen transports. They would allocate no fighters; moreover, they suggested that the RCAF should abandon its most recent claim to 167 Hurricanes from the Fort William, Ont., plant.[79]

These proposals were slightly modified. Air Commodore Walsh was able to inform Breadner that the RCAF could plan for a thirty-squadron Home War Establishment and that a final decision in Washington would be delayed until Ottawa replied. Breadner disagreed, and on his specific instructions Walsh protested to Brigadier General W. Bedell Smith, secretary to the US Joint Chiefs.

Walsh informed Smith that the American recommendations would force the RCAF to disband units which were already forming, and to undertake a complex reassignment of roles for squadrons on active service. Canada would have no proper striking force, no torpedo-bombers, and an inadequate fighter force. But Smith promised nothing, and Walsh warned Breadner that the Home War Establishment would never be able even to approach forty-nine squadrons. He nevertheless advised Breadner to insist that existing squadrons must be maintained at strength and provided with suitable aircraft.[80]

Breadner faced up to the inevitable and modified the forty-nine squadron plan. Walsh informed Air Marshal Douglas Evill, head of the RAF Washington delegation, that Canada's objective was thirty-five squadrons with a maximum of 575 aircraft: fourteen fighter or army co-operation squadrons equipped with Kittyhawks or Mosquitoes; twenty bomber or general-reconnaissance squadrons; and one dive-bomber squadron. This seemed reasonable to Evill, except for the large number of fighter squadrons, but he was in no position to help. The RCAF's option on British orders placed in the United States had been cancelled as a result of Canada's decision to enter its bids in Washington. The British could not support these requests, Evill explained, because the dominions came under American strategic control.[81]

The aircraft supply situation became still more difficult in September 1942. Because of fighter requirements for 'Torch' (the Allied landings in North Africa), the Desert Air Force, and the Soviet Union through lend-lease, the RAF was unwilling to allocate any Canadian-made Hurricanes to the RCAF. Since production at Fort William was scheduled to cease in April 1943, the RCAF seemed about to lose this one domestic source completely. Yet, as so often before, Air Force Headquarters willingly released 200 of these aircraft to the Air Ministry on the understanding that replacements from the United States would be made available in the spring of 1943.[82] Troubled by aircraft shortages so severe that they were reducing reserve and wastage rates for their formations overseas, however, the Americans anticipated no surplus for many months. In fact, Walsh reported in September that the US Joint Chiefs were about to reassess RCAF home defence requirements. Thirty-five squadrons might become twenty-five, or even fewer.[83]

Faced with this depressing news, Group Captain Heakes, now director of operations, examined the options open to Air Force Headquarters. If the RCAF accepted Allied advice and simply deferred its hopes for expansion until the supply situation was better, it would take months, perhaps years, before Canada had an adequate maritime patrol force, its most pressing requirement. Appropriating Canadian production, now including the Mosquito as well as the Lancaster, Hurricane, Bolingbroke, and Canso, offered no solution. Canada, which still manufactured no aero-engines, would surely be removed from the Allied pool. Increasing Bolingbroke and Canso production would add maritime-patrol aircraft (if engines were available), but it would not alleviate the fighter problem. The only solution Heakes could offer was for the government to continue to press for Canadian representation on the combined board in the hope that something better could be worked out there.[84]

Comments on Canadian requirements by Air Vice-Marshal Slessor, assistant chief of the air staff (policy) at the Air Ministry, did not ease the air staff's frustration. While admitting that Canada was 'not obliged to accept [American] estimates of her requirements,' Slessor nevertheless hoped that the dominion could be reconciled to American strategic direction of its forces. After all, every Allied power had accepted 'some abdication of sovereignty' for the common good, and Canada should not expect preferential treatment. Slessor also hoped that Canada would not seize its own production, which 'was ... primarily to meet the requirements of ... active theatres of war' and not for home defence in North America. Although the United Kingdom would not 'make a stand on any legal grounds' and had 'at best only a moral claim to certain aircraft now being produced in Canada, notably the Hurricanes,' Slessor held that the dominion should still pool all its resources for allocation 'according to the vital strategic requirements of the time.' It was unthinkable that the Canadian government would consider only its own interests and stand aloof from 'any arrangements for the coordination of the war effort.'[85]

Slessor's remarks thoroughly annoyed the air staff. Terence Sheard, air member for supply, complained to Breadner that the memorandum was 'rather irritating', in its 'old Colonial Office attitude.' There was a vast difference, Sheard noted, between 'abdicating sovereignty' while retaining a seat on the most important Allied planning and supply councils, as was the case with both Britain and the United States, and surrendering control without a voice. Sheard was confident that Canadian industry would eventually manufacture additional types of aircraft for the Home War Establishment, but at the moment the country needed 'immediate assistance' because of misplaced confidence in British promises to supply those types if Canada would concentrate on the production of others more urgently required by the RAF for the fighting fronts. 'The practical nullification of these undertakings,' Sheard warned, was about to lead to 'dangerous inadequacy in the equipment available for home defence.' This was essentially a government problem, but he feared the result if the politicians failed to press others to live up to their commitments to the RCAF.[86]

Group Captain Heakes was equally disturbed by Slessor's remarks when he met Air Marshal Evill in Ottawa. Looking for a better offer than that made by the American joint planners, Heakes told Evill that Canada was willing to let the British have 200 Hurricanes now if the RCAF could be certain of having sufficient other fighters on hand to maintain ten home defence squadrons at full strength at all times – in other words, rather more than 200 machines. Evill expressed his customary 'sympathy,' but emphasized Britain's greater need for fighters in more active theatres.[87] Heakes tried again two days later. The British first asked for all the Canadian-made Hurricanes without guaranteeing their replacement. Heakes countered that the fighters would be released if the Americans supplied a substitute. He also raised the possibility that Canada might seize all domestic production for the RCAF. This was a 'drastic solution,' he admitted, but it was justifiable on the grounds that 'overseas operations must be predicated upon the principle of [a secure] home base.' The British, however, ignored Heakes' threat and he retreated, convinced that Canada was 'a beggar at a rich man's table.'[88]

Heakes complained acidly to Breadner that 'we are being asked ... to accept some abdication of sovereignty determined for us by third parties without ourselves having a voice.' The British would not even admit that Canada had a home defence problem. 'Without intending to be critical,' he went on, 'I do not believe that until the fall of Burma and Singapore, the UK ever appreciated that Australia and New Zealand had a basic Home Defence problem.' This had been a 'fundamental error' in British reasoning, and it would not be repeated. Canada was not going to be unprepared, and her determination to be ready could not 'be lightly passed over by a senior partner who does not share that responsibility.'[89] Notably, however, Heakes made no comment on the changing strategic balance after Midway. The threat to Canada was diminishing daily, the sole exception being U-boat attacks on shipping in the western Atlantic.

Heakes was especially critical of the British position on Hurricanes. Howe had ordered 400 on his own initiative to keep the Canadian Car and Foundry plant open until it began producing more modern types. When the RAF displayed no interest in these early models, Howe intended to export them to China, until the RCAF submitted its claim. It was then, Heakes thought, that the British decided to ask for the fighters as part of their lend-lease contribution to the Soviet Union. In Heakes' view, the RCAF had acted first, and its claim was stronger. In fact, as the Department of Munitions and Supply knew, the Air Ministry had made a prior claim, and there was a moral commitment to deliver the aeroplanes to Britain. Heakes proposed drastic measures on 25 September. Despite the fact that no aero-engines were manufactured in the country, the director of operations declared bluntly that 'if there is no possibility of Canada obtaining representation on reasonable terms, I am firmly convinced that we must exercise firm control of the only weapon we possess, namely the production of our own industry.' Compromise would be possible only if 'the security of our country was not at stake.' Sheard agreed.[90]

Breadner presented these views to the minister that same day. He also told Power that the government had not done enough to secure Canadian representation on the assignment boards, and he wanted to be sure that the minister understood that even limited participation in the combined board was worth whatever effort was involved. 'Canadian production,' he explained, '... is in effect pooled now in the sense that it is very difficult for us to resist pressure for allocations to other theatres. This is particularly true when such pressure comes from the United States, as it is certain to do with respect to future deliveries of operational aircraft. I believe we would be in a better position to meet such pressure if it were channeled through an official body. Even if our representation were limited ... our representative would at least have some opportunity of scrutinizing requests, which is more than we have now.'[91] Canada would gain some leverage, however limited, and obtain a broader understanding of the allocation process and the dominion's place within it. Power took the case to Cabinet, where he found that J.L. Ralston now shared Howe's reservations about pooling production because representation on the board would gain nothing for the land forces overseas. The question was deferred and never raised again.[92]

By October 1942 Air Council realized that aircraft would probably never be supplied for a balanced air force in Canada. They also admitted for the first time that the strategic assumptions that underlay the scheme were no longer valid. Canadian bids would not be accepted 'merely on the distant theory of attack on our coasts,' and the limited expansion plan for 1943 was in jeopardy.[93] The American General H.H. Arnold, in a letter to Walsh in Washington, confirmed this view by urging that air force establishments in North America should be kept 'at the lowest possible minimum.'[94] Walsh continued to seek Air Marshal Evill's support, but the British airman echoed Arnold's remarks, pointing out that the Canadians might enjoy greater success if they showed a more realistic appreciation of the Allies' overall supply problems. Ten Hurricane squadrons (with 165 aircraft), five P-40 squadrons (with 87 aircraft), four Hudson squadrons (with 22 aircraft), six Bolingbroke squadrons (with 68 aircraft), and eleven Canso squadrons (with 267 machines) was the maximum Evill was willing to concede. Walsh seems to have been convinced that the RCAF must reduce its demands, especially as they related to reserve and wastage estimates, both of which remained substantially higher than those adopted by the British and the Americans for their operational squadrons overseas.[95]

Air Force Headquarters in Ottawa did reduce its demands, but not by enough. Aside from U-boat attacks on shipping, after all, the only potential threats were shelling by a pocket battleship on the Atlantic coast, or operations by a small carrier task force off British Columbia. Neither was particularly likely. More damaging still from the point of view of the RCAF's credibility, the number of squadrons the air staff wanted had risen to forty-three, of which fewer than a third were for anti-submarine operations off the east coast.[96] General Arnold suggested that thirty squadrons of all types might be too many.

The combined board's tentative allocations of mid-November, which were not then revealed to the RCAF, fell far short of Canada's stated requirements. As against Canadian requests for the delivery of 783 aircraft during 1943, the combined board allowed that 455 might be provided. The biggest cuts were in fighters: the air staff in Ottawa wanted 342; the board believed that 143 would be enough. Still, the allocations were larger than might have been expected. The Canadian air staff's persistence may have helped, but British influence is more likely to have made the difference. By late fall the Air Ministry was becoming increasingly worried that American insistence on Canadian industrial self-reliance would endanger British orders in Canada. For this reason Air Marshal Evill informed Walsh that Britain would support Canadian bids for a significantly increased share of American production.[97] At the same time, the Air Ministry wanted to renegotiate the terms of the Arnold-Portal-Towers agreement because American production had increased, and because it was taking longer than anticipated to find aircrew for the US Army Air Forces in Europe. The British succeeded, persuading President Roosevelt to put aside his policy requiring American crews to fly the majority of American-built aircraft. 'If you can get at the enemy quicker and just as effectively as we can,' he wrote to Churchill, 'then I have no hesitancy in saying that you and the Russians should have the planes you need.'[98] Freer access to American production would reduce the RAF's need for Canadian-made machines, some of which the Home War Establishment could now use, and possibly persuade the British to release some American types to the RCAF. The combined board, however, was unwilling to grant Canada further concessions, and its January 1943 allocation to the RCAF simply repeated November's figures.

The air staff accepted the situation as gracefully as possible. Even if home defence squadrons remained short of fighters, the combined board's assignment of twenty Curtiss Helldivers would at least give the RCAF a dive-bomber squadron, while the 157 Lockheed Venturas allocated, although substantially fewer than the 288 requested by the RCAF, would be sufficient to form two new bomber-reconnaissance squadrons and modernize three others for both the strike role against enemy surface warships and anti-submarine duties. Eastern Air Command's most desperate need, however, was for additional maritime-patrol aircraft with much greater endurance than the Ventura. Deliveries of long-range Cansos from Canadian production, which were now beginning, would help, but there was an urgent requirement for very long-range [VLR] Consolidated B-24 Liberator four-engine bombers to counter the U-boats inflicting heavy losses on shipping south of Greenland. The RCAF had requested Liberators in a separate bid; these were undoubtedly the most important type that could be added to the Home War Establishment's inventory. Yet the air staff's only quibble with the combined board's decision was that it had not allotted more fighters.[99]

Given the virtual freeze on the delivery of American aircraft since May 1942 and the disappointing allocations since then, most of the Home War squadrons, other than anti-submarine units on the Atlantic coast, were only marginally better off in 1943 than they had been the year before. Eastern Air Command's priority made complaints from British Columbia inevitable. In June 1943, for example, the officer commanding 4 Group in Vancouver wrote to the air officer commanding Western Air Command pointing out that the air staff seemed to consider 'our line of defences as the Rocky Mountains and not the Pacific Coast,' and so was 'prepared to sacrifice the coast to the enemy and spend several years trying to dislodge him.'[100] Later that summer, and then again in the fall, the Joint Canadian-United States Services Committee, formed on the west coast to co-ordinate local defence planning, observed that 'A Japanese force consisting of an aircraft carrier, six or seven transports, possibly an army division with anti-aircraft and field guns, supported by one or two capital ships ... could quite easily launch an attack against the Queen Charlotte Islands and establish themselves and have sufficient equipment for their own protection to be able to construct aerodromes and operate aircraft at leisure in approximately three weeks.' The RCAF, if attacked, 'would have no alternative but to either endure the attack or evacuate the machines to an inland base or destroy them.'[101]

Subordinate regional headquarters were bound to focus on apparent local requirements, however extreme. But as Group Captain Heakes had reminded Breadner in October 1942, 'in matters of air strategy the local view must give way to the larger view.' This demanded a careful husbanding of the limited number of aircraft available. In addition, the Japanese had already been taught that they could not 'manoeuvre with impunity' and so were not expected to undertake major operations against the Pacific coast.[102] This optimistic view was corroborated by the Anglo-American Combined Staff planners on 16 January 1943. Their analysis confirmed that an invasion of North America in force by either the Germans or the Japanese was entirely 'out of the question,' and as the PJBD had done before Pearl Harbor they discounted the possibility of raids by more than 500 men. The continued presence of Japanese forces on American soil in the Aleutians remained a concern, as did the enemy's capability of mounting 'an occasional carrier-borne raid on profitable objectives' including Vancouver and the 'military installations and bases in the Alaskan-North Canadian area.' The staff planners nonetheless concluded that there was no requirement to strengthen the forces available to defend the west coast.[103]

In February 1943 the Canadian Joint Planning Sub-Committee had reviewed its own estimates of the forms and scales of attack anticipated on the Atlantic coast and determined once again that the 'lack of Axis shipping and the relative strengths of the enemy and the United Nations Naval forces prohibit an invasion in force ... [or] a sea-borne raid on a large scale ... The losses which the enemy would suffer would be out of all proportion to any temporary advantages that they might expect to gain.' Smaller raids were possible, as were sporadic air attacks, but the major threat was under the sea.[104]

The growing concern over the success of German U-boats was reflected in the new Air Defence of Canada Plan submitted by Air Marshal Breadner on 20 March 1943. The 'maximum effort' was to be made on the Atlantic coast to assist the Royal Canadian Navy in its anti-submarine operations and to build up an air striking force capable of attacking enemy shipping. This meant bringing all existing squadrons up to strength and the formation of two of the Canso bomber-reconnaissance squadrons authorized the year before. So far as the fighter force was concerned, the two squadrons still waiting to be formed were to be held in abeyance 'because of a diversion of fighter aircraft to the United Kingdom for ... more active theatres of war,' because of the need to economize, and because there had been 'some reduction in the possibility of air attack.' The Mosquito night-fighter detachments called for a year before could be dispensed with altogether. On the west coast, the chief of the air staff noted, there had been considerable progress in the construction of bases, but little improvement in the command's operational capabilities. He therefore proposed to form one new reconnaissance squadron and two striking force squadrons there, one of which could be posted to Eastern Air Command as required. Air raids were still held to be a possibility, even if remote, and so one new fighter squadron should be brought onto the active order of battle. As on the Atlantic coast, the night-fighter flights could be dispensed with.[105]

The air staff had significantly scaled down the projected expansion of the home air force. Breadner, however, continued to think in terms of a forty-one squadron Home War Establishment, six more than the authorities in Washington had approved as an absolute maximum, with hundreds more aircraft than the most optimistic forecasts: 401 Cansos, 244 Mosquitoes, 214 Hurricanes, 157 Lockheed Venturas, 45 Kittyhawks, 25 Curtiss Helldivers, and 15 VLR Liberators. This was excessive in view of the latest assessment of forms and scales of attack, and beyond the capacity of anticipated American production. Over the next few months the air staff reduced its bids for fighters while stepping up, with British support, the campaign for VLR Liberators and Ventura maritime-patrol aircraft. This made sense; the greatest contribution the Canadian Home War Establishment could now make to winning the war was protection of shipping in the north Atlantic.[106]

The authorities in Washington, even so, had another perspective. Canadian fighter bids were still regarded as excessive, and the request for maritime-patrol aircraft could not be filled either. The combined board offered only eighty-one aircraft for delivery in 1944, including just forty-three Venturas and no Liberators. These meagre numbers provoked a vigorous appeal from the Canadian air staff for 143 P-40 Kittyhawks (to replace the Lockheed P-38 Lightnings and North American P-51 Mustangs it had been refused), sixty additional Venturas, and a number of Liberators. The only additional offer from Washington was eighteen and perhaps as many as twenty-one Liberators for 1944. This helped, but the fact that the Ventura allotment for 1944 remained in doubt (the forty-three being supplied were for 1943) was particularly disturbing. Only the RCAF had been interested in this type when it was first placed in the Allied pool; however, when the British, Australians, and New Zealanders decided that they also wanted Venturas their higher priority meant that the supply to Canada had to be reduced. Air Vice-Marshal N.R. Anderson, the RCAF air member for air staff, thought that it was time for Canada to call in the British debt. A good many aircraft had been released to the RAF. Some reciprocity was called for.[107]

The air member for supply reacted to these developments by immediately preparing a new bid for forty-eight VLR Liberators (to replace the lost Venturas) and an additional fifty-two Kittyhawks. However, the Americans had already delayed the final promulgation of the 1944 allocation in order to accommodate the RCAF. They had made the supply problem as plain as possible and would not accept further delays. Sheard's request was ignored. Nevertheless, Walsh was soon able to report that additional Liberators might be obtained if they were requested separately from Canada's general bid. General Arnold had apparently agreed that, because of their experience in flying over the north Atlantic, RCAF squadrons should receive these aircraft before American units accustomed to operating further south. Air Force Headquarters gladly accepted the combined board's latest offer.[108]

Allied military successes through the rest of 1943 brought further changes in plans, especially after the last Japanese had been driven from the Aleutians in July. On 16 August the Combined Chiefs of Staff issued a new study of the scales of attack expected on North America (CCS 127/3) in which the threat to the east coast was considered to be very small. 'Submarine attacks on shipping and minelaying in the coastal zone' were 'continuing possibilities,' as were 'sporadic bombardment of shore installations' and the landing of 'commando raiders or saboteurs,' but 'only on a small scale.' Attacks by surface raiders were 'highly improbable' and air attacks even more unlikely. Scales for the west coast were generally similar, except that the risks of submarine operations were

maller and those by shipborne aircraft comparatively greater. Both of these
hreats, however, were considered 'very unlikely.'[109]

When Breadner issued his appreciation for 1944, he observed that the RCAF
iad to take 'full cognizance of the necessity for economy at home' while
iroviding forces 'adequate for the protection of the Dominion.' That meant that
ihe air force could for the moment afford to give priority to its overseas effort,
ind thus make 'some deletions and other modifications' to the Home War
istablishment.[110] Breadner's plan differed little from the Air Defence of Canada
'lan already approved. The chief of the air staff judged that there could be no
eduction in the seven anti-submarine reconnaissance squadrons in Eastern Air
ommand if daily sweeps and convoy escorts were to be maintained at existing
evels. Nor could there be any reduction in the striking force which, though
istablished to counter surface warships, in fact flew anti-submarine operations.
ndeed, Breadner hoped that one of the four Hudson and Ventura squadrons
night soon receive Liberators to strengthen Eastern Air Command's very
ong-range capability against both ships and U-boats. Similarly, the four fighter
quadrons still on the east coast (two had been selected for transfer overseas)
vould remain on strength, although there could be some reduction in the size of
ihe sector control staffs. The army co-operation squadron at Debert, NS, would
iroceed overseas, and the coast artillery detachments at Torbay, Sydney,
Dartmouth, and Yarmouth could be phased out now that there were radars to
issist the gunners.

For the west coast, Breadner now discounted the possibility of major Japanese
iperations and recommended reductions. Two bomber-reconnaissance squad-
ons would be struck off strength; the fighter-bomber unit planned for 1943-4
vould not be formed; the army co-operation squadron could be converted to
ighter, and the coast artillery co-operation detachment disbanded. The
icheduled increase in maritime-patrol squadron establishments from nine to
ifteen aircraft was cancelled, a move which decreased the planned anti-shipping
iorce by the equivalent of two squadrons. Breadner nevertheless believed that
ome enemy activity had to be 'guarded against' by pushing patrols farther out to
iea; presumably this would be possible because Western Air Command would
eceive modern aircraft in place of the obsolete Stranraers still flying. With three
inits approved for transfer overseas, Breadner would not consider reducing the
ighter squadrons in the west below the current level of four, despite Japan's
everses in the Aleutians and the south Pacific. Accordingly, after some
eorganization of the transport, communications, and composite squadrons,
Western Air Command would be left with sixteen squadrons and Eastern Air
ommand with eighteen, one squadron less than the 1942 American recommen-
iation of thirty-five.

The Cabinet approved and, as well, cancelled the Helldiver order and reduced
he Canso order to 187. The government, which had tended to exaggerate home
iefence requirements, was now showing some support for the idea, taken up so
ecently by Breadner, that the highest priority should go to the RCAF abroad.
Vhen J.L. Ilsey, the minister of finance, suggested that personnel from
iisbanded units ought to be kept at home and released to industry, his colleagues

decided that they should instead be sent to Britain to reinforce the squadron there.[111] Whether or not it had been intended by the air staff as far back as March 1942, Home War Establishment surpluses were helping to 'Canadianize' the RCAF effort overseas.

Since the beginning of 1943, Air Marshal Edwards, the air officer commanding-in-chief of the overseas air force, had been pressing for additional fighter squadrons. At this time the Air Ministry was forming new composite fighter groups to support the invasion of Europe, and Edwards wanted one of them designated RCAF to operate within the Canadian Army. Consequently, he advocated the diversion of RCAF Home War squadrons intact to No 8 Composite Group. To anticipate the more detailed discussion in the next volume of this history, six squadrons were dispatched overseas, beginning in October They formed Canadian wings, but Edward's goal of a Canadian group was never realized.[112]

At the end of 1943 the air staff set the RCAF's needs at forty-four Liberators and 101 Venturas by the end of 1944. Concerned about the war at sea, the air member for supply drafted a telegram to Washington underlining the importance of the Venturas to the Allied anti-submarine campaign. Breadner, however, was satisfied that the Hudsons on strength could still effectively serve in the bomber-reconnaissance role. Venturas were in very short supply, and he was convinced that the need for them was greater in other theatres. The air staff accepted a reduction in the VLR Liberator allotment from forty-two to thirty-three, and the Ventura allocation was also cut. Air Commodore S.G Tackaberry who, as senior equipment and engineering officer on the Canadian air staff in Washington, had laboured so long to acquire these aircraft, fought the reductions, but he was over-ruled by the new chief of the air staff, Air Marshal Robert Leckie. Tackaberry's complaint that the sudden cancellation of the request would be embarrassing in light of his campaign for the allocation was not persuasive. Leckie also cancelled Canada's bids for Lightnings, Hurricanes, Kittyhawks, and Mosquitoes, leaving only the Liberator and the Mustang. The latter, too, was subsequently dropped.[113]

Leckie had started to make far-reaching cuts in the Home War Establishment based on the improving strategic situation from the time he had first become chief of the air staff (on an acting basis) on 11 November 1943. Responding quickly to Allied victories over the U-boat fleet in the Atlantic during 1943 Leckie persuaded the Cabinet on 1 December to approve the disbandment of one east coast Canso squadron and the dispatch overseas of a second, thereby effectively reducing Eastern Air Command's Canso establishment by a third. Under his instructions, Air Commodore K.M. Guthrie, acting air member for air staff, reviewed the Air Defence of Canada Plan in January 1944 with an eye to further reductions.[114] Leckie refused to consider cutting yet another Eastern Air Command Canso squadron because of the continued U-boat threat to the Gulf of St Lawrence, but with this exception approved Guthrie's recommendations. As a result, four squadrons on the west coast (one fighter, two strike, and one Canso) and three on the east coast (two fighter and one strike) were disbanded in March-May 1944. The Western Hemisphere Operations [WHO] organization, a

he Home War Establishment had been renamed, now included twenty-five
quadrons, twelve in Western Air Command and thirteen in Eastern Air
Command (the Canso squadron that had recently gone overseas was still
dministered from Halifax, and therefore the command's order of battle
ominally included fourteen squadrons).[115] Home defence veterans also
ubstantially reinforced RCAF squadrons overseas in time for the Normandy
andings in June 1944. Thus the Home War Establishment contributed to the
levelopment of a larger Canadian air force in the European theatre, even though
he RCAF overseas remained under the operational command of, and integrated
nto, the Royal Air Force.

   During September 1944 five more RCAF home squadrons disappeared from the
rder of battle,[116] though the air staff promptly cancelled the disbandment of a
ixth, the last remaining strike squadron on the east coast, in response to revived
J-boat operations in Canadian waters. By later that fall, with Allied armies
dvancing in Italy, northwest Europe, eastern Europe, and in the Pacific, the
possibility of air attack on Canada's East Coast' was seen to have 'almost
ompletely passed' and the threat from surface raiders had disappeared
ntirely.[117] The number of squadrons in the west fell to eight by 1 May 1945, and
n Eastern Air Command to ten, seven of which were anti-submarine units, fully
ngaged in meeting the final U-boat offensive in the western Atlantic. All of
hese disappeared by 1 September 1945.

   In purely military terms, the provision of adequate air defences for Canada
vas never a difficult planning problem. As the Chiefs of Staff Committee
oncluded in their periodic assessments, the danger was minimal: raids by 500
nen at the most; bombardment by, at worst, a cruiser or pocket battleship;
poradic air raids by ship- or carrier-borne aircraft; and most dangerous of all (as
t turned out), sustained submarine operations off the Atlantic coast and along
he sea-lanes to Europe. Only during two periods – the summer of 1940 when
3ritain was in jeopardy, and the seven months after the Japanese attack on Pearl
Iarbor – were more serious attacks a possibility. Canada's needs, therefore,
ould have been met by a relatively modest home air force with a high proportion
f maritime-patrol squadrons, as had been envisioned in prewar planning.

   In making home defence policy, however, the air staff was subjected to
ressures unrelated to the actual danger to Canada's coastlines. The RCAF's
ommitment in the fall of 1939 to the huge and unforeseen task of building the
CATP in Canada superseded existing plans and, given the dearth of resources
vailable, threw into question how many squadrons could or should be raised for
ome defence, and how many for service overseas. Not until the latter part of
943, moreover, after the war had clearly turned in the Allies' favour, was the
ir staff able to give considerations of military necessity precedence over
olitical imperatives. The King government's predisposition to maintain large
orces in Canada was reinforced by public alarm that major attacks were
mminent, particularly after Pearl Harbor. Breadner's programme of 1940 for
ineteen squadrons therefore grew in March 1942 to forty-nine with a potential
or sixty-five. The air staff substantiated the expansion with inflated threat
ssessments and placed large aircraft bids against limited Allied supply pools,

infuriating the British and the Americans. If the air staff truly believed there wa a valid military need for so large a home defence air force, their judgment wa questionable. If they were carrying out the instructions of the government, thei actions become more understandable. It is an air staff's responsibility to provid independent advice, however, and to propose alternate courses of action eve while carrying out directions if overruled. There is no evidence of such advice

The forty-nine squadron plan is the more remarkable because senior Canadia officers had shown calm and sound judgment immediately following Pea Harbor. At that time, the chiefs of staff maintained their assessment of a modes threat to the west coast while the American army and army air forces exaggerate the danger and demanded excessively strong continental defences. By th summer of 1942, however, when the RCAF was proceeding with the vas expansion of the Home War Establishment, the US chiefs of staff determine they must concentrate their military resources overseas and convinced thei government not to impose onerous home defence responsibilities. One reason tha the air staff in Ottawa grasped strategic realities less surely than their America counterparts may have been that Canada had no voice in the higher direction c the war. The performance of the Canadian air staff may also have reflected th fact that the officers who rose to senior rank had not been properly prepared t organize, control, supply, and direct a large air force. That is always a dange when miniscule professional forces are compelled to expand quickly in wartime no matter how earnest, hard-working, and determined the air staff officers ma have been, their peacetime experience bore no relation to the demands made c them once the war began. Little wonder, then, that Air Force Headquarters a times seemed out of its depth.

Canadian airmen were caught between their government's insistence tha Canada be well defended, their own aspirations to construct a respectabl national air force, and the fact that they did not control the resources to mee either objective. Air Marshal Breadner could write seriously about building forty-nine or sixty-five squadron organization at the same time that his staf scrambled to put twenty under-strength squadrons on operations. The air staff' policy was never wholly coherent, and the Home War Establishment was alway very much the product of improvisation.

10

Eastern and Central Canada

Defending Canada with air forces was logical, but putting the idea into practice was not easy. In addition to the procurement problems described in the preceding chapter, the development of air stations, support services, and communications along the vast and rugged coastline was an enormous undertaking. The Joint Staff Committee at National Defence Headquarters, formed by the military heads of the three services, had defined the broad roles for the army, navy, and air force in the 1938 Defence of Canada Plan. Joint Service committees, comprising the senior army, navy, and air force officers in Halifax, NS, Saint John, NB, and Victoria, BC, co-ordinated local arrangements. They subdivided coastal zones for operational purposes and set down objectives for the forces involved. Permanent and auxiliary squadrons were allocated for war planning purposes to the commands and the army's mobile force. The air commands were to co-operate with naval forces in seaward defence and the protection of shipping, provide spotting aircraft to direct long-range fire by army coast artillery, and operate fighter squadrons for defence against air attack.[1]

Regional commands were established as the RCAF gained its independence from the army in 1938. Western Air Command came into being first, on 1 March, with Eastern Air Command following on 15 September.[2] Plans for the organization of a Central Air Command were never implemented. Air operations in central Canada, where the danger of enemy attack was minimal, remained under the general control of Air Force Headquarters.

The Munich Crisis of September 1938 shifted the focus of Canadian defence planning from the Pacific to the Atlantic coast, and brought a reallocation of squadrons to the Maritimes. Fortunately, site surveys begun in 1937 had identified several potential aerodrome locations in the region, and by January 1939 contracts had been signed for construction at Sydney, Yarmouth, and Debert, NS. The terrain was difficult, however, and none of these facilities was ready when war broke out.[3]

Partly because of the dearth of landing fields, only one permanent squadron, No 5 (General-Reconnaissance) at Dartmouth, NS, was at its war station at the end of August 1939. The others had to struggle east from various places across Canada. No 1 Squadron, with modern Hawker Hurricane fighters, staged smoothly from Calgary to St Hubert, Que., an interim base pending the

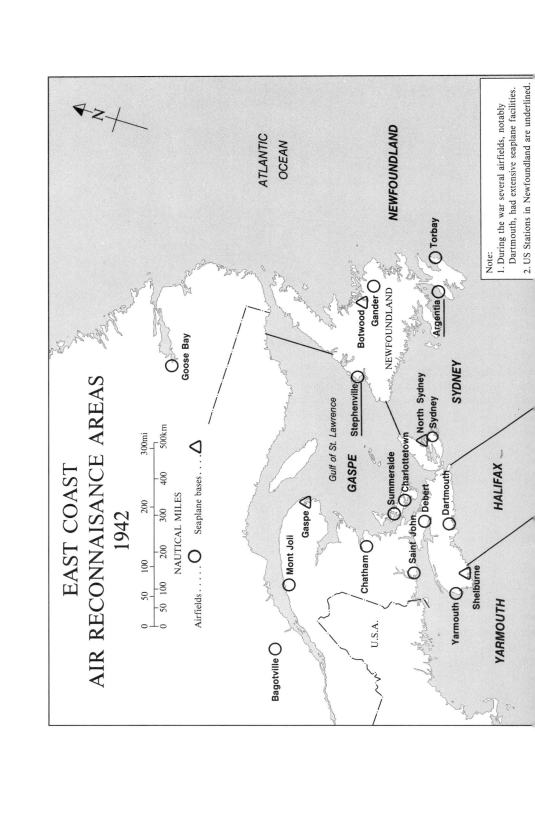

EAST COAST
AIR RECONNAISANCE AREAS
1942

NAUTICAL MILES

0   50   100   200   300mi
0 50 100 200 300 400 500km

Airfields..... ◯   Seaplane bases.... △

Bagotville ◯

Mont Joli ◯

Gaspe △

GASPE

Chatham ◯

Gulf of St. Lawrence

Summerside ◯

Charlottetown ◯

Saint John ◯

Debert ◯

Dartmouth ◯

HALIFAX

Yarmouth ◯

Shelburne △

YARMOUTH

Stephenville ◯

North Sydney △

Sydney ◯

SYDNEY

NEWFOUNDLAND

Botwood △

Gander ◯

Argentia ◯

Torbay ◯

NEWFOUNDLAND

Goose Bay ◯

ATLANTIC
OCEAN

N

Note:
1. During the war several airfields, notably
Dartmouth, had extensive seaplane facilities.
2. US Stations in Newfoundland are underlined.

completion of the Dartmouth aerodrome. Nos 2, 3, and 8 Squadrons, with older equipment, found the going more difficult. Since Canada was still at peace, all three took the direct route to the coast over American territory. No 3 Squadron had the most trying experience. Its obsolete Westland Wapitis flew from Calgary to Halifax in short hops, half the aircraft reached their destination by 1 September, but engine trouble forced the others down in Millinocket, Maine. Two of the three aircraft had to remain there until repaired, which meant that if war broke out there was every chance they would be interned. Though serviceable on 3 September – the day that the United Kingdom, but not Canada, declared war on Germany – poor weather kept them grounded until the 4th. They finally reached Halifax two days later. The squadron had been disbanded the previous day, but the aircraft and personnel were reorganized simultaneously as 10 (Bomber) Squadron, and assigned to the striking force role against enemy surface ships.[4]

Eastern Air Command's area of responsibility was immense – from eastern Quebec to the seas beyond Newfoundland – and there were no obvious transit routes for enemy ships and submarines comparable to the Shetlands-Iceland gap or the Bay of Biscay in the northeastern Atlantic. From the outset, on the basis of plans first drafted in September 1938 as a result of the Munich Crisis, the command's operational zone was subdivided into four air reconnaissance areas, Saint John (later Yarmouth), Halifax, Sydney, and Anticosti (later Gaspé), to guard against shore bombardment by ships and naval aircraft (which in 1939 seemed to be the most serious threat) and attacks on shipping and shore targets by submarines.[5] A main aircraft base was planned for each area, but only Dartmouth seaplane station was ready, and only its long-time resident permanent squadron, 5 (GR), was fully operational.

As other units arrived on the east coast they had to make do with the scanty facilities immediately at hand. No 10 (B) Squadron and a flight of 2 (Army Co-operation) Squadron took up station at the Halifax civil aerodrome, while the remainder of the latter unit moved into the Saint John civil aerodrome. Much more trying was the experience of 8 (General Purpose) Squadron, the reconnaissance unit for the Gulf of St Lawrence, which had to create its own seaplane base at the mouth of the Sydney River out of nothing. 'Aircraft are moored over two miles from the Squadron H.Q.,' the unit diarist noted on 29 August. 'All property along shore line is privately owned and great difficulty is expected in being able to establish a base from which to operate. To date movement of personnel to and from aircraft has been made in small row boat hired from Mrs. Georgia Piercey, from her property. Commanding Officer spent many hours attempting to find accommodation for personnel, a suitable building for flight office and right of way to shore.' Finally, a few days later, the diarist was able to record: 'Permission to use field adjacent to aircraft mooring area obtained. House rented for use as radio room and flight office. Small motor boat with operator rented by the day.'[6] Only in mid-December, when the freeze up had ended float-plane operations for the season, could the squadron move to the new seaplane base at Kelly Beach, North Sydney, but because the hangars were still under construction the aircraft had to be stored in the open along the station road.[7]

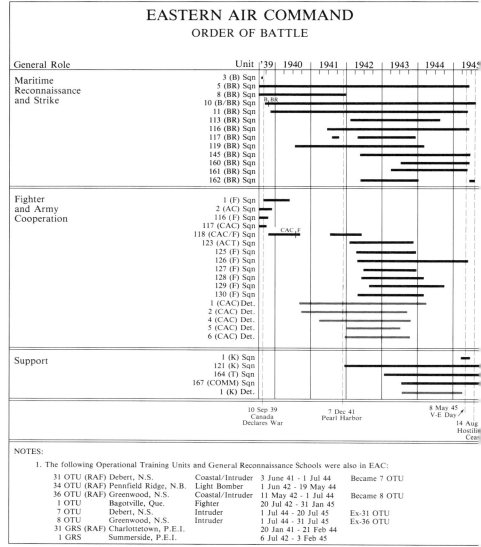

EASTERN AIR COMMAND
ORDER OF BATTLE

General Role	Unit	'39	1940	1941	1942	1943	1944	1945
Maritime Reconnaissance and Strike	3 (B) Sqn							
	5 (BR) Sqn							
	8 (BR) Sqn							
	10 (B/BR) Sqn							
	11 (BR) Sqn							
	113 (BR) Sqn							
	116 (BR) Sqn							
	117 (BR) Sqn							
	119 (BR) Sqn							
	145 (BR) Sqn							
	160 (BR) Sqn							
	161 (BR) Sqn							
	162 (BR) Sqn							
Fighter and Army Cooperation	1 (F) Sqn							
	2 (AC) Sqn							
	116 (F) Sqn							
	117 (CAC) Sqn							
	118 (CAC/F) Sqn							
	123 (ACT) Sqn							
	125 (F) Sqn							
	126 (F) Sqn							
	127 (F) Sqn							
	128 (F) Sqn							
	129 (F) Sqn							
	130 (F) Sqn							
	1 (CAC) Det.							
	2 (CAC) Det.							
	4 (CAC) Det.							
	5 (CAC) Det.							
	6 (CAC) Det.							
Support	1 (K) Sqn							
	121 (K) Sqn							
	164 (T) Sqn							
	167 (COMM) Sqn							
	1 (K) Det.							

10 Sep 39
Canada
Declares War

7 Dec 41
Pearl Harbor

8 May 45
V-E Day

14 Aug
Hostilities
Cease

NOTES:

1. The following Operational Training Units and General Reconnaissance Schools were also in EAC:

31 OTU (RAF)	Debert, N.S.	Coastal/Intruder	3 June 41 - 1 Jul 44	Became 7 OTU
34 OTU (RAF)	Pennfield Ridge, N.B.	Light Bomber	1 Jun 42 - 19 May 44	
36 OTU (RAF)	Greenwood, N.S.	Coastal/Intruder	11 May 42 - 1 Jul 44	Became 8 OTU
1 OTU	Bagotville, Que.	Fighter	20 Jul 42 - 31 Jan 45	
7 OTU	Debert, N.S.	Intruder	1 Jul 44 - 20 Jul 45	Ex-31 OTU
8 OTU	Greenwood, N.S.	Intruder	1 Jul 44 - 31 Jul 45	Ex-36 OTU
31 GRS (RAF)	Charlottetown, P.E.I.		20 Jan 41 - 21 Feb 44	
1 GRS	Summerside, P.E.I.		6 Jul 42 - 3 Feb 45	

Reproduced by Mapping and Charting Establishment.

EASTERN AIR COMMAND
ORDER OF BATTLE

General Role	Unit	'39	1940	1941	1942	1943	1944	1945
Radar Stations [2]	1 RU (TRU) Preston, N.S.							
	2 RU (CHL) Bell Lake, N.S.							
	3 RU (CHL) Tusket, N.S.							
	4 RU (CHL) Brooklyn, N.S.							
	5 RU (CHL) Queensport, N.S.							
	6 RU (CHL) Louisbourg, N.S.							
	12 RU (GCI) Bagotville, Que.							
	14 RU (CHL) St. John's, Nfld.							
	16 RU (GCI) Eastern Passage, N.S.							
	17 RU (GCI) Torbay, Nfld.							
	19 RU (GCI) Gander, Nfld.							
	20 RU (GCI) Sydney, N.S.							
	21 RU (GCI) Plymouth, N.S.							
	22 RU (CHL) Port Dufferin, N.S.							
	23 RU (GCI) Saint John, N.B.							
	24 RU (CHL) Tignish, N.S.							
	25 RU (CHL) St. Georges, Que.							
	29 RU (GCI) Goose Bay, Lab.							
	30 RU (CHL) Cape Bauld, Nfld.							
	32 RU (CHL) Port aux Basques, Nfld.							
	36 RU (CHL) Spotted Island, Lab.[3]							
	37 RU (CHL) Brig Harbour I., Lab.							
[4]	40 RU (US ew) Allan Island, Nfld.							
	41 RU (US ew) St. Brides, Nfld.							
	42 RU (US ew) Cape Spear, Nfld.							
	43 RU (US ew) Elliston, Nfld.							
	44 RU (US ew) Fogo Island, Nfld.							
	75 RU (MEW A/S) Fox River, Que.							
	76 RU (MEW A/S) St. Paul's Island, N.S.							
	77 RU (MEW A/S) Cape Ray, Nfld.							

10 Sep 39
Canada
Declares War

7 Dec 41
Pearl Harbor

8 May 45
V-E Day

14 Aug 45
Hostilities
Cease

NOTES:

2. Radio Detachments, renamed Radio Units 1 Sep 44:

TRU	High-flying early warning radar
CHL	Chain Home Low-flying, early warning radar
GCI	Ground Control Intercept radar
MEW A/S	Microwave Early Warning Anti-Submarine, surface radar
US ew	American SCR 270/271, early warning radar

3. No. 36 RU was never operational.

4. Nos. 40-44 RUs were ex-US radar stations orginally established in 1942.

AC	Army Cooperation	CAC	Coast Artillery Cooperation	T	Transport
ACT	Army Cooperation Training	COMM	Communications		
B	Bomber	F	Fighter		
BR	Bomber-Reconnaissance	K	Composite		

©Compiled and drawn by the Directorate of History.

Maritime defence, Eastern Air Command's principal task, required initimate co-operation with the RCN. In fact, as will be seen in Chapter 12, prewar British exercises in coast and shipping defence suggested that the responsible air and navy commanders should work together in a common operations room so there would be no delay in making a concerted response to enemy movements Impressed by these developments, in May 1939 the Canadian Chiefs of Staff Committee had instructed the east and west coast commanders to select sites for combined operations rooms. However, the most suitable accommodation Group Captain N.R. Anderson, commanding Eastern Air Command, could find when he moved his headquarters from the original, temporary offices in late August was the Navy League Building, some two miles from HMC Dockyard. Neither Anderson, nor Commander H.E. Reid, his naval counterpart, would consider leaving his headquarters to work in a combined operations room located elsewhere. The only solution the air commander could offer was to build an entirely new air headquarters adjacent to naval headquarters at the dockyard with the combined operations room located on neutral ground between the two buildings. Anderson was adamant; 'The individuality of the Air Command must be preserved by insisting on our own Headquarter's [sic] building with Flag Staff.'[8] The stalemate would continue for over three years, and it revealed attitudes that go far to explain the slow development of effective co-operation between air and sea forces in Canadian waters.

While the command staff settled into its new quarters, the squadrons quickly took up what became the home air force's pre-eminently important task: the defence of trade. When on 3 September 1939, the German submarine U-30 sank Athenia, a British liner, northwest of Ireland, the Admiralty immediately implemented prewar plans to sail north Atlantic shipping in defended convoys At Halifax, the western terminus, the Royal Navy stationed major warships to sail as escorts against German surface raiders, while the RCN's tiny fleet supplied anti-submarine escorts in the focal area off Nova Scotia. RCAF aircraft flew patrols around the convoys to locate enemy vessels and assist the surface escort in countering them.[9]

When the first HX (Halifax-United Kingdom) convoy put to sea on 16 September 1939, a pattern for the future was established. No 5 (GR) Squadron provided flying boats to search for submarines off Halifax harbour prior to the convoy's departure and an anti-submarine escort by day up to the limit of the Supermarine Stranraer's operational radius, approximately 250 miles seaward.

The term operational radius – also referred to as patrol range or effective range – requires some explanation because of its fundamental importance to maritime air operations. It was the distance from base at which an aircraft could linger for a useful amount of time to escort shipping or search for enemy vessels with enough fuel remaining for the return trip. Allowing a safety margin for headwinds and the possibility that deteriorating weather at base would force diversion of the returning aircraft to another station, the effective range was roughly a third – frequently much less – of the total distance the aircraft could fly without refuelling. The latter figure for a Stranraer carrying 1000 lbs of bombs was approximately 720 miles. As will be seen in Part IV of this volume, the weight of armament and equipment and number of crew members significantly altered aircraft performance, while the difficult weather conditions on the Canadian coasts often greatly reduced operational ranges.

Flying patrols of five hours and thirty minutes each between dawn and dusk, the Stranraers accompanied all departing and incoming Halifax convoys. Towards the end of October, 5 Squadron also began daily harbour-entrance patrols. In these early operations the Stranraers proved to be sturdy and dependable, if somewhat out of date. At Sydney, the Northrop Deltas of 8 Squadron carried out reconnaissance patrols and supported convoys in the area,[10] though the use of these converted civilian machines was never considered more than a temporary measure.

By the end of September 1939 the maritime patrol squadrons of the Home War Establishment had undergone a change in designation. Existing nomenclature, borrowed from the RAF for the most part, included 'Bomber,' 'Torpedo Bomber,' 'General Reconnaissance,' and 'General Purpose' squadrons, reflecting the functional specialization possible in a large air force. These terms were now replaced with the broader and uniquely Canadian designation 'Bomber Reconnaissance' or 'BR,' which more accurately described the various tasks carried out by each of the RCAF's small number of maritime squadrons.

Nos 5 and 8 (BR) Squadron were the only units in eastern Canada equipped to undertake the vital maritime reconnaissance role. When 1 (Fighter) Squadron's short-ranged Hurricanes moved from St Hubert to Dartmouth airfield in November, they were employed in coastal sweeps, the occasional patrol for convoys close inshore, and dive-bombing exercises with army batteries and naval anti-aircraft gunners. Earmarked for attachment to the army's mobile force, 2 (AC) Squadron was replaced at Halifax by the embryonic 118 (Coast Artillery Co-operation) Squadron, which joined the command from Montreal on 23 October 1939. Taking over 2 Squadron's aging Armstrong Whitworth Atlas aircraft, No 118's nucleus was reinforced by personnel transferred from other units and, on 28 October, the squadron's 'A' Flight was ready to begin operations. In the meantime, 10 (BR)'s Wapitis had proved so unsuitable for maritime reconnaissance that the squadron seldom flew operations.[11] It was undoubtedly a blessing that the first German incursion into the northwest Atlantic, the pocket battleship *Deutschland*'s cruise to the south of Greenland in October, never came within range of land-based aircraft.

The arrival of 11 (BR) Squadron at Dartmouth on 3 November added significantly to the command's capabilities. Organized at Ottawa the preceding month, the unit had been equipped with ten Lockheed Hudsons as they were delivered from their American manufacturer. These were the east coast's first modern maritime-patrol aircraft, with a maximum speed of 230 knots, as compared to the Stranraer's 130 knots, and an effective range of 350 miles. The re-equipment of 10 Squadron with Douglas Digbys was a further, major improvement. In December 1939 the squadron sent a detachment to St Hubert, Que., to begin conversion training as the aircraft started to arrive from the United States. The detachment moved to Dartmouth in April with the first five Digbys, and in June the whole squadron deployed there; Halifax municipal airport, whose runways were beginning to break through and cause damage to aircraft ceased to be an RCAF station. With the Digby, which could patrol to ranges o• over 350 miles and remain airborne for some twelve hours (the Hudson' maximum endurance was about seven hours), 10 Squadron was finally able t• take up its role as the east coast strike force.[12]

Accelerated construction programmes had greatly expanded ground facilitie: by the late spring of 1940. The Dartmouth aerodrome, which included a repai• depot, was fully operational; the aerodrome at Yarmouth would soon be able t• receive aircraft; and although the runways at the Sydney aerodrome would not b• ready until the end of the year, the new buildings at the North Sydney seaplan• station were virtually complete. Other new facilities included an equipmen• depot at Moncton, NB, and an explosives depot at Debert, NS.[13]

Additional support services were also organized, or grew in scope. The smal• clutch of RCAF marine craft on the east coast prior to the outbreak of war had bee• augmented by at least nine vessels thirty-five feet in length and larger fo• transporting equipment and supplies. In addition, six high-speed rescu• launches had been ordered for service on both coasts.[14] Another requirement which had been provided for in prewar planning, was to arrange for civilians t• notify the air force of any unusual activity in the air or at sea. These reports• particularly in the years before coastal radar stations were established later in th• war, might have been the only early warning of an attack. Organization of th• Aircraft Detection Corps began in May 1940, Eastern Air Command bein; responsible for the area east of the 100th meridian, which runs throug• Manitoba, and Western Air Command for the rest of the country. Staff at th• command headquarters contacted civilian volunteers, who served withou• compensation, distributed literature on aircraft recognition, and arranged fo• local telephone companies to route reports to RCAF stations.[15]

Eastern Air Command's responsibilities, however, would continue to grow• and at a faster rate than the improvement in its capabilities. Although th• Canadian government had specifically forbidden the military to discuss join• defence measures with Newfoundland before the war for fear that these woul• escalate into broader imperial commitments, Ottawa began to assume som• responsibility for the island's security during the first eight months of hostilities• a natural development in view of Newfoundland's geographical position astrid• the air and sea routes to Canada's Atlantic coast. On 4 September 1939, tw• Deltas from Sydney made a reconnaissance of the south coast of Newfoundlan• at the request of the Royal Navy, and during the next two days the government in St John's and Ottawa agreed that the RCAF should have free access t• Newfoundland's air space and ground facilities. By 13 March 1940 th• Canadian Cabinet was finally persuaded by British and Newfoundland argu• ments that the Canadian Army should provide coast guns to protect Bell Island i• Conception Bay, the source of iron ore for the steel industry at Sydney, NS• Meanwhile, the RCAF and the authorities in St John's began to mak• arrangements for Eastern Air Command to station aircraft in Newfoundland.[1•] In the event, a substantial Canadian commitment was to come much sooner tha• anyone had imagined.

The German conquest of France and the Low Countries in May-June 1940 increased the possibility of attacks on the Canadian Atlantic coast at the very moment the United Kingdom, now isolated and subject to invasion, urgently needed all possible assistance. The effects of the disasters in Europe on Eastern Air Command were sudden and far-reaching. Concerned that the Germans might seize Newfoundland Airport at Gander, thereby gaining control of the island's communications and acquiring a base for air strikes against the Canadian seaboard, on 27 May 1940 the Joint Service Committee Halifax urged that a detachment of 10 Squadron be sent there immediately.[17] The authorities in Ottawa and St John's agreed, and five Digbys landed at the airport on 17 June. In addition, the chiefs of staff planning subcommittee recommended sending a flight of fighters when suitable aircraft became available, as well as committing an infantry battalion for the ground defence of the airport and the seaplane anchorage nearby at Botwood.

The RCAF also rushed Home War Establishment aircrew and aircraft overseas. No 1 (F) Squadron, after amalgamation with 115 (F), left for England complete with Hurricanes and other equipment in June. This matériel was hastily crated by Dartmouth groundcrew, who also dismantled and loaded American aircraft aboard the French carrier *Béarn*. She sailed on 16 June, with RCAF personnel still working aboard, only to dock at Martinique after the French collapse. It took several changes of vessel before the RCAF party could get back to Halifax in mid-July.[18]

The departure of 1 (F) Squadron left the east coast with no fighter aircraft, forcing the Hudsons of 11 Squadron to fill the gap despite their unsuitability for this role. In early August, 118 (CAC) Squadron was redesignated as a fighter unit with the intention of posting most of its experienced personnel to new coast artillery co-operation detachments, and then bringing the squadron up to fighter strength. The conversion did not take place. No 118 broke up in late September, its flights becoming coast artillery co-operation detachments at Saint John, NB, and Halifax. No 11 Squadron's Hudsons had to continue as substitutes for fighter aircraft in the Halifax area until July 1941 when a reconstituted 118 (F) Squadron, flying obsolete Grumman Goblin biplanes, arrived in the command.[19]

The drain on Eastern Air Command's resources during the spring and summer of 1940 included maritime-reconnaissance bombers, at a time when its commitments to the defence of shipping were increasing. Thirteen Bristol Blenheim IVs, earmarked to replace 8 Squadron's Deltas, arrived from their British manufacturer, but were immediately returned to the United Kingdom where they were desperately needed. In July 8 Squadron lost its Blenheim/Bolingbroke training detachment to 119 (BR) Squadron, a new unit scheduled to move to Yarmouth, NS. At the end of the month 8 Squadron's 'A' Flight was then uprooted from North Sydney to Dartmouth to make room for a detachment of 5 Squadron Stranraers; a new series of slow transatlantic convoys started sailing from Sydney in mid-August and the Stranraers were needed to fly escort missions beyond the short reach of the Deltas.[20]

Despite the setbacks resulting from the crisis in Europe, Eastern Air

Command continued to expand. Air Force Headquarters responded to pressing aircrew shortages by giving the east coast priority over the west for recent graduates from training and by posting some personnel from Western Air Command to squadrons in the Maritimes. Deliveries of Digbys from the United States brought 10 Squadron up to full strength – fifteen aircraft – by August, and Canadian-built Bristol Bolingbrokes, a variant of the Bristol Blenheim twin-engine bomber with an effective range of about 200 miles, became available in numbers. Thus, 119 Squadron at Yarmouth reached its establishment of fifteen aircraft during the fall, and 8 Squadron began to rebuild in December, receiving its first Bolingbrokes while moving from Dartmouth and North Sydney to the new Sydney aerodrome.[21]

During the summer of 1940 the Canadian government and the armed forces also made more comprehensive arrangements for the defence of Newfoundland. The army created a new Atlantic Command on 1 August 1940 that embraced the island, Labrador, the Maritime provinces, and eastern Quebec. Later that month, the new minister of national defence for air, C.G. Power, the new chief of the air staff, Air Vice-Marshal L.S. Breadner, and the east coast commander met in St John's with the governor and his officials, described the defence Canada was prepared to provide, and won agreement that Newfoundland military forces would be placed under Canadian command. On 28 August the Joint Service Committee Halifax was redesignated the Joint Service Committee Atlantic Coast and its responsibilities extended to Newfoundland and Labrador. As a result of the subsequent expansion of the Canadian effort, on 4 July 1941 the commanders of the three services there formed the Joint Service Sub-Committee Newfoundland which reported to the JSC Atlantic Coast.[22]

The revised Defence of Canada Plan of August 1940 sought to strengthen the command structure in the Atlantic region. Unlike the plan of 1938-9 that had merely alluded to the desirability of close co-ordination among the three services, the 1940 version directed the army, navy, and air force commanders at Halifax to establish a joint operations room and to exercise collective as well as individual control over their commands.[23] None of these measures provided for unity of command – one service designated to exercise control over the other two – because this was alien to Canadian doctrine and practice; the Canadian Army, Royal Canadian Navy, and Royal Canadian Air Force insisted that they could achieve the desired degree of co-operation without the formal subordination of two of them to a third. As we shall see, however, it was not always possible to suppress service independence or to quell interservice rivalries simply by redrawing the organization charts to include joint service committees and joint command facilities. In Halifax, most notably, disputes over the location of the combined operations room continued to prevent its realization. Close, harmonious, and effective co-ordination of effort among the army, navy, and air force was discussed much more frequently than it was achieved.

Canada was not alone in its concern for the security of the east coast. The defence of the western hemisphere against incursions by overseas powers was a historic and fundamental American concern. Even though the United States was not at war her leaders were determined that a potentially hostile power should not gain a foothold in the Americas. President Roosevelt and Prime Minister Mackenzie King agreed that their two countries should co-operate in the defence of North America at the Ogdensburg summit of 17 August 1940 and, in the first two meetings of the Permanent Joint Board on Defence held on 26-7 August, attention quickly focused on the Atlantic. Representatives from both countries urged the strengthening of defences in the region, agreeing that the United States would make available urgently needed coast artillery and anti-aircraft guns (to be manned by Canadians) and that the Americans would be prepared to operate in the Maritimes and Newfoundland in the event of attack. Canada was to increase its garrison in Newfoundland and to prepare facilities there and on the mainland for use by American forces if an attack was imminent. These responsibilities were defined more precisely in the Joint Canadian-US Basic Defence Plan of October 1940 – the so-called 'Black Plan' – which postulated a German victory over Britain, the disappearance of the Royal Navy as an effective fighting force, and a concerted Axis effort against North America. Canadian authorities did not envisage that American troops would be stationed in Newfoundland or on Canadian territory except in a crisis, and at no time considered leasing or selling bases to the United States.[24] Indeed, as 1940 drew to a close and Hitler still had not crossed the English Channel, Canadian attention began to shift away from home defence to operations overseas.

Although the United States lent increasing assistance to Great Britain, its main interest was in strengthening and extending hemispheric defences. Accordingly, the British and Americans entered into an agreement which offered the United States a ninety-nine year lease on bases in Newfoundland. Not anxious to see a permanent American presence on the island, Canadian leaders and officials, like some Newfoundlanders, were wary of the arrangement. Nevertheless, when the first US troops arrived in January 1941 they did so without incident, while an Anglo-Canadian-American protocol signed in London on 27 March indicated Canadian acceptance of the situation.[25] The Canadian government remained suspicious of American intentions, however, and watched developments closely as the strength of US forces in Newfoundland grew steadily after April 1941. Canadian service personnel were similarly cautious despite the outwardly cordial working relationships they developed with their US counterparts.

The underlying tensions were particularly evident during discussions about Canadian-American command relationships in the spring of 1941. Two plans were being drafted. 'Joint Operational Plan No. 1,' which implemented the 'Black Plan' of October 1940, was to come into force if the United Kingdom fell and a major assault on North America was imminent. Under these desperate circumstances, the Canadian government agreed, the chief of staff of the United States Army could, with Canadian consent, exercise 'strategic direction' over Canadian land and air forces. The 'Joint Operational Plan No. 2' was an entirely different matter. Based on the assumption of Britain's survival, the plan was to come into effect when the United States entered the war to join the Commonwealth in striking back at the Axis powers. British and American military staffs had laid the groundwork for this contingency in meetings at Washington in January-March 1941 that resulted in the 'ABC-1' plan. Accordingly, the ancillary Canadian-American 'Joint Operational Plan No. 2' became known by the short title 'ABC-22.' Because ABC-22 would take effect when the threat to North America was much less grave than that foreseen in the 'Black Plan,' the Canadian Cabinet and chiefs of staff stoutly resisted determined American efforts to include the provision that the US chiefs of staff would exercise strategic direction over the Canadian forces. The issue caused some bad moments in the PJBD, but in the end the Americans relented. Under ABC-22, which received President Roosevelt's approval on 29 August 1941, and that of the Canadian Cabinet on 15 October, Canadian and American forces were to work together through 'mutual co-operation.'[26] Command relationships in Newfoundland and on the Canadian Atlantic coast, however, continued to cause serious difficulties until the creation of the Canadian Northwest Atlantic theatre of operations in 1943.[27]

Despite these disagreements, US help was welcome since the threat was very real. German surface commerce raiders had broken into the Atlantic again in the spring and summer of 1940, and on 5 November the pocket battleship *Admiral Scheer* encountered convoy HX 84 in mid-ocean, sinking five out of thirty-seven ships and HMS *Jervis Bay*, an armed merchant cruiser that was the sole escort. While *Scheer* moved out of range, aircraft from Sydney and Gander flew extensive but fruitless searches to locate the raider.[28]

This great sea drama, and its grave implications for the north Atlantic convoy routes, receives less attention in the records of Eastern Air Command than the practical day-to-day problems of airmen in the region. Still struggling with inadequate facilities, they had a natural tendency to be preoccupied with domestic problems. The inhospitable environment seemed to be the enemy. Airmen were in constant contact with it, closer to hand and much more persistent than the occasional German predator far out at sea. On 24 October 1940 Sydney's war diarist recorded, for example: 'At 2300 hours three shots were heard near the D.F. [direction-finding] Station and on investigation it was found that two guards had mired in the mud up to about their waists and were helpless, not being able to extricate themselves. They had fired all their shells, 10 rounds and only the last three were heard. It was necessary to dig them out and they were put in hospital suffering from shock and exposure.'[29] Such were the daily realities of war.

Poor operating conditions could not, however, explain the command's dismal performance when enemy warships lingered within range for the first time. On 22 February 1941 the Digbys of 10 Squadron's 'A' Flight at Gander were searching for the crashed Hudson in which Sir Frederick Banting, the Canadian co-discoverer of insulin, lost his life. While some of the aircraft were still air-borne, word arrived that the German battlecruisers *Scharnhorst* and *Gneisenau* had sunk five ships recently dispersed from a westbound convoy 500 miles east of Newfoundland. The Digbys had to refuel, and night fell before they could take off. The next day the raiders steamed out of range. On 15-16 March they returned to a position about 350 miles southeast of St John's, sinking or capturing some sixteen vessels from two convoys.[30] Two Digbys, en route to join the outer, or southerly, convoy learned from an armed merchant cruiser that an attack was in progress. In spite of this warning, 'both aircraft flew away without bothering to learn the position at which the shelling was taking place and, to make matters worse, proceeded to escort the wrong convoy [already escorted by a capital ship] with the result that several ships of the unescorted *outer* convoy were sunk and the R.C.A.F. failed to locate the two large raiders, a few miles away.'[31] *Scharnhorst* and *Gneisenau* withdrew unscathed and made for Brest, France.

The failure to press on towards the enemy and pass appropriate information was a grievous error that raises questions about the training of the air crews and the efficiency of the ground staff who had briefed them. Perhaps the routine of flying patrols in a theatre which experienced only rare and fleeting enemy encroachments had dulled operational perspectives and readiness. In that case, commanders at all levels had not exercised proper leadership and supervision. If senior commanders took prompt corrective action, no record has survived. Ten months later, however, a similar but much less serious failure by 10 Squadron aircrew to communicate with an American warship brought Eastern Air Command headquarters to recall the earlier incident and censure the station commander, his briefing officers, and the Digby pilots.[32]

The U-boat campaign was also moving westward and gaining in strength. The summer and fall of 1940 had brought German submariners their first 'Happy Time,' when packs of U-boats prowling the surface struck with impunity at mercantile convoys close in to the British Isles. British countermeasures, principally the extension of air and naval anti-submarine escort to mid-ocean, sharply checked German successes in the early months of 1941, but the increasing effectiveness of defences in the eastern Atlantic assured the continued westward migration of German attacks.

In March the Admiralty warned the Canadian authorities about the possible extension of the submarine war into the western Atlantic and enquired as to the strength of the available defences. The RCAF took the opportunity to once again raise the need for longer range aircraft on the Atlantic coast. Although the PJBD had recommended at its first meeting in 1940 that Canada receive twelve Consolidated PBY (Catalina) flying boats, subsequent Anglo-American discussion had reduced the number to six and then disagreements over allocation of the aircraft stalled delivery. By March 1941 none had yet arrived, nor were any deliveries from the RCAF's own contracts with Consolidated, and with Boeing in Vancouver (the Canadian builder), expected before the autumn. The British enquiry into Canadian preparedness now allowed the chief of the air staff, Air Vice-Marshal Breadner, to inform the Air Ministry that the RCAF needed three additional long-range squadrons of twelve flying boats each in order to meet its responsibilities. For the moment, the campaign for Catalinas rested there. In the meantime, Air Commodore Anderson proceeded overseas in early April for three months' duty with Coastal Command to learn first-hand of the latest methods and equipment.[33]

As spring approached, Eastern Air Command prepared to cover the Gulf of St Lawrence during the navigation season and to meet increased enemy activity in the northwest Atlantic. By mid-March the RCAF had established an advanced landing ground and refuelling base at Mont Joli, Que., which would be available to support operations in the upper Gulf. So serious was the shortage of combat aircraft, however, that an operational detachment could not be stationed in the region, either at the new aerodrome or the flying-boat base at Gaspé, during the 1941 season. For improved coverage of the ocean routes north and east of Newfoundland, in early April the main body of 10 (BR) Squadron moved from Dartmouth to join the unit's 'A' Flight at Gander. Nos 5 and 11 (BR) Squadrons carried on at Dartmouth, backed by a small detachment of two 119 Squadron Bolingbrokes from Yarmouth. At the end of May, 5 Squadron dispatched three Stranraers to the North Sydney seaplane station to assist 8 Squadron's Bolingbrokes at the Sydney aerodrome in escorting convoys and patrolling the Cabot Strait as navigation began in the area.[34] These were timely changes, but pitifully inadequate.

By early May the Germans, searching out the extended limits of British sea and air escort, were attacking convoys west of 35° west. On 20 May, the day convoy HX 126 was heavily attacked 680 miles east of Newfoundland, Air Commodore A.E. Godfrey, who commanded Eastern Air Command during Anderson's absence overseas, pressed again for immediate delivery of Catalinas. His plea was strengthened by the fact that a number of these aircraft were lying idle in the United States and Bermuda waiting to be ferried across the Atlantic. The next day, the command learned from the navy that bearings on German radio transmissions placed a U-boat at 55° north, 50° west – just barely within reach of RCAF aircraft at Gander. The aircrew of 10 Squadron pushed their Digbys to extreme range, over 500 miles, but at this distance from base were able to patrol only briefly over the suspected area. Godfrey immediately reported these developments in another bid for Catalinas, which, with an effective range of 600 miles, could have made a thorough search. The appearance of U-boats off Newfoundland quickly broke the bureaucratic logjam: on 24 May the Air Ministry informed the RCAF authorities in London that nine Catalinas on order for the RAF were being diverted to Eastern Air Command. The aircraft were being lent subject to replacement from the first deliveries of Catalinas from the RCAF's own orders.[35]

As the British agreed to release the flying boats, a great sea action was unfolding that further underscored Eastern Air Command's need for more effective aircraft. The German battleship *Bismarck* and heavy cruiser *Prinz Eugen* sortied from the Baltic on 18 May and, after destroying HMS *Hood* in the Denmark Strait between Iceland and Greenland on the 24th, succeeded in breaking contact with shadowing Royal Navy cruisers. The Admiralty presumed the Germans were headed for the convoy routes, and Eastern Air Command went on general alert. No 10 Squadron stood in readiness as an air-striking force, and on 26 and 27 May the Digbys patrolled to extreme range, but *Bismarck* had in fact made for France.[36] She met her end at the hands of the Royal Navy southeast of Ireland. On the 28th Eastern Air Command's aircraft searched for *Prinz Eugen*, which had continued to cruise in the western Atlantic, but well beyond range of the available land-based aircraft. The RAF eventually found her, safely back in harbour at the French port of Brest. Nonetheless, German surface ships never again attempted to hunt in the north Atlantic.

It was the spreading U-boat menace rather than the surface raider threat that brought Air Chief Marshal Sir Philip Joubert de la Ferté, the new air officer commanding-in-chief Coastal Command, to urge the need for air protection of shipping across the whole expanse of the north Atlantic in June and July. As will be seen in Chapter 12, an RCAF delegation attended meetings at Coastal Command to co-ordinate operations from the two sides of the ocean. Air Commodore Anderson, who was still on duty in England, played a prominent part, making the case for supplying Eastern Air Command with the best equipment and more adequate flow of aircrew. The hope, which detailed study soon proved to be illusory, was that by pushing Catalinas to the limit, transatlantic patrols could be made between Newfoundland and Iceland. The real answer, as both Anderson and Joubert de la Ferté recognized, was for the Canadians to operate four-engine Consolidated Liberators from Gander, an ambition which in the event took two years to realize (see Chapter 15).[37]

The nine loaned Catalinas were promptly delivered to the main body of 5 (BR) Squadron at Dartmouth in June. Having already sent personnel to Bermuda for training on the type, by the end of the month 5 (BR) was well advanced in converting to the new machines. The squadron was considerably shaken, therefore, by orders to transfer its most experienced personnel and all the Catalinas to 116 (BR), a new squadron organizing at Dartmouth. By the end of July the latter unit had dispatched a detachment of four aircraft to the seaplane station at Botwood, Nfld, which carried out the important task of escorting convoys routed through the Strait of Belle Isle. In the meantime, 5 Squadron reactivated the Stranraers.[38]

The RCAF's expanding commitment in Newfoundland brought the organization of 1 Group headquarters at St John's on 10 July 1941. Group Captain C.M. McEwen assumed command on 15 August. His responsibilities were to include control of all RCAF units in Newfoundland and, more particularly, of air operations in support of the RCN's Newfoundland Escort Force, formed at the end of May to complete the system for continuous naval escort of transatlantic convoys. For the time being, however, Eastern Air Command retained tactical control of the Newfoundland squadrons, passing orders through 1 Group. In the first months of its existence, the new headquarters was fully occupied with the development of command communications and in overseeing the construction of a new aerodrome at Torbay, near St John's.[39]

Allied command relationships also changed in the summer of 1941. Following Anglo-American staff talks, the US Navy assumed responsibility in July for the defence of American and Icelandic merchantmen moving between North America and Iceland. A few weeks later in the 'Riviera' meeting between Churchill and Roosevelt at Argentia, Nfld, the two leaders agreed to adopt the US Navy's Hemisphere Defence Plan No 4, more commonly known as WPL-51, placing Canadian naval forces in the area under American direction. This did not sit well with the Canadian navy, which thought its men more experienced, but a degree of RCN autonomy was ensured by the creation of all-Canadian escort groups.[40]

The situation facing the air force was more ambiguous. WPL-51 had applied only to the RCN, but since the American doctrine of unity of command assumed naval control and direction of maritime air operations far from shore, the US Navy was inclined to exercise command over the RCAF for these purposes as well. This had never been Canadian practice, but on 21 September Eastern Air Command learned that the senior American officer in Newfoundland, Rear Admiral A.L. Bristol, had received instructions that the RCAF was not to escort any more convoys out to sea. Naval Service Headquarters interpreted this to mean that RCAF escort duties were confined to Canadian and Newfoundland coastal waters, and that all long-range work would be left to the US Navy and US Army Air Forces.[41] Anderson was indignant: 'Since September 1939 this command has been providing anti-submarine patrols and sweeps in [the] protection [of] ocean convoys often 600 to 800 miles to sea. Many of our personnel have lost their lives in devotion to this the most honourable duty they could perform while serving in Canada. If any BR squadrons retained in this command [are] capable of undertaking general reconnaissance and convoy patrols and anti-submarine sweeps far to sea, [it is] strongly recommended [that] as air defence, protection Atlantic coast, and as means [of] maintaining high spirit [sic] de corps within the command, these squadrons be permitted to take part [in] such operations and not restricted coastal zones.'[42]

This was hyperbole, but national interests were at stake. Eastern Air Command's chief of staff, Group Captain F.V. Heakes, made a personal visit in early October to Admiral Bristol. On 17 October Anderson went to Argentia to meet with Bristol, in company with Group Captain McEwen and Commodore L.W. Murray, commanding the navy's Newfoundland Escort Force. Joint Canadian and American arrangements for operational responsibilities took shape as a result of this meeting. They were as flexible as conditions allowed. Generally speaking, US Navy aircraft were to escort all convoys east of 55° west and south of 48° north; Canadian aircraft would cover shipping in the Canadian Coastal Zone west of 55° west, and to extreme range off Newfoundland north of 48° north. The RCAF thus ensured that its squadrons would not be superseded by Newfoundland-based US forces in long-range ocean tasks. Anderson had also succeeded in defining a Canadian zone under Eastern Air Command control and thereby made it more difficult for the Americans to extend their influence over the RCAF. He also persuaded his US colleagues that communications between Argentia and St John's were too slow and clumsy for Admiral Bristol's headquarters to exercise operational control over 1 Group.[43]

These agreements did not fully resolve the problem of air force command and control. A revision of WPL-51, WPL-52, appeared to apply the principle of unity of command by the US Navy to all the forces involved in defending the east coast of North America. To have unity of command, which was unacceptable within the Canadian armed forces, imposed by a foreign service, contrary to the provisions of ABC-22, struck a raw nerve at Air Force Headquarters. In an attempt to mollify the chief of the air staff, on 20 October Admiral H.R. Stark, US chief of naval operations, wrote to explain that WPL-52 allowed the commander-in-chief of the US Fleet to exercise strategic direction over Canadian naval and air forces only outside the Canadian coastal zone. As the RCN had already agreed to this provision, Stark invited Breadner to do the same 'subject to the limitations contained in ABC-22.'[44] This was awkward. The reference to ABC-22 seemed, on the surface, to satisfy all the demands made by the Canadian government to protect Canadian interests. How could the RCAF refuse, particularly when the RCN was satisfied? The Cabinet War Committee concluded that the air force should follow suit unless it could demonstrate valid operational objections.[45]

Air Vice-Marshal G.O. Johnson, who as deputy chief of the air staff was responsible at this time for the Home War Establishment, offered a sufficiently convincing argument. He pointed out that the RCAF had agreed to unified command under the terms of ABC-22 only in cases of extreme urgency. 'We operate here successfully *in co-operation* with the RN and RCN, just as Coastal Command does. As far as we know there has never been an occasion where it has been deemed necessary to change this relationship.' He went on to suggest that being placed under American command would lower the morale of flying personnel, while the Canadian public would find it anomalous 'that our active forces are operating under the command of forces of a foreign power which, technically speaking, is not yet a belligerent.' In responding to Admiral Stark, Breadner assured him that 'all possible RCAF strength' would be committed to convoy protection, but, noting the successful co-operation between Eastern Air Command and the Commonwealth navies, rejected unified command. Stark accepted the rebuff, while making it clear that the responsibility for the divided command in the northwest Atlantic lay with the RCAF.[46]

Although the air staff's position had weight from a nationalistic perspective, Breadner, Johnson, and other senior RCAF officers had misinterpreted the precedents set by Coastal Command and would continue to do so. Difficult as it was for Canadian airmen to accept, Coastal Command did come under the operational control of the Admiralty, and its air groups responded directly to the commanders-in-chief of the Royal Navy's home commands (see Chapter 12).[47] If anything, the British example suggested that the RCAF's coastal formations could function well under naval direction. Although Naval Service Headquarters in Ottawa was not an operational headquarters like the Admiralty, neither did Eastern Air Command fall under the control of the east coast naval command. There was some justification for the independence of the RCAF on the Atlantic coast, however, for, unlike Coastal Command, its responsibilities were wider than maritime warfare, including fighter defence and co-operation with the army.

The air staff was on firmer ground when it opposed a fresh American attempt to impose unified command in Newfoundland during December 1941, following the United States' entry into the war. No 1 Group could not be divorced from Eastern Air Command because of Newfoundland's intimate geographical connection, especially from the air point of view, with the defence of the Canadian Atlantic coast. The whole of the command's resources had to be immediately available to reinforce stations in any part of the region where the enemy struck. Group Captain Heakes also astutely predicted that the American presence in Newfoundland might soon be greatly reduced if ships and aircraft were withdrawn to the Pacific, and he further pointed out that with the introduction in the near future of aircraft able to make transatlantic patrols, it would become increasingly important for the RCAF to work with Coastal Command rather than the US Navy. With these arguments, and others from the army and the navy, the Chiefs of Staff Committee ruled out a unified command. On 20 January 1942, however, Eastern Air Command turned tactical control of the RCAF squadrons in Newfoundland over to No 1 Group, whose organization was nearing completion; henceforth command headquarters gave only general directives to the headquarters in St John's.[48] As will be seen in Part IV of this volume, serious tensions would continue to inhibit co-operation between the Canadian and American air forces in Newfoundland for some months to come, but the way had been cleared for No 1 Group to develop an effective relationship with its American counterparts.

Although, as so often in coalition warfare, large and powerful allies sometimes seemed to pose the greatest threat, the real enemy was pressing closer to Canadian shores – U-boats made a second foray off Newfoundland in October-November 1941 – and Eastern Air Command's most urgent concern was to become more battle-ready. Hudsons, Bolingbrokes, and Digbys were adequate patrol bombers, but lacked range. Additional Catalinas (PBYS) were the obvious requirement. Delivery of thirty-six PBY5 flying boats from a Canadian order in the United States had begun in late August; fourteen PBY5As, the new amphibious model that would be more useful in the north west Atlantic, were due to arrive at the end of the year and in early 1942. These fifty aircraft incorporated modifications laid down by the Canadian air staff and were the first of the type to be designated Canso – Canso 'A' for the amphibious version – in the RCAF (the nine Catalinas on loan from the RAF had been built to somewhat different British specifications and therefore continued to carry that name). No 116 (BR) Squadron began ferrying Cansos from Rockcliffe to the Atlantic coast in September, while 5 Squadron flew its Stranraers to Western Air Command and converted to the new type.

However great the RCAF's need, the government responded generously to a British appeal for aircraft from the Canadian order in September. Over the next two months twenty-nine of the thirty-six Cansos were lent to the RAF. The Canadian air staff was also willing to send 5 and 116 Squadrons overseas to operate the aircraft, an offer the Air Ministry declined because the machines were needed to replace wastage in existing RAF units. The two governments did agree that when the fourteen Canso 'A' amphibians were delivered to the RCAF in early 1942 the remaining seven Canso flying boats would be transferred to the RAF, and the borrowed Catalinas returned. The outbreak of the Pacific war ultimately forced Canada to cancel this arrangement; nevertheless, the RCAF had already surrendered enough flying boats to equip two squadrons.[49]

While 5 Squadron re-equipped with Cansos during the fall of 1941, 118 (F) Squadron ferried Curtiss Kittyhawks to Dartmouth. By December the unit had replaced its Goblin biplanes with fourteen of the new fighters, at last giving the east coast effective air defence equipment. The aircraft situation was improving, but shortages continued to plague the command. The supply of well-trained aircrew was another continuing problem. Although the east coast did have priority over the west, large numbers of personnel were being sent overseas. On balance, the greatest progress was in the development of ground facilities. Eastern Air Command now had six operational aerodromes: Dartmouth, by far the biggest, Sydney, Yarmouth, Gander, Torbay, and Saint John. A new land base at Goose Bay, Labrador, was in the early stages of construction. Seaplane stations had been completed or were under construction at Botwood, Gaspé, North Sydney, Dartmouth, and Shelburne.[50]

Eastern Air Command had, to a large extent, been built up at the expense of its western counterpart, but that was no longer possible after the Japanese attack on Pearl Harbor. Simultaneously, the command faced a much greater threat. Germany, standing loyally by the Axis alliance, declared war on the United States in the immediate aftermath of Pearl Harbor. Previously Hitler had forbidden submarine operations in North American waters south of Newfoundland for fear of embroilment with the United States, but now the heavy shipping traffic off the Canadian and American coasts was fair game. In January 1942, U-boats opened an offensive in the northwest Atlantic, the subject of Part IV of the present volume, whose last actions would not be fought until after the German capitulation in May 1945.

The possibility that Germany might also make air raids on North America raised the issue of defences for central Canada, where the RCAF had no operational command. There were numerous potential targets of critical importance to the country's war effort in the canal locks and steel mill at Sault Ste Marie, mines in northern Ontario, and industrial areas further south. Before the war, members of parliament had worried about the danger of air attacks from Hudson and James bays, while Canadian and, more particularly, American military plans had taken account of raids against inland centres by aircraft operating from ships or temporary bases on isolated coastlines. But the threat was exceedingly remote, and the resources available to the RCAF desperately scarce. The August 1940 revision of the defence of Canada plan had directed No 1 Training Command to make emergency defence plans for the region, but an air staff initiative of late 1940 to have the command organize the Aircraft Detection Corps around Hudson Bay (which still came under Eastern Air Command's control) was not pursued energetically. After Pearl Harbor it was impossible to give the central region such a low priority. Municipal leaders and industrial officials in the vicinity of the Sault and Sudbury demanded air defences, but more importantly, American authorities pressed for action. At a meeting of the PJBD on 25-6 February 1942, the US members announced that an army anti-aircraft regiment, less a battalion, would be deployed south of the border at Sault Ste Marie and, at their insistence, the board urged the RCAF to make a 'comprehensive' study of the threat to the area.[51]

The air staff was reluctant to provide local defences, noting that equally vital industries and canal bottlenecks existed elsewhere in central Canada. Attacks 'by small numbers of aircraft' were possible but unlikely. To reach the targets, the enemy would either have to cross Eastern Air Command's coastal defences or launch aircraft from temporary bases or ships in Hudson or James bays. This latter possibility was 'most improbable and quite impossible except for

approximately three months of the year, namely mid-July to mid-October.'
Under the circumstances, it seemed reasonable to deploy anti-aircraft guns at
Sault Ste Marie, but not to use scarce air defence equipment to surround the
many individual targets far inland. Better, the air staff advised, to strengthen and
deepen coastal radar warning coverage and interception defences by installing
radar along the Labrador coast and providing fighter aircraft for Goose Bay,
Gander, and Torbay.[52] This extra fighter strength, stretching westwards to
include a station at Bagotville which covered the vital aluminum industry at
Arvida, Que., was soon approved by the Canadian government as part of the
forty-nine squadron plan put forward by Air Marshal L.S. Breadner on 16 March
1942.[53]

The United States continued to be concerned with the vulnerability of the
Sault Ste Marie locks. In March the US government designated the air space
around the locks on the American side as a restricted zone and asked Canada to
institute similar measures on her side. Canada did so. At a PJBD meeting on 7
April, Lieutenant-General Embick, the US Army representative, won agreement
that Canada should immediately organize the Aircraft Detection Corps around
Hudson and James bays. Arrangements were made that month to feed
information from the few Aircraft Detection Corps posts then operating in the
area to the US Army headquarters co-ordinating the Sault Ste Marie defences.
The RCAF organized a conference held on 6-7 May at Sault Ste Marie, Ont.,
where representatives of the Canadian and American services, commercial
communications companies, the Ontario and Manitoba governments, and other
agencies from both sides of the international border laid plans greatly to increase
the number of ADC posts, establish filter centres to correlate observer reports at
Winnipeg, Sault Ste Marie (at Fort Brady, Michigan), and Ottawa, and maintain
twenty-four-hour listening watches on observer radio links. To administer the
expanded Canadian system, a separate Central Area Aircraft Detection corps
was finally organized on 15 June, under the control of the air member for air staff
at Air Force Headquarters.[54]

The United States hoped that Canada would also conduct reconnaissance
flights over Hudson and James bays and their approaches during the danger
period after 25 July 1942, but Eastern Air Command could not spare aircraft
from its vital anti-submarine duties, and there were no other Canadian resources
available. For its part, the US Army established and manned radar units at
Cochrane, Hearst, Nakina, Armstrong, and Kapuskasing, Ont., with a
headquarters and filter room at the latter, in addition to supplying ground forces
to defend the Sault. Canadian flying restrictions, originally limited to the
immediate vicinity of the locks, were extended in early 1943 to a radius of 100
miles to correspond with the larger zone in effect in the United States, thereby
giving timely warning of the approach of unidentified aircraft. The Sault
defences were maintained throughout that year. Canada never regarded the
threat as seriously as did the United States, but willingly co-operated with US
plans. At the end of 1943 the United States decided to abolish its Central Defense
Command and remove its troops from Sault Ste Marie. Air Force Headquarters
disbanded the Central Area Aircraft Detection Corps, which had grown to

include 9077 observers, at the same time. Between February and April 1944 the restricted flying areas over the Sault on both sides of the border were abolished.[55]

However reluctant to commit resources at inland centres, the RCAF gave a leading priority to defences against enemy aircraft on the east coast. The forty-nine squadron plan of March 1942 called for no fewer than eight fighter squadrons in Eastern Air Command, each augmented by a night-fighter flight, as compared to the one unit, 118 (F), actually in existence. By the time the latter squadron moved to Alaska in June 1942, six others had organized or were about to do so. Procurement problems prevented the formation of the remaining two squadrons and the night-fighter flights, but during the latter part of 1943, all but one of the formed units had on strength or approached a full establishment of fifteen Hawker Hurricane XIIs, including immediate reserves.[56] This was nine fewer machines in each squadron than the over generous scale in the March 1942 plan, but aircraft for wastage replacement were available in Canada. The air staff, as has been seen, had always wanted a longer-range fighter than the Hurricane and was still attempting, without success, to procure more suitable types like the North American Mustang.[57]

The ground organization necessary to conduct fighter operations was also created in 1942 and 1943. The most ambitious part of the project was the development of a chain of radio (radar) stations or detachments to give early warning of enemy aircraft and control night-fighters. Radio detachments, renamed radio units on 1 September 1944, were of three types: early warning high flying (TRU) and early warning low flying (CHL), each with an approximate range of 100 miles; and ground control intercept (GCI), with a range of fifty miles. Filter centres at command and 1 Group headquarters plotted information from the radio units, Aircraft Detection Corps, and other sources, and fed the intelligence to sector control rooms at the fighter aerodromes which, in the event of an attack, would have directed the aircraft onto target.[58]

The increased threat to North America after Pearl Harbor also brought revisions in command arrangements. Concerned primarily to assure the public that everything possible was being done to improve the efficiency of the defences, in March 1942 the Cabinet War Committee overruled objections by the chiefs of staff and approved a system of unified command as between the Canadian services on the coasts. The senior members of the two Joint Service committees became commanders-in-chief, East and West Coast Defences, having authority to exercise overall strategic direction in their areas while retaining tactical command of their own particular service. Responsible to the commander-in-chief, East Coast Defences, the senior member of the Joint Service Sub-Committee in St John's was also now designated as 'commanding Newfoundland defences.' In practice, however, all that changed were the titles. The commanders-in-chief did not interfere in the operations of the other services.[59]

The real and pressing requirement, in fact, was for closer integration of the air and naval forces on the Atlantic coast to counter the U-boat offensive. It proved difficult to achieve. Not until the spring of 1943, when Great Britain and the United States agreed to the creation of the Canadian Northwest Atlantic theatre, under the command of the RCN admiral at Halifax, was there a single controlling authority. More strikingly, although 1 Group and Flag Officer Newfoundland had begun to work together in a combined headquarters at St John's in October 1942, interservice wrangling continued to prevent the organization of a combined headquarters at Halifax until July 1943.[60]

Eastern Air Command approached its zenith in the fall of 1943. There were, in November, eighteen combat squadrons on the order of battle, including eleven bomber-reconnaissance (four in the strike role, and seven anti-submarine), six fighter, and one army co-operation training. The air staff's forty-nine squadron programme of March 1942 had allocated twenty-three combat squadrons to the east coast but, as already noted, the large fighter organization planned had been cut back substantially; two glider squadrons, intended to support the army in countering enemy landings, were never formed. In terms of the number of squadrons and aeroplanes immediately available for operations, the target set for the critical maritime-reconnaissance role – five strike and seven anti-submarine units – had nearly been realized. Ten bomber-reconnaissance squadrons had fifteen machines on strength, or were only a few short of that number, and the eleventh was in the process of converting from outdated Digbys to Cansos. However, the Hudsons of two strike squadrons had not been replaced by more modern Lockheed Venturas, and no squadron had access to the nine reserve and twelve wastage replacement aircraft envisioned for each unit in the air staff's calculations. Liberators had not featured in the March 1942 plan, but their delivery to 10 Squadron during the spring of 1943 had dramatically increased Eastern Air Command's capabilities.[61]

During 1943, the command's many stations and support units finally achieved a stable organizational life. Among the latter was the Eastern Air Command Marine Squadron, which was formed in June from the vessels and crews that had previously been attached to the various air stations. Based on a central administrative home at Dartmouth, the command's 'fleet' included nine high-speed rescue launches, four supply and salvage vessels, the largest being the 600-ton ship *Beaver*, and over seventy smaller craft. The squadron assisted the repair depots in recovering wrecked aircraft (the unit's establishment included a section of divers who had the unpleasant and dangerous jobs of retrieving bodies and unexploded weapons), transported stores to the command's many isolated stations and detachments, and carried out rescue missions. By early 1944 the last service had been put on a more effective basis through the integration of the rescue vessels on both coasts with the flying control organization that monitored the movements of all aircraft in operational areas.[62]

When at the end of January 1944 Eastern Air Command reached its peak strength of 21,234 officers and airmen, reductions had already started in response to Allied successes in every theatre of war. The first units to go had been the coast artillery detachments, made redundant by army radar equipment. At the end of 1943, only 1 (CAC) Detachment at Saint John, NB, remained. During 1943, as well, Air Force Headquarters began regularly to post experienced pilots overseas from home fighter units. Of greater impact was the government's approval, in September 1943, of the air staff's proposal to reinforce the RCAF Overseas from the Home War Establishment by dispatching six fighter squadrons to No 83 Composite Group, Second Tactical Air Force, RAF, which at that time was earmarked as the air support formation for the First Canadian Army after the invasion of France in the spring of 1944. Three squadrons were withdrawn from Eastern Air Command, welcome news in units for which there had been little exitement in the way of enemy air attacks or landings, and whose only opportunity for action had been inshore anti-submarine patrols, a task for which the aircraft were ill-suited. No 123 (Army Co-operation Training) went overseas before Christmas 1943, reorganizing as 439 (Fighter-Bomber) Squadron; 125 (F) and 127 (F), which followed early in the New Year, became 441 (F) and 443 (F) Squadron, respectively.[63]

By this time, Air Marshal Robert Leckie, Air Marshal Breadner's successor as chief of the air staff, had made further cuts. One Canso squadron, 117 (BR), disbanded in December 1943, and another, 162 (BR), moved to Iceland in January 1944 to serve with Coastal Command. Air Force Headquarters also started to dispatch seasoned bomber-reconnaissance aircrew overseas (see Chapter 16). During March-April, 119 (BR) Squadron (Hudsons), 128 (F) Squadron, 130 (F) Squadron, and 1 (CAC) Detachment disbanded, and RCAF Stations Saint John, Botwood, Shelburne, and North Sydney were closed or placed under care and maintenance. To compensate for the loss in fighter strength, the establishments of the command's two remaining fighter units, Nos 126 and 129, were raised from fifteen to eighteen aircraft, and 1 OTU, Bagotville, was ordered to have twelve fighters available for operations at thirty minutes' notice.[64]

Other squadrons disappeared from the order of battle during the summer and early fall of 1944, but the long awaited delivery of additional Liberators strengthened Eastern Air Command's maritime-reconnaissance capability. A fighter squadron and both Ventura-equipped strike units were to have disbanded; the selection of the latter squadrons reflected the urgent need for aircrew with twin-engine qualifications to man two new transport squadrons forming for service in Southeast Asia. Nos 113 (BR) and 129 (F) broke up in August and September, but 145 (BR) was spared by the reluctance of the east coast commanders to give up entirely the fast and versatile Venturas, and by an upsurge in U-boat activity. In the meantime, 11 Squadron retired its Hudsons as the new Liberators arrived, and in the fall began operations as the command's second very long-range squadron.[65]

Development of ground radar facilities and associated airborne equipment continued until the end of the war. By 1945 there were twenty-two radar stations on the east coast for early warning or ground control, including five in Newfoundland that had been taken over from the US forces in late 1944. Although the units had no opportunity to serve in their primary air defence role, they were immensely valuable in locating friendly aircraft that were lost or in distress. The range at which flights could be tracked, moreover, had been greatly extended by Identification Friend or Foe (IFF) equipment, first fitted in

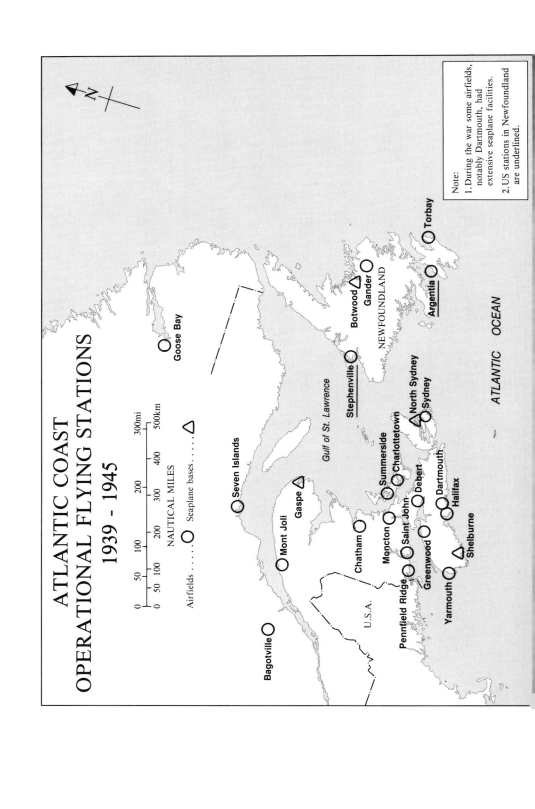

ATLANTIC COAST
OPERATIONAL FLYING STATIONS
1939 - 1945

Airfields . . . . . ○   Seaplane bases . . . . . △

NAUTICAL MILES

| 0 | 50 | 100 | 200 | 300mi |

| 0 | 50 100 | 200 | 300 | 400 | 500km |

Note:
1. During the war some airfields,
   notably Dartmouth, had
   extensive seaplane facilities.
2. US stations in Newfoundland
   are underlined.

Bagotville ○

Mont Joli ○

Seven Islands ○

Gaspé △

Chatham ○

Moncton ○

Saint John ○

Pennfield Ridge ○

Greenwood ○

Yarmouth ○

Shelburne △

Summerside ○

Charlottetown ○

Debert ○

Dartmouth ○

Halifax ○

North Sydney △

Sydney ○

Stephenville △

Goose Bay ○

Botwood △

Gander ○

NEWFOUNDLAND

Argentia ○

Torbay ○

Gulf of St. Lawrence

U.S.A.

ATLANTIC   OCEAN

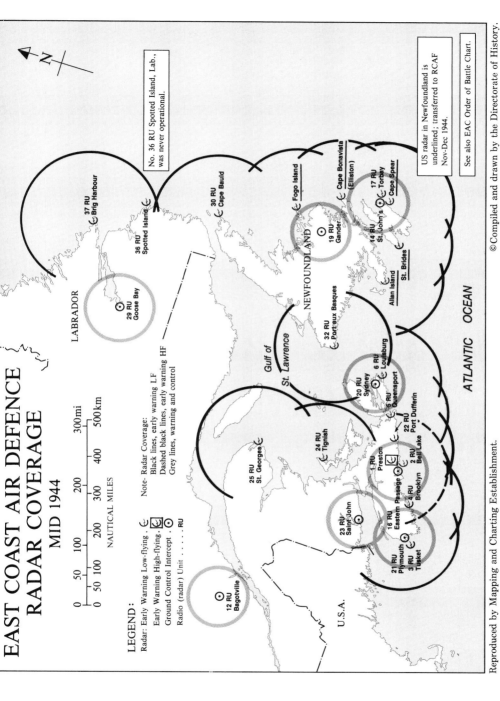

EAST COAST AIR DEFENCE RADAR COVERAGE

MID 1944

LEGEND:

Radar: Early Warning Low-flying . ⊂
Early Warning High-flying.
Ground Control Intercept . ⊙
Radio (radar) Unit . . . . . RU

Note- Radar Coverage:
Black lines, early warning LF
Dashed black lines, early warning HF
Grey lines, warning and control

No. 36 RU Spotted Island, Lab., was never operational.

US radar in Newfoundland is underlined ; transferred to RCAF Nov-Dec 1944.

See also EAC Order of Battle Chart.

37 RU Brig Harbour

LABRADOR

29 RU Goose Bay

36 RU Spotted Island

30 RU Cape Bauld

Fogo Island

Cape Bonavista (Elliston)

17 RU Torbay

Cape Spear

19 RU Gander

14 RU St John's

NEWFOUNDLAND

St. Brides

Allan Island

32 RU Port aux Basques

Gulf of St. Lawrence

20 RU Sydney

6 RU Louisburg

5 RU Queensport

22 RU Port Dufferin

24 RU Tignish

25 RU St. Georges

1 RU Preston

2 RU Bell Lake

4 RU Brooklyn

23 RU Saint John

16 RU Eastern Passage

21 RU Plymouth

3 RU Tusket

12 RU Bagotville

U.S.A.

ATLANTIC OCEAN

©Compiled and drawn by the Directorate of History.

Reproduced by Mapping and Charting Establishment.

Eastern Air Command aircraft during 1943. These airborne sets responded to signals from complimentary equipment at radar stations, and could also transmit a specially coded signal if the aircraft were in distress.[66]

Further aids to navigation were provided by three other ground radar systems, two of which worked in conjunction with air-to-surface vessel (ASV) radar that had become a standard fitting in the command's aircraft since 1942. The first was a beacon that responded to radiation from an ASV set with a strong pulse, enabling the aircraft to home on a known position. Twenty-five beacons were installed on the east coast by January 1945, each duplicated so that there would be no interruption in the event of equipment failure. The RAF's Blind Approach Beacon System, which was installed at eight Eastern Air Command airfields starting with Gander in 1942, functioned in much the same way. Pulses from a ground transmitter registered on airborne ASV sets, permitting pilots to align their aircraft with the runway in conditions of poor visibility. Finally, the US Navy had built LORAN stations, the American long-range navigation system for obtaining position by pulse signals, in Iceland, Newfoundland, and on the Canadian east coast. By late 1944 the necessary airborne equipment had been installed in Eastern Air Command's Liberators, but fitting in other types was still proceeding at the end of the war.[67]

In an entirely different category were the RCAF's anti-submarine radar stations in the Gulf of St Lawrence. As a result of the U-boat campaign in the Gulf during 1942, early in 1943 the air force ordered eight microwave early warning (MEW) sets, modified to detect surfaced submarines. Only one station, No 77 Radio Unit at Cape Ray, Nfld, was ready for operations during the 1944 shipping season; two others, No 75 at Fox River, Que., and No 76 on St Paul's Island, NS, were completed by 1945. The remaining sets were never installed because the navy did not develop facilities to plot the thousands of contacts made by the stations, and U-boats virtually abandoned surfaced operations in coastal waters.[68]

The radar networks largely superseded the Aircraft Detection Corps. In November 1944 the chief of the air staff ordered the organization, which had reached a peak enrolment of 30,000 members in December 1943 and still had 23,000 observers on strength, to be disbanded. Radar could not entirely replace the ground observer, however, and shortly afterwards former coastal observers and lighthouse keepers in the eastern area were asked to pass information on aircraft in distress, or on any other untoward incident, to the nearest RCAF station. They continued to do so for the rest of the war.[69]

On 4 May 1945 Admiral Doenitz ordered the U-boats to break off action. The official German surrender came two days later. In Eastern Air Command there was celebration for some and business as usual for others. A small handful, from RCAF Station Dartmouth and No 8 Construction and Maintenance Unit, became directly involved in the Halifax VE-Day Riots, though all charges against them were subsequently dropped. For many it was difficult to believe that victory had really been achieved, but within seven weeks much of Eastern Air Command's fighting strength had been dispersed.[70] By the end of June 1 Group headquarters at St John's had closed down, six squadrons had disbanded, and a seventh, 11

(BR), had moved to the west coast, which was still on a war footing. Two anti-submarine squadrons remained – 10 (BR) at Torbay and 162 (BR), recently returned from Iceland, at Sydney – in case 'rogue' U-boats refused to surrender. Both units were disbanded during the first half of August.

11

The Pacific Coast

Although the possibility of war with Japan was allowed for after September 1939, it was assumed that a strong and effective American fleet would stand between the Japanese and whatever Canadian forces were available in British Columbia. The unexpected damage done to the US Navy at Pearl Harbor altered Canadian perceptions of the threat to the Pacific coast. For a time it seemed that the Japanese might actually be capable of mounting a large-scale attack on North America, and because of this threat rather larger forces were stationed in British Columbia until 1945 than had been anticipated in pre-December 1941 plans.

West Coast defence during the Second World War, however, was never merely a simple military problem. British Columbia demanded an extra measure of protection, in part because of local hostility to the Japanese (including the Nisei in Canada) and in part because of the province's sense of isolation on the far side of the Rocky Mountains. These feelings of insecurity were not assuaged, even after the Japanese began to suffer defeat in the Pacific, and the government in Ottawa was compelled to offer greater insurance to the region than the military situation dictated. Few, therefore, of the thousands of Canadians who stood on guard on the west coast until August 1945 were expected to meet the enemy, and few did. Their presence was due very largely to political considerations, yet it was no less legitimate for that.

Army, navy, and air force planners actually began to look seriously at the problem of west coast defence in the late 1920s, when it seemed that Canada might be called upon to use force to assert its neutrality in an American-Japanese war. By the late 1930s, at the specific urging of the government, the army made an effort to improve its coastal defences in the region, the navy prepared to conduct off-shore patrols with the few ships at its disposal, and the air force selected sites for airfields and seaplane bases to facilitate reconnaissance along the entire coast and to provide a limited strike and air defence capability in the Victoria-Vancouver area. The air force was the 'predominant partner' in Pacific defence for reasons of geography. Aeroplanes could respond quickly and at great range to any incursion into Canadian territory or territorial waters. Thus, even before the RCAF obtained its independence from the army, a separate Western Air Command under Group Captain G.O. Johnson had been established on 1 March 1938 answering directly to Air Commodore G.M. Croil, the senior air officer in

Ottawa. Johnson's command included all RCAF units in British Columbia, Alberta, Saskatchewan, and Manitoba.[1] He was responsible for 'all phases of air action in the defence of the Western Canadian coast line and waters ... and for the air defence of vulnerable points within the confines of his operational zone.'[2] After the Munich Crisis of September 1938, the focus of Canadian defence preparations swung towards the Atlantic, however, and several units originally allocated to the west coast, and still physically located in western Canada, were removed from the command's war establishment.[3] This transfer left two permanent and three auxiliary squadrons for employment when war broke out in September 1939.

The Joint Service Committee Pacific Coast had divided the region, with its more than 1000 miles of coastline, into five defended areas. To cover them, the available squadrons had a total of eight serviceable operational aircraft, all obsolescent. No 4 (General Reconnaissance) Squadron flew one Supermarine Stranraer and two Vickers Vancouvers; No 6 (Torpedo Bomber) operated five Blackburn Sharks. The auxiliary squadrons – Nos 111 (Coast Artillery Co-operation), 113 (Fighter), and 120 (Bomber), the latter not immediately available for use – had no effective machines. There was not even the prospect of manning and equipping 113 Squadron, and it was disbanded in October.[4] The command did not receive any further allocation of fighter support until late 1941.

The one positive note in this gloomy recital was that the two permanent squadrons were already at their initial wartime station of Vancouver. On 2 September, the day after the precautionary defensive order against Germany came from Air Force Headquarters, two Blackburn Sharks of 6 (TB) Squadron flew the first ship identification patrols. Ten days later, 4 (GR) Squadron sent its first two aircraft out on coastal patrols,[5] while No 6 stopped its routine flights. 'As from today no search patrols will be carried out,' 6 Squadron's diarist noted, '... unless some definite job is to be done. Aircraft to stand by as striking force.'[6]

Pressed by the army for effective air spotting assistance to the coast artillery, Johnson in desperation suggested taking over 'Ginger Coote Airways,' a local commercial operator of several radio-equipped floatplanes. Croil rejected this idea and directed that 111 Squadron carry out its assigned role as best it could from the partially constructed runways at Patricia Bay. An Armstrong Whitworth Atlas with neither guns nor radio was all that could be spared to reinforce No 111's single Avro 626 trainer. The permanent squadrons found their tasks as the strike and reconnaissance force equally bizarre.[7] 'Stranraer "912 is the only aircraft in the Command which is suitable for search and patrol duty,' wrote Johnson, now an air commodore, on 10 September. 'The two serviceable Vancouver[s], due to their unreliability and poor performance, are unsuitable for operations except under fairly favourable conditions and should be kept within easy reach of adequate repair facilities. To operate them in remote areas, such as the Queen Charlotte Islands, is to invite disaster. The Shark II aircraft are continually becoming unserviceable ... The Shark III aircraft have not been in service sufficiently long nor in sufficient numbers to determine whether or not they are more reliable than the Shark II.'[8]

It was fortunate there was no enemy on the coast and Western Air Command

WESTERN AIR COMMAND
ORDER OF BATTLE

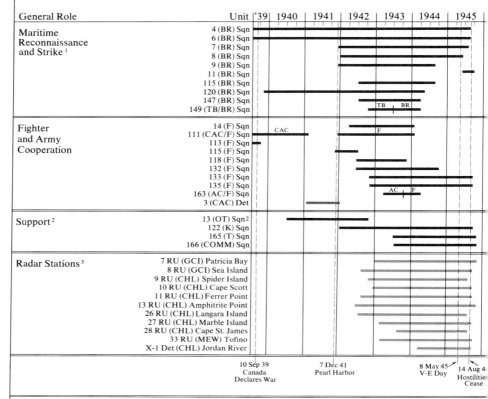

General Role	Unit	'39	1940	1941	1942	1943	1944	1945
Maritime Reconnaissance and Strike [1]	4 (BR) Sqn							
	6 (BR) Sqn							
	7 (BR) Sqn							
	8 (BR) Sqn							
	9 (BR) Sqn							
	11 (BR) Sqn							
	115 (BR) Sqn							
	120 (BR) Sqn							
	147 (BR) Sqn							
	149 (TB/BR) Sqn					TB	BR	
Fighter and Army Cooperation	14 (F) Sqn		CAC			F		
	111 (CAC/F) Sqn							
	113 (F) Sqn							
	115 (F) Sqn							
	118 (F) Sqn							
	132 (F) Sqn							
	133 (F) Sqn							
	135 (F) Sqn							
	163 (AC/F) Sqn					AC	F	
	3 (CAC) Det							
Support [2]	13 (OT) Sqn [2]							
	122 (K) Sqn							
	165 (T) Sqn							
	166 (COMM) Sqn							
Radar Stations [3]	7 RU (GCI) Patricia Bay							
	8 RU (GCI) Sea Island							
	9 RU (CHL) Spider Island							
	10 RU (CHL) Cape Scott							
	11 RU (CHL) Ferrer Point							
	13 RU (CHL) Amphitrite Point							
	26 RU (CHL) Langara Island							
	27 RU (CHL) Marble Island							
	28 RU (CHL) Cape St. James							
	33 RU (MEW) Tofino							
	X-1 Det (CHL) Jordan River							

10 Sep 39
Canada
Declares War

7 Dec 41
Pearl Harbor

8 May 45
V-E Day

14 Aug 4
Hostilitie
Cease

NOTES:

1. Nos. 119 (BR) and 160 (BR) Sqns organized and trained at Sea Island for brief periods in 1940 and 1943 respectively before joining EAC. No. 117 (BR) Sqn transferred from EAC to WAC in late 1941, but was disbanded to provide reinforcements to other squadrons.

2. In addition to 13 (OT) Sqn, the following Operational Training Units were in WAC:

32 OTU (RAF)	Patricia Bay/Comox	Torpedo-Bomber/Transport	1 Sep 41 - 31 May 44	Became 6 OTU
3 OTU	Patricia Bay	Flying-Boat	1 Nov 42 - 3 Aug 45	Absorbed 13 (OT) Sqn
5 OTU	Boundary Bay/Abbotsford	Heavy Bomber	1 Apr 44 - 31 Oct 45	
6 OTU	Comox	Transport	1 Jun 44 - 15 Jan 46	Ex - 32 OTU

3. Radio Detachments, renamed Radio Units 1 Sep 44:

    CHL   Chain Home Low-flying. Early warning radar.
    MEW Microwave Early Warning / Ground Control Intercept
    GCI   Ground Control Intercept

AC	Army Cooperation	COMM	Communications	OT	Operational Training
BR	Bomber–Reconnaissance	F	Fighter	TB	Torpedo Bomber
CAC	Coast Artillery Cooperation	K	Composite	T	Transport

had time to continue the interrupted prewar construction and rearmament process. Work began on a planned seaplane base at Prince Rupert in December, and on facilities at Coal Harbour and Bella Bella in 1940 (see map, front endplate). Although the stations were still far from complete, in May 1940 No 111 (CAC) concentrated at Patricia Bay, previously the site of only its advanced detachment, while 4 and 6 (Bomber-Reconnaissance) Squadrons moved fully to their war bases at Ucluelet and Alliford Bay, hitherto manned only on a skeleton basis. No 13 (Operational Training) Squadron occupied Sea Island, the site of the prewar Vancouver civic airport, while 120 (BR) Squadron followed No 111 from that site to Patricia Bay.[9]

After a year of war, the command's operational reconnaissance strength had grown to two Stranraers, fourteen Sharks, and four Northrop Deltas. Qualified aircrew were in short supply, and in September 1940, when Air Force Headquarters ordered the three west coast bomber-reconnaissance squadrons reduced to a cadre basis in order to bring similar east coast squadrons up to full strength, the shortage became chronic. No 111 Squadron, redesignated but not converted to a fighter role, had to be disbanded instead on 31 January 1941 and replaced by the smaller No 3 (CAC) Detachment.[10]

There was some encouraging progress, however. The RCAF Marine Squadron, vital for the support of isolated coastal stations, built up a collection of small search-and-rescue, supply, and working craft, and gave increasingly effective support to the command throughout the war. Starting in May 1940 the Aircraft Detection Corps began to enrol its unpaid volunteer civilian observers along the coast and throughout the countryside.[11] In January 1941 American requests for improved coastal air defences, and Mackenzie King's crucial opinion that 'such expenditures would be insurance ... [against] attack from the East,' persuaded the minister of finance, J.L. Ilsley – who even after a year of war expressed shock at the great expenditure on defence projects – to withdraw his objections to new facilities at Ucluelet.[12]

In the Joint Canadian-United States Basic Defence Plan – 1940 against 'direct attack by European and/or Asiatic Powers,' the Permanent Joint Board on Defence specified two joint tasks along the Pacific coast: one for the defence of Alaska, British Columbia, and the northwestern United States; and one for the protection of their vital sea communications. Mutual support was to be given if needed, although except for the possible early backup of Alaskan garrisons by Canadian forces from British Columbia, the board's report on the plan implied that it would usually be a case of American assistance to Canada. PJBD recommendations of mid-November included the completion of the North West Staging Route from Alberta to Alaska and the construction of a landplane aerodrome near the Ucluelet seaplane station, to extend fighter and bomber support northward towards the Queen Charlotte Islands.[13]

In the meantime, the command's air officer commanding from October 1939, Air Commodore A.E. Godfrey, and the Joint Service Committee Pacific Coast kept an anxious eye on the growing threat from Japan. The air staff in Ottawa was not in tune with their fears, but did recognize many of Western Air Command's shortcomings and difficulties. In the fall of 1941 a reconstituted

115 (F) Squadron, equipped with long-range, modified, twin-engined Bristo
Bolingbrokes, moved out west to provide a measure of fighter support, thoug
some imagination was required to see the Bolingbroke – designed as a ligł
bomber – in an air defence role. If active hostilities occurred, a modern fighte
squadron might be sent from the east for short-range work. Stranraers from th
east coast and others expected for future delivery promised to give Western Ai
Command enough aircraft to fill under-strength squadrons at Ucluelet, Coa
Harbour, Bella Bella (where a new 9 (BR) Squadron would be located), an
Alliford Bay. Supporting them in early December would be Sharks flown by
new 7 (BR) Squadron at Prince Rupert and, if needed, the service aircraft of 1
(OT) Squadron at Patricia Bay. Emergency air reconnaissance and strikin
strength off the southern half of the west coast was also increased considerabl
by the fifty-six Bristol Beauforts of 32 Operational Training Unit, RAF, a
Patricia Bay, to be available by mid-December. These forces would finall
allow limited coastal and seaward coverage up to approximately 250 miles.[14]

On 29 November 1941 the chief of the air staff told Western Air Command t
maintain the 'closest collaboration' with both of the other Canadian services an
with American west coast forces. A few days later, on 5 December, Lieutenan
General John L. DeWitt, commanding the American Western Defense Com
mand, suggested a combined meeting to draw up a tentative area defence pla
based on ABC-22, the successor to the 1940 Joint Defence Plan. On 7 Decembe
before such a meeting could be held, Japanese aircraft bombed Pearl Harbor
Canada declared war on Japan that night, the United States and Great Britai
followed suit on 8 December, and ABC-22 immediately came into force in th
Pacific.[15]

As these great events unfolded all forces went to a high degree of readiness
Aircraft flew continuous patrols by day. Reinforcements rushed west to fil
personnel shortages. No 111 (F) Squadron (Curtiss P-40 Kittyhawks), reforme
the previous month at Rockcliffe, Ont., transferred to Sea Island for fighte
defence. No 8 (BR) Squadron (Bolingbrokes) joined No 111 at the beginning o
1942 after a flight from Sydney, NS – the first time a complete squadron ha
flown from coast to coast – in unheated aircraft in the dead of winter. Bases a
Prince Rupert, Bella Bella, and Coal Harbour became operational, manned i
part by two new squadrons, 7 and 9 (BR).[16]

Effecting this reinforcement demanded immense efforts from many quarters
The kind of difficulty encountered is nowhere better illustrated than in the office
of the Canadian Department of Munitions and Supply's purchasing agents i
Washington. On 8 December the United States froze the export of all militar
equipment, just as eight new Curtiss Kittyhawks were about to depart for thei
Canadian destination from Buffalo. They could not be pried from the grip o
American officials until, two days later on 10 December, someone managed t
get through to the office of the commander of the United States Army Air Forces
Major General H.H. Arnold. Since these aircraft were for the defence of Nortł
America their release did not require too much persuasion at that level. Far mor
difficult was the release of spare parts and ammunition without which the aircraf
were useless. Unfortunately, this decision required co-operation from the RA

delegation in Washington. It took several days of personal telephoning and negotiating for Arnold's long-suffering aide to obtain the necessary release for matériel ready to be shipped.[17]

Another complicating factor was public anxiety on the west coast. In mid-December the Chiefs of Staff Committee advised the Cabinet War Committee that fears of an impending Japanese assault on British Columbia were unwarranted. Not only was a large-scale assault beyond Japanese resources, but the full involvement of the United States would help Canada's defensive situation. This was borne out by the American draft area defence plan which provided the basis for the Joint Canadian-United States Pacific Coastal Frontier Plan No 2, or ABC-Pacific-22, formally approved by all Allied west coast commanders on 23 January 1942. Based on the provisions of ABC-1 and ABC-22, the plan was designed to protect sea communications and territory from Alaska to the northwestern United States. Committed to mutual assistance, Canadians nevertheless visualized very little demand for their services outside their own borders. The Joint Service Committee Pacific Coast assessed the threat at the end of 1941 as consisting of possible hit-and-run attacks by carrier-borne aircraft, submarines, and minelaying ships; small-scale bombardment by one or two warships; and at the most strikes against important targets by air or sea-borne raiding parties.[18] There was no change in established RCAF roles.

Air Commodore L.F. Stevenson, who had been a prewar senior staff officer on the west coast under Johnson, returned from overseas as air officer commanding at this critical period. The state in which he found his command can be seen in a report by his old commander who, as deputy chief of the air staff, visited early in 1942. Despite the latest reinforcements, Air Vice-Marshal Johnson judged there were still serious shortcomings. Stranraers were restricted to patrolling no further than 150 miles from base because there was an insufficient number of these aircraft even to cover the inshore areas adequately. If enemy ships should close the coast during darkness for dawn attacks, the sixteen Bolingbrokes of 8 (BR) Squadron comprised the only really effective strike force; 7 (BR)'s Sharks were obsolete and vulnerable floatplanes, and the only other strike aircraft, being with training units, were unavailable for quick reaction. No 115 (F) Squadron's twin-engined Bolingbrokes were slow and unhandy fighter aircraft, so 111 (F)'s Kittyhawks had to bear most of the air defence burden in the Victoria-Vancouver area. There were not enough fighters to maintain continuous patrols, and air defence relied heavily on the Aircraft Detection Corps' scattered volunteers for early warning and tracking. Nothing better was available until radar was installed later in 1942. North of the Victoria-Vancouver area the situation was even worse. Airfields for strike and fighter aircraft would not be complete for many months. At Prince Rupert, the second most vital area, no suitable site for an airstrip had yet been found. Even at that, the Canadian coast was better defended than the United States, which Stevenson found 'not half as well equipped to repel attack on the Pacific Coast' as Canada. There were so few flying boats that the RCAF had to supplement the US Navy's distant sea patrols.[19]

It is not surprising that Canada turned down renewed demands in the PJBD for

American control in the Pacific region. This would have required a reorganiza tion of Western Air Command along the lines of the division of responsibilit between the US Army Air Forces and the US Navy, which gave the navy tactica command and responsibility for over-water operations. The Canadian chiefs c staff successfully maintained that ABC-22, amplified by the Joint Board' twenty-second recommendation that local commanders co-ordinate their ow efforts, was adequate. After more than a month's negotiations the America members let the matter drop.[20]

Liaison officers, as well as the telephone and teleprinter lines available, did i fact serve their purpose, but relations were prickly. Air Vice-Marshal Johnso reported in March 1942 that 'The various United States forces are trying t co-operate with the corresponding Canadian forces but it is apparent that they ar not co-operating with each other.' The American army and navy representative rarely met, he noted, while the US Army Air Forces interceptor and bombe commands normally dealt with each other through their general commanding i San Francisco, although their offices were in the same building in Seattle.[21] Suc criticism was returned in kind. From the date of the appointment of a Canadia commander-in-chief West Coast Defences that same month, almost a yea passed before a joint headquarters organization was created whose effectiv ness, even then, 'seemed doubtful to U.S. observers because of unco-operativ service attitudes.'[22]

Yet Canadian-American co-operation there was, and it led to an importai early benefit in the form of radar equipment. Immediately after the Pearl Harbo attack, the US War Department asked permission to install what the Canadiar still called 'radio direction finding' equipment at two sites on Vancouver Islanc The RCAF had been aware of British radar developments since early 1939, bu nothing had been done to install RDF equipment on west coast sites. Th Canadian government accepted the American offer, stipulating that th detachments be under Western Air Command and that Canadian personnel tak over as soon as they were trained. In July, after installing the sets, the America technicians departed. Canada, it should be noted, simultaneously returned th favour. C.D. Howe is said to have insisted on this action, somewhat to th dismay of the Air Council, when he received US requests for radar equipment t improve that in the Panama Canal Zone. Thus the first few early warning sets o Canadian production lines – more effective than existing American equipment went to the United States, and in February 1942 a small RCAF party went to th Panama Canal to install them and instruct American operators in their use.[23]

In February Stevenson also revived an earlier scheme for RCAF coast watche along the uninhabited west coast of the Queen Charlotte Islands as an earl warning network for Prince Rupert. Each manned by a woodsman, two radi operators, and 'a man with some cooking and camping ability,' eigl detachments of No 1 Coast Watch Unit were put ashore in isolated areas th provided a good seaward view and covered harbour entrances suitable for enem landing operations.[24] The coastline was rugged, the weather often poor, and th sites reflected these difficult conditions. Typical was tiny Hibben Island, whe the lookout and radio cabin were perched on the edge of a high cliff, and whe

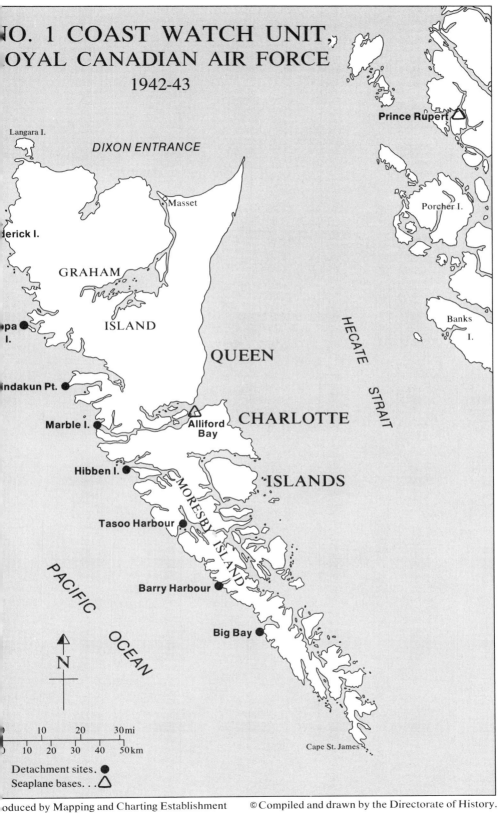

NO. 1 COAST WATCH UNIT,
ROYAL CANADIAN AIR FORCE
1942-43

Langara I.

DIXON ENTRANCE

Prince Rupert △

Masset

Porcher I.

erick I.

GRAHAM

ISLAND

pa ●
I.

Banks
I.

QUEEN

HECATE

ndakun Pt. ●

Marble I. ●

△ Alliford
Bay

CHARLOTTE

STRAIT

Hibben I. ●

ISLANDS

MORESBY ISLAND

Tasoo Harbour ●

PACIFIC

Barry Harbour ●

OCEAN

Big Bay ●

↑
N

| | | | | |
10 | 20 | 30mi
10 | 20 | 30 | 40 | 50km

Cape St. James

Detachment sites . ●
Seaplane bases . . . △

oduced by Mapping and Charting Establishment   © Compiled and drawn by the Directorate of History.

there were many 'successive days when landing with any safety for man, boat, or cargo was impossible.'[25]

Enemy activities were conspicuous by their absence. Other than some attack on merchantmen off California in late December 1941, there had been no interference with trade. The only Japanese warships off North America were large submarines, I-boats, each carrying a two-seat folding seaplane, which occasionally watched US ports for naval activity. There was a shore bombard ment by I-17 near Santa Barbara, California, on 23 February 1942, followed the next night by jittery gunners firing over 1400 rounds of anti-aircraft ammunition against imaginary targets in the 'Battle of Los Angeles.' Among other false alarms the minesweeper HMCS *Outarde* reported a submarine off the north end of Vancouver Island on 1 January 1942, and a Bolingbroke of 8 (BR) Squadron reported another on 5 February. Later that month the RCAF went on alert because the US Army in Honolulu reported the approach of a large air fleet that was actually US Navy planes arriving ahead of schedule.[26] Ships continued to move independently and relatively safely without convoys or escorts. At the navy' request, apparently more with an eye to intelligence gathering than the defence of shipping, the RCAF photographed all vessels in coastal waters hoping to identify any submarines disguised as surface vessels.

As early as mid-1941 RCAF intelligence officers in British Columbia had been questioning the wisdom of 'taking a chance' on Japanese loyalty.[27] New RCAF stations were for the most part in isolated areas and lacked adequate defence arrangements. Western Air Command, in spite of advice given by the chiefs of staff, was accordingly more sensitive than the army and navy on the west coast to possible espionage and sabotage. After Pearl Harbor, on 2 January 1942 Stevenson bypassed the Joint Service Committee and wrote directly to Air Force Headquarters to recommend removal of all Axis aliens from the coast. Security he argued, 'cannot rest on precarious discernment between those who would actively support Japan and those who might at present be apathetic.'[28]

Civilian reaction to the presumed Japanese threat paralleled that of Stevenson persuading the Cabinet War Committee to authorize the removal of the entire Japanese population from the west coast in late February 1942.[29] Indeed feelings in British Columbia were at such a high pitch that they overcame the best advice the chiefs of staff could give the government. There was a strong popular belief that Ottawa was out of touch with the real danger of enemy attack on the Pacific coast; public concern was fired by the media, with their vested interest in crisis and simplistic analysis. The Canadian general staff, Bruce Hutchison wrote scathingly in the Vancouver *Sun*, still had not grasped that the Axis powers were pursuing a strategy of global encirclement. British Columbia was in the front line and the government refused to send reinforcements. In mid-March the *Sun* ran another series of articles, in the local news section of the paper, that purported to reveal serious differences between west coast commanders and their superiors in Ottawa. British Columbia, forecast the author, Alan Morley would never be defended because the politicians did not understand military affairs. As for the military men, they were 'in awe of the politicians and [were]... aged, ineffective, mentally incapable of initiative or strong action, [and had]...

resolutely persisted in "paper-war" routine when they should have been organizing this coast for total war defense.'[30] As C.P. Stacey has observed in the official history of Canadian war policies, *Arms, Men and Governments*, the frightened voters of British Columbia forced the military advisers of the government, through the Cabinet, to sanction much more defence effort in western Canada than was necessary.[31]

Probably only the RCAF – forming the first line of defence – needed bolstering, and even there the threat was not great, so that only a limited response was required. When Stevenson declared himself on the Japanese question in January, drawing a reprimand because he had not gone through the Joint Service Committee as he should have done, he had been faced with a particularly vexing tactical problem. The scenario he painted in February 1942, of enemy aircraft carriers making a night approach, launching bombers at dawn very close to shore, and running to seaward to be overtaken by returning aircraft and covered by ship-borne Japanese fighters, was well within the bounds of possibility. As Air Vice-Marshal Johnson agreed, Western Air Command could have done virtually nothing about it.[32] Still, even after receiving reinforcements, airmen on the west coast again accused Air Force Headquarters of deliberately sacrificing Pacific coast defence to satisfy other priorities. Removed by such a great distance from Ottawa, the airmen (and no doubt the soldiers and sailors as well) had absorbed some of the local malaise.

In April the Joint Service Committee on the west coast issued a new appreciation of the situation, the language of which indicates a compromise between the acknowledged strategic priorities of the Allies and the demands of the local population.

The Japanese people are now flushed with victory and the consciousness of a crushing military and moral defeat inflicted by them on the Anglo-Saxon nations will undoubtedly have induced the peculiar form of savage exhaltation to which they are prone ...

The Naval, Military and Air strength which the United Nations dispose in the Eastern Pacific, and on the Pacific Seaboard of the North American continent, is based upon the fundamental premise that the decisive theatre of war is not in the Pacific and that diversion, beyond the minimum necessary for reasonable security, would be the result which the enemy is everywhere striving to attain.

Complex considerations of national prestige and public morale demand, however, the allocation of sufficient force to provide reasonable insurance against all predictable scales of attack and, at the same time, to satisfy public opinion.[33]

The first component of such insurance, 14 (F) Squadron (Kittyhawks), arrived at Sea Island in early April in place of No 111 (F), which had moved to Patricia Bay in January. These and later squadrons were to benefit from greatly improved facilities. Construction was now under way for two new airfields on Vancouver Island, at Tofino near the Ucluelet seaplane station, and at Port Hardy near Coal Harbour. At Comox and Cassidy on the east side of Vancouver Island, and at Boundary Bay, Abbotsford, Dog Creek, Williams Lake, Quesnel, Prince

George, Vanderhoof, Smithers, Woodcock. and Terrace on the mainland, more airfields and landing strips were in various stages of planning or building.[34]

Stevenson did his best to match these developments with improved co-ordination of operational control. In accordance with Chiefs of Staff Committee policy, the command's headquarters had moved from its original Vancouver location to Belmont House, Victoria, on 24 November 1939 in order to be near the local naval staff, but as on the east coast, the joint operations room ordered by the committee had still not been created. In February 1942 the Joint Service Committee agreed on the need for this facility, and the Cabinet War Committee approved the proposal for both coasts on 18 March when it created the position of commander-in-chief West Coast Defences.[35]

There was no easy agreement on the room's location. Stevenson doubted the suitability of Victoria, connected as it was to Vancouver by three vulnerable underwater cables and far removed from such key areas as Prince Rupert, but on 10 April the committee voted against moving to the mainland because of the possible adverse effect on public morale. Two months later the committee agreed to construct a headquarters in the Colquitz area of Victoria. Lieutenant-General K. Stuart, the chief of the general staff, was then in Victoria and discussed the problem with Stevenson and others; he opted for a move to Vancouver because it was on the mainland. He implemented this change after he personally took over the position of commander-in-chief West Coast a few days later. The Colquitz site was developed as a smaller tri-service headquarters for the forces on Vancouver Island only.[36]

In Vancouver, three separate operational headquarters sprang up in close proximity, each with its own operations room, and the only combined operations room was one created for the service chiefs. These final arrangements were far from satisfactory, and after Major-General G.R. Pearkes took over as commander-in-chief in September the Joint Service Committee 'noted with regret ... that the close physical contact between the Operations Staff of the Services which had been aimed at and which was considered so desirable' did not exist.[37]

In the meantime at the 'Arcadia' meetings in Washington from late December 1941 to early January 1942, British and American staffs judged there would be little likelihood of a Japanese attack in force upon the North American west coast. American reinforcements could therefore safely be sent to advanced posts in Hawaii and Alaska.[38] Prince Rupert, BC, was an excellent harbour with the most northerly coastal railhead in the west, and ABC-Pacific-22 specifically authorized the United States Army 'to establish such facilities as may be required at Prince Rupert for the supply of US Troops in Alaska ...'[39] The Canadians gave this project their wholehearted support, and on 5 April 1942 Prince Rupert officially became an American subembarkation port.[40]

Canadians had been concerned about the inadequacy of Prince Rupert's air defences even before this time. There was an RCAF seaplane base at Seal Cove only a mile north of the port, but without a land runway there could be no fighter protection. A long and exhaustive search had revealed no suitable site on Canadian territory. Concerned about defence of the Alaskan Panhandle, the

Americans had developed an airfield on Annette Island, about sixty miles northwest of Prince Rupert, but could not spare any air combat units to man it. Now the interests of the two countries coincided. The senior Canadian and American west coast service commanders discussed Prince Rupert's defences in Seattle on 6 March 1942. Stevenson tentatively suggested that it might be possible to deploy an RCAF fighter squadron to Annette as an interim measure. Lieutenant General DeWitt, whose Western Defense Command included Alaska as a subordinate command, welcomed this proposal, and within a month it was agreed to by both sides.[41]

No 115 (F) Squadron, under the command of Squadron Leader E. Reyno, went to Annette Island. Still equipped with twin-engined Bolingbrokes modified by the fitting of a belly-pack of forward-firing machine-guns, the squadron completed the move by 5 May and assumed responsibility for the fighter defence of Prince Rupert and its approaches. Western Air Command recognized that these aircraft had limited fighter value, but felt that the airfield conditions at Annette made it undesirable initially to transfer a more suitable type such as Kittyhawks.[42] The squadron enjoyed a special distinction nevertheless: it was the first Canadian force ever based in US territory to assist directly in American defence, a situation that created some unusual problems. The question of American customs duties on equipment and supplies, for instance, had to be solved by US Secretary of State Cordell Hull designating all personnel of the unit as 'distinguished foreign visitors' and so granting free entry of goods. The 'distinguished visitors' were themselves unaware and unaffected by this customs dispute. Their work remained under the operational control of the Canadian officer commanding, Prince Rupert Defences.[43]

As 115 (F) Squadron took up its new duties, the Japanese were preparing a strike against Alaska. In order to establish a defensive perimeter around newly conquered territory and force a decisive engagement with the American fleet, strategic points in the Aleutians, at Midway Island, and on the Hawaii-Australia supply line were to be seized to allow the detection and interception of American forays from Pearl Harbor. In addition to diverting American attention from the central Pacific, the Aleutian occupations would also prevent the United States from launching an offensive from the north Pacific and obstruct American-Soviet collaboration. Patrol planes from these islands would be able to detect any force raiding Japan's inner defences.[44]

The key position was Midway Island. On 5 May 1942 Imperial General Headquarters in Tokyo radioed the order for the Second Mobile Force to strike the Aleutians first in early June, followed a day later by the main force attack on Midway. United States Intelligence intercepted and decoded most of this message, obtained vital supplementary information on 20 May and over the following few days, and dispatched naval task forces to meet the threat. Most strength went to the defence of Midway, but a small North Pacific Force, Task Force 8 under the command of Rear Admiral Robert A. Theobald, steamed north for the protection of Alaska. All local army and navy forces were placed under Theobald's command.[45] Air reinforcements urgently needed to repel the attack, and not to be found in sufficient strength from the limited resources of the United States, had to come from the RCAF.

President Roosevelt already had implied that Canada ought to play a larger part in Pacific defence, especially in Alaska and the Aleutian Islands, and on 27 April the PJBD had agreed that local commanders, US and Canadian, should be ready to send air units to Alaska if necessary. The chief of the air staff ordered Western Air Command to comply, but he was uneasy about the decision in view of the Joint Service Committee's appreciation of 1 April. The RCAF barely had enough strength to protect Prince Rupert and to escort American coastal convoys, and Breadner emphasized that Canadian reinforcements should be limited to the Panhandle.[46] Tentatively, one Bolingbroke and two Kittyhawk squadrons were available in an emergency. Circumstances permitting, 111 (F) Squadron would go to Annette Island; 14 (F) and 8 (BR) Squadrons to Whitehorse for onward dispatch to Alaska. There was a planning meeting with the local American air staff,[47] a PJBD meeting on 27-8 May 1942, and an apparent consensus that 'there was no intention of affecting the basic responsibilities for the defence of Alaska as defined in Plan ABC-22.'[48] By then, however, strategic developments of which the Canadians were not fully aware had overtaken events.

If the Canadian chiefs of staff had been kept fully in the intelligence picture, the complicated and occasionally irascible negotiations that now took place could probably have been concluded with far less difficulty than they were. As the Chiefs of Staff Committee observed, the only information they received about Japanese intentions was at second hand or from US Navy dispatches. When news arrived from the west coast on 21 May, relaying American warnings of the day before that Japan was to attack Midway Island and the Aleutians, the Canadians' immediate concern was for Prince Rupert. Over the next eight days Stevenson, in consultation with the commander-in-chief West Coast, Major-General Alexander, devoted his efforts to reinforcing Annette Island. At the same time Stevenson's and Alexander's American counterparts, Brigadier General Simon B. Buckner, Jr, commanding Alaska Defense Command, and Brigadier General William Butler, commander of the subordinate Eleventh Air Force, had ordered all spare US combat aircraft forward to meet the known threat to Dutch Harbor.[49] They wanted to fill the resulting gap in Alaskan air defences with two Canadian squadrons at Yakutat, half way between Annette Island and Anchorage. This the Canadian chiefs of staff refused to do. Why leave Prince Rupert exposed to a raid which, so far as Mackenzie King was concerned, was 'about to be made on Alaska and probably on our Pacific Coast'?[50]

The chiefs decided that 8 (BR) (Bolingbroke) and 111 (F) (Kittyhawk) Squadrons would move from Patricia Bay and Sea Island to Annette Island where they would provide a striking force and effective fighter protection for the Prince Rupert area; two Kittyhawk squadrons, 118 (F) from Dartmouth, NS, and 132 (F) from Rockcliffe, Ont., were to move west to Patricia Bay and Sea Island. If the squadrons at Annette should be required to move yet further north, where they would be under American control, 118 Squadron would shift to Annette No 14 (F) Squadron from Sea Island would replace No 118 at Patricia Bay.[51]

General DeWitt was upset when Stevenson informed him of these plans. He and Buckner asked that 8 and 111 Squadrons be sent straight to Yakutat, and Buckner also wanted authority to move them to Kodiak, Anchorage, Cordova, or Cold Bay if necessary. It so happened that these conversations coincided with the arrival in Victoria of the Canadian chief of the general staff, Lieutenant-General Stuart. When he heard of the requests on 30 May Stuart agreed that complying with them would deprive British Columbia of adequate air defence. He telephoned his opinion to Air Force Headquarters, and received assurance that no such move would take place until the situation became clearer and the reinforcing squadrons had reached the coast.[52] It was a logjam, and not until 1 June, two days later, could it be cleared.

DeWitt had telephoned the War Department in Washington after hearing of Stuart's position, asking for help in arranging for the Canadian squadrons at Annette to be sent to Yakutat, at least until 8 June. This appears to have been the first mention of a time limit on the commitment. On 1 June, Lieutenant General S.D. Embick, an American member of the PJBD, phoned Air Marshal Johnson to request formally the move to Yakutat in accordance with the provisions of ABC-22, stating with some irritation that American forces in Alaska were being moved further out and implying that new US squadrons would be available to replace RCAF units after 8 June. After discussing the possible effects of the move, and taking into consideration the time limit mentioned, the Canadian chiefs of staff agreed that the RCAF should comply with the American request. Within a few hours orders were on their way to move the squadrons to Yakutat. Behind them, 118 (F) Squadron left Nova Scotia during the first week in June for Patricia Bay. En route its destination was changed to Annette Island.[53]

No 8 Squadron moved first. On 2 June the Bolingbrokes departed Sea Island for Yakutat by way of Annette Island and Juneau, followed by two Stranraers carrying groundcrew and essential spares. There were no air navigation maps of the terrain north of Prince Rupert, and the squadron made do with a few Admiralty charts as far as Juneau. There the last leg of the route had to be traced from local maps before the aircraft could fly on. Ten Bolingbrokes and the two Stranraers arrived at Yakutat on 3 June, the day the Japanese attacked Dutch Harbor. On the request of the local American commander, one Bolingbroke carried out a short patrol of Yakutat Bay, the first operational mission in support of Alaska Defense Command.[54]

On 4 June Wing Commander G.R. McGregor, who had previously won the Distinguished Flying Cross during the Battle of Britain, arrived to assume command of all local RCAF personnel. That day the squadron received its first direct operational order from Alaska Defense Command: all aircraft were to stand by armed with bombs. The armourers immediately discovered that the bomb shackle adapter rings – designed by 3 Repair Depot in Vancouver to take US ordnance – would only fit one size of American bomb, one that was not stocked in Alaska. New adapter rings were hurriedly made in Canada and flown north to reach the squadron of 8 June.[55]

Dutch Harbor, in the Aleutians, was now under attack. The enemy force launched air strikes from carriers against the port on 3 and 4 June. The crushing

defeat suffered by the Japanese main force at Midway on the 4th, which mad·
impracticable any Japanese major offensive beyond the original conques
perimeter, undermined the strategic purpose of the Aleutian operation
Nevertheless, the commander of the Northern Area Force, Vice-Admira
Boshiro Hosogaya, received orders to finish what he had begun. His force
occupied the islands of Kiska and Attu, far out in the Aleutian chain, on 6 and ·
June, respectively. At first the Japanese saw their presence as temporary, witl
the force to be withdrawn before winter. Without Midway, the islands had littl·
value for patrolling the ocean approaches to Japan from Hawaii. They did bloc
any (unlikely) American use of the Aleutian route to Japan, however, had
nuisance value, and doubtless helped to boost Japanese morale after the defeat a
Midway. By the end of the month, the Japanese had decided to stay.[56]

Buckner now redeployed his resources, and on 5 June ordered the Canadian·
(who comprised no less than a fourth of his air combat units) to move at once t·
Elmendorf Field, Fort Richardson, outside of Anchorage. This served as th·
final staging base for squadrons moving forward to carry the offensive agains
the new Japanese positions. McGregor immediately signalled Western Ai
Command for authority to comply. If the wing was to get into battle, h·
explained, it would have to advance. It was less difficult to get authority than t·
exercise it. Neither 8 Squadron nor the Yakutat airfield staff had maps of th·
route north or knew the necessary recognition signals. In response t·
McGregor's urgent request both arrived the next day, but bad weather scattere·
the Bolingbrokes during the trip north. All finally gathered at Elmendorf Fiel·
on the 7th, where the squadron diarist reported: 'Air Base Headquarters requir·
Blbks to be held in readiness twenty-four hours per day.'[57]

No 111 (F) Squadron had only one suitable map available, so its aircraft stage·
through Prince George and Watson Lake to Whitehorse, where they were me·
with maps for the rest of the trip. On the 8th the Kittyhawks flew on t·
Anchorage, with a stop at Yakutat. More Kittyhawks, equipped with bell·
tanks, flew north along the coast a few days later, to bring the squadron up t·
strength on the 24th. The deployment of the two squadrons had quickly brough·
home to the Canadians the greatest hazards of Alaskan operations: lon·
distances between bases and generally poor weather conditions, compounded b·
inadequate meteorological information, especially in route forecasts.[58]

McGregor established 'x' Wing Headquarters as a contact point between th·
RCAF and Alaska Defense Command. At Elmendorf Field the Canadians wer·
part of the force assigned to protect Anchorage from Japanese bombing raids·
but there were no such raids nor any great likelihood of them. It would have bee·
a foolhardy Japanese carrier force that ventured into the Gulf of Alaska afte·
Midway. All the action in that theatre was therefore concentrated against th·
enemy outposts on Kiska and Attu, and that was where the Canadians no·
wanted to be. As early as 11 June, 8 Squadron daily diary recorded that th·
'possibilities of unit seeing combat whilst based here seems extremely remote·
McGregor agreed, and expressed his reservations to Air Vice-Marshal Steven·
son, who visited Elmendorf on 18-19 June. Stevenson could give no estimate c·
how long the RCAF would stay in Alaska but he instructed the two squadrons t·

be kept together as a composite wing if possible, and gave McGregor discretion to transfer the units within Alaska as necessary.[59]

On 13 June, after a week on ground alert, 8 (BR) Squadron started anti-submarine patrols of the Gulf of Alaska from Kodiak to the east, and then back to Anchorage by way of Prince William Sound. Kodiak was better sited for these tasks, and occasionally a detachment worked out of that field when a convoy was in the area. By the end of the first month it was evident that the squadron's real problem was supply and maintenance for its British-designed Bolingbrokes, because only American spares were readily available. Spark-plug shortages were especially critical. By 13 July there were only enough to change the plugs on two aircraft, and on the 23rd only one of the seven aircraft at Elmendorf was serviceable, three others having been sent to Nome. Four days of total unserviceability followed, during a rare period of fine flying weather. In October, the Elmendorf aircraft were grounded again for over a week because there were no felt elements for oil filters.[60] Without a reliable supply system for its special parts, the squadron was never able to become fully operational.

In Washington the Joint Chiefs of Staff met on 15 June to discuss the Japanese occupation of Attu and Kiska. They concluded that these bases could be part of a screen for a northward thrust into the USSR's maritime provinces and Kamchatka Peninsula. Even though climate and topography made large-scale operations quite impracticable, the Joint Chiefs warned that additional Japanese objectives might include St Lawrence Island and Nome and its adjacent airfields. American air force reinforcements were immediately sent to Nome. On 27 June 'x' Wing was also warned for Nome, but then told a few days later that it would probably not be needed since an additional USAAF squadron was available if required. This incident seemed to substantiate the opinion already formed by Wing Commander McGregor that the Canadians were seen essentially as a convenient rear-area security force.[61] 'It is again evident,' he wrote to Stevenson at the end of the month, 'that Canadian Squadrons will only find themselves in a location likely to result in active operations as a result of some completely unforeseen enemy attack ... the greatest care will be taken to insure the Canadian Squadrons will not see action if it is possible to place U.S. Army Air Corps Squadrons in a position to participate in such action, even if the said U.S. Squadrons are much more recent arrivals in Alaska.'[62] McGregor recognized the useful role played by 'x' Wing in freeing American units from Anchorage's defence, but wondered if this use of two scarce Home War Establishment operational squadrons was in the best interests of the RCAF.[63] The Canadians had to move forward if they were to meet the enemy.

The minister of national defence for air, C.G. Power, the chief of the air staff, Air Marshal L.S. Breadner, and Stevenson supported this position in discussions with the American commanders when they visited Anchorage on 4 July, and General Butler expressed his willingness to comply. On the 6th he proposed that all of 111 (F) Squadron's pilots and selected groundcrew members, over half the unit, go forward to Fort Glenn on Umnak Island, the most advanced of the American bases. There they would relieve an equivalent number of personnel from the P-40 equipped 11th Fighter Squadron, USAAF.[64]

On 13 July 1942 Wing Commander McGregor and the first group of six pilot started west in Kittyhawks via Naknek and Cold Bay, followed by transport carrying extra pilots, groundcrew, and support staff. It was an unlucky trip. On Kittyhawk was accidently lost and another damaged on the first leg, bu fortunately both pilots were saved, and two replacement fighters were brough forward to join the others. Bad weather delayed the last two legs until the 16th and then tragedy struck. Shortly after passing Dutch Harbor the fighters ran int more bad weather, and McGregor ordered them to turn back. As the othe aircraft followed him in the turn they lost contact. Squadron Leader J.W Kerwin, Pilot Officer D.E. Whiteside, Flight Sergeant F.R. Lennon, Sergean S.R. Maxmen, and Flight Sergeant G.D. Baird disappeared in the fog. The firs four crashed into Unalaska Island; Baird was never found. McGregor himsel later narrowly missed a rocky ledge as he circled low on the fog's edge for half a hour calling them. Only one answered. This fighter continued on to Umnak an landed through the only available break in the cloud cover, while McGrego returned to Cold Bay to organize a search. The transports completed the tri safely.[65]

Umnak was a bare, treeless island, covered in volcanic ash and tundra. At th American base, Fort Glenn, the runway had been operational for less than tw months, the men slept under canvas (five to a tent with a sleeping bag and fou blankets each), and for the first month did without tent floors. Commanding th 11th Fighter Squadron was Major John S. Chennault, the son of Major Genera Claire Chennault, who had led the American volunteer group in China – th famous Flying Tigers. He and McGregor, together with General Butler, an with the approval of Air Vice-Marshal Stevenson, agreed that the Canadian would work with the 11th Squadron using USAAF machines. There would be n more ferrying of Canadian Kittyhawks until they had belly tanks fitted. On 2 July, after several days of familiarization flights, and the day after forming a all-Canadian 'F' Flight, the RCAF pilots began flying their own defensive patrols By 15 August Canadians had begun taking their turn on fighters flying from new satellite field ten miles away.

On 20 August Squadron Leader K.A. Boomer, accompanied by fou replacement pilots, arrived at Elmendorf Field to take command of the squadron By this time 8 (BR) Squadron had moved a detachment of three Bolingbrokes t Nome for patrols over Norton Sound and the Bering Sea. A small ground part from No 8 departed by air transport on 13 July, but bad weather prevented th Bolingbrokes from attempting the trip until the 17th and 18th.[66]

Nome was a small, isolated, turn-of-the-century gold-rush town, situated i low, rolling tundra. There were two gravel runways, no hangars, and canva accommodation. At this dreary place the Canadian detachment shared patr duties with the air echelon of the 404th Bombardment Squadron (Consolidate B-24 Liberators), while the Bell P-39 Airacobras of the 56th Fighter Squadro carried out local fighter protection until October. At first two Bolingbroke stood by as an anti-submarine striking force, while the detachment flew daily single-aircraft patrols southwards to Nunivak Island, returning by way of Stua Island and Norton Sound. Soon, coastal patrols northwards were added. On 2

August the 404th Squadron's B-24s, which had been carrying out distant patrols to St Lawrence Island, withdrew for operations in the Aleutian chain, and 8 Squadron's detachment took over their task as well.[67]

In the meantime American and Japanese commanders in the Aleutians were at a standoff. Both were starved of material because other war theatres enjoyed higher priorities; both struggled against vile weather. Of twenty-four 'Rufes' – seaplane versions of the 'Zero' fighter – brought out in July, only two were operational. The only other Japanese combat aircraft in the theatre, flying boats, had no noticeable effect on operations. Believing Kiska threatened because of repeated air attacks during the summer, the Japanese had reinforced that island from Attu. The Americans, in order to keep up the pressure, stepped down the Aleutian chain to Adak Island, just over 200 miles from Kiska. They moved in on 30 August and had an airstrip of perforated steel planking in place fifteen days later. On 14 September aircraft were taking off for raids on Kiska. Over the next week or so, reinforcements flew in from Umnak, including Canadians from 111 (F) Squadron: Squadron Leader K.A. Boomer, Flying Officers J.G. Gohl and R. Lynch, and Pilot Officer H.O. Gooding, flying P-40Ks with long-range tanks. A Canadian-American attack went in on the 25th, with fighters providing close and top cover; all strafed naval craft and ground targets after the bombers had finished their run.[68]

At approximately 1000 hours the Canadians swept low across little Kiska Island towards the North Head of Kiska Harbor. There they struck gun positions and then the main Japanese camp area and radar installations. Coming back for a second pass they met the two 'Rufe' seaplanes which had taken off to meet the attackers. The enemy leader attacked an American P-40, and was attacked in turn by Boomer. 'I climbed to a stall practically, pulled up right under him. I just poured it into him from underneath. He flamed up and went down.' The Japanese pilot jumped from his aircraft just before it hit the sea. Shortly after, Major Chennault downed the other Rufe. Then the Canadians joined some Americans attacking a surfaced submarine. Having expended their ammunition, the fighters rejoined the bombers and returned to Adak. Both the main island and Little Kiska had been thoroughly strafed, causing fires and explosions. Claims included the two Rufes, and five to eight float biplanes probably destroyed. All the Canadian and American P-40 pilots were awarded US Air Medals for this 'hazardous five hundred mile overwater flight' in single-engine aircraft. Boomer was also awarded the DFC. He had won the only air victory by a member of the Home War Establishment, and became the only member of an RCAF squadron to be credited with air victories against both the Germans and the Japanese. He was later killed in action over Germany in 1944.[69]

Canadians took no further part in offensive operations in 1942. In mid-October 111 Squadron moved back to Kodiak where on some days 'conditions were so poor that even the birds were walking.' When they could, the airmen flew defensive patrols from both the main Fort Greely air strip and a satellite field at Chiniak Point. At other times they endured the winter weather, and were able to break the tedium with squadron dances, USO shows, nightly films, sports parades, and, in some cases, semi-annual leave in Canada.[70]

At Nome the 8 Squadron detachment gradually found life more comfortable. Food improved, USO entertainers passed through, and the tented accommodation was replaced by three Quonset Huts the RCAF personnel erected themselves. The detachment's patrols covered the northern Bering Sea, intersecting at Nunivak Island those of the 406th Bombardment Squadron flying from Naknek. The remainder of 8 (BR) picked up the coverage again in the Gulf of Alaska, flying over Cook Inlet, between Kodiak and Middleton Island, and Prince William Sound, turning over responsibility to the 406th Bombardment Squadron near Cape St Elias. South of Yakutat the Alaska Panhandle was patrolled by Annette Island's 115 (BR) Squadron, RCAF, though the squadron came under the operational control of Western Air Command rather than the Eleventh Army Air Force. In the Aleutian chain to the west, the task of covering the North Pacific and Bering Sea approaches to Kiska and Adak belonged to US Navy PBYS.[71]

On 21 October 1942 General Butler ordered patrols from Nome to be discontinued for the winter, and the patrol system was reorganized in November. No 8 Squadron's Nome detachment returned to Elmendorf, and the squadron was given new patrol routes, Red and Blue, which roughly divided the old Elmendorf route in two. As the winter deepened and the cold intensified, there was great difficulty in completing even these tasks. Satisfactory winterization had not been developed for the Bolingbroke, and engine temperatures could not be maintained. Regulators and compressor lines froze. Finally it was decided to base a detachment of three aircraft at Kodiak, where the weather was milder, and carry out all future patrols from there. The detachment arrived at Kodiak on 30 December 1942 and flew its first missions on New Year's Day.[72]

Preparing for the spring campaign, on 12 January 1943 the Americans established a new base on Amchitka, just over fifty miles from the enemy at Kiska. Over the winter Canadian and American commanders took the opportunity to reorganize RCAF forces in Alaska. In March 14 (F) Squadron, with Kittyhawks, replaced 8 (BR) with its obsolescent, inappropriate, and increasingly tired Bolingbrokes. The pleased response of Generals DeWitt and Buckner, as Stevenson thought at the time, probably arose from their desire for a more elaborate air defence of Alaska than Washington was prepared to support. Stevenson agreed to keep the two fighter squadrons in northern Alaska until May, and in the event was to keep them there a few months longer.[73]

As the first of No 8's various air and sea parties started their slow journey south to Sea Island in February, No 14's Kittyhawks began a typical odyssey, dogged by bad weather all the way, to Umnak. The air party was grounded for four days at Port Hardy and another nine at Annette before flying on towards Yakutat. Conditions then were a rare CAVU – 'Ceiling and Visibility Unlimited' – until they reached their destination. Yakutat was closed by fog. With fuel running low, the Kittyhawks pressed on to an emergency strip at Yakutaga, eighty miles away. There was no fuel there, and another four days were spent transferring gasoline from Yakutat before they could get to Anchorage. Poor weather further delayed the Kittyhawks' departure from Elmendorf and hindered their progress through Naknek and Cold Bay so that they took more than a month in all to reach Umnak Island on 18 March. The ground party quickly turned out to watch the welcome sight as 'the whole Squadron of 15 Kittyhawks arrived over the aerodrome.' The Canadians shared accommodation with the 344th Fighter Squadron, USAAF, until April, when they moved the few miles to Berry Field, a satellite of Fort Glenn. There they became part of General Butler's shore-based air task group (as the Americans called their maritime formations) still under the overall direction of the US Navy's North Pacific Force, now commanded by Rear Admiral Thomas C. Kincaid.[74]

Air Vice-Marshal Stevenson and Wing Commander R.E. Morrow, an overseas veteran who had won a DFC in Europe and had taken over 'X' Wing from McGregor on 1 March, had persuaded the Americans to accept a 'pilots only' Canadian flight on the crowded Amchitka fighter strip. No 14 Squadron was assigned the first monthly tour, and on 31 March twelve selected pilots flew to Adak Island as passengers aboard an American transport. There they spent a few days in final training, broken by ten days of bad weather which culminated in a blizzard on 7 April with winds over 106 mph. The cups on the airstrip's anemometer were blown off. On the 17th the pilots flew forward to Amchitka and offensive operations.[75]

Kinkaid's first objective was Attu Island because intelligence reported that it was less well defended than Kiska. Even against his limited resources he expected that the Japanese, who were having difficulty reinforcing the island and had not been able to complete their planned landing strips, would hold out for no more than three days. The plan was to precede the assault with daily air bombardments against both Attu and Kiska in order to leave the Japanese uncertain as to the point of attack.[76]

So that Canadian airmen could play a part, pilots from 14 Squadron formed a fourth flight in the 18th Fighter Squadron, USAAF. The P-40s did not have the range to attack Attu, and all their offensive sorties were directed against Kiska. This was an important role, supposed to help gain tactical surprise and prevent Attu's reinforcement.[77] Since there was no enemy air opposition, the fighters carried bombs which they dropped on the fixed Japanese installations, and they then carried out as many strafing runs as ammunition and endurance would allow. The pilots established a four-day cycle: the first on operations, the second on rest, the third on alert, and the fourth on defensive patrols or 'flagpole flying.'[78]

The first sortie against Kiska took place on 18 April 1943, and for the next few weeks by far the greatest weight of Kinkaid's air bombardments fell on that island. Not only was this part of the plan, but weather often closed in Attu and led bombers directed there to hit Kiska instead during their return flight. In the last eleven days before the scheduled assault only ninety-five tons of bombs fell on Attu. From 7 to 11 May weather delayed the landing and prevented any further air attack, and when the assault went in on 11 May the Japanese were much better prepared than expected. It took three weeks of intense and bloody fighting, at the cost of over 560 American and 2350 Japanese dead, to recapture Attu.[79]

In mid-May a detachment from 111 Squadron relieved the pilots from No 14, remaining until early in July when another 14 Squadron detachment arrived in turn. An attempt was made to give as many pilots as possible the opportunity for combat flying while the campaign moved towards its conclusion. Over 34,000 men were assembled for the very stiff fight expected on Kiska. The Japanese, however, evacuated the island on 28 July. Unaware of the withdrawal, the Allies continued to carry out bombing attacks during a break in the weather between 29 July and 4 August climaxing, on the last day, with 134 sorties and 152 tons of bombs dropped. The assault went in as scheduled on 15 August, against a non-existent enemy. With the acquiescence of General DeWitt, 111 (F) Squadron had already started its move back to Canada on 8 August, and 14 Squadron followed on 21 September 1943.[80] The RCAF's Alaskan adventure was over.

Throughout the Aleutian campaign the air force had been careful to meet all obligations for the defence of British Columbia. On 16 June 1942 Western Air Command had raised readiness states and formed No 4 Group Headquarters in Prince Rupert to exercise command and tactical control over the northern RCAF stations at Bella Bella, Alliford Bay, and Prince Rupert, as well as the two squadrons (regrouped on 14 June as 'Y' Wing) on Annette Island. Some Stranraers received long-range tanks under each wing to permit a patrol radius of up to 500 miles. The Bolingbroke fighter squadron on Annette Island, No 115, converted to bomber-reconnaissance, a more suitable role for its aircraft, and a new Bolingbroke squadron, 147 (BR), was formed at Sea Island. The command also obtained three more fighter squadrons in June for air defence: No 132 (Kittyhawks) from Rockcliffe, Ont.; and two new Hurricane units, Nos 133 and 135, formed at Lethbridge, Alta, and Mossbank, Sask., respectively.[81]

Japanese submarine activity in 1942 pointed up the need for such changes. Submarines I-25 and I-26 arrived off the coast in the first week of June to monitor US-Canadian naval reaction to the Aleutian attack; I-26, in the Vancouver-Seattle area, torpedoed the American merchantman SS *Coast Trader* on 7 June west-southwest of the entrance to the Strait of Juan de Fuca, the only such sinking near western Canadian coastal waters during the war. In the early hours of 20 June, I-25 torpedoed and badly damaged the British SS *Fort Camosun* a little further south. That night I-26, on her way home, shelled the lighthouse and radio station at Estevan Point on the west side of Vancouver Island between Ucluelet and Coal Harbour. The submarine commander's regretful note that 'there was not a single effective hit that night'[82] is open to debate. He could not have known that his were the only enemy shells to fall on Canadian soil during the war, nor of the ensuing comedy of errors. Despite a full alert, only one Stranraer squadron, No 9 at Bella Bella, sent off a search aircraft. Because of topographical restrictions, night flying was out of the question at Ucluelet and Coal Harbour, the closest stations. No 32 Operational Training Unit at Patricia Bay dispatched its duty aircraft, a Beaufort bomber, but it crashed on take-off. The Stranraer finally arrived over Estevan Point later that night. Those on the ground could only hear, not see it. And the airmen, still without radar, had no real hope of sighting anything. After an uneventful flight of two hours and twenty minutes, the Stranraer flew home again.[83]

Stevenson could do nothing about equipment so he concentrated on technique. He cut out routine long-range (400 nautical miles) patrols, reduced the activity of each Stranraer squadron to one daily patrol 100 miles deep, and instructed the Bolingbrokes of 115 (BR) Squadron at Annette and the Sharks of 7 (BR) at Prince Rupert to supplement this action with two daily coastal patrols.[84] The time and effort saved was to be devoted to training. Group Captain A.H. Hull, the senior air staff officer, warned the stations that 'certain mishaps have given the impression at Western Air Command Headquarters, that either pilots are not being well trained, or are very inexperienced.'[85] This 'rocket' had the desired effect. An RAF Coastal Command visitor in November reported: 'Although there are very few U/BS in that area the pilots had far greater knowledge than those of E.A.C. This is due to A.O.C. W.A.C. detailing certain of his staff as A/S staff and distributing Tactical Memoranda and Instructions to the various squadrons. The situation of aircraft in this area is appalling though and, if the Japanese ever thought of sending submarines or surface craft over, the matter would be very difficult.'[86] Appalling aircraft in appalling conditions inevitably took a serious toll. A series of Stranraer forced landings occurred, caused by aircraft overloading, or failure of crews to jettison bombs or excess fuel when in difficulties. On 26 August 1942 all long-range patrols, except for training or special requirements, were discontinued.[87]

On 1 January 1943 No 2 Group Headquarters was formed in Victoria to assume tactical control along the southern BC coast, and the command's main headquarters then made its planned move to Jericho Beach, Vancouver. Because of the expansion of the Home War Establishment, Western Air Command had become a fairly strong and well-balanced force by this time. The three new fighter squadrons – Nos 132, 133, and 135 – were based at Patricia Bay and the new stations of Boundary Bay and Tofino, all for the air defence of the Victoria-Vancouver area. A new 163 Squadron, originally army co-operation and, from October 1943, fighter, was at Sea Island. A torpedo-bomber squadron, No 149, had been formed in October 1942 for anti-surface ship strike duties, but it was redesignated bomber-reconnaissance in July 1943 when it was clear that the Japanese threat had receded. In support were three non-combat squadrons: 122 (Composite), with a mixture of aircraft types; 165 (Heavy Transport), under operational control of Air Force Headquarters; and 166 (Communications) Squadron. No 13 (OT) Squadron had disappeared in late 1942, its personnel and flying boats forming the nucleus of 3 Operational Training Unit, under the command of Western Air Command for all purposes except training.[88]

During the same period, all but one of the command's bomber-reconnaissance squadrons re-equipped with more effective aircraft. As a Christmas present, 4 (BR) Squadron took delivery of the west coast's first operational Canso 'A' amphibian in December 1942. By April 1943 each of the five seaplane squadrons – Nos 4, 6, 7, 9, and 120 – operated a few of these long-range aircraft, permitting improved coverage of their patrol areas.[89] Three strike squadrons – Nos 8, 115, and 149 – converted to the twin-engined Lockheed-Vega

Ventura GR Mk V bomber. Only 147 (BR) Squadron retained the aging Bolingbroke, 'a troublesome aircraft to maintain' after years of service on both coasts.[90] It was no longer fun to fly, with 'a nasty habit of running short of oil before running out of gas. The first indication of this is when a propellor flies off. There have been five cases of this ... On frequent occasions, dinghies have come out of their stowage in flight, which is most dangerous ... [In one instance] The tail assembly was apparently damaged by the dinghy, and the aircraft spun inverted into the ground, killing the crew. This naturally does little to increase the aircrew's confidence in their aircraft.'[91]

The chain of radar stations along the coast, interlocking with American coverage, was almost complete by November 1943. The detachments of No 1 Coast Watch Unit were withdrawn after radar coverage of the western approaches to the Queen Charlotte Islands was established. The radar stations provided early warnings of the approach of aircraft to filter rooms located in Victoria and Prince Rupert, where plots could be maintained of enemy locations and courses, and warnings and interception orders sent out as needed. Local control of fighters was exercised from sector control rooms at airfields with fighter aircraft, and two radar stations, at Patricia Bay and Sea Island, were equipped to control night fighters in the air defence of the Victoria-Vancouver area. No enemy ever tested this system, but the radar proved its value in tracking Allied aircraft when they were in difficulty and in passing information to navigators or the search and rescue organization.[92]

The command's airfield-building programme in 1943 largely shifted to a second line of facilities deep in British Columbia, a north-south chain of aerodromes known as the Interior Staging Route. On 1 January 1944 the command also took over responsibility for the North West Staging Route from No 4 Training Command, No 2 Wing Headquarters, Edmonton, being established for this purpose. The wing became a separate command – North West Air Command – on 1 June 1944. A solution had also been found to the last airfield problem in the coastal defence programme: the location of a Canadian fighter strip near Prince Rupert. In fact, there were soon two strips, a steel-mat one near Massett, on the north shore of the Queen Charlottes, and later a second one at Sandspit, near the entrance to Skidegate Inlet, for the support and defence of the seaplane base at Alliford Bay.[93] Both airstrips were alternates for emergency use rather than permanent bases, but they provided vital landplane facilities in the area if needed and permitted the return to Canada of the Annette Island squadrons assigned to the defence of Prince Rupert.

The role of the Annette squadrons had become increasingly inconsequential. After a year out of Canada at the isolated station, the original squadrons were replaced in August 1943 by Nos 135 (F) and 149 (BR). These did not stay long, withdrawing to Terrace, BC, east of Prince Rupert, in November. With the likely scale of attack against the coast now greatly reduced, the command recommended to Air Force Headquarters that squadrons surplus to the new requirements be transferred overseas, converted to an operational training role, or disbanded. Thus, as the Annette squadrons prepared to move back into British Columbia, Nos 14, 111, and 118 (F) prepared to move out. Later taking the new

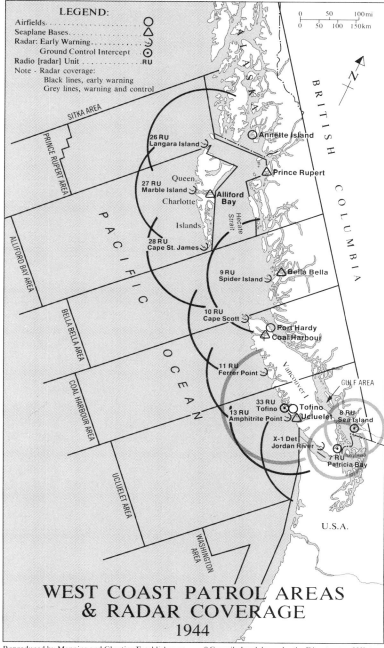

numbers 442, 440, and 438, respectively, they joined three fighter squadrons from Eastern Air Command to form part of the composite group providing tactical support for the army in Europe. They sailed for England between November 1943 and January 1944.[94] At the same time, because the 1944 Air Defence of Canada Plan took 'full cognizance of the necessity for economy at Home,' the establishment of flying-boat reconnaissance units was also cut back to the 1941 strength of nine aircraft each, for a loss equivalent to two fifteen-aircraft squadrons.[95]

There was some danger of reduced efficiency in this climate of retrenchment. In January 1944 Air Marshal Robert Leckie, the new chief of the air staff, expressed his concern that for the past six months the command's aircraft and crew had only averaged twenty-five and twenty-three operational hours, respectively, and could not understand why long-range patrols averaged no more than 140 miles. He ordered Stevenson to extend this to 500 miles, even though the risk of enemy activity was very small.[96] 'We have the alternatives,' wrote Leckie, 'of removing the bulk of our force and accepting the risk, or of keeping the force there and using it to reduce the risk from a small one to as near nil as possible.'[97] He was, he said, adopting the second alternative, but in reality he had already begun to implement the first.

Stevenson received word of a revised Air Defence of Canada Plan in February 1944. He and the other members of the Joint Service Committee Pacific Coast were understandably annoyed at not being consulted first, for the plan laid down extensive strength and facility reductions. Nos 2 and 4 Group Headquarters were to disband, leaving only their filter rooms active, and return operational control to Command Headquarters. One reconnaissance, two strike, and one fighter squadron were also to go. Stations at Port Hardy, Prince Rupert, Smithers, and Terrace were to be reduced to care and maintenance, and Boundary Bay reallocated to training duties. As a result, 147 (BR), 149 (BR), and 163 (F) Squadrons disbanded on 15 March, and No 120 (BR) followed on 1 May. With Prince Rupert considered less likely to be an enemy target than the Vancouver-Victoria area, the remaining strike and fighter squadrons redeployed to the latter, the fighter aircraft establishment being raised to eighteen for each unit. Port Hardy, Smithers, and Terrace were reclassified as staging units, and Prince Rupert became an administrative unit.[98] Stevenson was able to oversee these changes before turning his command over to Air Vice-Marshal F.V. Heakes in June 1944.

The next month the Chiefs of Staff Committee re-examined the defence of Canada once more and reduced their assessments of enemy scales of attack. Some form of submarine assault, including the use of small landing parties, remained the most likely danger, either against shipping in the approaches to Victoria and Prince Rupert or against coastal installations and ports, though occasional raids by carrier-borne aircraft or by surface raiders against seaborne trade in the Canadian Zone could not be entirely discounted. This time the Joint Service Committee Pacific Coast was asked to comment. Heakes recommended that aircraft only patrol the approaches to Victoria and Prince Rupert from the west and southwest, and the standard seaward patrol be reduced to 300 miles.

The area in between would not be covered. He proposed closing Bella Bella and Ucluelet. Anti-submarine squadrons would be retained at Alliford Bay, Coal Harbour, and Tofino, and all strike and fighter strength would be concentrated at Patricia Bay. This advice was accepted without reservation, and its effects were soon felt. Nos 9 (BR), 115 (BR), and 132 (F) Squadrons disbanded in September and October. No 4 (BR) moved to Tofino, and 133 (F) and 135 (F) Squadrons, re-equipped with Kittyhawks, were stationed at Patricia Bay along with the Venturas of No 8 (BR), the single remaining strike squadron. Bella Bella went to reduced operational status, and Ucluelet closed down. In an emergency the command could be reinforced by twelve heavy bombers – Liberators from 5 OTU, Boundary Bay – and any reinforcements from the east coast arranged by Air Force Headquarters.[99]

For the rest of the war Western Air Command emphasized training for quick tactical response to any attack. 'The basis of our work is mobility,' wrote Heakes, who acted very much as a 'new broom.' All squadrons were kept at short notice to move for operations from other bases. The command centralized operational control, a procedural change made possible by the introduction of a new Pacific coast communication system that also proved of considerable value to the other two services, and by the establishment of a high frequency/direction-finding system controlled from the combined operations room in Vancouver. Exercises were run regularly, with US forces participating in some and with the RCN joining in others for simulated convoy operations.[100]

An unpleasant interruption to this routine occurred in November 1944, when the Canadian government reluctantly approved the dispatch overseas of army conscripts, and disturbances broke out throughout the country. The worst incident was at Terrace, BC, where approximately 1600 men of 15 Infantry Brigade armed themselves and took over the camp on 25-6 November. On the 28th, the brigade requested an unarmed flight over Terrace to demonstrate that force was available if required. An eight-aircraft detachment of 8 (BR) Squadron flew to Smithers the following day, ostensibly on one of the command's 'mobility' exercises. They carried no bombs, but Dakotas transporting the groundcrew also brought ammunition. Immediately after arrival the Venturas were sent out on a 'training flight,' but were forced to turn back because of bad weather. The next day crews were maintained at one-hour notice until the flight over the army camp was cancelled on orders from the chief of the general staff. At Terrace, the brigade's senior officers, who had been at a meeting in Vancouver, returned and regained control. The air party returned to the coast, well nourished with moose meat, a highlight of the daily menu at Smithers.[101]

The Japanese, though pressed back towards their homeland, had one more offensive weapon to use against North America: armed balloons. In January 1945, as a defensive measure against these weapons, the fighter squadrons of Western Air Command took turns stationing two aircraft at Patricia Bay and two at Tofino in a condition of constant readiness. Further east, No 2 Air Command kept a handful of Hurricanes on alert at scattered stations in Alberta and Saskatchewan. The origin of this threat lay in a Japanese decision to retaliate for the USAAF Tokyo air raid of mid-1942 by attacking North American forests with incendiaries. The submarine I-25 had launched two partially successful seaplane bombing missions over Oregon in September 1942, mere pin pricks, but the long-term objective was to be achieved by free-flying balloons. Thousands of them, made of paper, were to fly at an average altitude of 30,000 feet carrying four small incendiaries and one anti-personnel bomb, dropped sequentially by an altitude regulating device. The campaign finally began in November 1944, because upper air currents between November and March were ideal for the purpose.[102]

This time of year was also, of course, the worst for igniting forests, since they were rain soaked or snow covered. The first incidents occurred in the United States in December, and a balloon came down with its payload near Minton, Sask., on 12 January. Officials, fearing that the balloons might soon be used to transport biological weapons, tried to deny the Japanese all knowledge of the effectiveness of the balloons by instituting tight press censorship.[103]

In Canada the army became the chief co-ordinating agency to deal with Japanese balloons, supported by the RCAF, RCMP, and various research institutions. The RCAF's job was to shoot down balloons where possible, fly army bomb disposal experts to incident sites, and transport recovered material to Ottawa. The Aircraft Detection Corps had been disbanded on 15 November 1944, but the west coast radar stations and filter centres (unlike those in the United States) were still fully operational. Unfortunately they were not much use against these high altitude targets, paper not being a good reflector of radio waves and the metal components being very small. Detection therefore was haphazard. On 21 February 1945 a Kittyhawk of 133 (F) Squadron shot down a balloon near Sumas, BC. On 10 March another aircraft of this squadron got one of two 'Papers' spotted at Galiano Island, in the Strait of Georgia. Two days later, a 6 (BR) Canso forced down a partially deflated balloon drifting at 500 feet over the Rupert Inlet near Coal Harbour. Wartime reports claim another interception in March near Strathmore, Alta, but it cannot be verified in any unit or station diary.[104]

By then the campaign was already near its end. Peak balloon-launching months were February and March, with a corresponding rise in balloon reports in North America. The final balloon was launched no later than April 1945. Faced by silence in North American news sources, and suffering production disruptions caused by more traditional American bombing, the Japanese cancelled the campaign. There had been no fires attributed to balloon bombs and only one incident of injury or death (in the United States). Although civil and military authorities prepared for incendiary and biological defence, there was no real increase in the resources committed to west coast defence.[105]

The end was in sight by July. One by one the units of Western Air Command began to stand down. Japan surrendered on 14 August. One month later, on 15 September 1945, 11 (BR) Squadron, a Liberator-equipped veteran of the Battle of the Atlantic which joined the command's order of battle on 25 May, disbanded. It was the last operational squadron of the two home defence commands.

In his postwar report, Air Vice-Marshal Heakes wrote: 'The chief difficulties encountered in all operations was weather, due to limited weather reporting facilities in the Pacific and the mountains with their local weather effects. Throughout the summer months a blanket of fog usually extended out over the Pacific up to a distance of 500 miles, thus curtailing effective visual search and requiring greater dependency upon radar. In this connection, the best types were not available for search.'[106]

The airmen of Western Air Command, with their frequently old and worn-out equipment, had performed a tedious and dangerous service, dangerous because weather and terrain put aircrew constantly at risk. There had been, however, little threat of enemy attack. The large establishment on the west coast was more to provide insurance against the possibility of Japanese raids than to carry the war to the enemy. Despite a creditable showing in the Aleutians in 1942-3, Western Air Command's principal function had been to give the population of British Columbia peace of mind. It may be regarded at this distance as a questionable use of scarce resources, but there were two useful military consequences: the exercise of sovereignty in Canadian coastal regions and the creation of a trained fighting force to reinforce other regions if and when needed.

PART FOUR

The North Atlantic Lifeline

The focus of all Eastern Air Command activity: RCAF Station Dartmouth, 1943, as seen from the southwest. Hangars and slipways for flying-boat operations are in the foreground. (REA 132-53)

Douglas Digby No 740 of 10 (BR) Squadron, the machine in which Squadron Leader C.L. Annis made the first attack on a U-boat by an RCAF aircraft, in October 1941. Digbys were the mainstay of 1 Group's operations until the end of 1942. (PA 140642)

The first of Eastern Air Command's Catalinas, a Mark I of 116 (BR) Squadron, undergoes a close inspection by RCAF personnel at Dartmouth, September 1941. (PL 5952)

First arrivals at Torbay, Nfld, October 1941: two B-17s of the USAAF and a Digby of 10 (BR) Squadron. (RE 64-1382)

Bombing up a 10 (BR) Squadron Digby at Gander in early 1942, by Paul Goranson. The trolley carries the ineffective anti-submarine bombs and, at the back, three 450-lb Amatol-filled depth charges – the first really effective anti-submarine weapon in the Eastern Air Command inventory. This significant piece of Canadian war art 'disappeared' in the immediate postwar years. Anyone knowing its location is invited to contact the Canadian War Museum. (PL 13418)

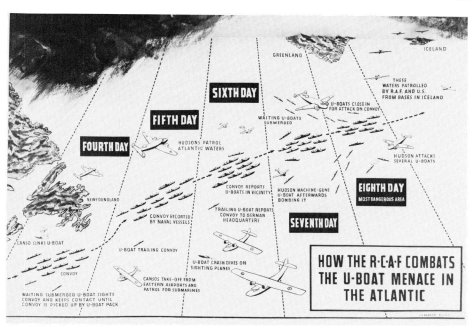

A misleading wartime representation of the RCAF's role in the defence of convoys. It was the Cansos which ranged far to seaward and tackled the U-boat packs, while the medium-range Hudsons operated closer to land. (PL 13802)

434

Depth charges falling away from a 116 (BR) Squadron Catalina during an exercise, April 1943. (RE 64-1044)

Squadron Leader N.E. Small, the officer responsible for 113 (BR) Squadron's remarkable success during the 1942 U-boat campaign in Canadian waters. (PL 12610)

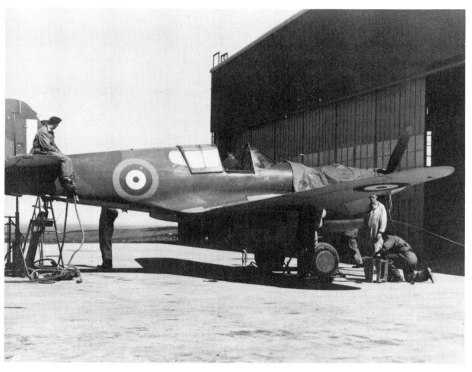

One of 130 (F) Squadron's Kittyhawks at Mont Joli, Que., June 1942. (PMR 75-620)

Loading a 250-lb depth charge into the bomb-bay of a Hudson, which sports the white camouflage scheme adopted by Eastern Air Command for anti-submarine aircraft in 1942. (PMR 77-192)

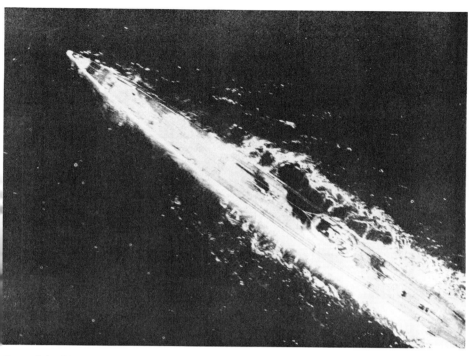

One of the U-boats attacked by aircraft from 113 (BR) Squadron: U-165 as seen from Flight Lieutenant R.S. Keetley's Hudson on 9 September 1942, just south of Anti-costi Island. (PL 12814)

Three pilots of 113 (BR) Squadron who made attacks on U-boats during 1942: left to right, Flight Sergeant A.S. White, Flight Lieutenant R.S. Keetley, and the squadron commanding officer, Squadron Leader N.E. Small. A wartime censor has crudely blotted out the wall map of the Atlantic coast. (PL 12609)

U-517 plunges to safety on 29 September 1942, as Flying Officer M.J. Belanger and crew of 113 (BR) Squadron make an attack run in their Hudson. The Gaspé coast is clearly visible in the background. (PMR 83-26)

Flying Officer M.J. Belanger, second from right, and his crew being debriefed by a squadron intelligence officer. Belanger's three attacks in four days on U-517 in September 1942 were spoiled by the lack of effective shallow-set depth charges. (PL 12628)

A 145 (BR) Squadron Hudson Mk I on 1 October 1942, its new camouflage scheme so recently – and quickly – applied that even the tires are coated. (PL 117987)

Beaching a Canso, in this instance on the west coast in November 1943. (PL 21928)

Operations plot, Eastern Air Command Headquarters, Halifax, 9 January 1943. (PL 14623)

Wing Commander C.L. Annis as commander of 10 (BR) Squadron, with one of the 'North Atlantic Squadron's' new Liberators behind him. Spring 1943. (PL 21786)

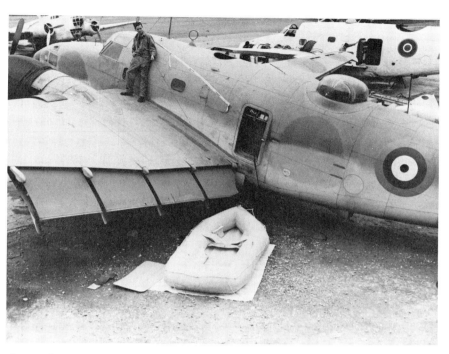

A must for over-ocean operations: the life raft of a Lockheed Ventura, demonstrated at Sydney in August 1943. In the background is a Digby of 161 (BR) Squadron; to the right a Hudson Mk I is being stripped of its useable parts. (RE 69-1562)

Refuelling a 10 (BR) Squadron Liberator at Gander in the summer of 1943. This particular aircraft has had most of its secondary armament removed in order to conserve weight and thereby increase range. (PL 21169)

One that got away. A U-boat of Group Leuthen, its guns still trained on the aircraft, as seen from Flight Lieutenant R.R. Inghams's Liberator on 23 September 1943 during the battle for convoys ONS 18/ON 202. (RE 64-1034)

Liberator P of 10 (BR) Squadron over the bleak Newfoundland landscape in the spring of 1943. The bulge under the aircraft's nose housed its 'Dumbo' radar set. (PL 36938)

Flying Officer W. Howes and Flight Sergeant A.J. Marion of 10 (BR) Squadron at the controls of a Liberator, 1 August 1943. (PL 21783)

A Lockheed Ventura of 145 (BR) Squadron, still in its United States Navy colour scheme, taking off from Torbay, Nfld, September 1943. (PA 141394)

A 10 (BR) Squadron Liberator at Gander, during the winter of 1943–4. (WRF 979)

Night operations at Gander, 11 November 1943. Just visible to the right of centre is a row of 10 (BR) Liberators. (PL 21727)

The two flying boats which saw the RCAF through the war at sea: a Catalina of an unidentified RAF unit alongside the larger RCAF Sunderlands of 422 and 423 Squadrons on the ramp at Castle Archdale, Northern Ireland, July 1942. (PL 41166)

Castle Archdale, Northern Ireland, the picturesque home station of the RCAF's two Sunderland-equipped Coastal Command flying-boat squadrons. (PMR 75-585)

A well-weathered Sunderland of 422 Squadron, RCAF, April 1943. (PL 15752)

U-625 in its last moments, under attack by Sunderland 'U' of 422 Squadron, 10 March 1944. (RE 68-587)

452

A 162 (BR) Squadron Canso 'A' at Reykjavik, Iceland, 25 October 1944. (PL 33838)

The destruction of U-342 by Flying Officer T.C. Cooke of 162 (BR) Squadron on 17 April 1944. The plume of the first depth charge has reached its apex, the dome of the second has just begun to rise, while the entry splash from the third charge in visible in the foreground. (PL 25259)

A somewhat fanciful rendering of Flight Lieutenant D.E. Hornell's VC action by the British war artist, de Grineau. The Canso's engine did not fall from the aircraft until the attacking pass was completed. (PL 47810)

A Canso 'A' of 162 (BR) Squadron undergoes a major overhaul by ground crews at Reykjavik, Iceland, September 1944. (PL 117246)

A 162 (BR) Squadron Canso clears the runway at Camp Maple Leaf, the RCAF establishment at Reykjavik, Iceland, in October 1944. (PL 33839)

An artist's impression of a 407 Squadron Wellington in the snow at Chivenor, England, January 1945. (PL 47368)

Four Liberators of 10 (BR) Squadron were lost when this fire raged through a hangar at Gander in June 1944. (PA 145400)

A 161 (BR) Squadron Canso 'A' arrives at Gaspé on 9 May 1944, in response to the renewed German campaign in Canadian waters. (RE 64-1638)

In late 1944 a second Eastern Air Command squadron, No 11 (BR), was equipped with Liberators, one of which is seen here arriving at Yarmouth on 8 September. (RE 64-1563)

The Lockheed Ventura was a direct descendant of the Hudson, which it closely resembled, although its performance was substantially better. The Ventura could transit to its patrol area at more than 300 miles per hour, and could carry nearly twice the bomb load of a Hudson. (PL 24711)

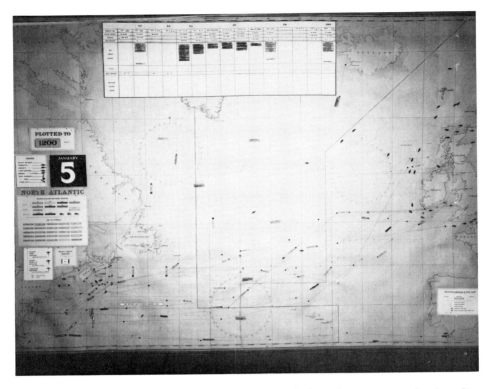

The Royal Canadian Navy's plot of the North Atlantic for 5 January 1945, the day after U-1232 sank two ships off Egg Island. The arcs of 'Otter' areas off Nova Scotia show clearly, as does the concentration of German efforts off the United Kingdom. (RE 84-1205)

A Liberator of 11 (BR) Squadron practising its radar operators on the dummy schnorkel of the British submarine *Unseen* in the Bay of Fundy, March 1945. (PA 141384)

A Canso 'A' at Dartmouth in June 1945. Note the ASV radar antennae on the starboard side and an acoustic homing torpedo, 'Proctor,' under its port wing. (PMR 77-550)

Wing Commander R.R. Ingrams, left, Eastern Air Command staff operations officer, and Wing Commander D.F. Manders and Squadron Leader C.A. Robinson, both radar officers, inspecting U-889's schnorkel shortly after her surrender. The square-patterned rubber coating of the schnorkel head was intended to absorb radar waves, while the basket-shaped search receiver on the top could detect radar transmissions of 8–12 cm, a range that included the 10 cm sets of RCAF Liberators. (PL 36520)

Introduction

The North Atlantic sea lanes were Britain's lifeline throughout the Second World War, important to the Soviet Union's survival and subsequent successes on the Eastern Front and the prosecution of the war in the Mediterranean, and vital to the successful liberation of northwest Europe. Air cover was essential for the protection of Allied shipping against submarine attacks, and the RCAF contributed heavily to that task, since Canada's (and Newfoundland's) geographic proximity to the key areas of the northwest Atlantic placed it in the forefront of the battle.

Both the technology and tactics in the fight against the U-boats changed repeatedly and rapidly. As has already been noted in this book, the number of modern aircraft available to the RCAF's Eastern Air Command became more than adequate in 1944 and 1945. Until then, however, the Canadians fought at a grave disadvantage. Challenged by some of the worst flying weather in the world, plagued by fog and ice, they coaxed their under-powered, poorly equipped machines to exceed all normal limits of performance, knowing too well that the prevailing westerly winds would often make their return flights the most hazardous part of each mission. Dependent upon reluctant British and American sources for most of their aircraft and much of their equipment, the Canadians were frequently many months behind in acquiring 'state-of-the-art' technical devices that might give them a tactical edge over the enemy. Command and control in the relatively undeveloped conditions which prevailed in Newfoundland and along much of the east coast – particularly between Halifax and St John's – presented major difficulties. Inevitably, Canadian results often failed to match those of the RAF's Coastal Command, the model they tried to emulate.

Canadian airmen did enjoy certain advantages through their close ties with Coastal Command, at that time certainly the most innovative and successful maritime air force in the world. But they did not derive as much benefit as they might have done, largely because the senior officers of Eastern Air Command were overly parochial in outlook and too often failed to get their priorities right, while Air Force Headquarters in Ottawa permitted them too much leeway. Eastern Air Command was slow to adopt new refinements of Coastal Command's battle-tested tactics and, as a result, squandered scarce resources on much less effective methods. Poor tactics sometimes resulted in missed sightings, and certainly prevented the destruction of several U-boats, notably during the German offensive of 1942 in the Gulf of St Lawrence.

There was also a problem with inter-service rivalry. The RCAF was most reluctant to accept the fundamental principle of British anti-submarine practice – that air forces should operate under the appropriate naval direction. Even when the Royal Canadian Navy came under the authority of an American admiral, based at Argentia, Nfld, in the fall of 1941, the RCAF fiercely maintained its independent stance. Eventually, early in 1943, the RCAF helped the RCN clinch its bid for control of the northwest Atlantic by agreeing that the Canadian admiral at Halifax should exercise operational direction of Eastern Air Command, but the anti-submarine forces of the two Canadian services were never as closely integrated as their British counterparts.

However much these shortcomings reduced the effectiveness of Eastern Air Command's operation, the RCAF's record in the Battle of the Atlantic was one of substantial achievement. Incapable of doing more than patrol the approaches to Halifax and Sydney with obsolete aircraft carrying totally inadequate armament at the outbreak of war, its aircraft were effectively striking at the enemy in mid-ocean by the latter part of 1943. Eastern Air Command squadrons destroyed six submarines between July 1942 – their first success – and October 1943. Thereafter, U-boats became virtually immune to air attack by running submerged during the hours of daylight. The RCAF did not get the centimetric radar and Leigh Light technology which made night attacks practicable until very late in the war.

Even when no submarines were being sunk, however, the importance of air escorts cannot be too strongly emphasized. While submerged, the U-boats' speeds were so slow that they found it difficult to get into position for attacks. Their response was to introduce 'wolf pack' tactics, in which teams of U-boats endeavoured to intercept convoys under circumstances which enabled them to launch co-ordinated night attacks, and there were times when that approach enjoyed success. Nevertheless, the success of air escorts must be measured as much by the number of merchantmen not sunk as the number of U-boats that were, and the ratio between ships sunk and submarines destroyed eventually proved too hard on the enemy. The presence of even a single aircraft with a convoy was enough to frustrate the intentions of a large wolf pack. Slowed by the necessity to move submerged, the U-boats were often unable to achieve good tactical positions.

Once the wolf packs were defeated, the strategic and tactical difficulties posed by improved U-boats (fitted with *schnorkel* tubes which enabled them to 'breathe' underwater), lurking in waters where SONAR detection was inhibited by temperature and salinity gradients, created challenges remarkably similar to those faced by postwar anti-submarine forces. No one found a solution in the last eighteen months of the Second World War, but efforts to solve the problem were instructive. The evidence about British decryption of U-boat signal traffic shows the important part it played in combatting the threat. This is a subject of absorbing interest, about which new information continues to appear from the study of previously closed wartime files. Enough is now known to confirm that

Canadian airmen used this intelligence to advantage. Because of problems inherent in the combined operations of naval and air forces for which there was no joint training, however, the RCAF was unable to carry many of its efforts through to a satisfactory conclusion.

Eastern Air Command's effort was only part of the RCAF contribution to the Battle of the Atlantic. Under the BCATP agreements, six RCAF squadrons formed in Coastal Command, and sank, or shared in the destruction of, nine U-boats in the eastern Atlantic. Large numbers of Canadian aircrew also served in RAF squadrons of Coastal Command and participated in many of its victories; during the last two years of the war, experienced crews from the Home War Establishment reinforced RCAF and RAF units in Coastal Command. Meanwhile Eastern Air Command's 162 Squadron operated from Iceland under British control and, in a three-month period, sank five U-boats, shared in the destruction of a sixth, and saw the gallantry of one of its pilots rewarded with a posthumous Victoria Cross.

12

The Beginnings of Anti-Submarine Warfare

Prior to the outbreak of war, neither the British nor the Canadians (who relied on British appreciations) anticipated the extent to which submarines would threaten the Atlantic shipping lifeline or the decisive part that aircraft would play in countering the U-boat. These developments should not have come as a surprise, however, given the precedents of the First World War. The U-boat offensive against merchant shipping in 1917 had nearly brought Britain to her knees, but the Royal Navy successfully met that challenge by sailing merchantmen in convoys, escorted in Home Waters by shore-based aircraft. Canada, too, had had first-hand experience of this new form of maritime warfare. When U-boats came to North American waters in 1918 the Canadian government had used United States Navy air units loaned to the short-lived Royal Canadian Naval Air Service to carry out anti-submarine patrols off Halifax and Sydney.[1]

Although during the First World War anti-submarine bombs were not very effective, even unarmed aircraft 'rendered convoys virtually immune from attack'[2] by severely limiting the mobility of U-boats. Capable of a sustained underwater speed of only a few knots, submarines could not follow the slowest convoy, let alone get into position for an attack, unless the convoy blundered on to them; U-boats therefore operated mostly on the surface where their diesel engines could deliver speeds of up to eighteen knots while the batteries for the electrical underwater propulsion motors were recharged.[3] The appearance of an aircraft was a signal to submerge immediately, for although the risk of destruction was slight, aircrew could summon anti-submarine vessels. In diving the U-boat lost a chance to attack the ships it was pursuing, and might also be unable to regain contact with them.

During most of the Second World War, U-boats were able to submerge to much greater depths than their predecessors, but had little more underwater speed or endurance. The lessons of 1917-18 had been forgotten. The development of underwater detection equipment – ASDIC, as SONAR (Sound Navigation and Ranging) was originally known in the Commonwealth navies – seemed to promise mastery of the submarine threat without the need of air support. For its part, the RAF was determined to preserve its independence from the army and the navy by emphasizing the strategic bombing mission. Not until the summer of 1937 did the British government override Air Ministry objections to rule that co-operation with the Royal Navy should be the principal task of Coastal Command, which had been organized in the preceding year. Even then, the Command's main role was to provide reconnaissance for the fleet against enemy surface warships.[4]

In terms of matériel, Coastal Command was ill-prepared for anti-submarine warfare in September 1939. A total of 298 aircraft were on strength, of which 171 were available for operations, a ratio governed by maintenance requirements which would generally hold true for maritime air forces throughout the war. Most, however, like the Avro Ansons that equipped ten of the eleven land-based general-reconnaissance squadrons and were capable of a maximum effective patrol radius of 200 miles, lacked the endurance necessary to give extended coverage to shipping to the west of the British Isles where ocean-going U-boats patrolled. Nor could the Ansons, whose bomb load at extreme range was only 200 lbs, carry the armament necessary to sink a U-boat. Only the American-built Lockheed Hudsons coming into service in a single general-reconnaissance squadron and the Short Sunderlands in three of the six flying-boat squadrons had adequate patrol ranges (approximately 350 and 550 miles, respectively) and weapon capacity (1000 and 2000 lbs). For many months, however, the latter capability was largely of academic interest, for the anti-submarine bombs available proved to be nearly useless. Attacks in September 1939 saw the bombs skip off the water and detonate in mid-air, fatally damaging the aircraft. Catching so elusive and small a target as a U-boat, moreover, required that a carpet, or a 'stick' of several regularly spaced bombs, should be dropped to produce a chain of explosions across the narrow and rapidly manoeuvring hull of the submarine. At the outbreak of war, only the Hudsons had suitable weapons-release mechanisms.[5]

Nevertheless, Coastal Command's aircraft quickly proved themselves to be valuable in the 'scarecrow' role. The unexpected success of aircraft in sighting U-boats in the North Sea, thus delaying their arrival in the operational areas by forcing them to run submerged, brought the Admiralty to direct, on 13 November 1939, that Coastal Command should now give anti-submarine warfare a priority equal to that of action against the enemy surface fleet.[6]

Much of the credit for the effectiveness of air operations was due to the excellent organization for the command and control of naval and maritime air forces that had been established in 1937-8. Coastal Command squadrons served under three (and later four) group headquarters, each of which was responsible for the waters off a section of the British coast. The order of battle was very flexible; squadrons or detachments could be freely moved from group to group according to operational requirements. Group boundaries closely followed those of the Royal Navy's home commands but, more importantly, the group headquarters were located with the corresponding naval headquarters to form three (later four) Area Combined Headquarters [ACHQ], where the staffs of the two services shared a common operations room. Air and naval commanders worked side by side with a common body of information, so that each service was able to respond rapidly to the requests of the other. At a higher level, Coastal Command Headquarters near London maintained close liaison with the

Admiralty, which functioned as an operational headquarters directing the general disposition of Britain's maritime forces. Naval officers assigned to Coastal Command ensured that air plans and operations were firmly rooted in the realities of sea warfare. When in April 1941 the Admiralty assumed operational control over Coastal Command, the agreement merely set down on paper a system already matured in practice: nearly all operations were controlled by the ACHQs where the air group commanders ordered flying programmes in accordance with the broad requirements laid down by the corresponding naval commanders-in-chief.[7]

Effective gathering and dissemination of intelligence was one of the great benefits of the intimate association of Coastal Command with the Admiralty. Much of the power of naval forces, submarines in particular, derives from the mobility that enables them to strike when and where they are not expected. Information concerning the enemy's whereabouts is a vital weapon, but only if it is processed and dispatched to operational ships and aircraft before the deployment of the opposing force changes significantly. During the last years of peace, the Admiralty laid the foundation for an effective intelligence organiza tion by establishing an Operational Intelligence Centre [OIC], including a Submarine Tracking Room, through which data from all sources was chan nelled. Every scrap of information was therefore placed in the hands of the experts best qualified to evaluate it. The centre, moreover, was able to communicate directly with naval operational commands, ships at sea, and Coastal Command, thereby supplying the maritime forces with the best information available as quickly as possible.

Initially, in 1939-40, the OIC could provide relatively little, but the situation improved as the Admiralty expanded its network of stations for intercepting radio traffic, and for locating enemy warships by taking cross-bearings on their transmissions, a technique known as direction finding (DF). The Royal Canadian Navy helped by developing a system of DF stations in Canada and Newfoundland that was controlled by Naval Service Headquarters in Ottawa. Patterns and call signs that could be gleaned from German signals provided useful information, but the value of the intercepted messages increased greatly in May-June 1941 when the Government Code and Cypher School at Bletchley Park in England 'broke' the enemy naval code and supplied decryptions of current messages to the OIC.[8]

Organizational excellence, however, could not make good the material weakness of the British anti-submarine forces when, in the summer and fall of 1940, the U-boat campaign became deadly in its effectiveness. From September 1939 to May 1940 U-boats had sunk 200 merchant ships, but only thirteen had been in convoys, and the Germans had lost twenty-three boats, over half of the operational force that had been available in September 1939. This balance was shattered by the German conquest of France in May-June 1940. Immediately U-boats began to operate from ports on the Bay of Biscay, which offered great advantages in striking at the Atlantic sea lanes upon which Britain was now almost completely dependent. No longer did submarines have to make the 450-mile journey around the north of Scotland, slowed by the sweeps of Coastal

Command aircraft. As a result Admiral Karl Dönitz, the commander of Germany's U-boat arm (*Befehlshaber der Unterseeboote* or BdU), was able once again to maintain fifteen boats on operations in the Atlantic despite the fact that wartime construction would not be able to make good his losses until 1941.[9]

The Admiralty soon rerouted shipping onto a northern course towards Iceland, as far as possible from the Biscay ports. Yet it took time to develop naval and air operating facilities to cover the new route, while the shortage of aircraft and escorts became more serious because of the necessity of withdrawing forces from anti-submarine duty to guard against a German invasion. Only in October was the Royal Navy able to extend the anti-submarine escort of convoys from 17 degrees west to 19 degrees west, that is, from roughly 350 to about 425 miles off the coast of Northern Ireland. At that time Coastal Command's aircraft situation had not greatly improved since the outbreak of war. Four squadrons and parts of two others still flew Avro Ansons, while design and production problems, and the priority given to fighters to meet Hitler's air offensive, was delaying the provision of multi-engine types.[10]

Although air patrols forced back German attempts to close in on the new focal point of transatlantic traffic off the North Channel between Northern Ireland and Scotland, the U-boats scored stunning successes from June to October 1940. During these months, submarines sank 217 ships, while losing only six boats to British action. Most alarmingly, seventy-three of the vessels were sunk in escorted convoys, the majority between August and October when Dönitz originated the first 'wolf pack' attacks. Previously, individual submarines had usually chased unescorted ships and struck in daylight. German submarine headquarters now ordered several boats to form a 'patrol line' across the likely convoy course. The U-boat that made contact with the ships (usually in daylight) would shadow them at a distance, beyond the visual range of the escorts. With the assistance of BdU it would then 'home in' the rest of the pack. Once the submarines had concentrated, they would attack simultaneously at night and on the surface. The British defences were helpless: Coastal Command's aircraft were blind at night, ASDIC could not normally detect surfaced submarines whose low silhouettes made them virtually invisible in the darkness, and the surface speed of the boats enabled them to outrun many of the escorts.[11] But had there been long-range air cover over the convoy by daylight, then the U-boats might well have been forced to submerge, either failing to make contact – in the case of the original 'spotter' – or being unable to concentrate in time.

The disasters in the summer and fall of 1940 brought the British government to give first priority to the expansion and improvement of the anti-submarine forces. On one point the Admiralty was adamant: greatly increased long-range air support was essential. In November 1940 Coastal Command had had fewer than five squadrons of long-range aircraft; by June 1941, despite the deployment of maritime aircraft to other theatres, there were nine long-range squadrons in the United Kingdom groups. The development of air and naval bases in Northern Ireland and Iceland permitted a much more effective deployment of the strengthened forces. In April 1941 the Royal Navy extended anti-submarine escort to 35 degrees west longitude and in that same month Coastal Command began to operate a squadron of Sunderlands and a detachment of Hudsons from Iceland.[12]

Tactics were also developed to counter the wolf packs. The large number of convoys attacked at night after air cover was supplied the preceding day demonstrated that the existing policy of providing as many convoys as possible with at least a few hours' escort by a single aircraft was failing to drive off shadowing submarines. If the shadowers could be suppressed, however, the whole pack could be thrown off the scent. Coastal Command arrived at a satisfactory solution by introducing 'offensive tactics' in April-May 1941. Each day several aircraft flew out to maximum range over the convoy routes. Studies of past operations suggested that aircraft with this roving commission were three times as likely to find U-boats as aircraft closely circling a particular convoy. Nevertheless, constant escort remained essential for convoys that were being shadowed, especially in the hours before sunset when the U-boats were closing to attack positions. Fortunately, pack operations required heavy radio traffic that enabled the Admiralty to judge which convoys were in danger. Coastal Command was therefore able to withdraw support from convoys not at risk, and provide more thorough coverage for those that were.[13]

The strengthening of British anti-submarine forces and their offensive air tactics had telling results when the Germans renewed their assault in the northwestern approaches in 1941. Until late in 1940 the U-boats had concentrated east of 15 degrees, but in the new year did not venture much beyond 17 degrees, about 350 miles from the air bases in Northern Ireland, the range to which Coastal Command aircraft regularly patrolled. The squadrons that began to operate from Iceland in April helped to drive U-boats some 350 miles further out, into mid-ocean; and as the U-boats were forced away from the focal areas of shipping near the British Isles the Admiralty gained sea room in which to route convoys around the packs, whose positions could often be accurately plotted by intelligence. It was the increasing effectiveness of the defences in the northeastern Atlantic that twice brought the U-boats to hunt off Newfoundland in 1941.[14] The British responded to the first of these forays by calling for Canadian support: the creation of the Newfoundland Escort Force at St John's by the Royal Canadian Navy to provide anti-submarine escorts in the western Atlantic from the end of May 1941, and the expansion of Eastern Air Command's operation from Newfoundland.

Great Britain and her allies kept the U-boat menace in check during 1941, destroying thirty-one U-boats as compared to eighteen in the preceding year. Even though the strength of the operational U-boat fleet grew from twenty-two in February to eighty-six in December, the heaviest monthly shipping losses approached but never quite equalled those of the latter part of 1940. Nevertheless, German submarines sank 427 ships in 1941, only a dozen fewer than in 1940, and prospects for the future were uncertain, given the accelerating pace at which the U-boat fleet was expanding. Most particularly, the evasive routing that had saved many north Atlantic convoys from detection would not be so effective as increasing numbers of submarines were deployed on the shipping lanes, or if, as was to happen in 1942, the Germans gained the upper hand in the battle for naval intelligence.[15]

Experience in 1941 bore out the case made by the Admiralty and Coastal Command that airpower was now a vital component of trade defence. In June, for example, only six out of fifty-seven ships sunk by U-boats had been attacked within 350 miles of Coastal Command bases. Sinkings increased dramatically at greater ranges, where the existing aircraft were able to make only occasional patrols, and in mid-ocean, beyond the reach of air cover. Even a few hours' air support at extreme range, however, could help to throw off a wolf pack or blunt the severity of its attack. The requirement, as Coastal Command realized in the spring and summer of 1941, was to station long-range aircraft in Northern Ireland, Iceland, and Newfoundland, so that a convoy being shadowed or attacked could receive support throughout its entire passage. The American-built Consolidated B-24 Liberator bomber answered nicely; when the heavy self-sealing material was removed from the fuel tanks it could patrol to a radius of 700 miles and more. No 120 Squadron, RAF, with nine modified Liberators, began to fly from Nutt's Corner in Northern Ireland in September 1941.[16] Almost immediately, however, it appeared that the Air Ministry was prepared to let the squadron 'die out' by allocating replacement aircraft to transport and bomber operations. As will be seen, Coastal Command and the RCAF had to fight a long and difficult battle for additional Liberators.

Convoy support was only one way of defeating the U-boat. The success of the North Sea patrols of 1939-40 in locating enemy submarines in transit suggested another approach. Renewed coverage of the waters north and northeast of Scotland (the 'Northern Transit Area' as it was now known) during 1941 yielded meagre results because only a small number of newly commissioned boats used the route after completing their work-ups in the Baltic. More encouraging were frequent submarine sightings by air patrols over the Bay of Biscay that began in the summer of 1941, as the U-boats approached or left their operational bases on the French Atlantic coast.[17] In 1942, as the Atlantic packs formed up beyond the reach of all but the longest range shore-based aircraft, the bay offensive became Coastal Command's major commitment, along with a substantial effort in the Northern Transit Area.

However impressive Coastal Command's contribution had been in suppressing U-boats during the first two years of war, aircraft had been singularly unsuccessful in destroying them. To ensure the 'safe and timely arrival of shipping' was the primary mission of Britain's maritime forces, but it was also necessary to sink submarines so that the expanding U-boat fleet would not eventually overwhelm the defences by sheer weight of numbers. Certainly the driving ambition of every member of Coastal Command was to destroy and not merely harrass the enemy.

Most important was the development of an effective aerial anti-submarine weapon. The first big breakthrough was the supply of Mark VII, 450-lb naval depth charges to operational squadrons in July-August 1940. However, the weight and shape of these depth charges restricted their use to flying boats. The answer was the development of the new Mark VIII 250-lb depth charge, which was issued to squadrons in the spring of 1941. Kills still eluded Coastal Command, whose score by September 1941, despite some 245 attacks since the beginning of the war, stood at three sinkings shared with surface escorts, one boat that had surrendered to aircraft, and a handful of boats damaged.[18]

Study of the problem in the summer of 1941 revealed that aircraft would have a good chance of inflicting serious damage only if they attacked the submarine while it was still surfaced, or, at the latest, within fifteen seconds of submergence; thereafter the unpredictable movements of the boat left little possibility of the explosives having any effect. Existing depth settings of 100-150 feet on aerial depth charges were obsolete. The ideal setting for destroying a surfaced submarine was twenty-five feet, but the naval detonators then in use could be set no shallower than fifty feet. One solution was to use stronger explosives. Most of Coastal Command's depth charges had been filled with Amatol, which included a high proportion of TNT and had about the same power. At the end of April 1942 squadrons began to receive charges filled with Torpex, which gave the charges 30-50 per cent more power than those filled with Amatol. By this time, an improved detonator, the Mark XIII, had been developed, but its minimum setting of thirty-four feet was still not shallow enough to deal with a fully surfaced submarine given the Torpex charge's lethal radius of nineteen feet. Additional refinements were required to counteract the tendency of the depth charge to plane across the water after impact and to prevent the formation of air bubbles that delayed the action of water pressure on the pistol. By July 1942 the Mark VIII depth charge had been further modified with the Mark XIII Star pistol, a break-away tail and concave nose spoiler; these improvements were also incorporated in a new Mark XI aerial depth charge that was also in production by July 1942. The weapons detonated at fifteen to twenty-five feet: at last Coastal Command had the means with which to sink submarines.[19]

Lethal attacks with shallow-set depth charges had to be swift, accurate, and heavy as a U-boat could dive within twenty-five seconds. To this end, Coastal Command Headquarters promulgated the first standard anti-submarine attack instructions in July 1941. These matured in a version revised for fully modified Mark VIII and Mark XI depth charges that appeared a year later. Aircraft were now to patrol at greater altitudes – 5000 feet in clear conditions, and close to the cloud ceiling otherwise. High-flying aircraft were more likely to make a sighting at long range, and to catch a boat unawares, for the lookout on the conning tower could comfortably scan the lower sky but had to strain his neck to sweep the upper altitudes. There was no advantage in flying above 5000 feet, as the unwieldy anti-submarine machines could not then descend to the attack level of fifty feet quickly enough to avoid alerting the enemy in ample time for them to dive. On making a sighting, the aircraft was to swoop in as swiftly as possible and drop all of its depth charges (with the exception of the largest types, like the Liberator, that could carry very heavy weapon loads) spaced at intervals of thirty-six feet (this spacing was later increased to one hundred feet when it became clear that most crews could not deliver a tightly packed 'stick' with sufficient accuracy).[20]

The realization that surprise was essential to successful air attacks made the need for effective camouflage obvious. The undersurfaces of many Coastal

Command aircraft had been matt black until trials in the summer of 1941 demonstrated that U-boat lookouts were unlikely to spot white-painted aircraft until they were 20 per cent closer than those with black paint.[21] When, in late 1941 and early 1942, Coastal Command's anti-submarine aircraft were painted white it was, in the words of one author, 'a tacit recognition of the advantages of a colour scheme gulls and other sea birds had adopted some millions of years earlier.'[22]

Camouflage was an ancient technique, but the notion of locating surfaced U-boats by electronic means was thoroughly modern. Shortly before the war, British research into radio direction finding, or 'radar' to use the later name, had produced airborne equipment that could detect ships. ASV (air-to-surface vessel) sets were first fitted in Coastal Command aircraft in early 1940, but their performance was so limited that they were of no use against the small targets presented by submarines. Night attacks by surfaced U-boats in the summer and fall of 1940 brought accelerated work on the ASV Mark II, which, like the original type, worked on a wavelength of 1.5 metres; by the end of June 1941 about half of Coastal Command's 272 principal anti-submarine aircraft carried the improved equipment. Hudsons were fitted with forward-looking aerial arrays only; larger aircraft also had arrays along the fuselage that covered the areas on either side. Great things were expected of the equipment both for night patrols and for surprising U-boats when daytime visibility was limited. Although operational experience showed that ASV Mark II could regularly locate surfaced boats at ranges of six miles and more, results were disappointing; only an insignificant number of contacts were initially made by ASV, and the human eye continued to be Coastal Command's principal search device. Most frequently, ASV registered false contacts on floating debris, whales, and icebergs; the equipment, moreover, was difficult to use and prone to failure without careful maintenance. At night it was impossible to home on a contact, because at ranges of a mile or less waves on the surface of the sea gave strong returns that masked the target.[23]

The solution to the night attack problem was the 'Leigh Light,' a twenty-four-inch aerial searchlight named for its inventor, Squadron Leader H. De V. Leigh, a staff officer at Coastal Command Headquarters. This lightweight equipment could produce a powerful beam for thirty seconds, long enough to illuminate a target during the last mile of approach. Although Leigh first produced the design in late 1940, bureaucratic inertia and competing proposals delayed installation of the device (initially in Vickers Wellington aircraft for operations in the Bay of Biscay) until the spring of 1942. When the Wellingtons began night patrols in early June the results quickly showed that ASV and the Leigh Light were a lethal combination, damaging two submarines and destroying another.[24]

Although a second victory for the Leigh Light would not come for another seven months, this achievement marked the beginning of a period when Coastal Command's improved training, tactics, and equipment came together to make shore-based aircraft the most effective U-boat killers. During the first six months of 1942 Coastal Command aircraft made eighty-two attacks but sank only two boats and shared a third victory with the Royal Navy. In July to December 1942,

299 attacks produced twenty-four kills (five in the Mediterranean, five in the Bay of Biscay, two in the Northern Transit Area, and twelve while supporting convoys in the Atlantic). Including victories by American aircraft and the RCAF's Eastern Air Command, shore-based aircraft sank thirty-four German and Italian submarines in the last half of 1942 as against thirty-one destroyed by ships.[25]

Coastal Command had revolutionized anti-submarine warfare from the spring of 1941 to the summer of 1942. It was during those months, and in no small part for that reason, that the U-boats came to Canadian waters. From a predictable routine of flying close escort for convoys, and making patrols in response to almost invariably erroneous reports of enemy activity, Eastern Air Command had suddenly to adapt to a new form of warfare, whose weapons and tactics changed rapidly, always in the direction of more sophisticated technology and more rigorous demands on groundcrew and aircrew alike. At the same time the command had to endure severe growing pains, struggling with fundamental problems of organization, matériel, and personnel (including the complex questions of co-ordination posed by the presence of American air forces in Newfoundland). The reader will recall from Chapter 10 that difficulties of rugged terrain and inhospitable weather presented the air force with major problems; Eastern Air Command had had to build from virtually nothing and with meagre resources in the shadow of the Canadian overseas war effort.

Eastern Air Command had received the first firm intelligence of a U-boat within extreme aircraft range of Newfoundland on 20 May 1941. The need to strengthen air operations from the island was obvious, but so too were the difficulties. The only operational maritime patrol aircraft in Newfoundland were fifteen Douglas Digbys of 10 (Bomber-Reconnaissance) Squadron based at Gander, with a maximum effective range of about 350 miles. In bad weather – something that was impossible to predict accurately more than twelve hours in advance – there was no alternate landing field. Canadian attempts to acquire a more suitable aircraft – the Consolidated PBY/Catalina flying boat which had an effective range of about 600 miles and no dependency on airfields – had failed because all evidence at the time pointed to a continued concentration of U-boats in the eastern Atlantic. As seen in Chapter 10, however, the German thrust towards Newfoundland persuaded the British to divert nine Catalinas to Eastern Air Command in late May. By early July personnel had been transferred from 5 (BR) Squadron to man the new aircraft and the first long-range RCAF squadron -116 (BR) – had come into existence at Dartmouth, NS.[26]

On 7 July Squadron Leader F.S. Carpenter flew the first Catalina into Botwood, near Gander, and three others soon followed. This four-boat detachment of 116 Squadron provided the only long-range capability over the northwest Atlantic and even this would have to be withdrawn with the onset of winter when ice-prone Botwood could no longer be used by flying boats. Eighteen US Navy PBYs (Catalinas) based at Argentia and the six Digbys of the US Army Air Forces' 21st Squadron at Gander continued to patrol the Atlantic but could not be counted upon to defend trade or attack German forces. The Americans, after all, were not at war. Their operations were not co-ordinated with those of the RCAF and, lacking common codes and radio frequencies, the Americans and Canadians could not even talk to one another.[27]

The more numerous RCAF squadrons on the mainland were, of course, well beyond the range of U-boat operations in 1941, and by the time the first Catalinas arrived at Botwood this was also true of Newfoundland-based squadrons. The U-boat foray into the northwest Atlantic had been in search of soft spots in the shipping defences, but it had coincided with the first British intelligence penetration of the German naval Enigma code. The result was the warning of 20 May that U-boats were within range of Newfoundland-based aircraft and information accurate enough to route all convoys clear of danger. By the end of June Dönitz had pulled back all his boats in frustration. But the cipher breakthrough had by then set in motion a sequence of events which thrust upon the Canadians unexpectedly heavy responsibilities.[28]

The allocation of Canadian air and naval forces to ocean escort and long-range patrols did not come within the terms of either ABC-1 (the result of British-American staff talks between January and March 1941) or ABC-22, the joint Canadian-American plan for hemispheric defence. Canada's responsibilities in both cases had been for the local defence of Canadian territory and territorial waters. The creation of the RCN's Newfoundland Escort Force in May was a stopgap measure to provide ocean escort in the western Atlantic until the US Navy could bring its great strength to bear in the region. Similarly, it is doubtful whether the RAF would have given up even nine flying boats without proof of U-boats in the western Atlantic, and it is certain that once American long-range aircraft and ocean escorts arrived in Newfoundland both the British and American governments expected Canada to turn over responsibility for trade protection to US forces, resuming the limited function of local defence. Canadians had very different ideas.[29]

The RCAF and RCN were already seeking to develop a trade defence system along the lines of Coastal Command and the Royal Navy. The RCAF sent observers to Coastal Command, first among whom was Air Commodore N.R. Anderson, air officer commanding Eastern Air Command, a future air member for air staff and deputy chief of the air staff. On 5 June he signalled home:

Understand Naval Sub-Command will be established St. John's, Newfoundland, control Convoy Ocean Escort ships based same point. As E.A.C. aircraft based Newfoundland will be co-operating, recommend Group HQ be established St. John's at once, forming combined HQ with Navy ... Essential Group HQ St. John's and Operational bases, Newfoundland, be linked HQ E.A.C., HALIFAX, by teletype. Operational and Intelligence reports must pass quickly between Coastal Command RAF and Eastern Air Command, Air Ministry Newfoundland-Birdlip W/T link available this purpose. Also essential aircraft operational frequencies used by both Air Commands Atlantic operations should now be standardized to facilitate co-operation and ensure enemy sighting reports sent by aircraft either Command be received immediately by escort ships, Naval forces and Shore Bases. Recommend frequencies used by Coastal Command be adopted at once by E.A.C. if equipment permits. Coastal Command and Admiralty concur with communication recommendations. Advise if you concur with proposals and give strength ground to air W/T Stations E.A.C.[30]

Unfortunately, direct radio links with Coastal Command and effective long-range ground-to-air communications were not practicable with the equipment available. And Anderson's later proposal to put four Catalina squadrons in Newfoundland during the summer and a squadron of Liberators all year long was also impossible. The RAF was after every long-range aircraft that could be produced. The RCAF, moreover, could only have found the necessary aircrew and groundcrew by robbing the BCATP; article 14 of the agreement committed all but 136 pilots, thirty-four air observers, and fifty-eight wireless operators (air gunner) every year to RAF or RCAF squadrons overseas. Anderson would have welcomed a change in this policy in order to concentrate on winning the battle against the U-boats in the north Atlantic. 'It is more important *now*,' he wrote, 'that personnel be posted to fill Eastern Air Command G.R. [General Reconnaissance] Squadrons than to fill Bomber and Fighter Squadrons of the R.A.F.'[31]

On 9 July a delegation from the RCAF met the new air officer commanding-in-chief Coastal Command, Air Chief Marshal Sir Philip Joubert de la Ferté, and some of his staff in London to discuss co-operation between the two commands. The need for a Liberator squadron based on Newfoundland in order to provide year-round long-range coverage was also clear to all. The long-range Liberator of that time had about the same range as a Catalina, but its cruising speed of 200 knots was twice that of the flying boat and it could carry eight depth charges to maximum range instead of the two carried by Catalinas. The faster and more heavily armed Liberator, with an endurance of sixteen and one-half hours, was therefore much preferred to the lumbering Catalina which could, on occasion, keep its crew aloft for up to twenty-eight hours. Joubert actually offered to transfer his only Liberator squadron to Newfoundland after Iceland operations ceased for the winter, but the Canadians had to decline the offer. There were no hangars at Gander capable of handling the large aircraft and, because work on other air commitments, such as transatlantic ferry operations, had priority, none could be built in 1941.[32]

The meeting of 9 July was also attended by the minister of national defence for air, C.G. Power, the chief of the air staff, Air Marshal L.S. Breadner, and Air Commodores Anderson, G.O. Johnson (deputy chief of the air staff, on temporary attachment to the Air Ministry), and L.F. Stevenson (air officer commanding RCAF in Great Britain). Anderson and Johnson were the present and future air officers commanding Eastern Air Command; Stevenson was about to become the air officer commanding Western Air Command. All the most vitally concerned authorities were aware from the start, then, of the conflict in priorities that would plague Eastern and Western Air commands for the next two years. The operational squadrons of the Home War Establishment had low priority in all essential areas – personnel, equipment, facilities, and even labour. Anderson, possibly as an alternative to having a Coastal Command squadron in Newfoundland, tried to establish an exchange of aircrew that would at least have allowed the RCAF to benefit from RAF experience. The shortage of qualified Canadian aircrew scotched this idea very quickly, and his proposal that five squadrons exchange crews for one year gave way to Power's of exchanging one Catalina crew for a much shorter term. That suggestion went nowhere either. In

November there was some talk of obtaining 'war-weary' crews from the RAF, but this suggestion was never pursued seriously. The northwest Atlantic was no place for a rest.[33]

A start was made, however, in establishing an intelligence organization like the one in the United Kingdom. The Admiralty's 'Y' service – radio intelligence – provided accurate and timely U-boat location reports, which allowed the RAF to organize air searches around known positions of enemy submarines. This was exactly what was needed by a force with very few aircraft and, in June, after visiting Coastal Command, Group Captain F.V. Heakes went to Naval Service Headquarters to see what the RCN's newly formed OIC could do for Eastern Air Command. After several meetings between naval and air force officers in Ottawa the navy agreed to transmit results from the analyses of all direction-finding bearings obtained in Ottawa to operational headquarters on the east coast. 'These analyses,' observed the naval memorandum, 'are based on somewhat less information than is available to the Admiralty and the results obtained by Ottawa are subject, therefore, to correction by the Admiralty.'[34]

Without a single controlling authority a cumbersome system of communication existed between the air and naval services involved in the same maritime battle. Fortunately, airmen and naval officers at lower levels were able to discuss some of their mutual problems and, as a consequence, Heakes persuaded Commander J.M. de Marbois, in charge of the OIC, to set up a direct telephone line to the air station at Dartmouth for passing direction-finding bearings as soon as they were received. This approach certainly bore fruit the following year, when U-boats started penetrating Canadian territorial waters, and it may have been through this channel that information reached 10 (BR) Squadron in mid-June about a U-boat off the coast of Newfoundland. That alert occurred just as U-111 was completing a reconnaissance of the Strait of Belle Isle and proceeding south to join Dönitz's western patrol line a few days before its dispersal. In the following month, however, intelligence from Naval Service Headquarters was useless. The delays were interminable until, in late August, the Admiralty's daily promulgation of submarine positions started arriving regularly and in good time.[35]

The United States Navy's assumption of strategic control over the forces operating in the western half of the north Atlantic in September 1941 raised more fundamental questions about the nature of the Canadian trade-defence effort. Although the RCN's escorts now operated under the general direction of Rear Admiral A. LeRoy Bristol, USN, at Argentia, Nfld, the RCAF would surrender neither its independence nor its commitment to long-range maritime reconnaissance. As seen in Chapter 10, representatives of the RCAF made an arrangement with Admiral Bristol in October whereby USN aircraft operating from Newfoundland flew escort missions for convoys south and east of Cape Race, while 1 Group provided similar coverage to the north of this area. Significantly, representatives of the United States Army Air Forces in Newfoundland did not participate in these discussions.[36]

The infrequent appearance of submarines within range of aircraft on the east coast until late 1941 was a mixed blessing. Without sure evidence of the enemy's presence it was difficult to motivate the crews. The increased number of convoys sailing in late 1941 made little difference to the airman's dreary routine. Aircrew exposed themselves day after day to hardship and danger with no tangible results. It was a triumph of sorts simply to return safely to base. And, as if natural conditions were not enough, they worked alongside a service which had very little understanding of air operations. After the first Newfoundland Escort Force operation in June 1941, the RCN complained that because an air escort was not provided it took more than twenty-four hours for convoys HX 132 and SC 34 to rendezvous. It was true that in the clear visibility an aircraft would have been useful to the convoy commodores and their escorts, but the available Digbys were, quite correctly, committed to the search for U-111, the only submarine in the vicinity. Although the RCAF soon posted a liaison officer to the staff of Commodore L.W. Murray, who commanded the Newfoundland Escort Force, effective co-operation would not be possible until plans for improvement of communications between St John's and Gander and for the establishment of a combined naval and air headquarters could be carried out.[37] Even then, the complaint of seamen that they could see no escorting aircraft would be heard time and again.

With only a small number of aircraft available and the great distances involved, long-range air operations from Newfoundland were extremely limited in 1941. Although the Catalinas now at Botwood had an endurance of twenty-four hours at ninety-five knots, giving a total range of 2400 miles and a patrol radius of 800 miles, operational conditions greatly reduced these figures. In theory, it took eight and one-half hours for a Catalina to reach a convoy 800 miles to seaward, and once there it could only devote four hours to patrolling. The remaining eleven and one-half hours were needed to combat the average twenty-two knot westerly winds prevalent on the homeward leg, during which ground speed was reduced to seventy knots. It was estimated that if headwinds in excess of twenty-two knots were encountered following a four-hour patrol at 800 miles, the aircraft would not get home at all. In any event, four hours of patrolling in a twenty-four hour flight was considered a misapplication of effort. Eight hours around a convoy, in practice, was the break-even point for a full day's flying, and that period limited ranges to 600 miles. However, it was necessary to retain at least 20 per cent of an aircraft's endurance against the need to land at an alternate base, the nearest of which was frequently North Sydney, NS. This reservation in turn cut effective ranges to 450–500 miles at best. No 1 Group was occasionally able to mount operations to extreme range, but only large, specially modified, four-engine aircraft, such as later versions of the Liberator, could effectively patrol at ranges of 700–900 miles and thereby close the mid-ocean gap in air coverage from Newfoundland and Coastal Command's base in Iceland.[38]

The limits of aircraft operating from both sides of the Atlantic were graphically illustrated in early September 1941, when Dönitz pushed his U-boat packs to the south of Greenland in hopes of better hunting. Between 9 and 13 September, Group *Markgraf* finally made contact with SC 42. It was the only convoy the Admiralty had not been able to reroute successfully around the danger areas, and it had been deprived of air cover from Newfoundland by several days of extremely heavy gales and low visibility. The convoy, escorted by an RCN group of the Newfoundland Escort Force, lost fifteen ships before air and surface reinforcements arrived from Iceland to end the struggle.[39]

The battle for SC 42 took place well beyond the maximum range of the Botwood-based Catalinas, and the historian will search in vain among squadron records for mention of the desperate fight raging off Greenland. The Catalinas were simply not able to respond to such distant operations. Nor was 116 Squadron up to the task in other respects. By the end of August the inability to make up full aircraft crews on a permanent basis, together with the absence of specialist officers, persuaded the officer commanding to shelve all thought of training, a blow to morale and efficiency. In hindsight, one may wonder if it would not have been possible for a hard-driving officer commanding to do something to improve the efficiency of his squadron or formation. Yet, in September the visit of the Duke of Kent to the Newfoundland bases was the most noteworthy event. And even two months later, when a large number of U-boats were within striking distance of aircraft at Botwood and Gander, comments in 116 (BR)'s diary on operations remained cryptic, while an elaborate description of the marriage of one of the squadron's aircrew to a nursing sister is included. The records of Newfoundland's other BR squadron, No 10, were not much better. Apparently commanders were content for the moment with simply having established air bases in the inhospitable natural surroundings. Effective operations demanded much more.[40]

In the meantime Dönitz, having learned from U-111 that convoy traffic passed through the Strait of Belle Isle, initiated an operation in that region. In late October the OIC in Ottawa began to receive information from the Admiralty on the westward movement of several U-boats, and it was confirmed on the 24th that four were just to the east of the strait. The Digbys of 10 (BR) Squadron were alerted and the next day all available aircraft were in the air, two to provide escort for a westbound convoy, ON 26, steaming into the danger area, and the rest in search patrols. Seven of 10 (BR)'s aircraft and the only two Catalinas available from 116 (BR)'s four-plane detachment at Botwood spent more than eighty hours aloft that day, and the result was the first sighting and attack made by an Eastern Air Command aircraft. The episode unfolded so as to illustrate most vividly the handicaps then afflicting anti-submarine squadrons.[41]

Squadron Leader C.L. Annis, the command armament officer, was visiting Gander when the alert came in and, since 10 (BR) had more serviceable aircraft than it had qualified pilots, took a Digby up on patrol himself. Annis was familiar with the aircraft type and had about 300 hours flying over the ocean, but he had to establish rapport with the crew at very short notice. His second pilot doubled as navigator, and three wireless operator/air gunners manned the rear and nose turrets as well as the wireless operator's seat. Annis's own account describes the flight in detail:

I took off ... at approximately 0750 hours ... As I crossed the coast, outbound, the air gunners proceeded to their look-out posts in the nose and rear turrets ... I instructed (the nose gunner) to 'arm' the bombs – an act which can be carried out only at the bomb aimer's controls in this compartment. In a few moments he returned and stated that they were armed.

The patrol ordered was a parallel track search consisting of an outward leg of some 40 miles from the Newfoundland coast on a north east heading, then a beat of roughly 270 miles almost due north, a westward flight of 18 miles and the return leg almost due south to base. The wind at patrol height, which was maintained at 900-1000 feet, was established as averaging approximately 45 knots from a little to the west of south. The sea was the roughest I have ever seen it ... I was actually quite surprised to find that a submarine could surface under such sea conditions ...

At approximately 1450 hours ... I sighted a submarine. Until that time all search for shipping of any description had been negative. I had noticed the air gunners exchanging lookout posts at approximately two-hour intervals but beyond being satisfied that they were carrying out their post-manning and search duties, I paid no particular attention to them. The air was unusually bumpy, and I was fully occupied in holding a steady course against an oscillating compass, looking after the engines, and scanning the sea. To add to the difficulties salt spray had been depositing on the wind screen from time to time throughout the flight and it now formed a not inconsiderable haze obstructing vision.

As I watched a wave drew away from the submarine towards me leaving its conning tower and upper hull completely exposed and dispelling any doubt as to its character ...

I at once threw out the auto pilot control and started a slight turn to the right in order to keep it in sight. I turned to Redman who was in the navigator's seat behind me, pointed and said: 'Thats a submarine.' He jumped up, looked over my shoulder and said: 'It sure is.' He practically flew into the second pilot's seat as I told him to put the engines into 'manual rich.' At the same time I reached down and jerked open the bomb doors with the pilot's emergency release handle. As Redman adjusted the mixture I increased the boost and r.p.m. on the engines. The engines gave a slight cough and I looked to see that Redman in his excitement hadn't put the mixture into 'idle cut-off' position. When I looked up again I couldn't see the submarine. I yelled 'where is it?' and he pointed ... Only its conning tower was visible and it disappeared into a wave as I watched. The vortex of its dive was plainly visible and the shadowy darkness of its hull showed for a few seconds. As the vortex and bubbles built up towards the east I was able to decide what had been troubling me all along – the direction it was moving and therefore at which point to aim in the attack.

By this time, which I should judge to be 20-30 seconds after first sighting, we were in a 30-40 degree dive as I turned to the left ... to make a quartering astern attack. Remembering to aim short and ahead and estimating a six-second interval between release and detonation, I released the bombs in salvo, by means of the pilot's emergency release, when at a little less than 300 feet indicated on the altimeter, and in an angle of dive of approximately 20 degrees ... The strong wind ... had caused me to undershoot somewhat.[42]

This attack failed because an inexperienced crew member had switched the bomb-arming release lever back to the 'safe' position at some point during the outward flight. It was the kind of mistake that crew training in operational training units [OTUS] was designed to avert, but Eastern Air Command had no

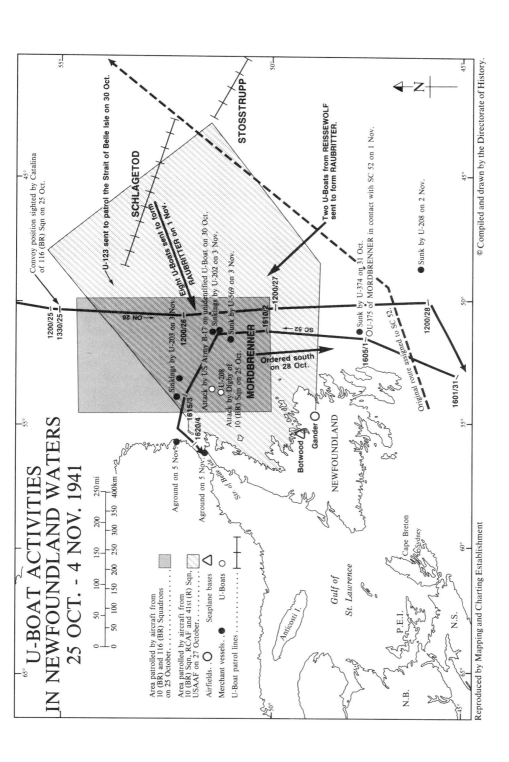

U-BOAT ACTIVITIES
IN NEWFOUNDLAND WATERS
25 OCT. - 4 NOV. 1941

Area patrolled by aircraft from
10 (BR) and 116 (BR) Squadrons
on 25 October.

Area patrolled by aircraft from
10 (BR) Sqn, RCAF and 41st (R) Sqn,
USAAF on 27 October.

Airfields. . . . . ◯

Seaplane bases . . . . △

Merchant vessels. . . . . ●

U-Boat patrol lines . . . .

U-Boats . . . . ◯

0 50 100 150 200 250mi
0 50 100 150 200 250 300 350 400km

Convoy position sighted by Catalina
of 116 (BR) Sqn on 25 Oct.

U-123 sent to patrol the Strait of Belle Isle on 30 Oct.

SCHLAGETOD

STOSSTRUPP

Eight U-Boats sent to form
RAUBRITTER on 1 Nov.

Two U-Boats from REISSEWOLF
sent to form RAUBRITTER.

OU-375 of MORDBRENNER in contact with SC 52 on 1 Nov.

Sunk by U-208 on 2 Nov.

1200/25
1330/25

1200/26

ON 26

Attack by US Army B-17 on unidentified U-Boat on 30 Oct.

Sinkings by U-203 on 3 Nov.

Sinkings by U-202 on 3 Nov.

Sunk by U-569 on 3 Nov.

1610/2

1200/27

MORDBRENNER

Ordered south
on 28 Oct.

SC 52

Sunk by U-374 on 31 Oct.

1605/1

Original route assigned to SC 52.

1200/28

1601/31

OU-208

Attack by Digby of
10 (BR) Sqn on 25 Oct.

1615/3

1620/4

Aground on 5 Nov.

Aground on 5 Nov.

St. of Belle Isle

Botwood △
Gander ◯

NEWFOUNDLAND

Gulf of
St. Lawrence

Anticosti I.

P.E.I.

Cape Breton

Sydney

N.B.

N.S.

65° 55° 45°

50° 55° 60° 65°

43° 45° 50° 55°

N

Reproduced by Mapping and Charting Establishment

© Compiled and drawn by the Directorate of History.

resources for OTUs. Squadron commanders were merely urged to advance aircrew effectiveness by any means available. It was clear that such instructions were not easy to implement even if the will to do so existed. The BCATP and its quota for overseas squadrons was leaving the Home War Establishment desperately short of aircrew.[43]

Attempts by 1 Group to locate and attack U-boats operating off Newfoundland were sharply curtailed after 26 October by deteriorating weather. In the meantime, yet more U-boats moved into the area until there were eighteen submarines within striking distance of Eastern Air Command aircraft. While Admiral Dönitz received permission to attack south of the Grand Banks, an area previously forbidden to his U-boats because of its proximity to US territorial waters, 1 Group waited for the weather to clear. Before it did U-374 intercepted the eastbound convoy SC 52 just east of St John's, and eleven nearby U-boats were brought together as Group *Raubritter* to attack it. On 3 November orders went out to have every available aircraft flying in support of SC 52, but it was not until two days later that the weather improved enough to make flying possible. By then the battle of SC 52 had been decided. After the loss of four ships the convoy was ordered to return to Canada through the Strait of Belle Isle, where two further ships were lost through grounding in fog.[44]

There was little Canadian airmen could do but pray for better weather, and there was precious little of that in Newfoundland during the first weeks of November. No 116 (BR)'s detachment at Botwood, crippled by the unserviceability of three of its four aircraft, received two reinforcements from Dartmouth but remained hamstrung by poor weather conditions. Finally, on the 19th, the day one of the serviceable aircraft was driven ashore and damaged in a blizzard, the detachment received orders to withdraw to Nova Scotia for the winter. Conditions in 10 (BR) were better, but not much better. By late in the month six of its fifteen Digbys were under repair, while the squadron had only seven crews for the remaining nine aircraft. Not surprisingly, No 1 Group was unprepared when it heard, on 24 November, that U-boats were once again bound for Newfoundland. Three Digbys were held in readiness armed with depth charges, while the remaining RCAF and US Navy aircraft flew patrols to seaward. Four Hudsons from 11 Squadron were hurriedly dispatched to the newly completed aerodrome at Torbay to provide harbour patrols for St John's and Wabana, anchorages which the U-boats were expected to attack. By the time the RCAF had made its dispositions and plans to meet the latest threat it had already passed. On 22 November Dönitz had been forced to satisfy Hitler's demand for U-boats in the Mediterranean in response to the British offensive in North Africa. Much to the German admiral's disgust every U-boat in the Atlantic headed for Gibraltar.[45]

As 1941 drew to a relatively quiet close the state of readiness in Newfoundland still left much to be desired, though the RCAF had far better anti-submarine facilities than could have been imagined a year before. The order of battle included 10 (BR) Squadron with its fifteen Digbys, and a USAAF squadron with six B-17s at Gander. On 14 October, as already noted, the airfield at Torbay, near St John's, had been opened with two runways available, and four Hudsons from

11 (BR) Squadron flew over from Dartmouth, NS, in November. The US Navy also had Catalina detachments of three navy and one marine squadrons at Argentia. Air control remained poor, however. The absence of a land line between 1 Group Headquarters at St John's and the station at Gander forced air controllers to improvise when atmospheric conditions prevented radio communication, as they often did, and aircraft sometimes had to curtail patrols because of a complete radio blackout caused by the *aurora borealis*. Furthermore, the teletype circuits to Halifax were severely overburdened with traffic.[46]

During the fall of 1941, 5 and 116 Squadrons had begun to receive the first PBY5 (Catalina) flying boats from Canadian orders in the United States. In December these aircraft received the RCAF designation 'Canso.' During that same month the first Canso 'A' (amphibians) arrived at 5 Squadron and, by the end of February 1942, thirteen Canso 'A's were on strength. In the meantime, the Canso flying boats had been concentrated in 116 Squadron, which by the end of February had seven of these machines and five of the Catalina boats that had been borrowed from the RAF the previous spring.[47]

The late fall also brought a clarification of Canadian and American operational responsibilities in the northwest Atlantic. In November, largely as a result of urgent questions from the US Navy Department through the Canadian air attaché in Washington, Air Vice-Marshal Anderson and Admiral Bristol promulgated their agreement of 17 October in formal terms. The Canadians were to cover two ocean areas, one north of a line drawn out from Newfoundland along the 48th parallel of latitude, and the other west of a line drawn out from Newfoundland along the 55th meridian of longtitude in to the Canadian coastline. In effect this meant that Eastern Air Command aircraft escorted convoys to the Western Ocean Meeting Point [WESTOMP] about 49 degrees west, while 1 Group Hudsons and Digbys from Gander and Torbay accompanied them for 200 and 400 miles, respectively, north of 48 degrees north. For anti-submarine sweeps and general reconnaissance patrols in the northern sector these ranges for the Newfoundland aircraft were extended further, the Hudsons going to 300 miles and the Digbys up to 600 miles. The latter stretched the Digby to the limit and would not in fact produce satisfactory results.[48]

While Eastern Air Command strove to match the effective ranges of air cover provided in the eastern Atlantic by Coastal Command, the RCAF also followed developments in British aircraft armament. In mid 1941 AFHQ arranged for Canadian production of the new Mark VIII 250-lb Amatol-filled aerial depth charge, and ordered fittings from the United Kingdom to convert naval 450-lb Mark VII depth charges for use in aircraft. By the end of the year the weapons had replaced the undependable anti-submarine bomb in most squadrons.[49]

Thanks to Air Vice-Marshal Anderson's visit to Coastal Command in the summer the sharing of knowledge on technical developments – as evidenced by Canadian production and adoption of the British aerial depth charge – was part of a growing understanding between the two commands. 'Long experience, training and scientific investigation of Coastal Command in maritime air operations,' Anderson wrote, 'has evolved a sound operational policy and procedure which is being continuously advanced to keep ahead of enemy methods. Any information for guidance which Coastal Command can give Eastern Air Command on advances in operational methods, equipment or procedure will be treated with the degree of secrecy desired and used in the manner most likely to ensure pursuit of a common operational doctrine in the Battle of the Atlantic.'[50]

Air Chief Marshal Joubert de la Ferté had responded personally to the Canadian overture in July with the first of a series of monthly letters between himself and Anderson on matters of mutual interest. But time for such discussion was fast running out. The brief calm following the withdrawal of U-boats in November was shattered by the news of Pearl Harbor on 7 December. This great turning point meant that not only squadrons based on Newfoundland, but also those in Nova Scotia would now be in the front line of anti-submarine warfare. The next move in Dönitz's strategy, Operation *Paukenschlag*, would suddenly and graphically illustrate all the quantitative and qualitative weaknesses of Eastern Air Command. As an immediate reinforcement for the west, 8 (BR) Squadron was moved hurriedly to Sea Island, Vancouver, BC, and its place taken at Sydney, NS, by another Bolingbroke squadron, 119 (BR), from Yarmouth, NS.[51] By early January 1942 the command still had only five principal anti-submarine squadrons deployed for the anticipated upsurge in German U-boat activity.

The timing of Japan's entry into the war came as a surprise to the Germans. Five weeks passed before they were able to send out five large Type IXB submarines, U-66, U-109, U-123, U-125, and U-130, to execute *Paukenschlag*. It was to be a 'tremendous and sudden blow' against merchantmen of over 10,000 tons between the St Lawrence and New York, planned to start, simultaneously, on 13 January. At the same time, seven Type VIIC U-boats, working independently of the main operation, formed Group *Ziethen* and spread themselves out in contiguous attack zones reaching out 250 miles from the south coast of Newfoundland.[52]

On 2 January the British Admiralty issued its first warnings of the offensive, based on Enigma decrypts. Canadian squadrons at Dartmouth, Sydney, Gander, and Torbay, US naval aircraft at Argentia, and the USAAF squadron at Gander accordingly increased their patrol activity. On 9 January HX 169, the convoy nearest to the approaching U-boats, was diverted northeastward towards Newfoundland 'to fight its way,' with a reinforced escort group of nine warships, through the danger area off Cape Race, and thus take advantage of the 'golden opportunity for destroying U-boats in which ... the strength of the air escort will play a large part.'[53] Mercifully for the convoy, the U-boats did not make contact.

Korvettenkapitän R. Hardegen of U-123 struck the opening beat of *Paukenschlag* on the night of 11/12 January. He torpedoed and sank the British ship *Cyclops* 180 miles south of Nova Scotia, the first merchant ship to be sunk in North American waters south of Newfoundland. Some hours later, on a clear, cold morning, Sergeant R.L. Parker of 119 (BR) Squadron took off from Sydney in a Bolingbroke. About forty miles north, while on a routine harbour entrance patrol, the aircraft's crew spotted U-130 'three miles away and awash, conning tower plainly visible.'[54] In the ensuing attack two 250-lb bombs were released one hundred feet ahead of the diving submarine to produce satisfying explosions. But, as Eastern Air Command correctly surmised, the effort was a 'complete miss,' because the bombs would have fallen short and detonated above the target.[55] Five Bolingbrokes mounted an extensive search of the area, twice came within visibility distance of their quarry, but made no detections. The U-boat slipped away. In the next twenty-four hours it sent to the bottom two independently routed ships, *Frisco* and *Friar Rock*. The latter, a Panamanian-registered vessel delayed at Sydney, had been trying to overtake the last convoy leaving that harbour until spring.[56]

Although U-boats near the mainland of Canada and the United States reported 'Enemy air patrols heavy but not dangerous because of inexperience,' they chose not to tangle with escorted shipping: of the twenty-one merchantmen destroyed north of latitude 40 degrees north and west of longitude 40 degrees west in January 1942, twenty were sunk while sailing independently or after having lost their convoy, and only one was sent to the bottom while under naval escort.[57]

On 19 January a Digby of 10 (BR) Squadron was on a coastal patrol from Gander when the conning tower and upper deck of a fully surfaced submarine lying in the trough of the waves appeared through the snow. The boat was U-86, fresh from inflicting torpedo damage on *Toorak* from convoy ON 52 and sinking *Dimitrios G. Thermiotis*, a straggler from SC 63. Flight Lieutenant J.M. Young brought his aircraft down to an approach course at right angles to that of the target, released the right bank of three 250-lb Amatol charges set to detonate at fifty feet, wheeled round, and dropped the left stick set to one hundred feet at forty-five degrees to the submerging U-boat's presumed course. It was a good attack with disappointing results, splitting welded seams but not sinking the U-boat.[58]

Three days later, when returning to base from a patrol in support of SC 65, another Digby of 10 Squadron encountered U-84. The submarine was moving fast on the surface three miles ahead on the port bow. Flight Lieutenant E.M. Williams started his run in from 1100 feet with his charges set to explode at a depth of fifty feet, but it turned out to be a botched effort. As the official report charitably put it: 'Only one of 3 D.C.'s released due to over keenness of first gunner,' who, in the excitement of the moment, forgot that all the depth charges had to be released manually because a twelve-volt distributor had not been available for the aircraft back at Gander. Williams, who won the Air Force Cross later that year for the quality and dedication of his work, made two more attacks that were obviously out of range. German records confirm a 'near miss.'[59]

Aircraft more often found survivors of sinkings, and led rescue ships to the position. The airman's view of this role is typified by an incident on 24 January. The Catalinas of 116 Squadron, after hours of flying, located all that remained of *Empire Wildbeeste*, a 6000-ton steamer torpedoed by U-106 360 miles southeast of Halifax:

The two boats were connected by a line and contained approximately 8 survivors in one and 12 in the other. They were signalled first by Aldis lamp and ... a message was dropped in a water tight container ... They were informed a rescue vessel was on its way.

Later on the same day ... a lifeboat with four or five survivors, with sail up, was sighted ... Messages, water, cigarettes, and flares were dropped in a rubber dinghy.[60]

In February Dönitz allowed his most northerly boats to move gradually southward from Cape Race, escaping the bad weather and intense cold that was forcing them to dive every two or three hours or risk the freeze-up of their diesel exhaust valves.[61] Here again, the majority of vessels they intercepted were alone, without sea or air escort, eight of the month's total of ten being caught in the approaches to the Nova Scotia coast.

To some degree the last ships were the victims of two major Allied setbacks in radio intelligence. On 1 February the Germans introduced a change to the Enigma machine by adding a fourth wheel for communications with U-boats in the Atlantic and Mediterranean. Bletchley Park was unable, except for a few days in February and March, to decrypt such messages for the next ten months. The German cryptanalytical service (*Beobachtungsdienst* or *B-Dienst*) moreover, had finally mastered British Naval Cypher No 3 so that, until June 1943, it was 'reading' a significant percentage of Allied signals concerning North Atlantic convoys.[62] The abrupt end to an important source of information on the submarine fleet, compensated for to some extent by Dönitz's preoccupation with North American coastal shipping, was to have its most serious consequences when a growing force of U-boats returned to the mid-ocean convoy routes later in the year. But the effect on operations in February was bad enough.

On 19 February *Kapitänleutnant* H. Lehmann-Willenbrock, an 'ace' U-boat commander known as *Der Recke* by the Germans, started a series of successful attacks off Halifax with the destruction of *Empire Seal*. By the 23rd his U-96 had accounted for three more vessels, one of them within fifteen miles of the port. On 24 February, following one of the last 'readings' of naval Enigma in 1942, the Admiralty's submarine report noted '1 or 2 off Halifax' but with unmistakeable local evidence of attacks this came as no surprise to Eastern Air Command.[63] On 23 February the merchant ship *Empire Union* had signalled she was being shelled south of the Halifax approaches, and forces had scurried to her aid from all directions. Shortly before 1800 hours Lysander 449, of No 2 Coast Artillery Co-operation [CAC] Detachment, Dartmouth, a most unlikely instrument of vengeance, had left the tarmac. The wireless operator/air gunner, Sergeant R.H. Smith, recorded the ensuing events:

headed approximately south for ... 20 minutes. We were flying parallel to a Catalina until we passed over a freighter coming up the coast. We went on beside the Catalina for another 10 miles then it climbed and turned to sweep back the way it had come. We turned and followed back to the freighter then turned and headed into the setting sun. We flew this course for possibly 15 minutes. Then F/O Humphreys pointed out the periscope of a submarine a mile or so ahead. The periscope was clearly visible, also a swirling around what was possibly the conning tower. As we approached, the submarine started to go under so that it was invisible for the last 30 seconds of our run on it. We passed over the spot where it had disappeared and dropped the depth charges. No air bubbles or oil observed ... We did a climbing turn and the charges went off about 5 sec. after dropping.[64]

Lehmann-Willenbrock had been saved by the alertness of his conning-tower look-outs in spotting the high-wing monoplane, and he was lucky to suffer only minor damage from two well- placed depth charges.[65]

Sinkings so close to the main assembly point for shipping put further strain on the anti-submarine squadrons, which also had to provide air cover for a growing network of local convoys in the Canadian Zone. CAC detachments from Saint John and Sydney were therefore shifted to Dartmouth to fly a continuous harbour entrance patrol in daylight hours. As it happened, this was unnecessary. Even as the RCAF strengthened patrols in the Halifax area, U-boat activity temporarily moved out from the coast. On 22 February U-155, on passage to American waters, fell in with ONS 67, a convoy of forty ships under American escort heading on a southwesterly course towards Cape Race, and still beyond aircraft range. U-boats homed in by U-155 were able to sink eight ships, most of them tankers, and damage another.[66]

The storms and generally foul weather continued into March, hampering U-boat operations. U-404, unsuccessfully depth-charged on the 2nd by a Hudson of 11 (BR) Squadron,[67] reported 'medium air activity, off Halifax a little traffic ... A great deal of fog, freighter *Collamer* sunk ...'[68] Lehmann-Willenbrock in U-96 also noted on 8 March, the day he was engaged for the second time by a Canadian aircraft: 'Traffic very spread out. Much fog and bad weather.'[69] Flight Lieutenant T.V.L. Mahon, who later won a Distinguished Flying Cross for bomber operations with 433 Squadron, made the second attack on U-96 in a 5 (BR) Canso 'A' and believed he 'must have been very close,' since his depth charges caused a gush of oil that was still welling up over an hour later. In fact *Der Recke* suffered very slight damage (there is no explanation of the oil) and the next day torpedoed the unescorted *Tyr* before heading back to St Nazaire.[70]

For two weeks there were no more sightings. Then on 23 March a straggler from HX 181, *Bayou Chico*, saw and reported U-754. Flying a Bolingbroke from 119 (BR) Squadron at Sydney, Sergeant C.S. Buchanan and his four-man crew subsequently spotted the U-boat fully surfaced, moving northward from the area where it had recently destroyed *British Prudence*. The ensuing attack was a disappointment. The airmen claimed to have blown the submarine to the surface, and it is true that the U-boat log records well-placed bombs, but once again there was no serious damage.[71]

Partly as a result of the bad weather but also owing to a dearth of easy targets, Admiral Dönitz now directed his Type VII U-boats to the more profitable areas off New York, while the Type IXs began a fresh round of successful operations against the unprotected fleet of tankers and bauxite carriers sailing independently in the Gulf of Mexico and Caribbean.[72]

The loss of U-656 and U-503 to US Navy Hudsons from Argentia on 1 March and 15 March, respectively, the first Allied air victories over U-boats in North American waters, failed to disconcert Dönitz, who confided to his war diary that

Sea defense measures so far met with (except area off Halifax and Cape Race) are small, badly organized and untrained.
Air defence in many areas (Aruba, Hatteras and Halifax) is there in sufficient strength

it is true, but inexperienced, and in comparison to the English air escort can only be described as *bad*.[73]

Thanks to U-boat successes further south the Canadian zone was comparatively quiet through April and May. The volume of offshore flying increased significantly with milder weather and the growing number of aircraft. A special detachment (formed after the sharp rise in sinkings south and west of Nova Scotia) of three Canso 'A's with crews from 10 (BR) Squadron and Hudsons of the new 113 (BR) Squadron made their first sorties from Yarmouth air station in April. From Dartmouth other Hudsons of No 31 Operational Training Unit, and Fairey Swordfish of the RN Fleet Air Arm, took their turn on harbour entrance and anti-submarine patrols, while Avro Ansons of No 2 Air Navigation School flew out of Pennfield Ridge, NB. Little was seen or heard of the enemy. Aircraft made two attacks, neither of which is substantiated by U-boat records, even though one was in the area where a U-boat transmission had been detected by shore-based DF.[74] The total of merchant ships sunk in the Canadian coastal zone fell to six in March, declined further in April to four, and rose again to six in May, including two in the Gulf of St Lawrence (which initiated a phase of activities discussed in Chapter 13).

Air Vice-Marshal A.A.L. Cuffe, who had arrived in Halifax on 11 February 1942 to replace Air Vice-Marshal Anderson as air officer commanding, was aware of the shortcomings in Eastern Air Command and brought some remedies. The British advisory teams touring American and Canadian anti-submarine commands early in 1942 found that 'the Canadians had been at great pains to extract all the lessons they could draw from the Battle of the Atlantic, and from our experience on this [the British] side.'[75] Then, on 13 April, the command adopted a modified version of the Manual of Coastal Command Operational Control. A few weeks later the command controller's staff moved to a new operations room in Halifax, imperfectly modelled on its British counterpart at Coastal Command Headquarters, having military and naval liaison officers but inadequate naval input. Reflecting Eastern Air Command's diverse responsibilities, the operations room also housed the facilities for fighter control and air-raid warning. The aim was to establish close operational links with Canadian air, sea, and land forces; the commander Eastern Sea Frontier, USN, whose New York headquarters was also that of the 1st Bomber Command, USAAF; and various American air bases in the northeastern United States and Newfoundland. A combined air-navy headquarters, however, had not yet been organized at Halifax; the interservice stalemate continued with both Cuffe and Rear-Admiral G.C. Jones, commanding officer Atlantic Coast, refusing to budge from their respective operations rooms. Because of distance and poor communications, Cuffe had delegated tactical command in Newfoundland to the commanding officer, No 1 Group.[76] At St John's the staff of Air Commodore McEwen (he received the acting rank in December 1941) was located in a centralized control room similar to but smaller than the one in Halifax, pending the completion of a combined headquarters building, and liaison officers were exchanged between the American and Canadian forces.

Inexperience and insufficient training – there was still no operational training unit specifically established for the command's maritime reconnaissance squadrons in 1942 – undoubtedly played a large part in the failure of aircraft to give U-boats the *coup de grâce*. To raise the level of efficiency of pilots and their crews, the RCAF instituted a syllabus on armament at training establishments and introduced a policy of 'on the job' training in operational units, geared to an up-to-date instructional programme. Aircraft on regular patrols carried addition-al bombs and gun ammunition for practice purposes, and each squadron assigned one flight commander, who had completed the eight-week armament course for pilots, the responsibility of propagating the training syllabus.[77]

In at least four of seven confirmed brushes with the enemy in early 1942, however, inadequate weapons rather than faulty technique had probably prevented a more successful outcome. Good marksmanship in the attacks on 19 January and 23 March had gone for naught because the depth charges carried the fifty-foot setting that Coastal Command's experience had shown to be ineffective. The latest detonator, the Mark XIII pistol, giving a depth setting of thirty-four feet, arrived in Eastern Air Command in February, many months after Coastal Command had introduced it. It was used in the Lysander's attack on the 23rd of that month, and by 11 (BR) on 2 March. Still, the Amatol-filled 250-lb charges lacked killing power, as Coastal Command's scoreless record in early 1942 also demonstrated. Air Force Headquarters ordered Torpex-filled charges from the United Kingdom early in May, pending the organization of Canadian production, but these were not delivered until late in the year, six months after Coastal Command began to receive the weapon. There were similar delays in the supply of Mark XIII Star pistols that provided the essential shallow setting. In the meantime, the most promising weapon in Eastern Air Command's arsenal was the Mark VII 450-lb Amatol-filled depth charge, whose power was equivalent to that of the 250-lb Torpex weapon, but it could only be carried in the larger aircraft.[78]

To solve the problem of detecting a surfaced U-boat quickly enough to make an effective attack, the RCAF equipped as many aircraft as possible with ASV Mark II radar. By the end of April 1942 the first half-dozen sets had been fitted, but Eastern Air Command's early experience with the equipment in detecting U-boats was as disappointing as Coastal Command's had been. Continued improvements in base facilities, deliveries of modern aircraft, and the organization of new squadrons were more tangible additions to Eastern Air Command's effectiveness. In mid-April there were six bomber-reconnaissance squadrons, one equipped with Digbys, two with Catalinas, Cansos and Canso 'A's, and three with Hudsons, including 119 (BR) which was converting from the less-capable Bolingbrokes. No 117 (BR) Squadron, having been disbanded shortly after mobilization in 1939, reformed and broken up in 1941, reactivated at Kelly Beach, North Sydney, on 27 April 1942, and soon began to receive Canso flying boats. No 162 (BR) Squadron, created at Yarmouth from 10 (BR)'s Canso 'A' detachment on 19 May, and 145 (BR) Squadron, formed at Torbay eleven days later from the former Hudson detachment of 11 (BR) Squadron, were further welcome acquisitions, though 162 Squadron would remain at detachment strength for many months to come.[79] At Argentia the US Navy replaced its Hudson squadron with two PBY squadrons. But at the same time, the Germans were about to expand their operations. The U-boat campaign in the Gulf of St Lawrence – with its wreckage and victims strewn along the Gaspé shore – would finally bring the war home to Canadians and precipitate a bitter domestic debate over the preparedness and capabilities of the RCAF and the RCN.

13
The Battle of the St Lawrence

The marked expansion of Eastern Air Command's strength in the late spring and early summer of 1942 was concentrated around its oceanic anti-submarine capabilities; but between May and the end of that year two waves of U-boats penetrated the Gulf of St Lawrence, adding a new dimension to the command's – and the RCN's – responsibilities. The harbinger of this new campaign was U-553, which slipped quietly through the Cabot Strait into the Gulf of St Lawrence on 8 May 1942,[1] the first enemy warship in those waters since Canada had become a nation seventy-five years before. Others soon followed, and sea and air resources were so scarce that this additional threat could not be properly countered without dangerously weakening the north Atlantic lifeline to the United Kingdom. To the credit of the Canadian government, it resisted this temptation, even though the U-boats scored a clear tactical victory. Without the loss of a single submarine the U-boats sank twenty-one ships in the gulf and forced its closure to ocean shipping in September 1942. By then the RCN was providing nearly half the escorts between Halifax and the United Kingdom, escorts for virtually all convoys between Boston and Halifax, and eight corvettes for oil convoys in the Caribbean. Armed yachts, a few Bangor minesweepers, corvettes, and Fairmile launches had to defend the gulf as best they could, in co-operation with whatever air forces could be spared after ocean requirements had been met.

With Newfoundland and Cape Breton on the east, the Quebec shore to the north, and Nova Scotia, Prince Edward Island, New Brunswick, and the Gaspé shore of Quebec to the south, the Gulf of St Lawrence is actually an enclosed sea about 250 nautical miles across at its widest point. Anticosti and the Magdalen Islands funnel shipping into pre-determined channels while the St Lawrence River itself, with its broad lower reaches, is navigable as far up as Montreal. The mouth of the river, where tidal effects, temperature gradients, river currents, and the mixing of fresh and salt water cause complex layering that often enabled submerged U-boats to escape detection by ASDIC, proved a fruitful hunting ground for bold submariners.

There had been no defence plan for the gulf until late 1938. During the Munich crisis of that year, the Joint Staff Committee in Ottawa had envisaged seaplane bases at Gaspé and at Port Menier, on Anticosti Island, to guard the western half of the region, with a seaplane base and aerodrome at Sydney to cover the eastern section and its seaward approaches. However, as mobilization began in late August 1939, Eastern Air Command decided it was more important to cover the Strait of Belle Isle, the northern entrance to the gulf, from a small base at Red Bay, Labrador, than to develop a station on Anticosti Island. Aircraft from Gaspé would cover the gulf, and those from Sydney the Cabot Strait and the waters south of Newfoundland. Only the last part of the plan was immediately practicable since no more than six Northrop Delta floatplanes of 8 (General Purpose) Squadron were available, flying from an improvised base at Sydney River until, in December 1939, new accommodation became available at Kelly Beach.[2]

Naval plans were even slower to develop and it was not until March 1940 that the RCN made provision for an establishment at Gaspé able to support up to seven anti-submarine vessels, including two destroyers. These ships would be kept 'at strategic points along the routes, and rely upon air patrols, with their high mobility and wide arcs of visibility to find and report submarines, and then keep them down until the arrival of the hunting force.'[3]

With no immediate threat and aircraft in short supply, operations in the region were extremely limited during the first two-and-a-half years of the war. The only operational unit stationed within the gulf prior to 1942 was a detachment of 5 Squadron Supermarine Stranraers that flew from an improvised base at Gaspé during the 1940 shipping season. Work began in 1941 on the Gaspé flying-boat station, but the arrival of Douglas Digbys from 10 Squadron at Gander in June 1940 had made the base planned for Red Bay, Labrador, unnecessary: the RCAF in Newfoundland became responsible for guarding the Strait of Belle Isle. As recorded in the preceding chapter, a summer detachment of 116 Squadron Consolidated Catalinas at Botwood assumed a major share of this task during the 1941 shipping season.[4]

By early 1942 Eastern Air Command was able to allocate considerably stronger forces to the gulf and its approaches. However, U-553 appeared soon after navigation opened in the southern gulf when defensive preparations were far from complete. Much work remained to be done at the Gaspé air station; 119 Squadron at Sydney aerodrome would not complete its conversion from Bristol Bolingbrokes to Lockheed Hudsons until early June; and 117 Squadron at North Sydney, the unit that was to provide the Gaspé detachment, was in the preliminary stages of organization. The squadrons at Dartmouth were able temporarily to deploy aircraft to the St Lawrence in an emergency, but at the cost of a serious strain on their resources. Not so pressing was the defence of the Strait of Belle Isle where the ice cleared more slowly. The movement of 116 Squadron at Botwood from its winter station at Dartmouth began with a detachment of four Catalinas at the end of May; the remaining four flying boats arrived in July.[5]

Substantial resources of No 3 Training Command were available to assist the operational forces. By May 1942 RAF schools at Charlottetown, PEI, and Debert and Greenwood, NS, had over 150 Avro Ansons and Lockheed Hudsons on strength. RCAF schools at Summerside, PEI, Chatham, NB, and Mont Joli, Que., had fewer aircraft available, but the bases were well placed and would prove invaluable.[6] Some of the Training Command Ansons were fitted with bomb-racks and machine-guns, and, carrying a maximum load of 500 lbs of bombs, had an operational radius of 200 miles. The airmen of training establishments, even instructional staff, could not normally be expected to perform as well as experienced operational crews, yet they were still a force to be reckoned with.

These were considerable air resources, but no coherent plan of air operations was in place to meet a real crisis. From the first it was clear that *ad hoc* measures would have to do, while co-ordination with the RCN – which forged ahead with its own plan for defence of shipping in the gulf – was almost non-existent. The navy's plan to work in conjunction with the RCAF to track and attack U-boats which penetrated the gulf had given way to a much narrower scheme simply to escort shipping. Some airmen thought this left the RCAF to carry altogether too much of the load.[7] Naval planners had worked on the assumption of sudden and unheralded attacks in the gulf. 'It is important,' wrote Commodore L.W. Murray when he was deputy chief of the naval staff in April 1941, 'that the officers who will be putting this scheme [on which the 1942 plans had been based] into operation should be firmly in a state of mind which will prevent "panic" when a ship has been sunk. They must remember that there may be one, perhaps two and at the very most three submarines, all of which must leave for Germany at an early date.'[8] The only fault in this prediction was Murray's failure to anticipate the six-week patrols which sometimes took place. In the meantime, the navy's Operational Intelligence Centre [OIC] in Ottawa, here as elsewhere, provided indispensable information on enemy activities. Apart from confirming the presence of a U-boat, high frequency direction finding [HF/DF] turned out to be 'often hopeless' in the gulf, but HF/DF was supplemented by other forms of intelligence and by visual sightings, many of which were made by members of the Aircraft Detection Corps [ADC].[9]

The ADC spread to Newfoundland and Labrador in July 1941, thus encompassing the entire gulf. These unpaid civilian volunteers, keen, diligent, and inexperienced as they were, passed their sightings to a 'reporting centre,' usually the nearest RCAF station, by telephone and telegraph. Their reports, which could never be ignored, were often false alarms. When they were not, communications were sometimes subject to fatal delays. On the Gaspé shore between Ste-Anne-des-Monts and Fox River there was no telephone, only a telegraph line with offices as far as twenty miles apart. At Gaspé itself the RCAF station had neither the personnel nor the accommodation to function properly as a reporting centre. Regional army headquarters was only dimly aware of the ADC system, and in at least one instance told civilians they had to report everything to army intelligence. All too often the first indication of the presence of a U-boat was the news that a ship had been sunk.[10]

Poor communications also hampered the control of military operations. Linkages between the headquarters of the three services in Halifax with the gulf bases were incomplete, leaving no alternative but reliance on the inadequate commercial telephone lines. The situation was particularly difficult for the air force, whose job it was to respond quickly to U-boat reports, a task which required frequent redeployments of aircraft among widely scattered stations.[11]

It was this combination of circumstances, not any particular sin of omission on the part of a navy and air force distracted by competing demands elsewhere, that opened the way to U-553's apparently easy successes. The first to enter the gulf, and the first to sink shipping there, *Korvettenkapitän* Karl Thurmann set the pattern for the battle that he set in motion: U-553's appearance, as a distinguished British airman once said of Eastern Air Command operations, was like putting 'a fox in a flock of hens,'[12] an unkind comparison, but not entirely inappropriate.

The initial air search for the boat was triggered by a false sighting by a civilian observer at Cape Ray, Nfld, on 9 May, the day after U-553 had passed through the area. A USAAF Boeing B-17 Flying Fortress from Gander made an unsuccessful attack on the submarine south of Anticosti Island early on the evening of the 10th. Major General C.G. Brant, commanding the United States Army Air Forces in Newfoundland, did not receive news of the attack until the following morning and then failed to pass it to No 1 Group, RCAF. Air Commodore C.M. McEwen, never friendly with Brant, reported that 'I had to extract it myself' and the news eventually reached Halifax late on the evening of 11 May.[13]

Two Canso 'A's from 5 Squadron at Dartmouth swept the gulf very early on 11 May, while 31 General Reconnaissance School at Charlottetown arranged exercise areas for its Ansons that covered the probable route of the U-boat. That night, however, during the early hours of the 12th, U-553 torpedoed and sank the steamers *Leto* and *Nicoya* north of the Gaspé coast. Before dawn the navy instructed ships due to sail through the gulf to remain in port, and a 5 Squadron Canso 'A' took off from Dartmouth to search the vicinity of the sinkings in miserable weather conditions. Later that day, five Hudsons – three from 31 Operational Training Unit [OTU] at Debert and two from 11 Squadron at Dartmouth – swept the area and twenty-four Ansons from Charlottetown exercised over the central gulf. The Canso 'A' and 11 Squadron Hudsons landed at Mont Joli where they were joined on the 14th by a second 5 Squadron Canso 'A'. This detachment operated over the river and western gulf until early June.

Meanwhile, 119 Squadron maintained a heavy schedule of patrols over the Cabot Strait, and 116 Squadron at Dartmouth began to transfer experienced personnel and Canso flying boats to 117 Squadron at North Sydney. By early June, with seven aircraft on strength, the latter unit was able to fly its full share of operations in the Sydney area, and on the 10th of that month dispatched two flying boats to form the detachment at Gaspé.[14] Warships based on Gaspé and Sydney by the end of May for gulf operations included six Bangor minesweepers (with a seventh joining in early June) three armed yachts and nine Fairmile launches.[15]

These modest air and naval forces had large responsibilities for the defence of shipping. Sydney-Quebec City [SQ–QS] convoys got under way on 17 May, following a route south of the Magdalen Islands so that they would be well within range of RAF Ansons at Charlottetown. On 19 May the first SB-BS convoys between Sydney and Cornerbrook, Nfld, sailed. RCAF squadrons from Sydney provided protection for the ferries *Caribou* and *Burgeo*, on the Sydney-Port aux Basques run, until in June the RCN took full responsibility for guarding these so-called SPAB convoys. Finally, the RCAF assisted in the protection of two other convoy routes, the LN-NL series between Quebec City and the new air base at Goose Bay, Labrador, and the SG-GS series between Sydney and US bases in Greenland.[16]

No doubt the sinking of two merchant ships seemed an adequate return to the Germans, but the results for the U-boat campaign as a whole would have been more spectacular had the sinkings propelled the Canadians into a large-scale redisposition of forces away from the strategically vital oceanic routes. This the naval and air staffs steadfastly refused to do. As it was, the presence of U-553 kept the gulf in an uproar until the end of May. The all-out air effort did not, in the event, achieve even a single sighting for, after his brief encounter with the Flying Fortress on the 10th, Thurmann played his hand very cautiously, surfacing only at night. Caution, however, deprived him of any further opportunities to attack as the naval control of shipping came into force: only a really enterprising submariner, boldly operating on the surface, could expect to locate and strike at convoys. In addition to the disappearance of steamer traffic, Thurmann also reported the 'very careful air patrol' over the gulf, but BdU did not appear to take that warning very seriously.[17]

U-553's departure on 22 May, accurately estimated by naval intelligence, was accompanied by some sober reflection. War had suddenly come close to home at a time when acute national controversy over conscription for overseas service was still simmering. The plebiscite of 27 April had split the country on this issue, the nation as a whole supporting the concept but Quebec responding with a resounding 'no.' In Ottawa, Prime Minister Mackenzie King had been about to go into a Liberal party caucus to explain how he would respond to that contradictory mandate when he received the news of the first sinkings. French-Canadian opponents of conscription, he believed, would now see that the war was not a remote affair, and that Canada could not limit its contribution. At the same time enemy operations in Canadian waters created arguments for a stronger emphasis on home defence. He might even be able to avoid sending conscripts overseas. Had Dönitz and the German High Command been privy to King's thoughts they would have marvelled at an unexpected bonus from their strategy; and had there been an enemy spy in caucus he would have listened with delight to King's efforts in presenting the news as dramatically as possible. The day after these events the prime minister reflected that 'Several lives have been lost which would bring home the whole situation to the people as nothing else ...'[18]

He was right. The minister of national defence for naval services, Angus L. Macdonald, announced the loss of one ship to the press on 12 May, and of the second to the House of Commons on 13 May. He did so not because he shared the prime minister's opinions, but because the survivors who streamed ashore on the Gaspé coast had divulged every detail to the press, including the dismal news that the ships had received no warning of a U-boat in the gulf. An additional consequence was that newspaper reports revealed facts likely to be of value to German naval authorities. Macdonald vowed never again to acknowledge such sinkings so soon after the event, and the navy distributed a pamphlet by the

Directorate of Naval Intelligence explaining to the press the ways in which unrestricted publication of news stories could help the enemy.[19] The government of course could not clothe disasters on the St Lawrence in a pall of silence. People living on the shores of the gulf wanted reassurance; they wanted to see troops, ships, and aircraft sent to protect them. Local MPs, especially the Independent member for Gaspé, J.-S. Roy, were bound to point out the long-standing failure to give the Gaspé region any real benefits from the booming wartime economy. For years Roy had been complaining about this neglect; now, albeit with a leap in logic, he could document horrifying results. For its part the Tory opposition, by no means in sympathy with Roy, was glad to seize such a useful opportunity to ridicule the government's war effort.[20]

It was more than a month before the next blow was delivered: U-132 passed through the Cabot Strait on the night of 29/30 June, and following U-553's example, *Korvettenkapitän* Ernst Vogelsang steered directly for the mouth of the St Lawrence River. By the early evening of 5 July U-132 was off Cap Chat, ninety miles upstream from the position of U-553's attacks of 12 May. Air patrols over the area during the day had been restricted to support for convoy SQ 16 in the morning by one of the two Cansos of 117 Squadron available at Gaspé. Shortly after the lone serviceable aircraft returned to base, convoy QS 15 departed its Bic Island assembly area for Sydney; the staff at Eastern Air Command, caught off guard by the convoy's early sailing, made hasty plans to provide air escort at first light on the 6th. Unfortunately, the Germans got there first. In the lingering summer twilight U-132 put torpedoes into two of the convoy's ships, retained contact despite the naval escort's efforts, and two hours later (2307 local time, which was three hours behind GMT and which will be used throughout this chapter) hit another ship, which subsequently sank. HMCS *Drummondville* depth-charged U-132 as it crash-dived following the second attack, but no report of the two attacks reached shore authorities until 0230 – six hours after the first torpedoes had struck.[21]

Because Eastern Air Command usually depended on commercial telephone for communication with the Gaspé region, the air officer commanding, Air Vice-Marshal A.A.L. Cuffe, had decentralized authority, instructing the commanders of Gaspé and Mont Joli to 'take whatever immediate action is necessary on all reports of sightings, in addition to performing the normal functions of a well-coordinated plan.'[22] However, on 5/6 July this system simply was not working. The first thing Gaspé knew of the attack was a phone call from Halifax ordering the two Cansos on detachment from Sydney to take off just before 0300 hours on the 6th. Fog prevented flying until after noon. At Mont Joli a telephone call from the naval detachment at Rimouski prompted some hasty action which turned out to be of a futile and ultimately tragic nature. The most suitable available aircraft were Curtiss P-40 Kittyhawks of 130 (Fighter) Squadron, temporarily based at the station. Groundcrew rushed to fuel and arm the fighters, and four of them took off into the darkness an hour later. Squadron Leader J.A.J. Chevrier, the first to be airborne, never returned, and civilian reports suggest he crashed into the sea near Cap Chat. In the meantime, the groundcrew had to install racks and a pair of depth charges on two Fairey Battles

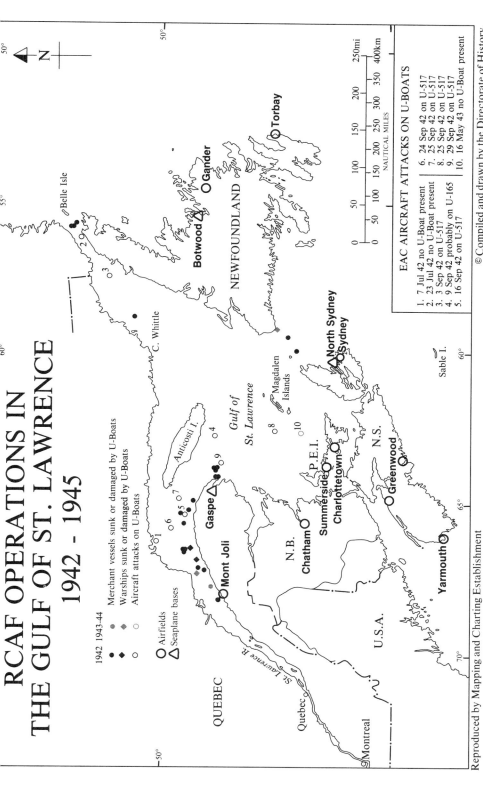

RCAF OPERATIONS IN
THE GULF OF ST. LAWRENCE
1942 - 1945

Merchant vessels sunk or damaged by U-Boats

Warships sunk or damaged by U-Boats

Aircraft attacks on U-Boats

	1942	1943-44
Merchant vessels	●	◆
Warships	●	◆
Aircraft attacks	○	○

○ Airfields
△ Seaplane bases

EAC AIRCRAFT ATTACKS ON U-BOATS

1. 7 Jul 42 no U-Boat present   6. 24 Sep 42 on U-517
2. 23 Jul 42 no U-Boat present   7. 25 Sep 42 on U-517
3. 3 Sep 42 on U-517   8. 25 Sep 42 on U-517
4. 9 Sep 42 probably on U-165   9. 29 Sep 42 on U-517
5. 16 Sep 42 on U-517   10. 16 May 43 no U-Boat present

© Compiled and drawn by the Directorate of History.

NAUTICAL MILES

Reproduced by Mapping and Charting Establishment

QUEBEC

Montreal

Quebec

Mont Joli

Gaspe

Anticosti I.

C. Whittle

Belle Isle

Botwood

Gander

NEWFOUNDLAND

Torbay

Gulf of
St. Lawrence

Magdalen
Islands

N.B.

Chatham

P.E.I.

Summerside

Charlottetown

North Sydney

Sydney

N.S.

Greenwood

Sable I.

Yarmouth

U.S.A.

St. Lawrence R.

of 9 Bombing and Gunnery School. At 0445 two pilots took off, knowing that the engines in the aircraft were not dependable; there may not even have been radio equipment on board. None of these brave efforts was successful, and it was adding insult to injury when the RCAF had to respond two weeks later to rumours reaching the House of Commons 'that the pilots at Mont Joli were all drunk and out with women at the time of the sinking.'[23]

In the wake of the new disasters the navy assigned six corvettes to the gulf, while three Hudsons from 119 Squadron at Sydney and three from 113 Squadron at Yarmouth, NS, went to Mont Joli, where for the remainder of the navigation season there was always a detachment from one of these squadrons or from 11 (BR) at Dartmouth. On 7 July an Aircraft Detection Corps report from Sept Iles resulted in the apparent sighting by a Hudson of 119 Squadron of a periscope feather – the spray thrown up behind the periscope of a moving submarine -and the aircraft attacked. U-132 was far away, however, near the Gaspé coast, and German records do not reveal any other U-boat in the gulf at this time. Whatever the aircrew had seen, it was not a submarine.[24]

The first U-boat campaign in the gulf was also, of course, an extraordinary situation for the remote and peaceful communities along the Gaspé coast. Even though the press obediently kept silent, word spread like wildfire through southeastern Quebec after the survivors came ashore on 6 July. J.-S. Roy could contain himself no longer and rose in Parliament on 12 July to announce that three ships had been sunk in convoy. He then repeated the demand he had been making since May for a secret session of the House of Commons. Angus L. Macdonald was furious. Roy was committing a breach of security, and he was undermining the government's well-considered war policies. 'If he [Roy] thinks for one moment that the whole Canadian navy is going to line up along his shores only, letting the convoy system we have and the protection we have for all the rest of Canada go to the dogs, he is making a tremendous mistake. I am not ready to change the disposition of one ship of the Canadian navy,' Macdonald concluded, 'for him or all the questions he may ask from now until doomsday.'[25]

The intensity of the minister's language reflected his commitment to his service and its intention not to be distracted by the gulf campaign, and perhaps echoed some of the bitterness surrounding the recent conscription controversy. He was evidently against a secret session of Parliament, but cooler heads prevailed: members of all parties, including a number of Quebec Liberals, endorsed the idea.[26] Adélard Godbout, the Liberal premier of Quebec, warned the prime minister that 'a perilous situation exists' because the population was bewildered and nervous, and rumours were legion. Godbout had it from 'two reliable sources' that two men, possibly landed from a submarine, had attacked the wireless station at the Mont Joli aerodrome. King, always sensitive to what Godbout legitimately called 'incalculable elements of danger to the safety and security of Canada,' ordered the secret session for 18 July. This allowed Macdonald and C.G. Power, the air minister, to reassure members about the naval and air measures to defend the gulf, Power seizing upon the Hudson attack on a false contact of 7 July as a 'probable sinking.'[27] For the time being the critics were silenced; they did not react strongly when U-132, attacking QS 19 off Cape Magdalen on 20 July, sank another freighter.[28]

It was the success of anti-submarine measures elsewhere on the eastern seaboard of Canada and the United States that exposed the gulf to its next and worst ordeal. Searching for soft spots in the shipping defences, Dönitz had deployed three U-boats off the Strait of Belle Isle by the last week of August 1942. Two of them, U-517 and U-165, proceeded into the gulf where, over the next six weeks, they carried out the most successful German patrols of the war in gulf waters.[29]

Air coverage of the gulf and its shipping at this time was largely unchanged from what it had been at the time of U-132's cruise. The Newfoundland squadrons continued to guard the Strait of Belle Isle, and 117 Squadron operated three Cansos from Gaspé, while at Mont Joli the 113 Squadron detachment, which had been expanded to seven aircraft after the sinking on 20 July, was reduced to four Hudsons on 1 August. (On the 3rd these were replaced by four similar aircraft from 119 Squadron.) But in confined waters and narrow channels, air coverage of shipping, even when it was almost continuous, was no protection against submarines lying in wait, as evidenced by U-165's and U-517's first successes in the northern reaches of the gulf. The prey was LN 6, a tiny Quebec-Goose Bay convoy, and SG 6, a group of American ships bound from Sydney to Greenland under US navy escort and, at the time of the attack, a Digby from 10 Squadron. The US Army transport *Chatham* was faster than the other ships of SG 6 and was permitted to forge ahead under naval escort but beyond the circuits flown by the convoy's air escort. *Chatham* was torpedoed and sunk by *Kapitänleutnant* Paul Hartwig's U-517 in broad daylight on 27 August, just as the two convoys were entering the Strait of Belle Isle. HMCS *Trail*, the escort of LN 6, which had slipped in between the main body of SG 6 and *Chatham*, sent its two charges to shelter in Forteau Bay while it conducted rescue work. Meanwhile, SG 6 sailed on under continuous air cover. At 2130 that night, when the 116 Squadron Catalina on task was apparently patrolling at some distance from the convoy, U-165 (*Korvettenkapitän* Eberhard Hoffman) and U-517 torpedoed the merchantmen *Laramie* and *Arlyn*. *Arlyn* sank, but *Laramie* was able to limp back to Sydney.[30]

LN 6 now turned back to Gaspé to join up with the two ships of LN 7, and the combined convoy sailed on 2 September with two escorting corvettes. The OIC warned them that day that the U-boats had detected them. The Canso on task from Gaspé lost the convoy in heavy fog about midday. U-517, lying in wait about one hundred miles southwest of the Strait of Belle Isle, sank the freighter *Donald Stewart* in the early morning hours of 3 September.

At daybreak a Hudson from Sydney, with a Digby and a USAAF B-17 from Gander, provided air cover, sweeping the strait in daylight hours. This led to the first actual RCAF air attack in the gulf. Flying Officer J.H. Sanderson of 10 Squadron sighted U-517 in the southern approaches to the strait a few minutes after noon. The submarine had been on the surface for hours and had dived several times because of aircraft: better air search techniques would no doubt have resulted in an earlier detection. Now the Digby, descending from a search altitude of 900 feet, attacked from 150 feet. The U-boat had been submerged for twenty seconds and the only damage inflicted was on the aircraft, from the premature explosion of a depth charge. Hardly a model attempt, the effort at least saved the convoy from further loss.[31]

At the other end of the gulf U-165 was on the prowl, penetrating the mouth of the river, and by 7 September U-517 had arrived off the Gaspé. The OIC concluded from a number of sources that two U-boats were operating in the gulf and air activity increased as a result. The 119 Squadron detachment at Mont Joli was reinforced by aircraft from 11 Squadron to a total strength of six Hudsons, and Eastern Air Command made extensive use of the Hudsons and Ansons of the OTUs at Greenwood and Debert, NS, and the general reconnaissance schools at Summerside and Charlottetown, PEI. Despite these efforts not every convoy was effectively screened. Weather prevented proper support for QS 33 during its passage of the lower St Lawrence River and although nine sorties were flown in the general area, U-165 and U-517 were able to sink four ships and the armed yacht *Raccoon* off Cap Chat on 6 and 7 September.[32] Without radar, which, even if fitted, was little more than a navigational aid at this time, the airmen were almost blind in conditions of poor visibility.

Eastern Air Command responded by sending three more Hudsons from 113 Squadron, Yarmouth, to Chatham, NB, and a Canso 'A' from 5 Squadron, Dartmouth, to Sydney. The Chatham aircraft, described as 'a special Submarine Hunting Detachment,' acted as a striking force in the central gulf.[33] On 8 September DF bearings, sightings, and a radar contact by the corvette *Summerside* indicated a U-boat off Gaspé and another northeast of Anticosti. Intensive air searches began again, with the Chatham Hudsons performing a 'general A/S [anti-submarine] Search' east of Gaspé.

No 113 Squadron had been the first Eastern Air Command unit to implement Coastal Command's recent tactical innovations by adopting white aircraft camouflage and high patrol altitudes of up to 5000 feet instead of 1500 feet or less; the new methods had quickly proved their value in the squadron's operations from Yarmouth, and did so again in the gulf. On the forenoon of 9 September, Hudson 403, flown by Pilot Officer R.S. Keetley, swooped down from 4000 feet on U-165 about twenty miles south of Anticosti. Because he first mistook it for a sailing boat – 'The conning tower was painted white and the hull sea green,' he claimed incorrectly – Keetley's first pass was too high and the submarine dived eight seconds before the attack.[34] However, his report brought out two corvettes and a Bangor minesweeper to search the area. Subsequent sightings and attacks, although unsuccessful, were enough to make U-165's captain report that air patrols made it difficult to contact convoys east of Gaspé and south of Anticosti.[35] In the narrow confines of the gulf it was still easy for U-boats to locate and attack targets. The very boldness of the submarines furthered their success. On 11 September U-517 was seen off Cap Chat by onlookers on shore just a few minutes before she sank the corvette *Charlottetown* in broad daylight, but Hartwig had gone before aircraft arrived on the scene.[36] On 15 and 16 September, in the same region, U-517 and U-165 had a field-day with SQ 36, a large convoy of twenty-two ships. Undetected by the Canso of 11 Squadron flying patrols ahead of the convoy in clear bright weather, U-517 was spotted by an ADC observer on the surface an hour and a half before she attacked

By the time the observer's report, transmitted through army channels, had been received, Hartwig had submerged ahead of the convoy, sinking two ships in the afternoon. Subjected to heavy counter attack by the large naval escort – seven ships in all, including a British destroyer – U-517 sustained only minor damage.[37] Air coverage for SQ 36 was taken over by a Canso 'A' from 5 Squadron which stayed on through the night but was unable to prevent further loss when SQ 36 encountered U-165 lying in wait, submerged, off Cap Chat, to sink two more ships and damage a third just before dawn.[38]

Eleven ships sunk in two weeks was a staggering blow, and the U-boats still appeared to be in full cry. DF bearings brought out the Hudsons from Chatham on 16 September and Pilot Officer Keetley spotted U-517 north of Cape Magdalen at about 1000 hours. Keetley reported bracketing the surfaced U-boat with four Amatol charges, but perhaps because they were spaced too far apart, or because they simply were not powerful enough, the charges caused no serious damage. Then for about a week no more was heard from the Germans.[39]

It was at this difficult time that the British government asked for Canadian escort vessels to support Operation 'Torch,' the North African landings. Compliance would mean withdrawing most of the naval escorts from the Gulf of St Lawrence and the west coast, thus shifting much more responsibility on to the air force. There is evidence that the navy had been leaning towards such a solution for some time, because they lacked the escorts necessary to protect gulf convoys adequately in 1942 and saw no improvement on the horizon for 1943. Shipping authorities, too, preferred to eliminate the movement of ocean traffic through the gulf because the thousand-mile passage to Montreal was a drain on critically short merchant tonnage and cargoes could always be moved by rail to east-coast ports. On 9 September the Cabinet War Committee approved a naval staff recommendation to meet the request for 'Torch' escorts by closing the St Lawrence to overseas shipping. The prime minister, moved by Winston Churchill's personal appeal, supported the step with grave reservations. He was sure it would mean more sinkings, and he argued perceptively that the corvettes so important to home defence might prove to be a relatively insignificant contribution to the 'Torch' landings. Even though the chief of the naval staff insisted the ships be returned by April 1943, King's 'fear and guess was that they will all either be gone or be kept by British for continental purposes for an early offensive when Spring comes.'[40]

Within hours of the Cabinet decision Naval Service Headquarters signalled the Admiralty that all ocean shipping bound for the St Lawrence should be diverted to Halifax, Sydney, or Saint John, NB. The navy had hoped to phase out the SQ-QS series, but this proved to be impossible because 40 per cent of the ships that sailed in the convoys were engaged in coastal trade that was essential both to the economy of the region and to the operation of major industries there. Immediate steps, however, almost halved the convoy cycle, and all but one corvette, which was being refitted in Nova Scotia, two Bangors, and the flotilla of six Fairmiles, ceased operations in the gulf in the following month. Shipping control authorities compensated by bringing in more varied and flexible convoy routes.[41] Slim pickings and unpredictable patterns would, it was believed, encourage U-boats to look elsewhere for their prey.

Eastern Air Command did not share that optimism. In spite of severe demands on Canso and Hudson squadrons in Nova Scotia, explained Group Captain M. Costello, senior air staff officer in Eastern Air Command, the air force had failed to achieve a sufficient 'concentration of operational aircraft to drive the enemy from the area.'[42] Air Vice-Marshal Cuffe, who was proposing a temporary withdrawal of all Hudsons and Cansos from Yarmouth in order to reinforce the gulf, had directed Costello to request authority from Air Force Headquarters 'to ask the Americans to take over the air protection of all convoys west of latitude 65 ... as long as is necessary for us to concentrate in the Gulf area.' On 17 September Air Marshal Breadner approved, 'as a temporary measure only, subject to US forces using Yarmouth for refuelling and to their not otherwise using the base ...' The US First Air Force moved into the Yarmouth patrol area on 18 September, and North American B-25 Mitchell bombers from Westover Field, Massachusetts, periodically landed at Yarmouth to refuel until late in October. Although the Canso 'A's of 162 Squadron did not leave Nova Scotia for the time being, 113 Squadron, commanded by Squadron Leader N.E. Small, immediately sent its remaining Hudsons to Chatham.[43]

Small was Eastern Air Command's outstanding pilot and its most conscientious student of maritime airpower. A prewar sergeant pilot in the RCAF, Small had left the service in 1937 to fly commercially before rejoining in 1939 as a pilot officer. His early wartime career was spent as an advanced flying instructor and, in the spring of 1941, as a ferry pilot. His five transatlantic flights in Catalinas marked him for assignment to 116 Squadron in July 1941, as that squadron took delivery of the type. Described by senior officers as a 'master pilot' and 'excellent tactician' possessed of a 'burning desire "to get on with the job,"' Small had received command of the newly organized 162 Squadron in May 1942. A month later he took over 113 Squadron and was awarded the Air Force Cross.[44] Under his inspired leadership, the unit soon achieved great things at Yarmouth (see Chapter 14) and, as already noted, its Chatham detachment made two of the three confirmed attacks on U-boats in the gulf. With the reinforcement of the detachment in late September, the squadron's exploits would considerably brighten the otherwise gloomy record of the effort to defend the St Lawrence.

On 25 September Hartwig, in U-517, reported the reduction in convoy cycles and the 'constantly strengthened' air patrols. The last observation was made with some feeling, no doubt. Only the day before a Hudson of 113 Squadron, escorting convoy QS 37, sighted the U-boat southeast of Sept Iles. Dropping sea markers, Flight Sergeant A.S. White flew back to warn the convoy and on returning was able to attack U-517 about five seconds after the conning tower had disappeared under the sea. A blown fuse prevented the release of three depth charges, and only one dropped. But U-517 had been put down, and after dark the largest night operation yet undertaken saw at least five aircraft on task for search and escort duties. About an hour before midnight another Hudson from Chatham, flown by Flying Officer M.J. Belanger, carried out a fine moonlight attack, catching U-517 completely by surprise and shaking the submarine with two 'violent' explosions close astern. After daybreak the next morning another Chatham-based Hudson in support of convoy QS 37, piloted by Flight Sergeant

M.S. Wallace, sighted and forced U-517 to dive on two occasions. Later that afternoon Belanger, patrolling just below cloud cover, attacked the U-boat again, this time with slightly less accuracy, as U-517 crash-dived. No sign of damage appeared and airmen began to feel that the fault lay with the Amatol-filled Mark VIII depth charges. Nevertheless, the crews of 113 Squadron's Hudsons had scored a remarkable seven sightings and three well-executed attacks on U-517 in twenty-four hours.[45]

That U-517's captain persisted through these constant alarms speaks volumes for his determination, but Eastern Air Command was equally determined in its pursuit. Six Ansons from the RAF's 31 General Reconnaissance School, Charlottetown, flew the school's first extended night patrols on 25/26 September. According to the station diary, 'A large convoy on its way through our area was threatened by three [naval intelligence actually estimated two] enemy submarines. The unit volunteered to escort all night. There was a full moon and a clear sky. Escort with aircraft armed with two 250-lb bombs was maintained till dawn.'[46] As it happened, the Germans had shifted their attention to the Cabot Strait, but they were back a few days later. Before dawn on 28 September U-517 attacked QS 38 off Gaspé without success. In the meantime, 113 Squadron once again began to fly sweeps over the operating area, taking their Hudsons to 5000 feet and once again the new tactics paid dividends; on 29 September Flying Officer Belanger surprised U-517 twenty miles off the Gaspé coast. Diving from the high patrol altitude, Belanger attacked the fully surfaced U-boat with four depth charges. He described the result in some detail: 'The charges were seen to explode all around the hull slightly ahead of the conning tower. One large explosion occurred around the hull ... The U-boat's bow came up out of the water and all forward action stopped. It then appeared to settle straight down. The sea was very rough under the influence of a 31 knot wind and no evidence of wreckage, oil or air bubbles was observed in the one hour and 55 minutes that the aircraft remained in the area.'[47] Like so many before him, Belanger had been deceived by appearances. Hartwig acknowledged that the depth charges were 'well-placed,' but Squadron Leader Small's belief that Belanger had destroyed U-517 was ill-founded. US naval analysts concluded from the photographs on which Small based his assessment that there had probably been an 'overshoot.' Their assessment, 'probable slight damage,' was correct.[48]

Nevertheless, Belanger was later awarded the Distinguished Flying Cross for his service in Eastern Air Command, and he subsequently added a Bar to it for his achievements in the RAF's Bomber Command during 1944.

Momentum was beginning to shift away from the U-boat commanders, but to Admiral Dönitz it still appeared that 'Defences proved comparatively weak and were limited to direct convoy escorts.'[49] More U-boats were already on their way to the region, and there were plans to send further reinforcements. Of the two assigned to the St Lawrence, only U-69, a minelayer which had been operating in Chesapeake Bay, actually entered the gulf, passing through the Cabot Strait on 30 September. By 5 October it was north of Gaspé, shadowing QS 39, but intelligence received at Eastern Air Command three days earlier had indicated there was a submarine in the vicinity of the convoy and there was constant air cover, including night escorts on 4-6 October. The navy diverted the convoy from the usual shipping route to one north of the Magdalen Islands.[50]

DF bearings obtained on 5 and 6 October suggested that a U-boat was now as far up river as Rimouski. Other intelligence reports on the 6th and 7th indicating that a submarine was off Gaspé and the Baie de Chaleur led the Hudsons at Chatham to investigate, but they came up empty handed. There was no U-boat in the central gulf. Once again, the real danger lay in the river, as convoy NL 9 discovered when, bound from Goose Bay for Quebec, it approached Rimouski on the night of 8/9 October. The air escort remained only until nightfall. A Hudson from 113 Squadron's detachment at Mont Joli flew a sweep beginning at midnight on the 9th but was not assigned to the convoy, and was not present an hour later when U-69 torpedoed and sank the merchantman *Carolus*. Naval escorts counter-attacked with depth charges, and Hudsons from Chatham searched for the submarine from before dawn on the 9th until the afternoon of the 11th, but U-69 slipped out of their grasp.[51]

Eastern Air Command strengthened the defences at Mont Joli on 10-11 October with two Canso 'A's from 162 Squadron at Yarmouth, but by then U-43 and U-106 were presenting a new threat in the Cabot Strait. At risk were two merchantmen escorted by the armed yacht HMCS *Vison*, which had just sailed from Cornerbrook, Nfld, for Sydney on 10 October. A Canso from 117 Squadron at North Sydney met the convoy at daylight on the 11th, and began to fly an inner anti-submarine patrol a half mile from the ships at an altitude of only 750 feet. Conditions were miserable – low visibility, drizzle, rough seas, and low clouds. About an hour before noon U-106 torpedoed ss *Waterton* in a submerged attack near the centre of the Cabot Strait; *Waterton* went down in eight minutes. The Canso, diving down through debris from the cargo of paper thrown up by the explosion, saw no trace of a torpedo track or periscope in the high seas.[52]

Three days later the ferry *Caribou* departed from Sydney for an overnight passage to Port aux Basques, Nfld, with the usual escort of a Bangor minesweeper, HMCS *Grandmère*, but without air cover. Shortly after midnight in 'fair' weather and 'very good' visibility, U-69 fired a torpedo into the ferry in a surface attack. *Caribou*, only forty miles from her destination, quickly sank. *Grandmère* sighted U-69 and increased to full speed to ram, but the submarine crash-dived. *Grandmère* then dropped eighteen depth charges, but raised only a small amount of oil. She rescued 103 survivors from the ferry, of whom two died subsequently, bringing the number of lives lost to 136, including seventy-nine civilians and fifty-seven service personnel. This tragedy resulted in a twenty-four-hour sweep of the Cabot Strait, by Hudsons of 119 Squadron and a 117 Squadron Canso, all from Sydney, but again U-69 made good its escape. From 30 October to about 8 November three Hudsons from 113 Squadron's Chatham detachment operated from Sydney to strengthen air cover over the entrance to the gulf. Regular air escort was also provided for ss *Burgeo*, the remaining ferry on the Sydney–Port aux Basques run.[53]

After sinking *Caribou*, U-69 left the gulf, reporting by radio to U-boat headquarters that the attack on *Carolus* in the St Lawrence River on 9 October had brought down quite formidable defences: 'strong sea patrol and constant patrol by aircraft with radar ...' On 22 October U-106 confirmed this report on leaving the area, signalling, 'Nothing sighted in ... [the St Lawrence River]. Heavy defence since 16 October.' U-69, located south of Newfoundland by HF/DF after unsuccessfully attacking the freighter *Rose Castle*, was in turn attacked without success on 21 October by a Hudson from 145 (BR) Squadron, Torbay. At the end of the month BdU recorded that U-43 had patrolled the mouth of the St Lawrence 'for seventeen days and operated on two convoys without success.' As Admiral Dönitz went on to note, 'Sea escort in co-operation with air [was present] on a larger scale.' Frustrated by vastly improved defences and more effective routing of shipping, U-43 left the gulf by 10 November.[54]

In the meantime, on 8 November U-518 (*Kapitänleutnant* Friedrich-Wilhelm Wismann) arrived off New Carlisle, PQ, on the north shore of Baie de Chaleur, to land a spy, Werner Janowski, who was promptly arrested by the Quebec Provincial Police. Wismann then slipped away to operate off Gaspé, unaware that the gulf was now closed to all but local traffic. There, in the words of the BdU war diary, U-518 found 'only occasional single ships sailing close to land. Slight surface patrols, no night air patrols. Meagre prospects of success.' Consequently, by 17 November the boat had gone to patrol off Halifax.

It is worth noting that Janowski was the second German agent to land in Canada. Six months earlier, on the night of 13-14 May 1942, U-213 had put ashore an agent named Langbein, about 30 miles south west of Saint John, NB. The Canadian services did not receive any intelligence concerning this mission, but no harm resulted. Langbein buried his radio transmitter near the landing site and undertook no subversive activities. Having lived innocuously in Montreal and Ottawa for two-and-a-half years, he turned himself in to the RCMP in November 1944.[55]

So long as U-boats still appeared to be in the gulf in late 1942, Eastern Air Command did not reduce the strength of the gulf detachments very much. Aircraft still provided escorts for convoys, performing regular sweeps, as well as searching areas where submarines had been sighted or located by DF bearings. Early in December the Gaspé Canso detachment finally left for North Sydney. On 13 December the 113 Squadron detachment at Chatham set out for Yarmouth. Part of the Mont Joli detachment remained until 23 December. QS 46, the last of the gulf convoys for the season, arrived at Sydney on 7 December.[56]

With the sinking of *Caribou* on 14 October the U-boats had drawn their last blood for 1942. But even before news of her destruction and the heavy loss of life was released, public outcry over the handling of gulf defences had boiled up again in the press. Three articles by Edouard Laurent in *L'Action catholique* of Quebec City on 14-20 October 1942, under the title 'Ce qui se passe en Gaspésie,' made particularly grave accusations. At least forty ships had been sunk in the St Lawrence, he claimed, while Gaspesians had never seen an aircraft escorting a convoy. Perhaps the federal government's 'red tape' had hamstrung the defences. When Mayor Louis Keable of Mechins had reported a U-boat close off shore near the RCAF Station at Mont Joli, Laurent reported, the air force had then asked Ottawa for instructions and waited until two members of the RCMP travelled twenty-eight miles from Matane to confirm the sighting: an aircraft arrived over Mechins a full eight hours after the initial report. With such stories Laurent captured the 'atmosphère de malaise et d'angoisse' in the Gaspé region, and raised a fundamental question: Why was Canada incapable of defending her own shores when she had raised so many thousands of soldiers, sailors, and airmen to fight overseas?[57]

The director of public relations in the Department of National Defence considered it 'significant' that Laurent 'is or has been associated with Mr. Duplessis,' leader of the Union Nationale opposition.[58] But it was Duplessis's opponent and nemesis, Premier Godbout, who sent copies of all three articles to King with the recommendation that they were 'the most complete and objective articles I have seen on the subject.'[59] A major English-language paper, the *Toronto Telegram*, printed one of the articles in translation and heartily endorsed Laurent's position. Laurent's timing was excellent: he published just as news of the October sinkings became public. When on 15 October Angus L. Macdonald announced the sinking of *Carolus*, detailed accounts in the press emphasized that the ship had gone down only 200 miles from Quebec City; news of the *Caribou*'s demise and the heavy loss of life was in the papers by 17-18 October. J.-S. Roy profited from all these revelations by renewing his public campaign to have the government strengthen the St Lawrence defences, receiving support from Jean-Francois Pouliot, a renegade Liberal MP for Temiscouata, and at least two Union Nationale members of the Quebec legislature.[60]

The government moved quickly to rebut the charge that the gulf had been incompetently and weakly defended. Air minister Power supplied Godbout with AFHQ's detailed response to Laurent's articles. The latter were clearly an exaggeration. For example, in the incident concerning Mayor Keable of Mechins, which took place on 19 July, the mayor had informed the RCMP, not the RCAF. The RCMP had phoned the Mont Joli station and fifty-six minutes after the report, not 'a full eight hours,' the aircraft was over the position of the sighting.[61] Power also asked a Liberal organizer in Rimouski to approach Laurent and *L'Action catholique* with evidence disproving allegations of the navy's negligence. On 2 November Louis St Laurent, King's minister of justice, publicly declared that not forty, but only ten to fifteen ships had been sunk in the gulf, and on 24 November Macdonald announced that fourteen had been sunk in the gulf and another six in the Strait of Belle Isle and the Cabot Strait. No doubt to counterbalance the bad news, in mid-December Power released a colourful and detailed account of Pilot Officer R.S. Keetley's two attacks during September.[62]

Whatever the alarm and despondency, and however justified, one thing was certain: the RCAF had exerted enormous efforts to defend the gulf in 1942. Approximate figures compiled at command headquarters in December show that between May and October a total of 5126 operational flights took place in Eastern Air Command, of which 1590, or 31 per cent, were over the gulf.[63] Even this estimate does not reflect the full scale of gulf air operations, as it does not include flights over the Strait of Belle Isle, or the thousands of training flights from Summerside and Charlottetown. During the same period there were twenty-four air attacks on U-boats in Eastern Air Command. Of these, seven were in the gulf and two more in the Strait of Belle Isle. If the defence of the St Lawrence was a commitment the navy did not want, then the air force, to an important extent, stood in for the senior service.

There is no doubt that the German campaign in the gulf during 1942 scored a clear victory for Admiral Dönitz. Nineteen merchant ships and two escorts were sunk and the Canadians were forced to restrict the movement of ships to and from St Lawrence ports. In exchange, no U-boats had been destroyed and, despite the remarkable efforts of 113 (BR) Squadron, the air force and the navy proved unable to inflict lasting damage on a resourceful enemy. Ineffective tactical procedures and the unavailability of shallow-set Torpex depth charges prevented the sinking of a single submarine, but German records show it was air patrols more than any other single factor that kept the U-boats at bay in the Gulf of St Lawrence for three weeks after 16 September, and from 14 October until the end of the shipping season.

As the 1942 shipping season drew to a close the lessons of the year's campaign – including those bearing on domestic politics – were already shaping plans for the defence of the gulf in 1943. To co-ordinate the efforts of the three services and ensure co-operation with other federal departments and provincial authorities, in December 1942 the chiefs of staff appointed a committee under the chairmanship of Air Vice-Marshal N.R. Anderson, air member for air staff, with representatives from army and naval headquarters.[64]

The navy, determined to avoid an expanded commitment in the gulf, continued to restrict ocean-going traffic to the barest minimum during 1943. It was not possible, though, to stop the shipment from gulf ports of minerals, timber, and pulp and paper that were vital to the Allied war effort, nor to close down the coastal traffic that sustained much of the region.[65] The naval staff expected the air force to carry a heavy share of the inevitable burden. Captain H.N. Lay, director of the Operations Division at Naval Service Headquarters, reminded his air force counterparts that 'although in 1939 and 1940 U-Boats were operating principally in coastal waters around the British Isles, now, due to the excellent work of the RAF Coastal Command and many successful air attacks against U-boats, there were practically no U-Boats operating in these waters.' Lay concluded that 'provided adequate aircraft and suitable bases were available [the RCAF] could produce the same results in the Gulf ...'[66]

Air Vice-Marshal Anderson did not need to be given this advice; he certainly had every intention of emulating RAF Coastal Command, and prepared to make available almost double the forty-eight aircraft that had been in the area during periods of peak activity in the previous year, including those at Gander and Botwood, Nfld. The plan was to increase the strength of each squadron from between eight and twelve to fifteen aircraft, to send a Canso 'A' squadron (No 162) into the gulf and move 113 (BR), a Hudson squadron, from Yarmouth to Sydney, where it would reinforce the Catalina and Canso flying boats of No 117 and the Hudsons of 119 (BR). If required, 113 (BR) would send a detachment of five aircraft to Chatham, NB. Improved aircraft would also be available. No 113 was scheduled to re-equip with Lockheed Venturas, a medium-range bomber that resembled the Hudson but could fly faster (a maximum of 318 mph as compared to 250 mph for the Hudson) and carry six 250-lb depth charges in place of the Hudson's four. In the event of a major U-boat assault, the St Lawrence defences could be further strengthened by 150 Squadron, with fifteen Venturas, which was slated to organize at Yarmouth and earmarked for service in Western Air Command. The number of training aircraft at schools around the gulf would also rise; 386 would be available in 1943 as compared to 259 in 1942.[67]

This ambitious scheme depended on squadrons as yet unformed or in the early stages of organization, and there were differences between the views of the staffs in Halifax and Ottawa. Headquarters intended to concentrate the weight of the St Lawrence defences at Sydney, while Eastern Air Command wanted to distribute aircraft more evenly through the gulf, and use the additional Canso 'A' squadron, 162 (BR), elsewhere in the command. When aircraft began to move to the gulf at the end of April and the beginning of May 1943, the command view prevailed because it reflected the resources actually available.[68]

There was much more to do in preparing defences than allocating aircraft and warships. Experience in 1942 had shown that a stronger command structure and better interservice co-operation were essential. From the beginning of the 1943 season the station headquarters at Gaspé controlled Eastern Air Command units within the gulf, which were now known as No 5 or the 'Gulf' Group. No separate group headquarters was established, command being exercised by the station commander at Gaspé, which became a group captain's rather than a wing commander's appointment, and additional staff was provided to carry the increased operational responsibilities. The Gaspé headquarters, which had no control over the squadrons at Sydney and Botwood, possessed nothing like the independence of No 1 Group in Newfoundland, and in fact functioned as an advanced controller for Eastern Air Command.[69] The naval and air staffs at Gaspé continued to share a single operations building, but a combined operations room, like those in St John's and Halifax, appears never to have been established.

While both services professed that the arrangements at Gaspé were satisfactory, the logs of the gulf air controller for 1943-5 refer to the navy as a remote entity, and leave the impression that relations were still not so close as they might have been.[70] At Sydney, which played as large a role in gulf operations as Gaspé, Captain C.M.R. Schwerdt, the naval officer in charge, pressed for the establishment of a combined operations room. Because the air and navy operations rooms were miles apart, there was a greater need than at Gaspé, but Eastern Air Command balked, apparently because the navy wished the air force operations staff to move to the Point Edward naval base. Finally, in June 1943, at Admiral Murray's urging, the air force promised to send a liaison officer to the naval operations room.[71] Meanwhile, to improve co-operation at lower levels, aircraft from the squadrons allotted to the gulf participated in exercises with Fairmile flotillas, primarily in St Margarets Bay, from February to April 1943.[72]

Failures in communication had seriously hindered operations during 1942. On the advice of the army, navy, and air signals staffs, Anderson's co-ordinating committee recommended a far-reaching programme at the end of January 1943 that included over-lapping wireless, telephone, and teletype systems linking the gulf stations with Halifax (and in some cases Ottawa) for each of the three services. In addition, wireless communication was to be provided for the Aircraft Detection Corps and the units of the Reserve Army on coast watching duty, and civilian telephone and telegraph systems refurbished and extended throughout the gulf.[73]

The report of the Anderson committee received the Cabinet War Committee's approval in principle on 18 February 1943. By this time the Department of Munitions and Supply had formed a crown company, Defence Communications Limited, to carry out many projects in the vast Atlantic coast communications programme, of which the gulf's requirements were only a part.[74] Difficulties in dealing with many small telephone companies, unavailability of equipment, winter weather, and the physical isolation of much of the coastline frustrated the Anderson committee's hope that the principal improvements in the gulf communications could be completed by 1 May 1943. Nevertheless, good progress was made. On 19 May 1943, for example, the army, which was in charge of the construction of landlines along the north shore of the Gaspé peninsula, reported that work was well under way on the western sector, was about to begin on the eastern sector, and that a chain of wireless stations for interim communication was nearly ready for service. In the event, the landlines were finally reported complete in mid-September.[75]

Observers on shore were at best uncertain sources of information. In the narrow waters of the gulf, shore-based radar stations offered the promise of better reliability. The air force had no suitable equipment, but the National Research Council advised that the army's GL Mark III sets, normally used to control anti-aircraft artillery, would do the trick; tests suggested that a surfaced U-boat could be followed at ranges of 25,000 yards. At the end of March the army responded to the air force's request by allocating ten GL sets for deployment at intervals of roughly ten miles along the coast between Matane and Gaspé, and organizing No 1 Radio Direction Finding Operating Unit, Royal Canadian Artillery, to man the installations. On 1 June the first two sets began to operate and by July six were in service while another three were nearly complete. The stations reported by telephone to the air force operations room at Mont Joli.[76]

In the meantime the National Research Council was completing an experimental 'Microwave Early Warning' radar set which, by working on a short 10.7 centimetre wavelength, could detect surfaced submarines at greater ranges than existing equipment. By May the Treasury Board had approved an air force order for eight sets which were to be placed to cover the Cabot Strait, Strait of Belle Isle, and the Gaspé passage. Work rushed ahead in a crash programme; an experimental set was erected near Fox River on the Gaspé peninsula for tests during the 1943 season. As noted in Chapter 10, by the time the first operational sets were installed in 1944-5, the adoption of submerged tactics by U-boats had rendered them virtually useless and the programme was never completed.[77]

In making plans for the defence of the gulf the services could not ignore public alarm and anger in Quebec. In March 1943 controversy flared up again when

Onésime Gagnon, a Union Nationale member of the Quebec Legislative Assembly, declared that more than thirty ships had been sunk in the St Lawrence in 1942, rather than the twenty admitted by the navy. The Conservatives and members from Quebec in the House of Commons pressed Gagnon's allegations on the government and revived stories that had circulated in 1942 about the inadequacy and ineffiency of the gulf's defences. Once again the press both in Quebec and other provinces showed great interest in the disasters of 1942 and the squabbling among the politicians. J.-S. Roy, the unruly Independent member for Gaspé, cut closest to the quick with a detailed account of how the lighthouse keeper at Cap des Rosiers had vainly attempted to warn the air force about the presence of U-517 an hour and a half before it sank two ships on 15 September 1942.[78] Angus L. Macdonald counter-attacked as vigorously as he had the year before, pointing out that many more ships had been sunk in the gulf of Mexico than in the St Lawrence, and yet no American had suggested that 'the whole United States fleet should be diverted from its other duties to protect the gulf of Mexico.'[79] More sharply still, he referred to the failure of the British services in preventing the escape of the German battlecruisers *Scharnhorst* and *Gneisenau* up the English Channel: 'the St Lawrence river, at the point furthest inland where an attack was made last year, is thirty miles wide. This is almost like the open sea. It is wider than the straits of Dover between England and France. If the great British navy with all its experience and skill and strength and devotion to duty has not succeeded in making the straits of Dover absolutely safe from submarines – indeed only a year ago it was unable to prevent certain great enemy ships from going through the straits – if that cannot be done there, is it to be wondered at that we cannot guarantee complete immunity to ships in the river St Lawrence?'[80] Macdonald also tried to silence the government's critics by divulging a good deal of information. He named all of the ships that had been sunk in 1942, including *Charlottetown* and *Raccoon*, revealed that aircraft had made eight depth-charge attacks, admitted there was no confirmation that a U-boat had been destroyed, and went a considerable way towards confessing that communications had gone wrong on 15 September 1942. At the same time, he explained in some detail the offensive capabilities of U-boats and the difficulties of anti-submarine operations, including the undependability of most reports from shore observers.[81]

Even though there was no further serious controversy about the defence of the gulf, because of the low level of U-boat activity, the services were now fully alive to the importance of public relations in the areas around the gulf. As in 1942, the military attempted to soothe nerves and gain useful assistance by enlisting citizens in such organizations as the Reserve Army and the Aircraft Detection Corps, but that was not all. The government emphasized the need for close co-operation with the provincial and local authorities. On 12 March Anderson's committee met in Ottawa with representatives of the Quebec Provincial Police, the Royal Canadian Mounted Police, and the Air Raid Precaution organization to co-ordinate the work of those agencies, particularly in educating and winning the co-operation of the public. Later in the month, Air Commodore K.M. Guthrie, deputy air member for air staff, who had chaired the

Ottawa meeting on Anderson's behalf, travelled to Quebec City for a conference with the provincial and local service authorities on 26-7 March. Although Guthrie spoke little French, he had lived and served in Quebec and was sensitive to the language issue. He and his staff assured the conference that all members of the expanded Aircraft Detection Corps organization who had to work with the public would be bilingual, and that publicity would be conducted in both French and English. Commissioner Marcel Gaboury of the Quebec Provincial Police persuaded the conference that the Aircraft Detection Corps should have a highly visible liaison office in Quebec City, as Eastern Air Command Headquarters was too remote from the province. Aware of the central place of the Roman Catholic church, especially in rural Quebec, Guthrie also met with Cardinal Villeneuve, who confirmed that the clergy would support the various volunteer defence organizations.[82]

The Chiefs of Staff Committee agreed that an ADC liaison office should be set up in Quebec City, and nominated Wing Commander E.B. Goodspeed, deputy director of the ADC at AFHQ, for the task.[83] The Cabinet War Committee, however, asked the chiefs of staff to reconsider the appointment in light of 'language as well as technical qualifications.'[84] As a result, Squadron Leader J.P. Desloges, who had served in Canada since being injured in combat during the Battle of Britain while flying with 1 (F) Squadron, RCAF, was appointed 'Defence Co-ordination Officer.' Desloges was responsible for supervising the expansion of the ADC, and reporting to the chiefs of staff on co-operation between the services and provincial authorities 'in the Gaspe and lower St Lawrence River districts.'[85] His office also became the centre for publicity by all three services through radio broadcasts, press releases, and other publications.[86]

Experience showed that only through personal contact could citizens be interested in defence work. From the early spring through the fall of 1942, field parties of ADC officers travelled the Atlantic coast and Newfoundland giving talks illustrated by slides and distributing literature. By 30 September there were over 15,000 observers in the Maritimes, Quebec, and Newfoundland. Although no specific figures are available, Eastern Air Command must have come close to realizing its objective of increasing the number of observers in the gulf area from 3968 in December 1942 to 9943 by the end of 1943.[87]

In May 1943 the RCN started again the system of gulf convoys that had been developed in 1942. To escort the SQ-QS series and the Newfoundland convoys, three Bangor minesweepers and eight anti-submarine trawlers were based at Sydney. At Quebec City were four corvettes which escorted the NL-LN convoys to Goose Bay. Naval policy, however, was to take the offensive against the U-boats, using a support force of five Bangors, and a striking force comprising four flotillas of six Fairmile motor launches each. The Bangors, based at Gaspé, patrolled in pairs along routes which enabled them rapidly to reinforce a convoy under attack, or to pursue a submarine contact. With limited sea endurance, Fairmiles patrolled less often but were held ready to strike at a contact. One flotilla was based on Sydney, the other three at Gaspé.[88]

While staff officers worked out the last details of the plans, aircraft rushed to the gulf somewhat earlier than had been anticipated. In the late morning of 24

April a reliable observer – he was described as a 'broadcasting engineer' – at New Carlisle, PQ, sighted something suspicious about a mile out on the Baie de Chaleur. He checked with binoculars and was sure he saw a submarine. The ADC reported the sighting to Eastern Air Command, which diverted a Canso from 117 Squadron, Dartmouth, then on ice patrol, to the area. The Canso arrived two hours and thirty-nine minutes after the sighting, and was soon relieved by a Hudson of 11 Squadron which had flown direct from Dartmouth to perform a thorough search.[89]

Nothing turned up. Staff officers at Halifax judged that the sighting had to be 'viewed with reserve.'[90] Nevertheless, within an hour and a half, they ordered 119 Squadron at Sydney to send two Hudsons to Mont Joli and two to Chatham. Ice was clearing from the St Lawrence more quickly than had been expected, and therefore Eastern Air Command decided that personnel for the group organization and the rest of the squadron should move into the gulf as soon as possible. The Gulf Group controller began to operate at Gaspé on 1 May, and on 3-5 May the main body of 119 Squadron travelled to its new stations by rail. Mont Joli, where more accommodation was available than at Chatham, became squadron headquarters.[91]

By 11 May 113 Squadron's move from Yarmouth to Sydney was nearly complete and on 14 May 117 Squadron began to migrate from Dartmouth to North Sydney, establishing a detachment of three Cansos and a Catalina at Gaspé on 18-21 May. At the end of the month the operational aircraft at the gulf stations included No 119's twelve Hudsons at Mont Joli and Chatham, No 113's thirteen Venturas and five Hudsons (the latter were slated for disposal, in part to 119 Squadron) at Sydney, and No 117's four Cansos and eleven Catalinas at North Sydney and Gaspé.[92]

The build-up had been hastened by intelligence received from Naval Service Headquarters on 29 April, derived no doubt from decrypted German signals, that a U-boat would enter the gulf during the first week in May, 'presumably to land or pick up enemy agents.'[93] Unfortunately, there was no hint as to the boat's specific destination. Sighting reports on 30 April by fishermen at the northern entrance to the Northumberland Strait and by an Anson trainer to the east of Prince Edward Island's North Point – both, in fact, false – suggested that the submarine had come in early. Operational and training aircraft scoured the area, and during the following days, as squadrons earmarked for the gulf arrived at their stations, regular sweeps from the mouth of the St Lawrence River to the Cabot Strait were mounted. U-262 had entered through the Cabot Strait on the night of 26/27 April, and after a harrowing journey through pack ice that seriously damaged the boat, arrived off North Point, PEI, before dawn on 2 May, where, paradoxically, aircraft had been searching three days before. Here U-262, surfacing for only brief periods at night, waited in vain to pick up German prisoners of war who had failed to escape from their Canadian camp, and then left through the Cabot Strait on the night of 8/9 May.[94]

The air and sea forces in the gulf were active through the summer escorting convoys and responding to false alarms, but a second submarine, U-536, did not enter until 24 September. Its task, like that of U-262, was to rescue escaped prisoners of war. Alerted to the scheme by excellent intelligence, the navy made elaborate, though ultimately unsuccessful plans to trap the boat with a hunting group at the pick-up point in the Baie de Chaleur, but did not bring the RCAF into the picture. On 26 September a Catalina from 117 Squadron's Gaspé detachment did carry out a special sweep in the area at the navy's request, but during the following ten days the Gaspé and Chatham aircraft carried on with their normal sweeps in the central gulf.[95] Both U-262 and U-536 had failed in their missions, but their success in evading detection demonstrated that if submarines did not press attacks against shipping and did not operate on the surface they were as good as invisible to aircraft and warships.

Air sweeps and convoy escort operations continued until shipping stopped in mid-November for the freeze up. Eastern Air Command and Air Force Headquarters had continued to argue about the deployment of squadrons until late in the season. Headquarters' intention of quickly transferring 162 Squadron to the gulf, and thereby bringing the 1943 plan into effect, was frustrated by equipment and personnel problems that made the recently organized 160 Squadron unable to take over operations at Yarmouth until September. At that time I Group urgently needed reinforcements to support embattled ocean convoys; on 24 September 162 Squadron detached aircraft for operations from Gander and the American base at Stephenville, Nfld, and then on 5 October dispatched all available aircraft to Goose Bay, Labrador.[96] Important as the gulf was to Canada, the critical fight was on the ocean routes, and it was here that Eastern Air Command made its greatest contribution to Allied victory in the Battle of the Atlantic.

14

Ocean Operations, 1942

Although the scale of Eastern Air Command's commitment to shipping protection increased during 1942, the geographical scope of its northwest Atlantic operations remained within the agreements reached with the Americans the previous fall. Nova Scotia-based aircraft ranged southward to the limits of the US Eastern Sea Frontier and northeastwards to the Western Ocean Meeting Point off Newfoundland, where the naval escorts exchanged convoys. From Newfoundland to the north and east as far as its Douglas Digbys and Consolidated Cansos could reach, 1 Group took charge, while wedged in between the two Canadian zones was a pie-shaped sector to the southeast of Argentia where US Navy aircraft guarded shipping. The Boeing B-17 Flying Fortresses of the US Army Air Forces at Gander remained committed solely to the role of reconnaissance rather than defence of shipping and, because U-boat density was so low, made few detections. Their contribution to the anti-submarine battle was therefore only marginal. Although fewer U-boats hunted close in to Nova Scotia and Newfoundland after July, when Dönitz shifted his main effort to mid-ocean, Eastern Air Command could not let down its guard in coastal waters, or in the Gulf of St Lawrence, while the enemy continued to pick off victims in both theatres. The RCAF had to stretch its meagre resources to the limit to meet all these threats in the second half of the year, but its problems were certainly made worse by the failure to adopt Coastal Command's proven and more economical tactics until the end of October.

In the summer of 1942 the gap between effective land-based airpower on either side of the Atlantic had not yet been bridged. Coastal Command aircraft pushed patrols and escorts westward to about 600 miles from their British and Icelandic bases, while aircraft of No 1 Group in Newfoundland ranged eastward to somewhat lesser distances. The intervening 'air gap' ran in a funnel shape from its neck in the north, where air patrols from Newfoundland and Iceland left a relatively short distance uncovered, broadening to the south where a great expanse of ocean lay beyond the limits of land-based aircraft. Several factors complicated 1 Group's efforts to support shipping moving through this gap. In the prevailing westerly winds Cansos and Digbys lumbering home after a patrol were frequently reduced to desperately slow ground speed, thus reducing the operational radius even more than usual. Airmen of 1 Group learned to fly in conditions that were well below the minimums tolerated in Coastal Command.[1] Weather, both at the airfields and over the operational area, limited the effectiveness of Newfoundland-based aircraft in other ways as well. The mixing of warm Gulf Stream water and the icy Labrador Current produced almost perpetual fog on the Grand Banks, and the fog zone extended to about the maximum range of 1 Group aircraft. Thus U-boat packs were able to begin and continue attacks on convoys which were technically within an area where constant air patrols might otherwise have eliminated pack operations entirely. The story of the group's operations in the latter half of 1942 is one of inability to close the air gap and stop the carnage in that area, and also to prevent fog-shrouded submarines from operating with impunity even within range of its Cansos, Digbys, and Lockheed Hudsons.

These problems first manifested themselves in May and June, when Group *Hecht* moved into the northwest Atlantic to mount attacks on ocean convoys at the very limits of Newfoundland-based airpower. The RCAF responded by flying sweeps whenever the patrol line came within range, and by making attempts to escort threatened convoys. But the heavy fog which blunted *Hecht*'s persistent efforts to attack westbound convoys as they passed the Grand Banks also severely hampered flying operations. None of 1 Group's sweeps made contact with the wolf pack; indeed few of the aircraft flying escort missions were able to find the convoys they had been assigned to protect. The westbound slow convoy ONS 94 was located in the danger area by two Digbys on 20 May, and ONS 96 by a single aircraft eleven days later. But in both instances the U-boats' operations were hindered by heavy fog and the convoys were never attacked. On 11 June ONS 100 arrived off the Grand Banks, having already lost a corvette and two merchantmen and with the pack on its heels. For the next three days dense fog over the area prevented Catalinas from Botwood and US Navy aircraft from locating the convoy. Two more ships were lost before *Hecht* became embroiled with ONS 102 on the 16th. On the 18th, as a Botwood Catalina tried unsuccessfully to find the convoy in the fog, U-124 torpedoed *Seattle Spirit*. Heavy reinforcements, including effective air cover, arrived the next day and the enemy abandoned the chase. In all, the group was able to sink twelve ships during its brief stay on the main trade routes without loss or serious damage to its U-boats.[2] Much worse was yet to come, but for the moment the action shifted southward, where a handful of submarines cruising independently south and west of Nova Scotia were creating havoc.

On 30 May U-432 sank the small steamer *Sonia* south of Yarmouth. Three days afterwards Flying Officer J.M. Greer of 113 (BR) Squadron, escorting BX 23, a Boston-to-Halifax coastal convoy, depth-charged the same submarine while it was in pursuit of the convoy. The U-boat reported it had been 'Driven off by a strong air escort.'[3] Another Yarmouth Hudson and a USN 'blimp' airship were less successful on 9 June when U-432 attacked the Boston-to-Halifax convoy BX 23A, torpedoing the cargo ship *Kronprinsen*, which reached Shelburne under tow. A week later, in a night encounter with the Halifax-to-Boston convoy XB 25 off Cape Sable on 16 June, U-87 sank *Port Nicholson* and *Cherokee*. She then moved northeastward towards Halifax and was spotted on

22 June by a Hudson of 11 Squadron, whose depth-charge attack was far too late to have any effect. From first light on 23 June the squadron mounted an extensive five-aircraft search. A few hours later Pilot Officer W. Graham sighted U-87, surfaced and stopped. Upon sighting the aircraft the U-boat dived, but the conning tower and stern were still visible when Graham straddled the hull with four 250-lb depth charges. The U-boat log recorded the effects of Graham's attack:

Aircraft comes directly out of the sun which is just rising above the layer of fog and has a very strong dazzle effect. Submerged, as the Diesel is ... not working.
     After 25 seconds three well-placed aerial bombs drop astern below the U-boat. Boat falls steeply down by the head and drops rapidly. Checked fall by blowing out diving tank 3. Boat rises up to A-65 (65 metres below periscope depth). The electric motors won't start because, as was later established a number of spare parts and tools fell from their mountings into the electric motors. By means of trimming by the head U-boat brought up to depth. Went to A ± 0 (periscope depth) and made repairs. The boat is not leaking too badly ... Both compressor supports are cracked. The port compressor bearing bracket has been torn off. The flange of torpedo tube V is leaking. Torpedo tube V is warped. In the electric torpedo lying in this tube the battery has been pushed backward, the bolts on the thrust bearings are either broken or loosened; the port-side diesel engine-bed bolts are for the most part broken, the engine has been shifted sideways. The electric engine-bed bolts have been loosened; the shaft flange port-side bolt heads have been ripped off in some cases; 5 cells of the after battery have leaked out; most of the spare parts fastened to the overhead deck have been sprung out of their mountings (a hazard for the crew). Injuries: Machinist's Mate Haferbier a bruised foot. When the door between the electric engine room and the diesel compartment was ripped off he fell into the diesel compartment.[4]

This description is adequate testimony to the toughness of a U-boat and its crew. Only perfectly placed and powerful depth charges were likely to destroy such a target.
     Aircraft continued to hunt for one or more submarines suspected of being off Halifax, and on 28 June Squadron Leader W.C. Van Camp, the officer commanding 11 Squadron, found what was probably U-215 whilst on patrol with two other Hudsons of his unit. It was not the kind of night favoured by U-boat commanders, the sea being flat calm under a bright moon. Three of Van Camp's crew thought they saw 'The silhouette ... of something on the water up the moonbeam ... too short to be a ship.'[5] Turning and slipping off height he headed towards it. Four depth charges were dropped from the Hudson at 100 feet, spaced sixty feet apart, and set to explode at twenty-four feet. If the target was U-215 only her crew would have known how close the charges detonated, for the boat was lost with all hands on 3 July, sunk by the British trawler HMS Le Tigre during an attack on BX 27.
     Except in the St Lawrence River, there were no more sinkings of merchantmen or attacks on U-boats in the Canadian zone for some three weeks, but the first six months of 1942 had been disastrous. The magnitude of losses in the

Western Hemisphere in the first half of 1942 – a staggering 505 ships, 95 per cent of them steaming independently and for the most part in US waters, had been lost in exchange for only eleven U-boats – was never repeated, thanks to the progressive extension of the coastal convoy system.[6]

Declining U-boat successes eventually brought Dönitz to redeploy his forces. On 19 July he began to withdraw submarines from the US seaboard, instructing those that were able to do so to operate further south; a few continued to operate off southern Nova Scotia. Dönitz had also become aware that convoys along the main mid-Atlantic route adhered closely to the great circle route and could therefore be readily intercepted by wolf packs. On 9 July he had initiated a duplication of *Hecht*'s successful operation, ordering outward-bound boats to form Group *Wolf*, in the air gap, beyond the range of Allied aircraft.[7]

ON 113 was the first victim. It had just crossed the meridian of 40 degrees west when Group *Wolf* made contact on 25 July. Fog had grounded the Catalinas at Botwood, and although HMCS *St Croix* destroyed U-90, the submarines sank one ship and damaged another. A Digby from Gander arrived the next day and met the convoy far beyond the normal operational limits of that aircraft with the aid of radar, while USN aircraft from Argentia provided air escort from 26 to 28 July. One more ship from the convoy was sunk in this period, and another on 29 July south of Sable Island by U-132, operating off Nova Scotia after her victories in the St Lawrence. A Hudson crew of 11 Squadron on task in the poor visibility and gathering darkness 'had the rather harrassing experience of seeing a ship (*Pacific Pioneer*) torpedoed before their eyes ... without being able to make reprisals.'[8]

The next convoy to come under attack, ON 115, was intercepted by U-boats as it left the range of Coastal Command air cover on 29 July. It was harried all the way across the gap but the RCN escort was able to prevent losses and break contact. However, Group *Pirat* was placed ahead of ON 115 just outside the range of 1 Group aircraft and on 1 August re-established contact. *Pirat* pursued the convoy to well within reach of Eastern Air Command but under the cover of dense fog. The convoy lost two ships and had a third damaged in what should have been protected waters. The same bad weather allowed *Steinbrinck* and remnants of *Pirat* to locate the eastbound SC 94 northeast of St John's on 5 August. Without air support and lacking modern radar, the Canadian escort group was unable to break up the U-boat concentration or shake it off. On 6 August, when beyond range of Catalinas and Cansos, SC 94 began to suffer heavy losses – ten ships in exchange for two U-boats – until Coastal Command aircraft drove off the wolf packs and brought the engagement to a close on 10 August.[9]

While 1 Group was being frustrated in its attempts to influence the battle on the ocean routes, the Hudson squadrons in Nova Scotia struck at every one of the four boats still operating inshore. Pilot Officer Graham opened the run of attacks when he unsuccessfully depth-charged U-89 off Halifax on 30 July. Eastern Air Command knew that the submarine was in the vicinity, but Graham's crew only detected the boat because they kept a sharp lookout in pouring rain while making a routine harbour entrance patrol. Command Headquarters had in fact failed to pass on information confirming U-89's presence that had been provided by a new system for promulgating naval intelligence.[10]

Since the introduction of the *Triton* cipher (known to British cryptanalysts as *Shark*) in February 1942, which Bletchley Park could not immediately penetrate, Allied intelligence had been largely dependent on high frequency direction finding [HF/DF], and Canadian capabilities with this technique were improving dramatically. The RCN's Operational Intelligence Centre [OIC] in Ottawa, using the HD/DF organization developed in co-operation with the Department of Transport, and to a lesser extent the RCAF, had become one of the two U-boat plotting centres for the Western Atlantic in April 1942. (The other was the US Navy's OP-20-G in Washington.) However, until July 1942 HF/DF information transmitted by signals tended to arrive in Halifax too late to have any operational value. Air Force Headquarters [AFHQ] in Ottawa therefore set up a system of passing immediate DF information received from the OIC to Eastern Air Command's operations room by commercial telephone, using a simple plain language 'Vitamin' code (words like 'pear,' 'apple,' 'grapefruit') to identify U-boats and the word 'ripe' to indicate warships or raiders.[11] At the same time, because of powerful new transmitters provided by the RAF at St John's and Halifax, it was now possible to maintain contact with aircraft at great distances and to communicate directly with Coastal Command in the United Kingdom.[12]

Within twenty-four hours of Graham's attack on U-89, the telephone link brought success for 113 Squadron at Yarmouth. Squadron Leader N.E. Small, who had assumed command of the unit only five weeks before, was an enthusiastic proponent of naval intelligence, designing patrols to cover probable U-boat locations and maintaining aircraft at base on immediate alert to respond to 'hot' DF bearings. As mentioned in the preceding chapter, Small was also the first squadron commander in Eastern Air Command to introduce white aircraft camouflage and high patrol altitudes in accordance with the latest British methods.[13]

All of these elements came together on 31 July when Small himself surprised U-754 south of Yarmouth. He and his crew, Pilot Officer G.E. Francis, observer, and Sergeants R.A. Coulter and D.P. Rogers, wireless operators (air gunner), were on a special sweep at an altitude of 3000 feet in response to fresh intelligence. The weather was ideal, a slight summer haze making visibility poor from the surface of the water. Three miles ahead the U-boat, quietly cruising along, was taken quite unawares as the Hudson dived to the attack. Sailors were seen scrambling for the hatch, and most of the boat was still visible when the depth charges went tumbling down around it. Small stayed over the spot for almost an hour. On the third circuit the front gunner opened fire when the conning tower briefly reappeared. Large air bubbles continued to surface until a heavy underwater explosion brought a large quantity of oil swirling up to mark the grave of U-754 – Eastern Air Command's first kill.[14]

A few hours later Pilot Officer G.T. Sayre of 113 Squadron attacked U-132, and Small also attacked U-458 on 2 August and U-89 on 5 August. None of these strikes was successful, but all had resulted from recent DF bearings on U-boat transmissions.[15] The chief of the air staff immediately began to dispatch the navy's daily estimates of submarine locations to Eastern Air Command Headquarters and No 1 Group so that airmen on the east coast could plan patrols on the basis of the fullest possible picture of enemy movements. AFHQ also organized a course on U-boat intelligence at the navy's OIC for those airmen most initimately concerned with bomber-reconnaissance operations. The air officer commanding [AOC], Air Vice-Marshal A.A.L. Cuffe, in the meantime, posted Small to Eastern Air Command Headquarters as controller to ensure that the staff in the operations room never again failed to promulgate intelligence as they had done on 30 July. Yet Cuffe's eminently sensible suggestion for a closed and secure telephone line between Naval Service Headquarters and Eastern Air Command operations switchboards, with connections to other air force and navy exchanges, was not acted upon for four months.[16] Despite 113 Squadron's success off Yarmouth, moreover, the Coastal Command techniques that the unit had adopted were not generally applied throughout Eastern Air Command until mid-autmnn.

An experiment that enjoyed much less success than the new methods for employing intelligence came to an abrupt halt in August. Because of sightings and DF reports of submarines in the vicinity of Sable Island, a Royal Navy Fleet Air Arm detachment with a radar-equipped Supermarine Walrus had been sent there in May, the RCAF providing a work party to build the 'station' and, later, an observer for the aircraft. The Walrus, affectionately known as the 'Shagbat,' was an amphibian biplane of prewar vintage that derived its motive power from a single pusher propeller. During flight, 'She wallows in the trough of the rough airs like a heifer knee deep in a boggy meadow,' wrote one Fleet Air Arm pilot. Under the orders of the Dartmouth controller, the Walrus flew daily patrols from a small lake on the island whenever the weather permitted, which was not often, until 20 August when it came to grief. After spending three days floating around, the crew was rescued by ships of convoy HX 204; the aircraft subsequently sank whilst under tow by the corvette *Napanee*. It was then decided to abandon the Sable Island patrol for the rest of the 1942 season and the detachment withdrew.[17]

For the rest of August Eastern Air Command only heard the faint echoes of convoy battles beyond the reach of its aircraft. Not until the end of the month did three Type IX U-boats, on passage south of Iceland, move westward to test the summer traffic in the Belle Isle Strait, an area previously left in peace. Two of them, U-517 and U-165, entered the Gulf of St Lawrence, an episode discussed in Chapter 13. The other, U-513, patrolled southeast of Newfoundland and on 5 September sank *Saganaga* and *Lord Strathcona* in short order as they lay off Bell Island, in Conception Bay. Gunfire was directed at U-513 and she reported having her 'conning-tower damaged as a result of ramming.'[18] A Hudson of 145 Squadron and two Digbys of 10 Squadron were quickly on the scene, but with a ceiling of only 200 feet over the anchorage they could do little to assist in the counterattack. U-513 made its presence felt again by damaging the freighter *Ocean Vagabond* in a torpedo attack a few miles off St John's on 29 September.

No 1 Group meanwhile ordered patrols at extreme range to reach convoys threatened by large U-boat groups. On 10 September the westbound ON 127 passed the southern end of a long line of thirteen submarines, Group *Vorwärts*, and there ensued an orgy of sinkings. At 1605 hours GMT on 13 September,

Flying Officer R.M. MacLennan, piloting a Catalina from Botwood, spotted the partially surfaced U-96, unfortunately too far away to attack before she submerged. Three-quarters of an hour later in 'the farthest east sighting' yet made, 550 miles east of St John's, the Catalina made contact with the beleaguered ON 127. A second Catalina picked up the convoy and its RCN escort at 2050 hours GMT and commenced a radar patrol around it in the darkness. Meanwhile, the ships responded to a U-boat alarm by firing illumination rockets, the standard procedure during night attack. The aircraft tried to help the escorts but 'due to faulty connection the parachute flares which were dropped ... failed to light,' and 'no attack could be made.'[19] At 0400 hours GMT on 14 September the Catalina had to depart thirty-five minutes after helplessly watching the destroyer *Ottawa*, stationed five miles ahead of the convoy, being torpedoed and sunk by U-91. Dönitz took note, for the first time and with some surprise, of the existence of long-range aircraft based in Newfoundland.[20]

What the RCAF really wanted was very long-range [VLR] Consolidated B-24 Liberators, such as those now being developed and operated from Iceland by 120 Squadron, RAF. In fact, on 11 September a 120 Squadron Liberator, benefiting from modifications that gave it extended endurance, had penetrated further into the air gap than any of its predecessors, although with no discernible result. Because the VLR Liberator came to play such an important part in the fortunes of Eastern Air Command, and because it is easy to confuse the various types of long and very long-range Liberators, it is important to understand what 120 Squadron was doing with its aircraft to obtain such greatly enhanced performance. The standard Liberator heavy bomber of the day had a maximum operational range of about 1700 nautical miles, which gave it an operational radius of about 700 miles. Modifications begun in 1942 eventually took two forms. Class 'A' VLR aircraft were to be Mark V Liberators from which the rubberized self-sealing compounds had been removed from inside the main wing tanks, and which were fitted with auxiliary wing tanks. Class 'B' conversions took various forms, the first of which was a modification of the Mark III Liberators whose delivery to Coastal Command had begun in late 1942. This type was not equipped with auxiliary wing tanks, nor was it possible to remove the self-sealing material from the main tanks. Extended range was therefore obtained by placing two fuel tanks in the bomb bay and removing equipment not strictly necessary for anti-submarine work including the tail and mid-upper gun turrets, much of the armour, oxygen equipment, bomb winches, all but the barest minimum of de-icing equipment, and the auxiliary power unit. These were probably the modifications done by 120 Squadron to give its Mark I Liberators a total range of 2300 miles with a depth-charge load of 1500 pounds and enable them to operate 700-1000 miles from shore bases. In 1943 the class 'B' conversions had the same capabilities, and, with a total range of 2600 miles, the class 'A' conversions had a somewhat greater endurance in the air gap.[21]

When asked by the British in the late summer of 1942 to extend air patrols to 800 miles from Newfoundland, Air Marshal L.S. Breadner, the chief of the air staff, pointed out the need for VLR aircraft in Eastern Air Command. Why neither the United States nor the United Kingdom would spare Liberators for the

RCAF, even after the need became obvious, is a complicated question that will be discussed in the next chapter.

The organization and performance of existing anti-submarine forces on the east coast still left much room for improvement, however. The first visitors to point this out, in July 1942, were Wing Commanders S.R. Gibbs and P.F. Canning of the RAF, who had recently spent eight months advising the USAAF on the organization of operational control, the creation of combined operations rooms, and the establishment of an anti-submarine command along the lines of RAF Coastal Command. Gibbs found two principal matters of concern in the organization of Eastern Air Command. First, he thought the organization was far too complex 'due to responsibility ... for [the] total air defence of Eastern Canada.'[22] Second, although liaison with the navy seemed to be as good as the system allowed, the lack of a combined services headquarters was a severe limitation.

In October Commander P.B. Martineau, RN, a staff officer from Coastal Command HQ, also on the last leg of a long advisory tour in America, found more to criticize in his report: 'Generally speaking the Eastern Air Command is a very long way behind any other place I visited in either Canada or the United States ...'[23] First and foremost, he recommended the adoption of Coastal Command's 'Offensive Tactics'; Eastern Air Command's efforts to escort every convoy whether it was threatened or not followed the tactical practice that the RAF had abandoned eighteen months before.

Martineau was not the first to acquaint Canadian air force authorities with offensive methods. As early as November 1941, Air Chief Marshal P.B. Joubert de la Ferté had described the new tactics to Air Vice-Marshal N.R. Anderson, then commanding Eastern Air Command, in a personal letter. Thereafter, RCAF headquarters in both Ottawa and Halifax had received memoranda and studies that evaluated the success of offensive methods in pushing the U-boats back 350 miles from Coastal Command bases. In March 1942 J.P.T. Pearman of the Coastal Command operational research section had visited Eastern Air Command to make statistical analyses of the RCAF's effort. Reports he completed for the Canadians in March and August showed that most of Eastern Air Command's flying was within 200 miles of base, thereby failing to strike at U-boats until they had actually reached focal areas of trade and coastal routes, where they could to the most damage. However, perhaps because the RCAF was not yet attuned to mathematical analysis – Eastern Air Command's own operational research section began to organize only in November 1942 – the personal arguments of Commander Martineau were required in order to bring a change. His advice was accepted immediately, perhaps because changes were in the offing anyway. When, in July, Naval Service Headquarters had begun to provide timely U-boat intelligence to Eastern Air Command, airmen had seen that operations ought to be concentrated on the probable locations of U-boats, if this could be done without unduly prejudicing the safety of convoys. Indeed, the RCAF's 'offensive' in the central Gulf of St Lawrence in late September had been an attempt at implementing this principle.[24]

With the concurrence of the RCN, Eastern Air Command applied offensive tactics off the Newfoundland coast for the first time on 30 October 1942. Coverage of areas where intelligence reported U-boats was to have a high priority. Convoy protection would now take the form of sweeps along parallel tracks fifty miles on either side of the mean line of advance, fifty miles to the rear and one hundred miles ahead, preferably in the last hours of daylight or immediately after sunrise when submarines were manoeuvring for attack or shadowing positions. Close escort was to be provided only to convoys known to be in danger and to shipping in confined waters such as the Gulf of St Lawrence. To make this new system work properly Martineau persuaded Ottawa to install what Cuffe had suggested in August, a direct telephone line from Naval Service Headquarters to Eastern Air Command. The 'Vitamin' code was also improved so that more than just the simple details of a DF fix could be passed quickly to the coast.[25]

Other criticisms concerned general procedures. There appeared, Commander Martineau reported, 'to be no decided policy of how to carry out A/S warfare from aircraft.' And in the same context, he 'was horrified to find on visiting the various airports how backward the pilots were.'[26] The Canadians emphatically denied the first charge: the command's squadrons were directed by the 'Manual of Eastern Air Command Operational Control,' and Coastal Command material, they said, was promulgated regularly thoughout the organization. This was true up to a point. Initially, tactical memoranda and instructions from overseas were sent around with a general order that they were to be followed. Subsequent instructions, however, circulated in their original Coastal Command format and never took the form of Eastern Air Command operational orders. The initial general order to adopt practices outlined in the memorandum and instructions was quickly forgotten and squadrons believed that the material was being circulated for 'information only.' Moreover, circulation among aircrew was slow and the adoption of the new tactics was totally dependent on the initiative of individual squadron commanders. In 1942 Squadron Leader Small's 113 Squadron was the only one in Eastern Air Command successfully applying the latest Coastal Command tactics. Martineau blamed the senior officers of Eastern Air Command for this general lack of leadership, and with that it is hard to disagree.[27]

On the second point regarding the backwardness of pilots, Cuffe did admit that standards were low in some of the operational squadrons because the command was still being 'bled' of experienced pilots and their replacements in many cases came straight from service flying training schools [SFTS]. The real problem, he felt, was that 'we have not enough aircraft and crews either for training or operations.'[28] To prove his point, a spot check on 15 October showed that only eighty-nine of the command's establishment of 135 bomber-reconnaissance aircraft were actually on strength. Of these aircraft, nine were allotted to training duties. Serviceability among the eighty remaining aircraft was about 60 per cent (a not unreasonable figure by the standards of the time), which left only about fifty aircraft normally available for operations on the whole east coast of Canada and off Newfoundland.[29] Ironically, the adverse effects of the lack of aircraft for operations and training might have been far less if the offensive method, which was designed to save hours of wasted flying, had been adopted earlier.

A paper by Martineau outlining all his findings and proposals was discussed at interservice staff meetings in Ottawa on 1 and 3 November. The Canadian officers present, Wing Commander C.L. Annis and, from Naval Service Headquarters, Captain H.N. Lay, director of Operations Division, Captain H.G. DeWolf, director of Plans Division, Commander G.A. Worth, director of Signals Division, and Lieutenant-Commander J.S. Stead, staff officer (air), urged that the northwest Atlantic finally be upgraded to the status of an important war zone for the allocation of equipment and well-trained personnel and that it be 'recognized as a joint commitment of the RCN and RCAF.'[30]

While the Canadians accepted most of the recommendations made by Martineau, Gibbs, and Canning, they balked at giving anti-submarine operational control on the east coast to one single authority. Senior officers cited as their reason the present 'excellent co-operation between C.O.A.C. [commanding officer Atlantic Coast], F.O.N.F. [flag officer Newfoundland], and A.O.C., E.A.C.,'[31] ignoring the well-established need for a still closer relationship. There was excellent co-operation between air force and naval authorities on the other side of the Atlantic, but they still found it necessary to place their anti-submarine resources under one operational commander. On the more specific points raised by Martineau, the meeting was in full agreement with the adoption of an offensive/defensive policy, based on anti-submarine intelligence, joint operations being conducted from a temporary facility until a new combined operations room could be provided in Halifax.

Despite the agreement in Ottawa, the creation of a combined operations room in Halifax was still fraught with difficulties. Air Vice-Marshal Cuffe, noting that several British area combined headquarters were located at some distance from naval dockyards, invited Rear-Admiral L.W. Murray, commanding officer Atlantic Coast, to move to Eastern Air Command's operations room. Murray responded that his broad responsibilites for naval operations and the control of merchant shipping made it impossible for him to do so, and he in turn invited Cuffe to come to the dockyard. Thus the manoeuvres begun in 1939 continued, with positions now so entrenched that the vice-chief of the naval staff urged that the whole question had to be approached 'most tactfully.'[32]

The development of further interservice co-operation in Ottawa was stalled as well. Commander C. Thompson, RN, a destroyer captain in the RCN's Western Local Escort Force who had had extensive experience in air operations and accompanied Martineau on his tour, emphasized the need for standard and comprehensive instructions to guide co-operation between aircraft and warships. For this purpose, and to address related interservice questions of tactics, equipment and training, the chiefs of the air and naval staffs agreed in January 1943 to the formation of a joint RCN-RCAF anti-submarine warfare committee with representatives from the interested divisions and directorates at Naval Service and Air Force Headquarters. Neither service took any action.[33]

More encouragingly, an RCAF operational research organization was taking shape. Impressed with the achievements of the RAF operational research sections, such senior officers as Air Marshal H. Edwards, Air Vice-Marshal N.R. Anderson, and Air Vice-Marshal E.W. Stedman promoted similar ideas in Canada. During his tour of duty in North America, J.P.T. Pearman, the Coastal Command operational researcher, lent assistance, and advised the USN on the organization of its Anti-Submarine Warfare Operations Research Group [ASWORG] as well. In August 1942 Professor J.O. Wilhelm, a physicist from the University of Toronto, established an operational research centre at AFHQ and Professor Colin Barnes, another University of Toronto physicist, organized an operational research section in Halifax at the end of November. Barnes, and the two other scientists who joined his staff, had visited the United Kingdom to learn RAF methods, and in August 1943 Ottawa posted a scientific liaison officer to RCAF Overseas Headquarters in London. Such was British leadership in the field that the USN researchers also depended upon advice and data from the United Kingdom. Like their American and British counterparts, Barnes and his colleagues at Eastern Air Command Headquarters worked closely with the intelligence staff to produce analytical statistical reports on air operations, and also undertook special studies in such areas as bombing accuracy, the employment of airborne radar, and sea-air radio homing to improve the command's effectiveness.[34]

However haltingly the Canadians adopted British models for command and control, the new anti-submarine tactics quickly proved themselves in the northwest Atlantic. During October 1942 No 1 Group participated in the defence of two eastbound convoys, SC 104 and SC 107, which were intercepted by submarine wolf packs. In the first case air support took the old form of close escort by aircraft flying at an altitude of around 1000 feet and had little effect. In the second, aircraft patrolling at high altitudes also covered areas where intelligence had located U-boats, and swept the tracks of the convoy in accordance with the new offensive methods. The result was the first successes by the RCAF in Newfoundland.

By the second week in October 1942 the Germans realized that convoys were no longer strictly following the great circle route. Group *Wotan* lay in wait 300 miles northeast of Newfoundland. Further east eight boats had just been detached from another line to form a new Group *Leopard* to hit ONS 136, an attack which failed. The *Leopard* line then came around to a westerly course in search of the luckless SC 104.

Air protection for the convoy was provided by US Navy PBYs from Argentia on 9 October, and the next day by two Hudsons from 145 Squadron, Torbay. On 11 October, as shore authorities attempted to edge the convoy around the northern tip of Group *Wotan*, Digbys of 10 Squadron provided continuous coverage for over fourteen hours. Unfortunately, they did not prevent U-258 catching sight of one of the escort vessels slipping away to the northeast, although in a failure of German communications the boat's report was delayed for twelve hours. In the meantime, attempts by 1 Group to renew air support on the 12th were frustrated by bad weather, and the lone 116 Squadron Catalina to reach SC 104 failed to make contact and was reduced to flying sweeps in the general area. On the same day the first member of *Wotan* drawn northward by the sighting report, U-221, made contact and over the next two nights, as U-607 and U-661 joined in the attack, eight ships were sunk. By the time RCAF aircraft were once again able to reach the scene of the battle, on the 14th, the airmen could only drop emergency kits to survivors as SC 104 steamed out of range into the air gap, through seas whipped up by a westerly gale, which sharply reduced the efficacy of escort vessels' radar and ASDIC equipment. Moreover, by now SC 104 was also in contact with Group *Leopard*. Improving weather enabled naval escorts to prevent any further losses until the convoy came under the protection of 120 Squadron Liberators from Iceland. The combined air and sea escorts accounted for three U-boats in the last days of the battle, and the remaining U-boats finally turned westward again on 19 October to form Group *Veilchen*, 400 miles east of Newfoundland.[35]

By 29 October the thirteen U-boats of *Veilchen* were on station on the Grand Banks. In addition, three large Type IX boats, U-522, U-520, and U-521, bound for the St Lawrence and Halifax areas, were south of Newfoundland. That day the southernmost boat of *Veilchen* sighted a westbound convoy and the line was shifted slightly to the southwest. Dönitz also received a decryption from German naval intelligence indicating that the eastbound SC 107 would be steering northeast from the Western Ocean Meeting Point off Cape Race.[36]

The gathering concentration of U-boats off Newfoundland provided Eastern Air Command with an opportunity to put offensive tactics to the test. At 0905 hours GMT on 30 October, 1 Group sent out two Hudsons of 145 Squadron on an anti-submarine sweep ahead of SC 107 to cover an area identified in NSHQ's routine U-boat forecast of the previous day.[37] Almost at the limit of their endurance, some 290 miles northeast of Torbay, they sighted a conning tower breaking surface two miles ahead at 1205 hours GMT. Flying Officer E.L. Robinson immediately began his run in from 2000 feet. It was one of those rare occasions when everything clicked into place: 'at the time the depth-charges were released the U-boat was almost fully surfaced. Four 250-lbs Mk. VIII depth-charges with Mk. XIII pistol set to 25 feet at an angle of 30 [degrees] across the U-boat from port astern to starboard bow. All the charges functioned correctly and explosions were noted bracketing the U-boat, the center two charges on opposite sides of the hull and very close to it. The explosion raised the U-boat in the water and 60 feet of its stern raised on an angle of 40° to the horizontal. The U-boat then settled and a large oil slick and air bubbles merging with the rough sea appeared immediately.'[38] Both Hudsons remained over the spot for fifty minutes before they had to fly home, a relief aircraft being on its way. Robinson and his crew had sent U-658 to the bottom in 2000 fathoms,[39] a feat which brought the pilot the Distinguished Flying Cross.

Another success was only hours away. At 2002 hours GMT a Digby of 10 Squadron, on the way back to Gander from an outer anti-submarine patrol with ON 140, came upon U-520 115 miles due east of St John's. Flying Officer D.F. Raymes made his approach directly along its track from astern, descending from an altitude of 3200 feet. After the explosion of the four 450-lb Mark VII Amatol-filled charges, the co-pilot, Pilot Officer J. Leigh, watched huge air bubbles and large quantities of oil come to the surface until darkness fell some

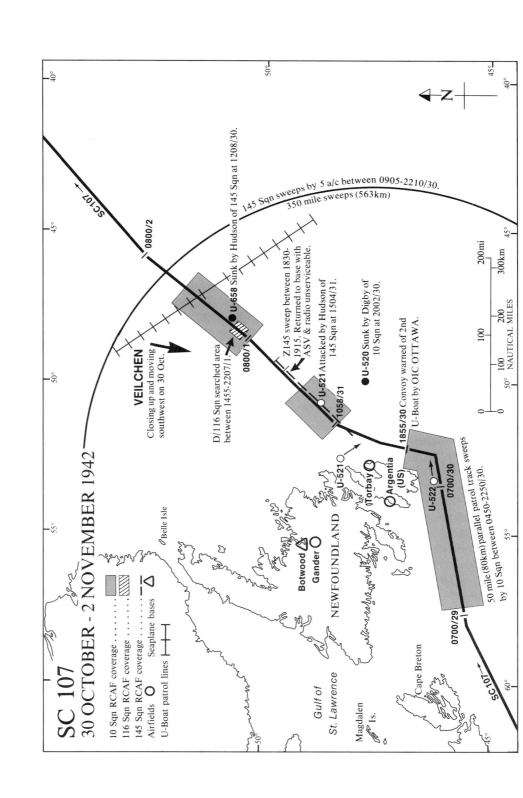

SC 107
30 OCTOBER - 2 NOVEMBER 1942

10 Sqn RCAF coverage . . . .
116 Sqn RCAF coverage . . . .
145 Sqn RCAF coverage . . . .
Airfields   ○
Seaplane bases   △
U-Boat patrol lines

N

40°   45°   50°   55°   60°

50°
45°
45°

SC-107

0800/2

U-658 Sunk by Hudson of 145 Sqn at 1208/30.

145 Sqn sweeps by 5 a/c between 0905-2210/30.
350 mile sweeps (563km)

VEILCHEN

Closing up and moving
southwest on 30 Oct.

Z145 sweep between 1830-
1915. Returned to base with
ASV & radio unserviceable.

D/116 Sqn searched area
between 1455-2207/1.

0800/1

U-521 Attacked by Hudson of
145 Sqn at 1504/31.

1058/31

U-520 Sunk by Digby of
10 Sqn at 2002/30.

1855/30 Convoy warned of 2nd
U-Boat by OIC OTTAWA.

0700/30

50 mile (80km) parallel patrol track sweeps
by 10 Sqn between 0450-2250/30.

0700/29

U-521 ○

Torbay ○

Argentia
(US) ○

U-522 ○

Botwood △
Gander ○

NEWFOUNDLAND

Gulf of
St. Lawrence

Magdalen
Is.

Cape Breton

Belle Isle

SC-107

0   50   100   200   NAUTICAL MILES
0   100   100   200   200mi
0   300km

thirty minutes later. His conclusion that 'the submarine was at a dead stop directly below' was only too true; they had destroyed U-520.[40]

Unfortunately for SC 107, the destruction of two U-boats did not materially alter the course of the battle. On 31 October 145 Squadron had four Hudsons sweeping the track of SC 107 between 0915 hours GMT and 2155 hours GMT in steadily deteriorating weather conditions of rain squalls and high wind. An object sighted after a radar detection by one of them, flying parallel to the convoy and eleven miles to port of its track, appeared at first to be a destroyer. But from 5000 yards Pilot Officer L.T. Ross recognized it to be a fully surfaced submarine and as he passed close over it, too quickly to deliver an attack, a single oilskin-clad member of the crew was seen on the conning tower. Turning steeply to port Ross came at the submarine again while it was taking a 90 degree evasive turn to starboard so that he attacked at right angles to its starboard beam. At 1505 hours GMT the depth charges appeared to explode within lethal range; it was, the assessors later observed, an 'excellent attack deserving of more concrete evidence of damage.'[41] U-521, however, survived. A hunt by other Hudsons and the corvette *Moose Jaw* on her way to join SC 107 found only streaks of oil, probably squeezed out of the compression valves on the U-boat's fuel tanks.

Meanwhile, SC 107 was approaching the U-boat concentration with HX 213 also steaming into danger not too far behind. The first of two 116 Squadron Catalinas from Botwood sent out on 1 November to support SC 107 and its RCN escort group briefly contacted the convoy in the dark and then lost it when the aircraft's radar broke down.[42] The convoy crossed the German line through the gap left by the sinking of U-658 two days earlier, but it did not go unseen. Nine miles away U-381 surfaced to send off her first sighting report, which was intercepted by the DF operators in HMCS *Restigouche* and the rescue ship *Stockport*; because the Catalina on task could not find the convoy, no aircraft was on hand to drive off the submarine. On the following days weather conditions prevented the Catalinas from flying, and since no other aircraft had the range to cover the convoy, it found itself effectively in the air gap when only 400 miles from Newfoundland. On the night of 1/2 November the U-boats began to pick off merchantmen and by the time Liberators from Iceland finally drove them away on 5 November they had sunk fifteen out of the forty-two ships originally in SC 107.[43]

Although the battle for SC 107 had ended in a defeat it marked an important turning point in the fortunes of Eastern Air Command. In contrast to the recent battle for SC 104, Canadian airmen had demonstrated that when properly directed they were more than a match for U-boats that ventured within range. Hudsons sweeping ahead of the convoy in search of *Veilchen* had sunk one submarine and driven off a key shadowing U-boat. As a bonus, one U-boat had also been sunk along the main convoy lanes by a Digby returning from a distant patrol.

The fundamental change in RCAF methods that occurred at the end of October 1942 caused repercussions in the complex Canadian-American air operational control system in Newfoundland. In accordance with the agreements reached in late 1941, Rear Admiral R.M. Brainard (who had taken command at Argentia after the death of Admiral Bristol in April 1942) controlled air forces in the northwest Atlantic by means of a daily signal covering flying activities from Newfoundland bases for the following day. His wording deferred to the niceties of the situation. There were 'orders' for Brainard's own USN squadrons, 'proposals' for 1 Group, RCAF, and, from October onwards when the US Army made available four B-17s for convoy duty, 'requests' for the employment of USAAF aircraft. The three commands then replied that they would comply, or comply with exceptions or additions.[44]

Operations by 1 Group during the period 30 October-2 November satisfied both American demands and the new Canadian tactics: Hudsons and Catalinas took care of SC 107 while Digbys of 10 Squadron supported other threatened convoys.[45] But once the *Veilchen* boats moved out beyond the reach of aircraft and were no longer a menace to shipping in the Newfoundland area, the RCAF increasingly failed to provide all the patrols proposed by the American admiral. The matter came to a head on 12 November when 1 Group refused to supply air cover for SG 12 as Brainard had asked because there were 'no submarines within 200 miles according to NSHQ estimates.'[46] Brainard believed that the Canadian's problem was simply a shortage of aircraft. The American command at Argentia was in fact becoming an obstacle to Canadian efforts to introduce proven British methods.

Brainard, however, was right about the shortage of aircraft in 1 Group. By the second week of November three of the four Catalinas of 116 Squadron's Botwood detachment were unserviceable. Even after the arrival of two relief aircraft from Dartmouth, severe winter weather precluded operations, and on 19 November the detachment was recalled. Its responsibilities were assigned to 145 Squadron Hudsons from Torbay, but the Hudsons also suffered from a shortage of spares and unserviceable aircraft as did 10 Squadron's Digbys at Gander. Not surprisingly, then, Brainard had asked that he 'be advised daily as to the number and type of aircraft ... available the following day for air coverage assignment thus permitting ... proposals being ... issued in a form that permits of accomplishment.'[47] The matter rested there for the moment.

As SC 107 departed, German pressure eased on ocean convoys in the Canadian zone. Four submarines only, U-518, U-106, U-43, and U-183, remained, with roving commissions inshore and operations by the first three of these boats included patrols in the Gulf of St Lawrence, described separately in Chapter 13. Outside the gulf, U-518 struck first. In the early morning of 2 November the submarine dodged a Bangor class minesweeper and two Fairmiles on patrol in the Wabana anchorage to sink two vessels and slightly damage a third alongside the loading wharf. Unscathed, U-518 continued its cruise down the east coast of Newfoundland to an unexpected rendezvous a day later with a Digby on an offensive sweep from Gander. Flying Officer J.H. Sanderson came in across the submarine's starboard bow at eighty feet, dropping four Mark VII charges spaced twenty feet apart.[48] But, as so often happened, the U-boat had spotted the aircraft first and was well out of danger in the depths.

On 17 November aircraft found two more of the U-boats operating inshore. An offensive sweep in support of ON 142 by a Digby of 10 Squadron revealed what appeared to be a Fairmile motor launch throwing up a strong wake. The fact that there were no binoculars on board the aircraft did not help identification and U-183 was well submerged before six Mark VIII depth charges hurtled down on its final swirl. The aircraft had nevertheless done what was required; ON 142 was not attacked. A Canso 'A' from 5 Squadron, recently deployed to Gander, had already prevented U-boats from establishing firm contact with another convoy off Newfoundland earlier in the day by forcing U-43 to submerge ten miles astern of SC 109.[49] Unfortunately, U-43 regained contact and torpedoed the freighter *Brilliant* the following morning, but the RCN escort was able to hold the U-boats at bay after that.

No air cover, however, had been provided when U-518 fell in with convoy ON 145 a few days later, and that unhappy fact demonstrated the weakness of divided Canadian and American control in the northwest Atlantic. In the early hours of 21 November, the submarine sank one ship in the convoy and damaged two others about 200 miles south of Placentia Bay. This almost certainly could have been avoided if aircraft had provided cover all day on the 20th, especially during the vital period at dusk. Argentia, in whose flying area the convoy was travelling, was fog-bound; three aircraft from Sydney, NS, carried out an offensive sweep as far east as 55 degrees west, but the USAAF's Gander-based B-17s allocated to convoy defence failed to respond to RCAF requests for assistance. This lamentable lack of co-operation between US and Canadian forces gave further impetus to the campaign, now underway in Ottawa and discussed in Chapter 15, to have all sea and air anti-submarine forces on the east coast brought under one Canadian authority.[50]

Autumn ended with the inconclusive depth-charging of an unidentified U-boat by a Hudson of 145 Squadron on 26 November.[51] The last, scattered clashes of the year were fought as the command deployed its squadrons to their winter stations. From Botwood the flying boats of 116 Squadron again moved to Dartmouth while their headquarters was set up at the new RCAF station in Shelburne, NS. The early icing over of the harbour quickly proved Shelburne to be useless for flying-boat operations and the whole squadron was then relocated at Dartmouth, using moorings in Eastern Passage, at the southeast extremity of Halifax harbour.

The closing down of flying-boat operations in Newfoundland left 1 Group with accommodation for only one, land-based, long-range squadron. No 10 Squadron's aging and often unserviceable Digbys occupying that billet at Gander were therefore replaced by the Canso 'A's of 5 (BR). The Digbys joined the pilgrimage to Dartmouth, which, by early December, included the Cansos of 117 Squadron when Gaspé and Kelly Beach, North Sydney, cut back to winter establishments. The movement brought an influx of men and aircraft to the command's main base, whose complement of anti-submarine operational squadrons now consisted of 10 (BR), 11 (BR), 116 (BR), and 117 (BR). By contrast, 1 Group's maritime patrol strength had been reduced to only 145 Squadron's Hudsons at Torbay and 5 Squadron's Canso 'A's at Gander, which, at the end of December, were reinforced by a small detachment of similar aircraft from the still incomplete 162 Squadron.[52]

The unbalanced winter deployments, dictated as they were by the limitations of available equipment rather than the course of the war at sea, highlighted Eastern Air Command's most critical shortcoming: a lack of land-based aircraft able to reach the mid-ocean air gap where U-boats intercepted and attacked convoys. Now that RAF VLR Liberators from Iceland were able to patrol to 35 degrees west, closing the eastern part of the gap, the danger lay in the western portion, between 35 and 50 degrees west, as the battles for SC 104 and SC 107 had demonstrated. Only the twelve Canso 'A's of 5 and 162 Squadrons had the potential – and that at the extreme limits of endurance – to reach the zone of heavy U-boat activity. RCAF aircrews coaxed their amphibians to extraordinary performance, but the only truly effective answer was to station VLR aircraft in Newfoundland.

Any lingering doubt about the crucial importance of the converted Liberators should have been swept away by events in early December. During the first week of the month convoy HX 217 was harried by twenty-two U-boats during its passage of the air gap. The naval escort was able to keep the pack at bay until 8 December, when three RAF VLR Liberators arrived to support it 800 miles from their Iceland base. The aircraft forced thirteen U-boats to submerge, attacked eleven, and broke German contact with HX 217. Weather prevented flying on the 9th and, although the Germans regained contact, the RN escort vessels were able to keep losses down to one ship. The assault ended on the 11th in the face of increasingly effective air cover. Nevertheless, debates in the Allied high command about the allocation of air resources continued to delay the assignment of additional Liberators to the north Atlantic convoy routes.[53]

By December 1942 Eastern Air Command had completed its first year of direct contact with U-boats. On the eve of a new phase, when the advantage of having full decryptions of German Enigma radio traffic was soon to be restored, it is a suitable moment to assess the campaign thus far.

The Hudson made up the bulk of Eastern Air Command's anti-submarine strength and had proved itself in the role. A comparatively heavy aircraft, it was light to handle on the controls, highly manoeuvrable, and had a clear, all-round view from the pilot's seat that made it very suitable for low-level depth-charge attacks in a period when 'eyeballing' was still the method of aiming.[54] Shortness of range was the Hudson's main handicap. The Catalina/Canso flying boat, although it had better range and had flown approximately 35 per cent of the hours flown by all types combined, did not perform well in the Canadian conditions of 1942. For a start, it could only carry 1000 lbs of depth charges with a regular seven-man crew and a full load of fuel. It was said about flying the noisy Catalina that the pilot 'required good training, much practice and plenty of muscle.'[55] Stamina was also important, because of the length of time it took to get out to the patrol area; efficiency was likely to suffer by the time the aircraft arrived on station. The flying boat also had a poor rate of climb so that it often could not get through the fog quickly enough to avoid wing icing. Consequently, a forecast of heavy 'icing' conditions meant that the Catalina could not be sent out above the overcast to rendezvous with convoys that were themselves beyond the fog belt. Once in the operational area the pilot's view of the ocean forward and downward was obstructed by the nose of the aircraft while, below, the U-boat's look-outs had plenty of time to give the alarm on spotting the large silhouette of the slow-moving flying boat.[56]

Until the advent of the Canso 'A' amphibian, the ungainly Digby was the only aircraft in Eastern Air Command able to make sustained patrols at ranges of over 300 miles that could operate during the winter from Newfoundland. As a result, it had formed the backbone of No 1 Group for nearly two years. Although Digbys made only five confirmed attacks on U-boats, one of these destroyed U-520 in October 1942. By that time, nine of the original twenty Digbys had either been written-off in crashes or had disappeared over the north Atlantic, and the remaining aircraft were no longer reliable enough for sustained long-range operations. Slated for transport duties, the surviving Digbys were actually passed to the newly formed 161 Squadron in the spring of 1943 as an interim measure pending the arrival of the squadron's Canso 'A's. And so the Digby flew on, in declining numbers, until the end of 1943 when it was finally withdrawn from operational employment.[57]

Looking at the general tactical situation in late 1942 it is clear that Eastern Air Command made full use of naval intelligence and that the majority of sweeps were organized on the basis of DF positions and estimates of U-boat locations derived from this and other sources of information. In addition, the command now had its own Operational Research Section to monitor and assess the efficiency of its operations as well as to make recommendations for more effective methods. These innovations quickly proved their worth, but the same could not be said of locating submarines with airborne radar. 'We can draw a very definite conclusion,' wrote the chief of the air staff two years later, 'which is that so far as the detection of submarines is concerned it would have made little difference if our aircraft had not been fitted with ASV Mark II.'[58] Indifferent serviceability, the fact that the equipment had to be switched off when radio transmissions were being made, and suspicions that U-boats were able to detect emissions had all combined to restrict the optimum use of radar. Aerial photography, to confirm U-boat sightings and record depth-charge attacks both for the assessment of results and as an aid to training in accurate bombing, was another matter requiring great improvement. Still, these were domestic air force problems, and the means existed within the service to find solutions. That was not true of the most serious shortcoming of Canadian anti-submarine operations: the failure of the RCN and RCAF to co-ordinate various instructions for co-operation between aircraft and escort ships into a common system understood by all. The requisite interservice co-operation was notable by its absence, belying Canadian claims that relations between the navy and the air force were all that could be desired.

The primary responsibility and main task of the anti-submarine air and sea forces during the five-and-a-half-year war of attrition on supply lines known as the 'Battle of the Atlantic' was the safe passage of merchant shipping. In that light, 1942 was by far the most perilous year for the Allies. Almost 1000 ships totalling more than 5 million tons were destroyed by U-boats. The losses in the northwest Atlantic (north of 40° north and west of 40° west) and including the Gulf of St Lawrence accounted for a shade under 12 per cent of those figures.

Eastern Air Command responded with some 8000 sorties. Aircraft logged approximately 50,000 flying hours (including those flown over the Gulf of St Lawrence and Strait of Belle Isle), starting with 591 hours in December 1941, rising to a high mark of 6448 hours in October 1942, before declining to 4602 hours in November after the command had adopted offensive tactics.[59] The defensive tactics involved in providing air cover to coastal convoys established early in the year had been an effective response to the heavy sinkings among independently sailed shipping, and had limited the extent of the German victory in the Gulf of St Lawrence. The problem with these tactics was that they made such heavy demands that it was impossible to provide constant air escort for all shipping. Nor, under these circumstances, could aircraft intervene when U-boats took up submerged attack positions on well-travelled routes or struck on dark nights and when weather prevented flying. Had the RCAF adopted offensive methods earlier, the German thrust into coastal waters could almost certainly have been blunted three to four hundred miles out to sea, and with significantly less wear on aircrew and aircraft than resulted from the policy of indiscriminate close escort.

For the assault on shipping the Germans had twenty-two U-boats directed to the north Atlantic at the start of Operation *Paukenschlag* out of a total of 248 submarines in commission on 1 January 1942. By 1 December the respective figures had grown to ninety-five and 582.[60] From Canadian and German records an educated guess would be that a total of thirty-five U-boats operated in waters covered by Eastern Air Command over the twelve-month period starting 1 December 1941. RCAF aircraft struck back with forty depth-charge attacks. The presence of a U-boat can be confirmed from German records as positive in twenty-six cases, possible in five, and unlikely in nine. Canadian aircrew attacked three boats twice, and one, U-517 in the Gulf of St Lawrence, six times. They destroyed three U-boats, half of the total Allied score in the northwest Atlantic; USN aircraft accounted for two and a Royal Navy trawler sank one.

The RCAF's ratio of kills to attacks, 7.7 per cent, was comparable to that of Coastal Command whose aircraft made 26.5 kills in 381 attacks during 1942,[61] although the resulting ratio of 7 per cent is unrepresentatively low because the British statistics included many strikes with machine-guns only. Undoubtedly, several Eastern Air Command attacks that were close to the mark would have resulted in serious damage or kills if the Canadian aircraft had carried the latest armament. Most of Coastal Command's sinkings were achieved between July and December with Torpex depth charges; the Mark XIII Star and Mark XVI shallow-depth pistols that became available through the fall further increased the effectiveness of the RAF attacks by about 25 per cent over those made with the Mark XIII pistols.[62] The RCAF must be given credit for achieving two of its successes with the inadequate 250-lb Amatol charge, one with the more effective 450-lb version, and all with the Mark XIII pistol. Torpex charges only became available for the last two attacks in November, in neither of which can the presence of a U-boat be confirmed, and the improved pistols did not arrive at RCAF squadrons until the beginning of 1943. That many attacks were marred by faulty tactics despite Coastal Command's prompt promulgation of more effective methods, reflected less on aircrew than on the senior commanders.

There were also fewer opportunities for attack, because Eastern Air Command did not match Coastal Command's operational performance in the number of sightings made – the Canadian average of one U-boat sighting for every 134 aircraft sorties was only about a quarter of the Coastal Command ratio of one to thirty or forty – yet this should not be taken to reflect discredit on the RCAF. In 1942 U-boats in the Canadian zone averaged about one every 40,000 square miles, 'often much less.'[63] Dönitz, speculating from the German side why there was more harassment from the air in the east than in the west, wrote: 'Reasons for this are probably the small number of air bases in Newfoundland and Greenland and the fact that fewer U-boats have operated in this area,' and he expected 'if U-boats were transfered to the West Atlantic, there would shortly be a stronger air patrol there ...'[64]

The second significant difference between operational conditions in the two commands was that the weather was generally far worse for air operations off the Canadian coast. Again, Dönitz, after his U-boats had had a particularly frustrating encounter with a convoy off Newfoundland, pointed out the problem: 'It has again been proved that the weather situation which is affected by seasonal and local conditions, permits only chance successes.'[65] That was as true of one side as it was of the other. Fog, as we have seen, frequently disrupted air searches off the Grand Banks. Amongst the hazards for pilots flying in overcast conditions was the difficulty of knowing how far their aircraft were from the surface of the water; altimeter readings, accurate at the point of departure, could vary significantly over a long flight because of changes in atmospheric pressure. Even if the altimeter was reading correctly, the radar operator could receive an echo that might be a surfaced U-boat, but might equally be an iceberg 100 feet or more in height so that it was impossible for the pilot to make the low attack approach essential for success if the contact was indeed the enemy.[66] Although the fogs and icebergs were seasonal, there was another danger always at the back of the minds of pilots on long patrols. A slow Digby or Canso struggling back against the prevailing westerly wind from far out in the Atlantic could easily run out of fuel, particularly if it had to divert to another airfield because of a sudden weather change at the home base. This factor, perhaps more than any other, restricted RCAF aircraft in their attempt to find submarines.

Difficult operating conditions still did not excuse Eastern Air Command for being slow in adopting Coastal Command tactics. Canadian experience showed that British methods were effective in the northwest Atlantic. Of the twenty-six attacks where the presence of a U-boat can be confirmed, half were made by aircraft patrolling at altitudes of 2000 feet and over. Significantly, 113 Squadron was responsible for the first successful attack shortly after adopting the higher altitudes and white camouflage advocated by the RAF, and made more attacks than the rest of the squadrons combined. In October and early November 10 and 145 Squadrons added to the RCAF's total of U-boat sinkings shortly after those squadrons belatedly employed the new methods. The RCAF's record also proved Coastal Command's conclusion that close escort of unthreatened convoys was the least effective way to make contact with the enemy. Only four confirmed attacks were made by aircraft on escort missions; by contrast, sweeps of suspected U-boat positions and over convoy tracks yielded seventeen attacks, two of which destroyed the U-boats. The third kill was made by an aircraft returning from escort duty, confirming British experience that sweeps to and from convoys were often more likely to locate submarines than patrols around the convoy itself. Had the RCAF followed Coastal Command's methods sooner and with greater care, the achievements of Eastern Air Command, both in strikes against the enemy and the defence of trade, would have been more impressive.

Contemporary British critics, who laid the blame for Canadian shortcomings squarely on senior officers for failing to provide adequate leadership, were undoubtedly right. Rather than ensuring the application of improved techniques and doctrines, senior officers were preoccupied with mundane day-to-day needs and the requirement simply to find enough men and equipment to fly the necessary number of sorties. A dearth of specialist knowledge compounded the problem. No one in senior command had any first-hand experience of anti-submarine operations. Until late 1942 that restriction also applied to senior staff officers. Wing Commander C.L. Annis, who took over as director of (BR) operations at AFHQ in August 1942, was the first man in that office who had such experience.[67] The excellent RAF suggestion in November 1942 to send four senior pilots at a time on a four-week course with Coastal Command, to benefit from British expertise, was not taken up. Instead, the RCAF had to depend on the ability of Canadian airmen themselves to rise above their difficulties.

15

Defeating the Wolf Packs

The RCAF renewed its agitation for Liberator aircraft in late 1942. It was necessary to bypass the normal procurement process because the Anglo-American Combined Munitions Assignment Board refused to consider the question, and the Canadian government was not prepared to pursue the matter through political channels (see Chapter 9). RCAF requests were, however, unceremoniously rejected in London and Washington. The British Air Ministry, supported by Winston Churchill, rebuffed repeated attempts by the Admiralty and Coastal Command to divert aircraft from strategic bombing to anti-submarine work. The US Army Air Forces, which had a virtual monopoly on long-range types in the United States, similarly objected to the allocation of heavy bombers to other roles in its determination to 'keep the mass of air striking power in the hands of one force.'[1]

It was an important step forward for the advocates of very long-range [VLR] operations when the British Cabinet's Anti-U-Boat Committee finally addressed the problem, and in November 1942 formally selected the Consolidated B-24 Liberator – a type already operating successfully in the depth of the air gap with 120 Squadron, RAF – as the most suitable heavy bomber for conversion to the VLR role. Even then, emphasis on operations in the Bay of Biscay delayed the conversion of Liberators for VLR convoy protection on the northern Atlantic routes.[2]

Within range of both medium- and long-range aircraft, the bay was an attractive and apparently logical killing ground for Coastal Command. The density of U-boats there was always high, since their bases lay along the French Atlantic shore. Moreover, because the Germans still relied on the old *Hydra* code for coastal operations, which included support for U-boats in transit, it was possible to direct operations with the aid of special intelligence. Enigma intercepts could provide precise U-boat positions in the bay, something which was not possible in mid-ocean areas in 1942 because the code for Atlantic U-boats remained unbroken. Perhaps understandably, therefore, great things were expected from these operations. The Admiralty and Coastal Command preached the doctrine that constant attacks on U-boats in the bay would break the morale of U-boat crews and defeat the enemy attack on shipping. Operational researchers in Coastal Command had also established a positive correlation between the speed of aircraft and the number of U-boat sightings. It was that principle that made the Liberator, with its speed and endurance, a much desired aircraft for the Bay of Biscay.[3]

Only after convoy losses became desperate in late 1942, and the USAAF reluctantly provided replacement aircraft for the bay offensive in January 1943, did the British Anti-U-Boat Warfare Committee decide to convert some of the Liberators that had been operating off the French coast to a VLR configuration for work in the mid-ocean gap. Nonetheless, even though there were more sightings in relation to hours flown by convoy escort than bay patrols – one every twenty-nine hours compared to one every 312 hours – the British clung to their preference for operations in the transit area. In early February 1943 the arguments of the British operational researcher P.M.S. Blackett, that shipping losses in the Atlantic could be reduced by a startling 64 per cent simply by closing the air gap, still failed to convince the decision-makers.[4] They saw the role of airpower as that of taking the war to the enemy – as in the bay offensive. In the meantime, the fledgling operational research team in Eastern Air Command was also demonstrating with 1942 statistics the links between U-boat density, the number of sightings, and the speed and endurance of an aircraft.[5]

On 11 November 1942, just after the battles for SC 104 and SC 107 which began with great losses less than 600 miles from Newfoundland, the chief of the air staff, Air Marshal L.S. Breadner, had instructed Air Vice-Marshal G.V. Walsh of the Canadian joint staff in Washington to ask for fifteen Liberators that had been superseded by an improved type. Walsh wrote on 18 December, and again on 5 January, to General H.H. Arnold, the chief of the US Army Air Forces. The replies from Arnold and his chief of staff, Major General George E. Stratemeyer, made it quite clear that the United States would not allocate any of these aircraft to Canada.[6]

After this rebuff Ottawa tried, without much success, to obtain a contact in Washington who might persuade senior American officers to change their minds. It was decided in February to let Wing Commander Clare Annis, director of (BR) operations, write a report based on his own extensive first-hand knowledge of anti-submarine warfare, spelling out the need for an aircraft with minimum cruising speed of 150 knots, an endurance of at least twenty hours, and a depth-charge load of at least one-and-a-half tons. A persuasive document, it found its way to Dr E.L. Bowles, a special assistant to the secretary of war, engaged in analysing the anti-submarine problem in the north Atlantic. Whether this report had the desired effect is impossible to say. Bowles was said to have been extremely impressed, and if so may well have passed on his views to his superiors; but by the time Annis heard that the report had reached Bowles, other and much more significant influences had come to bear on the American chiefs of staff.[7]

Between November 1942 and March 1943 Allied shipping losses reached their highest levels. Even though in statistical terms Admiral Dönitz had failed to win his tonnage war when new ship construction overtook the number of ships lost at sea in November 1942, he had not suffered the U-boat losses which might force him to give up his efforts.[8] Moreover, although Allied shipbuilding as a whole had well surpassed the loss rate, the German effort was directed primarily at shipping assigned to Britain. The U-boat campaign therefore struck at British war industry, and seriously threatened 'Bolero,' the Allied build-up in Great Britain for the eventual invasion of Europe.[9] The Allies needed to overcome the alarming losses to north Atlantic shipping and, at the same time, ensure that an ever-increasing flow of war materials reached Britain in 1943. Not surprisingly, then, at the Casablanca Conference in January President Roosevelt, Prime Minister Churchill, and the Anglo-American combined chiefs of staff placed defeat of the U-boat at the top of Allied priorities for 1943. Soon afterwards the British Admiralty and the United States Navy agreed to form the Allied Anti-Submarine Survey Board to examine the problems of anti-submarine forces in the Atlantic and make recommendations for improvement. Moreover, in February Admiral E.J. King, commander-in-chief of the US fleet, responded to the RCN's campaign for control of shipping protection operations in the northwest Atlantic by calling an Allied conference on command and control in the whole of the Atlantic.[10] Events were therefore moving very quickly in early 1943. The deepening crisis in the Atlantic added weight to the RCAF's pleas for VLR aircraft and forced a review of the command relationships in the northwest Atlantic. It also brought Allied war leaders to realize that the successful conduct of all future operations in Europe ultimately depended on securing the main trade routes.

These developments focussed attention on the efficacy of the escort forces engaged, including the RCAF, and during 1943 the Canadians would come under close scrutiny by their senior partners. The evaluation process began in February when two exceptionally qualified young aircrew officers in Coastal Command, Squadron Leader T.M. Bulloch, RAF, and Flying Officer M.S. Layton, RCAF, visited and reported on Eastern Air Command. Their orders had been not only to examine communications, aircraft control, and other support facilities for operations by RAF Liberators from Newfoundland as had been agreed to by the Canadian government in late 1942, but also to survey the state of the command as a whole. To the air staff in Ottawa the selection of such junior officers had almost looked like a calculated snub. 'We thought,' said Breadner and Anderson in a draft signal they decided not to send, 'more senior RAF representation might possibly be sent to discuss any policy questions involved,' but there is no evidence a snub was intended. More accomplished veterans of the anti-submarine war in the north Atlantic could not have been found. Layton had been Bulloch's navigator in 120 Squadron, RAF, in Iceland, and together they had sunk two U-boats and damaged several others. Both were members of the Distinguished Service Order and Layton had been awarded the DFC as well.[11]

These two very experienced airmen thought that existing facilities and personnel could handle VLR squadrons. They seem to have shared the local opinion that Eastern Air Command should have had a Liberator squadron long before. Like earlier visitors they saw much that was wrong, but an important difference was that they saw it through the eyes of aircrew rather than staff. RCAF aircrew they found capable and keen, even though inadequately briefed on the latest requirements. Partly because of a breakdown in communication between instructors at general-reconnaissance [GR] schools and operational personnel, Coastal Command tactical memoranda had not been getting through to the people who needed them. Airmen in Eastern Air Command were unaware of the latest doctrine, and the navigational syllabus in GR schools tended to push tactics into the background. Instructors believed the situation was aggravated because too many pupils were being selected who did not have the inclination for this type of work. Graduates of the schools went to squadrons which for the most part used outdated procedures and often suffered from a desperate shortage of adequate weapons and equipment.

For example, there was apparently still only one squadron, 113 (BR), consistently flying at the recommended search height of 4000-5000 feet or just below the cloud ceiling, although other squadrons had used it on occasion with marked success. Nor had white camouflage been widely adopted in Eastern Air Command. When radar was fitted (still not always the case), there was too much reliance on it, so that U-boats, using search receivers, got ample warning to dive before being detected. Visual lookouts, moreover, often merely scanned the horizon instead of searching the sea up to ten miles ahead of aircraft where there was the best chance of sighting a submarine in time to make an attack. When aircraft did strike, there was still little use of photography to analyze the accuracy and effect.

According to Bulloch and Layton, Eastern Air Command placed too much emphasis on distant anti-submarine sweeps, and not enough on searches near convoys. 'Most of the work they do is searching for a U-boat which has been D.F'd from shore stations and this they manage to carry out in bad visibility, in which we would consider an A/S patrol a waste of time.' This reflected Bulloch and Layton's specialized experience in VLR operations at mid-ocean. As Coastal Command Headquarters later explained, with only a handful of modified Liberators available close escort of threatened convoys had of necessity to take precedence over sweeps of convoy tracks and areas where intelligence located U-boats. The Canadian command's shortcoming was in fact very nearly the reverse of that identified by the visiting airmen: a tendency to escort unthreatened convoys at the expense of offensive sweeps.[12]

Bulloch and Layton's other criticisms, however, were undoubtedly on target. There was excessive reliance on the square search, a patrol usually of thirty- to forty-mile legs in the shape of a box, and the crews in one squadron had got hold of the extraordinary idea that they were not supposed to leave their track to identify suspicious objects. There was no policy for operational fatigue, no standard signals procedures, and no standard enemy reporting system.[13]

The most glaring problem of all was the lack of material. In 10 Squadron Digby pilots had a home-made device for releasing depth charges, and navigators had no astrodomes from which to take star shots, relied on an old type of compass not accurate within less than five degrees, used home-made 'Tail Drift Sights,' and only enjoyed the luxury of radar in three of their aircraft. Throughout the command there was a need to replace outdated depth charges, marine markers, sextants, photography and radio equipment. Radio telephone sets were an urgent necessity for communication with warships and airmen had to have better flying clothing. It astonished Bulloch and Layton that Cansos, which were particularly cold, were not equipped with electrically heated flying suits.[14]

For their part aircrew in Newfoundland and the Canadian Maritime provinces benefited from exchanging information with the two visitors from the other side of the ocean. 'Gen,' the air force slang for information, from brothers in arms is always more credible than staff memoranda, and it is likely that Bulloch and Layton also instilled some badly needed confidence.[15] That was important, because the RAF was bound to take Canadian operational efficiency into account before deciding on the allocation of Liberators.

Whatever faults Bulloch and Layton were able to find in Canadian anti-submarine operations, in the winter of 1942-3 (the worst on record for the war years) No 1 Group did well to fly at all. In January and a good part of February, weather exerted more influence than warfare on operations; it impeded flying, battered the convoys, and left U-boats almost helpless. Dönitz recalls in his memoirs that 'the elements seemed to rage in uncontrolled fury ... Systematic search for shipping became impossible; and when it was located by luck the weather gravely hampered attack.'[16] So he bided his time and built up his strength.

During this period Eastern Air Command endeavoured, with the resources available, to improve both the scale and the range of 1 Group's operations in an attempt to affect events in the air gap. In the process they went some way towards demonstrating the results they might have achieved with Liberators. At the end of December 1942 Canso 'A's of 5 (BR) were joined at Gander by two similar aircraft from 162 Squadron based in Yarmouth. Along with the 162 (BR) detachment came Eastern Air Command's most capable officer and the squadron's new CO, Squadron Leader N.E. Small. In order to extend the operational range of the Cansos beyond their normal 500 miles, 5 Squadron personnel, under Small's direction, began to strip some aircraft of excess weight, including extra guns, ammunition, and stores. In all, about 1200 lbs was removed, which permitted the Cansos to operate out to about 700 miles. Thus, as officers of 5 Squadron readily admitted, it was largely due to the efforts of Small that Gander-based Cansos were able to make a series of promising attacks at maximum range during the early weeks of February. Tragically, Small was killed when his Canso crashed while taking off on 8 January, a result of equipment failure.[17]

By the end of January there were no fewer than 100 U-boats at sea, more than forty in the mid-ocean gap. In Group *Haudegen* twenty-one boats formed a line attempting to intercept convoys south of Greenland, twenty in Group *Landsknecht* remaining further to the east. On 1 February ten of these boats moved west, some of them eventually to form Group *Pfeil* in mid-ocean, south of *Haudegen*. Dönitz then ordered Group *Haudegen* to move southwest and form a line as close as possible to the Newfoundland Bank. This brought the group within range of Gander, Torbay, and Argentia. On 4 February sightings and attacks by RCAF, USN, and USAAF aircraft began to take place with the assistance of special intelligence, which at this time was usually no more than one day old, the *Triton* code used by submarine headquarters for north Atlantic operations having at last been broken by Bletchley Park at the end of 1942.[18]

A Canso 'A' of 5 Squadron based on Gander made the first sighting, on 4 February. Flight Lieutenant J.M. Viau attacked what was probably U-414 with inconclusive results. Two days later a USN PBY from Argentia and a Canso 'A' from 5 Squadron flown by Flight Lieutenant F.C. Colborne both appear to have attacked U-403, a couple of hours apart. Neither attack caused significant damage; the Canso scarcely made an impression, presumably because the U-boat had dived in plenty of time. Several other sightings that day, though they produced no conclusive results, had a noticeably beneficial effect on squadron morale. More important, the U-boats did not attack any convoys within aircraft range of Newfoundland.[19]

There was, in fact, little enemy activity in the area in mid-February. Several convoys ran into U-boat attacks, but only after they steamed out of range of Canadian aircraft. Several others received complete air cover to the limits of Eastern Air Command resources under difficult circumstances, but there is no evidence that this had a direct effect on German attempts to intercept and attack. Convoy SC 118 had fought its way eastward through the air gap in early February, losing eleven ships before Liberators of 120 Squadron, RAF, were able to reach it and drive off the submarines.

The battle for SC 118 proved decisive in the Royal Navy's efforts to reorganize and strengthen escort forces operating in the air gap. It resulted in the Admiralty's approval for the formation of support groups, comprised of escorts drawn from existing groups and destroyers from the Home Fleet. These groups were to range the mid-ocean, reinforcing threatened convoys and chasing down submarine contacts with a determined hunt, something which convoy escorts could not do without endangering the merchant ships in their charge. This development, coupled with the extension of air support from land bases and escort aircraft carriers, ultimately decided the issue. But there were many more battles to fight before these forces could be deployed.[20]

The westbound convoy ON 166, escorted by the only American group left on the main trade route, had already lost nine of its forty-eight ships by the time it reached the outer limits of 1 Group's coverage on 23 February. Early on the 24th two more ships were torpedoed; of the eighteen U-boats concentrated against the convoy, seven were in contact that morning. Some confusion on the German side had interfered with co-ordination of the wolf pack, but air support was still urgently needed. No 1 Group had issued instructions for air coverage from Gander to tie in with USN coverage from Argentia, and USN PBYs swept towards the convoy, but it was beyond their range. Consequently, only the Cansos sent from 5 Squadron, their ranges significantly increased by Small's modifications, managed to provide some help. The first to arrive met the convoy and successfully completed a patrol; the second attacked a U-boat ahead of the convoy; the third failed to meet the convoy and made no sightings or attacks; and the last made an attack at dusk astern of ON 166.[21]

The two attacks on the 24th blunted the U-boat onslaught. The first incident involved the same crew flying the same aircraft that had encountered U-403

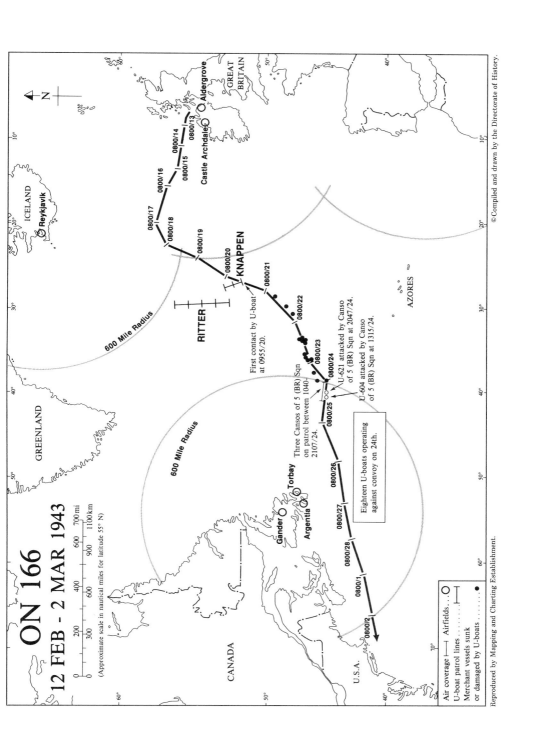

ON 166
12 FEB - 2 MAR 1943

0   200   400   600   700 mi
0   300   600   900   1100 km
(Approximate scale in nautical miles for latitude 55° N)

GREENLAND

600 Mile Radius

ICELAND
Reykjavik

CANADA

Gander
Torbay
Argentia

600 Mile Radius

U.S.A.

RITTER

KNAPPEN

First contact by U-boat
at 0955/20.

Three Cansos of 5 (BR) Sqn
on patrol between 1040-
2107/24.

U-621 attacked by Canso
of 5 (BR) Sqn at 2047/24.

U-604 attacked by Canso
of 5 (BR) Sqn at 1315/24.

Eighteen U-boats operating
against convoy on 24th.

AZORES

GREAT
BRITAIN

Castle Archdale
Aldergrove

0800/13
0800/14
0800/15
0800/16
0800/17
0800/18
0800/19
0800/20
0800/21
0800/22
0800/23
0800/24
0800/25
0800/26
0800/27
0800/28
0800/1
0800/2

N

Air coverage ....⊢—⊣   Airfields....○
U-boat patrol lines ....
Merchant vessels sunk
or damaged by U-boats ....●

Reproduced by Mapping and Charting Establishment.

© Compiled and drawn by the Directorate of History.

earlier in the month. Flight Lieutenant F.C. Colborne, approaching his rendezvous with fresh information from group headquarters that one of the ships in the convoy had been torpedoed and six U-boats sighted, came upon U-604 on the surface. From an altitude of 3000 feet, and in perfect visibility, he sighted the U-boat about six miles ahead. Colborne immediately applied throttle and put the nose down. At 800 feet and with an air speed of 200 knots he cut the throttles and began a steep diving attack as the U-boat began to submerge.[22]

A series of colourful accounts from the crew members describe the last moments of the run in. It seemed to them a complete success, several recalling with Colborne 'what appeared to be the conning tower wallowing through the swirling water – it sank and then came air bubbles a large boiling mass of them! These lasted for about ten minutes, then oil spread over the area with bits of debris.' In inimitable comic book style the second engineer, Leading Aircraftman John Watson, reported: 'The danger was all over and Hitler's little pet was blown to peases [sic].'[23] In fact, U-604 survived. *Kapitänleutnant* Holtring described the damage to his boat in calm professional language: 'Both compressors torn off. Shafts displaced in axial direction. Diesel clutches are pounding hard. Main clutches cannot be fully disengaged. Main ballast tank V has 50 cm long crack. Tank vents air very rapidly. Moved off ... to make repairs.' He arrived at Brest on 9 March after a slow journey home, out of action for the time being.[24] Colborne received the Distinguished Flying Cross later in the year.

Some seven hours after the first attack, a Canso flown by Flying Officer D.G. Baldwin sighted U-621. The navigator's account describes the action that followed. The aircraft, flying at 1000 feet just below a heavy bank of cumulus cloud, arrived over the convoy at dusk.

Its track had been searched forward 20 miles and 20 miles to starboard and now the aircraft was approaching from a position 30 miles behind it, maintaining an alert watch at all station[s] for the possible shadower. A long intercom silence was broken by [second pilot] F/O [L.J.] Murray, who was sweeping ahead and to starboard with the binoculars, reporting a streak in the water ahead about 5 miles. F/O Baldwin immediately made slight course adjustment and commenced to dive ... At 200 feet the binoculars clouded and the wake was lost. F/O Baldwin jumped from 100 feet to 300 feet and resighted the wake, by this time about 60° to starboard and still noticeably moving – and turned on to attack. Not wanting to make a straight beam attack he turned again, up the submarine's track, just as he approached the swirl dropping the four depth charges in the turn where they were observed to land in close diamond pattern 50-60 feet ahead of the swirl ...[25]

The light was fading fast and photography was impossible. All that could be done was to inform the escort commander by radio telephone, while setting course for base 'and opening another bottle of champagne.'[26] U-621, which had been frustrated in attempts to get at the convoy during the afternoon by some or all of the other Cansos, suffered slight damage, enough to put it out of action for the moment. Both attacks had been achieved at the extremity of Canso endurance.[27]

The next day fog grounded all aircraft and U-boats were again able to close the convoy. They sank one more ship, then Dönitz ordered them to withdraw before they came within range of further air coverage from Newfoundland. Liberators based at Gander might have been able to force such a withdrawal much earlier, almost certainly before the U-boat attacks of 22 and 23 February, which caused such severe losses. As the USN official historian subsequently noted, it was because of this shortfall that 'the wolf packs got in their dirty work.'[28] The increasing effectiveness of RAF Liberators of 120 Squadron in the eastern portion of the air gap confirms his opinion, and the subsequent heavy losses in the western part focused attention on the need to base VLR aircraft in Newfoundland.

The Canadians realized that even the aircraft they had were not being used to their best advantage because efforts were not properly co-ordinated with other air and naval forces. 'As matters now stand,' wrote Wing Commander Clare Annis, from his perspective in Ottawa, 'each service [the RCN and RCAF] is publishing a set of operational instructions and including in them their interpretation of the role the other service will play in the conduct of the joint operation of convoy escort.' He went on:

Neither set of instructions carries executive authority in the other's Service. Each Service has depended only on liaison with the other to ensure that their interpretation of the other Service's function will not conflict with its own ideas. This has resulted, it seems, in the issuing of two sets of orders which are neither complete in themselves nor even when combined. Moreover, as our control and administrative machinery now stands, it is necessary for the service wishing to introduce a new order or alter an old one to raise a special memorandum and/or arrange for a special conference. This allowed for delay, oversight, misunderstandings and considerable inefficiency.[29]

There were a number of possible solutions. The most obvious was to adopt, with amendments as necessary, the Admiralty's *Atlantic Convoy Instructions*. These already governed RN and RCN escorts and, through the Air Operations Section, Coastal Command as well. Or the RCN and RCAF could develop and adhere to their own joint tactics under the aegis of the Joint RCN-RCAF Anti-Submarine Warfare [ASW] Committee, a body which had been established but not yet convened. Some published doctrine, promulgated simultaneously through each service, was definitely needed.[30]

What made this co-ordination particularly urgent was the plethora of methods and ideas governing air operations in Newfoundland by USN and USAAF as well as RCAF forces. The American naval commander at Argentia, inhibited by inadequate telephone links with St John's and the Canadian mainland, had suggested a conference to discuss standard operating procedures between the USN, RCN, USAAF, and RCAF, and in doing so had in fact prompted Annis to offer his appreciation of the problem. From 26 to 29 February a meeting was held at Argentia between senior air authorities during which Air Commodore F.V. Heakes and key personnel from all three separate air commands thrashed out a great number of differences. Largely technical in nature, they were by no means resolved during the conference, but they pin-pointed the problems and contained the germ of fundamental reforms.[31]

Perhaps the most important outcome of the meeting was the further integration of USAAF operations with those of the USN and RCAF. Although the US Army's Newfoundland Base Command had made its four Boeing B-17 Flying Fortresses at Gander available for shipping defence in October 1942, control of these aircraft had in mid-February 1943 passed to the 25th Anti-Submarine Wing of the USAAF Anti-Submarine Command, a change that heralded a great expansion of the army air forces in Newfoundland. But the Anti-Submarine Command's mission, summed up in its motto 'to seek and to sink,' sharply contrasted with that of the USN and the RCAF. The latter services agreed that the protection of shipping was the principal task of anti-submarine squadrons; the location and destruction of U-boats, however necessary, took second place. It was therefore a remarkable concession when, at the Argentia conference, the USAAF representative announced the army would 'join in on the change of mission to agree with yours.' The USAAF in Newfoundland did make a significant effort to support convoys, but the late arrival of additional squadrons, all of which had to become acclimatized to the difficult operating conditions of the north Atlantic theatre, the fact that none of their aircraft had VLR capability, and a continued preference for the search and strike role limited the contribution of army aviation to the critical convoy battles of the early spring of 1943.[32]

In the meantime, the air officer commanding [AOC] Eastern Air Command, now Air Vice-Marshal G.O. Johnson, responded to the good work done at the Argentia meeting by bringing up the old problem of operational control or direction again, a reflection of the constant Canadian obsession with maintaining national control of their own forces, even at the expense of operational efficiency. In the flurry of signals that passed between St John's and Halifax after the Argentia meeting in late February the principal concern was a Canadian fear of subordinating Eastern Air Command to the USN task force commander [CTF 24]. Acting in the role of peacemaker, as he had done on a similar occasion in 1941, Heakes 'earnestly suggested' to Johnson, on 6 March, that the question not be raised again, because Eastern Air Command had enjoyed 'more than one years experience of satisfactory coordination ...' Heakes had 'rationalized' the co-ordination procedure from 'a haphazard method to a reasoned daily study of the situation insofar as RCAF is concerned.'[33]

A fundamental restructuring of command relations was, however, on the brink of achievement. In December 1942 the RCN had launched a campaign to assume control of convoy and anti-submarine operations in the northwest Atlantic. The intention of Naval Service Headquarters [NSHQ] was to elevate the commanding officer Atlantic Coast to commander-in-chief status, superseding the American admiral at Argentia in all matters relating to trade defence. Now that the RCN was supplying nearly 50 per cent of the escorts on the north Atlantic routes and all but a handful of USN warships had long since been withdrawn, CTF 24's responsibility for convoy protection not only needlessly complicated command but offended Canadian sensibilities.

Admiral King reluctantly agreed to the Canadian request for an interallied conference on Atlantic convoy arrangements, but the scope of the planned gathering soon expanded as a result of the crisis at sea and the priority given to the anti-U-boat war at the Casablanca conference. From the latter meeting emerged a proposal for a supreme Atlantic command, in order to rationalize the situation in the northwest part of the ocean where there were at least eight Canadian and us operational authorities. Because of the sensitive national interests involved, the supreme command was never realized; Anglo-American agreement in February 1943 on the creation of the purely advisory Allied Anti-Submarine Survey Board was the modest outcome of these efforts. Another, albeit indirect, result was the RCAF's retreat from its long-standing refusal to place Eastern Air Command under naval direction.[34]

Air Force Headquarters [AFHQ] became aware that great changes were in the making at the beginning of February. After the Casablanca conference, a subcommittee of the Anglo-American Combined Staff Planners in Washington had hurriedly prepared a preliminary report that envisioned a three-stage integration of command in the Atlantic. The air and sea anti-submarine forces of each nation would first be unified under a single national commander, all forces in the eastern Atlantic would then be placed under a British commander-in-chief, and those in the western ocean under an American officer; these steps would set the stage for the organization of a supreme command. The Canadian air attaché in Washington summarized this paper in a wire to Ottawa on 2 February. At that same time Wing Commander Clare Annis, who had recently returned from the American capital, reported that there were splendid opportunities for Canada in the rapidly developing situation if the RCAF would place Eastern Air Command under the RCN. The us services, Annis learned, might be willing to forego the installation of an American commander-in-chief if the Canadians were able to create a unified command (Admiral King, in fact, dispatched a signal to NSHQ and the Admiralty late on 2 February that proposed the removal of the Argentia command from convoy operations). In addition, the USN and the us Army would be more favourably disposed towards the allocation of Liberators to the RCAF.[35]

These exciting possibilities broke down the RCAF's resistance to naval direction with dizzying speed. Eastern Air Command's responsibility for the general defence of the Atlantic coast, including fighter operations and strikes against enemy landings as well as anti-submarine duties, had always proved an insuperable barrier to the subordination of maritime patrol aircraft to a naval command. Yet within forty-eight hours of the arrival of the news from Washington, AFHQ had found a solution. Anti-submarine squadrons would normally operate under the general direction of the naval commander-in-chief, though under the tactical control of the air officer commanding Eastern Air Command, as was the case in Coastal Command. The RCAF commander would, however, retain full control of other types of squadrons, and in the case of a major attack requiring a concentrated air effort, would also resume complete charge of the anti-submarine units. On 4 February officers from AFHQ and NSHQ began to work out the details of a unified command along these lines. Air Council gave its approval that same day, and on the 6th the chief of the naval staff, Admiral P.W. Nelles, was able to inform Admiral King of the speedy progress. Air Marshal Breadner, who was in London at this time, gave his assent to the proposed arrangements by signal the next day. Later in the month, NSHQ took the first step towards integration on the east coast by making flag officer Newfoundland, hitherto an independent command, subordinate to commanding officer Atlantic Coast with effect from 1 March, the opening day of the Atlantic Convoy Conference in Washington.[36]

As the delegates gathered in the American capital it was patently obvious that major changes were needed to check the U-boat offensive in mid-Atlantic. By the end of February, British intelligence was again encountering serious delays in its reading of north Atlantic U-boat signals. On 10 March German submarine headquarters compounded the problem by introducing a new code for weather reports, which effectively closed the cryptanalysts' 'back-door' into the more complex – and vital – operational cipher *Triton*, which had been broken only in December 1942. The cryptanalysts at Bletchley Park grimly predicted a two to three month delay in cracking this latest problem. In the event, Bletchley Park mastered the new *Triton* settings by 20 March, but in the meantime the lack of special intelligence proved disastrous. With a hundred U-boats at sea, and most of them in mid-ocean, the Germans were able to intercept every north Atlantic trade convoy, mount attacks against 54 per cent, and sink 22 per cent of ships convoyed in the first three weeks of March. Despite the presence of the auxiliary aircraft carrier USS *Bogue*, between 6 and 12 March westbound convoys lost fifteen of 119 ships and an escorting destroyer. Hard on the heels of these disasters came the wolf pack attacks on SC 122 and HX 229, which lost sixteen out of 149 ships, at the cost to Germany of only two U-boats. U-91 made the initial detection of HX 229 on 16 March about sixty miles east of 5 (BR) Squadron's most distant patrol, about 600 miles from Gander. As in the February battles, even one VLR Liberator, able to extend that patrol by another 200 miles, might have made a crucial difference.[37]

It was against this backdrop, the most serious crisis of the north Atlantic campaign, that the decisions at Washington were made. By closing ranks, the RCAF and the RCN had greatly strengthened the case for Canadian command. The conference approved the scheme the two services had worked out: there would be a separate Canadian Northwest Atlantic theatre, with Rear-Admiral L.W. Murray, RCN, at Halifax assuming the appointment of commander-in-chief. With respect to command relationships, it was agreed that anti-submarine air operations were now to be under the operational direction of the naval commander responsible for protecting shipping in any given area, the air officer commanding exercising general operational control. Canada was to be responsible for air cover of HX, SC, and ON convoys to the limit of aircraft range from Labrador, Newfoundland, and the Canadian Maritime provinces. The Washington conference's subcommittee on command, control, and responsibilities of air forces further explained in its report of 11 March: 'All ASW aviation of the Associated Powers based in this region to be under general operational control of the Canadian AOC EAC Halifax who, under general operational direction of Commander in Chief Northwest Atlantic, shall be responsible for the air coverage of all shipping within range including Greenland convoys and other shipping under US control.'[38] The new command structure came into force on 30

April when Admiral Murray took over responsibility for the defence of shipping from CTF 24.

Although the Canadian services had modelled their new organization on the relationship between the Royal Navy and Coastal Command, efforts to give substance to the framework were extremely tentative. While travelling to Washington, the Canadian delegates to the Atlantic Convoy Conference had realized they would be seriously embarrassed if the British or Americans asked precisely how the RCN and RCAF achieved co-operation. AFHQ and NSHQ therefore hurried the Joint RCN-RCAF ASW Committee into existence, and it met for the first time on 23 March. Although a valuable channel for sharing information, the committee did not realize its potential as a co-ordinating body for many months. Meanwhile, Eastern Air Command had attempted to resolve the problem of diverse instructions for co-operation between air and sea escorts by adopting the Admiralty's Atlantic Convoy Instructions on 16 March but, as will be seen, the requisite orders were not properly promulgated. More striking was the continued failure to form a joint operations room at Halifax. In February the two services had immediately agreed that such a facility would play a central role in the new Canadian command, and this requirement had been set down in the proceedings and conclusions of the Atlantic Convoy Conference. The naval staff had decided that Admiral Murray should go to Eastern Air Command Headquarters where better accommodation was available than in the dockyard, and where he would be free from routine administration. Still, Murray refused to move, believing that he could exercise direction over air operations through enlarged liaison staffs.[39]

Newfoundland, as always, posed some of the thorniest problems. The changeover in operational authority took place while the expansion of the US Army Air Forces on the island was under way. At the end of March a squadron of eleven B-17s joined the four B-17s already at Gander, and was followed in early April by another squadron equipped with B-24s (Liberators), although these were not converted to VLR and therefore restricted to an operational radius of about 650 miles, no better than the RCAF's modified Cansos. They were, however, a good deal faster and more powerful. In the meantime a team from the 25th Anti-Submarine Wing arrived at St John's and joined the Canadian combined headquarters. A liaison staff from the USN's air headquarters at Argentia was subsequently installed in the combined headquarters in early May, after the AOC 1 Group, Air Vice-Marshal Heakes, had assumed control over all air operations from Newfoundland related to the defence of shipping, under the direction of the flag officer Newfoundland Force and the air and naval commanders-in-chief in Halifax. Faced with the daunting problem of bringing together three air forces, each with it own operational procedures, Heakes adapted the system for co-operation that he had helped to develop under CTF 24. No 1 Group assigned missions to the American services, but left the execution – 'takeoff times, planes used, crews used, armament carried, diversions, or recall of planes on account of weather' – in the hands of the USN and USAAF staffs at the combined headquarters, and in Argentia and Gander.[40]

By accepting naval direction, the RCAF expected not merely to direct

American Liberator operations, but to advance its own bid for VLR aircraft. Canadian airmen seized the opportunity afforded by the Atlantic Convoy Conference to raise the issue once again at the highest levels. Just as the USN and RN were prepared at this time to support the Canadian naval case, both the RAF delegation in Washington and General Arnold had now accepted the reasonableness of the Canadian air force argument, but the RAF refused to support a proposal that would cut into British allocations from the United States, and Arnold, constrained by interservice disputes with the US Navy, refused to break previous agreements.[41]

Air Vice-Marshal N.R. Anderson, who represented Canada on the air forces subcommittee, in arguing for a Canadian VLR capability under the new command arrangements could find no documentary backing other than a memorandum of agreement with the combined chiefs of staff concerning allocations in which the United States undertook 'to assist in the equipping and maintaining of the RCAF.'[42] As he reported on 9 March, however, there was still cause for optimism:

Speaking to me privately AVM [A.] Durston [head of the RAF delegation, Washington] has more than once stated that UK might consider letting RCAF have twenty Liberators for GR [general reconnaissance] patrols North Atlantic and before yesterday's meeting stated that he would support our claim for VLR aircraft yet said nothing once the meeting had started. Allotment of Liberators to UK for 1943 is 398 of which 20 per month are modified in USA to VLR. These VLR aircraft are now going through Dorval en route UK. If UK would divert 5 per month to RCAF until squadron completely equipped we could collect them from Dorval at once with our experimental crews [and] establish VLR patrols in the Northwest Atlantic immediately in an effort to stop now the heavy ship losses being suffered. Proposal at yesterday's meeting that US Army Air Corps [sic] put VLR squadron at Gander in April is too indefinite. US Army Air Corps aircraft have still to be modified to VLR. Their crews do not know Northwest Atlantic weather conditions, are not familiar with GR operations and do not use our UK Canada communications procedure. Doubtful if they would be operational within one month of arrival at Gander.[43]

Breadner signalled immediately to the British chief of the air staff, Sir Charles Portal, 'I urge you to authorize the diversion at Dorval and re-allocation [of VLR Liberators] to the RCAF ... on the basis of 5 aircraft in March, 10 in April and 5 in May.' He informed Air Vice-Marshal Johnson in Eastern Air Command that Portal would agree.[44]

At first glance that seems to have been too optimistic. When in January the first sea lord, Admiral Sir Dudley Pound, had suggested at a British chiefs of staff meeting that Liberators should be allocated to Canada, the vice-chief of the air staff, Sir John Slessor, had been adamant that the RAF, not the RCAF, should take on the responsibility in the western Atlantic. The RAF's own need for VLR Liberators, and the reports received about Eastern Air Command's inefficiency, made him reluctant to spare any for the Canadians. Portal had agreed. Breadner, however, even if he was aware of this attitude, accurately sensed a softening in the British view. Portal replied on 11 March, after the bitter convoy battles of

February and as Allied fortunes in the air gap plummeted, that the Canadian proposal was under urgent examination.[45]

There now followed a series of negotiations between the RAF and General Arnold. Before deciding in favour of Breadner's request, the RAF entered into conversations with Washington. The RAF delegation there was instructed to find out:

a. When the United States think they would be in a position to allot G.R. Liberators to Canada and in what quantity.

b. Whether in your opinion diversions from current R.A.F. allocations as proposed ... would in fact be earlier than US allocations.

c. Whether US would be prepared to make good to us later in the year what we gave Canada and also provide attrition for the Canadian squadrons.[46]

The answers from Washington explained that there was no longer a shortage of aircraft (there were 653 Liberators then in the United States), but that the 'domestic difference of opinion' between the USAAF and USN continued to tie Arnold's hands. After the RAF delegation cabled on 23 March that Arnold had refused to alter his stand, the Cabinet Anti-U-Boat Warfare Committee met and 'In order to take advantage of experienced GR crews now available in Canada ... decided to divert from the RAF allocation to the RCAF the equivalent of one Coastal Command Liberator Squadron ... 5 Liberators will be made available this month, 5 in April and 5 in May.'[47] It is difficult to see how the British could have come to any other decision than it did.[48] It was eminently sensible – not to say urgently necessary – to put VLR aircraft into the hands of the RCAF. If the combined chiefs of staff had agreed at any time between November 1942 and February 1943 to base VLR Liberators in Newfoundland, there is little doubt the terrible north Atlantic convoy losses of March 1943 would have been dramatically reduced. In the event, the timely repenetration of the U-boat cipher *Triton* in late March, the advent of naval support groups and escort aircraft carriers, the onset of fairer spring weather, and the diversion of aircraft from the Bay of Biscay to the mid-ocean all combined to initiate an Allied offensive in the air gap and to reduce losses dramatically.

Unfortunately, the designated RCAF Liberator squadron, 10 (BR), did not complete conversion until June, by which time the battle had passed its peak. The only increment to 1 Group's strength in March was the dispatch of two 10 (BR) Digbys to Gander to augment the Cansos of 5 (BR) and the small 162 (BR) detachment. In the meantime, most of the decisive action took place well beyond the range of 1 Group's aircraft. The RCAF made few sightings and attacks in March and April, and it was only in the first week of May that a large number of German submarines once again came within range of Gander and Torbay. That provided a test which, on the eve of acquiring the new long-range capability, revealed both new strengths and old weaknesses.

With his usual tenacity Dönitz was using every resource, including excellent radio intelligence of Allied convoy movements, to force contact on the northern convoy routes. This had resulted in several hard-fought battles in mid-Atlantic

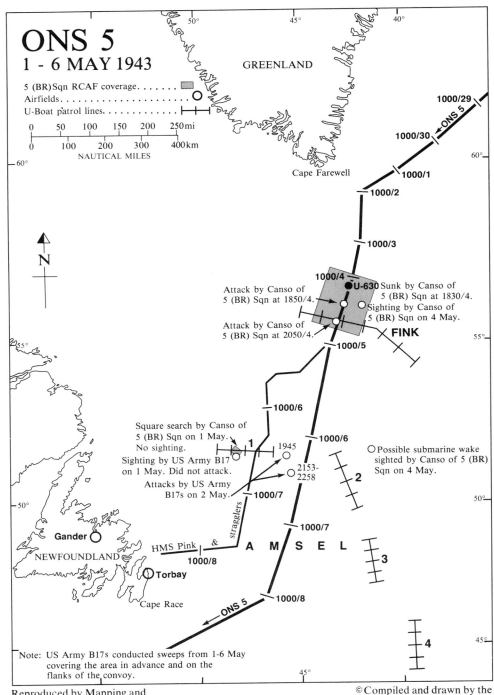

ONS 5
1 - 6 MAY 1943   GREENLAND

5 (BR)Sqn RCAF coverage . . . . . . ▨
Airfields . . . . ○
U-Boat patrol lines . . . . ⊢—⊣

0   50   100   150   200   250 mi
0   100   200   300   400 km
NAUTICAL MILES

Cape Farewell

N

Attack by Canso of
5 (BR) Sqn at 1850/4.

●U-630 Sunk by Canso of
5 (BR) Sqn at 1830/4.
Sighting by Canso of
5 (BR) Sqn on 4 May.

Attack by Canso of
5 (BR) Sqn at 2050/4.

FINK

Square search by Canso of
5 (BR) Sqn on 1 May.
No sighting.

Sighting by US Army B17
on 1 May. Did not attack.

Attacks by US Army
B17s on 2 May.

1945

2153-
2258

○ Possible submarine wake
sighted by Canso of 5 (BR)
Sqn on 4 May.

2

Gander ○
NEWFOUNDLAND

HMS Pink ⊣ &

A M S E L

3

○ Torbay

Cape Race

ONS 5

4

Note: US Army B17s conducted sweeps from 1-6 May
covering the area in advance and on the
flanks of the convoy.

1000/29
ONS 5
1000/30
1000/1
1000/2
1000/3
1000/4
1000/5
1000/6
1000/6
1000/7
1000/7
1000/8
1000/8

stragglers

during April. Ultimately, ONS 5, a storm-battered forty-three-ship westbound convoy that neither the Admiralty nor the Operational Intelligence Centre [OIC] in Ottawa were able to divert clear of two large patrol lines, *Fink* and *Amsel*, came under attack by forty U-boats within 400 miles of Newfoundland. During a co-ordinated Canadian and American sweep northeast of Newfoundland, one B-17 attacked three submarines in advance of the convoy on 2 May. A similar sweep on 3 May produced no results, but on 4 May a Canso 'A' of 5 Squadron sent out to cover the convoy at maximum range from the Torbay detachment – occasionally established to take advantage of better flying conditions when Gander was closed down – sank U-630 about thirty miles astern of the convoy, more than 650 miles from base.[49]

The destruction of U-630 resulted from an initial radar contact followed up by visual sighting at less than three miles. The pilot, Squadron Leader B.H. Moffit, AFC, apparently achieved total surprise, having 'just pushed the nose down and the throttles open' and experiencing 'the fastest ride I have ever had in a Canso ... Coming in straight on we let our depth charges go, and as the aircraft passed over the sub I could see two of the Jerries still on the conning tower platform. After that part of the show was over I was out of the picture, but the lads in the blister could see the depth charges striking ... two of them landed on the port side of the U-boat and one just off the conning tower. The fourth one ... missed as I attempted to bank to take another quick look.' The explosion in fact blew the submarine, which had crash-dived, back into a fully surfaced position for about ten seconds, before it finally sank. 'A thick oil slick immediately appeared, accompanied by a strong smell of oil ... Oil slick grew to 200 by 800 feet and wood in debris showing fresh breaks could be seen in it.'[50]

Moffit sighted another U-boat which escaped attack, but, some three hours later, Flight Lieutenant J.W.C. Langmuir in a second Canso flying at an altitude of 5500 feet, spotted what was probably U-438 fully surfaced about fifteen miles distant.[51] He placed himself up sun and also surprised the U-boat captain who, in this instance, decided to fight it out on the surface, a decision that saved him for the time being. (U-438 was sunk on 6 May by HMS *Pelican*.) Langmuir pressed on twenty feet above the waves and claimed a straddle with his depth charges: 'Jerry kept firing at us spasmodically while we hurriedly prepared the forward gun for a second attack. This time we came in on the starboard beam and the submarine opened fire at about 600 yards. He again missed us but explosives were coming mighty close ... Our front gunner ... held his fire until we were within 300 yards. Three of the sub crew were bowled over with this barrage ... Two other members could be seen seeking shelter of the conning tower ... In order to avoid further shellfire, I manoeuvred the aircraft well out of range taking slight evasive action. On taking a turn to take another look there was no sub.'[52] Both Moffit and Langmuir later received the Distinguished Flying Cross, the former in November 1943 for thirty-two months of outstanding service on anti-submarine patrols in which the destruction of a U-boat had been only the crowning achievement, and the latter, who subsequently served overseas in 422 Squadron, RCAF, in March 1945.

Unfortunately, the convoy was standing into further danger, in conditions that at first favoured the U-boats and which made it difficult for 5 Squadron to repeat its performance of 4 May. As a result, twelve merchant ships were lost over the next two days (5-6 May) in exchange for one submarine. One of the two aircraft scheduled to support ONS 5 on 5 May crashed on take-off, killing all but one of the crew. The other, apparently not where it should have been, did not see either the convoy or any of the submarines around it. One RAF VLR Liberator from 120 Squadron in Iceland, more than a thousand miles from base, actually met the convoy but the crew saw nothing through the fog patches for the short time they were on task. On 6 May thick fog, although it grounded all aircraft in the region, also brought an end to U-boat attacks. The low visibility enabled radar-equipped surface escorts to turn the tables and sink four more of their tormentors.

Weather and the modern radar of the naval escorts proved the decisive factors in this battle, while inadequate sea/air co-operation procedures by RCAF pilots lost them opportunities. This was clear from the failure to meet the convoy on 5 May, and even from the successful operation on 4 May. As the escort commander in HMS *Tay* pointed out, although he had heard Moffit's Canso reporting his attack on 4 May, and although he had continually attempted to establish communications with the Canso, not once had he been able to do so. Langmuir's machine, it is true, had co-operated quite well, employing standard searches ordered by the escort commander, but the aircraft 'arrived just too late.'[53]

Ever since aircraft have been used in military and naval operations the mental barrier between airmen and seamen, or soldiers, has weakened the effectiveness of the air weapon. It is noteworthy that nowhere in the operations record book, daily diary, or aircrew debriefings of 5 (BR) Squadron is there any reference to the threat posed by the U-boats to ONS 5. The weekly intelligence reports from 1 Group Headquarters in St John's show a great deal of concern for the convoys, but by comparison with entries several weeks later there was an absence of the kind of detailed information about convoy coverage, such as the close escort searches carried out, which indicates close co-operation with the ships. On 16 March Eastern Air Command, in a message to air controllers, ordered squadrons to comply with Atlantic Convoy Instructions, which governed the actions of naval escorts and Coastal Command as well, and the squadrons in Canada complied. However, 1 Group Headquarters in Newfoundland did not receive word until 18 May. The first tangible evidence of regular adherence to the instructions in Group intelligence reports did not appear until late June, fully ten months after the Admiralty had introduced them as the basis for north Atlantic convoy operations.[54]

A closer look at long-range operations, in which 5 Squadron and the B-17 squadrons from Gander had distinguished themselves on the few occasions that opportunity offered, shows that although ONS 5 benefited from the ability of Cansos, and to a lesser extent B-17s, to strike hard at great distances from base, this convoy may have suffered from a disposition of air power that resulted from faulty intelligence. As in late March, Ottawa was providing a good picture of submarine movements in the mid-ocean area. In spite of a brief Enigma 'blackout' that occurred at the end of April, the OIC knew of the arrival of Group

Amsel northeast of Newfoundland, athwart the tracks of several convoys. B-17 searches on 1 and 2 May paid off with the three positive sightings on 2 May already mentioned, but on 3 May the aircraft made no detections. Dönitz had ordered the U-boats in *Amsel* to split into four separate sections, leaving the impression there were no gaps in the patrol line.[55] Possibly this was why the search on 3 May, ordered to take place roughly in the gap between *Amsel* I and *Amsel* II, produced no results.

When deception succeeds in war it usually means the victim has a predisposition to believe what he sees; the battle for ONS 5 was no exception. The belief persisted until at least early June that Dönitz had stationed a permanent line of submarines northeast of Newfoundland as pickets to report on convoy movements. Logical so far as they went, these conclusions rested on partial and therefore dangerous information. As the OIC should have known from Enigma decrypts, there was no permament patrol line of the kind postulated. And as British codebreakers came to realize before June, German naval intelligence was reading Allied convoy signals; Dönitz had no need of a picket line that would have placed his U-boats at constant risk. Consequently, too much emphasis may have been placed on area searches for phantom U-boats, and too little on efficient co-operation with naval escorts to ensure the safe and timely arrival of convoys. The idea that some U-boats would be less likely to attack because they were on picket duty could even have led to the tragic assumption on 5 May that the westbound ONS 5 was past its greatest danger. Even if that was not in the minds of controlling authorities, the analysis of squadron activities recorded in weekly intelligence reports tends to support a conclusion that incomplete intelligence led to misemployment of air forces. Available evidence is not sufficiently complete to allow a firm opinion in this regard, but there is so much precedent for relating bad command decisions to faulty intelligence that the idea simply cannot be dismissed.[56]

On the German side it seems unlikely in May 1943, even had Dönitz been aware of a flaw in local intelligence, that he would have been able to exploit it further. U-boat losses that month, principally the result of convoy battles fought by naval escort and support groups (including some with auxiliary aircraft carriers) in the mid-ocean gap, continued at the rate set by ONS 5. Shaken on 7 May by the unacceptable exchange rate of seven submarines for what he believed were no more than sixteen merchant ships, Dönitz finally called off his mid-ocean boats on 21 May after losing a total of thirty-one in the first three weeks of the month.

The infusion of powerful new air and naval forces into the mid-Atlantic eliminated the last theatre where U-boats enjoyed the freedom of movement so essential to pack operations. In May 1943 these old tactics had brought stunning losses and ultimately collapse of the German campaign. The mystique of the wolf pack was shattered. Although British and American forces had scored the kills which prompted Dönitz's withdrawal, Canadians, too, celebrated the Allied victory in the early weeks of June. In the event, the final telling defeat of the U-boat packs did not come until September, and then Canadians would play a very prominent role. In the meantime the centre of gravity in anti-submarine warfare shifted to the Bay of Biscay transit routes. There and in the central Atlantic, using accurate intelligence to advantage, RAF Coastal Command and the Royal Navy, with elements of US Army anti-submarine command and US Navy land- and carrier-based aircraft, mounted an offensive against U-boats transiting from their Biscay bases.[57]

While operations to the south and east were achieving highly satisfactory results – between June and September Allied ships and aircraft accounted for twenty-one U-boats in the bay itself, and thirty-eight more in the central Atlantic – British and Canadian forces consolidated their position on the northern convoy routes, with more naval support groups, improved tactics and new methods of operational control, and additional US air units. As well, during the late spring and early summer 10 Squadron, RCAF, became fully operational at Gander with its new Liberators.[58]

To convert aircrews from the old twin-engine Digbys to heavy four-engine aircraft the RCAF brought in two experienced Trans Canada Air Lines pilots, J.L. Rood and G. Lothian. Between them these airmen put in 705 hours of air instruction from May to July, themselves learning the peculiarities and overcoming the problems of local flying in Newfoundland. In his memoirs Lothian described the treacherous conditions to be found in Newfoundland. 'Most Canadian airports are subject to the onslaughts of lows and fronts, usually predictable and short lived, but Gander was different than most ... For when the wind veered into the easterly quadrants at Gander and began to flow in from the ocean, carrying moisture-laden air toward the land, things could get gummed up with remarkable rapidity, often blotting out the place completely.' While training continued, 10 Squadron had already begun to fly operations, carrying out its first Liberator missions on 10 May.[59]

It was on that day that the Admiralty began to issue a daily message allocating four separate categories to convoys at sea: first those under attack or definite threat; second, those possibly in need of air cover in the near future; third, troop convoys or 'monsters' (fast independently routed ocean liners like the *Queen Elizabeth*) not under direct threat; and fourth, convoys that were standing out of danger. After dispatch of the message, prefixed with the word 'Stipple,' Coastal Command sent another with the prefix 'Tubular.' The Tubular messages outlined U-boat probability areas on the basis of the latest intelligence, especially Ultra, and was intended to help co-ordinate the air patrols by 15 Group, RAF (headquarters at Liverpool, England), Eastern Air Command Headquarters at Halifax, and 1 Group in Newfoundland. Based on the latest British intelligence – and it is important to remember that this system could only work so long as Bletchley Park continued to break the enemy's code – the Stipple and Tubular messages from now on governed Eastern Air Command's operations.[60]

As visiting staff authorities pointed out, however, Canadian organization and operating methods left a great deal of room for improvement. The Allied Anti-Submarine Survey Board came to Ottawa and then toured the east coast during the second week of May. The board's president, Rear Admiral J.L. Kauffman, USN, and the British naval member, Rear-Admiral J.M. Mansfield,

RN, had had extensive experience in Atlantic escort operations, as had the air representatives, Commander J.P.W. Vest, USN, and Group Captain P.F. Canning, RAF; Canning, it will be recalled, had already made a detailed report on Eastern Air Command in 1942. The board advised that NSHQ's role in co-ordinating anti-submarine operations should be strengthened by giving the assistant chief of the naval staff direct authority over Eastern Air Command, on the model of the relationship between the Admiralty and Coastal Command Headquarters. NSHQ and AFHQ rejected the suggestion, noting that Eastern Air Command already came under the direction of Admiral Murray; no useful purpose would be served by giving Air Vice-Marshal Johnson a second naval master. This argument would have been more persuasive if the Joint RCN-RCAF ASW Committee had been providing effective inter-service co-ordination.[61]

On the need for a combined headquarters at Halifax, the board was adamant. Admiral Murray should go to Eastern Air Command Headquarters 'with a minimum of delay,' certainly within the fortnight, the Allied officers urged, emphasizing 'most strongly that full operational efficiency cannot be realized until this is done.' Already losing patience with the slow progress in Halifax, NSHQ undoubtedly pressed Murray as a result of the board's report. He completed his move to the air headquarters on 20 July.[62]

As Group Captain Canning privately suggested to Air Chief Marshal Slessor, now air officer commanding-in-chief, [AOCinc] Coastal Command, the basic problem really lay with the RCN, which did not 'understand or appreciate the Air problem.'[63] Slessor was inclined to agree. In June he received a copy of Admiral Murray's operational directive to Eastern Air Command from the air member for air staff at AFHQ, Air Vice-Marshal Anderson, who observed that it appeared to assert excessive naval control over the employment of aircraft.[64] Slessor's 'candid opinion' was that the directive:

goes a very long way beyond anything which I could expect to receive from the Admiralty. I think that, in practically every paragraph, it encroaches on the sphere of tactics which, in Coastal Command, is entirely a matter for me or my group commanders. As I understand it (and I think the Admiralty now understand it) the definition of operational control is that the sailor tells us the effect he wants achieved and leaves it entirely to us how that result is achieved. For instance, I consider it entirely wrong for Murray to tell us that he wants close escort of any convoy; what he should tell us is that he wants that convoy protected; and he should give us an order of priority for the convoy; and he should tell us whether, in his view, convoy protection at any given place or time should have priority over offensive sweeps or patrols; but *how* you protect that convoy is entirely a matter for Johnson ...

How you deal with this matter is of course ... entirely for yourself [to decide]; if I may presume to advise on the basis of a certain amount of experience of dealing with the sailors, I should be inclined not to raise it as a policy issue in the first instance; but rather to gradually try and get the thing on the right lines by the ordinary informal day-to-day discussions which will become a matter of course as soon as Murray has been winkled out of his dock yard and put in the Combined H.Q. at Halifax.[65]

The RCAF followed this good advice, with the favourable results Slessor predicted.

The complicated situation in Newfoundland permitted no such straight-forward settlement of command relations. The anti-submarine board was extremely critical of the latitude Heakes allowed the Americans: 'Mutual Co-operation' was not an adequate substitute for the centralized 'Operational Control' envisaged by the Atlantic Convoy Conference. Although gladly accepting the board's detailed recommendations for improving the layout and procedures in the combined operations room at St John's, Heakes maintained that 'with such a mixed bag of tricks as we have the decentralized control has been fully justified ... Certain factors have tended to make this possible here,' he argued, 'namely, we have not the problem of enemy aircraft to contend with, nor the liability of our convoys being jumped by enemy sea forces other than submarines. Hence, we have a greater time factor to play with than they have on the other side. This gives us a working margin.'[66]

Air Vice-Marshal Johnson in Halifax shared Heakes's belief that the system in Newfoundland was 'working out very well.' Johnson's only concern was a lingering tendency in the USAAF squadrons to make anti-submarine sweeps unrelated to convoy protection when tasking from I Group did not fully employ the available aircraft. Nevertheless, the army airmen had readily complied when Heakes, on assuming control, endeavoured to employ additional aircraft on missions to support shipping. From 3 April to 2 May, the USAAF in Newfoundland flew 454 hours on convoy protection as compared to 588 hours on U-boat search patrols; by contrast, in the period 3-31 May, under the new Canadian régime, the squadrons flew 1161 hours in support of convoys and only 235 hours on search patrols. The problem had arisen, in part at least, because the army, in Johnson's words, 'have plugged Gander with three squadrons of long range aircraft which are more than really necessary.' When the AOCinC offered this opinion in mid-May the build-up was continuing with the replacement of the USAAF's B-17s at Gander by Liberators, and the arrival of a USN Liberator squadron at Argentia (although none of these aircraft had been modified to VLR). The extent of the Allied victory and of Dönitz's withdrawal from the north Atlantic was, however, quickly becoming evident. At the beginning of June two USN Lockheed Ventura squadrons returned from Newfoundland to the United States, and in late June to mid-August all three army squadrons and the USN Liberator squadron moved to England to join the Bay of Biscay offensive, leaving only a handful of PBYs at Argentia and solving the problem of divided control by default.[67]

The anti-submarine board's thorough investigations extended beyond the broad principles of organization to the details of tactics, equipment, and procedures, and here too there was much to criticize. Although impressed by the keenness and quality of the Canadian aircrews, Canning was dismayed by their ignorance of recent tactical innovations in Coastal Command and, especially, of the method for radio homing of aircraft to escorts. The latter, known as 'Procedure "B",' was laid down in Atlantic Convoy Instructions. Naval escorts were to take DF bearings on wireless signals from aircraft arriving on task, and then broadcast the information so that the aircrews could correct their courses; short-range, medium-frequency radio transmissions were used to reduce the chance of the enemy intercepting the signals. In their efforts to impress both Canadian services with the importance of sea-air radio homing, the members of the board were assisted by Commander Peter Gretton, one of the Royal Navy's outstanding escort commanders, who lectured on the subject and organized exercises in Newfoundland. The Allied officers also arranged for AFHQ to obtain immediately copies of Coastal Command tactical instructions and memoranda that were not readily to hand and urged the necessity, once again, of quickly distributing the material to squadrons. Eastern Air Command further benefited from a visit by Air Chief Marshal Slessor in early June to discuss means for improving the interchange of information between the RCAF and RAF, and increasing the range of 10 Squadron's new Liberators.[68]

Scrutiny by Allies and their good advice contributed to the efforts made by the RCN and RCAF during the summer months of 1943 to perfect the new organization in preparation for Dönitz's next onslaught. The schedule of exercises for co-operation between ships and aircraft was stepped up, with particular emphasis on radio homing; in addition, aircraft assigned to convoys were invariably to carry out Procedure 'B,' whether necessary or not, and establish communication with the senior officer of the naval escort before commencing sweeps in the area. Ashore, the naval and air commanders at Halifax and St John's began to hold daily conferences, with further consultation by signal between the two combined headquarters, to plan the programme of air coverage on the basis of the Tubular and Stipple signals from Coastal Command and other intelligence.

From 18 July, the OIC at NSHQ also provided the east coast commanders with a daily forecast of U-boat positions in or near the Canadian Northwest Atlantic. Called 'Otter' messages, they were designed to complement Stipple and Tubular information by providing more data about the Canadian coastal area, especially to assist in the planning of offensive sweeps by VLR aircraft based in Newfoundland. The signal gave an area of maximum probability for U-boats on patrol, and the likely course for the next twenty-four hours of U-boats on passage. Possibly trying to discourage decisions based on local intelligence estimates, besides tailoring information designed primarily for air searches to the needs of the navy, NSHQ decreed that 'No other authority is to originate a similar signal, except that C.-in-C., C.N.A., is authorized to promulgate a paraphrased version of relevant information contained in OTTER to sub- commands, if necessary, for establishment of searches for Naval Vessels.'[69]

Certainly there was marked progress in the Canadian organization for anti-submarine warfare. Commander P.B. Martineau made another tour, as the survey board had recommended, and on 6 August reported that 'The general situation has improved out of all recognition since my visit in October-November 1942 ... The co-operation between the RCN and the RCAF is excellent.' He did, however, emphasize two continuing weaknesses: the absence of any naval officer with a 'thorough understanding of air operations,' and a tendency on the part of the RCAF, despite its adoption of the offensive method, to waste flying time on the protection of unthreatened convoys.[70]

There were equally necessary technical developments. Having a squadron of VLR Liberators was one thing; maintaining and using it to best advantage was another. The first transatlantic flights by 10 (BR) Squadron did not occur until July, largely because, although modified in the United States, the aircraft still carried too much weight to achieve their required range of 2300 miles. Fortunately, 19 Sub Repair Depot at Gander had built up an excellent third-line maintenance team, and the friendly generosity of the USAAF personnel, so long as they remained at Gander, ensured there was never any want for spares. Consequently, when the Allied anti-submarine survey team visited in May and recommended removing tail turrets and armour from Liberators, it was possible to make modifications on the spot, although there is no evidence that the armour was ever removed.[71]

New equipment further improved Eastern Air Command's capabilities. No 10 Squadron's Liberators were fitted with American ASG radar; operating on a short wave-length of ten centimetres, it could locate surfaced submarines at ranges of fifteen miles and more. Unlike the ASV Mark II, which presented its data with 'blips' on a simple range scale that were very difficult to interpret accurately, the ASG 'scope' mapped all contacts precisely as the aerial scanned through 360 degrees, making it far more useful then the older sets for navigation and the location of shipping as well as U-boat hunting. The Ventura aircraft that were replacing the Hudsons in 113 and 145 Squadrons (see Chapter 13) carried another new American radar, the more compact 3 cm-band ASD, which, in theory, was capable of locating surfaced submarines at even greater ranges than ASG. The antennae, however, scanned only ahead of the aircraft, and although the scope mapped contacts, it distorted their relative positions. Serviceability problems, moreover, made the equipment unpopular with aircrews during its first months in service. ASD, like ASG, had the great advantage that its emissions could not be detected by search receivers that the Germans had developed to counter metric-band ASV radar.[72]

Another important acquisition was the 600-lb American homing torpedo that enabled aircraft to attack submarines which had already disappeared beneath the surface. Known affectionately as 'Fido' or 'Wandering Annie,' and by a number of code names (Project 'z,' the Mark XXIV Mine, and, later, 'Proctor'), the first of these torpedoes arrived in June 1943. Maintenance crews at Dartmouth, Sydney, North Sydney, Torbay, and Gander adapted Digbys, Venturas, Cansos, and Liberators to carry one and, in the case of the Liberator, two torpedoes, together with three or four depth charges. On 3 September a Digby of 161 (BR) Squadron based at Dartmouth made the first action drop, and a Ventura of 113 (BR) Squadron from Dartmouth made another the next day, but there is no evidence that a U-boat was present. The Liberators of 10 Squadron had their first opportunities later in the month. Like all new and complex weapons, this torpedo proved temperamental in its early stages, and these drops were unsuccessful.[73]

The United States Navy had developed the aerial homing torpedo in conjunction with the expendable radio sono-buoy. Dropped from aircraft in patterns of five, the radio-equipped buoys automatically deployed a hydrophone on a 24-foot cable and transmitted any sounds that were picked up. Using a multi-channel receiver, the aircrew could, with experience and luck, follow the track of a submerged U-boat, dropping a homing torpedo near the buoy that gave the strongest signals or directing surface escorts to the position. Because the non-directional hydrophones gave no indication of the position of the submarine relative to the buoy, however, they were very inaccurate, and if the submarine was running deeply or quietly it could not be detected at all. Even a moderate sea, moreover, could mask the sound of the U-boat with water noise. The equipment began to arrive at Eastern Air Command squadrons only at the end of 1943; technical problems and delays in the provision of training devices increased the inherent difficulty of using the buoys properly.[74]

In contrast to the teething troubles of the sophisticated underwater weapons systems, the RCAF's new Liberators and centimetric radars quickly demonstrated their effectiveness. When the eastbound convoy SC 135 sailed from Halifax on 27 June 1943, only a half-dozen U-boats remained in the north Atlantic, distributed in individual attack areas in the central and western portion of the ocean. To create the illusion that packs were still at large, they regularly broadcast messages on many wave-lengths. Even though Bletchley Park was encountering prolonged delays in breaking the *Triton* cipher during this period, Allied intelligence authorities were not deceived. That SC 135 nevertheless received massive land-based air protection was some measure of the surplus of long-range and very long-range aircraft now available in Newfoundland. In addition, the 1st Escort Group, a support group that included the escort carrier HMS *Biter*, reinforced the mid-ocean naval escort.[75]

On 3 July, when the convoy was some 500 miles northeast of Newfoundland, five 10 Squadron Liberators provided cover. During the afternoon, Liberator 'B,' with Pilot Officer R.R. Stevenson at the controls, made an ASG radar contact at a range of eighteen miles. As Stevenson closed, he dipped beneath the heavy cloud cover only long enough to make a quick visual contact at seven miles. The tactic worked. U-420 was caught completely by surprise as the bomber swept down through the clouds to make three attack runs. Dropping sticks of six, three, and one depth charges (the whole of the Liberator's load), the aircrew also poured machine-gun fire into the submarine. The U-boat's log describes the result: 'water columns dash together over the conning tower. Very violent vibration in the boat. On the second attack run upper MG [machine-gun] was destroyed ... Bosun's Mate Grosser killed, either by shell or bomb splinter. Able Seaman Noeske overboard ... Able Seaman Winn bullet entered right half of buttocks and a splinter in the upper thigh ... Crash dive! ... Large amount of water entered via the upper conning-tower hatch ... Damage ... Main periscope (bullet holes). Tubes I-IV mechanisms hard to work. Breech door tube IV broken off. Electric compressor, Junker compressor limited working capability. Forward horizontal rudder sticks ...'

Stevenson alerted the senior officer of the naval escort who dispatched the 1st Escort Group to the scene. Searches by the warships and *Biter*'s aircraft came up empty-handed, but Stevenson and his crew had knocked U-420 out of action; having scarcely begun its patrol, the submarine now limped back to port.[76]

Coverage of the convoy from Newfoundland continued until late on 5 July. RCAF, USN, and USAAF Liberators (the American aircraft having been converted to VLR) operated as far as 30 degrees west, some 1000 miles from base; one 10 Squadron aircraft was diverted to Iceland and another to Northern Ireland.[77] This was a convincing demonstration of the transatlantic support land-based aircraft could now provide, through such protection was still the exception rather than the rule.

Despite the quiet that settled over the north Atlantic during the rest of the summer as Dönitz withdrew the last of his boats, a renewed campaign at mid-ocean was expected.[78] 'The Battle of the Atlantic,' Heakes told the squadrons of 1 Group at the beginning of September, 'is of such importance to the German that he will make the most tremendous effort to regain control ... It is almost axiomatic to assume he will try again to catch the convoys in the western and middle part of the Atlantic ...' Months of fruitless patrol had sapped morale, and he tried to ginger up his aircrew: 'Let us get rid of this sense of frustration which has been growing through lack of action ... For though we have won the Battle, there undoubtedly, in my opinion, is another battle to be fought and won in these waters. And, beyond that battle, there is a long, long lane, branching out into many theatres, in which all will have the opportunity of their complete fill of action in this war.'[79]

Dönitz of course did not disappoint these expectations. Armed with the new *Zaunkönig* homing torpedo, or 'gnat' as it was called by the Allies, quadruple 20mm anti-aircraft cannons, and improved equipment for the detection of Allied radar transmissions, twenty-nine U-boats, including a 'milch cow' submarine tanker, sailed in the first weeks of September from bases in Norway, Germany, and the Bay of Biscay. By 19 September nineteen of them had formed Group *Leuthen* and lay seventeen miles apart on a north-south line west of the British Isles waiting for two westbound convoys, ONS 18 and, some distance astern, the fast convoy ON 202. However, Enigma intercepts enabled the Admiralty to order a diversion of the convoys to the northwest, take steps to reinforce their surface escort, and ensure the availability of air escort.[80]

It so happened that on 19 September three Canadian Liberators of 10 (BR) Squadron were at Reykjavik, Iceland, after providing the air escort for HMS *Renown*, bringing home Winston Churchill and the British chiefs of staff from the 'Quadrant' conference of Allied leaders at Quebec. Two of the aircraft covered ONS 18 on their return flight to Gander that day and the crew of Liberator A/10, piloted by Flight Lieutenant J.F. Fisher, sighted U-341 500 miles south of Iceland and 160 miles west of the convoy. On his first pass, Fisher was too high but the U-boat remained to fight it out on the surface and, on the second run, a straddle with six depth charges blew U-341's bow out of the water. As the conning tower disappeared four more charges were followed by a great eruption of oil and bubbles, which marked the end of the submarine. Fisher, who proceeded to Gander after remaining in the area for twenty-five minutes, was to die in a flying accident a month after achieving this first kill in a Canadian VLR aircraft.[81]

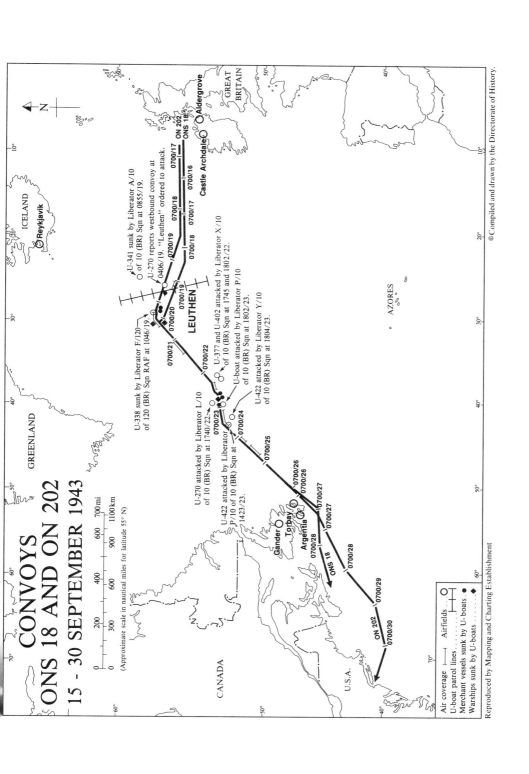

CONVOYS
ONS 18 AND ON 202
15 - 30 SEPTEMBER 1943

ICELAND

Reykjavik

GREENLAND

0   200   400   600   700 mi
0   300   600   900   1100 km
(Approximate scale in nautical miles for latitude 55° N)

CANADA

Gander

Torbay

Argentia

ONS 18

ON 202

0700/30

0700/29

0700/28

0700/28

0700/27

0700/27

0700/26

0700/26

0700/25

0700/24

0700/23

0700/22

U-422 attacked by Liberator
P/10 of 10 (BR) Sqn at
1423/23.

U-270 attacked by Liberator L/10
of 10 (BR) Sqn at 1740/22.

U-338 sunk by Liberator L/10
of 120 (BR) Sqn at 1740/22.

U-422 attacked by Liberator Y/10
of 10 (BR) Sqn at 1804/23.

U-boat attacked by Liberator P/10
of 10 (BR) Sqn at 1802/23.

U-377 and U-402 attacked by Liberator X/10
of 10 (BR) Sqn at 1745 and 1802/22.

0700/21

U-338 sunk by Liberator F/120
of 120 (BR) Sqn RAF at 1046/19.

LEUTHEN

0700/20

0700/19

U-341 sunk by Liberator A/10
of 10 (BR) Sqn at 0855/19.

U-270 reports westbound convoy at
0406/19. "Leuthen" ordered to attack.

0700/22

0700/19

0700/18

0700/18

0700/17

0700/17

0700/16

Castle Archdale

ON 202
ONS 18

Aldergrove

GREAT
BRITAIN

AZORES

U.S.A.

Air coverage .... | Airfields ... O
U-boat patrol lines ......
Merchant vessels sunk by U-boats .. ●
Warships sunk by U-boats .... ◆

Reproduced by Mapping and Charting Establishment

© Compiled and drawn by the Directorate of History.

During the next twenty-four hours ON 202 and ONS 18 gradually closed the distance between them until, on 20 September, they combined to form one large convoy. The night before the junction ON 202 had been successfully attacked, losing two ships. But throughout the 20th RAF Liberators from 120 Squadron provided air cover, attacking eight U-boats and sinking one, U-338. During the night of 20/21 September the escorts HMCS *St Croix* and HMS *Polyanthus* were sunk by 'gnats' before fog clamped down to restrict the activities on both sides. In the meantime, *Empire MacAlpine* – a grain ship fitted with a lightly built flight deck and known as a merchant aircraft carrier or MAC ship – launched a Fairey Swordfish to provide air cover for a few hours. Liberators were also sent to escort the convoy from both sides of the ocean: the air gap could now be closed at will. When the fog cleared more than 800 miles east of Newfoundland on the afternoon of 22 September, 'the air was filled with Liberators' of the RCAF's 10 Squadron.[82]

With the improved visibility, Liberator L/10 flown by Warrant Officer J. Billings, sighted and attacked U-270 with four depth charges in the face of accurate flak. One enemy round shot out an engine and another 'parted the hair above the Navigator's left eye and came to rest protruding half an inch out of one of the instruments in front of the Captain.' The Liberator circled the submarine, returning machine-gun fire and calling for assistance, but the convoy escorts were heavily engaged and Liberator X/10 some forty miles away replied 'I have a U-boat of my own on my hands.' Damaged, reaching the prudent limit of endurance, and unable to use his homing torpedo, the only main armament remaining, because the boat would not submerge, the aircraft left for home. U-270, however, had been badly damaged by Billings' near miss. A break in the pressure hull made it impossible for her to dive, so she retreated on the surface for port in France.[83] Billings was awarded the Distinguished Flying Cross in 1944.

Liberator X/10, flown by Flight Lieutenant J.R. Martin, who also received a Distinguished Flying Cross the next year, did indeed have a handful when her sister aircraft called for help. Dispatched by the senior officer of the naval escort to search an HF/DF bearing, Martin located U-377 on his radar and attacked through flak with machine-guns and four depth charges. The Liberator circled around the jinking U-boat and dropped two homing torpedoes twenty seconds after it disappeared beneath the surface. Neither the depth charges nor the acoustic torpedoes inflicted damage, but the machine-gun attack had left U-377's commander bleeding profusely from wounds in both arms. The boat therefore had to retreat from the battle and rendezvous with a second submarine for medical assistance en route to port.[84]

During the second attack on U-377 Martin sighted another U-boat, probably U-402, seven-and-a-half miles away. Having expended its main armament, the Liberator could only trade gunfire with the boat until it disappeared in a fog bank. Martin alerted the naval escort commander and maintained a patrol between the submarine's position and the ships he was protecting during the rest of his time on station. Shortly after this aircraft's departure in the late afternoon, Swordfish from *Empire MacAlpine* attacked an unidentified U-boat ahead of the convoy. Meanwhile, Liberator N/10 had been hampered by radio interference in its efforts to carry out homing procedure, possibly the result of German jamming. The aircraft was therefore only able to stay for an hour, when the pilot found the ships after twilight. In that brief time, the crew sighted a wake in the darkness and encountered anti-aircraft fire that confirmed the presence of U-275 some way ahead of the convoy. The escort commander, however, firmly refused permission to drop flares for a night attack, so the Liberator carried on with his orders to sweep around the convoy at visual distance to strengthen the inner defences against the closing pack. The aircraft had forced the submarine to submerge, but during the night at least seven U-boats which had escaped damage slipped through the screen, sinking four merchant ships and the escort HMS *Itchen*.[85]

The arrival before sunrise of a Liberator piloted by Flight Lieutenant J.F. Green undoubtedly prevented further losses. This was a flight of some note because the deputy inspector-general of the RCAF, Air Vice-Marshal A.E. Godfrey, whose most recent combat experience had been as a fighter 'ace' on the Western Front in 1918, was the 'acting waist gunner.' In the morning twilight Green sighted and briefly engaged with gunfire a U-boat that escaped in the low visibility. During the next six hours the aircraft succeeded in keeping the enemy submarines submerged. On the way back to base Green sighted U-422, giving Godfrey the opportunity to become the most senior RCAF officer to open fire directly against the foe during the Second World War. After a twenty-seven minute engagement the submarine dived. Green's attack with two homing torpedoes, like many other attempts to employ this temperamental weapon, was unsuccessful. Nearly four hours later Flight Lieutenant R.R. Ingrams, while on a close escort search in Liberator Y/10, attacked U-422, forcing it to submerge and inflicting casualties on the crew that demanded medical assistance from another submarine. Ingram's homing torpedoes missed their mark, but Dönitz ordered the U-boats to withdraw because of the onset of fog.[86]

Thus ended one of the most significant convoy battles of the war. The RCAF Liberators had acquitted themselves well. There was still room for improvement, especially in the technique of attacking surfaced submarines (there seems to have been a tendency, no doubt exaggerated by the U-boats' 20mm quad anti-aircraft cannon, to come in too high on the first run), and in perfecting the employment of homing torpedoes. The effectiveness of VLR Liberators at night was severely hampered without the Leigh Lights now available to Coastal Command aircraft operating in the Bay of Biscay. Nevertheless, the Canadians had been effective in protecting the convoys (there were no losses while aircraft were present), and had enjoyed notable success in sighting, attacking, and sinking U-boats. The senior officer with the naval escort group was highly impressed:

The dense fog which prevailed for such a large part of the passage made flying near the convoy very unpleasant, and at times I wondered if the aircraft were serving any really useful purpose in risking their lives to come so far, only to find nil visibility on arrival. I think this doubt was well answered when the instant the fog lifted three Liberators were not 'on the way' or 'expected in two hours,' but actually flying around the convoy and giving it valuable protection ...

On reaching St John's I learnt that aircraft had been taking off in dense fog at very great risk in order to provide us with full cover all the time. I can only say 'Thank you,' and assure them that their work is appreciated to the full, and their mere presence has an effect on the morale of both convoy and escorts which is invaluable.[87]

The exchange rate of three U-boats sunk for the loss of six ships and three escorts was a satisfactory result from the Allied point of view. Assessments based on inflated claims at first persuaded Dönitz that the battle was a German victory, but events of the next two months shattered the illusion. No more convoys were intercepted by U-boats until 7 October, when U-645 made contact with SC 143. In the early hours of 9 October this submarine sank one ship but was forced to remain submerged and lost contact, so that Dönitz had to call off the operation. From 15 to 17 October Group *Schlieffen* made contact with ONS 20 and ON 206, losing four U-boats to RAF Liberators and two more to the RN escort ships in exchange for one merchant ship in the latter convoy. Dönitz withdrew from this disastrous battle and formed a group, *Siegfried*, which, without even sighting the convoys it was supposed to attack, lost three U-boats.[88]

A Liberator of 10 Squadron was responsible for the destruction of one of the *Siegfried* boats on 26 October. Six Liberators flew close escort patrols for ON 207 and ONS 21 that day, and two others flew supporting sweeps. Flight Lieutenant R.M. Aldwinkle, just as he began his joining procedure with the convoy in Liberator A/10, sighted and attacked U-420, the same boat that had been so roughly handled by another squadron aircraft on 3 July. On the first run five of the six depth charges dropped failed to explode. There followed a protracted gun duel, after which the U-boat dived and Aldwinkle dropped his homing torpedo. Its explosion apparently forced U-420 back up to periscope depth, at which point the last two remaining depth charges caused another explosion that 'shot up like an oil gusher as though under great pressure and rose to a height of fifty or sixty feet' as the submarine was destroyed, probably by sympathetic detonation of torpedoes.[89] Aldwinkle received the Distinguished Flying Cross.

Groups *Jahn* and *Koerner*, formed from *Siegfried*, were taking up positions about 400 miles northeast and east of Newfoundland. On 29 October one of the boats joining up from the east was sunk by escort vessels about twenty miles ahead of convoy ON 208, and a few days later Dönitz adopted new tactics to deal with this menace of ubiquitous Allied sea and air forces. He dissolved existing groups, forming five small groups named *Tirpitz* 1-5 on the arc of a circle about 450 miles east of the southern tip of Newfoundland. By 8 November they had sighted no convoys and lost two U-boats to attack by a support group with an escort carrier, so Dönitz sent the *Tirpitz* boats in groups of three to a diamond-shaped patrol area southeast of Greenland. A Canso of 116 Squadron with convoy ON 209 sighted U-714 in one of these groups but did not make an attack owing to anti-aircraft fire; an investigation by No 1 Group concluded that there had been a serious failure of leadership in the unit and resulted in the relief of the squadron commander.

Two days later a discouraged Dönitz changed the disposition of the submarines yet again; the enemy, he said, 'has all our secrets and we have none of theirs.'[90] On 12 November he ordered another vain move, this time about 350 miles in a southeasterly direction.[91] Equally futile manoeuvres went on until the end of the year,

16

Securing the Lifeline, 1943-4

The defeat of the wolf packs in the fall of 1943 thrust Canadian airmen into a new era of anti-submarine warfare. During the last eighteen months of the war single U-boats returned to North American waters for inshore operations markedly different from those of 1942. Submariners were now cautious, sometimes to the extreme, intent upon a quick kill and getaway. No longer aggressively pursuing shipping on the surface, they employed 'ambush' tactics: lying submerged for extended periods, awaiting targets of opportunity. The U-boats also carried search receivers that could now detect radar transmissions on all Allied wave-lengths in time to dive before an aircraft was within visual range. Eastern Air Command's improved equipment – Lockheed Ventura and Consolidated Liberator aircraft, its first Leigh Lights, and the sonobuoy and acoustic torpedo – was in no sense a decisive answer to the new threat. For the aircrews, then, there were even more hours than before of tedious and exhausting patrols over vast expanses of ocean in search of an increasingly elusive enemy. Because the Germans initiated their 'ambush' methods in the northwest Atlantic, moreover, Canadians for the first time had to work out solutions to a tactical problem without the benefit of extensive British experience. How they responded to this challenge is an interesting measure of RCAF capabilities in the final months of the Second World War.

Although Admiral Dönitz had sustained a crushing defeat, the U-boat fleet was still formidable and a menace to the north Atlantic lifeline. In December 1943 there were 163 operational U-boats available, as compared to a peak strength of 239 in May, and new construction was making good the losses. Locating single U-boats scattered over large areas required just as many aircraft and ships as operations against whole wolf packs concentrated in the vicinity of convoys. It was possible, however, with the help of adroit intelligence, to keep the size of search areas within limits that could be saturated by the ships and aircraft to hand. Indeed, the new situation created opportunities to hunt U-boats at length, something which anti-submarine commands on both sides of the Atlantic had long desired, but had not been possible with the resources available. How long hunts should continue, and how far they should be allowed to interfere with routine convoy escorts – and therefore the number and disposition of ships and aircraft – were still matters for debate.[1]

Eastern Air Command's operational research section [ORS] had begun to examine the question of hunting submarines to exhaustion in February 1943. Canadian practice had been to abandon searches after losing contact, but Coastal Command aircraft had in some cases persisted for about six hours, and had achieved second sightings about 25 per cent of the time. Observing that most of Eastern Air Command's attacks had taken place within 200 miles of base, two-thirds of them in good flying weather, the ORS argued that extended searches would have been possible in most previous cases. British studies had concluded that a U-boat attempting to escape quickly was likely to surface and present a good target, and that when submerged the submarine's absolute limit of endurance was forty-eight hours.[2]

In mid 1943 the submerged U-boat could be expected to maintain a speed of about two knots, which meant that over two days it could not be more than one hundred miles from the last known position. Four aircraft on task at a time could, with the assistance of radar, cover such an area constantly for the whole period. Given good weather, a squadron of twenty aircraft could perform three 48-hour searches a week without extraordinary effort. This would prevent the submarine from surfacing to escape at speed, and ensure that naval forces could sweep the probability area thoroughly with ASDIC and radar.[3]

Hunts to exhaustion – quickly codenamed 'Salmons' in the Canadian environment – could only be carried out once a submarine had actually been sighted. Good intelligence was the key to making the initial contact and, in the northwest Atlantic, this was supplied by the daily Otter signals the Operational Intelligence Centre [OIC] at Naval Service Headquarters began to promulgate to the air authorities in Ottawa and on the east coast in July 1943. These signals, it will be recalled, contained the submarine tracking room's forecasts of the areas where U-boats would most probably be found on the following day; if further information became available the signal was amended immediately. The predicted locations were classified 'A,' 'B,' and 'C' in descending order of certainty. 'A' category estimates were based on fresh intelligence; a sighting, an attack on shipping, accurate direction-finding [DF] bearings, or German signals decrypted at Bletchley Park in England that revealed the boat's precise position. Air sweeps over 'A' areas had a priority second only to the defence of shipping at risk in the immediate vicinity. Predictions classified 'B' (and these were the vast majority) were based on contacts or DF bearings a few days old, and often on decrypted German signals that gave the route or destination of a boat. They also warranted air searches, provided threatened shipping was protected. There lay the essential difference between the old and the new offensive methods, for previously Eastern Air Command had generally made special sweeps only on the basis of information in the 'A' category. Class 'C' estimates were derived from information so old or vague that air searches were generally not worthwhile.[4]

Bletchley Park's speed in decrypting German wireless traffic by late 1943 enabled Naval Service Headquarters to make estimates of U-boat locations that were often as good as, or better, than BdU's own. Even forecasts based on recent information, however, had to allow for a wide margin of uncertainty: during the hours required to process the intelligence and dispatch aircraft to the position, the submarine could make off in any direction at an unknown speed. The submarine trackers in Ottawa therefore drew on their experience to pare down the area where, in theory, the boat might be located, to a smaller area where the boat was most likely to be found and which could be swept in a patrol by one or two radar-equipped aircraft.

Nevertheless, searching for single U-boats was still very much a game of chance. Otter areas were normally at least 15,000 square miles in size and often much larger, an area which a single aircraft could sweep only once during a patrol. If the air crew failed to maintain a sharp lookout at all times, a lapse that was inevitable during long and exhausting flights, if the ASV radar was not working properly or if the U-boat submerged, it would not be found. False, but convincing radar or visual contacts amidst the fog, ice-floes, and flotsam off the Canadian coast could put an air search on the wrong track for days. No matter how sound the intelligence, moreover, estimates could be wrong. Depending upon the weather, the state of a submarine's equipment, and the boldness of the commander, it could be several days ahead or behind the expected rate of advance, or even far off the course ordered by U-boat headquarters.[5]

Air searches that failed to sight the enemy were not necessarily wasted. As Coastal Command's offensive sweeps of 1941-2 that were based on much less complete intelligence had demonstrated, the constant presence of aircraft sapped the offensive spirit of all but the most extraordinary U-boat commanders, and rendered the submarine virtually immobile by forcing it to run submerged.

Otter signals enabled Eastern Air Command to take the initiative when in late 1943 single U-boats returned to Canadian waters in some numbers, but calculating the amount of effort that should be expended on the new offensive tactics was tricky. The tendency in Coastal Command and the Admiralty to overrate the value of offensive operations in the Bay of Biscay had, until September 1943, deprived convoys of adequate air coverage in the air gap. This was never the case in the northwest Atlantic. Offensive operations during the last nineteen months of the war seldom interfered with convoy defence. If Eastern Air Command were to err, it would be on the side of caution.

Naval co-operation, which was essential for hunts to exhaustion and became increasingly important for sweeping Otter areas once U-boats began to run submerged in daylight when within range of regular land-based air patrols, was a fundamental problem in the northwest Atlantic. Thorough coverage of a large expanse of ocean by combined air and sea forces required a higher degree of more sophisticated interservice co-operation than did the comparatively straightforward task of convoy escort. Unfortunately, because the RCN sent as many ships as possible to serve under British command in the eastern Atlantic after mid-1943, no permanently organized and well-trained naval group was available for offensive operations in the Canadian zone until the summer of 1944. All too often the RCN could provide only *ad hoc* groupings cobbled together from ships that had never worked as a team, let alone gained experience in co-ordinating their efforts with aircraft.

Quite aside from the shortage of ships neither the air nor the naval staffs in

Halifax enthusiastically embraced the new offensive methods. This hesitation reflected the same conservatism that brought the senior commanders to give a higher priority to convoy escort than did their British counterparts. Significantly, Air Force and Naval Service Headquarters in Ottawa took the initiative when Canadian forces first tried out the tactics; despite many months of discussion, little effort had been made on the coast to adapt the relevant British instructions for use in the northwest Atlantic.[6] When, on 29 October 1943, U-537's presence in the theatre became apparent, Ottawa seized upon the opportunity to put those instructions to the test.

The OIC had been unaware of U-537's specific destination or mission. This large Type IXA boat had already, on 22 October, visited Martin Bay, Labrador, where its crew had erected an automatic weather station that functioned for several months and remained undetected for thirty-seven years.[7] U-boat headquarters subsequently revealed the boat's position by ordering it to patrol within 150 miles of St John's to observe convoy traffic, information enough for naval headquarters to issue class 'A' Otter signals.[8] The OIC reminded Eastern Air Command that 'the highest possible priority' should be given to sweeps in 'A' areas,[9] while the air and naval staffs in Ottawa urged the east coast commanders to attempt their first hunt to exhaustion.

1. Code word 'Salmon' allotted this operation. Decision to execute at discretion CINC CNA [commander-in-chief Canadian Northwest Atlantic] and yourself but recommended as having strong chance of success under present favourable conditions. Conditions may remain suitable several days but operations should begin without fail on first sighting made in or near area …

2. General principle is if S/M [submarine] not attacked and killed on first sighting a/c [aircraft] continuously patrol area embracing all possible positions S/M. This area obviously increases steadily till next sighting when process begins again. Realize visual sighting or a/c attack impossible at night but ASV [radar] contact will fix position and surface vessels will co-operate. Time of first sighting will be zero hour and position will be datum position 'A.' Search area is circle with radius in nautical miles of twice number of hours since zero hour. During first eight hours cover area three times per hour. Next eight hours twice per hour. Third eight hours three times in two hours. Thereafter once per hour. Arrangements to be made for continuous intercommunication a/c and surface vessel by R/T [radio telephone] and also listening out for signals on convoy wave. R/T silence unnecessary after first sighting. Reckon this coverage will require for first eight hours one a/c. Next four hours two a/c. Next three hours three a/c and so forth. Second sighting when obtained … will bring operation back to zero hour. Position of second sighting to be datum point 'B' … Search is worthwhile up to 36 hours between sightings if sufficient a/c available … If operation Salmon seems profitable after executing it we must consider repeating it under same code name whenever similar favourable conditions arise in future.[10]

The commander-in-chief Canadian Northwest Atlantic, Rear-Admiral L.W. Murray, could not very well disregard such insistent pressure, and he sent out the necessary orders, with which the air officer commanding-in-chief [AOCinC]

Eastern Air Command, Air Vice-Marshal G.O. Johnson, complied. After sunrise on 31 October, the third day of the search, a Lockheed Hudson of 11 Squadron, flown by Flying Officer F.L. Burston (accompanied by his brother as navigator), sighted U-537 and carried out an unsuccessful attack. This was the only time rocket projectiles were used in action by an Eastern Air Command aircraft. The rockets, with solid steel semi-armour piercing warheads, had been delivered to 11 Squadron and 119 Squadron the month before. The Hudsons, fitted with eight of these projectiles, were supposed to aim twenty yards short of the submarine to hole it below the waterline, and in this instance the pilot probably undershot. No 1 Group dispatched or diverted three aircraft to carry out a Salmon, but the Hudson, its crew unaware of the importance of continual air coverage to keep the U-boat down and immobilize it until naval forces could reach the position, left the area after making its unsuccessful attack. Thus the operation had already been seriously compromised, even before deteriorating weather prevented further air support after warships arrived late in the day. Still, the effort had not been without effect. Mystified as to how he had been located and taken completely by surprise, U-537's captain concluded that 'this part of the coast has been made unhealthy' and retreated to the south.[11]

There was no further evidence as to the submarine's whereabouts until dusk on 10 November when a 5 Squadron Canso 'A,' escorting convoy HX 265 about 200 miles south of Cape Race, sighted the boat and made an unsuccessful depth-charge attack in the face of brisk flak. Admiral Murray promptly ordered another Salmon, but once again everything went wrong. The Canso thoroughly confused the warships escorting HX 265 by incorrectly reporting the position of the attack, and then departed before relief aircraft arrived. As a result, U-537 was able to escape by making a fast run on the surface for five-and-a-half hours.[12]

Nevertheless, another Canso 'A' participating in the Salmon search found U-537 on the surface, eighty miles to the south, the next morning. Despite accurate flak that blew a large hole in the leading edge of one of the wings, Pilot Officer R. Duncan placed four depth charges close enough to damage the boat slightly. He then lingered in the area to home in a relieving Canso, which in turn homed warships searching the vicinity of the previous evening's attack. The aircraft did not, however, perform a proper sweep of the expanding area where the submerged boat might be located prior to the arrival of the first surface escorts four-and-a-half hours after the attack. Fortunately, the senior ship was a British destroyer, HMS *Montgomery*, with an experienced captain and an Eastern Air Command pilot on board for a routine naval liaison cruise, who was able to advise the captain on communications with the aircraft. The ships searched within a radius of fifteen miles from the position of the attack, and the two 5 Squadron Canso 'A's now on task swept at radii of about five and twelve-and-a-half miles. Although the aircraft should have searched out to a twenty-mile radius, the operation did approximate a proper hunt to exhaustion. Within two hours, however, heavy fog rolled in, forcing the Cansos to return to base. A single relief aircraft was only able to make a few searches of specific areas before it too had to depart. The ships continued to hunt for three days in the swirling murk. With great effort two 5 Squadron Canso 'A's attempted to provide support for the ships on 13 November, while three 10 Squadron Liberators swept the whole Otter area, but the weather thwarted all further efforts.[13]

U-537 continued quietly to patrol east of Newfoundland, dropping out of sight until making a signal on 19 November that shore stations intercepted. Misinterpreting this signal as evidence that the submarine was homebound, the OIC plotted its track to mid-Atlantic, where 10 Squadron Liberators made four sweeps on 20-1 November, a week before U-537 actually departed.[14]

Although the air sweeps of the Otter 'A' areas had yielded the gratifying result of two attacks that effectively suppressed U-537, the attempts to trap the boat with Salmon operations on 31 October and 10 November had gone badly. The absence of Canadian orders for hunts to exhaustion was a large part of the reason, for the British instructions were unclear in some respects and, in others, inapplicable to practices in the northwest Atlantic. The only specific instructions had been suggested by the naval and air staffs in Ottawa on 29 October; these directions never reached the ships that made the search on 31 October, and it is clear that the aircrews that participated had been briefed poorly if at all. More generally, as Admiral Murray commented, air-sea communications were much worse than they should have been given the long time that Eastern Air Command and the RCN had worked together. Had fog not intervened, the Salmon on 11 November might have accomplished more, but the successful co-operation between ships and aircraft on that occasion had depended upon the presence of an exceptionally capable ship with an airman on board.[15] Circumstances would not always be so favourable.

The next U-boat to enter the Canadian zone, U-543, lingered in the vicinity of Flemish Cap from late December 1943 to early January 1944 to make weather reports and attack shipping. Decrypted German signals and DF bearings enabled the Operational Intelligence Centre to follow her with Otter 'A' signals.[16] A determined search for a boat some 400 miles out to sea was an ambitious undertaking, but the headquarters in Ottawa and Halifax decided it was worthwhile attempting to convince Admiral Dönitz that Canadian waters were not a soft spot. From 23 December to 6 January, 1 Group covered the area with twenty-one Liberator and seven Canso 'A' flights, including sweeps made in support of convoys in the area, none of which sighted the boat.[17] The OIC's estimates were accurate, however, for U-543 was in contact with the naval group that joined the search, made two unsuccessful attacks on the ships, and was detected on radar by one of the frigates, during the night of 2/3 January, when the weather had grounded 1 Group.[18]

The inexperience of the warships – most had only recently been commissioned and were still working up – largely accounted for the failure of the operation, but the air force had not done well either. In a blistering critical analysis of the search, Captain J.M. de Marbois, head of the OIC, found that 1 Group had devoted nearly twice as much flying time to protecting convoys, most of them not threatened, as to hunting for U-543. Only three night sweeps had been completed, despite the OIC's warning that the boat would likely submerge during daylight, and should therefore be pursued around the clock. On average, in fact, 1 Group covered only 76 per cent of the Otter area each day, and in most cases covered that portion no more than once. De Marbois calculated that a full commitment of resources could have produced three complete sweeps of the Otter area daily and one each night.[19]

A general review of Eastern Air Command's operations by the command's operational research section had brought Air Force Headquarters to much the same conclusion.[20] On 3 February Air Commodore K.M. Guthrie, acting air member for air staff, expressed the air staff's concern to Air Vice-Marshal Johnson that routine convoy escort was interfering with the imaginative use of air forces. Guthrie saw that the object was the safe and timely arrival of convoys, and placed this ahead of all other aims. When convoys were known to be clear of danger, however, and the position of U-boats could be fixed, convoy escort became a purely defensive mode of warfare. 'If we could give 100% protection to convoys so that no ships were ever sunk at all ... this, it is true, would render the enemy's submarines useless, and there would be no need to kill them. In fact, however, we can never give 100% protection and therefore we must fight the submarine and not merely try to ward it off.' Guthrie followed this sound piece of logic with another: 'It follows that we must try to improve our methods of seeking out and attacking submarines, and that wherever these methods have any chance of success, we should use for this purpose every aircraft that can be spared (with due regard to training requirements, etc.) from convoy escort. It is felt that serious consideration should be given to whether aircraft escort is sometimes wasted on convoys which are not threatened.' Thus setting forth the argument, but not intending 'to dictate operational policy, which must lie in the hands of yourself as the operational Commander ...' Ottawa left the decision for or against more offensive tactics in Air Vice-Marshal Johnson's hands.[21]

The arrival of Guthrie's missive just as another offensive operation was getting under way may have helped to spur Eastern Air Command on to greater efforts. Admiral Dönitz had ordered U-845, with U-539 following, to hunt close in to the southeastern coast of Newfoundland in the expectation that the boats would catch the Canadians by surprise. In fact, Bletchley Park knew at least the broad outline of the plan immediately through decrypted signals. On 23 January two Liberators from 10 Squadron flew out to mid-ocean at 38 degrees west to catch U-845 as it entered the Canadian zone, and from 29 January the squadron dispatched as many as five flights a day to sweep the Otter 'B' area.[22]

During the first week of February the trail grew cold and weather grounded aircraft on several days, but on the 6th a DF bearing that placed U-845 near Flemish Cap encouraged Admiral Murray to launch a strong naval search. When 1 Group was able to fly again on the 9th, the hunt had followed the estimated track into the vicinity of Cape Race. However, an estimated track was not an actual one, and the OIC had warned Halifax that U-845 might strike anywhere about the shores of the Avalon peninsula. That, in fact, was what happened. The U-boat had moved some eighty miles north of the estimated track and was lurking about ten miles off St John's on the morning of 9 February. By remaining submerged it had evaded aircraft, while the density layering of inshore waters greatly reduced the chance of surface vessels making an ASDIC contact. U-845 was thus able to torpedo the British steamer *Kelmscott*. The damaged ship was able to return to port but her attacker escaped unscathed despite a prompt air and sea search that included constant day and night coverage by 1 Group until the weather closed in on the 12th.[23] The same thing would happen many times again on the British and American as well as the Canadian seaboards. Although powerful anti-submarine forces had driven the wolf packs from the ocean routes, ships and aircraft were no more successful in detecting submerged boats in coastal waters than in the early years of the war.

During the hunt for U-845 from 9 to 12 February, 1 Group had also swept for U-539 as it came in south of Flemish Cap, but by the time the weather cleared on the 14th the locations of both boats were becoming uncertain, requiring the promulgation of four Otter areas. At dusk on 14 February Liberator 'Q' of 10 Squadron, flown by Flying Officer A.P.V. Cheater, was completing a sweep in one of these areas when the wireless operator was alerted by what appeared to be jamming from a nearby transmitter. In the failing light the crew spotted U-845; the boat put up heavy flak and the aircraft responded with accurate fire of its own. This was the first time the new low-level bomb sight that had recently been installed in 10 Squadron's aircraft was used in action, and the bomb aimer subsequently claimed that smoke from the nose gun blinded him, putting the six depth charges off target. On a second run he placed the remaining two depth charges close enough to lift the submarine in the water. Cheater made a third run to pour more machine-gun fire into the conning tower, and then released a homing torpedo without apparent result when U-845 dove. The depth charges had inflicted superficial damage at most, but the Liberator's guns had killed one member of the crew and slightly wounded two others.[24]

It proved impossible to organize a hunt to exhaustion on a contact so far out to sea. The relief aircraft could not reach the position until six hours after Liberator Q/10 at its prudent limit of endurance, had had to return to base; warships sweeping to the south of Newfoundland immediately made for Flemish Cap, but were ordered back by Admiral Murray as they were a full day's steaming from the position.[25]

Analysis of the Liberator's attack at Air Force Headquarters criticized the crew for not initially detecting the submarine with radar, a weakness that suggested the operator was not efficient, and for failing to drop radio sonobuoys as soon as U-845 dived. Although Group Captain C.L. Annis, now the station commander at Gander, admitted the crew had not been adequately briefed about sonobuoys, he properly commended the crew for their 'determination and coolness' in the face of heavy fire. Cheater and his navigator-bomb aimer, Flying Officer P.C.E. Lafond, received the Distinguished Flying Cross for the action.[26]

Air searches for U-845 and U-539 continued until the end of February in deteriorating weather. Without the benefit of any further intelligence, the Otter areas became increasingly inaccurate. The Nova Scotia squadrons participated in the last part of the operation, guarding against the possibility that one of the boats had made for Halifax. Like U-845, U-539 hunted close in to St John's, but left empty-handed, while U-845 made no more successful attacks and on 10 March was sunk by Canadian warships as it attempted to strike at a convoy in the eastern Atlantic.[27]

The operations of late January and February 1944 had marked the beginning of a stalemate in the northwest Atlantic which, despite the introduction of more sophisticated equipment and tactics by both protagonists, was to continue until the last days of the war. Eastern Air Command had for the first time made a whole-hearted commitment of its resources to the new offensive methods, at the expense of the effort devoted to protecting unthreatened convoys, as the following table of the crucial anti-submarine patrols flown out of Newfoundland demonstrates. Yet only once, on 14 February, had there been an opportunity to attack a U-boat.

U-Boat Searches, Canadian Northwest Atlantic
October 1943–February 1944[28]

		Convoy Protection		Offensive Sweeps	
	U-boat	No of missions	Flying hours	No of missions	Flying hours
1 Group 29 Oct.– 18 Nov. 1943	U-537	93	1035	60	555
24 Dec. 1943– 6 Jan. 1944	U-543	36	302	20	180
28 Jan.– 24 Feb. 1944	U-845 U-539	42	440	103	783

Although German signals provided timely information about a submarine's general course and destination, the OIC was still dependent upon aircraft sighting reports and DF bearings to pinpoint its position and accurately plot its movements. Cautious tactics, which included a policy of signalling as infrequently as possible from operational areas, and improved radar search receivers enabled U-boats to evade detection. At the same time, because the boats now submerged frequently and for extended periods while on patrol, they lost mobility and were seldom able to attack; hence the meagre result – one steamer damaged – of the long patrols by U-845 and U-539.

The frustrations suffered in pursuit of these two submarines were matched between early March and mid April, when U-802 arrived off Halifax. No 1 Group swept the estimated course soon after the submarine entered the northwest Atlantic, and 3 Group took over the search as the Otter areas approached Nova Scotia, but the intelligence picture remained cloudy as the boat began to patrol without betraying its position. A two-day Salmon triggered by false radar and radio sonobuoy contacts reported by a 161 Squadron Canso 'A' about 140 miles south of Halifax on 18 March did not locate the submarine. U-802 was in fact close in to the harbour and before dawn on the 22nd sank the small British steamer *Watuka* in the immediate eastern approaches.[29]

Admiral Murray immediately laid on an intense air and sea hunt that continued for four days, but a series of lapses and a bad guess by the shore command helped U-802 to escape unscathed. The boat surfaced about fifty miles southeast of

Halifax to make a victory signal during the night of 22/23 March, eighteen hours after sinking *Watuka*, and the OIC promptly plotted the submarine's track. One of the warships participating in the hunt, some twenty-five miles to the northeast, also obtained a bearing that would have fixed the position more precisely than had the shore DF stations but, failing to appreciate the importance of the information, was slow to pass it on. Meanwhile, a 145 Squadron Ventura had hastily taken off from Dartmouth to search the area, and it was probably this aircraft that, according to U-802's log, challenged the boat with a signal flare, forcing it to crash dive. Unfortunately, without the Leigh Light, which was never fitted on the command's Venturas, it was difficult to confirm night sightings, and the aircraft flew on unawares; the encounter is not mentioned in Canadian records. Soon after, promising but false radar and sonobuoy contacts by a 161 Squadron Canso 'A' brought Admiral Murray's headquarters to set the search onto the wrong track, to the west, for a critical four-and-a-half hours, while the submerged boat continued its southerly run.[30]

The squadrons at Yarmouth, Dartmouth, and Sydney continued to sweep day and night off southern Nova Scotia until 9 April without result. Eastern Air Command did, however, unknowingly score a notable success in defending HX 286, a convoy bound for the United Kingdom, that U-802 located on 8 April while departing from Nova Scotian waters. Venturas from 145 Squadron forced the boat to crash dive six times; when it was finally able to strike the next day the torpedoes were so far wide of the mark that none of the ships noticed the attack. DF bearings on U-802's convoy report signal enabled the OIC to promulgate fresh Otter areas for air searches of the boat's homebound track.[31]

During the hunt off Halifax, decrypted signals and DF bearings revealed the entry of U-550 and U-856 into the northwest Atlantic en route to patrol areas in American waters. From 20 to 27 March as many as four Liberator flights a day from Gander swept the Otter areas, with Canso 'A's from Yarmouth later picking up the trail after several days of bad weather. The only promising contact was by Liberator 'G' of 10 Squadron which, following a radar contact, claimed to have sighted a periscope about 450 miles south of St John's on 26 March. When the periscope disappeared before an attack could be made, the aircraft dropped sonobuoys and received positive returns, but further searches in the area brought no result. U-856 was in the general vicinity and U-550 may have been as well, but neither boat reported the incident, and since neither submarine survived its cruise, the encounter cannot be confirmed.[32]

Because both U-boats were headed south, on 26 March the USN detached the escort aircraft carrier USS *Croatan* and her five destroyer escorts from North African convoy routes to pick up the trail. Two additional destroyer groups joined. Before first light on 7 April one of *Croatan*'s Avengers closed on a radar echo about 250 miles southeast of Sable Island and U-856 gave itself away by putting up anti-aircraft fire. Destroyers later arrived, hunted the contact for ten hours, blew the submarine to the surface, and sank it by gunfire and ramming. Nine days later, on 16 April 1944, U-550 made a submerged attack on the tanker *Pan Pennsylvania* as convoy CU 21 formed up 200 miles off New York. Within two-and-a-half hours the three destroyer escorts present had made SONAR contact and sank U-550 within sight of the burning tanker.[33]

These operations may have benefited from better acoustic conditions in the waters south of Nova Scotia. They also demonstrated what could be done by experienced surface and air forces working in close harmony, especially in the case of U-856. By contrast, a large Canadian effort – 197 sweeps totalling 1756 hours and 158 flights of 1340 hours in support of convoys by Eastern Air Command in the period from 18 March to 6 April, and searches by as many as fifteen ships – had not produced even a single opportunity to attack. Rear-Admiral H.E. Reid, flag officer Newfoundland, writing his report of proceedings for March 1944, offered a blunt explanation from the navy's point of view: 'Recent unsuccessful hunts off Halifax and Newfoundland, where a U-boat was known to be present, by motley assortments of ships in various states of efficiency and training, lends emphasis to the fact that none but a highly trained, thoroughly co-ordinated and ably led team can hope to destroy U-boats at this stage of the campaign.'[34] Air force failures suggested that Reid's criticism applied as much to the RCAF as the RCN.

Dismal results in February and March had exhausted the patience of the new chief of the air staff, Air Marshal Robert Leckie. He decided to intervene directly after the failure, on 26 March, by 10 Squadron's Liberator 'G' to make an attack or achieve a second sighting after apparently detecting a periscope and receiving sonobuoy returns. An acoustic torpedo had apparently not been dropped because the crew had insufficient experience with the equipment. Training was obviously inadequate if that were the case. In Leckie's view, however, a far greater mistake had been made: the command had allowed several hours to elapse before the relief aircraft arrived on the scene. The weather had been good, and no extraordinary operational pressures had created a shortage of available aircraft:

It is most emphatically considered that whenever a submarine is definitely known to be in a small area, every possible effort should be made to cover this area continuously, day and night, and to extend it as necessary, with the object of obtaining a second sighting. An organized hunt to exhaustion may not always be possible, particularly if the sighting is a great distance from the nearest base, but at least continuous cover for the next 24 hours should be given. It is fully realized that an aircraft not equipped with the Leigh Light has perhaps little chance of making an attack by night, and that therefore night sweeps by such aircraft are not of great value unless they are based on very definite information; but when the position of a submarine is actually known with considerable accuracy, it should be of great value to patrol the area by night using ASV, in the hope either of obtaining a contact which will further fix the submarine's position, or of forcing the submarine to stay submerged throughout the night and thus increase the chances of sighting it on the surface next day.[35]

A common sense of purpose among air and sea forces, moreover, was still singularly lacking. In February Eastern Air Command had published the instructions for Salmon, but no one thought to distribute them to warships until

HMCS *New Glasgow* used improper procedures to home aircraft on 19 March during the first combined hunt for U-802.[36] Much more than such patchwork reform was needed to solve the problem; even though the RCN and RCAF were making a greater effort to hunt down U-boats, a more thoughtful, coordinated approach had to be developed, as well as a willingness to pay more attention to detail – particularly in training.

On 23 April, after the Canadian Northwest Atlantic had enjoyed a total absence of U-boats for about ten days, U-548 crossed 40 degrees west longitude en route for St John's. The OIC was aware both of its presence and destination. Canso 'A's from Torbay and Liberators from Gander began to hunt for the submarine that day. When by the OIC's estimates the U-boat should have been within one hundred miles of St John's, Hudsons from 11 Squadron at Torbay began local patrols. Towards the end of the month, however, bad weather restricted flying to a few hours a day, and on 1 May the enemy had reached Conception Bay undetected.[37]

That afternoon U-548 surfaced east of the bay to ventilate the boat with fresh air (see map ONS 236, 21-5 May 1944, below), and a Liberator of 10 Squadron, returning to base after a long convoy escort, saw the boat in the distance. U-548 crash dived. The U-boat captain thought, wrongly, that the aircraft had not sighted the submarine, but within two hours a Salmon had been ordered. The Liberator had in fact dropped sonobuoys and was able to follow the U-boat's course. Passing the limit of endurance, the aircraft then had to return to base before a Canso 'A' from 5 Squadron arrived on the scene, shortly to be relieved by another Liberator. The weather closed in, forcing this aircraft to leave as well, but over the next 44 hours twenty-one ships joined in the hunt, assisted when flying conditions permitted by two Liberator, three Canso, and six Hudson sorties.[38]

U-548 had seen the large number of ships and aircraft arriving late on 1 May and had shifted position to the south, miles away from the main search. The submarine surfaced after dusk the next day half way between St John's and Cape Race, to find the destroyer-escort HMS *Hargood* a little more than a mile away. The U-boat attacked the ship with a homing torpedo which missed just as a Liberator of 10 Squadron appeared on the scene. Having picked up *Hargood* on radar, the aircrew illuminated the vessel with their Leigh Light and then fired an identification flare that failed to function properly. However, the U-boat captain assumed he was under attack and immediately responded with 20mm flak, crash dived, and lay still on the sea bed to avoid detection. The airmen, incensed at being shot at, apparently by a friendly vessel, promptly flew away.[39] The British seamen on board *Hargood* were thoroughly bewildered. They appear to have searched for a U-boat, because the submarine's log records a 'shrill, undulating turbine noise' overhead for more than an hour, but they gained no contact. The whole affair was put down as an unsolved mystery. *Hargood* signalled to flag officer Newfoundland: 'At 0800Z aircraft circled ship in position 47 31N 52 02W when on bearing 045° appeared to have short bursts of Oerlikon [gunfire] fired at it ... Have you any information? Continuing patrol.'[40] The shore authorities had no information, failed to realize they had cornered U-548, and called off Salmon on 3 May.[41]

The submarine took up a position south of Cape Race, lying quietly among the ice clutter at periscope depth, a tactic that made it virtually impossible to detect. Meanwhile, Rear-Admiral Reid ordered an air and sea search of the area beginning early on 6 May; perhaps the shore authorities had belatedly realized the significance of *Hargood*'s strange encounter. Close to midnight on the 6th, a mid-ocean escort group crossed the search area, hurrying for St John's after a long spell of escort duty, and ran over U-548's hiding place. The U-boat fired a homing torpedo at HMCS *Valleyfield*, the nearest vessel in the group. Within three minutes the frigate had broken in half and sunk with only thirty-eight survivors from the 163 men on board. U-548 again descended to the bottom and did not move for four hours.[42]

It was more than thirty minutes before the other ships even realized that *Valleyfield* was missing. Then followed a search around the frigate's last known position and a counter attack that was too far away to damage the U-boat. Admiral Reid upgraded the search already in progress to Salmon status as soon as he received the report. A Canso 'A' had already joined the search by that time, and before dawn on the 7th, as RCN escorts arrived, 11 Squadron had begun the first of seven Hudson sorties that day. U-548 retreated to the southwest and after dark, as fog rolled in to halt further air searches, the submarine heard the last faint sounds of the hunt. Two days later on the afternoon of the 9th a transmission to U-boat headquarters, intercepted by at least two escorts, placed the submarine about 200 miles south of Cape Race. The escort from an American convoy nearby immediately searched the area, with support from a 10 Squadron Liberator and a 5 Squadron Canso. The ships and aircraft made no firm contacts, but U-548 believed it was under attack and slipped away as Canadian warships and additional aircraft from 1 Group arrived on 10 May.[43]

On 14 May the OIC ceased issuing Otter signals for U-548. The submarine went on to evade all further detection, swinging far to the south before arriving off Halifax on 17 May. It lingered there for ten days, making contact with two convoys and two independent steamers, but not striking. DF bearings on signals U-548 made on 30 May and 4 June, while departing from the Canadian zone, allowed 1 Group to renew the search despite very poor weather and a severe fire at Gander that destroyed a hangar and four Liberators. None of these flights was successful; U-548 returned to base at Lorient on the 24th.[44]

The failure to carry out a single effective attack on U-548, and the unnecessary loss of a frigate to this submarine, reveal a continuing inability to achieve adequate co-operation between air and sea forces. It stands in marked contrast, for example, to the concentration of force brought to bear on U-856 by the ships and aircraft of USS *Croatan*'s task group on 7 April 1944. That comparison also brings out other important considerations. US naval carrier forces had, since the spring of 1943, enjoyed far more opportunity than Canadian air and naval forces for joint operations against U-boats. They worked in continual close co-operation, and did not depend on interservice co-ordination ashore to develop joint tactics.

The same pattern of events with other U-boats in Canadian areas repeated itself between early May and mid July. Three submarines became the object of intense and prolonged searches – U-1222 from 10 May to 25 June, U-107 from 11 June to 4 July, and U-233 from 27 June to 5 July – and in spite of excellent intelligence, all escaped serious damage or destruction until USS *Card* and five destroyer escorts found U-233 on 5 July. The detection was made in one of the OIC's Otter areas, when two of the ships got SONAR contact. After a brisk forty-minute action the Americans blew U-233 to the surface, then sank it with a combination of gunfire, shallow depth charges, and ramming.[45]

Although they could not solve the problem posed by new U-boat tactics, Eastern Air Command and Canadian naval escorts did improve their conduct of convoy operations; and the safe and timely arrival of convoys, it must be remembered, remained the principal objective of the anti-submarine war. In order to place in context the RCAF's performance in the convoy escort role, it is necessary to describe certain organizational changes made between September 1943 and August 1944, as well as the activities of RCAF squadrons attached to Coastal Command during the period.

In September 1943 Eastern Air Command had needed all the long-range and VLR aircraft it could muster to parry Dönitz' final fling in the central north Atlantic – the one-time 'air gap'. But with the quick and decisive defeat of that thrust, there was soon a surplus of the long-range Cansos. There was still, however, a real need for more Cansos in other parts of the Atlantic theatre and the Canadians, who had hoped to place a squadron of them in the Azores, were persuaded by Coastal Command to send them to Iceland instead.[46] 'Although I am reluctant,' observed Johnson, 'to send a squadron from the Northwest Atlantic and its vile weather into the Northeast Atlantic and its similarly vile weather,' he advised Ottawa to agree.[47] Iceland had, besides the very successful 120 (VLR) Squadron, RAF, only one American Ventura squadron and a British Hudson squadron, neither of which had enough range to cover convoys on the northern routes or to catch U-boats as they debouched into the north Atlantic through the Iceland-United Kingdom gap.

Moreover, as then Air Vice-Marshal Robert Leckie pointed out to the minister of national defence for air, C.G. Power, it was unwise to hold surplus squadrons in Canada when the demand existed elsewhere for them. Not only would it make the RCAF vulnerable to Home War Establishment cutbacks, it would deprive airmen of the active and varied experiences they needed, and deserved, to keep up morale. These arguments told. On 1 December 1943 the Cabinet War Committee ordered the disbandment of 117 Squadron, whose eight Catalinas and four Cansos then flew out to reinforce Western Air Command, and approved the dispatch of 162 Squadron to Iceland.[48] At a stroke, twenty-seven flying boats and amphibians had disappeared from Eastern Air Command's order of battle.

The long, three-stage journey to Reykjavik through Goose Bay and Bluie West 1 in Greenland began for 162 Squadron on 1 January 1944. Already used to upheaval (in the past three months the squadron had been shunted around between Dartmouth, Newfoundland, Goose Bay, and Mont Joli, Que.), its long-suffering airmen took off in Canso 'A's loaded to maximum weight with passengers, personal kit, and spare parts. Coastal Command, it must be borne in mind, had no Cansos, so spare parts were essential. Among the passengers were sixty groundcrew. Another 114 groundcrew flew in Dakotas of 164 (Transport) Squadron to Goose Bay, thence to Reykjavik in 10 Squadron Liberators. Two modest wooden supply ships from the RCAF Marine Squadron at Dartmouth, the *Beaver* and the *Eskimo*, carried the squadron's heavy stores. Designed for coastal hauls, they had to battle violent mid-Atlantic storms to deliver their cargoes. By early February 1944 a total of 424 airmen had arrived in Iceland, and the squadron had already begun operational sorties with its fifteen Canso 'A's.[49]

This was the seventh RCAF squadron to serve in Coastal Command. Nos 404 (Coastal Fighter) and 415 (General Reconnaissance), were anti-shipping squadrons; No 413 (GR) Squadron, had taken its Catalinas to Ceylon in March 1942 to serve in a reconnaissance and anti-submarine role.[50] The three remaining GR squadrons, 407, 422, and 423, fought the U-boats in the eastern Atlantic.[51] No 407 Squadron had first become operational on 1 September 1941 as an anti-shipping (Coastal Strike) squadron. Early in 1943, after some unhappy Anglo-Canadian policy disputes (the full story of which will appear in the third volume of this series), the squadron converted to Vickers Wellingtons, and in April began offensive anti-submarine patrols over the Bay of Biscay from Chivenor, Devonshire, the unit's home station for all but brief periods during the rest of the war.[52]

Reference has been made in Chapter 15 to the British emphasis on operations over Biscay. Their object was to seize any opportunity for offensive action against the U-boats making for the open ocean from, or returning to, their bases on the French coast. The bay offensive did lead to a high rate of sightings and attacks. It did not, as its originators hoped, destroy the morale of U-boat crews, nor did it match the rate of sightings and attacks credited to aircraft escorting threatened convoys, but the Admiralty and Coastal Command continued to prosecute the campaign, because evidence indicated it was reducing the number of submarines on the convoy routes by about one-third.[53]

The RAF had first devoted special attention to the bay in April 1942. Not until the following June, when Leigh Lights fitted on Wellingtons using 1.5m-band ASV radar first came into their own, was there much success. In July the offensive had gone into high gear, until German development of *Metox* search receivers, which allowed U-boats to detect metric-band radar transmissions, frustrated Allied aircraft from September 1942 to March 1943. Then, however, the first airborne 10cm ASV sets thwarted the *Metox* system and left the submarines electronically blind again. In April 1943 new German tactics, by which U-boats moved in groups on the surface across the bay and depended on improved anti-aircraft weapons and shore-based air support to drive off Coastal Command aircraft, had resulted in another brief setback for the Allies. But from June to September 1943, when convoys were not threatened by wolf packs, the Admiralty was able to spare groups of surface vessels to co-operate with aircraft. In this period the offensive achieved its most impressive results. Thereafter, submarine sinkings in the area fell off significantly as the U-boats began to run submerged once again. An analysis of U-boat losses in 1943 shows that sea and air convoy escorts in the open ocean, even at the height of the bay offensive, actually sank more submarines than forces employed in the bay itself. Be that as it may, the airmen operating in those dangerous waters developed some of Coastal Command's more innovative tactics.[54]

The Wellingtons of 407 Squadron, equipped with Leigh Lights and among the first to have 10cm radar, began their bay patrols at a period when the U-boats had learned to evade detection by running submerged during the day, surfacing mostly at night, and using *Metox* to listen for metric radar transmissions. On the night of 21/22 April 1943 an RCAF Wellington unsuccessfully attacked two U-boats. Despite the advantage conferred by centimetric radar, over the next four months results for the squadron were similarly disappointing. Finally, on 2 August 1943, Wing Commander J.C. Archer, RAF, the squadron commander, swept down on U-106 from low clouds about 250 miles northwest of Finisterre, and straddled the target with six depth charges. Seriously damaged, and unable to submerge, the U-boat turned for home but that afternoon aircraft from 228 Squadron, RAF, and 461 Squadron, RAAF, found and sank it. A month later, on 7 September, Pilot Officer E.M. O'Donnell, RCAF, detected U-669 by radar northwest of Finisterre. He was able to illuminate the boat on his first pass, and on the second pass he destroyed it with a straddle of five depth charges.[55]

Two other RCAF contributions to the bay offensive must be mentioned. On 24 October 1942 405 Squadron of 4 Group, Bomber Command, moved temporarily from Topcliffe, Yorkshire, to Beaulieu, Hampshire, for a spell of operations in the Bay of Biscay aimed at suppressing German naval forces during the Allied invasion of North Africa. Its Handley Page Halifax aircraft made several strikes against enemy shipping, and two unsuccessful attacks on submarines; a third had some effect. During a daylight patrol off the northeastern coast of Spain on 27 November, a machine flown by Flight Lieutenant C.W. Palmer, DFC, sighted U-263, which, having previously been damaged, was proceeding on the surface with two escorts. Attacking through flak, the Halifax's first salvo of depth charges missed, but a second attack was officially credited with having inflicted further damage to the boat.[56] In June 1943, 415 Squadron, flying Handley Page Hampdens and based at St Eval, Cornwall, virtually abandoned its anti-shipping role to assist in the bay offensive. On 2 August one of its aircraft sighted U-706 and attacked with six depth charges. The U-boat escaped damage by violent evasive manoeuvres but, while the bridge watch was distracted by the circling Hampden, an American Liberator which had detected the boat on radar was able to slip in and sink the submarine with a stick of twelve charges.[57]

Nos 422 and 423 Squadrons, RCAF, were principally employed supporting transatlantic convoys to the west of the British Isles and covering the northern U-boat transit routes. The early operational history of 422 Squadron was chequered; equipped with Catalinas until early 1943, a small detachment was sent to North Russia to provide air cover for the Murmansk convoys. The squadron then converted to Short Sunderlands, and became operational on the west coast of Scotland on 1 March 1943. No 423 Squadron had in the meantime begun to operate its Sunderlands from Castle Archdale, on lower Lough Erne, in Northern Ireland, on 26 October 1942.[58]

The first three Sunderland attacks, by 423 Squadron, took place during the battle for HX 229 and SC 122 on 19 and 20 March 1943. Over the next seven months the squadron made six more attacks, in which three U-boats were destroyed. On 13 May Flight Lieutenant John Musgrave, RAF, escorting HX 237, homed HMS *Lagan* and HMCS *Drumheller* on to U-456 while attacking the submarine, which eventually fell victim to the ships. On 4 August 1943 Flying Officer A.A. Bishop (the son of W.A. Bishop, the First World War flying ace) attacked U-489 south of Iceland in the face of heavy flak. His machine was shot down and only six of the eleven men on board escaped by scrambling into an inflatable dingy. About twenty-five minutes later U-489, settling by the stern, approached the flyers. The submarine's crew took to rafts, and the Canadian survivors found themselves gazing across a hundred yards of water at the German survivors. The British destroyer HMS *Castleton* eventually came across this strange scene, picking up fifty-eight men from the U-boat and the remmants of the Sunderland crew. Both Musgrave and Bishop were awarded Distinguished Flying Crosses later that year, Bishop specifically for this action. Again on 8 October 1943, another 423 Squadron flying boat, captained by Flying Officer A.H. Russell, sighted U-610 while escorting an eastbound convoy and sank it with three depth charges.[59] Soon after, Russell received the Distinguished Flying Cross.

No 422 Squadron, which had had a less successful record than 423 Squadron, gave evidence on 17 October 1943 of at least equal determination. Flight Lieutenant P.T. Sargent, while supporting convoys ONS 20 and ON 206, encountered two U-boats travelling in company on the surface. He carried out two attacks in the face of heavy fire, damaging one of the boats on his second run. Flak killed two of his gunners and mortally wounded the navigator. Sargent ditched the badly damaged aircraft near HMS *Drury*, which rescued seven of his crew, but Sargent himself went down with the shattered wreckage of his Sunderland.[60]

Canadian air force contributions to the Battle of the Atlantic were clearly established on both sides of the Atlantic by the end of 1943. It is more difficult to assess their importance to national objectives: the assertion of Canadian political and military interests in the conduct of the war and the development of a recognizable national air force, considerations which are summed up in the term 'Canadianization.'

By December 1943 there were nearly 2000 Canadian airmen serving in Coastal Command. Of these, 903, mostly aircrew, were scattered among fifty RAF units, and 1036 – 540 groundcrew and 496 aircrew – were serving in the five RCAF squadrons based in the United Kingdom. There seems to have been little concern about Canadian groundcrew, who were being posted to form about 85 per cent of complement in RCAF squadrons, but aircrew numbered no more than 65 per cent. The most serious problem lay in 422 and 423 Squadrons, the Canadian component of whose large flying boat crews was only 51 per cent and 55 per cent respectively, a problem exacerbated by a total absence of wireless operator mechanics/air gunners and a grave shortage of flight engineers in the RCAF. Each Sunderland crew required two of the latter.[61]

Canadianization at the higher levels was particularly difficult to achieve in Coastal Command. Maritime operations, with their requirement for the frequent redeployment of individual squadrons to match the direction of German naval theats, did not favour the combination of RCAF units into larger formations that would have facilitated Canadian administrative control and given RCAF officers a chance to exercise senior command. There was, in any case, no prospect of forming a Canadian group from only five squadrons, and senior Canadian officers were unwilling to form additional maritime air units. Like many airmen, they looked upon Coastal operations as relatively dull and wanted Canadians employed in more glamorous roles. As early as August 1942, before RCAF Coastal Command squadrons became heavily involved in anti-submarine operations, Air Marshal H. Edwards, AOCinC RCAF Overseas, had urged that they should all be transferred to an RCAF group in Bomber Command; he subsequently pressed for three maritime squadrons – Nos 404, 407, and 415 – to be included within an RCAF composite group of the Tactical Air Force.[62]

Authorities in Ottawa were reluctant to support wholesale changes that would disrupt the RAF order of battle, but eventually, in July 1944, had 415 Squadron transferred to No 6 (RCAF) Group, Bomber Command, despite determined British resistance. Once a Hampden torpedo-bomber squadron, it had been flying unarmed Wellingtons and obsolete Albacore biplanes on 'odd jobs' against German torpedo-boats – the crews saw themselves as 'merely stooges' of the navy – since September 1943.[63] That sensitive issue, the allocation of second-rate equipment to Canadian squadrons in what were perceived to be second-rate roles, is inextricably bound up in the whole question of Canadianization, and it echoes through RCAF wartime records. The flying-boat squadrons, although by no means exempt from the problem, found themselves in a less vulnerable position because the RAF was perennially short of qualified flying-boat aircrew. In June 1943 Edwards won Ottawa's support for combining 413, 422, and 423 Squadrons into a Canadian flying-boat wing at Castle Archdale. The proposal itself came to nothing: the RAF did not want to bring 413 Squadron back from Ceylon, and there was no provision in Coastal Command for the kind of wing organization put forward by Edwards.[64]

Nevertheless, almost certainly as a result of Canadian pressure, the RAF agreed to an informal Canadianization of the RAF station at Castle Archdale. In October 1943 the Air Ministry appointed Group Captain Martin Costello, previously senior air staff officer at Eastern Air Command and then deputy air member for air staff in Ottawa, as the station commander. He remained with nine or ten Canadians on staff until August 1944, and after his departure there were at least a dozen Canadians at the Castle Archdale headquarters. Although 422 Squadron's aircraft – based in Scotland – had been flying many of their sorties from Archdale since the middle of June 1943, not until November did the ground organization move from the poorly sited and inadequately equipped station at Bowmore to Northern Ireland, and even then only part could be accommodated at Castle Archdale; the rest, including squadron headquarters, was several miles to the south at St Angelo, near Killadeas, until April 1944. RCAF Overseas Headquarters, moreover, did not pursue the formal reorganization of Archdale as an RCAF station because of the strong possibility that the Canadian squadrons might have to be moved elsewhere to meet the changing shape of the U-boat campaign.[65]

Another solution did present itself. When the pressure on Eastern Air Command lessened, in the winter of 1943-4, Canada formally proposed supplying 150 flying-boat crews a year to meet the needs of Coastal Command's Sunderland and Catalina squadrons. This number would be enough to maintain the three Canadian flying-boat squadrons (413, 422, and 423) and supply additional crews to the RAF. It would include experienced crews from Canada, and newly formed crews from 3 Operational Training Unit [OTU] at Patricia Bay, BC. Short of manpower, and particularly in need of flying-boat personnel, the Air Ministry accepted. There was a proviso that forty-four of the crews should be RAF (presumably recent graduates of the BCATP), so as to maintain national balance in the flow of reinforcements to maritime squadrons.[66]

By early February 1944 the first Canso crews had arrived in the United Kingdom. Staff officers at 17 Group, Coastal Command's training organization, interviewed one crew who had flown together for 500 hours and whose pilot had 1100 hours flying experience. By 17 Group's standards a lack of experience in water landings and take offs, and ignorance of Coastal Command signals, navigation, and tactical methods, required the crew to undergo the full twelve-week syllabus at 4 OTU. Coastal Command Headquarters balked, noting the urgent need for these Canadians with their 'quite considerable experience' of difficult north Atlantic conditions.'[67] The training authorities dug in their heels, and in the end the Canadians did the full OTU course, during which time an air gunner and a wireless operator mechanic/air gunner were added to each crew to make up the normal ten-man complement of the Sunderland. The first four crews were posted, two to 422 Squadron and two to 423 Squadron, in mid-May. The training staff was impressed by the keenness and high morale of the Canadians but thought that three of the crews lacked discipline. British and Canadian concepts of discipline were not infrequently at odds. The fourth crew – the same one that 17 Group headquarters had interviewed – was rated above average in all respects. By the end of August 1944 twenty-three more Canso crews had entered Coastal Command's No 4 OTU to reinforce both RCAF and RAF Sunderland squadrons. With the creation of this RCAF support stream, the percentage of Canadian aircrew in 422 Squadron increased from 51.3 at the end of January 1944 to 78.7 in January 1945 and 84.4 on 30 April; the figures for 423 Squadron on the same dates were 77.4, and 82.7, respectively.[68]

Other RCAF crews from Canada arrived at 131 OTU Coastal Command, at a rate of roughly two a month for conversion to Catalinas and posting to 413 Squadron in Ceylon. Support for 407 Squadron was provided by Ventura crews from Canada that, at a rate of two or three a month, converted to Wellingtons at 6 OTU.[69] Regular dispatch of such personnel stripped various Canadian home squadrons of their best aircrew, but in 1944 experienced men were also posted to the Home War Establishment from Coastal Command, something that Canadian commanders had been advocating for three years. The normal procedure for developing crew captains, in both Coastal Command and the Canadian home squadrons, was to send seasoned second pilots back to an OTU, where they would retrain as commanders of new crews. Beginning in March 1944 second pilots from the RCAF maritime squadrons overseas were sent to 3 OTU, Patricia Bay, where they became first pilots in the Home War Establishment. This was a sensible solution to the long-standing problem of imparting British operational experience to the Canadian commands.[70]

Although an acceptable degree of Canadianization was achieved in RCAF Coastal Command squadrons in 1944-5, there were still many Canadians serving in RAF units, and they were widely scattered. It had been intended to concentrate them in eight 'nominated' British squadrons, but less than 25 per cent of the Canadian personnel in RAF units were ever posted to these squadrons.

Despite the problems encountered in asserting the national identity of the Canadian contribution, that contribution was impressive. Comparison with the total complement of Coastal Command, which on 1 August 1944 amounted to 7635 aircrew, shows that the 1433 members of the RCAF formed almost 19 per cent of their numbers. The record of Canadians in RAF squadrons – nearly two-thirds of the total RCAF aircrew in Coastal Command – is a distinguished one that merits a study of its own. Because the subject bears only indirectly on the history of the RCAF as a national institution, no attempt has been made to describe their activities in this book. Pilot Officer M.S. Layton's contribution to a series of U-boat attacks in 1942 'unmatched in the annals of Coastal Command,' has already been noted. Flying Officer K.O. Moore also earned a DSO, and, in addition, received the United States Silver Star for destroying two U-boats within the space of twenty-two minutes on 7 June 1944.

Combining Coastal Command's Canadian aircrew with that of Eastern Air Command (1266), the RCAF's proportion of British Commonwealth aircrew engaged in the Battle of the Atlantic rises to about one-third.[71] This major effort resulted in the participation of RCAF squadrons, as well as Canadians in the RAF, in virtually every aspect of the North Atlantic war. In 1943 10 Squadron's VLR Liberators had been the first Eastern Air Command aircraft to operate from both sides of the Atlantic. By 1944 it would be fair to say that Eastern Air Command had, in the matter of convoy escort, become a western extension of Coastal Command. Escort procedures were being carried out in the same fashion as in Coastal Command, and with comparable success.

Procedures were based on the British Atlantic Convoy Instructions which Eastern Air Command had adopted in March 1943, and which were continually modified to suit Canadian conditions. Planning of air coverage began nearly twenty-four hours in advance with the arrival of the British Stipple and Canadian Otter signals for the following day. A few hours later flag officer Newfoundland and the air officer commanding 1 Group conferred at the Area Combined Headquarters [ACHQ] in St John's about what air operations would be needed; the naval and air commanders in Halifax held a similar conference at the same time. Both headquarters then issued orders for the following day to the air stations, so that crews could be scheduled and aircraft prepared. Meanwhile, Admiral Murray's headquarters sent a list of its priorities for air operations to St John's, where naval and air staffs had the opportunity to discuss any differences in the programmes decided upon at the two headquarters and amend orders to the stations accordingly. Aircrew who had to be on patrol by first light would be up most of the night before, having a preflight meal, and being briefed by specialist officers on details such as weather expected in the patrol area, the latest intelligence on the location of friendly shipping and U-boats, communications with naval vessels, and navigation procedures, before taking off in the small hours of the morning.[72]

The most difficult problem for escorting aircraft was to find ocean convoys that had been at sea for several days. Frequently the ships were not where they were supposed to be; foul weather and merchant vessels that were unable to keep pace meant unexpected delays. Similarly, incorrect estimates of wind strength and direction often caused aircraft to miscalculate their own positions. Procedure 'B,' the sea-air radio homing method the Canadian forces had adopted in the spring of 1943, had enabled 82 per cent of aircraft tasked as escorts to 'meet' their convoys during the following summer and fall, but Eastern Air Command's staff could still denounce as 'lamentable' the 'almost complete lack' of air-sea communications.[73] That winter, moreover, 1 Group's success rate plunged to a nadir of 58.3 per cent in December 1943. Further training in Procedure 'B' and rigorous investigation of failed rendezvous brought the proportion of convoys met to 96.1 per cent by May 1944, and with continued vigilance it remained at that high level.[74]

Eastern Air Command's improved efficiency in escort duties during the last year of the war is well illustrated by the western passage of ONS 236, with 113 merchant vessels and nine naval escorts, in the latter part of May 1944. On 8 May the OIC at NSHQ warned that U-1222 had crossed 40 degrees west latitude, and correctly plotted the boat into the Halifax approaches over the next two weeks while Eastern Air Command vainly hunted for it. Meanwhile, it will be recalled, the submarine trackers had lost any trace of U-548 after it sank HMCS *Valleyfield* on 7 May; on the 14th the OIC advised that all shipping west of Cape Race should receive as much air support as possible without prejudicing the search for U-1222.[75]

Just before 0100 in the morning, local time, on 20 May, a 5 Squadron Canso 'A' trundled into the darkness at Torbay to make the three-hour flight out to the convoy, then coming in to the north of Flemish Cap, over 300 miles east of the base. Homed on the ships in accordance with convoy instructions, the Canso remained in their vicinity for five hours, carrying out the orders of the senior naval officer of the escort for a patrol around the entire perimeter of the convoy at a distance of thirty miles and a search off the port quarter. Such search patterns, carefully designed from mathematical calculations related to the capabilities and limitations of U-boats, were identified by a 'reptile code.'[76]

At mid-day, three hours after the first aircraft departed, another Canso 'A' from Torbay was successfully homed and stayed for seven-and-a-half hours, performing patrols similar to those of its predecessor. This aircraft reported a 'suspicious swirl' about ten miles ahead of the convoy; ONS 236 made an emergency turn away from the position, while *Empire McAlpine*, one of three merchant aircraft carriers [MAC ships] in the convoy, flew off two Fairey Swordfish to join the Canso in patrolling the vicinity of the sighting. Two escort vessels closed on the circling aircraft and attacked an ASDIC contact, but the contact was uncertain. Shortly afterwards an American transport aircraft had

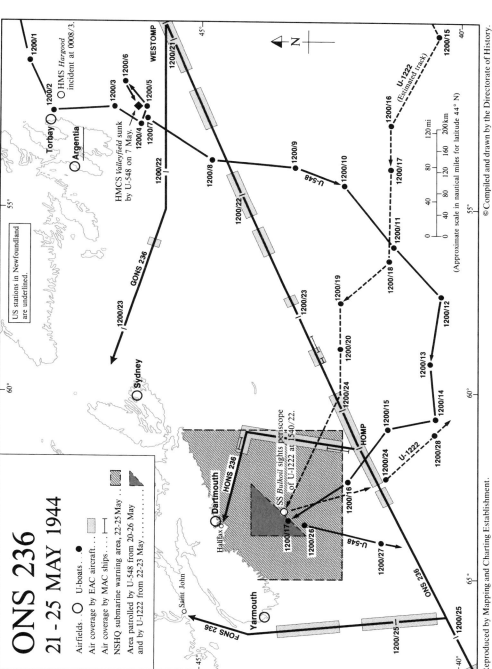

ONS 236
21 - 25 MAY 1944

Airfields. . . ○ U-boats. . . ●
Air coverage by EAC aircraft. . .
Air coverage by MAC ships. . . .
NSHQ submarine warning area, 22-25 May . .
Area patrolled by U-548 from 20-26 May
and by U-1222 from 22-23 May . . . .

US stations in Newfoundland
are underlined.

HMS *Hargood*
incident at 0008/3.

HMCS *Valleyfield* sunk
by U-548 on 7 May.

U-1222
(Estimated track)

Approximate scale in nautical miles for latitude 44° N)

0   40   80   120   160   200 km
0   40   80   120 mi

SS *Bulkoil* sights periscope
of U-1222 at 1540/22.

Reproduced by Mapping and Charting Establishment.

© Compiled and drawn by the Directorate of History.

reported two U-boats about 160 miles ahead of the convoy. Because transports flew at a much higher altitude their submarine sightings were notoriously unreliable, but with U-548 unlocated Admiral Reid was taking no chances. Two 5 Squadron Cansos watched over ONS 236 through the night of 20/21 May; one aircraft patrolled around the convoy at a distance of fifteen miles, while the other swept back and forth across the convoy's line of advance. At first light an 11 Squadron Hudson from Torbay patrolled for two-and-a-half hours.

At mid-day on the 21st eleven merchant vessels bound for Sydney and the gulf ports were detached under the escort of a corvette; GONS 236, as the group was designated, received three hours of coverage by a Hudson from Torbay at last light on the 21st, and arrived without incident off Sydney on the afternoon of the 23rd. The main body of ONS 236 continued to be guarded by a 5 Squadron Canso which remained on station until last light on the 21st. Next day two 10 Squadron Liberators, the first arriving before first light and the second departing after last light, provided nearly constant coverage during the passage south of Cape Race.

A Ventura from 113 Squadron at Sydney patrolled across the convoy's line of advance at first light on the 23rd, with a second Ventura, from 145 Squadron at Dartmouth, and four Swordfish from the MAC ships flying similar patrols at last light. Then, during the morning of the 24th, a 145 Squadron Ventura performed a first-light patrol as nine vessels, including the three MAC ships, detached for Halifax under the escort of two corvettes.

During the passage of ONS 236 off Nova Scotia a large-scale air and sea hunt had got under way about seventy-five miles south of Halifax when U-1222 revealed her presence through an unsuccessful attack on the American tanker *Bulkoil* on 22 May. For this reason the Halifax-bound ships, designated HONS 236, were given an indirect route, running eighty miles east of the port, clear of the area where U-1222 was being hunted. Two Canso 'A's from 160 Squadron at Yarmouth escorted the vessels until last light on the 24th; two Swordfish from the MAC ships also carried out patrols in the morning and at last light. No close air escort was provided during the early hours of the 25th as the convoy approached Halifax, but a Leigh Light Liberator from 10 Squadron's detachment at Sydney was employed in a night sweep in the area; HONS 236 entered port on the 25th without incident.

U-1222 had, in fact, escaped to the south. By the 24th, it was lurking near ONS 236's line of advance, but failed to make contact, while the Canadians had unwittingly suppressed U-548, whose presence was even not suspected. The captain reported in his log that he sighted aircraft seven times in four days, from 21 to 24 May, and during a seven-hour period on the 22nd noted that 'practically every half hour aerial bombs and depth charges seem nearby,' while HONS 236's long jaunt to the east of Halifax kept the convoy well clear of the boat.[77]

The main body of ONS 236 also received constant air cover on 24 May. A Canso 'A' relieved the Ventura that had flown at first light and stayed with the convoy until a second Ventura arrived for the last-light patrol. After sunrise the next morning, about 220 miles south of Yarmouth, thirteen ships bound for Boston, Portland, Maine, and Saint John, NB, parted company escorted by a corvette. Two patrols by Canso 'A's covered the detached ships, now known as

FONS 236, until last light; a third aircraft, possibly American, swept in the vicinity much of the afternoon. The Portland and Boston ships detached before sunset, and the main body arrived at Saint John on the 26th.

The passage of ONS 236 through Canadian waters had seen little drama, viewed through the eyes and ears of the mariners who sailed in it. They might have found it a great deal more stimulating, however, had it not been for the competence and dedication of Eastern Air Command. During the five days the convoy was in Canadian waters the main body was covered against possible submarine attack for a total of seventy-one hours by thirteen aircraft, while the three groups of ships that parted company were escorted by five aircraft for twenty-nine hours. Only once, with FONS 236, did Procedure 'B' fail (the escorting corvette appears not to have heard the Canso's transmissions), but the aircraft still located the convoy. The commanders of the naval escort groups that brought ONS 236 through the Canadian zone had high praise for Eastern Air Command: one noted that 'co-operation was excellent' and another remarked that 'The standard reached by RCAF planes in the matter of cooperation with Escorts of the W.E.F. [Western Escort Force] appears to be very good.' Progress had not only been marked but swift: only two months before a staff officer at Eastern Air Command had pondered why homing procedure appeared to fail most often with the ships of the Western Escort Force.[78]

Although in 1944 sea and air forces co-operated very effectively in escorting convoys, ships and aircraft on hunting operations not only failed to co-ordinate efficiently but often seemed at cross purposes. The principal reason for this contrast was the relative simplicity of standard operating procedures for convoy escort, compared to the complex, subtle skill needed to search a large ocean area thoroughly and, in the case of a contact, to conduct a hunt to exhaustion. It must be remembered, too, that naval escort groups with ocean convoys in 1944 had reached much higher levels of proficiency than the newly formed escort and support groups often committed to offensive operations in the northwest Atlantic.

While these developments were taking place in the Canadian theatre of operations, the RCAF squadrons on the other side of the ocean were, in 1944, fighting a very different kind of war. In the first three months of the year Admiral Dönitz again attempted to concentrate U-boat packs against convoys in the western approaches of the United Kingdom, a strategy that demanded rapid movements on the surface by submarines. The effort was a total failure. Nos 422 and 423 Squadrons, which were already operating from Castle Archdale in support of ocean shipping, and 407 Squadron, which moved to Limavady, Northern Ireland, at the end of January, participated in the operations that defeated Dönitz on this occasion.[79]

Night sweeps by No 407's Leigh Light-equipped Wellingtons brought immediate results. On 7 February two aircraft made radar contacts on U-762 running on the surface, west of Ireland. Each aircraft made a depth-charge attack that appeared to straddle the boat, but in fact inflicted no damage, and on the night of 10/11 February another squadron aircraft placed its depth charges wide of the mark on U-984 in the northern transit area, about midway between

Scotland and Iceland. Later that night, however, Flying Officer P.W. Heron sank U-283 in the same general area. The boat had already shot down a Wellington of 612 Squadron, RAF, when Heron swept in, turned on his Leigh Light at three-eighths of a mile, and dropped six depth charges, which destroyed the submarine. At the last moment he encountered flak, but by that time the U-boat's hull was showing a 'dull-red glow.'[80] Heron was awarded the Distinguished Flying Cross.

During a daylight sweep on 10 March a Sunderland of 422 Squadron, flown by Flight Lieutenant S.W. Butler, RAF, sighted U-625 five miles away. For at least ten minutes the submarine held off the aircraft with violent manoeuvres and anti-aircraft fire, until Butler was able to drop six depth charges. While the Sunderland circled, the U-boat submerged, but resurfaced three minutes later. An hour and twenty-eight minutes after the attack it's crew saluted the Sunderland with the visual signal 'FINE BOMBISH,' and then scrambled into dinghies shortly before the boat foundered. They were never seen again, but before abandoning their boat they had transmitted a distress signal and Dönitz dispatched U-741 and U-256 to the rescue. On the night of 11/12 March a Wellington of 407 Squadron, flown by Flying Officer E.M. O'Donnell, attacked U-256, which promptly shot it down; none of the Canadians survived.[81] For his successful attack on 10 March, Flight Lieutenant Butler received the Distinguished Flying Cross.

The other RCAF squadron in the northeastern Atlantic, No 162 flying out of Reykjavik, recorded an unsuccessful attack on 22 February 1944. The next opportunity arose on 17 April, when Flying Officer T.C. Cooke (recently returned from a Coastal Command anti-submarine course) was on a daylight meterological flight well to the west of Iceland, and the crew sighted U-342 six miles away. Against light flak, Cooke dropped three depth charges from a height of fifty feet. The U-boat seemed about to submerge nine minutes after the attack when there was a 'violent explosion' about fifteen feet forward of the conning tower and she 'sank instantly.' Cook received a Distinguished Flying Cross for this action and was later also awarded an Air Force Cross for ferry operations. A week later a Sunderland of 423 Squadron, on a daylight sweep with Flight Lieutenant F.G. Fellows at the controls, sighted U-672 sixteen miles away. During the attack run the aircraft's heavy nose armament (four fixed and two turret mounted machine-guns) was able entirely to neutralize the submarine's anti-aircraft defences. One of the six depth charges exploded prematurely and threw the Sunderland out of control for some minutes, so the crew could not clearly observe the fate of the boat, which submerged and left only traces of oil. It had, in fact, been seriously damaged.[82]

Dönitz's virtual abandonment of the attack on north Atlantic trade routes made it possible for 162 Squadron – still a part of Eastern Air Command for administrative and maintenance purposes, but under Coastal Command for operations – to move east and join in the offensive which Coastal Command had launched in the Arctic waters off Norway in May 1944. Between 23 and 25 May the first detachment of four Cansos arrived at Wick in northern Scotland; by the end of June all of the squadron's aircraft were flying from that base, having already compiled a most distinguished record. In the early hours of 3 June Flight Lieutenant R.E. McBride made a textbook attack through heavy flak on U-477. The 'U-boat appeared to lift bodily and swing to port losing almost all forward movement then submerged on even keel ... At least five survivors were seen in the water.' Oil slicks a mile long marked the grave of the boat when the Canso 'A' left the scene nearly four hours later. A week later, on the afternoon of 11 June, Flying Officer L. Sherman caught U-980 on the surface far to the north of the Shetlands, and despite accurate flak sank the boat with a perfect depth-charge attack.[83] McBride and Sherman were both awarded the Distinguished Flying Cross.

Less than two days later Sherman and his crew paid dearly for their offensive spirit. In the early hours of 13 June their Canso 'A' was so badly shot up in an unsuccessful attack on U-480 that the aircraft had to ditch. As the aircraft sank, five of her crew of eight managed to get into an inflatable dinghy. Flying Officer Sherman was not among them; he had been badly burned in the action, and was swept by the waves beyond the reach of those men in the raft. Perhaps he and the other two missing crew were the most fortunate. Control had picked up the Canso's U-boat sighting report and dispatched six aircraft to search the area from 13 to 15 June, but they saw nothing. The plight of the survivors was desperate; they were without food, water, or survival equipment, having to use a shoe to bail as the high seas repeatedly swamped the dinghy. After a week one man died of exposure; over the next few days or so three others, hallucinating and in despair, threw themselves over the side. Only Flight Sergeant J.E. Roberts survived, perhaps because he, unlike the others, had resisted the temptation to gulp sea water. On 22 June a Norwegian whaling vessel rescued Roberts about 135 miles off the Norwegian coast. After putting in at the port of Alesund, the Norwegian skipper's efforts to find a sympathetic doctor were foiled and he was 'obliged to turn you over to the German hangmen.' Actually the Canadian airman was well treated, and recovered almost completely before he was liberated from a prisoner-of-war camp near Berlin by the Russians and Americans in May 1945.[84]

The squadron's adventures on 13 June 1944 had only begun with Sherman's unfortunate encounter. During the late morning a Canso 'A' flown by Flying Officer J.M. McRae with Wing Commander C.G.W. Chapman, the squadron commander, as second pilot, sighted the periscope of U-715 north of the Shetlands. The conning tower broke the surface as the aircraft made its well-placed attack; machine-gun fire from the Canso killed three of the crew as they emerged on the bridge. The decks of the crippled submarine appeared, then she began to go down by the bow, then levelled out while a lone gunner brought the heavy 3.7cm gun into action, scoring a hit on the port engine of the aircraft. The Canso had to ditch. All the eight crew were uninjured, but one of two inflatable dinghies burst; two men got into the remaining dinghy while six hung on to the sides. Flying control in the Shetlands heard an sos from the Canso as she ditched and immediately ordered out a high-speed air-sea rescue launch, and diverted aircraft to the position. A Vickers Warwick of 281 Squadron, RAF, dropped a lifeboat two-and-a-half hours after the ditching when one of the flight engineers had already died of exposure. Pilot Officer J.C. Waterbury, the navigator of the downed crew, recovered the boat with a courageous swim, but it was leaking so badly that only constant bailing could keep the heads of the most exhausted men above water. The rescue launch arrived eight-and-a-half hours after they had gone into the water, too late to revive two of the wireless air gunners.[85] Chapman was made a member of the Distinguished Service Order in recognition of his 'high qualities of leadership and tenacity'; McRae and Waterbury were awarded the Distinguished Flying Cross, and two other members of the crew were decorated as well.

The squadron scored yet another victory on 24 June, but again with tragic losses. Late in the day, at the end of a twelve-hour patrol, a Canso 'A', flown by Flight Lieutenant David Hornell and Flying Officer B.C. Denomy, sighted U-1225 on the surface about 120 miles north of the Shetlands. As the aircraft made its attack run the boat put up intense and accurate fire which knocked out the starboard engine and started a fire on the starboard wing. Hornell held the violently vibrating Canso steady for a good depth-charge attack, but the starboard engine then fell right out of the wing and he had to ditch. As the crew abandoned the flaming wreck, one of the dinghies over inflated and burst, leaving only one dinghy for all eight men; two flyers at a time took turns in the water until, after several hours, everyone was somehow squeezed on board with limbs trailing over the side.[86]

Flak damage to the wireless equipment had prevented the Canso's sighting report and distress signals from being received. However, a Catalina of 333 (Norwegian) Squadron, RAF, flew over the dinghy five hours after the ditching, and the downed crew were able to attract its attention with flares from the survival equipment. They also sighted a large oil slick nearby in which there were thirty-five or forty bodies, sure evidence that the Canso had sunk U-1225. Again a high-speed launch from the Shetlands, and a Warwick of 281 Squadron, RAF, with an airborne lifeboat, were despatched to the rescue.

The ocean swell was too high for the Catalina to alight, but the Norwegians kept station over the dinghy all night. The rescue effort, however, was encountering heartbreaking delays. Heavy seas, and engine and wireless problems, were holding back the launch, while malfunctioning equipment helped to prevent aircraft from getting through until the late morning of the 25th, over fifteen hours after the ditching. When the airborne lifeboat was finally dropped, the seas carried it beyond the reach of the men in the dinghy. By this time one crewman had died, and Hornell, who was in the last stages of exhaustion, had to be restrained from swimming for the boat. Eventually the rescue launch did arrive, but by then the crew had been in the water twenty-one hours. A second man had died and Hornell, despite all-out efforts at resuscitation on board the launch, never revived. For his determined and skilful attack in the face of withering fire, and selfless conduct after the ditching, Hornell received the Victoria Cross, the first to be awarded to a member of the RCAF.[87] Denomy was awarded the Distinguished Service Order and four other members of the crew were decorated.

Less than a week later, while patrolling well to the northeast of the Shetlands on the afternoon of 30 June, a Canso flown by Flight Lieutenant R.E. McBride and his crew (responsible for sinking U-477 on the 3rd) sighted a periscope that submerged before an attack could be made. McBride homed in a Sunderland (which soon reached its prudent limit of endurance and had to depart) and two Liberators to saturate the area. Some three hours later the Canso saw U-478 on the surface eighteen miles away from the original sighting. The aircraft dived in through heavy flak that hit the port wing, made an excellent bombing run, and then had the depth charges 'hang up' in their racks. Not wishing to risk the lives of his crew on what might be a futile second run, McBride homed in one of the Liberators of 86 Squadron, RAF, which destroyed the boat with six depth charges. McBride's crew were officially credited with a share of the victory.[88]

It had been a remarkable month. Of the eight submarines destroyed in the northern transit area, 162 Squadron claimed four and shared in a fifth, at a cost of three aircraft downed, thirteen aircrew dead, and one taken prisoner. The air officer commanding 18 Group had no doubt as to the reason for the squadron's success: 'training and still more training. They had a magnificent system of training in that Squadron whereby every pilot at regular intervals went through a syllabus ... and then came back on to operations again. This was a perfect example of what training coupled with determination and bags of guts will do. It really got to the stage at one time when, if we had really good operational intelligence, we said, "Go on, we'll put 162 right in the middle."'[89]

Most of the Canadians' flying during July was from Wick, but squadron aircraft had no sightings as fewer boats made the transit, Dönitz reduced the strength of the patrols off Norway, and the boats at sea spent more time cautiously submerged. This was only a temporary lull, however. In August Allied victories in France forced the flotillas based on the Biscay ports to shift to Norwegian harbours, and schnorkel-equipped submarines began to penetrate close into the northern British Isles as the inshore campaign began. Nos 422 and 423 Squadrons now began to patrol over northern waters, while also supporting Atlantic shipping to the west of Ireland and hunting off the French coast. In the latter part of August both squadrons sent detachments to Sullom Voe for a brief period to try and catch Biscay boats making for Norway. On 26 August 407 Squadron moved the whole length of the British Isles from Chivenor to Wick for two months of duty in the north.[90]

On 6 August 162 Squadron's large detachment at Wick had returned to Iceland, to strengthen coverage of the western reaches of the northern transit area. The move had been precipitated by the appearance of U-300 southeast of the island two days before. During the late morning of 4 August a Canso 'A' flown by Flying Officer W.O. Marshall and Pilot Officer A.J. Beck, operating out of Iceland, caught the U-boat on the surface and attacked with three depth charges as it crash dived. A second Canso 'A', charges on an oil slick that the boat trailed. Sometime later U-300 surfaced, fired at her tormentors, and disappeared into the fog. Eleven hours after the first attack a Liberator of 59 Squadron, RAF, reinforcing the hunt, sighted the boat at the head of a long oil slick and again attacked as it dived. Further hunts by aircraft and warships turned up nothing more, but the three attacks had damaged the boat severely enough to send her back to port.[91]

The exciting and dangerous work of attacking surfaced U-boats, always more prevalent in the eastern than western Atlantic, was by the late summer of 1944 coming to an end, even for Coastal Command. Mundane escort duties, no less vital to defeat of the U-boats, would go on without pause. Atlantic convoy routes had become relatively safe since the air gap had been closed. In 1943 there had been 428 oceanic trade convoys between England and all other parts of the world, amounting to 13,788 ships. Of these, 124 ships had been sunk by U-boats. In 1944, of 476 trade convoys with 16,702 ships, only seventeen ships would have been sunk by U-boats before the end of the year. Many more ships were actually sunk, of course, but most of them were sailing independently, or separated from convoys. Convoy escort forces, therefore, played a large part in the reduced effectiveness of Dönitz's tonnage war.[92]

17

The Dawn of Modern ASW, 1944–5

By August 1944 Eastern Air Command, in conjunction with its naval counterparts, had achieved an effective co-ordinated defence of shipping. The successful protection of convoys continued for the balance of the war and, despite some singular accomplishments, the Germans found Canadian waters an unrewarding hunting ground. The RCAF, however, was still not responding adequately to the challenge of taking the offensive against solitary U-boats, ever more wary and elusive as they were. Its shortcomings became especially obvious when U-boats fitted with the new schnorkel breathing apparatus began to make regular visits to the western Atlantic.

The schnorkel, which was on a mast that could be raised hydraulically above the surface of the water when a submarine was at periscope depth, allowed a small amount of fresh air to pass into the submarine's hull and exhaust fumes to escape. Valves closed to prevent water from entering the schnorkel when waves washed over the mast. Thus the U-boat could use its air-breathing diesel engines, either for propulsion or charging batteries, without having to surface. Fitted in Type VII and Type IX boats, the schnorkel enhanced their underwater capabilities enabling them to achieve a sustained submerged speed of up to eight knots for as long as the crew could withstand the acute discomfort of pressure changes caused by the opening and closing of the valves and the dreadful stench from diesels and human bodies that built up over several days.

Sometimes the new equipment malfunctioned, forcing the boat to surface or switch to battery power; sometimes it seems to have tempted U-boat captains to lie inactive, or proceed with excessive caution, rather than pressing home attacks on vessels which were much more difficult to find through a periscope than from atop a conning tower. Such limitations notwithstanding, the schnorkel brought about a fundamental change in the character of anti-submarine warfare, often depriving aircraft of their principal means of detection (radar or visual sightings), and shifting the balance in favour of the submarine. How to project airpower effectively below the surface of the ocean was now the problem that air forces had to solve.

The schnorkel submarine made its first significant appearance in Canadian waters when Dönitz ordered U-802 and U-541 to the Gulf of St Lawrence in August 1944, hoping to repeat the successes of 1942. The chief of the air staff,

Air Marshal Robert Leckie, and the minister of national defence for air, C.G. Power, it will be recalled, had refused to entertain proposed reductions of strength in the gulf, so that 161 Squadron, with its Consolidated Canso 'A' amphibians at Summerside, Gaspé, and a new station at Sept Iles, supplemented the training Ansons at Charlottetown and Summerside. This was fortunate, because the disbandment of 31 General Reconnaissance School at Charlottetown, and the smaller requirement for new airmen in RAF Coastal Command, left fewer and less seasoned instructors and students on the scene than in previous years. With the expansion of the naval and air forces on the Atlantic coast since 1942 and the improvement of communications and base facilities in the gulf, large reinforcements could be deployed much more readily than had been possible two years before.[1] Still, layering of salt and fresh water and sharp temperature gradients made submerged U-boats singularly difficult to find.

The Operational Intelligence Centre [OIC] issued warnings about the threat to the Gulf of St Lawrence, estimating that U-802 might arrive off the Cabot Strait as early as 22 August. No 5 Squadron at Yarmouth immediately dispatched Canso 'A's to reinforce Sydney and the gulf stations where up to seven aircraft from the unit continued to operate for the next month. Heavy air coverage from the carrier USS *Bogue* on the Newfoundland Banks, however, had persuaded U-802 to dive on 19 August, and not to surface again until reaching the gulf eleven days later, on 30 August.[2] Poor flying weather allowed U-541, by contrast, to run on the surface at night, arriving in the Cabot Strait shortly after midnight on 3 September, more than a day earlier than the OIC had predicted. Before dawn, the boat torpedoed the British steamer *Livingstone*. Word of the sinking did not get out until nearly eight hours later when a coastal convoy happened upon the ship's survivors, and it was another three hours before a Canso 'A' could take off from Sydney to search beneath the 300-foot cloud ceiling. Soon, however, the strait was teeming with warships, from Fairmiles to frigates, supported by Canso 'A's and a Liberator of 10 Squadron so long as weather permitted. U-541 schnorkeled carefully through and arrived safely in the gulf by the morning of 5 September.[3]

The Canadian intelligence picture had by now become murky. The OIC was uncertain if U-802 had left the gulf and attacked *Livingstone* or if another submarine had arrived. Indeed, it was unclear whether there were now two boats in the gulf, or two boats patrolling outside the Cabot Strait south of Newfoundland. Fairmiles had reported contacts and attacked them near Gaspé (and in one instance came very close to U-802) but layering conditions in the water made all such contacts suspect, and the OIC did not pay them much attention.[4] At 2000 hrs local time on 7 September U-541 helped to clear up the picture by surfacing to attack an apparently unprotected freighter not far from Anticosti Island. The escorting corvette surprised the U-boat but, because the ship's four-inch gun jammed, only managed to make it dive and then lost contact.[5] Just after midnight, 7/8 September, when the commander-in-chief Canadian Northwest Atlantic, Rear-Admiral L.W. Murray, ordered 'Salmon,' every available ship and aircraft concentrated at the scene of U-541's attack. Flying was still limited by low ceilings and fog; none the less, from the afternoon of 8 September to mid-day on the 9th, when the commander-in-chief called off the operation, the gulf stations kept five Canso 'A's over the probability area at all times, and 10 Squadron at Gander allocated one Liberator to the same task. The Canso 'A's subsequently flew constant barrier patrols across estimated U-boat tracks until 11 September, when they began a heavy schedule of day and night sweeps in 'Otter' areas promulgated in the central gulf and Gaspé passage.[6] Although the OIC still could not be sure if there was more than one U-boat in the gulf, the massive sea and air search was paying dividends. The captain of U-802 recorded in his log: 'It appears that the enemy may after all have picked up some indication of my presence. After all, there hasn't been any other boat in this area for the last two years. Perhaps he was able to pick up my Schnorkel with his land-based equipment. It strikes me as odd that the aircraft are always flying back and forth over the area on a north-south course, while I have also been standing to and off land on north-south courses for the last 7 days. I therefore feel the right thing to do is leave the narrower entrance of the St. Lawrence R. and put myself ... southeast of the Island of Anticosti.'[7]

On 14 September U-802 encountered an RCN frigate group, and although the submarine escaped the ensuing attacks by hiding in the 'pronounced density layering,' the regular appearance of aircraft on 16 September convinced the commander that he dare not even schnorkel by daylight. The defences seemed so formidable that the U-boat drifted silently on the current on 17 September to avoid detection by ships. Neither U-802 nor U-541 found any merchant shipping, and both had left the gulf by 25 September.[8]

By this time U-1223 was on the way to replace them. Weather curtailed flying, so that there was no concentrated search for the new arrival until 4 October. Then OIC placed the submarine, accurately enough, in the approaches to the Strait of Canso, but the searching aircraft had no success. When weather again brought an end to flying three days later, a force of RCN frigates sailed for Gaspé to cover the mouth of the St Lawrence River. U-1223 evaded them all, and on 14 October attacked the gulf section of ONS 33 as it passed Pointe des Monts, en route to Montreal. A homing torpedo demolished the stern of HMCS *Magog*, while the defending forces, including a Canso 'A' that was soon joined by three others, were unable to find the submarine.[9]

Widespread hunts, so far as the weather permitted, continued until 18 October, when gulf activities began to wind down. Unfortunately, on 31 October the OIC mistakenly reported the area clear. In fact it was U-1221 which, after an uneventful four-week patrol off Nova Scotia, had signalled its departure, and the withdrawal of Canadian naval and air forces from the gulf left U-1223 free to roam. One of the submarine's torpedoes damaged the merchant ship *Fort Thompson* near Father Point on 2 November. Canso 'A's promptly flew back into the gulf and a number stayed until 18 November, but by that time the U-boat had slipped undetected out of their grasp.[10]

In relation to the number of U-boats in the region, there was now an enormous force of aircraft and ships ranged against them. But quantity alone was not enough. Though it might suppress them, it could not sink them, and suppression was a short-term solution.

There were in fact so many obvious shortcomings in the performance of ships and aircraft in the face of the new 'ambush' tactics that it was difficult to know where to begin correcting them. The Joint RCN/RCAF Anti-Submarine Warfare Committee, meeting in Ottawa on 19 September, confirmed the need, which had been under active consideration since July, for a joint tactical training school to improve search procedures in combined sea and air operations. It learned that the navy was acquiring a second group of frigates to create an adequate hunting force for the first time. In order that weaknesses could be identified the committee asked that naval and air authorities in Halifax submit an operational analysis of each search in which the presence of a U-boat had been established. Membership in the committee was expanded to include the directors of signals at Naval and Air Force Headquarters, as well as representatives from the staffs of commander-in-chief Canadian Northwest Atlantic, Eastern Air Command, 1 Group Newfoundland, and the joint tactical school, once it was formed. There were some prickly reactions from the coast about this. Eastern Air Command recognized that there were problems, but resented being told by Ottawa how to solve them; the air officer commanding-in-chief, Air Vice-Marshal G.O. Johnson, not for the first time, voiced the suspicion that Ottawa was trying to interfere with his conduct of operations. In the end, Eastern Air Command had to accept the assurance that mutual co-operation, not central control, lay behind the committee's recommendations.[11]

On the other side of the Atlantic, in Coastal Command, the schnorkel campaign off Britain's coast had opened when U-482 sank four merchant vessels and a corvette immediately to the north of Ireland between 30 August and 8 September 1944. The 'guerrilla' boats proved almost impossible to catch there, too. Saturation of the area with 7501 hours of flying during September did no damage to the enemy and produced only two sightings that postwar research has confirmed as authentic.[12]

Both 422 and 423 Squadrons, RCAF, made an all-out effort in the northern coastal waters, and the latter had more than its share of the limited amount of action. An hour after taking off from Castle Archdale on 3 September, Flying Officer J.K. Campbell attacked a submerged submarine after sighting its schnorkel, only to have the depth charges hang up. The armament failure was most unfortunate, because the Sunderland had actually been in contact with U-482. Campbell homed in anti-submarine vessels and scoured the area for the rest of the day in company with the warships, but without result.[13]

During September, 407 Squadron, RCAF, which continued to press the offensive into Norwegian waters, and 162 Squadron, RCAF, covering the western part of the northern transit area and Iceland's coastal waters, had no firm contact with the enemy, despite increased U-boat traffic. In October 407 Squadron made two contacts, however. Besides an unsuccessful night attack on 4 October, east of the Shetlands, against a surfaced U-boat, on 30 October Flying Officer J.E. Neelin attacked U-1061, a torpedo transport submarine plying Norwegian coastal waters, on the surface west of Bergen. Using its Leigh Light, the Wellington severely damaged the boat which, nevertheless, was able to dodge a second attack by a Liberator of 224 Squadron, RAF, and limp to port. Early in

November, informed by special intelligence that Dönitz was extending the inshore schnorkel campaign to the English Channel and southwest approaches, Coastal Command redeployed squadrons to the south. Leaving Castle Archdale behind, 422 Squadron began operations from Pembroke Dock on the 7th, while 407 Squadron returned from Wick to Chivenor where they began to fly again on the 12th.[14] Meanwhile, British intelligence, after this first experience with ambush tactics in British inshore waters, accepted that 'The evolution of the SNORT U/boat will be found to have affected profoundly the balance of power between hunter and hunted...'[15]

Decrypted signal traffic showed that the U-boat arm still had a generous measure of fighting spirit, and was developing alarming new technical capabilities. Type XXI U-boats 'working up' in the summer of 1944 had a sustained underwater speed of fifteen knots, enough to chase down convoys and outrun all but the fastest convoy escorts. It was small consolation that schnorkel and periscope masts would leave a much more noticeable wake when the boats were travelling at that speed. On 6 November the Admiralty's OIC predicted that as many as fifteen of these new submarines might be operational by 1 December, and seventy-four by 1 April 1945. Teething problems of a radically new design, and disruptions caused by the Allied bombing of Germany, did not in the end permit the fulfilment of this prophecy – only one Type XXI actually completed a war patrol – but in mid-1944 the threat seemed real.[16]

Coastal Command's experiences caused warnings to pour in to the authorities in Halifax late in 1944, perhaps the most interesting of which was a letter Air Chief Marshal Sir Sholto Douglas (the new air officer commanding-in-chief Coastal Command) wrote to Air Vice-Marshal Johnson, following a meeting between the two men. He referred to the unjustified optimism of those who believed the war would soon be over, and documented the signs of German plans for a renewed submarine offensive. This caution, and the demonstrated ability of U-boats to avoid detection by schnorkelling, left no room for complacency:

In my opinion it is definitely not the time when we can afford any relaxation of our efforts – in fact the reverse.

As I told you, we have put the scientists on to the problem and they are trying to find a quick means of improving the capacity of the various types of A.S.V. to pick up and home on the Schnorkel. Furthermore, I am starting an intensive training campaign designed to improve the capacity of our Radar operators to pick up and home on the Schnorkel by day and by night. But however successful we may be in effecting these improvements ... it seems clear that we shall never be able to pick up the Schnorkel at the range at which we used to be able to pick up a fully-surfaced U-Boat. As you are aware, the corollary to this is that more aircraft are required effectively to flood an area, since the number of aircraft required is directly related to the range of pick up. This again reinforces my conclusion that, on the assumption that the European war will continue for another six months, we shall if anything require more and better aircraft in order to achieve success against this new U-Boat threat.[17]

On 28 October Johnson conveyed Douglas's conclusions to C.G. Power and recommended special measures to sustain and expand the capabilities of Eastern Air Command.

Air Chief Marshal Douglas had urged the RCAF as early as June 1944 to replace the Canso 'A's in 162 Squadron with Liberators; by the time Air Marshal Leckie saw the proposal in November nothing had been done, and he decided that, since the war would probably be over before the squadron received new aircraft, it was now too late to implement the idea. Johnson did manage to convince him of the need for new ASD radar with a wave-length of 3cm for Cansos. Procurement difficulties had left these aircraft with the old 1.5m ASV Mark II, although Coastal Command had long before declared the set obsolete because of its poor definition of targets and its vulnerability to German metric-band search receivers. Moreover, the large aerial arrays tended to ice heavily enough to complicate flying in Canadian winter conditions, and even prevent the Cansos from flying at all on occasion. For that reason Air Force Headquarters [AFHQ] had in the fall of 1943 placed an order in the United States for ASB equipment, an interim design with a 50cm wavelength that featured a compact antenna. Despite assurances of early delivery, ASB was not available in quantity until the summer of 1944, by which time ASD – already in service in the command's Lockheed Venturas – had won much more popularity.[18] Coastal Command studies concluding that even the best centimetric radar was ineffective against schnorkels unless the sea was dead calm had not yet reached Ottawa. Johnson thus managed to overcome Leckie's sceptical view that expenditure of over $1 million on the new equipment was no more justified at this stage of the war than was the acquisition of new aircraft. As was so often the case, Leckie's instinct was the right one; a delay in designing ASD fittings for the Cansos meant that aircraft with the new set only began to reach squadrons in the last weeks of the war.[19]

The same story repeated itself with other modernization efforts. The flood of demands for the latest radio aids, such as LORAN, swamped technical units on the east coast. There had been, the air staff admitted, 'inadequate planning,' and delivery fell behind schedule. For example, the slow completion of a machine shop at No 1 Technical Signals Unit at Debert, NS, necessary to manufacture mounting brackets, left $2 million worth of radio equipment sitting in storage until at least April 1945. Such delays kept aircraft scheduled for refitting out of action. In January there would be an average of ninety-eight anti-submarine aircraft available for operations in the command; by March the number would slip to ninety. In the meantime, although squadrons continued to meet their training and operational commitments, the prospect of a sudden intensification of the U-boat offensive did not inspire great confidence either in Ottawa or in Eastern Air Command in the ability of their resources to meet it.[20] Only in aircrew strengths did the prospect look good. At the end of October 1944 Johnson reported that he had 200 aircrew needing replacement on completion of their operational tours and AFHQ promptly arranged for an increased flow of the required personnel. He had also persuaded AFHQ that 145 Squadron should not be disbanded as planned.

This continued vigilance was justified by events. In November 1944 U-boat headquarters assigned five U-boats to the Gulf of St Lawrence and Halifax approaches. German assessments of Canadian defensive capabilities were not flattering: despite reports by U-802 and U-1221 of 'efficient daytime air cover, increased day and night air cover during passage of convoy,' Dönitz chose to give more credence to U-541's account of 'little air activity' and 'Searching groups of destroyers and MLY-boats, not dangerous' in the gulf, and a claimed virtual absence of anti-submarine forces outside the gulf.[21]

The first three boats, U-1228, U-1231, and U-1230, if Dönitz had been right, should have achieved some remarkable successes. In fact, their isolated attacks on shipping were of limited significance. Canadian warships and aircraft were hunting for U-1228 on the basis of the OIC's predictions as the boat arrived in the approaches to the Cabot Strait on 15 November. Nursing a malfunctioning schnorkel, the submarine's commander would not risk entry into the gulf, but on the night of 24/25 November sighted HMCS *Shawinigan* in bright moonlight – it was probably the only clear night in that stormy month – off Port aux Basques, and sank the corvette with a single torpedo. Owing to the schnorkel defects the boat began its return passage on 4 December rather than joining the other boats ordered to the Halifax approaches. The second submarine, U-1231, reached Cabot Strait on 22 November and could hear the explosion when *Shawinigan* was attacked three days later. However, during two weeks of patrolling the strait and the gulf U-1231 found no targets. On 13 December the boat arrived off Halifax and displayed extreme caution for the next thirteen days before starting the return passage. Late in November the third boat, U-1230, landed two agents on the coast of Maine (who were picked up almost immediately by the FBI), and on 3 December sank the cargo ship *Cornwallis*, steaming independently in the Gulf of Maine. After successfully evading detection over the following three weeks the boat started for home, having made no more attacks on shipping as a result of technical defects that limited the ability to dive.[22]

This unimpressive performance owed as much to caution by U-boat commanders as it did to anything else. As later U-boat cruises would show, with advantages brought by the schnorkel they could have found plenty of targets in harbour approaches, especially off Halifax. But none of the first three boats pressed home such attacks, even though in November weather conditions severely limited the amount of air cover Eastern Air Command could put up. In November weather was so bad that Gander was closed for seventeen days and Sydney for ten; aircraft from Gander only completed their patrols on one day in the month, and those at Sydney and in the gulf only enjoyed seven decent flying days.[23] In December, by contrast, Eastern Air Command was able to mount massive sea and air searches. By the time the search for U-1230 in the Gulf of Maine and Bay of Fundy was called off on 13 December, RCAF aircraft had made more than forty-five sweeps and logged over 400 flying hours in addition to maintaining very strong air escort for shipping in the area. 'Some crews,' reported the diarist of 5 Squadron, 'were flying twelve hours and returning to the air again after twelve to eighteen hours off. The aircraft were used even more. At times crews were in the briefing room waiting to take off as soon as their Canso returned from patrol with another crew.'[24] On 17-18 December U-boat radio transmissions south of Sable Island, which the OIC interpreted, probably correctly, as evidence that U-1230 was homebound, provided direction-finding [DF] bearings that started up a hunt by aircraft from Sydney, Dartmouth, Yarmouth, and Gander in co-operation with two American destroyer groups placed under Canadian command. The search continued without result, often in miserable weather, until 23 December, when the submarine was approaching the eastern limits of the Canadian zone.[25]

The OIC continued to provide good intelligence of U-boat movements. There were periods of doubt, and some bad guesses, but command authorities ashore were not caught completely off guard by any of the first three boats. U-806 then gave the Canadians a rude shock. This was partly because Bletchley Park had identified, from a tasking message of 13 November, the 'approach point' south of Newfoundland, but not the operational area to which the U-boat was ordered on 4 December. Liberators from Gander spent three days searching for the submarine as it entered Canadian waters. Then, for some reason, on the 5th of the month the OIC removed U-806 from the Otter signal, and on 10 December placed the boat, incorrectly, in the Cabot Strait. Its presence off Halifax from 13 December went undetected until the torpedoing, on 21 December, of the Liberty ship *Samtucky*, in the Halifax section of convoy HX 327.

Inspection of the ship, after it was towed ashore, revealed that a torpedo rather than a mine had done the damage, yet remarkably little effort went into the subsequent search, the Dartmouth squadrons merely carrying out first- and last-light harbour entrance patrols. Whether through the continued failure to detect U-boats over a period of time, or from a lack of co-operation between RCAF authorities – documentary evidence sheds no light on the matter – there appears to have been a serious failure of confidence in Dartmouth-based squadrons during the last few months of the war.

On Christmas Eve, when all aircraft were grounded by weather, U-806 sank HMCS *Clayoquot*, escorting a Boston convoy just off the Sambro light vessel. Two hours later a Ventura of 145 Squadron was able to get off the icy runways at Dartmouth, while Canso 'A's from Yarmouth and Sydney were on the way to join the search.[26] In the meantime the submarine had simply waited on the bottom for twelve hours, then crept silently away to the south, not even putting up its schnorkel until late on 25 December. By that time an aircraft sighting and attack seventy-five miles south of Halifax had started another hunt, which made the OIC think U-1231 might have been detected as well, but that submarine was also patrolling close in to the harbour. For five days sea and air searches continued without success, and the U-boats lay low.

At the same time the fifth U-boat was entering the picture. Having accurately plotted U-1232's advance into the Canadian zone, a subsequent false sighting near Flemish Cap persuaded the submarine tracking room to place it much further east than was the case.[27] The U-boat arrived off Halifax on 31 December, nearly six days earlier than expected, and on 4 January, in spite of constant air cover, sank two ships of convoy SH 94, the *Nipiwan Park* and *Polarland*, about ten miles south of Egg Island. This started another massive sea and air search until 12 January, broken only by impossible flying conditions from 7 to 9 January. On 14 January, while aircraft were again grounded by weather, U-1232

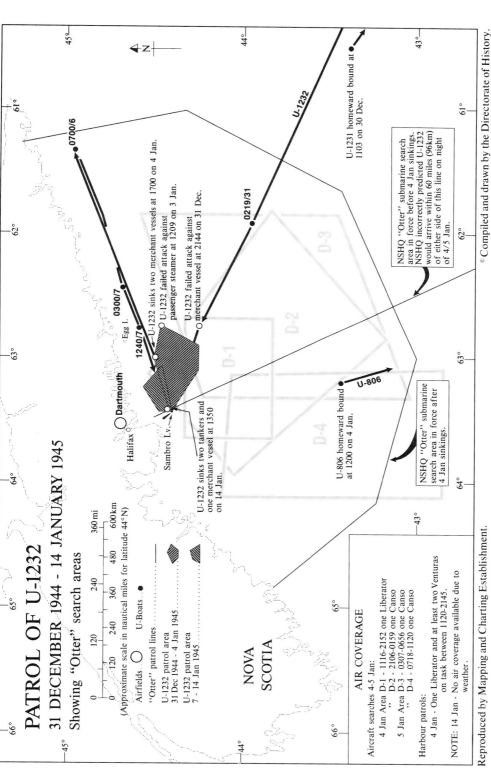

PATROL OF U-1232
31 DECEMBER 1944 - 14 JANUARY 1945
Showing "Otter" search areas

N

		360 mi	
0   120   240   480   600 km
0   120   240   360

(Approximate scale in nautical miles for latitude 44°N)

Airfields.. ◯   U-Boats.. ●

"Otter" patrol lines............

U-1232 patrol area
31 Dec 1944 - 4 Jan 1945............

U-1232 patrol area
7 - 14 Jan 1945............

NOVA
SCOTIA

AIR COVERAGE

Aircraft searches 4-5 Jan:
4 Jan Area D-1 - 1116-2152 one Liberator
  "   D-2 - 2106-0159 one Canso
5 Jan Area D-3 - 0307-0656 one Canso
  "   D-4 - 0718-1120 one Canso

Harbour patrols:
4 Jan - One Liberator and at least two Venturas
on task between 1120-2145.

NOTE: 14 Jan - No air coverage available due to
weather.

Halifax ◯   ◯ Dartmouth

Sambro Lv. ◯

Egg I.

1240/7

0300/7

0700/6

U-1232 sinks two merchant vessels at 1700 on 4 Jan.

U-1232 failed attack against
passenger steamer at 1209 on 3 Jan.

U-1232 failed attack against
merchant vessel at 2144 on 31 Dec.

U-1232 sinks two tankers and
one merchant vessel at 1350
on 14 Jan.

D-1

D-2

D-3

D-4

0219/31

U-1232

U-806

U-806 homeward bound
at 1200 on 4 Jan.

U-1231 homeward bound at
1103 on 30 Dec.

NSHQ "Otter" submarine search
area in force before 4 Jan sinkings.
NSHQ incorrectly predicted U-1232
would arrive within 60 miles (96km)
of either side of this line on night
of 4/5 Jan.

NSHQ "Otter" submarine
search area in force after
4 Jan sinkings.

© Compiled and drawn by the Directorate of History.

Reproduced by Mapping and Charting Establishment.

sank two tankers and a merchant ship, the *British Freedom*, *Athel Viking*, and *Martin van Buren* of convoy BX 141, as they passed Sambro light vessel towards the harbour.[28] Amid fog, sleet, and snow, ships and – when the weather improved briefly on 16 January and 20-2 January – aircraft from Dartmouth and Sydney tried in vain to hunt down the U-boat. On 23 January high frequency direction-finding operators in the searching ships and shore stations picked up U-1232's report that it was homebound and the OIC plotted the boat southeast of the Virgin Rocks, in the right vicinity, but somewhat to the west of its actual position. Searches conducted along its probable track, hampered by more bad flying weather, were no more successful than earlier ones.[29]

Although there were a number of false sightings in February, not until 5 March was there another confirmed incursion into the northwest Atlantic. On 5 March 1945 U-866, bound for Halifax, became the object of a combined sea and air search including both Canadian and US naval forces. On 18 March, after two weeks of surveillance along the estimated U-boat track by Canso 'A's and Liberators from Newfoundland and Nova Scotia, a formation of USN destroyers found U-866 with SONAR and after six hours of continual hunting destroyed the submarine with their underwater weapons. A Canso 'A' on task from Sydney during this hunt was forced to return to base by bad weather before U-866 met its end.[30]

Despite this success, prospects for the future were grim. Failure to find and destroy U-boats was becoming more frequent. A stalemate had been achieved in the eastern Atlantic only through the concentration of enormous forces in British home waters. On 1 January there were 426 escort vessels based on British ports, compared to the eighty-nine ships available to Admiral Murray in the Canadian Northwest Atlantic. Coastal Command's home groups, as they reached their peak wartime strength, mustered some twenty-seven anti-submarine squadrons with 389 aircraft. Eastern Air Command had ninety-four aircraft in seven bomber-reconnaissance squadrons.[31]

The first sea lord pointed out, in a paper dated 6 January 1945, that these large forces were tied down by a submarine fleet whose operational capacity was greatly reduced by the dislocations resulting from the loss of the French ports and the move to Norway. About thirty boats had been on patrol in the last months of 1944, of which only six or seven on average had been in British coastal waters. According to intelligence estimates, progress with construction programmes would enable the Germans, within a matter of weeks, to maintain seventy boats on patrol, including twenty-five of the new Type XXIs. By July 1945 the patrol strength would rise to ninety boats, of which thirty-three would be Type XXIs. Equally disturbing was the improved morale in the U-boat service revealed by recent determined attacks. A new offensive could be expected as early as mid-February, the first sea lord warned, and its effects would be so devastating that they could curtail land operations in northwest Europe. During the critical spring quarter of 1943 an average of sixty U-boats on patrol had sunk 184 ships. Now able to saturate inshore waters, and with the Type XXI to renew pack attacks on ocean shipping, the German submarine fleet might sink 248 ships during the spring quarter of 1945 and a further 296 ships in the summer quarter.[32]

Schnorkel boats continued to thwart the efforts of anti-submarine aircraft on both sides of the Atlantic until the end of the war. The Canadian anti-submarine squadrons with Coastal Command, like their sister British, American, and Allied units, did an enormous amount of flying in return for occasional fleeting glimpses of 'snorts' (which were bogus more often than not) and a few attacks that did no damage to such difficult targets. One of the few successes of the period was scored by 407 Squadron, RCAF. During the early hours of 30 December a Wellington, with Squadron Leader C.J.W. Taylor, DFC, at the controls, made a radar contact while on patrol about half way across the central part of the English Channel. As the aircraft closed, the crew could see a schnorkel on the calm sea in the moonlight, but had to make a second pass to lose altitude. Switching on the Leigh Light, Taylor straddled the tiny target with six depth charges. U-772, which the day before had sunk one merchant vessel and damaged another, now went to the bottom itself.[33] Taylor was subsequently awarded a bar to his Distinguished Flying Cross.

In Canadian waters a new offensive had been expected in the spring, and three more U-boats – the evidence suggests they were U-857, U-879, and U-190 – bore out the OIC's forecast. On 14 and 15 March Liberators from Gander patrolled over the estimated position of one boat about 500 miles east of Newfoundland, and on 15 March all available aircraft from 1 Group began three days of concentrated search in support of USN warships south of Virgin Rocks. Sydney's Canso 'A's joined on the 18th as the boat – probably U-857 – approached the mainland, and other Nova Scotia bases provided aircraft thereafter. In the meantime 10 Squadron's Liberators supported two more naval groups in pursuit of U-879 and U-190 east and south of Newfoundland, from 19 to 22 March. Weather prevented flying for the next several days, but on 26 March a Liberator from 10 Squadron, patrolling southeast of Sable Island, reported a strong disappearing radar contact which set off a combined sea/air operation lasting for over twenty-four hours. Available U-boat records are inadequate to determine whether this was a submarine, although U-190 could have been in the vicinity.[34]

U-857 and U-879, which the OIC estimated might be off the Halifax approaches by this time, had actually headed directly for Cape Hatteras. Nevertheless, the threat by these U-boats to Halifax shipping, and several spurious sightings in the Gulf of Maine, kept Eastern Air Command in a state of ferment until the end of the month, when a dozen submarines were found from Enigma radio intercepts to be heading for North America by way of the Canadian Northwest Atlantic. On 28 March one U-boat, possibly U-853, appeared on the OIC's plot near the eastern fringe of the zone. Two more boats, probably U-548 and U-530, followed on 7 April. Six more Type IXC U-boats, formed into Group *Seewolf*, were westbound north of the Azores in an attempt to revive pack attacks on the convoy routes before splitting up to work independently in North American waters. On 5 April U-889 sailed from Norway to work in Canadian waters, followed by U-881 and U-1228.[35]

Both Canada and the United States responded vigorously to the new threat, although Canadian operational authorities on the east coast did not appreciate the magnitude of the American effort until 24 April. On that day a USN ship visiting St John's brought news of the destruction of U-1235, U-880, U-518, and U-546 of Group *Seewolf* since 15 April.[36] Led to believe that the Germans were preparing to launch V-1 pilotless bombs and V-2 rockets from their U-boats (a possibility that the Canadian chiefs of staff discounted), commander-in-chief Atlantic Fleet, USN, had organized two massive barrier forces to intercept the boats as they approached North American waters. Operation 'Teardrop,' as this effort was called, devoted two escort carriers carrying thirty-two anti-submarine aircraft and six fighters, as well as twenty destroyers, to each of the barriers.

One U-boat, U-190, lurking near Halifax and never showing more than its schnorkel, evaded detection, and on 16 April torpedoed the minesweeper HMCS *Esquimalt* five miles east of Chebucto Head. In spite of good visibility, air activity in the vicinity, and considerable movement of shipping, this disaster went unnoticed for six hours, after which only twenty-six of seventy men in the ship's company were still alive. The sea and air search that followed again lacked conviction. All available ships engaged in the hunt until the forenoon of 18 April, but no special air coverage had been provided until first light on the day after the sinking, and even that had to be terminated when weather closed in a few hours later. U-190 remained, undetected, off the approaches of Halifax until 29 April. On that date the Canadians mounted a combined sweep by sea and air forces to meet the final wave of incoming submarines, but made no detections. The last attack carried out by Eastern Air Command occurred on 3 May 1945, when a Canso 'A' of 5 Squadron, escorting a convoy off Yarmouth, NS, followed up a radar and sonobuoy contact with an acoustic torpedo attack. There is no evidence that a U-boat was present;[37] perhaps a whale was the recipient of the last anti-submarine weapon to be launched in anger by Canadian forces in the Second World War.

The last enemy submarine to be destroyed in North American waters fell to a USN task force. On 6 May, before Bletchley Park had decrypted Dönitz's message of 5 May ordering all U-boats to cease operations against American and British forces, the destroyers escorting the carrier USS *Mission Bay* located and destroyed U-881 southeast of the Grand Banks.[38]

The USN had such enormous forces available that in April and May 1945, without denuding American waters, it could and did maintain nearly as many ships and aircraft in the Canadian zone as the entire naval and air strength normally available to the commander-in-chief Canadian Northwest Atlantic. That, and fog over the Grand Banks, help to account for the nugatory part played by Eastern Air Command in these final American triumphs against the enemy attack on shipping. Canadian aircraft still flew 3454 hours in anti-submarine operations elsewhere in the northwest Atlantic zone during April, and carried out extensive sweeps against U-853, U-530, and U-548. The Halifax approaches earned unusual attention. Of the 317 operational flights made by 3 Group in April 1945, ninety-two were sweeps off the port, forty-five were harbour entrance patrols, and forty-six were missions with RCN and USN support groups in the vicinity.[39] Only sixteen air sweeps from mainland bases ventured beyond the Halifax approaches in April. The remaining – and single largest component –

of the air effort was 138 flights in escort of convoys, the mission to which the Canadians continued to give first priority until the end of the war.

VE day brought only a gradual lessening of activity because U-boats still at sea might not have received, or could choose to ignore, surrender instructions. In accordance with the terms of the German capitulation, U-boat headquarters began to broadcast those instructions in plain language on 8 May. Canadians in Coastal Command carried out their last missions between 31 May and 2 June. No 407 Squadron disbanded on 4 June; 162 Squadron left Iceland for Canada a few days later. Both 422 and 423 Squadrons transferred to Transport Command and began conversion training for Liberator operations in the Pacific, but disbanded on 3 and 4 September, respectively, with Japan's capitulation.[40]

The surrender orders also meant the end of the Atlantic battle in Canadian waters. On 9 May U-805, U-858, and U-1228 surrendered to US warships in the Canadian zone. On 11 May U-190 broadcast her position to the Cape Race radio station, and the escorts HMCS *Victoriaville* and *Thorlock* were detached from convoy ON 300 to bring the boat into Bay Bulls, Nfld.[41] For Eastern Air Command the final moment came on 10 May, when Liberator 'X' of 10 Squadron, flown by Flight Lieutenant G.F. Clement and Flight Lieutenant E.H. Bowser, was returning from an escort for SC 175. At 1755 GMT, about 250 miles south of Virgin Rocks, the crew sighted U-889, proceeding at full speed on the surface: 'Aircraft immediately went in to attack whereupon the sub ran up the black flag of surrender, and members of the enemy crew were seen running up the conning tower and frantically waving their hands. V[isual] S[ignal] "Halten Warteband" (Stop and Wait) was sent by "X" to the sub, and our a/c proceeded to contact surface vessels [escort group W6] previously sighted 50 miles away by W/T. Through perfect signals procedure "X" homed the ships to the sub. At 1950 GMT the escorts closed in and took the sub in tow [for Shelburne, NS]. After circling the area for a further two hours, and ascertaining that the surrender was complete, 'X' set course for Gander with a feeling of exuberance and elation at the day's work.'[42]

These surrenders may have been satisfying, but the boats' survival of the intensive hunts since March underlined the ability of schnorkel-equipped submarines to avoid detection by anti-submarine forces. The success of US ships and aircraft in the location and destruction of U-boats during the last year of the war, especially in the vicinity of areas covered by Eastern Air Command, resulted from exceptionally large task forces that almost always made their first contact on surfaced rather than submerged submarines. They also had the benefit of very close rapport between carrier pilots and the ships screening their carriers, a rapport built up over several years of continuous joint operations often in areas of heavy submarine density. U-boat successes off Halifax in the last few months of the war seem to have resulted, at least in part, from the lack of such a rapport between Canadian airmen and sailors.

At the same time, given the resources available to them, the RCAF and RCN did give security to the shipping under their protection. The sinkings of 1944 and 1945 in the Canadian Northwest Atlantic theatre, tragic as they were, represented only the smallest fraction of what Germany needed to justify the continued and desperate efforts of the U-boat arm. Only on two occasions in this period were there really successful U-boat attacks on convoys escorted by Canadian forces, those by U-1232 on 4 and 14 January 1945. That they were unusual feats is clear from the delight expressed by Grand Admiral Dönitz at the daring of *Kapitänleutnant* Kurt Dobratz, who achieved his results by penetrating farther than any other U-boat commander into the Halifax approaches. Dönitz signalled, in a message duly intercepted by British intelligence, 'I applied in person today to the Führer for the Knight's Cross for you. The Führer replied in one word: "Instantly!" I congratulate you.'[43]

In 1941 Canadian aspirations to play a major part in the Battle of the Atlantic had not struck a particularly responsive chord, either in Britain or the United States, but by 1945 developments in Eastern Air Command and Coastal Command reflected an expansion of forces that was very much in line with what the air staffs in Halifax and Ottawa had envisaged. The expansion had not come about in a very orderly fashion; as has been argued elsewhere in this book, RCAF planning in the Second World War was open to serious criticism. Emphasis on an excessive fighter establishment, when anti-submarine squadrons went short, suggests that the pressure of events rather than the foresight of planners was responsible for the acquisition of a respectable Canadian anti-submarine capability. Yet if British and American assumptions of 1941 had been allowed to stand, the RCAF would have turned over responsibility for all long-range operations from Newfoundland and Canada to the USAAF and USN. Resistance to that demand, and constant efforts in the face of British and American opposition to acquire the latest types of aircraft, lay behind the RCAF's status as one of the major participants in the defeat of the German attack on Allied shipping. In the process Canadian airmen had belatedly adopted tactics and technology from Coastal Command; in conjunction with the Operational Intelligence Centre in Ottawa, they also developed their own innovations to suit Canadian circumstances.

By the time of the German capitulation in May 1945, RCAF squadrons had accounted for, or participated in the destruction of twenty-one U-boats, over 10 per cent of the 197 credited to Commonwealth air forces and just under 9 per cent of the 245.5 destroyed by all Allied shore-based aircraft in almost six years of war. Eastern Air Command squadrons scored twelve of the RCAF's successes, six by units based in Canada and Newfoundland and six by 162 Squadron while operating from Iceland and Scotland.

The contribution to security of the north Atlantic lifeline had served both national and alliance interests, and earned a measure of respect from friends and enemies alike. Operational activities in the western hemisphere complemented the actions, some recounted in this book and more to be described in the third volume of this series, of the RCAF overseas. Air force accomplishments at home and abroad gave the service what its progenitors had understood it would eventually need, a strong political and military presence in Canada. By 1945 the RCAF was, in every sense of the term, a national air force.

Appendices

In the early days of Ferry Command, pilots, such as these Americans seen aboard ship in Montreal harbour in April 1941, returned to their starting points by steamer. (PA 141354)

Lines of aircraft awaiting delivery, like these at Dorval, Que., could be caused by a shortage of aircrew, bad weather, or the need for modifications. (PA 114759)

Air Chief Marshal Sir Frederick Bowhill, air officer commanding, RAF Ferry Command, in May 1942. (PA 141355)

A Douglas Dakota gets a change of markings at Dorval in October 1943. (PA 141357)

Patrolling a line of Liberators and Hudsons at Dorval. Cats were kept to catch mice which sometimes gnawed at the fabric of aircraft. (PA 114767)

A Royal Air Force flight lieutenant briefing crews at Dorval prior to a delivery flight. (PA 114611)

'Bomber Mail': loading mail bags into a 168 (HT) Squadron Flying Fortress for delivery to Canadian troops overseas. (PL 23230)

RAF and USAAF ferry crews returning to Nassau aboard a Liberator transport in July 1943. It was a long, tough trip sitting knee to knee or sleeping in the bomb-bay. The men signed each others' 'short-snorters' – strips of bills from the different countries visited. (PA 114612)

Air Vice-Marshal H. Edwards and General G. Brandy, United States Army Air Corps, toasting the Clayton Knight agreements in 1940. (PMR 80-64)

Whitehorse, Yukon, one of the Northwest Staging Route airfields, August 1944. (PL 25572)

Principal Air Force Appointments in Canada, 1920–45

Officers are shown with ranks held as of the day on which they relinquished the appointments concerned. No distinction is made between acting and confirmed ranks.

AIR BOARD, 1919–22

An Air Board was constituted on 23 June 1919 under the chairmanship of A.L. Sifton to make recommendations on the organization and administration of postwar aviation in Canada. After stating the case for the creation of a military Canadian Air Force as well as a civil government flying organization under the same head, board members resigned and were replaced on 19 April 1920 by a new Air Board responsible for both civil and military flying. The first two chairmen of this new Air Board were the ministers of militia and defence of the day. With the formation of the Department of National Defence on 1 January 1923, responsibility for the Canadian Air Force passed to that department. The appointments listed are those authorized for the Canadian Air Force headquarters during the period that it came under the Air Board.

Chairman of the Air Board
H. Guthrie   April 1920–Dec. 1921
G.P. Graham   Dec. 1921–April 1923

Inspector-General of the Canadian Air Force
Air Vice-Marshal Sir W.G. Gwatkin   April 1920–March 1922

Air Officer Commanding Canadian Air Force
Air Commodore A.K. Tylee   May 1920–March 1921

Officer Commanding Canadian Air Force
Wing Commander R.F. Redpath   March–July 1921
Wing Commander J.S. Scott   July 1921–July 1922

Director Canadian Air Force
Wing Commander J.L. Gordon (acting)   July 1922–March 1924

ROYAL CANADIAN AIR FORCE, 1923–38

The RCAF came into being on 12 March 1923, but did not formally adopt its new title until 1 April 1924. Its status from 1923 to November 1938 was as a semi-autonomous branch of the armed forces reporting to the militia chief of the general staff. Some of the appointments listed reflect a reorganization of Canadian Air Force headquarters in July 1922.

Minister of National Defence
G.P. Graham   Dec. 1921–April 1923
E.M. MacDonald   April 1923–June 1926
H. Guthrie   June–Sept. 1926
Colonel J.L. Ralston   Oct. 1926–Aug. 1930
Lieutenant-Colonel D.M. Sutherland   Aug. 1930–Nov. 1934
G. Stirling   Nov. 1934–Oct. 1935
I.A. Mackenzie   Oct. 1935–Sept. 1939

Deputy Minister of National Defence
G.J. Desbarats   Jan. 1922–Nov. 1932
Lieutenant-Colonel (later Major-General) L.R. LaFlèche   Nov. 1932–Sept. 1939

Director Royal Canadian Air Force
Wing Commander J.L. Gordon (acting)   July 1922–March 1924
Wing Commander W.G. Barker (acting)   April–May 1924
Group Captain J.S. Scott   May 1924–Feb. 1928 (acting until April 1925)
Wing Commander L.S. Breadner (acting)   Feb. 1928–April 1932
Squadron Leader A.A.L. Cuffe (acting)   April–Oct. 1932

Senior Air Officer
Group Captain J.L. Gordon (acting)   Nov. 1932–May 1933
Wing Commander G.O. Johnson (acting)   June–Dec. 1933
Air Vice-Marshal G.M. Croil   Jan. 1934–Dec. 1938

Assistant Director Organization,
Training, Operations, and Personnel
Wing Commander J.L. Gordon   July–Dec. 1922

Assistant Director of Air Staff and Personnel
Squadron Leader G.O. Johnson   Jan. 1923–May 1925
Wing Commander J.L. Gordon   June 1925–June 1927

Assistant Director Supply and Research
Wing Commander E.W. Stedman   July 1922–July 1927

Chief of Aeronautical Engineering
Air Commodore E.W. Stedman   July 1927–Oct. 1939

Assistant Director and Secretary (Civil)
J.A. Wilson   July 1922–July 1927

Controller of Civil Aviation
J.A. Wilson   July 1927–Oct. 1936

Director of Civil Government Air Operations
Group Captain J.L. Gordon   June 1927–May 1933

Air Personnel Staff Officer
Wing Commander N.R. Anderson   Nov. 1932–June 1938
Group Captain W.R. Kenny   July 1938–Oct. 1939

Assistant Director of Air Staff Duties
Squadron Leader A.A.L. Cuffe   Jan. 1930–April 1932

Air Staff Officer
Wing Commander G.O. Johnson   Oct. 1932–Jan. 1934
Squadron Leader G.V. Walsh   Jan. 1934–Feb. 1936
Air Commodore L.S. Breadner   March 1936–Oct. 1939

ROYAL CANADIAN AIR FORCE, 1938–45:
MEMBERS OF AIR COUNCIL AND SENIOR STAFF OFFICERS
AT AIR FORCE HEADQUARTERS

Minister of National Defence
I.A. Mackenzie   Oct. 1935–Sept. 1939
N.McL. Rogers   Sept. 1939–May 1940
Colonel J.L. Ralston   July 1940–Nov. 1944
General A.G.L. McNaughton   Nov. 1944–Aug. 1945
D.C. Abbott   Aug. 1945–Dec. 1946

Minister of National Defence for Air
Major C.G. Power   May 1940–Nov. 1944
General A.G.L. McNaughton (acting)   Nov. 1944–Mar. 1945
C.W.G. Gibson   Mar. 1945–Dec. 1946

Deputy Minister of National Defence
Major-General L.R. LaFlèche   Nov. 1932–Sept. 1939

Deputy Minister of National Defence (Navy and Air)
Lieutenant-Colonel K.S. Maclachlan   Sept. 1939–April 1940

Deputy Minister of National Defence (Air)
J.S. Duncan   April 1940–Jan. 1941
S.L. DeCarteret   Feb. 1941–April 1944
H.F. Gordon   April 1944–Aug. 1947

Senior Air Officer
Air Vice-Marshal G.M. Croil   Jan. 1934–Dec. 1938

Chief of the Air Staff
Air Vice-Marshal G.M. Croil   Dec. 1938–May 1940
Air Marshal L.S. Breadner   May 1940–Dec. 1943
Air Marshal R. Leckie   Jan. 1944–Aug. 1947

Assistant Chief of the Air Staff
Air Commodore H.L. Campbell   Jan. 1944–April 1945
Air Commodore M. Costello   April 1945–Dec. 1946

Deputy Chief of the Air Staff
Air Vice-Marshal G.O. Johnson   Nov. 1940–July 1942
Air Vice-Marshal N.R. Anderson   Aug. 1942–Jan. 1944

Air Member for Air Staff
Air Commodore L.S. Breadner   Oct. 1939–May 1940
Air Vice-Marshal A.A.L. Cuffe   June 1940–Feb. 1942
Air Vice-Marshal N.R. Anderson   Feb. 1942–Jan. 1944
Air Vice-Marshal W.A. Curtis   Jan. 1944–July 1946

Air Member for Personnel
Air Commodore W.R. Kenny   Oct. 1939–Feb. 1940
Air Vice-Marshal H. Edwards   Feb. 1940–Nov. 1941
Air Vice-Marshal J.A. Sully   Nov. 1941–April 1945
Air Vice-Marshal H.L. Campbell   April 1945–Nov. 1947

Air Member for Aeronautical Engineering and Supply
Air Vice-Marshal E.W. Stedman   Oct. 1939–Nov. 1940

Air Member for Aeronautical Engineering
Air Vice-Marshal E.W. Stedman   Nov. 1940–March 1942*
Air Vice-Marshal A. Ferrier   March 1942–Sept. 1944

Air Member for Research and Development
Air Vice-Marshal E.W. Stedman   May 1945–Jan. 1946

Air Member for Supply
Air Commodore S.G. Tackaberry   Nov. 1940–Feb. 1942
T. Sheard   Feb. 1942–Aug. 1944

Air Member for Organization and Training
Air Commodore G.O. Johnson   March–Nov. 1940

* From March 1942 to May 1945 Air Vice-Marshal Stedman was director general of air research.

Air Member for Training
Air Vice-Marshal R. Leckie   Nov. 1940–Jan. 1944
Air Vice-Marshal J.L.E.A. deNiverville   Jan. 1944–July 1945

Air Member for Organization
Air Vice-Marshal A.T.N. Cowley   March 1942–Dec. 1943
Air Vice-Marshal F.S. McGill   Dec. 1943–Nov. 1944

Air Member for Supply and Organization
Air Vice-Marshal F.S. McGill   Nov. 1944–Oct. 1945

Air Member for Accounts and Finance
Air Vice-Marshal K.G. Nairn   Dec. 1941–Nov. 1944

Air Member for Works and Buildings
Air Vice-Marshal R.R. Collard   Jan.–April 1944

Air Member for Construction Engineering
Air Vice-Marshal R.R. Collard   April–Nov. 1944

*Inspector-General**
Air Vice-Marshal G.M. Croil   June 1940–Jan. 1944

Deputy Inspector-General
Air Vice-Marshal A.E. Godfrey†   Jan. 1942–Jan. 1944
Air Vice-Marshal A.A.L. Cuffe†   Jan. 1943–Jan. 1944

COMMANDERS OF TRAINING COMMANDS AND GROUPS, RCAF AND BCATP, 1938–45

AIR TRAINING COMMAND

Officer Commanding
Group Captain A.E. Godfrey   Oct.–Dec. 1938
Group Captain A.A.L. Cuffe   Dec. 1938–Aug. 1939

Air Officer Commanding
Air Commodore A.A.L. Cuffe   Sept.–Dec. 1939

---

* The inspector-general stood outside the formal air force chain of command. His duties were to report to the minister on the state of the RCAF as he found it. While free to offer advice, he had no power to give effect to his recommendations, and no responsibility for the implementation of policy.
† From January 1943 Air Vice-Marshal Godfrey was responsible for eastern Canada and Air Vice-Marshal Cuffe for western Canada.

NO 1 TRAINING COMMAND

Air Officer Commanding
Air Commodore A.A.L. Cuffe Jan.–June 1940
Air Vice-Marshal G.E. Brookes June 1940–July 1942
Air Vice-Marshal G.O. Johnson July 1942–Jan. 1943
Air Vice-Marshal F.S. McGill Jan.–Dec. 1943
Air Vice-Marshal A.T.N. Cowley Dec. 1943–Jan. 1945

NO 2 TRAINING COMMAND

Air Officer Commanding
Air Vice-Marshal A.B. Shearer April 1940–Jan. 1943
Air Vice-Marshal T.A. Lawrence Jan. 1943–June 1944
Air Vice-Marshal K.M. Guthrie June 1944–Nov. 1944

NO 3 TRAINING COMMAND

Air Officer Commanding
Air Commodore C.M. McEwen April 1940–March 1941
Air Commodore G.V. Walsh March–Nov. 1941
Air Vice-Marshal J.L.E.A. deNiverville Nov. 1941–Nov. 1943
Air Vice-Marshal A. Raymond Nov. 1943–Jan. 1945

NO 4 TRAINING COMMAND

Air Officer Commanding
Air Commodore L.F. Stevenson April–Sept. 1940
Air Commodore A.T.N. Cowley Oct. 1940–March 1942
Air Vice-Marshal G. Howsam March 1942–Nov. 1944

NO 1 AIR COMMAND
(formed 15 Jan. 1945 following amalgamation of
Nos 1 and 3 Training Commands)
Air Officer Commanding
Air Vice-Marshal A. Raymond Jan.–June 1945
Air Vice-Marshal E.E. Middleton June 1945–Feb. 1947

NO 2 AIR COMMAND
(formed 1 Dec. 1944 following amalgamation of
Nos 2 and 4 Training Commands)
Air Officer Commanding
Air Vice-Marshal K.M. Guthrie Dec. 1944–Feb. 1946

NO 12 OPERATIONAL TRAINING GROUP

Air Officer Commanding
Air Commodore L.L. MacLean, RAF July 1942–May 1943
Air Commodore W.J. Seward, RAF May 1943–Oct. 1944
Group Captain G.T. Richardson, RAF Oct. 1944–Jan. 1945

RCAF OPERATIONAL COMMANDS
AND GROUPS IN CANADA, 1938–45

EASTERN AIR COMMAND

Officer Commanding
Group Captain N.R. Anderson　Dec. 1938–Aug. 1939

Air Officer Commanding
Air Commodore N.R. Anderson　Sept. 1939–March 1941
Air Commodore A.E. Godfrey　March–July 1941
Air Vice-Marshal N.R. Anderson　Aug. 1941–Feb. 1942
Air Vice-Marshal A.A.L. Cuffe　Feb. 1942–Jan. 1943
Air Vice-Marshal G.O. Johnson　Jan. 1943–April 1943

Air Officer Commanding-in-Chief
Air Vice-Marshal G.O. Johnson　April 1943–March 1945
Air Vice-Marshal A.L. Morfee　March 1945–March 1947

NO I GROUP

Air Officer Commanding
Air Commodore C.M. McEwen　Aug. 1941–Dec. 1942
Air Vice-Marshal F.V. Heakes　Dec. 1942–May 1944
Air Vice-Marshal A.L. Morfee　May 1944–March 1945
Air Commodore F.G. Wait　March–June 1945

NO 5 GULF GROUP*

Officer Commanding
Group Captain W.A. Orr　May–Nov. 1943
Wing Commander F.J. Ewart　May–Nov. 1944
Group Captain W.E. Kennedy　April–July 1945

WESTERN AIR COMMAND

Officer Commanding
Group Captain G.O. Johnson　April 1938–Aug. 1939

Air Officer Commanding
Air Commodore G.O. Johnson　Sept.–Oct. 1939
Air Commodore A.E. Godfrey　Oct. 1939–March 1941
Group Captain C.R. Slemon　March–July 1941

* No separate No 5 Group Headquarters was established. RCAF Station Gaspé functioned in this role during the shipping season, with the station commanding officer acting as group commander.

　　Squadrons in Nova Scotia were organized into a 'No 3 Group' in 1943-5, but no separate group headquarters was established. Command headquarters fulfilled this function.

Air Commodore A.E. Godfrey   July 1941–Dec. 1941
Air Vice-Marshal L.F. Stevenson   Jan. 1942–June 1944
Air Vice-Marshal F.V. Heakes   June 1944–Feb. 1946

NO 2 GROUP

Air Officer Commanding
Air Commodore E.L. Macleod   Jan. 1943–March 1944

NO 4 GROUP

Officer Commanding
Group Captain R.C. Gordon   Jan. 1942–Jan. 1943
Group Captain R.H. Foss   Jan. 1943–March 1944

NORTHWEST AIR COMMAND

Air Officer Commanding
Air Vice-Marshal T.A. Lawrence   June 1944-Sept. 1946

NO 9 (TRANSPORT) GROUP, RCAF STATION ROCKCLIFFE

Air Officer Commanding
Group Captain Z.L. Leigh (acting)   Feb.–June 1945
Air Commodore J.L. Plant   June 1945–Feb. 1946

APPENDIX B

Defence Expenditures, 1919-47

TABLE 1
Department of National Defence Expenditure, April 1919–August 1939 ($)

Fiscal year	RCAF (service)	RCAF (civil)	Total air services	Total militia services	Total naval services	Total DND expenditure[a]
1919–20			109,464	4,630,573	2,635,292	337,971,818[b]
1920–21			2,007,728	9,892,754	3,387,523	32,799,493[b]
1921–22			1,659,842	11,015,824	3,356,477	25,517,983[b]
1922–23			1,004,983	9,796,291	1,390,892	15,467,472
1923–24			1,249,178	9,674,226	1,360,807	14,283,210
1924–25			1,377,328	8,820,243	1,400,132	13,386,999
1925–26			1,880,615	9,131,260	1,448,907	14,462,912
1926–27			2,197,645	9,158,593	1,667,848	15,077,346
1927–28	1,669,639	2,222,222	3,891,861	10,166,706	1,725,195	17,696,760
1928–29	1,697,653	3,342,852	5,040,505	11,047,233	1,836,488	19,787,754
1929–30	1,947,347	3,973,323	5,920,670	11,163,170	3,013,396	21,981,754
1930–31	2,342,033	4,804,985	7,147,018	11,026,363	3,597,591	23,732,151
1931–32	1,934,532	2,185,258	4,129,790	9,700,464	3,043,201	18,372,563
1932–33	1,554,400	176,820	1,731,220	8,718,880	2,167,328	14,145,361
1933–34	1,402,885	281,677	1,684,562	8,773,545	2,171,210	19,629,498
1934–35	1,926,684	331,458	2,258,142	8,888,030	2,226,439	22,305,299
1935–36	2,875,817	901,503	3,777,320	10,141,230	2,380,018	27,378,541
1936–37	4,208,579	1,613,245	5,821,824	11,345,751	4,763,294	26,669,942
1937–38	9,664,515	353,589	10,108,104	17,222,804	4,371,981	32,835,289
1938–39	10,863,372	352,683	11,216,055	15,768,166	6,589,714	34,799,192
1939–40[c]	4,835,277	16,266	4,851,503	5,977,312	1,869,162	13,327,451

SOURCE: Canada, Department of the Naval Service, *Report of the Department of the Naval Service, 1920-22* (Ottawa 1920-22); Canada, Department of National Defence, *Report of the Department of National Defence, 1923-47* (Ottawa 1923-47)

a Includes demobilization, general services, and administrative costs of the Department

b Total is for the Department of the Naval Service and the Department of Militia and Defence.

c Most expenditure is for 1 April to 31 August 1939 only.

TABLE 2

Defence expenditure, 1939–1947 ($)

Fiscal year	Western Hemisphere operations	Overseas air services	British Commonwealth Air Training Plan	Total air services[a]	Total army and general services	Total naval services	total defence expenditures[b]
1939–40	28,561,303		4,257,081	32,818,384	68,192,594	11,341,459	125,679,888
1940–41	49,415,465	5,362,067	121,501,922	176,279,454	383,234,590	88,162,512	647,922,940
1941–42	108,768,628	13,699,336	248,067,693	370,648,736	511,169,248	129,367,632	1,011,451,064
1942–43	226,550,150	23,665,980	366,895,831	617,234,635	1,037,790,407	210,182,445	1,865,622,615
1943–44	312,760,999	383,888,079	233,893,142	930,665,808	1,328,804,799	369,556,013	2,629,094,792
1944–45	227,942,394	759,069,682	272,341,805	1,259,456,625	1,261,754,887	417,098,883	2,938,377,688
1945–46	108,031,379	197,075,936		524,329,032	949,578,204	241,759,022	1,715,792,801
1946–47	37,697,311	4,799,181		99,267,176	218,877,539	64,848,288	387,336,198

SOURCE: Canada, Department of National Defence, *Report of the Department of National Defence, 1947* (Ottawa 1947), 78–81

a Includes departmental administration and miscellaneous costs

b Includes departmental administration, defence research, and miscellaneous costs

TABLE 3
Relative expenditures

Fiscal year	Total federal government expenditure (to nearest $100,000)	Defence expenditure as percentage of total government expenditure	Total air services as percentage of total government expenditure	Air service expenditure as percentage of defence expenditure	Militia service (1919–39) and army and general services (1940–47) expenditure as percentage of defence expenditure	Naval service expenditure as percentage of defence expenditure
1919–20	740,100,000	45.7	.01	.03	1.4	.8
1920–21	528,900,000	6.2	.4	6.1	30.2	10.3
1921–22	476,300,000	5.4	.4	6.5	43.2	13.2
1922–23	441,200,000	3.5	.2	6.5	63.3	9.0
1923–24	371,800,000	3.8	.4	8.7	67.7	9.5
1924–25	352,200,000	3.8	.4	10.2	65.8	10.5
1925–26	355,600,000	4.1	.5	13.0	63.1	10.0
1926–27	359,200,000	4.2	.6	14.6	60.7	11.1
1927–28	379,800,000	4.7	1.0	22.0	57.5	9.7
1928–29	394,100,000	5.0	1.3	25.2	55.8	9.3
1929–30	405,300,000	5.4	1.5	26.9	50.8	13.7
1930–31	441,600,000	5.4	1.6	30.1	46.5	15.2
1931–32	448,700,000	4.1	.9	22.5	52.8	16.6
1932–33	532,400,000	4.1	.3	12.2	61.6	15.3
1933–34	458,200,000	2.6	.4	8.6	44.7	11.1
1934–35	478,100,000	4.3	.5	10.1	39.8	10.0
1935–36	532,600,000	4.7	.7	13.8	37.0	8.7
1936–37	532,000,000	5.1	1.1	21.8	42.5	17.9
1937–38	534,400,000	6.1	1.9	30.8	52.5	13.3
1938–39	553,100,000	6.3	2.0	32.2	45.3	18.9
1939–40	680,800,000	18.5	5.5	30.0	59.0	10.5
1940–41	1,246,600,000	52.0	14.1	27.2	59.2	13.6
1941–42	1,885,000,000	53.7	19.7	36.7	50.5	12.8
1942–43	4,387,100,000	42.5	14.1	33.1	55.6	11.3
1943–44	5,322,200,000	49.4	17.5	35.4	50.5	14.1
1944–45	5,245,600,000	56.0	24.0	42.9	43.0	14.2
1945–46	5,136,200,000	33.4	10.2	30.6	55.4	14.1
1946–47	2,634,200,000	14.7	3.8	25.6	56.5	16.7

SOURCE: M.C. Urquhart, ed., *Historical Statistics of Canada* (Toronto 1965), 202

The Clayton Knight Committee

When President Franklin Delano Roosevelt declared on 3 September 1939 that the United States would remain neutral, he neither expected nor demanded that 'every American remain neutral in thought.' 'Even a neutral has a right to take account of facts,' he declared in his 'Fireside Chat' to the nation. 'Even a neutral cannot be asked to close his mind or conscience.'[1] The direction in which the president would be led by his conscience was no mystery. He was unambiguously anti-fascist, pro-French, and pro-British, but he could not easily translate his private feelings into public policy. Besides the significant opposition to American belligerency throughout the country, not the least in Congress, there were also those who did not agree that the preservation of the United States and its values depended upon an Allied victory. Roosevelt could, at best, hope only to make American neutrality as benevolent to the British and French as possible.[2]

Other Americans, some perhaps no more than adventurers, some truly concerned about the survival of democratic values, had their own way of demonstrating support for the Allies. Following in the footsteps of the thousands of US nationals who volunteered to fight against Germany in the First World War (including some 1500 in the British flying services), recruits began to move north across the border into Canada shortly after the dominion declared war. The existence of this potential source of manpower for the RCAF and RAF had been recognized before the war, in particular by W.A. Bishop, the Canadian First World War fighter ace. Convinced that there would be no problem with the numbers who would come forward, Bishop was concerned primarily with tapping the American talent pool as efficiently as possible without violating US law which forbade the recruiting of Americans into foreign armed forces. However, when a visit to the White House in March 1939 left him with the impression that these legal barriers might not be unsurmountable, Bishop began to work on problems of organization and administration.[3]

At some point – the date is not clear – Bishop contacted Homer Smith, a Canadian veteran of the Royal Naval Air Service who had fallen heir to an oil fortune, obtaining his promise of financial backing. Bishop also spoke to Clayton Knight, an American aviation artist who had flown with the British on the Western Front in the First World War. With his broad ties to the US flying fraternity, Knight would be a valuable asset in public relations work and in ascertaining the current of American opinion. Given the likelihood of an enthusiastic response, the three agreed, it would be important to impose order by screening all applicants before channelling them across the border.[4]

On 4 September 1939, the day after Great Britain declared war and six days before Canada followed suit, Bishop telephoned Clayton Knight, who was attending the Cleveland air races, advising him that it was time to begin work. Despite the warning of his dinner companion, Ohio attorney general Thomas J. White, that a scheme to 'smuggle' pilots to Canada was unquestionably illegal, Knight found general enthusiasm for the idea among his colleagues but cautioned Bishop that it would be wise to undertake a more general survey of opinion among American airmen before making any commitments. On 9 September defence minister Ian Mackenzie granted Homer Smith a commission as a wing commander in the RCAF, and charged him with responsibility for Knight's survey. Shortly thereafter Smith rented a suite of rooms at the Waldorf Astoria Hotel in New York as his main base, and then accompanied Clayton Knight on a tour of American flying schools.[5]

The enthusiasm for the project displayed by Bishop, Smith, Knight (and perhaps by Ian Mackenzie) was not matched by official Ottawa. The government wished to avoid any activity that might embarrass President Roosevelt and, apart from Smith's appointment and some 'cloak-and-daggerish' communications between Knight and 'Mrs. Bishop' and 'Mr. P. Jones' (the code-name for Group Captain Harold Edwards, then the RCAF's senior personnel staff officer), the Department of National Defence remained steadfastly aloof.[6]

Throughout the period of the 'Phoney War' there was still no sense of urgency in Air Force Headquarters about securing the services of American flyers. This 'unsettled' state of affairs annoyed Clayton Knight, who had already begun to recruit volunteers, albeit informally, and he complained bitterly to New York Mayor Fiorella LaGuardia – another First World War flyer – as well as to Ottawa. His protests achieved nothing. The embryonic organization he and Smith had established would remain precisely that for the time being, depending entirely on Smith's largesse to keep it going.[7]

The air battles that followed the German assault on France in May 1940 changed everything. The development of the BCATP was accelerated, creating a dire shortage of flying instructors in the dominion, especially those with experience on twin-engined aircraft. Called to a special meeting of the Air Council, along with representatives of Canada's major airlines, Smith and Knight listened quietly as the air staff was informed that perhaps two dozen instructors could be made available from Canadian sources. They then broke the silence that followed this sombre disclosure with the announcement that they already had a list of 300 Americans, experienced pilots all, who were eager to come to Canada. Sceptical at first, the air staff eventually accepted this solution, and the Clayton Knight Committee was born. Its instructions were simple: to find qualified American pilots and direct them to Canada once it was settled that such activities would not upset the United States government.[8]

This was a sensible precaution. Although the German attack on Western

Europe had mobilized pro-Allied forces in the United States more strongly behind the president, there was still considerable opposition to greater co-operation with the British and the French lest it draw America into the war. Some, including officials in the War Department, had already begun to write off the British and French as lost causes, arguing that it would be irresponsible to weaken American war potential by diverting resources to them. Stronger hemispheric defence, they contended, was the key to national security.[9]

This was not the view in the White House or the State Department. In May the British ambassador in Washington had asked what the American reaction would be to Allied recruiting of pilots and was reassured that there would be little difficulty if the undertaking was discreet. The Canadian minister was told the same story a few days later; the information, it was claimed, came from the 'highest quarter.' All the State Department asked was that us nationals not be forced to swear an oath of allegiance that would forfeit their citizenship. The Canadian Privy Council waived this requirement, substituting an oath of obedience to superior officers; then, in November, it was agreed that Americans in all British Commonwealth forces should have the right to transfer to their own services should the United States become a belligerent.[10]

Knight discovered, nevertheless, that the law against recruiting still stood. He travelled to Washington to see Major General H.H. Arnold, chief of the us Army Air Corps, and Admiral J.H. Towers, who headed the navy's Bureau of Aeronautics. Both were exceedingly helpful, despite the fact that they were beginning to expand their pilot training programmes. Knight discovered that standards were so high that a considerable pool of talent acceptable to the RAF and RCAF was unemployable in the American flying services, and he was also told by Arnold to take a good look at those 'washed-out' from us flying programmes. Whether they had an occasional drink too many, were inveterate 'stunters,' or had proved just a touch unruly, Arnold confessed, these men were 'the kind I'd want to keep ... if I was fighting a war.' As a token of good faith he promised to supply Knight with a list of the air force's failed candidates.[11]

With such generous co-operation, if not formal acceptance of its activities, the Clayton Knight Committee began to work in earnest, its first task being to secure the one hundred pilots Breadner had requested in April. Headquarters would remain in the palatine Waldorf-Astoria – Smith did not want to hide in a 'hole-in-the-wall' – while other offices were opened in Spokane, San Francisco, Los Angeles, Dallas, San Antonio, Kansas City, Cleveland, Atlanta, and Memphis, all in luxury hotels, and all headed by Knight's flyer friends. Secretaries were hired at $20-50 per week, and recruiter-interviewers appointed at $100-150 a week. By December, the number of paid, full-time staff had risen to thirty-four. Expenses were met by the RCAF through a bank account opened in Homer Smith's name.[12]

Unable to advertise in the media, the committee's recruiters depended on word-of-mouth references and brochures sent to aviation schools and airports which noted simply that the Clayton Knight Committee would assist applicants interested in the many positions available in both British and Canadian aviation. It would, for example, arrange for medical exams and flying tests, and complete the documentation required before anyone could be accepted for Allied service. Publicly, it was always emphasized that the committee was looking for civilians to serve as flying instructors or staff pilots in the elementary flying training schools and air observer schools of the BCATP. It was understood, however, that many Americans would prefer to join the RCAF and serve at a more advanced level, as instructors/staff pilots at service flying training and bombing and gunnery schools, or even fly in combat. For that reason all applicants were to be judged on their fitness for a service commission.[13]

Finding men willing to enlist, however, was not the committee's priority in these early months. Indeed, Knight and his colleagues had nothing to do with the raising of the first Eagle squadron, a group of fighter pilots who enlisted directly in the RAF, and they objected strenuously to continuing that practice. For one thing, the publicity that surrounded them could upset isolationist elements and lead to legal recriminations against the Clayton Knight Committee. For another, there was the possibility that romantic appeals for fighter pilots might do damage to the comparatively dull, but nevertheless vital, work of recruiting mere instructors.[14]

Although the RCAF's basic age, medical, and educational standards were more liberal than those of the American services, the expertise and experience demanded of potential flying instructors and staff pilots was understandably high. To be considered for immediate employment, volunteers had to have a current US Civil Aviation Authority certificate and a minimum of 300 hours of logged flying time, including a considerable amount of twin-engine hours. For those interested in either the British or transatlantic ferry service – lucrative jobs both – pilots had to be fully qualified on instrument flying. Those who had logged fewer than 300 but more than 100 hours were turned away with the promise that their names would be kept on file in case Canadian standards were reduced. The age limit was 18-40 (the US upper limit was 30), and Canada would accept married men. Where the US forces required two years of university and 20/20 vision without glasses, Canada required only a high school diploma and 20/40 vision correctable to 20/20. Pay for the British ferry (between factory and airfields) was $150 (US) a week; for the transatlantic ferry, $600 per trip for group leaders, $500 for aircraft captains, $400 for co-pilots, and $300 for radio operators, with two trips guaranteed per month, plus expenses.[15]

By September 1940, 197 civilian pilots had been sent to Canada and accepted for service there (forty-four would eventually become part of the ferry service), and hundreds more had applied. By the end of the year the number of volunteers accepted by Canadian authorities had reached 321 (with an additional 105 rejected); a further forty-one destined for the RAF had been posted to refresher courses organized in conjunction with a handful of flying schools in the United States. The cost for all this had been $213,738.26, some for salaries and overhead, but most for medical and flight tests, transportation allowances, and the $5 per diem provided potential recruits awaiting a decision after they had reached Canada. Given the promise of 300 a year made in May, this six-month effort was an outstanding achievement.[16]

There was no reason to believe that the numbers coming forward would decrease in the foreseeable future. Word of the Clayton Knight Committee's activities was still spreading, while the response of those sent to Canada was overwhelmingly favourable. This was the best kind of publicity, and recruits' letters, applauding the way in which Canadians were treating American volunteers 'as ... princes,' were copied for the use of all offices.[17]

Canadian authorities were genuinely happy with this early success, but they still urged caution until the November 1940 American elections had been held. Roosevelt was seeking a third term, and must not be embarrassed before the election. Despite the apparent popularity of the destroyers-for-bases deal, the increasingly bitter and isolationist campaign of Republican candidate Wendell Wilkie appeared to be gaining momentum. In mid-October Charles Lindbergh made a strong anti-Roosevelt speech on the day the president's controversial peacetime draft was begun: the Democrats, he charged, would lead the country into the war within months of their re-election. Wilkie followed with an equally critical attack two days later; on 25 October John L. Lewis, leader of the Congress of Industrial Organizations, and formerly a stalwart supporter of Roosevelt and the New Deal, promised to resign if organized labour did not vote Republican. Nevertheless, the president won handily in November, and felt secure enough after his victory to ask for considerably increased aid for Britain, declaring in his 'Fireside Chat' of 29 December that, by providing all help short of war, the United States would become the 'arsenal of democracy.'[18]

What should have been a green light for Clayton Knight and his colleagues was not. In late November the State Department complained that the open solicitation of American pilots was becoming a problem. Ever mindful of Washington's feelings, Mackenzie King's government gave serious consideration to disbanding Knight's organization, going so far as to draft a Cabinet order to that effect. On the advice, however, of deputy air minister J.S. Duncan, who insisted that a steady flow of American pilots was crucial to the BCATP's future, a final decision was deferred. Further investigation indicated that the State Department officials concerned had acted on their own, without consulting the White House. Nevertheless, recruiting activities must remain circumspect even though numerous and mostly favourable newspaper articles had made the committee well known. 'Damn careless' was the way one State Department officer, who knew Roosevelt's views, described some of these reports. His advice that the Knight organization should 'slow down and pull in their horns,' if only for appearances, was taken seriously. That being done, the senior Canadian consul general in Washington reported that the American government would continue to turn a blind eye to activities that stretched the law 'a little,' while isolationist complaints would receive a 'meaningless bureaucratic answer.'[19]

Still concerned about American opinion, and perhaps, persuaded that Ottawa should have greater control over American recruiting, the Canadian government went further than Washington required. The Dominion Aeronautical Association, a crown corporation with Homer Smith as chief executive officer and Clayton Knight as director of publicity, was established as a buffer between the committee and the RCAF. Since volunteers would now be passed on for employment with the DAA, a civilian agency, it would be easier to sustain the argument that Clayton Knight was not breaking American law. The fact that the DAA's offices were located next door to Air Force Headquarters in Ottawa – tailor-made for applicants who wished to join the RCAF, or for whom civilian jobs were not available – was not advertised, and carefully cultivated American press coverage emphasized the need for civilian pilots.[20]

Though the Eagle squadrons and other volunteers who had made their own way to military service in Britain and Canada made the best stories, Clayton Knight and his colleagues preached the view that staff pilots and flying instructors assigned to the training plan were making an equally valuable contribution to the war effort by freeing Canadians for overseas service.[21]

By May 1941 it was apparent that there had been a distinct falling off in the quality (but not the quantity) of American volunteers coming forward. The reasons for this are not entirely clear, but two factors seem to have been involved. The number of pilots who had 300 hours of flying experience and who were willing to serve in Britain or Canada was obviously limited, and the recruiters may well have already seen most of those who were interested. At the same time President Roosevelt had begun to move the United States closer to active participation in the war; some potential recruits may have preferred to wait for what they considered to be the United States' inevitable entry into the war.[22]

Whatever the reason, Stuart Armour, managing director of the DAA, was worried by the Clayton Knight Committee's diminishing returns. The solution, he thought, was to begin taking in volunteers for general aircrew training rather than restricting applications to experienced pilots. Having already cleared the idea with General Arnold and Admiral Towers, he also proposed that the RCAF make a concerted effort to recruit recent graduates from the US Civil Aviation Authority's pilot training programme. If implemented, Armour's proposal would represent a bold change of direction for the Clayton Knight Committee. Air Commodore Robert Leckie, the air member for training, agreed that the idea was worth consideration, but would not take immediate action despite growing indications that the RCAF was suffering from an acute shortage of aircrew. There were, he pointed out, still a good number of Canadians on the force's waiting list, and they must be accommodated first.[23] Leckie's hesitancy angered many of the Clayton Knight Committee's stalwarts, who appear to have had complete knowledge of Armour's plan. Bogart Rogers, head of the Los Angeles office, protested that 'We're daring, dashing fellows who want to get things done the quick way – pilots for Britain – and we really think that if we can build up a little we can help you a lot in shoving things down the Canadian throats which they might not have swallowed previously.'[24]

It was not long before Leckie's attitude changed. By June 1941 there was statistical evidence that a manpower shortage was a probability rather than a possibility. That same month President Roosevelt reassured his countrymen that the Neutrality Act did not prevent US nationals from going to Canada to enlist. He even pointed out that volunteers for the Commonwealth armed forces would be given a US draft deferment subject to recall if their services were eventually required by the United States.[25]

Armour took advantage of Roosevelt's pronouncements and the recent drop in enlistments to press again for the adoption of his scheme. Questioning the need to continue the Clayton Knight Committee's activities if it sought out only experienced pilots – who were now in demand in the United States as well – he asked Air Commodore Leckie (now acting chief of the air staff in Air Vice-Marshal L.S. Breadner's absence) to call a special meeting of the Air Council to decide the committee's future. The meeting was held on 9 July. Leckie acknowledged that trained staff pilots and flying instructors were no longer in short supply, and agreed that recruiting pilots was no longer the vital issue which it had once been. Because of this, he was prepared to accept the case made by Armour and Group Captain J.A. Sully (director of air personnel) that the Clayton Knight Committee should begin to recruit Americans for general aircrew training, aiming for 2500 by September. Since high policy was involved, however, Leckie would not act until Breadner and the minister of national defence for air, C.G. Power, had returned from the United Kingdom. In the interim the Clayton Knight Committee was to change its name to the Canadian Aviation Bureau to mask its forthcoming efforts at more direct recruiting.[26]

Armour, meanwhile, set off for Washington. Anxious to make Power's decision as uncomplicated as possible, he wanted to confirm that there would be no official opposition to the RCAF's recruiting of US nationals for active service. He discovered that, as had been the case in May 1940, the president's recent pronouncements had not changed the law. Clayton Knight could still be prosecuted, particularly if it could be shown that volunteers were paid to travel to Canada; however, the Roosevelt administration would not precipitate legal action against the committee. Armour then visited the Civil Aviation Authority headquarters, where he received a much warmer welcome. The CAA was prepared to hand over a list of 55,000 college students who had recently completed elementary flying training courses. There were only two qualifications to the CAA's co-operation: the RCAF should not contact the graduates of more advanced programmes, in whom both the air corps and the navy had an interest, and potential recruits must be seen to be paying their own way to Canada.[27]

Armour's report was enough to convince Leckie, Breadner, Power, and deputy minister Sydney de Carteret to go ahead. Early in August 1941 the mandate for the Clayton Knight Committee (the new name 'Canadian Aviation Bureau' never caught on outside the bureaucracy) was changed to include recruitment of combat pilots and other aircrew in the United States, and letters advertising the new policy were soon sent out to the thousands of young men who had received primary flying certificates from the CAA's civilian pilot training scheme.[28]

Complaints about this undisguised recruiting of Americans were voiced almost immediately, the most serious coming from an Oregon congressman, who demanded a full-scale investigation of the RCAF's activities.[29] Aiming to defuse the situation before the State or Justice departments were forced to take action, the Clayton Knight Committee took to the offensive, and within days the American press was full of disclaimers. 'Most of the men we contact go to civilian organizations,' the papers were told.[30] The State Department, for its part, quoted the president's June invitation to Americans to join the forces of the British Commonwealth. With that response, opposition seems to have crumbled, and for the next few months questions about the propriety of the committee's recruiting were raised only on the odd occasion when distraught parents sought congressional help to convince their underage offspring to return home. Perhaps the significance of individual foreign enlistments had paled in comparison to the near belligerency of the US Navy in the north Atlantic or to the statement of joint war aims issued by President Roosevelt and Prime Minister Churchill after their meeting at Argentia, Nfld, late that summer.

The main problem for the Clayton Knight Committee was to keep potential volunteers happy. This had been of little concern before because, with experienced pilots in such short supply, recruits had been sent north without delay once the required examinations had been completed and the paperwork was in order. While some grumbled about having to spend time at Manning Depots – to learn the ways of RCAF officers and gentlemen – and others, mainly the civilian instructors and staff pilots, were upset by the difficulties they had in finding accommodation for their wives, the majority of these early volunteers appear to have been well-satisfied.

After August 1941, however, the RCAF had set quotas on the number of Americans to be accepted, hoping that its American agents could regulate the flow. This soon proved unrealistic. When Knight's recruiters played by the rules, they found that many of those who turned out to be 'over quota' either lost interest or declared that they would make their own way to Canada secure in the knowledge that the RCAF could not afford to turn them away. Common sense persuaded Knight and his colleagues to dispense with the quota and let the air force worry about the consequences.[31]

This decision may have exacerbated the overloading from which the BCATP from time to time suffered. American volunteers soon found themselves marking time in non-flying jobs, 'sweeping hangars or acting as general flunkies,' and some threatened to return home.[32] For others, the prospect of permanent assignment to a flying school was a crushing disappointment. Clayton Knight recalled the slowly drawled warning given by one young Texan: 'Best they do something about my request to get over where the fighting is ... I did not enlist to be a damn elevator operator taking students up, day in and day out.'[33] As one young American reported, there was always a minority of his fellow-countrymen who felt that their special status as neutrals and the USA on their shoulders gave them 'priority on attention and a license for undue boasting, disregard for authority ... and an intolerable sense of "holier than thou"...'[34] Some American visitors, in addition, suffered mild culture shock. One volunteer complained that Canadian society was 'so conservative it's obnoxious,'[35] while another remarked that though he was 'quite pleased with Canada and the people' he nevertheless felt conspicuous 'without a mustache, pipe and drab grey suit.' 'These people seem to make a hobby of subduing excess emotion,' he continued, 'or excess anything.'[36]

All of this may have contributed to the 248 desertions that were recorded among the 3009 volunteers sent north. On the whole, however, testimonials in the files of the Clayton Knight Committee usually referred to the RCAF in glowing terms ('the best air force in the world'); the training seemed to be the finest available; and the people were 'swell.' The majority, in short, were quite happy with their treatment.[37]

After Japan's attack on Pearl Harbor in December 1941, American flyers who wanted to take an active part in the conflict could join their own armed forces. As agreed beforehand, all of the 6129 American aircrew serving in the RCAF were also given the opportunity to return home. About 2000 requested transfer, and in May a special train left Washington to make a cross-Canada journey gathering the flock. By the time it crossed the border again it had collected 1759 new members of the American forces, including most of the staff pilots and civilian instructors (who, it seems, were eager for less routine work and the higher rates of pay in the US forces). By the end of the war a further 2000 US nationals of the 8864 who had enlisted in the RCAF had transferred. However, 5067 Americans completed their service in the Royal Canadian Air Force, a foreign service with lower rates of pay. Whether they had listened to President Roosevelt when he argued that they could serve America's cause just as well by remaining in Canada, or whether they had developed a sense of commitment and belonging, or whether they simply did not want to risk what the US air services might offer is impossible to say.[38]

Nor did Washington prohibit Americans from volunteering for the RCAF or RAF after Pearl Harbor. In fact, from time to time the US government urged the RCAF to keep its lists open to American volunteers. By the spring of 1942 the average number of applications being received by the Canadian Aviation Bureau had risen to 3000 a month, many of them from those who wished to avoid the US ground forces and believed they would find no place in the American air force or navy. As far as Air Commodore G.V. Walsh, Canadian air attaché in Washington, was concerned, there would be a deplorable waste of potential flying talent if the RCAF ignored these men. Accordingly, he urged that Canadian and American authorities work out some means of preventing their underemployment in the US Army. Air Force Headquarters was not interested in Walsh's plan. There were sufficient Canadians to meet future requirements, Breadner maintained, and in any event the Permanent Joint Board on Defence had recently recommended against further recruiting of Americans into the RCAF. In fact, Breadner seems almost to have been primarily concerned about the bad risk involved in training more American volunteers. What, he asked, was to prevent them from demanding a transfer to their own services after the Canadian air force had spent time and money putting them through flying schools?[39]

As a result, the Clayton Knight Committee's Canadian operation effectively closed down from February 1942, and was not reopened despite the RCAF's manpower shortage about a year later. The British continued to make use of the organization's resources until May 1942, when it was agreed at the Ottawa Air Training Conference that the RAF could take a last 600 recruits with appropriate draft deferments from those applicants already accepted for its American training wing.[40] The Clayton Knight branch offices were shut down the following month, with New York headquarters remaining open only to tidy up accounts and, as it turned out, to send apologetic replies to the hundreds of Americans who still wished to join the RCAF and RAF – mainly to avoid non-flying military service in the US armed forces.

The significance of the Clayton Knight Committee's recruiting activities is told partially by statistics. According to its own estimates, the committee dealt with some 49,000 Americans, and by February 1942 had sent 900 experienced aircrew and 1450 trainees, most with some aviation experience, to the RCAF. An additional 300 pilots were sent to Canada for the RAF, and a few dozen more had been posted to flying schools in the United States before assignment to Britain.[41] Perhaps more significantly, there were the hundreds of civilian flying instructors and staff pilots who allowed the BCATP to operate at greater capacity much sooner than anticipated.

Ferry Command

One of the remarkable achievements of the Second World War, the ferrying of aircraft across the Atlantic Ocean, does not properly constitute part of the RCAF story. Nevertheless, its impact on both civil and military aviation in Canada was notable, and no account of the RCAF would be complete without reference to the origins, development, and impact of Ferry Command.

Consistent with the traditional practice of the British services, the Air Ministry encouraged a policy of domestic aircraft procurement between the wars. While the possibility of using British orders to build up the aviation industry in the several dominions (and particularly Canada) was raised from time to time, the other logical alternative – the United States – was less appealing. There was no guarantee that peacetime orders would be filled once war began and that uncertainty alone meant that the British were reluctant to commit themselves to American production. But necessity drives policy more vigorously than desire, and this attitude changed abruptly in 1938, especially after the war scare that preceded the Munich agreement. Confronted by an expanding German air force already thought to be much larger than the RAF, and faced with the prospect that domestic industrial capacity would soon be stretched to the limit, British authorities had no choice but to turn to the United States for help. Accordingly, the Air Ministry ordered 250 Lockheed Hudson reconnaissance aircraft and 400 North American Harvard trainers. Although shipments continued after the start of the war, further orders were out of the question until November 1939, when President Franklin Delano Roosevelt persuaded Congress to amend his country's neutrality laws to permit a cash-and-carry trade in war matériel. Both the British and the French were quick to take advantage of this shift in policy, and by late spring 1940 they had ordered some 10,800 aircraft and an even larger number of aero-engines from American sources.[1]

The German victories of May 1940 resulted in the French rejecting their commitment, but the RAF took over the undelivered balance of the French contracts and placed an order for 4200 additional aircraft. When it was clear that even this was insufficient the Air Ministry requested another 12,000 machines, emphasizing that this was only the first installment of a much larger expansion scheme. All told, by the summer of 1940 British orders in the United States amounted to over 26,000 aeroplanes, to be delivered at the rate of one thousand a month. The figures increased still more when the Americans indicated their willingness to open new plants capable of producing a further 3000 aircraft a month.[2] It was a logistician's nightmare. Sea transport was no longer a secure or efficient method of delivery. U-boats prowled the Atlantic; there was a great demand for the limited cargo space available to ship other critical war supplies; and the delay involved in dismantling, crating, loading, unloading, unpacking, and reassembling aeroplanes sent by sea was becoming unacceptable.

One answer was to fly as many aircraft to Britain as possible. Air Commodore N.R. Anderson, commanding the RCAF's Eastern Air Command, put forward such a recommendation in April 1940, pointing out the advantages of using Newfoundland Airport (as Gander was then known) as a staging base. Nothing came of his proposal, or of a similar plan suggested in England. The Air Ministry and the RAF held that it would be 'absolute suicide' to ferry aircraft from North America, particularly in winter. Transatlantic flying was still in its infancy, and the difficulties involved in piloting aircraft across the ocean with few navigation aids and no emergency fields en route seemed overwhelming.[3]

Neither the Air Ministry nor the RAF had counted on the intervention of the minister of aircraft production, the Canadian-born press baron, Lord Beaverbrook. A notoriously hard driver, contemptuous of bureaucracy and officialdom, he was eager to control the delivery of aeroplanes as well as their manufacture. As a result, he met with G.E. Woods Humphery, former managing director of Imperial Airways, to seek his opinion on a transatlantic ferry service. When the latter said that it could be done and even agreed to organize it if he could work within an existing structure, Beaverbrook needed no further encouragement. In July he formally approached the Canadian Pacific Railway without so much as a courteous nod to Canadian authorities.[4]

Why Beaverbrook chose the CPR, and whether he had the British Cabinet's (or Churchill's) authority to do so, are open questions. Beaverbrook, however, was probably influenced by his long-standing friendship with Sir Edward Beatty, Canadian Pacific's president, as well as by the company's growing interest in aviation. For his part Beatty was undoubtedly intrigued by the opportunity to break into the monopoly on transatlantic flying then held by British Overseas Airways Corporation (as Imperial Airways had recently been renamed) and Pan American Airways. In the event, an agreement to set up a transatlantic ferry was signed by representatives of the Ministry of Aircraft Production, CPR, and Woods Humphery on 16 August 1940. The latter would organize the service; Canadian Pacific was to engage all ground personnel, procure supplies, and furnish administrative support; Beaverbrook's ministry would provide experienced aviation executives and aircrew as well as reimburse CP for all expenditures except salaries.[5]

Preliminary work which had begun two weeks previously under Colonel H. Burchall, former general manager of Imperial Airways, now accelerated. D.C.T. Bennett and A.S. Wilcockson, both experienced Imperial Airways flying-boat captains, appointed flying superintendent and superintendent of operations, respectively, got down to work in CPR offices in the Windsor Street train station and at St Hubert airfield, east of Montreal. At about the same time

Squadron Leader G.J. Powell, chief navigation officer of Eastern Air Command and another Imperial Airways' veteran, was dispatched to Gander to survey facilities there. Shortly thereafter the Department of Transport made available its meteorological section, one of whom – P.D. McTaggart-Cowan – became the ferry service's pre-eminent North American weather forecaster.[6]

Canada's official contribution during these initial phases was minor. C.D. Howe, the minister of munitions and supply, and C.G. Power, the minister of national defence for air, were both eager to help, but Beaverbrook so dominated the affair they had almost no contact with the British, and certainly no detailed knowledge of future plans.[7] Eventually, however, the RCAF was able to open up hangar space at St Hubert and Gander and recruit aircrew volunteers from the United States through the Clayton Knight Committee (see Appendix C). The Department of Transport's immediate contributions were a number of radio operators (over 200 by 1944). Sometime later the department undertook the construction of a major airfield at Dorval, just west of Montreal, the future headquarters of the ferry service. Nevertheless, the part played by the Department of Transport, Canadian Pacific, and the RCAF did not alter the fact that Beaverbrook's creation was a British organization from start to finish.

It was a mark of Beaverbrook's drive, his positive outlook, and his faith in the American aviation industry that the first Hudsons were scheduled to fly the Atlantic at the end of August, barely two weeks after the ferry agreement was signed. Events proved this prediction wildly optimistic. In fact, Hudsons did not begin to arrive in Montreal until mid-October, and none were ready to leave on the next leg of the journey to Britain until the end of the month.

The level of risk was regarded as very considerable. Some of the scheme's proponents were ready to claim success if only three of the first seven aircraft arrived safely. Bennett, preparing diligently to lead the first group across the ocean, was sure he could do better than that. The Hudsons' de-icing equipment was supplemented by an anti-freezing compound smeared on the leading edges; the aircraft would fly in formation, within sight of each other, to compensate for the fact that only the lead plane carried a navigator; and, if heavy weather forced pilots to break formation, they were to do so according to a carefully prearranged plan designed to limit the possibility of collision. After that, however, they would be on their own, trusting in whatever talents they had at setting and keeping to the required course, and deciding whether to turn back or continue to press on towards Northern Ireland or Scotland.[8]

Fair weather, clear moonlit skies, and welcome tail winds favoured Bennett's flight as it left Newfoundland, late on 10 November 1940, but these almost ideal conditions did not last long. An active weather system covered the last two-thirds of the route and caused some pilots to break formation. Bennett and three others stayed together. Despite the rough and tumble skies this group put down at Aldergrove, near Belfast, Northern Ireland, just over eleven hours after take-off. The others, who had finished the trip independently, arrived about an hour later.[9] This success demonstrated that ferrying was feasible, given adequate training, thorough preparation, and qualified aircrew. Bennett fretted nonetheless. Luck, he knew, had played a large part in the safe arrival of his flight. Yet no one, least of all Beaverbrook, shared his concern that there would be trouble ahead if pilots had no navigators to help them.

Only after the fourth formation flight on 28/29 December 1940, when a Hudson crushed on take-off, without fatality, blocking the runway for another, and a third turned back to Gander with engine trouble, did 'The Beaver' admit that he was asking too much. Henceforth each aircraft would carry a navigator recently graduated from the BCATP and given additional training by BOAC personnel in Montreal. Three months later Bennett felt confident enough to call a halt to formation flying, which could be dangerous because it forced aircraft to fly so close to one another.[10] Accidents did occur. Major Sir Frederick Banting, the Nobel Prize winning co-discoverer of insulin, became one of the ferry service's first three fatal casualties when the aircraft in which he was hitching a ride went down near Gander on the night of 20/21 February 1941.[11] Still, with only a handful of fatal crashes for the rest of 1941, ferry operations remained much less costly than even the optimists had predicted.

The New Year also witnessed major changes in personnel and organization. Woods Humphery and Burchall resigned in January, partly because of a falling-out over the routing of Consolidated PBY Catalina flying boats through Canada during winter when the danger of icing was severe. A former bush pilot and general superintendent of northern operations for Canadian Airways, C.H. Dickins, became vice-president of the Canadian Pacific Air Services Department and deputy director general of the British Air Commission in Washington.[12] Illness then forced Beatty to retire, his place being taken in March by Beaverbrook's special North American representative, Morris Wilson, president of the Royal Bank of Canada. With some of its pioneers gone, and the size of the project mushrooming, in May the Ministry of Aircraft Production cancelled its agreement with the CPR and assumed direct control of the Atlantic Ferry Organization, or ATFERO as it was known to the employees.[13]

For the next few months the service's main preoccupation was with numbers. Although Beaverbrook had always counted on finding his crews outside the United Kingdom, recruiting drives in Canada and the United States proved major disappointments. The war effort had already attracted most Canadian pilots of military age, while few of the remainder qualified for long-distance ocean flying. In the United States, meanwhile, the Clayton Knight Committee was having little difficulty finding pilots, but it could pass on only a few to Beaverbrook. Most seemed to prefer joining the air force (despite the minimum US $1,000 a month paid to civilian transatlantic ferry pilots), while the majority of those who showed an interest in the ferry service did not meet Bennett's minimum standards. Thus, for 1940 at least, ATFERO had to make do with aircrew from BOAC, from the domestic British Air Transport Auxiliary, and from a very reluctant RAF. However, with an estimated 674 Hudsons, eighty-three Catalinas, fifty-eight Consolidated B-24 Liberators, and twenty Boeing B-17 Fortresses due to be received by June 1941, it was obvious that the three group leaders, thirty-five first pilots, and eleven second pilots on the ferry roster in January 1941 would be hard-pressed to keep pace with the anticipated explosion in American production.[14]

Shipping all but four-engined bombers by sea – as recommended by the RAF's chief of the air staff, Sir Charles Portal – would have alleviated pressure, as would employing BCATP aircrew graduates posted overseas (thus getting both aircraft and aircrews to the operational theatre), but Beaverbrook rejected both options. Relying once again on surface transport – now even more scarce than before – was unthinkable, while using air training plan crews would have given the Air Ministry more influence over the ferry service than Beaverbrook was prepared to accept. Churchill stood by his mercurial colleague, reaffirming on 1 March 1941 that the ferry service remained 'The Beaver's' preserve. By May, however, Beaverbrook's differences with the Air Ministry over aircraft production had finally brought his often threatened resignation.[15] Now that the driving force behind the civilian transatlantic ferry had departed, it seemed inevitable that the RAF would take over.

Other voices had to be heard before this decision was taken. Though the US government was, by and large, successful in handling criticism of its support for Britain, Roosevelt was embarrassed by reports of hundreds of American aircraft sitting idly on Canadian airfields waiting for crews to fly them overseas. If these machines were really so vital, his opponents asked, how could the British tolerate such delay? Would they not be of greater use in the US armed services than being lent, leased, sold, or given to a country that apparently did not know how to take advantage of them? Was American rearmament suffering because of misguided American generosity? So long as the Liberators, Fortresses, Catalinas, and Hudsons remained on the tarmac at Montreal and Gander – often awaiting essential modifications not done by the manufacturers – there was no convincing reply to be made. For their part the American service chiefs worried that in its attempt to reduce the backlog of undelivered aeroplanes the RAF might dissipate its operational strength. After lengthy discussions, during which the Americans did not hide their concern, agreement was reached to have US service pilots deliver the aircraft from the factories to Canada while the RAF would fly them across the Atlantic.[16]

The RAF officially took over ATFERO's role with the formation of Ferry Command, under Air Chief Marshal Sir Frederick Bowhill, on 20 July 1941. Although this reorganization led to Bennett's resignation – he felt his position untenable in the proposed military set-up, under a man who had at first strongly opposed the ferry service – there were few others, and Bowhill's command retained much of its civilian character. The uniformed component at the Dorval headquarters was kept small; of the 400 aircrew on strength just after the change-over, 207 were civilians.[17] Their numbers were soon augmented by American civilian pilots whose jobs delivering aeroplanes to Canada had been lost to the military, but by far the largest infusion of new talent in the latter half of 1941 came from the BCATP. After a series of false starts, it was finally decided to give selected graduates destined for Coastal Command some practical experience at long-range flying and navigation by having them take part in ferry operations before their first operational posting. Following intensive training at No 31 General Reconnaissance School, Charlottetown, and the RAF's No 31 Operational Training Unit (OTU) at Debert, NS, pilots, navigators, and wireless operators made one or two crossings before transfer to their squadrons.[18]

Some experienced RCAF aircrew, many from Eastern Air Command, also worked their way to overseas postings by delivering aircraft. Another source of supply came from the air observer schools, which maintained a large staff of civilian pilots to fly BCATP trainees on navigation practice flights. After a year or two of acting as taxi drivers for navigator trainees, many of these pilots offered their services to Ferry Command. With operational crews loaned by Coastal Command from time to time, the combination of direct American involvement and more complete exploitation of available Commonwealth resources allowed Ferry Command to cope with increased production by American manufacturers. As expected, the number of accidents increased with the influx of less experienced flyers, but never to the point of challenging the concept of ferrying.[19]

The size of the project continued to grow. In fact, by the spring of 1941 the need to ferry medium-range aircraft like the Douglas DB-7 Boston and the Martin B-26 Marauder had stimulated interest in establishing a second route, with shorter stages, through Greenland and Iceland. Britain already had bases at Reykjavik and Kaldaharnes in Iceland, but Greenland possessed no airfields and providing them required diplomatic as well as engineering solutions. Following complicated international negotiations the United States established a protectorate over Greenland and built landing fields there.[20] Both the British and Canadian governments bristled at the US initiative, but the two were eager to assist because Greenland airfields would speed the delivery of aircraft. Although the large airport at Narssarssuaq (code-named Bluie West 1) was almost exclusively an American project, Canadians were intimately involved in the survey that identified Goose Bay, Labrador, as the major North American terminus of this second ferry route, and Ottawa contributed $20 million and supervised the construction of the landing field.[21]

Work was well under way at Goose Bay by the time the United States entered the war. In the summer of 1942 some 650 aircraft of the US Eighth Air Force passed through Goose Bay, Bluie West 1, and Reykjavik on their way to Britain, most flown by regular squadron pilots rather than by ferry specialists. By the end of the year 882 of the 920 American service aircraft to attempt the transatlantic crossing reached the United Kingdom safely. The British total for the year was 994.[22]

The delivery of over 1900 aircraft in 1942 meant that the Anglo-American ferry was beginning to have an appreciable impact on the air war in Europe. Along with the fighters and bombers of the Eighth Air Force, replacement aeroplanes for the US Twelfth Air Force had also been staged through Goose Bay, while almost half of Coastal Command's aircraft establishment at the end of 1942 had been flown to Britain. The following year saw an even greater effort, the British alone ferrying more than 2000 machines across the ocean. At the same time the North Atlantic airway was being used more and more to transport passengers, mail, and vital war supplies, including medicine, technical equipment, food, and sometimes even ammunition.[23]

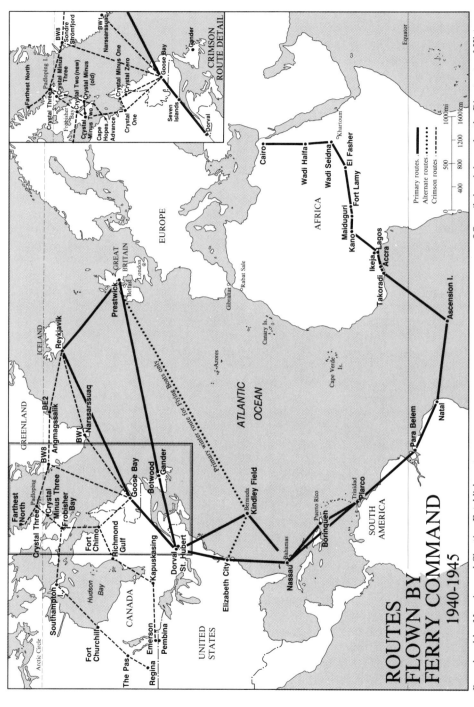

ROUTES FLOWN BY FERRY COMMAND
1940-1945

CRIMSON ROUTE DETAIL

Primary routes.
Alternate routes.
Crimson routes.

0   400   500   1000mi
0   800   1200   1600km

©Compiled and drawn by the Directorate of History.

Reproduced by Mapping and Charting Establishment.

This increase and broadening of function led to the last major change in the original organization. Recognizing that the aircraft ferry and the delivery of cargo and passengers were, in effect, two sides of the same coin, in March 1943 the RAF chose to amalgamate all air transport operations under one functional headquarters. As a result Ferry Command became 45 Group in the new RAF Transport Command, with subordinate wings and squadrons throughout North America. In addition, a second OTU (originally No 32 RAF, and then No 6 RCAF) was established at Patricia Bay, BC, to prepare additional crews for long-range transport, supply, and ferry operations.[24]

The continually expanding project required more aircrew. American production for the RAF was nearly at its peak – 3726 aircraft would be delivered in 1944 – and 390 Avro Lancaster XS and 626 de Havilland Mosquitoes on order in Canada were beginning to roll off production lines in Toronto and London, Ont. As these Canadian-built aeroplanes made their way to Britain, the proportion of Canadians in 45 Group increased. Along with the 200 or so Department of Transport radio operators and the remaining Canadian civilian pilots, by June 1944, 634 of the Group's 1330 uniformed aircrew belonged to the RCAF.[25] Nevertheless, these air force personnel continued to be part of a British operation.

As it turned out, however, the dominion's formal entry into the field of international aviation grew out of the ferry service. C.D. Howe failed in his initial bid to have Trans-Canada Airlines participate in the 'return' ferry bringing pilots back to North America. The United States, he was told, might protest the use of lend-lease Liberators to benefit a civilian airline, particularly one publicly owned. It was therefore wise to keep TCA and BOAC out of the picture for the moment at least. When BOAC eventually gained responsibility for the return ferry it offered TCA a share at some unspecified date in the future. Howe, however, did not like the idea of the Canadian airline acting as a satellite of a British parent – by using BOAC equipment overpainted with TCA markings, for example, or flying according to BOAC schedules laid down in London.[26]

All Canadian attempts to purchase transport aircraft from the United States also failed. It was not until March 1943, when the Air Ministry gave Canada the Lancaster bomber sent to Victory Aircraft as a production pattern, that prospects for an independent Canadian transatlantic air service improved. Modified to carry passengers and freight, and with TCA markings, this aircraft made its inaugural flight to England on 22 July 1943. Acquiring two more transport versions of the bomber, the airline embarked upon a thrice-weekly round-trip schedule in 1944. By the end of the year it had carried over one million pounds of mail and 2000 passengers between Canada and the United Kingdom, paving the way for a postwar network of international air routes.[27]

The RCAF's military transport service was no less an offspring of Ferry Command. Beginning the war with only one light transport flight (upgraded to 12 (Communications) Squadron in June 1940) used to fly senior officers from headquarters to the various commands, the RCAF evinced no interest in expanding this role until Canada accepted responsibility for developing Goose Bay in the summer of 1942. Though most construction materials could be taken in by water during the warm weather, the site was accessible only by air during the long Labrador winter, and once plans for an American freight service fell through it was up to the RCAF to assume the burden.[28] In July Wing Commander Z.L. Leigh, a veteran bush pilot and TCA instructor, was hastily brought to headquarters and ordered 'to get busy on the organization of a specialized transport service.'[29] In the beginning the Combined Munitions Assignment Board hesitated to allocate suitable aircraft: transports, like everything else, were in short supply in operational theatres, all of which had a higher priority than the RCAF's Home War Establishment. In January 1943, however, a number of Lockheed Lodestars were made available to the recently formed 164 (Transport) Squadron, which immediately started moving the backlog of 663,200 pounds of freight destined for Goose Bay. In the spring the squadron upgraded to Douglas C-47 Dakotas (military versions of the DC-3), enabling it to carry as much as one million pounds of supplies and mail and 2200 passengers a month.[30] A second transport squadron, No 165, had been established in April, and in time these two units, plus 12, 166, and 167 (Communications) Squadrons, and 70 and 124 (Ferry) Squadrons combined under the RCAF's Directorate of Air Transport Command. Despite their considerable achievements, the RCAF's domestic transport and ferry units were soon eclipsed by the operations of 168 (Heavy Transport) Squadron, formed in October 1943 specifically to provide dependable 'bomber mail' service to the Canadian forces overseas. By the end of the war its Dakotas, Liberators, and Fortresses had flown to Scotland, Gibraltar, Italy, North West Europe, Morocco, and Egypt, crossing the Atlantic 636 times.[31]

In 1945, thanks largely to ferry and transport operations, transoceanic flying was almost routine – a tremendous development in less than five years. In addition to this general legacy, the British ferry organization made a significant contribution to the RAF war effort that can be illustrated in statistical terms. The 9027 aircraft ferried to the bomber, fighter, transport, and maritime patrol squadrons in Europe, Africa, the Middle East, India, and Southeast Asia represented 8.9 per cent of total British aircraft production from January 1939 to September 1945, and 12.8 per cent of this total less trainers and miscellaneous aircraft. From a slightly different perspective, the total number of aeroplanes ferried across the Atlantic was a little more than a quarter of all aircraft delivered to the United Kingdom and British overseas commands from North America, and 35 per cent of this total once trainers are subtracted from it.[32]

While the BCATP provided a network of improved airfields in southern and central Canada, ferry and transport needs did the same in the north. In the northwest, the need to deliver American lend-lease aircraft to the Soviet Union, and to supply and defend Alaska, brought US assistance in upgrading the landing fields at Grand Prairie, Alta; Fort St John, Fort Nelson, Smeaton River, and Smith River, BC; and Watson, Whitehorse, Teslin, Aislik, and Snag in the Yukon – the North West Staging Route.[33] In the east, the success of Goose Bay convinced the US Army Air Forces that small fighter aircraft could be ferried across the north Atlantic by staging through central and eastern Canada and the Northwest Territories to Greenland and Iceland. Although very few aircraft were delivered this way, the American initiative produced a series of three airways known as the Crimson or North East Staging Route, built by the United States at a cost of $40 million: Fort Chimo, Que. – Frobisher Bay – Padloping Island; Regina – The Pas – Fort Churchill – Southhampton Island; and Kapuskasing – Richmond Gulf.[34] When the RCAF once again began to assist in opening up the Canadian north near the end of the war, it found that many of these strips could be put to good use. Some were prominent in the early plans for the postwar air defence of North America.

Home War Operational Stations, 1939-45

This appendix lists Home War Establishment operational flying stations, with the squadrons [sqn], flights, and detachments [det] on their establishments.

Aircraft from operational training units and general reconnaissance schools, though not part of the Home War Establishment, also flew occasional missions from the following stations:

Debert, NS   Bagotville, Que.
Greenwood, NS   Patricia Bay, BC
Pennfield Ridge, NB   Comox, BC
Charlottetown, PEI   Boundary Bay, BC
Summerside, PEI   Abbotsford, BC

NEWFOUNDLAND AND LABRADOR

Botwood	7 July–15 Nov. 1941	Det, 116 (BR) Sqn (from sqn at Dartmouth, NS)
	31 May–31 July 1942	Det, 116 (BR) Sqn (from sqn at Dartmouth, NS)
	1 Aug.–12 Nov. 1942	116 (BR) Sqn
	12 June–14 Nov. 1943	116 (BR) Sqn
	4 May–7 June 1944	Det, 116 (BR) Sqn (all aircraft from sqn at Gander, Nfld)
Gander	16 June 1940–10 April 1941	Det, 10 (BR) Sqn (from sqn at Dartmouth, NS)
	11 April 1941–15 Nov. 1942	10 (BR) Sqn (see also Yarmouth, NS)
	20 Aug. 1942–23 July 1943	127 (F) Sqn

	2 Nov. 1942–9 May 1943	5 (BR) Sqn (see also Torbay, Nfld)
	27 Dec. 1942–28 Feb. 1943	Det, 162 (BR) Sqn (from sqn at Yarmouth, NS)
	15 March–7 May 1943	Det, 10 (BR) Sqn (from sqn at Dartmouth, NS)
	8 May 1943–10 June 1945	10 (BR) Sqn
	27 July 1943–31 May 1944	126 (F) Sqn (see also Bagotville, Que.)
	15 Nov. 1943–7 June 1944	116 (BR) Sqn (see also Goose Bay, Lab., and Botwood, Nfld)
	3 June–30 Sept. 1944	129 (F) Sqn (see also Quebec City, Que.)
Goose Bay	9 April–15 Oct. 1943	129 (F) Sqn
	28 July–9 Aug. 1943	Det, 5 (BR) Sqn (from sqn at Torbay, Nfld)
	6–23 Oct. 1943	Det, 162 (BR) Sqn (from sqn at Dartmouth, NS)
	26 Oct. 1943–15 March 1944	130 (F) Sqn
	15 Nov. 1943–7 June 1944	Det, 116 (BR) Sqn (from sqn at Gander, Nfld)
Stephenville (US station)	24 Sept.–6 Oct. 1943	Det, 162 (BR) Sqn (from sqn at Yarmouth and Dartmouth, NS)
Torbay	26 Nov. 1941–31 May 1942	Det, 11 (BR) Sqn (from sqn at Dartmouth, NS)
	1 Jan. 1942–15 July 1943	5 (CAC) Flight
	18 May 1942–19 Oct. 1943	145 (BR) Sqn
	9 June 1942–25 June 1943	125 (F) Sqn
	winter 1942–3	occasional dets, 5 (BR) Sqn (from sqn at Gander, Nfld)
	24 April–9 May 1943	Det, 5 (BR) Sqn (from sqn at Gander, Nfld)

	10 May 1943–31 July 1944	5 (BR) Sqn (see also Goose Bay, Lab.)
	26 June 1943–15 March 1944	128 (F) Sqn
	15 July 1943–1 April 1945	1 (K) Det
	28 Oct. 1943–17 June 1944	11 (BR) Sqn
	21 June–23 Aug. 1944	113 (BR) Sqn
	3 Aug. 1944–15 June 1945	160 (BR) Sqn
	17 Aug. 1944–10 May 1945	Det, 145 (BR) Sqn (from sqn at Dartmouth, NS)
	1 April–30 June 1945	1 (K) Sqn
	11 June–15 Aug. 1945	10 (BR) Sqn (see also Yarmouth, NS)

PRINCE EDWARD ISLAND

Summerside	30 April–30 Nov. 1944	Det, 161 (BR) Sqn (from sqn at Gaspé, Que.)

NOVA SCOTIA

Dartmouth	prewar–1 Nov. 1942	5 (BR) Sqn (see also Gaspé, Que., North Sydney, and Sydney, NS)
	4 Nov. 1939–27 Oct. 1943	11 (BR) Sqn (see also Torbay, Nfld, and Mont Joli, Que.)
	6 Nov. 1939–8 June 1940	1 (F) Sqn
	31 March–27 Sept. 1940	Det, 118 (F) Sqn (from sqn at Saint John, NB)
	15 June 1940–10 April 1941	10 (BR) Sqn (see also Gander, Nfld)
	27 Sept. 1940–15 Aug. 1943	2 (CAC) Flight
	7 June–14 Aug. 1941	Det, 119 (BR) Sqn (from sqn at Yarmouth, NS)
	28 June 1941–31 July 1942	116 (BR) Sqn (see also Botwood, Nfld)

	16 July 1941–5 June 1942	118 (F) Sqn
	15 Dec. 1941–30 Sept. 1945	121 (K) Sqn
	27 April 1942–26 July 1943	126 (F) Sqn (see also Bagotville, Que.)
	1 July–17 Aug. 1942	127 (F) Sqn
	28 Aug. 1942–8 April 1943	129 (F) Sqn
	4 Nov.–28 Dec. 1942	Det, 116 (BR) Sqn (from sqn at Shelburne, NS)
	16 Nov. 1942–7 May 1943	10 (BR) Sqn (see also Gander, Nfld)
	1 Dec. 1942–30 April 1943	117 (BR) Sqn
	29 Dec. 1942–13 Feb. 1943	116 (BR) Sqn
	1 April 1943–8 May 1944	161 (BR) Sqn
	24 July–23 Dec. 1943	127 (F) Sqn
	15 Aug. 1943–1 Oct. 1945	167 (Comm) Sqn
	1 Oct. 1943–4 Jan. 1944	162 (BR) Sqn (see also Goose Bay and Stephenville, Nfld, and Mont Joli, Que.)
	30 Oct. 1943–30 June 1945	145 (BR) Sqn (see also Torbay, Nfld and Yarmouth, NS)
	30 Dec. 1943–1 June 1944	129 (F) Sqn
	1 June 1944–30 May 1945	126 (F) Sqn
	18 June 1944–19 May 1945	11 (BR) Sqn
	1 Oct. 1945–postwar	164 (T) Sqn
Debert	18 Feb. 1942–29 Nov. 1943	123 (ACT) Sqn (see also Sydney, NS)
Halifax	27–31 Aug. 1939	2 (AC) Sqn
	1–5 Sept. 1939	3 (F) Sqn
	1 Sept.–30 Oct. 1939	Det, 2 (AC) Sqn (from sqn at Saint John, NB)
	5 Sept. 1939–14 June 1940	10 (BR) Sqn
	28 Oct. 1939–30 March 1940	Det, 118 (F) Sqn (from sqn at Saint John, NB)
North Sydney	27 Aug. 1939–8 Feb. 1941	8 (BR) Sqn (det deployed to St John's Nfld, not then a station, 4–13 Sept. 1939)

	30 July–18 Dec. 1940	Det, 5 (BR) Sqn (from sqn at Dartmouth, NS)
	1 Aug.–27 Oct. 1941	117 (BR) Sqn
	27 April–30 Nov. 1942	117 (BR) Sqn (see also Gaspé, Que.)
	1 May–28 Nov. 1943	117 (BR) Sqn (see also Gaspé, Que.)
Shelburne	13 Nov.–28 Dec. 1942	116 (BR) Sqn (see also Dartmouth, NS)
	14 Feb.–11 June 1943	116 (BR) Sqn
	29 Nov.–15 Dec. 1943	117 (BR) Sqn
Sydney	9 Feb.–26 Dec. 1941	8 (BR) Sqn
	1 April 1941–1 Nov. 1943	4 (CAC) Flight
	26 May–24 Sept. 1941	Det, 5 (BR) Sqn (from sqn at Dartmouth, NS)
	7 June–8 Aug. 1941	Det, 119 (BR) Sqn (from sqn at Yarmouth, NS)
	31 Dec. 1941–9 Jan. 1942	Det, 119 (BR) Sqn (from sqn at Yarmouth, NS)
	10 Jan. 1942–3 May 1943	119 (BR) Sqn (see also Chatham, NB, and Mont Joli, Que.)
	20 April–8 June 1942	125 (F) Sqn
	7 June 1942–25 June 1943	128 (F) Sqn
	8 Oct. 1942–27 Jan. 1943	Det, 123 (ACT) Sqn (from sqn at Debert, NS)
	10 May 1943–20 June 1944	113 (BR) Sqn
	26 June–22 Dec. 1943	125 (F) Sqn
	1 Dec. 1943–15 March 1944	119 (BR) Sqn (see also Chatham, NB)
	8 June 1944–20 June 1945	116 (BR) Sqn
	1 Nov. 1944–25 April 1945	Det, 161 (BR) Sqn (from sqn at Yarmouth, NS)
	22 May–10 June 1945	Det, 5 (BR) Sqn (from sqn at Gaspé, Que.)
	14 June–7 Aug. 1945	162 (BR) Sqn

Yarmouth	18 July 1940–10 Jan. 1942	119 (BR) Sqn (see also Sydney and Dartmouth, NS)
	15 Dec. 1941–1 Nov. 1943	6 (CAC) Flight
	15 Feb. 1942–9 May 1943	113 (BR) Sqn (see also Chatham, NB, and Mont Joli, Que.)
	20 March–9 June 1942	Det, 10 (BR) Sqn (from sqn at Gander, Nfld)
	19 May 1942–30 Sept. 1943	162 (BR) Sqn (see also Gander and Stephenville, Nfld, and Mont Joli, Que.)
	4 July 1943–2 Aug. 1944	160 (BR) Sqn
	26 May–9 June 1944	Det, 161 (BR) Sqn (from sqn at Gaspé, Que.)
	1 Aug. 1944–8 May 1945	5 (BR) Sqn (see also Mont Joli, Que.)
	5 Nov. 1944–31 May 1945	161 (BR) Sqn (see also Sydney, NS)
	11 May–8 June 1945	Det, 145 (BR) Sqn (from sqn at Dartmouth, NS)
	17–31 July 1945	Det, 10 (BR) Sqn (from sqn at Torbay, Nfld)

NEW BRUNSWICK

Chatham	9 Sept.–13 Dec. 1942	Det, 113 (BR) Sqn (from sqn at Yarmouth, NS)
	24 April–2 Dec. 1943	Det, 119 (BR) Sqn from sqn at Sydney, NS, and Mont Joli, Que.)
Moncton	20 Jan. 1943–30 Sept. 1945	164 (T) Sqn
Saint John	1 Sept.–1 Nov. 1939	2 (AC) Sqn (see also Halifax, NS)
	1 Nov. 1939–27 Sept. 1940	118 (F) Sqn (see also Halifax and Dartmouth, NS)
	1 Sept. 1940–1 April 1944	1 (CAC) Flight

QUEBEC

Bagotville	14 June–31 July 1942	Det, 126 (F) Sqn (from sqn at Dartmouth, NS, and Gander, Nfld)
	14 July 1942–24 Oct. 1943	130 (F) Sqn
	26 Oct.–28 Dec. 1943	129 (F) Sqn
Gaspé	17 June–25 Oct. 1940	Det, 5 (BR) Sqn (from sqn at Dartmouth, NS)
	10 June–23 Nov. 1942	Det, 117 (BR) Sqn (from sqn at North Sydney, NS)
	18 May–31 Oct. 1943	Det, 117 (BR) Sqn (from sqn at North Sydney, NS)
	9 May–3 Nov. 1944	161 (BR) Sqn (see also Summerside, PEI, Seven Islands, Que., and Yarmouth, NS)
	9 May–15 June 1945	5 (BR) Sqn (see also Mont Joli, Que., and Sydney, NS)
Mont Joli	1 May–13 July 1942	130 (F) Sqn
	12 May–11 June 1942	Det, 11 (BR) Sqn (from sqn at Dartmouth, NS)
	6 July–3 Aug. 1942	Det, 113 (BR) Sqn (from sqn at Yarmouth, NS)
	2 Aug.–1 Nov. 1942	Det, 119 (BR) Sqn (from sqn at Sydney, NS)
	16 Sept.–23 Dec. 1942	Det, 113 (BR) Sqn (from sqn at Yarmouth, NS)
	10 Oct.–30 Nov. 1942	Det, 162 (BR) Sqn (from sqn at Yarmouth, NS)
	24 April–3 May 1943	Det, 119 (BR) Sqn (from sqn at Sydney, NS)
	4 May–30 Nov. 1943	119 (BR) Sqn (see also Chatham, NB)

	24 Oct.–26 Nov. 1943	Det, 162 (BR) Sqn (from sqn at Dartmouth, NS)
	19 April–21 May 1945	Det, 5 (BR) Sqn (from sqn at Yarmouth, NS, and Gaspé, Que.)
Montreal	prewar–31 Oct. 1939	118 (F) Sqn
	prewar–26 May 1940	115 (F) Sqn
Quebec City	2–23 Sept. 1944	Det, 129 (F) Sqn (from sqn at Gander, Nfld)
Seven Islands	4 July–1 Nov. 1944	Det, 161 (BR) Sqn from sqn at Gaspé, Que.)
St Hubert	10 Sept.–5 Nov. 1939	1 (F) Sqn
	1 March 1944–postwar	124 (FY) Sqn

ONTARIO

Hamilton	prewar–4 Jan. 1940	119 (BR) Sqn
Rockcliffe (Ottawa)	prewar–10 Sept. 1939	7 (GP) Sqn
	3–20 Oct. 1939	11 (BR) Sqn
	2 Nov.–16 Dec. 1939	2 (AC) Sqn
	17 Dec. 1939–13 Feb. 1940	110 (AC) Sqn
	7 Feb.–7 June 1940	112 (AC) Sqn
	28 June 1940–postwar	12 (Comm) Sqn
	13 Dec. 1940–15 July 1941	118 (F) Sqn
	1 Aug.–10 Oct. 1941	115 (F) Sqn
	ca.22 Oct. 1941–16 Feb. 1942	123 (ACT) Sqn
	1 Nov.–13 Dec. 1941	111 (F) Sqn
	1 Jan. 1942–29 Feb. 1944	124 (FY) Sqn (see also Winnipeg, Man.)
	2 Jan.–25 March 1942	14 (F) Sqn
	14 April–3 June 1942	132 (F) Sqn
	18 Oct. 1943–postwar	168 (HT) Sqn
	12 June 1944–postwar	14 (Photo) Sqn
Uplands (Ottawa)	21 Oct.–3 Nov. 1939	11 (BR) Sqn
Weston	prewar–16 Dec. 1939	110 (AC) Sqn

MANITOBA

Winnipeg	prewar–6 Feb. 1940	112 (AC) Sqn
	15 Nov. 1942–28 Feb. 1944	Det, 124 (FY) Sqn (from sqn at Rockcliffe, Ont.)

	1 March 1944–30 Sept. 1945	170 (FY) Sqn

SASKATCHEWAN

Mossbank	15 June–3 Oct. 1942	135 (F) Sqn
Regina	prewar–6 Nov. 1939	120 (BR) Sqn

ALBERTA

Calgary	prewar–2 Sept. 1939	1 (F) Sqn
	prewar–1 Oct. 1939	113 (F) Sqn
Lethbridge	3 June–4 Oct. 1942	133 (F) Sqn

BRITISH COLUMBIA

Alliford Bay	15 May 1940–22 April 1944	6 (BR) Sqn (see also Bella Bella, BC)
	19 Nov.–2 Dec. 1942	9 (BR) Sqn (mobility exercise from Bella Bella, BC)
	23 April 1944–25 July 1945	7 (BR) Sqn
Bella Bella	8 Dec. 1941–1 Sept. 1944	9 (BR) Sqn (see also Alliford Bay, BC)
	19 Nov.–2 Dec. 1942	6 (BR) Sqn (mobility exercise from Alliford Bay, BC)
Boundary Bay	5 Oct. 1942–30 June 1943	133 (F) Sqn
	1 July 1943–9 March 1944	132 (F) Sqn
	24 Sept. 1943–20 Jan. 1944	14 (F) Sqn
Coal Harbour	11 Dec. 1941–1 May 1944	120 (BR) Sqn (see also Ucluelet, BC)
	26 Jan.–8 Feb. 1943	4 (BR) Sqn (mobility exercise from Ucluelet, BC)
	23 April 1944–7 Aug. 1945	6 (BR) Sqn
Patricia Bay	22 Oct. 1939–15 May 1940	Det, 111 (CAC) Sqn (from sqn at Sea Island, BC)
	16 May 1940–1 Feb. 1941	111 (CAC/F) Sqn
	1 Aug. 1940–10 Dec. 1941	120 (BR) Sqn

	1 Nov. 1940–1 Nov. 1942	13 (OT) Sqn
	15 Feb. 1941–9 Jan. 1942	3 (CAC) Flt
	15 Oct. 1941–25 April 1942	115 (F) Sqn
	10 Jan. 1942–30 April 1945	122 (K) Sqn (see also Sea Island and Port Hardy, BC)
	19 Jan.–3 June 1942	111 (F) Sqn
	18 July–15 Oct. 1942	132 (F) Sqn
	1 Oct. 1942–16 Aug. 1943	149 (TB/BR) Sqn
	8 Oct. 1942–14 Aug. 1943	135 (F) Sqn
	19 Aug. 1943–20 Jan. 1944	111 (F) Sqn
	21 Aug. 1943–16 March 1944	115 (BR) Sqn
	10 Jan.–15 March 1944	163 (F) Sqn
	12 March 1944–10 Sept. 1945	135 (F) Sqn (see also Tofino, BC)
	20 March 1944–25 May 1945	8 (BR) Sqn (see also Terrace, BC)
	18–21 Aug. 1944	132 (F) Sqn
	22 Aug. 1944–10 Sept. 1945	133 (F) Sqn (see also Tofino, BC)
	20 May–15 Sept. 1945	11 (BR) Sqn
	27 Aug.–15 Sept. 1945	122 (K) Sqn
Port Hardy	14 May 1943–30 April 1945	Det, 122 (K) Sqn (from sqn at Patricia Bay, BC)
	19 Oct.–11 Dec. 1943	Det, 8 (BR) Sqn (from sqn at Sea Island, BC)
	11 Dec. 1943–19 March 1944	8 (BR) Sqn
	1 May–26 Aug. 1945	122 (K) Sqn
Prince Rupert	8 Dec. 1941–22 April 1944	7 (BR) Sqn
Sea Island (see also Vancouver, Jericho Beach)	prewar–15 May 1940	111 (CAC) Sqn (see also Patricia Bay, BC)
	7 Nov. 1939–31 July 1940	120 (BR) Sqn
	1 May–31 Oct. 1940	13 (OT) Sqn
	14 Dec. 1941–18 Jan. 1942	111 (F) Sqn
	1 Jan.–2 June 1942	8 (BR) Sqn
	27 March 1942–16 Feb. 1943	14 (F) Sqn
	4 June–17 July 1942	132 (F) Sqn
	1 July 1942–1 March 1943	147 (BR) Sqn (see also Tofino, BC)
	1 March–10 Dec. 1943	8 (BR) Sqn (see also Tofino and Port Hardy, BC)

	1 March 1943–9 Jan. 1944	163 (AC/F) Sqn (det deployed to Wainwright, Alta, not a station, 27 July–15 Oct. 1943)
	15 March–14 July 1943	Det, 122 (K) Sqn (from sqn at Patricia Bay, BC)
	3 May–28 June 1943	160 (BR) Sqn
	13 July 1943–31 Oct. 1945	165 (T) Sqn
	15 July 1943–1 Nov. 1945	166 (Comm) Sqn
	20 Aug.–1 Nov. 1943	118 (F) Sqn
	11 March–21 Aug. 1944	133 (F) Sqn
	22 Aug.–30 Sept. 1944	132 (F) Sqn
Smithers	20 Jan.–1 March 1944	Det, 149 (BR) Sqn (from sqn at Terrace, BC)
	20 Jan.–9 March 1944	Det, 135 (F) Sqn (from sqn at Terrace, BC)
Terrace	17 Nov. 1943–11 March 1944	135 (F) Sqn (see also Smithers, BC)
	18 Nov. 1943–15 March 1944	149 (BR) Sqn (see also Smithers, BC)
	22–27 June 1944	8 (BR) Sqn (mobility exercise from Patricia Bay, BC)
Tofino	16 Oct. 1942–30 June 1943	132 (F) Sqn
	4 Nov. 1942–1 March 1943	Det, 147 (BR) Sqn (from sqn at Sea Island, BC)
	2 March 1943–15 March 1944	147 (BR) Sqn
	1 July 1943–10 March 1944	133 (F) Sqn
	14–25 Oct. 1943	Det, 8 (BR) Sqn (from sqn at Sea Island, BC)
	10 March–17 Aug. 1944	132 (F) Sqn
	17 March–23 Aug. 1944	115 (BR) Sqn
	18–24 Aug. 1944	135 (F) Sqn (mobility exercise from Patricia Bay, BC)
	27 Aug. 1944–7 Aug. 1945	4 (BR) Sqn

	8 Oct. 1944–5 Aug. 1945	Det, 135 (F) Sqn (from sqn at Patricia Bay, BC; alternate every four weeks with 133 Sqn Det)
	11 Oct. 1944–30 June 1945	Det, 133 (F) Sqn (from sqn at Patricia Bay, BC; alternate every four weeks with 135 Sqn Det)
Ucluelet	12 Sept. 1939–30 April 1940	Det, 6 (BR) Sqn (from sqn at Jericho Beach, Vancouver, BC)
	3 May 1940–26 Aug. 1944	(BR) Sqn (see also Coal Harbour, BC)
	26 Jan.–8 Feb. 1943	120 (BR) Sqn (mobility exercise from Coal Harbour, BC)
Vancouver (Jericho Beach) (see also Sea Island)	prewar–2 May 1940	4 (BR) Sqn
	prewar–13 May 1940	6 (BR) Sqn (see also Ucluelet, BC)
	8 Jan.–15 July 1940	119 (BR) Sqn
	31 Oct.–20 Nov. 1941	117 (BR) Sqn

ALASKA

Adak Island	21 Sept.–8 Oct. 1942	Sub–det, 111 (F) Sqn (from Det at Fort Glenn, Umnak Island)
	31 March–16 April 1943	Det, 14 (F) Sqn (from sqn at Fort Glenn)
	4–14 May 1943	Det, 111 (F) Sqn (from sqn at Kodiak)
	3–8 July 1943	Det, 14 (F) Sqn (from sqn at Fort Glenn)

Amchitka Island	17 April–15 May 1943	Det, 14 (F) Sqn (from sqn at Fort Glenn)
	15 May–9 July 1943	Det, 111 (F) Sqn (from sqn at Kodiak)
	9 July–26 Aug. 1943	Det, 14 (F) Sqn (from sqn at Fort Glenn)
Annette Island	5 May 1942–18 Aug. 1943	115 (F/BR) Sqn
	21 June 1942–15 Aug. 1943	118 (F) Sqn
	15 Aug.–17 Nov. 1943	135 (F) Sqn
	15 Aug.–17 Nov. 1943	149 (BR) Sqn
Chiniak Point	6 Nov. 1942–24 April 1943	Det, 111 (F) Sqn (from sqn at Kodiak)
Elmendorf Field (Anchorage)	7 June 1942–27 Feb. 1943	8 (BR) Sqn (see also Kodiak, Nome, Yakutat)
	8 June–30 Oct. 1942	111 (F) Sqn (see also Fort Glenn, Umnak Island; Adak Island)
Fort Glenn, Umnak Island	16 July–10 Oct. 1942	Det, 111 (F) Sqn (from sqn at Elmendorf Field; see also Adak Island)
	18 March–21 Sept. 1943	14 (F) Sqn (see also Adak and Amchitka Islands)
Kodiak	31 Oct. 1942–12 Aug. 1943	111 (F) Sqn (see also Adak and Amchitka Islands, and Chiniak Point)
	30 Dec. 1942–4 Feb. 1943	Det, 8 (BR) Sqn (from sqn at Elmendorf Field)
Nome	18 July–5 Dec. 1942	Det, 8 (BR) Sqn (from sqn at Elmendorf)
Yakutat	3–6 June 1942	8 (BR) Sqn
	26 Oct.–2 Nov. 1942	Det, 8 (BR) Sqn (from sqn at Elmendorf)

ICELAND

| Reykjavik | 6 Jan. 1944–13 July 1945 | 162 (BR) Sqn (see also Wick, Scotland) |

SCOTLAND

| Wick | 24 May–7 Aug. 1944 | Det, 162 (BR) Sqn (from sqn at Reykjavik, Iceland) |

Notes

CHAPTER I: THE BIRTH OF THE RCAF

1 See S.F. Wise, *Canadian Airmen and the First World War* (Official History of the Royal Canadian Air Force, I; Toronto 1980), 579-620.
2 Wilson to Kennedy, 12 July 1919, HQ 866-1-53 pt I, PAC, RG 24, vol. 3577
3 C.C. MacLaurin, 'Memorandum Regarding the Formation of a National Canadian Air Service,' 28 Jan. 1919, HQ 866-25-8, ibid., vol. 3525
4 Lott to Gibson, 14 June 1919, OS 10-9-27 pt 3, PAC, RG 9 III, vol. 81
5 Biggar to Gibson, 7 July 1919, HQ 866-25-16 pt I, PAC, RG 24, vol. 3526
6 Borden to Montagu, 15 Dec. 1917, R.L. Borden Papers, PAC, MG 26 H, vol. 80, file OC 374(I). See also Robert Craig Brown, *Robert Laird Borden: a Biography*, II: *1914-1937* (Toronto 1980), 131; Robert Laird Borden, *Robert Laird Borden: His Memoirs*, Henry Borden, ed. (Toronto 1938), II, 759.
7 Borden to Montagu, 15 Dec. 1917, Borden Papers, PAC, MG 26 H, vol. 80, file OC 374(I)
8 Telegram, Borden to Ballantyne, 24 Nov. 1918, NS 63-10-1, DHist 77/58, vol. 20
9 Borden to Kemp, 24 Feb. 1919, A.E. Kemp Papers, PAC, MG 27 II D 9, vol. 132, file C-18
10 'Memorandum by Minister of Customs and Inland Revenue,' 29 April 1919, R.A. McKay, ed., *Documents on Canadian External Relations*, II: *The Paris Peace Conference of 1919* (Ottawa 1969), 136-8
11 'Memorandum by Minister of Customs and Inland Revenue,' 3 May 1919, ibid., 143. See also Margaret S. Mattson, 'The Growth and Protection of Canadian Civil and Commercial Aviation, 1918-1930' (PH D thesis, University of Western Ontario, 1978).
12 'Convention Relating to International Air Navigation,' and the Canadian regulations adapted from it, Canada, *Air Regulations, 1920* (Ottawa 1920)
13 Aero Club of Canada to White (acting prime minister), 5 Feb. 1919, Borden Papers, PAC, MG 26 H, vol. 74, file OC 329(2). The correspondence on wartime regulation is in HQ 6978-2-57, PAC, RG 24, vol. 2036.
14 Flavelle to Gwatkin, 7 Jan. 1919, HQ C2841 pt 5, DHist 77/57
15 See Frank Ellis, *Canada's Flying Heritage* (Toronto 1954).
16 O'Reilley to Gwatkin, 2 June 1919, HQ C2841 pt 5, DHist 77/57

17 Air Board minutes, 28 July 1919, DHist 181.009 (D6780)

18 Gwatkin to military secretary, 9 Jan. 1919, HQ C2841 pt 5, DHist 77/57

19 Privy Council dormant orders-in-council, PC 461, 26 Feb. 1919, PAC, RG 2, series 3, vol. 221. See also Mewburn to White, 23 Feb. 1919, HQ C2841 pt 5, DHist 77/57.

20 Gwatkin, 'Memorandum Relating to the Proposed Formation of a Canadian Flying Corps,' nd, in Kemp to Borden, 22 June 1917, P-5-94, PAC, RG 25 A 2, vol. 267

21 Gwatkin to Macallum, 8 Feb. 1919, HQ C2841 pt 5, DHist 77/57

22 Agent general for Ontario to Gibson, 10 Feb. 1919, Lott to Gibson, 24 Feb. 1919, OS 10-9-27 pt 2, PAC, RG 9 III, vol. 81; Pattullo to minister of militia and defence, 9 Jan. 1920, NS 63-1-1 pt I, PAC, RG 24, vol. 5666

23 Deville to deputy minister, 14 Nov. 1918, NS 63-1-5, DHist 77/58, vol. 3; Macallum to Gwatkin, 8 Jan. 1919, HQ C2841 pt 5, DHist 77/57

24 McArthur to Meighen, 29 March 1919, NS 63-1-5, DHist 77/58, vol. 3

25 Canada, Parliament, House of Commons, *Debates*, 7 March 1919, 317

26 A copy of Wilson's paper is in HQ 045-4 pt I, PARC 826453. MacLaurin sent a copy of his paper to the chairman of the Commission of Industrial Research and another, later, to the Privy Council. For the former see HQ C2841 pt 5, DHist 77/57; the latter, HQ 866-25-8, PAC, RG 24, vol. 3525.

27 Wilson to Grey, 12 June 1923, J.A. Wilson Papers, PAC, MG 30 E 243, copy in DHist 76/271, file E2

28 J.A. Wilson, 'Civil Aviation To-Day,' *Canadian Defence Quarterly*, I, April 1924, 23-4

29 Wilson, 'Air Policy,' nd, Wilson Papers, DHist 76/271, file E3

30 Reprinted in *Ottawa Citizen*, 24 April 1919

31 The correspondence and draft bill are in HQ 866-25-8, PAC, RG 24, vol. 3525. See also the 'Proceedings of the Naval and Military Committee,' 11 April 1919, HQS 1009 pt 3, PARC 394884.

32 Canada, *Statutes*, 9 and 10 Geo. V, c. 2 (1919), 'An Act to Authorize the Appointment of an Air Board for the Control of Aeronautics,' copy, as given Royal Assent on 6 June 1919, in 'Statutory Authorities,' DHist 77/451

33 House of Commons, *Debates*, 5 May 1919, 2133

34 See Sifton to Borden, 29 Nov. 1919, Borden Papers, PAC, MG 26 H, vol. 74, file 329(2).

35 Air Board minutes, 25 June 1919, DHist 181.009 (D6780)

36 Wilson, 'Proposed Air Board Act,' 2 April 1919, HQ 866-25-8, PAC, RG 24, vol. 3525

37 Telegram, Biggar to Gibson, 23 July 1919, HQ 866-25-16 pt I, ibid., vol. 3526

38 Biggar to Gibson, 7 July 1919, Biggar to Sifton, 4 July 1919, ibid.

39 Mulock to de Dombasle, 13 June 1919, R.H. Mulock biographical file, DHist

40 James Eayrs, *In Defence of Canada*, I: *From the Great War to the Great Depression* (Toronto 1964), 194-6

41 House of Commons, *Debates*, 4 April 1922, 685

42 See H. Montgomery Hyde, *British Air Policy between the Wars, 1918-1939* (London 1976), 56-61; and Robin Higham, *Armed Forces in Peacetime: Britain, 1918-1939, a Case Study* (London 1962), 147-8.

43 Secretary of state for the colonies to governor general, 4 June 1919, HQ 6978-2-159, PAC, RG 24, vol. 2045
44 Wise, *Canadian Airmen*, 614-20
45 Turner to Gibson, 25 June 1919, OS 10-9-27 pt 3, PAC, RG 9 III, vol. 81
46 Gibson to Biggar, 16 July 1919, HQ 866-25-16 pt I, PAC, RG 24, vol. 3526
47 MacLaren to Gibson, 25 July 1919, OS 10-9-27 pt 3, PAC, RG 9 III, vol. 81
48 MacLaren to Gibson, 25 July 1919, ibid. This is a second letter of the same date.
49 Wilson to Biggar, 16 Oct. 1919, Wilson Papers, DHist 76/271, file AII
50 Biggar to Cominster, 11 July 1919, HQ 866-25-16 pt I, PAC, RG 24, vol. 3526. See also Biggar to Mewburn, 22 March 1919, Borden Papers, PAC, MG 26 H, vol. 80, file OC 374(1), and MacLaren to chief of the general staff [CGS], 13 Sept. 1919, OS 19-9-27 pt 4, PAC, RG 9 III, vol. 81.
51 As relayed by Lott to director of air services, 15 July 1919, OS 10-9-27 pt 3, PAC, RG 9 III, vol. 81
52 MacLaren to Wilson, 23 Oct. 1919, Wilson Papers, DHist 76/271, file AII
53 Headquarters section Canadian Air Force [CAF] to Canadian liaison officer (London), 12 May 1921, HQ 1021-3-12, PAC, RG 24, vol. 5087. These numbers are taken from what appears to be the final inventory of equipment packed and shipped to Canada by the CAF and differ from those in Wise, *Canadian Airmen*, 614, and in F.H. Hitchins, *Air Board, Canadian Air Force and Royal Canadian Air Force* (Mercury Series, Canadian War Museum Paper No 2; Ottawa 1972), 407.
54 Air Board minutes, 28 July 1919, DHist 181.009 (D6780)
55 Biggar to Gibson, 7 July 1919, HQ 866-25-16 pt I, PAC, RG 24, vol. 3526
56 House of Commons, *Debates*, 16 June 1920, 3646
57 Air Board minutes, 28 Nov. 1919, DHist 181.009 (D6780)
58 PC 395, 18 Feb. 1920
59 Ibid.
60 Ibid.
61 Stephens to director of the naval service, 22 June 1921, DHist 181.009 (D5685)
62 Wise, *Canadian Airmen*, 314-20
63 Air Board minutes, 17 May 1920, DHist 181.009 (D6780); Mulock biographical file, DHist; Hitchins, *Air Board*, 12
64 Hitchins, *Air Board*, 12
65 'The Air Board, General Progress Report No 3, Part II, Canadian Air Force,' nd, DHist 75/300; Air Board minutes, 19 Aug. 1920, DHist 181.009 (D6780)
66 *Regulations for the Canadian Air Force, 1920* (Ottawa 1920), sections 19-20, quoted in Hitchins, *Air Board*, 17
67 Air Board minutes, 21 June 1920, DHist 181.009 (D6780)
68 Canadian Air Force Association [CAFA] Maritimes Branch minutes, DHist 181.003 (D4713)
69 Quoted in Hitchins, *Air Board*, 13. See also Air Board minutes, 19 Aug. 1920, DHist 181.009 (D6780).
70 *Regulations, 1920*, section 68, quoted in Hitchins, *Air Board*, 19
71 'Minutes of Meeting of Delegates of Provincial Executive Committees, CAFA, Winnipeg, 3 July 1920,' DHist 75/524
72 Hitchins, *Air Board*, 18

73 *Regulations, 1920*, sections 109-10; Weekly Order Da l, DHist
74 Hitchins, *Air Board*, 19-20
75 'Minutes of Meeting of Delegates of Provincial Executive Committees, CAFA, Winnipeg, 3 July 1920, DHist 75/524
76 Logan to Manning, 29 June 1960, R.A. Logan Papers, DHist 75/117, file 26. See also Logan to Hitchins, 12 July 1955, ibid.
77 Wise, *Canadian Airmen*, 18-19
78 Air Board minutes, 28 July, 24 Dec. 1919, DHist 181.009 (D6780). The official transfer was delayed until 5 July. Hitchins, *Air Board*, 16
79 'General Progress Report, Camp Borden Air Station,' 62, HQ 889-2-8 pt 2, DHist 74/284
80 Weekly progress reports, ibid.
81 Hitchins, *Air Board*, 17
82 R.A. Logan, 'Ground Instructional Section, CAF,' Logan Papers, DHist 75/117, file 26
83 Wise, *Canadian Airmen*, 105
84 Hitchins, *Air Board*, 21; *Report of the Air Board, 1921* (Ottawa 1922), 20
85 Logan to Hitchins, 6 Aug. 1955, Logan Papers, DHist 75/117, file 26. See also Logan to Manning, 30 May 1960, ibid.
86 Logan to Manning, 30 March 1960, ibid.
87 *Report of the Air Board, 1921*, 11; Hitchins, *Air Board*, 22
88 'Proceedings of CAFA Convention, Camp Borden, 22-6-1921,' DHist 181.003 (D2716)
89 Harris and Leonard to Guthrie, 3 Feb. 1921, DHist 74/273
90 Departmental Committee (Air) minutes, 4 April 1921, DHist 181.003 (D5392)
91 Wilson to inspector general CAF, 8 Feb. 1921, DHist 74/273
92 'Proceedings of CAFA Convention, Camp Borden, 22-6-1921,' DHist 181.003 (D2716)
93 Ibid.
94 Air Board minutes, 14 March 1921, submission no 145, DHist 181.009 (D6780)
95 'Proceedings of CAFA Convention, Camp Borden, 22-6-1921,' DHist 181.003 (D2716)
96 PC 395, 18 Feb. 1920
97 House of Commons, *Debates*, 30 June 1920, 4553-6
98 Gwatkin to Trenchard, 14 Dec. 1921, 601-43-8 pt 1, PAC, RG 24, vol. 4964
99 Eayrs, *In Defence of Canada*, I, 224-5; MacBrien to minister, 'Memorandum on Necessity for Ministry of Defence,' 19 Dec. 1921, W.L.M. King Papers, PAC, MG 26 J 1, vol. 60; MacBrien, 'Memorandum on a Future Military Force for Canada,' nd, OS 10-8-57, PAC, RG 9 III, vol. 78; 'Minutes of Defence Committee,' 15 Dec. 1921, HQS 1009 pt 3, PARC 394884
100 Currie to King, 19 Dec. 1921, King Papers, PAC, MG 26 J 1, vol. 59
101 Fiset to King, 15 Dec. 1921, ibid., vol. 60
102 King Diary, 15 Dec. 1921, King Papers, PAC, MG 26 J 13
103 Ibid., 28 Dec. 1921
104 Ibid., 13 Feb. 1922
105 House of Commons, *Debates*, 4 April 1922, 695

106 Canada, *Statutes*, 12 and 13 Geo. v, c. 34, s. 1 (1922), 'An Act Respecting the Department of National Defence.' See also PC 2445, 24 Nov. 1922.

107 Wilson to Leckie, 19 Feb. 1922, Wilson Papers, DHist 76/271, file A11

108 Canada, *Statutes*, 12 and 13 Geo. V., c. 34, s. 7 (1922), 'An Act to Authorize the Control of Aeronautics'

109 The National Defence Act, 1922, paras. 4-6

110 Gwatkin to Biggar, 14 Jan. 1920, Biggar to Gwatkin, 27 Jan. 1920, Gwatkin to Biggar, 29 Jan. 1920, Gwatkin to secretary Naval and Military Committee, 17 Sept. 1920, MacBrien to Gwatkin, 9 Oct. 1920, HQ 866-17-3, PAC, RG 24, vol. 3517

111 Gwatkin to MacBrien, 20 Aug. 1921, HQ 186-1-1, PAC, RG 24, vol. 5937. See also 'Minutes of Defence Committee,' 15 Dec. 1921, HQS 1009 pt 3, PARC 394884.

112 Gwatkin to Trenchard, 14 Dec. 1921, 601-43-8 pt 1, PAC, RG 24, vol. 4964

113 Gwatkin to MacBrien, 31 Dec. 1921, HQ 186-1-1, ibid., vol. 5937

114 MacBrien, 'Memorandum on a Future Military Force for Canada,' OS 10-8-57, PAC, RG 9 III, vol. 78. See also McNaughton to CGS, 4 March 1922, A.G.L. McNaughton Papers, PAC, MG 30 E 133, vol. 109.

115 Memorandum, 'Reorganization of the Canadian Air Force,' Jan. 1922, McNaughton Papers, PAC, MG 30 E 133, vol. 109

116 MacBrien to Gwatkin, 4 Jan. 1922, HQ 186-1-1, PAC, RG 24, vol. 5937

117 McNaughton to CGS, 4 March 1922, McNaughton Papers, PAC, MG 30 E 133, vol. 109

118 Ibid.

119 Memorandum, 'Reorganization of Canadian Air Force,' 26 Jan. 1922, ibid. See also Eayrs, *In Defence of Canada*, I, 224-56; and Norman Hillmer and William McAndrew, 'The Cunning of Restraint: General J.H. MacBrien and the Problems of Peacetime Soldiering,' *Canadian Defence Quarterly*, VIII, spring 1979, 40-7.

120 McNaughton to CGS, 27 Jan. 1922, McNaughton Papers, PAC, MG 30 E 133, vol. 109

121 Departmental Committee (Air) minutes, 9 Jan. 1922, DHist 181.003 (D5392)

122 Graham to Desbarats, 14 Feb. 1922, quoted in Eayrs, *In Defence of Canada*, I, 232. See also Diaries, 15 Feb. 1922, G.J. Desbarats Papers, PAC, MG 30 E 89, vol. 6.

123 Graham to Biggar, 24 Feb. 1922, quoted in Eayrs, *In Defence of Canada*, I, 233

124 Graham to deputy minister and CAS, 13 March 1922, McNaughton Papers, PAC, MG 30 E 133, vol 109. See also Departmental Committee (Air) minutes, 8 March 1922, DHist 181.003 (D5392).

125 Canada, Department of National Defence, *Report of the Department of National Defence, 1923* (Ottawa 1923), 5-8, 37-45; McNaughton memorandum, 'Steps Recommended for the Reorganization of the Canadian Air Force,' nd, McNaughton Papers, PAC, MG 30 E 133, vol. 109; MacBrien to deputy minister, 8 Aug. 1923, HQ 045-4 pt 1, PARC 826453; Hitchins, *Air Board*, 93-5

126 Quoted in Andrew Boyle, *Trenchard* (New York 1962), 415. See also Hyde, *British Air Policy*, 105-6.

127 Gwatkin to MacBrien, 11 April 1922, Wilson Papers, DHist 76/271, file A11
128 Judge advocate general [JAG] to CGS, 24 Oct. 1922, HQ 420-18-74, PAC, RG 24, vol. 6522
129 Ibid.
130 Ibid.
131 CGS to JAG, 12 Dec. 1922, HQ 462-23-1, PAC, RG 24, vol. 6523
132 Clarke to adjutant general, 10 Jan. 1922, ibid.
133 CGS to adjutant general, 23 Jan. 1923, ibid. See also JAG to director of supply and transport, 27 Feb. 1923, ibid.
134 Chief of staff to minister, 14 Sept. 1923, DHist 76/37
135 Chief of staff, 'Memorandum Respecting the Royal Canadian Air Force,' 30 Jan. 1924, ibid.
136 'Proceedings of the CAFA Convention, Camp Borden, 22-6-1921,' DHist 181.003 (D2716); Departmental Committee (Air) minutes, 4 and 8 July 1921, DHist 181.003 (D5392)
137 Gwatkin to MacBrien, 10 May 1922, AFHQ file 045-3, quoted in Hitchins, *Air Board*, 98
138 Acting deputy minister to undersecretary of state for external affairs, 5 Jan. 1923, quoted in ibid.
139 CAF/RCAF Weekly Orders, Nos 21/23, 26/23, 38/23, DHist; PRO, Air 2/337/857405/28. See also Hitchins, *Air Board*, 99.
140 C.F. Hamilton, 'Lieut.-General Sir Willoughby Gwatkin, An Appreciation,' *Canadian Defence Quarterly*, II, April 1925, 229
141 Hitchins, *Air Board*, 71
142 See, in particular, Barker to chief of staff, 26 March 1924, W.G. Barker biographical file, DHist.
143 Career information from biographical files, DHist. See also Hitchins, *Air Board*, 116-21, 208, 264, 280.
144 'Organization and Policy of the Royal Canadian Air Force, 1924,' DHist 180.009 (D21)

CHAPTER 2: THE RCAF AND CIVIL AVIATION

1 Biggar to Leckie, 6 March 1920, HQ 866-8-1 pt 1, PAC, RG 24, vol. 2929; Air Board minutes, 25 June 1919, DHist 181.009 (D6780)
2 Ellwood Wilson, report, nd, 28-31, DHist 77/58, vol 4; Ellwood Wilson, 'The Use of Aircraft in Forestry and Logging,' *Aeroplane*, XIX, Nov. 1920, 730-6
3 *Report of the Air Board, 1920* (Ottawa 1920), 6
4 Department of Militia and Defence, 'Flight, Trans-Canada, 1920,' HQ 1008-1-35, PAC, RG 24, vol. 4888; R.V. Manning, 'The First Trans-Canada Flight – 1920,' *Canadian Geographical Journal*, LXIX, Sept. 1964, 78-87, drafts, comments, photographs, and background material in DHist 75/311; F.H. Hitchins, *Air Board, Canadian Air Force and Royal Canadian Air Force* (Mercury Series, Canadian War Museum Paper No 2; Ottawa 1972), 41-53
5 Canadian Air Board, Progress Reports, 1921-2, Report No 5, DHist 74/285. See also controller of civil aviation to officer commanding Canadian Air Force [CAF], 3 Jan. 1921, HQ 866-1-13 pt 1, PAC, RG 24, vol. 2929.

6 International Joint Commission, 'St. Lawrence River Investigation,' DHist 76/102; *Report of the Air Board, 1921*, 11; Hitchins, *Air Board*, 56-64, 69-83

7 Gwatkin to MacBrien, 28 March 1922, J.A. Wilson Papers, PAC, MG 30 E 243, copy in DHist 76/271, file A11

8 Wilson to Mulock, 14 Aug. 1922, ibid.

9 'Reorganization of the Canadian Air Force,' 26 Feb. 1922, A.G.L. McNaughton Papers, PAC, MG 30 E 133, vol. 109

10 'Departmental Committee Minutes,' 28 April 1922, HQ 866-17-1, PAC, RG 24, vol. 3517; John Swettenham, *McNaughton*, I: *1887-1939* (Toronto 1968), 212ff

11 Canada, Parliament, House of Commons, *Debates*, 12 May 1922, 1722

12 Ibid., 1725

13 Ibid., 1732

14 King Diary, 26 Oct. 1923, W.L.M. King Papers, PAC, MG 26 J 13

15 Interdepartmental Committee minutes, 15 Nov. 1923, HQ 866-25-19, PAC, RG 24, vol. 3577

16 Wilson to Grey, 15 Nov. 1923, Wilson Papers, DHist 76/271, file E2

17 *Report on Civil Aviation, 1923* (Ottawa 1924), 27

18 Interdepartmental Committee minutes, 15 Nov. 1923, HQ 866-25-19, PAC, RG 24, vol. 3577

19 Ibid.

20 Ibid.

21 Quoted in Hitchins, *Air Board*, 167

22 William Arthur Bishop, *The Courage of the Early Morning: the Story of Billy Bishop* (Toronto 1965), 168

23 'Air Board Statement on Development of Civil Aviation in Canada,' May 1921, HQ 866-1-13 pt 1, PAC, RG 24, vol. 2928

24 Memorandum, 'Development of Civil Aviaton,' with Biggar to Wilson, 27 May 1921, HQ 866-20-2, ibid., vol. 2930

25 Senate of Canada, 2nd Session, 13th Parliament, 1919, Bill 22, 'An Act Resurrecting the Canadian Pacific Railway Company,' 29 May 1919

26 *Report on Civil Aviation, 1928* (Ottawa 1929), 14; *1930* (Ottawa 1931), 16-18; *1931* (Ottawa 1932), 17

27 D.R. MacLaren, 'Development and Control of Civil Aviation in Canada,' 1926, HQ 866-1-13 pt 1, PAC, RG 24, vol. 2928

28 Wilson to director RCAF, 11 March and 27 Dec. 1926, ibid.

29 Ibid.; Wilson to director RCAF, 26 Oct. 1926, McNaughton to director RCAF, 2 Nov. 1926, HQ 866-1-13 pt 2, PAC, RG 24, vol. 2929

30 Scott to MacBrien, 18 March 1927, Wilson Papers, DHist 76/271, file B2

31 PC 1878, 24 Sept. 1927; *Report on Civil Aviation, 1928*, 41; *1929*, 37; *1930*, 41; L.B. Stevenson, 'The Cape Breton Flying Club,' *CAHS Journal*, VI, fall 1978, 68-70

32 Scott to MacBrien, 24 Sept. 1926, draft, HQ 1008-2-6 pt 9, PAC, RG 24, vol. 4901

33 Ibid.

34 MacBrien to judge advocate general [JAG], 29 Sept. 1926, and JAG to chief of staff, 1 Oct. 1926, with minute to director RCAF, 3 Oct. 1926, ibid.

35 Gordon minute to Scott, 18 Jan. 1927, HQ 1008-1-185, PAC, RG 24, vol. 4898

36 Scott to MacBrien, 18 Jan. 1927, ibid.

37 Scott memorandum, 5 Aug. 1927, HQ 895-1 pt 1, PARC 429218. See also Norman
    Hillmer, 'The RCAF in 1927: Organizing for the Air Defence of Canada,' *High
    Flight*, II, 3, 86-90.

38 MacBrien to minister, 28 Jan. 1927, HQ 1008-1-185, PAC, RG 24, vol. 4898

39 Salisbury memorandum, 2 Oct. 1923, Cambridge University Library, Baldwin
    Papers, vol. 96, fol. 31-2. See also King Diary, 1 Oct. 1923, PAC, MG 26 J 13,
    and Norman Hillmer, 'Mackenzie King, Canadian Air Policy, and the Imperial
    Conference of 1923,' *High Flight*, I, 5, 189-93, 196.

40 King Diary, 25 Oct. 1926, PAC, MG 26 J 13

41 Imperial Conference, extracts from minutes, 28 Oct. 1926, A.I. Inglis, ed., *Docu-
    ments on Canadian External Relations* [DCER], IV: *1926-1930* (Ottawa 1971),
    112

42 House of Commons, *Debates*, 11 April 1927, 2278-80; Hitchins, *Air Board*, 179

43 King Diary, 12 Feb. 1927, PAC, MG 26 J 13

44 House of Commons, *Debates*, 11 April 1927, 2278-80

45 See Norman Hillmer and William McAndrew, 'The Cunning of Restraint: General
    J.H. MacBrien and the Problems of Peacetime Soldiering,' *Canadian Defence
    Quarterly*, VIII, spring 1979, 40-7.

46 MacBrien to minister, 11 April 1927, HQ 895-1 pt 1, PARC 829218

47 Wilson to Grey, 11 Aug. 1927, Wilson Papers, DHist 76/271, file E2

48 On the division of aircraft and equipment between branches see the correspondence
    in HQ 1021-1-19 pts 2 and 3, PAC, RG 24, vol. 5062, and Hitchins, *Air Board*, 181-2.

49 Air Force General Order no 51, 9 July 1927, quoted in Hitchins, *Air Board*, 181

50 Hitchins, *Air Board*, 177ff

51 *Report on Civil Aviation, 1927* (Ottawa 1928), 6-7

52 House of Commons, *Debates*, 4 June 1929, 3221-2

53 R.F. Futrell, *Ideas, Concepts, Doctrines: a Study of Basic Thinking in the United
    States Air Force* (Maxwell Air Force Base, Alabama 1971), 55

54 'Aileron,' 'Air Transportation,' *Canadian Defence Quarterly*, Jan. 1927, 150

55 Quoted in K.M. Molson, *Pioneering in Canadian Air Transport* (np 1974), 59

56 J.A. Wilson, 'Air Transport Policy,' 17 March 1933, Wilson Papers, DHist 76/
    271, file B16

57 Wilson to MacBrien, 17 April 1922, HQ 866-1-13 pt 1, PAC, RG 24, vol. 2928

58 'Aileron,' 'Air Transportation,' 150

59 See, for example, Wilson to deputy minister, memorandum on 'Airway Develop-
    ment,' 25 Nov. 1929, Wilson Papers, DHist 76/271, file B19; also 'Minutes of a
    Meeting Held at 8:30 am, on Wednesday, Feb. 1, 1928, in the Office of the
    Postmaster General,' ibid., file B3.

60 Wilson to director, 27 Dec. 1926, Wilson Papers, DHist 76/271, file B2, and
    Wilson to deputy minister, 'Airway Development,' 25 Nov. 1929, ibid., file
    B19

61 See James Eayrs, *In Defence of Canada*, I: *From the Great War to the Great
    Depression* (Toronto 1964), 221-2.

62 *Report on Civil Aviation, 1927*, 33-5; Wilson, 'Civil Aviation in Canada,' Wilson
    Papers, DHist 76/271, file B19. See also Francis W. Rowse, 'Air Mail Develop-
    ment in Canada,' *Canadian Air Review*, Nov. 1930, 12-39.

63 'Air Mail Services – Historical,' 30 March 1932, 'Air Mail Service – Maritime Provinces,' 4 June 1932, and Wilson to deputy minister, 30 Nov. 1932, Wilson Papers, DHist 76/271, file BB1

64 Wilson to deputy minister, 'St. Hubert Airport and Airship Base,' 18 Sept. 1931, ibid., file B19; *Report on Civil Aviation, 1929*, 62-4

65 'The Trans-Canada Airway System,' nd, 'Air Mail Services – Historical,' 30 March 1932, 'Air Mail Service – Maritime Provinces,' 4 June 1932, and Wilson to deputy minister, 19 Nov. 1928, Wilson Papers, DHist 76/271, files BB1, B14, C10. See also *Report on Civil Aviation, 1929*, 11-13.

66 Quoted in Molson, *Pioneering in Canadian Air Transport*, 98

67 *Report on Civil Aviation, 1926* (Ottawa 1927), 40-2; *1930*, 14-16

68 Wilson to deputy minister, 25 Nov. 1929, Wilson Papers, DHist 76/271, file B19

69 'Minutes of the Inter-Departmental Committee on Civil Government Air Operations,' 15 Jan. 1932, Wilson Papers, DHist 76/271, file C6

70 Ibid.

71 Reported by Mulock to Richardson, 2 April 1930, as quoted in Molson, *Pioneering in Canadian Air Transport*, 130

72 Wilson, 'Civil Government Air Operations,' 19 Jan. 1932, Wilson Papers, DHist 76/271, file BB1

73 'Belle Isle Air Mail Services,' 25 June 1932, and 'Air Mail Connection with Trans-Atlantic Mail Steamers in the Straits of Belle Isle,' 9 May 1932, ibid.; F.J. Hatch, 'The Ship-to-Shore Air Mail Service of the 1920s,' *Canadian Geographic Journal*, XCVII, Aug.-Sept. 1978, 56-61

74 Hitchins, *Air Board*, 246-7

75 Department of National Defence, *Report, 1933* (Ottawa 1934), 77

76 Desbarats memorandum, 2 March 1932, HQ 895-1 pt 1, PARC 829218; chief of the general staff [CGS] memorandum, 24 Oct. 1932, DHist 76/37; Hitchins, *Air Board*, 263-5

77 Interdepartmental Committee on Air Mails, minutes, Wilson Papers, DHist 76/271, file B3

78 Wilson to deputy minister, 16 July, 21 Oct., 27 Nov. 1931, ibid., files B15 and B19; G.M. LeFresne, 'The Royal Twenty Centers: the Department of National Defence and Federal Unemployment Relief, 1932-1936' (BA thesis, Royal Military College of Canada, 1962), passim

79 'Conversation with Admiral Sir Roger Keyes, Memorandum, 10 September 1934,' quoted in Norman Hillmer, 'Canadian Air Policy, 1923-1939, II: 1930-1935, The Bennett Years,' unpublished narrative [1977], 78, DHist 85/281

CHAPTER 3: BUSH PILOTS IN UNIFORM

1 C.R. Slemon interview, 20 Oct. 1978, DHist 79/128

2 Lawrence interview, 11 Oct. 1973, T.A. Lawrence biographical file, DHist

3 Canada, Department of National Defence [DND], RCAF, 'Information Relating to Pay, Allowances, Qualifications, General Conditions of Service, Future Prospects, etc.,' (Ottawa 1928), copy in DHist 181.009 (D21); PC 1655, 26 Sept. 1925, copy in DHist 181.006 (D68); 'Technical Training of Boys and Airmen by

Technical Schools,' nd, ibid.; F.H. Hitchins, *Air Board, Canadian Air Force and Royal Canadian Air Force* (Mercury Series, Canadian War Museum Paper No 2; Ottawa 1972), 184

4 Croil memorandum, 21 Dec. 1928, HQ 886-9-8 pt 1, PAC, RG 24, vol. 3512

5 Hitchins, *Air Board*, 99-100; Canada, DND, *Report of the Department of National Defence, 1923* (Ottawa 1923), 38; *1924* (Ottawa 1924), 50; *1925* (Ottawa 1925), 51-3

6 Hitchins, *Air Board*, 184

7 Scott to liaison officer, 26 Aug. 1927, liaison officer to secretary DND, 28 Sept. 1927, DHist 74/282

8 *The Canada Year Book, 1922-1923* (Ottawa 1924), 310-41; 'Memorandum, Conference on Forest Conservation,' 12 Jan. 1924, DHist 75/151

9 Wilson to Grey, 2 Feb. 1923, J.A. Wilson Papers, PAC, MG 30 E 243, copy in DHist 76/271, file E2

10 'Memorandum, Conference on Forest Conservation,' 12 Jan. 1924, DHist 75/151; Department of the Interior, 'Report of Departmental Committee on Air Operations,' 14 Nov. 1924, DHist 75/152

11 Earl MacLeod, 'Early Flying in British Columbia,' *CAHS Journal*, XII, winter 1974, 100-13, 127; Department of the Interior, Forestry Branch, 'Memorandum,' 15 Jan. 1923, DHist 75/152; Canada, DND, *Report on Civil Aviation, 1924* (Ottawa 1925), 56-65; *1926* (Ottawa 1927), 50-3; *1929* (Ottawa 1930), 44

12 Department of the Interior, Forestry Branch, 'Memorandum,' 15 Jan. 1923, DHist 75/152

13 Department of the Interior, 'Report of the Departmental Committee on Air Operations,' 14 Nov. 1924, ibid.; Air Vice-Marshal L.F. Stevenson's recollections, Feb. 1970, DHist 74/242

14 Stevenson to commanding officer [CO] RCAF Station Victoria Beach, 18 June 1924, DHist 75/151

15 Stedman to chief of staff, 20 Nov. 1923, HQ 1021-1-19 pt 1, PAC, RG 24, vol. 5061

16 Leckie memorandum, 31 May 1921, HQ 1008-6-3 pt 1, ibid., vol. 4907

17 Howsam interview, Aug. 1975, DHist 76/120

18 Stedman to director RCAF, 13 Nov. 1923, HQ 1021-1-19 pt 1, PAC, RG 24, vol. 5061

19 'Progress Report,' 16 Oct. 1921, Station Vancouver, operations record book [ORB] daily diary, DHist

20 Stedman to chief of staff, 20 Nov. 1923, HQ 1021-1-19 pt 1, PAC, RG 24, vol. 5061

21 Robert Leckie, 'Flying Conditions in Canada and Class of Work upon which Aircraft will be Employed,' 11 Aug. 1920, Stedman to Leckie, 20 Dec. 1920, Leckie to Stedman, 22 Dec. 1920, HQ 1021-1-15 pt 1, ibid., vol. 5059

22 Vickers Ltd to secretary Air Board, 29 Dec. 1920, HQ 1021-1-5, ibid.; C.F. Andrews, *Vickers Aircraft since 1908* (New York 1969), 489-94

23 Stedman and Leckie minutes, 17 Jan. 1921, HQ 1021-1-5, PAC, RG 24, vol. 5059

24 Wilson to Vickers Ltd, 3 Feb. 1921, ibid.

25 Wilson to Vickers' Aviation Dept, 14 Feb. 1921, Acland to Wilson, 25 Feb. 1921, Vickers Ltd to Scott, 19 Aug. 1921, Scott to Caddell, 26 Nov. 1921, and Caddell to Scott, 12 Dec. 1921, ibid.

26 E.W. Stedman, *From Boxkite to Jet: the Memoirs of an Aeronautical Engineer* (Mercury Series, Canadian War Museum Paper No 1; Ottawa 1972), 70

27 Stedman to chief of staff, 20 Nov. 1923, HQ 1021-1-19 pt 1, PAC, RG 24, vol. 5061

28 Gordon to chief of the general staff [CGS], 4 Oct. 1922, HQ 1021-1-15 pt 2, ibid., vol. 5059

29 'Canadian Air Force, Conference No. 2,' 18 Oct. 1922, Gordon to CGS, 19 Oct. 1922, CGS to minister, memorandum, 'Canadian Air Force Estimates, 1923-4,' 27 Oct. 1922, ibid.

30 PC 2417, 20 Nov. 1922; Stedman to director of contracts, 29 Nov. 1922, HQ 1021-1-15 pt 2, PAC, RG 24, vol. 5059; Ottawa Car Manufacturing Co to director of contracts, 13 Jan. 1923, Stedman to chief of staff, 5 Feb. 1923, HQ 1021-1-15 pt 3, ibid., vol. 5060

31 Stedman to chief of staff, 5 and 9 Feb. 1923, HQ 1021-1-15 pt 3, PAC, RG 24, vol. 5060

32 Scott to director RCAF, 19 March 1923, HQ 1021-1-15 pt 4, ibid.

33 M. Wright, 'Vickers "Viking" V, No 156, Handling Report,' 22 Dec. 1922, HQ 1021-1-15 pt 3, ibid.

34 Scott to director RCAF, 9 March 1923, ibid.

35 T.F. Cooper, 'Trials and Tribulations of the Ground Crew: Reflections on the 1920's and '30's by a "Jack of All Trades,"' Roundel, XI, Jan.-Feb. 1959, 9

36 Alex J. Milne, 'Pioneer Survey Flights in Northern Manitoba and Saskatchewan,' CAHS Journal, XXI, winter 1983, 104

37 Stedman to chief of staff, 25 Oct. 1923, Higgins to director, 14 Nov. 1923, HQ 1021-1-19 pt 1, PAC, RG 24, vol. 5061

38 Stedman to director, 8 Oct. and 13 Nov. 1923, Stedman to chief of staff, 25 and 16 Oct. and 20 Nov. 1923, Johnson to director, 3 Nov. 1923, ibid.; Canada, Parliament, House of Commons, Debates, 11 April 1923, 1748-51, 12 April 1923, 1774-8, 21 May 1923, 2970; Hitchins, Air Board, 206; Norman Hillmer, 'Mackenzie King, Canadian Air Policy, and the Imperial Conference of 1923,' High Flight, I, 5, 189-93, 196

39 K.M. Molson, 'Canadian Vickers Vedette,' Canadian Aeronautics and Space Journal, X, Oct. 1964, 253-8; Andrews, Vickers Aircraft, 489-90; Wilson to Winterbotham, 28 May 1926, Wilson Papers, DHist 76/271, file A6

40 Stedman, 'Specifications for Forestry Survey and Fire Detection Seaplane,' HQ 1021-2-18, PAC, RG 24, vol. 5075; copy of specification C4/24, Stedman to director of contracts, 17 April 1924, general manager, Canadian Vickers Ltd to director of contracts, 7 May 1924, HQ 1021-1-19 pt 1, ibid., vol. 5061

41 Stedman, 'Specifications for Forestry Survey and Fire Detection Seaplane,' HQ 1021-2-28 pt 1, PAC, RG 24, vol. 5075; Molson, 'Canadian Vickers Vedette,' 254-5

42 Stedman to director, 18 Sept. 1926, HQ 1021-2-47 pt 1, PAC, RG 24, vol. 5076; Cowley to secretary RCAF, 10 Nov. 1925, HQ 1021-1-28, ibid., vol. 5065; Hobbs to director, 7 Nov. 1924, HQ 1021-2-29 pt 1, ibid., vol. 5075

43 Hobbs to director, 14 May 1925, HQ 1025-2-29 pt 2, PAC, RG 24, vol. 5075

44 Wait to Canadian Vickers Ltd, 1 Oct. 1925, HQ 1021-2-46, ibid., vol. 5076; Tackaberry to CO Winnipeg Air Station, 7 Feb. 1930, HQ 1021-2-47 pt 5, ibid., vol. 5077; Molson, 'Canadian Vickers Vedette,' 256

45 Scott to Barker, 7 Jan. 1925, HQ 1021-2-47 pt 5, PAC, RG 24, vol. 5077; Scott to chief of staff, 19 Sept. 1924, HQ 1021-1-19 pt 2, ibid., vol. 5062; Hume to

director, 15 Dec. 1924, HQ 1021-1-19 pt 1, ibid., vol. 5061; Hitchins, *Air Board*,
156

46 T.F. Cooper, 'Trials and Tribulations,' *Roundel*, XI, Jan.-Feb. 1959, 10

47 Department of the Interior, Forestry Branch, 'Memorandum,' 15 Jan. 1923, DHist
75/151

48 Department of the Interior, 'Report of the Departmental Committee on Air Operations,' 14 Nov. 1924, DHist 75/152

49 Ibid.; Department of the Interior, 'Report of Departmental Committee on Air
Operations,' 14 Dec. 1926, DHist 75/24; *Report on Civil Aviation, 1924*,
92-103

50 B.F. Johnson, 'Air Operations and Air Routes in Canada,' lecture to the RAF Staff
College, 1934, DHist 75/325

51 Canada, DND, *Report on Civil Aviation, 1927* (Ottawa 1928), 43-4

52 Canada, DND, *Report on Civil Aviation, 1931* (Ottawa 1932), 55-62

53 Station Winnipeg, Annual Reports, 1928-30, Station Winnipeg, ORB daily diary,
DHist

54 Hitchins, *Air Board*, 228; H.A. Halliday, 'Wings over the Wilderness: Forestry
Patrols and Aerial Surveys,' unpublished narrative [1968], DHist 74/279

55 The above account, and that which follows, compiled from the Station Winnipeg,
Annual Reports, 1925-6, Station Winnipeg, ORB daily diary, DHist

56 Ibid.

57 'Memorandum re Ice Patrol on Hudson Straits,' 22 Jan. 1920, HQ 1008-1-29 pt 1,
PAC, RG 24, vol. 4884; R.A. Logan, 'Report of Investigations on Aviation in the
Arctic Archipelago carried out during the Summer of 1922,' DHist 74/414

58 Logan, 'Report of Investigations,' DHist 74/414

59 PC 85, 22 Jan. 1927. See also A. Lewis, 'Adrift on Ice-Floes: a Story of the Hudson
Straits Expedition,' DHist 181.001 (D6); Stedman to director, 18 Feb. 1927, HQ
1008-1-29 pt 1, Lawrence to director, 8 March 1927, HQ 1008-1-29 pt 2, PAC, RG
24, vol. 4884; T.A. Lawrence, 'Report to the Director Civil Government Air
Operations, Department of National Defence, on the Hudson Strait Expedition,
1927-28,' DHist 73/1018; T.A. Lawrence interview, 12 April 1973, DHist
73/1411; Lawrence interview, June 1980, T.A. Lawrence biographical file, DHist.

60 Lawrence, 'Report ... on the Hudson Strait Expedition,' DHist 73/1018; Lawrence
interview, June 1980, T.A. Lawrence biographical file, DHist

61 RCAF Headquarters, Orders R37, 13 April 1927, HQ 1008-1-29 pt 4, Lawrence to
officer commanding [OC] No 1 Flying Training School, Camp Borden, 1 April
1927, HQ 1008-1-29 pt 8, PAC, RG 24, vol. 4885; Lawrence, 'Report ... on the
Hudson Strait Expedition,' DHist 73/1018

62 Lawrence interview, June 1980, T.A. Lawrence biographical file, DHist

63 Lawrence, 'Report ... on the Hudson Strait Expedition,' DHist 73/1018

64 Lewis, 'Adrift on Ice-floes,' DHist 181.001 (D6)

65 Lawrence, 'Report ... on the Hudson Strait Expedition,' DHist 73/1018

66 Ibid.

67 Ibid.

68 Lewis, 'Adrift on Ice-floes,' DHist 181.001 (D6)

69 Ibid.

70 Ibid.
71 Lawrence, 'Report ... on the Hudson Strait Expedition,' DHist 73/1018
72 Ibid.
73 'Aircraft Construction Programme,' 16 Aug. 1927, HQ 1021-1-19 pt 2, PAC, RG 24, vol. 5062
74 Ibid.; Hitchins, *Air Board*, 174, 220
75 Gordon to liaison officer, London, 4 July 1929, and reply of 23 July, deputy minister to Field, 17 Dec. 1929, HQ 1021-1-19 pt 3, PAC, RG 24, vol. 5062
76 K.M. Molson and H.A. Taylor, *Canadian Aircraft since 1909* (Stittsville, Ont. 1982), 305
77 Hitchins, *Air Board*, 211
78 Molson and Taylor, *Canadian Aircraft*, 308, 310-11
79 Hitchins, *Air Board*, 242
80 F.J. Mawdesley biographical file, DHist; Molson and Taylor, *Canadian Aircraft*, 313
81 Molson and Taylor, *Canadian Aircraft*, 104-6; Hitchins, *Air Board*, 254
82 Morfee to Bowdery, 1 April 1962, A.L. Morfee biographical file, DHist
83 J.M. Swaine, 'Memorandum on a Proposed Plan for Airplane Dusting on a Spruce Bud Worm Outbreak in Cape Breton Island of Nova Scotia during the Summer of 1927,' 20 Jan. 1927, HQ 1008-17-2 pt 2, PAC, RG 24, vol. 4912; William J. McAndrew, 'RCAF Crop Dusting in the Early Days,' *CAHS Journal*, XXIII, winter 1985, 106-11
84 See the exchange of memoranda between the director RCAF and the chief of staff in February and early March 1927, in HQ 1008-17-2 pt 2, PAC, RG 24, vol. 4912.
85 Stedman to Mutt-Doland Airplanes, Inc., 4 March 1927, Coad to Wilson, 25 April 1927, ibid.
86 *Report on Civil Aviation, 1927*, 64-72
87 Bath to director, 'Report on Use of Keystone Puffer for Dusting the Forests,' 28 March 1928, HQ 1008-17-2 pt 2, PAC, RG 24, vol. 4912
88 D.L. Bailey and F.J. Greaney, 'Aeroplane Dusting in Manitoba for the Control of Wheat Stem Rust,' *Report on Civil Aviation, 1927*, 73-4
89 RCAF records of the Preventive Service are in HQ 1008-19-1, PARC 826309; copies of the relevant RCMP files are in DHist 73/615. See also D.R. Keane, 'Royal Canadian Air Force Assistance to the Royal Canadian Mounted Police, 1927-1939,' unpublished narrative [1968], DHist 74/35; 'The History of Eastern Air Command,' unpublished narrative [1945], DHist 74/2: Robin Bassett, 'Liquor Smuggling in the Maritimes, 1932-1938,' unpublished paper in the files of the RCMP historian; Air Commodore W. Clements, 'Preventive Operations by the RCAF for the RCMP, 1932-36,' *CAHS Journal*, XVII, spring 1979, 3-10; and Grey to Wilson, 24 March 1933, Wilson Papers, DHist 76/271, file E2.
90 Johnson to RCMP commissioner, 22 Nov. 1933, HQ 1008-19-1, PARC 826309
91 Commanding officer 'H' Division to commissioner, RCMP, 29 Jan. 1936, DHist 73/615
92 Leckie to Wilson, 8 Aug. 1924, Wilson Papers, DHist 76/271, file A12

CHAPTER 4: TOWARDS A MILITARY AIR FORCE

1 F.H. Sykes, *Aviation in Peace and War* (London 1922), 100 and 103
2 Guilio Douhet, *The Command of the Air*, trans. Dino Ferrari (Washington 1983), 20 and 23
3 Ibid., 5 and 213
4 'Memorandum by the Chief of the Air Staff for the Chiefs of Staff Sub-Committee, on the War Object of an Air Force,' 2 May 1928, in Charles Webster and Noble Frankland, *The Strategic Air Offensive against Germany, 1939-1945*, IV: *Annexes and Appendices* (History of the Second World War, United Kingdom Military Series; London 1961), 72
5 Douhet, *The Command of the Air*, 179
6 J.L. Gordon, 'Air Superiority,' *Canadian Defence Quarterly*, IV, July 1927, 480-2. See also Gordon's 'Limitations of Aircraft in Naval Warfare: a Reply to Lieutenant-Commander Ballou,' ibid., III, July 1926, 413-19.
7 G.E. Wait, 'Aims and Objects: a Study in Doctrines,' *Canadian Defence Quarterly*, X, April 1933, 349-53
8 G.R. Howsam, 'Canada's Problem of Air Defence,' ibid., VIII, April 1931, 356-60
9 G.R. Howsam interview, Aug. 1975, DHist 76/120
10 Director RCAF to chief of the general staff [CGS], 5 Aug. 1927, quoted in James Eayrs, *In Defence of Canada*, I: *From the Great War to the Great Depression* (Toronto 1964), 216
11 F.M. Gobeil, 'Siskin Pilot,' *CAHS Journal*, XV, spring 1977, 3-9
12 E.A. McNab biographical file, DHist
13 McNaughton memoranda, 21 Dec. 1931 and 29 Jan. 1932, HQS 5902 pt 1, PAC, RG 24, vol. 2740
14 Sir Maurice Hankey, 'Impressions of Canadian Defence Policy – December 1934,' PRO, Cab 63/81. See also R.A. Preston, *The Defence of the Undefended Border: Planning for War in North America, 1867-1939* (Montreal 1977).
15 Department of National Defence [DND], 'Geneva Disarmament Conference: Analysis of Draft Convention and Summary of Discussion before Preparatory Commission,' 1931-3, DHist 73/664; Donald Clarke Story, 'The Foreign Policy of the Government of R.B. Bennett: Canada and the League of Nations, 1930-1935' (PHD thesis, University of Toronto, 1971)
16 Gordon to CGS, 11 May 1933, 045-4 pt 1, PARC 826453
17 Deputy minister to minister, 2 March 1932, 895-1 pt 1, PARC 829217
18 Walsh to Gordon, 'Memorandum – Peace Organization and Establishment of the RCAF Considered Necessary to Meet Minimum Requirements for National Defence,' 18 July 1932, DHist 76/46
19 Ibid.
20 McNaughton memorandum, 29 Jan. 1932, HQS 5902 pt 1, PAC, RG 24, vol. 2740
21 Walsh, 'Memorandum,' DHist 76/46
22 Hankey, 'Impressions,' PRO, Cab 63/81
23 'Minutes of a Special Meeting of the Joint Staff Committee,' 8 Aug. 1929, PARC 266198
24 Matthews to McNaughton, 19 Feb. 1932, quoted in Eayrs, *In Defence of Canada*, I, 290

25 Quoted in ibid., 274-5
26 Ibid.
27 Ibid.
28 Senior air officer [SAO] to deputy minister, 7 July 1938, I.A. Mackenzie Papers, PAC, MG 27 III B 5, vol. 31, X-47. See also deputy minister to Canadian high commissioner, London, HQ 1021-1-19, PAC, RG 24, vol. 5062.
29 McNaughton, 'The Defence of Canada,' 28 May 1935, DHist 74/256, vol. 1
30 Ibid.
31 Ibid.
32 'Hearings before the Committee on Military Affairs, House of Representatives, 74th Congress, First Session on H.R. 6621 and H.R. 4130. Air Defence Bases; to Authorize the Selection, Construction, Installation and Modification of Permanent Stations and Depots for the Army, Air Corps, and Frontier Air-Defence Bases generally. February 11, 12, 13, 1935.' SAO file, DHist 74/256, vol. 2. See also William J. McAndrew, 'Canadian Defence Planning between the Wars: the Royal Canadian Air Force Comes of Age,' *Aerospace Historian*, XXIX, 2, summer/June 1982, 81-9; and John F. Shiner, *Foulois and the U.S. Army Air Corps, 1931-1935* (Washington 1983), 252.
33 'Report of Inspection of Brig General Wm. Mitchell, Assistant Chief of Air Service during Winter-1923,' nd, DHist 82/982
34 'Hearings before the Committee on Military Affairs,' 72, DHist 74/256, vol. 2
35 Ibid., 51-6
36 Ibid., 17, 22
37 External Affairs correspondence in PAC, RG 25 G 1, vol. 1746, file 408
38 'Note, from a Canadian Aspect, on a Report of the Hearings before the Committee on Military Affairs, House of Representatives, on H.R. 7022, 14 May 1935,' DHist 74/256, vol. 2
39 *Ottawa Evening Citizen*, 30 April 1935
40 H.H. Arnold, *Global Mission* (New York 1949), 145-7; Ray H. Crone, 'The Bombers are Coming,' *CAHS Journal*, XVII, spring 1979, 24-30; James N. Eastman, Jr, 'The Development of Big Bombers,' *Aerospace Historian*, XXV, winter/Dec. 1978, 211-19
41 'Appreciation of Canada's Obligations with Respect to the Maintenance of Neutrality in Event of War between the United States of America and Japan,' 14 Oct. 1936, 13-14, DHist 74/ 256, vol. 2
42 'Conversations on Defence Questions,' 25 Jan. 1938, DHist 112.3M2009 (D22). See also C.P. Stacey, *Arms, Men and Governments: the War Policies of Canada, 1939-1945* (Ottawa 1970), 95-8.
43 M.A. Pope, *Soldiers and Politicians: the Memoirs of Lt.-Gen. Maurice A. Pope* (Toronto 1962), 91
44 'The Co-ordination of Canadian Defence,' 28 Sept. 1935, 3, DHist 74/256, vol. 1
45 'Canada's Present Defence Policy,' July 1938, DHist 181.002 (D107)
46 Canada, Parliament, House of Commons, *Debates*, 19 Feb. 1937, 1050-1
47 King Diary, 25 Aug. 1936, W.L.M. King Papers, PAC, MG 26 J 13
48 H.B. Neatby, *William Lyon Mackenzie King*, III: *1932-1939: the Prism of Unity* (Toronto 1976), 170-85

49 Ibid., 180
50 King Diary, 26 Aug. 1936, PAC, MG 26 J 13
51 Ibid., 23 Oct. 1936
52 C.P. Stacey, *Canada and the Age of Conflict: a History of Canadian External Policies*, II: *1921-1948, The Mackenzie King Era* (Toronto 1981), 201
53 King Diary, 24 Nov. 1936, PAC, MG 26 J 13
54 Joint Staff Committee minutes, 27 July 1936, DHist 193.009 (D53)
55 James Eayrs, *In Defence of Canada*, II: *Appeasement and Rearmament* (Toronto 1965), 138
56 King Diary, 26 Nov. 1936, PAC, MG 26 J 13
57 C.P. Stacey, *Six Years of War: the Army in Canada, Britain and the Pacific* (Official History of the Canadian Army in the Second World War, I; Ottawa 1955), 11-12
58 House of Commons, *Debates*, 15 Feb. 1937, 893, 896
59 Ibid., 19 Feb. 1938, 1050
60 Stacey, *Arms, Men and Governments*, 71
61 Pope, *Soldiers and Politicians*, 124
62 Chief of staff to minister, 14 Sept. 1923, DHist 76/37; William McAndrew, 'From Integration to Separation: the RCAF Evolution to Independence,' *Revue internationale d'histoire militaire*, no 54 (misnumbered 51), 1982, 131-58
63 Quartermaster-general [QMG] to CGS, 11 July 1935, DHist 76/37
64 QMG to CGS, 15 Jan. 1936, with CGS's minute, ibid.
65 'An Outline of a Plan Recommended and Basis for a General Scheme of Mobilization,' and Walsh's responses of 13 and 18 March 1935, HQC 1050-71, PAC, RG 24, vol. 2500
66 SAO to CGS, 27 Aug. 1935, HQ 895-1 pt 1, PARC 829218
67 Ibid.
68 Adjutant-general [AG] to district officer commanding Military District No 4, 16 Nov. 1935, DHist 76/37
69 SAO to minister, 19 Sept. 1938, HQC 7674, PAC, RG 24, microfilm reel C5103
70 Ibid.
71 AG to deputy minister, 29 April 1936, with minutes of CGS, QMG, and master-general of the ordnance, HQ 650-77-1, PAC, RG 24, vol. 6541. On the Defence Council see Stacey, *Arms, Men and Governments*, 67-8.
72 Chief of the naval staff to deputy minister, 22 May 1936, HQ 650-77-1, PAC, RG 24, vol. 6541
73 SAO to deputy minister, 27 May 1936, ibid.
74 CGS to minister, 9 July 1936, DHist 112.1 (D77); PC 1742, 17 July 1936
75 SAO to CGS, 16 April 1937, copy in DHist 76/37
76 CGS minute on ibid.
77 'Memorandum on a Canadian Organization for the Higher Direction of National Defence,' drafted by Lieutenant-Colonels M.A. Pope and H.D.G. Crerar, 8 March 1937, HQS 5199K, PAC, RG 24, vol. 2697
78 Croil to chairman Joint Staff Committee, nd, ibid.
79 Ibid.
80 Memorandum to the minister, 1 June 1937, DHist 112.3M2 (D511)

81 SAO to CGS, 27 Aug. 1935, and to deputy minister, 3 Nov. 1937, quoted in 'Western Air Command,' unpublished narrative, 1945, DHist 74/3, vol. I

82 Meetings were held 16 Feb., 5 March, and 21 July 1938, ibid.

83 General Order No 30 of 15 March 1938 authorized the formation of Western Air Command. See SAO to air officer commanding Western Air Command, 21 July 1938, copy in ibid.

84 'Minutes of Meeting of Defence Council, 12 September 1938,' Mackenzie Papers, PAC, MG 27 III B 5, vol. 32, x-52

85 Ibid.

86 SAO to deputy minister (through CGS), 21 Sept. 1938, with draft general order enclosed, copy in 045-4 pt I, PARC 826453

87 Approved draft of Air Force General Order No 2, in HQ 895-1 pt I, PARC 829218. AFGO No I, issued at the same time, authorized the RCAF to publish General Orders.

88 Copy in ibid.

89 Joint Staff Committee memorandum, 13 Dec. 1938, ibid.

90 SAO to CGS, 'The Direct Defence of Canada Considered from an Air Force Aspect,' 22 April 1937, DHist 74/256, vol. I

91 SAO to deputy minister, 16 Sept. 1938, with enclosed memorandum, DHist 76/40

92 'The Direct Defence of Canada Considered from an Air Force Aspect,' DHist 74/256, vol. I

93 SAO to minister, 2 Dec. 1938, F.S. McGill Papers, DHist 74/628, file A4

94 Ibid.

95 'The Direct Defence of Canada Considered from an Air Force Aspect,' DHist 74/256, vol. I

96 SAO to minister, 2 Dec. 1938, McGill Papers, DHist 74/628, file A4

97 'Wapitis,' 9 May 1973, C.R. Dunlap biographical file, DHist

98 Carl Vincent, *The Blackburn Shark* (Canada's Wings, I; Stittsville, Ont. 1974); K.M. Molson and H.A. Taylor, *Canadian Aircraft since 1909* (Stittsville, Ont. 1982), 109-10

99 Molson and Taylor, *Canadian Aircraft*, 438-41

100 Ibid., 120-6, 449-54; air staff officer to SAO, 17 Jan. 1939, DHist 76/198

101 SAO to minister, 7 Oct. 1938, Mackenzie Papers, PAC, MG 27 III B 5, vol. 31, x-47

102 Joint Staff Committee minutes, 15 Sept. 1938, DHist 193.009 (D53); 'Canadian Defence Requirements,' 15 July 1938, Mackenzie Papers, PAC, MG 27 III B 5, vol. 29, x-4

103 Joint Staff Committee minutes, 13, 15, 17 and 29 Sept., I and 6 Oct. 1938, DHist 193.009 (D53)

104 SAO to minister, 7 Oct. 1938, Mackenzie Papers, PAC, MG 27 III B 5, vol. 31, x-47

105 Stedman, notes for Thursday, 29 Sept. 1938, in 'Daily Diary, 1st Air Mission to the United States re: Purchase of Military Aircraft,' DHist 78/477

106 Ibid.; SAO to minister, 7 Oct. 1938, Mackenzie Papers, PAC, MG 27 III B 5, vol. 31, x-47

107 Croil to Stedman, 29 Sept. 1938, DHist 78/477

108 Breadner (for SAO) to minister, 26 Jan. 1939, Mackenzie Papers, PAC, MG 27 III B 5, vol. 32, x-52A. See also Croil to Pirie, 2 June 1939, G.M. Croil Papers, DHist 79/104, file C.

109 Secretary of state for air, 'Creation of a War Potential for Aircraft Production in Canada; C.P. 224 (38),' 13 Oct. 1938, PRO, Cab 21/671

110 Stacey, *Arms, Men and Governments*, 82-5, 105-7; H. Duncan Hall, *North American Supply* (History of the Second World War, United Kingdom Civil Series; London 1955), 24-37; King Diary, 16 May 1938, PAC, MG 26 J 13

111 Bell-Irving to Curtis, 8 March 1939, DHist 76/122. See also PC 1903, 10 Aug. 1938.

112 See, for example, Bell-Irving to Curtis, 13 Feb. 1939, McGill to Bell-Irving, 20 July 1939, DHist 76/122, and McGill to Bishop, 12 Dec. 1938, McGill Papers, DHist 74/628, file A2.

113 Slemon interview, 26 Sept. 1976, C.R. Slemon biographical file, DHist

114 Croil to district officer commanding Military District No 10, 15 Aug. 1935, HQ 898-1-113, PAC, RG 24, vol. 3505

115 'Royal Canadian Air Force Officers – Permanent Who are Qualified in Specialist Duties,' nd, DHist 74/256, vol. 2

116 F.H. Hitchins, *Air Board, Canadian Air Force and Royal Canadian Air Force* (Mercury Series, Canadian War Museum Paper No 2; Ottawa 1972), 267, 282, 337, 366

117 Sampson report of period 1 Sept.-1 Nov. 1937, HQ 1004-3-33-3, PAC, RG 24, vol. 3568

118 Ibid., Sept.-Dec. 1937 and March-Sept. 1938; F.A. Sampson biographical file, DHist

119 Lewis reports, 12 May 1936, HQ 1004-3-33, PAC, RG 24, vol. 3567; and 9 March 1937, HQ 1004-3-33-1, ibid., vol. 3568

120 Lewis report, 9 March 1937, HQ 1004-3-33-1, PAC, RG 24, vol. 3568; 3 Squadron, 1938 Annual Report, HQ 2019-3-29, ibid., vol. 3572

121 Croil to liaison officer, 27 Sept. 1937, HQ 1004-3-33-3, PAC, RG 24, vol. 3568. See also M.M. Hendricks biographical file, DHist.

122 H.R. Allen, *The Legacy of Lord Trenchard* (London 1972), 201

123 H.J. Parkam and E.M. Belfield, *Unarmed into Battle* (Winchester 1956), 9

124 Shelford Bidwell and Dominick Graham, *Fire-Power: British Army Weapons and Theories of War, 1904-1945* (London 1982), 260-75

125 McNab's reports are in HQ 1044-3-33-2, PAC, RG 24, vol. 3568, copies in DHist 75/360.

126 SAO to deputy minister, 16 Sept. 1938, and enclosed memorandum, DHist 76/40; R.S. Reid, 'The Development of the Royal Canadian Air Force as a Military Service during the 1930s,' unpublished narrative, Feb. 1970, DHist 74/34

127 CAS, 'Development of the RCAF – Bulletin No. 4,' 30 March 1939, Bulletin No 6, 29 May 1939, DHist 181.009 (D2); Hitchins, *Air Board*, 364

128 See M.M. Hendricks biographical file, DHist.

129 The basic RAF training manual was Air Publication 847 which was issued in December 1928. See also the collection of syllabi in DHist 181.006 (D524-540): 'Bombing Syllabus for 1938,' 'Air Firing Syllabus for 1938,' and 'Training Syllabus for Pilots of Army Cooperation Squadrons.'

130 DND, *Report, 1938* (Ottawa 1939), 96-102. See also the training files in DHist 181.006 (D530-534) on 1 (F), 2 (AC), 3 (B), 4 (FB), and 4 (GR) Squadrons.

131 No 7 Squadron, 1938 Annual Report, HQ 2019-7-29, PAC, RG 24, vol. 3572
132 No 8 Squadron, 1938 Annual Report, HQ 2019-8-29, ibid.
133 No 3 Squadron, 1938 Annual Report, HQ 2019-2-29, ibid.
134 No 2 Squadron, 1938 Annual Report, HQ 2019-2-21,ibid.
135 See the quarterly reports of 2 Squadron in ibid.
136 Hitchins, *Air Board*, 380-1; air officer commanding Western Air Command to secretary DND, 4 March 1939, copy in McGill Papers, DHist 74/628, file A18
137 CAS, 'Development of the RCAF – Bulletin No. 8,' 31 July 1939, DHist 181.009 (D2)
138 Hitchins, *Air Board*, 381
139 'Joint Staff Committee Plan for the Defence of Canada,' 27 June 1938, App. IV, DHist 181.004 (D39)
140 E.W. Stedman, *From Boxkite to Jet: the Memoirs of an Aeronautical Engineer* (Mercury Series, Canadian War Museum Paper No 1; Ottawa 1972), 171
141 PC 2500, 2 Sept. 1939; PC 2511, 3 Sept. 1939; PC 2532, 5 Sept. 1939; Air Force General Orders 43 and 45, 1939; air staff officer to CAS, 12 Sept. 1939, DHist 181.009 (D2)

CHAPTER 5: ORIGINS

1 S.F. Wise, *Canadian Airmen and the First World War* (Official History of the Royal Canadian Air Force, 1; Toronto 1980), xi, 117, 120, 593, 634
2 King Diary, 20 Oct. 1923, W.L.M. King Papers, PAC, MG 26 J 13. See also Norman Hillmer, 'Mackenzie King, Canadian Air Policy, and the Imperial Conference of 1923,' *High Flight*, 1, 5, 190.
3 Imperial Conference 1923, meeting 10 of principal delegates, 19 Oct. 1923, King Papers, PAC, MG 26 J 4, vol. 82, file 'Imperial Conference, 1923,' c62784
4 Heakes, 'Liaison Notes,' 8 Feb. 1939, Heakes Papers, DHist 77/51
5 Quoted in Heakes, 'Canadianization,' nd, ibid.
6 J.A. Wilson, *Development of Aviation in Canada, 1879-1948* (Ottawa nd), 59. See also dominions secretary to governor general, 19 March 1927, enclosed in telegram, PRO, DO 114/13.
7 'Report of the Chief of the General Staff on the Imperial Conference 1930,' 2 Dec. 1930, DHist 112.1 (D142)
8 F.J. Hatch, 'The British Commonwealth Air Training Plan, 1939-1945' (PHD thesis, University of Ottawa, 1969), 22; dominions secretary to governor general, 19 March 1927, PRO, DO 114/13; C.P. Stacey, *Arms, Men and Governments: the War Policies of Canada, 1939-1945* (Ottawa 1970), 81; Dominions Office to Government of Canada, 22 Oct. 1929, PRO, DO 114/23
9 Grandy to secretary Department of National Defence [DND], 22 Oct. 1931, DHist 78/502
10 Lawrence to secretary DND, 4 Aug. 1932, and summary of files regarding RAF commissions, ibid.
11 Canada, DND, *Report of the Department of National Defence, 1933* (Ottawa 1934), 47; *1934* (Ottawa 1934), 82

12 'Note of a Meeting held at the Dominions Office on the 25th March, 1936,' PRO, DO 35/174

13 Thomas to Government of Canada, 3 Nov. 1934, PRO, DO 114/52; undersecretary of state for external affairs to dominions secretary, no 154, 5 June 1935, Alex I. Inglis, ed., *Documents on Canadian External Relations* [DCER], V: *1931-1935* (Ottawa 1973), 100-1

14 Dominions secretary to secretary of state for external affairs, no 486, 28 Nov. 1935, PRO, DO 114/60, printed in DCER, V, 104-5; Christie memorandum, 'Canadian Defence Commitments,' 3 March 1936, PAC, RG 25 D 1, vol. 755, file 243 pt 1 (II-B-84); Air Ministry memorandum, 'Training in Canada of Pilots for the Royal Air Force, Revised Proposals,' 5 Nov. 1938, PRO, Air 20/331

15 Dominions secretary to secretary of state for external affairs, no 486, 28 Nov. 1935, PRO, DO 114/60, DCER, V, 105

16 Memorandum, 'Canadian Defence Commitments; Canadian Government Coopera- tion in Recruiting Canadians for Royal Air Force,' 5 May 1936, enclosed in Christie to Skelton, 5 May 1936, John A. Munro, ed., DCER, VI: *1936-1939* (Otta- wa 1972), 173-5

17 Massey to Skelton, 27 March 1936, ibid., 173

18 'Canadian Defence Commitments,' 5 May 1936, ibid., 174-5

19 Christie to Skelton, 5 May 1936, ibid., 173

20 Leckie memorandum [May 1936], Tedder memorandum, 23 May 1936, 'A Back- ground to History,' *Roundel*, II, Dec. 1949, 14-15

21 Tedder memorandum [March 1936], Ian Mackenzie biographical file, DHist; Mac- kenzie to King, 4 Sept. 1936, King Papers, PAC, MG 26 J 1, vol. 220, 189790; Norman Hillmer, 'Defence and Ideology, the Anglo-Canadian Military "Alliance" in the 1930s,' *International Journal*, summer 1978, 604-5

22 Mackenzie to King, 4 Sept. 1936, King Papers, PAC, MG 26 J 1, vol. 220, 189790

23 Pickering memorandum, 11 Sept. 1936, ibid., J 4 series, vol. 151, file F1274, C109341

24 Joint Staff Committee memoranda, 6 and 19 May 1937, ibid., vol. 178, file F1641, C126700-2, and C126729-31; James Eayrs, *In Defence of Canada*, II: *Appease- ment and Rearmament* (Toronto 1965), 92

25 Dominions secretary, memorandum, 'Canadian Co-operation in Defence,' 3 June 1936, PRO, DO 35/174

26 Batterbee minute, 3 June 1936, ibid.

27 Secretary of state for external affairs to dominions secretary, 25 March 1937, DCER, VI, 179-80. See also PRO, DO 114/78, and Breadner to district officer commanding Military District No 2, 23 June 1937, DHist 78/502.

28 Dominions secretary to secretary of state for external affairs, 22 April 1937, DCER, VI, 192. See also PRO, DO 114/78.

29 Acting secretary of state for external affairs to Massey, 21 May 1937, Massey to secretary of state for external affairs, 21 June 1937, DCER, VI, 195-6, 203-4

30 Stacey, *Arms, Men and Governments*, 82; Massey to secretary of state for external affairs, 23 Nov. 1937, DCER, VI, 204

31 Government of Canada to Dominions Office, 21 Dec. 1937, PRO, DO 114/78

32 Skelton to King, 'Recruitment of Canadians for U.K. Air Force (Short Service Commissions),' 19 March 1938, DCER, VI, 204-5

33 Secretary of state for external affairs to dominions secretary, 22 March 1938, ibid., 205

34 Canada, DND, *Report of the Department of National Defence, 1939* (Ottawa 1939), 108-9

35 F.J. Hatch, *The Aerodrome of Democracy: Canada and the British Commonwealth Air Training Plan, 1939-1945* (Department of National Defence, Directorate of History, Monograph Series No 1; Ottawa 1983), 5. See also DHist 181.005 (D270), which lists 446 Canadian officers and 441 airmen.

36 Charles Webster and Noble Frankland, *The Strategic Air Offensive against Germany, 1939-1945*, I: *Preparation* (History of the Second World War, United Kingdom Military Series; London 1961), 109

37 Leckie memorandum [May 1936], 'A Background to History,' *Roundel*, II, Dec. 1949, 15

38 Cabinet minutes, 30 March 1938, PRO, Cab 23/93

39 Cabinet minutes, 29 June 1938, PRO, Cab 23/94

40 Dominions Office to Floud, 13 May 1938, PRO, DO 114/85

41 King memorandum, 13 [sic] May 1938, DCER, VI, 206-8

42 Floud to Dominions Office, 16 May 1938, PRO, DO 127/28

43 King memorandum, 13 [sic] May 1938, DCER, VI, 206-8

44 Ibid.; King Diary, 16 May 1938, PAC, MG 26 J 13. See also Street, 'Training of RAF Pilots in Canada,' 11 Nov. 1938, PRO, Prem 1/397.

45 Floud to Dominions Office, 16 May 1938, PRO, DO 114/85

46 Ibid.

47 Cabinet minutes, 29 June 1938, PRO, Cab 23/94

48 Dominions Office to Floud, 18 May 1938, PRO, DO 127/28

49 Floud to Dominions Office, 18 May 1938, ibid.

50 Batterbee to Floud, 20 May 1938, PRO, DO 127/30

51 Dominions Office minute, 29 Nov. 1938, PRO, DO 127/34

52 King memorandum, 13 [sic] May 1938, DCER, VI, 206-8. See also Floud to King, 24 June 1938, PRO, DO 127/31.

53 King Diary, 15 June 1938, PAC, MG 26 J 13; Canada, Parliament, Senate, *Debates*, June 1938, 502-3, 520-1

54 DCER, VI, 211-19; Floud to Dominions Office, 24 June 1938, PRO, DO 35/547

55 King Diary, 24 June 1938, PAC, MG 26 J 13

56 Ibid., 27 June 1938. See also Skelton memorandum, 2 July 1938, DCER, VI, 217-18.

57 King Diary, 1 July 1938, PAC, MG 26 J 13

58 Ibid.

59 Canada, Parliament, House of Commons, *Debates*, 1 July 1938, 4527, 4529. See also King's copy of Christie memorandum, 'The Imperial-Flying School-in-Canada Idea,' 19 June 1938, King Papers, PAC, MG 26 J 4, vol. 151, file F1274.

60 Floud to Dominions Office, 5 July 1938, PRO, DO 14/85. See also 'RAF Scheme – Introductory Note,' nd, Mackenzie Papers, PAC, MG 27 III B 5, vol. 31, file X-41.

61 Cited in [Christie] memorandum, 'Air Force Training Schools Question,' 12 Aug. 1938, PAC, RG 25 D 1, vol. 755, file 243 pt 1 (II-B-84); Floud to King, 7 July 1938, DCER, VI, 218-19

62 Street memorandum, 11 Nov. 1938, PRO, Prem 1/397. See also Dominions Office minute, 29 Nov. 1938, PRO, DO 127/34.

63 Skelton memorandum, 'Training of Air Pilots,' 11 Aug. 1938, DCER, VI, 219-20

64 Ibid.

65 King to Floud (draft), 15 Aug. 1938, PAC, RG 25 D I, vol. 755, file 243 pt I (II-B-84)

66 Croil to deputy minister, 'Training Scheme of Pilots for the R.A.F.,' 19 July 1938, DHist 76/144

67 LaFlèche to Skelton, 8 Aug. 1938, PAC, RG 25 D I, vol. 755, file 243, vol. I (II-B-84)

68 King Diary, 9 Aug. 1938, PAC, MG 26 J 13

69 Floud to King, 3 Sept. 1938, DCER, VI, 222-3. See King memorandum, 'Re: U.K. Training Scheme,' 5 Sept. 1938, ibid., 223-4. For the Robb report itself see 'Summary of Plan for Training of Pilots for Royal Air Force in Canada,' 2 Sept. 1938, PAC, RG 25 D I, vol. 755, file 243 pt I (II-B-84), and PRO, Air 20/434.

70 Street memorandum, 'Training of R.A.F. Pilots in Canada,' 11 Nov. 1938, PRO, Prem 1/397; King to Floud, 6 Sept. 1938, Skelton memorandum, 'Training of Air Pilots,' 9 Sept. 1938, DCER, VI, 225-7

71 Skelton memorandum, 'Training of Air Pilots,' 9 Sept. 1938, DCER, VI, 226-7

72 [Christie] memorandum, 'Canadian Air Force Program,' 5 Sept. 1938, PAC, RG 25 D I, vol. 755, file 243 pt I (II-B-84)

73 Croil memorandum to the minister, 15 Sept. 1938, DHist 76/40

74 DND memorandum, 'R.A.F. Scheme: Introductory Note,' nd, Mackenzie Papers, PAC, MG 27 III B 5, vol. 31, file X-41

75 Street memorandum, 'Training of R.A.F. Pilots in Canada,' 11 Nov. 1938, PRO, Prem 1/397

76 Dominions Office minute, 29 Nov. 1938, PRO, DO 127/34

77 Webster and Frankland, *The Strategic Air Offensive against Germany*, I, 110

78 Campbell to King, 9 Dec. 1938, and enclosed memorandum, PRO, DO 114/85, printed in DCER, VI, 228-30

79 King Diary, 15 Dec. 1938, PAC, MG 26 J 13

80 Ibid., 15 and 16 Dec. 1938

81 King to Campbell, 31 Dec. 1938, Campbell to King, 10 Jan. 1939, DCER, VI, 230-2, 233-4

82 W.K. Stevenson, 'The Origins of the British Commonwealth Air Training Scheme from 1923 to December 1939' (PHD thesis, Birkbeck College, 1980), 172-3; Croil to deputy minister, 5 and 19 July 1938, DHist 76/144; House of Commons, *Debates*, 26 April 1939, 3258-9; LaFlèche to Campbell, 11 April 1939, DHist 78/483. For the negotiations leading to the agreement see this file and DND memorandum, 'R.A.F. Scheme: Introductory Note,' nd, Mackenzie Papers, PAC, MG 27 III B 5, vol. 31, file X-41.

83 Air Ministry, 'Memorandum on the Possibility of Increasing Training in Canada for the Royal Air Force,' 2 Sept. 1939, PRO, Air 2/3206

84 Secretary of state for external affairs to dominions secretary, 3 Sept. 1939, dominions secretary to secretary of state for external affairs, 6 Sept. 1939, UK high commissioner to undersecretary of state for external affairs, 6 Sept. 1939,

Campbell to Skelton, and enclosed, 6 Sept. 1939, DCER, VI, 1287-8 and 1301-5

85 Croil memorandum for minister, 10 Sept. 1939, 5199-5 pt 1, PARC; Mackenzie to Skelton, 10 Sept. 1939, DCER, VI, 1314; King to Campbell, 12 Sept. 1939, quoted in Stacey, *Arms, Men and Governments*, 18

86 'Minutes of a Meeting ... on September 10th, 1939, to Discuss Flying Training Expansion,' PRO, Air 20/331

87 [Croil] memorandum for minister, 15 Sept. 1939, 5199-5 pt 1, PARC; King Diary, 18 Sept. 1939, PAC, MG 26 J 13; Chiefs of Staff Committee, 'Action by the Armed Forces of Canada,' 17 Sept. 1939, App. C, DHist 112.3M2009 (D36)

88 PRO, DO 121/6; Vincent Massey Diary, 23 Sept. 1939, Massey College, University of Toronto; Vincent Massey, *What's Past is Prologue: the Memoirs of the Right Honourable Vincent Massey, C.H.* (Toronto 1963), 303-6; Earl of Avon, *The Eden Memoirs: the Reckoning* (London 1965), 70; Cecil Edwards, *Bruce of Melbourne: Man of Two Worlds* (London 1965), 257-8, 278-80; Paul Hasluck, *The Government and the People, 1939-1941* (Canberra 1952), 70

89 'Note of Meeting on ... Dominion Training Scheme,' 22 Sept. 1939, 'Notes of a Meeting...' 4 Oct. 1939, PRO, Air 2/3206; 'Notes of a Special Meeting ...' 23 Sept. 1939, PRO, Air 20/333; Massey Diary, 25, 29 Sept. 1939; dominions secretary to Chamberlain, 25 Sept. 1939, PRO, Prem 1/397

90 Stacey, *Arms, Men and Governments*, 19

91 Massey Diary, 23 and 25 Sept. 1939. King remained ignorant of Massey's role until 1946, when Anthony Eden referred to it in a newspaper article. King wrote in his diary: 'The outrageous part is that Massey, as representative of the government, should not have made the suggestion to the administration here in the first instance.' King Diary, 9 March 1946, PAC, MG 26 J 13. See also Norman Hillmer, 'Vincent Massey and the Origins of the British Commonwealth Air Training Plan,' *CAHS Journal* (forthcoming).

92 J.L. Granatstein, *Canada's War: the Politics of the Mackenzie King Government, 1939-1945* (Toronto 1975), 59

93 King Diary, 27 Sept. 1939, PAC, MG 26 J 13

94 King to Chamberlain, 28 Sept. 1939, David R. Murray, ed., DCER, VII: *1939-1941, Part 1* (Ottawa 1974), 556-7

95 'Minutes of Emergency Council (Committee on General Policy) of Cabinet,' 28 Sept. 1939, ibid., 552-5

96 Skelton to King, memorandum, 'Air Training Scheme,' 29 Sept. 1939, ibid., 557-9

97 'Minutes of Emergency Council ... of Cabinet,' 28 Sept. 1939, ibid., 554

98 Skelton to UK high commissioner, 8 Oct. 1939, 'Memorandum by USSEA,' 8 Oct. 1939, ibid., 569

99 War Cabinet minutes, 10 Oct. 1939, PRO, Cab 65/1

100 Campbell to Skelton, 9 Oct. 1939, Skelton to Campbell, 9 Oct. 1939, Skelton memorandum, 10 Oct. 1939, DCER, VII, 574-8

101 War Cabinet minutes, 10 Oct. 1939, PRO, Cab 65/1

102 'Air Training Statement,' 10 Oct. 1939, DCER, VII, 577-8

103 'The War Finance of Canada,' nd, copy in PRO, T 160/1340. See also Stacey, *Arms, Men and Governments*, 12.

104 Quoted in Granatstein, *Canada's War*, 62. See also, Hector Mackenzie, 'Mutual Assistance: the Finance of British Requirements in Canada during the Second World War' (PHD thesis, University of Oxford, 1981), chap. 2; and 'Note of a meeting held in the Secretary of State's room at 6:30 p.m. on Tuesday, September 26th, to discuss the co-ordination of United Kingdom purchases and financial requirements in Canada,' PRO, DO 35/1069.

105 Harold Balfour, *Wings over Westminster* (London 1973), 114

106 'Memorandum from Chairman, Air Mission of Great Britain to Prime Minister,' 13 Oct. 1939, DCER, VII, 580-1. See also Riverdale's report to the minister for air, 19 Oct. 1939, PRO, Air 20/338.

107 Stedman, 'The British Commonwealth Air Training Plan,' 2, DHist 80/412

108 Ibid., 4

109 Dominions secretary to UK high commissioner, 27 Oct. 1939, PRO, DO 35/1028

110 UK high commissioner to dominions secretary, 1 Nov. 1939, ibid.

111 Gilbert, 'Dominion Air Training Scheme,' 28 Oct. 1939, PRO, T 160/987

112 UK high commissioner to dominions secretary, 24 Oct. 1939, PRO, DO 35/1028

113 Same to same, 27 Oct. 1939, PRO, T 160/987

114 Campbell to Machtig, 19 Oct. 1939, PRO, DO 35/1028

115 UK high commissioner to secretary of state for dominion affairs, 24 Oct. 1939, ibid.

116 Gilbert, 'Dominion Air Training School,' 28 Oct. 1939, PRO, T 160/987; Simon minute, 30 Oct. 1939, ibid.; War Cabinet minutes, WM65(39), PRO, Cab 65/1

117 'Revised Record of an Informal Meeting held on 25th October, 1939 ... to discuss arrangements for British and French purchases in Canada,' nd, PRO, DO 35/1028

118 Street to Machtig, 27 Oct. 1939, ibid.

119 Riverdale to Wood, 19 Oct. 1939, PRO, Air 20/338

120 Same to same, 6 Nov. 1939, ibid.

121 Memorandum from undersecretary of state for external affairs to prime minister, 1 Nov. 1939, DCER, VII, 592. See also Eayrs, *In Defence of Canada*, II, 108; Arnold Heeney, *The Things that are Caesar's* (Toronto 1972), 61; and Dexter to Ferguson, 7 Nov. 1939, J.W. Dafoe Papers, PAC, MG 30 D 45, vol. 11.

122 King Diary, 17 Oct. 1939, PAC, MG 26 J 13

123 UK Air Mission, 'Notes of meeting on 31 October with members of the Canadian War Cabinet,' DHist 181.009 (D786); 'Minutes of Emergency Council (Committee on General Policy) of Cabinet,' 31 Oct. 1939, DCER, VII, 586-91

124 J.W. Pickersgill, *The Mackenzie King Record*, I: *1939-1944* (Toronto 1960), 42-3

125 'Minutes of Emergency Council ... of Cabinet,' 31 Oct. 1939, secretary of state for external affairs to dominions secretary, 3 Nov. 1939, DCER, VII, 590, 598

126 Riverdale to Wood, 30 Nov. 1939, PRO, Air 20/338; Riverdale, 'Office Memorandum,' nd, PRO, Air 8/280

127 'Memorandum for United Kingdom Mission presented on behalf of Australian Mission and submitted to Canadian sub-committee on 22 November 1939,' copy in DHist 181.009 (D786); 'Minutes of Emergency Council ... of Cabinet,' 14 Nov. 1939, 'Memorandum by Prime Minister,' 25 Nov. 1939, DCER, VII, 604-7, 612-18

128 Stedman's draft estimates of costs are in DHist 80/462. See also Riverdale to Wood, 30 Nov. 1939, PRO, Air 20/338, which incorrectly counts part of the UK contribution twice.

129 'Minutes of Emergency Council ... of Cabinet,' 27 Nov. 1939, DCER, VII, 623-7; Granatstein, *Canada's War*, 65; Mackenzie, 'Mutual Assistance,' chap. 2; Phillips, 'Note of Interview with Graham Towers, 1 Dec. 1939,' PRO, T 160/1340

130 'Memorandum by Prime Minister,' 25 Nov. 1939, DCER, VII, 612-18

131 'Minutes of Emergency Council ... of Cabinet,' 27 Nov. 1939, ibid., 623-7

132 War Cabinet minutes, WM94(39) and WM96(39), PRO, Cab 65/2. See also Gilbert, 'The Finance of the Dominion Air Training Scheme,' 17 Nov. 1939, PRO, T 160/987; and Stacey, *Arms, Men and Governments*, 24.

133 Wood, 'Dominion Air Training Scheme,' 18 Nov. 1939, PRO, Cab 67/2; War Cabinet minutes, WM94(39), PRO, Cab 65/2

134 UK high commissioner to dominions secretary, 5 Dec. 1939, PRO, T 160/987

135 War Cabinet minutes, WM96(39), PRO, Cab 65/2

136 Chamberlain to King, 27 Nov. 1939, DCER, VII, 622-3. For the Crerar discussions on wheat, see R.J. Hammond, *Food*, III: *Studies in Administration and Control* (History of the Second World War, United Kingdom Civil Series; London 1962), 522.

137 'Minutes of Emergency Council ... of Cabinet,' 27 Nov. 1939, DCER, VII, 623-7; King to Chamberlain, 28 Nov. 1939, ibid., 635-6

138 Chamberlain to King, 1 Dec. 1939, DCER, VII, 637; King to Chamberlain, 5 Dec. 1939, Chamberlain to King, 7 Dec. 1939, ibid., 640-1; Stacey, *Arms, Men and Governments*, 24-5

139 Air Mission of New Zealand to Chairman, Air Mission of Great Britain, 28 Nov. 1939, 'Draft Memorandum of Agreement between Great Britain, Canada, Australia and New Zealand,' nd, DCER, VII, 628-634

140 Riverdale, 'Office Memorandum,' nd, PRO, Air 8/280

141 Chamberlain to King, 26 Sept. 1939, DCER, VII, 549-52

142 Street to Barlow, 24 Sept. 1939, 'Notes of a Special Meeting ...' 23 Sept. 1939, PRO, T 160/987

143 UK high commissioner to dominions secretary, 19 Dec. 1939, PRO, Prem 1/397

144 'Minutes of Emergency Council ... of Cabinet,' 6 Nov. 1939, DCER, VII, 600-3

145 Chief of the air staff [CAS] to minister, 23 Nov. 1939, AFHQ 927-1-1 pt 2, copy in DHist 180.009 (D12)

146 Stacey, *Arms, Men and Governments*, 18

147 CAS to minister, 23 Nov. 1939, AFHQ 927-1-1 pt 2, copy in DHist 180.009 (D12)

148 Memorandum from undersecretary of state for external affairs to prime minister, 13 Dec. 1939, DCER, VII, 648

149 Rogers to Riverdale, 8 Dec. 1939, Riverdale to Rogers, 8 Dec. 1939, ibid., 641-2

150 Heeney, 'Air Training Scheme – Organization of Canadians in R.C.A.F. Units and Formations,' 11 Dec. 1939, ibid., 642-5

151 Ibid.

152 'Minutes of the Cabinet War Committee,' 14 Dec. 1939, ibid., VII, 649-52

153 Ibid. See also Heeney, *The Things that are Caesar's*, 62-3.

154 'Minutes of Cabinet War Committee,' 14 Dec. 1939, DCER, VII, 649-52; Brooke-

Popham to MacLachlan, 15 Dec. 1939, AFHQ 927-1-1 pt 2, copy in DHist
180.009 (D12)

155 Heeney, *The Things that are Caesar's*, 63

156 C.G. Power, *A Party Politician: the Memoirs of Chubby Power*, Norman Ward,
ed. (Toronto 1966), 204

157 'Minutes of Cabinet War Committee,' 14 Dec. 1939, DCER, VII, 649-52; Heeney,
The Things that are Caesar's, 63

158 King to Chamberlain, 16 Dec. 1939, Chamberlain to King, 21 Dec. 1939, DCER,
VII, 662, 667. See also ibid., 660-2.

159 Pickersgill, *The Mackenzie King Record*, I, 53

160 Heeney, 'Re: British Commonwealth Air Training Plan, Negotiations of December 15-16, 1939,' 22 Dec. 1939, DCER, VII, 667-71

161 Pickersgill, *The Mackenzie King Record*, I, 50

162 Heeney, 'Re: British Commonwealth Air Training Plan ...' 22 Dec. 1939, DCER,
VII, 667

163 Ibid., 668

164 Ibid.; Pickersgill, *The Mackenzie King Record*, I, 50; Stacey, *Arms, Men and
Governments*, 25-8

165 War Cabinet minutes, WM118(39), PRO, Cab 65/2

166 Riverdale to King, nd, reprinted in secretary of state for external affairs to dominions secretary, 16 Dec. 1939, DCER, VII, 658

167 L.B. Pearson, *Mike: the Memoirs of the Rt. Hon. Lester B. Pearson* (Toronto
1972-5), I, 152

168 King to Chamberlain, 16 Dec. 1939, DCER, VII, 656-9. See also Pickersgill, *The
Mackenzie King Record*, I, 51.

169 Heeney, 'Re: British Commonwealth Air Training Plan ...' 22 Dec. 1939, DCER,
VII, 669-71

170 Pickersgill, *The Mackenzie King Record*, I, 54

171 King, 'Comments by Col. Ralston,' 16 Dec. 1939, DCER, VII, 662-4

172 Pickersgill, *The Mackenzie King Record*, I, 56

173 Ibid., 57. The final version is in Riverdale to Rogers, 16 Dec. 1939, DCER, VII,
664. On the detailed drafting of the letter see 'Memorandum by Prime Minister,' 16 Dec. 1939, ibid., 662-4.

174 Pickersgill, *The Mackenzie King Record*, I, 58

CHAPTER 6: BUILDING THE PLAN

1 Canada, Air Historical Section, *RCAF Logbook: a Chronological Outline of the
Origin, Growth and Achievement of the Royal Canadian Air Force* (Ottawa
1949), 58-60; J.R.M. Butler, *Grand Strategy*, II: *September 1939-June 1941*
(History of the Second World War, United Kingdom Military Series; London
1957), 33, 39; Canada, *Agreement Relating to Training of Pilots and Aircraft
Crews in Canada and their Subsequent Service between the United Kingdom,
Canada, Australia and New Zealand signed at Ottawa, December 17, 1939*
(Ottawa 1941), Table F (hereafter cited as *BCATP Agreement, 1939*; reprinted in
C.P. Stacey, *Arms, Men and Governments: the War Policies of Canada, 1939-*

1945, Ottawa 1970, Appendix D). For cost estimates, see E.W. Stedman's working notes, DHist 80/462, vol. 3.

2 J.A. Wilson, 'Aerodrome Construction for the British Commonwealth Air Training Plan 1940,' in Canada, Department of Transport, *Development of Aviation in Canada, 1879-1948: Articles by J.A. Wilson, C.B.E.* (np nd), 27, 30-1, copy in DHist 75/114

3 Memorandum attached to Croil to deputy minister, 14 Oct. 1939, HQ 103-74/68 pt 1, PAC, RG 24, vol. 4775

4 Wilson, 'Aerodrome Construction,' 30-1

5 Canada, Air Force, *Notes for the Information of Men Desirous of Enlisting in the Royal Canadian Air Force, (Permanent)* (Ottawa 1935), copy in DHist 75/29; F.H. Hitchins, *Air Board, Canadian Air Force and Royal Canadian Air Force* (Mercury Series, Canadian War Museum Paper No 2; Ottawa 1972), 331-2; 'Airmen's Technical Training, 1920-1944,' unpublished narrative [1945], 6-21, DHist 74/21; 'Technical Training, Pre-entry, Dominion-Provincial Youth Training, 1939-1944,' unpublished narrative [1945], ibid.; Christie interview, 22 Aug. 1981, A.G. Christie biographical file, DHist

6 'History of the RCAF (Women's Division), 1941-1971,' unpublished narrative, 26 May 1971, DHist 78/517

7 *BCATP Agreement, 1939*, articles 4, 5, 9, 14, 16 and App. I (EFTS, AOS, WS intake figures)

8 Ibid., App. II; Maclachlan to secretary UK Air Mission, 21 Dec. 1939, Jones to deputy minister and enclosed 'Extracts from Air Ministry Memorandum ...' 29 Jan. 1940, Breadner to chief of the air staff [CAS], 3 Feb. 1940, HQ 927-1-1, DHist 80/408, vol. 1

9 Canada, Air Force, *Final Report of the Chief of the Air Staff to the Members of the Supervisory Board British Commonwealth Air Training Plan* (Ottawa, 16 April 1945), 26, copy in DHist 81/221; Great Britain, Air Ministry, air member for training, *Notes on the History of RAF Training, 1939-44* (np Jan. 1945), 119, 287, copy in DHist 81/720; Supervisory Board minutes, 8 July 1940, 4-5, DHist 73/1558, vol. 2; Jerrold Morris, *Canadian Artists and Airmen, 1940-45* (Toronto nd), 32

10 Stacey, *Arms, Men and Governments*, 120-1; C.G. Power, *A Party Politician: the Memoirs of Chubby Power*, Norman Ward, ed. (Toronto 1966)

11 Great Britain, Air Ministry, *Flying Training*, I: *Policy and Planning* (np 1952), 69; Empire Air Training Scheme [EATS] Committee minutes, PRO, Air 20/1379A

12 Correspondence, 27 Nov. 1939-16 Jan. 1940, attached as Appendices 3 and 4 to Supervisory Board minutes, 24 Jan. 1940, DHist 73/1558, vol. 1; L.D.D. McKean, 'History of the U.K.A.L.M. – Canada,' unpublished narrative, 30 March 1945, 1-2, DHist 80/395

13 S.F. Wise, *Canadian Airmen and the First World War* (Official History of the Royal Canadian Air Force, I; Toronto 1980), chap. 4; Seymour interview, 14-15 May 1975, M.A. Seymour biographical file, DHist; A.G. Sutherland, *Canada's Aviation Pioneers: 50 Years of McKee Trophy Winners* (Toronto 1978), 115-21

14 G.L. Apedaile, 'History of Civil Flying Schools,' unpublished narrative, 30 Dec. 1946, DHist 181.009 (D3); 'BCATP Flying Training,' nd, 'The Elementary Flying Training Schools: the Civilian-Operated Schools,' 2-3, DHist 181.009

(D89A); Supervisory Board minutes, 24 Jan. 1940, App. 5, 8 April 1940, App.
III, Report of CAS, App. F, DHist 73/1558, vol. I

15 Supervisory Board minutes, 8 July 1940, App. I, Report of CAS, 3, DHist 75/1558,
vol. 2; 'Canadian Flying Clubs Association Annual Report For the Year 1940,'
29 Nov. 1940, 3-4, DHist 75/252, folder 5; Rayner to Douglas, 19 June 1981,
G.B. Rayner biographical file, DHist

16 Apedaile, 'History of Civil Flying Schools'; Supervisory Board minutes, 8 April
1940, App. III, Report of CAS, App. G, 6 May 1940, 3, DHist 73/1558, vol. I;
J.J.B. Pariseau, 'My BCATP Experience,' 1979, Pariseau biographical file, DHist;
J.R. Wood, 'My War Memoirs,' 4 Dec. 1980, Wood biographical file, DHist

17 Great Britain, *History of RAF Training*, 24, 33-4; 'BCATP Flying Training,' nd,
'The Elementary Flying Training Schools: Syllabus of Instruction,' I, 'Service
Flying Training: Syllabus of Instruction,' 2, DHist 181.009 (D89A)

18 Supervisory Board minutes, 24 Jan. 1940, App. 5, Report of CAS, 2, DHist 73/
1558, vol. I; 'Central Flying School,' nd, CFS permanent reference file, DHist

19 Senator Godfrey interview, 22 Feb. 1977, J.M. Godfrey biographical file, DHist

20 Great Britain, *History of RAF Training*, 5-6, 87-90, 118; W.G. Goddard, 'The
History of Air Navigation Training in Canada,' unpublished narrative [1945],
3-5, 41, DHist 74/17

21 Wilson, 'Aerodrome Construction,' 29-31; Canada, Department of Transport,
'The Selection and Development of Airports,' nd, 2-9, DHist 80/395; 'Armament Activity,' unpublished narrative, 4 April 1945, 13-17, ibid.

22 F.J. Hatch, 'Mackenzie King and No. 6 Air Observer School,' *High Flight*, II, 2,
66-71

23 'History of Construction Engineering,' unpublished narrative [1945], sect. I, 1-3,
sect. 12, I, DHist 74/20; R.R. Collard biographical file, DHist

24 'Development of the Equipment or Supply Branch,' unpublished narrative, April
1945, 14, 16, DHist 74/21; Supervisory Board minutes, 19 Feb. 1940, App. 2,
Report of CAS, App. A, DHist 73/1558, vol. I

25 Croil to minister, 9 April 1940, correspondence labelled 'Problems of Supply of
the RCAF,' cited in F.J. Hatch, 'The British Commonwealth Air Training Plan,
1939 to 1945' (PHD thesis, University of Ottawa, 1969), 173-4

26 Supervisory Board minutes, 8 July 1940, App. 2, DHist 73/1558, vol. 2

27 Canada, RCAF Logbook, 45, 53, 62; Supervisory Board minutes, 8 April 1940,
App. III, Report of CAS, 3-5, DHist 73/1558, vol. I

28 Rogers to Balfour, 27 Nov. 1939, attached as App. 3 to Supervisory Board minutes, 24 Jan. 1940, DHist 73/1558, vol. I

29 Brooke-Popham to Maclachlan, 29 Dec. 1939 and 8 Jan. 1940, Kenny to director
of air personnel, 3 Jan. 1940, HQ 927-1-1, DHist 80/408, vol. I; Johnson to CAS,
26 Nov. 1939, Croil to Mackworth, 19 Jan. 1940, ibid., vol. 2; McKean, 'History
of the U.K.A.L.M. – Canada,' 12

30 Wise, *Canadian Airmen*, 612-13; R. Leckie biographical file, DHist

31 CAS to Canadian Liaison Office [CLO], London, Edwards to air member for personnel [AMP], 18 Jan. 1940, CLO to CAS, 19 Jan. 1940, Kenny to director of air
personnel, 20 Jan. 1940, CAS to CLO, 21 Jan. 1940, CLO to CAS, 22 Jan. 1940,
Tyrell-Beck to judge advocate general and minute 2, 24 Jan. 1940, Croil to

liaison officer in chief, 30 Jan. 1940, and minute 2 to AMP, 31 Jan. 1940, HQ 927-1-1 pt 2, DHist 80/408, vol. 2

32 Supervisory Board minutes, 9 Dec. 1940, App. 1, Report of CAS, 4, DHist 73/1558, vol. 2; 'R.C.A.F. Personnel History,' unpublished narrative [1945], 855, 857, DHist 74/7, vol. 4

33 M.V. Bezeau, 'The Role and Organization of Canadian Military Staffs, 1904-1945' (MA thesis, Royal Military College of Canada, 1978), 100, 104-5, 124-6; R. Leckie biographical file, DHist

34 Department of National Defence [DND], *Report*, 1940, 95; 'R.C.A.F. Personnel History,' 14-15, 119, 127-8, DHist 74/7, vol. 1

35 'R.C.A.F. Personnel History,' 119, 124, 128

36 Farley Mowat, *And No Birds Sang* (Toronto 1979), 16-17

37 Supervisory Board minutes, 6 May 1940, 3, DHist 73/1558, vol. 1; 'BCATP Flying Training,' nd, 'The Elementary Flying Training School: Instructor Policy,' 1-5, DHist 181.009 (D89A)

38 Wise, *Canadian Airmen*, 89; 'R.C.A.F. Personnel History,' 542, 547, 612, DHist 74/7, vol. 3; PC 2399, 7 June 1940; Canada, Air Force, *The King's Regulations and Orders for the Royal Canadian Air Force, 1924* (Ottawa 1924), amendment of June 1940

39 Canadian minister to the United States to secretary of state for external affairs, 18 May 1940, HQ 45-10-2, PAC, RG 24, vol. 5368

40 King to Campbell, 9 Jan. 1941, David R. Murray, ed., *Documents on Canadian External Relations* [DCER], VII: *1939-1941, Part 1* (Ottawa 1974), 916-17; Christie to Skelton, 4 Nov. 1940, 'Clayton Knight-Homer Smith Committee,' 12 Nov. 1940, 'Recruiting of Pilots in the United States,' 19 Nov. 1940, 'Clayton Knight Agency,' 21 Nov. 1940, Skelton to Mahoney, 25 Nov. 1940, Mahoney to Skelton, 27 Nov. 1940, 'Clayton Knight Committee,' 18 Dec. 1940, David R. Murray, ed., DCER, VIII: *1939-1941, Part 2* (Ottawa 1976), 49-65; Seymour interview, May 1975, 11-15, M.A. Seymour biographical file, DHist

41 'R.C.A.F. Personnel History', 128-9, DHist 74/7, vol. 1; 1 Initial Training School, operations record book [ORB] daily diary, 29 April 1940, DHist; Supervisory Board minutes, 6 May 1940, App. 1, Report of CAS, 1, DHist 73/1558, vol. 1

42 Power, *A Party Politician*, 210-11; Canada, Parliament, House of Commons, *Debates*, 29 July 1940, 2108; Campbell to Rogers, 20 May 1940, HQ 927-1-1, DHist 80/408, vol. 3; Supervisory Board minutes, 10 May 1940, 2-3, DHist 73/1558, vol. 1

43 Dominions secretary to secretary of state for external affairs, 23 May 1940, DCER, VII, 680-1

44 Ibid; Supervisory Board minutes, 8 July 1940, App. 1, Report of CAS, 8-9, 5 Aug. 1940, App. 1, Report of CAS, 2, App. C, DHist 73/1558, vol. 2

45 Croil to minister, 24 May 1940, C.G. Power Papers, Queen's University Archives, box 54, file D1011; dominions secretary to secretary of state for external affairs, 23 May 1940, DCER, VII, 680-1; Supervisory Board minutes, 10 June 1940, App. 1, Report of CAS, 9, 8 July 1940, App. 1, Report of CAS, 8-10, 5 Aug. 1940, App. 1, Report of CAS, 2, 11 Nov. 1940, App. 1, Report of CAS, 2, 9 Dec. 1940, App. 1, Report of CAS, 4, DHist 73/1558, vol. 2; Supervisory Board minutes, 10 Feb.

1941, App. 1, Report of CAS, 8, ibid., vol. 3; Tackaberry to director of air organiza-
tion, 11 Sept. 1940, Long to personal staff officer, 12 Sept. 1940, HQ 927-1-1,
DHist 80/408, vol. 3; 'Dominion Training Scheme, Ratio of Single Engine to Twin
Engine Pilots, Note by A.M.S.O.,' 24 Jan. 1940, PRO, Air 20/1374

46 See, for example, Supervisory Board minutes, 10 March 1941, 2, App. 1, Report
of CAS, 9, DHist 73/1558, vol. 3.

47 Duncan to Power, 28 May 1940, HQ 927-1-1, DHist 80/408, vol. 2; secretary of
state for external affairs to dominions secretary, 13 June 1940, Power Papers,
box 53, file D1002; Canada, Department of Reconstruction and Supply, 'A Report
on the Canadian Programme of Aircraft Production and Maintenance,' nd, 83-4,
DHist 72/652

48 Supervisory Board minutes, 10 June 1940, 2, App. 1, Report of CAS, 1-2, 5 Aug.
1940, App. 1, Report of CAS, 2, DHist 73/1558, vol. 2; Supervisory Board
minutes, 13 Jan. 1941, Report of CAS, 1, App. B, ibid., vol. 3

49 Great Britain, *History of RAF Training*, 34, 72-3, 120-1, 154-5, 159; 'BCATP Flying
Training,' nd, 'Service Flying Training: Syllabus of Instruction,' 3, DHist
181.009 (D89A)

50 'BCATP Flying Training,' nd, 'Service Flying Training: Organization and Administration,' 1, 'Syllabus of Instruction,' 2-3, DHist 181.009 (D89A); BCATP *Agreement, 1939*, App. 1, Table A; Supervisory Board minutes, 5 Aug. 1940, App. 1,
Report of CAS, 2, 9 Sept. 1940, App. 1, Report of CAS, 2-3, 11 Nov. 1940, App.
1, Report of CAS, DHist 73/1558, vol. 2; Supervisory Board minutes, 19 Jan. 1942,
App. 1, Report of CAS, 7, ibid., vol. 4; Canada, *Final Report of the Chief of the
Air Staff*, 46

51 Supervisory Board minutes, 10 June 1940, App. 1, Report of CAS, 5, DHist 73/
1558, vol. 2; Supervisory Board minutes, 13 Jan. 1941, App. 1, Report of CAS,
5, ibid., vol. 3; Croil to minister, 18 and 24 May 1940, Power Papers, box 54, file
D1011

52 Supervisory Board minutes, 9 Oct. 1940, App. 1, Report of CAS, 3, 11 Nov. 1940,
App. 1, Report of CAS, 3, 6, 9 Dec. 1940, App. 1, Report of CAS, 6, DHist
73/1558, vol. 2; Berry to Manning, 7 March 1960, Lagace to Manning, 9 March
1960, DHist 74/486

53 Supervisory Board minutes, 15 July 1940, 1-4, 5 Aug. 1940, App. 1, Report of
CAS, 4, 16 Aug. 1940, 6, DHist 73/1558, vol. 2; dominions secretary to UK high
commissioner, 13 July 1940, UK high commissioner to dominions secretary, 16
and 19 July 1940, Churchill to King, 5 Sept. 1940, PRO, Air 46/8

54 J. de N. Kennedy, *History of the Department of Munitions and Supply, Canada in
the Second World War*, I: *Production Branches and Crown Companies* (Ottawa
1950), 147-9; Wilson, 'Aerodrome Construction,' 35; Supervisory Board minutes,
15 July 1940, 3, DHist 73/1558, vol. 2; 'History of the British Commonwealth
Air Training Plan,' March 1942, 3, HQ 927-1-1, DHist 80/408, vol. 6

55 No 31 General Reconnaissance School, ORB daily diary, 29 Dec. 1940, DHist; 31
Service Flying Training School [SFTS], ORB daily diary, 28 Aug. 1940 to 23 Feb.
1941, DHist

56 Stacey, *Arms, Men and Governments*, 34-5; draft 'Memorandum of Agreement in
Respect of the Administration of R.C.A.F. Squadrons in the United Kingdom,'

and of R.A.F. Schools in Canada,' 3 June 1941, HQ 19-10-11, PAC, RG 24, vol. 5229; Supervisory Board minutes, 5 Aug. 1940, 2, 16 Aug. 1940, 4-5, DHist 73/1558, vol. 2; Supervisory Board minutes, 15 Sept. 1941, App. I, Report of CAS, I, ibid., vol. 4

57 McKean to Garrod, 24 Feb. 1941, PRO, Air 20/1375

58 McKean to Garrod, 3 April 1941, Howard memorandum, 25 March 1941, ibid.

59 F.J. Hatch, 'The Spirit of Little Norway,' *High Flight*, I, 5, 171-80; H.W. Looseley, 'History of the Royal Norwegian Air Force in Canada,' unpublished narrative, 23 July 1945, DHist 74/22

60 Canadian high commissioner to secretary of state for external affairs, 8 July 1940, Breadner to deputy minister (Air), 18 July 1940, Canadian high commissioner to secretary of state for external affairs, 19 Aug. 1940, Chevrier to Mayrand, 19 Sept. 1940, de Gaulle to Canadian high commissioner, 24 Feb. 1941, Gough to CAS, 15 May 1941, de Carteret to assistant undersecretary of state for external affairs, 26 Sept. 1941, Frederick Hudd to secretary of state for external affairs, 14 Jan. 1942, HQ 15-21-2 pt I, PAC, RG 24, vol. 5197; secretary of state for external affairs to Canadian high commissioner, 17 Oct. 1941, DCER, VIII, 621-2

61 No 32 SFTS, ORB, 12 April 1942, DHist

62 No 2 SFTS, ORB daily diary, I Oct. 1940, App. A, DHist

63 R.V. Manning, 'Graduation of the First Pilot Course, B.C.A.T.P.' *Roundel*, XII, Sept. 1960, 18-20; Supervisory Board minutes, 13 Jan. 1941, App. I, Report of CAS, 5, DHist 73/1558, vol. 3

64 R.V. Manning, 'Graduation of the First Observer Course, BCATP,' *Roundel*, XII, Oct. 1960, 14-15; I Air Navigation School, ORB daily diary, 25 Oct. 1940, DHist; Supervisory Board minutes, 9 Dec. 1940, App. I, Report of CAS, 6, DHist 73/1558, vol. 2; Supervisory Board minutes, 13 Jan. 1941, App. I, Report of CAS, 5-6, ibid., vol. 3

65 Power, *A Party Politician*, 206-7

66 R.S. Malone, *Portrait of a War, 1939-1943* (Toronto 1983), 17-18

67 Dominions secretary to secretary of state for external affairs, 20 Nov. 1940, DCER, VII, 692; Robert Bothwell and William Kilbourn, *C.D. Howe: a Biography* (Toronto 1979), 9-12

68 RCAF Overseas Headquarters, London, to CAS, message A.91, 26 Dec. 1940, Pearson to Stevenson and enclosed memorandum of agreement, 7 Jan. 1941, OSHQ s.1-6, DHist 80/481, vol. I; Stacey, *Arms, Men and Government*, 263, App. I

69 Dominions Office to Government of Canada, no 178, 9 Dec. 1940, Sinclair to Ralston and attached aide-memoire, 7 Jan. 1941, RCAF Overseas Headquarters to CAS, A.117, 8 Jan. 1941, OSHQ 5.1-6, DHist 80/481, vol. I

70 House of Commons, *Debates*, 28 Feb. 1941, 1119-42

71 Supervisory Board minutes, 13 Jan. 1941, App. I, Report of deputy CAS, 7, 10 Feb. 1941, App. I, Report of CAS, 9, DHist 73/1558, vol. 3; Supervisory Board minutes, 15 Sept. 1941, App. I, Report of CAS, 11, 12 Oct. 1941, App. I, Report of CAS, 13-14, 10 Nov. 1941, App. I, Report of CAS, 13, 15 Dec. 1941, App. I, Report of CAS, 13, 19 Jan. 1942, App. I, Report of CAS, 12, ibid., vol. 4; House of Commons, *Debates*, 26 Feb. 1941, 1053

72 Secretary of state for external affairs to dominions secretary, 13 April 1941,

dominions secretary to secretary of state for external affairs, 6 May 1941, DCER, VII, 713-14; Supervisory Board minutes, 19 Jan. 1942, App. I, Report of CAS, 13, DHist 73/1558, vol. 4

73 John Slessor, *The Central Blue: Recollections and Reflections* (London 1956), 308; secretary of state for external affairs to Canadian high commissioner, 13 Nov. 1941, Canadian high commissioner to secretary of state for external affairs, 20 Nov. 1941, DCER, VII, 719-22

74 House of Commons, *Debates*, 17 March 1941, 1606; Stevenson to secretary DND for Air, 28 Jan. 1941, OSHQ S.1-6, DHist 80/481, vol. I

75 'R.C.A.F. Personnel History,' 130, 188-9, DHist 74/7, vol. I; Supervisory Board minutes, 9 Oct. 1940, App. I, Report of CAS, 5, DHist 73/1558, vol. 2; 'The History of the A.M.P. Division,' unpublished narrative, 1944, 166, DHist 74/14

76 'R.C.A.F. Personnel History,' 515-32, DHist 74/7, vol. 3; Supervisory Board minutes, 20 Oct. 1941, App. I, Report of CAS, 11, DHist 73/1558, vol. 4; Supervisory Board minutes, 15 June 1942, App. I, Report of CAS, 15, ibid., vol. 5; Supervisory Board minutes, 18 Jan. 1943, App. I, Report of CAS, 9, ibid., vol. 6

77 'The History of the A.M.P. Division,' 42-59, DHist 74/14; 'Manning the R.C.A.F.: a Short History of the Directorate of Manning,' unpublished narrative, nd, 9, DHist 74/15; Supervisory Board minutes, 20 Oct. 1941, App. I, Report of CAS, 12, DHist 73/1558, vol. 4; Supervisory Board minutes, 20 April 1942, App. I, Report of CAS, 10, ibid., vol. 5; Sully to air member for organization, 8 Aug. 1942, 'Organization and Establishments Committee, Submission No. 516,' 9 Sept. 1942, HQ 282-2-1, pt I, PAC, RG 24, vol. 3310

78 'R.C.A.F. Personnel History,' 544, 574-5, 582, 584-5, 588, 591, 609, App. D, DHist 74/7, vol. 3; Canadian minister in Washington to secretary of state for external affairs, 26 June 1941, HQ 45-10-2, PAC, RG 24, vol. 5368; Armour to Dominion Aeronautical Association, 22 July 1941, Clayton Knight Papers, DHist 80/68, file 44; J.M. Hitsman, 'Manpower Problems of the Royal Canadian Air Force during the Second World War,' unpublished narrative, 1953, 42-4, DHist 74/12

79 RCAF Overseas Headquarters to CAS, message A.391, 26 April 1941, CAS to RCAF Overseas Headquarters, X.38, 3 May 1941, OSHQ S.1-6, DHist 80/481, vol. I; Supervisory Board minutes, 9 June 1941, App. I, Report of CAS, 5, DHist 73/1558, vol. 3; Supervisory Board minutes, 14 July 1941, App. I, Report of CAS, 5, 20 Oct. 1941, App. I, Report of CAS, 5, ibid., vol. 4

80 Supervisory Board minutes, 11 May 1942, App. I, Report of CAS, 5, DHist 73/1558, vol. 5; Goddard, 'The History of Air Navigation Training in Canada,' 8, DHist 74/17

81 Great Britain, *History of RAF Training*, 74-5, 144; '(Pilot) Advanced Flying Units,' 23 Jan. 1942, PRO, Air 20/1382

82 Supervisory Board minutes, 15 Sept. 1941, 3, 10 Nov. 1941, App. I, Report of CAS, 3-5, 15 Dec. 1941, App. I, Report of CAS, 2, 19 Jan. 1942, App. I, Report of CAS, 4, DHist 73/1558, vol. 4; Supervisory Board minutes, 16 Feb. 1942, App. I, Report of CAS, 6, ibid., vol. 5; Canada, *Final Report of the Chief of the Air Staff*, 46-7

83 *BCATP Agreement, 1939*, article 10b, Table D; Supervisory Board minutes, 14 July

1941, App. 1, Report of CAS, 3-4, 19 Jan. 1942, App. 1, Report of CAS, 1, 6, App. A, DHist 73/1558, vol. 4; McKean to Garrod, 24 Feb. 1941, PRO, Air 46/10

84 Supervisory Board minutes, 11 May 1942, App. 1, Report of CAS, 15-16, DHist 73/1558, vol. 5

85 Murray Peden, *A Thousand Shall Fall* (Stittsville, Ont. 1979), 2; Supervisory Board minutes, 9 Oct. 1940, App. 1, Report of CAS, 4, 9 Dec. 1940, App. 1, Report of CAS, 2, DHist 73/1558, vol. 2; 'BCATP Flying Training,' nd, 'Initial Training Schools: Syllabus of Instruction,' DHist 181.009 (D89A)

86 'BCATP Flying Training,' nd, 'Initial Training Schools: Introduction,' 1, 'Initial Training Schools: Syllabus of Instruction,' 6, DHist 181.009 (D89A); 'Synthetic Training, the Visual Link Trainer,' unpublished narrative, nd, 1-37, DHist 74/19, vol. 1; Avant to Douglas, 2 June 1981, A.F. Avant biographical file, DHist

87 'BCATP Flying Training,' nd, 'Initial Training Schools: Quality of Instruction,' 'Initial Training Schools: Syllabus of Instruction,' 1, 4-5, DHist 181.009 (D89A)

88 Supervisory Board minutes, 11 Nov. 1940, App. 1, Report of CAS, 2, 10 Nov. 1941, App. 1, Report of CAS, 4, 15 Dec. 1941, App. 1, Report of CAS, 2, App. A, DHist 73/1558, vol. 4; 'BCATP Flying Training,' nd, 'The Elementary Flying Training School: Syllabus of Instruction,' 1-2, 4-7, 10, 'Training Aircraft,' 5-6, DHist 181.009 (D89A); Morris, *Artists and Airmen*, 23; Baker letter, 15 Sept. 1981, 3, R.E. Baker biographical file, DHist

89 'BCATP Flying Training,' nd, 'The Elementary Flying Training School: Syllabus of Instruction,' 4, 6-7, DHist 181.009 (D89A)

90 Leckie to No 1 Training Command, 20 Jan. 1941, HQ 306-100-A65 pt 1, quoted in Histman 'Manpower Problems of the Royal Canadian Air Force in the Second World War,' 39, DHist 74/12

91 Richard Gentil, *Trained to Intrude* (London 1974), 44, 46; 'BCATP Flying Training,' nd, 'The Elementary Flying Training School: Syllabus of Instruction,' 4, DHist 181.009 (D89A)

92 Morris, *Artists and Airmen*, 25; Peden, *A Thousand Shall Fall*, 36; Senator Godfrey interview, 22 Feb. 1977, J.M. Godfrey biographical file, DHist

93 'BCATP Flying Training,' nd, 'The Elementary Flying Training School: Syllabus of Instruction,' 1-2, 4-7, 10, 'Training Aircraft,' 5-6, DHist 181.009 (D89A); Supervisory Board minutes, 10 Nov. 1941, App. 1, Report of CAS, 4, DHist 73/1558, vol. 4; Peden, *A Thousand Shall Fall*, 47; Baker letter, 15 Sept. 1981, 6, R.E. Baker biographical file, DHist

94 'BCATP Flying Training,' nd, 'The Elementary Flying Training Schools: Instructor Policy,' 9-12, DHist 181.009 (D89A)

95 Ibid., 5-6

96 Ibid., 6

97 Ibid., 6-8, 12

98 Ibid., 8, 12; Supervisory Board minutes, 11 May 1942, App. 1, Report of CAS, 2, DHist 73/1558, vol. 5; Supervisory Board minutes, 15 Nov. 1943, 5, App. III, ibid., vol. 8; 'BCATP Flying Training,' nd, 'The Elementary Flying Training Schools: The Civilian Operated Schools,' 7, 'Instructor Policy,' 6, DHist 181.009 (D89A)

99 'BCATP Flying Training,' nd, 'The Service Flying Training Schools: Organization and Administration,' 1, 3-4, 7, DHist 181.009 (D89A)

100 'BCATP Flying Training,' nd, 'The Service Flying Training Schools: Syllabus of Instruction,' 4, 'Training Aircraft,' 5, DHist 181.009 (D89A); Great Britain, *History of RAF Training*, 71

101 Samuel Kostenuk and John Griffin, *RCAF Squadron Histories and Aircraft, 1924-1968* (Toronto 1977), 229-30

102 Peden, *A Thousand Shall Fall*, 31; Len Morgan, *The AT-6 Harvard* (Famous Aircraft Series; New York 1965), 11; 'BCATP Flying Training,' nd, 'Service Flying Training: Training Aircraft,' 6, DHist 181.009 (D89A)

103 'Flying Training,' nd, 'Service Flying Training, BCATP Syllabus of Instruction,' 4, table, DHist 181.009 (D89A); Great Britain, *History of RAF Training*, 34

104 Morgan, *AT-6 Harvard*, 13-14

105 Great Britain, *History of RAF Training*, 90; J.R. Wood, 'My War Memoirs,' Dec. 1980, 3, J.R. Wood biographical file, DHist

106 Goddard, 'The History of Air Navigation Training in Canada,' 15, 27-8, App. V: 'Air Observers School (14 weeks),' DHist 74/17; Supervisory Board minutes, 21 Sept. 1942, App. I, Report of CAS, App. D, DHist 73/1558, vol. 6; *BCATP Agreement, 1939*, Table D

107 Canada, *Final Report of the Chief of the Air Staff*, 17; Goddard, 'The History of Air Navigation Training in Canada,' 18-19

108 Goddard, 'The History of Air Navigation Training in Canada,' 21-3, 42-3

109 'No 6 Group, Points for A.M.T.'s Visit – 3rd August, 1941,' PRO, Air 20/1385; Supervisory Board minutes, 5 Aug. 1940, App. I, Report of CAS, 3, 9 Dec. 1940, App. I, Report of CAS, 2, DHist 73/1558, vol. 2; Canada, *Final Report of the Chief of the Air Staff*, 17-18

110 Supervisory Board minutes, 9 Oct. 1940, App. I, Report of CAS, 4, 9 Dec. 1940, App. I, Report of CAS, 3, DHist 73/1558, vol. 2; Thompson to Bezeau, 23 Sept. 1981, M.W. Thompson biographical file, DHist; Corey to Bezeau, 19 July 1982, H.L. Corey biographical file, DHist

111 Canada, *Final Report of the Chief of the Air Staff*, 17-18; Smith to Bezeau, 25 Aug. 1981, J.K. Smith biographical file, DHist

112 'Notes on Meetings Held in A.M.T.'s Room on 4th and 7th April 1941,' PRO, Air 20/1385; Supervisory Board minutes, 12 May 1941, App. I, Report of CAS, 6, 9 June 1941, App. I, Report of CAS, 6, DHist 73/1558, vol. 3

113 UK high commissioner to undersecretary of state for external affairs, 23 Oct. 1941, DCER, VII, 716-17

114 Great Britain, *Flying Training*, I, App. 2; Canada, *Final Report of the Chief of the Air Staff*, 47; Supervisory Board minutes, 20 July 1942, App. I, Report of CAS, 7, DHist 73/1558, vol. 5 (cf 13 Aug. 1942, App. I, Report of CAS, 9, ibid., vol. 6)

CHAPTER 7: MID-WAR MODIFICATIONS

1 C.P. Stacey, *Arms, Men and Governments: the War Policies of Canada, 1939-1945* (Ottawa 1970), 257-8. See also Queen's University Archives, C.G. Power Papers, box 58, folder D1028.

2 'The Ralston-Sinclair Agreement,' Stacey, *Arms, Men and Governments*, App. I. See also HQS 15-1-440, PAC, RG 24, vol. 5178.

3 Power's report on his meetings in the United Kingdom, 30 July 1941, W.L.M. King Papers, PAC, MG 26 J 4, vol. 347, file 3765; Stacey, *Arms, Men and Governments*, 265-8

4 Cabinet War Committee minutes, 9 Oct. 1941, PAC, RG 2, series 7c, vol. 6, microfilm reel c4654

5 Chief of the air staff [CAS] appreciation, 30 Oct. 1941, 12, DHist 112.3M2 (D477)

6 CAS to RCAF Overseas Headquarters, London, 4 Aug. 1941, no P507, HQC 20-3-1A pt 1, PAC, RG 24, vol. 5255

7 Power Papers, box 66, folder D1016, vols. 1 and 2; Breadner to Power, 16 Feb. 1942, HQC 20-3-1A pt 1, PAC, RG 24, vol. 5255

8 Power's report, King Papers, PAC, MG 26 J 4, vol. 347, file 3756

9 Air member for personnel [AMP] to minister of national defence for air, 10 Oct. 1941, HQC 20-3-1A pt 1, PAC, RG 24, vol. 5255

10 Stedman to minister of national defence for air, 7 April 1941, Power Papers, box 54, folder D1015

11 Power to King, 23 June 1941, ibid., box 58, folder D1028

12 Power's report, King Papers, PAC, MG 26 J 4, vol. 347, file 3765

13 MacDonald to Robertson, 23 Oct. 1941, HQS 55-1-1, PAC, RG 24, vol. 5387

14 Cabinet War Committee minutes, 29 Oct. 1941, PAC, RG 2, series 7c, vol. 6, microfilm reel c4654

15 Power to MacDonald, 13 March 1942, Power Papers, box 54, folder D1014

16 MacDonald to Robertson, 20 Jan. 1942, HQS 55-1-1, PAC, RG 24, vol. 5387

17 Empire Air Training Scheme [EATS] Committee minutes, 2 and 16 Jan. 1942, PRO, Air 20/1379A

18 Cabinet War Committee minutes, 23 Jan. 1942, PAC, RG 2, series 7c, vol. 6, microfilm reel c4654

19 De Carteret to undersecretary of state for external affairs, 2 Feb. 1942, sent to United Kingdom on 7 Feb., Power Papers, box 53, folder D1004

20 Permanent Joint Board on Defence [PJBD] 23rd Recommendation, in Stanley W. Dziuban, *Military Relations between the United States and Canada, 1939-1945* (United States Army in World War II, Special Studies; Washington 1959), 356

21 CAS to minister, 21 Jan. 1942, HQS 45-9-26, PAC, RG 24, vol. 5366

22 Cabinet War Committee minutes, 23 Jan. 1942, PAC, RG 2, series 7c, vol. 8, microfilm reel c4874

23 Canadian air attaché, Washington, to Air Force Headquarters [AFHQ], 10 March 1942, no A4, and same to same, 25 March 1942, no A370, HQS 45-9-26, PAC, RG 24, vol. 5366

24 Anderson to deputy CAS (signed by Heakes), 2 March 1942, and copy of Stark to Little, 20 Feb. 1942, ibid.

25 Power to Robertson, 2 March 1942, ibid.

26 Dominions secretary to UK high commissioner, 28 Feb. 1942, no 418, ibid.

27 Power to Robertson, 2 March 1942, ibid.

28 Canadian air attaché, Washington, to AFHQ, 10 March 1942, no A4, ibid.

29 Cabinet War Committee minutes, 5 March 1942, PAC, RG 2, series 7c, vol. 8, microfilm reel c4874

30 MacDonald to Robertson, 10 March 1942, Power Papers, box 53, folder D1004

31 Cabinet War Committee minutes, 18 March 1942, PAC, RG 2, series 7c, vol. 8, microfilm reel C4874

32 Dominions Office to Government of Canada, 19 March 1942, no 4 (secret and personal), secretary of state to Mackenzie King, HQS 15-1-166 pt 5, PAC, RG 24, vol. 5173, copy in PRO, Air 19/339

33 Power, notes to file, 24 March 1942, Power Papers, box 63, folder D1077

34 Robertson to MacDonald, draft, 24 March 1942, ibid., box 53, folder D1004

35 Breadner to Power, 24 March 1942, ibid., box 66, folder D1106, vol. 1

36 UK high commissioner to Dominions Office, 24 March 1942, no 570, and 25 March 1942, no 575 and no 576, PRO, Air 2/8181

37 Balfour to AMP, air member for training [AMT], air member for supply and organization, permanent undersecretary, director general organization, 27 March 1942, Dominions Office to UK high commissioner, 9 April 1942, no 714, PRO, Air 19/339

38 Dominions Office to UK high commissioner, 3 April 1942, no 677, PRO, Air 2/8181; Duff to Robertson, 4 April 1942, HQS 55-1-1, PAC, RG 24, vol. 5387

39 Robertson to King, 6 April 1942, King Papers, PAC, MG 26 J 4, vol. 237, file 2348, Cabinet War Committee minutes, 9 April 1942, PAC, RG 2, series 7c, vol. 9, microfilm reel C4874; UK high commissioner to Dominions Office, 10 April 1942, no 706, PRO, Air 2/8181

40 UK high commissioner to Dominions Office, 11 April 1942, no 717, PRO, Air 19/339

41 Dominions Office to UK high commissioner, 11 April 1942, no 736, PRO, Air 2/8181

42 UK high commissioner to Dominions Office, 11 April 1942, no 725, ibid.

43 Arnold to Breadner, 2 April 1942, HQS 45-9-26, PAC, RG 24, vol. 5366

44 Heakes to CAS, 9 April 1942, ibid.

45 Same to same, 13 April 1942, ibid.

46 Breadner to Arnold, 11 April 1942, in CAS to Canadian air attaché, Washington, 11 April 1942, no 206, same to same, 13 April 1942, no C207, ibid.,

47 J.W. Pickersgill, *The Mackenzie King Record*, I: *1939-1944* (Toronto 1960), 409-10

48 Stacey, *Arms, Men and Governments*, 279

49 Prime minister's personal telegram, no T588/2, president to former naval person (Churchill), cable no 136, received 18 April 1942, PRO, Air 19/339

50 Text of release in Canadian minister in the United States to secretary of state for external affairs, 16 April 1942, no WA675, HQS 55-1-10, PAC, RG 24, vol. 5388

51 Robertson to Pearson, 16 April 1942, ibid.,

52 Pearson to King, 25 April 1942, King Papers, PAC, MG 26 J 4, vol. 237, file 2348

53 Department of External Affairs to Canadian high commissioner in London, 28 April 1942, no 839, 29 April 1942, no 850, External Affairs draft on conference procedure, 6 May 1942, HQS 55-1-1, PAC, RG 24, vol. 5387

54 Heeney to King, 13 April 1942, King Papers, PAC, MG 26 J 4, vol. 347, file 3768

55 UK high commissioner to Dominions Office, 22 April 1942, no 781, PRO, Air 2/8181; 'Notes on Proposals for a Training Conference' for secretary of state, 19 April 1942, PRO, Air 19/339; Duff to Robertson, 4 May 1942, Duff to Pearson, 12

May 1942, HQS 55-2-1, PAC, RG 24, vol. 5388. See also Canadian minister in Washington to secretary of state for external affairs, 5 May 1942, no WA888, and Pearson to Duff, 6 May 1942, HQS 55-1-1, PAC, RG 24, vol. 5387.

56 De Carteret to Robertson, 5 May 1942, HQS 55-2-1, PAC, RG 24, vol. 5388; UK high commissioner to Dominions Office, 22 April 1942, no 787, PRO, Air 2/8181

57 RCAF Overseas Headquarters to CAS, 7 May 1942, no X5695073, HQS 55-1-1, PAC, RG 24, vol. 5387

58 Record of meeting in AMP's room, 8 May 1942, PRO, Air 2/8181. See also 'Ottawa Air Training Conference: Minutes and Agreement, May-June 1942,' 129ff, DHist 181.003 (D4776).

59 *Ottawa Air Training Conference, May 1942: Report of the Conference* (Ottawa 1942), 10-13, 22-3, copy in DHist 77/515

60 'Ottawa Air Training Conference,' 16 April 1943, HQS 55-1-10, PAC, RG 24, vol. 5388

61 UK high commissioner to Dominions Office, 19 May 1942, no 996, 22 May 1942, no 1021, PRO, Air 2/8181. See also the unpublished conference report and minutes, 'Ottawa Air Training Conference,' 65-90, copy in DHist 181.003 (D4776).

62 'Ottawa Air Training Conference,' minutes of meeting of Committee on Co-ordination of Training Capacity, 19 May 1942, 112-17, DHist 181.003 (D4776)

63 'Ottawa Air Training Conference,' report of the Conference Committee to the final plenary session of the conference, 43-4, ibid.

64 *Ottawa Air Training Conference, May 1942: Report of the Conference*, 24

65 Cumyn to BCATP Supervisory Board, 30 June 1942, HQS 15-9-85 pt 1, PAC, RG 24, vol. 5185

66 Robertson to de Carteret, 28 July 1942, Walsh to Leckie, 13 Aug. 1942, ibid.

67 Moffat to secretary of state for external affairs, 28 Sept. 1942, ibid.

68 Air Ministry to RAF Delegation, Washington, Garrod to Foster, 21 Nov. 1942, Webber W398, PRO, Air 19/339

69 Walsh to AFHQ, 5 Jan. 1943, no A193, Walsh to Breadner, 11 Jan. 1943, no A418, HQS 15-9-58 pt 1, PAC, RG 24, vol. 5185

70 Stacey, *Arms, Men and Governments*, 281-2

71 Quoted, ibid.

72 'Ottawa Air Training Conference,' App. 1, 24 May 1942, 189-90, DHist 181.003 (D4776)

73 'Agreement Amending and Extending the British Commonwealth Air Training Plan Agreement of December 17, 1939, Relating to the Training of Pilots and Aircraft Crews in Canada and their Subsequent Service, between the United Kingdom, Canada, Australia and New Zealand, Dated at Ottawa, June 5, 1942' (Ottawa 1942), 9, copy in DHist 181.003 (D4776)

74 Ibid., 10; EATS Committee minutes, 13 March 1942, PRO, Air 20/1379A

75 Canada, Parliament, House of Commons, *Debates*, 13 May 1942, 2410-11

76 'Ottawa Air Training Conference,' App. M, 196-9, DHist 181.003 (D4776)

77 MacDonald to Attlee, 16 June 1942, PRO, Air 19/339

78 'Ottawa Air Training Conference,' 174-5, DHist 181.003 (D4776)

79 'Agreement Amending and Extending the British Commonwealth Air Training
    Plan Agreement of December 17, 1939,' 5 June 1942, copy in DHist 73/1558,
    vol. 10; 34 Service Flying Training School, operations record book daily diary, 12
    April 1942, DHist
80 'Agreement Amending and Extending the British Commonwealth Air Training
    Plan Agreement of December 17, 1939,' 5 June 1942, App. III, DHist 73/1558,
    vol. 10; 'Agreement Amending and Extending the Empire Air Training Scheme
    Agreement of 27th November, 1939 ... between the United Kingdom and Aus-
    tralia,' 31 March 1943, DHist 83/193; 'Agreement Amending and Extending the
    Empire Air Training Scheme Agreement of November 27th, 1939 ... between the
    United Kingdom and New Zealand,' March 1943, DHist 83/192; Canada, Air
    Force, *Final Report of the Chief of the Air Staff to the Members of the
    Supervisory Board British Commonwealth Air Training Plan* (Ottawa, 16 April
    1945), 26, copy in DHist 81/221
81 'Final Minutes of a Meeting Held on April 3rd to Discuss the Future Expansion of
    Bomber Command,' 5 April 1941, 'Notes of Meeting Held in the Air Council
    Room ... 12th February 1942,' Garrod to CAS, 19 March 1942, Harris to Group HQ,
    6 April 1942, PRO, Air 20/1385
82 Laing to AMT, 4 March 1942, Garrod to CAS, 19 March 1942, 'Note of a Meeting
    ... 29th March, 1942,' letter to air officer commanding Bomber Command, 5
    April 1942, ibid; Canada, *Final Report of the Chief of the Air Staff*, 18-19
83 Canada, *Final Report of the Chief of the Air Staff*, 18-19
84 'Notes of a Meeting ... 29th March, 1942,' PRO, Air 20/1385
85 Canada, *Final Report of the Chief of the Air Staff*, 16
86 Ibid., 19-20
87 Ibid., 19, 48; Supervisory Board minutes, 16 Nov. 1942, App. I, Report of CAS,
    DHist 73/1558, vol. 6
88 Canada, *Final Report of the Chief of the Air Staff*, 20

CHAPTER 8: THE PLAN IN MATURITY

1 Central Flying School, operations record book [ORB] daily diary, 5 Aug. 1940,
    DHist
2 Carling-Kelly to secretary Department of National Defence [DND] for Air, 5 March
    1942, HQ 233-7-8 pt I, PAC, RG 24, vol. 3266. See also chief of the air staff
    [CAS] to air officer commanding [AOC] RCAF in Great Britain, 5 June 1941, HQS
    45-9-10, ibid., vol. 5366.
3 Carling-Kelly to secretary DND for Air, 20 April 1943, and enclosures, HQ 233-7-8
    pt 2, PAC, RG 24, vol. 3267
4 Great Britain, Air Ministry, air member for training, *Notes on the History of RAF
    Training, 1939-44* (np Jan. 1945), 193
5 Carling-Kelly to secretary DND for Air, 20 April 1943, and enclosures, HQ 233-7-8
    pt 2, PAC, RG 24, vol. 3267
6 CAS to AOC, 15 July 1941, HQ 233-7-8 pt I, ibid.
7 Report on staff pilots, 18 Nov. 1944, HQ 233-7-6, ibid., vol. 3266
8 Carling-Kelly to secretary DND for Air, 20 April 1943, and enclosures, HQ 233-7-8
    pt 2, ibid., vol. 3267

9 Ibid.

10 Great Britain, RAF *Training, 1939-44*, 74-5; Great Britain, Air Ministry, *Flying Training*, I: *Policy and Planning* (Air Publication 3233; np 1952), 161-3

11 Empire Air Training Scheme [EATS] Committee minutes, 21 Nov. 1941, PRO, Air 20/1379A

12 RCAF Overseas Headquarters to CAS, 31 Jan. 1941, HQ 927-1-1, DHist 80/408, vol. 5

13 Leckie to Garrod, 13 Feb. 1941, PRO, Air 2/8086

14 Breadner to Leckie, 28 April 1941, HQS 45-9-10, PAC, RG 24, vol. 5366

15 Air Ministry to RCAF Headquarters, 3 June 1941, ibid.

16 Cameron to air member for training [AMT], 28 Aug. 1942, HQ 45-8-39, ibid.

17 Director of flying training to air officer commanding-in-chief [AOCinC] Flying Training Command, 12 May 1943, PRO, Air 2/8236

18 AOCinC Flying Training Command to undersecretary of state for air, 26 June 1943, and enclosure, ibid.

19 EATS Committee minutes, 16 April 1943, PRO, Air 20/1379A; Carnegie to McKean, 17 July 1944, PRO, Air 2/8236

20 AOCinC Flying Training Command to undersecretary of state for air, 26 June 1943, and enclosures, PRO, Air 2/8236

21 Max Hastings, *Bomber Command* (London 1979), 215

22 Quoted in ibid.

23 Ibid. See also John Terraine, *The Right of the Line: the Royal Air Force in the European War, 1939-1945* (Toronto 1985), 464-7

24 Loose minute, 12 July 1943, PRO, Air 2/8236

25 Air Ministry, 'Empire Air Training Scheme: an Investigation of the Standards Reached by Pilots Drawn from Different Theatres of Training,' Aug. 1944, Table I, PRO, Air 20/1379B

26 'Observations on Quality of Pilots Destined for Bomber Command,' nd, PRO, Air 14/3519

27 Drummond to Harris, draft reply, Dec. 1943, ibid.

28 Carnegie to McKean, 17 July 1944, PRO, Air 2/8236

29 Minute, nd, ibid.

30 AOCinC Flying Training Command to undersecretary of state for air, 26 June 1943, and enclosures, ibid.

31 'Consolidated Quarterly Report on Standard of Overseas Trained Pilots ... July-September 1943,' nd, ibid.

32 Air Ministry, 'Empire Air Training Scheme: an Investigation ...' Aug. 1944, PRO, Air 20/1379B

33 Ibid., 7

34 Ibid., 11

35 Based on monthly reported strengths of service flying training schools [SFTSS] in Canada, SFTS ORB daily diaries, DHist

36 Empire Central Flying School report, Aug. 1944, 17, PRO, Air 20/1379B

37 Carnegie to McKean, 17 July 1944, PRO, Air 2/8236

38 'Consolidated Quarterly Report on Standard of Overseas Trained Pilots ... July-September, 1943,' nd, ibid.

39 Carnegie to McKean, 17 July 1944, ibid.

40 Same to same, 4 Oct. 1944, ibid.

41 EATS Committee, 'Minutes of the 90th (Special) Meeting,' 2 July 1943, PRO, Air 20/1379A

42 Great Britain, *Flying Training*, I, 255-7; Air Intelligence Security Branch [AIS 8], 'RAF Personnel in Canada – Curtailment of Flying Training,' 26 Aug. 1944, PRO, Air 40/1

43 Pringle to CAS, Ottawa, 14 Sept. 1944, HQS 45-9-10, PAC, RG 24, vol. 5366

44 Lawrence interview, 4 May 1982, T.A. Lawrence biographical file, DHist

45 Seward, AOC 12 Operational Training Group, to commanding officers, 1 and 31 General Reconnaissance schools, 6 Aug. 1943, HQ 450-19/0, PAC, RG 24, vol. 3394

46 Director of operational training to director of training plans and requirements, 27 Oct. 1942, ibid.

47 CAS to AOCs training commands, 24 June and 12 Oct. 1942, HQ 450-21/0 pt 1, ibid.

48 AOC No 1 Training Command to secretary DND for Air, 1 Oct. 1942, HQ 450-21/0 pt 2, ibid.

49 CAS to AOCs training commands, 31 May 1943, ibid.

50 AMT to air member for personnel, 16 April 1943, ibid.

51 Garrod to CAS, 18 June 1941, PRO, Air 20/2769; Garrod to air member for supply and organization [AMSO], 18 June 1941, PRO, Air 20/1385

52 AMSO, 'No. 6 Group, Points for A.M.T.'s Visit – 3rd August 1941,' PRO, Air 20/1385

53 AMSO, 'Notes on Meetings held in A.M.T.s Room on 4th and 7th April 1941,' ibid.

54 Quarterly summaries of air exercises, bombing and gunnery schools [B&GS], 2 March 1942-8 June 1942, HQ 450-21/0 pt 1, and 29 June 1942-23 Oct. 1942, HQ 450-21/0 pt 2, PAC, RG 24, vol. 3394

55 Liaison officer-in-chief, London, to CAS, 14 Dec. 1942, ibid.

56 Cameron to Leckie, 14 Sept. 1942, HQ 45-8-39, PAC, RG 24, vol. 5366

57 Liaison officer-in-chief, London, to CAS, 14 Dec. 1942, HQ 450-21/0 pt 2, ibid., vol. 3394

58 Leckie to UK Air Liaison Mission, 14 June 1943, ibid.

59 AOCinC Flying Training Command to undersecretary of state for air, 27 Sept. 1944, and enclosures, PRO, Air 2/8236

60 Ibid.

61 F.J. Hatch, *The Aerodrome of Democracy: Canada and the British Commonwealth Air Training Plan, 1939-1945* (Department of National Defence, Directorate of History, Monograph Series No 1; Ottawa 1983)

62 Material and quotations from interview transcripts in the A.R. MacKenzie biographical file, DHist, unless otherwise noted

63 No 31 SFTS, ORB daily diary, 28 Jan. 1941, DHist. See also Brereton Greenhous and Norman Hillmer, 'The Impact of the British Commonwealth Air Training Plan on Western Canada: Some Saskatchewan Case Studies,' *Journal of Canadian Studies/Revue d' études canadiennes*, XVI, fall/winter 1981, 133-44.

64 'BCATP – Record of Accidents by Students,' Jan. 1942, 4, PAC, RG 24, acc. 83-4/164 (formerly DHist 181.009 (D4761) and PARC acc. 69G2)

65 Material and quotations from interview transcripts in the S.F. Wise biographical file, DHist, unless otherwise noted

66 K.M. Molson and H.A. Taylor, *Canadian Aircraft since 1909* (Stittsville, Ont. 1982), 330

67 Arthur B. Wahlroth, 'Wellington Pilot,' *CAHS Journal*, xix, summer 1981, 49

68 Canada, Air Force, *Final Report of the Chief of the Air Staff to the Members of the Supervisory Board, British Commonwealth Air Training Plan* (Ottawa, 16 April 1945), 41, copy in DHist 81/221

69 Owen Thetford, *Aircraft of the Royal Air Force since 1918* (New York 1968), 46-7, 298-9, 440

70 Great Britain, RAF *Training, 1939-44*, 147

71 Great Britain, *Flying Training*, I, 39-40, 48, 58-9

72 S. Kostenuk and J. Griffin, RCAF *Squadron Histories and Aircraft, 1924-1968* (Toronto 1977), 36-7; 'A Brief History of 13 Operational Training Squadron,' DHist 181.009 (D5039)

73 'Report: Chief of Air Staff's Mission to United Kingdom,' 3 Feb. 1941, App. I, 'Notes of a Discussion in A.M.T.'s Room on 27th December 1940,' HQS 45-8-27, PAC, RG 24, vol. 5366

74 UK high commissioner to Dominions Office, CAS from Slessor, 4 Jan. 1941, PRO, Air 19/247

75 Minute, 7 Jan. 1941, ibid.

76 No 31 Operational Training Unit [OTU], ORB daily diary, DHist

77 Ibid.

78 Ibid., April 1942

79 No 32 OTU, ORB daily diary, Nov. and Dec. 1941, DHist

80 Ibid., Dec. 1941

81 Ibid., Nov. 1942 summary

82 No 34 OTU, ORB daily diary, 11 Sept. 1942, DHist

83 RCAF file S.42-9-1 pt I, fol. 39, cited by Flying Officer Hodgins, 'No. 36 O.T.U.,' in 'O.T.U.'s under the B.C.A.T.P,' unpublished narrative [1945], 17, DHist 74/13. The files relating to OTUs seem to have figured largely among the approximately 80 per cent of RCAF HQ central registry files destroyed, according to the introduction to the RG 24 Air Force Finding Aid prepared by the PAC. It appears that Hodgins's undated report on OTUs was prepared from those documents before they were destroyed.

84 W.F. Craven and J.L. Cate, eds., *The Army Air Forces in World War II*, I: *Plans and Early Operations, January 1939 to August 1942* (Chicago 1948), 631

85 'Ottawa Air Training Conference, Minutes and Proceedings, May-June, 1942,' vol. v, App. I, 189, 'Minute by AMO R.C.A.F. & DGO Air Ministry on B.C.A.T.P. Training Capacity in Canada ...' 24 May 1942, DHist 181.003 (D4776)

86 Great Britain, RAF *Training, 1939-44*, 162

87 Cowley to CAS, 28 April 1942, HQS 19-7-38, PAC, RG 24, vol. 5221

88 Hodgins, 'No. 1 Operational Training Unit,' chart, 'O.T.U.'s under the B.C.A.T.P.,' DHist 74/13

89 'Notes on Points discussed between D.T.O., Group Captain Oliver and Air Commodore Brown ... on 18 June, 1943,' PRO, Air 2/3124

90 Ibid.

91 Beisiegel to AOC EAC, 31 Dec. 1943, S 42-4-1, fol. 3, cited in Hodgins, 'No. 1 Operational Training Unit,' 1, DHist 74/13

92 CAS to chief of the general staff, nd, S 42-4-1, fol. 4, cited in ibid.; 1 OTU, ORB daily diary, Feb.-Aug. 1944, DHist

93 Leckie to Air Ministry, nd, S 42-4-1, cited in Hodgins, 'No. 1 Operational Training Unit,' 3, DHist 74/13

94 Supervisory Board minutes, 18 Oct. 1943, DHist 73/1558, vol. 8

95 Supervisory Board minutes, 20 Dec. 1943, App. 1, Report of CAS, 1, ibid.

96 'Agreements and Decisions Recorded as the Result of Discussions Held in Ottawa February 7th to February 16th, between: Capt. the Rt. Hon. H.H. Balfour ... and Air Marshal Sir Peter Drummond ... Representing the United Kingdom, and the Hon. C.G. Power and Air Marshal R. Leckie ... Representing Canada,' 16 Feb. 1943, DHist 181.009 (D878)

97 J.R. Smith and Anthony Kay, *German Aircraft of the Second World War* (London 1972), 516-19, 543-6

98 Quoted (from HQS 20-1-15) in J.M. Hitsman, 'Manpower Problems of the Royal Canadian Air Force during the Second World War,' unpublished narrative, 1953, 23, DHist 74/12

99 Power to MacDonald, 20 Oct. 1944, ibid.

100 Great Britain, *Flying Training*, 1, 267

101 Canada, *Final Report of the Chief of the Air Staff*, 54-5

CHAPTER 9: POLICY AND PROCUREMENT

1 W.L.M. King Diary, 24 Aug. 1939, King Papers, PAC, MG 26 J 13, quoted in C.P. Stacey, *Arms, Men and Governments: the War Policies of Canada, 1939-1945* (Ottawa 1970), 8. See also J.W. Pickersgill, *The Mackenzie King Record*, 1: *1939-1944* (Toronto 1960), 15-16.

2 Stuart to Anderson, 26 Aug. 1939, and Anderson, 'Canada's National Effort in the Early Stages of a Major War,' 27 Aug. 1939, HQS 3498 pt 13 and pt 22, PAC, RG 24, vol. 2648; Chiefs of Staff Committee, 'Canada's National Effort (Armed Forces) in the Early Stages of a Major War,' 29 Aug. 1939, DHist 181.006 (D276)

3 National Defence Headquarters, Bulletins on the Development of the RCAF, 25 Aug.-31 Dec. 1939, DHist 181.003 (D3868)

4 Chief of the air staff [CAS] to military secretary to governor general, 8 Oct. 1939, 'Policy of Distribution, War Establishment & Duties of RCAF Sqs,' DHist 77/543

5 Daily Diary, 2nd Air Mission to the United States, 24 Aug.-2 Sept. 1939, and Stedman to CAS, 3 Sept. 1939, DHist 78/478; Croil to deputy minister, 15 March 1939, S60-9-11 pt 1, PAC, RG 24, vol. 5395; Breadner to senior air officer [SAO], 'Recommendations for the Purchase of Aircraft in 1939/40 Estimates,' 17 Jan. 1939, DHist 76/198; SAO to minister of national defence, 15 Sept. 1938, DHist 76/40; Stedman to CAS, 27 Sept. 1939, HQS 5199S pt 1, PARC 395072; James Eayrs, *In Defence of Canada*, II: *Appeasement and Rearmament* (Toronto 1965), 140; Stacey, *Arms, Men and Governments*, ii. See also DHist 181.009 (D3658), passim.

6 Stacey, *Arms, Men and Governments*, 11-12; 'Department of National Defence Estimates, 1939-1940,' DHist 181.009 (D3658)

7 Croil memorandum, 'Policy Respecting the Distribution, War Establishment and

Duties of RCAF Squadrons,' 25 Sept. 1939, s8098, DHist 77/543; S. Kostenuk and J. Griffin, *RCAF Squadron Histories and Aircraft, 1924-1968* (Toronto 1977)

8 Cabinet War Committee minutes, 5 and 15 Sept. 1939, PAC, RG 2, series 7c, vol. 1, microfilm reel C4653A; Defence Council minutes, 14 Sept. 1939, DHist 112.1 (D77); Croil memorandum, 15 Sept. 1939, HQS 5199S pt 1, PARC 395072; Chiefs of Staff Committee, 'Action by the Armed Forces of Canada,' 17 Sept. 1939, App. C, DHist 112.3M2009 (D36); Croil, 'Policy Respecting the Distribution, War Establishment, and Duties of RCAF Squadrons,' 25 Sept. 1939, s8098, DHist 77/543

9 Cabinet War Committee minutes, 3 Oct. 1939, PAC, RG 2, series 7c, vol. 1, microfilm reel C4653A; Defence Council minutes, 10 Oct. 1939, DHist 112.1 (D77)

10 Croil to Rogers, 23 Nov. 1939, DHist 180.009 (D12)

11 Stacey, *Arms, Men and Governments*, 29-30

12 Cabinet War Committee minutes, 5 Sept. 1939, PAC, RG 2, series 7c, vol. 1, microfilm reel C4653A; CAS to RCAF liaison officer London, 21 Dec. 1939, s8161, DHist 181.002 (D460); estimates for 1940-1, DHist 181.003 (D2319)

13 Annis interview [1977], C.L. Annis biographical file, DHist

14 No 10 Squadron, ORB daily diary, DHist

15 J. de N. Kennedy, *History of the Department of Munitions and Supply* (Ottawa 1950), I, 4-6; Stacey, *Arms, Men and Governments*, 30, 102

16 Croil to minister, 16 March and 9 April 1940, s15-1-50 pt 1, PAC, RG 24, vol. 5170

17 Norman Ward, ed., *A Party Politician: the Memoirs of Chubby Power* (Toronto 1965), 206-7; PC 2665, 20 June 1940; Stacey, *Arms, Men and Governments*, 119-26

18 UK high commissioner in Canada to Dominions Office, no 1058, 19 May 1940, and draft reply, PRO, Air 2/3157; Cabinet War Committee minutes, 22, 23, 29 May, 3, 14, 20, 27 June, 9 July 1940, PAC, RG 2, series 7c, vol. 1, microfilm reel C4653A; King Diary for same period, PAC, MG 26 J 13

19 Appreciation by inspector general, 9 June 1940, with Defence Scheme No 3, Major War, App. B, and CAS to minister of national defence for air, 20 June 1940, approved 22 June 1940, DHist 181.002 (D107); air member for air staff [AMAS] weekly summary, DHist 79/30, vol. 1; AMAS to director of plans and operations [DPO], 21 May 1940, and air attaché Washington to AMAS, 8 June 1940, s60-3-11 pt 2, PAC, RG 24, vol. 5395

20 CAS to minister, July 1940, DHist 112.3M2 (D493)

21 Chiefs of Staff Committee, 'Defence of Canada Plan,' Aug. 1940, ibid.; Stacey, *Arms, Men and Governments*, 342ff; Joint Canada-US Defence Plan No 1, planning paper, and Stuart to Crerar, 10 Oct. 1940, DHist 112.11 (D1A)

22 CAS to minister, drafted by Johnson, 1 Oct. 1940, DHist 181.003 (D15)

23 M.M. Postan, *British War Production* (History of the Second World War, United Kingdom Civil Series; London 1952), 164-5; draft telegram, Dominions Office to UK high commissioner in Canada, 10 Nov. 1940, sent PM to PM, 25 Nov. 1940, and Dominions Office to UK high commissioner in Canada, no 2354, 30 Nov. 1940, PRO, Air 2/5260

24 Memorandum to UK high commissioner, drafted by Johnson, deputy chief of the air staff [DCAS], 28 Dec. 1940, DHist 181.002 (D107); Campbell to Dominions Office, no 2489, 30 Dec. 1940, PRO, Air 2/5260

25 PRO, Prem 3/458, Prem 3/459, Prem 3/478, Prem 3/485, passim; Cab 122/1582

26 Ralston to Power, 19 Jan. 1941, J.L. Ralston Papers, PAC, MG 27 III B 11, vol. 37; Power to Ralston, 28 Jan. 1941, s60-3-14 pt 1, PAC, RG 24, vol. 5396. See also files 60-3-9 and 60-3-15, ibid., vols. 5395 and 5397.

27 Chiefs of Staff Committee appreciation, 25 Feb. 1941, DHist 112.3M2 (D497); Cabinet War Committee minutes, 27 Feb. 1941, PAC, RG 2, series 7c, vol. 1, microfilm reel c4653A; Air Council minutes, 27 Jan. 1941, s840-108 pt 1, PARC 828985

28 Secretary of state for external affairs to dominions secretary, PM for PM, no 35, 2 March 1941, copy in DHist 193.009 (D2)

29 Dominions secretary to secretary of state for external affairs, PM for PM, no 48, 24 March 1941, ibid.

30 Slessor to dominions air liaison officer, 27 April 1941, PRO, Air 2/5260

31 Air member for supply [AMS] report, 13 June 1941, DHist 79/428, vol. 1; Kennan, minute no 54, 1 July 1941, PRO, Air 2/5260; 'Notes of a Discussion held in Air Member for Training's Room,' 5 July 1941, App. to Breadner's report on mission to the UK, 45-8-27, PAC, RG 24, vol. 5366

32 Air Council minutes, 13 Dec. 1940, 5, 10 Feb., 30 Oct. 1941, s840-108 pt 1, 2, and 3, PARC 828985; secretary of state for external affairs to dominions secretary, no 187, and reply, no 169, 27 Sept. 1941, s60-3-12 pt 1, PAC, RG 24, vol. 5395

33 See RCAF files s60-3-9, s60-3-11, and s60-3-15, PAC, RG 24, vols. 5305, 5395, and 5397.

34 I.B. Holley, *Buying Aircraft Material: Procurement for the Army Air Forces* (Washington 1964), 266

35 US and British chiefs of staff meeting, 11 Aug. 1941, PRO, Prem 3/485/5; RCAF laison officer, Ferry Command, to CAS, 15 Sept. 1941, External Affairs to Dominions Office, no 187, 18 Sept. 1941, and reply, no 163, 21 Sept. 1941, and no 169, 27 Sept. 1941, s60-3-12 pt 1, PAC, RG 24, vol. 5395; Report of Permanent Joint Board on Defence [PJBD] meeting, 10-11 Nov. 1941, PJBD Journal, vol. 2, DHist 955.013 (D10)

36 Croil report, 28 Oct. 1941, King Papers, PAC, MG 26 J 4, vol. 455

37 Breadner to Power, 28 Oct. 1941, ibid., vol. 425

38 Breadner to Power, 22 Nov. 1941, Cabinet War Committee document no 38, ibid.

39 Chiefs of Staff Committee appreciation, 10 Dec. 1941, DHist 112.3M2 (D497)

40 Ibid. See also Breadner's appreciation of 7 Dec. 1941, copy in Queen's University Archives, C.G. Power Papers, box 59, file D1030.

41 Stanley W. Dziuban, *Military Relations between the United States and Canada, 1939-1945* (United States Army in World War II, Special Studies; Washington 1959), 120

42 Pope, 'Notes on Question of United States-Canada Unity of Command,' 18 Dec. 1941, DHist 112.3M2 (D495)

43 Pope to chief of the general staff, 22 Dec. 1941, and 21 Jan. 1942, DHist 112.11 (D1A), vol. 3; PJBD Journal, 20 Jan. and 25-6 Feb. 1942, DHist 955.013 (D10); Stacey, *Arms, Men and Governments*, 349-54, 378-9

44 Officer commanding [OC] 1 Group, RCAF, memorandum, 3 March 1942, DHist 181.009 (D4655)

45 Chiefs of Staff Committee appreciation, 19 Feb. 1942, DHist 112.3M2 (D497)
46 Air officer commanding [AOC] Western Air Command [WAC] to Air Force Headquarters [AFHQ], 21 Feb. 1942, Joint Services Committee (Pacific) appreciation, 18 Feb. 1942, S201-9-1 pt 2, DHist 181.009 (D3334)
47 Heakes to AMAS, 24 Feb. 1942, S15-24-6 pt 1, PAC, RG 24, vol. 5198
48 Heakes (for AMAS) to DCAS, 12 Feb. 1942, S60-3-11 pt 2, ibid., vol. 5395
49 Power to Cabinet War Committee, 2 March 1942, King Papers, PAC, MG 26 J 4, vol. 425; Nairn to deputy minister, 10 March 1942, DHist 181.009 (D3455)
50 Chiefs of Staff Committee appreciation, 19 Feb. 1942, DHist 112.3M2 (D497)
51 Stacey, *Arms, Men and Governments*, 133-4; Mackenzie to PM, 14 Feb. 1942, I.A. Mackenzie Papers, PAC, MG 27 III B 5, vol. 47, file CNS 57. See also Gallup Poll of 5 Aug. 1942, which indicated that 65 per cent of BC residents considered 'an air raid on this province' was 'likely.'
52 Cabinet War Committee minutes, 20 Feb. 1942, PAC, RG 2, series 7c, vol. 8, microfilm reel C4874
53 Pickersgill, *The Mackenzie King Record*, I; 355; King to Cabinet War Committee, 20 Feb. 1942, King Papers, PAC, MG 26 J 4, vol. 124; King Diary, 24 Feb. 1942, PAC, MG 26 J 13
54 Robertson to Keenleyside, 2 March 1942, and Keenleyside to Robertson, 4 March 1942, Robertson to King, 2 March 1942, L.B. Pearson Papers, PAC, MG 26 N 1, vol. 25; Cabinet War Committee minutes, 5 March 1942, PAC, RG 2, series 7c, vol. 8, microfilm reel C4874
55 Stacey, *Arms, Men and Governments*, 47n, 48, 133-4; Cabinet War Committee minutes, 6 Jan., 5, 6, and 18 March 1942, PAC, RG 2, series 7c, vol. 8, microfilm reel C4874
56 Stacey, *Arms, Men and Governments*, 273-4
57 Cabinet War Committee minutes, 18 March 1942, PAC, RG 2, series 7c, vol. 8, microfilm reel C4874
58 Air member for organization [AMO] to AMAS, 29 April 1942, S19-7-38, PAC, RG 24, vol. 5221
59 Balfour to Sinclair, 26 May 1942, PRO, Air 19/339; Stacey, *Arms, Men and Governments*, 273-4
60 Breadner, 'The Air Defence of Canada,' 16 March 1942, copy in King Papers, PAC, MG 26 J 4, vol. 424
61 Ibid.
62 See 'Emergency and Reserve Squadrons (VANQUO Plan) – Organization of,' HQS 15-24-27, PAC, RG 24, vol. 5200.
63 Joint Planning Sub-Committee appreciation, first draft, 4 June 1942, and final draft, 15 June 1942, DHist 193.009 (D8)
64 Chiefs of Staff Committee appreciation, July 1942, DHist 193.009 (D9)
65 See the records of the conference in S55-2-18, PAC, RG 24, vol. 5387, and CAS report to BCATP Supervisory Board, 20 July and 30 Sept. 1942, DHist 181.003 (D2639).
66 Dickson to Edwards, 14 April 1941, PRO, Air 2/5260
67 J.M.A. Gwyer, *Grand Strategy*, III: *June 1941-August 1942*, Part I (History of the Second World War, United Kingdom Military Series; London 1964), 398; J.R.H. Butler, *Grand Strategy*, III: *June 1941-August 1942*, Part II (History of the Second

World War, United Kingdom Military Series; London 1964), 556; Christopher Thorne, *Allies of a Kind: the United States, Great Britain, and the War Against Japan, 1941-1945* (New York 1978), 63, 112

68 See the handwritten minutes on Edwards to Dickson, 28 April 1942, covering Breadner's memorandum of 16 March 1942, PRO, Air 2/5260; RCAF Overseas Headquarters to CAS, X5077/Q314, 11 April 1942, S15-9-35 pt 1, PAC, RG 24, vol. 5183.

69 Cabinet War Committee minutes, 4 Feb., 11 and 18 March 1942, PAC, RG 2, series 7c, vol. 8, microfilm reel C4874; Chiefs of Staff to ministers of national defence, 29 Jan. 1942, correspondence between London and Ottawa and Ottawa and Washington, 18 Feb.-14 March 1942, secretary of state for external affairs to Canadian high commissioner in London, no 502, 14 March 1942, and same to same, no 508, 16 March 1942, S15-9-35, PAC, RG 24, vol. 5183

70 Cabinet War Committee minutes, 18 March 1942, PAC, RG 2, series 7c, vol. 8, microfilm reel C4874

71 Copy of US Joint Chiefs' evaluation, and Walsh to AFHQ, 15 May 1942, S15-9-59 pt 1, PAC, RG 24, vol. 5187; Air Council minutes, 1 June 1942, S840-108 pt 4, PARC 828985

72 Butler, *Grand Strategy*, III, Part II, 557; H. Duncan Hall, *North American Supply* (History of the Second World War, United Kingdom Civil Series; London 1955), 362ff; Richard M. Leighton and Robert W. Coakley, *The War Department: Global Logistics and Strategy, 1940-1943* (Washington 1953), 276

73 Walsh to AFHQ, no A397, 27 June 1942, S15-9-55 pt 1, PAC, RG 24, vol. 5167; Tackaberry to AMAS, 24 June 1942, S59-9-59 pt 1, ibid., vol. 5187

74 Combined Planning Staff, 'Report by Special Sub-Committee: Strategic Policy and Deployment of US and British Forces,' 4 July 1942, National Archives, Washington [USNA], RG 165 (Records of the War Department General and Special Staffs), ABC 381 (9-25-41) Section 1

75 Walsh to AFHQ, no A1010, 30 June 1942, S15-9-59 pt 1, PAC, RG 24, vol. 5187; Canadian Joint Staff (Washington) to Chiefs of Staff, no JS1, 11 July 1942, and no JS4, 12 July 1942, ibid.; same to same, no JS3, 11 July 1942, Power Papers, box 66, file D1103

76 Combined Planning Staff, 'Report by Special Sub-Committee,' USNA, RG 165, ABC 381 (9-25-41) Section 1

77 Canadian Joint Staff (Washington) telegrams, especially Walsh to AFHQ, no A1010, 30 June 1942, and same to same, no A57, 9 July 1942, S15-9-59 pt 1, PAC, RG 24, vol. 5187; Breadner to Power, 15 July 1942, and private secretary to Power to CAS, 17 July 1942, S15-9-35 pt 1, ibid., vol. 5183. See also Robert Bothwell and William Kilbourn, *C.D. Howe: a Biography* (Toronto 1979), 171.

78 Walsh to AFHQ, for CAS, no A432, 18 July 1942, S15-9-35 pt 1, PAC, RG 24, vol. 5183

79 Joint US Staff Planners, 'Dominion Air Forces,' JPS 37/1, 3 Aug. 1942, USNA, RG 218 (Records of the United States Joint Chiefs of Staff), CCS 452 (6-26-42) (SCC.1)

80 Walsh to Bedell Smith, 13 Aug. 1942, Walsh to CAS, 14 Aug. 1942, ibid.

81 Walsh to Breadner (personal), 4 Sept. 1942, and Air Force Combined Staff, Washington [AFCS], to CAS, no A16, 21 Sept. 1942, S15-9-59 pt 1, PAC, RG 24, vol. 5187. See also RAF Delegation Washington to Air Ministry, 28 Aug. 1942, telegram TROON 15 28/8, Slessor from Evill, PRO, Air 8/673.

82 See telegrams, 28 Aug. to Oct. 1942, in PRO, Air 8/673.

83 AFCS to CAS, no A16, 21 Sept. 1942, referring to Arnold to Walsh, S15-9-59 pt 1, PAC, RG 24, vol. 5187

84 Heakes to AMAS, 24 Sept. 1942, ibid.

85 Slessor, 'Notes on Canadian Air Requirements,' Aug. 1942, copy to AMAS, 18 Sept. 1942, S15-9-35 pt 1, ibid., vol. 5183

86 Sheard to CAS, 'Notes on Slessor's memorandum,' 21 Sept. 1942, S15-9-59 pt 1, ibid., vol. 5187

87 Heakes (A/AMAS) to CAS, 22 Sept. 1942, S15-9-56 pt 1, ibid, vol. 5185

88 Heakes to CAS, 24 Sept. 1942, S15-9-35, ibid., vol. 5183

89 Heakes to Breadner, 25 Sept. 1942, ibid.

90 Heakes to Breadner (second memorandum), and Sheard to Breadner, both 25 Sept. 1942, ibid.

91 Breadner to Power, 26 Sept. 1942, DHist 193.009 (D12)

92 Cabinet War Committee minutes, 19 Aug., 4 Sept., 7 Oct. 1942, PAC, RG 2, series 7c, vols. 10 and 11, microfilm reel C4874; Heakes to CAS, 25 Sept. 1942 (the basis for Power's and Breadner's presentations), S15-9-35, PAC, RG 24, vol. 5183

93 Air Council minutes, 7 Oct. 1942, S840-108 pt 5, PARC 828985

94 Arnold to Walsh, 22 Oct. 1942, S19-9-59 pt 3, PAC, RG 24, vol. 5187

95 Walsh to Evill, 24 Oct. 1942, S25-9-56, ibid., vol. 5185; Walsh to AFHQ, Nov. 1942, S15-9-59 pt 3, ibid., vol. 5187

96 'Memorandum for Sub-Committee on Airplane Allocation from US 1943 Production,' USNA, RG 165, ABC 452.1, sect. 3 (1-22-42); 'Squadron Programme – Home War,' attached to Breadner to minister, 'Air Defence of Canada Plan, 1943-44,' 20 March 1943, S096-105 pt 3, PARC 826793

97 'Memorandum for Sub-Committee on Airplane Allocation from US 1943 Production,' USNA, RG 165, ABC 452.1 sect. 3 (1-22-42); Tackaberry to AMS, 24 and 27 Nov. 1942, and Walsh to CAS, no A398, 2 Dec. 1942, S15-9-59 pt 3, PAC, RG 24, vol. 5187

98 Quoted in Hall, *North American Supply*, 392

99 AMAS to CAS, 17 Jan. 1943, S15-9-59 pt 4, PAC, RG 24, vol. 5187. See also memorandum on anti-submarine operations prepared for Air Officers Commanding Conference, 15 Oct. 1942, DHist 79/184.

100 OC 4 Group, RCAF, to AOC WAC, 19 June 1942, S262-1-2, DHist 181.009 (D3583)

101 See the memoranda drafted at the special meetings of 7 July and 22 Sept. 1942, DHist 181.009 (D2740).

102 Heakes to CAS, 14 Oct. 1942, copy in Power Papers, box 69, file D2018

103 Combined Chiefs of Staff, 'Probable Scale of Attack on the West Coast of North America reported by the Combined Staff Planners,' CCS 127/1, 16 Jan. 1943, DHist 112.3M2 (D495)

104 Joint Planning Sub-Committee minutes, 26 Feb. 1943, ibid.

105 Breadner, 'Air Defence of Canada Plan, 1943-44,' 20 March 1943, DHist 181.009 (D6611)

106 See the correspondence from 20 April to July 1943 in S15-9-59 pt 4, PAC, RG 24, vol. 5187.

107 Walsh to CAS, no Q39, 15 July, AMAS to CAS, 22 July 1943, ibid.

108 See AFHQ (Sheard) to AFCS (Walsh), no A1061, 28 July 1943, and AFCS (Walsh) to AFHQ (Sheard), no A30, ibid.

109 Combined Chiefs of Staff, 'Scale of Attack on the East and West Coasts of North America,' CCS 127/3, 16 Aug. 1943, USNA, OPD 380 Axis (SCC.II) (Cases 37-61)
110 'Air Defence of Canada Plan,' 24 Sept. 1943, DHist 181.009 (D6277)
111 Cabinet War Committee minutes, 22 Sept. 1943, PAC, RG 2, series 7c, vol. 14, microfilm reel C4875
112 Breadner to Edwards, signal A202, 14 Aug. 1943, DHist 181.009 (D717)
113 Guthrie minute on draft telegram to AFCS (Walsh), 9 Nov. 1943, not sent, and revised telegram, no A1076, 9 Nov. 1943, AFHQ (Leckie) to AFCS (Walsh), no A1, 3 Jan. 1944, and reply, no 150, 5 Jan. 1944, S15-9-59 pt 4, PAC, RG 24, vol. 5187
114 Leckie to minister, 27 Nov. 1944, S096-105 pt 5, PARC 826793; Cabinet War Committee minutes, 1 Dec. 1943, PAC, RG 2, series 7c, vol. 14, microfilm reel C4875; Guthrie to CAS, 22 Jan. 1944, Power Papers, box 69, file D2018
115 Revised 'Air Defence of Canada Plan,' 10 Feb. 1944, DHist 181.009 (D6277)
116 Cabinet War Committee minutes, 31 Aug. 1944, PAC, RG 2, series 7c, vol. 16, microfilm reel D4876
117 'Air Defence of Canada Plan, 1944' (Second Revision), 25 Oct. 1944, and 'Air Defence of Canada Plan, 1945,' 18 Nov. 1944, DHist 181.009 (D6277)

CHAPTER 10: EASTERN AND CENTRAL CANADA

1 Officer commanding [OC] Eastern Air Command [EAC] to district officer commanding [DOC] Military District [MD] No 6, 22 Aug. 1939, DHist 181.009 (D4979)
2 General Order 151/1938, DHist; Canada, Air Historical Section, *RCAF Logbook: a Chronological Outline of the Origin, Growth and Achievement of the Royal Canadian Air Force* (Ottawa 1949), 52-3
3 Senior air officer to OC EAC, 12 Jan. 1939, S.11-2, DHist 181.002 (D446)
4 F.H. Hitchins, *Air Board, Canadian Air Force and Royal Canadian Air Force* (Mercury Series, Canadian War Museum Paper No 2; Ottawa 1972), 389-91
5 OC EAC to DOC MD No 6, 22 Aug. 1939, DHist 181.009 (D4979); 'Chiefs of Staff Committee Plan for the Defence of Canada,' 27 June 1938, as amended to June 1939, DHist 181.004 (D39)
6 No 8 Squadron, operations record book [ORB] daily diary, 29 and 31 Aug. 1939, DHist
7 'The History of Eastern Air Command,' unpublished narrative [1945], 105-10, 131-3, DHist 74/2, vol. 1
8 Anderson to Breadner, 23 Aug. 1939, chief of the air staff [CAS] to OC Western Air Command, 14 Sept. 1939, DHist 181.009 (D4979)
9 Great Britain, Admiralty, Historical Section, *Defeat of the Enemy Attack on Shipping, 1939-1945: a Study of Policy and Operations*, (BR 1736 (51) (1), Naval Staff History Second World War; np 1957), IA, 29
10 EAC operation instruction no 1, 16 Sept. 1939, S.30-2 pt 1, DHist 181.006 (D357); National Defence Headquarters, Bulletins on the Development of the RCAF, 25 Aug.-31 Dec. 1939, S.52, DHist 181.003 (D3868); 'The History of Eastern Air Command,' 106-7, DHist 74/2, vol. 1
11 'The History of Eastern Air Command,' 83, 102-3, 118-20, 129-30, 289, DHist 74/2, vols. 1 and 2; S. Kostenuk and J. Griffin, *RCAF Squadron Histories and Aircraft, 1924-1968* (Toronto 1977), 51

12 No 11 Squadron, ORB, Nov. 1939, DHist; 'The History of Eastern Air Command,' 123, 129-30, 147-8, DHist 74/2, vol. 1; EAC operation order 3/40, 25 May 1940, 501-1-13, PAC, RG 24, vol. 11123

13 'The History of Eastern Air Command,' 70, 179-83, 212, DHist 74/2, vol. 1

14 CAS to assistant deputy minister (air), 20 Nov. 1940, DHist 181.009 (D6771); Breadner to deputy minister (air), 22 Oct. 1940, Queen's University Archives, C.G. Power Papers, box 71, file D2033

15 OC EAC to DOC MD No 6, 22 Aug. 1939, DHist 181.009 (D4979); 'Aircraft Detection Corps, July 1940-March 1941,' DHist 181.009 (D123)

16 Secretary of state for external affairs to governor of Newfoundland, 5 Sept. 1939, and reply, 6 Sept. 1939, Paul Bridle, ed., *Documents on Relations between Canada and Newfoundland*, I: *1935-1949: Defence, Civil Aviation and Economic Affairs* (Ottawa 1974), 41-3; 'The History of Eastern Air Command,' 56-73, 105-6, DHist 74/2, vol. 1. See also C.P. Stacey, *Arms, Men and Governments: the War Policies of Canada, 1939-1945* (Ottawa 1970), 134-5.

17 Air officer commanding [AOC] EAC to CAS, 27 May 1940, AOC EAC to secretary Department of National Defence [DND], 29 May 1940, 'The History of Eastern Air Command,' 194-5, DHist 74/2, vol. 1; 'An Appreciation of Air Force Defence of Canada Atlantic Coast,' 9 June 1940, DHist 181.002 (D107)

18 Commanding officer [CO] 118 (CAC) Squadron to AOC EAC and enclosure, 23 July 1940, HQS 14-2, DHist 181.002 (D176)

19 'The History of Eastern Air Command,' 167, 187-9, DHist 74/2, vol. 1; organization order no 6, 15 Nov. 1940, copy in 118 Squadron, ORB daily diary, DHist; Kostenuk and Griffin, *RCAF Squadron Histories*, 51-2

20 CAS to AOC EAC, 1 April 1940, same to same, amendment no 1, 19 April 1940, HQS 3-5-2, DHist 181.003 (D4095); 'The History of Eastern Air Command,' 139, 171-2, DHist 74/2, vol. 1; memorandum to AOC EAC, 28 July 1940, DHist 181.002 (D154)

21 AOC EAC to secretary DND, 7 Aug. 1940, air member for air staff [AMAS] to CAS, 5 Sept. 1940, 'The History of Eastern Air Command,' 161-3, 209-11, DHist 74/2, vol. 1; 'Operational Units – RCAF,' 15 Aug., 15 Nov. 1940, DHist 181.002 (D460) pt 1; K.M. Molson and H.A. Taylor, *Canadian Aircraft since 1909* (Stittsville, Ont. 1982), 120-4

22 'Minutes of Meeting Held at Government House on August 20th, 1940, at 10 am,' DHist 355.013 (D1); 'Minutes of Meeting at St John's to Discuss Bilateral Defence Questions,' 20 Aug. 1940, governor of Newfoundland to dominions secretary, 23 Aug. 1940, Bridle, ed., *Canada and Newfoundland*, I, 159-64; secretary Chiefs of Staff Committee to CO Atlantic Coast, 28 Aug. 1940, HQS 5199-2 pt 1, PARC 395072; Stacey, *Arms, Men and Governments*, 132

23 'Defence of Canada Plan, August 1940,' pt III, para 19, DHist 112.3M2 (D497)

24 Stacey, *Arms, Men and Governments*, 344-5, 347, 349

25 Ibid., 129; R.A. MacKay, *Newfoundland: Economic, Diplomatic, and Strategic Studies* (Toronto 1946), App. C

26 Stacey, *Arms, Men and Governments*, 349-54, 360; S.W. Dziuban, *Military Relationships between the United States and Canada, 1939-1945* (United States Army in World War II, Special Studies; Washington 1959), 104-6

27 W.A.B. Douglas, 'Alliance Warfare, 1939-45: Canada's Maritime Forces,'

Revue internationale d'histoire militaire, No 54 (misnumbered 51), 1982, 159-80

28 'The History of Eastern Air Command,' 198, DHist 74/2, vol. 1; S.W. Roskill, *The War at Sea, 1939-1945*, I: *The Defensive* (History of the Second World War, United Kingdom Military Series; London 1954), 288-9

29 Station Sydney, ORB daily diary, 24 Oct. 1940, DHist

30 'The History of Eastern Air Command,' 235, DHist 74/2, vol. 2; 10 Squadron, ORB daily diary, 22 Feb. 1941, DHist; Roskill, *War at Sea*, I, 373-8

31 AOC EAC to CO Station Gander, 20 Jan. 1942, DHist 181.009 (D1192)

32 Ibid.

33 Admiralty to Naval Service Headquarters [NSHQ], Ottawa, 15 March 1941, CAS to chief of the naval staff, 15 March 1941, AMAS to CAS, 21 May 1941, HQS 3-5-2, DHist 181.003 (D4095); N.R. Anderson biographical file, DHist; 1941 correspondence, DHist 181.009 (D6734)

34 'The History of Eastern Air Command,' 256, 265, 304-5, DHist 74/2, vol. 2; EAC operation order 3/41, 26 March 1941, AOC EAC to Air Force Headquarters [AFHQ], signal A879, 29 May 1941, DHist 181.002 (D58); AOC EAC to COS Yarmouth, Dartmouth, and Sydney, 6 June 1941, HQS 30-5, DHist 181.002 (D154)

35 AOC EAC to AFHQ, 20 May 1941, DHist 181.003 (D4095); 'The History of Eastern Air Command,' 251, DHist 74/2, vol. 2; director of plans, Air Ministry, to AOC RCAF Overseas, 24 May 1941, PRO, Air 8/461

36 'Summary of Service Flying,' 31 May 1941, 10 Squadron, ORB daily diary, App. C, DHist

37 Great Britain, Air Ministry, Air Historical Branch, 'The R.A.F. in Maritime War, III: The Atlantic and Home Waters, the Preparative Phase, July 1941 to February 1943,' nd, 22-3, 35-6, DHist 79/599; Anderson to CAS, 9 July 1941, DHist 181.009 (D6734)

38 AOC EAC to AFHQ, 29 May 1941, DHist 181.002 (D58); 5 Squadron, ORB daily diary, 30 June and 1 July 1941, DHist; 'The History of Eastern Air Command,' 274, 277, 290-4, DHist 74/2, vol. 2; 'Convoys S.C. 37 and H.X. 138 – Orders for Ocean and Local Escort,' 10 July 1941, DHist 181.002 (D121)

39 EAC secret organization order no 17, 8 July 1941, No 1 Group, ORB daily diary, DHist; 'The History of Eastern Air Command, 299-301, 324-5, DHist 74/2, vol. 2

40 Stacey, *Arms, Men and Governments*, 312, 362; Dziuban, *Military Relations*, 122-3; Roskill, *The War at Sea*, I, 470-1; Admiralty general message, 13 Sept. 1941, S4-10-A, DHist 181.002 (D156)

41 Little to Pound, 1 Oct. 1941, PRO, Adm 205/9; AOC EAC to AFHQ, 21 Sept. 1941, 15-1-350 pt 1, PAC, RG 24, vol. 5177; NSHQ to commodore commanding Newfoundland Force, 17 Sept. 1941, DHist 181.002 (D121)

42 AOC EAC to AFHQ, 21 Sept. 1941, 15-1-350 pt 1, PAC, RG 24, vol. 5177

43 Heakes to AFHQ, 23 Sept. 1941, Anderson to AFHQ, 14 Feb. 1942, ibid.

44 Stark to Breadner, 2 Oct. 1941, ibid.

45 Douglas, 'Alliance Warfare,' 166-7

46 Papers concerning WPL-52, 2-27 Oct. 1941, 151-350 pt 1, PAC, RG 24, vol. 5177

47 'Committee on Coastal Command Report,' 19 March 1941, PRO, Air 15/227

48 Chiefs of Staff Committee memorandum, 31 Dec. 1941, DHist 193.009 (D3); Stacey, *Arms, Men and Governments*, 363-4; 'The History of Eastern Air Command,' 363, DHist 74/2, vol. 3

49 Department of Munitions and Supply to British Purchasing Commission, 12 Aug. 1940, 1021-9-95, PAC, RG 24, vol. 5133; Johnson to Power, 14 Oct. 1941, Breadner to vice-chief of the air staff, RAF, 26 Feb. 1942, S.60-3-12 pt 3, ibid., vol. 5395; Air Council minutes, 5 Dec. 1941, 840-108 pt 3, PARC 828985; J.A. Griffin, *Canadian Military Aircraft: Serials & Photographs, 1920-1968* (National Museum of Man, Canadian War Museum Publication No 69-2; Ottawa 1969), 362-3, 511; Roger Sarty, 'The RCAF's First Catalinas and Cansos,' (forthcoming)

50 'The History of Eastern Air Command,' 274, 336, DHist 74/2, vol. 2; EAC movement order 1/41, 22 Sept. 1941, DHist 181.006 (D13); Anderson to AOC RCAF London, 9 July 1941, DHist 181.009 (D6734); Chiefs of Staff Committee, Joint Planning Sub-Committee, 'Northwest River Aerodrome – Defence,' nd, 'Information Regarding Northwest River Area Labrador,' 27 Aug. 1941, DHist 193.009 (D3)

51 'Air Defence of Central Canada,' 1-4, 20, DHist 74/4; Canada, Parliament, House of Commons, *Debates*, 13 Feb. 1939, 861-2; 'Defence of Hudson Bay and Hudson Strait, Report of Sub-Committee appointed by the Chiefs of Staff Committee on 6th March 1939,' 11 April 1939, HQC 5199 pt 5, PAC, RG 24, vol. 2685; AOC EAC to AOC No 1 Training Command, 10 Feb. 1941, DHist 181.009 (D123); 'Report on Aircraft Detection Corps – Eastern Canada,' 27 Feb. 1942, DHist 321.009 (D94)

52 'Appreciation of Potentialities of Air Raids on Sault Ste Marie,' 17 March 1942, Heakes to Douglas, 2 April 1942, 'Air Defence of Central Canada,' 4-7, 18-19, DHist 74/4

53 CAS to minister, 16 March 1942, AMAS to various authorities, 23 March 1942, PRO, Air 2/5260

54 'Air Defence of Central Canada,' 7-11, DHist 74/4; 'Plan of Organization, Aircraft Detection Corps, Central Canada Area,' draft, 7 May 1942, quoted in ibid., 19-28; secret organization order no 76, 11 June 1942, DHist 181.009 (D216)

55 'Air Defence of Central Canada,' 15-17, 29-32, 38-41, DHist 74/4; 'History and Review of the Aircraft Detection Corps,' July 1944, 5, DHist 80/395

56 CAS to minister, 'Air Defence of Canada,' 16 March 1942, CAS to minister, 'Air Defence of Canada Plan, 1943-44,' 20 March 1943, DHist 181.009 (D6277); 'The History of Eastern Air Command,' 468-71, DHist 74/2, vol. 3; 'Operational Units-RCAF,' 14 June, 15 Nov. 1943, DHist 181.002 (D460) pt 5

57 Nesbitt to AMAS, 2 July 1943, Clements to AMAS, 13 July 1943, S17-1-1 pt 1, DHist 181.009 (D826); Millard to AMAS, 9 July 1943, CAS to minister, 'Air Defence of Canada Plan – 1944,' 24 Sept. 1943, S096-105 pt 4, PARC 826793

58 'Radar in the Royal Canadian Air Force,' nd, 17-22, DHist 80/395; 'Narrative History of the Formation and Development of the Fighter and Filter Control System of The Royal Canadian Air Force,' 25 Sept. 1944, ibid; organization order no 215, 12 Sept. 1944, DHist 181.003 (D257); 'Air Defence of Canada Plan – 1944/45 (Second Revision),' DHist 322.019 (D11); 'Maps of Radar Beacons and

Stations,' May 1945, DHist 181.004 (D102); 'Monthly Review of RCAF Operations,' I, no I, June 1943, 28-33; ibid., I, no 3, Aug. 1943, 43-5
59 Chiefs of staff to ministers, 10 March 1942, Chiefs of Staff Committee minutes, 10
March 1942, HQS 5199 pt II, DHist 193.009 (D53); Stacey, *Arms, Men and
Governments*, 134
60 P.B. Martineau, nd, PRO, Air 15/217, encl. 38G
61 CAS to minister, 'Air Defence of Canada,' 16 March 1942, DHist 181.009 (D6277);
'Operational Units – RCAF,' 15 Nov. 1943, DHist 181.002 (D460) pt 5
62 Organization order no 237, 21 March 1945, DHist 181.009 (D5484); RCAF EAC
Marine Squadron establishments, DHist 181.005 (D937); 'The History of Eastern Air Command,' 501-2, DHist 74/2, vol. 3; Guthrie to air member for organization, 'Report on Western Hemisphere Operations,' 31 Jan. 1944, DHist 181.003
(D17); 'EAC Marine Squadron,' permanent reference file, DHist; 'Flying Control,'
14 Feb. 1944, DHist 181.009 (D6823); 'Monthly Review of RCAF Operations,' I,
no 7, Dec. 1943, 3-4
63 'RCAF Monthly Summary of Strength by Location,' 31 Jan. 1944, DHist 181.005
(D1965); 'The History of Eastern Air Command,' 686-7, 741, 744, DHist 74/2,
vol. 4; Link to director of staff duties, 8 Feb. 1944, DHist 181.003 (D17); Stacey,
Arms, Men and Governments, 295-6; Kostenuk and Griffin, RCAF *Squadron
Histories*, 58-60
64 'The History of Eastern Air Command,' 717-8, 761, 784-5, 824, DHist 74/2, vol.
4; Station Shelburne, ORB daily diary, 4 March 1944, DHist; 'Air Defence of
Canada Plan – 1944 (Revised),' 10 Feb. 1944, 2, DHist 181.009 (D6277)
65 Chiefs of Staff Committee, 'Extract from Mins 298th Meeting,' 25 Aug. 1944,
DHist 193.009 (D34); T.W. Melnyk, *Canadian Flying Operations in South East
Asia, 1941-1945* (Department of National Defence, Directorate of History, Occasional Paper No I; Ottawa 1976), 106-7; I Group to EAC, signal A14, 28 July
1944, DHist 181.009 (D4656); AOCinC EAC to secretary DND for Air, 5 Sept. 1944,
S096-105 pt 5, PARC 826793; 113 Squadron, ORB daily diary, Aug. 1944, DHist;
129 Squadron, ORB daily diary, Sept. 1944, DHist; 11 Squadron, ORB daily diary,
July to Oct. 1944, DHist
66 'Radar in the Royal Canadian Air Force,' 20-2, 26, DHist 80/395; organization
order no 215, 12 Sept. 1944, DHist 181.003 (D257); 'Air Defence of Canada Plan
– 1944/45 (Second Revision),' DHist 181.009 (D6277); 'Minutes of Meeting Joint
Service Sub-Committee (RDF) Atlantic Coast,' 27 April, 7 June, 6 Oct. 1943,
DHist 79/177
67 'Radar in the Royal Canadian Air Force,' 228, DHist 80/395; 'Monthly Review of
RCAF Operations,' I, no 6, Nov. 1943, 12-13; 'Air Force Headquarters – Eastern
Air Command Meeting – Brief,' nd [Nov. or Dec. 1944], DHist 181.009 (D3217);
Harrison to senior air staff officer, 13 March 1945, DHist 181.009 (D4557)
68 'Radar in The Royal Canadian Air Force,' 20-1, DHist 80/395; NSHQ attack and
sighting reports, 12 Sept. 1944, NSS 8910-23 pt 3, PAC, RG 24, vol. 6897; Joint
RCN-RCAF Anti-Submarine Warfare Committee minutes, 11 Jan., 22 Feb. 1945,
DHist 181.002 (D399); JSC Atlantic Coast minutes, 15 March 1945, DHist
323.009 (D160)
69 Leckie to members Aircraft Detection Corps, 15 Nov. 1944, DHist 193.009 (D38);

'History and Review of the Aircraft Detection Corps of the Royal Canadian Air Force,' 2, DHist 80/395; HQ EAC to secretary Chiefs of Staff Committee, 21 Dec. 1944, DHist 193.009 (D38)

70 AOC EAC to director of provost and security services, 19 Oct. 1945, DHist 181.009 (D2628); CAS to secretary Chiefs of Staff Committee, 9 May 1945, DHist 193.009 (D43); secretary Chiefs of Staff Committee to secretary Joint Service Committee Atlantic and secretary Joint Service Committee Pacific, 10 May 1945, DHist 322.019 (DI1)

CHAPTER 11: THE PACIFIC COAST

1 Croil to deputy minister, 3 Nov. 1937, Mackenzie minute, 22 Dec. 1937, General Order no 30, 15 March 1938, Croil to Johnson, nd, in 'Western Air Command,' unpublished narrative, 1945, sec. 2, 4-5, 13, DHist 74/3, vol. 1; senior air officer [SAO] to officer commanding [OC] Western Air Command [WAC], 21 Nov. 1938, WAC S.11 pt 1, DHist 181.009 (D5945)

2 Chiefs of Staff Committee, operational and administrative memorandum no 1, 15 Aug. 1938, DHist 181.004 (D39)

3 SAO to OC WAC, 10 Dec. 1938, air officer commanding [AOC] WAC to secretary Department of National Defence [DND], 30 Aug. 1939, WAC S.11 pt 1, DHist 181.009 (D5945)

4 District officer commanding Military District No 11 to OC WAC, 4 April 1939, ibid.; 'Notes for C.A.S.,' 12 Sept. 1939, DHist 181.009 (D2); WAC, operations record book [ORB] daily diary, Oct. 1939 summary, DHist

5 F.H. Hitchins, *Air Board, Canadian Air Force and Royal Canadian Air Force* (Mercury Series, Canadian War Museum Paper No 2; Ottawa 1972), 389; Canada, Air Historical Section, *RCAF Logbook: a Chronological Outline of the Origin, Growth and Achievement of the Royal Canadian Air Force* (Ottawa 1949), 58-60; chief of the air staff [CAS] to WAC, 31 Aug. and 10 Sept. 1939, CAS to officers commanding, messages 18-1/9 and 20-1/9, 1 Sept. 1939, DHist 181.009 (D2); 6 Squadron, ORB daily diary, 2 and 8 Sept. 1939, DHist; 4 Squadron, ORB daily diary, 12 Sept. 1939, DHist

6 No 6 Squadron, ORB daily diary, 12 Sept. 1939, DHist

7 WAC to secretary and Croil minute, 4 Sept. 1939, DHist 181.009 (D2); Croil to AOC WAC, 7 Sept. 1939, AOC WAC to secretary DND, 10 Sept. 1939, WAC operation orders 6/39 and 7/39, 1 Sept. 1939, WAC S.11 pt 1, DHist 181.009 (D5945)

8 AOC WAC to secretary DND, 10 Sept. 1939, WAC S.11 pt 1, DHist 181.009 (D5945)

9 'Western Air Command,' sec. 6, 3-4, DHist 74/3, vol. 1; sec. 23, 5, ibid., vol. 2; S. Kostenuk and J. Griffin, *RCAF Squadron Histories and Aircraft, 1924-1968* (Toronto 1977), 24, 27, 36, 42, 55; squadron ORB daily diaries, DHist

10 Breadner to minister, 20 June 1940, DHist 181.002 (D107); AOC Eastern Air Command to secretary DND, 7 Aug. 1940, air member for air staff [AMAS] to CAS, 5 Sept. 1940, in 'The History of Eastern Air Command,' unpublished narrative [1945], 161-3, DHist 74/2, vol. 1; 'Western Air Command,' sec. 31, 2, sec. 42, DHist 74/3, vol. 2

11 'Summary of Marine Craft and Outboard Motors – 1939-40,' nd, DHist 181.005

(D1238); 'Report on Operational Procedure, Western Air Command,' 10 Nov.
1945, 14a, WAC S.204-1-1 pt 3, DHist 181.002 (D149); 'History and Review of the
Aircraft Detection Corps of the Royal Canadian Air Force,' July 1944, 4-5,
App. F, DHist 80/395

12 Cabinet War Committee minutes, 24 Oct. 1940 and 28 Jan. 1941, PAC, RG 2, series
7c, vols. 2 and 3, microfilm reel C4653A

13 S.W. Dziuban, *Military Relations between the United States and Canada, 1939-
1945* (United States Army in World War II, Special Studies; Washington 1959),
86-90, 351-2, 366-9; C.P. Stacey, *Arms, Men and Governments: the War Policies
of Canada, 1939-1945* (Ottawa 1970), 344-5

14 Croil to Power, 11 Sept. 1941, Slemon to Breadner, 2 Oct. 1941, Breadner to
minister, 28 Oct. 1941, in W.G. Goddard, 'Air Defence of the West Coast of
Canada,' unpublished narrative [1945], 6-9, DHist 74/4; EAC movement order
1/41, 22 Sept. 1941, EAC S.325-19, DHist 181.006 (D13)

15 CAS to AOC WAC, 29 Nov. 1941, 'R.C.A.F. in the Aleutians, 1942-43,' chap. 1, 8,
DHist 74/3, vol. 1; Freeman to western regional commanders, 18 Dec. 1941,
HQS 638-1-1-20-2, DHist 169.009 (D138); Stacey, *Arms, Men and Governments*,
45; Dziuban, *Military Relations*, 107-8

16 WAC, ORB daily diary, Dec. 1941, DHist; 'Blackout Orders,' 8 Dec. 1941, AOC WAC
to Air Force Headquarters [AFHQ], A141, 8 Jan. 1942, DHist 181.009 (D1281);
8 and 111 Squadrons, ORB daily diaries, Dec. 1941 and Jan. 1942, DHist; 'Reinforcement of Western and Eastern Air Commands,' 23 Dec. 1941, DHist
181.002 (D107)

17 Telephone conversations, Smye-Vanaman, 10 Dec. 1941, and Carswell-Vanaman,
11 Dec. 1941, US Library of Congress, H.H. Arnold Papers, box 185, copy in
DHist 82/970

18 Chiefs of Staff Committee minutes, 9 Dec. 1941, HQS 5199 pt 10, DHist 193.009
(D53); Freeman to western regional commanders, 18 Dec. 1941, DeWitt to
liaison officer 13th Naval District, 21 Dec. 1941, Alexander to secretary DND, 23
Dec. 1941, HQS 638-1-1-20-2, DHist 169.009 (D138); Joint Service Committee
Pacific Coast, minutes, 19 Dec. 1941, 'Appreciation of the Situation as at 1st
January 1942,' nd, DHist 193.009 (D3); ABC-Pacific-22, 23 Jan. 1942, DHist
112.3M2 (D500)

19 AOC WAC to secretary DND, 21 Feb. 1942, Johnson to CAS, 16 March 1942, Anderson to Breadner, 25 March 1942, Goddard, 'Air Defence of the West Coast,'
26-8, sec. 13, DHist 74/4; Plant to AOC, 20 Feb. 1942, WAC S.262-1-2 pt 1, DHist
181.009 (D3583); W.F. Craven and J.L. Cate, eds., *The Army Air Forces in
World War II*, I: *Plans and Early Operations, January 1939 to August 1942*
(Chicago 1948), 294-6

20 Dziuban, *Military Relations*, 120, 356; Stacey, *Arms, Men and Governments*,
349-54

21 Johnson to CAS, 16 March 1942, Goddard, 'Air Defence of the West Coast,' sec.
13, DHist 74/4

22 Dziuban, *Military Relations*, 122, 122n

23 'Western Air Command,' sec. 11, 2-3, DHist 74/3, vol. 1; 'Fighter-Filter Control,'
25 Sept. 1944, 1, 3, 7-8, DHist 80/395; 'Radar in the Royal Canadian Air

Force,' 19, ibid; Sheard interview, 17 Jan. 1984, Terence Sheard biographical file, DHist; Stetson Conn, Rose C. Engelman, and Byron Fairchild, *Guarding the United States and its Outposts* (United States Army in World War II, The Western Hemisphere; Washington 1964), 427-8

24 Stevenson to secretary DND for Air, 27 Feb. 1942, Hollingum to commanding officer [CO] Pacific Coast, 21 Dec. 1942, WAC S.202-1-32, DHist 181.009 (D2688)

25 Slinger to senior air staff officer [SASO], 9 Nov. 1942, ibid.

26 'Western Air Command,' sec. 8, 1-2, DHist 74/3, vol. 1; Samuel Eliot Morison, *History of United States Naval Operations in World War II, IV: Coral Sea, Midway and Submarine Actions, May 1942-August 1942* (Boston 1950), 169-70; A.J. Watts and B.G. Gordon, *The Imperial Japanese Navy* (London 1971), 332-3; Bert Webber, *Retaliation: Japanese Attacks and Allied Countermeasures on the Pacific Coast in World War II* (Corvallis, Oregon 1975), 11-12, 14, 16, 29-32; Clarke G. Reynolds, 'Submarine Attacks on the Pacific Coast, 1942,' *Pacific Historical Review*, XXXIII, May 1964, 183-93

27 'Resolutions of a Police-Military Conference in Victoria,' 1 Oct. 1940, 'Report on the State of Intelligence on the Pacific Coast with Particular Reference to the Problem of the Japanese Minority,' 27 July 1941, WAC S.76-3, DHist 181.009 (D5546)

28 Stevenson to secretary DND for Air, 2 Jan., CAS to AOC WAC, 6 Jan. 1942, ibid.

29 Cabinet War Committee minutes, 26 Feb. 1942, PAC, RG 2, series 7c, vol. 8, microfilm reel C4874; Klaus H. Pringsheim, *Neighbours across the Pacific: Canadian-Japanese Relations 1870-1982* (Oakville, Ont. 1983), 72-3

30 Vancouver *Sun*, 17, 18, 19 Feb., and 13, 14, and 16 March 1942

31 C.P. Stacey, *Six Years of War: the Army in Canada, Britain and the Pacific* (Official History of the Canadian Army in the Second World War, I; Ottawa 1955), 170; Stacey, *Arms, Men and Governments*, 133

32 Stevenson to AFHQ, 21 Feb. 1942, WAC S.201-9-1 pt 1, DHist 181.009 (D3334); Johnson to CAS, 16 March 1942, Goddard, 'Air Defence of the West Coast,' sec. 13, DHist 74/4

33 Joint Service Committee Pacific Coast, 'Appreciation of the Situation as at 1st April 1942,' nd, DHist 193.009 (D6)

34 'Transfer of 14 Squadron,' organization order no 48, 24 March 1942, DHist 181.009 (D2702); 111 Squadron, ORB daily diary, June 1942, DHist; 14 Squadron, ORB daily diary, 27 March and 4 April 1942, DHist; Breadner to minister, 9 March 1943, DHist 181.009 (D6823)

35 CAS to AOC WAC, 14 Sept. 1939, DHist 181.009 (D4979); Cabinet War Committee minutes, 18 March 1942, PAC, RG 2, series 7c, vol. 8, microfilm reel C4874

36 Stevenson interview, 18 June 1982, 18-21, L.F. Stevenson biographical file, DHist; Joint Service Committee Pacific Coast minutes, 10 April and 5 June 1942, HQS 201-1-3 pt 1 and 2, DHist 181.009 (D2740); secretary Joint Service Committee Pacific Coast to CO Pacific Coast and AOC WAC, 20 June 1942, ibid.

37 Joint Service Committee Pacific Coast minutes, 8 Sept. 1942, DHist 181.009 (D2740)

38 Craven and Cate, eds., *The Army Air Forces*, I, 237-41; Conn, Engelman, and Fairchild, *Guarding the United States*, 6-7

39 ABC-Pacific-22, annex IV, sec. III, 23 Jan. 1942, DHist 112.3M2 (D500)

40 Permanent Joint Board on Defence [PJBD] meeting, 25-6 Feb. 1942, W.L.M. King Papers, PAC, MG 26 J 4, vol. 319, file 3369; Dziuban, *Military Relations*, 239-40

41 'R.C.A.F. in the Aleutians,' chap. 2, 4, DHist 74/3, vol. 1; US Eleventh Air Force, 'History of the Eleventh Army Air Force,' unpublished narrative, nd, 14, 53, 66-8, 128-9, DHist 80/176, file 12; 'Report of Meeting,' 6 March 1942, Joint Service Committee Pacific Coast minutes, 12 March 1942, DHist 193.009 (D5); Dziuban, *Military Relations*, 252; Journal of Discussions, PJBD meeting, 7 April 1942, King Papers, PAC, MG 26 J 4, vol. 319, file 3369

42 AOC WAC to AFHQ, 27 May 1942, Queen's University Archives, C.G. Power Papers, box 69, file D2019; 'R.C.A.F. in the Aleutians,' chap. 2, 4, DHist 74/3, vol. 1; Clarke interview, 25 Oct. 1979, H.P. Clarke biographical file, DHist

43 Dziuban, *Military Relations*, 252, 254; correspondence, July 1942, HQ 035-11-1 pt 1, PAC, RG 24, vol. 17634; Clarke interview, 25 Oct. 1979, H.P. Clarke biographical file, DHist; letter, 29 Nov. 1979, J.Y. Scallon biographical file, DHist; Stacey, *Arms, Men and Governments*, 388

44 Morison, *Naval Operations*, IV, 4-6; Conn, Engelman, and Fairchild, *Guarding the United States*, 219, 258; Paul S. Dull, *A Battle History of the Imperial Japanese Navy, 1941-1945* (Annapolis, Md 1978), 7, 133-4; J.H. Belote and W.M. Belote, *Titans of the Seas: the Development and Operations of Japanese and American Carrier Task Forces During World War II* (New York 1975), 80-1

45 Conn, Engelman, and Fairchild, *Guarding the United States*, 221; R.W. Clark, *The Man Who Broke Purple: the Life of the World's Greatest Cryptologist, Colonel William F. Friedman* (London 1977), 146-7; Dull, *Japanese Navy*, 168, 170; Morison, *Naval Operations*, IV, 76-7, 165-6; Ronald Lewin, *The American Magic* (London 1982), 99-111; Craven and Cate, eds., *The Army Air Forces*, I, 464

46 Wrong to Robertson, 1 April, and extract from Cabinet War Committee minutes, 14 May 1942, in J.F. Hilliker, ed., *Documents on Canadian External Relations* [DCER], IX: *1942-1943* (Ottawa 1980), 1164-5, 1169-70; PJBD meeting, 27 April 1942, King Papers, PAC, MG 26 J 4, vol. 319, file 3369; 'R.C.A.F. in the Aleutians,' chap. 3, 1, DHist 74/3, vol. 1; 'Appreciation of the Situation as at 1st April 1942,' nd, DHist 193.009 (D6)

47 'R.C.A.F. in the Aleutians,' chap. 3, 1, DHist 74/3, vol. 1; Macdonald interview, 7 Feb. 1980, 17, J.K.F. Macdonald biographical file, DHist

48 PJBD meeting, 27 May 1942, King Papers, PAC, MG 26 J 4, vol. 319, file 3368

49 Chiefs of Staff Committee minutes, 29 May 1942, DHist 193.009 (D53); Stacey, *Six Years of War*, 173; AOC WAC to AFHQ, 21 May 1942, Power Papers, box 69, file D2019; Craven and Cate, eds., *The Army Air Forces*, I, 276, 306-7, 464-5

50 King Diary, 30 May 1942, PAC, MG 26 J 13

51 Johnston to minister, CAS to commander-in-chief [CINC] West Coast Defences, 29 May 1942, Power Papers, box 69, file D2019

52 AOC WAC to AFHQ (A63 and A465), 'Memorandum of Telephone Call,' 30 May 1942, minutes of conference in minister's office, 'Memorandum for Record,' AFHQ to AOC WAC, 31 May 1942, ibid.

53 Dziuban, *Military Relations*, 253; 'Report of Telephone Conversation,' 'Diary of

Action by DCAS in Respect of Alaskan Situation,' CAS to CINC West Coast Defences, 1 June 1942, Power Papers, box 69, file D2019; 118 Squadron, ORB daily diary, 30 May to 6 June 1942, DHist

54 No 8 Squadron, ORB daily diary, 1-3 June 1942, DHist; Watkins interview, 16 Aug. 1979, E.J. Watkins biographical file, DHist; Smith to Bezeau, 22 Oct. 1979, W.J. Smith biographical file, DHist; Tingley to Bezeau, 16 Nov. 1979, S.A. Tingley biographical file, DHist

55 No 8 Squadron, ORB daily diary, 4-5 June 1942, DHist; RCAF Wing Elmendorf Field, ORB daily diary, 8 June 1942, DHist

56 'History of the Eleventh Army Air Force,' 146-8, DHist 80/176, file 12; Morison, *Naval Operations*, IV, 139-40, 175, 178, 180-1; Craven and Cate, eds., *The Army Air Forces*, I, 466-9; Conn, Engelman, and Fairchild, *Guarding the United States*, 220-1, 261-3; Dull, *Japanese Navy*, 168-71; United States, Army Historical Section, 'The Aleutian Islands Campaign' (Japanese Studies of World War II, no 51; unpublished narrative, nd), 29-33, copy in DHist 80/192

57 Johnson to AMAS, WAC to AFHQ and minute, CAS to CINC West Coast Defences, 'Memorandum for Record,' 5 June 1942, Power Papers, box 69, file D2019; 8 Squadron and RCAF Wing Elmendorf, ORB daily diaries, 5-7 June 1942, DHist; R.E. Morrow, 'Historical Summary of the Activities of the Royal Canadian Air Force in Northern Alaska, June 1942-September 1943,' nd, 5-6, R.E. Morrow biographical file, DHist; '11 AF Assigned and Attached Units,' Courtney to CO XI Bomber Command, 12 June 1943, DHist 80/176, files 2 and 4

58 No 111 Squadron, ORB daily diary, June 1942, DHist; Gooding to Bezeau, 6 Feb. 1980, H.O. Gooding biographical file, DHist; 'Narrative,' attached to McGregor to AOC WAC, 9 June 1942, and entry for 24 June 1942, RCAF Wing Elmendorf, ORB daily diary, DHist

59 No 8 Squadron, ORB daily diary, 11 June 1942, DHist; RCAF Wing, Elmendorf, ORB daily diary, 18-20 June 1942, DHist; McGregor to AOC WAC, 30 June 1942, ibid.

60 No 8 Squadron, ORB daily diary, 7-23, 27-8 June, 4, 8, 13, 23-8 July, 31 Aug., 17 Sept., and 6, 12-21 Oct. 1942, DHist; 'Memorandum for Record,' 5 June 1942, Power Papers, box 69, file D2019

61 Morison, *Naval Operations*, IV, 259; Conn, Engelman, and Fairchild, *Guarding the United States*, 264; Courtney to HQ Eleventh Air Force, 3 Dec. 1942, and '11 AF Assigned and Attached Units,' DHist 80/176, files 2 and 4; McGregor to AOC WAC, 30 June 1942, and entry for 27 June 1942, in RCAF Wing Elmendorf, ORB daily diary, DHist

62 McGregor to AOC WAC, 30 June 1942, RCAF Wing Elmendorf, ORB daily diary, DHist

63 Ibid.

64 'Report by the Minister for Air to the Cabinet War Committee,' 11 July 1942, Power Papers, box 63, file D1078; RCAF Wing Elmendorf, ORB daily diary, 4-8 July 1942, DHist

65 No 111 Squadron, ORB daily diary, 16-17, 22 July, 17 Sept. 1942, DHist; RCAF Wing Elmendorf, ORB daily diary, 13-16 July 1942, DHist; Eskil's 'Report of Events ...' 18 July 1942, ibid.

66 RCAF Wing Elmendorf, ORB daily diary, 20-2, 25, 28 Aug. and 3 Sept. 1942, DHist
67 'History of the 404th Bombardment Squadron (H),' 14 June 1944, 10-12, DHist 80/176, file 3; Courtney to HQ Eleventh Air Force, 3 Dec. 1942, ibid., file 4; '11 AF Assigned and Attached Units,' ibid., file 2; 8 Squadron, ORB daily diary, 12 July 1942, Nome Detachment, daily diary, 18-23 July and Aug. 1942, DHist
68 Morison, *Naval Operations*, IV, 183-4; S.E. Morison, *History of United States Naval Operations in World War II*, VII: *Aleutians, Gilberts and Marshalls, June 1942-April 1944* (Boston 1951), 4, 8, 12-13; Conn, Engelman, and Fairchild, *Guarding the United States*, 264-6, 270-2; W.F. Craven and J.L. Cate, eds., *The Army Air Forces in World War II*, IV: *The Pacific: Guadalcanal to Saipan, August 1942 to July 1944* (Chicago 1950), 364-6, 369-70; W.F. Craven and J.L. Cate, eds., *The Army Air Forces in World War II*, VII: *Services around the World* (Chicago 1958), 294; 111 Squadron, ORB daily diary, 18 and 21 Sept. 1942, App. 3, 25 Sept. 1942, DHist; 'History of the Eleventh Army Air Force,' 166, 173-86, 195-6, 203, DHist 80/176, file 12; United States, 11th Fighter Squadron, 'History of Eleventh Fighter Squadron' [June 1944], 47-9, 136, docs. 56, 58, ibid., file 11; United States, Army Historical Section, 'The Aleutian Campaign,' nd, 5, 42, copy in DHist 80/192
69 'Squadron Leader K.A. Boomer,' nd, K.A. Boomer biographical file, DHist; 111 Squadron, ORB daily diary, App. 3 and 4, 25 Sept. 1942, DHist; 'History of Eleventh Fighter Squadron,' 48-9, DHist 80/176, file 11; Craven and Cate, eds., *The Army Air Forces*, IV, 371
70 No 111 Squadron, ORB daily diary, 17 April 1943, DHist; 'History of Eleventh Fighter Squadron,' 48, DHist 80/176, file 11; 'History of the Eleventh Army Air Force,' 198, DHist 80/176, file 12; Gooding to Bezeau, 26 Feb. 1980, H.O. Gooding biographical file, DHist; 'Historical Summary,' 10-14, R.E. Morrow biographical file, DHist
71 No 8 Squadron, ORB daily diary, App. B, Sept. 1942, DHist; 8 Squadron Nome Detachment, ORB daily diary, 13 Aug., 8, 14, 16, 20, 21 and 25 Sept. 1942, DHist; 'History of the Eleventh Army Air Force,' 192-5, DHist 80/176, file 12; Clarke interview, 25 Oct. 1979, H.P. Clarke biographical file, DHist
72 No 8 Squadron Nome Detachment, ORB daily diary, 27 Sept. 1942, 8 Squadron, ORB daily diary, 1, 5, 8, 17 and 23 Nov., App. C, 5, 15, 19-30 Dec. 1942, App., Dec. 1942, 8 Squadron Kodiak Detachment, ORB daily diary, 1 Jan. 1943, DHist; RCAF Wing Elmendorf, ORB daily diary, 21 Oct. and 29 Dec. 1942, DHist; Courtney to HQ Eleventh Air Force, 3 Dec. 1943, DHist 80/176, file 4
73 'History of the Eleventh Army Air Force,' 221, DHist 80/176, file 12; Louis Morton, *Strategy and Command: the First Two Years* (United States Army in World War II, The War in the Pacific; Washington 1962), 424-9; Morison, *Naval Operations*, VII, 17-18; Craven and Cate, eds., *The Army Air Forces*, IV, 374-6; Conn, Engelman, and Fairchild, *Guarding the United States*, 275-6; RCAF Wing, Elmendorf, ORB daily diary, App. 1, Jan. 1943, DHist; holographic note on draft of Stevenson to commanding general [CG] Western Defense Command, 13 Jan. 1943, Butler to Stevenson, 23 Jan. 1943, Stevenson to Butler, 9 Feb. 1943, and Stevenson to secretary DND for Air, 9 Feb. 1943, DHist 181.002 (D433)

74 No 8 Squadron, ORB daily diary, 28 Jan.-15 March 1943, DHist; 14 Squadron, ORB daily diary, 5 Feb.-20 March, 12 and 22 April 1943, DHist; RCAF Wing Elmendorf, ORB daily diary, Feb. 1943, App. A, DHist; United States, United States Fleet, 'Battle Experience: Assault and Occupation of Attu Island, May 1943,' 48-1, 5 Oct. 1943, DHist 112.3M1009 (D73); 'History of the Eleventh Army Air Force,' 226, 259, DHist 80/176, file 12; Craven and Cate, eds., *The Army Air Forces*, IV, 378-9

75 DeWitt to Stevenson, and enclosure, 16 Feb. 1943, DHist 181.002 (D433); Morrow to Bezeau, 29 Feb. 1980, 'Historical Summary,' 21-2, R.E. Morrow biographical file, DHist; handing-over certificate, 1 March 1943, AFHQ 804-8/27, PAC, RG 24, vol. 17721; 14 Squadron, ORB daily diary, 31 March, 1-17 April 1943, DHist

76 Morison, *Naval Operations*, VII, 20-1; Craven and Cate, eds., *The Army Air Forces*, IV, 378-81; Conn, Engelman, and Fairchild, *Guarding the United States*, 279-80, 284; 'History of the Eleventh Army Air Force,' nd, 257-8, DHist 80/176, file 12; '11 AF Assigned and Attached Units,' ibid., file 2; 'History of Eleventh Fighter Squadron,' 77, ibid., file 11

77 'History of the Eleventh Army Air Force,' 266, 268-70, DHist 80/176, file 12

78 'Historical Summary,' 21, R.E. Morrow biographical file, DHist

79 No 14 Squadron, ORB daily diary and operations record, 17, 18, 19 April 1943, DHist; Craven and Cate, eds., *The Army Air Forces*, IV, 379-81; 'History of the Eleventh Army Air Force,' 269-71, DHist 80/176, file 12; Morison, *Naval Operations*, VII, 41-51; Conn, Engelman, and Fairchild, *Guarding the United States*, 294-5

80 No 14 Squadron, ORB daily diary, 15 May, 3 July, and Sept. 1943, DHist; Conn, Engelman, and Fairchild, *Guarding the United States*, 296; Stacey, *Six Years of War*, 500-3; Craven and Cate, eds., *The Army Air Forces*, IV, 389-90; 'History of the Eleventh Army Air Force,' 307, DHist 80/176, file 12; DeWitt to Stevenson, 24 June 1943, AOC WAC to AFHQ, A496, 15 July 1943, AOC WAC to CG Western Defense Command, A497, 15 July 1943, WAC S.201-8-1 pt 1, DHist 181.002 (D433); 111 Squadron, ORB daily diary, 12-22 July and 1-20 Aug. 1943, DHist

81 Organization order no 50, 6 April 1942, No 4 Group HQ, ORB daily diary, DHist; 'R.C.A.F. in the Aleutians,' chap. 2, 6, DHist 74/3, vol. 1; CAS to AOC WAC, X161, 30 May 1942, WAC S.262-1-2 pt 2, DHist 181.009 (D3583); organization order no 82, 18 June 1942, WAC S.202-1-17, DHist 181.002 (D248); Kostenuk and Griffin, *RCAF Squadron Histories*, 62-3, 65

82 Webber, *Retaliation*, 18-20, 36-40

83 Ibid., 38; Anderson to Ralston, 2 July 1942, HQ 15-24-6, PAC, RG 24, vol. 5198; Breadner to Portal, 22 Feb. 1943, PRO, Air 2/5365; Anderson to minister, 2 July 1942, Goddard, 'Air Defence of the West Coast,' sec. 14, DHist 74/4; 9 Squadron, ORB daily diary, 20 June 1942, DHist

84 Amendment to patrol chart no 2, 4 Aug. 1942, HQS 204-5-1 pt 1, DHist 181.009 (D3468)

85 AOC to station COs, 4 Aug. 1942, ibid.

86 Martineau report on visits to Canadian and US air commands, nd, PRO, Air 15/217

87 AOC WAC to No 4 Group and stations, 26 Aug. 1942, HQS 204-5-1 pt 1, DHist 181.009 (D3468)

88 Organization order no 102, 26 Nov. 1942, No 2 Group HQ, ORB daily diary, 1 Jan. 1943, DHist; WAC, ORB daily diary, Jan. 1943, App. 26, DHist; 'Western Air Command,' secs. 32-4, 40, 43-6, DHist 74/3, vol. 2

89 No 4 Squadron, ORB daily diary, 22 Dec. 1942, DHist; Kostenuk and Griffin, *RCAF Squadron Histories*, 24, 27-8, 31, 55

90 Ibid., 30, 48, 66; inspector general's [IG] report, RCAF Station Tofino, June 1943, 2-3, Station Tofino s.641-9, DHist 181.003 (D2366)

91 CO Tofino to AOC WAC, 12 Oct. 1943, s.641-9, DHist 181.003 (D2366)

92 WAC to No 4 Group, Alliford Bay, 3 Nov. 1943, WAC s.202-1-32, DHist 181.009 (D2688); 'Fighter-Filter Control,' 25 Sept. 1944, 8-9, DHist 80/395; 'Radar in the Royal Canadian Air Force,' nd, 19-20, ibid.; IG's report, RCAF Station Tofino, June 1943, 12-4, Station Tofino s.641-9, DHist 181.003 (D2366)

93 'Western Air Command,' sec. 28, DHist 74/3, vol. 2; W.G. Goddard, 'North West Air Command,' unpublished narrative [1945], secs. 28-30, DHist 74/6; correspondence, HQS 19-5-7 pt 1, PAC, RG 24, vol. 5215

94 Stevenson to secretary DND for Air, 17 June 1943, DHist 181.002 (D433); 'R.C.A.F. in the Aleutians,' chap. 2, 8-9, DHist 74/3, vol. 1; Stevenson to AFHQ, 19 and 30 Oct. 1943, AFHQ to WAC, 31 Oct. 1943, Cornblat to AOC WAC, 9 Nov. 1943, WAC s.202-1-1 pt 1, DHist 181.002 (D421); Stacey, *Arms, Men and Governments*, 294-6

95 Breadner to minister, 'Air Defence of Canada Plan – 1944,' 24 Sept. 1943, 1, 4-5, DHist 181.004 (D3)

96 Leckie to AOC WAC, 12 Jan. 1944, WAC s.204-1-1 pt 1, DHist 181.002 (D149)

97 Curtis for CAS to AOC WAC, 16 March 1944, ibid.

98 'Air Defence of Canada Plan – 1944 (revised),' 10 Feb. 1944, WAC base summaries, nd, Mullaly to secretary Chiefs of Staff Committee, 23 Feb. 1944, Mullaly to brigadier general staff Pacific Command, 25 Feb. 1944, PCS 508-1-1-4, folder 6d, DHist 322.019 (D11); organization order no 165, 28 Feb. 1944, No 2 Group HQ, ORB daily diary, DHist

99 Secretary Chiefs of Staff Committee to secretary Joint Service Committee Pacific Command and enclosure, 31 July 1944, Joint Service Committee Pacific Command minutes, 31 July 1944, s.201-3-1 pt 4, DHist 181.003 (D4019); extract from minutes of Chiefs of Staff Committee meeting, 25 Aug. 1944, DHist 193.009 (D34); WAC operations order nos 32 and 33, 19 Aug. 1944, WAC s.604-1-1, DHist 181.003 (D258); organization order nos 218 and 222, 21 Sept. and 19 Oct. 1944, Station Bella Bella, ORB daily diary, DHist; organization order no 440, 21 Sept. 1944, Station Ucluelet, ORB daily diary, DHist; 'Air Defence of Canada Plan – 1944/45 (2nd rev.),' 25 Oct. 1944, PCS 508-1-1-4, folder 62, DHist 322.019 (D11)

100 Bennett to CO Tofino, 21 Sept. 1944, WAC s.604-1-1, DHist 181.003 (D258); Heakes to secretary DND for Air, 1 Feb. 1945, WAC s.204-1-1 pt 2, DHist 181.002 (D149)

101 No 8 Squadron, ORB daily diary, Nov.-Dec. 1944, DHist; Stacey, *Arms, Men and Governments*, 474-84

102 'Conference Held at Western Air Command,' 3 May 1945, NWAC S.204-9, DHist
181.002 (D269); Guthrie to COS, 21 April 1945, WAC S.3-4, DHist 74/715;
Webber, *Retaliation*, 65-8, 99-100, 103-8, 113; Yasushi Hidagi, 'Attack Against
the US Heartland,' *Aerospace Historian*, XXVII, summer 1981, 87-93; Corne-
lius W. Conley, 'The Great Japanese Balloon Offensive,' *Air University Review*,
XIX, Jan.-Feb. 1968, 69-74

103 Military District No 12, 'Japanese Balloons; RS 4-7-45,' DHist 168.009 (D11);
Webber, *Retaliation*, 99, 110-12, 136-7, 171-2; Stewart to AOC North West
Air Command, 26 May 1945, DHist 181.009 (D6416); Conley, 'Balloon Offensive,' 75-6, 81-3; Hidagi, 'Heartland,' 9; Robert Harris and Jeremy Paxman, *A
Higher Form of Killing: the Secret Story of Gas and Germ Warfare* (London
1982), 140-1, 152-3; 'The Shame of Japan,' Fifth Estate television programme, Canadian Broadcasting Corporation, 25 Jan. 1983

104 Canada, National Defence Headquarters, Directorate of Military Operations and
Planning, 'General Summary, Japanese Balloons in Canada,' 15 March 1945,
1, 9-10, copy, DHist 74/715; 'Japanese Balloon Incidents, Summary No 8,' 4
April 1945, WAC S.3-4, ibid.; Conley, 'Balloon Offensive,' 80-1; minute to
SASO, on AFHQ to WAC, 13 March 1945, WAC S.232-2-1 pt 1, DHist 181.009
(D6417); 'Conference Held at Western Air Command,' 3 May 1945, NWAC
S.204-9, DHist 181.002 (D269); Canada, *RCAF Logbook*, 81; 133 Squadron, ORB
daily diary, 21 Feb. and 10 March 1945, DHist; 6 Squadron, ORB daily diary,
12 March 1945, DHist

105 'Japanese Balloon Incidents, Summary No 8,' 4 April 1945, App. A, 11, DHist
74/715; Conley, 'Balloon Offensive,' 76-7, 79, 81; Hidagi, 'Heartland,' 92-3.
Webber, *Retaliation*, 108, 110, 122-3, 136-47, 172, lists two other balloons shot
down over Canadian territory. Canadian records do not substantiate this
assertion.

106 'Report on Operational Procedure, Western Air Command,' 21 Nov. 1945, 21,
WAC S.204-1-1 pt 3, DHist 181.002 (D149)

CHAPTER 12: THE BEGINNINGS OF ANTI-SUBMARINE WARFARE

1 S.F. Wise, *Canadian Airmen and the First World War* (Official History of the
Royal Canadian Air Force, I; Toronto 1980), 603-9; J.D.F. Kealy and E.C.
Russell, *A History of Canadian Naval Aviation, 1918-1962* (Ottawa 1965), 1-10

2 Wise, *Canadian Airmen*, 226

3 Eberhard Rossler, *The U-Boat: the Evolution and Technical History of German
Submarines* (Annapolis, Md 1981), 328-30

4 Ibid., 335-8; Arthur Marder, *From the Dardanelles to Oran: Studies of the Royal
Navy in War and Peace, 1915-1940* (London 1974), 38-48; Basil Collier, *The
Defence of the United Kingdom* (History of the Second World War, United Kingdom Military Series; London 1957), 55-6; Alfred Price, *Aircraft versus Submarine: the Evolution of the Anti-Submarine Aircraft, 1912-1972* (London 1973),
32-42

5 Great Britain, Air Ministry, Air Historical Branch, 'The R.A.F. in Maritime War,
II: The Atlantic and Home Waters, the Defensive Phase, September 1939 to

June 1941,' nd, 50 n 1, 371-2, DHist 79/599; Price, *Aircraft versus Submarine*, 39, 43-4

6 Air Ministry 'The R.A.F. in Maritime War,' II, 50; S.W. Roskill, *The War at Sea, 1939-1945*, I: *The Defensive* (History of the Second World War, United Kingdom Military Series; London 1954), 104-5

7 Great Britain, Air Ministry, Air Historical Branch, 'The R.A.F. in Maritime War, I: The Atlantic and Home Waters, the Prelude, April 1918 to September 1939,' nd, 212-19, 232-4, DHist 79/599; ibid., II, 285-8, 394-5; Roskill, *War at Sea*, I, 361

8 F.H. Hinsley et al, *British Intelligence in the Second World War: Its Influence on Strategy and Operations* (New York 1979-84), II, 12-13, 23-45; Patrick Beesly, *Very Special Intelligence: the Story of the Admiralty's Operational Intelligence Centre, 1939-1945* (London 1977), 1-41; 'History and Activities of the Operational Intelligence Centre, NSHQ, 1939-45,' NSS 1440-18, DHist

9 Great Britain, Admiralty, Historical Section, *Defeat of the Enemy Attack on Shipping, 1939-1945: a Study of Policy and Operations* (BR 1736 (51) (1), Naval Staff History Second World War; np [1957]), IA, 251; ibid., IB, Table 13; Air Ministry, 'The R.A.F. in Maritime War,' II, App. XIX

10 Air Ministry, 'The R.A.F. in Maritime War,' II, 49, 371-3

11 Great Britain, Admiralty, Tactical and Staff Duties Division, *The U-Boat War in the Atlantic*, I: *1939-1941* (BR 305 (1), German Naval History Series; np [1950]), 49; Admiralty, *Defeat of the Enemy Attack on Shipping*, IA, 61-6

12 Air Ministry, 'The R.A.F. in Maritime War,' II, 274-81, 294-5, 372-5

13 Ibid., 302-4; Hinsley, *British Intelligence in the Second World War*, I, 336-9

14 Air Ministry, 'The R.A.F. in Maritime War,' II, 302; Admiralty, *U-Boat War*, I, 73, 82-3; Admiral Karl Dönitz, *Memoirs: Ten Years and Twenty Days* (Westport, Ct 1978), 131, 175, 177

15 Admiralty, *Defeat of the Enemy Attack on Shipping*, IA, 245; ibid., IB, Table 13

16 RAF Coastal Command, Operational Research Section, 'A Simple Analysis of the Results of A/S Warfare,' report no 169, 31 Jan. 1942, DHist 181.003 (D929); *Coastal Command Review*, March-April 1942, 23-6; Great Britain, Air Ministry, Air Historical Branch, 'The R.A.F. in Maritime War, III: The Atlantic and Home Waters, the Preparative Phase, July 1941 to February 1943,' nd, 10 n 1, 29, 35-6, DHist 79/599; ibid., II, 304; Admiralty, *Defeat of the Enemy Attack on Shipping*, IA, 73

17 Air Ministry, 'The R.A.F. in Maritime War,' III, 48-51

18 Ibid., II, 40, 380-1, and III, 42-3

19 *Coastal Command Review*, I, Jan.-Feb. 1942, 34-5; RAF Coastal Command, Operational Research Section, 'Attacks on U-Boats by Aircraft,' report no 248, Aug. 1943, DHist 181.003 (D929); Air Ministry, 'The R.A.F. in Maritime War,' III, 40-2, 80-1; Admiralty, Anti-Submarine Warfare Division of the Naval Staff, *Monthly Anti-Submarine Report, July 1942* (CB 04050/42(7), 15 Aug. 1942), 45

20 Admiralty, Anti-Submarine Warfare Division of the Naval Staff, *Monthly Anti-Submarine Report, June 1941* (CB 04050/41(6), 15 July 1941), 13-15; Coastal Command Tactical Instruction no 31, 24 July 1942, S.28-5-11 pt I, PAC, RG 24, vol. 5272; Coastal Command, 'Submarine and Anti-Submarine,' Oct. 1942, PRO, Air 15/155/4080

21 Air Ministry, 'The R.A.F. in Maritime War,' II, 403-4; *Coastal Command Review*, I, March-April 1942, 27-9

22 Price, *Aircraft versus Submarine*, 70

23 Air Ministry, 'The R.A.F. in Maritime War,' III, 44-7; RAF Coastal Command, Operational Research Section, 'A Review of ASV Performance,' report no 201, 14 Oct. 1942, DHist 181.003 (D929); Price, *Aircraft versus Submarine*, 36-8, 53-9

24 Price, *Aircraft versus Submarine*, 59-65; Air Ministry, 'The R.A.F. in Maritime War,' III, 83-7

25 Air Ministry, 'The R.A.F. in Maritime War,' III, App. XXXIV; Admiralty, *Defeat of the Enemy Attack on Shipping*, IA, 254-6, 280-1

26 Eastern Air Command [EAC] to Air Force Headquarters [AFHQ], 20 May 1941, AFHQ to RCAF Overseas, 21 May 1941, EAC to AFHQ, 22 May 1941, 15-1-350 pt I, PAC, RG 24, vol. 5177; Admiralty to naval officer in charge St John's, no 171B/20, 20 May 1941, in Paul Bridle, ed., *Documents on Relations between Canada and Newfoundland*, I: *1935-1949, Defence, Civil Aviation and Economic Affairs* (Ottawa 1974), 558; Air Ministry to Dominions Office, 29 May 1941, PRO, Air 2/5260; Air Ministry to Ministry of Aircraft Production, 26 May 1941, PRO, Air 1/461

27 No 116 Squadron, operations record book [ORB] daily diary, DHist; EAC to AFHQ, 28 May 1941, DHist 181.002 (D124); Naval Service Headquarters [NSHQ] to Admiralty, 28 May 1941, air attaché Washington to AFHQ, 28 May 1941, 15-1-350 pt I, PAC, RG 24, vol. 5177; special naval observer London to British Chiefs of Staff Committee, 3 Aug. 1941, A.205/9, PRO, Adm 205/9

28 Naval Section, 'U-Boat Methods of Combined Attack on Convoys, from February 1st to October 31st 1941,' 10 Nov. 1941, PRO, Adm 223/1; *Befehlshaber der Unterseeboote* [BdU] war diary, translation, 6-20 May 1941, DHist 79/446; BdU teletype, 22 June 1941, DHist SGR II, 197, reel II

29 C.P. Stacey, *Arms, Men and Governments: the War Policies of Canada, 1939-1945* (Ottawa 1970), 125-36, 349-53, 361-5; S.W. Dziuban, *Military Relations between the United States and Canada, 1939-1945* (United States Army in World War II, Special Studies; Washington 1959), 104-5; Maurice Matloff and Edwin M. Snell, *Strategic Planning for Coalition Warfare, 1941-1942* (United States Army in World War II, The War Department; Washington 1953), 40-8; Admiralty, first sea lord's papers, PRO, Adm 205, vols. 9 and 10; US Naval History Division, Strategic Plans Division, VII, box 147G, and XIII, box 187; W.A.B. Douglas, 'Kanadas Marine und Luftwaffe in der Atlantikschlacht,' *Marine Rundschau*, March 1980, 151-64

30 Anderson to Breadner, 5 June 1941, DHist 181.009 (D6734)

31 Ibid.

32 Anderson to Joubert de la Ferté, 4 July 1941, DHist 181.002 (D121); Portal to Pound, 12 Feb. 1942, PRO, Adm 205/17; Consolidated Liberator permanent reference file, DHist

33 Anderson to Stevenson, 9 July 1941, DHist 181.009 (D6734); RCAF London to AFHQ, 26 July 1941, Power to Breadner, 25 Aug. 1941, 17-1-26, PAC, RG 24, vol. 5210; RCAF London to AFHQ, 13 Nov. 1941, 519-6-10, ibid., vol. 5218

34 'History and Activities of the Operational Intelligence Centre, NSHQ, 1939-45,' NSS 1440-18, DHist; Heakes interview, 26 Feb. 1976, F.V. Heakes Papers, DHist

77/51; meeting, 19 June 1941, chief of the naval staff [CNS] to chief of the air staff [CAS], 30 June 1941, 66-2-2, PAC, RG 24, vol. 5410

35 'History and Activities of the Operational Intelligence Centre, NSHQ, 1939-45,' NSS 1440-18, DHist; BdU war diary, June 1941, DHist 79/446; EAC intelligence file, s.22-4 pt 1, DHist 78/471; 10 Squadron, ORB daily diary, June 1941, DHist

36 Heakes to AFHQ, 23 Sept. 1941, Anderson to AFHQ, 14 Feb. 1942, 15-1-350 pt 1, PAC, RG 24, vol. 5177

37 NSS 8280-HX 132, DHist mfm; BdU war diary, June 1941, DHist 79/446

38 CAS to air officer commanding [AOC] EAC, 11 Nov. 1942, Anderson to air officer commanding-in-chief [AOCinC] Coastal Command, 4 July 1941, DHist 181.002 (D121)

39 BdU war diary, 9-13 Sept. 1941, DHist 79/446; 116 Squadron, ORB daily diary, DHist; NSS 8280-HX 133, DHist mfm; PRO, Adm 199/718

40 EAC, 1 Group, 10 and 116 Squadrons, ORB daily diaries, 9-13 Sept. 1941, DHist

41 BdU war diary, DHist 79/446; RCAF Station Gander weekly intelligence report, 1 Dec. 1941, DHist 181.002 (D178); 'Report of 1 Group Operations,' 25 Oct. 1941, DHist 181.002 (D173)

42 'Report of Investigation,' 1 Nov. 1941, DHist 181.002 (D173)

43 AOC EAC to commanding officer [CO] RCAF Station Gander, 3 Dec. 1941, AOC EAC to all BR Squadrons, 5 Dec. 1941, ibid.

44 BdU war diary, DHist 79/446; DHist 181.002 (D173); Admiralty, Anti-Submarine Warfare Division of the Naval Staff, *Monthly Anti-Submarine Report, November 1941* (CB 04050/41(11), 15 Dec. 1941)

45 Admiralty to CO Atlantic Coast, and commodore commanding Newfoundland Force, 24 Nov. 1941, DHist 181.002 (D173); BdU war diary, 22 Nov. 1941, DHist 79/446; Dönitz, *Memoirs*, 159

46 No 1 Group weekly intelligence reports, DHist 181.003 (D2178); RCAF Station Gander weekly intelligence reports, DHist 181.002 (D178); 10 and 116 Squadrons, ORB daily diaries, DHist; DHist 80/15

47 EAC movement order no 1-41, 22 Sept. 1941, DHist 181.006 (D13); 5 and 116 Squadrons, ORB daily diaries, Oct. 1941-Feb. 1942, DHist; air force routine order [AFRO] 1549, 19 Dec. 1941

48 'The History of Eastern Air Command,' unpublished narrative [1945], 249, 270, 301, 339, DHist 74/2, vol. 2

49 Summary of activities, air member for air staff, weeks ending 30 June, 10 Aug., 5 Oct., 30 Nov. 1941, DHist 79/430, pt 1; No 16 'X' Depot, Debert, NS, daily diary, 20 Sept. and 27 Oct. 1941, DHist; J.S. Gunn, 'History of Armament Activities,' unpublished narrative, 1945, DHist 80/395; AOC EAC to air attaché Washington, 30 Nov. 1941, AOC EAC to AFHQ, 3 Dec. 1941, DHist 181.002 (D173)

50 Chiefs of staff to AOC RCAF London, 21 Nov. 1940, HQS 452-4-41, PAC, RG 24, vol. 5432; Annis interview, 10 Sept. 1979, C.L. Annis biographical file, DHist

51 Anderson to AOCinC Coastal Command, 4 July 1941, DHist 181.002 (D123); EAC movement order no 3, 6 Jan. 1942, DHist 181.006 (D13)

52 BdU war diary, 7 Jan. 1942, DHist 79/446

53 Admiralty to ships and authorities in area 'A,' message, 9 Jan. 1942, DHist 78/471, vol. 2

54 EAC anti-submarine [A/S] report, Jan. 1942, DHist 181.003 (D25); RCAF attack report, 28 Feb. 1942, DHist 181.003 (D1300)

55 RCAF attack report, 12 Jan. 1942, DHist 76/278

56 No 119 Squadron, ORB daily diary, 12 Jan. 1942, DHist; U-130 log, copy and translation, DHist 85/77, pt 5; 1 Group weekly intelligence reports, 10 and 17 Jan. 1942, DHist 181.003 (D2178)

57 Commander Task Unit 4.1.8 to commander Task Force Four, 'Report of Escort Operations with Convoy ON 51 – December 30th to January 11th,' 13 Jan. 1942, PRO, Adm 199/729; 'ON Convoys General,' DHist 81/520/8280, box 5ON; BdU war diary, 11 Jan. 1942, DHist 79/446

58 AOC EAC to secretary Department of National Defence for Air, 'Air Intelligence,' serial no 45, 15 Jan. 1942, DHist 181.003 (D624), vol. 1; Jürgen Rohwer, *Die U-Boot-Erfolge der Achsenmächte, 1939-1945* (München 1968), 74; RCAF attack report, 19 Jan. 1942, DHist 76/278; U-86 log, DHist 85/77, pt 8

59 RCAF attack report, 22 Jan. 1942, DHist 76/278; U-84 log, DHist 85/77, pt 9

60 EAC A/S report, Jan. 1942, DHist. 181.003 (D25)

61 Great Britain, Admiralty, *The U-Boat War in the Atlantic*, II: *January 1942-May 1943* (BR 305 (2), German Naval History Series; London 1952), 4

62 Hinsley, *British Intelligence in the Second World War*, II, 179, 230-1, 543

63 Ibid., 228; Rohwer, *Die U-Boot-Erfolge*, 79-80; records of U-boat officers, DHist NHS 1650; Admiralty to ships and authorities in area 'A,' message, 24 Feb. 1942, DHist 78/471, vol. 2

64 RCAF Station Dartmouth weekly intelligence report, 27 Feb. 1942, DHist 181.003 (D4096)

65 U-96 log, DHist 85/77, pt 10

66 RCAF Station Dartmouth weekly intelligence report, 27 Feb. 1942, DHist 181.003 (D4096); 1 Group weekly intelligence report, 28 Feb. 1942, DHist 181.003 (D2178); NSS 8280-ON 67, DHist mfm

67 RCAF attack report, 2 March 1942, DHist 76/278

68 BdU war diary, 6 March 1942, DHist 79/446

69 Ibid., 8 March 1942

70 RCAF attack report, 8 March 1942, DHist 76/278; U-96 log, DHist 85/77, pt 12

71 RCAF attack report, 23 March 1942, DHist 181.003 (D1309); U-754 log, DHist 85/77, pt 13

72 Admiralty, *U-Boat War*, II, 4-7; Admiralty, *Defeat of the Enemy Attack on Shipping*, IA, 59

73 BdU war diary, 13 March 1942, DHist 79/446

74 AOC EAC to CO 31 Operational Training Unit, 13 April 1942, HQ 450-22/31 pt 2, PAC, RG 24, vol. 3397; EAC A/S report, April 1942, DHist 181.003 (D2649); RCAF attack reports, 8 and 28 April 1942, DHist 181.003 (D1310) and (D1311)

75 AOC 19 Group, RAF, to AOCinC Coastal Command, 5 March 1942, 'Air Vice-Marshal Bromet's Report on his visit to the United States and Canada, January-February, 1942,' PRO, Air 2/1040

76 Chiefs of staff minutes, 17 March 1942, DHist 193.009 (D53); AOC EAC to AFHQ, message, 22 Dec. 1941, S.314-4, DHist 79/237

77 AOC EAC to AOC 1 Group, 'Anti-U-boat Warfare,' 13 Feb. 1942, AOC EAC to 1

Group HQ repeat stations, signal, 13 March 1942, DHist 181.009 (DI 147); Gunn, 'History of Armament Activities,' DHist 80/395

78 RCAF attack reports, DHist 181.003 (DI 302), (DI 304), (DI 305), (DI 306), (DI 308), (DI 309); Joubert de la Ferté to Anderson, 7 May 1942, PRO, Air 15/368; air member for air staff weekly summary of activities, 8 May 1942, DHist 79/430, pt 1

79 C.B. Limbrick, 'Radar in the RCAF in the Second Great War,' unpublished narrative [1961], DHist 72/376; 'Monthly S.I. Operations Reports,' April 1942, DHist 181.003 (D3369); 'Operational Units – RCAF,' 15 April 1942, DHist 181.002 (D460), pt 2; 117 Squadron, ORB daily diary, 27 April–31 May 1942, DHist; S. Kostenuk and J. Griffin, *RCAF Squadron Histories and Aircraft, 1924-1968* (Toronto 1977), 64, 68

CHAPTER 13: THE BATTLE OF THE ST LAWRENCE

1 U-553 log, 8 Sept. 1942, DHist mfm 83/665

2 Joint Staff Committee, 'Emergency Plan for the Defence of the Eastern Coast of Canada,' 16 Sept. 1938, HQS 5199-0 pt 1, PAC, RG 24, vol. 2700; Anderson to secretary Department of National Defence [DND], 29 Aug. 1939, S.19-6-5 pt 1, ibid., vol. 2517; 'The History of Eastern Air Command,' unpublished narrative [1945], 104-9, DHist 74/2, vol. 1

3 Director of Plans Division to Chiefs of Staff Committee, 14 March 1940, HQS 5199-V, PAC, RG 24, vol. 2722; naval secretary, 'Memorandum: Defence of Shipping in Gulf of St. Lawrence,' 501-9-3, ibid., vol. 11124; 'Fort Ramsay (Base),' DHist NHS 8000

4 'The History of Eastern Air Command,' 143-4, 166, 207, DHist 74/2, vol. 1; Pate to air officer commanding [AOC] Eastern Air Command [EAC], 18 Nov. 1942, RCAF Station Gaspé, daily diary, DHist; EAC operation order 3/40, 25 May 1940, App. K (revised), 501-1-13, PAC, RG 24, vol. 11123

5 Chief of the air staff [CAS] to AOC EAC, signal A.184, 18 May 1942, S.19-6-5 pt 4, PAC, RG 24, vol. 5217; 119 Squadron, operations record book [ORB] daily diary, 1-6 June 1942, DHist; 116 Squadron, ORB daily diary, 31 May-1 Aug. 1942, DHist

6 No 1 General Reconnaissance School [GRS], 31 GRS, 31 Operational Training Unit [OTU], and 36 OTU, ORB daily diaries, 1941-2, passim, DHist; commanding officer [CO] 31 GRS to AOC EAC, 22 March and 5 April 1941, DHist 181.002 (D58), 287-9; 9 Bombing and Gunnery School [B&GS], ORB daily diary, 15 Dec. 1941, DHist; 'The History of Eastern Air Command,' 304-5, DHist 74/2, vol. 2

7 Naval staff minutes, 30 March 1942, DHist; CAS to AOC EAC, 10 April 1942, S.19-5-6 pt 1, PAC, RG 24, vol. 5217; 'Minutes of St. Lawrence Operations Conference held in Ottawa, February 22nd-24th, 1943,' DHist 79/179

8 Minute by deputy chief of the naval staff, 22 April 1941, NSS 8280-166/16 pt 1, PAC, RG 24, vol. 6788

9 Director of Plans Division to Chiefs of Staff Committee, 14 March 1940, HQS 5199-V, PAC, RG 24, vol. 2722; naval secretary, 'Defence of Shipping – Gulf of St. Lawrence,' draft plan, 18 April 1941, NSS 8280-166/16 pt 1, ibid., vol. 6788; 'History and Activities of the Operational Intelligence Centre, NSHQ, 1939-45,' annex 'W/T Intelligence (W/T "Y") – German,' 1942, NSS 1440-18, DHist

10 'History and Review of the Aircraft Detection Corps [ADC],' unpublished narrative, 1944, DHist 80/395; reports on ADC, DHist 321.009 (D94); Boucher memorandum, 18 Sept. 1942, deputy director ADC to air member for air staff [AMAS] (operations), 23 July 1942, Boucher to Goodspeed, 22 Sept. 1942, 460-7-1 pt 2, PAC, RG 24, vol. 3404

11 CAS to AOC EAC, signal A.184, 18 May 1942, S.19-6-5 pt 4, PAC, RG 24, vol. 5217; K.M. Guthrie, 'Air Aspect of the Defence of the Gulf and River of St. Lawrence,' 16 Dec. 1942, NSS 1037-2-6 pt 1, ibid., vol. 3901

12 John Slessor, *The Central Blue* (London 1956), 497

13 'The St. Lawrence Incident, May 1942,' nd, DHist NHS 1650-239/16B pt 1; AOC 1 Group to AOC EAC, signal A.219, 11 May 1942, DHist 181.002 (D124)

14 RCN commanding officer Atlantic Coast [COAC] to HMS *Vanquisher*, signal 0630Z, 12 May 1942, NSS 8280-ON 91, DHist mfm; COAC to HNMS *Lincoln*, signal 0730Z, 12 May 1942, NSS 8280-ON 90, DHist mfm; EAC operations summaries, 11 May-10 June 1942, S.19-6-5 pt 4, PAC, RG 24, vol. 5217; 5 Squadron, ORB daily diary, 11-15 May 1942, DHist; 31 GRS, ORB daily diary, 10-12 May 1942, DHist; 11 Squadron, ORB daily diary, 12 May 1942, DHist; 116 Squadron, ORB daily diary, 12 May-5 June 1942, DHist; 117 Squadron, ORB daily diary, 27 April-10 June 1942, DHist

15 Secretary Naval Board, 1 April 1942, 'Defence of Shipping – Gulf of St. Lawrence – 1942 (Short Title GL2),' H1002-1-8 pt 1, PAC, RG 24, vol. 11692; RCN daily states, 30 May, 13 June 1942, DHist NHS 1650-DS

16 G.N. Tucker, *The Naval Service of Canada: Its Official History*, II: *Activities on Shore during the Second World War* (Ottawa 1952), 538-9; NS 1048-48-32, PAC, RG 24, vol. 3976; NSS 8280-116/16 pt 3, ibid., vol. 6789; file 48-2-5, ibid., vol. 11098; file 1-14-2, ibid., vol. 11503

17 U-553 log, DHist mfm 83/665; *Befehlshaber der Unterseeboote* [BdU] war diary, translation, 20 May 1942, DHist 79/446; 'Report Made by BdU to Fuehrer on 14 May 1942,' annex to BdU war diary entry for 15 July 1942, ibid.

18 King Diary, 13 May 1942, W.L.M. King Papers, PAC, MG 26 J 13

19 Director of Naval Intelligence [DNI], 'St. Lawrence Incident, 11 May 1942, Notes on Consequences of Publicity,' nd, DHist NHS 1650-239/16B pt 2. See also 'Outline History of Trade Division, NSHQ, Ottawa,' 35, DHist 81/520/8280, box 1, 8280B, vol. 2; and newspaper clippings in DHist 73/912 and in DHist 81/531, box 180, file 144.

20 Canada, Parliament, House of Commons, *Debates*, 13 May 1942, 2389-90; minister's private secretary to chief of the naval staff, 11 Sept. 1940, NS 1065-2-3, PAC, RG 24, vol. 4030; Queen's University Archives, C.G. Power Papers, box 70, file D2032

21 Great Britain, Admiralty, Tactical and Staff Duties Division, *The U-Boat War in the Atlantic*, II: *January 1942-May 1943* (BR 305(2), German Naval History Series; np [1952]), 19; 117 Squadron, ORB, July summary, DHist; COAC to secretary Naval Board, 28 July 1942, DHist 81/520/8280 QS 15; BdU war diary, 20 July 1942, DHist 79/446; director Operations Division [DOD] weekly report, 9 July 1942, DHist 85/251

22 Guthrie, 'Air Aspect of the Defence of the Gulf and River of St. Lawrence,' NSS

1037-2-6 pt I, PAC, RG 24, vol. 3901; F.V. Heakes, 'Review of Article in L'Action Catholique, October 14th, 1942 entitled "What is Happening in Gaspé,"' 27 Oct. 1942, DHist 181.002 (D107)

23 EAC to Air Force Headquarters [AFHQ], signal A.39, 15 July 1942, DHist 181.009 (D121); 130 Squadron, ORB daily diary, 6 July 1942, DHist; 'Summary of Accident Investigation No 326,' 4 Aug. 1942, DHist 181.003 (D3898); 9 B&GS, ORB daily diary, 6 July 1942, DHist; Little to Anderson, 18 July 1942, S.19-6-5 pt 5, PAC, RG 24, vol. 5217

24 RCN daily states, 18 July 1942, DHist NHS 1650-DS; 113 and 119 Squadrons, ORBs, 6 July 1942, DHist; DHist 181.009 (D121); DHist 181.009 (D304); EAC anti-submarine [A/S] report, July 1942, DHist 181.003 (D25); RCAF attack report, 7 July 1942, DHist 181.003 (D1317); U-132 log, copy and translation, 7 July 1942, DHist 85/77, pt 18

25 House of Commons, *Debates*, 12-13 July 1942, 4098, 4124-6

26 Ibid., 13 and 16 July 1942, 4124-6, 4278-90

27 Godbout to King, 15 July 1942, King Papers, PAC, MG 26 J 1, reel C-6806, 276149-276149A; King Diary, 18 July 1942, PAC, MG 26 J 13

28 NSS 8280-QS 19, DHist mfm; EAC operations summaries for 19-20 July 1942, DHist 181.003 (D304)

29 Admiralty, *U-Boat War*, II, 37

30 S.E. Morrison, *History of United States Naval Operations in World War II, I: The Battle of the Atlantic, September 1939-May 1943* (Boston 1947), 330-1; AOC EAC to AFHQ, signal A.90, 29 Aug. 1942, DHist 181.003 (D304); I Group weekly intelligence report, 28 Aug. 1942, DHist 181.003 (D2178); AOC EAC to Anderson, 29 Aug. 1942, EAC to AFHQ, signal A.122, 3 Oct. 1942, DHist 181.009 (D121)

31 DOD weekly report, 3 Sept. 1942, DHist 85/251; coastal convoy signals, 'LN 6,' 'LN 7,' DHist; EAC operations summaries for 2-3 Sept. 1942, DHist 181.003 (D304); U-517 log, 3 Sept. 1942, DHist 85/77, pt 24

32 DOD weekly report, 10 Sept. 1942, DHist 85/251; staff A/S officer COAC, 'Analysis of U-Boat Attack on Convoy QS 33, 7th Sept. 1942,' 16 Nov. 1942, 21-1-14, PAC, RG 24, vol. 11504; BdU war diary, 6 Sept. 1942, DHist 79/446; EAC operations summaries for 6-7 Sept. 1942, DHist 181.003 (D304)

33 Nos 5 and 113 Squadrons, ORB daily diaries, DHist; CAS to minister of national defence for the naval service, 4 Nov. 1942 and encl., DHist 181.002 (D107)

34 Staff officer (operations) COAC, Report of Proceedings, Sept. 1942, NSS 1000-5-13 pt 14, DHist; COAC to Naval Service Headquarters [NSHQ], signal 1545Z, 12 Sept. 1942, and other material in RCAF attack report, 9 Sept. 1942, DHist 181.003 (D1321)

35 COAC to commander-in-chief US Fleet [COMINCH], 3 Oct. 1942, 21-1-14, PAC, RG 24, vol. 11504; BdU war diary, 17 Sept. 1942, DHist 79/446

36 Staff officer (operations) COAC, Report of Proceedings, Sept. 1942, NSS 1000-5-13 pt 14, DHist; EAC operations summaries for 11 Sept. 1942, DHist 181.003 (D304); COAC to COMINCH, 8 Oct. 1942, 21-1-14, PAC, RG 24, vol. 11504

37 EAC A/S report, Sept. 1942, DHist 181.003 (D25); Report of Proceedings, SQ 36 and QS 35, DHist 81/520/8280, box 10; staff A/S officer, 'Analysis of Attacks ... on Convoy SQ 36 ...' 3 Nov. 1942, 21-1-14, PAC, RG 24, vol. 11504; Naval Intelli-

gence Division, 'U-517, Interrogation of Crew,' BR 1907 (55), DHist 80/582, pt
16; U-517 log, DHist 85/77, pt 24; H.M. Boucher, memorandum and correspondence, 18 and 22 Sept. 1942, 460-7-1 pt 2, PAC, RG 24, vol. 3404

38 BdU war diary, 16 Sept. 1942, DHist 79/446; EAC weekly intelligence report, 17
Sept. 1942, DHist 181.003 (D423); coastal convoy signals, 'QS,' DHist

39 No 113 Squadron Chatham Detachment, ORB daily diary, 16 Sept. 1942, DHist;
EAC weekly intelligence report, 17 Sept. 1942, DHist 181.003 (D423)

40 Huband to director general military war transport, 30 July 1942, PRO 59/592, copy
in DHist 81/742; Cabinet War Committee minutes, 9 Sept. 1942, PAC, RG 2,
series 7c, vol. 10,.microfilm reel C4874; King Diary, 9 Sept. 1942, PAC, MG 26 J 13

41 NSS 8280-166/16 pt 3, PAC, RG 24, vol. 6789; naval officer in charge [NOIC] Sydney
to COAC, 15 Sept. 1942, COAC to NOIC Sydney and NOIC Quebec, repeated to
NOIC Gaspé, 19 Sept. 1942, 'NOIC Gaspé Misc. 2,' ibid., vol. 11504; naval control
service officer Quebec to NOIC Quebec, 28 Sept. 1942, NSS 8280-QS, DHist
mfm. See also coastal convoy signals, 'SQ,' 'QS,' DHist.

42 Senior air staff officer [SASO] EAC to deputy air member for air staff [D/AMAS]
(Plans), 17 Sept. 1942, DHist 181.009 (D121)

43 Ibid.; EAC weekly intelligence reports, 18 Sept.-22 Oct. 1942, DHist 181.003
(D423); 113 Squadron, ORB daily diary, 26 Sept. 1942, DHist

44 Air force routine order [AFRO] 1000-1001, 1942, DHist; RAF Ferry Command
records, DHist 84/44

45 BdU war diary, 25 Sept., 6-7 Oct. 1942, DHist 79/446; U-517 log, 25 Sept. 1942,
DHist 85/77, pt 24; RCAF attack reports, 24-5 Sept. 1942, DHist 181.003
(D1323), (D1324), and (D1325); EAC operations summary for 24 Sept. 1942, DHist
181.003 (D304); EAC A/S report, Sept. 1942, DHist 181.003 (D25); EAC weekly
intelligence report, 8 Oct. 1942, DHist 181.003 (D423); 113 Squadron, ORB daily
diary, 24-5 Sept. 1942, DHist

46 No 31 GRS, ORB daily diary, 25 Sept. 1942, DHist

47 Coastal convoy signals, 'QS,' DHist; RCAF attack report, 29 Sept. 1942, DHist
181.003 (D1326)

48 RCAF attack report, 29 Sept. 1942, DHist 181.003 (D1326); U-517 log, 29 Sept.
1942, DHist 85/77, pt 24

49 BdU war diary, 19 Sept. 1942, and 'Submarine Situation and Intended Operations'
following entry for 30 Sept. 1942, DHist 79/446

50 Admiralty, *U-Boat War*, II, 57; BdU war diary, 19, 30 Sept., and 6 Oct. 1942,
DHist 79/446; EAC weekly intelligence report, 9 Oct. 1942, DHist 181.003
(D423); EAC operations summaries for 6-7 Oct. 1942, DHist 181.003 (D304);
coastal convoy signals, 'QS,' DHist

51 EAC weekly intelligence reports, 9 and 16 Oct. 1942, DHist 181.003 (D423); EAC
operations summary for 9 Oct. 1942, DHist 181.003 (D304); DOD weekly report,
15 Oct. 1942, DHist 85/251; BdU war diary, 9 Oct. 1942, DHist 79/446; Jürgen
Rohwer, *Die U-Boot-Erfolge der Achsenmächte, 1939-1945* (München 1968),
127; [Handwritten note, misdated 4 Oct. 1942], DHist NHS 8000, '*Arrowhead*';
113 Squadron, ORB daily diary, Mont Joli Detachment, 9 Oct. 1942, Chatham Detachment, 9-11 Oct. 1942, DHist. There may have been additional flights from
Mont Joli, but only the records for the 113 (BR) detachment are available.

52 No 162 Squadron, ORB daily diary, 10-11 Oct. 1942, DHist; BdU war diary, 11 and 22 Oct. 1942, DHist 79/446; NRO Cornerbrook to Admiralty, signal 1918z, 9 Oct. 1942, DHist; coastal convoy signals, 'BS,' DHist; EAC weekly intelligence report, 9 Oct. 1942, paras 60-1, DHist 181.003 (D423); AOC EAC to AFHQ, signal A.451, 19 Oct. 1942, S.19-6-5 pt 5, PAC, RG 24, vol. 5217; Rohwer, *Die U-Boot-Erfolge*, 127; CO HMCS *Vison* to NOIC Sydney, 13 Oct. 1942, Report of Proceedings, 10-11 Oct. 1942, DHist NHS 8000, HMCS *Vison*

53 Nos 117 and 119 Squadrons, ORB daily diaries, 13-14 Oct. 1942, DHist; 113 Squadron, Chatham Detachment, 30 Oct.-8 Nov. 1942, DHist; EAC weekly intelligence report, 16 Oct. 1942, DHist 181.003 (D423); summaries of EAC operations, 13-29 Oct. 1942, DHist 181.003 (D999); DHist NHS 8000, HMCS *Grandmère*; staff officer (operations) COAC, Report of Proceedings, Oct. 1942, para 31, NSS 1000-5-13 pt 15, DHist; DOD weekly report, 15 Oct. 1942, DHist 85/251; EAC operations summaries for 1-8 Nov. 1942, DHist 181.003 (D304); RCAF Station Sydney, daily diary, 31 Oct. 1942, strength return, DHist

54 BdU war diary, 15, 22, and 31 Oct., and 10 Nov. 1942, DHist 79/446; DHist 181.003 (D5)

55 BdU war diary, 17 Nov. 1942, DHist 79/446; MS 0011, PAC, RG 24, vol. 11127; Michael L. Hadley, *U-Boats against Canada: German Submarines in Canadian Waters* (Kingston and Montreal 1985), 145-8

56 No 113 Squadron, daily diary, 13 and 23 Dec. 1942, Mont Joli and Chatham Detachments, ORB daily diary, 1-7 Nov. 1942, DHist; 117 Squadron, ORB, 1-7 Nov. and 1 Dec. 1942, DHist; 162 Squadron, ORB, 1-11 Nov. 1942, DHist; 113 and 162 Detachments at Mont Joli, weekly intelligence reports, 30 Oct.-11 Dec. 1942, DHist 181.003 (D4494); 'QS,' DHist 81/520/8280, box 8

57 Heakes, 'A Review of Article in L'Action Catholique,' DHist 181.002 (D107)

58 Director of Public Relations to Power and Macdonald, 17 Oct. 1942, Power Papers, box 70, file D2032

59 Godbout to King, 21 Oct. 1942, King Papers, PAC, MG 26 J 1, reel C-6806, 276171

60 Roy to King, 13 Oct. 1942, and 'What is Going on in Gaspé, and What in Ottawa?,' and 'Convoy Ships Sunk While Ottawa Guarded *Sportsmen*,' *Toronto Telegram*, 20-1 Oct. 1942, copies in Power Papers, box 70, file D2032; *Toronto Telegram*, 16 Oct. 1942, *New York Times*, 18 Oct. 1942, *Hamilton Spectator*, 14, 15, 26 Oct. 1942, *Globe and Mail*, 16, 22, 30 Oct. 1942, copies in DHist 81/531, box 180

61 Power to Godbout, 9 Nov. 1942, with enclosed ms, 'Memorandum re Sinkings in St Lawrence and Editorial in "L'Action Catholique" 14 October 1942,' 29 Oct. 1942, Power Papers, box 70, file D3032; Heakes, 'A Review of Article in L'Action Catholique,' DHist 181.002 (D107)

62 Power to Brillant, 17 Oct. 1942, DHist 181.002 (D107); *Hamilton Spectator*, 16 Sept., 2, 14 Nov. 1942, *Globe and Mail*, 16 Dec. 1942, DHist 81/531, box 180; *Ottawa Citizen*, 24 Nov. 1942, DHist NHS 1650-239/16B pt 2

63 Cuffe to secretary DND for Air, 21 Dec. 1942, S.15-24-20, PAC, RG 24, vol. 5200

64 Chiefs of Staff Committee, 4 Dec. 1942, DHist 193.099 (D53)

65 NSHQ, Trade Division, 'Review of General Trade Situation in Canadian Coastal Zones 1942-3,' 23 Jan. 1943, DHist NHS 1650-239/16B pt 1; Hurcombe

to Huband, 10 March 1943, NSS 8280-166/16 pt 4, PAC, RG 24, vol. 6789

66 Lay to Anderson, 11 Dec. 1942, enclosing 'Naval Aspect of the Defence of the Gulf of St. Lawrence,' DHist NHS 1650-239/16B pt 2

67 Anderson et al, 'General Review and Report upon Defences in the Gulf and River St. Lawrence ...' 30 Jan. 1943, App. C, DHist 181.003 (D4723); CAS to minister, 'Air Defence of Canada Plan 1943-44,' 20 March 1943, S.096-105 pt 3, PARC 826793

68 'Plans-Air Defence of Shipping – St. Lawrence Area,' Jan.-April 1943 passim, DHist 181.004 (D54); SASO EAC to [EAC staff], 'Gulf Operations – 1943,' 16 April 1943, DHist 181.002 (D151)

69 Amendment list no 1 to secret organization order no 85, 'Formation of RCAF Station, Gaspé, PQ,' 13 April 1943, Gaspé daily diary, DHist; SASO EAC to [EAC staff], 'Gulf Operations – 1943,' 16 April 1943, DHist 181.002 (D151)

70 Deputy CAS to minister, 21 May 1943, Power Papers, box 70, file D2032; K.M. Guthrie, 'Report upon Defences in the Gulf and River St. Lawrence ...' 4 April 1943, App. H, DHist 181.003 (D4723); 'The History of Eastern Air Command,' 601, DHist 74/2, vol. 3; 'Gaspé Operations Narrative,' 27 June to 28 Nov. 1943, DHist 181.005 (D1565); RCAF, 'Gulf of St. Lawrence Controller Logs,' DHist 181.005 (D1555)

71 'Minutes of St. Lawrence Operations Conference ... February 22nd-24th, 1943,' para. 14, DHist NHS 1605-239/16B pt 2; correspondence, 5 April-9 June 1943, 38-2-1B, PAC, RG 24, vol. 11064

72 'Minutes of Meeting to Discuss Coming Anti-Submarine Operations in the Gulf of St. Lawrence,' 30 Jan. 1943, DHist 181.004 (D54); officer commanding [OC] 113 Squadron to AOC EAC, 8 March 1943, DHist 181.002 (D68A), vol. 3; EAC, daily diary, 25 March 1943, DHist; 119 Squadron, ORB, 27 March, 4 and 8 April 1943, DHist

73 'General Review and Report upon Defences in the Gulf and River St. Lawrence Areas by a Committee formed under direction of the Chiefs of Staff Committee,' 30 Jan. 1943, 6-7, App. G and G1, DHist 181.003 (D4723)

74 Cabinet War Committee minutes, 18 Feb. 1943, PAC, RG 2, series 7c, vol. 12, microfilm reel C4875; 'Defence Communications Limited,' DHist 74/18

75 Memorandum to director signals, 'Communications, Gaspé Peninsula,' 19 May 1943, DHist 193.009 (D20); Guthrie, 'Report upon Defences in the Gulf and River St. Lawrence ...' App. F, DHist 181.003 (D4723); papers on 'Atlantic Communications Programme' for Chiefs of Staff Committee, DHist 193.009 (D19), passim; Joint RCN/RCAF A/S Warfare Committee, 30 March 1943, DHist 181.002 (D399); CAS to air officer commanding-in-chief [AOCinC], EAC, 10 June 1943, DHist 79/179; 'Third Report of the Defence Coordination Officer for the Gaspé and Lower St. Lawrence Area,' 14 Sept. 1943, DHist 193.009 (D25)

76 AMAS to CAS, 18 March 1943, NSS 1037-2-6 pt 1, PAC, RG 24, vol. 3901; OC Radio Wing, Coast and Anti-Aircraft Artillery Training Centre, 'Summary of Report on GL Mark IIIC Equipment Employed in an Anti-Surface Vessel role,' nd, DHist 112.3M2 (D509); No 1 Radio Direction Finding Unit, Royal Canadian Artillery, progress reports, May/Nov. 1943, DHist 142.98009 (D2)

77 AMAS to CAS, 14 Feb. 1944, NSS 1037-2-6 pt 2, PAC, RG 24, vol. 3901; C.B. Limbrick, 'Radar in the Royal Canadian Air Force,' unpublished narrative, nd, 20-1, DHist 80/395; W.E. Knowles Middleton, *Radar Development in Canada: the Radio Branch of the National Research Council of Canada, 1939-1946* (Waterloo, Ont. 1981), 101-5

78 House of Commons, *Debates*, 5 March 1943, 933, 10 March 1943, 1129-32, 11 March 1943, 1191-2, 1200-2, 15 March 1943, 1267-71, 25 March 1943, 1587; press clippings, March 1943, in DHist 81/531, box 180, and DHist 73/912

79 House of Commons, *Debates*, 10 March 1943, 1131

80 Ibid., 17 March 1943, 1344

81 Ibid., 10 March 1943, 1131, 17 March 1943, 1337-44

82 Guthrie, 'Report upon Defences in the Gulf and River St. Lawrence Areas by meeting held at Quebec City on 26-27th March, 1943,' N.R. Anderson et al, 'Second Report upon Defences in the Gulf and River St. Lawrence Areas ...' 18 April 1943, DHist 181.003 (D4723); Guthrie, 'Note re RCAF History – 1920/45 era,' 29 Jan. 1982, K.M. Guthrie biographical file, DHist

83 Chiefs of Staff Committee minutes, 11 May 1943, DHist 193.009 (D53)

84 Cabinet War Committee minutes, 13 May 1943, PAC, RG 2, series 7c, vol. 12, microfilm reel C4875

85 J.P.J. Desloges biographical file, DHist; Chiefs of Staff Committee to ministers, 11 May 1943, DHist 193.009 (D19); secretary Chiefs of Staff Committee to District Officer Commanding Military District No 5, 8 June 1943, DHist 181.003 (D4723)

86 CAS to minister of national defence for air, 1 Nov. 1943, Savard to Power, 29 Oct. 1943, Power Papers, box 70, file D2032; defence co-ordination officer, first report, 3 July 1943, DHist 193.009 (D21)

87 Defence co-ordination officer, third report, 14 Sept. 1943, DHist 193.009 (D25); E.G. Goodspeed, 'Air Craft Detection Corps Report of Activities Months of July, August, September 1943,' nd, DHist 321.009 (D94); N.R. Anderson et al, 'General Review and Report upon Defences in the Gulf and River St Lawrence ...' 30 Jan. 1943, App. E, DHist 181.003 (D4723)

88 CO HMCS *Ganonoque* to NOIC Quebec, 5 May 1943, NHS Sydney files 48-2-2 pt 11, DHist; 'SQ,' DHist 81/520/8280, box 10; RCN daily state, 15 June 1943, DHist NHS 1650-DS; commander-in-chief Canadian Northwest Atlantic [CINC CNA], 'Defence of Gulf of St. Lawrence 1943 ... Short Title GL43,' 25 May 1943, 38-2-1A, PAC, RG 24, vol. 11064

89 EAC weekly intelligence report, 30 April 1943, para. 5, DHist 181.003 (D423), pt 1; EAC operational intelligence summary, 25 April 1943, S.28-5-12 pt 1, PAC, RG 24, vol. 5272

90 EAC operational intelligence summary, 25 April 1943, S.28-5-12 pt 1, PAC, RG 24, vol. 5272

91 EAC weekly intelligence report, 14 May 1943, para. 17, 21 May 1943, para. 18, DHist 181.003 (D423); minutes of staff officers' meeting, 24 April 1943, EAC, daily diary, April 1943, App. 20, DHist; 'Orders Issued by Gulf Group Controller,' DHist 181.005 (D1556)

92 Nos 119, 117, 113 Squadrons, daily diaries, May 1943, DHist

93 NSHQ to CinC CNA, signal, 2258Z 29 April 1943, DHist 181.002 (D68A), vol. 1

94 EAC operational intelligence summary, 2 May 1943, DHist 181.003 (D1530); 31
    General Reconnaissance School, ORB daily diary, 30 April 1943, DHist; EAC
    operations summaries for 30 April–11 May 1943, DHist 181.003 (D3254); informa-
    tion from M. Hadley based on U-262 log

95 BdU war diary, 24 Sept. 1943, DHist 79/446; 'War Log "U-536" Final Report,'
    DHist mfm 83/665; 'U-536, Interrogation of Survivors, Jan 44,' DHist NHS
    1650-U536; Piers interview, 7 Jan. 1982, D.W. Piers biographical file, DHist;
    ships' movement cards, HMS *Chelsea*, 25 Sept.-10 Oct. 1943, DHist; EAC week-
    ly intelligence reports, 30 Sept. 1943, para. 23, 7 Oct. 1943, para. 24, DHist
    181.003 (D423); RCAF Station Gaspé, ORB daily diary, 26 Sept. 1943, DHist;
    'Gaspé Operations Narrative,' 26 Sept. 1943, DHist 181.005 (D1565)

96 Nos 116, 117, and 119 Squadrons, ORB daily diaries, Nov. 1943, DHist; AOCinC
    EAC to secretary DND for Air, 21 July 1943, S.096-105 pt 4, PARC 826793; SCB to
    AOCinC EAC, 26 Aug. 1943, DHist 181.006 (D13); 162 Squadron, ORB daily diary,
    Sept.-Oct. 1943, DHist; EAC, daily diary, 25 Sept. 1943, DHist; EAC to 1
    Group, signal A.238, 27 Sept. 1943, DHist 181.002 (D170); EAC to Dartmouth,
    signal A.395, 5 Oct. 1943, DHist 181.006 (D133)

CHAPTER 14: OCEAN OPERATIONS, 1942

1 Staff officer anti-submarine [A/S], Western Approaches Command, comment
   on Eastern Air Command [EAC] air operations, as quoted in Marc Milner, *North
   Atlantic Run: the Royal Canadian Navy and the Battle for the Convoys* (Toronto
   1985), 140-1

2 Commander Task Unit 24.1.3 to Commander Task Force Twenty-Four [CTF 24],
   'Report of Operations of Task Unit 24.1.3, Escort for Convoy ONS 102,' 28
   June 1942, PRO, Adm 199/729; RCAF Station Gander weekly intelligence reports,
   16 May-16 Oct. 1942, DHist 181.003 (D4099); Great Britain, Admiralty, Tacti-
   cal and Staff Duties Division, *The U-Boat War in the Atlantic*, II: *January 1942-
   May 1943* (BR 305 (2), German Naval History Series; London 1952), 23-4;
   Milner, *North Atlantic Run*, 113-22

3 *Befehlshaber der Unterseeboote* [BdU] war diary, translation, 3 June 1942, DHist
   79/446; U-432 log, copy and translation, 2 June 1942, DHist 85/77, pt 15

4 U-87 log, 23 June 1942, DHist 85/77, pt 16. See also RCAF attack report, 23 June
   1942, DHist 181.003 (D1314).

5 RCAF attack report, 28 June 1942, DHist 181.003 (D1315)

6 Great Britain, Admiralty, Historical Section, *Defeat of the Enemy Attack on Shipping, 1939-1945: a Study of Policy and Operations* (BR 1736 (51) (1), Naval
   Staff History Second World War; np [1957]), IB, plan 16 (4)

7 BdU war diary, 9 July 1942, DHist 79/446; Admiralty, *U-Boat War*, II, 37, 51

8 RCAF Station Dartmouth weekly intelligence report, 31 July 1942, DHist 181.003
   (D4096); Milner; *North Atlantic Run*, 125-7

9 BdU war diary, 29 July-1 Aug. 1942, DHist 79/446; 1 Group weekly intelligence
   report, 7 Aug. 1942, DHist 181.003 (D2178); Milner, *North Atlantic Run*,
   131-47

10 RCAF attack report, 30 July 1942, DHist 181.003 (DI104); U-89 log, 30 July 1942, DHist 85/77, pt 19; Anderson to air officer commanding [AOC] EAC, 31 July 1942, AOC EAC to secretary Department of National Defence [DND] for Air, 5 Aug. 1942, DHist 181.009 (DI147), pt 2

11 'History and Activities of the Operational Intelligence Centre, NSHQ, 1939-45,' NSS 1440-18, DHist

12 Power visit to UK, report, Aug./Sept. 1942, HQS 45-8-31, PAC, RG 24, vol. 5266; chief of the air staff [CAS] to AOC EAC, 'Convoy Patrols-Eastern Air Command,' 2 Jan. 1943, DHist 181.002 (DI23)

13 'The History of Eastern Air Command,' unpublished narrative [1945], 434-5, DHist 74/2, vol. 3; Small to AOC EAC, 24 Dec. 1942, DHist 181.002 (D68A); Annis interview, 10 Sept. 1979, C.L. Annis biographical file, DHist

14 RCAF attack report, 31 July 1943, DHist 181.003 (DI319)

15 RCAF attack reports, 31 July, 2 and 5 Aug. 1943, DHist 181.003 (DI089), (DI090), (DI091)

16 CAS to AOC EAC, signal, 5 Aug. 1942, S.15-24-12, PAC, RG 24, vol. 5199; 'History and Activities of the Operational Intelligence Centre, NSHQ, 1939-45,' '1942,' 6, NSS 1440-18, DHist; AOC EAC to secretary DND for Air, 5 Aug. 1942, DHist 181.009 (DI147), pt 2; Ruttan to AOC 1 Group, 31 Oct. 1942, S.28-5-10, PAC, RG 24, vol. 5272

17 Terence Horsley, *Find Fix and Strike* (London 1943), 33; AOC EAC to secretary DND, 25 June 1942, DHist 181.002 (DI80); EAC A/S report, Aug. 1942, DHist 181.003 (D25)

18 BdU war diary, 5 Sept. 1942, DHist 79/446; Admiralty, *U-Boat War*, II, 37

19 No 116 Squadron, operations record book [ORB] daily diary, 13 Sept. 1942, DHist; EAC A/S report, Sept. 1942, DHist 181.003 (D25); Milner, *North Atlantic Run*, 159-67

20 BdU war diary, 13 Sept. 1942, DHist 79/446

21 Vice-chief of the air staff to Coastal Command, 31 May 1943, App. I and II, PRO, Air 20/1065; Foster to Arnold, 17 April 1943, Library of Congress, H.H. Arnold Papers, container 39

22 S.R Gibbs, 'Report on Visit of EAC Halifax and RCAF Station Dartmouth, NS,' [July 1942], PRO, Air 15/217

23 Martineau report, 31 Oct. 1942, PRO, Air 2/8400

24 Joubert de la Ferté to Anderson, 18 Nov. 1941, DHist 181.009 (D6734); J.P.T. Pearman, 'Summary of Anti-Submarine Air Effort of Eastern Air Command, Halifax, N.S.,' 29 March 1942, DHist 181.009 (DI147); 'Intelligence – Operational Research Section Reports – Coastal Command,' 1-35, DHist 181.003 (D929), pt 1; command controller to 1 Group controller, message, 29 Oct. 1942, DHist 181.002 (DI23)

25 Ruttan to AOC 1 Group, 'Report-Course of Instruction, Naval "Y" Intelligence, Ottawa,' 31 Oct. 1942, HQS 28-5-4, PAC, RG 24, vol. 5272; CAS to AOC EAC, 'Air Operations against Submarines, D/F Fixes-Vitamin Code,' 14 Oct. 1942, AOC EAC to AOC 1 Group, 21 Oct. 1942, DHist 181.009 (DI147), pt 2

26 Martineau to staff, memorandum, 'Re Anti-Submarine Warfare,' 31 Oct. 1942, PRO, Air 2/8400

27 CAS to chief of the naval staff [CNS], 13 Dec. 1942, DHist 79/184; RCAF file, 'Operations-Anti U-Boat Warfare, S.25-25,' DHist 181.009 (D1147); RCAF liaison officer London to Air Force Headquarters [AFHQ], 19 March 1943, DHist 181.002 (D90)

28 AOC EAC to secretary DND for Air, 20 Nov. 1942, DHist 79/184

29 Senior air staff officer [SASO] to AOC, 15 Oct. 1942, ibid. For similar figures a month later, see air member for air staff [AMAS] to CAS, 25 Nov. 1942, DHist 79/84.

30 Minutes of a meeting on A/S warfare, 1-3 Nov. 1942, PRO, Air 2/8400

31 Ibid.

32 Commanding officer [CO] Atlantic Coast to CNS, 30 Nov. 1942, DHist 193.009 (D14); naval staff minutes, 23 Nov. 1942, DHist

33 Bliss to director Operations Division, 5 Jan. 1943, NSS 1271-24 pt 1, PAC, RG 24, vol. 8080; CAS to CNS, 5 Jan. 1943, CNS to CAS, 18 Jan. 1943, S.28-1-7, ibid., vol. 5270

34 J.O. Wilhelm, 'Operational Research Progress Report, Activities up to Aug. 31st, 1943,' 20 Aug. 1943, DHist 181.003 (D4033); P.M. Millman, 'Operational Research in the RCAF during World War II,' 2 Aug. 1947, DHist 77/510; J.W. Mayne, *Operational Research in the Canadian Armed Forces during the Second World War* (Department of National Defence, Operational Research and Analysis Establishment, Report No R68, June 1978), I, 15-26; Keith R. Tidman, *The Operations Evaluation Group: History of Naval Operations Analysis* (Annapolis, Md 1984) 51-4, 64-5

35 No 1 Group weekly intelligence report, 16 Oct. 1942, DHist 181.003 (D2178); BdU war diary, 12 Oct. 1942, DHist 79/446; Jürgen Rohwer, *Die U-Boot-Erfolge der Achsenmächte, 1939-1945* (München 1968), 128; Milner, *North Atlantic Run*, 171-4

36 Admiralty, *U-Boat War*, II, 56

37 EAC A/S report, Oct. 1942, DHist 181.003 (D25)

38 RCAF attack report, 30 Oct. 1942, DHist 181.003 (D1328)

39 Admiralty, *Defeat of the Enemy Attack on Shipping*, IA, 255

40 Ibid.; EAC weekly intelligence report, 30 Oct. 1942, DHist 181.003 (D423); RCAF attack report, 31 Oct. 1942, DHist 181.003 (D1329)

41 RCAF attack report, 31 Oct. 1942, DHist 181.003 (D1330)

42 No 116 (BR) Squadron, ORB daily diary, 1 Nov. 1942, DHist

43 W.A.B. Douglas and J. Rohwer, '"The Most Thankless Task" Revisited: Convoys, Escorts and Radio Intelligence in the Western Atlantic, 1941-43,' in J.A. Boutilier, ed., *The RCN in Retrospect, 1910-1968* (Vancouver 1982), 187-234; Milner, *North Atlantic Run*, 177-80

44 CTF 24 to commanding general, Newfoundland Base Command, US Army, 'Employment of U.S. Army B-17 Aircraft for Protection of Shipping,' 2 Oct. 1942, DHist 181.003 (D123)

45 EAC weekly intelligence reports, 30 Oct. and 6 Nov. 1942, DHist 181.003 (D423); EAC operations summaries, 30 Oct.-2 Nov. 1942, DHist 181.003 (D304)

46 Staff officer (operations) to AOC 1 Group, memorandum, 16 Nov. 1942, DHist 181.002 (D123)

47 CTF 24 to AOC 1 Group, 12 Nov. 1942, ibid.; 'The History of Eastern Air Command,' 505-15, DHist 74/2, vol. 3; ORBs and daily diaries of the various squadrons, DHist

48 Flag officer Newfoundland [FONF] report, Nov. 1942, NS 1000-5-20 pt 2, DHist; RCAF attack report, 3 Nov. 1943, DHist 181.003 (D1332)

49 RCAF attack report, 17 Nov. 1942, DHist 181.003 (D1333); EAC A/S report, Nov. 1942, 7, DHist 181.003 (D25)

50 Rohwer, *Die U-Boot-Erfolge*, 138; CNS to CAS, 'Report on Proceedings Convoy O.N. 145,' 18 Jan. 1943, DHist 181.002 (D123); W.G. Lund, 'The Royal Canadian Navy's Quest for Autonomy in the North West Atlantic, 1941-1943' (MA thesis, Queen's University, Kingston 1974)

51 RCAF attack report, 26 Nov. 1942, DHist 181.003 (D1335)

52 'The History of Eastern Air Command,' 507-24, DHist 74/2, vol. 3

53 Great Britain, Air Ministry, Air Historical Branch, 'The R.A.F. in Maritime War, III: The Atlantic and Home Waters, the Preparative Phase, July 1941 to February 1943,' nd, 514-17, DHist 79/599; Milner, *North Atlantic Run*, 194-5

54 RAF Coastal Command, 'The Last Hudson,' July 1943, App. J, Coastal Command ORB, July 1943, DHist 181.009 (D590)

55 W.E. Scarborough, 'Cause a PBY Don't Fly That High,' *United States Naval Institute Proceedings*, CIV, April 1978, 59-73

56 C.L. Annis, 'Submarine Warfare, World War II,' 29 Jan. 1943, DHist 181.003 (D309)

57 Carl Vincent, 'Distended Douglas: the Story of the Douglas Digby in Canadian Service,' *High Flight*, II, no 5, 179-84, no 6, 219-22, III, no 1, 17-27, no 2, 65-6; S. Kostenuk and J. Griffin, *RCAF Squadron Histories and Aircraft, 1924-1968* (Toronto 1977), 31-2

58 CAS to air officer commanding-in-chief [AOCinC] EAC, 3 Feb. 1944, 'A/S Warfare Operational Research and Analysis,' DHist 77/540

59 EAC A/S report, Nov. 1942, DHist 181.003 (D25)

60 BdU war diary, 1 Jan. and 1 Dec. 1942, DHist 79/446

61 Air Ministry, 'The R.A.F. in Maritime War,' III, App. XXXIV

62 RAF Coastal Command, Operational Research Section, 'Attacks on U-boats by Aircraft,' report no 24, Aug. 1943, fig. 4, DHist 181.003 (D929), pt 2

63 EAC, Operational Research Section, 'Comments on Anti-Submarine Effort, 1941-42, E.A.C.' 15 March 1943, DHist 77/540

64 BdU war diary, 3 Sept. 1942, DHist 79/446

65 Ibid., 2 Aug. 1942

66 Annis interview, 10 Sept. 1979, C.L. Annis biographical file, DHist

67 Annis to deputy AMAS (operations), 25 Feb. 1943, S.28-1-1, PAC, RG 24, vol. 5269

CHAPTER 15: DEFEATING THE WOLF PACKS

1 Arnold to King, 25 Feb. 1942, US Naval History Division, Strategic Plans, box 101, A21, 'Aviation'

2 Great Britain, War Cabinet Anti-U-Boat Committee minutes, 4 and 13 Nov. 1942,

PRO, Cab 86/2; secretary of state for air, 'Modification of Aircraft to Provide an Operational Range of 2,500 Miles,' 12 Nov. 1942, PRO, Cab 86/3; S.W. Roskill, *The War at Sea, 1939-1945*, II: *The Period of Balance* (History of the Second World War, United Kingdom Military Series; London 1956), 88

3 Air officer commanding-in-chief [AOCinC] Coastal Command, 'The Value of Bay of Biscay Patrols,' 22 March 1943, AU(43)84, PRO, Cab 86/3; first sea lord, notes for a meeting, 31 March 1943, PRO, Adm 205/30

4 First sea lord, notes for a meeting, 31 March 1943, PRO, Adm 205/30; PRO, Cab 86/2; P.M.S. Blackett, 'Progress of Analysis of the Value of Escort Vessels and Aircraft in the Anti U-Boat Campaign,' 5 March 1943, PRO, Prem 3/414/1

5 'Comment on Eastern Air Command Anti-Submarine Effort,' 14 Feb. 1943, S.28-5-11, PAC, RG 24, vol. 5272. See also R. Baglow and J.D.F. Kealy, 'A Statistical Analysis of the Performance of RCAF Maritime Aircraft, Dec 42-Nov 43,' unpublished narrative, 1980, DHist 80/151.

6 Breadner to Walsh, 11 Nov. 1942, 1-15-350, PAC, RG 24, vol. 5177; Walsh to Arnold, 18 Dec. 1942 and 5 Jan. 1943, DHist 76/259; Arnold to Walsh, 13 Jan. 1943, Library of Congress, H.H. Arnold Papers, extracts in DHist 82/970

7 Deputy air member for air staff [D/AMAS] to air member for air staff [AMAS], 9 Feb. 1943, Hobson to Annis, 13 and 26 March 1943, DHist 76/259; C.L. Annis, 'Submarine Warfare, World War II,' 29 Jan. 1943, DHist 181.003 (D309)

8 Philip Lundeberg, 'La réplique des états unis à la guerre au tonnage,' *Revue d'histoire de la Deuxième Guerre Mondiale*, XVIII (1968), 67-96; Michael Salewski, 'The Submarine War: a Historical Essay,' in Lothar-Gunther von Buchheim, *U-Boat War* (New York 1978)

9 See R.M. Leighton, 'US Merchant Shipping and the British Import Crisis,' in K.R. Greenfield, ed., *Command Decisions* (Washington 1960), 199-224.

10 Roskill, *War at Sea*, II, 252; Admiralty, 'Review of Proceedings of Anti-U-Boat Warfare Committee,' 20 Aug. 1943, Annex I, Section VIII, PRO, Adm 205/30, file no 8; US Naval History Division, A 16-3(9), 'Anti-Submarine Warfare'; W.G.D. Lund, 'Command Relations in the Northwest Atlantic: the Royal Canadian Navy's Perspective' (MA thesis, Queen's University Kingston, 1972), 41; G.N. Tucker, *The Naval Service of Canada*, II: *Activities on Shore during the Second World War* (Ottawa 1952), 402-17

11 Draft signal 'not to be despatched but to be used as basis for further discussion between [chief of the air staff] CAS and AMAS,' 12 Jan. 1943, Bulloch and Layton report, 1 March 1943, 1-15-350 pt 3, PAC, RG 24, vol. 5177

12 Bulloch and Layton report, 1 March 1943, 1-15-350 pt 3, PAC, RG 24, vol. 5177; AOCinC Coastal Command, 'Policy for the Employment of V.L.R. Aircraft in the North Atlantic in the Present and Near Future,' 27 March 1943, DHist 181.002 (D122)

13 Bulloch and Layton report, 1 March 1943, 1-15-350 pt 3, PAC, RG 24, vol. 5177; Eastern Air Command [EAC] weekly intelligence report, 26 Nov. 1942, App. H, DHist 181.003 (D264)

14 Bulloch and Layton report, 1 March 1943, 1-15-350 pt 3, PAC, RG 24, vol. 5177

15 See daily diaries of EAC squadrons, Feb. 1943 passim, DHist.

16 Admiral Karl Dönitz, *Memoirs: Ten Years and Twenty Days*, trans. R.H. Stevens
   (Westport, Ct. 1976), 316
17 Nos 5 and 162 Squadrons, daily diaries, Dec. 1942 and Jan. 1943, DHist
18 *Befehlshaber der Unterseeboote* [BdU] war diary, 1-4 Feb. 1943, DHist 79/446;
   PRO, Adm 223/16; F.H. Hinsley et al, *British Intelligence in the Second World
   War: Its Influence on Strategy and Operations* (New York 1979-84), II, 543
19 No 1 Group weekly intelligence report, Feb. 1943, DHist 181.003 (D423); U-414
   and U-403 logs, 4 and 6 Feb. 1943, copy and translation, DHist 85/77, pt 31 and
   pt 32; 5 Squadron, operations record book [ORB] daily diary, 6 Feb. 1943, DHist
20 Roskill, *War at Sea*, II, 201, 357-8, 366-8; Marc Milner, *North Atlantic Run:
   the Royal Canadian Navy and the Battle for the Convoys* (Toronto 1985),
   224
21 RCAF attack report, 24 Feb. 1943, DHist 181.003 (D1338); 1 Group weekly intelligence report, 5 March 1943, DHist 181.003 (D423)
22 RCAF attack report, 24 Feb. 1943, DHist 181.003 (D1338)
23 Ibid.
24 U-604 log, 24 Feb. 1943, DHist 85/77, pt 33; BdU war diary, DHist 79/446
25 No 5 Squadron, ORB daily diary, 24 Feb. 1943, DHist
26 Ibid.
27 U-621 log, 24 Feb. 1943, DHist 85/77, pt 34; 5 Squadron, ORB daily diary, 24 Feb.
   1943, DHist; RCAF Station Gander, daily diary, 24 Feb. 1943, DHist
28 Samuel Eliot Morison, *History of United States Naval Operations in World War II*,
   I: *The Battle of the Atlantic, September 1939-May 1943* (Boston 1947), 338
29 Annis to D/AMAS (operations), 16 Feb. 1943, 1-15-35 pt 2, PAC, RG 24, vol. 5177
30 Ibid.
31 Commander Task Force [CTF] 24 to EAC and US Army Newfoundland Base Command, 12 Feb. 1943, ibid.; report of conference, 26-7 Feb. 1943, DHist
   181.003 (D96)
32 Report of conference, 26-7 Feb. 1943, DHist 181.002 (D96); CTF 24 to Newfoundland Base Command, 2 Oct. 1942, DHist 181.002 (D123); EAC and 1 Group
   weekly intelligence reports, March-May 1943, DHist 181.003 (D264) and (D423);
   1 Group to EAC, 30 March 1943, DHist 181.002 (D124); US Antisubmarine
   Command, 'Missions, Sightings, Attacks, Hours Flown, Nov. 1942-July 1943,'
   Maxwell Air Force Base, microfilm reel BO934, fol. 0031, copy in DHist
   80/208; 'Review of Anti-Submarine Intelligence in Area 40 to 60N, 30 to 60W,
   3-31 May 43,' para. 5a, reel BO 933, fol. 1568-9, ibid.
33 AOC 1 Group to AOC EAC, 6 March 1943, DHist 181.002 (D96); Canning to Slessor,
   27 May 1943, PRO, Air 2/8400
34 Lund, 'Command Relations in the Northwest Atlantic,' 41-8; Tucker, *Naval Service
   of Canada*, II, 406-8; Great Britain, Air Ministry, Air Historical Branch, 'The
   R.A.F. in Maritime War, IV: The Atlantic and Home Waters, the Offensive Phase,
   February 1943 to May 1944,' nd, 2-3, DHist 79/599
35 Air Force Combined Staff [AFCS] Washington to Air Force Headquarters [AFHQ],
   signal A432, 2 Feb. 1943, AFHQ to ROYCANAIRF, signal C477, 4 Feb. 1943,
   s.28-1-2, PAC, RG 24, vol. 5270; Air Ministry, 'The R.A.F. in Maritime War,' IV, 7
36 Deputy CAS to minister, 4 Feb. 1943, Air Council minutes, 4 Feb. 1943, AFHQ to

AFCS Washington, signal C479, 5 Feb. 1943, S.28-1-2, PAC, RG 24, vol. 5270; Tucker, *Naval Service of Canada*, II, 409; Air Ministry, 'The R.A.F. in Maritime War,' IV, 7; CAS to chief of the naval staff [CNS], 21 Feb. 1943, Queen's University Archives, C.G. Power Papers, box 71, file D2034; Naval Board minutes, 22 Feb. 1943, DHist

37 Jürgen Rohwer, *The Critical Convoy Battles of March 1943* (Annapolis, Md 1978); J. Rohwer and G. Hümmelchen, *Chronology of the War at Sea, 1939-1945*, trans. Derek Masters (London 1978), 308-10; PRO, Adm 223/16, fol. 73, 77; EAC weekly intelligence report, 23 March 1943, DHist 181.003 (D308); Hinsley, *British Intelligence*, II, 750

38 'Report of Sub-Committee on Command, Control and Responsibilities of Air Forces, 8-9 March 1943,' N.R. Anderson, 'Report on Convoy Conference 8-9 March 1943,' 1-15-350 pt 3, PAC, RG 24, vol. 5177

39 Director of Operations Division to vice-CNS and CNS, 5 March 1943, NSS 1271-24 pt 1, PAC, RG 24, vol. 8080; CNS to commanding officer Atlantic Coast [COAC], signal 1440Z, 4 Feb. 1943, AFHQ to AFCS Washington, signal C479, 5 Feb. 1943, EAC to AFHQ, signal A359, 5 Feb. 1943, S.28-1-2, ibid., vol. 5270; COAC to secretary Naval Board, 8 Feb. 1943, DHist NHS 8000, 'Flag Officer Atlantic Coast'

40 'The Nineteenth Antisubmarine Squadron Diary,' 1132-4, Maxwell Air Force Base, microfilm reel A0523, copy in DHist 80/207; chief of staff, Army Air Forces Antisubmarine Command, movement order no 8, 31 March 1943, 0884-7, reel B0993; ibid.; 'History of Antisubmarine Squadrons, 25th Antisubmarine Wing,' 0749, reel B093, ibid.; 1 Group to EAC, signal A127, 30 March 1943, DHist 181.002 (D124); 'Fleet Air Wing Seven History Narrative,' 37-8, DHist 80/15

41 RAF delegation Washington [RAFDEL] to Air Ministry, 20 March 1943, PRO, Air 20/848. See also Air Ministry, 'The R.A.F. in Maritime War,' IV, 20.

42 Anderson to Breadner, 8 March 1943, citing Combined Chiefs of Staff memorandum 61/1, 1-15-350 pt 3, PAC, RG 24, vol. 5177

43 Anderson to Breadner, 9 March 1943, ibid.

44 Breadner to Portal, 9 March 1943, Breadner to Johnson, 10 March 1943, ibid.

45 Portal to Breadner, 11 March 1943, ibid.; 'Extract from Minutes of C.O.S. (43) 21st Meeting held 25th January, 1943,' and minute to CAS, 28 Jan. 1943, PRO, Air 8/673

46 Air Ministry to RAFDEL, 19 March 1943, PRO, Air 20/848

47 Portal to Breadner, 25 March 1943, 1-15-350 pt 3, PAC, RG 24, vol. 5177

48 Adjutant general US Army Antisubmarine Command HQ to commanding general Army Air Forces Washington, 16 May 1943, Maxwell Air Force Base, microfilm reel A0523, fol. 1259-60, DHist 80/207; note by the chief of the air staff, Sir Charles Portal, 'Reequipment of Coastal Command Squadrons with Liberators,' AU(43)93, PRO, Cab 86/3

49 J. Rohwer and W.A.B. Douglas, '"The Most Thankless Task" Revisited: Convoys, Escorts and Radio Intelligence in the Western Atlantic, 1941-43,' in J.A. Boutilier, ed., *The RCN in Retrospect, 1910-1968* (Vancouver 1982), 187-234; USAAF Gander periodic intelligence report, 1-8 May 1943, 1 Group weekly intelligence report, 10 May 1943, DHist 181.003 (D308); 5 Squadron, ORB daily diary, 4 May 1943, DHist; RCAF attack report, 4 May 1943, DHist 181.003 (D1341)

50 RCAF attack report, 4 May 1943, DHist 181.003 (D1341)
51 U-438 to BdU, signal of 5 May 1943, DHist 85/77, pt 41
52 RCAF attack report, 4 May 1943, DHist 181.003 (D1342)
53 No 5 Squadron, ORB daily diary, 5-6 May 1943, DHist; 1 Group weekly intelligence report, 10 May 1943, DHist 181.003 (D308); comments by Commander Peter Gretton, NSS 8280 ONS 5, PAC, RG 24, vol. 11329
54 AOC EAC to controllers, 16 March 1943, AOC EAC to AOC 1 Group, 10 May 1943, and Heakes minute, 24 May 1943, DHist 181.002 (D125)
55 BdU war diary, 3 May 1943, DHist 79/446
56 No 1 Group weekly intelligence report, 24 May 1943, DHist 181.003 (D308); review of anti-submarine intelligence, DHist 80/208; Hinsley, British Intelligence, II, 636-7
57 Dönitz, Memoirs, 339; BdU war diary, 6 and 24 May 1943, DHist 79/446; Hilary St George Saunders, Royal Air Force 1939-45, III: The Fight is Won (London 1954, paperback edition 1975), 50-7
58 Saunders, Royal Air Force, III, 57; Great Britain, Admiralty, Historical Section, Defeat of the Enemy Attack on Shipping, 1939-1945: a Study of Policy and Operations (BR 1736 (51) (1), Naval Staff History Second World War; np [1957]), IA, App. 2; 10 Squadron, ORB daily diary, DHist
59 George Lothian, Flight Deck: Memoirs of an Airline Pilot (Toronto 1979), 104-5; 10 Squadron, ORB daily diary, 10 May, 25 July 1943, DHist
60 AOCinC Coastal Command, messages, 7 May, 1 June 1943, DHist 181.002 (D121); 1 Group to EAC, 23 July 1943, DHist 181.002 (D122)
61 Allied Anti-Submarine Survey Board to CNS, 18 May 1943, CAS to AOCinC, 15 June 1943, S.28-6-7 pt 1, PAC, RG 24, vol. 5274; Joint RCN-RCAF Anti-Submarine Warfare Committee minutes, 22 June 1943, DHist 181.002 (D145)
62 Allied Anti-Submarine Survey Board to CNS, 18 May 1943, S.28-6-7 pt 1, PAC, RG 24, vol. 5274; Naval Staff minutes, 3 June 1943, DHist; commander-in-chief Canadian Northwest Atlantic [CinC CNA] to NSHQ, signal 1620Z, 12 July 1943, DHist NHS 8000, 'Flag officer Atlantic Coast'; EAC HQ, daily diary, 20 July 1943, DHist
63 Canning to Slessor, 27 May 1943, PRO, Air 2/8400
64 Anderson to Slessor, 21 June 1943, DHist 181.009 (D6734)
65 Slessor to Anderson, 24 June 1943; ibid.
66 Allied Anti-Submarine Survey Board to CNS, 19 May 1943, S.28-6-7 pt 1, PAC, RG 24, vol. 5274; Heakes to Baker, 9 Aug. 1943, DHist 181.009 (D4656)
67 EAC HQ to AFHQ, signal A295, 15 May 1943, DHist 181.002 (D96); 'Review of Antisubmarine Intelligence ... 0001Z May 3, 1943 to 2400Z May 31, 1943,' 1568-9, Maxwell Air Force Base, microfilm reel B0933, DHist 80/208; 'History of Antisubmarine Squadrons, 25th Antisubmarine Wing,' 0723-6, ibid.; 'The Nineteenth Antisubmarine Squadron Diary,' 1137-41, reel A0523, DHist 80/207; 'Fleet Air Wing Seven History Narrative,' 38-43, 'War Diary of Bombing Squadron One Hundred Three,' DHist 80/15; minute on EAC HQ to 1 Group, signal A337, 1 Sept. 1943, DHist 74/372
68 Canning to Slessor, 27 May 1943, PRO, Air 2/8400; 'Minutes of Meeting of A.M.A.S. Division with Members of Kauffman Board, 8 May 1943,' S.28-6-7 pt

1, PAC, RG 24, vol. 5274; Peter Gretton, *Convoy Escort Commander* (London 1964), 153; 'Allied Anti-Submarine Survey Board Meeting Held at 1500 Hours, 7th May, 1943 in Ottawa,' PRO, Adm 1/13756

69 'Operations-Naval Co-operation,' DHist 181.002 (D464); 'ASW Training – D/F Homing – Comments on Exercises,' DHist 181.003 (D36); 1 Group to EAC, signal A829, 23 July 1943, 1 Group-EAC teletype conversation, 24 July 1943, DHist 181.009 (D4656); AOCinC EAC to 1 Group, Gulf Group, signal A873, 26 July 1943, DHist 181.002 (D122); secretary Naval Board, 'Daily Forecast of U-Boat Positions,' 14 July 1943, NSS 8910-9 pt 1, PAC, RG 24, vol. 6895; McDiarmid to officer in charge Operational Intelligence Centre, 10 July 1945, NSS 8910-20 pt 2, ibid., vol. 6896

70 Martineau to CinC CNA, 6 Aug. 1943, 7-6-2, PAC, RG 24, vol. 11022

71 Canning to Slessor, 27 May 1943, PRO, Air 2/8400; Carl Vincent, *Consolidated Liberator & Boeing Fortress* (Canada's Wings, vol. 2; Stittsville, Ont. 1975), 31; Annis interview, 10 Sept. 1979, C.L. Annis biographical file, DHist

72 Great Britain, Air Ministry, Air Historical Branch, 'The R.A.F. in Maritime War, III: The Atlantic and Home Waters, the Preparative Phase, July 1941 to February 1943,' nd, 489-92, DHist 79/599; Coastal Command, Operational Research Section, 'A Review of s-Band ASV Performance in Detecting U-Boats,' report no 308, 2 Nov. 1944, PRO, Air 15/133; *Monthly Review of RCAF Operations, North America*, I, Nov. 1943, 12, II, June 1944, 6-8, II, July 1944, 21-3

73 'Eastern Air Command-Project "z" ... Supply and Use of Same in Anti-Submarine Warfare,' DHist 181.009 (D1519); Mark 24 Mine instructions, 4 June and 16 Sept. 1943, DHist 181.003 (D4421); RCAF attack reports, 3 and 4 Sept. 1943, DHist 181.003 (D1099) and (D1100); 'List of RCAF Sightings and Attacks on U-Boats,' DHist 85/77, pt 1

74 Alfred Price, *Aircraft versus Submarine: the Evolution of the Anti-Submarine Aircraft, 1912 to 1972* (London 1973), 107-8; '"z" Project-Equipment,' DHist 181.002 (D39); Deshaw, 'Report on Expendable Radio Sonic Buoys,' 6 June 1944, DHist 181.003 (D3302); Thomas to commanding officer [CO] RCAF Station Dartmouth, 7 Dec. 1944, DHist 181.003 (D3738)

75 BdU war diary, 25 June 1943, DHist 79/446; Admiralty, Operational Intelligence Centre, special intelligence summary, 28 June 1943, PRO, Adm 223/15; NSS 8280-SC 135, DHist mfm

76 RCAF attack report, 3 July 1943, DHist 181.003 (D1347); U-420 log, 3 July 1943, DHist 85/77, pt 42

77 No 1 Group weekly intelligence report, 8 July 1943, DHist 181.003 (D308); 10 Squadron, ORB daily diary, 4-5 July 1943, DHist

78 CinC CNA to AOCinC EAC, signal 1535Z, 6 July 1943, DHist 181.002 (D123)

79 Heakes to 1 Group squadron COs, 1 Sept. 1943, 1-15-350 pt 5, PAC, RG 24, vol. 5177

80 BdU war diary, 10-16 Sept. 1943, DHist 79/446; Dönitz, *Memoirs*, 418-9; Air Ministry, 'The R.A.F. in Maritime War,' IV, 177

81 No 10 Squadron, ORB daily diary, 16-19 Sept., 20 Oct. 1943, DHist; RCAF attack report, 19 Sept. 1943, DHist 181.003 (D1349)

82 S.W. Roskill, *The War at Sea, 1939-1945*, III: *The Offensive, Part I, 1st June 1943*

– *31st May 1944* (History of the Second World War, United Kingdom Military Series; London 1960), 40

83 *Coastal Command Review*, II, Sept. 1943, 6, DHist 181.003 (D1096); U-270 log, 22 Sept. 1943, DHist 85/77, pt 47; BdU war diary, 22-4 and 27 Sept. 1943, DHist 79/446

84 RCAF attack report, 22 Sept. 1943, DHist 181.003 (D1350); U-377 log, 22 Sept. 1943, DHist 85/77, pt 46; BdU war diary, 23, 26, 27 Sept. 1943, DHist 79/446; Anti-U-Boat Division of the naval staff, 'Analysis of U-Boat Operations in the Vicinity of Convoys ONS 18 and ON 202, 19th-24 Sept. 1943,' 15 Nov. 1943, 106, PRO, Adm 199/1491

85 RCAF attack report, 22 Sept. 1943, DHist 181.003 (D1350); U-275 log, 22 Sept. 1943, Forstner (U-402) to BdU, signal 846, 2030 hrs, 22 Sept. 1943, DHist 85/77, pt 44 and pt 45; 'Analysis of U-Boat Operations ... ONS 18 and ON 202,' 107, 113-16, PRO, Adm 199/1491; *Coastal Command Review*, II, Sept. 1943, 6, DHist 181.003 (D1096); I Group weekly intelligence report, 23 Sept. 1943, DHist 181.003 (D308); Air Ministry, 'The R.A.F. in Maritime War,' IV, 179; Joseph Schull, *The Far Distant Ships: an Official Account of Canadian Naval Operations in the Second World War* (Ottawa 1952), 181

86 RCAF attack reports, 23 Sept. 1943, DHist 181.003 (D1352) and (D1353); BdU war diary, DHist 79/446. See also Admiralty, Anti-U-Boat Division of the Naval Staff, *Monthly Anti-Submarine Report, September 1943* (CB 04050/43(9), 15 Oct. 1943), 7.

87 Senior officer B3 Group, report of proceedings, nd, section 3, DHist 81/520/8280 ONS18

88 Air Ministry, 'The R.A.F. in Maritime War,' IV, 182-8

89 RCAF attack report, 26 Oct. 1943, DHist 181.003 (D1354)

90 BdU war diary, 15 Nov. 1943, DHist 79/446

91 Air Ministry, 'The R.A.F. in Maritime War,' IV, 194-5; RCAF attack report, 8 Nov. 1943, DHist 181.003 (D1356); Orr to secretary DND for Air, 22 Nov. 1943, DHist 181.003 (D1123)

CHAPTER 16: SECURING THE LIFELINE, 1943-4

1 Great Britain, Air Ministry, Air Historical Branch, 'The R.A.F. in Maritime War, IV: The Atlantic and Home Waters, the Offensive Phase, February 1943 to May 1944,' nd, App. xiii, DHist 79/599. The basic source on the anti-submarine war in the Canadian Northwest Atlantic, October 1943 to July 1944, is the war diary of the commander-in-chief, Canadian Northwest Atlantic for those months, NSS 1000-5-13 pts 20-22 and NSC 1926-102/1, DHist. For a more detailed account of the operations described in this chapter see Roger Sarty, 'The RCAF and Anti-Submarine Warfare, October 1943-May 1945,' unpublished narrative, 1984, DHist.

2 'Comment on Eastern Air Command Anti-Submarine Effort,' 17 Feb. 1943, s.28-5-11 pt I, PAC, RG 24, vol. 5272; Eastern Air Command [EAC] Operational Research Section [ORS], 'Comments on Anti-Submarine Effort, 1941-42, EAC,' 15 March 1943, DHist 77/540; air member for air staff [AMAS] to deputy air mem-

ber for air staff (operations) [D/AMAS(Ops)], 26 March 1943, with enclosures, S.19-17-4 pt 1, PAC, RG 24, vol. 5233

3 AMAS to D/AMAS(Ops), 26 March 1943, with enclosures, S.19-17-4 pt 1, PAC, RG 24, vol. 5233

4 Secretary Naval Board, 'Daily Forecast of U-Boat Positions,' 14 July 1943, NSS 8910-9, PAC, RG 24, vol. 6895; F.H. Hinsley et al, *British Intelligence in the Second World War: Its Influence on Strategy and Operations* (London 1979-84), II, 551n; Patrick Beesly, *Very Special Intelligence: the Story of the Admiralty's Operational Intelligence Centre, 1939-1945* (London 1977), 169; air officer commanding [AOC] EAC to AOC 1 Group, signal A178, 20 March 1943, DHist 181.003 (D123)

5 See, for example, de Marbois to assistant chief of the naval staff [ACNS], 'Sweeps by No 1 Group V.L.R. and L.R. A/C during U-Boat Hunt Vicinity Flemish Cap, 23/12/43-9/1/44,' 27 Jan. 1944, DHist NHS 1650 – 'Salmon.'

6 Wilhelm to AOC EAC, 9 Nov. 1943, S.19-17-4 pt 2, PAC, RG 24, vol. 5233

7 W.A.B. Douglas, 'The Nazi Weather Station in Labrador,' *Canadian Geographic*, 101, Dec. 1981-Jan. 1982, 42-7

8 Naval Service Headquarters [NSHQ] to commander-in-chief Canadian Northwest Atlantic [CINC CNA], air officer commanding-in-chief [AOCINC] EAC et al, signal 2154Z, 28 Oct. 1943, NSS 8910-20 pt 1, PAC, RG 24, vol. 6896; U-537 log, 17 Oct. 1943, DHist mfm 83/665, vol. 15

9 NSHQ to CINC CNA, AOCINC EAC et al, signal 0002Z, 28 Oct. 1943, NSS 8910-20 pt 1, PAC, RG 24, vol. 6896

10 Air Force Headquarters [AFHQ] to EAC, signal X320 A2308, 29 Oct. 1943, S.28-9-3, ibid., vol. 5274

11 U-537 log, 31 Oct. 1943, DHist mfm 83/665; RCAF attack report, 31 Oct. 1943, DHist 181.003 (D1355); 1 Group weekly intelligence report, 4 Nov. 1943, DHist 181.003 (D308); 5 Squadron, operations record book [ORB] daily diary, 31 Oct. 1943, DHist; de Marbois to ACNS, 'Operation Salmon: Air Cover during Escape Interval,' 27 Jan. 1944, DHist NHS 1650 – 'Salmon'; Alfred Price, *Aircraft versus Submarine: the Evolution of the Anti-Submarine Aircraft, 1912 to 1972* (London 1973), 108

12 RCAF attack report, 10 Nov. 1943, DHist 181.003 (D1357); NSS 8280 – HX 265, DHist mfm

13 DHist 181.003 (D1093); RCAF Station Torbay, daily diary, 11-14 Nov. 1943, DHist; 1 Group weekly intelligence report, 18 Nov. 1943, DHist 181.003 (D308); senior officer W6, 'Operation Salmon II,' 16 Nov. 1943, 7-6-7, PAC, RG 24, vol. 11023; de Marbois to ACNS, 'Operation Salmon ...' 27 Jan. 1944, DHist NHS 1650 – 'Salmon'; *RCN-RCAF Monthly Operational Review*, 1, Dec. 1943, 13; U-537 log, 11-13 Nov. 1943, DHist mfm 83/665

14 U-537 log, 14-28 Nov. 1943, DHist mfm 83/665; Otter signals for 14-20 Nov. 1943, NSS 8910-20 pt 1, PAC, RG 24, vol. 6896; ZTPGU/19379, 19 Nov. 1943, PRO, Defe 3/724; EAC proposed operations for 20-1 Nov. 1943, DHist 181.003 (D3254); EAC weekly intelligence report, 25 Nov. 1943, DHist 181.003 (D423)

15 Wilhelm to AOCINC EAC, 9 Nov. 1943, S.19-17-4 pt 2, PAC, RG 24, vol. 5233; *RCN-RCAF Monthly Operational Review*, 1, Dec. 1943, 13-14; Murray to secre-

tary Naval Board, 11 Dec. 1943, 7-6-6, PAC, RG 24, vol. 11023; de Marbois to ACNS, director of operations division [DOD], and director of operational research [DOR], 27 Jan. 1944, DHist NHS 1650 – 'Salmon'

16 ZTPGU signals 20266-20747, 16 Dec. 1943-3 Jan. 1944, PRO, Defe 3/725; Otter signals for 23 Dec. 1943-8 Jan. 1944, NSS 8910-20 pt 1, PAC, RG 24, vol. 6896

17 De Marbois to ACNS, 'Sweeps by No 1 Group ...' 27 Jan. 1944, DHist NHS 1650 – 'Salmon'; EAC weekly intelligence report, 30 Dec. 1943, 6 Jan. 1944, DHist 181.003 (D423); EAC HQ, daily diary, Dec. 1943 and Jan. 1944, DHist

18 U-543 log, copy and translation, 30 Dec. 1943, 2-3 Jan. 1944, DHist 5/77, pt 53; commanding officer [CO] HMCS *St Laurent* to captain (D) Halifax, report of proceedings, 10 Jan. 1944, CO HMCS *Swansea* to captain (D) Halifax, 9 Jan. 1944, 7-6-7, PAC, RG 24, vol. 11023

19 De Marbois to ACNS, 'Sweeps by No 1 Group ...' 27 Jan. 1944, DHist NHS 1650 – 'Salmon'; Murray to secretary Naval Board, 13 Feb. 1944, 7-6-7, PAC, RG 24, vol. 11023

20 *RCN-RCAF Monthly Operational Review*, 2, Jan. 1944, 29-33

21 Guthrie to AOCinC EAC, 3 Feb. 1944, S.28-3-1, PAC, RG 24, vol. 5270

22 ZTPGU/21250, 16 Jan. 1944, ZTPGU/21537, 26 Jan. 1944, ZTPGU/21723, 1 Feb. 1944, PRO, Defe 3/726; Otter signals for 21-5 Jan., 28 Jan.-6 Feb. 1944, NSS 8910-20 pt 1, PAC, RG 24, vol. 6896; EAC proposed operations signals for 23-4 Jan., 28 Jan.-5 Feb. 1944, DHist 181.003 (D3254); 10 Squadron, ORB daily diary, 23 Jan.-3 Feb. 1944, DHist

23 Flag Officer Newfoundland [FONF], war diary, Feb. 1944, NSS 1926-112/3 pt 1, DHist; EAC weekly intelligence reports, 10 and 17 Feb. 1944, DHist 181.003 (D423); DHist NHS 1650 – 'U-845'; Otter signals for 9-10 Feb. 1944, NSS 8910-20 pt 1, PAC, RG 24, vol. 6896; McDiarmid to officer in charge, Operational Intelligence Centre [OIC], NSS 8910 pt 2, ibid.; EAC proposed operations for 9 Feb. 1944, DHist 181.003 (D3254); 5 and 11 Squadrons, ORB daily diaries, 9-12 Feb. 1944, DHist; 128 Squadron, ORB daily diary, 9 Feb. 1944, DHist

24 RCAF attack report, 14 Feb. 1943, DHist 181.003 (D1359)

25 FONF, war diary, Feb. 1944, NSS 1926-112/3 pt 1, DHist

26 Otter signals for 9-14 Feb. 1944, NSS 8910-20 pt 2, PAC, RG 24, vol. 6896; EAC weekly intelligence report, 10, 17 Feb. 1944, DHist 181.003 (D423); RCAF attack report, 14 Feb. 1943, DHist 181.003 (D1359); ZTPGU/22245, 15 Feb. 1944, PRO, Defe 3/727; Air Force Routine Orders [AFRO] 874/44, 1133/44

27 Otter signals for 15 Feb.-4 March 1944, NSS 8910 pt 1, PAC, RG 24, vol. 6896; EAC weekly intelligence report, 2 March 1944, DHist 181.003 (D423); U-539 log, 10 Feb.-4 March 1944, DHist 85/77, pt 54; ZTPGU/21878, 6 Feb. 1944, ZTPGU/21939, 7 Feb. 1944, PRO, Defe 3/726; DHist NHS 1650 – 'U-845'

28 No 1 Group weekly intelligence reports, 3 Nov. 1943-24 Feb. 1944, DHist 181.003 (D308)

29 ZTPGU signals 22514-22782, 22 Feb.-3 March 1944, PRO, Defe 3/727; Otter signals for 3-17 March 1944, NSS 8910-20 pt 1, PAC, RG 24, vol. 6896; EAC proposed operations and operations summaries for 4-21 March 1944, DHist 181.003 (D3254); EAC weekly intelligence reports, 9 and 16 March 1944, DHist 181.003 (D423); N.J. Chaplin, 'Operational Use of Radio Sono-Buoy Equipment

by Canso "A" 9837, 18 March/44,' nd, DHist 181.009 (D5985); CO HMCS *New Glasgow* to captain (D) Halifax, report of proceedings, 25 March 1944, 7-6-6, PAC, RG 24, vol. 11023; U-802 log, 17-22 March 1944, DHist 85/77, pt 55; NSS 8280 – SH 125, DHist mfm

30 EAC anti-submarine [A/S] operations intelligence summary, 26 March 1944, EAC HQ, daily diary, March 1944, DHist; U-802 log, 22-3 March 1944, DHist 85/77, pt 55; NSHQ to HMCS *Wentworth*, (R) CinC CNA, signals, 0335Z 23 March 1944, 0940Z 23 March 1944, 1330Z 23 March 1944, HMCS *Wentworth* to CinC CNA, (R) NSHQ, signal 0345Z, 23 March 1944, DHist NHS 1650 – 'Salmon'; de Marbois memorandum, 2 May 1944, director of warfare and training [DWT]/Tactics to DWT, 2 May 1944, DHist NHS 8440 – 'W-10'; AFHQ to EAC HQ, signal HAC-569, 23 March 1944, EAC operations summary for 23 March 1944, DHist 181.003 (D3254); 145 Squadron, ORB, 23 March 1944, DHist; Chaplin, 'Operational Use of Radio Sono-Buoy Equipment by Canso 9840, 161 Squadron, March 23,' nd, DHist 181.009 (D5985)

31 EAC proposed operations and operations summaries, 26 March-13 April 1944, DHist 181.003 (D3254); U-802 log, 8-9 April 1944, DHist 85/77, pt 55; NSS 8280 – HX 286, DHist mfm; NSHQ to CinC CNA, AOCinC EAC, signal 2254Z, 8 April 1944, NSS 8910-20 pt 1, PAC, RG 24, vol. 6896; 1 Group weekly intelligence summary, 13 April 1944, DHist 181.003 (D308)

32 ZTPGU signals 23162-23492, 17-25 March 1944, PRO, Defe 3/728; Otter signals for 16 March-7 April 1944, NSS 8910-20 pt 1, PAC, RG 24, vol. 6896; FONF, war diary, March 1944, NSC 1926-112/3 pt 1, DHist; EAC proposed operations and operations summaries for 19 March-7 April 1944, DHist 181.003 (D3254); EAC weekly intelligence reports, 23 and 30 March 1944, DHist 181.003 (D423); T.P. Boyle, 'Report on E.R.S.B. Investigating Action by Aircraft,' 27 March 1944, DHist 181.003 (D3300); *Befehlshaber der Unterseeboote* [BdU] war diary, 25-6 March 1944, DHist 79/446

33 *United States Fleet Anti-Submarine Bulletin*, I, May 1944, 28-31, II, June 1944, 21-3; William T. Y'Blood, *Hunter Killer: U.S. Escort Carriers in the Battle of the Atlantic* (Annapolis, Md 1983), 160-2

34 FONF, war diary, March 1944, NSC 1926-112/3 pt 1, DHist; EAC weekly intelligence report, 23 and 30 March, 6 April 1944, DHist 181.003 (D423)

35 Chief of the air staff [CAS] to AOCinC EAC, 12 April 1944, DHist 181.009 (D3217)

36 EAC operational instructions BR operations, 'Hunt to Exhaustion ('Salmon'),' 20 Feb. 1944, CO HMCS *New Glasgow* to captain (D) Halifax, report of proceedings, 25 March 1944, and attached minutes, DWT/Tactics to DWT, 10 May 1944, DHist NHS 8440 – 'W-10'; Coastal Command tactical instruction no 42, App. A, 5 Jan. 1944, DHist 181.009 (D213)

37 U-548 log, 23 April-1 May 1944, DHist SGR II 240; Otter signals for 24 April-1 May 1944, NSS 8910-20, PAC, RG 24, vol. 6896; EAC proposed operations for 23 April-1 May 1944, DHist 181.003 (D3254); 5 and 11 Squadrons, ORB daily diaries, 23 April-1 May 1944, DHist

38 U-548 log, 1 May 1944, DHist SGR II 240; EAC A/S operational intelligence summary, 7 May 1944, DHist 181.003 (D1555); operational research staff officer [ORSO] Halifax to chief of staff (operations), 6 May 1944, DHist NHS 1650 'Salm-

on'; 5, 10, and 11 Squadrons, ORB daily diaries, 2-3 May 1944, DHist; EAC proposed operations for 2-3 May 1944, DHist 181.003 (D3254)

39 Officer commanding [OC] 10 Squadron to CO RCAF Station Gander, 3 May 1944, DHist 181.003 (D1167)

40 HMS *Hargood* to FONF, signal 0140Z, 3 May 1944, DHist NHS 8000 'Valleyfield'

41 Nos 5, 10, and 11 Squadrons, ORB daily diaries, 3-5 May 1944, DHist; U-548 log, 3 May 1944, DHist SGR II 240

42 No 11 Squadron, ORB daily diary, 6 May 1944, DHist; EAC proposed operations for 6 May 1944, DHist 181.003 (D3254); U-548 log, 7 May 1944, DHist SGR II 240; DWT/Tactics to DWT and ACNS, 31 May, 9 June 1944, DHist NHS 8440 – ' C-1'; FONF to W-2, signal 051319Z, May 1944, 'Signals, 1.5.44 to 17.5.44,' naval secretary to commodore, RCN Barracks, Halifax, 28 Oct. 1952, 'Loss of HMC Ships Valleyfield and Shawinigan,' DHist NHS 8000 'Valleyfield'

43 CO HMCS *New Glasgow* to captain (D) Newfoundland, report of proceedings, 12 May 1944, 7-6-6, PAC, RG 24, vol. 11023; DWT/Tactics to DWT and ACNS, 15 June 1944, DHist NHS 8440 – 'C-1'; 5, 10, and 11 Squadrons, ORB daily diaries, 7-12 May 1944, DHist; FONF to W-11, signal 1944Z, 7 May 1944, signals, 9-11 May 1944, DHist NHS 8000 'Valleyfield'; U-548 log, 7-9 May 1944, DHist SGR II 240; EAC proposed operations for 9-12 May 1944, DHist 181.003 (D3254)

44 Nos 5 and 10 Squadrons, ORB daily diaries, 30 May-5 June 1944, DHist; U-548 log, 17 May-24 June 1944, DHist SGR II 240; EAC weekly intelligence report, 8 June 1944, DHist 181.003 (D423); Otter signals for 30 May-5 June 1944, NSS 8910-20 pt 1, PAC, RG 24, vol. 6896; ZTPGU/25025, 4 June 1944, PRO, Defe 3/740

45 EAC operations summaries for 21 May-5 July 1944, DHist 181.003 (D3254); FONF, war diary, NSC 1926-112/3 pt 1, DHist; HMCS *Wallaceburg*, report of proceedings, 16 June 1944, DHist NHS 8440 – 'W-10'; EAC A/S operations intelligence summary, 28 May-18 June 1944, DHist 321.009 (D8A); 10, 113, 116, and 145 Squadrons, ORB daily diaries, May, June, July 1944, DHist; Otter signals for 8 May-5 July 1944, NSS 8910-20 pts 1-2, PAC, RG 24, vol. 6896; U-107 log, DHist 85/77, pt 56; BdU memorandum, 'Submarine Situation 1.6.1944,' and generally, BdU war diary, DHist 79/446; *United States Fleet Anti-Submarine Bulletin*, II, Aug. 1944, 22-3

46 Coastal Command HQ to AFHQ Ottawa, signal, 1823Z 6 Oct. 1943, PRO, Air 15/355/4094, encl. 51; Air Ministry, 'The R.A.F. in Maritime War,' IV, 191; Slessor to Johnson, 3 Nov. 1943, DHist 181.002 (D175)

47 EAC to Coastal Command HQ, personal for Slessor from Johnson, signal, 2018Z 19 Nov. 1943, DHist 181.002 (D175); Air Ministry, 'The R.A.F. in Maritime War,' IV, 218

48 Leckie to minister, 27 Nov. 1943, S.096-105 pt 5, PARC 826793; Cabinet War Committee minutes, 1 Dec. 1943, PAC, RG 2, series 7c, vol. 14, microfilm reel C4875

49 No 162 Squadron, ORB daily diary, Jan. and Feb. 1944, DHist; EAC Marine Squadron, ORB daily diary, Feb. 1944, App. A, DHist; Jack Birt, 'RCAF Sailors Ride a Gale,' *Star Weekly*, 17 June 1944, 4-5; Sheard interview, 20 Jan. 1984, Terence Sheard biographical file, DHist

50 T.W. Melnyk, *Canadian Flying Operations in South East Asia, 1941-1945* (Department of National Defence, Directorate of History, Occasional Paper No 1; Ottawa, 1976)

51 Samuel Kostenuk and John Griffin, RCAF *Squadron Histories and Aircraft, 1924-1968* (Toronto 1977)

52 Ibid.

53 Coastal Command, ORS, 'Air Offensive against U-Boats in Transit,' report no 204, 12 Oct. 1942, PRO, Air 15/732; Coastal Command, 'Manual of Anti-U-Boat Warfare,' May 1944, PRO, Air 15/295

54 Denis Richards and Hilary St George Saunders, *Royal Air Force, 1939-45*, II: *The Fight Avails* (London 1954), 107-10; Hilary St George Saunders, *Royal Air Force, 1939-45*, III: *The Fight is Won* (London 1954), 34-68; Coastal Command, ORS, 'Air Operations in Support of Convoys 1942-May 1943,' report no 256, 24 Sept. 1943, PRO, Air 15/732; Coastal Command, ORS, 'Air Operations in Support of Convoys (Part II) Sept.-Oct. 1943,' report no 266, 20 Dec. 1943, PRO, Air 15/733; Eberhard Rössler, *The U-Boat: the Evolution and Technical History of German Submarines* (Annapolis, Md 1981), 188-94

55 AFHQ, Air Historical Section, 'No. 407 Squadron: a Narrative History,' unpublished narrative, 1953, 93, 99-100, DHist 74/308; Air Ministry, 'The R.A.F. in Maritime War,' IV, 131-2; RCAF Coastal Command ORB, Aug. 1943, App. B, and Sept. 1943, App. E, DHist 181.003 (D886); Great Britain, Admiralty, Historical Section, *Defeat of the Enemy Attack on Shipping, 1939-1945: a Study of Policy and Operations* (BR 1736 (51) (1), Naval Staff History Second World War; np [1957]), IA, 262

56 No 405 Squadron, ORB daily diary, Oct. 1942-Feb. 1943, DHist; Great Britain, Air Ministry, Air Historical Branch, 'The R.A.F. in Maritime War, III: The Atlantic and Home Waters, the Preparative Phase, July 1941 to February 1943,' nd, 501, DHist 79/599; 405 Squadron, progress reports, DHist 181.003 (D3111); *Coastal Command Review*, I, Nov. 1942, 8; DHist 181.003 (D3282)

57 No 415 Squadron, ORB daily diary, June-Aug. 1943, DHist; Air Ministry, 'The R.A.F. in Maritime War,' IV, 131; *Coastal Command Review*, II, Aug. 1943, 9; Admiralty, reports on interrogation of German prisoners of war (BR 1907), copy in DHist 80/582, item 41, 3

58 AFHQ, Air Historical Section, 'No. 422 Squadron: a Narrative History,' unpublished narrative, 1953, DHist 74/333

59 Air Ministry, 'The R.A.F. in Maritime War,' IV, 72, 149, 183; AFHQ, Air Historical Section, 'No. 423 Squadron,' unpublished narrative [1953], 21-52, DHist 74/334; Form UBAT, RCAF Coastal Command ORB, Aug. 1943, App. E, DHist 181.003 (D886)

60 'No. 422 Squadron,' 26-8, DHist 74/333; Air Ministry, 'The R.A.F. in Maritime War,' IV, 187; Form UBAT, RCAF Coastal Command ORB, Oct. 1943, App. E, DHist 181.003 (D886)

61 RCAF Coastal Command ORB, Dec. 1943, App. C, DHist 181.003 (D886); DHist 181.003 (D3596)

62 Edwards to Power, 18 Aug. 1942, DHist 181.009 (D4741); Edwards to minister, 27 May 1943, DHist 181.009 (D719), pt 1

63 Minister to ROYCANAIRF, signal x384c2143, 17 Feb. 1944, DHist 181.006 (D295). See also PRO, Air 20/1325; and PRO, Air 15/487.

64 Melnyk, *Canadian Flying Operations in South East Asia*, 33; Edwards to Breadner, 13 June 1943, Edwards to Slessor, 29 June 1943, DHist 181.009 (D719), pt 1; Air Ministry (director general organization [DG Org]) to Edwards, 16 July 1943, DHist 181.006 (D295)

65 DHist 181.003 (D1192); 'No. 422 Squadron,' 32, 85, DHist 74/333; RCAF Coastal Command ORB, Nov. 1943-Jan. 1945, App. C, DHist 181.003 (D886); RCAF Overseas Headquarters, daily diary, 1 Feb. 1944, DHist

66 DG Org to Coastal Command HQ, 26 Jan. 1944, PRO, Air 15/575/137

67 Coastal Command HQ to 17 Group HQ, 2 March 1944, PRO, Air 15/575, encl. 156

68 No 17 Group HQ to Coastal Command HQ, signal AT558, 16 May 1944, group captain commanding RAF Station Alness to 17 Group HQ, 28 May 1944, ibid.; 422 and 423 Squadrons ORB daily diaries, 31 Jan. 1944, 31 Jan., and 30 April 1945, DHist

69 Macfarlane to director of personnel, 24 June 1944, DHist 181.009 (D4163)

70 RCAF Overseas HQ, daily diary, 2 March 1944, DHist; 'No. 423 Squadron,' 64, DHist 74/334

71 RCAF Coastal Command ORB, July 1943, Sept. 1944, and Jan. 1945, App. C, DHist 181.003 (D886); DDO(P), 6 June 1944, 'Squadrons Nominated for Reception of RCAF Air Crews ...' DHist 181.009 (D6723); DHist 181.003 (D931); strength returns for 31 July 1944 in ORBs of EAC bomber-reconnaissance and fighter squadrons, DHist

72 AOCinC EAC to Dartmouth controller, Yarmouth controller et al, signal, 16 March 1943, DHist 181.002 (D125); J.D.F. Kealy, 'Command and Control of Naval and Air A/S Forces in the Northwest Atlantic 1943: a Study based on the Passages of HX 229/SC 122 and ONS 18/ON 202,' unpublished narrative [1977], DHist; 1 Group to EAC, signal A829, 23 July 1943, 1 Group-EAC teletype conversation, 24 July 1943, AOCinC EAC to 1 Group, Gulf Group, signal, 26 July 1943, DHist 181.003 (D122)

73 Kenyon to OBR, 29 Sept. 1943, Williams to CO RCAF Station Sydney, 1 Oct. 1943, DHist 181.002 (D464)

74 *Monthly Review of RCAF Operations North America*, 1 (July 1943-May 1944), tables 3 and 4; EAC, 'Six Month Summary of BR Operations in Eastern Air Command July to December, 1944,' report no 17, 21 March 1945, 3, DHist 181.002 (D379); J.W. Mayne, *Operational Research in the Canadian Armed Forces during the Second World War* (Department of National Defence, Operational Research and Analysis Establishment, Report No R68, June 1978), 1, 18, 24; EAC operational instructions BR operations, section P, App. II (March 1944), DHist 181.002 (D125)

75 The account of ONS 236 is based on the following sources: reports of proceedings for C.4, W.6, and W.2 groups, NSS 8280 – ONS 236, DHist mfm; EAC proposed operations and operations summaries for 21-5 May 1944, DHist 181.003 (D3254); ORB daily diaries for 5 Squadron, 20-1 May 1944, 11 Squadron, 21 May 1944, 10 Squadron, 22 May 1944, 113 Squadron, 23 May 1944, 145 Squadron, 23-4 May 1944, 160 Squadron, 24-5 May 1944, DHist; Otter signals for 8-22 May 1944, NSS 8910-20 pt 1, PAC, RG 24, vol. 6896.

76 David Syrett and Alec Douglas, 'The "Reptile" Searches: Defence of Convoys by British and Canadian Aircraft during the Battle of the Atlantic,' *Mariner's Mirror* (forthcoming)

77 U-548 log, 21-4 May 1944, DHist SGR II 240; BdU war diary, 27 May 1944, DHist 79/446

78 Rutledge to AOCinC EAC, 22 March 1944, DHist 181.002 (D98)

79 'No. 407 Squadron,' 111-12, DHist 74/308

80 Coastal Command HQ, intelligence summary, 12 Feb. 1944, RCAF Coastal Command ORB, Feb. 1944, App. B and App. E, Form UBAT, DHist 181.003 (D886); Air Ministry, 'The R.A.F. in Maritime War,' IV, 457-9

81 RCAF Coastal Command ORB, March 1944, App. E, Form UBAT, DHist 181.003 (D886); 'No. 407 Squadron,' 116, DHist 74/308; Air Ministry, 'The R.A.F. in Maritime War,' IV, 463-4

82 No 162 (BR) Squadron, ORB daily diary, 22 Feb., 12 and 17 April 1944, DHist; RCAF Coastal Command ORB, Feb. and April 1944, App. E, Form UBAT, DHist 181.003 (D886); 'No. 423 Squadron,' 66-8, DHist 74/334; 423 Squadron, ORB, 24 April 1944, DHist; BdU war diary, 24 April 1944, DHist 79/446; Coppock to Douglas, 10 March 1986, DHist

83 '162 (RCAF) Squadron Operations with 18 Group from Wick,' unpublished narrative [1945], 3, DHist 74/1; 162 Squadron, ORB daily diary, summary for June 1944, Form UBAT, July 1944, DHist; Great Britain, Air Ministry, Air Historical Branch, 'The R.A.F. in Maritime War, V: The Atlantic and Home Waters, the Victorious Phase, June 1944-May 1945,' nd, 2, 17, DHist 79/599; ibid., IV, 486-7

84 '162 (RCAF) Squadron Operations with 18 Group from Wick,' 13, DHist 74/1; Air Ministry, 'The R.A.F. in Maritime War,' V, 17n4; Remö to Roberts, 8 March 1946, 162 Squadron daily diary, June 1944, App.; DHist 77/366

85 No 162 Squadron, ORB, July 1944, Form UBAT, DHist; *Coastal Command Review*, III, July 1944, 8, 19; 'Questionnaire Regarding Forced Alighting of Aircraft on Water,' DHist 181.009 (D2441)

86 No 162 Squadron, ORB, July 1944, Form UBAT, DHist

87 Denomy to air force historian, nd, ibid., June 1944; *Coastal Command Review*, III, July 1944, 19-20, a useful account of the rescue that contains some errors; Hugh Halliday, *Target U-Boat: Canadians with Coastal Command in the Battle of the Atlantic, 1939-45* (Stittsville, Ont. forthcoming); 'Crash Alighting of Flying Boat,' DHist 181.009 (D2441)

88 '162 (RCAF) Squadron Operations with 18 Group from Wick,' 15-16, DHist 74/1; Coastal Command HQ, intelligence summary, 1 July 1944, RCAF Coastal Command, ORB, June 1944, App. B, DHist 181.003 (D886)

89 'Extract from Station and Squadron Commander's Conference held at Coastal Command Headquarters on 20th December, 1944,' 162 Squadron, ORB, March 1945, App. A, DHist

90 Air Ministry, 'The R.A.F. in Maritime War,' V, 37-8, 53-5, 58-61; 'No. 422 Squadron,' 56-8, DHist 74/333; 'No. 423 Squadron,' 81-4, DHist 74/334

91 No 162 Squadron, ORB daily diary, 4 and 6 Aug. 1944, DHist; Coastal Command HQ, intelligence summary, 5 Aug. 1944, Coastal Command HQ, narrative no 19 and no 20, 4 and 5 Aug. 1944, RCAF Coastal Command ORB, Aug. 1944, App. B

and App. H, DHist 181.003 (D886); *Coastal Command Review*, III, Aug. 1944, 2, 5; Air Ministry, 'The R.A.F. in Maritime War,' V, 59

92 Admiralty, *Defeat of the Enemy Attack on Shipping*, IB, Table 12 (ii)

CHAPTER 17: THE DAWN OF MODERN ASW, 1944-5

1 BCATP progress report no 51, 20 March 1944, DHist 73/1558, vol. 8; 161 Squadron, operations record book [ORB] daily diary, July 1944, DHist; 'The History of Eastern Air Command,' unpublished narrative [1945], 809-13, DHist 74/2, vol. 4; RCN weekly state, 2 May-10 June 1944, DHist, NHS 1650 – 'DS'

2 U-802 log, copy and translation, 19 Aug.-3 Sept. 1944, DHist 85/77, pt 57; 5 Squadron, ORB daily diary, 22 Aug.-27 Sept. 1944, DHist; Otter signals for 23-7 Aug. 1944, NSS 8910-20 pt 2, PAC, RG 24 vol. 6896. The basic source on the anti-submarine war in the Canadian Northwest Atlantic, Aug. 1944-May 1945, is the war diary of the commander-in-chief Canadian Northwest Atlantic [CINC CNA] for those months, NSC 1926-102/1, DHist. For a more detailed account of the operations described in this chapter see Roger Sarty, 'The RCAF and Anti-Submarine Warfare, October 1943-May 1945,' unpublished narrative, 1984, DHist.

3 U-541 log, 6, 11, 24, 29 Aug. and 3-5 Sept. 1944, DHist 85/77, pt 58; RCAF Station Sydney, weekly intelligence report, 7 Sept. 1944, DHist 181.003 (D267); HJF 28 report of proceedings and supporting letters, NSS 8280 – 'HJF 28,' DHist mfm; Eastern Air Command [EAC] operations summaries, 4-5 Sept. 1944, DHist 181.003 (D3254)

4 Otter signals for 3-5 Sept. 1944, NSS 8910-20 pt 2, PAC, RG 24, vol. 6896; Naval Service Headquarters [NSHQ] sighting and attack reports, 4 Sept. 1944, NSS 8910-23 pt 3, ibid., vol. 6897; U-802 log, 4 Sept. 1944, DHist 85/77, pt 57

5 HNMS *King Haakon VII*, report of proceedings, NSS 8280 – 'QS 89,' DHist mfm; NSHQ sighting and attack reports, 8 Sept. 1944, NSS 8910-23 pt 3, PAC, RG 24, vol. 6897; U-541 log, 7-8 Sept. 1944, DHist 85/77, pt 58

6 EAC operations summaries for 8-13 Sept. 1944, DHist 181.003 (D3254); 1 General Reconnaissance School, daily diary, 8 Sept. 1944, DHist; EAC, daily diary, Sept. 1944, App. 11, DHist

7 U-802 log, 13 Sept. 1944, DHist 85/77, pt 57

8 Ibid., 14-25 Sept. 1944; U-541 log, 18-27 Sept. 1944, ibid., pt 58

9 *Befehlshaber der Unterseeboote* [Bdu] war diary, translation, 22 Sept., 1-6 Oct. 1944, DHist 79/446; Otter signals for 1-13 Oct. 1944, NSS 8910-20 pt 2, PAC, RG 24, vol. 6896; commanding officer [CO] HMCS *Magog* to captain (D) Halifax, 15 Oct. 1944, NSS 8340-381/29, ibid., vol. 6790; sonobuoy report, 14 Oct. 1944, DHist 181.003 (D3385)

10 U-1221 log, Sept.-Oct. 1944, DHist 85/77, pt 59; BdU war diary, 26 Nov. 1944, DHist 79/446; master, *Fort Thompson* to Ministry of War Transport representative Quebec, 5 Nov. 1944, NSC 834-3995, PAC, RG 24, vol. 6791; EAC operations summaries for 3-18 Nov. 1944, DHist 181.003 (D274)

11 Joint RCN/RCAF Anti-Submarine Warfare Committee minutes, 19 Sept. 1944, DHist 181.009 (D3188); air officer commanding-in-chief [AOCinC] EAC to secre-

tary Department of National Defence [DND] for Air, 4 Oct. 1944, CinC CNA to secretary Naval Board, 4 Oct. 1944, Curtis to Johnson, 17 Oct. 1944, S.28-6-4, PAC, RG 24, vol. 5273

12 Great Britain, Air Ministry, Air Historical Branch, 'The R.A.F. in Maritime War, V: The Atlantic and Home Waters, the Victorious Phase, June 1944-May 1945,' nd, 83-5, DHist 79/599

13 Ibid., 83; 423 Squadron, ORB daily diary, 3 Sept. 1944, DHist

14 No 407 Squadron, ORB daily diary, 4-5 and 29-30 Oct. 1944, DHist; Air Ministry, 'The R.A.F. in Maritime War,' V, 95-6, 100; Admiralty, Operational Intelligence Centre [OIC], special intelligence summary, 16 and 23 Oct. 1944, PRO, Adm 223/21; Air Force Headquarters [AFHQ], Air Historical Section, 'No. 407 Squadron: a Narrative History,' unpublished narrative, 1953, 132, DHist, 74/308; AFHQ, Air Historical Section, 'No. 422 Squadron: a Narrative History,' unpublished narrative, 1953, 85, DHist 74/333

15 Admiralty, OIC, special intelligence summary, week ending 28 Aug. 1944, PRO, Adm 223/21

16 Ibid., 7 Aug., 23 and 30 Oct., 6 Nov. 1944; Eberhard Rössler, *The U-Boat: the Evolution and Technical History of German Submarines* (Annapolis, Md 1981) 214-32, 240-6, 248-65

17 Douglas to Johnson, 14 Oct. 1944, PRO, Air 15/345

18 Breadner to Power, signal C466, 30 June 1944, DHist 181.006 (D312); chief of the air staff [CAS] to minister, 8 Nov. 1944, S.19-6-5 pt 6, PAC, RG 24, vol. 5217; Leckie to Portal, liaison letters, 19 Nov. 1943, 17 May 1944, PRO, Air 15/356; *RCN-RCAF Monthly Operational Review*, Aug. 1944, 24, DHist; S.34-51-1, PAC, RG 24, vol. 5346

19 Coastal Command, Operational Research Section [ORS], 'A Review of S-Band ASV Performance in Detecting U-Boats,' report no 308, 2 Nov. 1944, PRO, Air 15/733; *RCN-RCAF Monthly Operational Review*, II, Dec. 1944, 20-2, DHist; director of signals to air member for air staff [AMAS], 7 Nov. 1944, acting AMAS to assistant CAS, 9 Nov. 1944, assistant CAS to AMAS, 14 Nov. 1944, director of signals to AMAS, 17 Nov. 1944, S.19-6-5 pt 6, PAC, RG 24, vol. 5217; EAC equipment situation report no 15, 30 April 1945, S.28-4-9, ibid., vol. 5271; AMAS Division, summary of activities for Jan., March, April 1945, DHist 79/430, vol. 3

20 EAC ORS, 'Five Month Summary of BR Operations in Eastern Air Command January to May, 1945,' report no 21, 13 Aug. 1945, table II, DHist 181.002 (D379); AMAS to air member for supply and organization [AMSO], 23 March 1945, director of aeronautical engineering [DAE] to AMSO, minute, 10 April 1945, S.19-6-5 pt 7, PAC, RG 24, vol. 5217

21 BdU war diary, 8 Oct. and 12 Nov. 1944, DHist 79/446; U-1221 log, 5 Nov. 1944, U-541 log, summary of operations Aug.-Nov. 1944, DHist 85/77, pts 59 and 58

22 U-1228 log, 3 Nov. 1944-5 Jan. 1945, U-1231 log, 12 Nov. 1944-2 Feb. 1945, DHist 85/77, pts 60 and 62; BdU war diary, Nov.-Dec. 1944, DHist 79/446; ZTPGU signals 35045-6, 3 Jan. 1945, PRO, Defe 3/740

23 EAC monthly operational report, Nov. 1944, EAC daily diary, DHist

24 EAC weekly intelligence report, 7 Dec. 1944, DHist 181.003 (D4863)

25 EAC anti-submarine operations intelligence summary, 24 Dec. 1944, EAC daily diary, DHist; EAC operations summaries for 17-23 Dec. 1944, DHist 181.003 (D274); 10 Squadron, ORB daily diary, 18-19 Dec. 1944, DHist; CINC CNA to commander-in-chief Atlantic, signal, 1520Z 1 Dec. 1944, NSS 8910-166/10, PAC, RG 24, vol. 6901; BdU war diary, 28 Dec. 1944, DHist 79/446

26 ZTPGU/33333, 13 Nov. 1944, ZTPGU/33822, 4 Dec. 1944, PRO, Defe 3/738; Otter signals, 4-20 Dec. 1944, NSS 8910-20 pt 2, PAC, RG 24, vol. 6896, EAC operations summaries for 4-24 Dec. 1944, DHist 181.003 (D274); Michael Hadley, 'U-Boot-Begegnung vor Halifax: Die Versenkung von HMCS *Clayoquot*,' *Marine Rundschau*, March and April 1982, translation in DHist SGR II 258 (an excellent account of U-806's cruise); U-806 log, 13-21 Dec. 1944, DHist SGR II 257; commander of the port Halifax to CINC CNA, 29 Dec. 1944, 7-12 pt 1, PAC, RG 24, vol. 11023; NSS 8280 – 'HHX 327,' DHist mfm; 145 and 11 Squadrons, ORB daily diary, and RCAF Station Dartmouth, daily diary, 21-4 Dec. 1944, DHist

27 U-806 log, 24-5 Dec. 1944, DHist SGR II, 257; U-1231 log, 24-6 Dec. 1944, DHist 85/77, pt 62; EAC operations summaries for 25-9 Dec. 1944, DHist 181.003 (D274); Otter signals for 22-4 Dec. 1944, NSS 8910-20 pt 2, PAC, RG 24, vol. 6896; Admiralty OIC, special intelligence summary, 27 Nov. 1944, PRO, Adm 223/21

28 Otter signals for 22-6 Dec. 1944, NSS 8910-20 pt 2, PAC, RG 24, vol. 6896; EAC operations summaries for 2-14 Jan. 1945, DHist 181.003 (D274); NSS 8280 – 'SH 194,' DHist mfm; 11 Squadron, ORB daily diary, 4 Jan. 1945, DHist

29 NSS 8280 – 'BX 141,' DHist mfm; EAC operations summaries for 15-23 Jan. 1944, DHist 181.003 (D274); ZTPGU/35648, 23 Jan. 1945, PRO, Defe 3/740; 10 Squadron, ORB daily diary, 24 Jan. 1945, DHist; 27th Escort Group report of proceedings, 24 Jan.-4 Feb. 1945, DHist NHS 8440 – 'EG 27'

30 Otter signals for 16-31 Jan. 1945, NSS 8910-20 pt 2, PAC, RG 24, vol. 6896; Admiralty OIC, special intelligence summary, 29 Jan.-12 Feb. 1945, PRO, Adm 223/21; DHist NHS – 1650 'U-866'; US *Fleet Anti-Submarine Bulletin*, II, April 1945, 31-2, DHist; 10 and 160 Squadrons, ORB daily diaries, DHist

31 S.W. Roskill, *The War at Sea, 1939-1945*, III: *The Offensive, Part II, 1st June 1944-14th August 1945* (History of the Second World War, United Kingdom Military Series; London 1961), 287; RCN weekly state, 2 Jan. 1945, DHist, NHS 1650 – 'DS'; Air Ministry, 'The R.A.F. in Maritime War,' V, App. 1, 20; EAC monthly operational report, Jan. 1945, figure 1, EAC, daily diary, Jan. 1945, DHist

32 Air Ministry, 'The R.A.F. in Maritime War,' V, 197-8; 'Draft: a Forecast of the "U" Boat Campaign during 1945, Note by the First Sea Lord,' nd, PRO, Air 20/1237/X/P 04895; 'Review of the Anti-U-boat War from 20th December, 1944, to 20th January, 1945,' 25 Jan. 1945, PRO, Adm 205/44/X/N 08723

33 RCAF attack report, 30 Dec. 1944, DHist 181.003 (D4417)

34 Nos 10 and 160 Squadrons, ORB daily diaries, March 1945, DHist; EAC operations summaries for March 1945, DHist 181.003 (D274); ZTPGU/37121, 10 March 1945, PRO, Defe 3/742

35 Air Ministry, 'The R.A.F. in Maritime War,' V, 185; EAC operations summaries for 25-7 March 1945, DHist 181.003 (D274); EAC monthly operations reports, April and May 1945, EAC, daily diary, DHist; Admiralty OIC, special intelligence summary, 26 March, 2 and 30 April 1945,' PRO, Adm 223/21; Admiralty, 'Fuehrer

Conferences on Naval Affairs, 1945,' (London 1947), 78-9, 89, 107-8; US Navy, 'OP-16-Z, P/W Weekly (German),' 19 and 26 May 1945, DHist NHS – 1650 'U-Boats 1939-45'

36 Flag officer Newfoundland Force, war diary, April 1945, NSS 1000-5-20 pt 5, DHist

37 Naval Intelligence Division, 'Report on an Interrogation of some members of the crew of U-190 ...,' 22 May 1945, DHist NHS – 1650 'U-190'; naval secretary to commodore RCN Barracks, Halifax, 'Loss of HMC Ship *Esquimalt*,' 8 Nov. 1952, DHist NHS 8000 'Esquimalt'; 'Report of Proceedings – EG 28, 3rd April to 19th April, 1945,' DHist NHS 8440 – 'EG 28' pt 1; RCAF attack report, 3 May 1945, DHist 181.003 (D1366)

38 United States, Department of the Navy, Naval Security Group Command Head-quarters, 'Intelligence Reports on the War in the Atlantic 1942-5,' II, 226-8, DHist mfm 80/206; S.E. Morison, *History of United States Naval Operations in World War II*, X: *The Atlantic Battle Won, May 1943 – May 1945* (Boston 1956), 330, 344-56; William T. Y'Blood, *Hunter-Killer: U.S. Escort Carriers in the Battle of the Atlantic* (Annapolis, Md 1983), 263-72

39 EAC operations summaries for April-May 1945, DHist 181.003 (D274); EAC anti-submarine operations intelligence summaries, April 1945, EAC daily diary, DHist

40 Intercepted signal, BdU to all U-boats, 1945Z 8 May 1945, DHist, NHS – 1650 'U-boats 1945' pt 2; 'No. 407 Squadron: a Narrative History,' 146, 148, DHist 74/308; 162 Squadron, ORB daily diary, June 1945, DHist; 'No. 422 Squadron: a Narrative History,' 96-107, DHist 74/333; AFHQ, Air Historical Section, 'No. 423 Squadron: a Narrative History,' unpublished narrative, 1953, 128-33, DHist 74/334

41 DHist NHS 1650 'U-190'

42 No 10 Squadron, ORB daily diary, 10 May 1945, DHist

43 ZTPGU/35677, 23 Jan 1945, PRO, Defe 3/740

APPENDIX C: THE CLAYTON KNIGHT COMMITTEE

1 Quoted in Robert Dallek, *Franklin D. Roosevelt and American Foreign Policy, 1932-1945* (New York 1979), 199

2 See ibid., Chap. 9, and Joseph P. Lash, *Roosevelt and Churchill, 1939-1941: the Partnership that Saved the West* (New York 1976), 63-74.

3 'Recruiting in the United States of America,' unpublished narrative [1945], DHist 74/7, vol. 3, 542; F.J. Hatch, 'Recruiting Americans for the Royal Canadian Air Force, 1939-1942,' *Aerospace Historian*, XVIII, March 1971, 12

4 Bishop to Thomas (former secretary to Clayton Knight Committee), 12 Sept. 1944, Clayton Knight Committee Papers, DHist 80/68, file 39. See also Clayton Knight, 'Contribution to Victory, 1939-1942,' ibid., file 2; and F.J. Hatch, *The Aerodrome of Democracy: Canada and the British Commonwealth Air Training Plan, 1939-1945* (Department of National Defence, Directorate of History, Monograph Series No 1; Ottawa 1983), 86-7, and, generally on this subject, 86-96.

5 Knight, 'Contribution to Victory,' DHist 80/68, file 2; Hatch, 'Recruiting Americans,' 13

6 Knight to Rogers, 30 June 1942, DHist 80/68, file 47

7 See Knight to LaGuardia, 20 Feb. 1940, ibid., file 5, and the list of contacts in ibid., file 4.

8 Knight, 'Contribution to Victory,' DHist 80/68, file 2; Curtis to air member for personnel, 31 May 1940, 'Enlistments in the U.S.A.,' HQ 45-10-2, PAC, RG 24, vol. 5368

9 Dallek, *Franklin D. Roosevelt*, 228-9; Lash, *Roosevelt and Churchill*, 150ff, especially 162

10 Hatch, 'Recruiting Americans,' 13; Canadian minister to the United States to undersecretary of state for external affairs, 18 May 1940, copy in HQ 45-10-2, PAC, RG 24, vol. 5368; Knight to Edwards, 22 Nov. 1940, DHist 80/68, file 9

11 Clayton Knight interview, 17 June 1965, DHist 80/68, file 3; Knight, 'Contribution to Victory,' ibid., file 2

12 Knight, 'Contribution to Victory,' DHist 80/68, file 2; 'Clayton Knight Committee Financial and Statistical Reports,' ibid., file 12; Hatch, *Aerodrome of Democracy*, 88

13 Hatch, *Aerodrome of Democracy*, 88-9

14 Knight, 'Contribution to Victory,' DHist 80/68, file 2; Knight interview, ibid., file 3

15 See correspondence in 'Ferry Pilots, etc.,' DHist 80/68, file 14, and Clayton Knight Committee, 'General Regulations,' April 1941, ibid., file 28.

16 'Clayton Knight Committee Financial and Statistical Reports,' DHist 80/68, file 12

17 Mudre to Renway (Los Angeles office), 6 Aug. 1940, ibid., file 6

18 Lash, *Roosevelt and Churchill*, 228ff, 264-5; Dallek, *Franklin D. Roosevelt*, 249ff

19 Hatch, *Aerodrome of Democracy*, 89-90

20 Ibid., 90

21 See, for example, Richard Thorelsen, 'Canada's Open Society,' *Saturday Evening Post*, 1 Feb. 1941, 18ff; 'Gateway to the R.A.F. – For U.S. Volunteers,' *Sunday Mirror Magazine Section*, 28 Sept. 1941, 6ff; Robert Tulley, 'Memphis Hell for Adolf,' (Memphis) *Commercial Appeal*, 17 Aug. 1941, all in DHist 80/68, file 36. See also transcript of E.L. Benway radio interview, March 1941, ibid., file 44.

22 Armour to president and directors of Dominion Aeronautical Association, 21 May 1941, DHist 80/68, file 44

23 Ibid.

24 Rogers to 'Air Marshal' [Knight?], 14 June 1941, ibid., folder 19

25 Hatch, 'Recruiting Americans,' 15, and *Aerodrome of Democracy*, 91-2

26 Armour to president and directors of Dominion Aeronautical Association, 22 July 1941, DHist 80/68, file 44; Hatch, 'Recruiting Americans,' 16

27 Hatch, 'Recruiting Americans,' 16

28 Ibid.

29 *New York Sun*, 12 Aug. 1941, copy in DHist 80/68, file 50

30 *Oregon Journal*, 16 Aug. 1941, copy in ibid., file 36

31 Hatch, 'Recruiting Americans,' 16, and *Aerodrome of Democracy*, 92

32 Gene to Jack, nd, DHist 80/68, file 7, pt 1

33 Knight, 'Contribution to Victory,' ibid., file 2
34 McNeil to Gilchrist, 4 Nov. 1941, ibid., file 7, pt 2
35 Gene to Jack, nd, ibid., file 7, pt 1
36 Juhan to Southwark et al, nd, ibid., file 8
37 Ibid., file 23
38 Hatch, 'Recruiting Americans,' 16-18, and *Aerodrome of Democracy*, 92-3
39 Walsh memorandum, 5 Feb. 1942, in DHist 80/68, file 31; Smith memorandum, 12 Feb. 1942, ibid., file 11
40 Smith memorandum, 2 June 1942, DHist 80/68, file 30
41 Ibid., file 41

APPENDIX D: FERRY COMMAND

1 H. Duncan Hall, *North American Supply* (History of the Second World War, United Kingdom Civil Series; London 1955), 105-9; H. Duncan Hall and C.C. Wrigley, *Studies of Overseas Supply* (History of the Second World War, United Kingdom Civil Series; London 1956), 4; W.K. Hancock, ed., *Statistical Digest of the War: Prepared in the Central Statistical Office* (History of the Second World War, United Kingdom Civil Series; London 1951), 156n; Edward R. Stettinius, Jr, *Lend-Lease, Weapon for Victory* (New York and London 1944), 22

2 Hall and Wrigley, *Studies of Overseas Supply*, 109-10; Hall, *North American Supply*, 170-3

3 Anderson to secretary Department of National Defence, 6 April 1940, S3-5-2, DHist 181.003 (D4095); Griffith Powell, *Ferryman: from Ferry Command to Silver City* (Shrewsbury, England 1982), 20; D.C.T. Bennett, *Pathfinder* (London 1958), 121

4 A.J.P. Taylor, *Beaverbrook* (London 1972), 428; Sholto Watt, *I'll Take the High Road: a History of the Beginning of the Atlantic Ferry in Wartime* (Fredericton, NB 1960), 8, 14; S.A. Dismore, 'Atlantic Ferrying Organization (ATFERO): the Past,' 22 May 1941, PRO, Air 8/474, Air 2/7508, and Air 20/6090; Great Britain, Ministry of Information, *Atlantic Bridge: the Official Account of R.A.F. Transport Command's Ocean Ferry* (London 1945), 7; W.P. Hildred, 'Report on ATFERO,' 1 July 1941, paragraph 3, PRO, Air 2/7508; Powell, *Ferryman*, 20-1

5 J.R.K. Main, *Voyageurs of the Air: a History of Civil Aviation in Canada, 1858-1967* (Ottawa 1967), 163; K.N. Molson, *Pioneering in Canadian Air Transport* (np 1974), 233; D.H. Miller-Barstow, *Beatty of the C.P.R.* (Toronto 1951), 170-1; Burchall to Dismore, 7 Oct. 1940, enclosing unsigned copy of the agreement, DHist 74/799. See especially paragraphs 1, 3, 4, and 5. For more detail on the development and history of the wartime ferry service, see C.A. Christie and F.J. Hatch, *Ocean Bridge* (Stittsville, Ont. forthcoming).

6 Bennett, *Pathfinder*, 97-100; Watt, *High Road*, 23; Powell, *Ferryman*, 25-6

7 Taylor, *Beaverbrook*, 414-45; Watt, *High Road*, 9

8 'Address by Dr P.D. McTaggart-Cowan on Early Trans-Atlantic Aviation in Newfoundland Given at the CAHS Meeting, 18 Nov. 1975,' transcript, 24-5, DHist 80/350; Bennett, *Pathfinder*, 103-4; V. Edward Smith, 'North Atlantic Ferry,'

Aviation, May 1941, 132-4; Bennett interview, 17 June 1976 (transcript), 5, D.C.T. Bennett biographical file, DHist; Watt, *High Road*, 45

9 *Atlantic Bridge*, 12-16; Bennett, *Pathfinder*, 103-6; Watt, *High Road*, 34-45; Reader's Digest, *The Canadians at War, 1939/45* (np 1969), I, 114-16; Smith, 'North Atlantic Ferry,' 132; Newfoundland Airport watch log, copy, DHist 79/1, vol. I

10 Bennett, *Pathfinder*, 107-10; 'Paper Dealing with the Past Functions of ATFERO under the Ministry of Aircraft Production and the Future Functions of the Royal Air Force Ferry Command,' 2 Aug. 1941, PRO, Air 2/8135

11 Michael Bliss, *Banting: a Biography* (Toronto 1984), 295-309; Bennett, *Pathfinder*, 113-5; Ralph Barker, *Survival in the Sky* (London 1976), 49-58; Newfoundland Airport watch log, DHist 79/1, vol. I

12 Bennett, *Pathfinder*, 107-8; British Air Commission to Ministry of Aircraft Production, 17 July 1941, PRO, Air 19/247; Powell, *Ferryman*, 33-4; Molson, *Pioneering*, 173, 207; Dismore, 'Atlantic Ferrying Organization (ATFERO): the Past,' PRO, Air 2/7508; Watt, *High Road*, 100; *Atlantic Bridge*, 22; A.G. Sutherland, *Canada's Aviation Pioneers: 50 Years of McKee Trophy Winners* (Toronto 1978), 35-6

13 Watt, *High Road*, 102; Bennett, *Pathfinder*, 97, 118; Dismore, 'Atlantic Ferrying Organization (ATFERO): the Past,' PRO, Air 2/7508; Molson, *Pioneering*, 237

14 Bennett to Bowhill, 28 June 1941, PRO, Air 2/8135; [Burchall] to H.S. [Self?], 26 Aug. 1940, Clayton Knight Papers, DHist 80/68, file 14; Sinclair-Beaverbrook correspondence, 30 July-5 Aug. 1940, Lord Beaverbrook Papers (copies), DHist 74/527, files A10-13; Air Member for Personnel Division, progress reports, 12 Feb.-3 Nov. 1940, DHist 73/1174, vol. 1B; Self to Westbrook, 1 Jan. 1941, PRO, Air 19/247

15 Taylor, *Beaverbrook*, 414-30, 467-9; Beaverbrook-Sinclair correspondence, Beaverbrook Papers, DHist 74/527, files A and A1, and PRO, Air 19/247 and Air 19/248; chief of the air staff to secretary of state for air, 6 Jan. 1941, encl. dated 7 Jan. 1941, PRO, Air 19/247; Churchill to secretary of state for air, 1 March 1941, PRO, Air 19/248

16 Portal to US military attaché London, 16 May 1941, PRO, Air 19/249; Sinclair to Beaverbrook, 25 March 1941, PRO, Air 19/248; president [Roosevelt] to former naval person [Churchill], 29 May 1941, PRO, Air 2/7508; reply to signal from president to prime minister, attached to Melville to Martin, 30 May 1941, former naval person to president, 31 May 1941, and 'Notes of a Meeting Held on 2-6-41 to Discuss the Future Organization of Trans-Atlantic Ferrying in the Light of the Telegram from the President of the USA,' PRO, Air 8/1369, Air 2/7508

17 Private secretary to the secretary of state for air to air member for personnel, 8 June 1941, PRO, Air 8/1369; Hildred to Street, 29 Aug. 1941, PRO, Air 2/7509; *Atlantic Bridge*, 24; Bennett, *Pathfinder*, 120-1; Bennett interview, 5-6, D.C.T. Bennett biographical file, DHist

18 Supervisory Board minutes, 12 May 1941, App. 1, 'Report No 17 by the Chief of the Air Staff to the Members of the Supervisory Board, British Commonwealth Air Training Plan,' DHist 73/1558, vol. 3; No 31 Operational Training Unit, daily

diary, May 1941-April 1943, DHist; F/O Hodgins, 'OTU's under the BCATP: No 31 OTU,' unpublished narrative [1945], DHist 74/13; *Atlantic Bridge*, 25

19 P.Y. Davoud and K.C.B. Hodson biographical files, DHist; Newfoundland Airport watch log, DHist 79/1; squadron diaries, DHist; Bowhill to Sinclair, 15 Aug. 1941, PRO, Air 2/7509; Bennett, *Pathfinder*, 122

20 C.P. Stacey, *Arms, Men and Governments: the War Policies of Canada, 1939-45* (Ottawa 1970), 367-70; Stanley W. Dziuban, *Military Relations between the United States and Canada, 1939-1945* (United States Army in World War II, Special Studies; Washington 1959), 149-52, 183-4, 353-4

21 Bennett, *Pathfinder*, 116-17; Watt, *High Road*, 121-2; *Atlantic Bridge*, 26-7; 'Development of R.C.A.F. Station Goose Bay, Lab.,' 26 May 1942, S.17-4, DHist 181.009 (D2941); 'North Atlantic Ferry Routes,' HQS 15-24-30 pts 1-7, PAC, RG 24, vol. 5201; 'Record of Conference Held in the Air Ministry on Wednesday, 9th July 1941,' PRO, Air 2/7509; '6th Weekly Letter from Air Marshal Harris to C.A.S. Week Ending 1800 hours, Saturday, August 2nd, 1941,' PRO, Air 45/12; Wesley Frank Craven and James Lea Cate, eds., *The Army Air Forces in World War II*, I: *Plans and Early Operations, January 1939 to August 1942* (Chicago 1948), 342-4

22 Craven and Cate, *Plans and Early Operations*, 639-45; RCAF Station Goose Bay, daily diary, June-July 1942, DHist; *Statistical Digest of the War*, 156-7; PRO, Air 38/23; 'Cumulative Monthly Receipts and Deliveries,' in PRO, Air 24/5493, Air 25/647, and Air 25/648

23 Air officer commanding [AOC] 45 (Trans-Atlantic) Group to air officer commanding-in-chief [AOCinC] Transport Command, 10 Oct. 1944, PRO, Air 25/648

24 Ibid.; Hodgins, 'OTU's under the BCATP: No. 32 OTU,' DHist 74/13; F.J. Hatch, *The Aerodrome of Democracy: Canada and the British Commonwealth Air Training Plan, 1939-1945* (Department of National Defence, Directorate of History, Monograph Series No 1; Ottawa 1983), 78-9

25 *Statistical Digest of the War*, 157-8; 45 Group, reports for Aug. 1943-Sept. 1945, PRO, Air 25/647 and Air 25/648; AOC 45 Group to AOCinC Transport Command, 4 July 1944, PRO, Air 25/648. See also various reports and returns Sept. 1941-Oct. 1945 in PRO, Air 24/5493, Air 25/647, and Air 25/648.

26 PRO, Air 2/5340, passim; Sinclair to Beaverbrook, 2 Sept. 1941, and subsequent correspondence, Beaverbrook Papers, DHist 74/527, file E7; Beaverbrook to Sinclair 10 Oct. 1941, Sinclair to Beaverbrook, 17 Oct. 1941, and further correspondence, PRO, Air 2/5362

27 Cabinet War Committee minutes, 21 Oct. 1942, PAC, RG 2, series 7c, vol. 11, microfilm reel C4874; Bruce Robertson, comp., *Lancaster: the Story of a Famous Bomber* (Letchworth, England 1964), 106, 148; Canada, Parliament, House of Commons, *Debates*, 16 June 1943, 3696-7; Ewart Young, 'Trans-Atlantic Service,' *Canadian Aviation*, Feb. 1945, 59

28 No 412 (12 Comm.) Squadron, daily diary, 10 Sept. 1939-30 Sept. 1941, DHist; McDougall to Pope, 30 Sept. 1942, DHist 181.009 (D4907)

29 Leigh's unpublished memoir, PAC, MG 31 G 11 and DHist 77/13. See also Air Transport Command, daily diary, 5 Feb. 1945-31 May 1949, 'RCAF Transport Organization, 1939-45,' nd, DHist.

30 Dziuban, *Military Relations*, 63-4, 82; Hall, *North American Supply*, 300; Stacey, *Arms, Men and Governments*, 167-74; Canadian Joint Staff Washington, RCAF Division, war diary, 1 Jan. 1942-Dec. 1943, DHist; secret organization order no 108, 3 Feb. 1943, 164 Squadron, daily diary, DHist; Air Force Headquarters [AFHQ], Air Historical Section, 'No 164 (T) Squadron,' unpublished narrative, nd, 5-8, 164 Squadron permanent reference file, DHist

31 'AFHQ Sectional Histories,' sect. 4, 'Historical Record of Directorate of Air Transport Command,' DHist 80/395; Air Transport Command, daily diary, 5 Feb. 1945-31 May 1949, 'RCAF Transport Organization, 1939-45,' and 'Summary of Operations Performed by No 168 (H.T.) Squadron,' nd, DHist; 168 Squadron, daily diary, 17 Oct. 1943-21 March 1946, DHist; RCAF working file, 'RCAF Postal Services Overseas: 168 Heavy Transport Squadron,' DHist

32 For the various aircraft totals see *Statistical Digest of the War*, 152-7; 'Cumulative Monthly Receipt and Deliveries ... North and South Atlantic to the U.K.,' nd, PRO, Air 38/23; monthly reports of 45 Group, PRO, Air 25/647 and Air 25/648.

33 Dziuban, *Military Relations*, 216, 351; Deane R. Brandon, 'ALSIB: the Northwest Ferrying Route through Alaska, 1942-1945,' *Journal, American Aviation Historical Society*, summer 1975; John Stewart, *Canada, the United States, and the Air Corridor to Alaska, 1935-1942* (undergraduate thesis, Mount Allison University, Sackville, NB, 1981), copy in DHist 81/332

34 Stacey, *Arms, Men and Governments*, 376; Dziuban, *Military Relations*, 186-7, 324, 334; K.C. Eyre, *Custos Borealis: the Military in the Canadian North* (PHD thesis, University of London, 1981), 112-20

Index

EASTERN AIR COMMAND OPERATIONS
(NORTH ATLANTIC OPERATIONS)
1939-1945

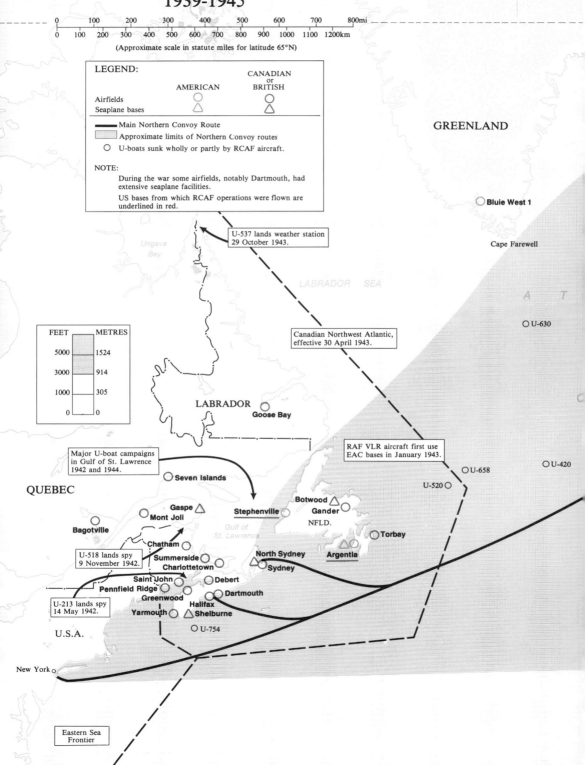

LEGEND:

	AMERICAN	CANADIAN or BRITISH
Airfields	○	○
Seaplane bases	△	△

— Main Northern Convoy Route

Approximate limits of Northern Convoy routes

○ U-boats sunk wholly or partly by RCAF aircraft.

NOTE:

During the war some airfields, notably Dartmouth, had extensive seaplane facilities.

US bases from which RCAF operations were flown are underlined in red.

GREENLAND

○ Bluie West 1

Cape Farewell

U-537 lands weather station 29 October 1943.

Ungava Bay

LABRADOR   SEA

Canadian Northwest Atlantic, effective 30 April 1943.

○ U-630

FEET	METRES
5000	1524
3000	914
1000	305
0	0

LABRADOR   ○ Goose Bay

Major U-boat campaigns in Gulf of St. Lawrence 1942 and 1944.

RAF VLR aircraft first use EAC bases in January 1943.

○ U-420

QUEBEC

○ Seven Islands

○ U-658

U-520 ○

○ Bagotville

Gaspe △
○ Mont Joli

Stephenville ○

Botwood △ ○
Gander ○

NFLD.

U-518 lands spy 9 November 1942.

Chatham ○

Summerside ○
Charlottetown ○

North Sydney   Argentia

○ Torbay

U-213 lands spy 14 May 1942.

Saint John ○
Pennfield Ridge ○
Greenwood ○

○ Debert

Sydney

Gulf of St. Lawrence

U.S.A.

Yarmouth ○

Halifax
△ Shelburne

○ Dartmouth

New York ○

○ U-754

Eastern Sea Frontier